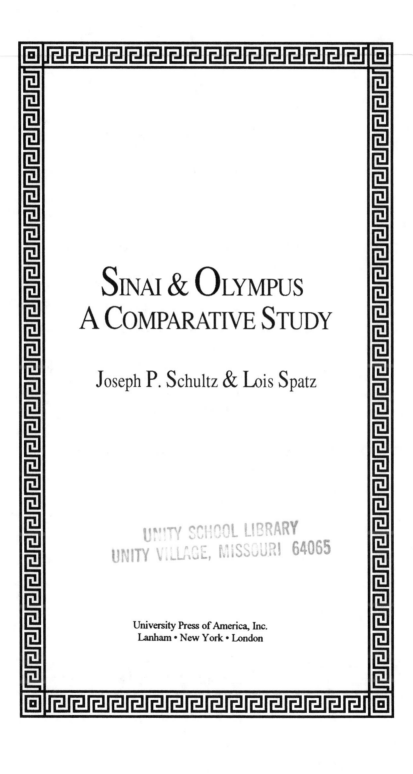

SINAI & OLYMPUS
A COMPARATIVE STUDY

Joseph P. Schultz & Lois Spatz

University Press of America, Inc.
Lanham • New York • London

Copyright © 1995 by
University Press of America,® Inc.
4720 Boston Way
Lanham, Maryland 20706

3 Henrietta Street
London, WC2E 8LU England

Library of Congress Cataloging-in-Publication Data

Schultz, Joseph P.
Sinai & Olympus : a comparative study / Joseph P. Schultz & Lois
Spatz.
p.   cm.
Includes bibliographical references and index.
1. Judaism--History--To 70 A.D. 2. Greece--Religion. 3. Hellenism.
I. Spatz, Lois. II. Title.
BM165.S35   1995   292--dc20   95-24240 CIP

ISBN 0-7618-0032-8 (cloth: alk ppr.)

10/97

$70.00

⊖™The paper used in this publication meets the minimum
requirements of American National Standard for Information
Sciences—Permanence of Paper for Printed Library Materials,
ANSI Z39.48—1984

For Abe J. Kaplan and his late beloved wife Catherine,
devotees of learning and patrons of scholarship.

Contents

Chapter 2: Creation: Genesis or Theogony?

Chapter 3: The Origin of Evil

Chapter 4: Is There a Moral Order in the Universe?

Chapter 5: Paradigms of Heroism

Chapter 6: Patterns of Piety

Chapter 7: Patterns of Public Worship

Chapter 8: Public Life—Law and the State

Chapter 9: The Concepts and the Methods of History

Chapter 10: The Endtime: Afterlife and Apocalypse

Acknowledgements

We would like to thank the Abe and Catherine Kaplan Philanthropic Fund of the Jewish Community Foundation of Greater Kansas City for helping to support the publication of this book.

We wish to thank the College of Arts and Sciences of the University of Missouri-Kansas City, as well as the Weldon Springs Fund of the University of Missouri, for the leaves and summer stipends which enabled us to do our research and writing.

For permission to reprint copyrighted materials, we thank the following:

The University of Chicago Press for permission to quote from *The Complete Greek Tragedies*, 4 volumes, David Grene and Richmond Lattimore, editors (Chicago: University of Chicago Press, 1959-60).

Cambridge University Press for permission to quote from G. S. Kirk, J. E. Raven, and M. Schofield, *The Presocratic Philosophers: A Critical History with a Selection of Texts,* 2nd edition (Cambridge: Cambridge University Press, 1983).

Dine Israel (Tel-Aviv University Law Journal) for permission to quote from "Max Weber and the Sociological Development of Jewish Law," *Dine Israel* 16 (1991-1992): 72-79.

Shofar: An Interdisciplinary Journal of Jewish Studies, Purdue University and Purdue Research Foundation, publisher, for permission to quote from "From Sacred Space to Sacred Object to Sacred Person in Jewish Antiquity," *Shofar*, Vol. 12, No. 1 (Fall, 1993):28-37.

Saint Paul School of Theology for permission to quote from "Three Jewish Perspectives on Suffering" in *The Meaning of Suffering: An Interreligious Symposium Sponsored by Saint Paul School of Theology* (Kansas City, Missouri: Saint Paul School of Theology, 1989): 45-53.

The various libraries utilized in the preparation of this work have been graciously accommodating and we wish to record our thanks to the staffs of the Miller-Nichols Library of the University of Missouri-Kansas City, the Asher Library of Spertus College, the Library of the Jewish Theological Seminary of America, the Library of Saint Paul School of Theology, and the Library of the Nazarene Theological Seminary.

For help in preparing the manuscript, we thank Carol Rust, Administrative Associate in the Dean's Office of the College of Arts and Sciences at the University of Missouri-Kansas City. For the preparation of our camera-ready copy, we thank Renée LaRoe and John LaRoe of Kansas City.

We are grateful for the advice and encouragement of our colleagues at the University of Missouri-Kansas City, and at the University of Missouri-Columbia and the University of Kansas, where we read excerpts from various chapters.

To the members of the Schultz and Spatz families we express our gratitude for their patience and support during the long time spent in preparation of this book.

Preface

"All the hopes we entertain in the midst of the confusion and dangers of the present are founded, directly or indirectly, positively or negatively, on the experiences of the past. Of these experiences, the broadest and deepest—so far as Western man is concerned—are indicated by the names of two cities: Jerusalem and Athens."

So begins Leo Strauss in his essay "Jerusalem and Athens," published in 1967. Recognition of the importance of both Greek and Hebraic cultures and their impact on each other goes back as far as the third century B.C.E. when the Hebrew Bible was translated into Greek for the Jewish diaspora. Later scholars and religious leaders such as Philo of Alexandria, the rabbis of the Talmud, and the founders of Christianity also knew about important aspects of Greek culture. In a discussion of whether a man should teach his sons the language or wisdom of the Greeks (b. Sotah 49b) it is said in the name of Rabbi Simeon ben Gamaliel that of the one thousand pupils in his father's house, five hundred studied the Torah and five hundred studied Greek wisdom. The tension between the Greek speaking and Aramaic speaking disciples in the early church (Acts 6:1) was eventually overcome in the merging of the Hebraic and Hellenistic strands of Christianity exemplified by the Church Fathers Origen and Jerome. In the Middle Ages, some scholars, like Moses Maimonides, championed the fusion of Greek thought, the product of reason, and Hebrew faith, the product of revelation, but others opposed it. Judah Halevi, for example, argued that Greek philosophy bore flowers but no fruit. Following in the footsteps of Halevi, the nineteenth century Jewish scholar Samuel David

xiii

Luzzato judged Hellenism, which he called Atticism, inferior to Judaism, which he called Abrahamism.

Writers as diverse as Matthew Arnold, Friedrich Nietzsche and Hermann Cohen have recognized that our own culture is a blending of the ideas handed down from Sinai and Olympus. All try to isolate and compare the essential characteristics. In his famous essay "Hebraism and Hellenism," Arnold distinguishes between the two, finding the main stream of Hellenism in the development of "clear intelligence" and of Judaism in the implementation of "firm obedience." Nietzsche focuses instead on the difference in emphasis between excellence and reverence. Comparing Plato and the prophets, Hermann Cohen views our modern culture as a unique synthesis of the scientific truth of the Greeks with the ethical truth of the Hebrews. To Leo Strauss, the essential ideals of both are summarized in the single word "wisdom."

Although all recognize the convergence of the distinct Hebrew and Greek currents in Western civilization, the two actually emerged from a common source: the polytheistic Mediterranean culture of the ancient Near East. They separated themselves from that background and from each other within a common chronological framework. The biblical culture of the Hebrews developed from Patriarchal origins some time in the first half of the second millennium B.C.E. through the monotheistic revolution associated with the Exodus (c. 1220 B.C.E.), culminating in the canonization of the Pentateuch and the early prophets in the time of Ezra and Nehemiah (445 B.C.E.). Greek civilization began essentially in the Mycenaean age (c. 1600-1100 B.C.E.), out of which the major myths developed, and then evolved its characteristic polis culture in the centuries between 800-322 B.C.E., culminating in the ideas of Plato, the near contemporary of Ezra, and Aristotle, who looked backward from the boundary marking the new Hellenistic age introduced by his pupil Alexander.

In the process of forming their distinct identities, Hebrew and Greek thinkers approached and answered a nest of fundamental questions common to both cultures: What is the world? What is God? What is the human being? What is the relation between them? How does the individual come to know this? What is expected of human beings? What religious, social, and political institutions help him or her to meet these expectations, and how do these institutions do that? What is humanity to expect in turn, in life, in history, and after death?

In this book we show how the responses to these questions within each culture are often interdependent; Hebrew monotheism provided the basic framework for examining fundamental questions whereas polytheism, which the Greeks retained, conditioned them toward pluralistic approaches to these issues. Thus there are clear differences. Yet there are similarities as well because the Greeks endeavored to find a unifying concept and to develop ethical standards based on it. The ideas transmitted through Greek myth and poetry demonstrate an increasing belief in Zeus as a just god who unified the anthropomorphic pantheon and established a moral order. Greek thinkers who demythologized or rebelled against the mythopoetic tradition attempted to discover a single principle in the natural realm to account for change and to educate their followers to live according to that principle. What is exciting about this work is that it reveals how the early movement of Hebrew culture to a monotheistic world view and the development of unifying views in Greek culture within a pluralistic framework affected so many intellectual and social aspects of each civilization.

Sinai & Olympus concentrates primarily on the myth and philosophy of archaic and classical Greece and the biblical-rabbinic legacy of classical Israel. Since rabbinic literature, philosophy, and mysticism continued far beyond the Hellenistic period, and sometimes reveal the impact of earlier Greek ideas, we occasionally discuss these later sources as well. We also introduce aspects of early Christianity that relate to our topics in Second Temple and talmudic Judaism. To treat the enormous question of the influence of Hellenistic Greek and Jewish culture on the development of Christianity is beyond the scope of our comparative study.

The book is divided into ten chapters focused on specific topics. Each chapter builds upon the preceding ones and the whole book reveals the interconnectedness of ideas and institutions in each society while at the same time relating one world view to the other topic by topic. To accomplish this, each chapter begins with a joint introduction which defines and limits the topic. We then present separate analyses, emphasizing the key concepts we are relating as we approach the topic from our own perspectives. We end each chapter with a joint comparision which both summarizes the similarities and differences and relates these specific conclusions to the other topics and the fundamental assumptions of each world view. Although we cannot cover the entire wealth of information and opinion among Judaic scholars, classicists, and comparativists on each of our topics, we provide notes and bibliography for those readers who are interested in further study of the details we introduce.

There have been many detailed scholarly examinations of the relations between the two cultures. Most, however, are interested in the Jewish-Greek encounter after Alexander's death. Some concentrate on specific personalities like Philo of Alexandria and Flavius Josephus, whose lives and works reflect the fusion of Greek and Hebrew values. Others have compared one facet of the two cultures: for example, thought processes, philosophy of religion, sacrifical rites, historiography. Many comparativists have analyzed differences in creation narratives or similarities between individual tales or rituals. Yet there have been very few comprehensive comparative studies of the ideas and institutions of the two cultures. In recent years, however, many exciting new studies of specific aspects of each civilization have been published. This specialized research has enabled us to present a fuller profile of each culture for the purposes of our comparison of topics intrinsic to both.

As we trace the different paths leading from Sinai and Olympus, we keep in mind the words of Matthew Arnold: "The final aim of both Hellenism and Hebraism, as of all great spiritual disciplines, is no doubt the same: man's perfection or salvation."

Comparative Chronology: Events and People

There is considerable debate about the dating of the events and people we discuss. For brevity and comparison, we have used a simple, single timeline and have marked few specific dates. There is general agreement, however, that the formative period for the transformation of Hebrew saga into a connected prose narrative began in the United Monarchy (1020-922 B.C.E.). The formative period for the transformation of Greek saga into a connected verse epic is generally agreed to have begun around the same time, after the destruction of Mycenaean Greece.

We have remained within the wide general consensus of scholarship, consulting primarily the chronologies in John Boardman, Jasper Griffin, and Oswyn Murray, editors, *The Oxford History of Greece and the Hellenistic World* (Oxford: Oxford University Press, 1991), pp. 475-507; Robert M. Seltzer, *Jewish People, Jewish Thought: The Jewish Experience in History* (New York: Collier Macmillan, 1980), pp. 2-5, 166-167; and Hershel Shanks, editor, *Christianity and Rabbinic Judaism: A Parallel History of their Origins and Early Development* (Washington, D.C.: Biblical Archaeology Society, 1992), pp. x-xi.

OLYMPUS CHRONOLOGY

Dates	Major Events	Important People
2200 - 1700 **B.C.E.**	3000 - 2000 Early Minoan, Cycladic, Helladic	
1600	2000 -1600 Middle Minoan, Cycladic, Helladic; Mycenaeans arrive in mainland Greece	
— 1500 —		anonymous bards who create, develop, and transmit oral tradition about deities, heroes, and heroines
1400 **1300**	1600 - 1100 Late Minoan, Cycladic, Helladic; also Mycenaean; probable origins of Greek heroic myths, Linear B	
1200	1200 - 1100 destruction of Mycenaean sites	
1100	1184 traditional date of Trojan War	
— 1000 —	1100 - 1000 Dorian Invasion; migration from mainland Greece to Aegean Islands and coast of Asia Minor; transformation of saga into epic begins	
900		continued

SINAI CHRONOLOGY

Dates	Major Events	Important People
2200 - 1700 B.C.E.	2200 - 1400 probable origins of patriarchal traditions	Abraham, Isaac, Jacob
1600	1678 - 1570 Hyksos in Egypt; possible descent of Hebrew clans	Joseph
1500		
	1570 - 1304 Egyptian New Kingdom	
1400		
1300		
	1275 - 1220 enslavement; Exodus	Moses, Aaron, Rameses II Pharaoh
1200	1250 - 1200 conquests in Canaan; tribal alliance; primitive democracy	Judges
1100	1100 - 1020 rise of Philistines	Samson to Samuel
1000	1020 - 922 United Monarchy; connecting prose narrative begins	Saul, David, Nathan, Solomon
	922 split into Northern Kingdom, Israel, and Southern Kingdom, Judah; unstable kingship in Israel; Davidic dynasty in Judah	Jeroboam, Rehoboam
900		

OLYMPUS CHRONOLOGY

Dates	Major Events	Important People
900		
800	800 Greek trading post at Al Mina in Syria 776 first Olympic Games colonization of W. Mediterranean begins	
750	750 - 700 formation and spread of Greek alphabet 725 stone temple at Sparta; colonization of n. Greece and Hellespont begins	Homer; Hesiod; beginning of epic cycle
700		
650	675 Lycurgan reforms at Sparta; 670 Zaleucus lawgiver at western Locris settlements on Black Sea begin; lyric poetry begins 621 Draco's Code in Athens	Archilochus; Tyrtaeus Homeric Hymn to Demeter; Mimnermus; Alcman
600	594 Solon's reforms in Athens 585 Thales predicts eclipse; philosophy begins in Miletus 582 Pythian Games; 581 Isthmian Games; beginning of cycles of panHellenic games; 580 first major temple of Athena at Athens	Solon; Thales; Anaximander
550		

SINAI CHRONOLOGY

Dates	Major Events	Important People
900		
	875 - 842 Omri dynasty in Israel	Elijah; Elisha; Ahab; Jezebel
800		
	785 - 745 Jeroboam II in Israel	Amos, Hosea
750	722 Assyria conquers Israel; Israelites deported	
	715-657 Hezekiah king of Judah; Assyrian siege of Jerusalem	Isaiah; Micah
700		
650		
	640 - 609 Josiah King of Judah; Book of Deuteronomy found; religious reform.	Jeremiah, Ezekiel
600		
	587 - 586 Babylonian conquest; destruction of First Temple; Babylonian exile	
550		

OLYMPUS CHRONOLOGY

Dates	Major Events	Important People
550 — **500** —	546 - 510 Pisistratids in Athens 545 Persians capture Sardis 534 first tragedy at City Dionysia in Athens 509 reforms of Clisthenes 499 Ionian Revolt against Persia 490 - 479 Persian Wars 487 first Old Comedy 478 Delian League 461 murder of Ephialtes 461-429 Pericles leads Athens	Xenophanes of Colophon; Croesus of Lydia; Cyrus the Great of Persia; Pythagoras; Theognis of Megara; Thespis; Pherycedes of Scyrus Alcmaeon; Hecataeus; Heraclitus Pindar; Aeschylus; Parmenides
450 **400** **350** **300**	454 Delian League treasury moved to Athens 447 Parthenon begun 431 - 404 Peloponnesian Wars history and rhetoric develop 404 Thirty Tyrants in Athens 403 Fall of Thirty; restoration of democracy in Athens 402 recodification of Athenian law code complete 399 death of Socrates 387 Plato founds Academy 338 Greeks defeated by Macedon; end of Greek independence 336-323 Alexander conquers East; Hellenization begins 335 Aristotle founds Lyceum	*dramatists* Sophocles; Euripides; Aristophanes; *historians* Herodotus; Hellanicus; Thucydides; *philosophers and rhetoricians* Protagoras; Gorgias; Anaxagoras; Empedocles; Democritus; Socrates; Antiphon the Sophist; Critias; Hippocrates; *artists* Phidias; Polygnotus Plato ; Xenophon Aristotle; Demosthenes; Isocrates

SINAI CHRONOLOGY

Dates	Major Events	Important People
550		Second Isaiah
	539 Persia captures Babylon; Judea under Persian control	
	538 Cyrus allows exiles to return	Zerubavel, Joshua, the High Priest
500	515 Second Temple completed	Haggai; Zechariah
450	450 - 400 B.C.E. new wave of returnees; canonization of Pentateuch; prophecy goes underground	
		Ezra and Nehemiah
400		Men of the Great Assembly
350	333 B.C.E. Alexander conquers Persia; Hellenization of Judea begins	
300	323-198 Judea under Ptolemies; Hebrew Bible translated into Greek	

OLYMPUS CHRONOLOGY

Dates	Major Events	Important People
300 **200**	Epicureanism begins; Stoicism begins; Museum created at Alexandria;Old Testament translated into Greek	Epicurus; Zeno the Stoic; Euhemerus; Euclid;Duris; Aristarchus of Samos Cleanthes the Stoic; Archimedes
100	167 Rome defeats Macedon, Macedon becomes Roman province Hellenized eastern culture spreads west as Rome conquers east	Polybius
	63 Pompey reorganizes east	Lucretius, Cicero
Common Era **B.C.E - 0 - C.E.** Begins	44 Death of Julius Caesar 31 Battle of Actium ends Roman Republic 31 B.C.E.- 14 C.E. Octavian rules Rome as Caesar Augustus, princeps	Virgil; Horace
	31 B.C.E. - 69 C.E. - Julio- Claudians	Philo; Seneca
100	69 - 96 Flavians 66 - 73 Jewish Revolt 70 - destruction of Second Temple 55 - 100 New Testament in Greek	Pliny the Elder; Josephus
200 **300**	96 - 192 Antonines 132 - 135 Bar Kokkbah revolt under Hadrian Jewish city of Jerusalem destroyed	Tacitus; Epictetus; Plutarch; Pliny the Younger; Lucian; Claudius Ptolemy; Pausanias; Aelius Aristides; Marcus Aurelius, Galen; Apuleius
400 - 600 **C.E.**	312 Constantine declares Christianity official religion of Roman Empire 527-565 Digest of Roman Law	Justinian

SINAI CHRONOLOGY

Dates	Major Events	Important People
300		Ecclesiastes
200	198 - 165 Judea under Seleucids	Joshua Ben Sira
	169 - 164 Maccabean Revolt; apocalyptic literature begins	Mattathias; Judah the Maccabee and brothers (the Hasmoneans)
100	140 - Judea independent state under high priest	
	63 Pompey intervenes in Judea	
	37 - 4 Herod the Great client king under Rome; culmination of Second Temple period	
Common Era B.C.E - **0** - C.E. Begins	0 - COMMON ERA BEGINS 6 - Judea becomes Roman province	Jesus; Paul; Philo of Alexandria (15 B.C.E. - 50 C.E. Hillel the Elder; Shammai
	66 - 70 First Jewish Revolt	
	70 Second Temple destroyed; Academy at Javneh founded; Rabbinic Judaism begins; Tannaim	Flavius Josephus; Rabban Johanan ben Zakkai
100	90 final cannonization at Javneh	Rabban Gamaliel
	135 Bar Kokkbah Revolt	Rabbi Akiba
200	200-300 *Amoraim*; completion of Mishnah	Rabbi Judah the Prince; Rav and Samuel
300		
400 - 600 C.E.	400 Jerusalem Talmud	
	500-600 Babylonian Talmud	

Chapter 1

The Nature of the Literary Sources

Introduction: From the Oral to the Written Word

Sinai and Olympus are arguably the two most famous mountains in the West. From their peaks have issued our common definitions of divine and human, the ideals which regulate society, the forms of our institutions, and the hopes for reunion with the divinity and the renewal of humanity. Archaeological discoveries, as well as the new disciplines of comparative anthropology, sociology, and religion, have greatly increased our understanding of the two civilizations which raised their eyes to these heights. This comparison, however, will be based primarily on their own words, the literature that the early Hebrews and Greeks produced as they evolved simultaneously out of a common background. For the Bible and the Greek corpus first spoke loudest to their respective communities when there were no mute stones, then later impressed each other, when the cultures met in the Hellenistic world, and even now communicate with us across time and space.

The two bodies of literature had similar beginnings in an oral culture. Long before the appearance of the written word, humans sought to define their place in the universe, record their past, and transmit their values to future generations. The skilled communicators of the ancient world, the poets, bards, or storytellers, developed techniques of spontaneous oral composition rather than devices associated with writing or the recitation of a fixed text. To facilitate their improvisations, they used verse or balanced prose stichs and built up and passed on a repertoire of stock phrases, syntactical constructions, and dramatic situations where nouns and verbs could be changed to meet their immediate needs. In addition, they used frequent repetitions of the same lines and summations of previously related incidents. Such devices were not only vital to the bards, they were also essential to the listeners, who could not refer back to a written text to fill in what they missed. To fix their words in the listeners' minds, the bards limited themselves to short pieces which matched their audience's attention span (as well as their own vocal stamina), and they infused their compositions with emotional impact. Regular rhythms and balanced phrases are pleasurable as well as memorable. Narrative myth and saga, with concrete situations and characters from life, impressed the heart as well as the mind.

By the introduction of writing, some of these short pieces were woven together into longer narratives which were eventually fixed in a text. Nevertheless they were still delivered orally to the community. Thus, the performer continued to adhere to the constraints of oral presentation and the same techniques of improvisation found their way into literature. It was a long time before the oral communicator of traditions was replaced by a writer of abstract ideas and even then the author frequently resorted to the techniques of poetry. The development from storyteller to thinker corresponded to the change in audience from listeners to readers. But for many centuries serious thought about religion, ethics, history, science, and philosophy was conveyed through the genres of prayer, song, epic, legend, and lyric poetry.

Despite the continuation of oral performance and the techniques of oral composition, the earliest materials were gradually refined and adapted to the changing thought patterns of the developing civilization and the growing number of writers and readers. In Greek literature, we can trace the attempt to synthesize and systematize the large body of stories which frequently contradicted one another. This very process engendered a reinterpretation of the old myths as well as criticism of myth itself as a medium for expressing truth. By the end of the fifth century, myth and poetry were supplemented by prose, and the newer genres of history and philosophy, as the vehicle for serious thought. In Israel, the monotheistic revolution compelled the systematization of all the ancient traditions and their adjustment to the new religious framework, with interpretation and reinterpretation continuing within this structure. Although the ancient narrative forms were kept, they were continuously filled with new content. Hebrew genres which supplemented the narrative never became as abstract as Greek philosophy and science.

On both Sinai and Olympus, this refinement led to two related phenomena: first, to methods of using older stories in new ways to validate historical change or abstract thinking, and second, to the development of a canon, unified in part by intertextual interpretation. But the motivation for a canon and the connection of old with new were very different in the two civilizations because the Hebrews and Greeks evolved different attitudes toward their literature, its communicators, and the means of dissemination.

Sinai: Unity and Prose

Israelite religion was born into a high cultural environment, into the mellowed civilizations of the Near East that had already developed theistic religions. A universalistic strain was present in the religions of Babylonia, Egypt and Canaan. Their gods were world creators and rulers, founders of culture and society, guardians of justice and morality. Israel inherited these concepts but expanded them in the framework of its unique ideas about monotheism. According to Yehezkel Kaufmann, the essence of Israelite monotheism is the concept "of a god who is the source of all being, not subject to a cosmic order, and not emergent from a pre-existent realm; a god free of the limitations of magic and mythology."[1] The concretization of this idea in every aspect of the life and literature of ancient Israel constituted the monotheistic revolution which in the words of Scripture made the Hebrews "a people dwelling apart, not reckoned among the nations" (Num. 23:9).

When did this momentous shift in spiritual consciousness occur? The Bible speaks of individuals who were monotheists beginning with Adam and continuing through the generations of Abraham and his descendants. But according to Kaufmann it was during the Exodus ca. 1280-1220 B.C.E. that Israel became a monotheistic people and it was during the stewardship of Moses that the prime religious phenomena associated with monotheism made their appearance. These phenomena, divine revelation (in which God makes His name and His commandments known to the people), apostolic prophecy and the battle against idolatry became the hallmarks of the religion of Israel and the central threads of the Hebrew Bible.

The ancient Hebrew writers who composed the books of the Bible, though working under the impact of the monotheistic revolution, continued to be surrounded by a vast and alluring sea of paganism. They understood the impossibility of sealing off their island of faith from polytheistic influences and the hopelessness of winning assent to an unprecedented message totally divorced from their readers' pagan past. So with consummate pedagogic and artistic skill they reworked elements of the pre-monotheistic oral tradition of the Hebrews and wove them into the tapestry depicting the story of God and humanity. This oral tradition was a synthesis compounded of religious and cultural elements from Babylonia, Egypt, Asia Minor and Canaan. It not only existed before the emergence of biblical literature but, though subject to careful screening to purify it of polytheistic dross, it continued throughout the biblical period and in the post-biblical era resurfaced in the apocryphal-pseudepigraphic literature and in rabbinic legend and folklore. In every culture a vigorous literature stands in direct relation to life and is constantly revitalized by the subterranean springs of popular oral tradition.

Separate Elements of the Oral Tradition

Though the pre-biblical history of ancient Israel is shrouded in mist, scholars have been able to reconstruct the form and content of the early Hebrew oral tradition from remnants in the Bible itself and from the corpus of ancient Near Eastern literature recovered by archaeological excavation.

Sayings— The simplest form of oral tradition is the word (*davar*) which in Hebrew possesses a wider sense that includes a short command, a divine threat or promise or even an account of events that have already taken place. The revelation of God to Moses was set out in ten *devarim*. The word of God, i.e., the single brief sentence comes to the prophet and he proclaims it. Chapter 22 of the Book of Genesis which describes the binding of Isaac begins: "After these *devarim*," i.e., after the events previously reported by the narrator, "God proved Abraham." As the form of everyday speech, the word can have as many shapes as there are ways of speaking.

The *mashal*, proverb is also found in a very simple form in the oral tradition. The range of the proverb is as comprehensive as life itself. In a very short sentence a universal experience is expressed and the shorter the form the greater the impact particularly when it is further enhanced by alliteration, by traces of rhyme, by employment of different forms of the same root or of similarly sounding words. The effect is also heightened by emphasizing an absolute or relative comparison such as: "As the mother, so her daughter" (Ezek. 16:44) or "As a living dog he is better than a dead lion" (Eccles. 9:4). An epigrammatic proverb such as "A good name (*shem tov*) is better than good ointment (*shemen tov* Eccles. 7:1) is not only a play on words but contains wisdom that is not to be dissociated from the words.

Closely related to the epigrammatic proverb is the riddle whose solution was as serious a business as the interpretation of dreams and visions (See Judg. 14:11-19). The riddle's punch came from its interrogative form combined with assertion and admonition. The numerical saying retains a form of the riddle that must have been very popular in the oral tradition of the pre-Israelite Hebrews for it brings together amazing or detestable things in such a way as to make it easy to remember or enumerate them as in Prov. 6:16-19: "There are six things that the Lord hates, seven that are an abomination to him" (cf. Prov. 30:15 ff.).

The experiences of the community were also summed up in sayings such as the lament of the people during the destruction of the First Temple and the exile to Babylonia: "The fathers have eaten sour grapes, And children's teeth are set on edge" (Jer. 31:29-30; Ezek. 18:24). The sayings could also be shaped into a parable or allegory. David's adultery with Bathsheba is interwoven into the illustration of the rich man with many sheep who stole the single lamb of the poor man in Nathan's parable (2 Sam. 12:1 ff.). The fable of Jotham caricatures the absurd pretensions to honor of something quite useless (i.e., the thorn bush that would rule over the trees, Judg. 9:7 ff.); its contempt for kingship marks it as belonging to a very early age. Equally old are the folk sayings crystallizing a truth garnered from the experiences of the individual and the community.[2] The human life cycle prompted many of these sayings preserved in the biblical text (marriage, Gen. 2:23; 24:60; children, Ps. 127:3; death, Job 1:21).

The Song— In ancient Israel, the song accompanied by instrumental music and often associated with dancing was a dramatically effective vehicle of oral tradition. From its very beginning this oral tradition of song shared with its contemporaries of the Near East highly developed artistic forms. The most common is parallelism, the hallmark of Hebrew poetry but also of the Canaanite tablets of Ras Shamra. Parallelism was enhanced by rhythm based on an elusive system of stressed syllables which follow the thought structure of the poetic line.

In the pre-monotheistic oral tradition no differentiation was made in form or content between secular and religious songs. The wedding song told not only of the union of man and woman but also of the marriage of the gods (the *hieros gamos*) the causes of fertility and life. Similarly, the dirge lamented not only the demise of mortals but also of the gods because they too must descend to the netherworld though they do not remain there. With the monotheistic revolution love songs and dirges became entirely secular due to the antagonism to the fertility cult and the cult of the dead.

The differentiation of the secular and religious songs in the biblical texts are the results of a long process of theological purification. Religious songs bearing the earmarks of this process but also the remnants of the pre-biblical tradition are the invocation of Ps. 29:1, the sacred formula of Ps. 91:1 and the question of Exod. 15:11. They suggest by their form an early period when the people were instructed orally as to the name by which they might call on the Lord and what they might expect of Him. Remnants of secular songs are the song of the well (Num. 21:17 ff.) in which prayer or pre-monotheistic incantation persuaded the water to rise, war songs and victory songs (Gen. 4:23 f; Isa. 37:22-29; 47:1 f. 1 Sam. 18:7); and wedding songs including the exhibition dance of the bride and bridegroom's praise of his beloved (Song of Songs 6:4 ff.; 6:13 ff.).

The Saga— An important oral source of biblical narrative was the saga of pre-biblical Israel. Sagas were connected with localities or other natural phenomena echoed in the Bible's description of the cities of Sodom and Gomorrah and their destruction. Sagas also developed around an individual or a human group as in the story of Tamar and Judah in Genesis 38.

The significance of the tribal or leader sagas is to be found in the belief of the ancients that all human communities have an ancestor or ancestress whose life and actions are decisive for the destiny of their descendants. As the Hebrew aphorist Immanuel of Rome (thirteenth/fourteenth century) expressed it, "*maaseh avot siman l'banim*, all that happened to the fathers is symbolic for their children." This perspective is identified by the term "typology" which sees in persons events or places a prototype, a foreshadowing of historical persons, events or places that follow it in time. Northrop Frye uses the term "antitypes" to define the present or future offspring of the prototypes which validate the "assumption that there is some meaning and point to history."[3]

The ancients believed that the ancestors did not merely belong to the past but lived on, in, with and beyond their descendants. An echo of this view is to be heard in Moses' concluding exhortation to Israel: "I make this covenant with its sanctions not with you alone, but both with those who are standing here with us this day before the Lord our God and with those who are not with us here this day" (Deut. 29:13). Thus there are always individual protagonists at the center of the tribal and national sagas that developed among the Hebrews. The degree for which the individual stands for the community varies. In the earlier stages of the oral tradition's development of the saga, it is quite apparent that the individual is only a symbol for tribes and peoples. The sketchiness of the saga of Keturah and her sons in Gen. 25:1-6 is very different from the more complex characterization and plot development in the Hagar stories of Gen. 6:4-14 and Gen. 21:8-21. In the later stages of the development of the oral tradition as the historical circumstances and conditions surrounding the origins of the tribe or nation receded into the distant past, interest in the tribal and national history declined while interest in the individual protagonists representing this history increased. The human traits and characteristics of these protagonists were now filled out and firmly fixed in the popular mind. As the protagonists ceased to be merely symbols for the nation or tribe but complex characters in their own right the door was open for them to become universal types and for the saga conditioned by historical actuality to become a supra-historical drama. This is indeed what happened to the Hebrew Bible and its characters after the monotheistic revolution. Thus, the patriarchs Abraham, Isaac and Jacob and the heroes Joseph, Moses and David became typological figures exemplifying moral traits and religious ideals.[4]

Unification and the Connected Prose Narrative

The narrative is the most sacred portion of biblical literature into which hallowed collections of *devarim* (words) such as the Ten Commandments and many songs, sayings, proverbs, parables and sagas have been incorporated. The purpose of the narrative is to relate the story of the interaction of God and humanity through successive generations. The formative era of Hebrew narrative was the First Commonwealth period ca. 1020-586 B.C.E. when the great sequence of works from Genesis to Kings was initially formulated. It is no coincidence that these books of the Bible are primarily prose and not epic poetry. In this case the medium is the message. The choice of a historicized prose narrative into which the building blocks of the oral tradition have been embedded proclaims a conscious opposition to the pluralistic poetic forms of paganism and emphasizes history rather than myth as the arena for the human-divine encounter.

The biographical typologies of the Hebrew Bible played an important role in converting the sagas into a continuous whole narrative. They were used to establish historical sequences and to structure thematic patterns. Thus, after the flood it is Noah who stands for the whole human race as Adam had done in the biblical creation saga. This connection is made by a genealogical link that places Noah in the tenth generation after Adam and by linguistic allusions to the fact that Noah was to repair the defects in nature caused by the divine curse directed at Adam (Gen. 5:29 and Gen. 3:17).

The puzzling repetitions of scenarios and narrative forms in the Bible begin to make sense when underneath them we see typology as a needle stitching together the separate and independent sagas. Type scenes were used in which the same basic situation is duplicated in story after story but with subtle shifts and transformations. There were certain fixed episodes which the storyteller was expected to include in his narrative and which he must present according to a prescribed order. The type-scenes used by the biblical narrator dealt with milestones in the lives of the heroes. Typical biblical type-scenes are the birth of the hero to a barren mother, the meeting with his future wife at a well, the revelation in the field, the initiatory trial, danger in the wilderness and the discovery of water or some other source of provision, and the testament of the dying hero. In the written text of Scripture this phenomenon appears as the somewhat distorted duplication of the same story. In reality the variations in the parallel story are not random scrambling but the conscious use of subtle changes to indicate changes in character, plot development and destiny.[5]

What made the biblical adaptation of the saga so interesting was that despite the lack of narrative detail and explicit judgment of character, the use of conversation and direct speech involved the listener in the recitation. In addition the biblical author's method of building up a narrative out of small self contained scenes is also rooted in the oral tradition's objective of maintaining the listener's interest. The patriarchal stories are a good example of this technique. Originally they may have been independent sagas but for artistic purposes they were linked. In an oral presentation or dramatization this linkage of independent sagas made possible a change of scene and actors, increased suspense by marking time, and permitted the presentation of contemporary events in different places without making the narration too retrospective. For the biblical author the joining of sagas had a religious as well as an artistic purpose—to show the spiritual development of the individual and the working out of the divine plan. It is the interaction of this plan and human free will through the twists and turns of history's corridors that is the central theme of the great sequence of works from Genesis through Kings.

As the linear history developed typologies became a device for interpreting the unfolding events. They were used, for example, to

spiritually legitimate the leaders of a later generation by showing
the links in life and in divine pronouncement to their earlier
forerunners. Abraham as a foreshadowing of David (i.e., Gen.
17:6 where the divine promise is made to Abraham that kings will issue
from him) and Joshua, Elijah and Ezekiel as reflections of Moses
(e.g., as Moses envisages the desert tabernacle as a heavenly
pattern, Exod. 25:9,40; 26:30; 27:8, so does Ezekiel as a new Moses
envisage the blueprint of a new Temple, Ezek. 40-47). Similarly
geographical locations separated in time and in space were
typologically linked both to legitimate them as sacred centers and
to provide historical allusions that wove disparate events and places
into the tapestry of sacred history. Thus, in defiance of historical
and geographical reality 2 Chron. 3:1 asserts that Solomon built the
Temple of the Lord in Jerusalem on Mount Moriah, the site of
Abraham's great test of faith in the near-sacrifice of his son Isaac
(Gen. 22:2, 14).[6]

This process of unification and reinterpretation is also evident in
ancient Israelite typological thinking in which cosmic, mythic
patterns from Israel's pre-history are interpreted typologically in
terms of later Hebrew history. Thus, the myths of divine combat
and victory prominent in the creation dramas of the Near East (see
ch. 2) that surface in Gen. 1 as the restive forces of chaos are
identified with the historical enemies of Israel in a later age (cf.
Ezek. 29: 1-12). But there is a counter movement to the typological
historicization of myth in the Hebrew Bible. It is the recognition
that underneath specific and unique historical events there are
recurrent divine patterns that place these events in a meta-historical
context. Thus the creation of the world, the exodus from Egypt, the
Sinaitic Revelation, the conquest of the Promised Land, the
Davidic and Solomonic empires, the destruction of the First and
Second Temples and the exiles are all to be seen as part of the
archetypes of Creation, Revelation and Redemption.[7]

If the classical prose narrative with its laconic style is dominant
from Genesis through Kings, poetry is the dominant form of the
prophetic books, Job and Psalms. Could it be that once the base of
monotheism had been secured in the Pentateuch and the early
prophets, the Hebrew literary imagination could be released without
fear of pagan dilution? Or perhaps, very simply, poetry is the
natural form for prophecy and prayer. After the destruction of the
First Temple in 586 B.C.E. instead of one dominant form, as in the
earlier period, there is a proliferation of forms from the
autobiographical writing of history in Ezra and Nehemiah to the
apocalyptic style of Daniel and the broad comedy contained in

Esther. Yet despite this heterogeneity there is unity in content and form created by developing and extending the existing typologies and by attributing increasing sacredness to the texts.

Canonization and the Continuing Oral Tradition

The monotheistic revolution gave rise in the course of time to the biblical canon. The process began with the purification of the oral tradition and the folk literature of ancient Israel in which Near Eastern mythological motifs predominated. Near Eastern mythology knew of a garden of the gods situated on a mountain containing stones of fire and magical trees bearing gold and precious stones. The biblical author eliminated from his Garden of Eden all aspects of magic. The fruit bearing trees of the biblical garden are natural, not magical.[8]

In content the refining process established the supra-mundane nature of God who is supreme, eliminated pagan mythology whose remnants in the Bible were taken only as similes and metaphors, replaced demonology and magic with a moral and natural order in the universe, and depicted the relationship of humanity and God in terms of the working out of divine purposes in history. In form, a sign of the unifying process, intrinsic to all the biblical texts is the widespread use of allusions. The numerous authoritative national traditions, fixed in particular verbal formulations to which later writers refer by incorporating them, elaborating on them, debating them or parodying them all point to a creative, consolidating and reinterpretive effort.

The bondage in Egypt and the exodus are reflected in almost every book of the Bible, in law codes, in historical narrative and in poetry. In addition, in the biblical texts there are recurrent symbols which taken together form large interpretive patterns, a unified way of conceiving the world and individual experience. The recurring polarities of chaos and order, heaven and earth, water and dry land describe God's creative power. The symbols of Promised Land and wilderness, homeland and exile mark the exodus. In the realm of history, Israel and the nations, and in the realm of time, the Sabbath and the six days of labor, mirror a persistent vision of reality that led to canonization.[9]

Theological expurgation, interpretation and literary refinement led to the hallowing of portions of the oral tradition and the literature which embodied it. The sanctification led to canonization. It was not the stamp of canonization that conferred holiness on a book but the reverse. The literature had already become hallowed and canonization made final a long standing situation. To be sure, admission to the canon reinforced, intensified and perpetuated the reverence, piety and authority attributed to a book. Not everything that was considered hallowed or revealed was canonized but clearly sanctity was an indispensable ingredient for admission. Since the process of canonization is shrouded in obscurity we can only speculate as to why certain works were included and others excluded. The element of chance in the preservation of a work cannot be excluded. The literary beauty of a work, its use by scribal and priestly schools or by Temple singers contributed to sanctification and canonization. So did national sentiment and pride evoked by the basic documents of the national religion employed in the cult.

The process of canonization is already mentioned in the Pentateuch (e.g., Exod. 24:4) and continued throughout the First Temple period and the Second Temple period until about the half of the first century C.E. The earliest connected pieces (J,E,P) were probably brought together to form the Tetrateuch by the time of the destruction of the Northern Kingdom of Israel in 722 B.C.E. The discovery of the "Book of the Torah" in 621 B.C.E. under King Josiah marks another important stage in the process of canonization because the book probably included Deuteronomy and the Former Prophets. After the Babylonian exile, the Pentateuch was promulgated as the binding law for the returned exiles by Ezra and Nehemiah (ca. 444 or 400 B.C.E.). Ezra and his priestly colleagues are generally credited with the final editing and arrangement of most of the Prophets and Writings regarded as sacred Scripture. After the destruction of the Second Temple, the rabbis made the last decisions about the books not yet included in the canon.[10]

The canon had porous boundaries. Its sanctification did not preclude reinterpretation or challenge of older Hebrew ideas as we have already seen. It only established the outside limits of revelation and the overarching principles of monotheism and morality. Within these boundaries there was room for variety. Every reader of the Hebrew Bible recognizes contradictory opinions of the monarchy in Judges through 2 Kings. A comparison of the creation accounts of Gen. 1-3, Prov. 8 where Wisdom personified is the first creation of God and Job 38-40 where the creation of humanity is ignored and God asks Job if he can do any better, illustrates the process. Deutero-Isaiah's spiritual critique (e.g., Isa. 40:28) of the anthropomorphic approach to creation in Gen. 1 that speaks of the human resemblance to the divine and the need for the deity to rest on the seventh day is another example of the ongoing interpretation and reinterpretation. So is Job's parody (Job 7:17-18) of Ps. 8:5-7 in which the psalmist's exaltation of the human being to near divine status is bitterly questioned.[11]

The interpretive activity became broader and deeper in the centuries after Ezra and was designated by the rabbis as the oral tradition that continued to flourish side by side with the canonical Scripture. In order to distinguish between the two, the rabbis ordained that oral material should not be written down. Their purpose was twofold: With respect to the rapidly developing oral legal tradition their intention was to keep the law fluid for once it was written down it became sacred and unchangeable. With respect to non-legal material that included legend, history, theology, myth and folklore, they were well aware that elements of the pre-monotheistic oral tradition, removed from biblical literature had resurfaced in this post-biblical lore and though neutralized and reinterpreted still could pose a danger to the works of Scripture. Thus, while Rabbi Akiba and his colleagues were interpreting the Song of Songs allegorically as dialogue between God and Israel, the carousing young men of the time, possibly in keeping with a very old folk tradition, were singing its love ditties in the cabarets and banquet halls treating it "as a kind of secular song."[12]   Finally, Rabbi Akiba set off the canonical books of the Bible from the apocryphal-pseudepigraphic literature by forbidding the reading of the latter.[13]

Notes

1. Yehezkel Kaufmann, *The Religion of Israel* trans. Moshe Greenberg (Chicago: University of Chicago Press, 1960), p. 29.

2. Other examples are the parable of King Jehoash of Israel in 2 Kings 14: 9-10 and Isaiah's Song of the Vineyard, Isa. 5: 1-7.

3. Northrop Frye, *The Great Code: The Bible and Literature* (New York: Harcourt Brace Jovanovich, 1982), pp. 81-82.

4. For an extended treatment of the pre-biblical narrative and other forms of the early oral tradition see Otto Eissfeldt, *The Old Testament: An Introduction*, rev. ed. trans. P. R. Ackroyd (New York: Harper and Row, 1965), pp. 9-86 and Johannes Hempel, "The Forms of Oral Tradition" and "The Contents of the Literature" in *Record and Revelation* ed. H. W. Robinson (Oxford: The Clarendon Press, 1938), pp. 28-73.

5. Robert Alter, *The Art of Biblical Narrative* (New York: Basic Books, 1981), p. 50 ff. On the intricate structure and highly refined art of repetition in the biblical narrative see the illuminating discussion in Meir Sternberg, *The Poetics of Biblical Narrative: Ideological Literature and the Drama of Reading* (Bloomington: Indiana University Press, 1987), pp. 365-436.

6. Michael Fishbane, *Biblical Interpretation in Ancient Israel* (Oxford and New York: Oxford University Press, 1988), pp. 368-379.

7. Ibid. 356-57.

8. Umberto Cassuto, *From Adam to Noah* (Jerusalem: The Magnes Press, 1953), pp. 48-53.

9. Robert Alter, "Introduction to the Old Testament" in *The Literary Guide to the Bible* ed. Robert Alter and Frank Kermod, (Cambridge, Mass.: Harvard University Press, 1987), pp. 13, 31.

10. *M. Yadaim*, 3:5; *Tosefta Yadaim* 2:14; *M. Eduyot* 5:3; *B. Megillah*, 7a. For the varying views of scholars on the biblical canon see Nahum M. Sarna, "Bible Canon," *Encyclopedia Judaica* 4:816-32; Harry M. Orlinsky, *Essays in Biblical Culture and Bible Translation* (New York: Ktav Publishing House, 1974), pp. 257-85; Sid Z. Leiman, *The Canonization of Hebrew Scripture: The Talmudic and Midrashic Evidence* (Hamden, Conn.: The Connecticut Academy of Arts and Sciences, Archon Books, 1976), pp. 16 - 35.

11. Fishbane, *Biblical Interpretation in Ancient Israel*, pp. 285, 411.

12. *Tosefta Sanhedrin* 12:10. On the relationship of the oral to the written law see Moshe David Herr, "Oral Law" *Encyclopedia Judaica* 12: 1442; Herman L. Strack, *Introduction to the Talmud and Midrash* (New York and Philadelphia: Jewish Publication Society of America, 1959); For an example of the resurfacing of pre-monotheistic ideas in the *aggadah* see the next chapter.

13. *M. Sanhedrin*, 10:1.

Olympus: Poetry and Plurality

Beginnings of the Oral Tradition

The earliest Greek languages and literature reveal a connection to the same high civilization of the Ancient Near East out of which the Hebrew Bible emerged. Moreover, the encounters which stimulated the unique development of the Greeks occurred within the same time frame as the Hebrews' reaction to their exodus from Egypt. Linguists and archaeologists concur that the proto-Greeks were Indo-Europeans from west of the Black Sea who migrated south into Anatolia before crossing the Aegean to the mainland.[1] Although they brought Indo-European speech and thought patterns, non-Greek elements in the language and similarities between early sites in Greece and Asia Minor suggest contact with the Eastern Mediterranean cultures prior to the Minoan-Mycenean period. After the Trojan War and the destruction of Mycenaean civilization (c. 1100 B.C.E.) Greek mainlanders fled east and established refugee communities on the Aegean islands and the coast of Asia Minor.[2] There the Greeks were reintroduced to the peoples, stories, gods, and institutions of the Ancient Near East. These different cultures influenced them as they developed new economic, social, political, and religious ideas to adapt to the new surroundings and the forced separation from the homeland. Tradition records that the anonymous author of the *Iliad* and *Odyssey*, later named as Homer, came from one or another such community.

In the period known as the Dark Ages (c. 1100-700), the new aspects of the culture made their way back to the Greek mainland. Hesiod's works, composed in Boeotia in the eighth century, show affinities with ancient Near Eastern texts.[3] *Theogony*, for example, describes battles between several generations of gods and the castration of father by son similar to those found in the Babylonian creation epic *Enuma Elish* and the Hurrian *Epic of Kumarbi* respectively. *Works and Days* resembles many collections of Wisdom Literature found in the Ancient Mediterranean area; couched as advice from an elder brother, it transmitted the proverbial and technical knowledge necessary for success in life. Like the Hebrew monotheists, however, Hesiod used familiar settings and story patterns, blending the eastern with the old and new western traditions, and adapting both to the Greek culture that was evolving in his own day.

The traditional material had first been framed in the same short oral forms, vestiges of which appear in the Hebrew Bible. From the earliest times, group activities such as daily labors and special ceremonies were organized and unified by group singing. Thus work songs, prayers, hymns of praise of gods and men, funeral dirges, victory celebrations, and epithalamia must have circulated in oral form for centuries. These popular types find their highest expression in the developed choral and monodic lyric of the poets of the seventh through fifth centuries. The age-old wisdom, too, must have been passed down in oral form through brief memorable sayings. Concise statements like the phrases inscribed on the temple of Apollo at Delphi (e.g., "Know thyself;" "Nothing in excess."), the proverbial sentences of Hesiod's *Works and Days* and the lyrics of Theognis, or the oracle-like fragments of the earliest philosophers, and the *gnomai* (maxims) ascribed to the seven sages illustrate this element of the oral tradition. Riddles too must have been an important vehicle for transmission (v. Athenaeus, 10.448b-459b). Like the popular Hebrew form, the riddle of the Sphinx uses numbers to pose the question "What walks on four feet in the morning, two at noon, and three in the evening?", and Oedipus' answer, "Man," summarizes the universal movement of human life. Oracular responses also were framed in enigmas which had to be solved by the petitioners.

We are most concerned, however, with the narration of stories or events from saga which were first performed in verse by singers trained to compose spontaneously and then transmitted from one such singer to the next through space and time. In the *Odyssey*, Homer depicts bards who entertain the public by recounting isolated incidents from saga and myth. Penelope, in Ithaca, begs that Phemius sing about something less painful to her than his account of the heroes' return from the Trojan War (*Od.* 1. 325-43). Odysseus, on the other hand, requests that Demodocus, the bard in the court of Phaeacia, sing the story of the wooden horse (*Od.* 8. 487-98). Both bards clearly have a repertoire to choose from; Phemius could turn to other "deeds of gods and men which singers make famous," (*Od.* 1. 337-8) whereas Demodocus has already sung of a quarrel between Achilles and Odysseus and of the time when Hephestus trapped his adulterous wife Aphrodite in a net with her lover Ares. The other songs of such bards probably included episodes from the lives of divine patrons, local heroes, and powerful relatives which, like Hebrew saga, were worthy of preserving as records of the group's sacred beginnings and exemplars for its present. Among the Greeks, the repeated performance of these traditional tales brought honor to the gods and immortality through song to the human subjects.

The movement of refugees from Mycenaean Greece c. 1100 B.C.E. to the islands and coast of Asia Minor precipitated the formation of relatively fixed legends in verse for refugees who wanted to remember their homeland's heroic past. Unusual features of both content and language in the *Iliad* and *Odyssey* suggest the continuous development of an oral tradition during this period.[4] Information about the remote past and the eighth century B.C.E., from the bronze age as well as the iron age, from the Mycenaean/Trojan feudal warrior society and the pastoral refugee communities, appear side by side in the verses of Homeric epic. Moreover, the language of the *Iliad* and *Odyssey* is poetic and artificial. Its diction contains an inseparable mixture of Greek dialects as well as archaic words whose meaning had been forgotten by historical times.[5] Its style is marked by formulae developed to facilitate improvisation: e.g., 1) intricate patterns of noun-epithet combinations which fit every theme, verse position, and grammatical requirement, 2) repeated lines and passages, 3) type scenes where important new developments occur in familiar dramatic contexts. This concatenation of disparate dialects, customs, descriptions, places, and ages, embedded in a long narrative which progresses by means of variations in the formulae, indicates that for centuries before Homer (c. 750 B.C.E.), bards who improvised their songs had been traveling through Greece, the Aegean islands, and Asia Minor sharing their materials, adding new pieces, and passing them on to the next generation. How far back into the past the process stretches is difficult to determine. Linguistic analysis of the form of Achilles' name and its relation to a word in Linear B suggests that the story pattern of a warrior who brings pain to his people not only predates the Trojan War, but goes back to Indo-European themes.[6]

Poetry: Epic as Connected Verse Narrative and Other Genres

By the time the Greeks had adopted the Phoenician alphabet and writing became a possibility, some of the separate pieces had been organized into two long chronological narratives which were assigned to a poet known as Homer, a name which Nagy translates as "he who fit the song together."[7] Homeric epic's main unifying device, as Aristotle notes in *Poetics* 1451a, is the construction of the individual episodes around a single action. The *Iliad* includes events from the entire Trojan war, the glorious deeds of many fighters, and even details about warriors and battles of past generations, as retold by old men like Nestor and Phoenix or young warriors vaunting their genealogies. From its first word, *menin*, however, the *Iliad* traces the wrath of Achilles from its beginning to end, in the tenth year of the Trojan War. Likewise the *Odyssey* contains different episodes from the Trojan War, sea tales, adventure stories, and descriptions of domestic life, all of which probably circulated independently before. Yet it is organized around Odysseus' journey home from Troy and ends only when the hero quells the disorder in Ithaca depicted at the beginning. Thus the unified plot of each epic is similar to the continuous prose narrative of the Bible.

To stitch the pieces together, the poet used the same repetitions and allusive devices as the shapers of the Hebrew Bible. For the very things which made simultaneous performance and improvisation possible also enabled the listeners to follow the longer story. Repetitions in new contexts clue the audience in to major developments and their relation to what has preceded. The Homeric type-scenes, like their Hebrew counterparts, place important occurrences in the settings most significant to the understanding of the unfolding story. But they differ in that they dramatize characteristic Greek political, military, and social behaviors, e.g., 1) the public meetings where issues are debated, conflicts arise, and decisions are made, for better or worse, 2) war scenes of arming, boasting and blaming, hand to hand combat, wholesale slaughter,' fighting over the bodies of the slain, 3) domestic scenes of strangers received, meals shared, rites and prayers performed, encounters between husbands, wives, children, and servants. There are also type-scenes which focus on the gods (e.g., the assemblies and feasts on Olympus, encounters between mortals and immortals, prayers and rituals directed to attentive deities). Such scenes generally represent the Greek gods as responding to human initiatives, whereas the Bible more often dramatizes the divine initiative and its human results.

Once the two Homeric epics became known, rhapsodes, called the Sons of Homer (*Homeridae*), memorized and recited these narratives, competing for prizes, at public gatherings. Several sagas preserved as the Epic Cycle filled in what Homer omitted, i.e., fuller stories of the events preceding the war and the quarrel between Agamemnon and Achilles (*Cypria*), the last days of Troy (*Aithiopis, Little Iliad, Sack of Ilion*), and the returns of other warriors. Although these works were ascribed to different poets, Homer's name was also assigned to several. By the late sixth century B.C.E., the Athenians, under Pisistratus the tyrant, had established an official text of the *Iliad* and *Odyssey* and initiated a contest of bards who recited the books of the epics in order at the Panathenaic Festival.[8] School children memorized the *Iliad* and the *Odyssey*, Aeschylus considered his plays "slices from Homer's banquet," (Athenaeus 8.347e), and Homer himself was known as "The Poet" to Plato, e.g., *Gorgias* 485d, and Aristotle, e.g., *Rhetoric* 1365a, 1380b.

To account for the importance the later Greeks attached to Homer, one must realize that oral epic was not literature in our sense of aesthetic entertainment or "belles lettres" to be appreciated in private by the educated few. Rather public performance was a political and social necessity. It was the most efficient means of mass communication of the information and values of an illiterate culture when that culture was being formulated, and it remained the most effective means of passing that culture on to succeeding generations. Into the narrative the poet wove and thus preserved beliefs about the gods, knowledge of the past, facts like birth and death records, muster lists, maps, and instructions for various procedures as well as accounts of major events in earlier generations.

Before literacy was common, the society learned about itself by oral recitation at public gatherings, even when facts and statistics were recorded in Linear B. After the alphabet facilitated the writing down of the texts of Homer, Hesiod, the poets of the Epic Cycle, and the lyric poets, performance remained the main means of communication. The dramatic poets, who probably composed by writing rather than by improvising, passed their plays on through the actors who had memorized them, so that there were no fixed texts for drama until the fourth century. Early philosophers like Xenophanes and Parmenides composed in verse, despite rejecting myth and narrative, and Solon defended his political ideas in iambic poetry which he recited to the citizens in the Athenian agora. Herodotus' prose history, which was also recited in public, used many of the devices of epic narrative. When prose and reading became more widespread in Athens, by the end of the fifth century, poetry lost its position as the sole medium of serious communication. Yet Plato's philosophic dialogues written for the general reader maintain the fiction of oral presentation and argue their abstract ideas by the device of a conversation, usually reported, between characters in a dramatic setting.

Oral recitation was an effective means of communication because it used pleasurable devices to convey and reinforce its message.[9] The rhythms of poetry aided the memory and stressed the importance of the words through the very repetitions demanded by the processes of improvisation. The music of the bard's lyre underlined the beat, increasing the pleasure without distracting from the sense. The bard himself was part actor, accompanying his words with gestures, and changing his voice to imitate the changing speaker and the variety of emotions expressed.

Moreover, the techniques of narrative transmitted the whole culture, its values, skills, and beliefs, in a way which personally involved the listeners. Heroic characters in action, particularly in conflict with one another, dramatized the ethics and customs of the society. Their dialogue articulated the primary attitudes and oppositions of social and political life in an engrossing way. Their very lives provided archetypes for excellence, and patterns of behavior in crises, illustrating what should be imitated or avoided, why anger must be controlled, or how to face death bravely. Thus, as in the Hebrew saga, so in the Greek, these characters became universalized as complex individuals exemplifying moral traits and behavior patterns which expanded the significance of the situational plot. Cause and effect too were explained in human terms; the change in seasons, weather, wars, catastrophes, even psychological motivations were attributed to various supernatural agents who behaved like men and women. (So too the transcendent God of Gen. 1 is made more immanent through anthropomorphized dialogue and metaphor for the purposes of the narrative.) The listeners, who were unable to study the written word and analyze the ideas, absorbed the information and values of their culture through an emotional identification with the characters.

Homeric epic is the closest Greek equivalent to the canonized Hebrew prose narrative. Both arose as the product, not the producers of an inherited cultural memory. At the same time as the Torah and former prophets were taking shape, traveling Greek bards were reciting the traditional tales the listeners expected, with set plots and characters which dramatized their culture. According to Nagy, as they moved from one community to the next, the bards refined their repertoires, de-emphasizing purely local tales or local variations in order to facilitate spontaneous performance and appeal to a general audience in competitive festival settings. The canonization occurred as an evolutionary process: "the pan-Hellenic diffusion of the Homeric traditions, concomitant with ongoing recomposition-in-performance at international festivals, led gradually to one convergent pan-Hellenic version."[10] Nagy connects this development, which reached its culmination in the eighth century, with further signs of the rise of pan-Hellenism in the same period: the establishment of the Delphic Oracle and the Olympic Games. The fact that Herodotus (Book 2.53) attributed the description of the major Greek divinities, and their genealogies and relationships, to Homer and Hesiod suggests the simultaneous unification of local mythic and religious traditions into an overarching pan-Hellenic culture which linked the diverse tales, practices, and institutions of the newly evolving individual Greek city-states.

The very process of synthesis led to a recognition of the confusion and contradictions in the body of tales. Hesiod began his *Theogony* by announcing that his muses direct him to tell the truth, "for we know how to tell many falsehoods that seem real," (1.27-8) a phrase which suggests that his own poetry will be a correction of previous songs.[11] Nagy analyzes Hesiod's words as an assertion of his freedom from dependence on the approval of each local audience for his bed and board; "all such local traditions are *pseudeia*, 'falsehoods,' in the face of *aletheia*, 'true things,' that the Muses impart specially to Hesiod. They have transformed him into a pan-Hellenic poet, "composing one overarching tradition capable of achieving something that is beyond the reach of individual local traditions . . . and acceptable to all."[12] The *Theogony* synthesized the myriad stories and names of divinities from various traditions into a careful genealogy which describes not only the progress from one generation to the next, but also the movement from an undelineated and barbarous universe into an orderly and natural and social organization presided over by Zeus.[13] For Hesiod, these tales are sacred truth, revealed by his divine muses; his poetry won him a prize and a place second to Homer. For us, however, his truth is a selection and refinement of earlier traditions in the light of new experiences.

This process of refinement continued as old myth was reworked in different genres of poetry, in a manner which resembles the allusiveness and intertextuality of the developing Hebrew canon.[14] Lyric poets like Bacchylides and Simonides recounted familiar narratives in choral song. To praise contemporary Greeks, Pindar culled from the mass of stories archetypal allusions which connected his patrons with the nobility and vitality of the mythic past when excellence flourished and songs brought immortality. His epinician odes equated the athletic victories of citizens and city-states to the glory of epic warriors, making the citizen/athletes true descendants of that earlier age, capable themselves of deeds worthy of eternal fame. The sagas of heroes like Oedipus, Orestes, and Heracles, mentioned as *obiter dicta* in Homer, passed through several transformations in epic, lyric, and drama, each with a new perspective on eternal questions about human life and theodicy. Out of the performance traditions of these various works, there developed a concept of a canon of genres and poets regarded as 'classics' by the Alexandrian period.[15]

Myth yielded fresh meanings relevant to each contemporary audience.[16] Through stories of the past with universalized characters, which transported the spectators above the trivia of their daily lives, the poet could examine the characters, responsibilities, problems, and assumptions of the citizens. The heroes and their situations must have provided paradigms for judging or praising present leaders. Athenian heroism at Marathon was associated with Theseus' victory over the Amazons and the Greek defeat of Troy on the Stoa Poikile. The Athenian audience is said to have recognized Aristides the Just in Aeschylus' portrait of Amphiarus in *Seven against Thebes* (Plutarch, Aristides, 3). If politicians and leading families manipulated the myths for propaganda, the poets also used them for criticism and admonition. Athena's speech to the jury/chorus as she founds the Areopagus in *Eumenides* 690-703 is a veiled warning against the kind of violent strife as dangerous to the city of Athens as to the House of Atreus. And Euripides' Trojan War plays (i.e., *Trojan Women* and *Iphigenia at Aulis*) are indictments of Athenian *Realpolitik*.

Unlike Hebrew Scripture, however, the Greek corpus had no all-encompassing organizing principles such as the covenant and the salvation history to link the individual elements and the on-going interpretation into a coherent whole. Unconnected to the concept of a historical continuum, the Greek heroes, fixed forever by their names and inevitable destinies, point backwards, not forward. They never broke as free from their original myths as the Hebrew typologies whose antitypes validate all future change by becoming mythic themselves (i.e., Abraham, Moses, David, Jesus).[17]

Most Greek poetry and plays based on myth confirm the age-old wisdom about the dangers of excess and ignorance. Yet the poets and playwrights chose only slices, each selecting an episode from a varied banquet and then adapting it to suit his particular theme, without aiming for consistency. Because heroic and divine behavior was so tied to the specific situation or theme, individual episodes or allusions often canceled each other out. In Euripides' *Trojan Women*, for example, Helen is a promiscuous woman who has caused all the destruction without suffering any of its consequences. Euripides' *Helen*, however, exploits the Spartan version in which the beautiful and innocent queen has been kidnapped from Sparta and left behind in Egypt while Aphrodite masquerades as Helen in Troy. Odysseus, glorified for his resilience in the *Odyssey* and for his flexibility and compassion in Sophocles' *Ajax*, is vilified as a political opportunist and moral relativist when he displays the same qualities in the war plays of Euripides and in Sophocles' *Philoctetes*. Thus, as the stories were reperformed and reexamined by succeeding generations, there were few clues to help the listeners discover absolute directives for ethics or belief from their comprehensive experience of poetry and myth.

Criticism and Prose

For those who began to demand a logically consistent or morally coherent explanation of the world, the ideas transmitted through myth and poetry were inadequate or downright wrong. The criticism of myth and the endeavor to make rational rather than poetic sense began very early. Hesiod's *Theogony* exemplifies the attempt to fit transmitted information into a system, yet he recorded crude and fantastic stories without skepticism. Theagenes of Rhegium and Pherycedes of Syros are reported to have found hidden meanings in the poets' stories and to have identified divinities with cosmic forces or human faculties. Thus began the process of demythologizing myth into allegory in order to provide continuity between new ideas and traditional beliefs.[18]

Other poets were not so willing to accept the barbarism or even the anthropomorphic descriptions of the divine. Xenophanes of Colophon (c. 570-473) wrote about the absurdity of creating god in man's image and tainting him with human faults.

> But if cattle and horses had hands or were able to draw with their hands and do the works that men do, horses would draw the forms of the gods like horses, and cattle like cattle and they would make their bodies such as they each had themselves. (Frag. 169)

> Homer and Hesiod have attributed to the gods everything that is a shame and reproach among men, stealing and committing adultery, and deceiving each other. (Frag. 166)[19]

Pindar refused to believe the tale about Demeter biting into Pelops' shoulder and substituted a version more acceptable to him (Olympia 1.35-54).

The general objections to poetry and myth can be summarized as follows.[20] In the first place, many of the stories seemed ridiculous to succeeding generations. The tales did not offer information that could be verified either by experience or by logical examination. Secondly, the presentation itself, with its music, dramatized dialogue, and exciting devices of plot, character and argument, was hypnotic; it provided patterns to be absorbed and imitated rather than examined and understood. Gorgias the Sophist defined tragedy and epic as *apate* or deceit because their pleasures robbed man of his reason, tempting him into an emotional or subjective state which prevented thought.[21]   Plato objected to poetry because performances of it appealed to the basest elements in the human soul, stimulated identification with unworthy characters and actions, and transmitted ideas without encouraging active conversation and argument.

Moreover, although the story form conveyed the psychological complexity of human behavior, it was too firmly grounded in the changing situations of the separate episodes to express a universal unchanging truth about god or an absolute moral standard for man. When Socrates proclaimed that "the unexamined life is not worth living," he was objecting to the oral culture where definitions of such important qualities as piety, justice and love had been transmitted as truths in story form without having been validated by careful analysis. Plato's Socratic dialogues begin with discussions which effectively demolish accepted definitions by proving them absurdly illogical, i.e., *Euthyphro, Lysis, Republic*. Only then could his Socrates reach for a new definition which would express the unchanging and eternal essence responsible for the ever-changing particular uses of the term.

Several different factors may explain why the Greeks began to demand rational examination and to search for an underlying principle which accounted for the variety they perceived in nature and in human life. Perhaps the contact with the myths and customs of different cultures led them to look for important common features. The increase in writing and reading made reflection easier; the examination of the tales as one corpus may have heightened the awareness of glaring contradictions and implausibilities. Moreover, the Greece which emerged from the Dark Ages was itself in a state of flux, with each local government developing new institutions to cope with economic change and social conflict. Faced with new problems, the city-states needed to understand the realities of their own time rather than to emulate the traditional situations of the heroic age. When the citizens were writing down laws and procedures to establish order, they could hardly accept less ethically consistent behavior from their patron gods than they were demanding from themselves.

Whatever the cause, there was a steady development of critical and rational thinking which was accompanied by a change in the medium of communication. Intellectuals began to reject the poetic vernacular of the oral tradition for a simple and straight forward account of their inquiries or investigations (*historia*) in prose.[22] The earliest geographers were called *logopoioi* or *logographoi* (from *logos* meaning 'account' or 'report') because they used prose to describe the places they saw and the customs they confronted in their travels. Pherecydes of Syros, whose *Cosmology* is an allegory lying somewhere between myth and philosophy, was considered among the first to write a book in prose. When the Milesian philosophers began searching for the underlying "stuff" which would account for the variety in nature and asked the questions "What?" and "How?" rather than "Who?," they expressed their conclusions about water, air or the "unlimited" and the processes by which they became particular things in short prose sentences. Anaximander too was credited with writing books.

Other philosophers found different principles to account for the variegated world perceived by the senses. Whether pluralists like Empedocles and Heraclitus, or monists like Parmenides, all, even those who wrote in verse, rejected the anthropomorphic/polytheistic explanations of myth and the subjective devices of poetry. The diction and syntax of the later prose writers like Thucydides and the Hippocratic corpus reveal their effort to record the facts precisely and evaluate them objectively. They pay careful attention to chronological sequence, reasoned argument, and clear statements of cause and effect. These writers abandoned the paratactic style of oral epic and early prose and developed instead the paragraph and the periodic construction, which expresses the relation between events or ideas by its careful subordination of clauses and its balanced antitheses. Plato chose the dramatic dialogue in prose as the medium for disseminating his dialectical method as well as his philosophy. He and Aristotle and later philosophers like the Stoics established the principles of logic in order to prove their hypotheses. They also attempted to organize all branches of human knowledge into a coherent system with a unified epistemology, metaphysics and ethic. All demanded an objective observation of the facts and

an unbiased rational examination of ideas. Thucydides berated
historians who used romantic tales to excite their audiences (Book
1.21) whereas Socrates criticized his jurors for being more moved
by pity than by truth (*Apology* 34c-35d).

Plurality and the Open Ended Corpus

During the period between Homer and Constantine, however,
there was never a time in which all intellectuals and artists rejected
myth and poetry absolutely. Poets continued to communicate new
perceptions through myth even after other poets and prose writers
had attacked the anthropomorphic explanation of the universe.
Aeschylus' dramas reveal his knowledge of the schools of medicine,
rhetoric and philosophy developing in Sicily. Yet, in his *Oresteia* of
458 B.C.E., he adapted the barbaric saga of the House of Atreus as a
vehicle for describing the evolution of cosmic and human justice
from savagery to civilization. More than four hundred years later,
when prose and philosophy were the most common media for
serious thought, Virgil incorporated the facts of recent Roman
history and contemporary Stoic and Neopythagorean ideas into his
Aeneid which imitated the *Iliad* and the *Odyssey* in story and style.
Such reinterpretations of myth were produced by different
individuals in different places and times and were all passed on as
part of the general culture.

Not even the prose writers completely rejected myth. The father
of history, Herodotus, was also called "father of lies" because he
included so many implausible folktales and used the divine and
anthropomorphic framework to explain cause and effect. Although
Plato banished the poets from his republic for lying about god and
providing bad examples for men, he resorted to "plausible fiction"
(*eikota muthon*, v. *Timaeus*, 29b and c) to discuss probable
hypotheses that could not be proved by logical argument. The
western picture of the afterlife, so vividly described by the poets
Virgil and Dante, had its literary beginnings in the prose dialogues
of Plato, i.e., the last section of the *Republic*, appropriately known
as the Myth of Er.

Nor were the philosophers any more able than the poets to agree
on a monolithic description of the world.[23] Plato's theory of forms
has been interpreted as his attempt to bring the contradictory
hypotheses of the monists and the pluralists into agreement. But
Aristotle could not accept this hypothesis of his great teacher and
substituted his own. In the Hellenistic period, several new schools
of philosophy developed different definitions of virtue and wisdom.

There were so many contradictory explanations of nature and ethics that the Academy itself, descended from Plato, despaired of finding the absolute truth and became indistinguishable from the Skeptics.

Thus, before the Romans made Christianity the state religion, there never was at any given time one single Hellenic world view or scripture which explained the universe rationally or defined all the individual divinities with consistency. Our term Olympus really refers to an entire mountain range with far more volcanoes than burning bushes. It must include not only the gods who inhabited that mountain top, but also the myriad deities on and beneath the earth and even the philosophers' diverse ideas of divinity itself. Out of this pluralistic culture emerged no single hereditary priesthood or set of laws to regulate relations between gods and mortals and to establish rules for human behavior. Although most Greeks traced their common moral imperatives and custom/laws back to the same set of gods and participated in several pan-Hellenic activities, the various political entities developed different institutions which reflected their particular histories, geographical conditions, and values.

The evidence about Olympus derives from such diverse sources and exhibits such variety that there can be no monolithic discussion of the topics to be examined in the following chapters. In fact, the existence of diverse views and modes of expression is one of the central characteristics of Olympus. It is derived from experiences which encouraged the Hellenes to free their intellects from the bonds of religious and political tradition and examine new ideas. That the Greeks tolerated such independence in each other and accepted their pluralistic society indicates how great a value they placed on human freedom. But they also saw its dangers. The pluralism was always threatening to lead to social and political chaos. Thus came the urge toward pan-Hellenism, the quest for underlying principles, and the moral imperative to know the limits of their freedom.

Notes

1.　See L. R. Palmer, *The Greek Language* (Atlantic Highlands, NJ: Humanities Press, 1980), pp. 3-26 for a summary of the evidence and the various hypotheses about the migrations. See also Gregory Nagy, *The Best of the Achaeans: Concepts of the Hero in Archaic Greek Poetry* (Baltimore: Johns Hopkins University Press, 1979), hereafter referred to as *Best,* and *Greek Mythology and Poetics* (Ithaca: Cornell University Press, 1990), hereafter referred to as *Greek M&P,* for traces of Indo-European language, themes, and religion in Greek literature and culture.

2.　For a detailed analysis of the kinds of developments that took place in this period *see* A. M. Snodgrass, *The Dark Ages of Greece: An Archaeological Survey of the Eleventh to the Eighth Centuries B.C.E.* (Edinburgh: Edinburgh University Press, 1971), Chester G. Starr, *The Origins of Greek Civilization, 1100-650 B.C.* (New York: Alfred A. Knopf, 1961) and P. Walcot, *Hesiod and the Ancient Near East* (Cardiff: University of Wales, 1966), as well as relevant volumes of *The Cambridge Ancient History.* Andrew Robert Burr, *The World of Hesiod: A Study of the Greek Middle Ages C. 900-700 B.C.* (New York: Benjamin Blum, 1966) discusses the difference between the world depicted by Homer and by Hesiod.

3.　Walcot discusses the many similarities and analyzes the theories of transmission as well as the reasons for differences. See also M. L. West's introductions to his Oxford University Press editions of *Theogony* (1966) and *Works and Days* (1978).

4.　The most important scholars connected with the discovery that Homeric epic derives from a long oral tradition are Milman Parry and Albert B. Lord who collected material from contemporary Yugoslav bards which exhibited the same characteristics. For further reading on the oral epic and Homer in particular, *see* A. B. Lord, *The Singer of Tales* (Cambridge: Harvard University Press, 1960) as well as C. M. Bowra, *Homer and His Forerunners* (Edinburgh, 1955) and G. S. Kirk, *Homer and the Oral Tradition* (Cambridge: Harvard University Press, 1978), T. B. L. Webster, *From Mycenae to Homer* (London: Norton, 1958) and C. H. Whitman, *Homer and the Heroic Tradition* (Cambridge: Harvard University Press, 1958). For a discussion of all aspects of Homeric studies, see A. J. B. Wace and F. Stubbings, *A Companion to Homer* (London: Macmillan, 1962). For specific analysis of the techniques of oral poetry see G. P. Edwards, *The Language of Hesiod in its Traditional Context* (Oxford: Basil Blackwell, 1971) and Gregory Nagy, *Comparative Studies in Greek and Indic Meter* (Cambridge: Harvard University Press, 1974), as well as Nagy, *Best,* and *Greek M&P,* and D. Gary Miller, *Improvisation, Typology, Culture, and the 'New Orthodoxy': How 'Oral' is Homer?* (Washington D.C.: University Press of America, 1982) which also includes responses to criticism or misunderstanding of the theory of oral composition, and William G. Thalmann, *Conventions of Form and Thought in Early Greek Epic Poetry* (Baltimore: The John Hopkins University Press, 1984)

5.　See Palmer, pp. 83-101.

6. See Palmer, pp. 37-8, as well as Nagy, *Best*, pp. 69-83.
7. The questions of why and how the material was put together and by whom are topics of serious debate. See the works in note 4 as well as H. T. Wade-Gerry, *The Poet of "The Iliad"* (Cambridge: Cambridge University Press, 1952). Other scholars doubt that Homer was a real person at all and have analyzed the name as meaning 'hostage,' 'blind,' or 'singer' (Miller, p. xii). Nagy relates the growth of this epic to the simultaneous development of the Greek hero cults and pan-Hellenism. In *Greek M&P*, he traces the Hellenization of Indo-European myth and ritual into uniquely Greek ideas and institutions.
8. See the chapter by J. A. Davidson, "The Transmission of the Text" in Wace and Stubbings, pp. 215-33. Scholars continue to debate how and when the epics were written down.
9. E. A. Havelock, *Preface to Plato* (Cambridge, Mass.: Belknapp Press, 1963), pp. 145-193.
10. In his essay, "Early Greek Views of Poets and Poetry," in George Kennedy, ed., *Cambridge History of Literary Criticism, Vol. 1: Classical Criticism* (Cambridge: Harvard University Press, 1989), pp. 1-77. The quote is taken from p. 16, where Nagy relates the term 'canonical' to 'pan-Hellenic'; on p. 44, he summarizes the growth of a Greek canon through pan-Hellenic diffusion. See also *Greek M&P*, p. 80, where he emphasizes Hesiodic poetry as the "product of the Greek poetic heritage."
11. See Nagy, *Greek M&P*, p.44, as well as Pietro Pucci, *Hesiod and the Language of Poetry* (Baltimore: Johns Hopkins Press, 1977), pp. 8-44.
12. Nagy, *Greek M&P*, p. 44.
13. For a summary of the progress implicit in *Theogony*, see Norman O. Brown's introduction to his translation (Indianapolis: Bobbs-Merill, 1953), pp. 7-49, as well as Wm. Blake Tyrrell and Frieda S. Brown, *Words in Action: Perspectives on Athenian Myths and Institutions*, (Oxford: Oxford University Press, 1991), pp. 15-39.
14. For a history of Greek literature, see Nagy, *Greek M&P* and "Early Views," as well as Albin Lesky, *A History of Greek Literature* trans. by James Willis and Cornelius de Heer (London: Methuen, 1966).
15. Nagy, "Early Views,' pp. 44-46.
16. For examples, see Tyrrell and Brown, and Nagy, *Greek M&P*.
17. See Northrop Frye, *The Great Code: The Bible and Literature* (New York: Harcourt Brace Jovanovich, 1982), pp. 78-101.
18. Rudolf Pfeiffer, *History of Classical Scholarship from the Beginnings to the End of the Hellenistic Age* (Oxford: Clarendon Press, 1968), pp. 9-10 and J. Tate, "On the History of Allegorism," *Classical Quarterly* 28 (1934): 105-114.
19. The quote is taken from G. S. Kirk and J. E. Raven, and M. Schofield, *The Presocratic Philosophers: A Critical History with a Selection of Texts* (Cambridge: Cambridge University Press, 1983), pp. 168-69. This text will be referred to as KRS throughout the rest of the book. Translations from the Presocratics have been quoted from KRS, unless

otherwise indicated, and will be cited in the text in parentheses by their KRS fragment number.

20. Both Havelock, *Preface to Plato*, pp. 197-253, and Walter J. Ong, *Orality and Literacy: The Technologizing of the Word* (London: Methuen, 1982), pp. 36-57, 139-147, discuss these characteristics of oral transmission. See also G. R. F. Ferrari, "Plato and Poetry," pp. 92-148 in *CambHistLitCrit1*.

21. See Kennedy's discussion of Gorgias' *Encomium on Helen, 8-14,* in his essay, "Language and Meaning in Archaic and Classical Greece," pp. 82-85 in *CambHistLitCrit1*, as well as Thomas Rosenmeyer, "Gorgias, Aeschylus, and *Apate*," *American Journal of Philosophy* 76 (1955), pp. 255-60.

22. For a history of the development of Greek prose, see J. D. Denniston, *Greek Prose Style* (Oxford: Clarendon Press, 1952) and George Kennedy, "The Evolution of a Theory of Artistic Prose," pp. 184-199 in *CambHistLitCrit*.

23. For a general history of Greek philosophy, see W. K. G. Guthrie, *A History of Greek Philosophy I-III* (Cambridge: Cambridge University Press, 1962-1969). For the Presocratics, see Jonathan Barnes, *The Presocratic Philosophers* (London, Boston: Routledge & Kegan Paul, 1982), as well as KRS.

Conclusions and Comparisons

The literatures of the Hebrews and the Greeks began in similar oral contexts and were influenced by the same Mediterranean cultural traditions. Both separated themselves from a common background within a similar time frame. The Exodus dated c. 1220 stimulated the monotheistic revolution of the Hebrews whereas the destruction of the Mycenaean kingdoms after the Trojan War c. 1200 catalyzed the unique development of the Greeks. The oral traditions of both cultures began to be organized and written down about the same time, in the First Commonwealth of Israel and in the Archaic Age in Greece. Moreover, Plato and Ezra, nearly contemporary, mark the ends of their respective classical periods.

Certainly the two cultures liberated themselves from their common background in distinct and original ways. Monotheism became the basis of all Israelite ideas and institutions, and fostered the Hebrews' geographical, political, and religious unity. The Greeks retained polytheism, and their city-states, separated geographically and politically, never could unite, although they shared a pan-Hellenic pantheon and a common sense of their 'Greekness.'

Despite the separate developments of the Sinai and Olympus traditions, both bodies of literature were subject to a continuous refining process which evolved toward a rational, moral and more spiritual concept of God and humanity. Such reinterpretation and spiritualization were not uncommon in the surrounding civilizations, but the Hebrew monotheism of Deutero-Isaiah and Platonic philosophy represent the apogee of this type of refinement in the Mediterranean area.[1]

This process took slightly different directions. The Hebrew writers of the Bible reworked the epic traditions of pre-monotheistic Israel into a historicized prose narrative in conscious opposition to the poetic genres of paganism. Into their narrative framework they wove the demythologized remnants of the oral culture. Once monotheism was secured, it was safe to add other poetic genres to the sacred literature. Alongside the verse epic, the Greeks developed new poetic genres as well as narrative and expository prose. Everything got passed along together as part of what Gilbert Murray refers to as the 'Inherited Conglomerate.'[2]

Differences in form are related to differences in content. The monotheistic revolution of the Hebrews established a unified world view. Its literary expression resulted in the sacralization of certain texts and then led gradually to their canonization. The canon established the overarching principles of monotheism and morality. Within these boundaries, however, there was room for different temperaments to emphasize different aspects of Hebrew religion. Through typology, allusion, and intertextuality, it was even possible for a later author to criticize or reinterpret older ideas and to introduce new ones. Yet the Bible maintains a unified way of conceiving the world and individual experience which makes it a single book as well as an entire library.

In contrast, the Greeks simultaneously produced several explanations of their world, some in clear opposition to each other. The urge to find a unifying cultural thread among the diverse Greek communities resulted in the identification of certain works as pan-Hellenic. The term 'canon' has been applied to them, but their contents are not circumscribed in the same way as the biblical books that entered the Hebrew canon. Though different authors also communicate with each other over time and space through intertextuality, repetition, and allusion, their opposition is much more open and the introduction of new ideas far less subtle. The clamor of new voices in the Bible never reached the pitch where a philosopher judged ritual sacrifice as sinful murder, a dramatist called the gods an invention of humans, or a historian ignored divine control of human events.

As they evolved, the two civilizations developed different attitudes to their bodies of literature. In the early oral contexts of the traditions of both, there was a fluid boundary between communicator and community; the conveyer of the tradition was viewed as a recipient of the divine revelation and a channel between the divine and human. Thus the individuality of the author was secondary to the message. Only later did names become attached to specific literary materials. For example, the Hebrew wisdom tradition was assigned to Solomon, whereas Greek epic and wisdom were passed on under the names of Homer, Hesiod, and Theognis.

As the Hebrew corpus grew, the dominant issue was not the name of the author of a particular work, but the place of the work in the hierarchy of sanctity. In the Bible itself, there is a tripartite division of sanctity attached to the three major sections. The Torah is considered most sacred because of God's direct revelation of this teaching to Moses, the Prophets are recipients of divine revelation second only to Moses, and the Writings are considered the work of divinely inspired authors. Many of the books are anonymous or pseudepigraphical. Even the classical prophets, who have names, personalities, and biographies, usually begin their compositions with the words: "Thus says the Lord!"

The Greeks also believed that poetic creation was a gift of the gods (e.g., see Plato's *Ion*). The poet called Homer is in fact an anonymous bard, an *aoidos* or inspired singer, who traces his words to Apollo and the Muses. According to Hesiod, the Heliconian Muses chose him as the prophet of their divine communication. But gradually the invocation to the gods or Muses and the claim of divine inspiration became literary conventions as literature grew increasingly desacrilized.[3] By the classical period, the composer of verse was referred to as *poietes*, himself a 'maker' skilled in the art of song. Even poets who announced their dependence on divine aid proclaimed their own names as well and felt free to express personal feelings and opinions. Parmenides attributed his compositions to the meeting with a goddess, in imitation of Hesiod, but his poem was a departure from a traditional theogony and a polemic against earlier philosophers.

Although Greek poets continued to be considered inspired because of their extraordinary talent or knowledge, their works were never revered as sacred or revealed in the way that the Hebrew Bible was perceived in Israel. They, however, received far more recognition and reward for their creativity than the Hebrew authors. The competitions for prizes among the poets indicates that the Greeks honored humans who excelled at literature almost as much as the divine patrons who inspired them. Moreover, they respected the judgment of the human beings who, representing their fellow citizens, selected the winners.

In both societies, the oral tradition must have continued side by side with the written one. But among the Hebrews it was elevated almost to the level of Scripture as a source of religious authority. It was divided into two distinct branches: the legal, *Halakhah*, which comprised continuing interpretations of biblical law and was considered binding, and the *Aggadah*, which preserved, interpreted and added to the lore and folklore of ancient Israel. The ongoing Midrash continued the process of reinterpretation as well as the reworking of pagan myth and philosophy.

This oral Torah was not written down for a variety of reasons: first and foremost, to distinguish it from the more sacred written Scripture; secondly, to prevent its sanctification as a written source, which would restrict its flexibility as a body of law applicable to life and its changes. This refusal to fix a text in writing, which precludes expansion or argument, recalls Plato's objections at *Phaedrus* 274b-276d (cf. 7th Epistle 328d). Only after the destruction of the Second Temple did the rabbis begin to commit the oral Torah to writing to preserve it for succeeding generations.

The different degrees of sacredness produced different means of disseminating the two literatures. Greek poetry, drama, and prose were frequently performed in sacred contexts and written works were sometimes deposited in temples, like the Hebrew Scriptures. But public debate on all kinds of topics occurred in many religious as well as social and political arenas and written works and laws were made available to all for reading, interpretation, and judgment (v. Plato's *Apology* 26d). Although Harris documents the thin veneer of literacy in Greece, he emphasizes that "its level was in a sense remarkably high, for literacy ceased to be scribal, and also went far beyond the circle of the wealthy."[4] He stresses how much the spread of reading and writing was connected with the self-governing citizens' rights and responsibilities. In the Bible, however, the people, because of their fear of direct confrontation with the divine, transfer to Moses the authority to receive the divine revelation. This action provided the paradigm for dissemination through priests, prophets and judges in biblical Israel. The texts were taught and read out, even to lay people who were literate.

Some Greeks, on the other hand, saw the need for censoring their literature. Plato reacted to the dangers of the open society in Athens by suggesting that certain poetry and music be excluded from his utopian republic. In part, his objections to the Greek lore were similar to the strictures of the Hebrew monotheistic revolution; stories about divinity must reflect its true nature. Plato wanted to exclude the tales about immoral or irrational human behavior as well because he thought that they appealed to the senses and projected dangerous models for developing minds. Ezra and the other editors of Scripture, however, retained similar narratives because they saw an affirmation of the divine moral order in the failures of humanity.

Although Plato and Ezra began with different experiences and assumptions, they arrived at surprisingly similar positions. Ezra and Nehemiah, with their Scriptures in hand, replaced the defeated Davidic kingdom with a theocratic commonwealth based on God's law. Plato, disillusioned with the democracy, provided a charter in *Laws* for a nomocratic state which reflected the divine order. Thus, Plato and Ezra represent a convergence of the process of refinement in the Sinai and Olympus traditions.

Notes

1.   Fishbane, pp. 323-4.
2.   *Greek Studies* (Oxford: Clarendon Press, 1946), pp. 66f, as cited in
E. R. Dodds, *The Greeks and the Irrational* (Berkeley: University of
California Press, 1959), p. 179.
3.   Nagy, "Early Views," pp. 23-29.
4.   William V. Harris, *Ancient Literacy* (Cambridge: Harvard University
Press, 1989), p. 114.

Chapter 2

Creation: Genesis or Theogony?

Introduction

According to Mircea Eliade, there is a universal need for man to explain his origins.[1] This impulse is undoubtedly the source for the variety of creation stories that have come down to us from civilizations all over the world. Among the great breakthroughs in Near Eastern Studies has been the discovery and interpretation of epics explaining the origins of the world and man.[2] Biblical and classical scholars, in comparing their own traditions to those finds, have realized that the Mesopotamian, Egyptian, and Hittite stories provide the springboard for the accounts in Genesis and Hesiod's *Theogony*. Because the scholarship is so voluminous and so easily accessible, we will summarize the main points of contrast and similarity in the conceptions of how the world and humanity came into existence.[3] With this as our starting point, we will progress to the ways in which Sinai and Olympus account for the reality of evil and confusion in a universe that was created according to the principles of goodness and order.

For our purposes, the most significant creation story is the Babylonian epic the *Enuma Elish*. Although clearly based on earlier Mesopotamian oral traditions, this version was produced in Babylon under Nebuchadnezzar I around 1100 B.C.E. during a revival of that city's political ascendancy. In this epic, the world resulted from a union between Sweet Water (Apsu) and Salt Water (Mummu-

Tiamat) which produced offspring who represent silt (Lahmu and Lahamu), the circular rims of the earth and sky itself (Anu) and fresh water (Ea). Because the tumult of the younger gods disturbed the rest of the oldest deities, there was a war between Apsu and Ea. After Ea defeated and killed Apsu, he built his sacred abode on his victim's carcass. Later, when Ea's son Marduk was born and the other gods were making things such as winds and streams, Tiamat too became disturbed by the activities of the younger gods. In response, she and her allies created monsters to do battle with her descendants. Her chief, Kingu, was so powerful that only Marduk could stand up against him. In exchange for Marduk's leadership, the other gods promised to cede him all authority. After his victory, Marduk cut the body of Tiamat in half. From one part, he made the sky, winds, and constellations and assigned positions on them, with ranks and functions, to the other deities. Next he created the earth itself out of the second half, using Tiamat's eyes for the Tigris and Euphrates, and her breasts for mountains. To serve the gods, he created man out of the dead monster Kingu's blood. After Marduk put the finishing touches on his world order, the gods proclaimed him supreme and established Babylon as his capital city and cultic center. They also promulgated the duties of the human race to provide sustenance to all the gods and homage to Marduk. The *Enuma Elish* concludes with a paeon of praise to Marduk.

This cosmology contains several concepts which will provide points of comparison and contrast with Hebrew and Greek ideas of creation. First of all, the Babylonians viewed their gods as a part of nature; they were the physical realities of sky, water, earth, and the constellations. At the same time, they were anthropomorphic, having human characteristics and passions. In the progress from the first parents to their descendants, scholars detect the evolution of nature from simple forms into more complex and detailed patterns. In the evolution of the anthropomorphic aspects, there is an increasing emphasis on the rise of intelligence over physicality. However, the process generates conflict which is only resolved by the total defeat of the old gods. And, in this Babylonian version, it is Marduk, rather than the earlier, more whimsical gods, who creates according to a plan. As part of this plan, the world and human beings are created out of the corpses of Marduk's enemies to serve the gods. The cult of Marduk and his capital city emerge as the religious and political center of the life of Mesopotamia.[4]

The *Enuma Elish* was much more than a simple creation story; it was also an integral part of a Babylonian festival whose central theme was the renewal of the cosmic order. The celebration centered in Babylon, the religious and political[5] nucleus of Mesopotamia, at the *Esagila*, the temple of Marduk and the focal point of his cult. The *akitu* festival was a New Year's rite that was marked during the first eleven days of the spring month *Nisan*. On the fourth day, the creation epic, the *Enuma Elish* was presented in reactualization of the primordial events that the great poem narrates. As a result of the inclusion of the *Enuma Elish* in the rites, the Babylonian New Year festival became more than the celebration of a calendrical milestone; it marked the re-creation of the ordered world.[6]

Notes

1. *See* Mircea Eliade, *Myth and Reality*, trans. W. R. Trask (New York: Harper and Row, 1963) for an explanation of his theory and its application to the mythological systems of many civilizations.

2. For a collection of ancient mythological texts from the Mediterranean area *see* James B. Pritchard, ed., *Ancient Near Eastern Texts Relating to the Old Testament*, 3rd ed. with Supplement (Princeton: Princeton University Press, 1969).

3. There are many books and articles which anthologize and compare creation stories. Joan O'Brien and Wilfred Major, *In the Beginning: Creation Myths from Mesopotamia, Ancient Israel and Greece* (Chico, Calif..: Scholars Press, 1982), analyze what the material reveals about the distinctive traits of each culture.

4. See the translation by Alexander Heidel, *The Babylonian Genesis*, 2nd ed. (Chicago: University of Chicago Press, 1963), pp. 18-60 and the fine analysis in Thorkild Jacobsen, *The Treasures of Darkness* (New Haven: Yale University Press, 1976), pp. 167-91.

5. This political aspect is unique to this Babylonian version.

6. *Encyclopedia Biblica,* s.v. "The New Year in Mesopotamia." Hayim Tadmor. Hebrew. (Jerusalem: Bialik Institute, 1967) 7: cols. 305.11.

Sinai I: Creation by the One

Genesis

Nowhere is the impact of the monotheistic revolution in Israel more apparent than in the first two chapters of the Hebrew Bible where the story of creation stands in stark contrast to the Babylonian cosmogonic epic. To begin with, the Mesopotamian gods are part of nature; more precisely, they are born through procreation out of a primordial aquatic substance. By linking cosmogony to theogony the *Enuma Elish* implies that the gods are subservient to the primordial realm that preceded them and gave them life. In Genesis God stands supreme outside all of nature which is His creation and entirely subservient to His will.[1] Not only is God removed from all aspects of nature but in Genesis 1, where He creates the universe, He is totally devoid of all human characteristics such as body, sex and a mate. Even in Genesis 2, where more anthropomorphisms appear as He enters into human relationship, He still lacks human form.

The Babylonian account of creation is characterized by sex and violence beginning with the sexual union of the gods and proceeding to its final phase through the violent conflict of parent gods and their offspring. In the course of this conflict monsters and demons are formed and released. The release of the monsters and demons by Tiamat during the combat preceding creation implies that there is a demonic aspect to primordial nature. The cosmos consists of demonic matter, the negative creation of Tiamat and divine form, the more positive contribution of Marduk.[2] The double nature of the cosmos implies a continuous struggle in which man and nature are involved. In the Bible, however, there is no active opposition to God's creative labor. Nature is demythologized and, having no independent power, follows the rational order God has imposed on it. In the Hebrew saga, creation is the result of God's word. Order is imposed on nature by divine fiat and everything is good from the very beginning.

It is true that the power of the word was a widespread notion in the ancient Near East but this power was essentially magical. The pronouncement of the right word like the performance of the right magical action actualized the divinity or the demonic inherent in matter.[3] In contrast, the divine word in Genesis is stripped of magic and the biblical author is silent as to the nature of those things upon which the divine word acted creatively. In the biblical view words, not magic, underlie reality. Humanity's capacity for using language sets it apart from other creatures and puts it in touch with the world as it is. Spoken language is the medium of everything human and divine that happens in the Bible and the biblical author converts even preverbal and nonverbal reactions into the spoken word because this is his way of getting at the essence of things.[4] Thus for example, when God enters into a covenant with Abraham he changes his name from Abram to Abraham and his wife's name from Sarai to Sarah to reify their new status as progenitors of the future nation.

In Genesis, the conflicts of the *Enuma Elish* are transmuted into a series of creative polarities each complementing the other. In the first half of chapter one creation is a series of bifurcations. God divides primordial light from primordial darkness, the upper waters from the lower waters, day from night, earth light from earth darkness. The symmetrical divisions point to coherence as the hallmark of creation. The sequence is logical and intelligible. Underlying the created order are four principles, place, separation, motion and life but particularly the last three. God brought order out of chaos mainly through acts of separation, division and distinction. Implicit in the first chapter of Genesis is a concept of hierarchical evolution in which higher forms have a greater degree of individuality (the result of separation, (motion, i.e., locomotion or mobility) and life. Human beings stand at the pinnacle of creation because they have the greatest potential for individuality exemplified by speech (which implies the making and recognition of separations and distinctions) mobility, the product of human intelligence and life whose quantitative and qualitative edge in humans is the product of speech and intelligence.[5]

The creation of humanity also highlights the differences between the biblical account and the Babylonian epic. Both accounts picture the deity as a sculptor working with flesh and bone (Gen. 2:7) but in the Babylonian narrative humans are fashioned as a kind of afterthought, as menials of the gods to provide them with nourishment and to generally satisfy their physical needs. The biblical text sees humanity as a crown of creation made in the image of God (Gen. 1:26-27). Only in the case of man is the material from which he is created explicitly mentioned implying his unique position among created things. Man alone has the breath of life blown into his nostrils by his Maker and man alone has the power of speech to name the animals. The creation of woman out of man's rib implies that she too is a crown of creation endowed with a divine image. The equality of Adam and Eve is further emphasized in the verses that speak of them as becoming one flesh (Gen. 2:23-24).

The stark contrasts between the Babylonian epic and the biblical creation narrative are like the contrasting colors in a great mural seen from a distance. On closer examination the finer nuances of shading become more apparent, for the biblical author subtly alludes to the *Enuma Elish* in his monotheistic reworking of the familiar story. My analysis follows the order of creation in the Bible.

Gen. 1:2 describes conditions before creation began as "the earth being unformed and void, with darkness over the surface of the deep and a wind from God sweeping over the water." Similarly, Marduk used the winds to overcome Tiamat and then paused to examine her dead body just before he split her in half to form the sky and the earth.[6] The latter action of Marduk is analogous to God's creation of the sky as a divider separating the supernal and the terrestrial waters, until now an undifferentiated mass. Then God commanded the terrestrial waters to "be gathered unto one area, that the dry land may appear (Gen. 1:6-9). Genesis 1 also makes a distinction between the light created on the first day and the heavenly luminaries that were not created until the fourth day. The same situation exists in the *Enuma Elish* where Apsu tells Tiamat that he can neither rest during the day nor sleep at night because of the noise of the young gods. Yet, the heavenly lights were set in the sky by Marduk only after the great victory over Tiamat.

Another biblical reworking of the combat myth is found in Gen. 1:21 which tells us that God created "the great sea monsters." But these mythological beings, who elsewhere in the Bible are described as continuing to rebel against God (Isa. 27:1; 51:9), are in Genesis not at all preexistent rivals of God but merely His own creatures. Nevertheless, the allusion to a continuing struggle extending into the apocalyptic end time in the Isaiah passages alerts us to an idea of the *Enuma Elish*, which though greatly muted in Genesis 1, appears again and again throughout the Bible. After defeat by Marduk, Tiamat does not disappear but is transformed into sky and earth. The influence of the defeated Tiamat continues, as mentioned above, in the demonic aspect of nature which constantly presses against the forms imposed on it by Marduk. In Genesis the demythologized primordial waters are confined to two places, the space above the sky and the seas on and below the earth. But like the demonic influences of Tiamat, the forces of chaos in the Bible are always poised to overrun the boundaries set by divine order.[7]

It is in this context that we can understand the narrative of Gen. 6:1-4, a reworking of the combat myth in its Hurrian variation, a variation indebted to the Mesopotamian version for a number of key elements. In Genesis 6 we are told of the *bene elohim*, the divine beings who, attracted by the beauty of human females, descended from heaven and mated with them producing an offspring of giants who were known as the men of renown. Of the sex and violence of the combat myth only the sex is present in this reworking but its depiction of the obliteration of the division between heaven and earth, between the divine and the human carries with it a tone of horror at such depravity. The juxtaposition of this section before the narrative of the great flood in the time of Noah is clearly intended to show a compelling motive for the impending disaster.[8] Just as the divine beings unleashed the forces of moral chaos by crossing the boundary separating the realm of heaven from the realm of earth, so measure for measure to restore the balance (see chapter 4) God removed the boundaries holding back the chaos of nature so that

> All the fountains of the great deep burst apart
> And the floodgates of the sky broke open (Gen. 7:11).

After the flood as the world is recreated around Noah and his family it is only the oath of God embodied in the Noahite Covenant that stands between order and chaos (Gen. 9:8-11). But the survival of chaos obliquely raises the possibility that it may again break through obliterating human civilization. To allay this anxiety the prophet asserts that though the benevolent world-ordering side of God may be temporarily eclipsed, it can never be uprooted or overthrown (Isa. 54:7-10). Yet the tension generated by the survival of chaos, which though banished by God still poses a threat, reverberates throughout the Bible (Pss. 29:3; 89:26; 93:3-4; 104:6-9: Job 38:8-11).

Tiamat, whose malevolent influence continues even after her demise, as we have just seen, has a philological equivalent which is rendered in the Hebrew original of Genesis 1 as *Tehom* (the deep, i.e. the depths of the Primeval sea). Although *Tehom* is not a feminine noun it is frequently followed by a feminine adjective or adverb as in Gen. 6:11 thus suggesting a transformation by the biblical writer of a female dragoness into a natural phenomenon. The Babylonian goddess is not only a female requiring a male to conceive but also possesses the male potency to impregnate herself, as well as the masculine, aggressive tendencies expressed in battle.

The verses in Genesis implying the androgynous nature of the first humans (Gen. 1:27; 2:23-24) suggest that the biblical author was not unaware of Tiamat's bisexuality. He simply transferred this characteristic from the level of deity to the plane of humanity.

The creation of the first humans, described so differently in the *Enuma Elish* and the Bible as noted above, proves, on closer examination of the biblical narrative, to contain a link, though ever so small, leading to the Mesopotamian cosmogony. In Genesis God proposes to create humanity, male and female together with this declaration: "Let us make man in our image, after our likeness" (Gen. 1:26). Since the "royal we" was not part of the vocabulary of kings or gods in the ancient Near East, God seems to be addressing other primordial divine beings. Because they do not object to His proposal to create human beings, we cannot determine whether God's initiative, like Marduk's involved an element of collegiality. But from other biblical accounts of the divine assembly in session (I Kings 22:19-23; Job 1:6-12; 2:1-6) it seems that the divine beings do advise and consent though God alone remains the final authority.[9] Thus, the divine beings of the Bible, like the other gods at the end of the *Enuma Elish*, are real and important but also subordinate and not individualized.

The creation narrative of Genesis 1 is concluded with God resting on the seventh day and hallowing it (Gen. 2:1-4) thus laying the ground for the institution of the Sabbath (Exod. 20:8-11). The *Enuma Elish* concludes, as we saw earlier, with the establishment of the cult of Marduk around his temple, the *Esagila*, in his capital city of Babylon, the site of the great New Year celebration at which the epic of creation was read and dramatically reenacted. Is there any connection between these two cultic conclusions to the Hebrew and Mesopotamian cosomogonies? It is clear that Genesis, unlike the *Enuman Elish* is silent about any relation between the creation of the world and the Israelite cult or political system. Thus it is not a text for the ritual reenactment of the birth of the universe at the Hebrew New Year festival nor is it used in any way to substantiate the development of the primitive democracy and the monarchy in ancient Israel. Nevertheless, the connection between creation and the Hebrew cult is not entirely absent from the Bible. The seven day creation-scheme of Genesis is, as scholars have suggested, implicitly associated in the Bible with the seven day Passover spring festival and the seven day *Sukkot* (Tabernacles) fall festival (which is an extension of the New Year and Day of Atonement observance). Post-biblical tradition has indicated that both the first day of the fall month Tishri and the first day of the spring month

Nisan were reckoned as New Year's days.[10] If this was the case in biblical times as well and if some biblical scholars are right in their conjecture that there were two New Year's festivals in early Israel, one in the fall and one in the spring,[11] then the connection between the seven days of creation and the seven days of the fall and spring festivals, each at one time associated with a New Year, is no coincidence. The parallel to the *akitu* festival of the Mesopotamian New Year celebration at which the *Enuma Elish* was presented, though tenuous, is nevertheless real. Similarly, the cosmic symbolism of the Tabernacle in the wilderness and the Jerusalem Temple (discussed in chapter 7) and the linguistic parallels between the biblical accounts of the creation of the world in Genesis and the building of the wilderness Tabernacle in Exodus suggest the idea that creation culminates in temple building. This is also a theme of the *Enuma Elish* in which the capstone of Marduk's cosmogony is the construction of the *Esagila*, his temple in Babylon.[12]

The Wisdom Literature

A striking parallel to the Torah account of creation in Genesis 1 is Ps. 104. In fact, some scholars argue that Ps. 104 preceded and influenced the creation narrative of Genesis.[13] In Genesis God's first creative act is the creation of light and Ps. 104 begins with an image of God donning in splendor his robe of light. The separation of supernal and terrestrial waters to make room for sky and land in Genesis is rendered poetically in Ps. 104:3-4 as God setting "the rafters of His lofts in the waters" and using the clouds as his chariot, moving "on the wings of the wind." The psalm then proceeds to dovetail with Genesis, though not exactly in every place, in describing the succeeding acts of creation concluding with a meditation on the dependence of all life upon God for food and for life itself (Ps. 104:27-30). Similarly, Genesis concludes the sixth and final day of active creation with God assigning the plants and fruits to humans and animals for food (Gen. 1: 29-31). There is also an overlap in vocabulary between Genesis 1 and Ps. 104 such as the use of the terms "fill", "full", and "fullness."[13]

Most interesting is the reference to the primordial sea monster, the daunting adversary of the combat myth, who is reduced in Gen. 1:21 to the anonymous sea monsters who are neither primordial or free of God's rule or an embarrassment to it. The monster in Ps. 104:26, however, is given a name the Leviathan whom God created for His personal diversion and amusement. The great beast never opposed its designer, maker and owner; it is just one more of the miracles of creation that prompts the psalmist to ecstatic praise of God's wisdom.

The only discordant note in this psalm of adoration appears in the last verse: "May sinners disappear from the earth and the wicked be no more" (Ps. 104:35). But this verse must be seen as a complement to verses 6-9. Just as God has set bounds to the waters of chaos but has not destroyed them and their continued survival represents a clear danger for the natural order, so has he set bounds to human evil but has not obliterated it and its continued existence poses a distinct threat to the moral order. The psalmist's hope is that some day the waters of chaos "will never again cover the earth" (verse 9) and that "sinners (will) disappear from the earth" (verse 35). In this context the interpretation of the latter verse by Beruryah, the scholarly wife of R. Meir is pertinent. When certain evil individuals antagonized her husband and he prayed for their death, she rebuked him interpreting Ps. 104:35 as expressive of God's desire for the destruction of sin (*hataim*) and not sinners (*hot'im*), and exhorting him to pray rather that they repent of their evil ways.[14]

The difference between Genesis 1 and Ps. 104 is that the latter does not concentrate on the *process* of creation but is a panoramic tour of the natural world undertaken for the purpose of praising the creator for his peerless wisdom in conceiving and fashioning such a marvelous place. In this respect Ps. 104 is strikingly similar to "The Hymn to the Aten", an Egyptian composition dated with certainty in the reign of the Pharaoh Amunhotpe IV in the mid-fourteenth century B.C.E.[15] Because of his quasi-monotheistic reform and his devotion to the solar disc, understood as a universal creator god, the Pharaoh changed his name to Akhenaton ("the effective spirit of Aten"). Not only are there verbal correspondences between the Hebrew psalm and the Egyptian hymn, but there are also parallel images such as the evocation of divine light, sunrise in "The Hymn to the Aten", and God's wrapping Himself "in a robe of light" in Ps. 104. The crucial difference between the two compositions is that the "Hymn to the Aten" regards the physical sun itself as a divine being[16] while Ps. 104:19 points to God's creation of the solar body.

Psalm 104 echoes a fundamental outlook of the wisdom books of the Bible and post-biblical literature in which the divine order of creation is raised to a revelatory experience which like the revelation of the Torah at Sinai endows human life with supreme happiness and sublime meaning. The revelation of law and salvational history promulgated at Sinai was mediated through priests and prophets but the revelation of God's order in the universe was mediated by the wisdom teachers of Israel (see chapter 6). According to these teachers the due order given by God to the mysterious works of creation can be summed up in the term "wisdom". Wisdom is both in the world but also separate from the work of creation. It is a kind of "meaning" or ordering principle implanted by God in creation.

In Prov. 8:30-31 wisdom is described as a darling child playing before God and delighting Him even before He created the world. This image is stylistically derived from Egyptian texts which describe the deity as a father who is embraced by a baby daughter, *Maat*. He kisses her after he has "set her at his nose." In Egyptian wisdom literature, *Maat* is a central concept embodying law, world order and justice.[17] But there are vast differences between the Egyptian *Maat* and the Hebrew wisdom. Wisdom has no divine status, nor is it a hypostasized attribute of God, but rather something created *by* God and assigned its proper function. Though wisdom is distinguished from the rest of creation (in Proverbs 8 and Job 28) it is an entity which belongs in the world even if it is the creature above all creatures.

The creation chapter of Proverbs 8 does not merely recapitulate the Genesis saga but introduces a new element: the world order turns as a person toward human beings and in direct address encourages them. The link between this chapter and the pragmatic advice for the conduct of human affairs in the rest of Proverbs is the principle discussed in detail in chapters 4 and 5 - the rule of wisdom in the natural order (in mysteries of creation) and in the moral order (in the affairs of men). Sometimes the wisdom in these two orders is contrasted. Thus in Job 28, the poet stresses that despite the extensive knowledge and ability of man, *homo faber*, who can mine gold and silver in the heart of a mountain, he cannot fathom the place where wisdom is found. But more often, as in the Book of Proverbs, the two forms of wisdom complement one another; the pursuit of the larger meanings of life represented by the mysteries of creation includes the wisdom required to order day-to-day affairs.

Wisdom personified is not always at the disposal of the individual seeking guidance whenever needed. She can also withdraw herself from those who do not heed her with catastrophic consequences. Horror, terror and distress descend upon human life (Prov. 1:24-31). This withdrawal is not motivated by jealousy or anger but is carried out with sadness in accordance with the laws of reciprocity (see chapter 4). In actuality wisdom has a deep and abiding love for man.

The idea that wisdom is not only immanent in the universe as an abstract principle but deeply loves and cares for human beings is found in a range of texts from the biblical Proverbs to the post biblical Joshua ben Sira and the Wisdom of Solomon. In these texts the motif of love of Creator and creation for the individual expressed by wisdom reinforces the axiom of the first chapter of Genesis that all that God had made was good. Wisdom's love is reciprocated by the wise man. The Wisdom of Solomon (6:12-16) describes how the wise man runs with delight toward a meaning which is already rushing towards him; he uncovers a mystery which was already on its way to reveal itself to him as a young wife reveals herself to her beloved. The surrender of the human being to the glories of existence, verging on the mystical, is found not only in this text but also as we have just seen, in the hymns and psalms of praise extolling the majesty, sublimity and mystery of the divine order (e.g., Pss. 8; 19:2; 97:6; 104; 145:10; 148). The instruction of nature, according to the wisdom teachers, is everywhere to be found and its purpose is to make evident the glory of God.

> But ask the beasts and they will teach you;
> The birds of the sky, they will tell you.
> Or speak to the earth, it will teach you;
> The fish of the sea, they will inform you.
> Who among all these does not know
> That the hand of the Lord has done this?
> (Job 12:7-9). [18]

Notes

1. Yehezkel Kaufmann, *The Religion of Israel*, trans. and abridged by Moshe Greenberg (Chicago: University of Chicago Press, 1960), pp. 21-25

2. Mircea Eliade, *A History of Religious Ideas*, 2 vols. (Chicago: The University of Chicago Press, 1978), pp. 1:72

3. Samuel N. Kramer, *History Begins at Sumer* (Toronto: Doubleday, 1959), pp. 79f.

4. Robert Alter, *The Art of Biblical Narrative* (New York: Basic Books, 1981), pp. 69-70

5. Leo Strauss, "On the Interpretation of Genesis," *L'Homme XXI* (1) (January-March, 1981): 5-20, Cf. Leon R. Kass, "Evolution and the Bible" *Commentary* 86:5 (November, 1988): 29-39.

6. Alexander Heidel, *The Babylonian Genesis* 2nd ed. (Chicago: University of Chicago Press, 1963), pp. 40, 42-43; W. G. Lambert, "A New Look at the Babylonian Background of Genesis," *Journal of Theological Studies* (1965): 287-300.

7. This ancient Near Eastern myth that haunted the Sinai consciousness for centuries has been treated extensively in modern scholarship. Cf. Umberto Cassuto, *The Goddess Anath: Canaanite Epics of the Patriarchal Age* trans. Israel Abrahams (Jerusalem: Magnes Press, 1971), pp. 33-34; Mary K. Wakeman, *God's Battle with the Monster: A Study in Biblical Imagery* (Leiden: E. J. Brill, 1973); Herman Gunkel, *Schopfung und Chaos in Urzeit und Endzeit: Eine religionsgeschichtliche Untersuchung uber Gen. 1 und Ap. Joh 12* (Gottingen: Vanderhoek and Ruprecht, 1895); Jon D. Levenson, *Creation and the Persistence of Evil* (San Francisco: Harper & Row, 1988), pp. 14-25; Adela Yarbro Collins, *The Combat Myth in the Book of Revelation* (Missoula: Scholars Press for Harvard Theological Review, 1976).

8. *The Anchor Bible*, Genesis, intro., trans. and notes by E. A. Speiser (Garden City, N.Y.: Doubleday & Company, 1964), pp. 44-46.

9. See the Commentary of Rashi to Gen. 1:26.

10. *M. Rosh Ha-Shanah* 1:1

11. Frank Moore Cross, *Canaanite Myth and Hebrew Epic* (Cambridge: Harvard University Press, 1973), p. 105, n. 48 and p. 123, n. 37.

12. Levenson, *Creation and the Persistence of Evil*, pp. 78-99.

13. *Ibid.* pp. 53-54; p. 59.

14. *b. Berakot*, 10a.

15. See Pritchard, *Ancient Near Eastern Texts*, pp. 369-371 for the translation of the texts.

16. Kaufmann, *The Religion of Israel*, p. 226, n.6.

17. Gerhard Von Rad, *Wisdom in Israel* (Nashville and New York: Abingdon Press, 1972), pp. 72-73.

18. *Ibid.*, 144-176.

Sinai II: Creation Interpreted

In the rabbinic legends of the Bible, particularly those stemming from the latter part of the tannaitic period and from the amoraic period, the Babylonian creation myths, whose remnants were kept alive and embellished in popular tales and folklore, reappear in a more full bodied form.[1] There we read that the masculine waters, the waters above, desired union with the feminine waters below and had not God separated them by means of the sky their union might have destroyed the world.[2] In another rabbinic legend Rahab, the Angel of the Sea, rebelled at the creation of the world. God had commanded Rahab to take in the water but when he refused he was punished by death and his body rests in the depths of the sea where the water dilutes the foul odor emanating from it.[3] Even in this more pronounced form the cosmic sexual union is attributed to the waters and the cosmic rebellion to the Angel of the Sea not to the Almighty who is supreme and exalted above all.

The concept of a preexistent struggle between the Creator and a mythological rival or rivals, characteristic of the combat myth, refined and transformed in the Bible, is further transmuted by the rabbis. Describing God as creating worlds and destroying them until He made the present universe and was satisfied, the rabbis imply that our world was formed out of a preexistent chaos.[4] The survival of this malevolent chaos into the present and the future, held in check only by God's covenant with Noah, a central theme of the Bible as mentioned above, is also echoed by the rabbis. Rabbi Simeon ben Lakish said: "What is the meaning of the verse, 'And there was evening and there was morning *the* sixth day' (Gen. 1:31)? This teaches us that the Holy One Blessed be He made a condition with the created world that he fashioned. He said: 'If Israel receives the Torah on Sinai everything will be fine but if not then I shall turn you back into chaos.'"[5]

According to R. Simeon, the definite article (i.e., *the* sixth day omitted from the enumeration of the other days of creation in the Bible) is superfluous in the verse but alludes to the sixth day of the Hebrew month *Sivan* on which, according to tradition, Israel received the Torah at Sinai. Here the biblical covenant with Noah has been replaced by the covenant of Sinai. By linking creation to revelation R. Simeon suggests that the natural order of creation is dependent on the moral order of the Torah which keeps the world from reverting to chaos. The concept of a continuing malevolent chaos, the residue of the worlds that were destroyed by God before

He created this world, as the source of evil in the universe passes into the Zohar, the great text of medieval Jewish mysticism.[6]

But there is also a talmudic tradition that views demons created by God as another source of evil in the universe. On the first Sabbath eve, at twilight, as God was bringing his work of creation to completion, He created these evil beings, who, though included in the plan, were left for last. God had just fashioned their souls when the hastening Sabbath overtook Him and He was compelled to cease His labors to hallow the first day of rest. For this reason the demons have no bodies but are composed entirely of spirit.[7] An element of the old Babylonian combat myth has resurfaced in this talmudic tradition although it has been reshaped in a changed context. There is an allusion here to the monsters created by Tiamat to do battle with the younger gods.

The biblical image suggesting that God, though retaining final authority, sought advice and consent from His heavenly retinue, a faint echo of Marduk's collegiality in the *Enuma Elish*, is expanded by the rabbis. In numerous legends they describe God as taking counsel with the angels.[8]

The rabbinic legends are also more explicit than the biblical narrative regarding the androgyny of Adam. Thus we find the statement that when the Holy One blessed be He created Adam he made him an androgynous being as Scripture states: "male and female he created them" (Gen. 5:1-2).[9] But as in the Bible, so too in the rabbinic legend this characteristic is removed from divinity and transferred to humanity.

Notes

1. M. D. Cassuto, "*Shirat ha-Alilah be-Yisrael,*" *Knesset* 8 (1943-44): 121-144.
2. Louis Ginzberg, *The Legends of the Jews* 7 vols. (Philadelphia: Jewish Publication Society, 1947): 1:15; 5:17-18, nn. 48, 59, 52. Henceforth referred to as Ginzberg, *Legends*.
3. *Ibid.* 1:18. Cf. Irving Jacobs, "Elements of Near-Eastern Mythology in Rabbinic Aggadah," *Journal of Jewish Studies* 28, No. 1 (1977): 1-11.
4. *Gen.* R. 3:7 (ed. Theodor-Albeck), p. 23; Ginzberg, *Legends*, 5:3-4, n. 5.
5. *b. Avodah Zarah*, 3a; Cf. *b. Shabbat*, 88a; *Deut. R.* 8:5; *Ruth R.* beginning; Ginzberg, *Legends* 1:52; 3:92; 5:67-68, n. 8.
6. G. Scholem, *Kabbalah* (New York: Quadrangle, 1974), p. 124.
7. *M. Avot*, 5:6; *Gen. R.* 7:7 (ed. Theodor-Albeck), p. 54; The commentary of *Hadar Zekenim* on Gen. 2:3 and Joshua Trachtenberg, *Jewish Magic and Superstition* (New York: Atheneum, 1974), p. 29.
8. Ginzberg, *Legends* 5:3, n. 3.
9. *Gen. R.* 8:1 (ed. Theodor-Albeck), p. 55 and parallels cited there. Ginzberg, *Legends* 5:88-89, n. 42.

Olympus I: Cosmogony as Theogony

Homer and Hesiod

The earliest Greek reference to creation appears in a Homeric epithet which describes Oceanus as "the source of the gods" (*theon genesin*, *Il.* 14.201, 246, 302). This notion that the cosmos developed out of anthropomorphized primordial waters corresponds to the priority of Tiamat and Apsu in the *Enuma Elish* and the use of *tehom* in Gen. 1:1. *The Iliad* (14. 258-61) also refers to Night as a personified goddess, the "mistress of gods and men", so powerful that Zeus himself dreaded to anger her. Perhaps Homer knew of a tale in which she too had cosmogonic significance, for Aristotle (*Metaphysics* 1091 b4) alludes to "those writers about the gods who generate from Night."[1] The fact that cosmogonies were attached to the names of poets, sages, and legendary holy men both before and after Homer indicates that theogonies were a traditional genre which may have originated in or been connected with some ritual.[2] But Homer was more interested in the deeds of heroes than in the birth of the gods. Nowhere does he elaborate upon the oral tradition which lay behind his references to Oceanus or Night.

Hesiod's *Theogony* is the first extant poem which describes the creation of the universe in detail. As the title indicates, the poem is about the birth of the gods. In the course of one thousand lines, the Greek divinities come into being, their positions, functions and personalities are described, and prominent features of a variety of cult practices are validated. There are no signs, however, either in the text of Hesiod's poem or in its subsequent history, that this cosmogony was ever connected directly or symbolically, to cultic New Year's festivities or symbolism, as were the Near Eastern epics and perhaps Genesis. *Theogony* was simply a poem intended for the entertainment as well as the education of the audience, in a setting similar to that of the bards described in the Odyssey.[3] The occasion for Hesiod's performance may have been a poetry contest at funeral games honoring a dead king. And perhaps Hesiod's choice of subject was motivated by an interest in human history, for the poet seems to have organized the relevant pieces of the oral tradition in an attempt to fill in the period from the beginning of time to the heroic age, just prior to his own, for listeners who were already familiar with Homeric kings interacting with a well defined Olympic pantheon.[4] Whether or not *Theogony* actually won the prize, for a long time the cosmogony "had no serious rivals and established itself as an acceptable statement of how the world and the gods came to be."[5]

Hesiod's *Theogony* brings together a long and diffuse oral tradition. Although composed around 730 B.C.E. in mainland Greece (Ascra, Boeotia), it includes themes, ideas, and descriptions reminiscent of Hurrian, Babylonian, Egyptian, and Hittite myths interwoven with native Greek traditions. It is difficult to separate out common motifs from direct borrowings and nearly impossible to determine which borrowings came from where and at what date.[6] It is clear, however, that, despite features similar to those found in Near Eastern tales, Hesiod's version of creation presents a different view of the evolution of the world order and a different end product.

As in the Near Eastern epics, cosmogony is equated with theogony. Out of Chaos, a gap or opening, come anthropomorphic deities who are also physical realities: e.g., Earth, Tartarus, a dark place in the depth of the earth, Night, and Darkness. Although Earth (Gaia) brings forth Sky (Ouranos), Hills (Ourea), and Sea (Pontos) without sexual union, through copulation with Sky she bears six sons and six daughters, some of whom are aspects of the natural world such as Ocean, Sun and Moon. These divinities mate to produce more specific parts of nature: springs, rivers, waves, winds, dawn, stars, etc.

The Greek theogony also produces deities who represent forces affecting the lives of individuals and societies. One of Chaos' first children is Love (Eros), the cosmic principle of harmony and sexual union which makes procreation possible for humans, gods, and nature. Night, another child of Chaos, produces deities who personify the limitations and perils of life: Death, Deceit, Old Age and Strife. Succeeding generations represent more distinct facets of social order or disorder—e.g., Law, Memory, Famine, Toil. The younger gods, Zeus and his siblings and children, have more specific human characteristics which reflect different age groups and personality types. Moreover, these newer divinities patronize the activities which not only make human survival possible but also endurable. As the opening hymn makes clear, the Muses and Apollo teach sweet music which alleviates sorrow, whereas Zeus guides princes' wise decisions and persuasive speeches. Thus, the Greek cosmogony/theogony traces the gradual development of a natural world which is essentially anthropocentric.[7] In fact, the *Theogony* ends with a catalogue of human heroes born from matings between divinities and mortals almost at the point where cosmic history is over and human history begins.[8]

The progress of the cosmos from Chaos to the Olympian pantheon and their semidivine descendants occurs over a series of generations. Just as in the Near Eastern tales, the proliferation of offspring produces conflict. When Sky refuses to release their children from Earth, the divine mother induces her son Cronus to castrate his father (thereby separating Sky and Earth to make further differentiation of the natural world possible). Cronus, fearing his own children's violence against him, swallows each one as it is born. His consort, Rhea, with Earth's help, saves her youngest son Zeus so that he can liberate his siblings. Before Zeus is able to gain eternal control of the natural and social order, he must in turn defeat threats against him - from the rebellious Titans or Giants, from Typho, the fiery dragon generated by Earth and Tartarus, from wily Prometheus, and from his first wife Metis (Wisdom) whom he swallows pregnant to insure his control over their "very wise" offspring (894). This series of conflicts has obvious affinities with the succession drama by which Marduk gains absolute control of heaven. It also resembles the Hurrian Epic of Kumarbi which contains the castration and swallowing motifs as well as the creation of a monster to oppose the storm god.

Although Zeus' swallowing of Metis prevents the birth of a child destined to overthrow him, their daughter Athena, "having strength equal to her father and sage in counsel" (896), is born from Zeus' own head, as if an extension of himself. Thus she is transformed from his rival into his adjutant. Athena's position as Zeus' favorite daughter calls to mind the Egyptian personification of Maat as the child of god and Wisdom as God's first creation in Proverbs. Her preeminence as the agent of her father's plans, with access to his lightning bolts, and her patronage of intelligence, persuasion, and craft among humans further link Athena with the personification of Wisdom in the Bible. But she is also a warrior goddess, "to whom clamor and battles and fighting are pleasing" (924-6). And Athena does not play any role as a cosmogonic deity. She functions rather as an intermediary between Zeus and mortals, and the guide toward the uses of intelligence in all aspects of life.[9]

In *Theogony,* most of the natural world is created by generational proliferation. Therefore, Zeus is not a creator god like Marduk and the world that human beings will eventually inhabit is not a lesser realm carved out of a defeated enemy's carcass. Rather, Earth, Sky, Hills, and Sea are primary divinities who came into being before the matings and violence, and Earth herself remains a revered goddess, a wise advisor to the younger gods including Zeus. Nor does Zeus arbitrarily impose his own will on the world which has developed prior to his ascension to the throne. Zeus' new order after the victory for the most part confirms the existing distribution of privileges and functions that Sky or Cronus tried to suppress (392-6). Thus nature has a validity and order of its own and is basically not capricious. The fact that the banishment of the Titans to Tartarus results in a symmetrical universe where earth is equidistant from heaven and Hades (720-21) underscores the rationality of the natural world.

The political order too is different and is validated by a different means. Unlike Marduk, whose allies are powerless without him, Zeus needs to find support among the earlier generations and cannot demand allegiance unless he makes concessions. So Zeus, following Earth's advice, releases potential enemies like the Cyclopes and the Hundred-handed Brothers from the punishment imposed by their father Sky "who was jealous of their superior manliness, beauty, and great size" (619-20). To get the help of the enemies of Cronus and the Titans, Zeus promises to restore their former privileges and functions in exchange for their loyalty. He makes new allies by offering equal shares to those who were positionless before. According to *Il.* 15.185-99, Zeus and his brothers, Hades and Poseidon, drew lots after the battle and divided up the domain equally so that although Zeus rules wide heaven and the earth beneath it, he cannot assert complete control over Hades' realm in the underworld or Poseidon's on the seas. Nor can Zeus fix his present power by suppressing his offspring as his father and grandfather did. His eager parenting of so many children who contribute new and positive elements to his order provides the encouragement for creativity and progress under his eternal aegis.

The different positions of Zeus and Marduk reflect the differences in the two societies which worshipped them.[10] At the end of the *Enuma Elish,* Marduk is an autocrat, even though his absolute power has been ceded to him in a democratic fashion. He enjoys his own cult center, his capital city, and copious eulogies from deities whose prerogatives he alone has determined. His autocracy validates the major features of the Babylonian despotism, highly organized under king and priesthood to maintain an economic system dependent on irrigation. Zeus, in contrast, presides over a multiplicity of gods and heroes whose own honors, cults, and localities are also legitimized in the *Theogony.* Although Zeus is "first in power" and "first in wisdom" and clearly has the authority to rule, he is the one god who organizes the many and maintains a harmony among them primarily by persuasion and compromise rather than by despotism. His cosmic order which incorporates and honors all parts of the whole validates the Greek ideal of unity without suppression, an ideal put forth by a loose union of city-states with a common language and cults, but each developing independently and facing its own problems of maintaining internal order.

Of course, those first divinities, Earth, Sky, and Sea, do produce some monstrous and violent descendants whose excessive might or unnatural physical features must be refined as nature achieves its complex final form and Zeus establishes a stable order. Their presence engenders such strife that even the victory over them threatens to return creation to its initial chaos. As in the biblical flood story, so in *Theogony,* god's weapon, here the fiery thunderbolt, nearly drives earth and heaven back together again (700-705). But the defeat of the rebellious monsters leads to a new stage in the cosmic order. When Zeus hurls his inveterate enemies beneath the earth, the Titans' imprisonment defines the limits of Tartarus and delineates the kingdom of Hades. Enceladus' eternal rage accounts for the activities of volcanoes whereas Typho's blasted body becomes the boisterous wind that causes men trouble.

Such development suggests that the demonic is not totally eliminated, but that, as in biblical poetry, it is controlled by the natural order and the divine authority. Although volcanoes and winds may threaten mortals, the depths of Tartarus prevent their violence from confounding high Olympus. Although strife may continue to occur among the immortals, Zeus' supreme authority and the power of the "dread" goddess Styx in Hades (776), plus the punishment for forswearing an oath made by her sacred water, will deter the catastrophic escalation of any divine quarrel (775-806). Most of the other hideous and unnatural monsters famed in Greek mythology are engendered by the sea (233-336), so closely associated with the demonic in muted biblical myth. In *Theogony,* however, they are either destroyed or given a proper place in the established order. Those beasts who threaten human communities, like the Sphinx, the Lernean Hydra, the Nemean Lion, and the Chimaera, succumb to the great heroes (e.g. Oedipus, Heracles, and Bellerophon) and enhance their glory. Cerberus, "the brazen-voiced, fifty-headed dog who eats raw flesh" (309-11) guards the entrance to Hades whereas his mother Echidna, the half-nymph, half snake who eats raw flesh, is given a "famous house" by the immortal gods, and protects Arima beneath the earth" (295-305). The winged horse Pegasus, son of Medusa, carries the thunder and lightning to Zeus on Olympus (284-6). The youngest offspring of Ceto (Sea Monster) is a dreadful snake whose task it is to guard the golden apples (333-5). The monstrous children of Earth and Sky, the One-eyed Cyclopes and Hundred-handed Brothers, become Zeus' weapon makers and defenders of his throne, respectively.

As the continued existence of the demonic suggests, the Greek cosmos retains a double nature even at its completion. Here too the bisexuality implicit in the activities of the earliest deities may reflect an initial unity. For Chaos, Earth, and Night, like Tiamat, can engender without a consort; Hera too bears Hephestus alone after Zeus gives birth to Athena. But Chaos' first series of births splits that unity into many. Their separation is organized according to a principle of polarity reminiscent of the bifurcations in Genesis and *Enuma Elish*.[11] The generational proliferation produces a series of opposites like light out of darkness, gentle breezes and fierce winds, nurturing springs and hideous sea monsters. From the castration of Sky came both Aphrodite, the beautiful goddess of love, and the Furies, the dreadful spirits of blood vengeance. As supreme ruler, Zeus must make a coherent whole by maintaining the proper balance among them. And Eros, one of Chaos' first born, represents a means to overcome this bifurcation and restore unity. The children of Zeus and Night, the Moirae (Fates) and Dike (Justice) offer a different, less physical means: apportionment as equal division and the measure for measure principle (see chapter four).

Yet the proliferating polarity of the divine world implies a human world which is not entirely good or beneficent. Its double nature is reflected in the personifications who represent aspects of human life. That life itself is limited from the beginning for Death comes into being very early. Thanatos (Death) is a child of Night with siblings who are synonyms for death - hateful Doom and black Fate. Night's other children, deceitful Old Age and strong-hearted Strife, and Strife's own offspring, Toil, Famine, Fighting, and Lawlessness, depict the grim realities of humans existence before humans even exist. But new principles by which these harsh aspects of life might be countered or diminished are also born. Night herself, for example, gives birth to Sleep, which is "kind to men" (763) and to Themis (Order) and Memory. When Zeus later mates with Themis, they produce Good Government, the Seasons, Justice and Peace. At every stage in the cosmic evolution, there is a balance of good and bad in the development of the moral and social order. In the story of Prometheus and Pandora, the notions of bifurcation and balance are stated explicitly; the first woman is created as the "beautiful evil" (*Kalon Kakon , Theogony* 585; see also, 570; *Works and Days* 57) meant to be the price for the good that is fire.[12]

Although Hesiod gives a detailed description of the origin of Pandora, he does not provide a precise account of the maker, material or motivation for the creation of man. Hesiod simply assumes his existence in *Theogony* 511 where he describes the banquet shared between gods and men in Mecone which resulted in the theft of fire and the formation of woman as a punishment. In *Works and Days,* in the allegory of the five ages, Hesiod says that gods and humans sprang from a common source (108), but "gods who dwell on Olympus" created the first two races, whereas Zeus created the others out of ash trees.[13]   Later accounts ascribe the creations of humans out of clay to Prometheus, the generation of a new group of men and women out of stones thrown upon earth, or the birth of soldiers from serpents' teeth in the soil. These tales suggest that human beings, like the rest of the cosmos, emerged from Mother Earth; in fact, Hesiod may not have named the first man simply because he knew of too many "first men," each an autochthonous founder of a different Greek community.[14]   Some scholars, however, speculate that the vagueness about the creation of the first man marks a suppression or distortion of the well-known but alien, Eastern tales where humans are shaped from Kingu's blood as a slave born to free the gods from menial labor. Perhaps the references to Zeus' unmotivated malevolence to man and Prometheus' position as man's champion in Aeschylus' *Prometheus Bound* reflect the influence of the tales of the controversy between the Babylonian gods Enlil and Enki over the destruction and status of human beings.[15]

If the Greeks' imprecision about the creation of mortals suggests they were unwilling to accept the Near Eastern idea of humanity's lowly position and limited potential, the polarity of the universe and the inevitability of death imply that humanity can never achieve the fullness of power and pleasure which belong only to the immortal gods. In the *Iliad,* where the human and divine planes are juxtaposed and linked to each other in various ways, the gods articulate the difference between them. Apollo, in 21.461-67, gives his reason for refusing to fight with Poseidon over Troy.

> Shaker of the earth, you would have me be as one without prudence
> if I am to fight you for the sake of insignificant
> mortals, who are as the leaves are, and now flourish and grow warm
> with life, and feed on what the ground gives, but then again
> fade away and are dead. Therefore let us with all speed
> give up this quarrel and let mortals fight their own battles.
> (Lattimore, trans.)[16]

And when the immortal horses Achilles brought to Troy mourn the death of Patroclus, Zeus himself pities their grief and says,

> . . . Poor wretches
> why then did we ever give you to the Lord Peleus,
> a mortal man, and you yourselves are immortal and ageless?
> since among all the creatures that breathe on earth and crawl on it
> there is not anywhere a thing more dismal than man is.
> (17.441-4, Lattimore, trans.)

At the end, Achilles and Priam temper their own grief by acknowledging that unhappiness is inevitable for mortals—that only the gods have no sorrow (*Il.* 24.525-526).

The Greek gods are not generally malevolent or capricious towards mortals, however. As we have seen, many of the divinities in the *Theogony* symbolize blessings and pleasures made available for humans. And we shall see that the gods validate and maintain a moral as well as a natural order in the human world. Nor do the gods disdain human beings. In the *Iliad*, they watch the struggles and affairs of the heroes with fierce partisan interest and even suffer when their favorites are endangered. Hesiod records many examples of early intercourse between mortals and gods that produced new divinities like Plutus and Dionysus as well as human heroes (e.g., Perseus, Memnon, Achilles, and Aeneas). In fact the poet asserts that at one time extraordinary mortals could themselves become immortals. Zeus made Dionysus' mother and wife divine, and of Heracles Hesiod comments,

> Happy he who has finished his great work and dwells among
> the immortal gods free from toil and ageless all his days.
> (954-55, White, trans.)[17]

Heracles' acceptance on Olympus suggests that the immortal gods respect and reward the courage and fortitude of "insignificant mortals."

Later Greek Theogonies

Pherecydes and Alcman— By the sixth century, other cosmogonies had appeared, perhaps under the influence of closer contact with Iranian and Indian ideas when the Persians began their move west.[18] Although they are clearly related to earlier creation tales, new ideas introduced in them reveal contradictory tendencies: on the one hand, the movement away from anthropomorphic myth toward abstraction and greater unity and, on the other, a closer connection between the description of creation and religious practice.

Pherecydes of Syros (c.550 B.C.E.) was said to be the first to call human souls immortal as well as the author of the first book in prose, which began, according to Diogenes Laertius (1.119), "Zas and Chronus always were and Chthonie; but Chthonie's name became Ge when Zas gave her the earth as a present." From the sparse fragments and references to Pherecydes, scholars have attempted to reconstruct and interpret his theogony.[19] Out of these three eternal deities, Time, Zeus, and the Earth, came the world as we know it. With his own seed, Time engendered Fire, Wind, and Water, from which new generations of gods developed. Zeus, however, married Chthonie and, as a wedding gift, wove a robe decorated with the terrestrial world, Ogenos (Ocean) and the mansions of Oganos (the places beyond the ocean). As in the other theogonies, generational proliferation produced strife, but in this case the leader of the battle against Chronos for the possession of heaven was Ophioneus whose name means "serpent" and he and his sons, the Ophionidai, were banished to the depths of the sea. Beneath the sea was the kingdom of the dead, where Pherecydes may have believed human souls went before they returned to earth. In the lowest depths was Tartarus, guarded by the daughters of Boreas, the Harpies, and Storm, to which "Zeus expels whosoever of the gods behaves insolently."[20]

From this brief and tentative summary, one can recognize similarities to Hesiod's *Theogony* as well as tales from the Near East and the suppressed theomachy in biblical poetry. The sections on the wedding and the battle of the gods may have developed out of or been used for bridal ceremonies and seasonal rituals. Pherecydes' Zeus resembles the craftsman/god of other creation stories, the divine weaver who, like a demiurge, fashions the world as a work of art.

But Pherecydes' tale also includes some notions which may account for Aristotle's statement that he was an intermediate kind of philosopher who didn't say everything in myth (*Metaphysics* 1091b8). Pherecydes' first cosmogonic god, the father of all, is the abstraction Time, so important to the later Greek philosophers and medical writers. Perhaps he was influenced by certain Iranian tales or was simply interested in the etymological link between the old god Cronus and *chronos*, the Greek word for time.[21] But an older poet Alcman had already displayed the same tendency toward abstraction. The few cosmogonic lines attributed to him relate that out of the waste of "trackless" and "featureless" waters arose Thetis and then Track and Feature, abstract and physical rather than anthropomorphic deities.[22]   Pherecydes also introduces the clearly physical abstraction when Time begets Air, Fire, and Water, three of the four primary elements of the nature philosophers (the fourth, Earth, is like Time, preexistent) and the constituents of semen, "being hot, wet and quickening."[23]

Pythagoras— By the end of the sixth century, B.C.E., other versions of creation were attributed to legendary poets like Orpheus and famous sages like Pythagoras, who was said to be the pupil of Pherecydes. It is hard for scholars to separate the person Pythagoras from the legends that accrued to him or to distinguish his own ideas from those of his followers or his interpreters.[24]   Our modern age generally associates Pythagoras with geometry, the ratios in musical harmonies, and the idea that number is the organizing principle of the universe.   In the cosmogony attributed to the Pythagoreans, the world was somehow generated from number, from the seed of the one, associated with the male and limit, which drew in from the unlimited, or female, time, breath, and the void to create distinctive things.[25]   The numbers one through ten were assigned certain qualities, some of which connected them to traditional religion, e.g.,

> 7 is opportunity (*Kairos*) and also Athena, as the "virginal" prime number [because among the first 10 it neither begets another nor is begotten by any] Ten is the perfect number and comprehends the whole nature of number and determines the structure of the cosmos. [26]

Certain geometric shapes were dedicated to certain deities: the angle of the triangle to the males Cronus, Hades, Ares, and Dionysus, the angle of the square to the female goddesses Rhea, Demeter, and Hestia, and the angle of the dodecagon to Zeus.[27] According to Walter Burkert, such symbolism is not really mathematics and can be paralleled in Greek poetry and cult as well as in other premathematical cultures. It developed from the urge to find correspondence and orderly arrangement in the world, to limit the unknowable and unlimited in time and space.

> Thus the multiplicity of the world is reduced to clearly articulated groups, whose mutual relationship is known to the "wise man"; and he "honors" this orderly arrangement in his practical activity.[28]

Pythagoras was such a "wise man", who believed in the reincarnation of the soul, and the kinship of all living things, and who founded a religious brotherhood which practiced abstinence and passed on his sayings (*akousmata*) and his number speculation as part of their secret knowledge.

Orpheus— By the end of the fifth century Pythagoras himself had become a legendary figure and was closely associated with Orpheus and the Orphics whose mystery religion offered initiates hope for their souls after death.[29] The theogony ascribed to Orpheus follows the familiar outline of a succession myth, but introduces changes which reflect different ideas about the unity and order of the universe and the relation between god and man. The universe began when Time coupled with Necessity and generated Aither and Night. From Aither, Time made an egg out of which emerged the winged god Phanes also known as Protoganos, the first born god. He carried within himself the seeds of all the other gods. By both autogenesis and matings with his offspring, Phanes produced a series of deities as well as the sun and moon and places for man and god. Such a demiurge born from Time has affinities with versions of creation developed in Phoenicia, Persia, and India, as well as the more abstract accounts of the activities of the Egyptian god of the Eternal Sun Re.[30]

As in the Egyptian tale, so in this Greek refinement of Hesiod, the last King God in the succession, Zeus, swallowed Protogonos/Phanes and the whole previous creation "became one with him." In an activity corresponding to creation by the word, Zeus brings everything out of his mouth in due order (except for Aphrodite who is born from his ejaculation). Not only are all aspects of the present world reborn as his creation, but he himself is the One who precedes and encompasses the Many, the polarities which the delineation of the cosmos necessitates. The Zeus proclaimed in a hymn ascribed to Orpheus resembles the unity of the one god of monotheism.

> Zeus was born first, Zeus last, god of the bright bolt:
> Zeus was male, Zeus was an immortal nymph.
> Zeus is the foundation of earth and starry heaven
> Zeus the king, Zeus the ruler of all, god of the bright bolt.[31]

Zeus' activity in engendering new deities concludes with the creation of humans and animals. In an allegory of the ages of man,

Phanes had already created a golden race and Cronus a silver. Now Zeus creates a new race of mortals out of a new material. When the Titans killed and devoured his infant son Dionysus, Zeus blasted them with his thunderbolt and reduced them to ashes. Dionysus' heart was saved by Athena so that he lived again (although his limbs were buried on Parnassus by Apollo). From the soot of the blasted Titans, Zeus created the animals, birds, and "the foolish human race that does not know good and evil."[32] Although humans have mortal bodies, they possess immortal souls which move from body to body. Unlike animal souls which float until a body catches them, after death the souls of mortals are led to the underworld for judgment. They are rewarded or punished for three hundred years before they are reborn into another body. To help humans achieve release from this cycle, Zeus ordained purification rites, sacrifices, and ceremonies which are under the special provenance of his child-mate Kore/Persephone and their son Dionysus.

Such a creation tale has a purpose. It traces the dual nature of man to the evil Titans and divine Dionysus so that the person who understands his origin may find his soul's release from mortal cycles through the proper rites. Unlike the poems of Hesiod and Homer, these tales were not sung to the general public by bards. Rather they were ascribed to a legendary poet like Orpheus and passed on as a sacred text, a *Hieros Logos,* which accompanied the secret rites of a mystery cult or were transmitted as the sacred lore of brotherhoods who established rules for this life in preparation for the soul's release.[33] But outsiders were familiar with the sacred texts, the general ideas in them, and the use to which they were put. Aristophanes' chorus of *Birds* (414 B.C.E.) bases their claim to priority over the Olympians on the birth of a winged god from the cosmic egg (693-703) and Plato alludes to

> . . . a whole farrago of books in which Musaeus and Orpheus, described as descendants of the Muses and the Moon, prescribe heir ritual; and they persuade entire communities, as well as individuals that both in this life and after death, wrongdoing may be absolved and purged away by means of sacrifices and agreeable performances which they are pleased to call rites of initiation. (*Republic* 2.364, Cornford, trans.)[34]

Participants in such rites believed that the immortal soul was imprisoned in a mortal body and exiled to earth as a punishment for a crime (as funerary inscriptions, the writings of Empedocles, and the maxims ascribed to Pythagoras, e.g., "Having come for punishment, we must be punished," suggest).[35] M. L. West conjectures that the immortal souls in humans are fallen *daimones*, beings intermediate between god and man, who Plato's pupil Xenocrates believed included the Titans. Familiar with Zeus' actions in the Orphic theogony, however, the Stoics moved away from the more chaotic pantheon of immortals towards a stabler monotheism. According to Cleanthes and Chrysippus, the other cosmic elements were gods but were not deathless. Zeus, the only eternal deity, periodically consumed and regenerated the rest out of himself.[36] The analogue in the biblical tradition is Genesis 6, where the conception of a class of "fallen angels" hints at a chaos which is ever threatening and at a divine hierarchy in which God rules supreme.

Notes

1.   See G. S. Kirk, J. E. Raven, and M. Schofield, *The Presocratic Philosophers: A Critical History with a Selection of Texts* (Cambridge: Cambridge University Press, 1983), pp. 7-74 for a summary of the earliest cosmogonic ideas. This text will be referred to in subsequent notes as KRS. Translations and fragment numbers for the Presocratics are quoted from KRS unless otherwise noted. Although most scholars consider that Hesiod followed Homer, M. L. West argues that Hesiod is the earliest Greek poet whose compositions have come down to us and that Homer is the later of the two. See West's edition, *Hesiod's "Theogony": Edited with Prolegomena and Commentary* (Oxford: Clarendon Press, 1966), pp. 40-48. The works of both poets are culminations of long oral traditions in separate genres, however, so that the unity of the texts and the dates or authenticity of individual verses or passages are subject to dispute.

2.   See West, *Theogony*, pp. 1-16 for a brief survey of theogonic poetry in other cultures and in Greece.

3.   The quote is from West, *Theogony*, p. 16. See pp. 43-46 as well as Hesiod, *Works and Days*, 654-9 for suppositions about the occasion for the performance.

4.   Thomas G. Rosenmeyer, "Hesiod and Historiography," *Hermes* 85 (1957): 267-85.

5.   M. L. West, *Early Greek Philosophy and the Orient* (Oxford: Clarendon Press, 1971), p. 203.

6.   Peter Walcot, *Hesiod and the Ancient Near East* (Cardiff: University of Wales, 1966) summarizes and compares the various stories and examines the evidence for Hesiod's date and the transmission from east to west. West, *Theogony*, pp. 1-48 summarizes the information. West's commentary has been used as a reference for the interpretation of Hesiod's text. See also Richard S. Caldwell, *Hesiod's "Theogony", Translated with Introduction, Commentary, and Interpretive Essay* (Cambridge: Focus Information Group, 1987).

7. Norman O. Brown, *Hesiod; "Theogony"*, *translated with an Introduction* (Indianapolis: Bobbs-Merrill, 1953), pp. 7-48, traces several aspects of this evolution. See also Linda S. Sussman, "The Birth of the Gods: Sexuality, Conflict and Cosmic Structure in Hesiod's *Theogony*," *Ramus* 7. 1 (1978): 61-77, which relates the physical evolution with the social and psychological and social aspects of human life.

8. Scholars disagree about where the authentic *Theogony* ended. See West, *Theogony*, pp. 48-52 and his commentary on lines 881-920.

9. Her roles as adjutant of her father Zeus and aid to men are best illustrated by her character in Aeschylus' *Eumenides*. For a structuralist analysis of the kinds of wisdom Athena and Metis represent, see Marcel Detienne and Jean-Pierre Vernant, *Cunning Intelligence in Greek Society and Culture*, trans. Janet Lloyd (Sussex: Harvester Press, 1978).

10. Brown, pp. 19-22, emphasizes the political nature of Zeus's regime and contrasts his rise to power with Marduk's, pp. 41-46.

11. Brown, pp. 27-29, 31-33.

12. See K. Olstein, "Pandora and Dike in Hesiod's *Works and Days*," *Emerita* 48 (1980): 295-312 for an interesting analysis of the oppositions and their implications.

13. West, *Theogony*, pp. 172-177; p. 187, comments on this belief. The different materials and creators underline the difference between the happy past in the age of Cronus and the more difficult present which came into existence in Zeus's reign.

14. W. K. C. Guthrie, *In the Beginning: Some Greek Views of the Origins of Life and the Early State of Man* (Ithaca, N.Y.: Cornell University Press, 1957), pp. 141 ff.

15. G. S. Kirk, *The Nature of Greek Myths* (Middlesex, Eng.: Penguin, 1974), pp. 268-275.

16. Translations from the *Iliad* are taken from Richmond Latttimore, "T*he Iliad" of Homer* (Chicago: University of Chicago Press, 1951).

17. Translations of Hesiod are taken from Hugh G. Evelyn White, *Hesiod, The Homeric Hymns, and* Homerica(Cambridge: Harvard University Press, 1914).

18. West argues for these new influences in *Early Greek Philosophy* which is a comparative study. KRS disagree. See pp. 22, 57.

19. See West, *Early Greek Philosophy*, pp. 1-75 as well as KRS, pp. 50-71. The quote is from fragment 49, p. 57.

20. KRS, fragment 59, p. 67.

21. See KRS, p. 57 and West, *Early Greek Philosophy*, pp. 28-36 for opposing views of Pherecydes' sources. KRS lists some later development.

22. West, *Early Greek Philosophy*, pp. 206-8, as well as KRS, pp. 47-9.

23. West, *Early Greek Philosophy*, p. 14. Although KRS ascribes these terms to later rationalizing interpreters (p. 58), West believes Pherecydes has combined a "theological idea with a physical rationale."

24. See Walter Burkert, *Lore and Science in Ancient Pythagoreanism* , trans. Edwin L. Minar, Jr. (Cambridge: Harvard University Press, 1972) for a presentation and interpretation of the sources, as well as an analysis of the

pre-scientific lore of the earliest Pythagoreans. See also KRS, pp. 214-38; 322-50.

25. KRS, pp. 338-342 as well as Burkert, *Lore*, pp. 30-38.

26. Burkert, *Lore*, pp. 467-8.

27. Burkert, *Lore*, pp. 349.

28. Burkert, *Lore*, pp. 477-8.

29. See M. West, *The Orphic Poems* (Oxford: Clarendon Press, 1983) for an analysis of the sources, the texts and the religion. KRS, pp. 21-33 presents a good summary of major texts, problems, and interpretations.

30. West, *Orphic*, pp. 101-107.

31. West, *Orphic*, pp. 89-90.

32. West, *Orphic*, p. 75.

33. West, *Orphic*, pp. 75-82.

34. The translation is taken from the edition by F. M. Cornford (New York and London: Oxford University Press, 1945).

35. West, *Orphic*, p. 22.

36. West, *Orphic*, p. 113.

Olympus II: Creation Demythologized

Such tales about gods swallowing gods or making love and war did not satisfy everyone. In the mid-sixth century, Xenophanes of Colophon, for example, objected to the anthropomorphism of Homer and Hesiod and posited a different definition of divinity: "one god, greatest among gods and men, in no way similar to mortals, either in body or in thought."[1] We have already noted signs of abstract thinking in Pherecydes, but he was closely associated with the mythmakers, those whom Aristotle called *theologoi*, "discoursers about the gods," (e.g. *Metaphysics* 983b24, 1000a9, 1071b27). Like the mythmakers, the other early thinkers whom we now call philosophers assumed that the gods existed and that the universe was divine because it was immortal. And they began by asking the same questions about origin as other mythmakers the world over; "how the first gods and earth came to be and rivers and the sea with its raging swell and the gleaming stars and the wide heaven above" (*Theogony* 108-110, White, trans.)[2] But they did not explain how things came to be what they are now in terms of an anthropomorphic theogony. Rather they looked to nature and the natural world for answers. Thus Aristotle called them *physiologoi*, "discoursers on nature *(pyusis)*" "investigators of natural causes and phenomena" (e.g., *Metaphysics* 986b14, 988b27, 940a3). The earliest Ionian *physiologoi* sought a fundamental and permanent material substance (rather than a deity) out of which all things originated and a process (other than sex and violence) by which each individual thing came into being, changed, and passed away. Later thinkers concentrated on principles that would explain the underlying unity and order in the ever changing natural world and the causes for its very existence and movement.

It is important to recognize that the *physiologoi* did not consider their activities irreligious.[3] Rather as they transferred to nature activities previously ascribed to the gods, they also transferred their faith and their reverence for the justice and wisdom associated with Zeus. Thus they viewed nature as divine and as the moral guide for human life. But Zeus and his pantheon were transcendent. Although they were in part nature gods and coexisted with the laws of nature, they were also able to suspend those laws for their own purposes to communicate with men through signs or to punish sinners with floods, storms, or plagues. The *physiologoi* conceived of nature, however, as a self-enclosed, self-regulating order which permitted no external interference with its laws. Thus their transfer of divinity to nature represented an enormous change. In the words of Gregory Vlastos,

> . . . the unique achievement of the pre-Socratics as religious thinkers . . . lies, in a word, in the fact that they and they alone, not only among the Greeks, but among all the peoples of the Mediterranean world, Semitic and Indo European, dared to transpose the name and function of divinity into a realm conceived of as a rigorous natural order, completely purged of miracle and magic . . . . Thus they presented deity as wholly immanent in the order of nature and therefore absolutely law abiding. [4]

To these *physiologoi*, G. E. R. Lloyd attributes the "discovery of nature" and thus the beginnings of science.[5] Their substitution of a naturalistic explanation for the random and arbitrary influences of individual supernatural divine wills and personalities involved the recognition that "natural phenomena . . . are regular and governed by a determinable sequence of cause and effect."[6] In studying this regularity, they focused on the general phenomenon; they investigated what was "universal and essential, not particular and accidental."[7] They then attempted to fit it all together into a coherent and systematic unified explanation. Their activities led them to discover and define fundamental problems (e.g., motion and change), and to develop methods for study as well as for proof (e.g., the application of mathematics and geometry to physics and astronomy, experimentation, deductive reasoning, and logic). Equally important, they introduced the practice of intellectual criticism and debate which led to the rejection or reformation of old theories and the development of new ones.[8]

How can we account for this Greek initiative which separates them so markedly from their eastern predecessors?[9] Clearly the impetus came from closer contacts with the east. Many of the early philosophers were born in Greek settlements in Asia Minor; ancient biographers report that they were active men of affairs who traveled to Babylonia and Egypt where they were introduced to many new ideas. These early non-professional thinkers were heirs not only to the accumulated myth of several different cultures, but also to the great individual advances in knowledge and technology (e.g., mathematics, geometry, astronomy, architecture, and medicine). But Greece of the sixth century was the perfect alembic for distilling the essence of Near-Eastern ideas and facts and elevating their position from ancillaries of cult and sacred lore to science. Greece's own mythopoetic tradition going back to Homer and Hesiod contained much that was both rational and rationalizing. No sacred writings, rigid dogmas, or powerful priesthoods with difficult hieratic scripts restricted the information available to the individual or the direction his thinking about it could take. Greek social institutions rewarded individuals for extraordinary creativity and fostered competition. The Greek adaptation of the Phoenician alphabet facilitated spreading ideas and educating the general citizenry. Their developing political freedom encouraged freedom of thought and stimulated intellectual debate about all kinds of questions related to social, political, religious and technological activities. Moreover, with the introduction of coinage, material culture had advanced to the level where there was enough leisure for Greek men to look beyond the most practical uses of knowledge toward the value of knowledge for its own sake. The large body of specific information must have encouraged the perception of commonalities, the definition of essential characteristics, and principles, and the search for a systematic organization. The effort to understand the world and the continuous exchange of ideas about it stimulated the growing belief that philosophy was the greatest gift of the gods to man (e.g., Plato, *Timaeus* 47c).

Most of the questions and some of the answers developed by the *physiologoi* are clearly related to the ideas expressed through myth.[10] The Milesians' search for a fundamental substance is similar to the Near Eastern concept of a primal realm out of which the gods are created and to the designation of a god as first parent in the theogonies. Thales' choice of water, so basic to the sustenance of life, parallels the early primacy of Oceanus in Homer and the marriage of Apsu and Tiamat in the *Enuma Elish* as well as Egyptian stories. The separation of the waters in Genesis and the separation of Earth and Heaven, either by castration or the sword of Marduk, in pagan myth reappear in the philosophical accounts in the significance of the primary process of *ekkrisis*, by which the other elements are separated out of the fundamental substance in motion.

The concentration on the origin of the heavens and the movement of the heavenly bodies, which led to the sciences of astronomy and meteorology, arose from the mythmakers' focus on heaven and the sea as the abode of the anthropomorphic gods. Natural phenomena like earthquakes, thunder, and lightning attracted attention precisely because of previous supernatural explanations, as signs of the wrath of Poseidon and Zeus. Theories that the universe is constructed out of a harmony of fundamental opposites (e.g., Anaximander, the Pythagoreans, Heraclitus, Anaxagoras) recall the bifurcation of creation in many of the myths (as well as the Bible), and the character of Zeus as harmonizer of conflicting personalities and principles. The idea of a *kosmos*, a harmonious arrangement of nature expressed in terms of proportion, number, and equality, which stimulated the development of theoretical mathematics, geometry, and acoustics, has been traced back to the mythmakers' conception of order as the division or apportionment of shares among the gods as well as to the Pythagorean (and archetypal) correspondence between number and natural phenomena.[11] Embedded here too is the notion of correspondence itself, which relates the matter, organization and processes of the divine and natural order to the physical, social, and moral world of mortals, the macrocosm to the microcosm so important to both philosophic and mythopoetic thinking (see Chapter 4).[12]

Nor did the language of myth disappear altogether. Parmenides began his hexameter poem with a proem claiming divine revelation, in a manner similar to Homer and Hesiod. Empedocles introduced the four primary elements he posited, earth, air, fire, and water, by the divine names Hera, Adoneus, Zeus, and Nestus, and he personified as Love (Aphrodite, Philotes, or Harmonia) and Strife the forces of attraction and repulsion which brought together and separated his elements.

But the nature philosophers removed the anthropomorphic personalities and motivations from their explanations. Most often, they removed the proper names as well, substituting ordinary nouns like air or neuter forms, e.g., *ta onta* "the things that exist," "the elemental powers."[13] They believed humans could discover nature's law by observation and thought. They took careful note of physical matter itself and of distinctions in quality like hot and cold and dry and moist. Anaxagoras, for example, described the sun, moon, and stars as red hot stones carried around by the rotation of air.[14] Some reasoned by analogy from processes they had observed, and developed theories of generation based on purely natural causes like the growth of an embryo from a seed or rarefication and condensation.[15] Empedocles explained why the earth, having come to the center, stays there by comparing it to the way water remains in a cup when the cup is given a circular motion.[16] Anaximander's description of the formation of the heavens out of a primary uniform mass, which he called the indefinite, in eternal motion, illustrates how different his explanation of process is from the anthropomorphism of the *Theogony* or the divine fiat of Genesis.

> He says that which is productive from the eternal of hot and cold was separated off at the coming to be of this world, and that a kind of sphere of flame from this was formed round the air surrounding the earth, like bark round a tree. When this was broken off and shut off in certain circles, the sun and the moon and the stars were formed.[17]

Parmenides, in contrast, depended upon pure thought instead of observation. In "The Way of Truth," he started with the premise "it is" and, for the first time, used logical deduction to arrive at the qualities of Being. Having proved that the statement "it is not" cannot be true, he concluded that Being cannot come into being and therefore must be uncreated, imperishable, indivisible, motionless, finite, and spherical. His reason had led him to deny reality to either sense perceptions or the things perceived by them.[18] Parmenides' methods and conclusions in turn forced all the later thinkers to take account of his questions about the source of motion and change, the void, and the relation between truth and the phenomena.

Many of the theories about nature posited that the present observable order of the universe has evolved by chance and necessity, through mechanical processes such as rarefaction and condensation, or forces of attraction and repulsion operating on the primary substance or substances. The randomness of the attraction of the four elements is clear from the following fragments about Empedocles.

> But as one divine element mingled with another, these things fell together as each chanced to meet other, and many other things beside these were constantly resulting.
>
> Whenever, then, everything turned out as it would have if it were happening for a purpose, there the creatures survived, being accidentally compounded in a suitable way; but where this did not happen, the creatures perished and are perishing still . . . .[19]

Democritus and Leucippus conjectured that atoms of different shapes and sizes, constantly moving in an infinite void, sometimes collide and become intertwined with one another to form compound bodies. (Although their collisions are not planned, there is an aspect of necessity in the mechanical laws of motion and resistance which cause the collisions and their reactions.)[20] The atomists even speculated that innumerable worlds had arisen in such a way and that these worlds might differ from ours: "some without a sun and moon," "some without living creatures or plants, or moisture."[21]

Most of the early thinkers, like the mythmakers, concluded that the earth was the source of human life. No god created humans from the clay, however, or destined them for an easy existence. Rather animal life resulted from spontaneous generation in the moist earth, stimulated by heat or putrefaction, and humans, being the weakest of infant animals, needed help to survive.[22] According to Anaximander,

> . . . the first living creatures were born in moisture, enclosed in thorny barks; . . . .as their age increased they came forth on to the dryer part and, when the bark had broken off, they lived a different kind of life for a short time.

> Further he says that in the beginning man was born from creatures of a different kind; because other creatures are soon self supporting, but man alone needs prolonged nursing. For this reason he would not have survived if this had been his original form.

> Anaximander of Miletus conceived that there arose from heated water and earth either fish or creatures very like fish; in these man grew, in the form of embryos retained within until puberty; then at last the fish-like creatures burst and men and women who were already able to nourish themselves stepped forth.[23]

This conception of a gradual evolution of the human race is echoed in several fragments of Empedocles. He divided the process of development into four progressive stages. In the first generation animals and plants were not complete and consisted of separate limbs, but, in the second the limbs were joined, and by the third there were whole natural forms.

> And the fourth arose no longer from the homogeneous substances such as earth or water, but, by intermingling, in some cases as the result of the condensation of their nourishment, in others because feminine beauty excited the sexual urge; and as the various species were distinguished by the quality of the mixture in them.[24]

Empedocles speculated that many monstrosities were formed as the parts came together at random, e.g., man-faced oxen and ox-faced men.

Theories which concentrate on nature as apprehended by observation explain from what and how without explaining why. And those which suggest evolution and survival of the fittest deny intelligent purpose to creation. Plato, heir to Socrates' ethics as well as to conflicting pre-Socratic ideas, considered such constructs inadequate. As Socrates explains in *Phaedo*, he had hoped that Anaxagoras, who posited Mind (*Nous*) as the force which causes and orders all things (by beginning the rotation of matter) would not only describe elements and processes, but would explain the cause for their being the way they are.

> I never thought that when he said that things are ordered by Mind, he would introduce any reason for their being as they are, except that they are best so. I thought that he would assign a cause to each thing, and a cause to the universe, and then would go on to explain to me what was best for each thing and what was the common good of all (98 ab, Church, trans.).[25]

Plato developed his own explanation of cause which brought together the various theories of his predecessors, but emphasized the ideas that the universe was created according to rational principles or proportions and that men had an immortal soul that was derived from and related to the eternal unchanging part of the universe.[26] Plato's Theory of Forms posits a real world of Being, made of perfect immutable essences called forms or ideas or absolutes. Our world of Becoming, in which things are born, change, and perish, exists as an imperfect copy perceptible through the senses but ultimately unknowable because of its constant flux. The soul, which is the seat of reason and originates in the world of Being, is, like Hebrew Wisdom, man's instrument for knowing the true reality and modeling his private and communal life according to it so he too can strive to be and do his best. This theory is alluded to in most of Plato's middle dialogues, but is spelled out in great detail in the figure of the divided line and the allegory of the cave in *Republic* 6.509d-7.521b. According to the theory, all the forms, mathematical objects, visible things, and images derive their existence from the highest form, the Good, which is compared to the sun.

> You will agree that the sun not only makes the things we see visible, but also brings them into existence and gives them growth and nourishment; yet he is not the same thing as existence. And so with the objects of knowledge: these derive from the Good not only their power of being known, but their very being and reality; and Goodness is not the same thing as being, but even beyond being, surpassing it in dignity and power.
> (*Republic* 6.508, Cornford, trans.)[27]

Plato could establish the existence of the forms and the immortality of the soul through the method of deduction which he called dialectic. It was difficult, however, to explain the process by which our sensible world, composed of many objects and qualities in flux, was generated by the perfect, unchanging single essences in the world of Being. He usually used the verb *metalambano* for "receiving a share," or "coming to partake," to describe how the many sensible objects can derive from the unique forms. In *Phaedo* 101d, however, he expressed his reluctance to be more precise.

> I hold to the doctrine that the thing is only made beautiful by the presence or communication, or whatever you please to call it, of absolute beauty—I do not wish to insist on the nature of the communication, but what I am sure of is that it is absolute beauty which makes all beautiful things beautiful. (Church, trans.)

Parmenides, in the dialogue Plato named after him, rejects "participation" as an explanation of the relationship between Being and Becoming, pointing out its logical fallacies.[28]

In the *Timaeus*, Plato employed a different method, myth, to express his conviction that the physical sensible world presupposes an intelligent and purposive creation according to the "best" plan.[29] Having established through deduction that the visible world is a changing likeness of an eternal model, Timeaus announces that for a likeness one can expect only a "likely story" (*ton eikota* and *mython*, 29d) an exceedingly plausible but not a precise account.[30] He proceeds to describe the creation of the universe by a divine artificer, the demiurge, whose only motive was that

> he desired that all things should come as near as possible to being like himself . . . . Desiring then that all things should be good, and, so far as they might be, nothing imperfect, the god took over all that is visible - not at rest, but in discordant and unordered motion - and brought it from disorder into order, since he judged that order was in every way better. (29a-30a, Cornford trans.)

Using the eternal model, the world of Forms, the demiurge acts upon a receptacle or space filled with undifferentiated agitated matter containing traces of the eventual nature of the four elements. "The god begins by giving them a distinct configuration by means of shapes and numbers" (53b, Cornford, trans.), applying intelligence and limit to direct the necessary movements and powers of matter to his purpose.[31] He makes it a smooth, uniform and complete world with a soul at the center and extended through the whole. He then shapes the sun, moon, and other planets as celestial gods, living creatures whose intelligent souls have voluntary motion.   The demiurge directs the created gods to create in turn, instructing them to make mortal creatures to whom he himself will grant the immortal element of soul.   After describing the genesis and activities of the physical, biological, and physiological aspects of the sensible world according to the theories of the Pre-Socratics, Timaeus tacks on an explanation of the origin of women and animals from men whose bodies and souls are not in proper harmony.   He concludes with the assertion that

> For having received in full its complement of living creatures, mortal and immortal, this world has thus become a visible living creature embracing all that are visible and an image of the intelligible, a perceptible god, supreme in greatness and excellence, in beauty and perfection, this Heaven single in its kind and one. (92c, Cornford, trans.)

As in Genesis the created natural world is good; although it has a lesser reality, it is a "perceptible god" and thus a revelation of god, as in Hebrew wisdom. In book 10 of the *Laws*, Kleinices the Cretan uses visible nature to argue for the existence of the gods

> First there's the earth, the sun, the stars, and all things and this beautiful orderliness of seasons, divided into years and months. [32]   (886a Pangle, trans.)

For the Athenian stranger, however, this truth is not as easily proved; he must go through more sophisticated arguments to refute the nature philosophers who attribute the world order only to mechanical principles. Using dialectic, he establishes the priority of the soul over matter, and soul as the source of notion, intelligence, and goodness in nature. He concludes his argument by equating souls with gods as the causes of all things. [33]

> And with regard to all the stars, and the moon, the years, months, and all the seasons, what other account will we give except this same one to the effect that since soul or souls are evidently the causes of all these things, and souls good with respect to every virtue, we will declare that they are gods - whether they order the entire heaven by existing within bodies, as living beings, or in whatever way and however they do it? Is there anyone who will agree to these things and maintain that all things are not full of gods?
> (899b, Pangle, trans.)

Notes

1. Fragment 170 in G. S. Kirk and J. E. Raven and M. Schofield, *The Presocratic Philosophers: A Critical History with a Selection of Texts* (Cambridge: Cambridge University Press, 1983²), p. 169. This text will be referred to in subsequent notes as KRS. Translations and fragment numbers for the Presocratics are quoted from KRS unless otherwise noted.

2. See Charles H. Kahn, *Anaximander and the Origins of Greek Cosmology* (Philadelphia: Centrum, 1985) and especially the chapter entitled "Milesian Speculation and the Greek Philosophy of Nature," pp. 199-215 for a discussion of the effects of cosmogonic questions on early philosophy.

3. See Gregory Vlastos, "Theology and Philosophy in Early Greek Thought, in David J. Furley and R. E. Allen, (eds.), *Studies in Presocratic Philosophy, Vol. 1 The Beginnings of Philosophy* (New York: Humanities Press, 1970, 92-129, referred to hereafter as Furley and Allen) for an excellent discussion of the question and bibliography.

4. Vlastos, "Theology", pp. 119-20.

5. G. E. R. Lloyd, *Early Greek Science from Thales to Aristotle* , (New York: W. W. Norton, 1970), pp. 8-15; pp. 125-146, for an analysis of these aspects of their contribution to science.

6. Lloyd, *Early Greek Science*, pp. 8.

7. Lloyd, *Early Greek Science*, pp. 10.

8. See G. R. Llyod, *The Revolutions of Wisdom: Studies in the Claims and Practice of Ancient Greek Science*. Sather Classical Lecture, 52 (Berkeley: University of California Press, 1987), pp. 83-102, for a discussion of the extent to which this debate took place, as well as a bibliography of primary and secondary references.

9. G. R. Lloyd, *Revolutions*, pp. 50-108, discusses various theories to account for it analyzing especially the role of egotism and competitiveness in the culture.

10. See W. K. C. Guthrie, *In the Beginning: Some Greek Views of the Origins of Life and the Early State of Man* (Ithaca, N.Y.: Cornell University Press, 1957), pp. 11-45 as well as Kahn, *Anaximander* and KRS, pp. 7-74.

11. Kahn, *Anaximander*, pp. 222-230 presents an excellent summary of the development of the concept of *kosmos*.

12. For this correspondence and sympathy between the divine, natural, and human world, see Walter Burkert, *Lore and Science in Ancient Pythagoreanism*, trans. Edwin L. Minar, Jr. (Cambridge, MA; Harvard University Press, 1972), pp. 37-40, as well as Anders Olerud, *L'idee de macrocosmos et microcosmos dans "Le Timee" de Platon. Etude de mythologie comparee* (Uppsala: Almquist & Wiksells, 1951) and Hans Kelson, *Society and Nature: Perspectives in Social Inquiry* (London: Kegan Paul, Trench, Trubner, and Co., 1946).

13. Kahn, *Anaximander*, p. 180.

14. KRS, p. 381.

15. The analogy of the embryo is important in myth as well as philosophy. See note 12, as well as H. C. Baldry, "Embryological Analogies in Pre-Socratic Cosmogony," *Classical Quarterly* 26 (1932): 27-34. For the importance and use of analogy in ancient thought, see Jonathan Barnes, *The Presocratic Philosophers* (London; Routledge and Kegan Paul, 1982), pp. 53-56.

16. Aristotle, *de caelo* B13, 295a13.

17. KRS, p. 131, fragment 121.

18. KRS, pp. 239-262.

19. KRS, p. 304, fragments 377 and 380.

20. KRS, pp. 418-427 for fragments about necessity in the movement of matter.

21. KRS, pp. 416-418, from fragment 565.

22. See Guthrie, *In the Beginning*, Chapter 2: "Mother Earth II The Scientific Approach," 29-45 and 6 "What is Man: The Philosophic Implications," for a survey of the developing concept.

23. KRS, p. 141, fragments 133, 134, 135.

24. KRS, p. 303, from fragment 375.

25. *Phaedo*. New York: Liberal Arts Press, 1951.

26. For a general study of Plato, see A. E. Taylor, *Plato: The Man and His Work*, (Cleveland and New York: Meridian, 1956). The collection of essays, *Studies in Plato's Metaphysics*, edited by R. E. Allen (Routledge & Kegan Paul in London and Humanities Press: New York, 1965) contains important articles on aspects of Plato's ideas relevant to this discussion.

27. Translations of the *Republic* come from Francis MacDonald Cornford, *"The Republic" of Plato* (New York and London: Oxford University Press, 1945). This passage appears on p. 220.

28. For a discussion of the problem, see F. M. Cornford, *Plato and Parmenides: Parmenides' "Way of Truth" and Plato's "Parmenides,"* *translated with an Introduction and Running Commentary* (New York: Liberal Arts Press, 1957), as well as R. E. Allen, "Participation and Prediction in Plato's Middle Dialogues," pp. 43-60 and the essays on *Parmenides* in the Allen collection.

29. See F. M. Cornford, *Plato's Cosmology: "The Timaeus" of Plato translated with a Running Commentary*, (London: Routledge and Kegan Paul, 1957), for an analysis of the entire dialogue. Translations are quoted from this edition.

30. For the seriousness of the verisimilar account, where the emphasis is on the *EIKOS*, see Anne Freire Ashbrugh, *Plato's Theory of Explanation: A Study of the Cosmological Account in the "Timaeus"*, (Albany: State University of New York Press, 1988), as well as Gregory Vlastos, "The Disorderly Motion in the *Timaeus*," pp. 379-419 in Allen and the commentary on the phrase in Cornford, 28-32.

31. Glen R. Morrow, "Necessity and Persuasion in Plato's *Timaeus*", pp. 421-437, in Allen, argues for the way in which the Demiurge or *Nous* pulls together the materials and powers of necessity to produce the complex structures of nature.

32. The translation is taken from the edition by Thomas L. Pangle, *"The Laws" of Plato* (New York: Basic Books, 1980).

33. Although scholars have argued about the contradiction between the function of the demiurge in the *Timaeus* and the soul in *Laws* (see Vlastos, "Disorderly Motion", p. 393, as well as R. Hackford, "Plato's Theism," pp. 439-447 in Allen), here the point is that in both dialogues the visible universe is a revelation of the divine.

Sinai III: The Rejoinder to Philosophy

Though the Greek philosophers had appeared and their impact had been felt throughout the Mediterranean world by the time the rabbis of the Talmud had formulated their teachings, the rabbinic sages were not familiar with formal philosophy.[1] The names of the major philosophers are absent from the rabbinic writings; the only philosophers mentioned by name are Epicurus and the obscure second century Cynic Oenomaus of Gadara. Harry A. Wolfson claimed that he was unable to find a single technical Greek philosophical term in rabbinic literature.[2] Nevertheless, the rabbis did have some acquaintance with Greek philosophical ideas, particularly those of the Stoics, which must have reached them through their co-religionists in Alexandria, Rome and other Mediterranean centers or through contact with Hellenistic scholars and popular orators. Many of these ideas, centering on the concept of creation, penetrated rabbinic circles generating controversy and polemic but nevertheless influencing rabbinic thought.

"A philosopher said to Rabban Gamaliel that God found materials which he used in the creation of the world, *Tohu. Bohu* darkness, water, wind and the deep, to which R. Gamaliel vigorously replied 'Woe to that man! The term creation is explicitly used of them'".[3] We do not know who the philosopher was but the fact that he upholds the doctrine of the eternity of matter and the view that God was not the sole creator, both of which he seeks to prove from Scripture, suggests that he was a Jewish heretic deeply influenced by Greek and Gnostic views.[4] Rabban Gamaliel refutes both views. Rabbi Joshua ben Hananyah, the contemporary of Rabban Gamaliel, who spent a great deal of time in Alexandria and was familiar with the many philosophical currents of the age was reputed to have debated issues of creation with Hellenistic scholars and particularly with the Roman emperor Hadrian.[5]

The Greek philosophers' views of a fundamental substance out of which all things originated are paralleled in rabbinic sources which view water, air and fire as the primeval elements out of which created things are formed.[6] The comment of Rav, the leading Babylonian scholar of the third century C.E. on Genesis 1:8 "God called the expanse Sky" (*Shamayim*) that the Hebrew word *shamayim* is composed to two words *esh*, fire and *mayim*[7] water is strikingly analogous to the Greek theories that the universe is constructed out of a harmony of fundamental opposites. The four primary elements of Empedocles, earth, air, fire and water are also mentioned in rabbinic sources in connection with the miracle of the

Ten Plagues which involved God's interference with the natural order.[8]

The Platonic view of creation that the world as we know it, the world of Becoming, is an imperfect copy of the real world of Being, the world of ideas, is merged by Philo with biblical teaching. Philo, explaining where and how Plato's intelligible world of ideas exists, uses the following parable. A king seeking to build a city cannot build it by himself but must make use of the services of some skilled architect. The architect on receiving his commission devises a plan for the city he is about to build. He studies the site and in accordance with the terrain and climate he sketches the various parts which form in his mind a general image of the city as a whole. This image he carries in his soul as the impression of a seal is carved in wax and by the innate power of memory the architect recalls the various parts of the city as he proceeds to build it. In a similar way, says Philo, blending the Bible and Plato, God, in planning the creation of the world, conceived beforehand the models of its parts out of which he constituted the intelligible world as a whole.[9]

A similar parable by the third century Palestinian Amora, Rabbi Hoshayah the Great, reads: "According to the custom of the world, when a mortal king builds a palace he does not build it by his own skill but with the skill of an architect, and that architect does not build it out of his own head, but employs plans and diagrams to know how to arrange the chambers and the wicket doors. Thus the Holy One Blessed be He looked into the Torah and created the world.[10] The critical difference between the two parables is that Philo does not mention the architect's blueprints, which would destroy his Platonic analogy.

Philo and R. Hoshayah drew on a common tradition which derives from Near Eastern literature where the preexistence of wisdom is seen in a mythologial context.[11] As mentioned earlier, this conception was refined in Prov. 8:22-31 where wisdom has no divine status nor is it a hypostasized attribute of God but only a *creation* of God. The identification of wisdom with the Torah is very old[12] and is already suggested in the book of Joshua ben Sira where wisdom says: "The Creator of all things commanded me . . . and said: 'Let your dwelling place be in Jacob and in Israel take up your inheritance'" (Sira 24:8-9). Elsewhere in this work the author declares: "All wisdom is the fulfilling of the Law" (Sira 19:20; Cf. 21:11; 24:23; 34:8). Philo identified this conception of the pre-existence of the Torah with the Platonic theory of ideas; R. Hoshayah did not.[13] But even if R. Hoshayah's parable does not echo Platonic doctrine, the literary images used are strongly suggestive of Philo and Plato. It is interesting to note that in rabbinic lore the Torah is preexistent just as chaos is preexistent, in keeping with the folk saying that God prepares the remedy before the illness. As noted above, after the creation of the world, the observance of the Torah holds back the forces of chaos.

Plato, Philo and the rabbis are of one mind that the purpose of creation was God's desire to bestow his goodness on the world and to make it most perfect.[14] The tannaitic Midrash commenting on Deut. 32:4 "The Rock! -- His deeds are perfect!" states: "His work is perfect with regard to all creatures, and one should not second-guess His actions at all. Not one of the created beings can reflect and say: "If I only had three eyes, if I only had three hands, if I only had three feet, if I could only walk on my head, if my face were only turned around facing backward, how pleasant it would be for me.[15] The rabbis sought to show the purpose and the benefit of all created things, even the nuisances. In the words of Rav: "Whatever the Holy One blessed be He created in His world was not created without a purpose." Even flies, mosquitoes, snakes and snails have a purpose and a use.[16]

Finally, the first chapter of Genesis, the story of Creation (*Ma'aseh Bereshit*) and the first chapter of Ezekiel, the vision of God's Throne- chariot (the *"Merkabah"*) were, in the Second Temple period, favorite subjects of discussion and interpretation which it was apparently considered inadvisable to make public. The Mishnah ordained: ". . . the Story of Creation (may not be expounded) before two people nor the (chapter of) the Chariot before one, unless he is a Sage that understands of his own knowledge Whosoever gives his mind to four things it were better for him if he had not come into the world. What is above? What is beneath? What was beforetime? and what will be hereafter?"[17]

Notes

1. Saul Lieberman, "How Much Greek in Jewish Palestine?" in *Biblical and other Studies* ed. Alexander Altmann (Cambridge: Harvard University Press, 1963), pp. 123-141.

2. Harry A. Wolfson, *Philo* (Cambridge: Harvard University Press, 1947), 1:91.

3. *Gen. R.* 1:9. (ed. Theodor Albeck), p.8.

4. Ephraim E. Urbach, *The Sages* trans Israel Abrahams (Cambridge and London: Harvard University Press, 1987), p. 188.

5. *Gen. R.* 10:3 (ed. Theodor-Albeck), p. 75; *Gen. R.* 13;9 (ed. Theodor-Albeck), p. 1181; Moshe David Herr, "The Historical Significance of the Dialogues Between Jewish Sages and Roman Dignitaries,: in *Scripta Hierosolymitana* 22, *Studies in Aggadah and Folk Literature* ed. by Joseph Heinemann and Dov Noy (Jerusalem: The Magnes Press, 1971): 142-144.

6. *Exodus R.* 15:22; Ginzberg, *Legends*, 5:22, n. 93 where snow is also mentioned.

7. *Gen. R.* 4:8 (ed. Theodor-Albeck), p. 31.

8. Ginzberg, *Legends*, 2:341.

9. *De Opificio Mundi* 17-20; Harry A. Wolfson, *Philo: Foundations of Religious Philosophy in Judaism, Christianity and Islam*, 4th ed. revised (Cambridge: Harvard University Press, 1968): 1:244-246.

10. *Gen. R.* 1:1 (ed. Theodor-Albeck), p. 2; Wolfson, *Philo* 1:243.

11. *Enziklopedia Mikrait* 23: 130-131.

12. Harry A. Wolfson, *Philo* 1:20-24.

13. Urbach, *The Sages*, pp. 199-200.

14. *Timaeus* 293; *De opificio Mundi* 21.

15. *Sifre* to Deut. 307 (ed. Friedmann), pp. 132b-133a. Cf. *Midrash Tannaim* (ed. Hoffman), p. 187.

16. *b. Shabbat*, 77b.

17. *M. Hagigah* 2:1. For a detailed discussion see Chapter 10.

Conclusions and Comparisons

Both traditions describe the progression of the universe from chaos to order in developmental stages.   In Genesis order is accomplished by the divine word uttered over a period of seven carefully planned days while in the Greek theogonies it is the result of generational evolution.   The Greeks retain the Near Eastern theme of conflict as a result of the proliferation of offspring, but this entire complex of ideas is removed from Genesis where God is supreme and creation is an intellectual-spiritual process that results in a physical world.   Although the early Greek philosophers ascribed the development of the physical world to mechanical laws of nature which sometimes involve conflict either between opposites or between different elements, Plato, like the author of Genesis, describes creation in spiritual and intellectual terms.   His creator-god, the demiurge, forms the physical world in a series of developmental stages working from an ideal paradigm which is both rational and good.

Sinai and Olympus in contrast to the Mesopotamian myth do not view nature as capricious but as having a validity and order of its own.   In Genesis this validity and order come from God whose creation progresses according to inherent principles of hierarchical evolution; in the *Theogony* they are inherent in the gradual evolution of nature itself and are confirmed by Zeus when he becomes eternal ruler.   In the Bible and in the Greek mythological tradition the supremacy of the deity does not reduce subordinates and allies to powerlessness.   Zeus negotiates with the other gods, unlike Marduk whose allies are powerless without him. Likewise the biblical texts in a number of places and rabbinic legend (*Gen. R.* 8:4) commenting on the plural form of Gen. 1:26 "Let us make man in our image . . ." picture God as consulting the angels before the creation of Adam.   Nor does the supremacy of the deity preclude initiative and creative progress in the creatures.   The offspring of Zeus contribute new and positive elements to his order and their creativity is an extension of his. Similarly, Adam is given dominion over the earth and other created things (Gen. 1:28) implying that he too is to create under the eternal aegis of God.

The dynamism and validity of nature expressed in Greek myth carry over to Greek philosophy but the various philosophers view the process of creation and evolution from two opposite perspectives. Those who were interested in the physical world for its own sake saw the development as moving from disorder to order and from simple elements to complex compounds with imperfections gradually refined by necessity and chance as the universe progressed toward completion. Their view is most similar to that of the *Theogony*. For Plato, however, whose ethical ideas led him to posit an absolute standard of goodness, the development moves in the opposite direction. The model on which the physical universe is patterned is perfect and complete in itself. Once the demiurge sets creation in motion the physical world obeys the laws of nature, as described by the physical philosophers, to come into being as the copy of the perfect model. But the copy is necessarily less perfect than the model and the necessities of change and movement in the physical world lead to further deviations from the ideal pattern.

On Sinai and on Olympus, as in Mesopotamia, the heavens are a mirror image of the earth. The Hebrew and Greek concepts of a non-autocratic Creator, who though supreme, honors and legitimizes the activities of his creatures, reflect the political ideals in Israel and in Greece. In Plato's theory of forms the mirror image is transferred from heaven and earth to the world of being and the world of becoming. The visible universe is a reflection of the perfect and eternal realm from which it derives its very existence and its standards for personal and communal behavior. Both Genesis and the *Theogony* inherit from the *Enuma Elish* the idea of the double nature of the cosmos manifested in the polarities of creation. On Sinai as on Olympus the deity lends coherence to chaos by maintaining the proper balance between the polarities. The Greek philosophers as well conceived the process of creation as an initial separating out of opposites and then their combination according to universal principles such as proportion and balance.

The Greek and Hebrew traditions rejected the Babylonian epic's depiction of the creation of humans as menials to the gods albeit in different ways. The author of Genesis pictures the first humans as the crown of creation formed in the image of God. Hesiod remains deliberately vague about human creation but dramatizes the fellowship between mortals and immortals and proclaims human superiority over the other creatures because of his God-given sense of justice (*Works and Days* ll. 276-280). In contrast, the Greek philosophers see human beings as weaker creatures who need extra help at the beginning. According to Plato's myth in *Protagoras*, even though humans have been granted a spark of the divine, an immortal soul, Prometheus must later provide them with fire and still later Zeus must add justice so that humanity can survive by living peacefully together (322).

Both Hebrews and Greeks portray the world as essentially good though not without difficulties. Some of these difficulties arise from the persistence of chaotic elements which have been banished but not destroyed and which continually threaten the order of creation. It is a world in which the God of Sinai is deeply concerned with His creatures; he hears their cries, watches their struggles and suffers with them. Similarly, the gods on Olympus pity human mortality, concern themselves with human affairs and provide paradigms for human survival and pleasure. Those Greek philosophers who reject anthropomorphisms still see the world as basically good. For the concern of the gods they substitute natural law which is orderly and understandable rather than capricious and bewildering. Instead of picturing gods who act like humans they bestow reason on humans so that they can become wise and guide themselves in accordance with the highest good.

In the Greek as in the Hebrew tradition a very high value is placed on wisdom, the divine progenitor of human reason. For the Hebrews wisdom existed before the creation of the world and after creation it became a channel for the human perception of divine revelation in nature. Among the Greeks not only was wisdom personified and mythologized in the Olympian pantheon but among the philosophers it was depersonalized and abstracted into Mind and *Logos*, the intelligent principles behind divine nature and the essence of natural law. In both the Bible and Greek philosophy reason provides the human link to God and the metaphysical. For some Greek philosophers the immortal soul was, as in Hebrew wisdom, a principle agent of creation as well as the vehicle which led humans to the truths about nature and the reunion with the supernatural.

Hebrew wisdom writers and their rabbinic successors knew practical mathematics, science and technology. They knew the importance of observation, the methods of plant and animal classification and the movements of the heavenly bodies as well as the general principles derived from them on the basis of inductive and deductive reasoning. But the rabbis were interested in such knowledge and methodology only insofar as they contributed to the observance of the Mosaic law and its talmudic extensions that embraced all of life.[1] In contrast the Greeks, looking for the universal and the eternal in nature, went beyond useful knowledge and general principles to develop all embracing scientific theories and their philosophical implications. Although the rabbis prohibited lay speculation on "the above," "the beneath," "the beforetime," and "the hereafter," rabbinic mystics were as interested in these matters as were the Greek philosophers despite their different perspective.

This developing tradition, particularly the heavenly ascent, has striking similarities to Neoplatonism (see Chapter 10).

Plato's portrayal of a mythical creator has obvious affinities with the divine creator of Genesis. The demiurge is a transcendent divinity who formed the visible universe according to the highest principles of order and morality. For this reason it was possible for Philo to adapt Plato's view of creation to biblical teaching and for the rabbis to use images suggestive of Philo and Plato in their description of God's creation of the world.

There are, however, several important differences between Plato's demiurge and the biblical God of creation. The world of forms is prior to the demiurge. Although the demiurge is transcendent he is considered a lower form of divinity. He does not bring the visible world into being; he only imposes order on a formless matter that already exists. Nor is he omnipotent. The necessities of matter in motion prevent his imposing control over every part of the physical substratum and, once creation is complete, the laws of physical nature impose their own movements and changes which may lead to deviations from the ideal. In Genesis God precedes His creation, is supreme, and forms the world out of nothing. There are no limits to His power and the deviations from His plan of creation are still part of a divine design in which human free will plays a critical role. It is free will more than the imperfection of the material world, as Plato saw it, that accounts for the entrance of evil into a world created good.

Notes

1. *Julius Preuss' Biblical and Talmudic Medicine* trans. and ed. Fred Rosner (New York: Sanhedrin Press, 1978); I. Low, *Die Flora der Juden* (Vienna, 1926-1934); L. Lewysohn, *Zoologie des Talmuds* (Frankfurt am Main, 1858). For other works see Herman L. Strack, *Introduction to the Talmud and Midrash* (New York, Philadelphia: Meridian Books and The Jewish Publication Society of America, 1959), pp. 193-194. As yet, however, there is no single work examining thoroughly and methodically all the biblical and rabbinic material in this area. The basis for such a work is to be found in the chapter by Saul Lieberman, *Hellenism in Jewish Palestine* (New York: The Jewish Theological Seminary of America, 1950), pp. 180-193.

Chapter 3

The Origin of Evil

Introduction

Evil as a concept is the product of a late stage in the development of the human species—the stage of reason and reflection. In their earliest stages of maturation human beings experienced fear that was physiological in origin, fear of physical pain, unsatisfied hunger, death or some earthly calamity. Something of this primitive fear is reflected in the rabbinic legend that tells us how Adam and Eve were overcome by terror that they would be attacked by the serpent when the celestial light ceased because of their sin and they were plunged into darkness.[1] In Greek legend, at the beginning of Zeus' reign the world was similarly dark and frightening to his subjects. Io, Zeus' human victim in Aeschylus' *Prometheus Bound*, must travel through terrifying countries populated by monstrous hags and murderous races before the compromise between Zeus and Prometheus (Forethought) enables witless and helpless humanity to use the gift of fire, the symbol of intelligence, to develop a more secure existence. In an echo of the Prometheus legend Adam is endowed with the divine wisdom and he learns to rub two stones against each other to produce fire.[2]

From fear connected with physiological deprivation or pain there emerged a dread of what Rudolf Otto has called numinous phenomena, i.e., phenomena that are associated with a sense of mystery, awe, power and a mixture of fascination and terror.[3] Both Sinai and Olympus, despite their sophistication, exhibit belief in

this numinous quality of the deity. In the Bible, the Israelites are
warned on pain of death not to go up Mount Sinai or even touch it
during the revelation (Exod. 19:12-13) and Uzzah, who took hold of
the Ark of God to prevent it from falling, is struck dead (2 Sam. 6:6-
9). Even the most anthropomorphic Greek deities still retained their
otherness and were always capable of doing the unexpected and
inexplicable. Thus the gods had to be correctly addressed in prayer
and properly approached in their holy places lest their dreaded
power be aroused against the worshipper. The chorus of *Oedipus at
Colonus* describes the right way to pass by the sacred grove of the
Eumenides: with their eyes closed and in silent prayer (129-32).
The old, blind stranger has endangered them all by inadvertently
stumbling into the goddesses' space.

The belief in demons and the demonic is another result of
objectifying the numinous phenomena and in the words of Carl Jung
is the outgrowth of "a millenial process of symbol formation which
presses toward consciousness, beginning in the darkness of pre-
history with primordial or archetypal images, and gradually
developing and differentiating these images into conscious
creations."[4] According to Jung, the process is one of individuation
in which the undifferentiated, chaotic view we have of ourselves at
the beginning of life slowly develops into a good and evil side that
are differentiated from one another. Dissatisfied with the evil side
the human being represses it causing the growth of a shadow in the
unconscious. If the repression is carried too far, the shadow will
become gargantuan and may eventually burst forth and overwhelm
the personality. In the healthy person there is a third stage in which
the good and evil sides are both recognized, accepted for what they
are, reintegrated on a conscious level and, in the case of some
individuals, transcended on the super conscious or spiritual level.[5]

A similar development is to be found in the human perception of
God. At first God may appear undifferentiated. In the second stage
the benevolent deity and the monstrous devil are increasingly
separated and the devil is repressed and banished.   A good
illustration of this tendency is to be found in the narrative of
Genesis 6 (discussed in the previous chapter) where the *bene
elohim*, the divine beings, who copulated with the daughters of man
and begot a race of giants are demoted from immortality to
mortality and suffer a loss of power because of their sinfulness. The
psalmist echoes this drama when he describes how "God stands in
the divine assembly and among the divine beings He pronounces
judgment" and concludes with the Almighty's admonition: "I had
taken you for divine beings, sons of the Most High, all of you, but

you shall die as men do, fall like any prince" (Ps. 82:1-7). In the apocalyptic book of I Enoch or the Ethiopic Enoch (chapters 6-36) the evil nature of these fallen beings is delineated in detail. Another example is Satan, who makes his first appearance in the opening chapter of the Book of Job but is associated in rabbinic legend and folklore with the serpent in the Garden of Eden.[6] Hesiod's *Theogony* describes the many monsters like the Harpies, Gorgons and the Hydra (most of whom originate from the numinous sea) who are eventually defeated because they prevent the evolution of order and civilization. Typhon, the snaky, fire-breathing dragon brought forth by Earth and Tartarus in a desperate effort to overthrow Zeus is one Greek parallel to the serpent and Satan; Hesiod's Prometheus, who is both a trickster and a rebel, is another.[7] Finally, Jung posits a third stage which he felt had not yet appeared among the masses in the history of this idea (though it did appear among individuals of unique spiritual stature). In this stage there would be an integration of good and evil, the Lord and Devil, and we can even speak of a transcending of this duality altogether.[8]

Mircea Eliade comes to a similar conclusion from the perspective of the history of religions. Influenced by the fifteenth century philosopher Nicholas of Cusa's definition of God as a *coincidentia oppositorum*, Eliade claimed that polarity, duality, alternation, antithetical dyads, and *coincidentia oppositorum* are found throughout the world and at every level of culture. Oppositions later abstracted as the paradoxical coincidence of eternity and time, of being and becoming, of good and evil were resolved and articulated for archaic peoples by means of mythical thought and imagery. In the mythology of India, for example, the *devas* (gods) and *asuras* (demons) are locked in endless conflict as the powers of light and darkness respectively. But they are also brothers, sons of the same father, Prajapati. Thus what appears as contradictory in this world is unitary at a higher level.[9]

As culture grew, the expanding human powers of reason and abstraction conceptualized evil but, as Jung and others remind us, the symbol laden archetypes of the earlier eras remain, either as metaphors for evil or in their literal form, side by side with the higher concepts. The biblical story of the Garden of Eden represents a distinct progression in which rational moral teachings are clearly derived from a symbolic narrative but the echoes of the original pre-Israelite myths can still be heard in the reworked monotheistic version. Similarly, the rabbis in interpreting the narratives of Genesis 1 to 11 provided profound insights into the psychological and moral nature of man, yet some of them also believed in demons and the demonic who could trap the unwary.[10]

The progressive rationality of Greek myth did not banish the mysterious powers of the unnatural and irrational that still gripped the mind. Typhon, hurled deep into Tartarus by Zeus, remained an ever present source of fear to humanity, having become the "evil raging winds" on sea and land "against which man has no help" (*Theogony*, 869-880). In 458 B.C.E. Aeschylus terrified his audience by introducing a chorus of Furies as repulsive, Gorgon-like monsters dressed in black, oozing gore, and hastening to mutilate, impale and suck the blood from their victim. According to the ancient *Life of Aeschylus*, this spectacle was so frightening that youths fainted and pregnant women aborted at the sight. But once Aeschylus had established the distance between Zeus' cosmos and these Furies "born out of evil and inhabiting evil dark Tartarus" (*Eumenides*, 71-72) he used them to dramatize the efficacy of terror in preventing evil. Here the demonic archetype has been transformed to explicate a higher morality associated with the fear of punishment for sin. Thus evil has become a concept to be explained.

Notes

1. *Gen. R.* 11:1 and 12:6; Ginzberg, *Legends* 1:86; 5:112-113, n. 104.

2. *Ibid.*

3. Rudolf Otto, *The Idea of the Holy* (New York: Oxford University Press 1958), pp. 8-40.

4. C. G. Jung, *Psychology and Religion: West and East.* trans. by R. C. F. Hull Bollingen Series XX (New York: Pantheon Books, 1958), p. 312.

5. *Collected Works of C. G. Jung*, 2nd ed. (Princeton: Princeton University Press, 1968), Vol. 9, Part 2, pp. 8-10; *Collected Works*, 2nd ed., Vol. 9, Part 1, pp. 116-118; pp. 120-122; pp. 120-125.

6. Ginzberg, *Legends* 1:95, 98; 5:100, n.83; 121, n. 116; 123-24, n.131.

7. On the relation of Satan to Prometheus in legend (they are both conceived as jesters, for example) *see* R. J. Zwi Werblowsky, *Lucifer and Prometheus* (London: Routledge and Kegan Paul, 1952) and Jung's forward also found in *Collected Works of C. G. Jung* 2nd ed., Vol. 11, pp. 311-315.

8. This is Jung's third stage of the conjunction of the opposites, the *unus mundies.* See *Collected Works of C. G. Jung* 2nd ed., (Princeton: Princeton University Press, 1970), 14:533-543. Cf. Jeffrey Burton Russell, *The Devil: Perceptions of Evil from Antiquity to Primitive Christianity* (Ithaca and London: Cornell University Press, 1977), p. 31; pp. 184-187.

9. As Eliade expresses it: What is true of eternity is not necessarily true in time. The world came into existence as a result of the breaking of a primordial unity. The world's existence as well as existence in the world presupposes a separation of light and darkness, a distinction between good and evil, a choice and a tension. See *Mephistopholes and the Androgyne: Studied in Religious Myth and Symbol* (New York: Sheed and Ward 1965), p. 94; p. 88. See also Eliade, *History of Religious Ideas: From Gautama Buddha to the Triumph of Christianity* (Chicago: University of Chicago Press, 1982), p. 17. I am indebted to my student George Lawrence Israel for this point and its source.

10. Joshua Trachtenberg, *Jewish Magic and Superstition*, 2nd ed. (New York: Atheneum, 1974), pp. 25-28.

Sinai I: Evil—A Divine Creation

From its outset, the religion of Israel, because of its uncompromising monotheism, was faced with the fundamental question: What is the source of evil in all its manifestations? For the pagan faiths surrounding Israel the question, though troubling, was far less central because in essence these religions had a ready made explanation. Evil like the good has its source in a bifurcated divine realm in which there are gods appointed over the good in the cosmos and gods who hold sway over the realm of evil. This radical dualism (best exemplified by Zorastrianism in which Ahura Mazda is the god of good identified with the light and Ahriman the god of evil identified with the darkness) is categorically rejected by the Bible. Most explicit are the words of the prophet spoken in the name of God: "I form light and create darkness, I make weal and create woe—I the Lord do all these things". (Isa. 45:7)

Having taken its stand, the Bible had to explain how it came about that God who is the acme of all that is good created a world that is essentially good but contains evil.[1] This explanation is set forth in the early sections of the Book of Genesis where natural evil (suffering and death), moral evil (murder and robbery) and religious evil (idolatry) are explored not in a philosophical fashion but through a symbolic narrative infused with an intuitive vision. As noted in the previous chapter, the Bible in numerous places alludes to the idea that evil is embedded in the natural world. The malevolent forces of chaos were not destroyed in the process of creation but removed from those areas set off and governed by divine order. Thus they are always poised to overrun these boundaries and as such, constitute, from the human perspective, a source of potential evil in the universe.

In the Garden of Eden story evil enters the world through human sin and sin is made possible by humanity's freedom of choice, the gift of God. This freedom of choice presupposes the latent existence of evil which is activated by humans, in Genesis chapter three by the serpent enticing Eve to eat the forbidden fruit. The dialogue between Eve and the serpent is but a mirror image of the dialogue taking place within Eve herself, between her inclination to obey God and her inclination to disobey Him.[2] In essence the Garden of Eden story sees the root of evil as human rebellion against God caused by hubris, the desire to be like God, to know good and evil.

Prior to disobeying God's commandment, Adam, in the Garden of Eden, reflected the perfect unity of His Creator. This unity is suggested by the incorporation of male and female aspects in the first human (Gen. 1:27). Adam's profound realization of the unity of all things did not preclude an understanding of duality which is intertwined with the realm of experience. The naming of the animals, beasts and birds and the creation of Eve (Gen. 2:19-22) underscore Adam's understanding of that which exists apart from the self. But the underlying unity of the separate selves of the first man and woman was not lost on them: "This one at last is bone of my bones and flesh of my flesh" (Gen. 2:23). The sense of duality was also represented in the Garden of Eden by the two trees, the tree of the knowledge of good and evil and the tree of life. (It is interesting that in the mythologies of Europe and the Orient, the tree of knowledge is itself the tree of life and is still accessible to humans.[3] The Kabbalists saw Adam's sin as separating the tree of knowledge from the tree of life and the redemption of humanity as marked by their reunification.[4]) The prohibition of eating from the tree of knowledge of good and evil was intended to prevent a deepening of the sense of duality that would come with the intensification of human experience but at the expense of the heightened consciousness of unity. In other words, by deepening their experience of the opposites of good and evil in all their dimensions Adam and Eve would come to recognize that every boundary line that separates the self from the world is also a potential battle line and that conflict is the price for immersion in the war of opposites. Under such conditions, the consciousness of unity, which fosters serenity and tranquillity, must be substantially diminished. In the Garden of Eden dualistic experience was controlled so that Adam and Eve could use it in learning what earthly existence had to offer without at the same time losing the sense of unity which was part of their transcendent awareness.

What exactly was the kind of knowledge acquired by Adam and Eve on eating the forbidden fruit? It was a sudden awareness of the interconnectedness and the ramifications of good and evil in the world. Prior to eating from the tree of good and evil Adam and Eve had an intuitive understanding of moral choice, of good and evil but not an experiential, objective understanding. This intuitive knowledge was of a very high order and predisposed the first humans toward a yearning for and a desire to do the good. With the eating of the forbidden fruit came experiential, objective knowledge of good and evil in their totality and in all their intensity.[5] Taste and sex represent two of the most intense and direct kinds of human experience.[6] It is interesting that Genesis 3 begins with the verse: "the two of them were naked, the man and his wife, yet they felt no shame." Prior to their eating from the fruit of the forbidden tree their procreative sex had been blessed (Gen. 1:28) as had their eating and drinking (Gen. 2:9, 16); it was a natural, joyous uncomplicated function. But on eating the fruit Adam and Eve immediately became aware of their nakedness (Gen. 3:7), i.e., they knew the sense of shame associated with nakedness and sex. Henceforth human sexuality would be associated with shame, pain and conflict (Gen. 3:16) just as eating and drinking would now be a complicated, difficult achievement permeated by strife (Gen. 3:17-20).

With the acquisition of experiential, objective knowledge of good and evil in all its ramifications the first humans lost much of that higher intuitive understanding that predisposed them to yearn for the good and seek its actualization in the world. That intuitive knowledge was not entirely gone but henceforth human beings would have to struggle for it as they struggled for their food, and moral choice like physical sustenance and the procreation of the species would now be shot through with conflict.[7] This is the implication of God's message to Cain that "Sin couches at the door; Its urge is toward you, Yet you can be its master" (Gen. 4:7). The first humans sought to become like God by increasing and deepening their knowledge and experience of good and evil but being human they were unable to cope (without struggle) with the effects of this greater involvement and understanding. As the writer of the Book of Ecclesiastes, reflecting on the human condition, succinctly expressed it, "For as wisdom grows vexation grows; To increase learning is to increase heartache" (Eccles. 1:18)

By their expulsion from the Garden of Eden Adam and Eve were deprived of access to the tree of life so that the desire to become like God and achieve eternal life was lost to them. The concept of death as a punishment for the sin of rebellion against God becomes a major theme in the Bible and its variations appear also in post-biblical literature. But there is also another view of death inherent in the Garden of Eden narrative. Death and birth are parallel processes, both interwoven into the very fabric of nature. This is the implication of those verses (Gen. 1:27; 3:19) which state that God made man from the dust of the earth and to dust he must return.

Though the death of mortals by natural causes was a decree of God (Gen. 6:3) the destruction of life by murder and violence was the doing of humans. From Adam and Eve onward the rebellion against the fatherhood of God had as its corollary the rupture of the brotherhood of man beginning with the murder of Abel by his brother Cain. Like violence and murder, sexual irregularities also represent a rebellion against the divine order established by God at creation. This divine order ordained that the heavens and its creatures be separated from the earth and its creatures and that natural sexual intercourse take place only between members of the same species. Thus the divine beings who, following the desire of their eyes, mated with the daughters of man (Gen. 6: 1-7) opened the door to a reversion to primordial chaos and prepared the way for the corruption of the entire earth and its species in the days of Noah. This chaotic corruption necessitated a cleansing flood and a new beginning with Noah as a second Adam. The sexual code and the dietary regulations of the book of Leviticus (see Lev. 11 and 18 and the discussion in chapter 7) as well as the exhortation in the book of Numbers (Num. 15:39) to "not follow your heart and eyes in your lustful urge" are echoes of both the divine order of creation and its violation by the antediluvians.

Idolatry also is seen in the early Genesis narrative as an effect of and a punishment for rebellion against God. The story of the tower builders (Gen. 11:1-9) emphasizes that the result of the revolt against God was the splintering of humanity into various nations and tongues further rupturing human unity. Moreover, humanity's rejection of God caused them to rely on idols, as many and as different as the nations and the languages of the world. These idols, as the prophets were later to underscore, are as reliable for those thirsting for faith as a broken cistern is reliable for those thirsting for water (Jer. 2:13).

Surveying Genesis 1-11 makes clear that two opposite and contradictory movements are described in these chapters: divine creation contrasted with human decreation. In Genesis 1 God's creative acts unfold in a progression from initial chaos to ultimate order, unity and harmony. Obedience to the divine command is followed by the successful functioning of inorganic life and the bestowal of divine blessing, first upon living creatures and then upon humans. Genesis 2 marks the transition from creation to disintegration. In this chapter the network of essential relationships upholding order, unity and harmony among God, humans, animals and nature begins to disintegrate in the course of events leading from the Garden of Eden to the Tower of Babel. Finally in Genesis 3-11 the progression of creation is reversed and replaced by the process of decreation. The regression from harmony to chaos is punctuated by the expansion of sin and violence from the individual to all humanity and even to divine beings, followed, measure for measure, by expulsion, homelessness, the limitation on the length and quality of human life, the almost complete annihilation of creaturely existence and the rupture of the unity of humankind. The flood and Babel are the final stages in the process of human and cosmic disintegration that began in Eden.[8]

Though the opening chapters of Genesis posit human rebellion against God as *the* sin of humanity, there are other facets of sin illumined in other parts of the Bible. The basic meaning of the Hebrew word *het* is to miss the mark, to go astray. The concept of sin as erroneous action is to be found in the cultic laws (Lev. 4:2 ff.) and in the civil laws regarding unpremeditated offenses (Num. 35:1; Deut. 19:4-10; Josh. 20:3). Job in his argument with God suggests that the Almighty is responsible for human error (Job 12:16) while the prophet Isaiah sees this error as the effect of the debauched life of the false priests and prophets of his time (Isa. 28:7-8). The Psalmist declares that the Torah is the moral compass that keeps humans from going astray (Ps. 119:67). In the wisdom literature of the Bible and the post-biblical writings sin is equated with foolishness and righteousness with wisdom. The author of the Book of Proverbs states that "The fear of the Lord is the beginning of knowledge; Fools despise wisdom and discipline" (Prov. 1:7) and "The schemes of folly are sin" (Prov. 24:9). Hillel the Elder expressed in the rabbinic compendium of proverbs that which became axiomatic for the rabbis: "An uncultured man cannot really fear sin; an ignorant man cannot be truly pious" (M. Avot 2:5). But a distinction was made between the individual who though of simple mind did possess high qualities of moral character and the one who is devoid of intellectual as well as ethical virtues. The former (*peti*) could become religiously attuned when under the influence of God's teaching (Pss. 19:8;119:130) and merits divine protection (Ps. 116:6). The latter (*naval*) justifies his immoral ways by stupidly denying God and His moral order in the universe (Pss. 14:1; 92:7-8).

Notes

1. This problem was answered in a different way by the Lurianic Kabbalah of the sixteenth century. See G. Scholem, *Major Trends in Jewish Mysticism*, pp. 244-286 and *Kabbalah* (New York: Quadrangle, 1974), pp. 67-79; 122-144.

2. U. Cassuto, *From Adam to Noah* (Jerusalem: The Magnes Press, 1953), pp. 94-95.

3. Joseph Campbell, *The Masks of God: Occidental Mythology* (New York: The Viking Press, 1973), p. 106.

4. *Zohar* (ed. Margaliot), 1: 12 a-b, 35b-36a, 221 a-b; 3:182a, 240a. *Zohar Hadash*, Genesis (ed. Margaliot), p. 19a (*Midrash ha-ne'elam*);

Scholem, *Kabbalah*, p. 124 and *On the Kabbalah and Its Symbolism*, trans. Ralph Mannheim (New York: Schocken Books, 1965), pp. 68-77; 108. G. Scholem, *On The Mystical Shape of the Godhead*, trans. Joachim Neugroschel (New York: Schocken, 1991), pp. 56-87. On the psychological plane, the sin corresponds to the splitting off of consciousness from the unconscious. See Carl Jung, *The Structure and Dynamics of the Psyche* in *Collected Works* 8:157; Erich Neumann, *The Origins and History of Consciousness* (Princeton: Princeton University Press, 1970), pp. 102-27; Julian Jaynes, *The Origin of Consciousness in the Breakdown of the Bicameral Mind* (Boston: Houghton Miflin, 1976), p. 299.

5.   Scholem, *On the Kabbalah and Its Symbolism*, pp. 72-74; p. 90; Yehezkel Kaufmann, *Toledot ha-Emunah ha-Yisraelit* (Jerusalem, Tel Aviv: Mosad Bialik, 1953) 8 vols., 4:408-412.

6.   In the priestly Judaism of the Hebrew Bible eating and sex served as potent (in every sense of the term) signs for the social order as a whole. They performed the invaluable anthropological functions of preserving lineage, separating the holy from the profane and distinguishing men from women. Thus, for example, Leviticus 19:23 speaks of immature trees as 'uncircumcised" and calls their fruit "foreskin" (*orlah*), suggesting that just as other cultures frequently associated fruit with sexuality, the Israelites saw a direct analogy between pruning maturing fruit trees to increase their yield and pruning the male foreskin to enhance fertility. Similarly, the biblical prohibition of boiling a kid in its mother's milk can be viewed as a metaphor for incest. See Howard Eilberg-Schwartz, *The Savage in Judaism: An Anthropology of Israelite Religion and Ancient Judaism* (Bloomington and Indianapolis: Indiana University Press, 1990), pp. 130-131; 141-176 and below Chapter 7, Sinai: Priestly Piety, notes 30 and 31.

The idea that gluttony leads to sexual desire no doubt grew out of the interpretation of the Garden of Eden narrative. The rabbis of talmudic and medieval times associated sexual intercourse with eating and drinking and prescribed dietary regimens for procreation and for the curbing of sexual appetite. Cf., Ginzberg, *Legends* 6:208, n. 121 and 6:461, n. 88 and Joshua Trachtenberg, *Jewish Magic and Superstition*, pp. 184-85; 302-303, n. 6. In Greco-Roman medical literature eating and sexual intercourse are associated and in Christian ascetic writings sexual desires and temptation are cured by fasting and ascetic diets. C f. Michel Foucault, *The History of Sexuality*, vol. 3: *The Care of the Self* trans. Robert Hurley (New York: Pantheon Books, 1986), pp. 125-126; pp. 140-141; Aline Rouselle, *Pornea: On Desire and the Body in Antiquity* trans. Felicia Pheasant (Oxford and New York: Basil Blackwell, 1988), pp. 16-19; 169-178; Peter Brown, *The Body and Society: Men, Women and Sexual Renunciation in Early Christianity* (New York: Columbia University Press, 1988), pp. 78, 224-25; 419.

7.   Kaufmann, *Toledot ha-Emunah ha-Yisraelit*, 4:412-414. .Cf. Moses Maimonides, *Guide of the Perplexed*, trans. and intro. by Shlomoh Pines (Chicago: University of Chicago Press, 1963), pp. 23-26. Philo held that even after the Fall there were certain unique individuals (i.e., Melchizedek, Noah, Abraham, Isaac, Jacob and Moses) "to whom virtue was natural and

they needed not to toil in order to attain it." *Legum Allegoria* 3, 46, 134-135; 3: 24, 77; 25, 79-81; 27, 83-84; Wolfson, *Philo* 1: 450-452. The rabbinic sources also refer to the extraordinary physical, mental and spiritual powers of Adam which were somewhat diminished by his sin. See *b. Hagigah*, 12a; *b. Sanhedrin*, 38b; *Tanhuma B* Genesis 18 (ed. Buber), p. 7; Ginzberg, *Legends* 5:112, n. 104; Urbach, *The Sages* pp. 228-232, 421-422. The surmounting of dualism is also a central theme of the Gospel of Philip, one of the Nag Hammadi texts stemming from the Gnostic school of Valentinus and dating from the second century C.E. Cf. *The Gospel of Philip*, trans. with intro. and commentary R. McL. Wilson (New York and Evanston: Harper & Row, 1962), pp. 44 (saying 71); p. 46 (sayings 78-79); p. 134; p. 14; p. 29 (sayings 10-11). The contrasts of light and darkness, life and death, right and left in the latter passage is strikingly reminiscent of the rabbinic statement that for everything God had created He also created its counterpart. The contrast of opposites in the dualistic world in which we live is also depicted in the early kabbalistic work, the *Sefer Yezirah*, the *Book of Formation* (Warsaw, 1884), 4:1, 3-4; 5:2; 6:2, G. Scholem, *Kabbalah*, pp. 23-30 and is echoed in the oriental concept of the *Yin* and the *Yang*. Cf. Ernest Wood, *Zen Dictionary* (New York: Philosophical Library, 1962), pp. 155-56; Max Kaltenmark, *Lao Tzu and Taoism*, trans. Roger Greaves (Stanford: Standford University Press, 1969), pp. 24, 26-27; 41-46; 130-136. The difference between the Gnostic outlook and the views expressed in the biblical, rabbinic, and kabbalistic texts is that the latter, unlike Gnosticism, *do not* devalue dualistic earthly existence only an excessive immersion in it. To the contrary, from the Sinai perspective, this existence is *good* for human beings whose task is to maintain the proper balance between mundane dualism and transcendent unity.

8. Bernard Och, "The Garden of Eden: From Re-Creation to Reconciliation," *Judaism* 37, No. 3 (Summer, 1988): 340-351.

Sinai II: Evil in its Human Dimension

Like the Bible, so the rabbis defused the problem of good and evil for monotheistic faith by transferring it from the realm of God to the realm of humans, from the sphere of theology to the province of psychology. They portrayed the moral struggle of humanity after the Fall of Adam and Eve in terms of the good impulse (*yezer ha-tov*) and the evil impulse (*yezer ha-ra*). Thus the Talmud asserts: "Two inclinations did the Holy One Blessed be He create: the one is the good inclination, the other the evil inclination."[1] The inner man is the battleground of these two inclinations. The commandment "You shall love the Lord your God with all your heart" (Deut. 6:5) is interpreted as "with both your inclinations,"[2] for the heart pulls us in two directions.

Taking a cue from the Garden of Eden narrative, in which after the Fall humans lost their intuitive predisposition toward the good which could now only be attained by great struggle, rabbinic psychology sees the evil inclinations as innate. It develops in the mother's womb and is born with the child, or, according to an opposing opinion, becomes operative only at birth.[3] The good inclination appears thirteen years later at puberty.[4] It emerges as the product of a specifically human psychological development from a background of purely natural instinct, against which it must struggle, a concept strikingly akin to Freudian theory.[5]

The good inclination is often identified with the Torah. "The Holy One Blessed be He said to Israel: "My children I created the evil impulse but I also created the Torah as its antidote."[6] The Torah revealed by God is the introjected conscience of the Jew.[7] The good inclination identified with the Torah thus becomes a kind of regulative principle by which human beings through their consciences subjugates their nature (the evil inclination), master it, integrate it and sanctify it. It is now clear why the rabbis speak of the appearance of the good inclination at puberty, at age thirteen, for this coincides with the religious rite of Bar-Mitzvah in Judaism when the child attains religious adulthood and takes upon himself the responsibility for obeying God's commandments.[8]

But the evil impulse is not to be identified with sin. In the words of George Foot Moore: "The opportunity or the invitation to sin may come from without, but it is the response of the evil impulse in man that converts it into a temptation. It pictures in imagination the pleasures of sin, conceives the plan, seduces the will, incites to the act. It is thus primarily as the subjective origin of temptation or more correctly as the tempter within, that the *yezer ha-ra* (the evil impulse) is represented in Jewish literature. Since it compasses man's undoing by leading him into sin, it is thought of as maliciously seeking his ruin, a kind of malevolent second personality. Throughout his life, from infancy to old age, it pursues its deadly purpose, patiently biding its time."[9]

In fact, the evil impulse, though responsible for human struggle and suffering, also plays an important role in God's design for the world. At the conclusion of His work of creation, "God saw everything that He had made, and behold, it was very good" (Gen. 1:31). "Very good" comments the *Midrash*, "by that is meant the evil inclination, for had the evil inclination not existed, no man had built a house and no man had married a wife."[10]   In an ironical legend the Talmud relates that when the rabbis had one day succeeded in catching the (personified) evil inclination and chaining it up, the next day not so much as a fresh egg could be found even for a sick man, so they had to let the evil inclination—indispensable for men and cocks alike—go free again.[11]   The rabbinic view is that the impulses natural to human beings are not in themselves evil. The appetites and passions are an essential element in the constitution of human nature and necessary to the perpetuation of the human species and to the existence of civilization. For this reason they are not to be eradicated or suppressed but directed and controlled.

For the rabbis as for the biblical writer the primary sin of mankind is rebellion against God. The rabbis see this rebellion as expressed primarily through idolatry which is more deeply rooted in the nature of human beings than any other passion; it is even stronger than the sexual passion leading to adultery.[12]   But as the later books of the Bible, they also see sin as a result of human foolishness. The verses of Prov. 9:1-14 in which Wisdom personified invites the simple minded to enter her house is interpreted by Rabbi Jeremiah ben Eliezer as referring to Adam and Eve who thinking they could become like God deserted Him and followed the advice of the serpent.[13]   In a similar vein Rabbi Simeon ben Lakish said: "A person does not commit a transgression unless a spirit of folly enters into him."[14]   Rabbi Simeon identified Satan with the evil impulse responsible for human sin caused by folly and in rabbinic legend and folklore Satan in the guise of the serpent seduced Adam and Eve.[15]

Though foolishness and idolatry represent the ultimate causes of mortal sin, the rabbis also saw intermediate sources of human evil. In Gen. 4:8 we read: "Cain said to his brother Abel . . . and when they were in the field, Cain set upon his brother Abel and killed him." The biblical verse is elliptical. It begins with the statement that "Cain said to Abel" but it does not tell us what Cain said. The rabbis supplement the missing words and reconstruct the dispute that probably took place before Cain murdered Abel.[16] According to one explanation, Cain proposed to divide the world. Abel took the flocks and became a keeper of sheep, while Cain took the land and became a tiller of soil. Following this division of property and labor, a dispute emerged between the landowner and the shepherd. This materialistic explanation parallels and anticipates that of Karl Marx in the opening of chapter three in the third book of his *Das Kapital*, where the collapse of the primeval ideal commune is seen as the reason for man's fall.

A second explanation states that the dispute between the brothers revolved around the question: on whose territory will the Sanctuary be built? The dispute was a religious, idealistic one. According to this explanation differing ideals, contradictory religious dogmas, and competing holy places are the sources of evil and the urge to kill. Holy wars are justified by the need to annihilate societies or segments of societies upholding doctrines opposed to those regarded as the norm by the in-group. By extirpating the dissenters the world is purified and made exemplary.

A third explanation has it that the brothers' dispute was about possessing the father's first wife, the she-demon Lilith.[17] This would reflect the dark human instincts of depth psychology theories. The final explanation of the dispute is based on the oral tradition according to which a twin sister was born with Abel and each of the brothers claimed her for himself, using legal and logical reasoning. This would correspond to the Freudian theories of male competition over the possession of women in primitive societies.

The connection between sin and death established in the Bible is also echoed by the rabbis but the Bible's alternate view of death, that it is the culmination of a natural process, is likewise to be found in rabbinic literature. The latter view is reflected in the enigmatic comment of Rabbi Meir on Gen. 1:31, "And God saw all that He had made and found it very good." Remarked Rabbi Meir: "It was very good, that is death."[18] As Maimonides explained it, Rabbi Meir seems to say that death is an integral part of the natural order making way for new life and continued creation.[19] The naturalness of death is also specified in the rabbinic saying that the Angel of Death was created on the first day of creation.[20] On the other hand, the Talmud affirms that "there is no death without sin"[21] and it is the inevitable fate of humans in that no human being is sinless. But as the context in which this statement is found indicates, sin *per se* is not the cause of death among human beings but it does shorten the allotted years of an individual's life.[22]

Notes

1.   *b. Berakot*, 61a.
2.   *M. Berakot*, 9:5
3.   *b. Niddah*, 30b.
4.   *Ecclesiastes R.* 9:14; *Avot de Rabbi Natan* 16, ed. Schechter, p. 62; *The Fathers According to Rabbi Nathan*, trans. Judah Goldin (New Haven, Conn.: Yale University Press, 1955), p. 83.
5.   Sigmund Freud, *Three Essays on Sexuality*, in the standard ed., *Complete Psychological Works of Sigmund Freud*, trans. and ed. James Strachey (London: Hogarth Press, 1953) 7:192-193; Sigmund Freud, *Civilization and Its Discontents*, trans. Joan Riviere (London: Hogarth Press, 1953), pp. 10-13; on the influence of rabbinic thought on Freud *see* David Bakan, *Sigmund Freud and the Jewish Mystical Tradition* (New York: D. Van Nostrand Co., 1958).
6.   *b. Kiddushin*, 30b.
7.   This introduction of conscience is derived from an artificially construed contradiction in Ps. 1:2, where it is said of the righteous man that "His delight is in the Law of the Lord and in his law (construed by the rabbis as referring not to the Law of the Lord but to the righteous man's own law) does he meditate day and night.   According to this rabbinic interpretation, in the beginning of his religious development the righteous man views the Torah as God's law, but in the end it becomes his own law.
8.   *M. Avot*, 5:21.
9.   George Foot Moore, *Judaism* (Cambridge: Harvard University Press, 1950), pp. 481-482. See also Frank C. Porter, "The Yecer Hara, A Study in the Jewish Doctrine of Sin," in *Biblical and Semitic Studies* (New York: Charles Scribners & Sons, 1901), pp. 91-156.
10. *Gen. R.* 9:9, ed. Theodor-Albeck, p. 72.
11. *b. Yoma*, 69b.
12. *b. Yoma*, 69b; *Canticles R.* 7:13; *Yer. Avodah Zarah* (ed. Krotoschin, 1866), 40c; *Midrash Ha-Gadol*, Genesis (ed. S. Schechter, Cambridge, England 1902), p. 120.
13. *Lev. R.* 11:1 ed. M. Margaliot, Jerusalem, 1953-1958, p. 220.
14. *b. Sotah*, 3a.
15. Ephraim E. Urbach, *The Sages* (Cambridge and London: Harvard University Press, 1987), p. 170, p. 472. Louis Ginzberg, *The Legends of the Jews* 7 vols. (Philadelphia: The Jewish Publication Society of America, 1954) 1:95-96, 105, 5:121, n. 117, henceforth referred to as Ginzberg, *Legends*.
16. *Gen. R.* 22:7, ed. Theodor-Albeck, p. 212 and parallels in Ginzberg, *Legends* 5:138 ff. n. 17.
17. On Lilith see Gershom Scholem, *Kabbalah* (New York: Quadrange 1974), pp. 356-361 and the bibliography cited there.

18. *Genesis R.* 9:5 (ed. Theodor-Albeck), p. 70.

19. Moses Maimonides, *The Guide of the Perplexed* trans. with an intro. and notes by S. Pines (Chicago: University of Chicago Press, 1964) 3:10 p. 440. Cf. Urbach, *The Sages*, pp. 264-266.

20. *b. Bava Batra*, 10a; *Tanhuma*, Vayeshev, 4.

21. *b. Shabbat*, 55b. Urbach, *The Sages*, p. 266 claims this view is amoraic not tannaitic.

22. Urbach, *The Sages*, pp. 426-427. W. D. Davies, *Paul and Rabbinic Judaism* 3rd ed. (London: S.P.C.K. Press, 1970), pp. 24-31 rightly sees a connection between Romans 7 in which Paul divides his life into three periods and rabbinic views of sin. The first stage of Paul's life was an age of innocence in which sin, though latent in him, was "dead" and he was able to live a full life without restraint. This corresponds to the rabbinic view discussed earlier that the evil impulse operates unopposed from birth to the age of thirteen. In the second period of Paul's life, the commandment came to him and with it not only the awareness of the sinfulness of sin but also an impetus toward sin arising from the human tendency to regard forbidden fruits as the sweetest and the tendency toward self-righteousness if one observes the commandment. Until this point in his life sin was not known as sin; it was revealed to Paul as such by the Law (i.e., the Torah). This second stage corresponds to the rabbinic description of *bar-mitzvah*, when the commandment, i.e., the Torah, identified as the good impulse enters the individual's life and begins to battle with the evil impulse causing conflict. In the third period of Paul's life the Spirit came to deliver him. This corresponds to the rabbinic belief that the study of and meditation on the divine revelation contained in the Torah is the surest antidote to the internal conflict of the good and evil impulse, *b. Kiddushin*, 30b and 81a. For Paul the Torah commandments kept him from sin and the Spirit delivered him from self-righteousness. See the interpretation of Romans 7 by my former student Mark D. Nanos in the conclusion to his forthcoming book *From Zion to Rome: the Jewish Context of Paul's Letter to the Romans.* Paul's contrast of flesh and spirit is analogous to the rabbinic contrast of the evil impulse and the good impulse.

Olympus I: Evil "Beyond The Measure"

Hesiod describes a cosmos with divine prototypes for natural evils like death and old age as well as for the moral, social, and physical evils which make humans miserable. Yet he also posits an Eden-like time, in the age of the Greek fertility god Cronus, when people lived entirely blessed lives.[1]

> First of all the deathless gods who dwell on Olympus made a golden race of mortal men who lived in the time of Cronus when he was reigning in heaven. And they lived like gods without sorrow of heart, remote and free from toil and grief: miserable age rested not on them; but with legs and arms never failing they made merry with feasting beyond the reach of all evils.
>
> When they died it was as though they were overcome with sleep, and they had all good things; for the fruitful earth unforced bare them fruit abundantly and without stint. They dwelt in ease and peace upon their lands with many good things, rich in flocks and loved by the blessed gods. (*Works and Days* 109-120. White, trans.)

Inevitable death came upon them like a gentle transformation. When earth covered the earliest generations, they became spirits who remained close to earth watching over human affairs.

At the beginning of Zeus's reign, men were still able to live on intimate terms with the gods. *Theogony* describes them as sharing a common banquet whereas Pindar (*Olympian* 1, 38 & 60) relates that Tantalus invited gods to a feast at his home. But Hesiod knew from bitter experience that humans were no longer "beyond the reach of all evils." In fact, he acknowledged that in his own age, "men will never cease from work and suffering by day nor from being distressed at night for the gods will give grievous cares (*Works and Days* 176-178)." He even predicted that Zeus would eventually destroy the race of mortals because it would become so degenerate, so full of sin and violence that "right and reverence" would entirely cease to exist. (*Work and Days* 180-201). And the Greeks, like the Hebrews, remembered that creation had once nearly been annulled; Deucalion and Pyrrha correspond to Noah as virtuous mortals preserved from a destructive flood sent by the deity to punish human wickedness (Apollodorus 1.7. 1-2; Ovid *Metamorphosis* 1.318-415).

But why couldn't humans continue to live entirely blessed lives in harmony with the gods? On one level, the gods themselves are the source of misery. Achilles tells Priam in Book 24 of the *Iliad*,

Such is the way the gods spun life for unfortunate mortals,
that we live in unhappiness, but the gods themselves have no sorrows.
There are two urns that stand on the door-sill of Zeus. They are unlike
for the gifts they bestow: an urn of evils, an urn of blessings.
If Zeus who delights in thunder mingles these and bestows them
on man, he shifts, and moves now in evil, again in good fortune.
But when Zeus bestows from the urn of sorrows, he makes a failure
of man, and the evil hunger drives him over the shining
earth, and he wanders respected neither of gods nor mortals.
(24. 525-33, Lattimore, trans.)

Achilles' image of the two urns corresponds to the idea that the cosmic order has developed from a harmonizing of opposite forces and characters. Human life at its best is, of necessity, a balance of good and evil, and Zeus, the ultimate harmonizer, is responsible for both aspects of life.

The early Greeks, like other polytheists, believed that everything in the human realm derived its existence from the activities of immortal beings in the divine realm.[2] Hesiod's personifications are divine exemplars for the realities that existed in his world: e.g., toil, famine, disease, murder, war. The anthropomorphic gods, too, validate drives, types, relationships, and conflicts of human beings. Zeus functions as son, father, brother, lover, husband, warrior, and king whereas the lesser gods and goddesses have more restricted roles and personalities. Their interaction provides the divine pattern for human interaction among individuals, families, and social organizations.

Divine behavior, like the divine cosmos itself, is neither entirely good nor entirely perverse. No one Greek anthropomorphic god is an embodiment or symbol of evil in himself, like the Persian Ahriman or the Christian Satan. Hades, the king of the underworld, is not a rival of Zeus or a threat to his order. His kingdom is the general repository for the dead rather than a specific place for the punishment of sinners. Although no individual deity symbolizes villainy, most gods, like most humans, misbehave at one time or another, either out of lust, jealousy, anger, ambition, or divided loyalty. When they err, they must suffer the consequences. If a divinity swears falsely by Styx, for example, he must endure pain, hunger, disease, and exile for nine years (*Theogony* 775-819). The fact that Apollo, the patron of purification rites and laws for homicide, is himself a murderer (of Pytho and a Cyclops) who undergoes the prescribed punishments and rites illustrates how the anthropomorphic system validates both the reality of human evil and the existence of a moral system which does not condone it.

Although everything has its origin in the divine realm, humans bring more than their portion of suffering upon themselves. In the *Odyssey*, Zeus complains to the assembled gods,

> My, how mortal beings blame the gods.
> They say that evils come from us, but they
> themselves have grief beyond their measure
> because of their own reckless sins.
> (1. 32-34, Fitzgerald, trans.)[3]

The phrase "beyond their measure" refers to grief which exceeds the natural limits that separate humans from the deathless gods who can have no real sorrow. Old age and death are inevitable for mortals but they are part of the natural process of growth and decay. They can come gently as a blessed release (e.g., *Works and Days* 116; *Timaeus* 81e), but they can also bring with them the limitations and evils represented by the other children of Night (e.g., Blame, Grief, Retribution, and Strife). The children of Strife validate further kinds of evils which humans certainly bring on themselves: Toil, Negligence, Famine, Sorrow; Wars, Battles, Murders, Lawlessness, Madness, Feuds, Lying Words, and False Oaths.[4] These divine personifications exist as latent possibilities in the beginning of *Theogony*, but they become realities as the cosmos develops and human history begins, activated in the divine realm by strife initiated by the rebellious gods of *Theogony*, and then in the human world by the foolish men of *Works and Days*.

Several tales which account for the evils and miseries in human life point to hubris as a major cause. This term, usually translated as pride, implies the misuse of one's energy and power in a way which is self -indulgent and intends to shame as well as injure the victim.[5] In the Athenian law code, such behavior was considered an offense against the whole community; any citizen could bring a public suit (*graphe*) and the penalty paid by the party judged guilty went to the state instead of the victim. The egotistical mental attitude which led a person to satisfy his own wishes by infringing on the rights, honor and property of others distinguished hubris from other crimes which were private suits (e.g., rape, theft, assault). If the victim was a god, or if the behavior dishonored or damaged the moral customs or institutions supported by a god, the willful self-indulgence could be viewed as a religious sin as well as a secular crime. According to certain passages in tragedy, the gods were sure to punish those presumptuous individuals who insult or assault things worthy of honor to achieve excess honor or pleasure for themselves (e.g., Aeschylus *Persians* 807-31).

In both *Theogony* and *Works and Days*, Hesiod blames wily Prometheus' attempt to match wits with Zeus for the added sorrows of humanity. Prometheus is first introduced into *Theogony* as the clever sibling of "dauntless" (*kraterophron*a, 509) Atlas and "violent" (*hubristen*) Menoitios, who was punished "because of his wickedness and insolent prowess" (516). The details and the diction suggest that all three exhibited hubris; they demanded more than their portion of power, limited for them by the authority of Zeus, and resorted to violent or rebellious behavior to achieve their ends. Prometheus' brothers are members of the generation of Titans defeated and imprisoned by Zeus for their assault on his new regime. In Hesiod, Prometheus is not motivated by pity or altruism for man. He simply wants to trap Zeus and demonstrate his superior cunning. His trick at the sacrifice gave man an excessive portion of the animal to be shared with the gods. His theft of the fire Zeus denied to man presented a direct challenge to Zeus's authority. Not only did Zeus devise a cruel punishment for Prometheus, but he also ordered the creation of Pandora, the first woman, as a new evil, to balance the new blessing, fire. After relating the incident, Hesiod draws the following moral: "So it is not possible to deceive or go beyond the mind of Zeus" (613).

Although the poet emphasizes the Titan Prometheus' rebellion against Zeus, the parts of his tale relating to human beings contain the same elements of eating and sexuality which are the focal points of the Garden of Eden story. For, not only are food and sex vital to the survival of the human race but, for the Greeks, they are the very characteristics which separate mortals from the anthropomorphic but deathless gods. Prometheus' deception which validates the traditional division of the sacrificial animal gives the gods only the smoke and scent from the fat and bones and leaves the meat for the human participants because gods do not, in fact, require food whereas mortals must constantly consume it to stay alive.[6] And although immortals certainly engage in sexual activities, they do not need to procreate to insure their survival, as mortals must.

The desire to attack the gods and usurp their prerogatives is also exhibited by the first humans in Aristophanes' comic tale about the origin of Eros in Plato's *Symposium* (189d-193d). Originally, men and women had different, more powerful bodies and were much more mobile. But they had great ambition as well as great strength and vigor. Like Ephialtes and Otus, two giants who, according to Homer

(*Od.* 11. 305-320), piled Ossa on Pelion to scale Olympus, these humans tried to ascend to heaven and lay violent hands upon the gods. Therefore, Zeus changed the first humans' shapes and made them weaker in order to prevent them from further licentiousness and outrage.

But ignorance or foolishness is also deemed responsible for the loss of an easy life in harmony with the gods. Prometheus, whose name means "Forethinker," did not know his powers were limited by Zeus "whose wisdom is everlasting." In Hesiod's account," Zeus recognized and was not ignorant of the trick" (551) and responded with troubles that neither mortals nor Prometheus could overcome by themselves. But Epimetheus (Afterthinker), whose epithet is "erring in mind" (*hamartinon, Theogony* 5ll), shares the blame for the new human misery with his presumptuous brother Prometheus. According to *Works and Days*, Epimetheus did not think about Prometheus' warning not to accept any gift from Zeus (86). "When he had Pandora, the evil thing, however, he understood" (89). Pandora, a punishment in herself, brings further evils (e.g., countless diseases that stalk men) when she lifts the lid off a jar. Although the story in *Works and Days* is a conflation full of ellipsis, the fact that she stops the jar suggests that her opening it was a thoughtless action.[7]

Hesiod adds another tale in *Works and Days* to explain why suffering and hard work are necessary elements in man's life. In this allegory of the five ages, hubris is connected with ignorance or foolishness. After describing the golden race, quoted above, he introduces a second silver generation, "unlike the former in body or mind." This generation is characterized by its foolishness (*nepios*, 131; *aphradie*, 134) which brought them misery. Because they were unable to keep from sinful violence (*hubris*) against one another and were unwilling to serve or honor the gods, Zeus in his anger hid them away. The next age, the bronze age, was so violent (*hubries*) that the fierce warriors destroyed themselves. After a description of the age of heroes, Hesiod moves to his own iron age which is full of labor and sorrow because humans do not know veneration and fear of the gods (187) and will praise the doer of evils and hubris (191). Urging his brother to choose the path of justice, Hesiod warns Perses that Justice always defeats hubris in the end, but the fool (*nepios*) only knows this after suffering (*Works and Days* 217-18).

The ignorance of humans, which leads to violent and irreverent behavior, is two-fold. On the one hand, mortals are flawed by fate or necessity. That is, they do not, by definition, have either the eternal life outside time or the omniscience of gods like Zeus or

Apollo. Uncertain of the future or the consequences of their actions, they are destined to make mistakes. The Greek words most frequently connected with sin (e.g., *hamartanein, amplakein, sphallesthai*) imply an error which is not necessarily willful, such as missing a target or failing, but which may cause harm.[8] That Oedipus committed the very crimes he exerted his intelligence and effort to prevent illustrates how little control he really had over the events he tried to take charge of.

Human beings must always be mindful of this limit to their knowledge, always aware that they cannot place total confidence in their reason or ability to mould the future. As Haemon says when he tries to dissuade Creon from killing Antigone,

> Whoever thinks that he alone is wise,
> his eloquence, his mind, above the rest,
> come the unfolding, shows his emptiness.
> A man, though wise, should never be ashamed
> of learning more, and must unbend his mind . . . .
> I'd say it would be best if men were born
> perfect in wisdom, but that failing this
> (which often fails) it can be no dishonor
> to learn from others when they speak good sense.
> (*Antigone* 705-11; 720-23, Wycoff, trans.)[9]

After Antigone has been led to her underground prison, Tiresias also tries to change Creon's mind.

> Think of these things, my son. All men may err (*hamartanein*)
> but error once committed (*hamarte*), he's no fool
> nor yet unfortunate who gives up his stiffness
> and cures the trouble he has fallen in.
> Stubbornness and stupidity are twins. (1023-7, Wycoff, trans.)

Though Creon relents, he is too late to prevent the suicides of Antigone, Haemon and Eurydice. In the end, he accepts his own responsibility for these deaths, seeing them as punishments for his impiety. The concluding choral ode connects the sufferings of the "overproud" with their inability to "think correctly."

When a human being's portion of knowledge and understanding is limited by necessity, "thinking correctly" and avoiding error are not easy tasks. Epic poetry and tragedy concentrate on characters who are faced with a difficult but necessary choice, and must weigh rights and wrongs, moral and practical, before coming to decisions which affect their families, states and relations with the gods.[10]

Whatever the motives or causes for a wrong decision, the one who acts upon it must accept the responsibility for the deed and suffer the penalties exacted by god and mortal. Sometimes, heroes act out of fatal ignorance, as the old Oedipus insists he did when, as a younger man, he killed his father and married his mother (*Oedipus at Colonus* 270-274). Sometimes they act with full knowledge that their deed is not proper, as the old Oedipus charges that those who wronged him did (e.g., his parents, the two shepherds, his own sons and Creon) and as Creon dramatizes when he seizes Oedipus' defenseless daughters, even pulling Ismene from a shrine. More often, however, the hero is a good person, like the young Oedipus or like Creon in *Antigone*, struggling to make the proper choice between undesirable alternatives, but blinded by the very qualities which propel him toward greatness: high birth and position, as well as ambition, intelligence and self-confidence resulting from former successes. It is the paradox of the human condition that the great must push themselves to the limits and use their god-like powers to accomplish great things, but that these very assertions are often doomed to failure and bring down multiple disasters.

In such situations, the logic of the story precludes our blaming necessary ignorance alone because the person involved, like Adam and Eve, is warned beforehand. Prometheus told Epimetheus not to accept any gift from the gods. The gods themselves sent Hermes down to warn Aegisthus against the murder of Agamemnon and the adultery with Clytemnestra, predicting that Orestes would certainly avenge these crimes. Hesiod warns that there are two kinds of Strife, one fostering war and battle, and the other stimulating men to work hard in harmless competition with their neighbors.[11] It is up to greedy Perses not to choose the Strife in which evil men delight because he is bound to lose what he has already gained (*Works and Days*, 11-26). But men are so full of passion and life so full of temptation that humans foolishly disregard the voices of reason.

Deliberate choice is such an important element in bringing down disaster that epic poetry and drama often depict the process. Book 9 of the *Iliad* provides a good example of the type of scene. Odysseus, Phoenix, and Ajax all try to persuade Achilles to accept Agamemnon's apology and return to battle. Each advances specific arguments, related to his own position, and warns Achilles of the personal and social consequences of his refusal. Achilles' answers not only reveal that he has pondered over the problem; they also indicate his pride and the power of his wrath over his reason. He argues that he no longer needs honor from men, since he has honor from Zeus (608) and that, although he respects and loves his friends, he is just too angry to do what they require. Many tragic heroes, from Aeschylus' Eteocles, to Creon in *Antigone* and Pentheus in the *Bacchae*, remain as determined as Achilles to pursue a chosen course, despite attempts to dissuade them by relatives, priests, and citizens. As the hero defends his position, he exposes his rashness, rigidity, over-confidence, or excess of passion. Although he insists that his arguments are rational, his antagonists accuse him of madness and folly as well as hubris. Afterwards he acknowledges his own part in the catastrophe. So Achilles, when he learns of the death of Patroclus, blames himself and that strife "and gall which makes a man grow angry for all his great mind/that gall of anger that swarms like smoke inside of a man's heart/ and becomes a thing sweeter to him by far than the dripping of honey" (18. 107-110, Lattimore, trans.). In *Bacchae* 1120-21, Pentheus, face to face with his mother, both rejectors of Dionysus, cries out as she and her frenzied band of lionhunters pounce, "Do not kill me, your own son, for my sins (*hamartiaisi*)."

Notes

1. Hesiod's allegory of the five ages of man is a conflation of several stories from both the Near East and the Greek mainland. See M. L. West's commentary on line 11 as well as his introduction to the section on pages 172-177 in his edition of *Works and Days* (Oxford: Clarendon Press, 1978). Translations from Hesiod are quoted from Hugh G. Evelyn White, *Hesiod, the Homeric Hymns and Homerica*. Loeb Classical Library (Cambridge: Harvard University Press, 1914), unless otherwise noted.

2. For an excellent explication of this world view in relation to Mesopotamia, see Thorkild Jacobsen's description of Mesopotamian myth in Henri Frankfort, Mrs. H. A. Frankfort, John A. Wilson, Thorkild Jacobsen, *Before Philosophy: The Intellectual Adventure of Ancient Man* (Baltimore: Penguin, 1949), pp. 137-234.

3. I quote from Robert Fitzgerald, *Homer: "The Odyssey "*(Garden City, NY: Doubleday, 1961). Translations from the *Iliad* are quoted from Richmond Lattimore, *"The Iliad" of Homer*, (Chicago: University of Chicago Press, 1951).

4. Norman O. Brown, *"Theogony:" Hesiod translated with an Introduction* (Indianapolis: Bobbs Merrill, 1953), pp. 85-86.

5. Athens had a law against hubris which was loosely defined as abuse, slander or assault where the motive seems to be dishonor of the victim or abuse for one's own enjoyment. It was an offense that was very hard to prove. For a closer examination of the uses of the term in Greek literature and law see Douglas M. MacDowell, "Hybris in Athens," *Greece and Rome* 23 (1976): 14-31 and N. R. E. Fisher, "Hybris and Dishonor," *Greece and Rome* 23 (1976): 177-93 and 26 (1979): 32-47

6. For an analysis of the meaning of this myth, see Jean-Pierre Vernant, "Sacrifice and Alimentary Codes in Hesiod's Myth of Prometheus," reprinted in R. D. Gordon, Ed., *Myth, Religion, and Society: Structuralist Essays* (Cambridge: Cambridge University Press, 1981), pp. 57-79.

7. See West's commentary on these lines.

8. For an analysis of the terms and ideas associated with them, see J. M. Bremmer, *Hamartia: Tragic Error in the "Poetics" of Aristotle and in Greek Tragedy* (Amsterdam: Adolf M. Hakkert, 1969) and T. C. W. Stinton, *"Hamartia* in Aristotle and Greek Tragedy," *Classical Quarterly* n s. 25 (1975): 221-54.

9. All translations of Greek tragedies are quoted from *The Complete Greek Tragedies*, David Grene and Richmond Lattimore, eds. Vols. 1-4 (Chicago: University of Chicago Press, 1959-60) unless otherwise noted. They will be cited by tragedian, play, lines, and translator in the text rather than by volume and page in the notes.

10. Bruno Snell, *Discovery of the Mind: The Origins of European Thought*, trans. T. G. Rosenmeyer (New York: Harper Brothers, 1960), pp. 99-112. Snell attributes the development of tragedy to the growing consciousness that men are able to make decisions by themselves. See also Richmond Lattimore, *Story Patterns in Greek Tragedy* (Ann Arbor: University of Michigan Press, 1965) for an analysis of plays with focus on choice.

11. Gregory Nagy, *The Best of the Achaeans: Concepts of the Hero in Archaic Greek Poetry* (Baltimore: The Johns Hopkins University Press, 1979), pp. 214-221;309 -323, discusses the ambivalent role of Strife (*eris*) and its counterpart Might (*bie*).

Olympus II: Evil Demythologized

The mythmakers inculcated moral values and self control by dramatizing the divine punishment for violent or arrogant acts committed out of ignorance, hubris, or excess emotion. Yet the divinities themselves were either personifications of specific evils or anthropomorphic paradigms for the foolishness and overweening passions of mortals. Therefore, many of the early thinkers rejected these tales as outright lies. Socrates, in Plato's *Republic* 2.378, insisted that poets must "represent the divine nature as it really is and the truth is that nature is good . . . and cannot do harm . . . and so cannot be responsible for evil . . . . Whereas the good must be ascribed to heaven only, we must look elsewhere for the cause of evils."[1]

Most Greek proto-scientists located the cause in the disorder of physical nature instead, for the universe was good, or a *kosmos* , only so far as it was well-ordered, balanced, or harmonious.[2] The early thinkers (e.g., Anaximander, Heraclitus, Parmenides, Pythagoras, Empedocles, Anaxagoras) had defined the polarities they perceived in nature as a series of significant opposites. The Pythagoreans, for example, constructed a table of elemental polarities, arranged in pairs, out of which they conjectured the universe was generated: limited and unlimited, odd and even, unity and plurality, right and left, male and female, resting and moving, straight and curved, light and darkness, good and bad, square and oblong, considering that there was a good and a corresponding evil in each pair.[3] To them Aristotle attributed the idea that "Evil belongs to the unlimited and good is the limited (*Eth. Nic.* 1106b29).[4] Impressed by the way in which number organizes or orders things and particularly by the numerical ratios behind the musical scale, the Pythagoreans supposed the elements of numbers to be the elements of all things and the whole heaven to be an attunement (*harmonian*) and a number (Aristotle *Metaphysics* 985b23).[5] It was this harmony which locked together the limiters and the unlimited, essentially unlike and unequal, into an ordered universe.[6]

Other philosophers, too, connected the harmony of opposites with the good and sought to explain how this good was achieved. Anaximander, the first to posit the interplay of polarities like hot and cold and moist and dry, used an analogy from justice to demonstrate the constant interchange between opposed substances and qualities: "they pay penalty and retribution to each other according to the assessment of time."[7] His statement implies that the prevalence of one of a pair, like heat in summer, must be compensated by a defect at another time, as in winter, in order for an underlying balance or justice to be maintained.[8]   Heraclitus emphasized the principle of measure:

> The ordering (*kosmos*) is the same for all, no god nor man has made, but it ever was and is and will be fire everliving, kindled in measures and in measures going out. Sea pours out (from earth) and it measures up to the same amount (*logos*) before coming earth.[9]

As Kahn interprets, "the measures of equality are thus vigorously respected over the long run, no matter how dramatic the reversals may be at any given moment". The balance of the exchanges preserved over a sequence of transformations is connected to the concepts of both *kosmos* and *logos*, e.g., rationality which characterizes all things.[10]

The underlying harmony could explain away certain things usually judged as evils. According to Heraclitus, each pair of opposites was necessary and together formed a hidden divine unity.

> Disease makes health pleasant, evil makes good pleasant, want makes satiety pleasant.

> Things taken together are whole and not whole, something which is being brought together and brought apart, which is in tune and out of tune; out of all things there comes a unity, and out of a unity all things.[11]

By this explanation, evil is the necessary opposite of good; there can be no good unless there is also a corresponding evil. Socrates implied something similar in *Phaedo* 60 b-c when he discussed the relation between pleasure and pain as he removed his shackles. In this context, death (if not caused by disease or violence) is a part of the process of exchange and is not an evil: "The same . . . living and dead, and the waking and the sleeping, and the young and old. For these transposed are those and those transposed are these."[12] Socrates on his deathbed used the argument that "the living are generated from the dead no less than the dead from the living" to prove that the soul must have had a prior existence (*Phaedo* 72a). The Epicureans strongly disagreed about the immortality of the soul, but defined death as a dispersal of the indestructible atoms that assembled to compose the mind and body. "From this it follows that death is nothing and no concern of ours," for "when we shall be no more," "nothing will have the power to stir our senses," (*De Rerum Natura* 3.830-41). Nor was death an evil for the Stoics who also believed that it was but a dissolution of the elements which make up every life, although the elements of the immortal soul return to the divine fire from which it came. In fact, because the Stoics conceived of Nature as divine, rational, predetermined, and provident (called Zeus, or Fate, or Logos), they thought whatever humans perceived of as evil was a necessary part of the whole and thus a good misunderstood.[13]

If harmony is the good, excess and defect which disturb the harmony are the source of true evil. In nature as a whole, the balance of opposites is maintained over time, but in the individual body, any imbalance produces disease. According to early Greek physicians such as Alcmaeon of Croton

> [he] maintains that the bond of health is the 'equal rights' of the powers, moist and dry, cold and hot, bitter and sweet, and the rest, while the 'monarchy' of one of them is the cause of disease . . . . Illness comes about directly through the excess of heat or cold, indirectly through surfeit or deficiency of nourishment . . . Health on the other hand is the proportionate admixture of the qualities.[14]

Plato only changed the theory slightly when he attributed disease to the excess or defect of one of the elements (earth, air, fire, and water) or to the movement of one from its own place to a position contrary to nature (*Timaeus* 82a-b). Aristotle applied the same principle of measurement to moral virtue when he defined it as the individual's disposition to choose the mean (relative to the situation) between excess and defect which are both vices: e.g., courage is the midpoint between the vices rashness and cowardice; temperance between self-indulgence and insensibility; liberality between meanness and prodigality, etc. (*Eth. Nic* 1107-1109a).

But Empedocles and Plato took the concepts of order and measure one step further back from the balance between perceived opposites. For the former, the first stage in cosmic evolution was the best because it was a perfect sphere made up of a uniform mixture of the four elements, a perfect harmony ruled by Love, which is the source of all good things.[15] But when Strife entered, the elements began to be separated out and come together again into compounds. Empedocles envisioned a never-ending cosmic cycle which consisted of four stages, the first ruled by Love, a second transitional stage, a third of total chaos ruled by Strife, and a fourth transitional stage when Love returned and caused things to cohere again.

For Plato, however, the phenomenal world, because it is subject to transition, is deficient in the good by definition. Plato's demiurge, the divine creator in *Timaeus*, stands outside of matter, using intelligence and purpose to impose order and limit on an indistinct matrix which has no form or quality and is in disorderly motion. The order he imposes is good in so far as it resembles his perfect unchanging model, the World of Forms, but the creation itself cannot be entirely good, since the material out of which it is made has its own "necessity," its inherent powers of moving and being moved "without reason or measure." *(Timaeus* 47e-53c). Timaeus, the narrator, constantly uses qualifying adverbs like *hos*, meaning "as far as possible" to describe the necessary limitations to the demiurge's creation.

Thus a defect in the matter itself produces an inherent or unintentional evil.[16] Only the incorporeal World of Forms, with its unchanging perfect essences, could be entirely good. The matter out of which the created world was shaped is not fair and good in itself. According to a myth in Plato's *Statesman*, 269c-273e, when the rule of reason, imposed by the good, withdraws, the created world moves in a reverse direction and degenerates into its former chaotic condition.

> . . . and the reason for this was the material element in its composition *(somatoeides)*, because this element, which was inherent in the primeval nature, was infected with great disorder before the attainment of the existing orderly universe. For from its Composer, the universe has received only good things; but from its previous condition it retains in itself and creates in the animals all the elements of harshness and injustice which have their origin in the heavens.(273b, Fowler, trans.)[17]

The notion that the matter out of which the physical world is made is inherently inferior implies a cosmic dualism more profound than the principal polarities or the contrast between order and disorder.[18] It is connected to the age-old belief that the breath of life or soul *(psyche)* is made of the purest, dryest kind of invisible element, whether air or fire (usually called aether). The heavens, too, are composed of this purer matter and all living things contain a spark of it, by which they move and breathe. But the visible universe, the earth, seas, and animal bodies, are mainly composed of the coarser, heavier, moister matter which weighs the more divine part down. The popular belief is reflected in the epitaph of the Athenians who died at the Battle of Potidaea: "Aether received their souls; their bodies earth."[19] Philosophers from Heraclitus and Pythagoras through Empedocles, Plato, and the Stoics developed this dualism into the concept of the division between body and soul or matter and spirit, and related it to both natural and moral evil.

Plato is the most influential Greek spokesman for the dualism which accounts for moral or intentional evil. Humans, like the cosmos, have a dual nature. They are made out of physical matter, but they also have a kinship with the divine because they possess an immortal soul. Timaeus actually described them as having two kinds of souls which correspond to their two parts. The divine soul has to be separated from the body soul by the neck, however, because the mortal elements are

> . . . subject to terrible and irresistible affection-first of all, pleasure, the greatest incitement to evil; then, pain, which deters from good; also rashness and fear, two foolish counselors, anger hard to be appeased, and hope easily led astray-. . . mingled with irrational sense and with all-daring love and according to necessary laws, . . .
> (69c-d, Jowett, trans).[20]

After explaining humanity's nature, Timaeus could define good and evil in terms of immortal and mortal inclinations.

> And we should consider that God gave the sovereign part of the human soul to be the divinity of each one, being that part which, as we say, dwells at the top of the body, and inasmuch as we are plants not of an earthly but of a heavenly growth, raises us from earth to our kindred who are in heaven. And in this we say truly . . . . When a man is always occupied with the cravings of desire and ambition, and is eagerly striving to satisfy them, all his thoughts must be mortal, and, as far as it is possible altogether to become such, he must be mortal every whit because he has cherished the mortal part. But he who has been earnest in the love of knowledge and of true wisdom, and has exercised his intellect more than any part of him, must have thoughts immortal and divine, if he attain truth, and in so far as human nature is capable of sharing in immortality, he must altogether be immortal; and since he is ever cherishing the divine power and has divinity within him in perfect order, he will be perfectly happy. (90a-c, Jowett, trans.)

In this context, humans are capable of reason and choice and are thus held responsible for most of the evils in their lives, even though the world is only as good as it can possibly be. Empedocles, in his

Purifications, presented a mythic account of humanity's fall more similar to the events in the Garden of Eden or Genesis 6 than to the tales of Prometheus and Pandora.[21]   When Love was the sole ruler, humans lived a blessed and innocent life. Strife only entered because and after they committed the first acts of bloodshed. Empedocles postulated a cycle for the fallen soul which corresponded to his four cosmic cycles; from innocence the soul passed into the world and went through various incarnations and transformations before it could return to its blessed state. The Pythagoreans and Plato developed these theories of metempsychosis and connected them with good and evil and reward and punishment.[22]

The intellect and purpose which impose order on the matter in the phenomenal world have their parallel in the human realm. Humanity's divine element, the soul, modeled on and bestowed by the divine creator, has the capacity to reason and to impose order on its inferior mortal and disorderly parts, its passions, impulses and instincts. If a human being neglects his soul and allows his lesser drives to rule him, he will bring disorder and therefore misery to himself and his society. Plato's myth of the charioteer in the *Phaedrus* (253e-254e) conveys the struggle of the divided soul to make the right choices among good and bad impulses. Before birth the immortal soul possesses knowledge of the divine, but mortal existence necessitates forgetfulness. The natural world, however, is a visible model of the eternal; its beauty stimulates the soul and leads it to recollect its former knowledge. Senses and passions, when guided toward the proper goal, can aid in this endeavor. But the soul is like a charioteer (reason) trying to control two horses (spirit and appetite). One is fair and good and a lover of honor only when that may be joined with temperance and decency (spirit). The other is ugly and bad (appetite) and at the sight of a beautiful object which stimulates desire, forges ahead toward a "dreadful lawless thing" pulling the whole chariot with him. A closer look at the beloved, however, awakens in the charioteer the memory of True Beauty . . . seated beside Temperance (*sophrosynes*) on a holy throne." He regains control just in time and continues to battle until the bad horse is finally tamed and the soul can approach the beautiful with reverence and awe. Both the Stoics, who connected reason with the immortal soul, and the Epicureans, who rejected the immortality of the soul and absolute standards of morality, also attributed the greatest evils in human life to chaotic passion unrestrained by intellect.

To avoid evil, then, humans must know what their true goods are. Therefore, as in myth, so in philosophy, the bad person is also the ignorant person. Empedocles referred to bloodshed as "heedlessness of mind" and to the father who sacrifices his son as a "witless fool,"[23] Democritus, too, blamed evil on man's blind and ignorant mind."[24] Socrates' insistence that ignorance was the cause of evil led him to devote himself to pointing out that "the unexamined life is not worth living." (*Apology* 38a); for if one assumed he had knowledge he did not really possess, his ignorance could lead him to disaster. The Epicureans believed that those who did not know the universe was composed of atoms moving in a void were bound to suffer the greatest evils—mental anguish caused by pursuing meaningless goals, and fear of the gods, death, and the afterlife. Knowledge of the true nature of things would free humans from such pain and permit them to enjoy the highest good, pleasure, defined as mental tranquillity.

But Socrates emphasized a new dimension—that evil was involuntary because no one would knowingly choose to do wrong and thus harm not only others but also himself. Plato argued his case most effectively in *Protagoras* using the familiar concepts of measurement and defect.

> for you also admitted that men err in their choice of pleasures and pains; that is, in their choice of good and evil, from defect of knowledge; and you admitted further, that they err, not only from defect of knowledge in general, but of that particular knowledge which is called measuring. And you are also aware that the erring act which is done without knowledge is done in ignorance. This, therefore, is the meaning of being overcome by pleasure;—ignorance and that the greatest (357d-e, Lamb, trans).[25]

Having led them to agree that ignorance is "having a false opinion and being deceived about important matters," he makes the Sophists assent to his conclusion that

> No man voluntarily pursues evil, or that which he thinks to be evil. To prefer evil to good is not in human nature; and when a man is compelled to choose one of two evils, no one will choose the greater when he may have the less (358d, Lamb, trans).

Euripides disagreed with Socrates' conclusion that "virtue is knowledge," that if people know what is good for them, they will necessarily choose it. His great tragic heroines Phaedra and Medea lament that they understand full well the evil they are about to commit, but that their feelings are too strong to be restrained by their minds. They proclaim uncontrollable passion the source of the greatest human misery even as they lie and murder to satisfy their rage.[26]   But the dramatist's negative examples prove the philosopher's rules. Phaedra and Medea are souls out of harmony, so driven by excessive mortal passions that they cannot but act in ways that harm themselves and others. Despite Plato's desire to expel such poetry from his utopian polis, the powerful dramatization of the dangers of chaotic behavior could reinforce his own beliefs about the true good for man—prudent moderation or *sophrosyne*.

For the philosophers and poets agreed that humans should aim for balance and proportion in life, accepting limits and avoiding excess, in imitation of the cosmic harmony, whether it is maintained by rational natural laws or by Zeus' enlightened rule of a diverse pantheon. It is ignorance of this good which leads to evil. Therefore, both Apollo and the philosophers exhorted humans to seek knowledge. Delphi urged one to "know himself" in relation to the supernatural macrocosm which was only partially knowable. The philosophers had more confidence in human reason. They attempted to learn and describe all aspects of nature, its order and its laws, so that they could dispel ignorance. And they hoped that, by patterning themselves and society according to the eternal principles they discovered, they could mitigate the misery that human ignorance caused.

Notes

1. Translations of the *Republic* come from Francis MacDonald Cornford, *"The Republic" of Plato* (New York and London: Oxford University Press, 1945). This passage appears on p. 71.

2. See Charles H. Kahn, *Anaximander and the Origins of Greek Cosmology* (Philadelphia: Centrum, 1985), pp. 222-3 for the implications of goodness in the term *Kosmos*.

3. F. M. Cornford, *Plato and Parmenides: Parmenides' "Way of Truth" and Plato's "Parmenides*," *translated with an Introduction and Running Commentary*, (New York: Liberal Arts Press, 1957), pp. 6-7, G. S. Kirk, J. E. Raven, and M. Schofield, *The Presocratic Philosophers: A Critical History with a Selection of Texts* (Cambridge: Cambridge University Press, 1983), pp. 337-9. This text will be referred to in subsequent notes as KRS. Translations and fragment numbers for the Presocratics are quoted from KRS unless otherwise noted. See also Walter Burkert, *Lore and Science in Ancient Pythagoreanism*, trans. .Edwin L. Minar, Jr. (Cambridge: Harvard University Press, 1972), pp. 51-2.

4. KRS, p. 339, quoted as fragment 440.

5. KRS, p. 329, quoted as fragment 430.

6. KRS, pp. 327-8, fragment 429.

7. KRS, pp. 117-18, quoted as fragment 110.

8. KRS interprets the fragments, pp. 119-20. See also Kahn, *Anaximander*, pp. 166-96.

9. Charles Kahn, *The Art and Thought of Heraclitus: An Edition of the Fragments with Translation and Commentary* (Cambridge: Cambridge University Press, 1979), p. 139.

10. The quote is from Kahn, *Heraclitus*, p. 144. See also KRS, pp. 197-200.

11. KRS, p. 188 quoted as fragment 201 and p. 190, quoted as fragment 203 respectively.

12. Kahn, *Heraclitus*, quoted on p. 71 as fragment XC111. See also pp. 210-28 for a discussion of related fragments on death.

13. For a general work on the Stoics, see John Rist, *Stoic Philosophy* (Cambridge: Cambridge University Press, 1969).

14. KRS, p. 260, quoted as 310 in the chapter on Parmenides.

15. KRS, pp. 294-6 and 314-21.

16. See F. M. Cornford, *Plato's Cosmology: "The Timaeus" of Plato translated with a Running Commentary* (London: Routledge and Kegan Paul, 1957), pp. 160-210 as well as the articles by G. Vlastos, "The Disorderly Motion in the *Timaeus*," pp. 379-399, and Glen R. Morrow, "Necessity and Persuasion in the *Timaeus*," pp. 421-431 in R. E. Allen, ed., *Studies in Plato's Metaphysics* (Routledge & Kegan Paul in London and Humanities Press: New York, 1965). See also Harold Cherniss, "The Sources of Evil according to Plato," *Proceedings of the American Philosophical Society* 98 (1954): 23-29. Cherniss refers to the evil which is the obverse of the

goodness of the world of forms as negative evil in contrast to the intentional evil which he calls positive evil.

17. See the myth in *Statesman*, and especially 273b, for this statement. The term *somatoeides* is Pythagorean as well as Platonic. The passage is quoted from H. N. Fowler, *Plato III*. The Loeb Classical Library (Cambridge: Harvard University Press, 1939).

18. See W. K. C. Guthrie, *In the Beginning: Some Greek Views of the Origins of Life and the Early State of Man* (Ithaca, N.Y.: Cornell University Press, 1957). See especially "Body and Soul: The Kinship of Nature," pp. 46-62.

19. Guthrie, p. 53, with source in note 10, pp. 128-29, as well as On Soul.

20. The translations of *Timaeus* are quoted from the edition by Liberal Arts Press: New York, 1949.

21. KRS, pp. 314-21.

22. See the Myth of Er at the end of *The Republic*; KRS, pp. 346-8 and Burkert, *Lore*, pp. 120-66.

23. KRS, p. 319, quoted as fragments 414-415.

24. Fragment 175 in Hermann Diels, *Die Fragmente der Vorsokratiker* Vol. 2 (Berlin: Weidman, 1912), p. 96. The entire fragment actually says: "The gods have given all good things to men both long ago and now, except those things that are evil and harmful and profitless. These things, neither long ago nor now do the gods give men, but men themselves came near to them because of their own blindness and folly."

25. *Protagoras* quotes come from *Plato IV*. Loeb Classical Library (Cambridge: Harvard University Press, 1927).

26. See *Medea*, 1078-80, "I know what sort of evil I intend to do, but stronger than all my deliberations is my anger which is the greatest source of evil for mortals.", and *Hippolytus*, 377-381, "People seem to me not to do evil on account of the nature of their mind, for many know how to think correctly. We know the good and clearly recognize it, yet we do not achieve it, some on account of laziness, others because they prefer some other pleasure above virtue."

Conclusions and Comparisons

When the biblical narrative of the Garden of Eden and Hesiod's story of Pandora are examined in the context of similar accounts found in different cultures all over the world, certain common characteristics stand out. All these tales relate that humans once enjoyed a blissful existence with a deity or deities, free from toil and the anxieties that now trouble human life. As a group or individually, deliberately or unwittingly, humanity disobeyed some divine prohibition or warning. The result was that humankind was then cast into the state of conflict, illness, and death in which it now lives. The catalyzing agent for this misfortune was woman.[1] Since the societies in which the various versions of this common story emerged were all patriarchal, it is not surprising that woman became the culprit responsible for the evil afflicting the human race.

The cultural triumph of the patriarchal hero myths over the older mythologies of the goddess mother Earth corresponded to the historical triumph of nomadic warrior tribesmen who overran the area, whose traditions are preserved in the Hebrew Bible and in the myths of Greece. The patriarchal perspective is characterized by a tendency to see dualities, male and female, life and death, true and false, good and evil, as absolutes in themselves rather than as merely aspects of the larger unity of life. This absolutism of duality, which was a clear advance over the undifferentiated view of humanity and the universe characteristic of the goddess mother Earth myths, went hand in hand with a suppression (rather than a transcendence) of the older, and admittedly more primitive, less rational outlook.[2] But the reasons for blaming women had a more personal dimension. Women are the vehicle for burdening men with responsibilities, with dependents and with heirs whose survival must be insured by man's constant labor and vigilance. In addition, the biological structure of women, in which the menstrual cycle produces an outflow of blood symbolic of illness and death, and the psychological identification of the womb with the tomb are all part of the complex associations which connect women with the misfortunes of life.[3] Hesiod's misogynous description of Pandora, the "beautiful evil," suggests the paradox of the sex drive which engenders so many of the agonies of existence. A similar set of dynamics is present in the temptation of Eve by Satan, who, according to Hebrew folklore, desires to copulate with her.

Though Eve and Pandora are part of a universal archetype, the specific treatment they receive underscores the differences in the two perspectives. Eve is part of a good creation where the polarities are integrated. She, like Adam, is the crown of creation, made "in the image of God" and "very good". She is made as a blessing, in Genesis 2, as a helpmate for Adam, and their sex is also blessed, unblemished by the consciousness of separation or sin. Shame, clothes, separation, and the pain arising from the consequences of sex (e.g., childbirth, families to feed, children to raise) occur only after the couple has tasted the forbidden fruit and become involved in experiential knowledge. As in Genesis, so in the Prometheus tale, food is the medium which precipitates the separation of humans and gods, and the complications connected with sex symbolize the loss of that earlier harmony. Pandora, however, is introduced into an already polarized world where good and evil are held in equilibrium. She is a curse, an evil in herself, sent to men as a punishment which balances a good, the fire stolen from the gods. Described as a "beautiful evil", Pandora is symbolic of the paradoxes of human existence. As in Genesis, this paradox is dramatized through the experience of sexuality, but Pandora, unlike Eve, is created as a sex object, separate from man from the beginning, her feminine beauty and grace so heightened by alluring garments that gods and men are left "defenseless" at the sight of her (*Theogony* 589). According to Hesiod, human beings must marry to survive, but they will never again have peace.

In both narratives, rebellion against the divine is motivated by the desire to become like the deity. In the Sinai tradition, this is the equivalent of idolatry which seeks to destroy the uniqueness and oneness of God and make the human being like God. The significance of the prohibition against idolatry is clear from its position as the first of the Ten Commandments. For the Greeks, who worshipped anthropomorphic deities, the directive to "Know Thyself," inscribed on Apollo's temple and quoted by poets and philosophers, warned that there is a natural boundary between mortals and the gods which humans transgress at their peril. The ambition to be like the gods leads humans to think arrogant thoughts and engage in violent actions associated with the word hubris. The Greeks, though idolatrous in Hebrew terms, saw a connection between hubris and the failure to revere and serve the gods. The tales of the heroes and giants who attack Olympus in order to ascend to heaven and become like gods have their parallel in the biblical story of the tower builders of Babel.

In both traditions, folly and the misuse of free will are as important as rebellion. Humans, in their ignorance, misuse their freedom and learn from bitter experience the harsh contrast with their former state. Both Greeks and Hebrews use similar terms for sin which is error, connecting it with missing the mark or deviation from a straight path.[4] The knowledge gained as the result of the foolish choice and the divine response is different in the two traditions. For the Hebrews, the higher, non-dualistic, intuitive knowledge of good and evil which brought the first humans closer to God is exchanged for an immediate, intensified, dualistic, experiential understanding which ensnares humanity in endless conflicts which they can surmount only with great difficulty. The Greeks who follow Pandora or the golden race are also ensnared in endless conflict, but the knowledge they gain is a profounder understanding of human limitation.

In the Greek traditions that conceive of the human soul as originating in a higher realm, this soul already possesses before birth that intuitive knowledge of the good that, according to the Bible, Adam and Eve possessed between their creation and their fall.[5] In the Greek perspective, because the material elements imprison the soul and cause forgetfulness of the immortal realm, scientific and moral knowledge must be pursued in order to reawaken the memory of the higher reality and its truths. Only then would humans be able to avoid the snares of the lesser realm. This lesser realm is not a source of positive evil in itself. As a copy of the World of Being derived from the Good or fashioned by the demiurge, it imitates and reveals perfection while falling short of it. Positive evil results when man succumbs to the snares of the lesser realm.

For the Hebrews, the created world is not inferior to any immortal realm and there is no corresponding division between the human body and the human soul. But now after the fall, humans must use their dualistic knowledge and self control to tame the drives and impulses that have become more subject to temptation as a result of immersion in the experiential world. The rabbinic concept of the good and evil impulse is similar to Hesiod's two kinds of strife. It is also analogous to the Greek philosopher's idea of man's dual nature or tripartite soul. The equation of the good impulse with the Torah suggests the Platonic Doctrine of Recollection in which knowledge is the instrument leading man to recall his highest good.[6]

For both the Greeks and the Hebrews, the signs of sinfulness are the breaking of the harmony between God (gods), humans, and the natural world. Once Adam and Eve eat the forbidden fruit, they look at each other with shame and hide from God. When confronted by the deity, they blame each other and the serpent. The divine response is measure for measure; the blame which is passed by the three culprits from one to another is requited by conflict between man and wife, between humans and the serpent, and between humanity and the earth itself. Hesiod's silver race manifests its folly by neglecting to serve the gods and by killing one another. Again the gods respond in kind; an angry Zeus hides them away or kills them. Death, which is, in one sense, part of the natural process for both Sinai and Olympus, is also a divine punishment for a sinful humanity. (For the Greeks, who valued glory as a means to immortality, obscurity after death is a further punishment; the silver age was hidden away, while the more violent bronze race passed into icy Hades, leaving no name behind.) In both traditions, human corruption increases with the increasing complexity of society, since human desires and temptations are now exposed to an entire spectrum of possible fulfillments. Thus, the many variations of greed, lust, ambition, anger, and, for the Hebrews, religious conflict, threaten to overwhelm human spirituality, unless human passions are mastered.

Therefore, despite the Greek philosophers' emphasis on the elemental disorder or defect in the matter of uncreated nature and the biblical rabbinic-depiction of chaos that remains a threat to humanity and the cosmos, both traditions place the responsibility for most of the evil in human life on humans themselves. They have the freedom of choice between alternatives and must exercise it. And there are positive guidelines to chart their way. For the Hebrews, it is the obedience to God and his revealed teaching, as dramatized in the divine commandment not to eat the forbidden fruit. For the Greeks, it is the path of moderation, the principle of limit and proportion in human life which reflects the eternal order of the universe.

Notes

1.   See the treatment of this idea in John A. Phillips, *Eve: The History of An Idea* (New York and San Francisco: Harper & Row, 1984), pp. 70-87. Phyllis Trible, *God and the Rhetoric of Sexuality* 4th ed. Overture to Biblical Theology Series ed. Walter Brueggeman and John Donahue S.J. (Philadelphia: Fortress Press, 1985), pp. 72-144 interprets Genesis 2-3 as indicating the mutuality and equality of Adam and Eve before the Fall.

2.   Joseph Campbell, *The Masks of God: Occidental Mythology* (New York: The Viking Press, 1972), pp. 7-31; Eric Neumann, *The Origins and History of Consciousness* (Princeton, NJ: Princeton University Press, 1973), *passim.*

3.   H. R. Hays, *The Dangerous Sex: The Myth of Feminine Evil* (New York: Putnam, 1964), *passim*.

4.   See the discussion in *Theological Dictionary of the New Testament*, ed. G. Kittel (Grand Rapids, MI: Wm. B. Eerdmans Publishing Co., 1964), 1:267-289; 296-302.

5.   The idea that there is an aspect of divinity in man (a divine spark in the human soul) is to be found in Jewish thought beginning with Philo, continuing in the writings of the medieval Jewish poet-philosopher Solomon Ibn Gabirol and finally emerging in kabbalistic doctrine.   See Louis Jacobs, "The Doctrine of the 'Divine Spark in Man' in Jewish Sources," in *Studies in Rationalism, Judaism and Universalism* ed. Raphael Loewe (London: Routledge and Kegan Paul, 1966), pp. 87-103.

6.   Philo identifies Plato's concept of recollection with Hebrew prophecy, Harry A. Wolfson, *Philo* 2:10-11.

Chapter 4

Is There a Moral Order in the Universe?

Introduction

The universe as viewed from the heights of Sinai and Olympus is both coherent and orderly. All its parts are interconnected and function as an organic whole. Both physical nature and the moral realm are held in equilibrium under the system. In the Bible the various aspects of the universe are not only held in balance by God but have no independence except through His will. The Greek universe, in contrast, is composed of many diverse parts, natural, human and divine which operate together to maintain the balance. In myth, divinities have their own histories and portions of privileges and functions through which they participate in running the universe. Sometimes these complementary responsibilities come into conflict with one another, as when Apollo and the Furies fight over the punishment of Orestes. Zeus serves as arbitrator to preserve the harmony among these independent but less powerful entities. Greek philosophers too perceived the entire universe as interconnected, deriving from the same ultimate source and subject to the same processes, laws, and principles of order.

In both traditions moral and spiritual corruption of any degree disturbs this holistic balance. Because it breaks the harmony existing between God, humans, and nature, its effects are cosmic. To reestablish the balance, nature often acts as a cleansing agent, destroying the corruption and restoring the possibility of harmony.

The classical example in the Bible of the destructive reaction of nature to moral turpitude is the Flood story (Gen. 6:9; 9:28) which has its parallel in Hesiod and Ovid. According to the rabbis, the animals respected the image of God and feared the first human couple before the fall, but afterward the opposite was true.[1] On the other hand when there is an elevation in human morality and spirituality there is a corresponding elevation in the physical world. Isaiah's vision of nations beating their swords into ploughshares (Isa. 2:1-4) is extended to include the wolf dwelling with the lamb (Isa. 11:6-9). Isa. 65:17-25 shows the human and the non-human spiritual elevation within a single chapter. In *Eclogue* 4 Vergil uses the same vision of all nature at peace to describe his hopes for a moral rebirth of Rome under Augustus.

The principle involved in maintaining this moral and natural order is the doctrine of reciprocity. Though implicit in almost every biblical narrative and law code, the doctrine is formally expressed in the Talmud: "In the measure with which a man measures, is it meted out to him."[2] The 'measure for measure' principle is most clearly stated in the old Greek proverb cited in Seneca's *Apocolocynctosis* 14:

> What thou hast wrought thou shouldst suffer
> straight would justice be done.

Greek myth underscores this rule as operating in the lives of many of its heroes. According to the chorus in *Agamemnon*, "This law that the doer (i.e., the transgressor) must suffer remains in effect so long as Zeus in on his throne" (1563-64). In essence, it is the inevitably of punishment for sin and its obverse, the possibility of reward for merit, that preserves the balance. But this principle does not cover all possibilities. The suffering of the innocent as individuals or in groups exposes the inadequacies of the doctrine of reciprocity as the only explanation for human misery. Both civilizations struggled to account for these anomalies and still maintain their beliefs in a moral cosmic order.

Notes

1. Ginzberg, *Legends* 1:71, 79, 5:119-120, N. 113.

2   *M. Sotah* 3:7-9; *b. Sotah*, 8b; *b. Sanhedrin*, 90a; *b. Nedarim*, 32a; E. E. Urbach, *The Sages: Their Concepts and Beliefs* , trans. Israel Abrahams (Cambridge: Harvard University Press, 1987), pp. 371-73; 437-39, m. 68. The same idea is expressed in the New Testament in Matthew 7:2, "And the measure you give will be the measure you get."

Sinai: The Struggles of Theodicy

The interconnectedness of physical nature and the moral realm as conceived by the Hebraic mind has its roots in two facets of God's relationship to the cosmos: the Creator's ordering of nature and His supplying the needs of all created things as well as His scrutiny of the motives and the deeds of human beings. The ibn Tibbon family, who translated medieval Jewish philosophical works from Arabic to Hebrew, coined a term for this dual divine activity. They called it *hashgahah*, divine providence. The word is found with the same connotation, but in verbal form, in Ps. 33.

> The Lord looks down from heaven
> He views all the children of men;
> From His habitation He looks intently
> (*hishgiah*)
> Upon all the inhabitants of the earth.

The next two lines underscore the aspect of *hashgahah* (divine providence) concerned with the moral realm.

> He fashioned each man's nature
> He understands all their doings.
> (Ps. 33:13-15)

Ps. 139 expresses the moral dimension from the human perspective.

> O Lord You probe me; You discern thoughts
> Whether I sit or rise You know from afar
> You observe me walking or resting;
> You are aware of my every movement.
> (Ps. 139:1-2)

Ps. 104 glorifies God in His role of cosmic artisan and universe manager who provides for the needs of all living things, the aspect of divine providence related to the sphere of physical nature. Since the physical and moral orders are united in God they must be interrelated in the operation of the cosmos. As noted earlier, this operation, based on the doctrine of reciprocity, strives toward harmony and balance, and when thrown out of equilibrium by sin, seeks to neutralize the effects by restoring harmony throughout natural catastrophes—plague, famine, flood and earthquake and man-made upheavals—the devastations of war and captivity.[1] The sins demanding such redress are ethical transgressions between human beings and religious transgressions between humans and God.

The annihilation of Sodom and Gomorrah, through what biblical scholars now think was an earthquake and conflagration,[2] was caused by the inhabitants who grossly flouted God's universal laws of morality of which the forcing of sodomy on the strangers in their midst is cited as the most repulsive example (Gen. 19:1ff). After detailing the laws against incest and other sexual prohibitions the Book of Leviticus warns the Israelites: "Do not defile yourselves in any of those ways, for it is by such that the nations which I am casting out before you defiled themselves. Thus the land became defiled and I called it to account for its inequity, and the land spewed out its inhabitants" (Lev. 18:24-25). Very similar is the exhortation of the Book of Numbers: "You shall not pollute the land in which you live; for blood pollutes the land, and the land can have no expiation for blood that is shed on it, except by the blood of him who shed it" (Num. 25:33). The sin of idolatry also pollutes the holy land and Israel is warned that idol worship will bring about its destruction and exile as it brought the expulsion and extinction of the people who preceded the Hebrews. Measure for measure, the Book of Leviticus warns that if the Israelites will not observe the Sabbatical year (the seventh year) in which the land is to lie fallow they will be driven into exile and "then shall the land make up for its Sabbath years throughout the time that it is desolate and you are in the land of your enemies". . . (Lev. 26:34-35).[3]

There is, however, a crucial difference between humans and nature as agents of divine retribution in restoring the harmony of the cosmos. The human being, unlike nature, is prone to intent and thought that can be completely at odds with the thought and intent of God. As Isaiah pointed out, Assyria appears as the agent of God's retaliation against the nations that have violated His universal teachings. But Assyria, unmindful of its divine mission, regards only its own interests. It boasts of its conquests; its arrogant king, ignoring God, exalts himself (Isa. 10:5-15). King Sennacherib of Assyria went so far as to speak blasphemously against the Almighty (2 Kings 19:22ff.) Improper intent can also be expressed through unnecessary cruelty. Amos condemned the six Gentile nations for mass murder, ruthless exile and excessive brutality (Amos 1:3-2:1).

Whenever man serves as God's means of chastisement, there is always the danger that, without the proper intent and thought, he will seek to play God, the worst form of idolatry. The minute the intent is perverted, the stage is set for yet another round of killing and bloodshed as the agent of retribution now becomes its recipient.

In the present state of humanity the cycle of violence is bound to continue for the intent of the best people is ever subject to corruption. Only in the Messianic Era when the level of humanity will be raised so that "Nothing evil or vile shall be done; For the land shall be filled with devotion to the Lord, As water covers the sea" (Isa. 11:9) only then will universal peace reign on earth.[4]

The doctrine of reciprocity in its various permutations runs like a golden thread from Genesis to Chronicles. Adam and Eve ate the fruit of the forbidden tree and are driven from the Garden of Eden. Lot's scoffing sons-in-law, who did not believe the dire report of the angels who came to rescue Lot and his family, are destroyed with the evil cities of Sodom and Gomorrah. Jacob, who deceived his father and took his brother's blessing, is in turn deceived by Laban, who gives him in marriage to Leah instead of Rachel. Years later an aged Jacob is again deceived by his own sons who, after selling their brother into slavery, bring to their father Joseph's bloody garment and tell him that his favorite son has been killed by a wild beast. The Hebrew midwives, who saved the Hebrew male children, despite Pharaoh's order to kill them, are given families of their own. The generation of the wilderness, that refused to enter the Promised Land because of the distorted report of the spies sent by Moses, died in the wilderness. Caleb and Joshua, who alone among the spies exhorted the Israelites to enter the land and conquer it, are the only ones of that generation to survive to inherit the land. The biblical law of retaliation (*lex talionis* Exod. 21:23-25; Lev. 24:19-20; Deut. 19:21) is based on the measure for measure principle.[5]

In seeking to uphold the ideal of God's justice as expressed through the doctrine of reciprocity, the Bible links it to the concept of collective responsibility extending vertically down through the generations and horizontally across the corporate body of society. This collective responsibility is rooted in the Sinaitic Revelation and God's covenant with Israel. The community to which God reveals Himself becomes corporately responsible to uphold His covenant. The individual's responsibility derives from his membership in the Israelite community. The Mosaic Law addresses not the family, the tribe, the state, but the people of the covenant. The "you" form of address of the laws shifts imperceptibly from the individual to the people, and at times both are meant. The covenant is binding not only on the present generation but also on its descendants (Deut. 29:13-14). Thus there is vertical and horizontal accountability not only as applicable to the people of the covenant but as a universal law operative even among non-

Israelites. The guilt of the pagan king Abimelech, who almost committed adultery with Sarah because he thought she was Abraham's sister, would have enveloped his kingdom as well (Gen. 20:9). The non-Israelite sailors, on Jonah's request, cast him into the sea lest his guilt in fleeing from God overtake them, causing them to go down with him in the storm (Jon. 1:11-15).

The classical example of vertical retribution is the assertion of the Book of Exodus that God "visits the iniquity of fathers upon children and children's children upon the third and fourth generations (Exod. 34:7). Horizontal retribution is manifest in the total destruction that God intended to decree for the Israelites (Exod. 32:10) for worshipping the golden calf even though only three thousand people participated in the orgy (Exod. 32:28).

The positive corollary of collective retribution is collective merit that also extends vertically to posterity and horizontally to contemporaries. Abraham's blessing extends to his descendants (Gen. 13:16; 15:5; 17:6-8; 12:13; 26:3-5; 24; 28:13-14) as the reward of Caleb and Phinehas (Num. 14:24; 25:13) is transmitted to their posterity. Noah's family is saved from the flood because of his righteousness (Gen. 7:1) and Lot and his family are saved from the doomed cities of Sodom and Gomorrah because of Abraham's righteousness (Gen. 19:29). Similarly, Abraham's plea for the group of righteous people in Sodom and Gomorrah is a plea for horizontal merit.

On the other hand, the Deuteronomic law code legislates that "parents shall not be put to death for children, nor children be put to death for parents: a person shall be put to death for his own crime" (Deut. 24:16). This Deuteronomic judicial provision stands in sharp contrast to the non-Israelite legal systems of the Near East where the concept of collective responsibility was juridically implemented through vicarious punishment. The Bible indicates that individual and collective retribution were translated into actual practice (2 Kings 14:6; 2 Sam. 21:6ff.). However, the incidents of collective retribution were either irregular actions outside the domain of law (Judg. 18:25; 1 Sam. 22:18-19; 25:33; 2 Kings 9:26) or cases involving divine sanctions, not criminal law.[6] In Israel the dominant attitude was that collective retribution was the way of God's justice, not to be usurped by the limited flawed systems of human justice.

Though the Book of Deuteronomy emphasizes individual responsibility and punishment it also prescribes the rite that removes the stain of horizontal responsibility and retribution from the community. If a corpse is found near a town and the slayer is unknown, the elders of the town nearest the corpse shall go out into the field taking with them a young heifer that has never been worked. They shall break its neck and wash their hands over it intoning a declaration of absolution (Deut. 21:1-18).

But alongside the doctrine of reciprocity with its corollary of individual and collective retribution there emerged in the Bible another view which declared that human repentance can change the outcome of the doctrine of reciprocity. This is the main thrust of the Book of Jonah in which the prophet, believing in the strict doctrine of reciprocity, refused to bring the message of repentance to Nineveh. Forced by a series of catastrophes (including the famous sojourn in the belly of the great fish) to carry out his mission, Jonah was dismayed when the People of Nineveh did repent and God renounced punishment. This concept was embedded in the prophecies of Jeremiah and Ezekiel. Jeremiah quotes God as saying:

> If any time I declare concerning a nation or kingdom that I shall pluck up and break down and destroy it, and that nation . . . turns away from its evil, I shall renounce the evil I planned against it. And if at any time I declare concerning a nation that I shall build it and plant it, and it does evil in my sight, not listening to My voice, then I shall renounce the good which I planned for it. (Jer. 18:7-10).

With regard to the individual Ezekiel declared: "God wants not the death of the sinner, but that he turn away from evil and live" (Ezek. 18:23).[7]

Both Jeremiah and Ezekiel, unlike theologians, did not attempt to systematize the biblical teachings of individual and collective responsibility and retribution along with the doctrine of repentance but spoke to the needs of their generation. During the siege of Jerusalem and the destruction of the First Temple (586 B.C.E.) the concept of collective responsibility collided with the doctrine of personal responsibility and repentance. The generation of the destruction and the exile did not admit the justice of its fate. The Book of Lamentations records their complaint: "Our fathers sinned and are no more; And we must bear their guilt" (Lam. 5:7). This complaint gave rise to a popular parable of the time quoted by Jeremiah and Ezekiel: " . . . Parents have eaten sour grapes, and the children's teeth are blunted" (Jer. 31:29-30; Ezek. 18:2). In this way the survivors of the catastrophe shifted the blame for their present suffering to previous generations and sought to absolve themselves of responsibility for their fate. Jeremiah could not bring himself to reject the bitter complaint of his people that they suffered for the sins of their fathers. He could only promise that in the future there would be individual retribution. Not so the prophet Ezekiel. He sought to combat the popular parable and the state of mind that gave birth to it. He argued that children do not suffer for the sins of their fathers. The calamities of the age are thoroughly merited by the corruption of the present generation, which he describes in agonizing detail. Basing himself on Levitical tradition, that only if the children of wicked men sin do they bear both their own and their father's guilt (Lev. 26:39ff.), he argued that because the present generation did not purify themselves from sin, they harvested the punishment of previous generations as well. At the same time Ezekiel provided his audience with an opening for repentance. Though God had already decreed destruction, those who repent will be delivered from the judgment.[8]

Thus, Jeremiah and Ezekiel embraced the conflicting views without attempting to reconcile them or force upon them the strait-jacket of systematization. The religious outlook of the Bible unmediated by philosophical speculation or theological formulation looked upon divine providence as the ultimate source of human welfare and woe. It viewed the individual as part of the macrocosm, woven into the woof and web of society but also a microcosm, an individual who stands responsible before God. When the collective consciousness of the group was weak and the individual refused to participate in group activities for the good or protest group action for evil, Scripture stressed collective responsibility. But when the individual sought to avoid his duty by shifting responsibility to the group or to his ancestors the Bible stressed individual responsibility. For both the individual and the group repentance, according to the later teaching, was always operative. Thus from the organic perspective of the Bible the doctrines do not contradict but complement each other.[9]

The Book of Job represents the supreme challenge in the Bible to the doctrine of reciprocity because it explodes the connections between sin and suffering. The book is structured as a prose tale that frames a poetic dialogue and deals with the problem of the suffering of the righteous from a human-emotional point of view and a religious-philosophical perspective. It is Job's religious-philosophical problem that we address here leaving Job's human-emotional struggle for the next chapter.

The poetic dialogue that contains the intellectual dialectic typifies the wisdom strata of the Bible. Here Job is pictured as a wise man defending his righteousness by reasonable argument with his friends who seek to comfort him with traditional explanations that uphold the doctrine of reciprocity. The poetic dialogue poses

the question: Is there a moral order in the universe? For Job this is
not an abstract inquiry but a burning issue that cuts to the core of
his existence. He suffers doubly, agonizing over the miscarriage of
God's justice as well as bearing his own pain. Elihu, the third of
Job's friends, whose arguments the author presents just prior to the
God speeches thus indicating that they are second only to the divine
reply, seeks to refute Job's negation of the moral order in the
universe. Elihu focuses on the two facets of God's relationship to the
world (*Hashgahah*) that prove His abiding goodness and concern for
all creation: 1) He regulates the cosmos in an orderly fashion and
sustains all living things (Job 36: 26-33); 2) He has implanted moral
consciousness in human beings for their benefit since a human
being's good or evil neither profits God nor harms Him (Job 35:4-
11). The doctrine of reciprocity that does operate in the moral
realm (as in the realm of nature), if one only has eyes to see it,
argues Elihu, is the Almighty's gift to mortals (Job 34:24-37).[10]

The divine reply to Job's accusation of unfairness provides the
fullest answer that Job is capable of understanding.[11] Despite
appearances to the contrary, God (as Elihu claimed) cares enough
about humanity to reveal Himself to humans in order to give them
some intimation of the order and direction of His creation.[12]   The
imagery of life and light in the God speeches standing in contrast to
Job's images of death and darkness imply that Job has skewed the
relationship of the two. The delicate balance between light and
darkness is part of the infinite beauty of creation undetected by
finite creatures. This limitation pertains to the moral nature of man
as it does to the nature of the universe (Job 38:12-15). In another
image, echoing the Hebrew reworking of the Mesopotamian combat
myth, discussed earlier, God's creative power sets limits to the
primal sea so that the flood will not engulf the earth but the
pulsating surge of the waves transmits the energy of life (Job 38:8-
11).[13] In the description of the animal world, the God speeches
single out the most repulsive of creatures, the crocodile and the
hippopotamus, as evidence of the beauty of creation (Job 40:7-14).
Similarly, the Voice from the Whirlwind underscores the violence
and even the beauty of violence in the animal kingdom (Job 39:29-
30).[14]   Just as the esthetic imagination of the individual is
inadequate to comprehend the beauty with which God has endowed
crocodiles and hippopotamuses, so is human moral reasoning
deficient in understanding the paradox of how the tender care for
one's young may well mean their gulping the blood of freshly killed
creatures. Violence and nurture, destruction and creation are the
systole and diastole of the universe. This universe is not

anthropocentric. Chapters 38 and 39 of the Book of Job are parallels to the first chapter of Genesis but in Genesis man is the crown of creation, while in Job he is peripheral to the marvels of the cosmos that include the constant clash of warring forces.

The two aspects of God's relationship to the world implied by the term *hashgahah* (divine providence) were as axiomatic for the rabbis as for the biblical writers. In His capacity of universe Creator and director God feeds the whole world from the horned buffalo to the brood of vermin; everything has some purpose, even though this may not be apparent to humans. Even flies, fleas and mosquitoes are not superfluous.[15] As architect of the moral order the Almighty scrutinizes the deeds and the motives of the individual.[16] In the rabbinic lexicon of morality it is a cardinal sin to declare: "There is no judge and there is no justice,"[17] i.e., to deny a moral order in the universe. But they were not insensitive to Job's arguments and to the suffering that prompted his outbursts. There were many Jobs in their own generation. It was said of Elisha ben Avuyah, who became an apostate and was called *Aher*, a stranger, by the rabbis, that he lost his faith in God when he saw the tongue of a colleague, martyred during the Roman persecution under the emperor Hadrian, lying on a dung heap. Job's mental anguish would have been alleviated had he been able to believe in the afterlife (Job 14:7-14) and according to the rabbis the same belief would have enabled Elisha ben Avuyah to retain his faith.[18]

The belief in the afterlife, to be discussed in a later chapter, did not cancel out the older doctrines seeking to justify God's ways to humanity. As in the Bible, so in the Talmud nature and morality are seen as intertwined in the operation of the cosmos. Echoing the image in God's reply to Job where the divine power sets limits to the primal sea so that it will not inundate the earth (Job 38:8-11), Rabbi Simeon ben Lakish, as noted earlier, saw the Torah, the moral law, as holding back the powers of chaos from overrunning the world.[19]

As discussed in the introduction to this chapter the rabbis, like their biblical predecessors, understood the doctrine of reciprocity as fundamental to maintaining the equilibrium between nature and morality and they, too, connected this doctrine with collective retribution and merit extending horizontally to society and vertically to posterity. In a well known *Mishnah* we read: "Seven kinds of punishment come upon the world, to expiate for seven capital offenses . . . . Pestilence comes into the world to exact the death penalties mentioned in the Torah, the execution of which was not entrusted to the human tribunal, and for using the crops forbidden on the Sabbatical year. The sword descends upon the world because of a delay of justice or a perversion of justice, and because of the deliberate misinterpretation of the Torah. Wild beasts come ravaging the world because of false oaths, and because of a profanation of God's name. Exile comes upon the world because of idolatry, incest, bloodshed, and for denying rest to the soil on the Sabbatical year."[20] In this *Mishnah* ethical lapses (e.g., the perversion of justice) and ritual transgressions (e.g., using crops forbidden on the Sabbatical year) trigger the law of reciprocity so that nature responds in a negative fashion. But the converse is also true. The proper observance of the commandments causes nature to respond positively by adhering to its regular cycles thus maintaining the harmonious functioning of the cosmos. It has already been noted earlier that the normal functioning of the universe was, according to the rabbis, predicated on Israel's receiving the Torah (see above Ch. 2, Sinai II: Creation Interpreted, note 6). According to another source the sacrificial offerings of the Temple service gave the world a firm foundation and prevented it from tottering (possibly a reference to earthquakes).[21] A tradition preserved in the name of R. Jacob bar Aha held that "were it not for the Temple watches (*ma'amadot*, see Ch. 7 Sinai: Priestly Piety, notes 39-40) heaven and earth could not endure."[22] Both the positive and negative activities of humans that through the law of reciprocity interact with the cosmos are summed up in the rabbinic statement that the righteous maintain the world, while the wicked destroy it.[23]

These positive or negative actions have both a horizontal and a vertical effect. The biblical concept of horizontal merit is given talmudic expression by the rabbis through the belief that in every generation there are a fixed number of saintly people for whose sake the world is preserved.[24] Building on the biblical teaching of vertical responsibility, the rabbis claimed that vertical merit and demerit operate in reverse—not only do children die for the sins of their parents, but parents also die for the sins of their children.[25] For the rabbis, vertical merit meant primarily the merit of the patriarchs Abraham, Isaac and Jacob, whose faith and good deeds resulted in the splitting of the sea and the descent of the manna for their posterity, the generation of the Exodus.[26] The sounding of the shofar on Rosh Hashanah is intended to remind God of the virtue of Isaac who was ready to be sacrificed so that the Supreme Judge will render a favorable verdict for Isaac's descendants on the Day of Judgment. Not only the patriarchal fathers but even ordinary fathers can pass on to their children wisdom, beauty and wealth according to Rabbi Akiba.[27]

The conflict in the Bible between individual and collective responsibility and retribution was not lost on the talmudic sages. They sought to reconcile the two views in a variety of ways: 1) by invoking the doctrine of vertical retribution only when each succeeding generation follows in the evil footsteps of its fathers but not when there is an intermediate generation of righteous offspring or when the evil was committed by children, not responsible for their actions;[28] 2) by explaining that horizontal retribution encompasses those who have directly or indirectly aided the sinner, i.e., the family of the robber who cover up for him;[29] 3) by arguing that horizontal retribution is intended to serve as a deterrent to those who might be influenced by the example of the sinner or the criminal;[30] 4) by imaginatively depicting Moses as persuading God to rescind the declaration of vertical responsibility and punishment of Exod. 34:7 and replace it with the individual liability and punishment of Deut. 14:16;[31] 5) by simply stating that the prophet Ezekiel's emphasis on individual accountability canceled Moses' earlier declaration of vertical accountability in the Book of Exodus;[32] 6) by attributing collective and individual retribution to the ways of God (unknown to humans) which must be accepted on faith.[33]

Unlike the biblical writers the rabbis were more inclined to speculate on the relationship between the two aspects of divine providence (*hashgahah*) as they affected the course of human life. They sought to find the boundaries between God's direction of the universe through natural laws and His response to the moral choices of human beings. Their speculations can be framed by the following questions: To what extent do human choices determine human destiny? Are good and bad deeds as well as their reward and punishment merely part of the program (natural law constituting the other part) that is fed into the cosmic computer of universe operation? For Rabbi Akiba freedom of human choice and the concomitant responsibility for its effect was axiomatic.[34] But even he recognized that the human life span is predetermined by God and the individual's good deeds can only save him from unnatural kinds of death and allow him to live out his allotted years. Though bad deeds can shorten life, good deeds cannot extend it. The other sages, who differed with Rabbi Akiba, claimed that good deeds could extend one's life span.[35]

If religious and ethical conduct cannot extend one's life span, according to Rabbi Akiba, can they enhance the physical and material conditions of one's life? Are there rewards in this world for the good life as the Bible claims? Though the rabbis, including

Rabbi Akiba, upheld the promises of Scripture in teaching and preaching to the masses, to the more sophisticated they taught a higher truth which they rooted in Scripture—there is no connection between religious ethical behavior and physical-material attainments in the present life. Reward and punishment in the ultimate sense are on another level in the afterlife.[36] Rabbi Hanina summed up this view in the following epigram: "Everything is in the hands of Heaven but the fear of Heaven,"[37] i.e., only in the moral and religious realm is the human being a free agent; everything else is determined by God. But lest this outlook cause an individual to neglect the necessary caution in his daily actions, the rabbis also taught that God's will intersects with human choice and thus the individual bears the responsibility for his own welfare. Divine providence may determine our health, our wealth, our intelligence, our span of years, and even according to Rabbi Hanina, our natural inclination or lack of it toward piety and morality. But foolish would be the person who neglected his health, who squandered his wealth, who refused an education and turned a blind eye to religious-ethical requirements. Divine providence will not save him from the relentless action of the law of reciprocity in this world and in the next one.

The interlacing of the two strands of divine providence (*hashgahah*) in the functioning of nature and in the working of human conscience and the intersection of God's will and human choice is exemplified in this explanation by Rabbi Simeon bar Yohai. He taught that if on the New Year (*Rosh Ha-Shanah*) when God judges the entire world, Israel was found meritorious and much rain was decreed for them but subsequently they sinned, God cannot rescind the decree but He scatters the rain over the oceans and deserts and not on cultivable land. If the reverse is true, that on the New Year they were found lacking in merit and little rain was decreed for them but subsequently they repented, God does not rescind the decree but causes the rain to descend on cultivable land and increases its effect by means of dew and wind.[38] Rabbi Simeon's teaching also exemplifies how the rabbis, like the Bible, emphasized the power of repentance that can alter decrees based on the doctrine of reciprocity.[39]

Notes

1. Martin Buber, *Die Schrift und ihre Verdeutschung* (Berlin, 1936), p. 127 notes this holistic relationship between the moral and the physical realms in his explanation of vertical retribution in the second commandment of the Decalogue Exod. 20:5.

2. Nahum Sarna, *Understanding Genesis* (New York: The Jewish Theological Seminary of America and McGraw Hill, 1966), p.142.

3. Theodore H. Gaster, *Myth, Legend and Custom in the Old Testament*, (New York and Evanston: Harper and Row, 1969), pp. 71-72; M. Greenberg, "Bloodguilt" *Interpreter's Dictionary of the Bible* (New York and Nashville: Abingdon, 1962), 1:449-50. For the consequence of this conception in Mesopotamian religion *see* Henri Frankfort, *Kingship and the Gods* (Chicago: University of Chicago Press, 1948), pp. 278-79. On the principle of retribution in nature as viewed in archaic societies *see* Hans Kelsen, *Society and Nature: A Sociological Inquiry* in Perspectives in Social Inquiry Series (New York: Arno Press, 1974) reprint of 1943 edition. Cf. Raphael Patai, *Man and Temple: In Ancient Jewish Myth and Ritual* (New York: Ktav Publishing House, 1967), reprint of 1947 edition, Ch. 5-6.

4. Gerhard Von Rad, *The Message of the Prophets* (London: SCM Press, 1968), pp. 152-53. In the Second Temple period the Pharisaic author of the Psalms. of Solomon expresses similar ideas with regard to the Roman conquest of Jerusalem under Pompey. Psalms of Solomon 7:5-9; 2:32-41; 4:24. Cf. Adolf Buchler, *Types of Jewish Palestinian Piety: From 70 B.C.E. to 70 C.E. - The Ancient Pious Men* (New York: Ktav Publishing House, 1968; first published in 1922), pp. 146, 180-81.

5. The evolution of the *lex talionis* originates in the Code of Hammurabi in which the law of equivalence administered by the state and defining bodily injury as a crime replaced the older private law of monetary compensation defining bodily injury as a civil offense. The older, private law emerged in order to discourage the cycle of vengeance and counter-vengeance but it had in it an element of inequality. It is easier for the rich than for the poor to make pecuniary restitution. Hammurabi's *lex talionis* sought to introduce equity and exact justice, an emphasis on the seriousness of the offense (i.e., criminal not civil) and its removal from private negotiation to state control. Biblical law accepted the principle of monetary compensation. In the Book of Exodus the *lex talionis* is followed immediately by a law that orders the liberation of a slave in compensation for his loss of an eye or a tooth caused by his master (Exod. 21:26-27) and preceded by a law that orders only the payment of compensation and medical expenses for a wound inflicted in a fight (Exod. 21:18-19). But the Pentateuch retains the wording of the *lex talionis* to insure exact justice and equity in administering proportionate compensation and as the Book of Leviticus urges "not to render an unfair decision, not to favor the poor or show deference to the rich." (Lev. 19:15). Cf. A. S. Diamond, *Primitive Law* (London: Longmans, Green and Co., 1935), pp. 8-45; 102-26; W. G. Lambert, *Babylonian Wisdom Literature* (Oxford: Clarendon Press, 1960),

pp. 12-13; Nahum Sarna, *Exploring Exodus* (New York: Schocken Books, 1986), pp. 182-189 and my *Judaism and the Gentile Faiths* (Rutherford, Madison, Teaneck, NJ: Fairleigh Dickinson University Press, 1981), p. 52.

6.   Moshe Greenberg, "Some Postulates of Biblical Criminal Law" in *The Jewish Expression*, ed. Judah Golden (New York: Bantam Books, 1970), pp. 30-32 (reprinted from the *Yehezkel Kaufman Jubilee Volume* (Jerusalem 1960). In addition to the punishment of the sons of Saul just mentioned there was the punishment of the inhabitants of Yavesh Gilead (Judg. 21:10-11), and the children of Achan (Josh. 7:24-25).

7.   Elias J. Bickerman, *Four Strange Books of the Bible* (New York: Schocken, 1967), pp. 38, 43; Jacob Milgrom, "Vertical Retribution: Ruminations on *Parshat Shelah*" *Conservative Judaism* Vol. 34, No. 3 (Winter, 1981), p. 12 and more fully in *Interpreter's Dictionary of the Bible, Supplementary Volume*, ed. K. Crim et. al. (Nashville: Abingdon, 1976), pp. 736-38; Jeffrey H. Tigay, "The Book of Jonah and the Days of Awe," *Conservative Judaism* Vol. 38, No. 2 (Winter, 1985-86): 67-76.

8.   Yehezkel Kaufmann, *The Religion of Israel*, pp. 76, 282-85, 331. Ezekiel confines the range of individual responsibility to each and every action and abolishes the double standard, one for the human level and one for the divine level. In so doing he reinterprets the older doctrine. See the discussion in M. Fishbane, *Biblical Interpretation in Ancient Israel* (Oxford: Clarendon Press, 1989), pp. 337-341.

9.   Meir Weiss, *"Miba'ayot 'Torat ha-Gemul' ha-Mikrait,"* *Tarbiz* 31 (1961-62), 249-250; 256-259.

10.   Yehezkel Kaufmann, *Toledot ha-Emunah ha-Yisraelit*, 2nd ed. (Jerusalem-Tel Aviv; Mosad Bialik, 1953), Vol. 2, Book 2, pp. 605-612.

11.   Robert Gordis, *The Book of God and Man* (Chicago and London: University of Chicago Press, 1965), p. 132.

12.   Kaufmann, pp. 614-615.

13.   The biblical allusion to the Creator sheltering or shading His creatures from the divine power became an important theme in the interpretation of the Lurianic Kabbalah by the Habad movement in Hasidism, Cf. Louis Jacobs, *Seeker of Unity* (New York: Basic Books, 1966); p. 156, and my *Judaism and the Gentile Faiths , Comparative Studies in Religion* (Rutherford-Madison-Teaneck, NJ: Fairleigh Dickinson University Press, 1981), p. 94.

14.   Gordis, *The Book of God and Man*, p. 120; Robert Alter, *The Art of Biblical Poetry* (New York: Basic Books, 1985), p. 102. On the power and the mystery that transcend reason in God's reply to Job *see* Rudolf Otto, *The Idea of the Holy* (New York: Oxford University Press, 1958), pp. 77-80 and M. Tsevat, "The Meaning of the Book of Job," *Hebrew Union College Annual* 37 (1966), p. 99 ff.

15.   *b Avodah Zarah*, 3b, *Gen. R.*, 10:5 ed., Theodor-Albeck, p. 78.

16.   *M. Avot* 2:1.

17.   *Gen. R.* 26:6, ed. Theodor-Albeck, p. 252; *Lev. R.* 28:1; *Avot de Rabbi Natan*, Version A, Ch. 32, ed. S. Schechter, p. 47.

18.   *b. Hullin*, 142a.

19. See chapter 2

20. *M. Avot*, 5:45; *Avot de Rabbi Natan*, Version A, Ch. 38, ed. S. Schechter, p. 47. On the measure for measure principle in the human dimension alone, see *M. Sotah* 1:8-9.

21. *Pesikta De Rab Kahana* 19 trans. William G. Braude and Israel J. Kapstein (Philadelphia: The Jewish Publications Society of America, 1975), p. 329

22. *b. Ta'anit*, 27b; *b. Megillah*, 31b. Cf. Saul Lieberman, *Tosefta Ki-Feshuta* (New York: Jewish Theological Seminary of America, 1962), 5:1103.

23. *M. Avot*, 5:1. The Kabbalists greatly expanded this conception. Their outlook was succinctly expressed by R. Menahem Recanati: "It is incumbent upon man to contemplate the commandments of the Torah (to see) how many worlds he maintains by their performance and how many worlds he destroys by their neglect." *Commentary on Pentateuch*, fol. 51b; Moshe Idel, *Kabbalah: New Perspectives* (New Haven and London: Yale University Press, 1988), p. 172 and Idel's refutation of Scholem's contention that in Judaism the Law was dissociated from cosmic events, pp. 170-171.

24. *b. Hullin*, 92a; *b. Sukkah*, 45b; *b. Sanhedrin*, 97b. Urbach, *The Sages*, pp. 488-498. G. Scholem, *The Messianic Idea in Judaism* (New York: Schocken Books 1971), pp. 251-256.

25. A. Marmorstein, *The Doctrine of Merits in Old Rabbinical Literature* (New York: Ktav Publishing House, 1968), pp. 54, 185ff.

26. *Mekilta de Rabbi Ishmael*, Tractate *Vayehi Beshalah* 3, ed. Horowitz, p. 99; Tractate Vayasa 2, ed., Horowitz, p. 160.

27. *M. Eduyot* 2:9; *Yer. Berakot* 4:1; *b. Berakot*, 27b.

28. *Mekilta de Rabbi Ishmael*, Tractate *Bahodesh* 6, ed., Lauterbach, p. 246; b. *Berakot* 7a; *b. Sanhedrin*, 27b; *Midrash Tannaim*, Deut. 5:9, ed., Hoffman, p. 159.

29. *Sifra, Kedoshim*, 10 ed., Weiss, p. 91c; *b. Shevuot*, 39a; *Pirke de Rabbi Eliezer*, Ch. 38 on children of Achan.

30. *b. Sanhedrin* 44a, Rav Huna's reply to the Exilarch regarding the case of Achan in Josh. 7:24.

31. *Num. R.* 19:33.

32. *b. Makkot*, 24a. Isaac Heineman,, *Darke ha-Aggada* (Jerusalem: The Magnes Press, 1953), p. 89 claims that the sages could never conceive of canceling the divine words of the Torah but limited their meaning in keeping with the ideal of individual accountability. But J. M. Gutman, *Behinat Kiyum ha-Mizvot* (Breslau, 1931), p. 45, is of the opinion that the intention was indeed to cancel the concept of collective responsibility in keeping with the rabbinic views on the nature of the commandments.

33. *b. Yoma*, 22b; *Yer, Kiddushin* 4:1; *Yer, Sanhedrin* 6:10; Urbach, *The Sages*, pp. 516-17. There are times of plague and natural catastrophe in which the excessive imperfections of the world must be righted so that the cosmos may be brought back into equilibrium. The rabbis referred to such periods as *idan ritha*, times of divine anger though they understood these intervals as a recurrent phenomenon whose regularity may be likened to the

operation of natural laws. In such times of communal danger even the righteous must take extraordinary precautions since their merit, whether personal or ancestral, will be unavailing and even these extraordinary precautions may not save them. Under such conditions only in very rare instances will divine guidance serve to protect those in danger. See Yaakov Elman, "When Permission is Given: Aspects of Divine Providence," *Tradition* 24, no. 4 (Summer, 1989): 24-45.

34. *M. Avot* 3:15-16 and Urbach's interpretation in *The Sages*, 256-58.

35. *b. Yevamot*, 50a; *Eccles. R.* 3: 4: Cf. Urbach, *The Sages*, p. 265 n. 36.

36. *b. Menahot*, 29 b; *Tosefta Yoma* 2; 7; Urbach, *The Sages* p. 270, n. 47.

37. *b. Berakot* 33 b. Cf. *Maharsha* (R. Samuel Edels, d. 1631) *Hiddushe Halakot Va Aggadot* to *b. Berakot*, 33b. and Rashi to *b. Megillah* 25a. See Urbach's discussion in *The Sages*, pp. 280-81, n. 81.

38. *Yer. Rosh Ha-Shanah*, 1:3, *b. Rosh Ha-Shanah*, 17b.

39. The literature on the rabbinic concept of repentance is vast. The best summaries of the classical sources are to be found in Solomon Schechter, *Some Aspects of Rabbinic Theology* (New York: Macmillan, 1923): 313-343; George Foot Moore, *Judaism* (Cambridge, Ma.: Harvard University Press, 1950), 1:520-534; Urbach, *The Sages*, pp. 462-471. For more modern treatments see *Abraham Isaac Kook* trans. and intro. Ben Zion Bokser (New York, Ramsey, Toronto: Paulist Press, 1978): 39-128 and Pinchas H. Peli, *Soloveitchik On Repentance* (New York and Ramsey: Paulist Press, 1984).

Olympus: Cosmic Order as Moral Order

Because the Greeks have so many gods and the myths about those gods express the full range of human foibles, it may be difficult to recognize that those same divinities define and uphold a moral order comparable to that described in the Bible. Greek standards of morality and justice are all the harder to appreciate because the multiplicity of stories arose in different times and places to satisfy different needs. The corpus was never organized into a single, continuous, and fixed narrative illustrating a single belief like monotheism or the working out of one god's plan in the developing history of one nation. Although the individual city-states worshipped the same major deities, each had its own divine patrons and local sagas which illustrated the effect of the will of the gods on the life of its people. To complicate matters, by the early sixth century B.C.E., some thinkers had begun to demythologize traditional beliefs and to look to physical nature as a means of understanding the world and as a model for human behavior. Yet, when viewed together, the individual myths and theories emerge as particular illustrations of a consistent set of general beliefs which have affinities with the Hebrew conceptions of morality and justice. And the doctrine of reciprocity is spelled out as the mainstay of the system.

Most Greeks, like the Hebrews, conceived of the natural order and the moral order as an organic whole in perfect equilibrium, an idea which probably derives from the belief that the non-human world is basically the same as the human in substance and attitude.[1] According to the mythmakers, gods, nature and humans were made of the same stuff. Earth, one of the first divinities from Chaos, gives birth to Sky, Mountains, and Sea, out of which come a multitude of immortals who are also parts of nature; from them or by them mortals are eventually created. The world that Zeus rules as sky god is organized according to the principles of distribution. Each individual element, whether human, natural, or divine, has its own proper role in the harmonious functioning of the whole, its own *moira* or portion, with specific rights, honors, responsibilities, and limitations which necessarily accompany it.[2] When Hesiod narrates the birth of Aphrodite, for example, he adds the following verses:

> And with her went Eros and Comely Desire followed her at
> her birth at the first and as she went into the assembly of the
> gods. This honor she has from the beginning, and this is the
> portion (*moiran*) allotted to her amongst men and undying
> gods . . . (*Theogony* 201-4, Evelyn-White, trans.)[3]

So Mimnermus pities the sun god who has been "allotted daily labor
and gets no rest for himself or his horses" (E frag. 8). The black-
robed Furies or Erinyes of Aeschylus' *Eumenides* insist that at their
birth Destiny or *Moira* allotted them the duty of punishing kindred
murder. They add that no other immortal can interfere with their
function whereas they themselves can have no portion of the white
robes of the upper world (333-40, 347-53, 390-96). Plato captures
the essence of the mythological picture of a harmonious whole
divided into complementary parts in his image of the cosmos at the
end of the *Republic*. Er, a visitor to the afterlife, sees a spindle
which is the axis for all the heavenly orbits. Although each of the
eight whorls revolves at its own speed in its own direction, the
goddess Necessity moves the spindle as a whole so all parts also
revolve together at the same time.

The *physiologoi*, those who spoke about nature instead of gods,
agreed that everything derived from the same stuff, whether they
posited water, fire, the four elements, or air or the Boundless as the
ultimate matter. The order developed not out of sex and violence,
as in the theogonies, but out of natural processes like rarefaction
and condensation or the forces of attraction and repulsion. In the
words of Diogenes of Apollonia, for example,

> My view, to sum it up, is that all things are differentiated
> from the same thing and are the same thing . . . for, if the
> things which are now in this world - earth and water, and air
> and fire, and the other things which we see existing in this
> world - were different from any other . . . by having a
> substance peculiar to itself and if it were not the same thing
> which is often changed and differentiated, then things could
> not in any way mix with one another . . .

In *On Generation and Corruption* 1.6, Aristotle expresses a similar
idea: "Unless all things were derived from one, action and passion
could not have occurred."[4] The Stoics too traced everything back to
one substance, fiery *pneuma*.

The order which arose from the fundamental principle in process
was based on balanced proportions of elements so that nature was a
self-regulating equilibrium. To the *physiologoi* we owe the term

'cosmos' for the 'arrangement' of all things in which every natural power has its functions and its limits assigned.[5] For Plato, as for the Pythagoreans before and after, the concept implied a geometric equality which had moral overtones. A passage from *Gorgias* 508 illustrates the connection between the divine and human as well as the moral and natural realms.[6]

> The wise, Callicles, say that both heaven and earth and gods and men are held together by community and friendship, by orderliness (*kosmiotes*) and temperance and justice (*dikaiotes*) and for this reason they call this whole universe an Order (*kosmos*) . . . But you have noticed that geometric equality has great power both among men and among gods and you think one should practice excessive greed because you neglect geometry.

The ideas of apportionment and equilibrium are inextricably joined with notions of justice.[7] In fact, the interconnection between the moral, natural, and social orders is best exemplified by Plato's definition of justice achieved by the end of the *Republic*. Er's vision of the natural universe as parts in harmony corresponds to Socrates' definition of justice in the state which in turn corresponds to justice in the individual soul: each part does its own proper work without interfering with the others. Solon and Heraclitus apply the same principle to the natural world, respectively: the sea is "justest" (*dikaiotate*) when, being undisturbed by the wind, it does not disturb anyone or anything (frag. 12) and "the sun will not overstep his measures; otherwise, the Erinyes the ministers of Justice (*Dike*) will find him out." (KRS 226)[8]

For both the *theologoi* and the *physiologoi*, justice involved retribution or reciprocity since a failure to perform one's duty or an encroachment on another's portion destroyed the balance of the whole and necessitated restoration through compensation. In the philosophers' conception of 'cosmos', the universal order is seen as a process of balance or equality over time. Anaximander, for example, explains that all things arise from the Boundless and return to it, "for they pay penalty and retribution to each other for their injustice, according to the assessment of Time" (KRS 110). Thus the heat of summer is compensated for by the cold of winter, the dark of night by the light of day. Because nature operates according to such laws which balance out excess or encroachments, it is not conceived of as irrational, unjust, or ultimately unfathomable. Rather, precisely because its laws are rational, knowable, and predictable, its eternal regularity and equilibrium provide the model for moral and social virtue, as the passage from *Gorgias* indicates, and even for physical well-being, according to the ancient physicians who saw health as a proper balance of qualities or powers in the body (e.g., Alcmaeon, the authors of the Hippocratic corpus, Galen). To most, nature was good and provident; the study of its laws and the imitation of its order were the highest goods for mortals.

It is in myth, however, where the gods use nature to reward and punish, that we find the most powerful particular examples of the general principle of reciprocity which sustains the moral order. Zeus, the supreme deity on Olympus, possesses attributes which are similar to the providence of God. He has not, of course, created or arranged the natural world by himself. Once he stabilizes his reign, however, he functions as the highest authority who settles conflicts which disturb the harmony. Thus he, like God, provides for and orders all for all. The lesser divinities come to him, as if to a judge, and argue their cases before him and his council. In the Homeric Hymn to Hermes, for example, Apollo drags his younger brother to their father to accuse him of stealing his cattle, "for there were the scales of judgment set for them both" (324). With Zeus' help, the two work out a compromise which actually involves the delineation and confirmation of their separate responsibilities in the world. The Homeric Hymn to Demeter relates a far more serious disturbance of the cosmic order. Because Hades has kidnapped Demeter's daughter Persephone, the grieving mother, the goddess of grain, absents herself from Olympus and prevents seeds from sprouting on earth. Humans are starving and the gods lack honor until Zeus effects a compromise which satisfies all parties and ensures the continuing cycle of the seasons. Most divinities accept his judgment because his superior wisdom is backed by superior force (the thunder and lightning of the sky god). When the Furies reject the compromise suggested by Zeus' emissary, Athena, the goddess adds threats to her sweet persuasion:

> I have Zeus behind me.
> Do we need speak of that: I am the only god
> who knows the keys to where his thunderbolts are locked.
> We do not need such, do we? Be reasonable.
> (*Eumenides* 826-28, Lattimore, trans.)[9]

These examples suggest that Zeus' providence, like God's, is a dynamic rather than a static activity. When the old order fails to maintain harmony, Zeus intervenes in response to new developments and effects a modification.

His responsibility for the cosmic order includes his continuing concern for human events which occur in time. Although, unlike God, Zeus and the other Greek deities have individual histories of birth, youth, and romance, once they achieve their defined portion, they live as a group outside of time, immortal and therefore transcendent as well as immanent in nature. They watch over the concerns of humans from a distance and know not only the past and present, but also the future which stretches out in full view before them.[10] Those of the upper realm, Zeus the sky god and Apollo, associated with the sun by the fifth century, are especially identified with the power of prophecy and were worshipped at shrines such as Dodona and Delphi where people came to inquire about the future.

Although the gods could see what would happen in time and sent warnings in the form of omens or oracles, they were not solely responsible for causing those events. Sometimes they clearly effected what happened, as when Apollo told Croesus he postponed his defeat for three years out of love for him. But that defeat had been determined long ago, not by the whim of Apollo, but by the crime of regicide committed by Croesus' ancestor Gyges, to which the gods responded by a decree of punishment to his line (Herodotus *Histories* 1.91). And, as we shall see in the next chapter, Croesus' own foolishness also played a part in the disaster which befell him. These provident gods could forsee and did predict, but not until the Hellenistic period did the Greeks believe they also predetermined everything that happened on earth.

Rather, the omniscient Greek gods, particularly Zeus and Apollo, can, like God, see into the hearts and minds of human beings, and they are ever on the watch over all to ensure that justice is maintained throughout the earth.[11] As Hesiod interprets two proverbs in *Works and Days*:

> He does mischief to himself who does mischief to another
> and evil planned harms the plotter most.

> The eye of Zeus, seeing all and understanding all, beholds
> these things too, if he so will, and fails not to mark what sort
> of justice is this that the city keeps within it. (264-69,
> Evelyn-White, trans.)

Zeus also has "thrice 10,000 spirits" to observe the "deeds of wrong" and keeps his virgin daughter Justice (Dike) at his side to report to him so that punishment can be meted out (*Works and Days* 253-64). In a fragment from a lost play of Aeschylus, Dike herself proclaims her origin and function. She sits in glory by the throne of Zeus because he overthrew his father Cronus "by means of Justice," having justly repaid him for beginning the quarrel. Now it is her task to reward the just for their life of justice, but to make the reckless more moderate by "writing their offenses on the tablet of Zeus," so that the list of crimes can be unrolled "when the proper time brings the fulfillment of what is theirs by right."[12]

As in the Hebrew narrative, so in the Greek myths, the offenses which demand punishment are ethical transgressions between man and man and religious transgressions between man and god. The words for crime are very general and imply violence, presumption, ignorance, deviation from a straight path, or missing a target, but each crime itself stems from a reckless mental attitude which leads the person to think and do things "beyond mortality."[13]   Greek myth abounds with tales of proud people who boast of their superiority to one or another of the gods and receive dire punishment for their insolence *hubris* (see chapter 3). Niobe, for example, witnessed the death of her seven sons and daughters after she proclaimed her superiority to Leto, mother of only two (Artemis and Apollo). Anthropomorphic deities who react so swiftly to human challenges are called "jealous" (*phthonos*) and may seem petty for holding a grudge against weak and foolish mortals who can threaten only divine self-esteem.[14] But in fact the whole just division of the universe is also threatened by such encroachments on the established limits. Mortals who take their superiority to other mortals as a sign of their equality to the gods may be infatuate enough to assert that mental arrogance in concrete actions which destroy the justice and reverence that hold the universe together. When, for example, Creon has refused to bury the dead Polynices and has buried Antigone alive instead, Tiresias' words,

> For you've confused the upper and the lower worlds.
> You sent a life to settle in a tomb;
> You keep up here-that which belongs below,
> the corpse unburied robbed of its release.
> Not you nor any god that rules on high
> can claim him now.
> You rob the nether gods of what is theirs.
> So the pursuing horrors lie in wait
> to track you down. The Furies sent by Hades
> and by all the gods will even you with your victims.
> (1068-77, Elizabeth Wyckoff, trans.).

reveal that physical nature, the divine order and the moral realm have all been disturbed by his rash act. Only his punishment will "even" the account and restore the balance.

In plays, poetry, and prose, Greek writers demonstrate clearly what concrete actions upset the moral order and therefore demand retribution. Foremost among these crimes is murder, especially when kindred blood is shed. Aeschylus' *Oresteia* chronicles the vendetta that proceeded through three generations of the House of Atreus as family members requited murder with further murder. Despite the escalating savagery, which included cannibalism and child-sacrifice, the chorus of *Libation Bearers* proclaims the justice of the doctrine of reciprocity (in a passage which resembles God's words to Cain in Gen. 4):

> . . . The spirit of Right (Dike)
> cries aloud and extracts atonement due:
> blood stroke for the stroke of blood
> shall be paid. (310ff, Lattimore, trans.)

Although the younger gods, Zeus, Apollo, and Athena, modify the human procedures by which the principle is effected, none quarrels with the concept of punishment for such crime.

Taking advantage of the weak is a crime so serious that Zeus himself is patron and protector of guests and hosts, of suppliants, and of beggars.[15] As Zeus Xenios, the chief deity insists that strangers be able to eat and sleep together, at hearth or market, free from fear of theft or violence. As Zeus Ikesios, he protects those who appeal at the altars of the gods, granting the defenseless time to find support. Those who abuse these sacred bonds which civilize relations between humans are sure to be punished. The poet Theognis knows for certain that "no mortal man . . . ever escaped the notice of the immortal gods when he deceived a stranger or a suppliant" (143-4). In myth, Paris' abduction of his host's wife brought devastation to Troy, whereas Laius' rape of his host's son provoked the curse which destroyed his family and endangered his city. In several tragedies, sinners manifest their villainy by forcibly removing the weak from the altars they cling to in the name of Zeus—e.g., Aeschylus' *Suppliants*, Sophocles' *Oedipus at Colonus*, and Euripides' *Heracles*. Conversely, heroes like Pelasgus in the first play and Theseus in the second dramatize their reverence for both gods and humans by defending the suppliants despite the danger their protection may incur.

Other social crimes motivated by the desire for wealth or by disrespect for the family also anger Zeus and provoke him to lay on a "heavy requital for evil doing" (Hesiod *Works and Days* 332-3). Hesiod lists theft, adultery, offenses against orphans, and verbal abuse of parents as punishable actions. He condemns the crimes of bribery, perjury, and giving false judgments with special venom. Connected to the perversion of judicial procedures is the equally serious crime of breaking an oath. In reality as well as in myth, all important events, procedures, decisions, and agreements, public and private, were solemnized and sealed by the taking of sacred oaths. By virtue of the oath breaking involved in any misdeed, secular encroachments on the rights of others became sins against the gods.[16] Oaths were so important in maintaining order and justice that even the gods took them, swearing to each other by the sacred water of Styx. If ever they were forsworn, Hesiod relates, they suffered ten years of physical isolation and pain in a death-like state (*Theogony* 793-806).

From these examples, it is clear that many Greeks connected justice in society with reverence for the gods.[17] Hesiod's catalogue of sins in *Works and Days* ends with a warning to his brother Perseus not only to turn his "foolish" heart from these things, but also to "sacrifice to the deathless gods purely and cleanly" (334-6). Theognis warns,

> Honor and fear the gods, Cyrnus, for this prevents a man from doing or saying impious things. (1179-80) Beware of crooked speech of unjust men who having no reverence for immortal gods covet other men's possessions and make dishonorable plots for evil deeds. (1146-52, Edmonds, trans.)

Aeschylus' ambitious and overconfident heroes, Xerxes and Agamemnon, committed literal sacrilege as well as crimes against humanity. Darius voices outrage that his young and reckless son Xerxes actually shackled the sacred Hellespont, as if the divine river were a slave, and then went on, "restrained by no reverence for the gods", to savage their images and burn their temples on the Athenian Acropolis (*Persians* 809-10). Agamemnon too desecrated their altars in his wanton destruction of Troy. When he returned to Argos, he trampled the expensive tapestries intended for the honor of the gods alone. Watching him tread the blood red carpet, the audience must have connected this demonstrated violence against the sacred object with the violence and bloodshed he has previously committed.[18] He begs that no god's jealousy (*phthonos, Agamemnon*

947) strike him down for stepping upon cloth too rich for mortal feet, but it is clear that he deserves punishment for his *hubris*.

The Greeks, like the Hebrews, believed that all nature was affected by such crimes. In fact, nature's prompt reaction to Creon's unnatural burials drove the prophet to the king, for the birds became mad and violent, the sacrifices would not burn, and dogs were depositing their leavings at the altars of the gods. In other Greek myths as well, nature (or the gods identified with the natural world) responds to moral corruption by destroying the wicked and sometimes even the very soil defiled by their activities. According to a Homeric simile (*Il.* 16.384-93), which is reminiscent of the biblical flood story, Zeus, immanent in nature as the god of thunder, lightning, and rain, unleashes storms and floods "in deep rage against mortals after they stir him to anger/ because in violent assembly they pass decrees that are crooked/ and drive righteousness from among them and care nothing for what the gods think" (386-8, Lattimore, trans.). Poseidon and Athena, divinities associated with the sea and navigation respectively, conspired to destroy the victorious Greek fleet on its voyage home from Troy in retaliation for the many crimes and sacrileges committed there (v. Euripides *Trojan Women* 1-97). According to the Persian who describes the disastrous retreat from Salamis an unidentified god (*theos*) "roused winter before its time" to tempt the fleeing survivors across a frozen stream to safety - but only so the sun could melt the ice and drown the desperate troops mid-passage (Aeschylus *Persians* 495-6). In Hesiod's *Works and Days* (242-4), the gods send famine and plague to cities defiled by murder so that both the earth and its people become barren.

The idea that the land itself can be corrupted by sin, and suffer retaliation is prominent in Greek myth as well as in the Bible. When a serious crime has been committed, it is as if a stain or taint (often associated with the Greek word *miasma*) appears and obstructs the natural fecundity in the area.[19] In Sophocles' *Oedipus the King,* for example, Apollo sends a plague which the priest describes:

> A blight is on the fruitful plants of the earth,
> A blight is on the cattle in the fields,
> A blight is on our women, that no children
> are born to them . . . (25-28, Grene, trans.).

Thebes cannot be cleansed and healthy again until the murderer of King Laius is expelled from the land. In *Eumenides*, when the

Athenian court releases Orestes despite his confession of matricide, the Furies threaten to retaliate by spreading plague and blight throughout the land because they consider that the place which frees the murderer becomes itself defiled by the crime. The Athenian legal system took account of the danger of pollution to the land. It required a victim's family to accuse a murderer, prevented the accused from contact with citizens or public places before and during the trial, and insured that punishment was meted out to the condemned criminal. In the event of an unknown homicide or an animate or inanimate object that caused a death, the official in charge actually conducted a trial and expelled the condemned to remove any danger of pollution from Attica.[20]

In some cases, as in the Bible, a human being is assigned the role of avenger and the penalty is exacted through war or murder. Apollo actually compelled the reluctant Orestes to commit matricide by threatening him with dread disease if he didn't requite the death of his father Agamemnon. According to Herodotus, Themistocles, the Athenian general who master-minded the Persian defeat at Salamis, ascribed the Greek victory to the gods: "Indeed, we did not perform this deed; the gods and our divine protectors did, who begrudged that one man, unholy and rash, should be King of both Asia and Europe" (*Histories* 8.109.3). But, when human beings act as god's instruments of reciprocity, the situation is often more complex than the previous examples suggest. The chorus of *Agamemnon* asserts that the gods sent the general to punish Troy for Paris' violation of the sacred guest-host relationship. Yet Agamemnon sacrificed his daughter to enable his fleet to sail and then destroyed all the Trojans and the altars of their gods after his victory. Clytemnestra and Aegisthus eagerly exacted retribution from Agamemnon for his own and his father's crimes, claiming that they were instruments of Justice. But they, like Sennacherib of Assyria, had motives, thoughts, and deeds which were not just. Such human agents of divine retribution must also bear their own responsibility for crimes they have committed.

Like the Hebrews, the Greeks believed that the penalty could be exacted from the group as a whole. The Greeks have no concept of a covenant between God and his people which makes all individuals corporately responsible for infringements against His laws. Their myths and the practices associated with *miasma*, however, describe a similar type of horizontal reciprocity.[21] In the *Iliad*, Apollo shoots the arrows of plague at the entire Greek camp, including even its animals, because Agamemnon has dishonored the priest Chryses. When the murder of Laius goes unavenged, the plague strikes all Thebes indiscriminately. Such divine responses suggest that the group bears a corporate responsibility for the crime, since it harbors the criminal. After the Trojan priest has been appeased, the plague recedes, and, at the end of *Oedipus the King*, the patricide/regicide insists that he must leave to cleanse Thebes of his crime. When all Troy is destroyed because of Paris' adultery and violation of the guest-host relationship, the poet Aeschylus alludes to the group's complicity in the crime: "They sang the wedding song too loudly" (*Agamemnon* 705).

As in Exodus, so in Greek saga, the punishment could also be exacted vertically from the descendants of the guilty individual, as if members of the continuing lineage, connected by blood, could be surrogates for each other.[22]   Solon, for example, asserts that the wicked "who themselves flee and escape the pursuing destiny of Heaven . . . the price of their deeds is paid by their innocent children or else by their seed after them" (13.27-32, Edmonds trans.). In myth, the victims' curses, invoked against Atreus and Laius, bring disaster to the children and grandchildren of both their houses. Like Herodotus' Croesus, most of these individuals are also culpable because of their own aggressiveness or conceit. Clearly, however, Iphigenia is an innocent, paying for the murder of other innocents, Thyestes' children in the past and the Trojan children yet to be slaughtered when Agamemnon conquers Troy. The idea of vertical reciprocity is so prevalent that in Euripides' *Hippolytus* Theseus assumes that some avenging spirit is responsible for his wife Phaedra's death (820) and speculates that he must now be paying the gods' penalty for the crimes of one of his ancestors (830). Hippolytus, punished for the alleged rape, reaches the same conclusion: this evil has arisen from an ancient polluting murder committed by his ancestors (1379-82).

But Hippolytus is guilty (although not of the rape and adultery Theseus punished). Aphrodite and the aged servant both accuse the youth of disrespect for the goddess and Phaedra alleges the rape in response to his excessive chastity, misogyny, and self love. Thus his death is a just punishment for his own unacknowledged but demonstrated hubris. For Greek saga, like Hebrew law and narrative, developed the concept of individual responsibility alongside of the idea of corporate horizontal or vertical reciprocity. Perhaps the latter served the needs of the smaller more interdependent communities of earlier Greek history, whereas the idea of individual culpability emerged as societies became larger and more diffuse. Certainly the developed legal codes of the city-states exacted punishment only from those who had been judged guilty.[23]   Yet, the early epic the *Odyssey* opens with a clear statement of the theme of individual responsibility. The invocation asserts that Odysseus could not save his companions "who were destroyed by their own wild recklessness" (7). After Zeus proclaims that Aegisthus' crime was justly punished by Orestes, episode after episode, from the storm which avenges Odysseus' blinding of Polyphemus, to the drowning of the sailors who ate the cattle of the Sun, to Odysseus' slaughter of the suitors and separation of the loyal servants from the traitors in Ithaca, dramatizes how human beings are punished as individuals for their own foolishness and crime. Poets like Solon and Theognis develop this idea, attributing suffering beyond man's portion to individual greed, foolishness, and hubris.

> All things here are among the crows and perdition and none
> of the blest immortals, Cyrnus, is to blame. The violence of
> men and their base gains and their pride (*hubris*) have cast
> us from much good into evil
> (Theognis 833-6, Edmonds, trans.)

> If you suffer bitterly through your own fault, don't blame the
> gods for it (Solon 9,10, Edmonds, trans.)

Tragic heroes like Creon in *Antigone* (257), Oedipus in *Oedipus the King* (1370ff.) and Pentheus in *Bacchae* (1120-21) acknowledge their own responsibility as well as the gods' power at the moment of their ruin.

The Greeks recognized the difficulty of establishing divine justice on earth when human instruments and procedures were imperfect by definition. Great men, whose very mortality precluded sufficient knowledge, might also have personal motives for eliminating their rivals. And kings and judges were always in a position which might tempt them to pervert justice rather than preserve it. Out of the savage mechanism of self-help depicted in the sagas of powerful houses under a curse, the Greeks developed a legal system that protected the accused before trial, determined the degree of culpability, and insured appropriate punishment. Aeschylus' *Oresteia* dramatizes the stages in the process: from the Furies' automatic demand for further blood as atonement for blood shed, to the purification rites of Apollo which allowed the murderer to substitute animal sacrifice and exile for death, to the Athenian court system derived from Zeus and Athena. Although vendettas and excessive punishments were eliminated and the subjectivity of the judges was diminished, the basic principles of the doctrine of reciprocity remained unchanged. In the *Eumenides*, the detestable Furies argue that their very horror and the swift certainty of dread punishment deter crime and preserve order. Athena agrees and advises the citizens "not to cast fear utterly from your city. What man who fears nothing at all is ever righteous?" (698-9, Lattimore, trans.). She persuades the Furies to remain in Athens, for "In the terror upon the faces of these, I see great good for our citizens." (990-91, Lattimore, trans.).

Greek tradition also allowed for some mitigation of the absolute application of the doctrine of reciprocity. The *Iliad*, in books 9.632-36 and 18.497-508, refers to the fact that the relatives of a murdered man might accept a blood-price from the murderer as restitution for their slain kin (although this practice was prohibited in later law codes). The process described would prevent a blood vendetta from destroying a society that had not yet established fixed written procedures for determining the degree of guilt, the seriousness of the crime, or the appropriate penalty. Some myths, however, suggest the notion of divine mercy. Zeus, for example, freed Ixion, the first kindred murderer, as God protected Cain (although Ixion then committed a new crime for which he was severely punished). Both Apollo and Zeus protected the rights of a suppliant, even when accused of a capital crime. According to Aeschylus, Athena established the principle that the accused would be freed if the votes of the jury were equal. It remained in effect in the fourth century and was known as the "vote of Athena."

Divine mercy was also connected to the notion of human repentance. Phoenix, in *Iliad* 9.496-512, tries to arouse pity in Achilles by arguing that even the gods are not pitiless and sometimes forgive humans who do wrong if they venerate the spirits of Prayer the daughters of Zeus. Since these Prayers follow Ate (the delusion which is both the source of sin and the ruin which is its punishment) as possible healers, the personifications imply the effectiveness of words and actions that indicate repentance. By the third century B.C.E. the maxim "Repent when you do wrong" was connected with Apollo. Statues which show the god holding the Graces in his right hand and his bow of retribution in his weaker left were interpreted as indicating his reluctance to punish swiftly so that the evil-doer had a chance to repent.[24]

Perhaps the most optimistic statement of the doctrine of reciprocity is its reverse—the assurance that goodness and merit will be rewarded. Athena only emphasizes the positive corollary when she urges the Furies to "do good and receive good" in *Eumenides* 868. That aspect was part of the common man's definition of just behavior as early as Odysseus' wish to Nausikaa that she and her future husband be a grief to their foes and a joy to their friends (6.815) and as late as Plato's challenge of that maxim in *Republic* 1. Collective merit also corresponded to collective punishment. If a community has a good king who governs well, its soil is fertile, its sheep prolific, its seacoasts full of fish, and its people prosper (*Od.* 19. 108-114). Those places which accept the bones of the great heroes like Oedipus, Amphiarus, Diomedes, and others receive great blessings from their burial sites. In the compromise effected by Athena in the *Oresteia* the Furies become Eumenides, "Beneficent Ones," and agree to bring prosperity, fertility, and harmony to Athens in exchange for virtuous behavior and honor from the citizens.

But the Greeks had, of course, experienced enough of life's complexities to know that the simple equation of suffering with sin or blessing with goodness did not apply to every situation. In fact, being mortal, from the beginning, precluded living a life free from pain and suffering. Only a fool could expect an entirely happy life and the individual was responsible for only those evils he brought upon himself "beyond his portion" (e.g., *Od.* 1.34,35; *huper moron*). But the line dividing "his portion" from "beyond" was far less clear for polytheistic Greeks who had no guidelines equivalent to the Hebrews' Torah and covenant with their one God. Therefore, the Greeks suffered more acutely from their own ignorance about the gods' will than from disappointment over the suffering of the innocent. Many poets echo the pessimism expressed in the following lines ascribed to both Solon and Theognis.

> No man is himself the cause of loss and gain Cyrnus; the gods are the givers of them both; Nor does any man labor knowing in his heart whether he is moving toward a good end or a bad. For often expecting to make a bad end he makes good and expecting to make good he makes bad Nor does anyone get what he wishes for he has limits of difficult perplexity for we men believe vain things knowing nothing but the gods accomplish all things according to their own minds. (Theognis 133-42; see also Solon 17.5, 13.63-9, Edmonds, trans.)

Thus most of the famous victims in saga dramatize the inhumanity of humans to one another (e.g., Macaira, Megara and her children, Polyxena, Iphigenia) rather than impugn divine justice.

Still there are questions. What about the obvious fact that some heinous crimes appeared to go unpunished? The idea of vertical reciprocity, where justice takes its own time to restore the balance, offers a partial answer. Horizontal reciprocity too might explain those cases where catastrophes like flood, plague, storms, and earthquakes destroy whole groups. But these solutions are not entirely satisfactory, especially for those who insist on the principle of individual responsibility as emphasized as early as the *Odyssey*. Theognis protests punishing the children for the reckless deeds of the fathers and asks "How can it be just" (743)? and "What mortal, seeing this, would honor the immortal gods" (747-8)?

An innocent man's misery or a punishment so disproportionate to the crime called for further explanation. Sophocles' late plays *Philoctetes* (409 B.C.E.) and *Oedipus at Colonus* (406 B.C.E.) treat characters whose suffering is much greater than their deeds merit. The elder Oedipus, unlike his sons, sinned in ignorance; he never would have harmed his relatives if he had known who they were. Philoctetes, abandoned by the Greek warriors because of his wounds, is described by the sailor chorus as "one who wronged no one nor killed but lived just among the just and fell in trouble past his deserts" (683-5, Grene, trans.). He expresses the frustration and anger felt by those who personally experience the shortcomings of the doctrine of reciprocity:

> —nothing evil yet has perished.
> The Gods somehow give them most excellent care.
> They find their pleasure in turning back from Death
> the rogues and tricksters, but the just and good
> they are always sending out of the world.
> How can I reckon the score, how can I praise,
> when praising Heaven I find the Gods are bad?
> (446-52, Grene, trans.)

A character in Euripides' *Bellerophon* actually denies that there are any gods in heaven, reasoning from the obvious fact that tyrants and oath breakers reap rewards while pious citizens and their cities are overwhelmed (fragment 286).[25]

One solution to the problem of theodicy was the extension of the doctrine of reciprocity into an afterlife. Although most of the dead souls of the *Odyssey* (Books 11 and 24) have only a shadowy existence, Odysseus also sees the greatest sinners of the past, Tityus, Tantalus, and Sisyphus, suffering terrible agonies for their terrible crimes. In the centuries between Homer and Plato, the concept of reward and punishment after death had developed to such a degree that Plato in the *Republic* and *Phaedo* could describe the geography of the realms of the dead and stages of penalties and purification. These ideas will be discussed in detail in a later chapter.

Other solutions diminished or severed the relation between the cosmic order and human morality. The atomists and later the Epicureans, for example, reduced nature and the gods to atoms colliding as they moved through empty space, and denied that the gods had any control over the affairs of mortals. For divine providence and reciprocity, they substituted the avoidance of pain and the pursuit of mental tranquillity as the principles that would maintain individual well-being, if not a moral order.[26] Some sophists also theorized that reciprocity, morality, and law were not a part of nature; rather they were traditions developed by humans to insure social order. Yet most advised that such traditions should be obeyed because they were rational and had proven themselves effective.[27] Protagoras' famous proposition, "of everything the measure (*metron*) is humanity (*anthropos*) . . ." brings together the connotations of measure as assessment, mastery, and principle of harmony between the opposites in nature; it makes humans the judges of which opposites apply and renders the judgment relative to persons and contexts.[28] Thucydides traced the causes of events in the Peloponnesian Wars to basic human nature, with its drives of fear, honor and self interest, and to the resulting power politics, without reference to divine intervention and recompense.[29] In a fragment of a satyr play ascribed to the politician Critias, a character explains that law and religion were invented to keep the savage human race from destroying itself:

> There was a time when the life of men was unorganized,
> and brutish, and the servant of force;
> When there was no reward for the good,
> Nor again any punishment came to the bad.
> And then I think men set up laws
> as punishers, in order that justice might be ruler
> [of all alike] and hold violence a slave.
> And anyone who might transgress was penalized.
> Then, since the laws prevented them
> from performing overt acts by force,
> but they performed them secretly, then it seems to me
> [for the first time] some man, acute and wise in mind,
> invented the fear of the gods for mortals, so that
> there might be some terror for the bad even if in secret
> they do or think or say anything.
> Hence then, he introduced divinity . . .
> (*Sisyphus* 1-15)[30]

By the end of the fifth century, a few were considered godless men or atheists. Tradition reports that Diagoras of Melos, the most notorious, lost his faith when he was victimized by injustice.[31]

In the Hellenistic period, when the Greeks felt less control over their political and personal destinies, some groups proposed a universal determinism that separated the pains of life from moral evil.[32] Already in the late fifth century, the personification of Fortune, *Tuche*, previously allied with older divinities, came to the fore as a powerful goddess with a following of her own. She did not represent blind chance; she symbolized an order far beyond the comprehension of mortals and yet clearly at work in the vicissitudes of life.[33] Writers like Euripides, Menander, Theophrastus, and Polybius testify to her activity. But the belief in Fate as the absolute controller of an individual's life also became very popular - whether as blind as chance or as predictable as astrology, based on the mechanical movements of the heavens.[34]

Stoicism too was predicated on fate and determinism.[35] Its proponents believed that god (or nature as *logos*) was the provident, rational and efficient cause of the universe and not only created all things, but also permeated all things as *pneuma*. The Stoics asserted that all events were causally related as "stages in the history of a single, rational, continuously changing substance."[36] If god was directly responsible for everything and had providentially ordered the world, disease and disaster must have a *logos* too, and in some way be useful to the world . . . "For without it (*kakia*)", in the Stoic sage Chrysippus' words, "there could be no good." (Plutarch, *Comm. Not.* 1056b; *De Stoic. Rep.*: 1050f.).[37] Since evils were outside human control, they had to be accepted as the necessary consequences of the good. Therefore, they could have nothing to do with moral evil.

Critics of the Stoics attacked the apparent contradiction between their idea that everything is fated and their insistence that Stoic individuals could be wise and virtuous. For, they asked, isn't the character of the individual also fated? The Stoic response was a definition of moral evil based on man's particular *logos* which gave him alone the ability to reason and to make choices.[38] If one failed to exercise right reason when faced with external events and temptations, he would be deemed "foolish" and "evil" and therefore culpable, even if what he did had been predetermined by a divine, rational, and ultimately benevolent Nature.

Greek myth and philosophy projected a definition of human beings who had free will, despite external compulsions, and thus would be held accountable for actions which deviated from religious, social, and moral standards. All believed that fear was a necessary element in keeping the individual from stepping across the established lines. Retributive justice was the primary deterrent to transgression. But despite the universal belief in its efficacy and the rounding out of the roughest edges by threatening corporate, generational, and even eternal reciprocity, still people continued to test the limits and tried to extend the boundaries of their portions. The sagas of the great houses of Greece dramatize the characters and capacities of those whose ambitions and circumstances lead them to court the disasters which moderate men avoid. We turn next to them to discuss human heroism.

Notes

1. Hans Kelson develops this idea in detail and examines its appearance in a variety of cultures in *Society and Nature: Perspectives in Social Inquiry*. Classics. Staples and Precursors in Sociology (1946; reprint, New York: Arno, 1974). Charles Kahn refers to the notion as "panpsychism" in "Religion and Natural Philosophy in Empedocles' Doctrine of the Soul" *Archiv fur Geschichte der Philosophie* 42 (1960): 14. It is often called the "sympathy of nature" e.g., Cicero, *De Natura deorum* 2.19. See Anders Olerud. *L'idee de macrocosmos et de microcosmos dans "Le Timee" de Platon: Etude de mythologie comparee*, (Uppsala: Almqrista Wiksells Boktryckeri: AB, 1951), for a detailed examination of physiological, morphological, psychological, and sociological correspondence.

2. For an introduction to this concept, see W. C. Greene, *Moira: Fate, Good, and Evil in Greek Philosophy* (Cambridge: Harvard University Press, 1944).

3. The translations from the Homeric Hymns and Hesiod are taken from Hugh G. Evelyn-White, *Hesiod, the Homeric Hymns, and Homerica* (Cambridge: Harvard University Press, 1914).

4. Kelson provides many other examples of the homogeneity of nature in chapter two. In chapters four and five, he relates it to notions of retribution as justice in Greek religion and philosophy. He refers to these passages as well as several others. My translations are quoted from pp. 235-7.

5. See chapters two and three and notes.

6. The passage is quoted from Charles H. Kahn, *Anaximander and the Origins of Greek Cosmology* (Philadelphia: Centrum, 1982), p. 188, n.2. Kahn, on p. 188, refers to the "combined radiance of the moral and aesthetic ideals of early Greece," connected to the term *Kosmos*.

7. In addition to Kelson, see Gregory Vlastos, "Equality and Justice in Early Greek Cosmologies," *Classical Philology* 42 (1947): 156-78.

8. Translations of the Presocratics have been quoted from G. S. Kirk, J. E. Raven, and M. Schofield, *The Presocratic Philosophers: A Critical History with a Selection of Texts*, 2nd ed. (Cambridge: Cambridge University Press, 1983) (Referred to as KRS and cited by fragment number). Translations of Solon and Theognis have been quoted or translated by me from the text of J. M. Edmonds, *Elegy and Iambus* (Cambridge: Harvard University Press, 1931).

9. All translations of Greek tragedies are quoted from *The Complete Greek Tragedies*, David Grene and Richmond Lattimore, eds., Vols. 1-4 (Chicago: University of Chicago Press, 1959-60) unless otherwise noted. They are cited by translator in the text.

10. For a comparative study of this conception of deity, see R. Pettazzoni, *The All Knowing God*, trans. H. J. Rose (London: Methuen, 1956).

11.   I am indebted to two important studies which trace the development of the concept of justice: H. Lloyd-Jones, *The Justice of Zeus* (Berkeley: University of California Press, 1971) and E. A. Havelock, *The Greek Concept of Justice from Its Shadow in Homer to Its Substance in Plato* (Cambridge: Harvard University Press, 1978).

12.   The text of this fragment with interpretation and translation appears in Hugh Lloyd-Jones' appendix to the second edition of volume 2 of Herbert Weir Smyth, *Aeschylus: Plays and Fragments with an English Translation*. The Loeb Classical Library (Cambridge: Harvard University Press, 1963), pp. 576-81.

13.   J. M. Bremer studies all the terms in *Hamartia: Tragic Error in the "Poetics" of Aristotle and in Greek Tragedy* (Amsterdam: Adolf M. Hakkert, 1969).

14.   Peter Walcot analyzes the term and its use as well as the psychology behind its origin and development in *Envy and the Greeks: A Study of Human Behavior* (Warminster, Eng.: Aris and Phillips Ltd., 1978).

15.   See Robert Parker, *Miasma: Pollution and Purification in Early Greek Religion* (Oxford: Clarendon Press, 1983), pp. 181-186 for an analysis of the seriousness of these crimes.

16.   See K. J. Dover, *Athenian Popular Morality* (Oxford: B. Blackwell, 1974) and Jon D. Mikalson, *Athenian Popular Religion* (Chapel Hill: University of North Carolina Press, 1983), especially Chapter 5 "Gods and Oaths" for a discussion of the ways in which oaths made social fidelity a religious duty.

17.   Parker, *Miasma*, pp. 188-190, and p. 170, note 146.

18.   R. Goheen, "Aspects of Dramatic Symbolism: The Studies in the *Oresteia*," *American Journal of Philosophy* 72 (1955): 113-37.

19.   See Parker, *Miasma* for a thorough study of this phenomenon, as it is manifested in myth and history. The chapters "The Shedding of Blood," pp. 104-143, and "Purifying the City," pp. 257-280, are especially relevant to this discussion.

20.   On the relation of purification to the laws on homicide, see D. M. MacDowell, *Athenian Homicide Law in the Age of the Orators* (Manchester: University of Manchester Press, 1963), pp. 4-5, 141-150.

21.   Parker, *Miasma*, pp. 257-280, the chapter, "Purifying the City" analyzes both the mythological and historical examples of communal affliction.

22.   Parker, *Miasma*, pp. 190-206. The chapter on "Curses, Family Curses, and the Structure of Rights" considers the examples of and problems associated with vertical reciprocity.

23.   Parker, *Miasma*, pp. 278-79. Parker considers the phenomenon of corporate responsibility as most effective among restricted and clearly defined social groups. He notes that most of the Greek examples concern either an individual sinner whose crime endangers the whole group or a powerful individual like a king responsible for the welfare of the whole.

24.   R. Pfeiffer, "The Image of the Delian Apollo and Apolline Ethics," *Journal of the Warburg and Courtald Institute* 15 (1952): 20-32.

25. G. B. Kerford, *The Sophistic Movement* (Cambridge, Eng.: Cambridge University Press, 1981), p. 170 discusses the attitude and translates the fragment.

26. For a full analysis of their religious and ethical ideas, see Cyril Bailey, *The Greek Atomists and Epicurus* (New York: Russell & Russell, 1964), pp. 438-528; 588-594.

27. See Kerford, especially pp. 111-30 on the *nomos-physis* controversy and pp. 139-162 on the theory of society for a detailed analysis of the ideas of various individuals.

28. For translation and analysis of the proposition as well as bibliography on interpretation, see Edward Schiappa, *Protagoras and Logos: A Study in Greek Philosophy and Rhetoric* (Columbia: University of South Carolina Press, 1991), pp. 117-133; 190-196 and Mario Untersteiner, *The Sophists*, trans. Kathleen Freeman (New York: Philosophical Library, 1984), pp. 41-51; 77-91.

29. Thucydides does not ignore, however, the effect of religious institutions and beliefs on events. Nor does he give any indication that he himself denied the existence of the gods. See Borimir Jordon, "Religion in Thucydides," *American Journal of Philology* 116 (1986): 119-147 for analysis and bibliography.

30. Quoted from Jonathan Barnes, *The Presocratic Philosophers* (London: Routledge Kegan Paul, 1982), pp. 451-2, in a section on the Sophists and the origins of atheism.

31. Barnes, pp. 453-4.

32. For general surveys of Hellenistic culture, see Moses Hadas, *Hellenistic Culture: Fusion and Diffusion* (New York: Norton, 1959); Luther Martin, *Hellenistic Religions: An Introduction* (New York: Oxford University Press, 1987); W. W. Tarn, *Hellenistic Civilization* revised by G. T. Griffith, (Cleveland: Meridian, 1961).

33. Tarn, p. 340; Martin, pp. 21-23, in a discussion of Apuleius' *Golden Ass*. For further discussions of *Tuche*, see chapters 5 and 9.

34. Tarn, pp. 345-352.

35. For studies of Stoicism, see J. B. Gould, *The Philosophy of Chrysippus* (Leiden: E. J. Brill, 1970); A. A. Long, ed., *Problems in Stoicism* (London: Athlone, 1971); John Rist, *Stoic Philosophy* (Cambridge: Cambridge University Press, 1969) and Rist ed., *The Stoics* (Berkeley: University of California Press, 1978).

36. A. A. Long, "The Stoic Concept of Evil," *Philosophical Quarterly* 18(1968): 332.

37. *Ibid*, p. 331. In note 17, on p. 333, Long quotes similar ideas that some particular evils are necessary consequences of the good which preserves the whole in statements by Cicero, Marcus Aurelius, and Epictetus.

38. Long, *Ibid*, pp. 334-343, as well as Charlotte Stough, "Stoic Determinism and Moral Responsibility," in Rist, *The Stoics*, pp. 203-231 and Margaret Reesor, "Fate and Possibility in Early Stoic Philosophy," *Phoenix* 19(1965): 285-297.

Conclusions and Comparisons

Both in Greece and in Israel the cosmos was understood to be an organic whole in which the natural order and the moral order function as interdependent units. But the two civilizations gave different reasons for this interconnectedness of nature and morality. The Hebraic mind saw the root of this interdependence in the double pronged relationship of God to the universe-the Creator who systematizes nature and who scrutinizes the motives and the deeds of human beings. In applying the law of reciprocity to both the natural and the moral realms, God can interrupt the course of nature through miracles or catastrophes to restore equilibrium and to bring about a more profound harmony between the parts of his creation. In contrast, the Hellenic mind saw the correspondence between natural law and human morality as rooted in the homogeneity of all parts of the universe which evolved from the same substance(s) and were subject to the same principles of order. As immanent in nature the gods are subordinate to its laws, but as independent personalities in myth, they are able, like God, to assert their own natural power in applying the doctrine of reciprocity, as when Demeter prevents the seeds from sprouting to punish the rape of Persephone or when Poseidon rages against Odysseus by causing storm after storm at sea. Zeus gives the gods some free reign but pulls them back when their individual application of the doctrine does not serve the purposes of the cosmic order.

On Olympus as on Sinai the doctrine of reciprocity involves collective responsibility and merit extending horizontally across society and vertically down through the generations. The sins that trigger the operation of this law are offenses against human beings and offenses against the gods or God. Both traditions grapple with the problem of the innocent person's misery or punishment so disproportionate to any offense committed; a problem that defies the solutions of horizontal and vertical responsibility. The poets and philosophers of Athens like the prophets and sages of Jerusalem sought to unravel the painful knot by extending the doctrine of reciprocity into the afterlife. Yet even in this life the relentless operation of the doctrine of reciprocity could be mitigated by repentance and prayer.

But the theological edge to the problem of suffering of the innocent was far sharper in Israel than in Greece. In the Bible the doctrine of reciprocity is expressed through the formal but highly personal relationship of the covenant between God and Israel (the community and the individual). Thus there is a driving necessity for theodicy on Sinai in order to explain why God does not appear to be keeping his part of the covenant. On Olympus the gods have abiding and deep relationships with humans either as patrons of individual cities or of individual personality types and professions. The multiple examples of reward and punishment demonstrate the gods' concern for justice and the reality of a moral order in the universe. But the connections between the divine and the human are never as clearly spelled out either in law or in the unfolding historical process as in the Torah. Therefore, Greek heroes and heroines caught in the confusion of crisis often express their doubts whether the gods' will can be known at all. The chorus of *Oedipus the King* prays that Oedipus is not the killer and at the same time that Apollo's predictions are correct, "for if impious deeds foreseen go unpunished why is it necessary for me to dance in honor of the gods" (895). The chorus of *Hippolytus*, watching the destruction of the chaste youth, question whether there is any divine plan or cosmic morality at all.

> The care of God for us is a great thing
> if a man believes it at heart;
> it plucks the burden of sorrow from him.
> So I have a secret hope
> of someone, a God, who is wise and plans;
> but my hopes grow dim when I see
> the deeds of men and their destinies
> (1102-1110, Grene, trans.)

These questions are also found in the Book of Job and in the despairing utterance heard and rejected by the rabbis: "There is no Judge and there is no justice." But among the Greeks there is less sense of personal betrayal by god and more pessimism about the outcome of human endeavor. For the Hebrews, however, the seemingly clear specifications of the covenant lead man to indict God for His apparent violation of the agreement.

Another solution to the theological and personal dilemma of innocent suffering was provided in later ages by Jewish folk religion where the measure for measure principle is seen through a different prism. In the houses of mourning of Oriental Jews coming from Muslim countries it is customary for the mourners to be comforted by stories showing the ultimate justice of Divine Providence. In the typical plot of these Jewish theodicy tales the protagonist is a pious, God-fearing person who accompanies a religious authority, a prophet, a sage or a celestial being on a journey. A strange deed, often one of conspicuous injustice, is performed by the trusted authority in the presence of the confused onlooker. The latter attacks the neutrality and silence of the authority because he does not prevent a seeming perversion of justice though he is capable of doing so. The strange behavior is then explained very often by showing the pious individual a different temporal or spatial dimension in which the peculiar act becomes logical and an apt demonstration of the doctrine of reciprocity. Thus, for example, a good man who welcomes strangers is repaid by having his cow slaughtered but seen from the higher perspective the cow served as substitute for the good man's wife who, following a heavenly decree, would have died. Similarly, a miser who refused to give anything to the wayfarers who visited him sees a fallen wall in his house rebuild itself without having to expend any effort or money of his own. The reason is that had the miser done the building he would have found a hidden treasure. The three children born out of the union of a young man and the "daughter of an angel" perish shortly after birth. The grieving husband is comforted by his celestial wife who shows him their fate had they remained alive— they would have died a violent death. In all of these tales the pious onlooker, like Job, is silenced. He admits his ignorance of God's acts motivations and priorities.[1]

The "Hymn to Zeus" by Cleanthes, the third century B.C.E. Stoic philosopher, expresses a similar belief in the ultimate good of divine providence and the assurance that the seeming evils of earthly life are in fact good from the perspective of heaven and the whole.

> Nothing occurs on the earth apart from you O God,
> Nor in the heavenly regions nor on the sea
> except what hard men do in their folly;
> but you know how to make the odd even,
> and to harmonize what is dissonant, to
> you the alien is akin,
> And so you have wrought together
> into one all things that are good and bad
> So that there arises an eternal *logos*
> of all things . . . (11-21, A. A. Long trans.).[2]

Nevertheless, the dilemma of human suffering led the Stoic philosophers, like the rabbis, to speculate on whether the suffering of an individual is the result of his or her choices or the product of a predetermined destiny, as in a governing *hashgahah* (divine providence) or Stoic fate. Despite the great differences between the Stoic natural law and the biblical-rabbinic view expressed by the term *hashgahah*,[3] the rabbis would have no doubt agreed with the Stoics that human beings are unique creations endowed with the capacity for moral and rational choice and are therefore responsible for their actions though they cannot control the results.

At this point we turn from the divine to the human perspective to consider both the possibilities and pitfalls of human life because, despite external circumstances, we are ultimately responsible for what we do and what we become.

Notes

1.   Dov Noy, "The Jewish Theodicy Legend," *Fields of Offerings: Studies in Honor of Raphael Patai*, ed. by Victor D. Sanua (New York: Herzl Press, 1984), pp. 70-84.

2   A. A. Long, *Hellenistic Philosophy: Stoics, Epicureans, Sceptics* (New York: Scribners, 1974), p. 181.

3.   Philo blends the Stoic view of providence, the uniformity, unity, continuity and immutability of the universal laws of nature with the biblical-rabbinic view of individual providence (which the Stoics denied). He claims that providence is both universal, i.e., the operation of natural laws and individual i.e., the suspension of these laws by God for the sake of some individual. Cf. Harry A. Wolfson, *Philo*, 2:293.

Chapter 5

Paradigms of Heroism

Introduction

The literatures of ancient Israel and classical Greece not only define the divine realm but they also provide a wide spectrum of patterns for human life. In these traditional societies where values remained relatively stable for generation after generation, the lives of great men and women were used as educational vehicles for inculcating virtues. The stories concretized heroic role models who served as exemplars for young people to pattern themselves after. The approved model of virtue, taken from life or literature, might be a sage, a teacher, a valiant warrior or good king, a faithful wife or dutiful son, or an individual who bore suffering with courage. Against these examples of rectitude were arrayed the malefactors of society—the greedy, the self indulgent, the foolish, the vicious, the brutal, the disloyal, and the rebellious. Homer is quite explicit about the purpose of such pattern stories. In the *Odyssey*, for example, Telemachus is told again and again that he must do what Orestes did to set his house in order, whereas Phoenix, in *Iliad 9*, ends his advice to Achilles with the warning not to do what Meleager did (600-601).

The biblical narrative is furnished with typological characters for the guidance of future generations. Drawing from details of previous stories, later biblical writers created antitypes that recalled the prototypes but at the same time introduced new dimensions to accommodate the changing historical and cultural circumstances. The rabbis further developed an entire hermaneutical approach linked to typologies.[1] Their outlook was epitomized by the Hebrew aphorist Immanuel of Rome (13/14th century) in his statement that the deeds of the ancestors are a sign to the children[2] and in the midrashic expression that the Holy One blessed be He took the conversations of the fathers and made them the key to the redemption of the children.[3] For the biblical writers and the rabbis, typologies were best suited to their programmatic view of history.

The heroes and heroines of Greek myth exist outside the context of any broad historical continuum or teleological progression from creation. Fixed forever by name and position in a particular saga, the characters provided archetypes rather than typologies; by being continually re-presented, they became traditional, as "stable structural units or persistent themes, situations, and character-types."[4] These retold stories from the past with well known but remote characters allowed for the examination of current personalities, issues, and values *sub specie aeternitatis* without the trivia or the subjectivity associated with current events. According to Tyrrell and Brown, Greek myths

> constitute a discourse, a verbal medium, through which members of the community - those who share the same myths - use the past to talk about the present. They communicate with one another *through* but not *about* their past.[5]

Although the names and basic plots remained the same, the tales continued to be re-presented with variations and new emphases that yielded fresh meaning to each succeeding generation in an ever-changing society.

Alongside the depictions of the heroes and the heroines there are descriptions of the good life in which all the values of the two civilizations find expression: their aspirations, their great joys and their simple pleasures, the harmonious relationships which are the basis for tranquil families and communities. On his journey Odysseus visits an ideal society on the island of Phaeacia just before he returns to Ithaca to try to establish himself as good husband, good father, good son and good leader ruling a pious, peaceful, and prosperous kingdom. Adam and Eve, before the fall, represent the biblical ideal of humanity in harmony with one another, with nature and with God. This ideal is echoed in Isaiah's prophetic vision of peace in the end of days (Isa. 2:2-4; 11:1-5) and the psalmists' depiction of the Lord's blessing of the family circle (Ps. 128).

These pictures of contentment gain their strength because of the contrast with human failure and suffering. In both cultures the exemplars also demonstrate this dark side of human life. Not only are there villains but even the heroes overreach themselves, or act foolishly, or become victims of circumstances beyond their control. Their behavior in crisis and their choices in facing dilemmas provide patterns for imitation or warnings for avoidance. Those who triumph over difficulties offer models for courage, integrity, and patience in adversity. As the hero or heroine articulates what has been learned from the ordeal, the reader or observer gains a valuable insight into the self and the world without having to experience the pain.

Notes

1.   On the use of typology in rabbinic literature see I. Heinemann, *Darkhei ha-Aggadah* (Jerusalem: The Magnes Press, 1950), pp. 32-4. See also Ch.1, Sinai: Unity and Prose n.3 on "typology" "prototype" and "antitype".

2.   Immanuel's adage is cited in I. Davidson (Ed.) 2. *Ozar ha- Meshalim Veha-Pitgamim* (Jerusalem: Mosav Harav Kook, 1957), 2 with earlier authorities cited (pp. 2f., n. 40).

3.   *Gen R.* 70:5 (ed. Theodor-Albeck), p. 803.

4.   Quoted from Northrop Frye, *The Great Code: The Bible and Literature* (Harcourt Brace Jovanovich: New York, 1982), p. 48. See also his *Anatomy of Criticism: Four Essays* (Princeton: Princeton University Press, 1971) pp. 95 -112, 95n, and glossary, where he defines archetype as "a symbol, usually an image, which recurs often enough in literature to be recognizable as an element in one's literary experience as a whole." According to Carl Jung, archetypes occur independently in the dreams of different people and in the images of different cultures because they come from a common source in the unconscious on which all human beings draw.

5.   Wm. Blake Tyrrell and Frieda S. Brown, *Athenian Myths and Institutions: Words in Action* (Oxford: Oxford University Press, 1991), p. 8.

Sinai: Biblical—Rabbinic Typologies

The Setting for Prototypes and Antitypes

The biographical typologies of the Hebrew Bible focus on a wide variety of challenges that confront the heroes and heroines: divided loyalties in family conflict; the weak and idealistic versus the powerful and unscrupulous; foreigners in a strange land; a higher vision to be taught to a materialistic, rebellious people; personal excellence and personal failings; the trials of suffering and death. All of these difficulties have their source in the imperfection of the human being and the imperfection of the cosmos, despite which, God's will and purposes are to be implemented.

The basic problem as the rabbis saw it, was that human beings are midway between the animals and the angels, composed of physical and spiritual elements.[1] Their hearts, minds, and souls are the battlegrounds between the higher forces prompting upward and the lower forces pulling downward. The struggle continues throughout life and the intensity is such that, as Rabbi Gamaliel concluded, we cannot be sure of ourselves until we die.[2] In view of this continuous struggle and the suffering it engenders (which is often compounded by circumstances over which individuals have no control), the Schools of Hillel and Shammai debated for two and a half years the following question: Would it have been better if the human being had, or had not, been created? Finally they agreed that it would have been better had humans not been created, but since they have been created let them investigate their past doings and let them examine what they are about to do.[3] Nevertheless, the Bible and rabbinic literature tempered this pessimism with the conviction of God's special love for His creatures[4] and their unique role in His far reaching plan for the universe. The prototypical men and women in the Bible provide the mirror by which succeeding generations could measure their behavior

Abraham and Isaac

One of the assumptions concerning human existence implicit in the biblical narratives is that life represents a series of trials imposed by God for human growth. This pattern is most clearly represented in the life of the first patriarch, Abraham. The authors of the Apocrypha and the rabbis, basing themselves on the biblical text, list ten trials through which Abraham passed, emerging with

faith and integrity intact.[5]   Three trials are connected with
Abraham's rediscovery of the one God, his separation from his
pagan environment, his journey to Canaan, and his acceptance of
the covenant of circumcision (Gen. 12:2-5; 17:9-14).[6]

Three trials are connected with Abraham's forced departure from
Canaan because of the famine, his descent into Egypt, where Sarah
was taken into the Pharaoh's harem (Gen. 12:10-20) and then
released, and his journey to the land of the Philistines where an
identical episode involving Sarah occurred. The views of the post-
biblical commentators are divided regarding Abraham's actions.
Some see his descent to Egypt shortly after arriving in Canaan as an
act of faith without impatience toward God, who bade him abandon
his native land for a land of starvation. Others see Abraham's faith
faltering. He should have remained in Canaan and have faith that
God would supply his needs. When he did leave for foreign
countries he should have had faith that God would protect him and
not introduce Sarah as his sister, thus exposing her to possible
adultery out of fear of the inhabitants.[7]

Abraham's seventh trial was that of a warrior in combat and a
victor in war. He rescued his nephew Lot and his intervention
turned the tide of battle in favor of the coalition led by the kings of
Sodom and Gomorrah (Gen. 14).[8]

Particularly painful was the eighth trial Abraham had to undergo
in sending away Hagar and Ishmael. Not only did he love them
both deeply, but there were moral considerations. Sarah had
undertaken in advance to recognize as her own offspring sons born
of the union of Abraham and Hagar, which Sarah had initiated, in
the hope that this would remedy her own infertility.[9] In demanding
of Abraham that he send away the maidservant and her son she was,
in effect, repudiating her word. Moreover, by sending out Hagar and
Ishmael, Abraham was essentially depriving them of all claims to
the family estate.[10] On the other hand, Ishmael, of whom the angel
of the Lord predicted, "He shall be a wild ass of a man; his hand
against everyone and everyone's hand against him. . . " (Gen.
16:12), was a corrupting influence on Isaac. Torn by conflicting
loves and by the rival claims of what law and society allowed but
what righteousness demanded, Abraham, left to his own decision,
would have resisted Sarah and not sent away Hagar and Ishmael.
God, however, intervened, telling the reluctant patriarch to accede
to Sarah's demand. God sees what Abraham cannot see, that it is
through Isaac that Abraham's line is to be continued and the divine
mission carried forth while divine protection will be granted the

servant and her son, for he too will become a great nation (Gen. 21:12-13).

The culminating trials of Abraham's life were God's commandment to sacrifice his son Isaac on the heights of Mount Moriah and the death of Sarah caused, according to rabbinic tradition, by the impending death of her son.[11] It is no accident that when Erich Auerbach searched for a biblical narrative to illustrate the laconic style of the Bible, whose psychological and religious depth forces the reader to supply description and detail from his or her own imagination and experience, he selected Gen. 22, known in Hebrew as the *Akedah*, "the binding" (of Isaac to the altar).[12] The story of how God, without forewarning, commanded Abraham to offer Isaac as a sacrifice, and then, as the father "put out his hand and picked up the knife to slay his son," intervened to prevent the slaughter, substituting a ram for Isaac, has fixed itself in the religious imagination of Jews, Christians and Muslims.[13]

Abraham's ten trials foreshadow the tests of Moses in Egypt (Exod. 2:11-22), the trials of the Israelites in the wilderness (i.e., Exod. 15:22-26), and the trials of Job. In a wider sense, as scholars have suggested, the court circles of David established a typological link between Abraham and David and adapted their royal histories to the older patriarchal narratives. This antitype was set up anachronistically retrojecting to Abraham the divine promise that "kings shall come forth from you" (Gen. 17:6).[14] In the post-exilic period the life of Abraham served as a prototype for the promise of a blessing for those who heed God's command to return to the Promised Land. Just as Abraham was promised numerous descendants and bounty (Gen. 12:1-3), a blessing fulfilled in the course of time, so Israel, the antitypical heir of the patriarch, could anticipate renewal if the people returned to the land of their ancestors (Isa. 51:2).

Isaac, too, was torn by conflicting loves. He loved Esau, according to the rabbis, for his exemplary filial piety, and according to modern commentators, because he was drawn to the directness and the earthiness of his hunter-son, a man of the fields.[15] But the father was not unaware of his son's unfitness to carry forth the divine mission, the tradition of Abraham, and hence his love for the twin son Jacob, the continuer of that tradition. This antitype to Abraham's family conflict and divided loyalty is paralleled by an even more exact one in which Isaac's wife Rebecca is taken into the harem of Abimelech, the king of the Philistines, when Isaac passed her off as his sister duplicating the experience of his father and mother in the same court with the same king and in Pharaoh's court in Egypt.

Isaac himself became a prototype. The crucial image was his role in the *Akedah* on Mount Moriah, his faith and willingness to accept a destiny as victim which made him the martyr *par excellence*. The word "martyr" comes from the Greek meaning "to bear witness" and in post-biblical Jewish literature Isaac became the prototype of those bearing witness to the truth of their belief even at the cost of their lives. In the New Testament Isaac foreshadows the martyrdom of Jesus on the cross.[16]

Jacob

Jacob as biblical and rabbinic tradition portray him, was a quiet, thoughtful, sedentary man, a stranger to the rough and tumble of life and innocent of the violence that often accompanies it. He was a man who used his wits to survive among antagonists who were far more powerful than he. Aware of the uncertainties of life in a dangerous, corrupt world, Jacob anticipated the future, planned for it and worried about it. He took his brother's birthright with an eye to the future leadership of the household. He allowed his mother to persuade him to deceive his father and take his brother's blessing lest Esau, on the basis of that blessing, mistakenly consider himself to be the inheritor of the religious-ethical tradition of Abraham, so alien to his nature and way of life.[17] Jacob made stipulations in legal or quasi-legal terms with God, with Esau, with Laban and with his mysterious opponent concerning future circumstances. Legal agreements are the instruments of the weak to guarantee their rights; the powerful often disdain them. Jacob, unlike Esau, deferred his gratification fourteen years, until he could have his beloved Rachel as his wife. These are the qualities that made him the fit bearer of Abraham's covenant. Through the life of Jacob the biblical narrator reminds us that historical destiny is not completely in the hands of God; the individual also brings it about by keeping an eye on the distant horizon of present events.

But in the biblical perspective, covenantal privileges do not automatically bestow moral perfection. By stealing his brother's blessing and deceiving his father, Jacob set in motion the law of reciprocity (discussed in the previous chapter) so that his own life was blighted by deceptions perpetrated on him by Laban, his sons, and even his beloved wife Rachel (Gen. 31:25-35).[18] Jacob had other faults. He was a passionate man. The conflicting loves of his life tormented him and led him into error and tragedy. His love for Rachel was so overwhelming that he was unjust to Leah. His love for Joseph and Benjamin led him to slight the other sons.

Jacob's confrontation with the mysterious adversary (Gen. 32:25-30) was an epochal turning point in his life. The episode can be understood metaphorically as an internal struggle in which the patriarch overcame moral and intellectual flaws to rise to new heights of spirituality. But it can also be interpreted as an archetypal event foreshadowing the destiny of Jacob's descendants in their struggle with the non-Jewish world.[19] On the other hand, the prophet Hosea interprets Jacob's encounter with the divine being not as symbolic of the patriarch's spiritual growth but as a presage of his descendants' religious rebellion. In Hosea 12 the entire northern kingdom of Israel becomes the antitype to the prototype of the third patriarch. Drawing on a pentateuchal clue, the prophet narrows the focus on Jacob's life only to his personal deceptions seeing in them the foreshadowing of northern Israel's national misconduct. In a similar vein, the prophet Jeremiah, drawing on the Jacob narrative, makes the Hebrews of his time the antitypical target for accusations of dishonesty using the darts drawn from their prototypical ancestor's interpersonal relationships (Jer. 9:3-5).[20]

Joseph

According to rabbinic tradition the whole course of Joseph's life was but a recapitulation (with antitypical variations, of course) of the life of his father Jacob.[21] There is much truth in this assertion. Joseph's difficulties, like Jacob's, were the results of a combination of circumstance and character. He was brilliant, charming, handsome and so extraordinary a boy that Jacob, succumbing to the weakness of his father Isaac, could not resist showing preference. The favoritism, combined with an innate narcissism, made Joseph spoiled, proud of his brilliance, and a show-off. So arrogant did he become, and so insensitive to the feelings of others, that he made that unpardonable remark not once but twice to his brothers: "I dreamed that you bowed down to me" (Gen. 37:7-9).

Sold by his brothers as a slave and carried down to Egypt, Joseph like his father, found himself in a turbulent, corrupt, foreign environment in which he must survive among powerful antagonists through his industry, his integrity and his wits. Like his father, Joseph suffered from the relentless law of reciprocity. According to the biblical commentators, Joseph's dream of power and his narcissism reasserted themselves when as the chief steward in Potiphar's house "he began to eat and drink and curl his hair."[22] It was then that his master's wife tried to seduce him and because he rejected her advances, he was dismissed and thrown into prison.[23]

Like his father, Joseph surmounted his personal failings and overcame his adverse circumstances.

But Joseph was not a mere double of his father. Jacob, the tent dweller, was not driven by ambition for wealth and power. His needs were simple. Having achieved a measure of status and security after much struggle and suffering he would have been content to live among the sheiks of Canaan. Joseph, in contrast, was driven by the ambition for kingship. He saw how the descendants of Esau had become princes of fiefdoms and wielders of power (Gen. 36). Why should the sons of Jacob remain country bumpkins drifting in the backwater of history? Joseph's dreams were more than dreams of power. They suggest that it is possible for a man to bend the forces of nature and economics to serve him (a very modern idea) and ultimately Joseph, confounding the astrologers of Egypt, did just that.

Jewish tradition calls him *zaddik*, the righteous one, for ultimately resisting the allures and temptations of his Egyptian environment. On attaining power he used it wisely and humanely and became reconciled with his brothers, but only after he made them suffer measure for measure for the suffering they inflicted on him.[24] In the end, Joseph served to further the divine design by which the descendants of the patriarchs went down to Egypt as hungry refugees, to go up generations later to the land of Israel as God's chosen people.

If Joseph is the antitype of his father Jacob, Daniel is the antitype of Joseph. Like his prototype Joseph, Daniel is a foreigner in a strange land who survives by his wits and with divine help interprets dreams that enable him to rise to high rank in a monarch's court. Joseph's incarceration and providential release are paralleled by Daniel's confinement in the lions' den and his miraculous deliverance.

Moses

It was Moses who served as the catalyst in the transformation of the Hebrew clans into a nation. Moses was prophet, legislator and leader of a people. These various roles were not compartmentalized in his life but within the depths of his soul mingled into a most rare unity. This personal unification of seemingly disparate callings reflected a new ideal-the realization of the unity of religious, social and political life under God in the community of Israel.[25] Only the cultic aspect of religion was given to Aaron the High Priest, Moses' brother, so that religious unity was still symbolized by the family unit. In the implementation of this vision, in transferring the pattern of his own undivided human life (and that of Aaron) to the life of his people, Moses was met by unremitting resistance on the part of the Israelites. He did not want to use force nor did he wish to impose himself on his people. He wanted to bring them so far along that they themselves could become priests (Exod. 19:6) and prophets (Num. 11:29).

Moses, the Bible tells us, "was a humble man, more so than any other man on earth" (Num. 12:3). This humility mirrored his fundamental belief in spontaneity and freedom but it also provoked the rebellion of Korah and his followers (Num. 16). They sought to split the unity of the religious, social and political life embodied in Moses and his brother Aaron by demanding a portion of that authority for themselves.[26] Moreover, the rebels declared that the people were already holy so that they no longer needed to choose between good and evil using the Torah as their guide.[27] It was a declaration that challenged the essence of the divine plan. Moses called for the destruction of the rebels just as he ordered the levites to fight against the people after the sin of the Golden Calf (Exod. 32:25-28).

The destruction of Korah and his followers would have engulfed the entire community of Israel had not Moses interceded for them. The life of Moses is a vivid illustration of the dialectical tension the prophet undergoes between passive transmission of divine anger and pronouncements of doom for the people on the one hand and active intercession on behalf of the people in the name of prophetic love on the other hand. The prophet is not a mere channel for the transmission of the divine message; he is a sensitive personality who sympathetically identifies with the intensity of divine emotion and at the same time feels surging within him the emotional identification with his people. God expects this two-fold emotional response from the prophet who must see in two directions at once, from God's perspective and from the people's vantage point. At times the tension between the two becomes unbearable and in the life of Moses constituted his grandeur and his tragedy.[28]

That Joshua is the antitype of Moses is made explicit when God tells him that, "I will be with you as I was with Moses" (Josh. 3:7). It is further confirmed by the retrojective typology in which the crossing of the Sea of Reeds under Moses becomes the paradigm of the crossing of the Jordan under Joshua (Josh. 3:13; cf. Exod. 14:21-22; Exod. 15:8). It is finalized by the narrative voice in the Book of Joshua which reports that from that time on the people revered Joshua all his days as they revered Moses (Josh. 4:14). Elijah too becomes an antitype of Moses in a geographical typology that links the two prophets by God's revelation to them (described in similar language i.e., 1 Kings 19:11-12; Exod. 19:16, 18-19) at the same site, Mount Sinai (1 Kings 19:8-18). The new Temple envisioned by Ezekiel is the spatial typology that links him to Moses as an antitype. As Moses envisioned the wilderness Tabernacle as a blueprint of the heavenly shrine (Exod. 25:9, 40; 26:30; 27:8), so does Ezekiel's vision of the new Temple correspond to a heavenly model (Ezek. 40-43). Finally, the Deuteronomist makes Moses the prototype of all true prophets (Deut. 18:15), and the redactors of the prophetic traditions portray the prophets as being commissioned like Moses by having their mouths prepared to utter the divine word (Exod. 3:12; 4:10-16; Deut. 18:18; Jer. 1:9). But the antitype is expanded in the End of Days to include all Israel who will have God's word placed in their mouths (Isa. 59:21; Joel 3:1-2; cf. Num. 11:29).[29] In the New Testament, particularly in Matthew, Jesus is the antitype of Moses.

David

David, as portrayed by the chronicler of the books of Samuel and Kings, is the most universal man of the Bible. He was fighter, friend, lover, singer, statesman, man of God, and in each of these capacities he was outstanding, a classic example of what the Greeks call *arete*, excellence. Through a vast variety of human relationships David emerges a protean figure who, as the second king of Israel, was enshrined in Jewish tradition as the prototype of the messianic redeemer. All subsequent Hebrew kings and even post-biblical exilic leaders become antitypes of David.

The contrast with Saul is striking. Saul, the first king of. Israel, began his reign under the cloud of being that which Samuel had *not* wanted and which God had finally granted (1 Sam. 8:11-22). In the political history of ancient Israel Saul represents the transition from the charismatic but transient leadership of the judges, whose reigns were coterminous with the crises they were summoned to manage, to the dynastic rule of monarchy. As the first king, Saul had the disadvantages of a transitional leader appointed as a grudging concession to popular demand as well as the personal defects of a vacillating character, a clumsy political touch and, worst of all, an unstable emotional constitution. To this must be added Samuel's denunciation of Saul and the proclamation of the end of his dynasty after the king's first blunders, the secret anointing of a successor during Saul's lifetime, the rising popularity of David, whom everyone (including Saul) recognized as the successor, and finally the death of Saul and Jonathan in the final battle with the Philistines. The picture is one of many failures overwhelming a few successes. Saul was a tragic figure, the victim of seemingly unjust circumstances.

David, as the king of Israel, was not under the historic handicap of his predecessor. The monarchy was established in Israel and David was everything that Saul was not. He was brilliant on the battlefield and a public charmer. He was a shrewd political manipulator who adroitly handled friends and enemies and wove his way through political minefields to attain the crown of a united kingdom. He was a farseeing statesman who, in making Jerusalem his political capital and the religious center of the nation, forged an indissoluble bond between nationalism and religion. David was a God intoxicated man. Saul was, too, but the difference was that Saul's prophetic frenzy elicited from the people the derisive question: "Is Saul also among the prophets?" (1 Sam. 10:11-12; 19:24). When David danced before the Ark it evoked awe and exaltation (2 Sam. 6:12-15).

But the man who was possessed, haunted, inhabited and harassed by God consciousness was also driven, bewitched, ensnared and tormented by earthly passions. The rabbis expressed it this way: "He who is greater than his neighbor, his *yezer* (evil inclination) is also greater."[30] David's lust and love for Bathsheba brought him to compound adultery with murder when he arranged to have Uriah, her husband, put in the forefront of the hottest battle where he perished. As in the case of other biblical heroes, David's sin, as the prophet Nathan made painfully clear, set in motion the law of reciprocity that brought a series of calamities to David's family life and personal wretchedness to the king: the death of Bathsheba's child sinfully conceived; the rape of David's daughter by his son Amnon; the murder of Amnon by his brother Absalom's command; the rebellion and death of Absalom; the thwarting of David's dearest ambition to build the Temple (on the grounds that he had shed much blood); and even on his death bed, the rebellion of his son Adonijah, who sought to seize the throne. David, like Abraham, Isaac and Jacob, had a weakness for his sons, an overweening fondness for Absalom, for example, that made him close his eyes to the tremendous danger that Absalom posed to the throne. On the other hand, his hatreds were as passionate as his loves. David's last will and testament to his son Solomon is a catalogue of scores to be settled, evidence of a rage and blood-lust that persisted into old age.

What saved David's life from being completely overwhelmed by these demonic passions was an intelligence, an instinct to pull back before it was too late. He listened to those who sought to save him from the throes of his emotions. He listened to Abigail when she sought to prevent him from killing her husband, Nabal, who had insulted David and his guerillas. He listened to Nathan's denunciation of his adultery and murder by proxy, accepting punishment without protest, thus saving his kingdom through penitence. He listened to Joab, his general, and overcame his blind love for Absalom to put an end to the latter's rebellion.

The Heroines

In a patriarchal society in which women are limited in legal privileges and in institutional functions, social convention confines them to the home and the family. The idyllic picture of the family circle in Psalm 128, mentioned in the introduction to this chapter, pictures the wife as a "fruitful vine in a corner of your house." The capable wife of Proverbs 31 has a far more active role "making cloth and selling it" and seeing to it "that her business thrives." But it is "her husband" who "is prominent in the gates" and who "sits among the elders of the land."

On the other hand, the biblical writers and the rabbis were well aware that women can be not only worthy partners but also daunting adversaries. Commenting on Gen. 2:18: "The Lord God said: 'It is not good for man to be alone; I will make a fitting helper for him,'" the rabbis take the words "a fitting helper" (in Hebrew *ezer ke-negdo*, literally, "a helper opposite him") to mean if a man merits it she is *ezer*, a helper; if he does not merit it, *ke-negdo*, she is an adversary.[31]

In this alternate perspective women are quite the equals of men (Eve being made from Adam's rib is a sign of that equality), morally and psychologically capable of exerting just as much power through intelligent resourcefulness. These women are not content to exist in a corner of the house but when thwarted by the world of men, or finding it deficient in moral insight or practical initiative, they have no hesitation in taking their destiny or that of the nation into their own hands.

The prototype of this activist woman in the Bible was Rebecca, a superb manager of people and circumstances. From her subtle management of her betrothal (Gen. 24) to her handling of that involved and explosive situation of the embezzled blessing, in which murder was latent, Rebecca displayed competence and unerring instinct. The antitypes of Rebecca span the spectrum of good and evil, encompassing women of every rank and circumstance in life. Esther was a manager of the first order although her stage was a royal court rather than a family hearth. Her speech entreating the king to spare her and her people (Esther 7:3-4) is a masterpiece of diplomatic technique, the climax of a carefully orchestrated plan in which seductive beauty, flattery, political maneuvering and perfect timing are all unerringly combined. Tamar, Judah's daughter-in-law (Gen. 38), defies law and convention and as a disguised harlot manages to get herself pregnant by her father-in-law. When found out she confronts him with the evidence of his weakness and insensitivity and escapes condemnation and death. The Bible gives us to understand that this clever manipulation of people and circumstances was for a higher purpose-for one of the twins to whom she gave birth was Peretz, the progenitor of Jesse, from whom came the house of David.

A similar high purpose was served by another managerial woman, softer, gentler than her counterparts, a woman whose Hebrew name testifies to her goodness-Naomi (meaning pleasant). Naomi is the patron saint of matchmakers. Her daughter-in-law Ruth, a Moabite woman who, like Naomi, has lost a husband to sickness and death, refused to leave her mother-in-law and returned with her to the land of Israel. Ruth's loyalty to Naomi, that bridges the differences in their ethnic and religious backgrounds, is epitomized by her reply to her mother-in-law's plea that Ruth shall remain with her own people. "Do not urge me to leave you, to turn back and not follow you. For wherever you go, I will go; wherever you lodge, I will lodge; your people shall be my people, and your God my God" (Ruth 1:16).[32] It is this unusual woman whom Naomi subtly and delicately leads into marriage with her kinsman Boaz. The son born of the union is the grandfather of King David.

The considerable effectiveness of women for the good was counterbalanced by the utilization of the same abilities for the purposes of evil. The managerial qualities of a Rebecca and a Naomi in a woman like Jezebel produce a biblical counterpart to Lady Macbeth, but without the latter's pangs of conscience. Jezebel suffers not even a temporary emotional upset in planning and executing the most diabolical crimes.

The seductive wiles of a Tamar used to further the divine plan become, in a woman like Delilah, the trap in which Samson is destroyed and Israel's destiny imperiled. The biblical typology of the temptress, representing the fertile gods and goddesses of Near Eastern paganism that seduce Israel from the divine covenant, is

concretized in Hosea's harlot wife Gomer, in the loose woman of
the Book of Proverbs (Prov. 2:16-19), and in the Moabite women
who lure the Israelite men into the orgiastic cult of Ba'al Peor
(Num. 25:1-4).

Job

As mentioned in the previous chapter, the Book of Job contains a
prose tale that provides the framework for a poetic dialogue. In the
prose narrative Job is a righteous God-fearing man, a non-Jew, one
of the heroes of ancient Near Eastern folklore who is mentioned
along with Noah and Daniel in Ezek. 14:13-20. Job is blessed with
abundant possessions and a large and happy family but he is
unaware that in the heavenly assembly the Adversary (Satan) has
challenged God to test the disinterestedness of Job's piety by
afflicting him. In rapid succession Job loses his possessions, all his
children and is stricken with itching sores from head to foot.
Rejecting his wife's urging that he curse God and die in order to put
an end to his suffering, Job sits down in the dust, resigned to his
fate. The central question of the prose tale is: Will the righteous
man stand the test?

The prose tale in and of itself is not especially remarkable. It
echoes earlier portions of the Bible in which Abraham and Isaac,
the tribe of Levi as well as the entire community of Israel are all
tested by God (Gen. 22; Exod. 16:4; Deut. 8:2; 33:8; Judges 2:22;
3:1, 4).[33] Job, like Abraham, stands the test and is restored to
health, wealth, prestige and a new family as the almost martyred
Isaac is restored to his father. In this respect, Job is an antitype of
Abraham, Isaac and the community of Israel. But this is the only
link to biblical typology. The author of the Book of Job deliberately
removed his characters from any specific historical context so that
Job is the closest to a purely archetypal figure among the characters
of the Hebrew Bible. He hails from the "Land of Uz," a mythical
place which scholars have sought to identify with a variety of
locations. The members of Job's community are referred to as *B'nai
Kedem*, "people of the East," a generic term referring to the lands
east of the land of Israel. Job's friends come from places that do not
have historical or geographical specificity but are derived from
names of people listed in the genealogy of Esau in the Book of
Genesis.[34] Job is not a Hebrew and when he defends his integrity
against the accusations of sin by his friends, his protest of
innocence (Job 31) contains no reference to the observance of the
Jewish ritual law. His guiltless suffering makes him a universal

symbol for a suffering humanity, a view already articulated by a rabbi of the third century C.E., Resh Lakish, who declared: "Job was never created, nor did he ever exist but is simply a parable."[35]

The author of the Book of Job, with consummate artistry and profound spiritual insight, has intertwined the prose tale and the poetic dialogue in such a way that he has deepened the theme of the book to an extent that would have been impossible had the prose tale or the poetic dialogue stood alone. From this perspective, the Book of Job is the story of the spiritual transformation of a good man into a wise man.[36]

Job's piety, as described in the prose tale, though admirable, is based squarely on the doctrine of reciprocity. It is the piety of the Book of Proverbs (see chapter six) and it is significant that in the Hebrew Bible Job comes right after Proverbs.[37] Job avoids evil because he realizes the penalties. The moral order as he understands it is a *quid pro quo* between God and man. Wealth and the good life are given in exchange for religious ritual and good deeds. But Job harbors a lurking fear that in an unstable world this exquisite balance can be upset so that the Lord can deliver him to the forces of evil. He becomes anxious about making the slightest mistake and this leads him to make burnt offerings for each of his children not because they have committed any sins but because they *may* have had blasphemous thoughts. This is what William James has called "the religion of the sick soul." [38] The mirror of the state of Job's religion on earth is the dualism represented by the wager between God and Job's Accuser in heaven.

Job's fearful religiosity has deep psychological roots. Like his friends he has a driving need to posit an absolutely predictable moral world order directed by God. It stems from a desire for ultimate security, for perfect control over one's destiny. Just as the savage could never be sure that his proficiency in the hunt would guarantee food on his table and so he developed magical practices and later, moral and religious ones to extend his power over the unexpected, so does religious fundamentalism offer a seeming escape from the human predicament into a desired ultimate security through scrupulous attention to ritual and morality.[39]

Anxieties have a habit of projecting themselves from psychological into physical reality and no human being, no matter how pious, can have complete dominion over life's exigencies. In the poetic portion of the book at the climax of his first speech, Job admits that his fearful premonitions turned out to be accurate (Job 3:25). As the full weight of his calamity settles down on him, Job becomes too terrorized from within his anxiety to do anything *but* bless the Lord. Who knows what even more horrible consequences there might be in store for him? Before any spiritual transformation can occur, Job will have to be willing to let his hidden anxieties emerge. He will have to enter the storm of his own psychic chaos and go to the bottom of despair before his servile, fearful piety that masks a will to dominate will allow him initially to stand up for himself and shake his fist at God and finally accept in humility the inscrutable will of his Creator.

It is this emotional and spiritual cleansing that puts off his friends. In the beginning, with sensitivity and delicacy they sit with him in silence seeing how great is his suffering. But Job's active rebellion in anguish forces them to argue with him. They cannot understand that Job's curses and blasphemies are really cries of pain because they are locked into the rigid orthodoxy of the doctrine of reciprocity. Thus the dialogue is more psychological than theological. Ironically, the dualism of the prose prologue is carried into the poetic dialogue. The accusations of the Accuser are absorbed by Job and his friends. The more the friends become Job's accusers, the more Job becomes the accuser of God.

Purged psychologically and spiritually, Job is now ready to listen to his Creator. When the Voice speaks from the Whirlwind, the act of divine revelation confirms the humanity of Job. God, as Job's friend Elihu claimed, cares enough about humans to reveal Himself to them in order to give them some intimation of the nature of the universe and their place in it. As the psalmist says: "The Lord is near to all who call Him, to all who call Him with sincerity" (Ps. 145:18). God's answer to Job consists mostly of questions, a good Jewish trait but also characteristic of Zen Buddhism and psychoanalysis. Like the Hasidic or Zen master and the psychoanalyst, God's questions are intended to force Job to see the brilliant, intense light of reality; so intense that it hurts, and to prevent him from shading his eyes with the illusions of his ego and his comfortable grief. Job has made of his suffering a *cause celebre* and in so doing he has blotted out every aspect of existence and sought to focus God's attention only on himself. God's questions imply that Job can break through the self-centeredness of his suffering by contemplating the vast mysteries of the universe of which he is but an infinitesimal speck. This is not an answer that could be imposed from without; it could only come from within Job as he resonated to the questions from the Voice in the Whirlwind.

Job is spiritually transformed (Job 24:1-6). The prose epilogue confirms that Job's return to his former state of health, prosperity, family and possessions are but the visible sign of his inner transformation. Job's anxiety has vanished and so has the Accuser. The dualism of the prose prologue mirroring Job's former religious outlook has been replaced in the prose epilogue by a unified, integrated, tranquil spirituality reflecting the transformed Job. As we saw in the conclusion and comparison section of chapter three, dualism is connected with an absolutist patriarchal outlook that seeks to suppress the feminine mythology that preceded it. Thus in the prose prologue Job's daughters are hardly mentioned except to show that they are dependent on the hospitality and largesse of their brothers (Job 1:4). In the prose epilogue, where dualism has been greatly diminished, Job's daughters are on center stage (they are named and described while Job's sons remain anonymous, Job 42:13-15). They are dignified equally with their brothers by being given a share of their father's wealth.[40]

The Meaning of Suffering

What does the reader of the Bible learn about the meaning of suffering from the struggles of the biblical protagonists? Clearly, as noted in an earlier chapter, it is the danger of hubris, human arrogance, that is the prelude to some kinds of suffering. Men like David who have exceeded the limits instinctively pull back before suffering is converted into disaster. Others persist and in their persistence trigger what can be termed double motivation. One of the villains of the Bible, the Pharaoh of the Exodus, exemplifies this tendency. During the first half of the ten plagues Pharaoh's stubbornness in refusing to let the Israelites leave Egypt is self motivated. The Israelites were a valuable property and their slave labor contributed mightily to the grandiose projects of the despot. In the second half of the ten plagues and in the pursuit of the Israelites after the exodus (Exod. 7:22; 8:11,25,28; 9:7; 9:12; 10:20, 27; 11:10; 14:8), God is said to have hardened Pharaoh's heart. The rabbis explain it this way: "God gives warning a first, a second, a third time and if an individual does not repent He closes that person's heart to repentance in order to punish him(or her) for sin. Wicked Pharaoh received God's emissaries five times and ignored their warnings; so God said: 'You have chosen to stiffen your neck and harden your heart-now I on my part will add to your guilt.'"[41] Elsewhere the rabbis raise this idea to a life principle. "He who seeks to defile himself, the way is opened for him, he who seeks to purify himself receives (divine) help."[42]

Not only the vice of arrogance but even an excess of virtue leads to human anguish, if positive human emotions like love are allowed to run riot, without wisdom or moderation to restrain them. The unbridled loves of the patriarchs and of David for favorite sons are the examples the Bible underscores. Similarly, an excess of righteousness can lead to disaster. Commenting on Eccles. 7:16, "So don't overdo goodness and don't act the wise man to excess, or you may be dumbfounded," the rabbis cite the examples of Saul and Solomon. In the case of Saul the rabbis say that he who is merciful to the cruel will end up being cruel to the merciful. Saul, who could not bring himself to kill Agag, the murderous king of the savage Amalekites and his entourage-even though under divine command, he had gone to war to liquidate this ruthless enemy (1 Sam. 15:2-34)-was the same man who could give the order to kill all the people of Nob, the city of priests, men, women and children (1 Sam. 22:11-19).[43] Solomon's over reliance on his great wisdom led him to transgress the laws of the Torah by multiplying wives, amassing silver and gold, and increasing his horses and stables.[44] Saul was unable to secure the throne for his descendants and Solomon was unable to secure a united monarchy for his posterity.

Pain is also the product of the law of reciprocity but if the individual recognizes it, this understanding can lead him or her to higher levels of spirituality and illumination. There is some indication in the Bible and its commentaries that this was the case with Jacob and in the conflict of Joseph and his brothers. Even without a full understanding of its origin, pain can lead to what existential psychology today calls self-actualization. It can spur the individual to become more courageous, more loving, more compassionate, more spiritually wise. This clearly is one of the underlying themes of the Book of Ruth and the Book of Job.

The rabbis in discussing suffering, which they called *yissurin*, distilled its origins into five categories.[45]

1) Some are brought upon an individual as challenges or tests such as the trials by which Abraham and Job were tested. In meeting these challenges one rises to higher levels of spiritual and mental development.[46]

2) Some forms of *yissurin* come as an inevitable aspect of human frailty and the course of nature. The example used is that one who gathers myrrh must get his hands gummy.[47]

3) There are *yissurin* of love that are sent upon a person simply to increase his or her reward in the afterlife.

4) Some types of suffering are intended to wipe out sins and even the most righteous are not free of sin.

5) Other kinds of *yissurin* are visited upon the leaders in their role of responsibility for the people. Moses' anguished leadership is a

prime example. Moreover, the suffering of martyrdom by righteous leaders is intended to serve as a symbol to the community to raise its moral level and its dedication to God. Thus Rabbi Akiba, the post-biblical antitype *par excellence* of Isaac on the altar, suffered martyrdom at the hands of the Romans.[48]

In the final analysis the finite mind of a mortal cannot completely understand the infinite causes of human affliction. This emphasis on partitive knowledge as a given of the human condition makes the Book of Job a hallmark of biblical wisdom. The Hebrew wisdom literature, like its counterparts in the Far East and in the Occident, is not primarily concerned with objective knowledge but with living intelligently. Unlike the scientific philosophers of all ages who seek to embody truth in definitive theories or systems, the wisdom teachers, as Confucius put it, are interested "in watching truth affecting the way people grow." Growth means change and it requires a knowledge that is content with partitive claims, claims that are suitable for certain times, certain places, certain people, and certain circumstances. It is this open-ended knowledge that God commends to Job.

Though possessing only partial understanding, a human being can use it as a basis for a deeper faith. We are aware of the beauty and harmony in the natural world even though we cannot understand all its secrets, so must we believe in the rationality, the justice and the ultimate meaning of suffering even though we cannot fathom its depths. The rabbis understood this and that is why they looked upon *yissurin* as the burden of earthly toil, trial and struggle which everyone must shoulder on the ascending path that brings humanity closer to God.[49]

Notes

1.   *Gen. R.* 8:11 (ed. Theodor-Albeck), pp. 64-65.
2.   *M. Avot* 2:4; *Midrash Psalms* 16:2 (ed. Buber), p. 120.
3.   *b. Eruvin*, 13b.
4.   This love is epitomized by R. Akiba: "Beloved is man for he was created in the divine image." *M. Avot* 3:14.
5.   Jubilees 17:17; 19:3,8; *M. Avot* 5:3; *Avot de Rabbi Natan*, Ch. 33 (Version B, Ch. 36) ed. Schechter, p. 47b; *Gen. R.* 56:11 (ed. Theodor-Albeck), p. 609 and note thereon; *Midrash Psalms* 18 (ed. Buber), p. 153. cf. Louis Ginzberg, *Legends of the Jews* (Philadelphia: Jewish Publication Society of America, 1947), 5:218, n. 52.
6.   Adin Steinsaltz, *Biblical Images* (New York: Basic Books, 1989), pp. 14-19 insightfully points out that monotheism was the primary, basic and dominant belief of humanity as far back as human memory goes;

polytheism was a later development. In this respect Abraham was not an innovator but an ultraconservative calling for a renewal of a primary and ancient religious faith. Thus the Hebrew monotheistic revolution was restorative rather than innovative.

In the Second Temple period Abraham became a role model for proselytes to Judaism who, like him rediscovered the one God, separated from their pagan environment and in the case of men, underwent the rite of circumcision. *Yer. Bikurim*, 1:4; *M. Gerim* 4:3; *Gen. R.* 38:11 (ed. Theodor-Albeck), pp. 361-364; 46:2; Moses Maimonides, *Igrot u- She'elot u-Teshuvot*, (Warsaw, 1882), pp. 70-71 and "The Proselyte" in *The Judaic Tradition* ed. by Nahum M. Glatzer (Boston: Beacon Press, 1969), pp. 395-96. cf. my "Two Views of the Patriarchs: Noahides or Pre-Sinai Israelites" in *Texts and Responses: Studies in Honor of Nahum Glatzer* ed. by M. Fishbane and P. Flohr (Leiden: E. J. Brill, 1975),p. 56.

7.   *Gen. R.* 40:2 (ed. Theodor-Albeck), p. 382; Ginzberg, *Legends*, 1:221; 5:220; *Zohar*, Genesis (Vilna: Rom Publishers, 1882), p. 80b; Rabbi Moses ben Nachman (Nachmanides) *Commentary on the Torah*, ed. by C. B. Chavel (Jerusalem: Mosad ha-Rav Kook, 1962): 1:81. On the new light cast on this incident as a result of recent discoveries see E. A. Speiser, "The Wife-Sister Motif in the Patriarchal Narratives" in A. Altmann, ed. *Biblical and Other Studies* (Cambridge: Harvard University Press, 1963), pp. 15-28.

8.   Josephus, *Antiquities*, 1,10,1 and Philo *De Abrahamo*, 233 emphasize Abraham's military achievements due, according to Josephus, to his strategic skills and leadership abilities and, according to Philo, to a combination of skill and faith in God. The rabbis, in contrast, view the victory as a miraculous act of God. See the sources cited in Ginzberg, *Legends*, 5:216, n. 46 and 225, n. 97. Josephus and Philo seek to counter the charge of cowardice heaped upon the Jews in the Greek speaking world. The rabbis, living after the disasters of the Roman-Jewish War and the Bar Kokhba Rebellion sought to tone down the martial spirit. cf. Louis H. Feldman, "Abraham the General in Josephus" in *Nourished with Peace: Studies in Hellenistic Judaism in Memory of Samuel Sandmel* ed. by Frederick C. Greenspahn, Earl Hilgert and Burton L. Mack (Chico, Ca.: Scholars Press, 1984), p. 49.

9.   S. Kardimon, "Adoption as a Remedy for Infertility in the Period of the Patriarchs," *Journal of Semitic Studies* 3 (1958): 123-126. In Gen. 30:17-18, Leah gives expression to this popular belief.

10.   According to the laws of Hammurabi, the sons of a slave-wife are entitled to an equal share of the inheritance if the father legitimizes them. If he does not accept them as his sons, the mother and her sons must be given their freedom. See Nahum Sarna, *Understanding Genesis* (New York: McGraw Hill, 1966), p. 156.

11.   Ginzberg, *Legends* 3: 286-87.

12.   *Mimesis* (Princeton: Princeton University Press, 1953), pp. 15-16.

13.   In the Jewish and Christian traditions see Shalom Spiegel, *The Last Trial*, trans. with an intro. by Judah Goldin (New York: Pantheon Books, 1963) and the sources cited there. On Islam see Koran, Sura 37:99-100 and

the Hadith quoted by al-Tabari in *Ta'rikh* 1:184-85 and his *Tafsir* (commentary). Soren Kierkegaard, *Fear and Trembling*, trans. Walter Lowrie (Princeton: Princeton University Press, 1941) saw in the *Akedah*, a classical illustration of the truth that the demands of faith rise beyond ethical demands and sometimes the two are irreconcilable.

14. R. Clements, *Abraham and David: Genesis XV and its Meaning for Israelite Tradition* (London: SCM Press, 1967), pp. 55-60.

15. Ginzberg, *Legends* 1:332-33; 5:278, n. 51. Mark Van Doren and Maurice Samuel, *In the Beginning Love: Dialogues on the Bible*, ed. Edith Samuel (New York: The John Day Co., 1973), pp. 84-86.

16. II Maccabees, Ch. 7, the story of "The Woman and Her Seven Sons" who refused to bow down to the idol during the persecution of Antiochus IV and were killed as they hallowed God's name. The story was embellished and anachronistically transferred to the period of the Hadrianic persecution by the rabbis. During this time the legends arose that Isaac actually died on the altar but was resurrected. During the massacres and mass suicides of Jews, who, during the Crusades, preferred death to forced baptism, the image of the sacrifice of Isaac became a dominant motif of synagogue poetry. See Spiegel, *The Last Trial*, 28-37. In the New Testament Isaac foreshadows the martyrdom of Jesus on the cross. cf. Romans 3:23-26; 4:18-25; 5:8, 12, 18-19; 8:32; Galatians 1:4; 3:8,13-14; 4:28; I Corinthians 15:14, 20-21; Colossians 1:15-18. See also the Epistle of Barnabas VII,3; VII,10; ed. Kersopp Lake *The Apostolic Fathers* I (1925), p. 340 f.

17. Maurice Samuel argues in *Certain People of the Book* (New York: Alfred A. Knopf, 1955), pp. 166, 168, that Isaac never dreamed of bestowing the blessing, i.e., the charges, commandments, statutes and laws of Abraham on Esau and Rebecca never suspected him of such folly. What she feared was that Isaac would bless Esau with material things and Esau would claim this as the blessing of Abraham from which Jacob was excluded, thus distorting the legacy for future generations.

18. On the measure for measure of the deceptions see Nehamah Leibowitz, *Studies in Bereshit (Genesis)*, 4th revised ed. (Jerusalem: World Zionist Organization, 1981), pp. 322-24.

19. Ibid., 366-70.

20. cf. Fishbane, *Biblical Interpretation in Ancient Israel*, pp. 376-79.

21. Ginzberg, *Legends*, 2:4-5; 5:325, n. 4.

22. Commentary of Rashi to Gen. 39:6. cf. Leibowitz, *Studies in Bereshit (Genesis)*, pp. 413-15.

23. The Bible contrasts Joseph's sexual continence with Judah's sexual incontinence by juxtaposing Gen. chapters 38 and 39. cf. Alter, *The Art of Biblical Narrative*, p. 10.

24. In contrast to the rabbinic tradition and Thomas Mann in *Joseph and His Brothers*, Maurice Samuel indicts Joseph as a brilliant failure in *Certain People of the Book*, p. 10.

25. Martin Buber, *Moses: The Revelation and the Covenant* (New York: Harper Torchbook, 1958), p. 186.

26. The rabbis portray Moses as replying to Korah: "Other nations have many religions, many priests, and worship in many temples, but we have one God, one Torah, one law, one altar and one high priest." cf. Ginzberg, *Legends* 3:293.

27. Buber, *Moses:*, pp. 189-90.

28. Yochanan Muffs, *Love & Joy: Law. Language and Religion in Ancient Israel* (New York and Jerusalem: The Jewish Theological Seminary of America, 1992), pp. 9-48.

29. Fishbane, *Biblical Interpretation in Ancient Israel*, pp. 358, 371, 374.

30. *b. Sukkah*, 52a.

31. *Gen. R.* 17:2 (ed. Theodor Albeck), p. 152.

32. The rabbis take these words as an indication of Ruth's determination to accept the Jewish religion, despite what Naomi, in compliance with the Jewish injunction, told her of the difficulties of the Jewish law. See Ginzberg, *Legends* 4:32; 6:190, nn. 44-45. Ruth thus becomes a role model for female converts to Judaism just as Abraham became the prototype for male converts.

33. cf. Yehezkel Kaufmann, *Toledot ha-'Emunah ha-Yisraelit*, 2nd ed. (Jerusalem-Tel Aviv: Mosad Bialik, 1953) vol. 2, Bk. 2: 613-15.

34. Gordis, *The Book of God and Man*, pp. 66-7.

35. *b. Bava Batra*, 15a. A slight textual variant reads: "Job was created solely to serve as a parable." cf. Ginzberg, *Legends* 5:381, n. 3.

36. Moses Maimonides, *The Guide of the Perplexed* 3:22-32 (ed. Pines): 486-531. cf. *The Book of Job* trans. with and intro. by Stephen Mitchell (San Francisco: North Point Press, 1987), pp. vii-xxx.

37. In some translations of the Bible, Job precedes Proverbs. The Talmud (*b. Bava Batra*, 14b) has Job preceding Proverbs and following Psalms but also following Proverbs as we have it in our Hebrew editions (*b. Berakhot*, 57b). The custom of placing Job after Psalms and before Proverbs stems from a tradition assigning the book to the time of the Queen of Sheba (Job 1:15; *b. Bava Batra*, 15b.) The custom of placing Job after Proverbs was probably conditioned by the view that Job was among those who returned from the Babylonian exile (*b. Bava Batra*, 15a).

38. William James, *The Varieties of Religious Experience* (New York: Vintage Books, 1990), pp. 121-154.

39. John T. Wilcox, *The Bitterness of Job: A Philosophical Reading* (Ann Arbor: The University of Michigan Press, 1989), pp. 202-3. Henri Bergson, *The Two Sources of Morality and Religion*, trans. R. Ashley Audra and Cloudesley Bereton with the assistance of W. Horsfall Carter (New York: Holt, 1935), contrasts this conventional religion satisfying the need to control with mystical religion. Psychologists speak of the "illusion of control." See Ellen J. Langer, "The Illusion of Control," *Journal of Personality and Social Psychology* 32 (1975): 311-28.

40. William Blake (1757-1827) the English mystic, poet and artist understood that the central theme of the Book of Job is spiritual transformation. In his first illustration to Job portraying the atmosphere of the prologue, the patriarch and his wife are seated at evening prayer with

Bibles open on their laps, their children are kneeling around them while the sheep and the dogs are drowsing and they themselves look up to heaven in drowsy piety. The musical instruments of the family hang silently on a tree. In the last engraving portraying the epilogue, the whole family is standing up with faces illuminated exuberantly playing their favorite instruments. See *Blake's Job: William Blake's Illustrations of the Book of Job* intro. and commentary, S. Foster Damon (Providence, RI: Brown University Press, 1966), pp. 12, 52. The talmudic debate between R. Yohanan ben Zakkai who claimed that Job's piety was rooted in fear and R. Joshua ben Hananiah who argued that it was rooted in love (*M. Sotah* 5:5 and *b. Sotah*, 31a) is reconciled in this interpretation. In the prologue Job served the Lord from fear but in the epilogue he served God in love.

41. *Exod. R.* 13:3; Moshe Greenberg, *Understanding Exodus*, vol. 2, Part 1 of the Melton Research Center Series (New York: Behrman House, 1969), pp. 138-40.

42. *b. Yoma*, 38b; *b. Shabbat*, 104a and *Tosafot ad loc* s.v." *It d'garsinan*." According to Philo, an individual is free to choose good or evil but in his choice of the good he is not left completely on his own. Once he has demonstrated his strength in curbing his evil inclination and in recognizing that the strength to choose the good comes to him from God, God comes to his aid and helps him. In contrast, the choice of evil is completely in the hands of the individual. cf. Wolfson, *Philo* 1:448-50.

43. *b. Yoma*, 22b; cf. Steinsaltz, *Biblical Images*, pp. 137-43.

44. Ginzberg, *Legends* 4:129; 6:281-82, nn. 14-16 referring to Deut. 17: 16-17.

45. *Gen. R.* 92:1 (ed. Theodor- Albeck), pp. 1136-38. See also the commentary of *Yefeh Toar* (R. Abraham Yoffa) on these passages.

46. This idea was brilliantly developed into a dialectical theology of the human ascent toward God by the great Hasidic master R. Nahman of Bratslav. See Arthur Green, *Tormented Master: A Life of Rabbi Nahman of Bratslav* (Tuscaloosa, Ala.: University of Alabama Press, 1979).

47. *Canticles R.* 1:3.

48. *Semahot* 8; *b. Sanhedrin*, 39a; *Mekhilta de Rabbi Ishmael* on Exod. 22:22 (ed. Lauterbach) 3:141-43; Ephraim Urbach, "Ascesis and Suffering in Talmudic and Midrashic Sources (Hebrew) *Yitzhak Baer Jubilee Volume*, ed. S. W. Baron, B. Dinur, S. Ettinger, I. Halpern (Jerusalem: The Historical Society of Israel, 1960), pp. 57-61.

49. Matthew B. Schwartz, "The Meaning of Suffering, A Talmudic Response to Theodicy," *Judaism* 34, 4 (1983): 444-51; cf. David Kraemer, *Responses to Suffering in Classical Rabbinic Literature* (New York: Oxford University Press, 1994).

Olympus: Role Models From Myth

General Archetypes vs. Individual Typologies

The Greek myths are not unified by a singular goal like the human ascent toward God or a progression of typologies validating the movement of human history. Long before the Greeks became conscious of a meaning in the sequence of events (see chapter nine), they had been telling and retelling the same tales both in the limited but connected narratives of epic and in the shorter verse forms of lyric and drama. The traditional tales retold became archetypes rather than typologies, that is, universal characters or patterns independent of history rather than a series of prototypes and antitypes embedded in it. As archetypes, the traditional heroes and heroines from the remote past were unconnected to the lives of current leaders. Attached to isolated sagas of powerful families long dead, they were also removed from the fray of contemporary rivalries between city-states and could become pan-Hellenic and even universal symbols of the general human condition. So the individual archetypes, e.g., great warriors with names like Achilles, Ajax, or Hector, or wise leaders like Odysseus or Oedipus, could themselves be subsumed under a more general archetype—the good person who fails to lead a good life, a pattern which demonstrates the vulnerability of being human.[1]

Because the character patterns are more universal in themselves and because the actions and themes in their lives are so similar to each other and to the universal rhythm of human life, I will discuss general themes and archetypes, providing specific examples, rather than catalogue the individual Greek heroes and heroines, in the manner of the typologies which point forward and backward in the longer Hebrew history.

But the Greek archetypes also have a historical dimension. For, as Greek society evolved and went through its own characteristic changes, the traditional tales became the medium for examining issues in the present *sub specie aeternitatis*. Aeschylus, for example, could use the bloody saga of the house of Atreus to remind his audience, so recently fragmented by civil strife, that they themselves had developed from savagery to civilization because they were willing to submit to the rule of law. So too tragedians could use Thebes and the aberrant behavior in the Theban houses of Cadmus and Oedipus to define what was not Athenian and thereby direct Athens toward self-examination.[2] Thus the Greek archetypes have their own history which can be traced even to the twentieth century when, for example, French, Eastern European, Japanese, and Irish artists have re-presented *Antigone* with new emphases in order to examine such current cases of human failure as two World Wars, and the Irish Troubles.[3]

Pessimism, Humanism, and the Archetype of Vulnerability

Zeus was not a creator with a special love or far-reaching plan for human beings. In fact, he had once been malevolent enough to attempt their destruction and torture their savior (v. Aeschylus' *Prometheus Bound*). If the god eventually granted them justice and other blessings, still the human race was doomed not only to old age and death, but also to a life which included miseries by definition. Held responsible for one's actions and constantly warned to "know himself," "obey the limit," and "avoid excess," the human being had to beware of transgressing or offending a host of gods. Sometimes one could be caught between two opposing divinities, like Orestes between the Furies and Apollo. Although time might reveal the cosmic order through the working out of retributive justice, the ephemeral individual was perplexed about the gods' plan at the moment of crisis. The chorus of Aeschylus' *Suppliant Maidens* proclaims the mysteriousness of Zeus even as they pray to him as their kinsman and protector: "His will not easily traced . . . Dark are the devices of his council. His ways blind to our sight." (87-90).

From this perspective, human beings have little to expect from life beyond the certainty of punishment for transgression. The conversation between Glaukos and Diomedes on the battlefield of Troy reveals the fear of error and the pessimism about the value of one individual's life. Before he strikes, Diomedes asks the name of his enemy, lest in his zeal he assault a god by mistake. Glaukos replies with a simile that compares the generations of humans to the generations of leaves which the wind scatters on the ground (*Il.* 6.119-150). The riddle of the sphinx that Oedipus solved expresses the inevitable limits: Question - what is it that has one voice but is four footed, two footed and three footed:"; answer - Man, as crawling babe, self-sufficient adult, and old man too weak to support himself.[4]

If the mid-point leaves room for hope, it is also filled with danger. So Oedipus' previous good fortune only increases the Thebans' pessimism after his self-discovery. In words analogous to Rabbi Gamaliel's, the chorus of elders conclude "Count no mortal happy until he's completed his life without suffering pain" (Sophocles,

Oedipus the King, 1529-30).[5] The Greeks' awareness of their vulnerability to luck or fortune (*tuche*), to things which just happen to them, without their own responsibility or agency, led them to speculate on the safest paths to a good life and the ways to use reason to control the contingencies which might lead to a bad one.[6] Still the chorus of Sophocles' *Oedipus at Colonus* affirm that it would be best never to be born at all and next best to die quickly (1224-7; v. Herodotus 1.31).

But, like the Hebrews, the Greeks did place humanity in the middle, between the blessed gods whose immortality precludes real suffering and the animals who have not been granted *dike* (e.g., v. Hesiod *Works and Days* 276-280; Aristotle *Politics 1253a*). Heracles, who has both a divine (Zeus) and mortal (Amphitryon) father, embodies the human potential at all points on a scale. A hero of prodigious animal appetites, strength, and temper, he wears a lion skin symbolic of his triumph over animals as well as his own animality. With his club, a tool devised by man, he has civilized the world, ridding it of the monsters that threaten society, but in a fit of madness, he has also killed his own children. In comedy, he is depicted as a lusty gourmand (v. *Birds, Frogs*); in tragedy, he is capable of great sensitivity and intelligence (Euripides' *Alcestis, Heracles*). Several of his labors (e.g., bringing back the Golden Apples and Cerberus) suggest the mortal hero's conquest of death. Because of his extraordinary suffering and toil, the gods welcome him to Olympus as an immortal after he dies in excruciating pain.[7]

Human beings, in their lifetime, could become closer to the gods, or godlike, if they achieved excellence (*arete*) imitative of divine perfection in important endeavors or characteristics.[8] The Greek verb *aristeuein* may have originally meant "to be bravest in warfare", but the quest for achievement and the fierce competition for preeminent position as the best extended to all areas of physical, intellectual, and aesthetic human activity. Children were taught to be both "speakers of words and doers of deeds" (*Il.* 6.208), the best in council as well as in battle. Athenian festivals included contests between rhapsodes, poets, dramatists, actors, singers, dancers, and musicians, in addition to athletes. The division of some contestants into peer groups enabled young and old to compete for recognition.

Preeminence brought great rewards to the individual. On the one hand, he received honor (*time* or *kudos*) in the form of prizes (*gera*) from his peers. Epic sagas indicate that the rewards were more than pay or outward symbols of inner worth. Rather they were the actual equivalents of the real worth of the superior individual in the estimation of his group.[9] For this reason Achilles reacted as if Agamemnon had taken his honor away when he took his war prize.

Honor brought more than material rewards, however.[10] It might also confer a kind of immortality on the heroic mortal if his deeds were praised by the poets. The earliest Greeks thought of Hades only as a repository for dead shades, not as a place of punishment or blessed afterlife. If their names and glorious achievements were preserved in song, however, they would defeat death by attaining everlasting fame (*kleos*). Such excellence, worthy of an eternal reputation, raised the whole society further above the animals and closer to the perfection of the divine. The beautiful Helen, "so terribly like the immortal goddesses in appearance" (*Il.* 3.158), the health and strength of the prize-winning athlete, the courage and prowess of the godlike warrior, the reasoned argument of the cleverest speaker all exemplified the divine ideal and encouraged imitation of it. Praise of such excellence had its antithesis in blame (*ainos*), warning society against the 'don'ts' as well as encouraging the 'do's'. So Helen, aware of the destruction she and Paris have caused, laments that their shame will live on in song (*Il.* 6.356-358).

Those who excelled had a responsibility to the society that honored them above the others. They had to fulfill the duties expected in their preeminent position in order to merit the expected respect (*aidos*) in the form of prizes, honor, and appropriate behavior toward them. If one failed to perform his duty, he would feel shame (also *aidos*) and receive blame from his community who depended on him, as Hector explained when he rejected his wife's plea that he retreat to a safer position (*Il.* 6.442-3).[11] The harmony of society rested on such reciprocity between superior performance of duty and appropriate rewards for preeminent position.[12] It also rested on the sense of obligation to the group felt by the individual who was exalted by his community. The *Iliad* dramatizes the significance of the reciprocity by tracing the disasters that occur after Agamemnon dishonors both the priest and his best warrior and then his best warrior in turn dishonors his friends by demanding more honor at their expense.

In book 12 of the *Iliad*, Sarpedon's speech to rally his comrades articulates the connection between the performance of duty, the competition for excellence, and the quest for immortality.

> Glaukos, why is it you and I are honored before others
> with pride of place, the choice of meats and the filled wine cups
> in Lykia, and all men look on us as if we were immortals . . . .
> Therefore it is our duty in the forefront of the Lykians

to take our stand; and bear our part of the blazing of battle, . . .
Man, supposing you and I, escaping this battle,
Would be able to live on forever, ageless, immortal,
so neither would I myself go on fighting in the foremost
nor would I urge you into the fighting where men win glory.
But now, seeing that the spirits of death stand close about us
in their thousands, no man can turn aside nor escape them,
let us go on and win glory for ourselves, or yield it to other.
(310-328, Lattimore, trans.)

His words suggest that the inevitability of death gives all human actions real consequences and makes human excellence particularly beautiful.[13] Although the gods live on forever, their lives seem dull in comparison. Divine problems are ultimately trivialized by the absence of real stakes. Divine perfection precludes change and the excitement of striving to be the best. So the Greeks glorify their portion as struggling mortals and attack the problems of life with zest. Odysseus chooses his aging Penelope and the chaos in Ithaca over Calypso's eternal beauty and static life. Nor would the dead hesitate to return to their life of contingency, choice, and pain. After hearing of the honor and glory the Greeks have bestowed on him, the shade of Achilles in Hades assures Odysseus that he would rather be the live servant of a poor farmer than lord it over the house of the dead (*Od* 11. 488-491). Sophocles, friend of the sophist Protagoras and citizen of Athens at its zenith, summarizes the Greeks' pride in human rationality and art (*techne*) which helped them to survive and prosper.[14] The first stasimon of *Antigone* begins "Many the wonders but nothing is more wondrous than man" (1.332). After listing his conquest of the sea, the earth, the birds of the air, and animals, the chorus continues:

Language and thought like the wind
and the feelings that make the town,
he has taught himself, and shelter against the cold,
refuge from rain. He can always help himself.
He faces no future helpless. There's only death
that he cannot find an escape from. He has contrived
refuge from illnesses once beyond cure.
(353-61, Wyckoff, trans.)

From this perspective, the literature, and indeed the entire culture of the Greeks, may be considered anthropocentric. The power and the ultimate justice of the gods (or natural law) are almost always a given, but the authors generally concentrate on human beings. As Bruno Snell has written of the *Iliad*, "Human action does not serve a higher divine cause, but quite the reverse. The story of the gods contains only so much as is needed to make happenings on earth intelligible."[15] The interaction of the two planes both elevates and defines the life of mortals. The gods are the models, sources, and patrons of all physical, intellectual, and aesthetic abilities which make human life pleasurable as well as bearable. Their various anthropomorphic emotions, individual personalities, and professions, as well as their familial, social, and political roles on Olympus provide a metaphysical validation of the possibilities and problems of men and women in public and private. Yet their juxtaposition with humans underscores the contrasts. In the *Iliad* Agamemnon may be Zeus' surrogate among the Greeks at Troy, but his wisdom and power are limited. The human king cannot foresee the consequences of his behavior and he cannot control his opponent Achilles with a threat of violence. Zeus' quarrel with Hera on Olympus dissolves into laughter, feasting, and lovemaking, whereas Agamemnon and Achilles do not meet again until their argument has brought destruction to countless men in both camps.

Myths and sagas like the *Iliad* continued to be recited and reinterpreted for centuries because they dramatized the attempts of god-like human beings, "whose inventive craft may drive them at one time or another to good or ill" (*Antigone* 362-364), to comprehend and master themselves and their world without offending heaven. Most of the myths concentrate on characters whose preeminence in highly valued qualities such as strength, wisdom, beauty, integrity, power, and responsibility places them at the boundaries of human possibility. The various story patterns then illustrate how events outside their personal control, or conflicts between chosen values, or internal passions provoke actions which change the direction of their lives and illustrate, in Nussbaum's words, "the gap between our goodness and our good living, between what we are . . . and how humanly well we manage to live."[16]

The archetype is most familiar from Aristotles's definition and analysis in *Poetics*. The fact that the character is good but not perfect, and is, like the rest of us, prone to error (*hamartia*), leads the audience or reader to identify with him. When he suffers a misfortune all out of proportion to his intent or culpability, we feel both pity for him and fear for ourselves, recognizing that like misfortunes could happen in our lives as well, a kind of intellectual/emotional 'clarification' or 'illumination' which Aristotle called *catharsis*.[17] According to Oliver Taplin, the ordered sequence of events and the moral context in which social, intellectual, and theological conflict is set out and examined make the universal experience of suffering more concrete and comprehensible.[18]

Achilles' behavior in the *Iliad*, for example, dramatizes both the beast/man/god spectrum and the inevitable vulnerability in being human. He is godlike (*dios*) in his beauty, swiftness, and strength as well as in his prodigious wrath (*menis*). Although he has formerly been magnanimous to his inferiors and, like Saul, merciful to his enemies, he crosses the boundaries of human nature when aroused to fury by the death of Patroclus, for which he is partly responsible; his inhumanity is emphasized by the similes which compare him both to savage beasts and suprahuman fire. Yet once he has assuaged his rage, he discovers his common bonds with other mortals, articulates the new wisdom gained from his painful experience, and heroically faces his own death.[19]

This archetype has many specific variations in the plethora of Greek sagas. The Greeks could re-use such myths to talk about the present because the complexity of such great characters involved in equally complex situations enabled later generations to discover their own issues in them and through them express new perceptions about what it means to be human and how to lead a reasonably good life. Thus, without the antitypes offered by a program of history, the archetype Achilles could represent the heroic warrior of the noble past, on a quest for honor and glory, to a more cynical Athens whose current leaders acted only for their own political and material advancement (e.g., Sophocles, *Philoctetes*). For Socrates refusing to desert his post assigned by Apollo, Achilles was also a positive model: the steadfast soldier, who chose death rather than dishonor (*Apology* 28 b-d). In contrast, Plato pointed to Achilles' excessive emotions, greed for gifts, and irreverence to men and gods as egregious examples of all the wrong lessons in Homer (*Republic* 386c-391c).[20]

So too the main events and characters of the Trojan War, where men won glory, could be re-presented in the light of the power politics of the Peloponnesian War period (e.g., Euripides, *Trojan Women, Iphigenia at Aulis*; Sophocles, *Philoctetes*). Prometheus the trickster in Hesiod could be viewed by a later democratic society as humanity's savior from Zeus' tyranny and the divine source of all human technology in *Prometheus Bound* (v. Plato, *Protagoras*). Orestes the matricide, a positive role model for Telemachus in the *Odyssey*, became the prism for later examinations of divine justice, perversions of domestic and political relations, and the ingenuity of humans in crisis (e.g., Aeschylus, *Oresteia*; Sophocles, *Electra*; Euripides, *Electra, Orestes, Iphigenia at Taurus*). Sophocles retold the saga of the house of Oedipus three times from different perspectives at three different points in his life and the life of his city (*Antigone*, 442 B.C.E.; *Oedipus Tyrannus*, c 429, during the plague in Athens; and *Oedipus at Colonus*, 406, anticipating his own death and the final defeat of Athens).

Archetypes for Living, "Good or Ill': General Paradigms

Through stories of bold characters in action, the culture transmitted its guides to all important social roles, the accepted ways to achieve personal success and glory, and its definition of the limits to human endeavor. The corpus of Greek myth displays a plethora of role models for special skills, professions, social status, sexes, stages in life, and personalities. Their interactions demonstrate correct behavior in a variety of situations.

Some people had a unique place in society by virtue of their position or fortune. Hermes on Olympus and Talthybius and Eurybates in the Greek camp at Troy define and validate the crucial and therefore sacrosanct position of the herald. So too the skills and personality of the crippled Hephestus give dignity to those men who are relegated to the forges because they are unable to fight. Priests, seers, and poets deserved special respect because they were close to the gods and possessed extraordinary insight. Beggars, suppliants, and strangers too were special, as the unfortunates under the protection of Zeus.

Their appearance in the narrative reveals and transmits, through positive and negative example, the proper and civilized code of behavior toward one another. Agamemnon cannot insult a priest of Apollo with impunity. Nor will Polyphemus who eats his guests or Penelope's suitors who abuse their host and ridicule beggars go unpunished. The relationship between leaders and subordinates necessarily differs in peace and war. Thersites must not challenge the king's authority during a war, but the warrior Odysseus who beats him into silence in the *Iliad* shares his life and secrets with his loyal but lowly servants in the *Odyssey*.

Like the Hebrew typological figures, most of the deities and people belong to families and must confront all the complexities of domestic life. The variety of married couples (e.g., Zeus and Hera, Aphrodite and Hephestus, Heracles and Deianira, Priam and Hecuba, Hector and Andromache, Helen and Paris, Agamemnon and Clytemnestra, Penelope and Odysseus) presents a spectrum of possible patterns, some more fulfilling than others. The close bonding of parent and child is elevated by the parallels between

Thetis' suffering for Achilles and Priam's grief for Hector. Zeus' tears of blood for his dying son Sarpedon, or Hecuba's savagery after her last child's death testify to the depth of feeling possible. Although Zeus achieved power by rebelling against his parent, a similar succession drama will not be tolerated on the human plane. The proper transition between the generations is implicit in the maturation of Telemachus, who both aids and is aided by his father Odysseus, and the respect shown to the aged Laertes after he has removed himself from power. As in the sagas of Jacob and David, the consequences of dishonoring parents and destroying families by adultery, kindred murder, or sibling rivalry are clearly illustrated by the vertical reciprocity of the curses on the great houses of Laius at Thebes and Atreus in Mycenae.

The traditional tales offer a variety of role models for women.[21] The major goddesses—Artemis, Aphrodite, Hera, Demeter, Athena, and Hestia—validate the various stages and types in Greek women's lives as well as their skills and spheres of interest: maiden, nubile sex kitten, mature wife, mother, capable masculine woman, and spinster adjunct to the household. Myths such as the story of Demeter and Persephone, Cupid and Psyche, and the daughters of Danaus recount the painful transition from maidenhood to mature sexuality, the first two from the perspective of the mother and mother-in-law as well as the virgin. The pairs Demeter and Persephone and Clytemnestra and Electra personify the joys and miseries of the mother-daughter relationship whereas Electra and Antigone validate the affectionate relationship of brother and sister and father and daughter.

Although women were important as food providers, spinners, nurturers, and household managers, they contributed most as loyal wives and bearers of sons. Therefore the queens of the great houses are the most enduring female archetypes and their lives illustrate what women can and cannot achieve. Helen clearly has *arete*; her great beauty raises her closest to the gods. Even the Trojan men whose lives and city will perish on her account say "Surely it is no great shame to fight over such a woman" (*Il.* 3.156-57). But she is wretched and self-deprecating, dissatisfied with Paris and ashamed of herself in the *Iliad* and a villainess in Euripides' *Trojan Women*. The virtuous Phaedra, like Helen, has too much Aphrodite, an insatiable lust for her stepson which overcomes her will to be a good woman, a loyal wife, and an upright queen. Both she and Medea illustrate the dangers of female excess—immoderate passion, too much love turned too quickly to too much hate. Clytemnestra too is a negative model, threatening to men, like

Medea, because of her cleverness, but also a "man-counseling" (*Agamemnon* 11), ambitious, and treacherous woman, unnatural enough to choose a weakling as a lover, kill her husband, and hate her children.

All these, like Jezebel, Delilah, and Gomer, are *femmes fatales*, whose wiles entrap their men and threaten their communities. The goddesses who tempt Odysseus on his journey home, Circe, Calypso, and the Sirens, are simpler versions of the type. But the positive role models are inspiring. Penelope is the best wife, loyal through the long years. Like the activist biblical heroines Rebecca, Tamar, and Abigail, she uses her feminine wiles to save herself, her family, and her community; she is shrewd enough to put off her suitors and to test the authenticity of her husband with tricks, and yet modest enough to defer to men. Andromache is both the loving wife of Hector and a *mater dolorosa*. After her husband dies in battle and their young son Astyanax is murdered by the Greeks lest he grown up to be an enemy warrior like his father, she prefers death to the possibility that she might enjoy living with another man. In Euripides' *Trojan Women*, Andromache describes how she has been the best wife to Hector: aiming high at honor, she did all that brought her a reputation for discretion and she did not do what she longed to do, to leave the house, to display her wit, to dispute with her husband (643-56). Her self-restraint approaches the ideal for womanhood put forth by Pericles in the Funeral Oration: the greatest glory belongs to her "who is least talked of among the men whether for good or bad" (Thucydides 2.46).

Specific Types

Warriors— Among the myriad population of Olympus and the microcosm, certain male types stand out for their potential to be most godlike. Since brave warriors were essential to the survival of the group, those who possess strength, speed, and courage are most likely to achieve the kind of merit which wins the respect of their peers, the tangible prizes of honor, and everlasting glory. Almost all the important gods and warriors demonstrate their athletic ability, prowess in battle, their occasional cowardice, the enmity which makes them fight like savages, and the courtesies to opponents and loyalty to friends by which they maintain their humanity amidst the gore. Some men even get the opportunity to dramatize how to kill and die heroically.

Four heroes are outstanding warriors whose valor brings fame to them and safety to their companions: Diomedes, Ajax, Achilles, and Hector. The particular dangers of such great strength are revealed in their sagas, however. Achilles, respected and honored as the bravest and best of the Greeks, sets himself too far above the others to accept Agamemnon's offer to restore his honor with extra prizes and a public apology. Because he now believes that his honor comes from Zeus, not men, and is too angry at Agamemnon to give in, he rejects his friends' request to fight to save them and permits his weaker friend Patroclus to fight (and die) in his place. He returns to the battle too late, when his honor has become less important than his crazed need to avenge Patroclus' death. Hector, the valiant defender of doomed Troy, becomes deluded by his victories in Achilles' absence and forgets the limits to his own very great power. He foolishly forces a confrontation with Achilles which, as he recognizes too late, can end only in death for him and defeat for Troy. A similar delusion has led Patroclus to stay on the battlefield too long and venture too far from the Greek camp. Ajax, the equal of Hector, accepts his position as the fighter second to Achilles, but cannot endure the slight when the Greeks give the dead hero's weapons to Odysseus instead of to himself. Outraged, he tries to kill his fellow leaders, and, when he fails, he kills himself instead.

Wise Leaders— Good rulers who are wise and flexible are as essential as warriors to the survival of the community. In fact, the Greeks voted to give Achilles' arms to Odysseus because his cleverness was judged of greatest value to the group. Odysseus, "the man of many turnings," able to plan, speak, and do, as well as fight, is, like Jacob, never at a loss in any situation. Athena's patronage only confirms his own excellence as a man who thinks before he acts. His role as trusty advisor to the foolish Agamemnon in the *Iliad* is supplemented by his behavior as the leader of the expedition home where he displays his cunning and expertise in domestic, political, and economic situations. Older characters like Nestor complement Odysseus as archetypes for inactive men who can call upon their reason and experience to benefit the group. Those who reject the advice of a wiser or cooler head endanger themselves and their communities, as Hector learned when he disregarded Polydamus' warning to retreat before Achilles returned to battle. Epic or dramatic type-scenes of assemblies and councils or arguments in which intelligent men debate crucial issues find their parallels in Thucydides' account of the Athenian community where, according to Pericles, even ordinary citizens were able to follow intelligent discussion and make fair judgments about public matters (2.40).

But wisdom too has its dangers and its limits. Overproud of his successful strategems against Polyphemus, Odysseus flaunted his true name and thus brought the Cyclops' curse and Poseidon's enmity upon himself and his men. To the dramatists of the Second Peloponnesian War period (v. Sophocles, *Philoctetes*; Euripides' *Trojan Women, Iphigenia at Aulis*) Odysseus' "many turnings" looked suspiciously like the amoral expediency practiced by the new leadership. Sophocles' audience must have disapproved of Odysseus' situational ethics ("I am the one for whatever the occasion requires . . . . To win in every case is what I crave," *Philoctetes* 1049-52), especially when placed side by side with the integrity of the young Neoptolemus, whom he tries to corrupt, and the courage of the wounded warrior, Philoctetes, whom he had abandoned for the sake of victory. Those mythical kings who used their cunning for themselves instead of for their gods and subjects are exposed as vicious villains through juxtaposition with wiser and better men (e.g., Aegyptus' herald and Pelasgus in Aeschylus' *Suppliant Maidens*, Creon and Theseus in Sophocles' *Oedipus at Colonus*, and Lycus and Amphitryon in Euripides' *Heracles*). The lives of Oedipus, Creon in *Antigone*, and Pentheus demonstrate that too great confidence in human reason can lead even well-meaning, responsible leaders to catastrophe (see below).

Martyrs— Some characters are martyrs who choose to suffer for the sake of a principle. Antigone refused to betray her beliefs even at the threat of death. In the name of obedience to the unwritten laws of god, loyalty to the family, and love of her dead brother, she disobeyed Creon's decree and buried the traitor Polynices. Bold enough to defy the king and articulate her reasons clearly, she was bold enough to kill herself before Creon had time to rescue her. So too, the philosopher Socrates, described like a hero in the writings of Plato and Xenophon, preferred death to abandoning his mission from Apollo. Other martyrs of saga die to preserve the safety of their cities: the virgin daughters of Leos for Athens; Aristodemus' daughter for Messina; Menoeceus, the son of Creon, for Thebes.[22.] In at least three cases, the tale parallels the near-sacrifice of Isaac, where an animal was substituted for the victim at the last minute. According to Euripides' *Iphigenia at Tauris*, Artemis spirited away the virgin and left a stag on the altar to die in her place; Phrixus' father Aeolus provided a ram to replace his son; Pelopidas offered a mare to satisfy the gods' demand for an auburn-haired virgin as the price of victory. Whatever the external compulsions or responses, however, tragedy, like Plato's dialogues about Socrates' trial and death, concentrates on the reasons why the martyr chooses death. After first protesting, Euripides' Iphigenia accepts her sacrifice and rejoices in its consequences; she will be savior of Greece, protector of the guest-friend relationship, and avenger for the abduction of Helen as well as the obedient servant of divine Artemis (*Iphigenia at Aulis* 1378ff; cf. Macaria in Euripides *Heracleidai* 500-35).

Prophets— The prophets of saga are also essential to the community both because they receive knowledge from god more directly than others and because they can intercede to warn humans of error or ward off disaster. Calchas, seer and interpreter of the omens for the Argives, knows how to end the plague sent by Apollo by making Agamemnon return the girl and by instructing the men to perform the proper rites of propitiation. Tiresias, priest of Apollo at Thebes, knows the truth about Oedipus and can predict the future when warning Creon not to bury Antigone alive. His words lead Creon to repent and rescind his decree. Like the poet Homer, Tiresias is blind because he sees what other men cannot.

Interesting and necessary as these prophets are, however, they are not heroes in their own right, as Moses and his antitypes are to the Hebrews. Rather the Greek prophets are advisors to the preeminent, providing them with facts or conditions about the supernatural which will affect their success or failure. Like the Hebrew prophets, they are often endangered by the unpleasant truths they must proclaim, but the Greek prophets are only foils to the more powerful, whose misfortunes, improprieties, and ignorance they expose.

Complexities of the Archetypes: Characters in Action

Being the best was dangerous. As Artabanus warned Xerxes, "You know how god always hurls lightning bolts at the biggest buildings and tallest trees, for he loves to abuse the prominent" (Herodotus, *Histories* 7.10). The Greeks, like the rabbis, believed that those who were greater than their neighbors were also more inclined toward evil. Several passages of poetry describe the situation in which "too much (*koros*) of a good thing" (*olbos*, prosperity from god in the form of power, wealth, or honor) "gives birth to hubris" in men "whose minds are not sound" (Solon, frag. 5; cf. Aeschylus, *Agamemnon*, 763-71; Sophocles, *Oedipus the King*, 873-77). When such men act under the delusion (*ate*) that they can satisfy their own lust for more at the expense of others, they bring divine retribution (*Ate, nemesis, timia,* etc.) upon themselves.[23]

In *Persians*, Aeschylus reveals how Xerxes, mighty ruler of all Asia, in his rash attempt to shackle Greece to his empire, arrogantly shackled the divine waters separating the two continents. The ghost of Darius, Xerxes' father, recognizes a universal paradigm for failure in his son's defeat of Salamis.

> For hubris blossomed faith and grew a crop of ruin (*ate*),
> And from it gathered in a harvest full of tears.
> As you look upon these deeds and recompense (*timia*) for them,
> Remember Athens and Greece and let no man hereafter,
> Despising what he has from heaven, turn lustful eyes
> To others, and spill a store of great prosperity (*olbos*).
> For Zeus is standing by, the punisher of thoughts
> Too boastful, a harsh and careful scrutineer.
> (821-28, Podlecki, trans.)[24]

Still Xerxes' situation is more complicated than the sequence from *olbos* to *koros* to *ate* to hubris to Ate as nemesis suggests. The poet creates some sympathy for the hero because he is a youth who was poorly advised and because the gods tempted him toward the ruin which was the natural consequence of his folly. Darius summarizes the principle behind this divine/human complicity: "Whenever someone presses on, the gods join with him," (742). The chorus in Sophocles' *Antigone* echoes this idea: "Whoever confuses the evil with the good, the god leads toward *ate*" (622-4).

The notion that the gods cause men to sin resembles God's hardening of Pharaoh's heart, the evil spirit sent to Saul, and the *yezer ha-ra* (evil impulse) of the rabbis. Like the Hebrews, the Greeks believed that the divine compulsion was related to the individual's character so that human beings' actions are attributed to both an external force and an inner reality. This idea, termed double motivation or determination by classical scholars, appears as early as the earliest Greek literature.[25] In the *Iliad*, Agamemnon, for example, later blames Zeus for the insult to Achilles, claiming that the god hurled "savage delusion" into his heart (19.86-94; 134-138). Sometimes the divine compulsion and the individual "ethos" express the same reality, as when Helen, Paris, or Phaedra, whose passion overcomes their reason, are controlled by Aphrodite, the goddess of love (e.g., Euripides *Trojan Women* 981-990), or when Athena, goddess of wisdom, enters the scene as her favorites deliberate with themselves (e.g., *Il.* 1.195-221; *Od.*13.296-99). Often, however, the gods seem drawn to "the tallest trees" to place

them in situations where they will be able to err if hubris is
incipient in their characters. About Niobe, who was punished for an
excess pride in her children which led her to insult Leto, mother of
Artemis and Apollo, her nurse says

> A god causes a fault to grow in mortals, when he is minded
> utterly to ruin their estate. But none the less, a mortal must
> abstain from rash words, carefully nurturing the happiness
> that the gods give him. But in great prosperity, men never
> think they may stumble and fill the cup of their fortune. So it
> was that this woman, exultant . . . in beauty . . . (fragment
> from Aeschylus *Niobe*, Lloyd Jones, trans).[26]

In some cases the external force of gods and curses represents the
factors outside our own agency (*tuche*), which we might call
heredity or environment. All the characters in Aeschylus'
Agamemnon are trapped by the curse on the house of Atreus and the
failure of the blood vendetta to restore order. They see themselves
as instruments of divine Dike (Justice) who must punish violations
against god and man, as if they have become the spirits of
vengeance, the Furies or Erinyes, incarnate.

Yet if they think the gods will not punish their own impieties and
atrocities, they learn a hard lesson when they receive justice in
turn, as Agamemnon did. Or, if like Clytemnestra, they insist they
murder in the name of justice, while displaying the lust, jealousy,
and ambition which the murder satisfies, they will be held
accountable for their own motives and excesses. When
Clytemnestra claims to be a fury avenging the sacrifice of her
daughter Iphigenia, the chorus of elders agrees that her murder of
Agamemnon may avenge all the murders of innocent children in the
house of Atreus, but they refuse to proclaim her innocent (1505-
1512).

Their response implies that Agamemnon's murder has two
explanations—the divine compulsion of the fury and Clytemnestra's
own will. So too Oedipus' curse on his sons carries its own effective
power. Yet Antigone insists that Polynices has the power to defuse
the curse by refusing to fight his brother. "See how you fulfill his
prophecies," and "You go with open eyes to death", she cries as he
chooses kindred murder and suicide rather than disgrace in
Sophocles' *Oedipus at Colonus* (1426; 1440).

Like Polynices, Agamemnon, at the beginning of the *Oresteia*,
must make a choice between two injurious alternatives. His high
positions as general of the Argive army and head of his household
require him to decide between aborting the expedition to Troy and

sacrificing his daughter Iphigenia; to commit either act would be unthinkable in other circumstances. We cannot help but pity him when the chorus describes his agony. For, as Nussbaum points out, like Abraham, this "good (so far) innocent man must either kill an innocent child out of obedience to a divine command, or incur the heavier guilt of disobedience or impiety." [27]   In the biblical context, such a situation became a test of faith to which God responded by saving Isaac. In his deliberations, however, Agamemnon barely mentions the external forces which should affect his choice. Instead, he struggles between two different human values, love for his daughter and duty to his troops. And he chooses to sacrifice Iphigenia rather than abandon his men and expose himself to disgrace.

One cannot blame Agamemnon's decision; he has been forced to choose between two wrongs by contingencies outside his control. But one does not sympathize with his response or ensuing behavior. Instead of being repelled by murdering his child, Agamemnon judges it an act of piety (*themis*) and performs it willingly, optimistic about its outcome. Instead of learning from his painful experience, he is irreparably harmed by it and becomes a far worse person.[28]   The chorus makes clear that the situation and then the act itself brought out in Agamemnon boldness, recklessness, daring, infatuation—all the words for moral imperfection manifested later in the play by his total annihilation of Troy and its altars, his seizure of Cassandra, and his trampling of the blood-red carpet.

Other famous characters prove to be wiser and better men than Agamemnon, but, like him, they are endangered by their high positions in which they must make choices and be responsible for them even though they can't foresee the consequences. Aristotle chooses Sophocles' *Oedipus the King* as the best tragedy and Oedipus is probably the best example of a good man who falls through a combination of circumstances beyond his control and his own actions.[29]   On one level, his misfortunes were determined by his father's crimes which resulted in the curse on the house of Laius. Nor could Oedipus prevent his own birth and exposure, the herdsmen's acts which saved him, or the drunk's insults which aroused his curiosity about his true parents. His responses to the insult, to the oracle, to the old king's assault at the crossroads, to the sphinx, to the plague, and to the truth about himself are his own, however, even if Apollo could foresee and predict them. They stem from his curiosity, intelligence, self-confidence and sense of decency, as well as his rashness, all of which are displayed in Sophocles' play about his self-discovery. If in his zeal to save his city he gets angry and insults the priest who withholds vital information, if he draws the wrong conclusion from his facts and almost condemns Creon for conspiracy, we cannot find evidence here of a glaring fault that explains those heinous crimes he did commit. We can only blame his literal error in not knowing who his true parents were. In Sophocles' last play, Oedipus *at Colonus*, the old hero insists he sinned in ignorance. "In me myself you could not find such evil as made me sin against my own" (966-7). He is different from Creon, Polynices, and Eteocles who wronged and ruined him with full knowledge (166-75).

We cannot extrapolate a *koros hubris ate nemesis* pattern from Oedipus' story. Rather we must see his fall as an illustration of the vulnerability of even the best mortals because of the mutability of life and the limitations of human knowledge. Even the wisest of us does not know basic facts about himself and cannot comprehend or control all aspects of the situation. Therefore, all human beings must beware of placing too much confidence in either reason or success. Croesus, king of Lydia, assumed that the oracle of Delphi was predicting victory against Persia when it told him he would destroy a mighty empire. To his complaint that the oracle had misled him into defeat, Delphi responded that he should have asked which empire (Herodotus *Histories* 1.91). Perhaps if Oedipus had repeated his question, "but who are my real parents?" after the oracle responded the first time with a non-sequitur, "You will kill your father and marry your mother," he would have returned to Corinth and lived happily ever after. But he, paradigm for all good and reasonable men, reacted to the prophecy with horror, assumed it referred to the Polybus and Merope of his question, and fled toward Laius, the sphinx, and Jocasta.

The failure of the best human intelligence to perceive or control all pieces of a problem is a crucial element in the models of great suffering. Creon, in Sophocles' *Antigone*, for example, begins as a reasonable defender of principles that maintain civil order and public safety. When opposed, however, he betrays an insensitivity to religious traditions and family feelings as well as disrespect for individuals and excessive reliance on his own reason. Although other characters call his behavior hubris, this hubris alone does not cause the tragedy. He is flexible enough to change his mind, but he cannot prevent the suicides of the loved ones he has denigrated. In the end, he blames his failure on himself and acknowledges his ignorance. Nussbaum suggests that both Creon and Antigone suffer such great misfortune because they have attempted an impossible simplification of human life; they have tried to limit the tensions caused by conflicting values by selecting only one value to live by and ignoring all others.[30]

Some heroes are depicted as victims of circumstances or bad luck whose own conscious choices play little part in their suffering. After Philoctetes was bitten by a snake, he had to endure terrible agony. Because his cries of pain and foul odors from the festering wound disturbed his fellow soldiers, he was abandoned on a desolate island, left to loneliness and a constant struggle for bare survival. Heracles, hated by Hera even before his birth, was condemned to a life of labor in the service of others, compelled to kill his family in a fit of madness, and tricked, albeit accidentally, into an excruciating death by his jealous wife. The older Oedipus considered himself a victim of others, gods and humans; he was acted upon rather than one who acted with intent (*Oedipus at Colonus* 266-7; 963-4). Yet the way they responded to the uncontrollable events (*tuche*) and lived out their wretched lives also brought them extraordinary blessings at the end: Philoctetes a cure and glory as slayer of Paris, Oedipus a miraculous death, Heracles eternal life on Olympus.[31] Do such denouements mean that there is a corollary to "Count no man happy until he's dead," that one might also say "Count no man unhappy" because the full story, when understood, reveals that great adversity can also elevate the sufferer and instruct those who witness his suffering?

Lessons of Suffering

Almost all the life patterns illustrate how limited and vulnerable human beings are. Not only can they not control other people or events, but in crises they often cannot even control themselves or make good decisions, no matter how reasonable, or virtuous, or strong they might be in normal circumstances. So the stories of characters in action dramatize the mutability of life, the reversal of fortune implicit in the human condition.

According to Herodotus, a wise old Solon tried to explain this cold fact to Croesus who considered himself the most fortunate of men because he was the rich and powerful king of Lydia (*Histories* 1.30-33). Certain that nothing bad could ever befall him, the over-confident king dismissed the Athenian as a fool. Once Croesus had suffered the death of his son and the destruction of his kingdom, however, he recognized the wisdom of Solon's warning.

The proverbial phrase *pathei mathos* (wisdom through painful experience) expresses this idea, which is also illustrated by the book of Job: that one must feel suffering himself in order to fully understand what it means to be human.[32] According to the chorus of Aeschylus' *Agamemnon*,

> Zeus who guided men to think,
> who has laid it down that wisdom (*mathos*)
> comes alone through suffering. (*pathei*)
> Still there drips in sleep against the heart
> grief of memory; against
> our pleasure we are temperate.
> From the gods who sit in grandeur
> Grace comes somehow violent.
> (176-83, Lattimore, trans.)

The sufferer may have known his place intellectually, but only living through the emotion and the physical pain can produce full recognition, without denial or delusion. Not every fool learns to "know himself;" Agamemnon and Clytemnestra acknowledge neither their crimes nor their errors. But their children, Orestes and Electra, who are agents as well as victims of the blood vendetta in their family, recognize the horror of their own acts and are able to atone for them. Other heroes like Creon in *Antigone*, Achilles, and Pentheus proclaim the lesson clearly as they face disaster. Prometheus predicts that even Zeus will learn from suffering in the course of time (Aeschylus *Prometheus Bound* 186-92, 927, 931, 980-81).

Many sagas illustrate the individual's responsibility for "evil beyond the measure" to warn mortals of the dangers of hubris and overconfidence in human reason. Both lead to suffering, whether the source is *ate* or unintentional error, and teach the moderation which is often the good quality contrasted with hubris.

The sufferings of the great also illustrate the truth of *meden agan* "Nothing in excess," one of the cardinal principles of Apollo. We have seen how *koros*, too much of a good thing, frequently leads to *ate* or delusion. But excess passion too is dangerous, as the uncontrollable anger of Achilles, the excess love-turned-to-hate in Phaedra and Medea, and even the immoderate quest for virtue and chastity in Hippolytus teach. Phaedra's nurse, witness and catalyst to the unfolding disaster, praises moderation in all things:

> The ways of life that are most fanatical
> trip us up more, they say, than bring us joy.
> They're enemies to health. So I praise less
> the extreme than temperance in everything.
> The wise will hear me out.
> (Euripides *Hippolytus* 260-66, Grene, trans.)

Most witnesses to the sufferings of the preeminent pray to avoid too much wealth, responsibility, beauty, or good fortune because they are dangerous. But we admire the heroes, not their moderate foils. For those who aim high represent, even when they fail, our best qualities, the courage, intellect, and resilience that are uniquely human. They do not shy away from action in situations that demand bold leadership, they acknowledge their own mistakes, and they face their ruin bravely. Therefore, suffering, or witnessing it, teaches people an appreciation for human greatness which the realities of pain and the eternal separation in death make all the more significant. Neoptolemus and the soldiers who've been sent to drag Philoctetes back to Troy are awed by his heroic ingenuity in devising the means to survive his pain and his hostile environment. Their respect and pity prevent them from deceiving him.

Former enemies feel pity and affection for each other when they recognize their common lot as sufferers. Achilles and Priam in *Iliad* 24 and Theseus and the son he's rashly condemned to death at the end of *Hippolytus* commiserate together and express mutual respect as they try to mitigate each other's pain. The sight of the ruined Ajax moves Odysseus not only to pity, but also to self-knowledge.

> . . . yet I pity
> His wretchedness, though he is my enemy.
> For terrible is the yoke of blindness that is on him
> I think of him, yet also of myself;
> For I see the true state of all us that live—
> (Sophocles *Ajax* 121-6, Moore, trans.)

His perception enables him to defend his former friend's right to an honorable burial and "To recognize in him the bravest man of all that came to Troy, except Achilles" (1340-41).

Friends and family, too, are drawn closer together by their common grief, and recognize their kinship with the rest of suffering humanity. At the end of Euripides' play, the polluted Heracles, gratified for the support of Theseus, defines true heroism as facing necessity like other human beings and does not feel degraded by his tears. All the characters in Aeschylus' *Prometheus Bound* are immortals except Io, but their responses to the conflict between Prometheus and Zeus validate the emotional bonds between mortals. With the exception of Zeus' lackeys, Might, Force, and Hermes, everyone, even Hephestus whose fire was stolen, pities Prometheus because of his painful punishment on a desolate crag. Prometheus himself has acted out of pity for humanity's sorry state. Bound together by family ties as well as opposition to Zeus' new and unjust rule, his more moderate visitors express respect and gratitude for Prometheus' indomitable will to fight Zeus' indomitable force, at the same time as they urge him to desist from foolish actions that will cause him further pain. But Prometheus has a secret which will cause Zeus to suffer mental anguish. Once the king of men and gods has also suffered, he, too, will feel pity and affection for other sufferers as well as responsibilities of kinship with the human race, his progeny through Io.

Suffering also gives meaning to all struggles to preserve the best of the present and to develop what may be even better. Aeschylus' Prometheus has chosen his torment in order to bring about a better world. His gift of fire will enable humans to use their intelligence and craft to progress out of bewilderment and violence toward mastery of themselves and their environment. With the fire, he also bestowed the gift of hope, to give humanity the courage to face inevitable pain for the sake of the promise of the future. Because Prometheus could foresee the time when Zeus would temper his savagery and allow humans to develop, he was willing to endure and to encourage Io to endure the present cruelty of the god and the barbarity of fellow human beings.

If Greek sagas teach the grandeur and the limitations of humanity, they also increase awareness of the superhuman. For in confronting the outer edge of human possibility, the preeminent are brought face to face with what lies beyond. By book 24 of the *Iliad* godlike Achilles proclaims, for Priam and for us, his experiential knowledge of the vital differences between the gods' portion and his own. Aeschylus traces, in the macabre sagas of the greatest families, the history of the development of a just and provident universe presided over by an eternal, wise, and all powerful Zeus. The trilogy about the conflict between Zeus and Prometheus dramatizes the chief god's own family saga, in which the development out of savagery at the cosmic level validates both the suffering in history and the faith in a divine moral order.

Euripides' heroes and heroines, caught in catastrophe, articulate the new cosmic awareness of the last half of the fifth century. Several express real skepticism about the myths they are part of.

Hecuba, for example, does not permit Helen to blame the goddess for the seduction of Paris: she argues that Aphrodite is nothing but human lust (*Trojan Women* 987-89). But Heracles, archetype for the toils of mortality, will neither rationalize the gods or associate evil and injustice with them.

> Ah, all this has no bearing on my grief;
> but I do not believe the gods commit
> adultery, or bind each other in chains . . .
> If god is truly god, he is perfect,
> lacking nothing. These are the poets' wretched lies.
> (*Heracles* 1340-46, Arrowsmith, trans.)

These characters speak like the philosophers, Plato and his predecessors who rejected the anthropomorphism of myth and poetry.

But poetry's "wretched lies," with its sounds, figurative language, and passionate dialogue which arouse our emotions, help us empathize with the sufferers and gain an experiential, if vicarious, insight into the mystery and power of the divine. Both Greek tragedy and the poetic core of the biblical book of Job make us feel the characters' pain, anger, and despair, and enable us to share their illumination.

Like the characters in Job, the Thebans in Euripides' *Bacchae* begin with a very limited perception of divinity. Dionysus' aunts, out of jealousy, refused to accept their sister's account of his miraculous birth. Cadmus and Tiresias worship him in the appropriate way for inadequate reasons: the old king/grandfather because it's good politics to have a god in the family, and the priest of Apollo because he can rationalize away the ridiculous birth story and turn the god of wine into a philosophical abstraction–the Wet. Even the herdsman, who has witnessed the paradoxically divine and bestial powers of the women on the mountaintop, reduces Dionysus to the wine god and the great relaxer at the end of his terrifying report. Pentheus, the young king who wants to maintain civic order, is the greatest offender. He has repressed the physicality of the Dionysian in himself and he relies so much on his own rationality that he totally rejects the irrational and miraculous occurring all around him.

Audience and readers, like Job's comforters, may feel smug about their understanding and acceptance of the deity; we would never be such fools as Pentheus and the others. But as Dionysus changes from victim to victimizer, we witnesses pity Pentheus, Agave and Cadmus, so cruelly punished out of all proportion to their crime, and thus reject and feel revulsion for this inhuman god. And isn't that part of the point? For the divine is not human. The Thebans' suffering, which makes them acknowledge their error, has led us to see more of the divine than we want to, to recognize how perilous it is to reduce deity to our human categories, and to glimpse how far beyond our anthropocentric comprehension of the world the realities of nature and the cosmos actually are. Although the conceptions of divinity are different in the book of Job and the *Bacchae*, both force us to face the 'otherness' of the godhead and our own vulnerability.

Notes

1. For a thorough study of this pattern and its manifestations and effects, see Martha C. Nussbaum, *The Fragility of Goodness: Luck and Ethics in Greek Tragedy and Philosophy* (Cambridge: Cambridge University Press, 1986).

2. Froma I. Zeitlin, "Thebes: Theater of Self and Society in Athenian Drama," pp. 101-141 in *Greek Tragedy and Political Theory*, J. Peter Euben, ed. (Berkeley: University of California Press, 1986.)

3. For lists and analyses, see George Steiner, *Antigones* (Oxford: Oxford University Press, 1984) and Anthony Roche, "Ireland's *Antigone*s: Tragedy North and South," pp. 221-250 in *Cultural Contexts and Literary Idioms in Contemporary Irish Literature*. Studies in Contemporary Irish Literature 1. Irish Literary Studies 31 (Gerrards Cross: Colin Smythe, 1988).

4. The *Library* of Apollodorus, III.v. 7-8 contains a complete account of the riddle and its source. See the English translation by Sir James Frazer in the Loeb Classical Library (Cambridge: Harvard University Press, 1921), vol. 1, p. 347, n.2 for other references to the riddle.

5. The fact that this phrase occurs in other contexts (e.g., Aeschylus, *Agamemnon* 938, Euripides, *Andromache* 100, Herodotus, *Histories* 1.32) suggests it was a common notion.

6. Nussbaum, esp. pp. 3-8, 89-94, for definitions and analyses of *tuche*.

7. See Mark P. O. Morford and Robert V. Lenardon, "Heracles" in *Classical Mythology*, 4th ed. (New York: Longman, 1991), pp. 457-481 for an excellent summary of his saga with interpretation and bibliography.

8. Werner Jaeger, *Paideia: The Ideals of Greek Culture*, 3 vols., trans. G. Highet (New York: Oxford University Press, 1960) defines this concept of *arete*, its manifestation, aims, and influence on Greek culture from Homer to Plato. See chapters 1, "Nobility and Arete," and 2, "The Culture and Education of the Homeric Nobility," pp. 1-34, as well as the abundant notes to these chapters, pp. 415-26 for explication of the related terms as well as interpretation of their implications in Greek society. Gregory Nagy translates *arete* as merit,' e.g.., *The Best of the Achaeans: Concepts of the Hero in Archaic Greek Poetry* (Baltimore: The Johns Hopkins University Press, 1981), pp. 13-14, and judges that Achilles' superior might (*bie*) in the *Iliad* and Odysseus' superior artifice' (*metis*) in the *Odyssey* make them

222   *Sinai & Olympus: A Comparative Study*

best, e.g., pp. 35-38. Nussbaum, p. 6, summarizes her use of the term as "all features of persons in virtue of which they live and act well, i.e., so as to merit praise."

9.   Jaeger, pp. 9-10, as well as E. R. Dodds, "Agamemnon's Apology," in *The Greeks and the Irrational* (Berkeley: University of California Press, 1959), pp. 1-27.

10. For an analysis of *kleos* and *ainos*, and their relation to preeminence, death, and later cults of the *heros*, with copious notes and bibliography, see Nagy.

11. See Dodds, *loc. sit*, for an analysis of the Homeric "shame culture."

12. A. W. H. Adkins, *Merit and Responsibility: A Study in Greek Values* (New York: Oxford University Press, 1960) for an analysis of the interrelation of these ideas and their development.

13. Nussbaum, p.2. Translations of the *Iliad* have been quoted from Richmond Lattimore, *"The Iliad" of Homer* (Chicago: University of Chicago Press, 1951.)

14. Nussbaum, pp. 89-101, for definitions of *techne* and its relation to *tuche*; pp. 73-75 for her analysis of the ode from *Antigone*. All translations of Greek tragedies are quoted from *The Complete Greek Tragedies*, David Grene and Richmond Lattimore, eds. Vols. 1-4 (Chicago: University of Chicago Press 1959-60) unless otherwise noted. They will be cited by tragedian, play, lines, and translator in the text rather than by volume and page in the notes.

15. *The Discovery of the Mind: The Greek Origins of European Thought*, trans. T. G. Rosenmeyer (New York: Harper & Brothers, 1960), p. 37.

16. P. 382. See Nussbaum's summary, pp. 6-7.

17. For notes, bibliography and discussion, see James Hutton, *Aristotle's "Poetics"* (New York: W. W. Norton Co., 1982), as well as Nussbaum, pp. 378-391, esp. 388-391 for her discussion of *catharsis*. Andrew Brown, *A New Companion to Greek Tragedy* (Totowa, N.J.: Barnes and Noble, 1983) provides discussions and bibliography of all relevant terms.

18. Oliver Taplin, *Greek Tragedy in Action* (London: Methuen, 1978), pp. 169-70.

19. See Katherine Callen King, *Achilles: Paradigms of the War Hero from Homer to the Middle Ages* (Berkeley: University of California Press, 1987), pp. 1-47, for a succinct summary of the complexities of Achilles' character and actions, with excellent notes and bibliography.

20. King, pp. 50-109, analyzes classical uses of Achilles.

21. See Sarah B. Pomeroy, *Goddesses, Whores, Wives and Slaves: Women in Classical Antiquity* (New York: Schocken Books, 1975), pp. 1-16 for a summary of the various divine archetypes and interpretations of them. See also *Women in the Ancient World: The Arethusa Papers*, edited by J. Peradotto and J. P. Sullivan (Albany: State University of New York Press, 1984), pp. 362-365 for a selected bibliography of women in Greece.

22. See Shalom Spiegel, *The Last Trial* (New York: Pantheon, 1967), pp. 9-12 for a discussion of human sacrifice in Greek mythology and a bibliography of Greek and Roman sources.

23. See Dodds, *loc. sit* and Chapter 2, "From Shame Culture to Guilt Culture," pp. 28-63 as well as Brown; R. D. Dawe, "Some Reflections on *Ate* and *Hamartia*," *Proceedings of the Cambridge Philological Society*, 186 (1960): 19-31; and Anthony J. Podlecki. *"The Persians" by Aeschylus: A Translation with Commentary* (Englewood Cliffs, N.J.: Prentice Hall, 1970).

24. See Podlecki for analysis of terms and play.

25. A full discussion of double motivation appears in Albin Lesky, "Gottliche und menschliche Motivation in homerichen Epos," *Sitzungberichte der Heidelberg Akademie* 4 (1961). See also P. E. Easterling, "Presentation of Character in Aeschylus," *Greece and Rome* 20 (1973): 3-19; N. L. G. Hammond, "Personal Freedom and its Limitations in the *Oresteia*," *Journal of Hellenic Studies* 85 (1965): 42-55; Albin Lesky, "Decision and Responsibility in the Tragedy of Aeschylus," *Journal of Hellenic Studies* 86 (1966): 78-85; and R. P. Winnington-Ingram, "Tragedy and Greek Archaic Thought," pp. 29-50, in *Classical Drama and its Influence: Essays presented to H. D. F Kitto,* M. J. Anderson, ed. (London, 1965).

26. This fragment has been cited from Hugh Lloyd-Jones' appendix to Volume 2 (Cambridge.: Harvard University Press, 1963), p. 562, of Herbert Weir Smyth, *Aeschylus. Vol. 1 and 2: Plays and Fragments with an English Translation.* Loeb Classical Library. (New York: G. P. Putnam, 1922).

27. P. 35. See pp. 32-38, 41-50 for a discussion of his decision and its results.

28. Nussbaum, *op. cit.*

29. There are many excellent studies of Sophoclean Drama and *Oedipus the King.* See Bernard Knox, *The Heroic Temper*, (Berkeley: University of California Press, 1964); R. P. Winnington-Ingram, *Sophocles: An Interpretation.* (Cambridge: Cambridge University Press, 1980); M. J. O'Brien, ed., *Twentieth Century Interpretations of "Oedipus Rex"* (Englewood Cliffs, N.J.: Prentice Hall, 1968).

30. Pp. 31-82.

31. See Edmond Wilson's essay, "Philoctetes: The Wound and the Bow" in his collection *The Wound and the Bow: Seven Studies in Literature.* (Boston: Houghton Mifflin, 1941).

32. The meaning of the maxim *pathei mathos*, "wisdom through suffering" is a subject for debate. See Nussbaum's discussion of the term and the passage, pp. 45-47, as well as E. R. Dodds, "Morals and Politics in the Oresteia" in *The Ancient Concept of Progress and Other Essays* (Oxford: Clarendon Press, 1973); Michael Gagarin, *Aeschylean Drama* (Berkeley: University of California Press, 1976), pp. 139-50; Peter Smith, *On the Hymn to Zeus in Aeschylus' "Agamemnon"* (Chico, Calif.: Scholars Press, 1980); and Taplin, pp. 168-170.

Conclusions and Comparisons

Both the Greeks and the Hebrews envisioned imperfect humanity as aspiring to emulate the perfection of the divine model. On Sinai, the interaction of God, Israel, and the nations supplies a variety of scenarios that enable the rabbis to posit the ultimate typology. How can one become like God? By modeling one's self on God's attributes. "As God is merciful and gracious so must you be merciful; as God is righteous, so must you be righteous; as God shows loving kindness, so must you show loving kindness."[1] In a similar fashion, the gods who dwell on Olympus provided ideal paradigms for humans on earth. Although Plato rejected anthropomorphic religion, he theorized that the human world of flux and flow was an imperfect copy of an eternal and flawless realm of Being derived from the idea of the Good.

The biblical-rabbinic ideal lies somewhere between Plato and the Greek myths. God retains the vitality of the anthropomorphic deities because He is immanent as a personality and interacts with His creatures through dialogue, miracle, and revelation. But He is not a person. He has no body and He forbids making an image of His perfection in terms of physical beauty and strength. He has no sex and consequently no family history that can serve as a pattern for generation and change. Therefore, His attributes as a transcendent deity are strongly reminiscent of Plato's idea of the good.

The anthropomorphism of the Greek gods fostered an ideal which exalted all aspects of life—physical, aesthetic, and intellectual. Therefore, religious life was only one part of the whole rather than the main focus, as it was in the Bible shaped by the canonists. In the Bible, necessary aspects of human life such as eating, sex for reproduction, physical labor and the pleasure in its results, are blessed, but they are not exalted as ends in themselves. In contrast, sex, and food, so essential to human survival, are elevated by the lusty and zestful Greek gods' delight in them. In ancient Israel, music, dance, poetry, and physical prowess were means of celebration in the worship of God, but they were not selected by society as a way of demonstrating excellence. In Greece, however, such activities were esteemed as abilities of the gods themselves which they bestowed on humans, and competitions for the best mortals at these endeavors were part of the religious worship of divine patrons. Although, with the exception of the Song of Songs (later allegorized as referring to God and Israel) there are no extended descriptions of physical beauty in the Bible, nevertheless, beauty was prized in ancient Israel. One of the qualifications of the High Priest was superior beauty so that he would be the best representative of man to God and would be venerated by the people.[2] Lest beauty lead to idolatry, however, the second commandment prohibited the making of any human sculpture or pictorial form. In contrast, Greek literature is replete with descriptions of the external characteristics of deities which match the ubiquitous sculptures and paintings of bodies at rest and in motion, most reflecting the cohesion of external power, proportion, and beauty with the inner calm produced by reasoned reflection.

The Greek exaltation of the physical complements the esteem for the intellectual and the moral. The ideal of the Beautiful, *to kalon*, in myth, philosophy, and life, encompassed inner and outer qualities.[3] The leaders of society, at first noble by birth, were called *kalos kagathos* (beautiful and good) and their ability and magnanimity *kalokagathia*. To Plato, the sensual experience of an individual's beauty could lead the beholder up a ladder to inner beauty, to all manifestations of beauty, and finally to the highest eternal essence, called Beauty in the *Symposium*, but Goodness in the *Republic*.[4]

Despite these differences in the divine ideals for perfection, the human archetypes and typologies are surprisingly similar. Human behavior is both humanly motivated and divinely fostered, but human life is still vulnerable to contingencies beyond the individual's control. However these factors coalesce, a person is subject to the law of reciprocity. In both traditions, greater privilege brings greater responsibility and greater danger. So the tales of exemplars illustrate the need for moderation and the value of wisdom.

There are striking analogies between the two groups of exemplars. Jacob and Odysseus are brothers in cunning who must use their wits in struggling with superior adversaries on foreign soil. Joseph and Oedipus, though disparate in destiny, are alike in their reliance on wisdom and insight as well as in their sense of responsibility to the community. Saul and Agamemnon are good men made worse by conflicting public responsibilities; Saul is the greater sufferer because he knows, in his lucid moments, how far he has fallen. David encompasses many of the qualities of the Greek warrior, musician, and statesman. His battle with Goliath resembles all the duels of Greek epic; his friendship with Jonathan echoes the friendship of Achilles and Patroclus. Like the Greek tragic heroes, David overreaches himself at the height of his power. Both societies value the martyrs who bear witness to duty to man or faith in God. In fact, Plato's account of the trial and death of Socrates (v. *Apology, Crito, Phaedo*) provided the model for the martyrdoms of Eleazer in 2 Maccabees 7 and Polycarp in the Early Christian writings.[5] Just as Socrates' trial publicly demonstrated his duty from Apollo to examine life, so did Rabbi Akiba's martyrdom publicly demonstrate his belief in his duty to God to teach the Torah. On Sinai and Olympus, suffering is seen as integral to the life process, as stimulating human beings to greater effort and nobler feelings, and an increasing awareness, both of human limitations and divine transcendence.

Although the heroic types and their life patterns are analogous, they are not identical. The Hebrew perspective is ultimately theocentric and optimistic; the biblical heroes, though enmeshed in human conflict, are working out a divine design and can be certain of divine love. The Greeks, in contrast, have no salvational history to tie all the situational episodes together and move them forward toward a clearly defined transcendent goal. Their perspective is anthropocentric and less optimistic; although the world is divinely given and arranged, Greek heroes and heroines are less certain of the gods' design and love. The different results of the wisdom of Oedipus and Joseph exemplify the difference in *weltanschaung*. Oedipus' insufficient human wisdom cannot prevent catastrophe. Joseph's wisdom, ascribed to God, turns the evil of his brothers into good for the nation as he himself recognizes: "As for you, you meant evil against me; but God meant it for good, to bring it about that many people should be left alive as they are today" (Gen. 50:20).

The Hebrew hero is God-chosen and God chooses for His own reasons. He tells Samuel:

> For the Lord sees not as man sees. Man looks on the outward
> appearance, but the Lord looks into the heart (1 Samuel 16:7).

Unlike the insignificant shepherds, lowly slaves' sons lacking primogeniture, or even women, Greek heroes are usually noblemen whose families have achieved distinction through birth and accomplishment. They must struggle to retain preeminence which derives from recognition by their peers rather than by God. In the type-scenes of Greek literature, competitive heroes confront each other, either on the battlefield or in the assembly where they argue motives, issues, expediency, or justice, presenting both sides so they can make vital decisions without unambiguous directives. In contrast, interactions between Hebrew protagonists and their adversaries often take place against the background of a divine revelation or divine guidance. Thus the directives are clear and the heroes are reassured that despite their limitations they will be equal to their mission.

Of course Hebrew heroes have to struggle; God's choice is not unconditional, so they must raise themselves to merit its continuation. Competition among the Hebrews therefore arises over the correct reading of God's mandate and over the correct way to serve Him. This is the crux of the dispute between Korah and Moses (Numbers 16). The ideal of the covenant community, however, is cooperative rather than competitive.[6] This ideal stems partially from the belief in the equality of humanity under God, not equality in function but equality of intrinsic value. It is epitomized by the favorite saying of the rabbis of Yavneh, the architects of Talmudic Judaism:

> I am a creature of God
> My neighbor is also a creature of God;
> My work is in the city,
> His work is in the field;
> I rise early to my work,
> He rises early to his.
> Just as he is not overbearing in his calling,
> So am I not overbearing in my calling.
> Perhaps you will say:
> I do great things and he does small things.
> We have learnt:
> It matters not whether one does much or little,
> If only he directs his heart to heaven.[7]

The Hebrew view of competition is also rooted in the belief that achievement is ultimately elusive. The author of Ecclesiastes observed that:

> The race is not won by the swift.
> Nor the battle by the valiant,
> Nor is bread won by the wise,
> Nor wealth by the intelligent,
> Nor fame by the learned.
> (Eccles. 9:11)

The insignificant duration of life renders all success illusory. In a similar vein, the rabbis, commenting on Eccles. 1:13; note that no one departs this world without half of his or her desires and ambitions remaining unfulfilled.[8] What the individual does not achieve will be achieved by the group. Work is important, not achievement. Rabbi Tarfon summed it up succinctly. "It is not your duty to complete the work but neither may you desist from it."[9] Rabbi Israel Salanter, the renowned teacher of Jewish ethics in nineteenth century Eastern Europe, is said to have uttered this epigram: "There are three things which no one need do. One need not initiate, one need not complete, one need not accomplish."[10]

Similar reflections can be found in the writings of the Greek and Roman philosophers after the older social and political aspirations were radically transformed by the decline of the city-state and the growth of the Hellenistic empires.[11] The Epicureans shunned competition and public life if it threatened to disturb their peace of mind. More like the rabbis, the Stoics recognized the impossibility of fulfilling one's desires, and advised controlling the will to desire instead, but they insisted on the performance of duty, whatever that entailed. Epictetus, a former slave, used the metaphor of the stage to define the duty of every individual.

> Remember that you are an actor in a drama of such sort as the Author chooses—if short, then a short one, if long, then a long one. If it be his pleasure that you should enact a poor man, or a cripple, or a ruler, or a private citizen, see that you act it well. For this is your business, to act well the given part, but to choose it belongs to another.
> (*Enchiridion* 17, Higginson, trans.)[12]

Like the rabbis too, the Stoics found their peace of mind in the knowledge that the Author was divine and that each individual part had real value as a contribution to the perfection of the whole. As the Emperor Marcus Aurelius explained,

> All things are implicated with one another and the land is holy — for there is hardly anything unconnected with any other thing. For things have been coordinated and they combine to form the same universe. For there is one universe made up of all things, and one god who pervades all things, and one substance, and one law, one reason common to all intelligent animals.
> (*Meditations* 7.9, Long, trans.)[13]

Recognizing that he is thus related to all parts of the universe, he continues

> I shall be discontented with none of the things which are assigned to me out of the whole; for nothing is injurious to the part, if it is for the advantage of the whole. I shall do nothing unsocial, but I shall rather direct myself to the things which are of the same kind

with myself, and I shall turn all my efforts to the common interest, and divert them from the contrary. (*Meditations* 10.6, Long, trans.)

The Stoic ideal is best typified by Virgil's Aeneas, a new hero for a new world, after the fierce competition of the Roman leaders overrode all sense of social responsibility and finally destroyed the republican system entirely. When Augustus ended a century of civil war, the poet Virgil expressed the hopes and anxieties of his age in the Roman epic *The Aeneid*, modeled on the *Iliad* and the *Odyssey*.[14] Aeneas differs from the earlier Greek heroes, however. Compelled by fate to abandon Troy, the brave warrior gives up his urge to die Hector's glorious death defending his city. Wandering the seas like Odysseus, he cannot stay where he chooses or live with the woman of his choice. As he learns the predetermined future, he develops the will to subordinate his personal feelings to the greater good—the founding of Rome and the promised *pax Romana*. Virgil makes clear the difficulty of the self sacrifice and the suffering endured by all, but the heroic figures, like Dido and Turnus, whose private passions prevent their accepting their destinies, only increase the pain of all to no purpose. Individual virtue and happiness come from choosing to do what must be done, secure in the knowledge that it is fated by the gods for the good of the greater whole.

Both civilizations conceive of life as a school where one should learn to live intelligently, but the particular lessons learned are somewhat different. For the Hebrews, each life experience, from the highest to the lowest, in pain and pleasure, is intended to perfect the human being and enable him or her to come closer to God. For the Greeks, the struggle for perfection, which also takes place in a variety of human conditions, leads instead to the realization of the fullest human potential which both imitates and pleases the gods. In myth, however, the inevitable failure of the great fosters in them and in us a clearer realization of the gulf between man and god. Hebrews also are aware of the gulf. For this reason, knowledge in the Hebrew school is a means to an end; as Prov. 1.7 states, "Fear of the Lord is the beginning of knowledge."

To the Greeks, knowledge is the means to the realization of full human potential, but it also became an end in itself. Although Socrates, like the mythical heroes, is wisest when he knows what he does not know, the later Greek philosophers defined man as a rational animal and considered reason his most godlike quality. Therefore the realization of the fullest human potential meant knowing as much as possible, not only about the highest good for humans but also about the physical operation of the universe. If for the Hebrews *imitatio Dei* meant emulating God's ethical actions, for the Greeks it also meant knowing the first principles of divine nature.[15] The rabbis and the Jewish philosophers of a later age accepted Greek scientific knowledge because they believed that it was only through knowing God's world that one could come to know God. But on Sinai philosophy and science always remained the handmaidens of Scripture.

Notes

1.   *Mekilta de Rabbi Ishmael*, Tractate *Shirata* 3 (ed. Lauterbach) 2:25. cf. George Foot Moore, *Judaism: In the First Centuries of the Christian Era* (Cambridge: Harvard University Press, 1950), 2:109-111.

2.   *b. Yoma*, 19a.

3.   Jaeger, *Paideia*, pp. 3-4; 416 n. 4; pp. 11, 420, n. 35.

4.   A. E. Taylor, *Plato: The Man and His Work* (Cleveland: World Publishing Co., 1965), p. 231.

5.   Moses Hadas and Morton Smith, *Heroes and Gods: Spiritual Biographies in Antiquity* (New York: Harper and Row, 1965), pp. 87-97.

6.   Maurice Samuels, *The Gentleman and the Jew* (New York: Alfred Knopf, 1950) traced this tendency from the Hebrew Bible to the Israeli kibbutz which he argued is as much the product of the Hebraic spirit as it is the outgrowth of modern socialism.

7.   *b. Berakot*, 17a.   Yavneh was the seat of a famous academy of talmudic learning established by Rabban Yohanan ben Zakkai after the destruction of the Second Temple in the year 70 C.E.

8.   *Ecclesiastes R.* 1:34.

9.   *M. Avot* 2:15.

10.   Cited in Matthew J. Schwartz, "Koheleth and Camus: Two Views of Achievement," *Judaism*, Vol. 35, No. 1 (Winter, 1986): 34.

11.   *See*, P. E. More, *Hellenistic Philosophies* (Princeton: Princeton University Press, 1923) for a survey of the various schools.

12.   Quoted from *Epictetus: "The Enchiridion"* trans. by Thomas Higginson with an intro. by Albert Salomon (Indianapolis: Bobbs Merrill, 1955).

13.   Quoted from Moses Hadas ed., *The Essential Works of Stoicism* (New York: Bantam, 1965).

14.   For an examination of the conflict between hope and fear and the tensions between public and private in the epic, see Susan Ford Wiltshire, *Public and Private in Vergil's Aeneid*.   (Amherst: University of Massachusetts Press, 1989.)

15.   E.g., Aristotle *Metaphysics* 980-983a.

Chapter 6

Patterns of Piety

Introduction

On Sinai and Olympus, as we have just seen, wisdom both cognitive and intuitive was the avenue that led to *imitatio dei*. Therefore those individuals who possessed inspiration or special insight about God and His will for the cosmos and humanity were regarded as expositors of religion. Their words expressed the spiritual and intellectual dimensions of internalized piety. But this concept of piety stood in creative tension with an externalized piety represented by priests, temples, and organized rituals (to be discussed in the next chapter) which served to concretize the abstractions of religion by means of formalized cultic activities. This tension was analyzed by the modern Hebrew essayist Ahad Ha-Am in his well known essay "Priest and Prophet"[1] and was dramatized by the composer Arnold Schoenberg in his two act opera *Moses and Aaron.*

The prophets and wisdom teachers of old would have empathized with one of the greatest of our modern pianists of whom it was told that he sat for hours in solitude making inaudible music on an invisible piano. He had developed an obsession that the instrument was not so much a conveyor as an obstacle to the flow of pure music. Music was the stuff of the universe, in the air all about us. The human mind, if it became subtle enough, could evoke it from the spheres without the intrusion of a crude box of wood, ivory, and steel wire.

For the priest, it is the festival, the ritual, and the ritual objects that are the focal point of religion. The temple, the altar, the sacrifices, the holiday celebration, the priestly vestments, wine goblets, incense, candles—what would the worship of God be without these? If for a brief moment on Mount Sinai Moses entertained the idea that the Israelites would accept a religion dominantly prophetic, he was completely disabused of it when he came down from the mountain and found them worshipping the golden calf constructed under the supervision of his brother, Aaron the priest. Moses recognized the human limitation of his people, their inability to grasp essences, their desire for created forms which could suggest and evoke larger meanings and touch deeper significances. Moses' intuition was confirmed by God's command: "Let them make me a sanctuary that I may dwell among them" (Exod. 25:8).[2]

To the inheritors of the Judaeo-Christian tradition, Greek polytheism may seem to be a less serious religion centered almost exclusively on cult.[3] There are traces of more than 300 public festivals held in over 250 places for no less than 400 deities.[4] From the fragmentary descriptions of rites and ancient authors' attitudes toward them, some modern interpreters have concluded that Greek religion was "at bottom a question of doing, not of believing, of behavior rather than faith."[5] According to John Gould, the term *nomizein theous* "means not 'believe in the gods'; but 'acknowledge them', that is, pray to them, sacrifice to them, build temples to them, make them the object of cult and ritual."[6] Ordinary Greeks, like most of Moses' Israelites, probably participated in cult activities without understanding the essence of the gods they worshipped or the ethical demands implicit in their worship. But Greece, like Israel, also produced extraordinary individuals who articulated the spiritual and intellectual dimensions of religious behavior. And, as in Israel, some were closely connected, like Moses, Isaiah, and the Pythian priestess, with the centers of cult activity, whereas others, like Amos, Hesiod, and Plato, were not.

We must be careful, however, not to exaggerate and project on the ancients the modern tendency of atomizing religion into its various components, setting them in opposition to each other. Though the tension between internal and external piety was real, these two poles of religious life were often harmonized in an organic unity in societies of antiquity. For the ancient Hebrews and Greeks, life was unthinkable without the cult, but existence was unbearable without prophecy and wisdom which gave practical guidance, moral direction, and metaphysical meaning to human endeavor. To paraphrase Prov. 29:18, without vision the people are lost.

Such vision emanated from similar channels in Greece and Israel. Prophecy was manifested on several levels from the magician who changed the course of nature to the mantic who interpreted signs to the messenger who spoke the actual words of God. Wisdom could also be inspired but it drew its insights from all aspects of experience and learning: i.e., the observation of the movement of the heavens; the intricacies of human relationships; the workings of animate and inanimate nature. In Israel, due to historical circumstances, prophecy superseded wisdom as a higher form of revelation. The Greeks, who lacked a single divine authority, did not make the same distinctions between the two kinds of inspiration, and did not, in fact, value revelation as highly as the Hebrews did. The prophetic words, conveyed by poets and philosophers as well as seers, were subjected to critical judgment, interpretation and even correction.

Notes

1. *Selected Essays by Ahad Ha-Am*, trans. Leon Simon (Philadelphia: The Jewish Publication Society of America, 1948) , pp. 125-138.

2. The rabbis note that the Israelites poured out as much gold and silver for the construction of the sanctuary as they poured out for the building of the Golden Calf, *Yer. Shekalim*, 1:1. Moses Maimonides, *The Guide of the Perplexed*, trans. Shlomoh Pines (Chicago: University of Chicago Press, 1963) II, 32 writes that the whole command to build a temple and offer sacrifices was to wean the people away from idolatry. It was a concession to human frailty.

3. See John Gould, "On Making Sense of Greek Religion," pp. 1-33 in *Greek Religion and Society*, P. E. Esterling and J. V. Muir, eds. (Cambridge: Cambridge University Press, 1985), for an excellent discussion of the sources of information and the problems of comprehension by twentieth century interpreters. Robert Garland, "Priests and Power in Classical Athens," p. 75 in Mary Beard and John North, Eds. *Pagan Priests: Religion and Power in the Ancient World* (Ithaca: Cornell University Press, 1990), adds the additional point that the term 'religion' itself was not "part of the Greeks' own thought-world" and that the category is an analytical tool of modern scholarship, which may introduce false associations with systems of dogma and belief.

4. Paul Cartledge, "The Greek Religious Festivals," p. 98-99 in Easterling and Muir.

5. Cartledge, p. 98 in Easterling and Muir.

6. P. 7 in Easterling and Muir.

Sinai I: Prophetic Piety

The Hebrew prophet was a charismatic individual endowed with the divine gift of both receiving and communicating the message of God's revelation. The prophet did not choose to prophesy; he or she was chosen, and compelled inwardly (as in the case of Jeremiah) or outwardly (as in the case of Jonah) to deliver God's message and impart His will. Prophecy is not an inherent natural ability or a human faculty independent of God and divine revelation. Moses, the greatest of the prophets, was a stammerer by nature (Exod. 4:10; 6:12, 30) and Samuel, relying on his own judgment, failed to select the son of Jesse ordained for kingship for he, like all human beings, could see only outward appearances (1 Sam. 16:6ff). Nor was prophecy passed by inheritance from generation to generation as a power latent in the genes. On the contrary, in the two instances in the Bible where there was an attempt by a son to capitalize on his father's charismatic power (Abimelekh, the son of Jerubaal-Gideon in Judges 9) and by a father to pass on his prophetic authority to his sons (Samuel appointed his sons judges, 1 Sam. 8:1-3), both ended in failure.[1] Prophecy is not a science to be learned or mastered. Its very essence is provisional and tentative, totally dependent on the will of God. The provisional character of prophecy is underscored in the role of the prophet in performing miracles. The miracle of Hebrew prophecy was the monotheistic counterpart of pagan magic.

Generally speaking, the occult wisdom of ancient paganism consisted of the mantic (i.e., a body of knowledge and actions by which it was possible to fathom the will of the gods, the outcome of the future and the secrets of existence) and the magical (i.e., a body of rites and incantations through whose power the gods and nature can be coerced to fulfill the will of the individual). There were two main categories of magic, cultic magic and technical magic. Cultic magic consists of a system of fixed activities intended to bring about the beneficial and the good and to ward off the harmful and the evil. Cultic magic inserts itself into the workings of nature in order to repair some fault that has appeared in the natural order or to insure that the natural order continues without fault. The concept of the sanctity or impurity of certain substances or in the purifying effects of certain materials or actions (i.e., the red heifer rite of Num. 19) are part of cultic magic as are ceremonial regulations such as the proper age, sex or color of the animal to be sacrificed. Technical magic interrupts the natural order, causing unusual transformations to suddenly occur in mysterious ways. The ten plagues brought on the Egyptians by Moses' staff is strikingly reminiscent of Near Eastern technical magic.[2]

In prophetic circles there was a constant struggle to subordinate mantic and magical elements to the more characteristic expressions of Hebrew monotheism, prayer, meditation and faith in God. It is the servant of God, never God Himself, who uses the devices of cultic and technical magic as a pedagogical device in which the popular belief in the occult is used as a means for inculcating higher religious ideals and doctrines. Typically the prophet does not study the occult texts or engage in lengthy rites in preparation for the miracle. He prays and performs the required action and then awaits the will of God. Moses performs the technical aspects of the miracle with his staff and awaits God's action (Exodus 7,8).

But Moses at a later stage of his crisis-plagued leadership of Israel, under external provocation and internal emotional turmoil, crossed the fine line between miracle and magic and failed to superimpose the higher over the lower piety. Moses and Aaron are commanded by God to take the staff of Moses and order the rock to yield water for the Israelites to drink. But Moses struck the rock twice with his staff instead of speaking to it with the result that he and Aaron are told they shall not lead Israel into the Promised Land (Num. 20:7-13). Yet on a previous occasion in an exactly parallel circumstance Moses uses his staff in accordance with the express command of God to strike the rock and bring forth the water for the people to drink (Exod. 17:1-7). What is the difference between the two incidents? In Exodus the use of the staff in striking the rock is in accordance with the magical practice of the ancient Near East. In Numbers, however, there is a divine demand for progression to a higher level of piety in which the magical potency of the staff is to be subordinated to the prophetic word. Moses, in reverting to the older practice in which miracle and magic border closely on one another, failed in his prophetic calling to raise Israel to a higher religious plane. This interpretation is borne out by the emphasis in God's words to Moses: "Take along the staff with which you struck the Nile" (Exod. 17:5), i.e., the staff that is viewed by the people as magically potent. In the incident related in the Book of Numbers, the staff is mentioned without any additional words of explanation or emphasis, i.e., it is an ordinary staff without any magical potency.[3] In addition, the phrase referring to the affirmation of God's sanctity is repeated twice (Num. 20:12-13), i.e., affirming God's sanctity means to perceive Him from the higher perspective of prophecy rather than from the lower vantage point of magic. It is this context that explains the severity of the sin and its punishment.

Prayer is the hallmark of prophetic piety, particularly intercessory prayer. As prophetic miracle struggled to subordinate the mantic and magical elements of Near Eastern occult wisdom to the essentials of monotheistic faith, so did prophetic prayer struggle to elevate the worship of God above pagan incantation formulas. As alluded above, incantations are based on the principle that evil is an autonomous power, personified by demons and forces destructive to humans and gods, that can be coerced to fulfill the individual will. The pagan sorcerer developed an arrogant assurance that his manipulation of the incantation could coerce the gods and the mythological forces to which even the gods were subservient (Num. 22:5-6). In contrast, the prophet never knew whether his action would bring the desired result and his prayer would be answered. There are times when God's way remains an enigma even to him. Elisha, who correctly foretold that the barren Shunamite woman would bear a son (2 Kings 4:16-18), confesses, when the child dies, that "the Lord has hidden it from me, and has not told me" (2 Kings 4:17).

Incantations are often strictly formalized in style, each word having a precise magical potency. They must be recited at special times or seasons and in specified locations and by specific people (e.g., Balaam and Balak in Num. 22:39-41; 23:1-2).[4] In contrast, prophetic prayer, unlike sacrifice, did not have a specified location. The sanctuary was the preferred site of prayer but not the exclusive one.[5] Like the prophet, whose divine mission can take him anywhere, even beyond the borders of the land of Israel, prayer could be offered to God from every location. Jonah prays from the belly of the fish and Daniel, Ezra and Nehemiah pray from Babylon and Persia. Moreover, prayer is not the monopoly of the prophets. In ancient Israel anyone could pray and be heard, non-prophets and even non-Israelites. The heathen sailors on Jonah's ship, momentarily moved to acknowledge Israel's God, pray to Him (Jon. 1:14) and Solomon in his dedicatory prayer of the Temple petitions God to hear the prayer of the non-Israelite who directs his prayer toward the house of God in Jerusalem (1 Kings 8:41-43).

The word that best characterizes prophetic prayer is the same term that best describes the phenomenon of prophecy—spontaneity. As prophecy can theoretically be the province of all God's people (Num. 11:29), so prayer is accessible "to all who call Him with sincerity' (Ps. 145:18). The spontaneous prayers of the Bible are simple in form, consisting of an address invoking God's name, a petition and a motivating sentence offering a rationale for the petition that hopefully will bring divine compliance. There was a great deal of freedom to add or subtract elements and the content of the prayers arose from particular circumstances that prevented them from being repeated on different occasions. Typical is Moses' prayer for his sister Miriam: "O God, pray heal her!" (Num. 12:13). The patterns of the prayers reflect human conversation and are derived from the social and psychological dynamics of human situations of petitioning, confessing and expressing gratitude. The biblical writers thus imply that dialogue between the individual and God is analogous to communication between humans and in this way underscore the intensely personal conception of God in the Sinai tradition.[6]

Spontaneous prayer continued alongside the structured liturgical poems inside the temple and outside its precincts throughout the biblical period, but from the prophetic standpoint the former was superior to the latter. The spontaneous prayer was bound to be more sincere, more a matter of the heart and soul than the formalized utterance that could easily degenerate into the mouthing of words (Isa. 29:13). The refined spirituality of the prophets demanded conformity in speech, thought and deed because the prayer dialogue reflects the social intercourse of people (e.g., 2 Kings 10:15). Just as words cannot persuade another individual when one mistrusts the speaker, so is prayer unacceptable to God when it is unaccompanied by purity of thought and action.

It is in this context that we must understand the prophetic insistence on the primacy of morality over the cult. In the Torah and preclassical prophetic literature there is no sharp distinction made between cultic and moral requirements. Both are equally important and both are essential to the continued existence of the nation. In the Ten Commandments, the quintessential distillation of the Torah, the ritual obligations of the first five commandments are weighted equally with the ethical obligations of the last five. But for the prophets the essence of God's demand is not to be found in the cult but the ethical and moral spheres of life (Mic. 6:7-8; Amos 5:21ff.; Isa. 1:11ff). They were not unequivocally opposed to the cult, the psalm, the song or prayer, festival and Sabbath *per se*, all of which they included in their assault (Amos 5:23; Isa. 1:13-15). What they condemned was the absolutization of the ritual.

The underlying premises of this condemnation were that all forms of worship are, like prayer, a dialogue-relationship between man and God, mirroring the dialogue-relationship between people. This dialogue-relationship is completely removed from occult influences or any other form of compulsion. Unlike many human relationships it is a symbolic gesture of submission to the will of God, but like the human paradigm, it depends on the sincerity and the morality of both parties that make identification between them possible. For worship to be acceptable to God the worshiper must identify with God (know God in the biblical idiom) in the only way possible for humans—by imitating His moral conduct (Hos. 4:1f and Jer. 9:2). Thus, the gestures of submission made by the wicked are an abomination to the Almighty.[7]

Prophetic piety was not merely the religious experience of individual prophets but also a group phenomena. The prophets had disciples *(benei ha-neviim)* who may or may not have been located at a shrine. Though they had their meals in common (2 Kings 4:38) and traveled together (1 Sam. 10:1), some of their members were married and had families and others owned their own houses (1 Kings 13:15 F.). Elisha performed a miracle for the widow of one of the members of this order, (2 Kings 4.17).

It is quite possible that these groups, who no doubt had to meet rigorous standards of ethics and emotional control, were taught meditative methods by master prophets (Elisha is called their "father", 2 Kings 6:21) in order to attain a closeness to God and as a side effect of such meditation ecstatic states were achieved that sometimes produced authentic prophecy.[8] When Saul, on consulting the seer for his father's lost asses, is told that he will "become prince over his people" this prediction is substantiated by a second one. On arriving in Gibeah he will "meet a band of prophets coming down from the high place with harp, tambourine and lyre before them." And when Saul subsequently met them "a spirit of God gripped him and he spoke in ecstasy among them" (1 Sam. 10:5-10). On another occasion when Saul was already king and jealous of David, he sent his men to capture David, who was then in the company of Samuel. When the men "saw a band of prophets speaking in ecstasy with Samuel standing by as their leader . . . the spirit of God came upon Saul's messengers and they too began to speak in ecstasy" (1 Sam. 19:20). This incident is repeated two more times as subsequent messengers are overcome by the contact with the band of prophets.

The prophets themselves were subject to ecstatic trances and used music as a spiritual stimulus. Elijah sprinted before Ahab's chariots (1 Kings 18:46); Elisha requests a musician "and when the musician played" the power of the Lord came upon him." The ecstatic state sometimes appeared to outsiders as a frenzy associated with madness (2 Kings 9:11; Jer. 29:26; Hos. 9:7). But unlike pagan prophecy, in Israel ecstasy was only a preparation for prophecy not identical with it. Moreover many of the prophets prophesied without any signs of ecstasy whatsoever.[9]

Fasting was also part of the Israelite cult but the prophets continually underscored that fasting and mortification of the body in themselves are not pleasing to God, except insofar as they transform human moral actions (Isa. 58:3-7). Nevertheless we do find the prophet Ezekiel practicing mortification to induce a vision (Ezek. 4:4-15) and it is quite possible that the visionaries of the biblical period, like the mystics of the Second Temple and talmudic era, fasted in preparation for ecstatic trance.[10] The biblical laws regarding the Nazirite who abstained from wine and did not cut his hair (Lev. 21:6 and Num. 6:8) and the family of the Rechabites who followed Nazirite practices but in addition refused permanent agricultural settlement preferring the pastoral-nomadic way of life (2 Kings 10:15-17; Jer. 35) provided biblical models for ascetic forms of piety in post-biblical times.

If ecstasy and ascetic practices were preparatory stages for prophecy but not identical with it, the out of body experience was an integral part of the prophetic vision itself. Though this experience was far more characteristic of the visions of the apocalyptic visionaries of the Second Temple period, to be discussed in the last chapter, it was not unknown to the biblical prophets. It is implied in the famous Temple initiation of Isaiah which begins with a vision of the Lord on His throne surrounded by His heavenly retinue in the Temple (Isa. 6:1-7). Once the prophet has been purged of his sin, the scene shifts and he is permitted to sit in on the meeting of the divine council taking place in the heavenly realms where he volunteers his services (Isa. 6: 8-13 and parallels in 1 Kings 22:19-22; Job 1:6-12). Far more explicit is Ezek. 11:1 (cf. Ezek. 3:12; 8:2) where the prophet residing in Babylonia is lifted up and brought to the east gate of the Jerusalem Temple.

Notes

1. It is true that Solomon like his father David had a charismatic gift but in both instances it was a gift of God not an inherent talent passed on through heredity. The Bible (1 Kings 3:5-14) is most specific about this in the case of Solomon.

2. Yehezkel Kaufmann, *Toledot ha-'Emunah ha-Yisraelit* (Jerusalem-Tel-Aviv: Bialik Institute-Dvir, 1953) 1: 458-507 and *The Religion of Israel*, trans. Moshe Greenberg (Chicago: University of Chicago Press, 1960), pp. 80-84; Benjamin Uffenheimer, *Ancient Prophecy in Israel* (Hebrew) (Jerusalem: The Magnes Press, 1973), pp. 287-288.

3.   B. Uffenheimer, *Ancient Prophecy in Israel*, pp. 288-289. One need not accept Uffenheimer's view that Numbers 20:12-13 are a later addition. That miracle bordering on magic persisted in the framework of monotheism is evident from the fact that God is credited with the instruction to sculpt a bronze serpent with the power to heal snake bite (Num. 21:8-9), and with the ritual to topple the walls of Jericho (Josh. 6:2-5). There is a good measure of truth in David Sperling's assertion: "Whether an Israelite ritual was 'magical' or 'divine service' depended on its performers, on the group with which it was associated and on the writer responsible for its extant description." "Israel's Religion" in *Jewish Spirituality: From the Bible Through the Middle Ages* ed. by Arthur Green, World Spirituality: An Encyclopedic History of the Religious Quest vol. 13 (New York: Crossroad Publishing Co., 1986), p. 18.

4.   The rabbis commenting on Num. 24:16 state that Balaam knew precisely the hour in which the divine wrath could be kindled to bring down a curse on Israel, *b. Berakot*, 7a.

5.   Kaufmann, *The Religion of Israel*, pp. 109, 309.

6.   Moshe Greenberg, *Biblical Prose Prayer: As A Window to the Popular Religion of Ancient Israel*, The Taubman Lectures in Jewish Studies Sixth Series (Berkeley, Los Angeles, London: University of California Press, 1983), pp. 17, 36. At the opposite pole were stereotyped prayers which grew out of spontaneous prayers that were unusually expressive of personal need and private sentiment. Such individual prayers were imitated by others as voicing better than they could their own feelings. In time such prayers acquired a fixed form and were utilized repeatedly on similar occasions. They were distinguished by the distinct style, phraseology and vocabulary of liturgical poets and were used by worshippers who felt that a visit to the temple called for a more polished utterance than a commoner could supply. In these compositions for set occasions there is often a divergence between what is said and the personal circumstances of the sayer since no standardized prayer couched in general terms can accurately express the individual differences in the life situations of vast numbers of people. The Book of Psalms is such a collection of standardized prayers but it never deterred the devout who continue to pour out their souls to God through the Psalter, reading into the 150 psalms their own personal needs and desires. The use of standing prayers with stereotyped formulas for fixed occasions brought the psalms very close to incantations and in talmudic times and during the Middle Ages they were used as incantations to ward off disease and protect from danger. cf. Joshua Trachtenberg, *Jewish Magic and Superstition* (New York: Atheneum, 1974), pp. 109, 139, 156, 169, 170; M. Grunwald, "Bibliomancy" *Jewish Encyclopedia* (New York and London: Funk and Wagnalls, 1903) 3: 203-4; Joseph Dan, "Magic," *Encyclopedia Judaica* (Jerusalem: Keter Publishing House, 1972) 11:711; Kauffman, *The Religion of Israel*, p. 310; David Sperling, "Israel's Religion" in *Jewish Spirituality*: 19-20.

7.   M. Greenberg, *Biblical Prose Prayer*, pp. 55-56.

8.   Aryeh Kaplan, *Jewish Meditation: A Practical Guide* (New York: Schocken Books, 1985), p. 42.

9.   On ecstasy and prophecy see Kaufmann, *The Religion of Israel*, pp. 94-95; Abraham Joshua Heschel, *The Prophets* (New York and Philadelphia: The Jewish Publication Society of America and Harper & Row, 1963), pp. 324-366; Shalom M. Paul, "Prophets and Prophecy", *Encyclopedia Judaica* (Jerusalem: Keter Publishing House, 1972): 155-56.

10.   G. Scholem, *Major Trends in Jewish Mysticism* (New York: Schocken Books, 1961; first published in 1941), p. 49.   As to whether prophecy and mysticism are distinct phenomena or whether prophecy, though having distinct qualities, is part of the mystical spectrum, opinions differ.   Scholem, *On the Kabbalah and Its Symbolism*, trans. by Ralph Manheim (New York: Schocken Books, 1965), pp. 9-11 and Abraham Joshua Heschel, *God in Search of Man: A Philosophy of Judaism* (Philadelphia: Jewish Publication Society of America, 1956), pp. 198-199 hold they are distinct but Ben Zion Bokser, *The Jewish Mystical Tradition* (New York: The Pilgrim Press, 1981), pp. 6-7 citing Sidney Spencer and J. Abelson argues for the latter view.

Sinai II: The Charismatic Piety of the Second Temple and Talmudic Periods

One of the fundamental differences between the biblical and the post-biblical periods in the Sinai tradition is the dramatic change in the nature of prophecy. From Moses to Malachi there was an unbroken chain of apostle-prophets who appeared before the people bearing God's message. From Moses to Samuel the prophets also served as national leaders guiding the destiny of the Israelites in accordance with divine instruction. After the establishment of the monarchy the prophets served as advisors to the kings of Judah and Israel, ever seeking to bring the affairs of state into harmony with the mandate of heaven. But their power was far greater than that of mere consultants, for from Saul down to the last monarchs of the northern and southern kingdoms, no royal house was ever established or deposed without the authoritative word of the prophet.

After the destruction of the First Temple in 586 B.C.E., with the exception of the Second Isaiah, Haggai, Zechariah and Malachi, whose prophecies are related to the return from Babylonia and the rebuilding of the Second Temple, prophecy went underground. There were no more apostle-prophets who addressed the people as a whole and were directly involved in the affairs of state and the ebb and flow of daily life. Instead there were seers of the apocalypse such as the author of the book of Daniel who disguised themselves under pseudonyms.

There were also individuals who spoke clairvoyantly of the future, who interpreted dreams and whose charismatic gifts were such that their prayers inclined the divine will to grant their requests. But after the victory of Judah Maccabee and his guerrilla forces over the army of Antiochus Epiphanes and the liberation of Jerusalem in 165 B.C.E. there was no prophet who could decide the religious status of the stones of the Temple altar defiled by the Hellenists (1 Macc. 4:46) as Moses might have done. Similarly, there was no prophet to validate in the name of God the rule of Simeon (Judah's brother) over an independent Jewish kingdom in 142 B.C.E. (1 Macc. 14:41-42) as Samuel and his successors might have done.

What are the causes of this vast shift in religious perspective? Hebrew apostolic prophecy is not merely an individual phenomenon. It is a mass event. It is dependent not only on the will of God and the receptivity and personality of the prophet but also on the receptivity and belief system of the public to whom the message is addressed. In turn the belief system of the masses is conditioned not only by political, social, economic and religious changes, but also by the psychological response to these changes.

Throughout the centuries that the apostle-prophets brought God's message to Israel they were often reviled and maltreated but their divine authority was never questioned. To the contrary, prophecy was seen as a gift of God to His chosen people, a sign of His love, as were the land of Israel and the sovereignty of the Hebrew nation. Conversely, in the prophecies of catastrophe, not only was the land and national sovereignty to be taken from the Israelites but also access to God's word via his messengers was to be denied them (Amos 8:11-12: Mic. 3:6-7; Jer. 18:18; Ezek. 7:26, cf. 13:1-23; Zech. 13:2-6). With the destruction of Jerusalem and the exile of the nation the people were overwhelmed by a mass religious-psychological depression whose single conviction was: the anger of God and the eclipse of His presence from Israel. If the prophecies concerning destruction and exile had materialized then the prophecy concerning the shutting off of God's word to His people through the prophets was also a reality. Thus, in the belief system of the exiles and their remnants in Judea, the distance of the divine presence meant the interruption of apostle-prophecy just as the proximity of God in former times had meant its effervescence.[1]

This view is mirrored in the elegy of the destruction ". . . Her prophets, too, receive no vision from the Lord" (Lam. 2:9). An echo of it can be heard in the remark of the Maccabean chronicler describing the mourning of the people after the death of Judah: "There was great tribulation in Israel the like of which had not existed since the time that no prophet appeared unto them" (1 Macc. 9:27). A further echo is to be heard in the statement of the rabbis that prophecy has been taken from the prophets since the day the Temple was destroyed.[2]

There was another aspect of the belief system of the exilic and post-exilic Jews related to their conviction that the era of apostle prophecy had ended. This was their intuitive feeling that the great period of originality that inaugurated the religion of Israel, when the truth of the Sinai teachings was dramatically manifested in public divine revelations to the patriarchs, in the exodus, on the crossing of the Sea, at Sinai and in the land of Israel, was over. Now the great organizing periods were beginning, when all existing culture would be bent into obedience to the highest religious ideas already revealed. In this era the divine spark within the soul of the individual was the source of revelation and the focus was on the inner religious and ethical work that opens up the individual's spiritual channels to divine guidance. The change in the belief system of Israel from the Babylonian exile through the talmudic period and beyond is reflected in the conception of a descending order of divine revelation as follows:

1)   The public revelations of the Mosaic period.

2)   The revelations to the apostle-prophets who brought the message to the people.

3)   The revelation of the Holy Spirit to the authors of the Psalms and the other books of the third section of the Bible, the Writings.

4)   The revelation of the Heavenly Voice (*bat kol*) believed to have been audible to select rabbis of the talmudic era.

5)   The revelation of the prophet Elijah received by the rabbis and the kabbalists of a later period.[3]

An allusion to this conception is to be found in the statement of R. Eliezer ben Hyrcanus that "the maidservant at the crossing of the Sea (of Reeds) saw more than Ezekiel and all the other prophets",[4] i.e., the public revelations of the Mosaic period, though witnessed by ordinary people, take precedence over the visions of Isaiah and Ezekiel that are on a lower rung in the hierarchy of prophetic revelation. In turn, the revelations during the prophetic period are authoritatively higher than the revelations that followed. R. Reuben (third century C.E.) compared the prophetic period to the presence of the king in the city, the time thereafter to the presence of the statue of the king: "The statue cannot do what the king Himself can do."[5]

There were also social and political changes that contributed to the belief system which viewed apostolic-prophecy as a phenomenon of the past. The Persian period was the time of "small things," the concerns of the individual, not the destiny of the nation, which was the main focus of the prophets. Now the nation had dwindled to a small province of the Persian empire. The prophets through their activity were never bound up with any social class nor were they integrated into any religious or governmental institutions. But with the canonization of the Pentateuch by Ezra and his colleagues, Judaism became a religion of the book and a group of scholars emerged, the interpreters of Scripture, who were part of a distinct governing, aristocratic class.[6] When Alexander the Great brought Hellenism to Palestine other far reaching changes occurred, among them the development of parties or sects among the Jews (Pharisees, Sadducces, Essenes) patterned after the non-official, non-state social and religious societies of the Hellenistic world.[7] In the spirit of the time, conditioned by the Hellenistic outlook, reason became as important as revelation and in certain cases (as we shall see further on) even more important in guiding the people.[8] The rabbis state it clearly: "He is Alexander of Macedonia who ruled twelve years. Until then the prophets prophesied through the Holy Spirit, from that point onward incline your ear and listen to the words of the sages."[9]

Nevertheless, in the Jewish religious consciousness of the Second Temple and talmudic periods, revelation was not altogether a matter of the past. People believed that God spoke to human beings, not only through the medium of the Scriptures, but also in direct communications. But these communications were distinct from biblical prophecy. As mentioned earlier, Hebrew prophecy was completely spontaneous, the result of the will of God. It was independent of any personal characteristics of the prophet considered indispensable for the prophetic gift or any preparation on his part. But in the Second Temple period Josephus describes Essene clairvoyants whose skill was the product of training in a discipline or a personal characteristic bestowed as a gift for living a saintly life. Similarly, the rabbis speak of the "worthiness" of an individual to receive the Holy Spirit as the result of intellectual and moral preparation, of personal traits of character as well as certain specific, objective external conditions.[10] Thus we are told: "Once when the elders (Sages) gathered in the house of the family of Gadia in Jericho, and a heavenly voice (*bat kol*) came forth and said to them, "'There is among you a man worthy of the holy spirit only the generation is not worthy of it', all eyes turned to Hillel the elder."[11] In keeping with the analysis above concerning the reasons for the interruption of prophecy, what may be meant here is that the belief system of Hillel's generation had been so modified that it could no longer accept prophecy in the biblical sense and this external condition prevented the Holy Spirit from resting on him even though he personally was eminently qualified. However, during the celebration of the Waterdrawing Festival in the Temple, Hillel's exaltation, and his profoundly spiritual statements to the festive crowd, gave the impression even to his generation that they were witnessing a prophetic revelation though only for the duration of the celebration.[12]

By establishing worthiness as a condition for prophecy the post-biblical age reversed the biblical concept of divine revelation. In the Bible God's call to the prophet marked the beginning of a process in which the prophet, moved by a divine pathos, forced and controlled by a "strong hand," embarked on a mission that revolutionized his life. For the Essenes, as for the rabbis and the writers of the New Testament, God's call to the individual was the result of preparation achieved by study and good deeds. It was the culmination, the end of a process, not its beginning. When the Holy Spirit rested on an individual in the later era it was not conceived as a spontaneous experience overwhelming in its newness and immediateness. Rather it was an awareness of the divine presence entering the human sphere to help and to guide, establishing a more constant coordination and contact between God and man. In addition to other reasons mentioned above, the purpose was to control sudden outbreaks of prophetic spirit that might challenge the religious authority of the time and give new and unexpected direction to the established religious order.[13]

The idea that religious and moral preparation makes one worthy of the Holy Spirit is best epitomized by the statement of Rabbi Pinhas ben Yair, the fifth generation Tanna: "Heedfulness leads to cleanliness; cleanliness leads to purity; purity leads to abstinence; abstinence leads to holiness; holiness leads to humility; humility leads to fear of sin; fear of sin leads to piety (*hasidut*); piety (*hasidut*) leads to the Holy Spirit; the Holy Spirit leads to the resurrection of the dead; and the resurrection of the dead comes through Elijah of blessed memory."[14] The first four terms in this statement spell out the rabbinic requirement for complete observance of ritual purity in all areas of life, including sexual relationships, which is summed up in the fifth term, holiness. This pivotal word leads in turn to matters of ethics and character that have nothing ritual attached to them and no question of priestly cleanliness related to them. Careful observance of the laws of purity and cleanliness, all of which are matters of self-discipline and control of the human appetite, be it for food, sex, wealth or power, leads one to humility. The person has subordinated the individual will to the will of God. Thus humility in turn is the foundation for fear of sin. This is a negative virtue carrying the control that keeps one from ritual impurity, sexual immorality, greed and pride into the more advanced realm of separation from all sin, moral and ritual. All of this prepares one logically for the next step, *hasidut* (piety), the positive side of one's actions, those acts of special piety, ceremonial and ethical, that are the pinnacle of human conduct. Human effort can bring the self no higher than this and from this point on, the ladder no longer concerns itself with what an individual can do but with what can happen to him (or her).[15]

What can happen is that the individual is now potentially the recipient of charismatic gifts, but as in the case of the disciples of the prophets in the biblical period, there was no automatic guarantee that he would receive them. Honi the Circle Drawer (*ha-*

Me'aggel) was the recipient of such gifts some time during the first century B.C.E. We are told: "It once happened that the people turned to Honi the Circle Drawer and asked him to pray for rain. He said to them: 'Go and take in the ovens for the Passover sacrifice so that they may not be dissolved by the rain.' He prayed but no rain fell. What did he do? He drew a circle (or dug a pit) and stood within it and called to God: 'Master of the Universe Your children have turned to me because they believe me to be a member of Your household. I swear by Your great name that I will not move from here until You have mercy upon Your children.' Rain then began to fall. He said: 'It is not for this that I have prayed but for rain to fill cisterns ditches and pools.' The rain then began to come down in great force. He exclaimed: 'It is not for this that I have prayed but for rain of benevolence, blessing and bounty.' Rain then fell in the normal way . . . Thereupon Simeon ben Shetah sent to him this message: 'Were it not that you are Honi I would have placed you under the ban but what can I do to you who importune God and He accedes to your request as a son importunes his father and he accedes to his request."[16]

Unlike biblical prophecy, Honi's charismatic gifts were passed down in inheritance or possibly through instruction to his grandchildren. The fact that the Talmud describes their power to bring rain immediately after the description of their distinguished grandfather's exploits suggests this transmission of charisma. "Abba Hilkiya was a grandson of Honi the circle-Drawer and whenever the world was in need of rain the rabbis sent a message to him and he prayed and rain fell.[17] Another grandchild of Honi the Circle-Drawer was Hanan-who-hid-himself. "When the world was in need of rain the rabbis would send school-children to Hanan . . . and they would take hold of the hem of his garment and say to him, 'Father, father give us rain!' Thereupon he would plead with the Holy One Blessed be He: 'Master of the universe do it for the sake of these who cannot distinguish between the Father who gives rain and the Father who does not give rain.'"[18] Josephus calls this Hanan who successfully prayed for rain Onias and explains his name as coming from the fact that he "hid himself because he saw that the unrest in the country would last a great while."[19] It is quite clear from the talmudic narrative that Honi's grandchildren, like Honi, eminently fulfilled the rabbinic requirement of "worthiness" for their charismatic gifts.

Rabbi Hanina ben Dosa, who lived in the first century C.E., was another recipient of charismatic gifts. He was considered to be a man of very special powers of prayer and healing who could also control supernatural beings. The *Mishna* states that this first generation *tanna* was called upon to pray for the sick and could always predict who would live and who would die.[20] Both Rabban Yohanan ben Zakkai and Rabban Gamaliel called upon him to pray for the lives of their sons, who then recovered.[21] His manner of prayer was to place his head between his knees, a position strikingly similar to the meditative trance of Elijah on Mount Carmel and the visionary Riders of the Chariot.[22] Rabban Yohanan ben Zakkai remarked that he could have "put his head between his knees all day" without being answered and explained to his puzzled wife that it was not because Hanina was greater than he was, but because "he is like a servant before the king and I am like a high official before the king." The phrase is similar to that used by Simeon be Shetach, who spoke of Honi whose prayers were answered by God because he was like a spoiled child being indulged by his father. Like Honi, Hanina had special powers of praying for rain and caused it to rain or stop raining at the drop of a phrase.[23] Rabbi Haninah, like Honi, rose to the summit of the rabbinic ladder of perfection described by Rabbi Pinhas ben Yair and a heavenly voice proclaimed that "the whole world is sustained for the sake of My son Haninah."[24] He performed many miracles for others and many miracles were performed for him and his wife.[25]

Both Honi the Circle Drawer and Rabbi Hanina ben Dosa provide examples *par excellence* of the rabbinic attitude toward miracles and prayer. Simeon ben Shetah's threat to excommunicate Honi undoubtedly was based on the assumption that Honi's behavior was reminiscent of a magician certain of his powers and his intercessory prayer was perilously close to a magical incantation. Honi readily accepted without any hesitation the role of intercessor and when he ordered the people to remove from the open yards the earthen ovens set up for roasting the Pascal lambs on the eve of the Passover, he showed unseemly confidence in the immediate and full effect of his prayer. When he received no answer to his prayer, he drew the mandala-like circle (or dug the pit), an action with the earmarks of magic on it, and stood in it and swore by God's name (the rabbis were vehemently against such oaths) that he would not move until his prayer was answered. It was as though he intended or was able to force the Almighty to yield and send rain. The Talmud, like the Bible, considered such arrogance unseemly in a Hebrew prophet or in his charismatic descendant.[26]

In contrast, Rabbi Haninah ben Dosah seems to have been more subdued. In praying for the recovery of the sons of Rabban Johanan ben Zakkai and Rabban Gamaliel, R. Haninah did not have the patients brought before him, nor was he invited to see them, so that no personal influence was to be exercised upon the children. When the boys recovered and they asked him whether he was a prophet, he replied: "I am neither a prophet nor the son of a prophet (citing Amos 7:14) but I have the tradition that when my prayer is fluent in my mouth, I know that it is acceptable, and when it is not fluent it is rejected."[27]   R. Hanina's intercessory prayer had no force to compel God to yield. If God was willing to restore the patient to health, He granted a reassuring sign to R. Haninah and if it was God's will that the sick person not recover, this too was indicated to R. Hanina by the lack of fluency. In another incident when he was informed that the daughter of a pious man who was a digger of public pits had fallen into a deep pit, he clairvoyantly foretold her rescue. When asked how he knew it, he modestly declined any special abilities (again citing Amos 7:14) but pointed to God's law of reciprocity. "Should the daughter of the righteous man perish by the very thing that is his occupation?"[28]

The rabbis echoed the biblical opposition to magic but like their biblical predecessors they did not deny its efficacy.[29]   Rituals such as the rite of the red heifer (Num. 19), that resemble magic rites, were given a religious-moral interpretation. The miracle stories of the early and the later sages were used to justify the truth of the Sinai tradition and to validate its beliefs, practices and religious institutions. The rabbis underscored their belief that miracles were performed only for those of absolute faith and unimpeachable morality who were ready to sacrifice themselves for God. Miracles, as we saw above in the incident of R. Hanina ben Dosa, were also seen as validation of the doctrine of reciprocity. Throughout talmudic literature the view is expressed that miracles that take place outside the framework of natural law are less of a marvel than those that take place according to natural law—a clear attempt to rationalize the miraculous. Finally, in rabbinic miracle stories there is a conscious attempt to subordinate the personality of the miracle maker.[30]

If the rabbinic view of miracles, echoing the Bible, was that they are a spontaneous act of God that can be prayed for but never absolutely counted on, the rabbinic view of prayer, also echoing the Bible, was that it should be a spontaneous expression of man. In this respect the prayers of Honi the Circle-Drawer and R. Hanina ben Dosa are models of spontaneity. They are, like the prophetic prayers, conversations with God, reflecting human patterns of speech and the human contexts of petitioning, confessing and expressing gratitude. The moral integrity, the character of the one who prayed and the people for whom he prayed were as significant for the rabbis in determining God's response as they were for the prophets.[31] Similarly, the prayers of R. Hanina ben Dosa and others became stereotyped because ordinary people must have felt the prayers of these saintly men to be more effective than their own utterances. Standardized prayer was important to the rabbis who sought to unite the Jewish people around a distinct worship service in the synagogue, particularly after the destruction of the Second Temple in 70 C.E.[32] But they were also aware of the danger that conformity could be achieved at the expense of spontaneity. Thus R. Simeon said: "When you pray do not make your prayers a set routine (*keva*) but offer them as a plea for mercy and graciousness before God . . ."[33] and Rabbi Elezer said: "He who makes his prayer a set routine (*keva*), his prayer is not an act of grace."[34] How then did they meet these twin objectives?

> When the sages ordained the obligatory fixed prayers, they did not prescribe their exact wording . . . They prescribed a framework: the number of benedictions comprising each prayer—such as the eighteen of the week-day *amidah*, the seven of the Sabbath and festival, and so forth. They also prescribed the topic of each benediction; for example, in a given benediction one must ask for the rebuilding of Jerusalem; in another for the ingathering of the exiles. But they did not, nor did they ever seek to, prescribe the wording of any benediction or any prayer. That was left as a rule to the prayer-to be exact to the prayer-leader (a layman).[35]

In capsulizing the charismatic piety of the Second Temple and talmudic period we can describe it as carrying on the prophetic tradition of ecstatic prayer (such as the early pietists, *Hasidim ha-rishonim*, who meditated one hour before beginning to pray[36]) and the performance of miracles. These charismatics often participated in mystical experiences[37] and were scrupulous in the observance of the ritual and the moral law, going beyond the legal requirements in these areas. They were forgiving of wrongs done to them and would not insist on their legal rights in cases of civil law. There was a tendency toward asceticism in some charismatics who looked upon the Nazarite as a holy person.[38] This type of piety was not institutionalized. Its practitioners belonged to no organization in which there were vows and pledges or provisions for acceptance or expulsion. In the words of Solomon Schechter:

> In speaking of saints it should be premised that I am not
> referring to organizations or societies bearing the name. The
> references in Jewish literature to such organizations are few
> and of a doubtful nature, and will certainly not stand the test
> of any scientific criticism. Besides, one does not become a
> saint by reason of a corporate act, or by subscribing to a
> certain set of rules, though a man may be a saint despite his
> being a member of a society or community composed of
> professional saints.[39]

The charismatics described above were primarily associated with
the Pharisees and their rabbinic successors. There were, however,
in the Second Temple period, two types of charismatics whose
outlook and practices resembled in some respects that of their
Pharisaic counterparts but also distinctly differed from them—the
Essenes and Jesus. Josephus, the Jewish historian of the Second
Temple period, underscores the prophetic gifts among the Essenes
that included the interpretation of dreams and clairvoyant
predictions concerning the future.[40]   They sought to impart
instruction in this art to their disciples and, as noted above,
believed that "worthiness" for prophecy could be achieved by the
study of Scripture, ritual purifications, and scrupulous moral
integrity.[41]

Philo and Josephus described the Essenes as especially devout in
God's service but not by offering animal sacrifice but in sanctifying
their minds. They lived communally in villages, rejecting slavery
and despising wealth, preferring manual labor on the land. The
groups are described as celibate but not all of the Essene-like
groups followed this rule.[42]   The Essenes avoided all talk before
morning prayer, waiting silently for a long period to direct their
hearts to God and possibly waiting silently again after prayer. In
their Sabbath regulations they were stricter than other Jews. The
Essenes maintained the tradition of spontaneous prayer but over a
period of time undoubtedly some of their prayers became
stereotyped.[43] It should be noted that the Essenes were opposed to
sacrifice not because they rejected the cult *per se* but because they
opposed the temple priests of their time as corrupt and their service
in Jerusalem as illegitimate. The Essenes and Pharisees based their
patterns of piety on the model of the early charismatic pietists
(*hasidim ha-rishonim*) who lived before the Maccabean Era, but
both religious groups modified these beliefs and practices due to the
changed circumstances that were ushered in with the Maccabean
Revolt and the establishment of the Second Jewish Commonwealth.
The tight organizational structure of the Essenes and the Pharisaic

societies (*havurot*) are among the factors that differentiate these groups from the earlier pietists.[44]

The life and teachings of Jesus of Nazareth as recorded in the Gospels, originating during the Tannaitic period, have frequently been shown to contain strong resemblances to rabbinic models of piety and to rabbinic statements of the same period. There are also parallels to numerous rabbinic utterances which, though ascribed to later authorities, are based on earlier traditions.[45] The charismatic powers of Jesus are clearly evident in most of the major stories in the Gospels. He had the power to make anyone he wanted to follow him. Like Elijah and Elisha, he induced miraculous cures and like Elijah and Elisha, he miraculously provided food when it was needed. Like Jonah, Jesus could still storms. Jesus' prayers for the sick (that bring healing) are strikingly reminiscent of Rabbi Hanina ben Dosa, and like Rabbi Hanina, who is described as having power over demons to force them to leave the realm of earth,[46] Jesus overcame the devil and cast out demons.[47]

But these charismatic powers were but the by-product of a life devoted not only to the fulfillment of the biblical teachings but also to going beyond the strict demands of the written law.[48] Jesus' expansion of the biblical commandment "Love your neighbor as yourself" (Lev. 19:18) is explained by David Daube as follows: ". . . wider and deeper though it may be it is thought of as, in a sense, resulting from and certainly including the old rule, it is the revelation of a fuller meaning for a new age. The second member unfolds rather than sweeps away the first."[49] Daube has also explained Jesus' admonition: "You have heard that it was said: 'An eye for an eye and a tooth for a tooth.' But I say to you. Do not resist evil. But if anyone strikes you on the right cheek, turn to him the other also; and if anyone would sue you and take your coat, let him have your cloak as well" (Matt. 5:30-40). According to Daube, Jesus is against insisting upon rights of compensation for insult, of which striking the cheek is one instance. According to rabbinic law[50] one could receive payment for being shamed. Jesus, teaching the higher ethic of charismatic piety, urges that one should not stand on one's legal rights in such a matter.[51]

Jesus' preference for what the rabbis called private prayer (Matt. 6:5-6), which is direct and specific with regards to the condition of the worshiper, is a continuation of the prophetic tradition of spontaneous prayer. But with the development of institutionalized Christianity the Lord's prayer, like the psalms and the rabbinic liturgy, became standardized and stereotyped.[52] Spontaneity and the lack of formal organization also characterized Jesus' ministry. He lived as a wandering preacher with a circle of disciples, akin to the Hebrew prophets and their bands (*benei ha-neviim*), without formal rules, vows, pledges or by-laws, a situation that threatened to dissolve into chaos after his death.[53]

Though Jesus upheld the Torah he differed with the Pharisaic charismatics over their emphasis upon extreme care in fulfillment of ritual commands which to them were no less important than ethical demands, since ritual was seen as the foundation upon which morality was to be built. Jesus did not accept all the interpretations of the Scribes and the Pharisees which constituted the Oral Law and in this respect he somewhat resembled the Sadducees who also rejected the oral Law. But Jesus' differences with the Pharisees, unlike the Sadduceean objections, were not doctrinal. His negativism toward the more sophisticated, scholarly, urban Judean Pharisees reflect his Galilean origins. In the Galilee the Jews were rural, unsophisticated, and much more relaxed in their religious observances. The anti-scholastic feeling that Jesus sometimes exhibits was also to be found in a later generation in Akiba, who stated that before he entered the world of the scholars he passionately hated them.[54] Jesus also questioned the Pharisaic assumption that extreme punctiliousness in matters of ritual would lead to equal scrupulousness in matters of ethics. He felt that an exaggerated zealousness in ritual matters could lead to the kind of religious behaviorism denounced by the prophets (Isaiah 29:13) in which the routine of ritual eclipsed the spiritual and the ethical.

> Woe to you scribes and Pharisees hypocrites! for you tithe mint and dill and cumin, and have neglected the weightier matters of the law, justice and mercy and faith; these you ought to have done, without neglecting the others (Matt. 23:23).

The final phrase in this verse shows that Jesus did not say that the ritual law should not be observed, but that he feels that an excessive emphasis has been placed upon it. Finally, the emphasis upon sexual asceticism in the Gospels goes far beyond the modesty and propriety urged by the Pharisaic charismatics, pointing to the influence of the Essenes on Jesus and his circle.

Notes

1. Yehezkel Kaufmann, *Toledot ha-'Emunah ha-Yisraelit*, 4:389-390. According to Kaufmann, the exceptions of the Second Isaiah, Haggai, Zechariah and Malachi, apostle prophets who prophesied after the destruction of Jerusalem, prove the rule. For these prophecies were delivered under the impact of the Edict of Cyrus the Great as the hope of redemption and the promise of return to the land and the rebuilding of the Temple lifted the depression of the people and caused their belief system to revert once more to the faith in the divine presence that had returned to dwell in their midst. *Ibid.*, 391-392; 393-394.

2. b. *Bava Batra*, 12a-b.

3. Gershom Scholem, *On the Kabbalah and Its Symbolism*, pp. 19-20. The term *bat kol*, Heavenly Voice is used interchangeably with *ruah ha-kodesh* in talmudic literature, cf. Saul Lieberman, *Hellenism in Jewish Palestine* (New York: The Jewish Theological Seminary, 1950), pp. 203-208 and the pagan and Christian parallels cited there. With the advent of Christianity and its challenge of a competing revelation, the tendency became even more pronounced to derive all later prophecy from the prophecy of Moses. See Nahum N. Glatzer, "A Study of the Talmudic Interpretation of Prophecy," *The Review of Religion* (January, 1946): 116-118; 127. Cf. H. Parzen, "The Ruah ha-Kodesh in Tannaitic Literature," *Jewish Quarterly Review*, N.S. 20 (July, 1929): 51-76.

4. *Mekilta de Rabbi Ishmael* to Exod. 15:2, Tractate Shirata (ed. Lauterbach) 2:24-25.

5. *Cant. R.* 2:11.

6. During the time of Ezra, the governing body of the Jews was an organization called "The Community" composed primarily of various clans led by *Sarim* or heads of fathers' houses (Ezra 10:7, 8, 14, 16; Neh. 10:1; 11:1 ff.). The religious authorities were the Levites (Neh. 8:7, 9, 11; 9;4ff.). During the second half of the Persian period, the *Sarim* and Levites yielded their authority to a council of elders and prophets called in talmudic sources "The Men of the Great Synagogue" (*Anshe Knesset ha-Gedolah*). cf. Hugo Mantel, "The Development of the Oral Law During the Second Temple Period" in *The World History of the Jewish People* ed. by Michael Avi Yonah and Zvi Barras, vol. 8: *Society and Religion in the Second Temple Period* (Jerusalem: Masada Publishing Co., 1977), pp. 42-48.

7. Hugo Mantel "The Nature of the Great Synagogue," *Harvard Theological Review* 60 (1967): 75-91. And in expanded form, H. D. Mantel, *The Men of the Great Synagogue* (Hebrew) (Jerusalem: Dvir, 1983), Passim. The Hellenistic societies were the Greek world's counterpart of modern pluralism. With the triumph of Alexander the Great came the establishment of Greek religion as the official state cult but the voluntary religious associations were dedicated to the cult of deities other than those of the established state religion. Cf. M. N. Tod, *Sidelights on Greek History* (Oxford: Oxford University Press, 1932), p. 71 ff.; W. L. Westerman, "Entertainment in the Villages of Graeco-Roman Egypt," *The Journal of*

Egyptian Archaeology 18 (1932): 16-27 and H. D. Mantel "The Sadducees and the Pharisees" in *the World History of the Jewish People*, vol. 8: *Society and Religion in the Second Temple Period*, pp. 99-125. On the Essenes see J. Licht, "The Qumran Sect and Its Scrolls," *Ibid.*, pp. 125-152.

8. Yitzhak Baer, *Yisrael Ba-Amim* (Jerusalem: Bialik Institute, 1955), 37ff. On the impact of Greek civilization on Palestine and the Jewish Diaspora see Menahem Stern, "The Period of the Second Temple" in *A History of the Jewish People* ed. by H. H. Ben Sasson (Cambridge: Harvard University Press, 1976), pp. 185-238; 282-295; Salo W. Baron, *A Social and Religious History of the Jews* (New York: Columbia University Press, 1952) 2:3-56.

9. *Seder Olam Rabba*, Ch. 6 (ed, B. Ratner, Vilna, 1894-97), p. 70b. This change did not come about abruptly. After Malachi, the last of the classical prophets, according to talmudic tradition (*Tos. Sotah* 13, 2 (ed. Zuckermandl), p. 318; *b. Sotah*, 48b; *b. Yoma*, 9b; *b. Sanhedrin*, 11a; *Avot de Rabbi Natan*, version 1, Ch. 1, (ed. Schechter), p. 2; *The Fathers According to Rabbi Nathan* trans. Judah Goldin (New Haven: Yale University Press, 1955), p. 4, there evolved a group of scholar-prophets (to be discussed more fully below) who took the place of the levitical teachers in the time of Ezra. It is the end of the activity of the scholar-prophets to whom the *Seder Olam Rabba* refers, Mantel, "The Nature of the Great Synagogue," *Harvard Theological Review* 60 (1967): 71.

10. Flavius Josephus, *The Wars of the Jews* 2,8,12.; *Mekilta de Rabbi Ishmael*, Tractate *Pisha*, 11 (ed. Lauterbach), p. 89b; *b. Nedarim*, 38a (R. Johanan); *b. Shabbat*, 30b, 92a; *b. Pesahim*, 66b; 117a; *Sifre, Behaalotekah* 95 (ed. Friedman), p. 96; *Tanhuma, Mikez* 6 (ed. Buber), p. 192.

11. *b. Sotah*, 48b; *Yer. Sotah* 9:24b; *Tos. Sotah* 13:3. Adolf Buchler, *Types of Jewish-Palestinian Piety: From 70 B.C.E. to 70 C.E.* (New York: Ktav Publishing House, 1968), p. 9, n. 1 suggests that the contrast between Hillel and his generation reflects the feeling of his colleagues who "did not sufficiently appreciate his great qualities and did not think him worthy of the position he was holding." According to this interpretation the Heavenly Voice sought to dispel this attitude. Samuel the Little (*ha-Katan*) was also proclaimed by the Heavenly Voice (*bat kol*) as worthy of the Holy Spirit, *Tos. Sotah* 13:3, *b. Sanhedrin*, 11a.

12. *b Sukkah*, 53a; *Yer Sukkah* 5:7; E. E. Urbach, "Matay Paskah ha-Nevuah," *Tarbiz* 17 (1945), p. 7. Significant also is the comment of the Palestinian Amora R. Joshua b. Levi (3rd century), who himself was the recipient of revelations from the prophet Elijah: "Why was its name (i.e., the celebration) called *bet shoevah*, the drawing forth, because from that place they drew forth the Holy Spirit. *Yer. Sukkah* 5:1; *Pesikta Rabbati* 1:2 (ed. Friedman), p. 1b; *Tosafot* to *b. Sukkah*, 50b, s.v. *Had*.

13. Glatzer, "A Study of the Talmudic Interpretation of Prophecy," *Review of Religion*: 124.

14. *M. Sotah* 9:25; *b. Avodah Zarah*, 20b; *Yer. Shekalim* 3:4; *Yer. Shabbat* 1:3; *Midrash Tannaim* to Deut. 23:15 (ed. Hoffman); *Cant. R* 1:9. For an analysis of the different versions see Robert Alan Hammer, Hasidut in Early

Rabbinic Literature: A Study of the Pharisaic Concept of Piety, (Ph.D. Dissertation, Jewish Theological Seminary of America, 1969), Vol. 1, Ch. 5, pp. 6-7.

15. Hammer, Hasidut 1, Ch. 5, p. 9 rightly rejects Buchlers interpretation (*Types of Jewish-Palestinian Piety*, pp. 42-55) of these terms as referring primarily to sexual practices.

16. *M. Ta'anit*, 3:8; *b. Ta'anit*, 23a; *Yer. Ta'anit* 3:10-12. Honi, like the biblical prophets, had disciples who sought to learn his form of ecstatic prayer. Cf. *Tos. Rosh Ha-Shanah* 4:11; Buchler, *Types of Jewish-Palestinian Piety*, pp. 256-257.

17. *b. Ta'anit*, 23a.

18. *b. Ta'anit*, 23b. In the folk beliefs of many people drought is brought on by the sin of fornication. School children, who cannot as yet commit this sin, are considered to be effective intercessors in relieving drought. See Raphael Patai, *Man and Temple: In Ancient Jewish Myth and Ritual* (New York: Ktav Publishing House, 1967), reprint of 1947 ed., pp. 156-160.

19. Josephus, *Antiquities* 14,2,1.

20. *M. Berakot*, 5:5.

21. *b. Berakot*, 34b; *Yer. Berakot*, 5:5.

22. G. Scholem, *Major Trends in Jewish Mysticism* (New York: Schocken Books, 1941), pp. 49-50. So intense was R. Hanina's trance in prayer that he did not feel a snake bite and the snake was later found dead at the entrance to its den. *Yer. Berakot* 5:1. ·

23. *b. Ta'anit*, 24b.

24. *Ibid.*

25. See note 31 and Buchler, *Some Types of Jewish-Palestinian Piety*, pp. 96-100 and sources cited there. Hammer, Hasidut 1, Ch. 5, pp. 4-5 defines *anshe ma'aseh* as men of wondrous deeds, i.e., men of special powers.

26. Honi's prayer was not answered immediately because it lacked modesty, *Yer. Ta'anit* 3:9.

27. See note 30.

28. *b. Yevamot*, 121b; *Yer. Shekalim* 5:1 where the protagonist is R. Pinhas ben Yair.

29. *b. Sanhedrin*, 67b-68a and Trachtenberg, *Jewish Magic and Superstition*, pp. 19-23.

30. E. E. Urbach, *The Sages*, pp. 97-123. Philo sees miracles as implanted in the natural order by God at the time of creation. Though the ordinances of the natural order are immutable, God has "reserved for Himself, mentally, the right to upset the order of nature, at least temporarily, whenever there should be a need for it . . ." cf. Harry A. Wolfson, *Philo* 1:347-348.

31. Buchler, *Types of Jewish-Palestinian Piety*, pp. 214-221 and the sources cited there.

32. *Ibid.*, pp. 240-246.

33. *M. Avot* 2:18.

34. *M. Berakot*, 4:4. On the polarity of *keva*, set routine and *kavannah*, inner devotion (lit. the directing, the focusing of attention and

consciousness) see Abraham Joshua Heschel, *Man's Quest For God* (New York: Charles Scribner's Sons, 1954), pp. 64-70.

35. Joseph Heinemann, "Fixity and Renewal in Jewish Prayer" in Gabriel H. Cohen, ed. *Jewish Prayer: Continuity and Innovation* (Hebrew) (Jerusalem: Kedem, 1978), p. 79f. and Joseph Heineman, *Prayer in the Talmud: Forms and Patterns*, English version by Richard S. Sarason (Berlin, New York: de Gruyter, 1977), pp. 37-69. For the rabbis the prophetic ideal of completely spontaneous prayer which is direct and specific with regards to the condition of the worshipper was best realized in private prayer. For a comprehensive but more general treatment of the subject see Abraham Milgram, *Jewish Worship* (Philadelphia: The Jewish Publication Society of America, 1971).

36. *M. Berakot,* 5:1.

37. Among the Tannaim not already mentioned: R. Yohanan b. Zakkai, *Yer. Hagigah* 2:1; R. Yosi ha-Kohen, Ben Azzai, Ben Zoma, Elsiha b. Avuyah, R. Akiba, R. Joshua b. Hananyah, *M. Hagigah* 2:3; *b. Hagigah,* 14b; R. Eliezer b. Hyrcanus, *b. Sanhedrin,* 68a; R. Simeon b. Yohai, *b. Shabbat,* 33b. Among the Amoraim, R. Joshua b. Levi, *Yer Terumot* 8:10; Rav, *b. Kiddushin,* 71a; R. Shimon Hasida, *b. Yevamot* 60b; *b. Sanhedrin,* 16a; *b. Menahot,* 35b; *b. Sanhedrin,* 22a and the daughter of R. Nahman *b. Gettin,* 45a. Cf. Gershom Scholem, *Jewish Gnosticism, Merkabah Mysticism and Talmudic Tradition* (New York: The Jewish Theological Seminary of America, 1960). One type of mystical experience was connected with the thread of blue in the fringes on each corner of the garment mandated by biblical law (Num. 15:37-41; Deut. 22:12). The color blue was associated with the sky and the deity and the thread of blue became a focal point for meditation and a talisman guarding one from sin, injury and death. Cf. Ben Zion Bokser, "The Thread of Blue," *Proceedings of the American Academy for Jewish Research* 31 (1963): 1-31.

38. *b. Ta'anit,* 11a-b; *Tos. Nedarim* 1:1; *Yer. Nedarim* 1:1; *b. Nazir,* 3a; 22a; *b. Sotah,* 15a; *Numbers R.* 10:15.

39. Solomon Schechter, *Studies in Judaism* (New York: Atheneum, 1970), p. 127.

40. *Antiquities* 17,13,3; *Antiquities* 13,11,2.

41. *Antiquities* 13,11,2; *Wars* 1,3,5; *Wars* 2,8,12. On the moral scrupulousness of the Essenes see *The Dead Sea Manual of Discipline,* trans. by William H. Brownlee (New Haven: American Schools of Oriental Research Bulletin, Supplementary Studies, No. 10-12, 1951).

42. Philo, *Every Good Man Is Free,* ed. Loeb Classics, trans. by Colson-Whitaker (London: Heinemann; Cambridge: Harvard University Press, 1960), Vol. 9, p. 75f. cf. *Hypothetica* 11;1, ed. Loeb Classics, 9:437. Josephus, *Wars* 2,8:2-12 and par. 13 on Essenes who do marry: *Antiquities* 18,1,5. G. Vermes, *The Dead Sea Scrolls: Qumran in Perspective* (Philadelphia: Fortress, 1981), pp. 87-115. In recent years an inscription was discovered on a rocky hillside near Kashmir, dated about 250 B.C.E., and proclaiming the reforms of Asoka, the Buddhist missionary Emperor of India. Asoka, who reigned in India from 273 to 231 B.C.E. sought to spread

the Buddhist faith through missionaries whom he sent as far as Egypt, Syria and even Greece. Scholars are speculating as to whether the Essenes in Palestine and the Therapeutae in Egypt described by Philo and Josephus were influenced by Buddhist models. See G. Pugliese Caratelli and G. Levi Della Vide, "Un Editto Bilingue Greco-Aramico Di Asoka," *Serie Orientale Roma* 21 (1958): 1-34; A. Dupont Sommer, "L'Inscription Punique," *Journal Asiatique* 252, No. 3 (1964): 289-302.

43. Yigael Yadin, *The Message of the Scrolls* (New York: Grosset & Dunlap, 1962), pp. 105-111.

44. See above notes 17 and 40. Hammer, *Hasidut* vol. 1, Ch. 3, pp. 6-9. Baer, *Yisrael Ba-Amim*, p. 43ff states that the Essenes are the *hasidim harishonim*.

45. Morton Smith, *Tannaitic Parallels to the Gospels* (Philadelphia: Society of Biblical Literature, 1951) and Morton Smith, *Jesus the Magician* (New York: Harper & Row, 1977); Strack-Billerbeck, *Kommentar zum Neuen Testament aus Talmud und Midrasch* (Munich: Beck, 1922-1928); Israel Abrahams, *Studies in Pharisaism and the Gospels*, First and Second Series (Cambridge: University Press, 1917, 1924); David Flusser, *Jesus*, trans. by Ronald Walls (New York: Herder and Herder, 1969). Also important are the following articles in the *Hebrew Union College Annual* 1 (1924): Louis Ginzberg, "The Religion of Jews at the Time of Jesus," p. 307; Jacob Mann, "Rabbinic Studies in the Synoptic Gospels," p. 323; Solomon Zeitlin, "The Halaha in the Gospels and Its Relation to the Jewish Law at the Time of Jesus," p. 357.

46. *b. Pesahim*, 112b.

47. Matt. 4: 1-11; Matt. 8: 28-34. Cf. Morton Smith, *The Secret Gospel* (New York, Evanston, San Francisco, London: Harper & Row, 1973), pp. 105-106.

48. Matt. 5: 21-43 contains a list of biblical commandments that Jesus affirms but also calls for going beyond them. See also Matt. 5; 17-19 for Jesus' ringing affirmation of the Torah and Prophets.

49. David Daube, *The New Testament and Rabbinic Judaism* (London: Athlone Press, 1956), p. 60.

50. *M. Bava Kamma* 8:1.

51. Daube, *The New Testament and Rabbinic Judaism*, p. 254ff.

52. Joseph Heineman, "The Background of Jesus' Prayer in the Jewish Liturgical Tradition," and Jean Carmignac, "The Spiritual Wealth of the Lord's Prayer" in *The Lord's Prayer and Jewish Liturgy* ed. by Jakob J. Petuchowski and Michael Brocke (New York: Seabury Press, 1978), pp. 81-89; 137-146.

53. Elaine Pagels, *The Gnostic Gospels* (New York: Vintage Books, 1979), p. 7ff.

54. *b. Pesahim*, 49b.

Sinai III: The Older Biblical Wisdom Piety

Prophecy and Wisdom

Alongside the currents of prophetic piety (discussed above) and priestly piety (to be discussed in the next chapter) there flowed through Hebrew faith a third stream which the scholars have called the piety of wisdom. If prophetic piety derived its impetus from divine revelation and priestly piety its impulse from the cult, wisdom piety had its source in human experience. Its origins lie in the disintegration of an understanding of reality that has been described as pan-sacralism, i.e., the viewing of all existence in the framework of the holy. With the process of secularization the focus is shifted somewhat from the divine to the human, from revelation to the rational search for knowledge. It can be said that in the prophetic view God was in search of man, offering guidance on life's journey, while from the vantage point of wisdom, man, though constantly aware of God's presence, was in search of himself, mapping his course according to the guideposts of human culture.[1]

The prophets experienced God as a powerful, dynamic, living presence continually confronting humanity with critical choices. They felt a compelling urgency to articulate the meaning of that divine presence and its radically realistic demands of religion and morality. The wisdom teachers perceived God in the created order, in the workings of the world and in the moral order of human life and relationships. God was present in a structure of meaning that could and should be understood by those who have eyes to see and ears to hear. They were less urgent and forthright but more patient, since their primary task was to educate the minds and stimulate the consciences of young men who were learning about life. Their patience was also part of a lifelong habit of observation and the slow accumulation of knowledge rather than cataclysmic religious experience. The prophetic focus was on "the whole family which (God) had brought up from the land of Egypt" (Amos 3:1), while the wisdom teachers were concerned with man as an individual member of the human race. The overwhelming concern for the destiny of the nation combined with the overpowering impulse of the divine imperative made the prophets oblivious to the dangers of challenging the political establishment and the power structure. The wisdom teachers were far more prudent. Their attitude was best summed up by Ecclesiastes (known in Hebrew as *Kohelet*). "Obey the king's orders . . . inasmuch as a king's command is authoritative, and none can say to him 'What are you doing?' One who obeys orders will not suffer from the dangerous situation." (Eccles. 8:2-5).

Nevertheless, we must be careful not to dichotomize wisdom and prophecy since they had much in common and in the cultural and spiritual life of ancient Israel they interacted and influenced each other. Both prophets and wise men belonged to the intellectually active and articulate level of society, with the prophets rooted in the style and tradition of the charismatic orators and the wise men practicing the style and traditions of the scribes and teachers. Both drew on the common sources of ethical thinking prevalent throughout the Near East. The sages and prophets were not too distant from one another in their views of the cult, with the former (until Joshua ben Sira) viewing the cult with indifference (Prov. 21:3; 16:6 represent the spiritualization of cultic terms)[2] and the latter emphasizing its subordination to morality. The prophets used the literary forms of wisdom, the riddle, the parable and the proverbial saying, and the wisdom teacher's religious development was an outgrowth of prophetic faith. Some wisdom teachers such as Sira were even aware of their own prophetic gifts (Sira 1:10; 24:33). A clear example of the impact of prophecy on wisdom is the divine revelation with which the Book of Job reaches its climax.[3]

The Historical Development of Wisdom

The Hebrew term for wisdom is *hokmah* and the term for a wise man is *hakam*. The primary meaning underlying both terms is "superior mental ability or special skill." Thus Bezalel, the craftsman and designer of the tabernacle, was skillful "in wisdom" (Exod. 35:31-33). It is also noteworthy that Bezalel was inspired to teach (Exod. 35:34). One of the specialized skills was that of the scribe, who undoubtedly taught others and served not only the needs of the individual but also the needs of institutions, the courts, the temple and the monarchy. He was thus the wise man *par excellence*. There was also the specialized wisdom of farmers, merchants, musicians, soldiers, political counselors, astrologers, priests, judges and kings. A second meaning attached to the terms "wisdom and wise" is a *savoir faire* about life and its problems. This sagacity is part of the folk wisdom that appears spontaneously in traditional societies. It was formulated in proverbs and riddles and was passed on from parents to children as the heritage of "what wise men have told, and their fathers have not hidden." But this kind of wisdom was also transmitted in a more formal way, as part of the curriculum of the schools in which wisdom teachers instructed the young from texts and collections like the biblical Book of Proverbs. Finally, the terms "wisdom" and "wise" have the connotation of moral discernment and in its later stages wisdom is associated with metaphysical and theological thought.

The various meanings of the terms "wisdom" and "wise man" have also given us a glimpse of the circles in which the wise functioned. Broadly speaking, these wisdom circles can be divided into two categories, secular wisdom and religious wisdom. In the First Temple period secular wisdom was to be found in the political institutions of the monarchy, in the court counselors, the scribes and the remembrancer (the writer of the official histories of the kings). It is no accident that Solomon is reputed to have been a master of all forms of wisdom—political cunning (1 Kings 2:1-2; 5-6); moral discernment (1 Kings 3:9, 12); intellectual brilliance and encyclopedic knowledge (1 Kings 5:9-14); competent rules and administration (1 Kings 4 and 1 Kings 5:26). Secular wisdom was not only part of the professional class of ancient Israel described above, it was also the stock in trade of the educators in the schools. Even though the first direct reference to a school is not found until the very late book of Joshua ben Sira, scholars have assumed that these schools were in existence in Israel also during the First Temple period.[4] Secular wisdom was also embodied in the creations of the ballad singers and poets who entertained the people. The Song of Songs belonged to this genre until it was incorporated, through interpretation, into the canon of the Bible.

Religious wisdom was an integral part of the priestly schools, where questions of ritual and the complex distinctions between the clean and the unclean were taught. The priests in their roles of judges and medical experts also preserved the civil and commercial codes of society and the handbooks for the diagnosis of leprosy and other maladies. As late as the Second Temple period the prophets Haggai, Zechariah and Malachi point to the priests as the repositories of wisdom. "For the lips of a priest guard knowledge and men seek rulings from his mouth" (Mal. 2:7; cf. Hag. 2:11-15; Zech. 3:6-10; 7:2-6). Religious wisdom schools also included the Levites who were instructed in numerous skills concerned with the Temple including choral singing and the playing of musical instruments (Pss. 88, 89, and 92; 1 Chron. 15:19) as well as the interpretation and preaching of old traditions. There were scribes connected with the prophets such as Baruch, the amanuensis of Jeremiah, and there must have been wise men and women in the prophetic bands, the *benei ha-neviim*, the disciples of the prophets. There were also religious wisdom teachers who, like their secular counterparts, focused on teaching the individual to lead the good life as ordained by God.

A critical turning point in the development of religious wisdom was the appearance of Ezra in Jerusalem, in the fifth century B.C.E., with a copy of the Torah, which was not only a code of laws, but the book of Israel's covenant with God, the source and summation of religious wisdom. It was Ezra who, though a priest himself, inaugurated the first organized revolt against the authority of the high priest as a supreme judge of religious law. Under the tutelage of Ezra an entire class of non-priestly lay scribes and teachers emerged, incorporating the non-priestly religious wing of the older wisdom tradition, which had retained its concern for the life of the individual and kept aloof from the priests and the prophets and their salvational-history orientation. Now the study and exposition of the written Torah became the primary professional interest of this class which laid the foundation for the development of the oral law.[5] Accompanying this process was the emergence of a new form of piety that viewed the Torah as law code, the book of Israel's covenant with God and the summation of divine wisdom. The individual's purpose in life was to meditate on the divine will and wisdom as expressed in the Torah books. The older wisdom materials used by teachers for the instruction of youth were given a more specifically religious formulation. In the Hellenistic period the religious wisdom schools turned to theological reflection on the origin and nature of wisdom as an objective entity connected with the revelation of the Torah to Israel, and on the meaning of life, death and suffering.

The secular wisdom tradition also continued into the Second Temple period with popular sayings and maxims of the ancients expressing the insights on life of the anonymous observer modified and pressed into service to meet the changing conditions in society. The teacher's epigrams took on a more contemporary dress. Here, too, theological reflection commenced and the wisdom teacher, like Ecclesiastes, who taught the conventional wisdom of society and tradition to his students during the day, went home at night and penned his more radical thoughts in his private journal or diary. Sometimes he agreed with the conventional wisdom but at other times he was profoundly skeptical of its truths.[6] During the day he may have taught his students the upper middle class virtues of industry and diligence as expressed in the proverb: "See you a man diligent (or skilled) in his work - He shall attend upon kings; He shall not attend upon obscure men" (Prov. 22:29). But at night he

may have confided to his journal the melancholy observation borne
out by experience:

> The race is not won by the swift;
> Nor the battle by the valiant;
> Nor is bread won by the wise,
> Nor wealth by the intelligent,
> Nor favor by the learned (Eccles. 9:11)

It is difficult to delineate which books fall into the categories of
secular and religious wisdom since the impact of both schools is
evident in all the wisdom writings. Nevertheless, it would not be
wide of the mark to say that some of the wisdom psalms and the
post-biblical Wisdom of Solomon represent the far end of the
religious spectrum and Ecclesiastes is representative of the secular
wing. In the book of Joshua ben Sira (c.a. 190-170 B.C.E.), secular
proverbial wisdom, prophecy, priestly devotion to the cult and Torah
study and interpretation all converge.[7] This book, which was highly
valued by the rabbis, is the bridge from wisdom piety to the
intellectual piety of the talmudic age.

The Book of Proverbs

In H. Gressman's apt observation, "Palestine was a corridor for
ideas as well as for armies." Over the last half century or so
biblical scholarship has become increasingly aware that from the
Nile to the Tigris and Euphrates an international wisdom literature
came into existence and was cultivated. It was carried between
Egypt and Mesopotamia and through Palestine by a cosmopolitan
corps of professional scribes who traveled to and from the main
centers of the literary art and in transit earned some money by
practicing their craft in localities where it was less developed. Thus
their ideas germinated in places far removed from their origin. The
cross-pollinization of ideas also resulted from local scribes who,
having learned the rudiments of the profession, migrated to the
major centers for more advanced training, returning with new ideas
as well as advanced skills.[8]

The Book of Proverbs reflects the blending of ancient Near
Eastern wisdom with the unique perspective of Hebrew monotheism.
As in the wisdom literature of the ancient Near East, pragmatism
pervades Proverbs. Though adultery is a sin (Prov. 2:17) it also
depletes one's wealth (Prov. 29:3) and is ruinous to reputation and
personal happiness (Prov. 5). Drunkenness leads to quarrels, blows

and wounds (Prov. 23: 29-35). Even the fear of God, the religious foundation of the book's exhortations is colored by a degree of utilitarianism related to the doctrine of reciprocity. God requites human beings according to what they deserve. "Do not envy the prosperous wicked man," warns Proverbs, for "the lamp of the wicked will be extinguished" (Prov. 24:19 f.). Unlike the Torah, Proverbs grounds morality on prudence and "God-fearing" (a term for universal morality grounded in reason and life experience as discussed in chapter 7) rather than on a historical covenant.

The morality of Proverbs lacks a historical-national motive. Torah and wisdom are not yet identified as they are in the later wisdom literature from Ben Sira onward. As in oriental wisdom, Proverbs refers to *torah* and wisdom personified. Conspicuously absent is explicit reference to a revealed Torah concerning which a covenant has been made. The beginning chapters of Proverbs depict a father instructing his son to follow the paths of wisdom and understanding. But Exodus (Exod. 31:3 ff.) and Deuteronomy (Deut. 4:9) state that the Hebrew father must teach his children the story of the Exodus from Egypt and the laws given Israel at that time. The cultic aspects of Sabbath observance and its social-moral implications of giving rest to slave and animal are not discussed in Proverbs. Despite its concern for depressed classes, Proverbs does not have the great commandment of loving the stranger which the Torah grounds on the fact that the Israelites were themselves strangers in the land of Egypt.

Nevertheless, there are many points of contact between the Book of Proverbs and the Torah. All the rules of the Ten Commandments except the ban on idolatry and the law of the Sabbath are found here. The optimism of the Torah expressed by the repetition of the word "good" in the unfolding of divine creation in the first chapter of Genesis, is also found in Proverbs where the buoyant belief in God's just providence and a moral world order remains unclouded. Like the Torah, the Book of Proverbs posits faith in God as the cornerstone of religion. For the Torah it is the basis of Israel's national existence and for Proverbs it is the foundation of human happiness and success. Within this ideational framework the wisdom teachers, using the Book of Proverbs as their text, instructed the upper middle class youth of ancient Israel in the orders for correct social behavior and in the essentials for coping with reality.[9]

Notes

1. Gerhard Von Rad, *Wisdom in Israel* (Nashville and New York: Abingdon Press, 1972), pp. 58, 309.

2. *Ibid.*, pp. 187-188. Since the wisdom teachers were not in the main priests serving in the Temple, they were not particularly interested in cultic matters but as in the case of the prophets they were not opposed to ritual *per se.*

3. R. B. Y. Scott, *The Way of Wisdom, In The Old Testament* (New York: Macmillan, 1971), pp. 113-131.

4. G. Von Rad, *Wisdom In Israel*, p. 17.

5. I. H. Weiss, *Dor, Dor Ve-Dorshav* (New York and Berlin: Platt & Minkus, 1924) 1: 49-50; R. T. Herford, *The Pharisees* (London: G. Allen & Unwin, 1924), pp. 18-21; Louis Finkelstein, *The Pharisees* (Philadelphia: Jewish Publication Society of America, 1940) 1: 263f. See above Sinai I: Prophetic Piety, note 16.

6. On the use of quotations in Ecclesiastes in which the author modifies or even disagrees with conventional wisdom see Robert Gordis, *Koheleth-The Man and His World* (New York: The Jewish Theological Seminary of America, 1951), pp. 191, 212.

7. Scott, *The Way of Wisdom, In the Old Testament*, pp. 191, 212.

8. *Ibid.*, pp. 23-24

9. Kaufmann, *The Religion of Israel*, pp. 323-327.

Olympus: Piety from Another Perspective

In Greece the mantics, poets, and philosophers were the ones who articulated the spiritual and intellectual dimensions of religious behavior.[1] These men do not correspond exactly to the priests, prophets, rabbis, and sages of ancient Israel, however.[2] Their lives were not primarily dedicated to God; most were actively engaged in secular affairs and practiced poetry or philosophy as private individuals or citizens contributing to city life. Aeschylus, for example, composed more than ninety tragedies which dramatized the working out of divine justice, but his epitaph commemorated his valor at Marathon rather than his poetry.

Although the Greeks' words were often couched as revelation or inspiration, they did not come directly from Zeus nor did they have the same degrees of authority as the words of God's prophets, rabbis, and sages. Greek poets were inspired by the Muses or Apollo. Later poets were free to criticize the truth of their predecessors' words. Philosophers who introduced their speculations as revelations presented their new ideas in precise unpoetic language and defended them by cogent arguments rather than by appeals to authority. Neither speaker nor audience, nor reader and writer expected the words to be accepted without criticism and, by the fifth century, without rational debate.

Nevertheless, the mantics, poets, and philosophers were the spiritual leaders of Greece, for their words had clear moral and religious implications and their skill and creativity immortalized their thoughts.[3] The fact that the maxims of the seven sages (quoted below) were inscribed on tablets at the shrine of Apollo at Delphi testifies to the connection between their wisdom and the divine. Legend also enshrines the wide definition of wisdom and the humility of those accounted wise. The list of the seven fluctuates, but it includes the philosopher/statesman/scientist Thales, the poet/politician Solon, and the inspired healer Epimenides as well as the philosopher/mystic Pythagoras.[4] Tradition records that when a tripod fell out of heaven with the instructions to present it to the wisest of all, no one of the seven kept it for himself. Instead, each sent it on to the next, and, after it had been passed around, they dedicated the tripod to Apollo, the wisest of all.[5]

If some wise men, now called Sophists, wondered whether humans could really know the attributes of god and questioned the divine origins of human institutions, very few were atheists.[6] Most expressed the idea that the world was in some sense divine and viewed their speculations as compatible with their participation in the worship of traditional gods.[7] In fact, the author of the Hippocratic treatise "On the Sacred Disease" accused faithhealers of impious fraud for blaming the disease on gods and trying to heal it with religious purifications. Searching for the true cause and cure in nature instead, he still reaffirmed that natural causes—cold, sun, winds—were in themselves divine (21) and stressed the absolute purity of deity(4).[8] As Plato redefined the divine in his pursuit of truth, he developed a philosophy which was both spiritual and theological, with god and the good as the source of all that is good in man's world and the model of all human endeavor.

Prophecy

The Mantics and "Menial Science"— Plato defined the mantics as "those who have to do with divination and possess a portion of a certain menial science for they are supposed to be interpreters of the gods to men" (*Statesman* 290). In the *Phaedrus* he connects this "science (*mantike*) which foretells the future" with madness (*manike*) and asserts that it is a divine gift of divine origin associated particularly with Apollo (244c).[9] Pindar (*Olympian* 6.57-76) describes how the youth Iamus, having prayed to Poseidon and Apollo, was led to Olympia where he was endowed "with a gift of prophecy two-fold, first from that day he should hear the speech that knows not falsehood, and further . . . he bade him set up his oracle on the crown of the altar of Zeus." Calchas, prophet of the Argives, the Trojan Cassandra, and the sibyls also received their powers from Apollo. Tiresias, the Theban prophet of Apollo, was blinded for his error (either in revealing women's greater pleasure from sex or for seeing the goddess of wisdom, Athena, in the nude) but was compensated by Zeus with an inner light to see the future or by his mother, a nymph, with the power to understand birds.

As with the Hebrew prophets and charismatics, the possession of extraordinary knowledge and ability set the Greek seer apart from other men. Calchas understood why Apollo was so angry that he sent the plague to the Greek camp at Troy. Cassandra not only foresaw her own death, but recalled the whole grim history of the House of Atreus. It is god's truth that they convey - "speech that knows not falsehood" but it is also a knowledge of how to do things. From Homer's assertion that Calchas led the Achaean ships to Troy, Morrison infers that his mantic art of bird augury was complemented by the practical skills of navigation which enabled him to determine when to set out, when to seek port, and the best course to follow.[10]

Several of the seers, upon being touched by serpents, received the power to understand birds and animals, a gift which often enabled them to perform extraordinary acts and miraculous cures. Melampus, for example, whose ears were once licked by a snake, predicted the fall of a wall after overhearing the conversation of wood-worms; from vultures he learned of a charm worked against Iphiclus and was able to cure him of impotence.

Miraculous cures were especially connected to the *manteis*, perhaps because of their association with Apollo and his rites of purification, but also because of the general belief that severe diseases had divine or demonic sources.[11] Calchas and Tiresias knew the causes of the plagues and the means of lifting them by action and ritual. Epimenides, a legendary seer from Crete, was credited with purifying the city after the slaughter of Cylon's associates brought phantoms and plague on Athens. According to late sources, Epimenides claimed to have slept for fifty-seven years in a cave where truth and justice were revealed to him. He was said to have lived for more than three generations.

Some scholars connect certain holy men with the shamans of other cultures because they were reputed to quit their bodies and travel at will, to be able to contact the spirit world, to live without food or at least meat, and to perform miracles and healings in the name of gods.[12] Aristeas of Proconnessus, for example, was a servant of Apollo who was about to be buried in one place when he appeared in another at the same time. He is said to have accompanied Apollo in the form of a raven. Abaris the Hyperborean traveled around the world carrying the golden arrow emblematic of Apollo, prophesied at Athens, and cured a plague at Sparta. Similar legends accrued about Orpheus, Pythagoras, and Empedocles because of their ascetic practices and belief in the preexistence of the soul. These stories resemble the accounts of the visions, actions, and powers of several of the Hebrew prophets mentioned above.

In contrast to the Hebrews, however, Greek tradition maintained that mantic powers could be handed down from generation to generation. Iamus became the founder of the Iamidae, the family of prophets at Zeus' oracle at Olympia, whereas Melampus was the ancestor of the prophetic clan of Melampidae. The famous legendary seers of Argos, Amphiarus and Amphilochus, were descended from Melampus; Teisamenos, the seer who served the Spartans in the Peloponnesian War, traced himself back to Melampus as well. The names of fifth century mantics (Stilbides Brightson "and Lampon Shiner") suggest to Morrison that there were still mantic families in existence who named their children in accordance with their profession.[13]

Much of the art that was passed on depended on a "certain menial science," an inductive divination from omens.[14] Plato, in fact, distinguishes the type which reads signs as a lesser kind of prophecy because it comes from rational investigation (*Phaedrus* 245). The legendary seers Tiresias and Calchas divined by watching the flight of birds, judging favorable or unfavorable implications from their number or the direction from which they appeared. Sacrifice too was an important scene for signs from the gods. Mantics watched to see if the victim was willing, how quickly it bled to death, how the flames moved and affected the tail or bladder. They paid close attention to the entrails; any abnormality would be a portent of ill-fortune. The lobes of the liver, considered the source of blood and therefore the seat of life, received the closest inspection for their formation, color, and size.[15]

Manteis were also skilled in other ways of reading signs. Casting lots (kleromancy) was a common means of learning divine will.[16] Dreams, which were viewed as coming from the gods, needed the interpretation of experts. Clytemnestra's nightmare prefigured her death at the hands of her son Orestes, but the prophet's words revealed the relation of her past sin to the dream portent. (*Libation Bearers*, 37-40). Dreams could be signs of blessing as well, however. Worshippers at the shrines of Aesclepius, god of healing and son of Apollo, dreamed their cures when they slept overnight in the incubation rooms around the temple. The mantics also read signs in nature. At Dodona, the Selloi and the prophetess interpreted the sounds of the rustling leaves or the cries of birds circling about Zeus' oak (Herodotus 2.52 f). One might throw things into sacred water and determine a yes or no answer depending on whether the object sank or floated. Or one might read signs in the objects floating in water drawn from a sacred source.

Contact with the holy aided the mantic.[17] "The Selloi of the unwashed feet who slept on the ground" at Dodona (*Il.* 16.234) were probably literally keeping in touch with Mother Earth. Dream oracles were often situated by holy springs or waters and drinking from such waters might facilitate the prophecy. The Pythia at Delphi probably bathed in the Castalian spring or drank from Cassiotis before performing her duty. When she entered the sanctuary, she mounted the tripod to await the trance and held a branch of laurel from the god's sacred tree. The priestess at Didyma held the laurel wand of Apollo in her hand while wetting her feet in the sacred spring and breathing its vapors. As Halliday notes, the primary object of such activity was "union with the divinity."[18]

"Divine Madness"— The mantic art which depended purely on such union with the divinity was the one which Plato considered superior to "the rational investigation of futurity" described above. In *Phaedrus* 244, he terms it divine madness and the source of great blessings from gods to humans:

> . . . For prophecy is a madness, and the prophetess at Delphi and the priestesses at Dodona when out of their senses have conferred great benefits on Hellas, . . . but when in their senses Few or none. (Jowett, trans.).[19]

Dreams sent by god to willing or unwilling individuals fall into this category. So too do the symbolic visions of such legendary figures as Theoclymenus, Telemachus' companion who in *Odyssey* 20.351-7 foresees the death of the suitors. But the highest type relied on "enthusiasm" in its basic sense, where the god entered directly into his vehicle so that he or she became *entheos* and was used as the human spokesman of his divine communication.[20] As the Pythian priestess at Delphi explained in the opening of Aeschylus' *Eumenides*, Zeus made Apollo's mind *entheos* and full of prophetic craft when he established him as mantic on the throne of Delphi (17-18) "so that Loxias (Apollo) is the prophet of his father" (19) and she herself "prophesies only as the god may guide" (33). Although no one is certain how the Pythia was selected, the ancient sources emphasize that she was an ordinary woman, of no particular family or training, who possessed special knowledge only at the time when the god inspired her to speak his words. Like the Hebrew prophets, the ecstasy, trance, or frenzy was only a prelude to the all important message.

The sanctuaries where a god was considered to be present in order to offer the prophetic service (*chresmos*) were known as *chresteria* or *mantica*. (Our word oracle derives from the Latin *oraculum*). Many of these achieved an international reputation: the oracles of Apollo at Branchidae, Abae, and Delphi, of the heroes Amphiarus and Trophonius in Boetia, the oracle of Zeus at Dodona, and of Zeus-Ammon in Libya (Herodotus 1.6 ff. and 26 ff.) By the sixth century B.C.E, the oracle at Delphi was the most famous and influential of the Greek oracles and it is now the one about which the modern world has the most information.[21] The temple built on the ruins of earlier structures by the Alcmaeonid family of Athens became the center of an elaborate sanctuary which also included within its walls a theater, twenty-seven 'treasuries' built by different cities to house their gifts to Apollo, and fifty-nine statues and other offerings set up along the paths, as well as a gymnasium and stadium outside the walls for use during the Pythian games. The inhabitants of Delphi provided the personnel for the oracle, but the upkeep and administration were directed by an association of neighboring Greek city-states known as the Amphyctyonic League.

Although the details remain controversial, the general procedures for consulting the oracle can be described. In earliest times, responses were probably given only on the seventh day of one month in the spring, but later "the god occupied a mortal body once every month" (Plutarch *Moralia* 398 ab), except for the three winter months when Apollo was absent and a lot oracle may have been used. At the height of the oracle's popularity, two priestesses were employed in responding, with a third held in reserve. The preliminaries to the consultation, such as offerings, were handled by the priests.

Once the consultation began, the inquirer, having been warned to be silent and think pure thoughts, probably sat with the prophets, cult officials, and a representative of his polis at Delphi in a separate room (*oikos* or *megaron*) which prevented them from clearly viewing the priestess' performance. She herself preceded them into an inner sanctuary (*adyton*), which may have contained the Omphalos or navel stone marking the center of the earth, two statues of Apollo, the tomb of Dionysus, and a chasm over which she sat an Apollo's tripod. Although she was most likely a mature woman, she was dressed in the costume of a pure virgin. Having been informed of the question either orally or in writing by the *prophetes*, she awaited the inspiration. When possessed by the god, the Pythia did not speak normally, but neither did she rant and rave and utter gibberish which the *prophetes* overheard, interpreted, and translated into hexameter verse. More likely she spoke clearly enough for the inquirer and officials to hear and understand her. Perhaps the prophet transcribed the words, in prose or verse, for the record or for inquiries conducted through an agent.[22] In *Aeneid* 6.45-105, Virgil describes the frenzied agony of the Cumaean Sibyl as Apollo seizes possession of her mind and mouth. Despite her pallor, disheveled hair, and raging heart, however, she delivers the god's message so clearly that Aeneas instantly understands.

People traveled from all over the Greek and non-Greek world to seek the god's service and left lavish gifts as a sign of their gratitude for his responses. Representatives of cities and private individuals came to seek advice on various kinds of problems from personal matters, such as marriage or business, to religious questions about sacrilege and purification, to political issues, e.g., founding colonies, beginning war, defensive strategies. The responses appear to have been more than simple yes or no's.[23] The recipient was responsible for the correct interpretation. If the answer was unwelcome, he could find some way to evade it; if it was ambiguous or unclear or unfavorable, he could ask again. Thus the Pythia refused to accept the blame for Croesus' disastrous attack on Persia; when the god declared Croesus would bring down a mighty empire, Croesus should have inquired which empire was meant (Herodotus 1.92).

Herodotus' account of the Athenians' consultations with Delphi about the threatened Persian invasion provides an excellent illustration of the oracles and the problems and procedures of interpretation. The first prophecy of the priestess portended disaster. When a noted Delphian advised the despondent delegates to reenter as suppliants requesting a better fate, the prophetess gave a new response. Preferring the second answer, the envoys wrote it down and returned to Athens where the public came up with two mutually exclusive interpretations. Themistocles' reading was preferred to the one by the professional interpreters.

There is a considerable debate about whether all the oracles ascribed to Delphi by Greek writers are authentic in form and actually originated at that oracle. Most likely, many of the prophecies go back to a long oral tradition in which individual responses were gradually embellished and were attached to the names of famous shrines or mantics.[24] Books were attributed to Musaeus, Orpheus, and the Sibyl as well as to Bakis, whose collection Cleon boasts of possessing in Aristophanes' *Knights*. Herodotus mentions one Onomacritus who was banished from Athens for inserting a new prophecy into the oracles of Musaeus (7.6). There were also semi-official professional interpreters of oracles who were known as *chresmologoi*. In *Birds*, Aristophanes introduces an anonymous *chresmologos* who comes to Cloudcuckoo land and tries to bilk its founders. But the collections themselves were taken seriously by Herodotus. The prophecy ascribed to Bakis, Musaeus, and another soothsayer Lysimachus, "The Colian Women shall cook their food with oars," was proved true when the wreckage from the battle of Salamis was blown to the Colian Coast of Attica (8.96). The Euboeans suffered greatly when they ignored an oracle of Bakis (8.20). Before describing the battle of Salamis, the historian asserts the truth of prophecies, when expressed in clear language, citing Bakis' prediction of the Greek victory (8.77).

Skepticism and Belief— Herodotus' affirmation indicates that mantics and prophecy were viewed with suspicion by his day. The dramatists certainly depict accusations of greed and self-interest (against Tiresias, in *Oedipus the King, Antigone, Bacchae*). Jocasta tries to persuade Oedipus to disregard the oracle by showing how wrong it was about Laius' fate. Her conclusion "Give them no heed, I say; what God discovers need of easily he shows to us himself." (723) is similar to the messenger's words in Euripides' *Helen*:

> How rotten this business of prophets is, how full of lies . . . .
> Then . . . why consult the prophets? We should sacrifice
> to the gods, ask them for blessings, and let prophecy go.
> The art was invented as a bait for making money,
> but no man ever got rich on magic without work.
> The best prophet is common sense, our native wit.
> (745-57, Lattimore, trans) [25]

Plutarch, in his life of Pericles, recorded how Anaxagoras the philosopher's explanation of a one-horned ram was greatly preferred to Lampon the soothsayer's interpretation. The philosopher had dissected the head, like a scientist, and found the source of the prodigy in the animal's misshapen brain (6).

But Lampon turned out to be correct as well. He received his proper share of honor when Pericles became sole ruler of the state shortly after the seer's prediction based on the single horn. As Plutarch, a priest of Apollo at Delphi in the first century C.E., judged, both the scientist and the prophet were right:

> It was the business of the first to observe why something
> happens and how it becomes what it is, and of the second to
> foretell the purpose of an event and its significance.
> (*Pericles*, Scott-Kilvert, trans.) [26]

Despite the difficulty of the divine communication and the fallibility of its human instruments, most Greeks believed "Zeus and Apollo are wise and know mortal affairs" (*Oedipus the King* 499 ff.) and tried to maintain contact through signs and oracles. Armies took soothsayers with them when they marched out to battle (e.g., Herodotus 9.33-43; Xenophon *Anabasis* 6.1.23; 6.4:12-5.2). When city-states lost their power to make war or treaties, communities still consulted the oracle about other public questions and private individuals still asked about personal matters.

It is hard for the modern scientific age to account for the seriousness which the otherwise rational Greeks attached to the mantics. Plutarch's comment that the philosopher and the seer provide two different but necessary kinds of knowledge offers part of the explanation. Comparing Evan Pritchard's experience with the Azande's use of poison oracles, Price concludes that the Greeks consulted mantics and oracles when they were facing difficult problems they had already thought through carefully. If the imponderables appeared too great, and either alternative might lead to disaster, the consultation gave them the confidence to act.[27] Anthropologists who analyze the relation of the religion to the political culture, however, consider that the oracles' significance was tied to the growth of democracy in Greece. Their interpretation required no special charismatic figure with greater authority than any other citizen. Their words were in a common language accessible to all, despite the riddling, and their meaning could be decided by public debate.[28] Burkert speculates that "precisely because there are no revealed scriptures, the signs become a preeminent form of contact with the higher world and a mainstay of piety."[29] E. R. Dodds explains that Apollo, in the absence of Bible or Church, became "vicar on earth of the Heavenly Father" because life in the archaic age would have been unendurable:

> Without the assurance which such an omniscient divine counselor could give, the assurance that behind the seeming chaos, there was knowledge and purpose . . . .[30]

The Spiritual Dimension— Because the pious frequently inquired at oracles about matters of policy and conduct, Delphi, as the most famous oracle, became a moral authority in the ancient world.[31] A fourth century B.C.E. historian claimed that the shrine was founded by Apollo and Themis, the goddess of law, to benefit the human race, partly by issuing commands and prohibitions, partly by giving oracular responses, and again by refusing altogether to admit to the temple particular individuals.[32] The Pythia's responses to questions about purification rites and public matters such as constitutions for colonies provided effective support for prohibitions against murder and the value of human life as well as the importance of the rule of law.[33]

Whatever the original source of the sayings or legends, those which embodied a spiritual message became attached to Apollo and his shrine.[34]   Most famous are the maxims of moderation, "Know thyself" and "Nothing in excess" which were said to have been inscribed on the outside of the temple.   They epitomized the warnings against presumption in so many of the legends about those who considered themselves the most fortunate or wisest of men until the oracle and later events revealed the truth to them (e.g., Croesus of Lydia, of course [Herodotus I], but also Gyges [Pliny, *Natural History* 7.46.151] Chilan the Spartan and Anacharesis the Scythian, famous for wisdom [Diogenes Laertes 1.130; 1.9.106-7; Diodorus 9.52]).

The same lesson was applied to those who considered themselves most pious.   To a wealthy Magnesian who had just offered a hecatomb to Apollo, the Pythia named Clearchus the one who best honored the gods and made the most pleasing offerings.   Surprised, the Magnesian sought out this Clearchus and found a farmer who was very poor but scrupulous in his gifts to gods.   When the Pythia, however, preferred a poor man who offered a handful of barley from his wallet to a Thesssalian who sacrificed gilt-horned oxen, she scorned the same poor man after he then emptied the rest of his wallet at the altar.   He had antagonized Apollo twice as much by this ostentatious act as his first moderate gift had pleased him.

The moral exhortations of Delphi extended beyond warnings against presumption, and included intention as well as action. According to Herodotus, a Spartan named Glaucus asked Delphi whether he might perjure himself and keep money entrusted to him. When the priestess responded with the warning that the whole race of a perjured one is swiftly destroyed, the man apologized for the question and asked forgiveness.   The priestess' second response stated a more sophisticated moral judgment: "To seek God's approval of a sin came to the same thing as committing it" (6.86). Two oracles recorded only in later sources but considered much earlier emphasize the same point that the moral condition of the agent is as important the deed itself.   In this case, three young men were attacked by robbers on their way to consult the Pythia.   While one ran away the second killed his friend in an attempt to save him. The Pythia drove the one who ran away out of the shrine, for "when a friend was dying, though near at hand, you did not help."   She exonerated the other, however, with the words:

> You slew your comrade when defending him.   The blood has not stained you; you are now purer in hands than you were before.[35]

The extension of ritual piety to spiritual purity is also expressed by two elegaic couplets in the Greek Anthology (14,71) titled *chresmos* of the Pythia and addressed to worshippers entering the shrine.

> 1. Holy in spirit, stranger, come to the sanctuary of a pure divinity when you have touched the spring of the nymphs. A tiny drop then will suffice the good man. But the bad, all ocean could not wash with his springs.

> 2. The temple of the gods is open wide to good men and they have no need of purification. For no stain of guilt can touch virtue. But whoso is baneful in heart, stand aside. For washing of the body will never thoroughly clean your soul.[36]

Wisdom: Poets and Philosophers

Divine Inspiration and Secular Identity— The definitions of piety established by the prophets at Apollo's sanctuary never reached the heights articulated by the classical Hebrew prophets.[37] The oracle at Delphi did not initiate new ideas; it operated primarily to answer specific questions and usually responded by supporting the *nomos* (custom-law) of the inquirer's homeland. The emphasis was on ritual, although spiritual refinements were implicit in the pronouncements. The clearest articulation of thoughts about the gods, their nature, their relation to men, and proper behavior toward them comes from another source—the poets, sages, and philosophers, who were renowned for their extraordinary insight and knowledge and were called by an honorable title *Sophistes* or wise man.[38]

Their special abilities were often considered a gift from the gods.[39] Plato defined poetic inspiration as divine madness coming from the Muses "which taking hold of a delicate and virgin soul, and there inspiring frenzy, awakens lyrical and all other numbers; with these adorning the myriad actions of ancient heroes for the instruction of posterity." (*Phaedrus* 245f). The bards depicted by Homer do not go into trances to sing at court. The poet tells us, however, in *Odyssey* 8.488, that their gifts come from the Muses and Apollo, the children of Zeus; the former was probably associated with the power of memory, the latter with the power of prophetic words. Demodocus of Phaeacia is described as the god-like minstrel to whom "the god gave the special power of song" (44-5) and whom "the Muse cherished" but deprived of his sight when she gave him "sweet song" (63-4). Asked to sing, "the bard stirred by the god, expressed the song" (499).

But the song itself and the degree and authority of the revelation changed with the changing social organization and the position of the poet in relation to his audience.[40] Homer's singers are intimate members of the households of kings whose palaces are the center of community life. He entertains them with songs of their own heroic exploits and values, for which he receives honor and respect. Homer, an anonymous poet, does not separate himself from the upper class world of an idealized past in which aristocrats and the gods they interact with are the main interest.[41]

Hesiod asserts his authority to proclaim a different song when he describes the revelation he received from the Heliconian Muses, which begins *Theogony.*

> And one day they taught Hesiod glorious song while he was shepherding his lambs under holy Helicon . . . and they plucked and gave me a rod, a shoot of sturdy laurel, a marvelous thing, and breathed into me a divine voice to celebrate things that shall be and things that were aforetime; and they made me sing of the race of blessed gods that are eternally. . . (22-34, Evelyn-White, trans.)

The call of the shepherd-poet has been compared to the call of Amos the Hebrew prophet who was "but a herdsman and dresser of sycamore trees" before God directed him to prophesy to the people of Israel.[42] The vision itself, with the symbolic transfer of the word through the laurel and the breath, resembles the visions of Isaiah and Ezekiel.

In both *Theogony* and *Works and Days*, Hesiod's new position and own point of view are clear.[43] Whether persona or poet, the singer of these two didactic epics has separated himself from his rulers. Unlike Homer, he has his own name, a personal past, non-aristocratic interests like agriculture, trade, and navigation, and a new relationship to his audience. For one of his songs, he has won himself a victory in a contest at the funeral games of a noble, and also a prize, a tripod, which he dedicated to his patronesses, the Heliconian Muses, at the spot where they made him "tread the path of song." (*Works and Days* 653-9)

His detachment from his rulers affects the religious content of his song. As a member of the common people, he is incensed by the injustice he perceives all around him. As a recipient of the Muses' gift, "of things that shall be and things that were aforetime," he has a sense of the movement of history as well as a knowledge of the divine. So he can proclaim the disparity between his own iron age and the eternal standards for justice established by Zeus and his daughter Justice (*Dike*). *Theogony* traces the development of a just and stable order under Zeus while *Works and Days* urges just behavior by offering guides to successful life and warning that Zeus punishes those who practice violence, cruelty, and injustice (e.g., 238-9, 248-51). It has been suggested that Hesiod emphasized his meeting with the Muses because he, like Amos, was an unexpected source for an unexpected message.[44]

Later poets expressed similar ideas about the source of their art. For example, Theognis in the sixth century (769) and Pindar in the fifth (frag. 150 S [137B]; Paeon 6.6. [frag. 40B]; Pyth. 4.279) considered themselves servants and messengers of the Muses. Pindar even used the terms associated with Delphi and the Pythia's inspiration, calling on the Muse to pronounce her oracle and referring to himself as her prophet.[45] They and others (e.g., author of Homeric Hymn 4, Solon, Ibycus) called their art *sophia* or wisdom. Pindar attributed to the muse his first impulse, his sustained effort, the material itself, and the spirit in which he handled it.[46]

The archaic age was a period of great disturbance and innovation which effected a change in genre and context.[47] The shift in power and prosperity from the noble few to the people, coupled with the spread of literacy, produced many more educated individuals who aspired to compose poetry about themselves and their lives. They developed shorter forms of lyric for addressing groups with similar values, interests, and professions. Several (e.g., Tyrtaeus, Alcaeus, Solon) wrote about the political turmoil of their communities; others (e.g., Sappho, Archilochus) described such personal situations as love affairs or quarrels with friends. There were new private social contexts for the poets' oral performance—symposia where men met together unofficially, women's gatherings—as well as more public occasions like funerals, weddings, contests at religious festivals, and celebrations for victories in the games. Some poets (e.g., Pindar, Alcman, Xenophanes) became professional poets who traveled from city to city and supported themselves with their choral or personal songs.

The oral poet had always been viewed as the inspired teacher, and by now, the personal poet could expect to survive in written circulation. Therefore, lyric poetry overcame its immediate context to universalize feelings, attitudes, and aspirations and to pass on their moral context. Theognis and Solon, for example, were gnomic poets who repeated and extended the accumulated wisdom of earlier generations; like Hesiod they emphasized Zeus and Dike.

Politician/poets also formulated new ideas of social justice based on their understanding of divine will and cosmic order. Pindar glorified the winners of athletic contests by exploring their relation to the gods and examining the nature of divinity.

A new poetic form, drama, originated in democratic Athens as the artistic equivalent of its new political system.[48] The playwrights, unlike Hesiod and the lyric poets, had to speak through their characters in action; except in the parabasis of comedy, the poet had no voice or presence of his own. But he was a citizen, whose drama was judged by his fellow citizens, and he directed his themes to the purpose, according to Aristophanes' *Frogs* 1009, of offering the best advice to the city and making the citizens better. Exploiting dramatic situations from the sacred past, the tragedians could examine political issues and social tensions underlying the democratic union *sub specie aeternitatis*. Comedians, whose plots were topical, could poke fun at any institution, place, person, or god in the entire Greek world. The context for the performance, however, was the religious festival of Dionysus, in his sacred place during his sacred time, and both forms of drama, in their different ways, explored crucial religious topics such as the limits on human intelligence and power and the concern of gods for mortals.

A new kind of wisdom, philosophy, also took shape in the archaic age. Its development gave rise to new interests, new forms of communication, and new contexts of presentation to the audience or reader.[49] In simple terms, as cosmology based on investigation of nature replaced theogony inspired by the gods, prose gradually replaced poetry and wise men took on private pupils or opened schools. Most of the philosophers, however, transferred their faith in Zeus to belief in nature as divine, well ordered, and rational. Heraclitus of Ephesus, for example, equated god with *logos* as the principle of coherence underlying the flux and fire of all things, and dedicated his book in the temple of Artemis.[50] Several associated their wisdom with divine inspiration and couched it in the terms of religion. Parmenides, the early fifth century philosopher, introduced his poem, composed in the hexameters of the Pythia, by describing a revelation. He is driven in a chariot on a journey from darkness to light through the gates of night and day where a goddess teaches the poet/sage the "unshaken heart of well-rounded truth" and the "opinions of mortals" (KRS, p. 243). Perhaps, like Hesiod, he has emphasized the source of his inspiration to give authority and seriousness to his "way of truth" which undermined earlier ideas of cosmogony. Empedocles too calls on the gods to "pour forth a pure stream from their holy lips" and urges the muse to drive her "well-reigned chariot from Piety's hall" to teach what is lawful for men to hear, using dactylic verse as well as the imagery and language drawn from initiation into the Mysteries.[51] His natural philosophy is also moral and spiritual. The goddess Love, called Attraction (*Philotes*) and Harmony as well, is the source of the perfectly proportioned mixture of the four elements which forms the universal sphere and is the perfect primordial state of nature, "a rounded sphere rejoicing in its joyous solitude." The disturbance of the divine sphere by Strife leads not only to the formation of the phenomenal world, but also to the exile of the soul, the god-like element in man, which must now participate in cycles corresponding to cosmic cycles.

Later philosophers emphasized the piety implicit in their search for knowledge and understanding. Plato calls love of wisdom that madness from the gods in which the philosopher, seeing the beauty of the earth, seeks to learn the truth about the eternal realm. His doctrine of knowledge, termed *anamnesis* or recollection, presupposes an immortal soul which once possessed this truth before being born into a temporal body. The recollection of knowledge is valuable in itself and yields models for virtue, but it is also a religious experience.

> he [the philosopher] is always . . . clinging in recollection to those things in which God abides, and in beholding which He is what He is. And he who employs aright these memories is ever being initiated into perfect mysteries and alone becomes truly perfect. (*Phaedrus* 249 c-d, Jowett, trans.)

Other thinkers also used the language of religion to describe intellectual activities. Galen calls his studies of the parts of animals an "initiation" and says his entire work is a hymn to the creator, for piety consists in discovering his wisdom, power, and goodness and showing it to the rest of humankind.[52]

As the above examples illustrate, the Greek philosophers' quest for wisdom had a spiritual dimension similar to the poets'. Some scholars have referred to such thinkers as Pythagoras, Empedocles, and Plato as philosophical mystics.[53] But most philosophers' interests and methods gradually diverged from the poets. The development of Pythagorean ideas provides a case in point.[54] Although the truth about his life and teachings is buried in later legends or uses of his thought, Pythagoras seems to have been an extraordinary sage and personality who lived in Samos and later in Southern Italy in the last half of the sixth century. He wrote nothing himself; he founded a sect which practiced silence as well as asceticism and passed on a collection of sayings (*akousmata* "things heard") as a guide to living a pure life. The quest for purity was related to a belief in the survival of the soul after death. He was also credited with attaching enormous cosmological and moral significance to number and harmony as the principles of origin and order in the universe. After his death, his followers split into two groups: the *akousmati*, who obeyed the rules of abstinence in hopes of a blessed afterlife, and the *mathematici* who pursued the study of number and made contributions to geometry and the arithmetical theory of music.

The division of the Pythagoreans exemplifies the movement from inspired wise men to proto-scientists, for the philosophers soon differed from the poets and holy men. First of all, even those who attributed their inspiration to the gods did not present the details of their wisdom as revelation to be accepted because of its transcendent authority. Parmenides' goddess exhorts him clearly to "judge by reason (*logos*) the strife encompassed refutation spoken by me:"[55] His "Way of Truth" develops a rational sequence of argument which exposes the logical errors of his predecessors' cosmologies. Audience and readers must follow the stages of the argument to the conclusion reason demands. In place of poetry, most philosophers chose prose, the medium of discussion and debate in the political context, and attempted to present their points clearly, to offer proof from experience or reason, to critically examine the theories of others, and to respond to the criticism of their own theories.[56] They became well-known individuals who competed with their peers in writing, in reputation, and sometimes in debates staged in public places, where the audience judged the validity of their wisdom.[57] Forced to defend their inquiries and ideas, they honed their intellectual, logical, and rhetorical skills.

Out of their practices the scientific method developed, along with science's willingness to look into everything. For their attempt to understand the matter and processes of nature, the philosophers of the sixth century and later had at their disposal a huge body of fact and technology from the Ancient Near East. Beginning with their assumption that nature was rational, regular, and operated according to laws humans could comprehend, they inquired about many things—origin, mechanism, mathematical or geometrical proportion, movement of the heavenly bodies, the origins and behaviors of animals, man, the state, the law, the way human senses operate, the nature of health and disease. Because they also assumed an orderly relationship between all of the parts of the whole which composed the cosmos, they attempted to fit all their observations and ideas into a comprehensive system based on a general theory or fundamental set of assumptions. In the search for general principles, they transformed much earlier isolated bits of fact and know-how into knowledge.[58]

As in Israel, the position of the wise man changed with the developing political context.[59] The earliest philosophers like Thales and Anaximander were active citizens of their communities who recorded their ideas as amateurs, lovers of wisdom (the literal meaning of "philosophers"). In the upheavals of the late sixth century, however, some withdrew from their government activities to form sects of their own (e.g., Pythagoreans), or to become itinerant holy men (e.g., Orphics) or professional intellectuals who traveled around to teach and debate. When Athens developed into the center of the Greek world, many flocked to the city and stayed in the homes of wealthy citizens. Although they have been lumped together under the name "Sophists", they were varied individuals with different interests and theories.[60]

Some charged money to teach the principles of clear speech, argumentation, and persuasion, so necessary to success in the democracy, but they also pursued physical science, geometry, linguistics, and moral philosophy. Kerford suggests that Plato attempted to resolve many of the questions of epistemology and ontology that they defined for the first time.[61] But after the defeat of Athens and the year of the thirty tyrants, several of whom had been pupils of sophists or Socrates, and the execution of Socrates (399), philosophers moved away from the casual education of citizens and opened schools for students who wanted to pursue philosophy seriously. Plato founded the Academy in 385 B.C.E. as a religious brotherhood dedicated to Apollo and the Muses in a grove sacred to the hero Academus. Its purpose was to prepare future political leaders through a rigorous scientific and philosophical curriculum; the warning "Let no man ignorant of geometry enter here" was inscribed on its entrance. In 335 his former pupil Aristotle established a school of his own, in a grove sacred to Apollo Lyceius and the Muses, which became a center of research and scholarship on a wide variety of topics. In the Hellenistic period, other philosophical schools were founded, e.g., the Stoics, Epicureans, Sceptics. They were more loosely organized than the Academy or Lyceum, but they each had official leaders, a clearly distinct line of thought, and a long history of development. Although they attracted the serious few to the pursuit of esoteric studies and skills, they popularized their ideas through books, often in the interesting dialogue form, and public debates.

Wisdom and the Nature of the Divine— Over the centuries the poets and sages articulated and expanded the definitions of divinity. According to Herodotus, "Homer and Hesiod described the gods for us, giving them all their appropriate offices, titles, and powers" (2.53). Their epic synthesis of isolated myths paralleled the synthesis of cults which merged the diverse local mother goddesses, maidens, and males into the panhellenic Olympian pantheon, and helped to create a national Greek religion.[62]   As earlier chapters have shown, the Olympic paradigm provided the model not only for excellence in the various activities of human life, but also for social behavior and personal morality. Both implicitly and explicitly, the earliest poets connected the gods with justice in the universe and depicted the ways in which they enforce the measure for measure principle among men. Lyric poets like Pindar and the tragic poets of Athens found in the myths of the past a way to join their present world with the eternal. Aeschylus, who called all his plays "slices from the banquets of Homer" interpreted the violent sagas of Thebes, Argos, and Mycenae, and the struggles of Zeus and Prometheus as divine paradigms for the evolution of a more just cosmic and social order. Sophocles and Euripides concentrated primarily on single episodes from saga which exemplified the clash of man with the divine order, generally asserting its ultimate providence as well as its power, mystery, and majesty.

The mythpoetic conception of divinity was not beyond question by the poets themselves, however. Pindar rejected barbarous stories about the gods and heroes. Reacting against tales of Heracles' crude behavior, goaded by the gods, he sang

> Fling this tale away, my lips!
> For to revile the gods is an odious act
> And to boast beyond measure
> Is a tune for the song of madness
> (*Olympian* 9.369)[63]

He also changed the story of Tantalus so that he wouldn't accuse Demeter of eating Pelop's shoulder

I cannot say, not I
That any Blessed God has a gluttonous belly;
I stand aside.
Those who speak evil have troubles thick on them.
(*Olympian* 1.52-53)[64]

Sophocles dramatized Jocasta's skepticism of Apollo's oracles and priests *Oedipus Tyrannos*), Creon's disrespect for Tiresias (*Antigone*), and Philoctetes' disbelief in divine justice. Euripides, clearly influenced by the Sophists, allowed his characters to speculate on more abstract or rational definitions of divinity. Tiresias explained away the miracle of Dionysus' birth as a linguistic error and allegorized Dionysus as the Wet in opposition to Demeter the Dry (*Bacchae* 274-297) whereas Hecuba reduced Aphrodite to Helen's lust personified (*Trojan Women* 981-997). Euripides' Heracles expressed what Pindar's reservations could lead to: stories about cruel and immoral gods are only lies spread by the poets; true divinity is perfect (*Heracles*, 1341-46).

Euripides' verses resemble the different definition developed by the philosophers.[65] Although Thales abandoned mythical explanations of the movement and matter of the world around him, he did not abandon the idea of divinity as the source of life. He called the mind of the world god and considered that a divine power penetrates and moves the elemental moisture.[66] The late sixth century poet/sage Xenophanes of Colophon, who criticized the immorality and anthropomorphic conception of the poets' gods, posited:

One god, greatest among gods and men, in no way similar to mortals, either in body or in thought (fragment 23, KRS) Always he remains in the same place, moving not at all, nor is it fitting for him to go to different places at different times, but without toil he shakes all things by the thought of his mind. (Fragments 26 & 25, KRS) All of him sees, all thinks, and all hears. (Fragment 24, KRS).

The conception of a single imperishable reality beyond and accounting for the flux in the natural world was developed in various ways by later philosophers. For some, like Parmenides and Anaxagoras, the principle was not called god and had no moral attributes; for others, although it was divine in the sense of immortal, all powerful, imperishable, and life-giving, it was not personified as an object of worship or source of cult. Yet, according to Cornford, such ideas of divinity "laid one of the foundation for a monotheistic and universal religion in which the Logos of Heraclitus and the Mind of Anaxagoras could be fused with a spiritualized Zeus."[67]

Wisdom and the Nature of Worship— Both the poets and sages depict the various ways of worshipping the traditional gods. Epic is replete with spontaneous prayers and vows of individuals to their divine patrons, respectful confrontations between mortals and immortals, group sacrifices, atonement rituals, funeral rites, and athletic games. The hymns to the various gods (e.g., the Homeric Hymns, Sappho's private prayer to Aphrodite, Pindar's paeans to Apollo and Artemis, dithyrambs in honor of Dionysus, the choral lyric of comedy and tragedy) not only invoke them by their diverse names, attributes, and beloved places and relate incidents from their mythology, but also describe details peculiar to their worship, e.g., processions, dances, music (v. parodos of Euripides' *Bacchae* 67-82).

As the gods are themselves imagined as delighting in dance, music, feasting, sport, and physical beauty, so the Greeks both celebrated and entertained their gods by presenting their own best artistic and intellectual efforts in their deities' honor - at the dramatic festivals, the contests of bards, singers, dancers, debaters, and athletes, complete of course with hymns and the meal in which the sacrificial animals are shared by the god and his worshippers. For Pindar the poet, music on earth was part of a greater harmony; song had the power to bind the universe together in joy and calm and to bring humanity closer to its immortal patrons.[68]   From Pythagoras to Plato, the beauty, grace, joy and exquisite sound of the various divine singers, dancers, and musicians was demythologized into the harmony of the spheres, to be imitated, if not worshipped, in the harmony of the soul and the order of society, as well as in the music which enhanced and uplifted daily life.

The poets and sages also transmitted rules for proper behavior in the presence of divinity or for maintaining the holiness of human life which are in some ways similar to the legalism of the Priestly codes in the Bible and their rabbinic extensions.[69]   The gnomic sections of Hesiod's *Works and Days* contain strictures which are related to reverence for the ambivalent power of divinity.

> Do not stand upright facing the sun when you make water,
> but remember to do this when he has set and toward his rising
> . . . Never cross the sweet-flowing water of ever-rolling rivers
> afoot until you have prayed, gazing into the soft flood, and

washed your hands in the clear lovely water. Whoever
crosses a river with hand unwashed of wickedness, the gods
are angry with him and bring trouble upon him afterwards
(727-45, Evelyn-White, trans).

The Pythagorean sect and Orphic priests developed ascetic ways of
life which included dietary restrictions, sexual abstinence, ritual
purification, and communal meals with libations and incense as
well as the study of sacred books, presumably to purify the soul for
the next life.[70] The Orphic rules suggest that, once initiated,
followers had to reject all the normal good things of life in order to
atone for some great sin (the slaughter of Dionysus by the Titans?).
Many seem to have been wandering beggars. Because there were
levels and choices inherent in polytheism and no organized caste of
priests to impose such rules, legalism never became a general
feature of Greek religion. The poets narrated or dramatized the
most basic rules—the need to approach the gods with physical
purity and spiritual reverence, to maintain the sanctity of the holy
places, to respect those made holy by their relation to the gods
(e.g., priests, prophets, heralds, poets, suppliants, strangers,
beggars), and to honor oaths and laws.
     Some wise men criticized the blood sacrifice, the central act of
traditional worship, however. Although the Pythagorean *akousma*
named "Sacrifice" as "most just," ritual murder of a living being
seemed to contradict belief in the survival of the soul after death
and the kinship of all living things. The Pythagoreans did not reject
either sacrifice or the eating of certain parts of the animal, but they
rationalized their practice in various ways: e.g., "The only animals
to which the souls of men do not enter are those which may,
according to law, be sacrificed."[71] Heraclitus, however, objected
absolutely to sacrifices as purification rites, as well as to idolatry
(the latter in words similar to the Hebrew prophets' ridicule of
praying to a block of wood or stone):

They vainly purify themselves of blood
guilt by defiling themselves with blood,
as though one who stepped into mud were
to wash with mud; further, they pray to
these statues, as if one were to carry on
a conversation with houses, not recognizing
the true nature of gods or demi-gods.
(KRS, p. 209)

For Empedocles, blood sacrifice and the eating of flesh were the primal sins introduced by Strife for which the divine soul was banished from the perfect Sphere. To gain release from the cycles and return to the divine source, the human being had to purify his life by abstention from both.[72] Orphics substituted vegetarianism and a pure life for traditional forms of worship.

Although Plato accepted the traditional cults, properly supervised, (e.g. in *Laws*), in *Euthyphro* he asked the more profound question: What exactly is piety (*to hosion*)? Socrates, on his way to defend himself against the charge of impiety, meets Euthyphro the mantic hastening to court to accuse his own father of murder for the accidental death of a field hand. When Socrates expresses surprise that a charge against his father can ever be an act of piety, Euthyphro insists that he has a religious obligation to purify the house of murder, that pollution is pollution whether the murderer is a relative or not, and that it is impious for him to associate with a known murderer or avoid prosecuting him. Socrates modestly asks Euthyphro to define the general idea which makes all pious things pious. Socrates then proceeds to demolish the assertions of his friend one by one. Typically, Socrates has demonstrated the hazards of the unexamined life without substituting a more adequate definition of the term examined. He does, however, establish some very important ideas about piety: 1) Religion is not a *do ut des* exchange, for the gods are in no way dependent on men; 2) holiness consists of far more than ritual purity; and 3) the gods love justice in and of itself.

The poets and philosophers also explored the connection between piety and justice. Out of the corpus of speculation on the life-force animating men and the world, shadowy notions of death, growing belief in a rational soul which survived the body, and an increasing demand for theodicy as well as justice and law in civic government, there developed a concept of life after death with reward and punishment for the behavior of men on earth. The details of Greek eschatology will be discussed in a later chapter. It is from the pagan poets and sages, however, that the Christian picture of heaven and hell derived its basic shape. As early as the *nekyuia* in Homer's *Odyssey* ll, the abyss of the dead, a pit similar to the biblical Sheol, also included a place of punishment for the great mythological sinners Tityus, Tantalus, and Sisyphus. Although there are allusions to concepts of afterlife of the Blessed who have been initiated into the mysteries in the Hymn to Demeter 480-82, Pindar fragments 131,137 and Aristophanes' *Frogs*, the fullest pictures of life after death and its connection with cosmic and human justice occur in Plato, in the myths in *Gorgias, Phaedo*, the *Republic, Phaedrus*, and in the sixth book of Virgil's *Aeneid*.

The myth of Er at the end of the *Republic* underscores beliefs which Plato has argued through dialectic in earlier sections. The work itself, most often thought of as Plato's Utopia, is in fact, a conversation about justice in which Socrates demolishes the current unexamined definitions and discusses the crucial question similar to the one posed by Satan in the prologue to the Book of Job. Is man just because it is in his best interest, i.e., because he desires rewards and fears punishments? Or is man just because it is in his nature and the nature of things for him to be just? Once Socrates has proved that justice is the true behavior for the soul, which should do what is right, whether it can get away with wrong or not, he then brings up the question of rewards, forbidden earlier, and presents his poetic picture of the blessings or horrors of the afterlife for the individual soul. In *Phaedo*, when Socrates is about to drink the hemlock, he comforts his companions with the assurance that the man who has prepared his soul by seeking knowledge, justice, temperance, courage, and truth has nothing to fear from death (114e-115e).

The Nature of Human Wisdom and Piety— The transmission of the developing ideas of virtue, wisdom and the path to true happiness was the provenance of the poets and sages, who were called *sophos* "wise" and possessed *sophia* "wisdom".[74] In Homer *Iliad* 15.1412 *sophia* refers to the skill of a boat builder "who by Athena's inspiration, is well-versed in all his craft's subtlety" (Lattimore, trans.). For the early poets, practitioners of all such useful arts were inspired by their divine patrons, particularly Athena, Hephestus, and Prometheus. The poets' special knowledge included verses of instruction in the technology which fostered survival and progress. Hesiod's *Works and Days*, for example, contains an agricultural handbook (383-617), a manual on seafaring (618-694), both geared to the cycle of the seasons and describing what to do, when, and how, as well as a calendar of lucky and unlucky days for various activities. To Hesiod, too, were ascribed other didactic writings; his *Precepts of Chiron* may have contained verses on oaths, sacrifices, and the calendar, transmitted through the persona of the centaur who first, according to tradition, taught them to men.[75]

From earliest times *sophia* was also associated with extraordinary knowledge about "gods, man, and society".[76] The *sophoi* or wise men, (also called *sophistai* or sophists) passed on or participated in a wisdom tradition which has many parallels in other literatures and resembles Hebrew wisdom. The precepts of the Seven Sages, inscribed on a column in front of the temple of Apollo at Delphi, contain a similar mixture of pragmatic, moral, and religious advice, e.g., "Aid friends. Control anger. Shun unjust acts. Acknowledge sacred things. Control pleasure. Consider luck. . . . Do just acts. Return favor. . . . Keep from evil. . . . Guard your property. Oblige a friend. Hate violence. . . . Pity suppliants. Educate sons . . . . When you err, repent. Worship the divine."[77]

Other works of Greek wisdom are similar to Proverbs and Ecclesiastes.[78] Like the biblical books, many are couched in a dramatic form in which an experienced elder instructs a youth. Hesiod addresses *Works and Days* to his brother Perses who has tried to rob him of his share of an inheritance in order to get rich quick. So too Theognis instructs Cyrnus, his younger friend whereas in the *Precepts of Chiron*, the centaur speaks to his most famous pupil, the young Achilles. As in Proverbs, the genre itself combines short pithy sayings with longer passages and the advice covers social conduct as well as ethical behavior. Theognis' verses, composed in elegaic couplets, are very similar in structure and thought to the poetry of Proverbs.

> Never make though the bad thy friend, but flee him ever like an evil anchorage (113-114, Edmonds, trans.)

> Surely to drink much wine is an ill; yet if one drinks it with knowledge, wine is not bad, but good (211-212, Edmonds, trans.).

Although specific parallels are too numerous to list, similar attitudes pervade both the biblical and Greek sets of admonitions. Like Proverbs and Ecclesiastes, Hesiod emphasizes the moral value of work itself, which is of course god-given, and the practical and ethical dangers of idleness, in which the sluggard is equated with the evil fool and the hard worker with the good wise man who can achieve happiness through labor and its fruits. Hesiod is certain that the measure for measure principle will be enforced by the divine order in time. Like the Preacher, however, Theognis expresses his doubts:

> How then is it, Son of Cronus, that thy mind can bear to hold the wicked and the righteous in the same esteem, whether a man's mind be turned to temperateness, or, unrighteous work persuading, to wanton outrage? (377-380, Edmonds, trans.)

> Yet the wicked enjoy untroubled prosperity, such as keep
> their hearts from base deeds, nevertheless for all they may
> love what is righteous, receive Penury, the mother of
> perplexity . . . (383-385, Edmonds, trans.).

There is one significant difference between the two wisdom traditions, however. The Hebrews considered this kind of knowledge less holy than the Torah and the prophetic books because it was based on experience rather than direct revelation or inspiration and was thus available to all. The poets, however, saw the content of their verses, as well as their skills and the results of the activities described, as a gift of the gods. Hesiod's invocation to the Muses, *Works and Days* 1-10, makes Zeus the source of all these things.

The poet and the sages also transmitted and developed the political wisdom which articulated the ideal of the just society where the individual could achieve virtue and wisdom. From Homer to Callinus to Pindar to Euripides and Aristophanes, the epic, lyric, and dramatic poets were all concerned with procedures in the state, and the right relationship between the community and the gods. They denounced tyranny, the loss of individual rights, social upheaval, and unjust violence. They praised military valor, patriotic self-sacrifice, and the wisdom that helps the state. The elegaic poetry of Solon is perhaps the best example of the way in which the religious and moral precepts affected political ideas and activities. Both his criticisms of Athens' excessive greed and folly and the new laws he introduced, whose purpose he proclaimed in the Athenian agora,

> For I gave the common folk such privilege as is sufficient for
> them, neither adding nor taking away; and such as had power
> and were admired for their riches, I provided that they too
> should not suffer undue wrong. Nay I . . . would have neither
> to prevail unrighteously over the other. (Fragments 5, 6,
> Edmonds, trans.)

reflect the maxims of the wisdom tradition associated with Apollo and Delphi and the principle of justice as a balance of portions (e.g., nothing in excess) which can be traced from Hesiod through Plato. The political thoughts of Plato permeate all his works, but are the particular subject of the *Republic, Statesman, Laws,* and the *Seventh Epistle.* Aristotle too wrote on politics and collected information on the constitutions of various city-states. To the Stoics (and perhaps the Sophists before them) belongs the concept of cosmopolis, a universal brotherhood of citizens of the world.

The philosophers also examined nature and natural changes, as well as developing what Aristotle called metaphysics, the study of first principles and causes. Such knowledge was important to them in itself; Aristotle believed humanity is by nature eager to learn and derives pleasure from knowing and contemplating the truth and from exercising reason, which is unique to him. But they also equated wisdom with virtue; they believed that knowing the truth about nature and its unseen laws could direct humans towards their own best goods and happiness. The connection between theoretical knowledge and ethics is most clear in the systems of the atomists, and Epicureans, Heraclitus and the Stoics, and in Plato, who insisted that his philosopher king, although he might prefer to contemplate the vision of the Good, must be compelled to use his knowledge of Justice, Beauty, and Goodness to perfect the state (*Republic* 7.520). Aristotle considered philosophic or theoretical wisdom the most valuable, as the formal cause of happiness, but judged the practical wisdom analyzed in the *Ethics* and *Politics* the best means of effecting happiness (*Nichomachean Ethics* 6.1143).

Although most viewed the state as the vehicle for the education and maintenance of the wise, just, and good citizen, they were also concerned with the individual's virtue and happiness *per se*. The role models of epic and drama, caught up in the crises of life, articulated their inmost thoughts about success and failure and the possibilities for happiness. It was the philosophers, however, who deduced precise definitions of such concepts as the cardinal virtues—courage, temperance, wisdom and justice—and the *summum bonum*, the highest good for man. If Plato, in the *Republic*, sought the essence, the idea according to which all behavior could be called virtuous, Aristotle, in such works as the *Nichomachean Ethics*, examined human action in the actual situations of daily life. Not only did he consider such questions as the nature of friendship and pleasure, the necessity for material goods, and the importance of choice and responsibility, but he also illustrated what behavior would be courageous, temperate, wise, or just in a given situation and provided a general rule for action in all circumstances, known as the Golden Mean (1107a).

For all, wisdom either led to or was the highest good. Most Greeks considered that it was ignorance of the true goods for man that caused injustice and unhappiness. But they judged individuals responsible for their own lack of knowledge since it was possible for them either to learn for themselves or to follow the lead of wise men. The Stoics and Epicureans defined the *summum bonum* as tranquillity or mental calm which could be achieved only by those who understood what nature was and how it operated. The Stoic wise man could be happy and good regardless of his external circumstances because he could live in conformity with nature by restricting his will and his desire for things beyond his control. The Epicurean who knew that this world is made up of atoms and the void was free from fears of death or the gods and the compulsion to seek after vain things; therefore, he could find the least pain and the most personal pleasure in the simple contemplative life among true friends. Since the force animating the physical world was rational and the individual partook of that force through his rational part, it behooved man to develop that faculty to the highest degree. Thus, the exercise of reason, both in practical and intellectual pursuits, and the contemplative life itself, were the highest goods for human beings (e.g., Aristotle *Nichomachean Ethics* 1098-1099a). And the philosophers were teachers, preachers and missionaries, directing their fellow mortals to this highest good. Some like Socrates and the Cynics were gadflies, shocking men to examine themselves through harsh words and unusual behavior. Others like Pythagoreans, Plato, Aristotle, the Stoics, and Epicurus established brotherhoods or schools to help their followers find the truth. Almost all wrote books to educate the general public and shape the state according to their wisdom.

The question of whether all were capable of attaining the highest good was also considered. The Cynics preached that people needed very little but their knowledge to achieve happiness. Stoic philosophy freed even the slave and gave him the means to become a wise man despite his lowly state. Aristotle, ever more pragmatic, admitted that true happiness required external goods as well (*Nichomachean Ethics* 1.1099b). In the allegory of the cave, Plato insisted that the soul of every man has the power to learn, if only it is turned in the right direction (*Republic* 7.518). Yet the *Republic* is predicated on the fundamental principle that individuals are born into this world with different abilities and interests which fit them for different roles in society and different means of achieving happiness. Diotima's revelation of the ladder of love in *Symposium* illustrated how all individuals seek immortality, but some procreate children, write poetry, or establish institutions and laws, whereas the one who has seen immortal Beauty itself has achieved the highest good and happiness (208e-212c).

The lovers of wisdom attain the most happiness because it brings them closer to god. In the words of Pindar,

> Single is the race, single
> Of men and of gods:
> From a single mother we both draw breath
> But a difference of power in everything
> keeps us apart;
> For the one is as nothing, but the brazen sky
> Stays a fixed habitation forever.
> Yet we can in greatness of mind
> Or of body be like the Immortals,
> Tho' we know not to what goal
> By day or in the nights
> Fate has written that we shall run
> (*Nemean* 6.1-7 Bowra, trans.)

His phrase "greatness of mind" refers to the art with which he created beauty, honored the excellence of others, and taught men about the immortal gods, an art which he called wisdom (*sophia*).[79] Diotima ended her speech on love with a similar speculation.

> But what if the man had eyes to see the true beauty . . .
> Remember how in that communion only, beholding beauty
> with the eye of the mind, he will be enabled to bring forth,
> not images of beauty but realities (for he has hold not of an
> image but of a reality), and bringing forth and nourishing true
> virtue to become the friend of God and be immortal, if mortal
> man may (Plato *Symposium* 211 e-212a, Jowett, trans.).

Aristotle, whose ultimate reality was the Prime Mover composed of thought which has itself for an object (*Metaphysics* 12.1074), concluded his practical and theoretical proofs that the contemplative life is the *summum bonum* with the argument that it is the true *imitatio dei*.

> Now he who exercises his reason and cultivates it seems to be
> both in the best state of mind and most dear to the gods. . . . it
> would be reasonable both that they should delight in that
> which was best and most akin to them (i.e., reason) and that
> they should reward those who love and honor this most, as
> caring for the things that are dear to them and acting both
> rightly and nobly. . . . philosopher . . . therefore is the dearest to
> the gods. And he who is that presumably will also be happiest
> (*Nichomachean Ethics* 10.1179a, Ross, trans.)[80]

Notes

1. The connection of the mantics, poets, sages, and philosophers of Greece with religion is most fully developed by Francis Cornford in *Principium Sapientiae: The Origins of Greek Philosophic Thought* (Cambridge: Cambridge University Press, 1952). See also W. Jaeger, *The Theology of the Early Greek Philosophers*, trans. E. S. Robinson (Oxford: Oxford University Press, 1947) and E. R. Dodds, *The Greeks and the Irrational* (Berkeley: University of California Press, 1959), esp. Chapter 3, "The Blessings of Madness," pp. 64-103, and Chapter 5. "Greek Shamans and the Origins of Puritanism," pp. 135-178. Although E. R. Dodds and Cornford emphasize the similarities between the Greek figures and shamans of other cultures, several scholars are wary of drawing too close a parallel. See Walter Burkert's chapter, "Metempsychosis and Shamanism," esp. pp. 147-65 in *Lore and Science in Ancient Pythagoreanism* , trans. Edwin J. Minar, Jr. (Cambridge: Harvard University Press, 1972) as well as C. H. Kahn, "Religion and Natural Philosophy in Empedocles' Doctrine of the Soul," *Archiv fur Geschichte der Philosophie* 42 (1960): 30-35.

2. See the excellent summary in S. C. Humphreys, *Anthropology and the Greeks* (London: Routledge and Kegan Paul, 1978), p. 237. For a detailed analysis of the distinctions between theology and wisdom, see the articles by G. Vlastos, "Cornford's *Principium Sapientiae*," pp. 42-55, and "Theology and Philosophy in Early Greek Thought," pp. 97-123 in *Studies in Presocratic Philosophy. Vol. I. The Beginnings of Philosophy*, D. J. Furley and R. E. Allen, eds. (New York: Humanities Press, 1970). G. E. R. Lloyd, *The Revolutions of Wisdom; Studies in the Claims and Practices of Ancient Greek Science* (Berkeley: University of California Press, 1987), pp. 83-102 analyzes the public, competitive and critical nature of the development of Greek wisdom and provides abundant primary and secondary source material. Lloyd's earlier book *Magic, Reason and Experience: Studies in the Origin and Development of Greek Science* (Cambridge: Cambridge University Press, 1979) emphasizes the development of argumentation and research.

3. Humphreys, *Anthropology*, p. 220, 225-6, as well as G. B. Kerferd, *The Sophistic Movement* (Cambridge: Cambridge University Press, 1981), p. 24.

4. Lloyd, *Revolutions*, p. 84 with notes 120 and 121 for information on various lists and speculation on reasons for the inclusion of certain individuals. Humphreys, *Anthropology*, p. 263, emphasizes the political dimensions.

5. H. W. Parke and D. E. Wormell, *The Delphic Oracle*. Vol I. *The History* (Oxford: Basil Blackwell, 1956), pp. 387-88.

6. See Kerferd, *SM*, pp. 85-110, 165-69, for analysis of Protagoras' man-measure doctrine and its relation to ideas about the gods.

7. J. V. Muir, "Religion and the New Education: The Challenge of the Sophists", pp. 191-218 in P. E. Easterling and J. V. Muir, eds., *Greek Religion and Society* (Cambridge: Cambridge University Press, 1985).

8. Lloyd, *Magic*, pp. 15-58, discusses the criticism of religious views of disease and places it in its social and philosophical context.

9. Detailed discussions of Greek mantics appear in Walter Burkert, *Greek Religion*, trans. John Raffan (Cambridge: Harvard University Press, 1985), pp. 109-114; Cornford, pp. 73-76, as well as the chapter on Shamanism, pp. 88-106; Dodds, pp. 68-75, 135-178; W. R. Halliday. *Greek Divination. A Study of its Methods and Principles* (Chicago: Argonaut, Inc., 1967), J. S. Morrison, "The Classical World," in *Divination and Oracles*, Michael Loewe and Carmen Blaker, eds. (London: George Allen and Unwin, 1981); John Pollard, *Seers, Shrines, and Sirens* (South Brunswick, NJ: A. S. Barnes and Co., 1965), pp. 17-39, 106-116; Simon Price, "Delphi and Divination," pp. 128-154 in Easterling and Muir. See also Burkert, *Lore and Science*, pp. 147-65. In *Greek Religion*, p. 112, Burkert lists the terms associated with the art of the mantic which are derived from the word for god *theos*: e.g., seer - *theopropos*; interpreted sign - *theophaton*; to interpret or divine - *theiasein* or *entheazein*.

10. P. 91.

11. Lloyd, *Revolutions*, pp. 11-13, 84, and note 118.

12. See sources cited in note 9. Burkert, *Lore and Science*, pp. 120-165 analyzes these legends.

13. P. 104.

14. Halliday goes into great detail on all the various types of divination. See also Burkert, *Greek Religion*, pp. 112-114.

15. Halliday, pp. 198-200.

16. Morrison, p. 98. See Halliday, pp. 206-7., for examples.

17. Burkert, *Greek Religion*, pp. 114-116.

18. Halliday, p. 128, in Chapter on divination at sacred springs, pp. 116-144.

19. Quotations from Jowett's translation have been taken from the Modern Library College Edition: New York, 1927.

20. For a discussion of the phenomenon, see Dodds, pp. 68-75, including the notes, as well as p. 108; 116 f; 124, n. 24; 128 n. 62; 130; n. 82, and 131.

21. For detailed information on the oracle at Delphi, see Joseph Fontenrose, *The Delphic Oracle: Its Responses and Operation* (Berkeley: University of California Press, 1978); Parke and Wormell; Morrison, pp. 98-10; Pollard, pp. 17-39; and Price, who, on pp. 140-141, discusses Plutarch's speculations on the phenomenon in the first century C.E.

22. See Price, p. 142 for a succinct defense of this position.

23. Parke and Wormell, Vol. 2, contains a collection of the oracles in Greek. Fontenrose catalogues and translates them on pp. 240-416. See Price, pp. 143-152 for an excellent concise discussion of the types of oracles and the problems of interpreting them.

24. See Fontenrose, for an analysis of the forms and their development as well as Chapter V. "Chresmologues and Oracle Collections", pp. 145-165, and Martin Nilsson, *Greek Folk Religion* (New York: Harper and Brothers, 1961), pp. 121-139.

25.   Translations from Greek Tragedy have been quoted from *The Complete Greek Tragedies*, David Grene and Richmond Lattimore, eds., Vols. 1-4 (Chicago: University of Chicago Press, 1959-60), and are cited by translator in the text.

26.   *The Rise and Fall of Athens; Nine Greek Lives by Plutarch* (Middlesex England: Penguin Books, 1960), p. 170.

27.   Pp. 146.

28.   Humphreys, p. 237.

29.   *Greek Religion*, p. 111.

30.   P. 75.

31.   See especially Parke and Wormell, Vol. 1, pp. 378-392 for a discussion of this subject.

32.   As quoted in Park and Wormell, Vol. 1, p. 378.

33.   Nilsson, pp. 106-108.

34.   Fontenrose is particularly concerned with the authenticity of oracles ascribed to Delphi.

35.   Summaries and quotations are taken from Parke and Wormell, Vol. 1, pp. 382-3.

36.   Parke and Wormell, Vol. 1, p. 383. On p. 392, n. 13, the authors note that Wilamowitz has dated these verses to the Hellenistic age.

37.   Parke and Wormell, pp. 371-78.

38.   Kerferd, *SM*, p. 24, with reference to his earlier writings, establishes the respect implicit in the term *sophistes*, and, in the rest of his book, the types of wisdom to which it applied. Lloyd, *Revolutions*, pp. 92-139, and notes 152 and 153 summarizes the uses of the term to indicate both the breadth of its application and its positive connotations.

39.   Dodds, pp. 80-82 and Cornford, pp. 76-79. C. M. Bowra, *Pindar* (Oxford: Clarendon Press, 1964), pp. 1-16. Scholars argue that both the techniques of versification, and the content were thought to have derived from the gods.

40.   Structural anthropologists have studied these developments in detail. See Humphreys, pp. 209-241 for bibliography, summary, and analysis.

41.   Humphreys, pp. 213-15.

42.   Cornford, pp. 77; 91; 105. Quotations from Hesiod are taken from the Loeb Library edition: Cambridge, Mass., 1914.

43.   Humphreys, pp. 215-18.

44.   Humphreys, p. 217.

45.   Dodds, p. 101, notes 121 and 122;

46.   See Bowra, pp. 4-16, for an analysis of Pindar's theory of poetry, based on the poet's scattered references to his *sophia*, as well as for similar ideas expressed by other poets.

47.   Humphreys, pp. 218-221.

48.   See Gerald Else, *The Origin and Early Form of Greek Tragedy* (Cambridge: Harvard University Press, 1965), as well as the excellent summary of Athenian drama as a complement to politics in Humphreys, pp. 228-34.

49.   Humphreys, pp. 221-228; 235-6.

50. For a detailed study of Heraclitus, see Charles Kahn, *The Art and Thought of Heraclitus: An Edition of the Fragments with Translation and Commentary* (Cambridge: Cambridge University Press, 1979). G. S. Kirk, J. E. Raven, M. Schofield, *The Presocratic Philosophers: A Critical History with a Selection of Texts* (Cambridge: Cambridge University Press, 1983), pp. 181-184, discuss problems of biography and questions about the writing of a "book". Several quotations of the Presocratics have been taken from this edition, referred to as KRS. Humphreys, p. 224, emphasizes Heraclitus' religious orientation.

51. Kahn, "Religion and Natural Philosophy", pp. 6-8. The article analyzes the correspondence between Empedocles' two poems, *The Purifications* and *On Nature*.

52. Lloyd, *Revolution*, p. 48, n. 162. See also p. 334, n. 161 for a list of passages where Galen expresses similar ideas.

53. Kahn, "Religion and Natural Philosophy", p. 35.

54. Burkert, *Lore and Science*, is the major work on Pythagorean sources and ideas. KRS presents a summary and analysis of his conclusions in the chapters on Pythagoras and Philolaus.

55. KRS, p. 248. See note 2 as well for bibliography on differences between religion and philosophy.

56. Humphries, p. 221.

57. Lloyd, *Revolutions*, pp. 83-108, discusses debate and competition and its good and bad effects on the expansion of knowledge. See Humphreys, pp. 225-6, on the impact of the audience on style and content.

58. See G. E. R. Lloyd, *Early Greek Science: Thales to Aristotle* (New York: W. W. Norton & Co., 1970), pp. 1-15; 125-146 for a general statement of Greek contributions to the development of knowledge and science.

59. Humphreys, pp. 235-6.

60. See Kerford, *SM* for details on individual lives and teachings.

61. *SM* throughout, but esp. pp. 173-4.

62. Humphreys, p. 21.

63. Bowra, p. 55.

64. Bowra, p. 57.

65. Cornford, p. 146, calls this the philosophic conception in contrast to the poetic.

66. KRS, p. 97.

67. P. 154; See Cornford's discussion of the philosophical concept of god in Chapter 9, pp. 143-55.

68. Bowra, p. 40.

69. Nilsson, pp. 104-108.

70. Burkert distinguishes between the two and discusses their ways of life in "Craft versus Sect: The Problem of Orphics and Pythagoreans", pp. 1-22 in *Jewish and Christian Self Definition. Volume 3. Self Definition in the Greco-Roman World*, Ben F. Meyer and E. P. Sanders, eds. (Philadelphia: Fortress Press, 1982). Burkert's chapter on the *akousmata* in *Lore and Science*, pp. 166-92, discusses the Pythagorean restrictions in the context of similar regulations and analyses their motives and later interpretations. He

concludes, p. 180, that the rules for life "developed from living custom with all its complexity and paradox, rather than from clearly articulated doctrine," e.g., the confusing traditions about abstentions from meat and beans (pp. 180-85). See also *Greek Religion*, pp. 301-4, for a summary.

71. Burkert, *Lore and Science*, p. 182.

72. KRS, pp. 319-20, as well as Kahn, "Religion and Philosophy."

73. See Cornford's discussion of *Euthyphro*, pp. 137-40.

74. See George B. Kerford, "The Image of the Wise Man in Greece in the Period before Plato," pp. 17-28 in *Images of Man in Ancient and Medieval Thought: Studia Gerardo Verbeke ab amicis et collegis dicata*, F. Bossier et al., eds. (Leuven: Leuven University Press, 1976) for a summary of the development of wisdom, as well as his *SM*, pp. 20 & 24, and Lloyd, *Revolutions*, pp. 83-4, and 93, n.153.

75. M. L. West, *Hesiod's "Works and Days"* (Oxford: Clarendon Press, 1978), p. 23.

76. Kerford, *SM*, p. 20.

77. Quoted from David G. Rice and John E. Stambough, *Sources for the Study of Greek Religion* (Missoula, Mont.: Scholars Press, 1979), pp. 96-97.

78. For a survey of the Wisdom Tradition in several cultures, see West, *Hesiod's "Works and Days,"* pp. 1-25. For a comparison of Greek and Hebrew Wisdom, see Von Otto Plager, "Wahre die richtige Mitte: solche Massist in allem das Beste!", pp. 156-173 in *Gotteswort und Gottes Land* (Hans Wilhelm Hertzberg Festschrift) H. G. Reventlow, ed. (Gottingen: Vandenhoeck and Ruprecht, 1965) and Stella Lange, "The Wisdom of Solomon and Plato," *Journal of Biblical Literature* 55 (1936): 293-302. Translations from Theognis and Solon are quoted from J. M. Edmonds, *Elegy and Iambus*, Vol. I, Loeb Classical Library (Cambridge: Harvard University Press, 1944).

79. Bowra, p. 97.

80. Richard McKeon, ed. *Introduction to Aristotle* (New York: Random House, 1947).

Sinai IV: Wisdom Piety in the Hellenistic World

*The Book of Ecclesiastes (*Kohelet*)*

Of the wisdom books of the Bible, the Book of Ecclesiastes (*Kohelet*) shows Greek influence most decidedly. Written in Hebrew in Jerusalem, some time in the middle of the third century B.C.E., the author, though cloaked by a pseudonym, gives precedence to his "I" (Eccles. 1:12) for the first time in Hebrew wisdom literature with the exception of Prov. 24:32. Another first is the use of the term *darash* in the sense of investigating a problem (Eccles. 1:3) so characteristic of the age of Aristotle, a meaning that later became fundamental in the rabbinic schools and developed into a major form of Bible exegesis—*Midrash*. Throughout his book, *Kohelet* emphasizes his personal experience of life. In Greek fashion, he conducts a psychological experiment in which he puts to the test three types of life described by the Greek philosophers as pleasure, contemplation and action and is disappointed in all three (Eccles. 1:12; 2:1-11). His contact with Greek ideas probably came from the popular philosophical orators whom he heard in the port cities of Palestine. Kohelet breaks with the anonymous matter-of-fact optimism of the earlier wisdom tradition and reveals himself as a *critical* observer and independent thinker. The subject of his book is the meaning of life, a subject discussed by the Greek philosophers. They posited the highest good in life and explained how the world was governed but for them humanity remained at the center of the discussion.

Kohelet had to contend with the God of Israel and His covenant with the people of Israel. For the religious wing of the wisdom tradition meaning in life was based on the law of reciprocity implicit in the covenant and explicit in the Torah. From this vantage point meditation on God's teaching and observance of His commandments were the *summum bonum* of individual existence. The early Hellenistic period expressed growing skepticism about the classical Greek belief in the doctrine of reciprocity (discussed in Chapter 4).[1] Toward the end of the third century, when the Book of Ecclesiastes was composed, even the optimistic rationalism of the Hellenistic enlightenment began to wane.[2] Like his counterparts in Athens and Alexandria, the sage of Jerusalem could no longer derive meaning from traditional wisdom, piety and the cult, but he did not repudiate them (Eccles. 4:17-5:4). Neither did wisdom (though superior to folly) provide ultimate meaning for him (Eccles. 2:13-19). In the book of Ecclesiastes God loses the intensity of the personal covenant-relationship with humanity so characteristic of the Torah, the prophets and the religious wing of wisdom teachings. Kohelet's God is far removed from humanity ("For God is in heaven and you are on earth." Eccles. 5:1) who remains an isolated being. There is only a short distance between this *deus absconditus* and the impersonal fate of Stocicism.

The sharp sense of the limitations of life and happiness and a pervading feeling of futility often lead to hedonism, on the one hand, and to asceticism on the other. Kohelet is no hedonist. He advises his listeners to go to the house of mourning rather than to a house of feasting so that they might learn the inevitable end of human life (Eccles. 7:2). But neither is he an ascetic. For him *carpe diem* means enjoying the simple pleasures of life (Eccles. 2:24-9:7-10).

This emphasis on the enjoyment of life reflects a life style characteristic of the upper middle class of society who lived off their capital in the form of land or other investments (Eccles. 11:1 f.) and were the dominant force of the Hellenistic world, whether Greek or non-Greek. They had an active approach to life, but it was entirely directed toward security and pleasure and despite all its rationalism, was basically conservative.[3] Like the Stoics and Epicureans, Kohelet allowed gentlemen of his day to strive for health, riches, and other worldly goods. But like them he looked down on those who became greedy and put on airs. He speaks disdainfully of slaves who, becoming rich, mount horses (Eccles. 10:7), a sign of extraordinary wealth in a poor land like Judea. In the Ptolemaic monarchy which controlled Palestine, the political activity of the middle class was considerably limited. Thus a man like Kohelet, though acutely aware of the social injustices engendered by the nihilism of the bourgeoisie of his time, shows none of the passionate commitment of the prophets to set society aright.

The Book of Joshua Ben Sira

The upper middle class assumptions of the Hellenistic world are also to be found in the wisdom work by Joshua ben Sira included in the Apocrypha. The author was both a scholar and a teacher of wisdom lore and piety, who gathered pupils about him in his own school. His book, composed in Jerusalem about 190-170 B.C.E., reformulates older proverbs, adds new ones and develops others into miniature essays. According to ben Sira the ideal scholar is a cultivated man who has broadened his mind by travel in foreign countries and by experiences with good as well as evil in men. He is a man of genteel qualities, at home in the highest company. His studies have a wide range. He devotes himself to the understanding of the divine law and is thus qualified to take a leading part in the assembly of the people, or to sit on the judge's bench and deliver just and right sentence. The ideal scholar seeks out the wisdom of all the ancients and preserves the utterances of famous men. He is also well versed in the elusive turns of parables and in interpreting enigmatical utterances. Ben Sira contrasts the situation and occupation of the scribe and the sage with the lower classes. Of the carpenter, the goldsmith, and the potter, ben Sira says: "All these are skilled with their hands and each is expert in his own work. Without them a city cannot be inhabited." Yet, unlike the Sage, "They are not sought out for the council of the people, nor do they attain eminence in the public assembly. They do not sit in the judge's seat, nor do they consider statute and judgment."[4] According to ben Sira, those who must give all their time and thought to making a living cannot possibly have wisdom, which only leisure for reflection and dedication to study can produce.[5] This anti-plebian line echoes the attitudes found in the Greco-Roman world toward labor.[6]

There are other signs of Greek influence on the writing of ben Sira. He carries Kohelet's emphasis on "the I" one step further by writing under his own name, a factor responsible for the exclusion of his book from the biblical canon. Ben Sira's "Hymn of the Fathers" (Sira 44-50) is strikingly reminiscent of the glorification of the heroes in the biographical genre of Hellenistic times.[7] The titles for individual sections of his work, the use of transitional passages from one theme to another and the fact that he rarely expresses his ideas in independent statements but treats his subject matter in larger units is also an indication of Greek literary influence on ben Sira and the difference in style between him and earlier wisdom teachers.

The difference, however, is only in style. In content and *weltanschaung*, ben Sira, as we have noted, is deeply rooted in the Torah, prophecy, the priestly ritual and the Torah piety of the religious wing of wisdom. Unlike Kohelet, in whom the Hellenistic intellectual climate inspired skepticism about life's meaning and a critical stance toward the older wisdom tradition and its pieties, ben Sira affirms life's meaning in terms of the older piety and dresses its traditions in Hellenistic garb. Thus, for example, he merges the older prophetic teaching of the rise and fall of nations due to their arrogance and ignorance of God's plan, discussed in Chapter 4, with the Greek tragic concept of hubris, also discussed in Chapter 4 (Sira 10:4,8). Rejecting a secular wisdom dissociated from piety, he upholds an educational ideal that merges the Hebrew concept of *musar*, divine instruction in the good life emphasized by the Book of Proverbs with the Greek concept of *paideia*, a term used by his grandson in translating ben Sira's work into Greek. This educational ideal resulted in an interiorized emotional piety in which the relationship with God is at the center. Ben Sira differs with Kohelet in believing that a human being *can*, with divine help, discover the right time (*kairos*) to undertake mundane tasks and to understand the ultimate questions of divine decrees. In the book of Joshua ben Sira, Torah study and wisdom are fused, as seen in the description above of the ideal sage, who is both wise man and Torah interpreter and judge.

The Wisdom of Solomon

Joshua ben Sira's counterpart in the Jewish Diaspora of the Hellenistic world is the unknown author of the Wisdom of Solomon. Composed in Alexandria in the first century B.C.E., this work unlike the biblical Book of Proverbs and Sira's work is not an instructional text for pupils in a wisdom school but an extended treatise addressed to both Jews and Gentiles. Its twofold aim is to strengthen Jewish faith against the distractions and temptations of Hellenistic culture and to champion the Hebrew concept of wisdom in the face of the challenges of Greek intellectualism and the continuing tradition of ancient paganism. Written in the form of a manifesto, addressed by King Solomon to his fellow monarchs throughout the world, the book uses Greek rhetorical forms and philosophical terminology.[8]

The Essence of Hebrew Wisdom

It was axiomatic for the religious outlook of the older wisdom tradition represented by the Book of Proverbs that right knowledge about God puts an individual into a right relationship with the objects of his or her perceptions. The search for knowledge can go wrong not so much as a result of individual errors in judgment or mistakes creeping in at different points, but through one single mistake at the very beginning—the failure to know God. If it was accepted that there was no understanding which did not include faith, it was also felt as certain that there was no faith which could not rest on insights and experiences. In ancient Israel, wisdom, like prophecy, was a charismatic gift from God. Thus, the first three kings of Israel were the recipients of such charismatic gifts—Saul prophesies under the spirit, David plays divine melodies (a form of wisdom as discussed above) and Solomon is given a wise and understanding heart. This concept of wisdom is still found in the books of Proverbs and in Job (Prov. 2:6, 10f; Job 4:12-17). But despite wisdom's roots in divine revelation the teachers were duty bound to be accurate in their reasoning and diligent in refuting erroneous opinions.

Finally, as discussed in a previous chapter, Hebrew wisdom was partitive. Unlike the Ionian nature—philosophers who were concerned with knowledge in the largest denominations with the principles of the world as a totality, the wisdom teachers dealt with much smaller currency, with partial insights into the ambiguities of life. To paraphrase Isaac Newton, they were aware that, like children at the seashore, they had discovered a few shells of knowledge while the vast ocean of truth lay before them. This awareness of the limitations of the human search for wisdom had a depressing effect on Kohelet and his book is an elegy to its futility. But for the authors of Proverbs and Job (in its concluding chapters) and for Joshua ben Sira, this limitation pointed to the mystery of God and the mysteries of creation which could lead the thoughtful individual to praise of the Creator and awe for His works.

That much remained unknown did not lead the wisdom teachers to belittle what could be and what had become known. But it did incline them toward a reticence in undertaking great, sweeping explanations of existence. Their hesitation was based on the intuition that the individual as part of creation could never assume an entirely objective position in relation to the world, the position of a mere observer. Thus *their* observations were expressed in an organic fashion which, like a kaleidoscope, constantly takes on new shapes, images and colors as the partitive truths jell differently under different circumstances. This structure of thought stands in striking contrast to the hierarchical thinking of the scientific philosophers in Greece and in the western world of our own time.

Notes

1. Martin Hengel, *Judaism and Hellenism* (London: SCM Press, 1974) 1: 121-123.

2. Elias Bickerman, *Four Strange Books of the Bible* (New York: Schocken Books, 1967), p. 156.

3. M. Rostovtzeff, *The Social and Economic History of the Hellenistic World* 3 vols. (Oxford: Oxford University Press, 1941) 2:1105, 1108 and 1116 ff.

4. The Wisdom of Joshua ben Sira 39: 4-6.

5. *Ibid.* 38: 24-39.

6. Aristotle was of the opinion that it was impossible for a poor man to govern well since he has no leisure. He cites an adage that there is no leisure for slaves and goes on to say that the best state will not make an artisan a citizen. See *Politics* in *The Works of Aristotle* (Oxford: The Clarendon Press, 1921) 10: 1273A, 1278A, 1334A.

7. G. Von Rad, *Wisdom In Israel*, pp. 257-58 and nn. 24-25, p. 258; Martin Hengel, *Judaism and Hellenism* 1:136; 2:90, n. 209.

8. See the introduction and commentary by David Winston to The Wisdom of Solomon, Anchor Bible ed. (Garden City: Doubleday & Co., 1979).

Sinai V: The Intellectual Piety of the Rabbis

The Socio-Economic Status of the Sages

As noted above, Joshua ben Sira and his work were the bridge leading from the wisdom piety of the Bible and the early post-biblical literature to the intellectual piety of the rabbis. The transition is evident in the gradual change in the social and economic status of the sage and his relationship to the community as well as in the shifting emphasis on the essentials of wisdom and piety. The upper class orientation of Sira, who envisioned the scholar as far above the laboring masses, a man who is praised by them but who is not close to them or active in their midst, is still echoed in the statements of some of the earliest rabbis.[1]

But as a result of the Maccabean rebellion, fueled by the energy, the religious loyalties and patriotism of the lower classes led by plebeian priests of the Hasmonean family who overthrew the aristocratic Jewish Hellenizers and their Syrian-Greek sponsors, a new type of sage emerged.[2] He maintained an independent attitude toward the rich upper classes and those in political power even though he may have belonged to their circle.[3] This independence was rooted in economics; the sage derived his livelihood from his own labor (often manual labor) and the popular support of the masses who saw in the study and the teaching of Torah a vehicle of upward mobility for themselves and their children and who in turn prevented the mandarinization of Jewish learning. Hillel the Elder criticized the Aristotelian-Greek view echoed by ben Sira that only the leisured class can study and his rabbinic descendant held up the ideal of Torah study combined with vocational training that leads to a practically useful occupation[4] Even after the destruction of the Second Temple, when the rabbis became more socially and economically dependent on the Patriarch (the rabbinic head of the Sanhedrin and the Jewish community in Palestine), who appointed them to communal positions and paid their salaries, there were still those who sought to maintain their economic independence, meager as it might be, so that they could openly disagree with the Patriarch on matters of law and administration.[5]

The Maccabean rebellion also ignited a social revolution. Not only had a new Jewish aristocracy replaced the traditional priestly and noble classes of the age of ben Sira, witness the rabbinic ruling "A learned bastard takes precedence over an ignorant high priest,"[6] but a new authority was introduced even into the family—the teacher. In the world of rabbinic Judaism, a new social hierarchy was created, analogous in some respects to the intellectual circles in Greece, in which learning replaced lineage as a measure of distinction. It did not matter a great deal whom you called your father. It mattered a great deal whom you called your teacher and how close you were in your relationship with him. The Roman historian Tacitus who complained that Jewish proselytism broke up stable Roman families[7] would have found a similar complaint in many Jewish homes in Palestine. According to rabbinic tradition, Rabbi Eliezer ben Hyrcanus, as a young man defied his wealthy father and went to study at the academy of R. Johanan ben Zakkai in Jerusalem. Years later his aged father came to Jerusalem to disinherit his rebellious son but when the father discovered that R. Eliezer had become a distinguished sage, father and son were reconciled.[8] If what counted was not only life, but a life of Torah study, then one's physical parents were hardly as important as one's spiritual masters. In fact the *Mishnah* incorporated this social revolution into law.[9] It is perhaps in the context of this social revolution that we can understand Jesus' statement: "Anyone who has given up houses or brothers or sisters or father or mother or children or land for my sake will receive many times as much, and shall inherit eternal life" (Matt. 19:29. Cf. Luke 14:33). In sum, as Max Weber noted: "Through the rabbinate there now ensued, in contrast to what had gone before, a tremendous expansion of lower middle class . . . intellectualism such as we do not find among any other people."[10]

The Tension Between Revelation and Reason

In the earlier discussion of the charismatic piety of the rabbis, it was pointed out that throughout the talmudic period and beyond, a descending hierarchy of divine revelation was established with the Mosaic revelation as the most authoritative, the prophets less so and so on. The authority of the Mosaic revelation included not only the law and commandments but also the authority to explain and interpret them. All of the later rulings of prophets and sages are but a later unfolding of that which already existed *in potentia* in the revelation of Sinai. Even innovative legislation introduced by talmudists of a later period, was understood as being derived from that which was implicit in the words of Scripture but was not made explicit until much later. Thus, beginning with the revelation to Moses and continuing with the prophets down through the talmudic rabbis and their medieval successors, there were two channels by which the oral law continued to develop—through succeeding revelations and through rational modes of argument, explanation and exegesis. The question debated by the rabbis was: What weight should be given to revelation and what importance attached to reason?

One group among the rabbis sought to limit revelational authority in legal development as well as in non-legal matters only to Moses.[11] According to this view even Moses did not add anything to that which he received on Sinai.[12] But what about the evidence in the Bible and in the oldest layers of the rabbinic tradition that the prophets after Moses did introduce laws and interpretations of existing commandments? Thus Elisha commands those battling the Moabites to "fell every good tree" (2 Kings 3:19) in opposition to the law of the Torah (Deut. 20:19), and Jeremiah warns the Jerusalemites not to carry burdens out of their houses and through the gates of Jerusalem on the Sabbath (Jer. 17:21-27), a law that is not specified in the Torah.[13]

This contradictory evidence was dealt with in two different ways by two different groups of sages.

1) One group argued that the new enactments by the prophets were not really new at all for they were all implicit in the Sinaitic revelation and made explicit at the time they were needed in the same way that the sages rational interpretations were also implicit in the Sinaitic revelation and made explicit later. The difference is only in the channel through which these interpretations made their way into the world—for the prophets, the channel was prophecy; for the rabbis, reason. Both channels are legitimate.

2) A second group of sages denied the legitimacy of the prophetic channel as a means for bringing new enactments into the world after the once-only revelation to Moses on Sinai. How then did the prophets arrive at these new legal interpretations or decisions? The answer is through reason and rational modes of argument and exegesis. In this view everyone after Moses is modeled on the image of the talmudic sage whose sole authority is his intellect and the words of the Torah.

It has already been noted that the tendency to derive all later prophecy from Moses was related to the advent of Christianity and Gnostic sects who claimed competing revelations. In this atmosphere it was necessary to restrain the immediacy of prophecy, with its unforeseen message breaking into the historic situation by introducing into it the element of tradition.[14] But within the framework of prophecy rooted in tradition there were the charismatics who saw its continuation in the development of law as both legitimate and desirable, not in the place of reason but alongside it, and there were the rationalists who ruled out the incursion of prophecy and revelation into the domain of law after the Sinaitic revelation.[15]

This conflict is epitomized in the debate between R. Eliezer ben Hyrcanus on one side and R. Joshua ben Hananya and the Sages on the other side.[16] After failing to convince his opponents on rational grounds, R. Eliezer resorted to calling for miracles as proof that his views were correct. When the walls of the academy began to buckle as a result of R. Eliezer's call, R. Joshua halted them by pointing out that when scholars are engaged in *halakic* (legal) dispute miracles have no right to interfere. When a Heavenly Voice (*bat kol*) cried out that in all matters of *halakah* (law) R. Elizer's authority prevailed, R. Joshua countered, citing Deut. 30:12, that since the Torah had been given at Sinai we pay no attention to a Heavenly Voice because the Torah itself states that in matters of law the majority view must prevail (Exod. 23:2).

There are a number of significant points in this remarkable narrative that pertain to our context. R. Eliezer did not seek to replace reason with psychic power, miracles and revelation. Only when rational argument failed to move his disputants did he resort to these means. On the other hand, R. Joshua did not deny the validity and the efficacy of psychic power, miracles and revelation. In fact he, too, used them to prevent the walls of the academy from falling. What he objected to was the inappropriate appeal to these powers after the Sinaitic revelation in a context of legal discussion in which only intellect, reason and majority rule should apply. Moreover, he underscores the fact that the Sinaitic Revelation is not only the source of latter day prophecy, miracles and revelations; it is also the source of rational argument that rests on majority rule. As noted above, R. Eliezer ben Hyracanus was noted for his charismatic power and abilities.[17] In contrast. R. Joshua was known to be highly adept in the forms and methods of Greek logic and rhetoric.[18] The Talmud concludes the narrative by telling us that when Elijah, the prophet, appeared to R. Nathan he informed the rabbi that at the time of the dispute, God laughed with joy and said: "My sons have defeated Me! My sons have defeated Me!" The argument of R. Joshua and the sages that reason prevail in the context of the legal discussion regarding these worldly matters, overcame God's inclination toward R. Eliezer. Indeed, R. Eliezer's stubborn refusal to accept the majority rule brought about his excommunication.[19] Nevertheless, R. Eliezer's position remained influential far beyond his time. His rabbinic successors continued to call upon and make use of psychic, charismatic and revelatory powers alongside their reason to determine matters of law and morality.[20]   Philo, like the rabbis, also has this unique blending of the mystical and the rational.   Describing Abraham, Jacob, Melchizedek, Levi and Moses as mystical voyagers he writes: "These no doubt are truly admirable persons and superior to the other classes. They have, as I said, advanced from down to up by a sort of heavenly ladder and by reason and reflection happily inferred the Creator from his works. But those, if such there be, who have had the power to apprehend Him through Himself without the cooperation of any reasoning process to lead them to the sight, must be recorded as holy and genuine worshippers and friends of God in truth."[21]

The Ethics of the Intelligentsia

Though the rabbis differed over the boundaries between rational and revelational sources of knowledge they were unanimous in their agreement that intelligence was indispensable for piety. Hillel's maxim also quoted in the name of R. Akiba "An uncultured man cannot really fear sin, an ignorant man cannot be truly pious"[22] has already been cited in an earlier chapter. The intelligent individual who is immersed in Torah study and its way of life is aware of ethical subtleties and refinements that are lost on those who lack both intelligence and intellectual training. For the average person the rabbis established the doctrine of reciprocity as the norm of justice. But they considered it the floor of ethics since it represents the minimal obligation of the law. On a higher level is the code of the rabbinic scholar and saint who adheres to a standard above that of the average man. This is the ethical ceiling which in rabbinic morality is called going beyond the limit of the law. The following incident related in the Talmud exemplifies this attitude:

> Raba bar bar Hana's porters broke his barrel of wine and their contract stipulated that they were liable for breakages, Raba took their cloaks as security for the compensation they owed him. The porters came to Rav (the head of the academy of Sura and one of the outstanding Babylonian Jewish scholars of the third century C.E.) to plead their case. Said Rav to the owner of the wine: "Give them back their cloaks," Bar Hana replied: "Is this the law?" "Yes," answered Rav, "In order that you may go in the way of the upright (Prov. 2:20).[23]

However, there is a question implicit in this narrative. When Raba bar bar Hana asked Rav, "Is this the law?", Rav should have answered him, "No, this is not the minimal obligation of the law; this is the ethical imperative that goes beyond the limit of the law." Why did Rav say this is the law? The answer is that Rav is saying to Raba bar bar Hana that the average man would consider this going beyond the limit of the law. But you and I are not average men. We are scholars. For us this is the law; anything less than this standard is contrary to the law. From the historical perspective it is also interesting that Rav reaches into the early wisdom piety of the Book of Proverbs to provide a basis in Scripture for the concept of a higher ethic for the intellectual.

Discussing a talmudic case involving a double standard of morality (one for the intelligentsia and one for ordinary people) in a life and death decision,[24] David Daube concludes from the entire discussion that we are dealing with "directions laid down for the mass of people which, however, a superior person should not rely on as his guides . . . . Where there is a double standard, the idea may be either that the general laws are adequate though the elite must do something extra, or that only the code of the elite is adequate while the general laws constitute a concession to the ordinary man's weakness."[25]

The pious individual who lacks intelligence will not only fail to understand the higher ethical demand of the scholar and saint, not to speak of the subtleties of ordinary ethics, but he or she will also grossly misunderstand moral priorities and fail to differentiate between the permitted and the prohibited, between the crucial and the less important in ritual as well as ethical matters. R. Joshua ben Hananya, who, as we saw above, put a particularly great premium on reason, lists the foolish pietist among those who ruin the world.[26] The Talmud gives the following example of what the rabbis considered a foolish pietist: A man who sees a woman drowning but will not save her because he does not think it proper to look upon her.[27] Though the rabbis were willing to accept the individual who adopted more strict rulings and attitudes than what they had ordained, they demanded that this strictness be based on learning and intelligence and be pure in motive. If such piety were motivated by self-pride or the desire to enhance one's reputation, it would easily degenerate into hypocrisy.[28]

The Polarities of Torah Study and Torah Practice

In a highly intellectualized piety there is always the danger of a gap developing between word and deed. If it is true that mindless piety can lead to a distortion of faith it is also true that a purely intellectual piety can lead to a sterility of faith. Thus R. Eliezer ben Azariah taught that an individual whose wisdom exceeded his good deeds was like a tree of many branches and few roots which could easily be overturned in the wind.[29]

The opposite pole was represented by R. Simeon bar Yohai, who believed that Torah study took precedence over everything, even to the exclusion of good deeds where it was impossible to do both. When a man in a fit of anger took a vow that he would not allow his wife any benefits unless she made two of the leading sages of the time, Rabbi Judah and Rabbi Simeon, eat of her cooking (which must have been very bad), Rabbi Judah went out of his way to eat in order to make peace between husband and wife, but Rabbi Simeon refused to budge from his study of Torah.[30]

During the Hadrianic persecution, when both study and practical observance were forbidden, the sages had to decide which of the two risks should sooner be taken. R. Tarfon argued that practical observance was greater, but R. Akiba maintained that study is greater because it leads to practical observance. R. Akiba's argument won the day[31] but in succeeding generations the balance between the life of the mind and religious-ethical practice was debated again and again.

Notes

1. *M. Avot*, 1:4-5. Yose ben Yohanan of Jerusalem is speaking of the poor as the object of aristocratic, philanthropic solicitude, not as a constituency on whose behalf and in whose midst one is active.

2   Victor Tcherikover, *Hellenistic Civilization and the Jews*, trans. S. Applebaum (Philadelphia and Jerusalem: The Jewish Publication Society of America, The Magnes Press, the Hebrew University, 1959), p. 207, p. 480, n. 6.

3.   *M. Avot*, 1:10. "Love work, hate domineering over others; and do not seek the intimacy of public officials."

4.   *M. Avot*, 2:4; 2:2.

5.   *b. Berakot*, 28a; See also Ephraim E. Urbach, "Class Status and Leadership in the World of the Palestinian Sages, "*Proceedings of the Israel Academy of Sciences and Humanities* (Jerusalem: Magnes Press, 1960) 2:46-47 and Urbach, *The Sages*, pp. 593-603.

6.   *M. Horayot*, 3:8.

7.   *Greek and Latin Authors on Jews and Judaism*, ed. with intro., trans. and commentary by Menahem Stern (Jerusalem: The Israel Academy of Sciences and Humanities, 1974) 2: Intro.

8.   *Avot de Rabbi Natan*, Version A, Ch. 6, Version B, Ch. 13 (ed. S. Schechter), pp. 15-16; *The Fathers According to Rabbi Nathan*, trans. Goldin,

pp. 43-44; *Gen. R.* 41(42) (ed. Theodor-Albeck), pp. 397-399; *Tanhuma B, Lekh Lekha* 10 (ed. Buber), pp. 34-35; Gerson D. Cohen, "The Talmudic Age" in *Great Ages and Ideas of the Jewish People*, ed. Leo W. Schwarz (New York: Random House, 1956), pp. 173-212.

9. *M. Bava Mezia*, 2:11. The commentators point out that if the father was a learned man his person and his property would take precedence, for where the advantage of learning is present in both teacher and father, filial peity decides the issue.

10. *The Sociology of Religion* (Boston: Beacon Press, 1963), p. 128. Cf. Urbach, *The Sages*, pp. 585-586. The rabbis gave an additional meaning to the term *am ha'arez*, the people of the land which both the Pharisaic *havurot* (societies) and the Essenes understood as those who could not be trusted in matters of ritual purity. For the rabbis the term also included the ignorant and the unlettered. Unlike the Essenes and even the Pharisaic *havurot* (societies) who sought to exclude the *am ha'arez*, the rabbis made every effort to educate the *am ha'arez* and to raise as many of the untutored masses to their level as they possibly could. Thus R. Judah ben Bathyra cautioned his colleagues to honor the children of the *am ha'arez* because from them the Torah would go forth, *b. Sanhedrin*, 96 a and Rashi's commentary *ad. loc.*

11. *Exod. R.* 28:4; *Exod. R.* 42:7; *Cant. R.* 1:29; *Tanhuma Yitro*, 11; *b. Berakot*, 5a.

12. *Sifre, Behaaloteka* 68; *Sifre, Shelah* 111; *Sifre Zuta, Shelah* 32 (ed. Horowitz), note 17; *b. Bava Batra*, 119a; *b. Sanhedrin*, 78b; Bernard J. Bamberger, "Revelations of Torah after Sinai," *Hebrew Union College Annual* 16 (1941): 97-114.

13. *b. Sukkah, 44a*. Other examples are that Ezekiel set forth the laws concerning the Temple to be reconstructed in the future, and the laws concerning the priests and the altar that he had received through a divine revelation (Ezek. 43:10-44; 31). According to R. Johanan the rite of the willow branch on *Sukkot* (the Feast of Tabernacles) was instituted by the prophets of the Second Temple Haggai, Zecharia and Malachi, to whom rabbinic tradition ascribed many legal enactments, see above Sinai II: note 16.

14. See above Sinai II: note 13.

15. Ephraim E. Urbach, "*Halakah U-Nevuah*", *Tarbiz* 18 (1946-47), pp. 1-27.

16. *b. Bava Mezia*, 59b. The debate concerned an oven, which instead of being made in one piece was made in a series of separate portions with a layer of sand between each. R. Eliezer maintained that since each portion in itself was not a utensil, the sand between prevented the whole structure from being regarded as a single utensil and thus not liable to ritual impurity. The Sages, however, held that the outer coating of mortar or cement unified the whole and made it a single utensil and thus liable to ritual impurity. See Maimonides commentary on *M. Kelim* 5:10.

17. See above Sinai II: note 47.

18. Saul Lieberman, *Hellenism in Jewish Palestine* (New York: The Jewish Theological Seminary of America, 1950), pp. 94-95.

19. *b. Bava Mezia*, 59b.

20. E. Urbach, "*Halakah U-Nevuah*," *Tarbiz* 18, pp. 19-27. On the use of these powers by Rabbi Joseph Karo see R. J. Zwi Werblowsky, *Joseph Karo: Lawyer and Mystic* (Philadelphia: The Jewish Publication Society of America, 1980) and on the Gaon Elijah of Vilna's acknowledgment of these powers but his refusal to use them see Appendix F as well as H. H. Ben Sasson, "The Personality of Elijah Gaon of Vilna and His Historical Influence," *Zion* 21, nos. 1-2, 3-4 (1966): 40-216. See also Abraham J. Heschel, *Prophetic Inspiration After the Prophets, Maimonides and Others* (Hoboken, NJ: Ktav Publishing House, 1994).

21. *De Praemiis et Poenis*, 43f.; ed. Loeb Classics, ed. and trans. Colson (Cambridge, Mass., and London, 1939): VIII, 337.

22. *M. Avot*, 2:5; *Avot de Rabbi Natan*, Version A, Ch. 26 (ed. Schechter), p. 41b; *The Fathers According to Rabbi Nathan*, trans. Goldin, p. 112.

23. *b. Bava Mezia*, 83a.

24. The case dealt with a city that is besieged because of a fugitive who is harbored within or in other sources a caravan is besieged because of a particular woman whom the besiegers want to rape. The question is shall the individual be surrendered so that the community can be saved particularly if the fugitive is named *Yer. Terumah* 8:10; *Tosefta Terumah* 7:20; *b. Makkot*, 11a; *Gen. R.* 94:9 (ed. Theodor-Albeck), pp. 1182-85; *M. Terumot*, 8:11-12; *Lev. R.* 19:6. Saul Lieberman, *Tosefta Ki-Fshuta, Zeraim* (New York: Jewish Theological Seminary, 1955), p. 422, n. 141. David Daube, *Collaboration With Tyranny In Rabbinic Law* (London: Oxford University, Press, 1965), pp. 19-26 points out that there are two different historical situations under consideration: 1) The besiegers are marauders and raiders of caravans. 2) Where specifically named individuals are demanded, governmental authorities such as the Romans are the besiegers. Thus the first situation reflects conditions toward the end of the first century C.E. when law and order had completely broken down in Palestine in the face of the undeclared war between Jews and non-Jews and different factions of non-Jews. Under such conditions there is an absolute prohibition against handing over any Israelite under any circumstances. But under governmental persecution as during the reign of the Roman Emperor Hadrian after the failure of the Bar Kokba revolt, the prohibition was relaxed somewhat to allow for the surrender of an individual to save the community.

25. Daube, *Collaboration With Tyranny In Rabbinic Law*, p. 12. Daube also points to these two views of the double standard in the New Testament: "Not all men can receive this saying, but they to whom it is given. For there are eunuchs, that were so born from their mother's womb; and there are eunuchs that were made eunuchs by men; and there are eunuchs, that made themselves eunuchs for the kingdom of heaven's sake. He that is able to receive it, let him receive it" (Matt. 19: 11-12). "Moses for your

hardness of heart suffered you to put away your wives . . ." (Matt. 19:8). In the first citation (Matt. 19: 11-12) "the elite do something extra," in the second citation (Matt. 19:8) the general norm is a concession. See David Daube, "Concessions to Sinfulness in Jewish Law," *Journal of Jewish Studies* 10 (1959): 1ff.

26. *M. Sotah*, 3:4.
27. *b. Sotah*, 21b; *Yer. Sotah*, 3:4.
28. *Avot de Rabbi Natan* Version B. Ch. 27 (ed. Schechter), p. 25b.
29. *M. Avot*, 3:17.
30. *b. Nedarim*, 66b.
31. *b. Kiddushin*, 49b; I. H. Weiss, *Dor, Dor Ve-Dorshav* 2:125.

Conclusions and Comparisons

Our discussions of piety among the Hebrews and the Greeks have exposed several similarities inherent in their common background. Like the other ancient civilizations around them, they developed various means of maintaining contact with the supernatural. Thus the most striking manifestations of prophecy—ecstasy, visions and out-of-body experiences, mantic and magical powers—were present on both Sinai and Olympus. In Israel, where prophecy was connected with a revealed Scripture, the mantic and magical devices were stripped of their pagan wrappings. The miracles performed by Moses, for example, are the counterpart of pagan mantic and magical practices, but Exodus clearly presents them as pedagogical devices to impress Pharaoh with the power of the one God and win over the Israelites to Him. Other mantic and magical arts such as the reading of signs were either forbidden outright (Lev. 19:26; Deut. 18:1-12) or pushed off to the periphery (1 Sam. 28:7-19). Prayer, meditation, and faith in God were always more important expressions of prophetic charisma than mantic devices. In the absence of a revealed Scripture in Greece, however, these arts, in the words of Burkert, "became a preeminent form of contact with the higher world and a mainstay of piety."[1]

For Plato as well as the Hebrews, mantic devices were inferior to the type of prophecy in which the deity directly inspired the human to become his messenger. Here the essence of the prophecy was its content - the word of God. Indeed, the later kabbalists interpreted the communication between God and Moses as a kind of union similar to the "divine madness" described by Plato.[2] But in biblical Israel, prophecy was an ad hoc gift of God independent of any personal characteristics of the prophet or his or her preparation for it. Once called, the prophet was a servant of God, dedicated to and dominated by his or her mission. Nor could the charisma be passed on by inheritance from generation to generation. Only in the Second Temple period, when the belief in direct revelation had waned, do we find charismatic gifts passed down in families such as the grandchildren of Honi the Circlemaker. Then too, in contrast to biblical times, there were clairvoyants, healers, and other charismatic types whose skills were clearly a product of training in a discipline or a personal characteristic bestowed as a gift for living a saintly life.

Greek prophecy does not have the same religious intensity or urgency as biblical prophecy. Not only were there more divine sources of inspiration and different types of messages, but the messengers themselves were frequently connected to the cult centers rather than recipients of an ad hoc gift from the Lord. The Pythian Priestess, for example, prophesied only in the manner and at the times established at Delphi. The oracles were not delivered as spontaneous messages from the god; rather they were responses to questions posed to the god by individuals or states. Once granted, some prophetic arts could be handed down through families such as the Iamidae and the Melampidae.

The poets or philosophers who best defined the divine were generally individuals without formal ties to cult. Even if someone like Hesiod or Parmenides described, in the manner of Amos, the moment of inspiration and reported the content of the divine message, he remained a poet or philosopher rather than a man of god. Whether or not the audience assumed divine inspiration behind their words, the presentation occurred most often at a festival administered by the state or through private performances and publications; and the reception depended as much on the political context or critical evaluation by the listeners as on the recognized authority of the author. Only Plato's Socrates closely resembles the Hebrew prophets in his sense that he was called to a life-long mission by Apollo and his awareness that a spirit (*daimon*) prevented him from taking actions contrary to his duty to god and man. Some Greeks, associated with charismatics such as Orpheus and Pythagoras, tried to live holy lives and advocated asceticism and training, in the manner of the Second Temple prophets, but primarily as a means of purifying the immortal soul from its earthly dross, in preparation for its journey home after the death of the body. Despite different degrees of revelation and different contexts, however, the Greeks' words offered their communities a religious vision like the Hebrew prophets', expressing faith in a divine order, meditating on its nature, and composing the prayers and hymns which helped the people to reach out toward their gods.

On Sinai and Olympus, the recipients of divine revelation were deeply concerned with the political and social problems that affected their respective societies and they measured the performance of the institutions dealing with those problems by a divine standard. On Sinai, the classical prophets arose, inspired by God to insist on the priority of morality over forms of cult and the primacy of ethics over political and economic expediency. On Olympus, the oracles of the gods promoted the value of human life and the rule of law as well as spiritual and moral purity. The early poets insisted that political leaders try to establish Zeus' justice on earth and later lyric and dramatic poets examined contemporary problems in the light of eternal paradigms (often in performances at religious festivals). Most philosophers were concerned with cosmic and human justice; many (e.g., the charismatic Pythagoras and Empedocles) were concerned with sin and purity as well. Like a Hebrew prophet, Socrates goaded his fellow citizens into examining their lives and seeking the true standards for behavior. Like Jesus, he discredited the common belief that justice necessitated revenge, but he proved it, in a characteristically Greek way, by reasoning that the one who harms his enemy ultimately harms himself (*Apology* 25c-26a) and that by definition a good man cannot harm a bad man (*Republic* 1.134-5).

From the beginning wisdom was an important element of both cultures and included the knowledge that came from human experience and the exercise of reason and judgment as well as inspired insight into divine matters. Its development went through similar stages in Israel and Greece. Wisdom began as an oral tradition in which technical skills, practical advice, proverbs, maxims, and folk beliefs were passed down from generation to generation and eventually appeared in such books as the biblical Proverbs and Hesiod's *Works and Days*.

In the second stage individual thinkers expressed original ideas or their own responses to tradition in new formats. In Israel, the wise men, the authors of Kohelet (Ecclesiastes), Job, and the Wisdom of Solomon, as well as Joshua Ben Sira, reexamined Hebraic attitudes toward life, society, suffering, and death, using the old wisdom tradition as a springboard. In Greece, lyric and dramatic poets examined the same issues through the medium of myth and conventional morality while amateur thinkers pursuing idiosyncratic interests popularized new theories about the divine, natural, and human realms through public readings and written work.

Professionalism and the emergence of schools which attracted those drawn to intellectual pursuits marks the third stage. The practical, secular wisdom schools of Israel were eventually superseded by the religious wisdom schools beginning with Ezra and the Men of the Great Synagogue known as Scribes and culminating in the rabbinic schools of the *Tannaim* (the early teachers) and the *Amoraim* (the later teachers). The religious wisdom schools focused their energy on interpreting Scripture and developing the oral law and eventually absorbed all previous expressions of Hebrew wisdom, assigning Kohelet (Ecclesiastes) and Job to the biblical canon while placing Joshua Ben Sira and the Wisdom of Solomon in the Apocrypha.

By the mid-fifth century in Greece some wise men were taking on pupils and charging money to teach them. In the fourth century several philosophers founded schools to examine intellectual questions in depth and published popular works to inform the general public. When the founders died, the schools continued, with new leaders studying, interpreting and extending their masters' theories.

The connection of Greek philosophy with piety may seem tenuous when compared to the ongoing religious wisdom tradition of the Hebrews. But even when the Greek philosophers no longer emphasized their divine inspiration, they were attempting to understand the divine and eternal and to examine the implications of their theories for human life. Several of the schools, e.g., the Academy and the Lyceum, were established in sacred places as religious brotherhoods, and some, like the Stoics, could be considered philosophic religions or religious philosophies. As we have seen, the questions, methods of examination, and answers of Greek philosophy influenced Hebrew Wisdom in the Hellenistic period. The later rabbis maintained the emphasis on wisdom and passed on and developed the tradition, but they, unlike their Hellenistic predecessors both Greek and Hebrew, had a lower middle class proletarian outlook; they held that manual labor and Torah study were an ideal combination.

Despite the similar esteem for wisdom, the Greeks and the Hebrews evaluated its types, sources, and possibilities differently. As already noted in our brief introduction to this chapter, the Hebrews considered the practical wisdom derived from experience or tradition less sacred than the wisdom of the Torah revealed by God or direct revelation to the prophets by God, though wisdom too constituted a revelation through nature and reason. Secular knowledge and philosophy remained the handmaiden of Scripture while Scripture itself remained the ultimate authority although later subjected to interpretation by inspired sages. Great value was attached to reason and judgment, but its efficacy was considered limited since human knowledge was organic and partitive and could at best be applied to particular times, particular places and particular situations, yet never capable of grasping the totality of life or God. Thus the rabbis depended on the clash of intellects and logical reasoning to arrive at approximate truth regarding the application of Scripture to the ambiguities and changing conditions of life.

The Greeks traced all types of knowledge and all things in their world back to the gods or the divine order, but without any central authority, Scripture, or tradition, there was no hierarchy implicit in religious practice to assume the position of ultimate authority and to guarantee the truth of prophecy or knowledge. They had to rely on their own powers of reason and judgment. Thus, on the one hand, they were more suspicious of the mediators between individuals and their gods than the Hebrews were of their prophets. Although Hebrew prophets and Second Temple charismatics also faced skeptics and challengers (e.g., Jeremiah and Jesus and their interlocutors), there is no parallel in the Sinai tradition to Croesus who felt the need to test the most famous oracles before choosing one to which he posed his questions. Similarly, many Greeks expressed doubts about the various professional interpreters of the gods' enigmatic pronouncements and even about the political biases of the oracles themselves. The ultimate resolution of an oracular riddle was often accomplished by debate in an assembly of citizens, a practice not found in Israel. So too the truth about God and nature was not self evident or revealed. It had to be argued for and defended against in debate or book form and the ultimate arbiter of all questions was the individual thinker or the majority of the citizens persuaded by reasoned proof.

If the absence of a clear line of authority necessitated confidence in human reason, the lack of hierarchy in the types of wisdom encouraged the Greeks to examine everything. Ironically, they sought the explicit universal that their polytheistic religion and pluralistic society lacked and unlike the Hebrews they were convinced that human reason and judgment could attain more than partitive knowledge. From the particular facts of their organic world they moved to general theories and attempted a universal, systematic and hierarchic explanation of the entire cosmos. Philosophy was not a handmaiden; it was the highest pursuit and the greatest pleasure for man. In this context, there is a contrast between the Sinai tradition where piety is the pinnacle of human conduct as stated in Prov. 1:7, "The fear of the Lord is the beginning of knowledge" and the Olympus tradition where the concept of piety itself was but one subject among many examined by the poets and philosophers.

The Socrates of the *Apology*, however, would probably have understood the Hebrew conception of partitive wisdom and would have agreed with Prov. 1:7. Living in the transitional period between the mythopoetic and the philosophical ages, Socrates embodied the religious attitude best exemplified by the statement "know thyself" (*gnothi seauton*) associated with Apollo and Delphi.

After investigating the meaning of the oracular response which named him the wisest of men, he concluded,

> I am called wise, for my hearers always imagine that I myself possess the wisdom which I find wanting in others: but the truth is, O men of Athens, that God only is wise; and by his answer he intends to show that the wisdom of men is worth little or nothing: he is not speaking of Socrates, he is only using my name by way of illustration, as if he said, He, O men, is the wisest who, like Socrates, knows that his wisdom is in truth worth nothing. (23a-b, Jowett, trans.)

Notes

1. See above Olympus: Piety from Another Perspective; *Greek Religion*, p. 111.

2. Aaron of Starosselje, *Sha' ar ha-Yihud Va-ha-'Emunah* (Shklov, 1820), chap. 3, pp. 9a-10a. Cf. Louis Jacobs, *Seeker of Unity* (New York: Basic Books, 1966), p. 93.

Chapter 7

Patterns of Public Worship

Introduction

In the earliest societies, places embodying numinous powers, discussed in the introduction to chapter 3, were set aside as sacred space. Since whatever was deemed holy was paradoxically capable of great beneficence or malevolence, these holy sites could be approached only in a prescribed and proper manner. The Book of Exodus describes Mount Sinai at the time of the revelation as having such power that special precautions had to be taken to prevent the death of man or beast (Exod. 19:12-13). Among the Greeks, places struck by the lightning of Zeus or the tombs of people killed by it emanated such dangerous divine energy that they were *abata*, forbidden to be tread upon. Taboos of approach, sight, and sound protected those who passed by sites or images which possessed especially ambiguous powers.[1]

The people of archaic communities tended to live in close proximity to the sacred space which they conceived as being at the center of the world. The concept of the center was connected with three complementary images:

1) The "sacred mountain: where heaven and earth meet is also part of the sacred center.

2) Every temple or palace, and by extension every sacred town and royal residence, is assimilated to "a sacred mountain" and thus becomes a center.

3) The Temple or sacred city, in turn, as the place through which the *Axis Mundi* (the center of the earth) passes, is held to be a point of junction between heaven, earth and hell.[2]

The impact of the numinous and the symbolism connected with sacred space are visible in the biblical account of Jacob's dream in which he saw a ladder reaching from earth to heaven with angels ascending and descending on it and its interpretation in the legend and lore of the Sinai tradition. The biblical description of Jacob's response to his dream, "Shaken, he exclaimed: 'How awesome is this place! This is none other than the abode of God, and that is the gateway to heaven'" (Gen. 28:17), is a typical reaction to the numinous.[3] The pillar that Jacob erected on the spot is also part of *axis mundi* symbolism since the pillar, like the ladder and the mountain, represents the direct line connecting heaven, earth and the underworld. The dream is also an archetypal event recalling the past and adumbrating the future. The site on which Jacob slept and dreamt was also the site on which Abraham bound Isaac for the sacrifice—it was Mount Moriah.[4] According to 2 Chron. 3:1, this was also the spot selected for the altar of the First Temple. In rabbinic legend the entire world is said to have been created from Zion.[5] Philo and the rabbis describe Jerusalem and the Temple as the center of the world and in rabbinic lore Jerusalem is also at the gates of heaven and hell.[6] In other rabbinic legends Mount Sinai, where the revelation took place, is identified as part of Mount Moriah confirming Eliade's view of the connection between theophanies, sacred mountains and temples.[7]

The connection between sacred mountain, temple and universe center is exemplified by Ps. 24 in which there is a shift in theme from the earth as the Lord's creation, to the religious and moral interrogation of those who seek to ascend the temple mount, to the entrance of the Ark and the enthronement of God. Scholars have concluded that Ps. 24 is a composite of at least two psalms.[8] But the unspoken assumption that links the first part of the psalm to what follows and maintains its unitary integrity is that the temple on its mount is both the center and the microcosm of the universe.[9]

Greek sacred spaces had similar geographic and symbolic associations.[10] Proximity to sacred mountains determined the location of many shrines. The temple of Apollo at Delphi was literally built on a ledge of Mount Parnassus, but other sacred sites such as the horns at the palace at Knossos, the altar of Zeus at Olympia, and the acropolis at Athens, itself a mountain top, all have sacred mountains as significant elements of the background. Delphi was reputed to be the literal center of the world; according to tradition, it was built on the very spot where Zeus' two eagles met after he had released them with instructions to fly in opposite directions. A stone worked in the shape of an *omphalos* or navel marked the site, connecting it with the earth goddess and creation. Depictions of Zeus' eagles linked it with heaven. The private shrines too, the hearths of individual households, were fixed in the earth but open to the sky, connecting the consecrated fire of domestic life to heaven, earth, and the underworld. The city-states of archaic and classical Greece had large common public hearth buildings which consecrated their political centers as *axes mundi*. Some spaces retained their sanctity throughout the whole of Greek history. The shrine in the palace of the Mycenaean king at Eleusis became the center of the later mysteries and remained the site of the Holy of Holies, which was called the Palace (*Anaktoron*), even as the *Telesterion*, the Hall of the mysteries, and the sacred precinct grew up around it.

Many ancient peoples also personified the numinous in varying degrees as another being of superhuman qualities. The distinction made between the human and the divine was accompanied by a recognition of the difference between the human and the animal. In Gen. 1:20 we are told that Adam gave names to all the animals, birds and wild beasts but could find no fitting helper for himself. The rabbis interpret this to mean that he became aware of his difference and isolation from the animal world.[11]

The Greeks also acknowledged their isolation from animals. Hesiod sang that it was justice, given by the gods to men but not to beasts, which separated the two species (*Works and Days* 274-280). According to structuralist scholars, Greek myths about systems of cooking their food and burying their dead became symbolic of their awareness of the distance between men and animals. But Greeks defined civilized men as "those who eat bread" (*siton edontes*), i.e., who must keep food in their bodies in order to remain alive. The gods who do not need to maintain themselves by constantly replenishing their lost energy with food, were in an entirely different category, requiring nothing, although delighting in nectar and ambrosia.[12]

The gulf between the human and the divine, and the sense of isolation one begins to feel as he cognitively separates himself from the natural world give rise to the numinous feeling of "little me", the primary sensation of awe and fear experienced by every individual when facing the mystery and vastness of the universe, as well as his own life and death. To assuage this feeling every society develops elaborate procedures for communicating with the deity and the forces of nature: sacrifice, prayer, vows, ritual reenactments, hymns of praise and thanksgiving and festival celebrations. Thus religious ritual and the cult are the bridges that enable human beings to overcome their sense of alienation and their existential anxieties.

The worship of the holy often centered on the ritual sacrifice of a living animal within the sacred precinct. Scholars have offered a variety of explanations to account for this blood rite so alien to modern ideas of what "the Lord doth require." According to the scapegoat theory, groups might have experienced the danger of aggressive instincts when internal feuds threatened to destroy the community. Sacrifice arose to prevent reciprocal violence from wiping out the entire group. The elaborate ritual in which a victim represents the whole group, and is killed together by all, controls aggressive impulses without necessitating retaliation from an individual or family.[13]

According to others, the danger of aggressive instincts is increased by humanity's guilt at spilling blood. A human being has a basic respect for life which conflicts with the need to kill, in hunting or in war, in order to survive. Feelings of anxiety, guilt and remorse may have crystallized into symbolic acts through which the individual tried to prevent his own destruction for having killed an animal or another human being. These symbolic acts were intended to restore the equilibrium disturbed by death at human hands, to stress the continuity of life through death and to restore the remains of slaughtered animals to the giver of life on whom survival depends. Features of the blood sacrifice such as the close identification between the victim (usually a prized domestic animal) and the sacrificer, the pretense that the victim either chose or deserved its death, and the symbolic restoration or return of the victim to his Maker (e.g., the draining of blood into the ground, the burning of bones and fats, the hanging of remains on sacred trees) suggest the reluctance to destroy life. The careful acts of the ritual in which meat is roasted or boiled rather than eaten raw, the blood (in the Bible conceived as identical with the soul) saved for the deity, the bones and fat burned, and the rest of the victim buried are intended to raise humans above the animals by underscoring the differences in their killing and consumption. Thus, the sacrifice mitigates internal violence, builds group solidarity, mediates the ambivalent emotions of humans, proving they are not beasts even when they kill, and ultimately brings them closer to the deity.[14]

Blood sacrifice could take place any time of year, independent of the season. However, with the development of agriculture came the establishment of annual lunar calendars of festivals associated with the yearly cycle of planting, tending and harvesting crops. (In Israel and in Greece the lunar calendar was adjusted to the solar year and its seasonal cycle.) Sacrifice remained the central rite of worship but the death of the animal was connected with the coming of winter or drought, both the nemeses of the fertile crop. The sacrificial death was symbolized in the mythical conflict between Baal and Mot or as the death of the old year to make room for the new (e.g., the dying gods Tammuz and Adonis, loved and lamented by fertility goddesses like Ishtar and Aphrodite).[15] In the ancient Near East and Greece the major feast days were associated with crucial periods in the agricultural year and their various elements have been interpreted as attempts to propitiate the divine to ensure animals and children for survival. The sacrifice itself and the spilling of blood on the ground have often been viewed as magical rites to induce rain.

Both societies transformed the sacrificial rituals and seasonal festivals in ways which expressed the uniqueness of their vision of humanity and its relation to divinity. In Israel the monotheistic revolution imposed a new perspective on festival celebrations. They not only commemorated the seasons of the agricultural year but also the historic events of the covenant people and its progenitors. Thus, for example, the New Year was connected to God's creation of the world and the three pilgrim festivals Passover, *Shavuot* (Pentecost) and *Sukkot* (Tabernacles) with the exodus from Egypt and the revelation on Mount Sinai.

In Greece the rites associated with sacrifice and agriculture also became connected with events in the lives of gods, heroes, and peoples. The three days of the Anthesteria or spring blossoming festival at Athens, for example, were linked not only to Dionysus' introduction of wine into Attica, but also to the god's marriage to Ariadne and the matricide Orestes' visit to Athens as well as the first meal of the survivors of the flood which nearly destroyed the world. Certain rites, however, developed into contests to please the gods and to perfect the potential of man. The great festivals became opportunities for exhibiting great talents in athletics, drama, poetry, music, dance and debate. The sites where the worshippers gathered became works of art in themselves, full of magnificent temples and sculptures dedicated to their divine patrons as *agalmata*, objects for the gods' eternal delight. Both the holy days and the holy places were organized as community projects with the whole group participating or contributing so that the unity in diversity represented by Zeus' pantheon was replicated in the solidarity created by the activities of worship.

Notes

1.   For a detailed discussion, see below, Olympus section "Access and Taboo" and notes 53-64.

2   Mircea Eliade, *Patterns in Comparative Religion*, trans. Rosemary Sheed (Cleveland and New York: World Publishing Co., 1958), p. 375. Cf. M. Eliade, *The Sacred and the Profane*, trans. Willard R. Trask, Bollingen Series 46 (New York: Pantheon Books, 1954), pp. 5-16. The critique of Eliade that pertains to our discussion focuses on the following elements: 1) Eliade's comparative studies tend to sever the symbolic pattern and its system from the concrete historical culture that produced it resulting in an overemphasis on similarity without a corresponding sensitivity to fine gradations of difference. 2) In focusing on the center Eliade has neglected the importance of periphery in certain religious traditions. 3)Eliade's contention that sacred space is non-homogeneous in contrast to the homogeneity of profane space does not hold up in regard to the Jerusalem Temple in the visions of Ezekiel 40-48. Cf. Jonathan Z. Smith, *Imagining Religion: From Babylon to Jonestown* (Chicago and London: The University of Chicago Press, 1982), pp. 26-29; *Map Is Not Territory: Studies in the History of Religions* (Leiden: E. J. Brill, 1978), pp. 96-99; p. 128; 292-293; *To Take Place: Toward Theory in Ritual* (Chicago and London: The University of Chicago Press, 1987), pp. 13-17; 57-70; 83-84. Though Smith's critique is an important corrective it does not invalidate Eliade's basic insights. See the article, by J. Schultz, "From Sacred Space to Sacred Object to Sacred Person in Jewish Antiquity," *Shofar: An Interdisciplinary Journal of Jewish Studies*, vol. 12, no. 1 (Fall, 1993): 28-37.

3.   Rudolph Otto, *The Idea of the Holy*, trans. John W. Harvey (New York: Oxford University Press, 1958), pp. 5-40.

4.   Ginzberg, *Legends*, 5:253, n. 253.

5.   *b. Yoma*, 54b.

6.   *Legation ad Gaium*, 294; *Tanhuma B*. Lev. (ed. Buber), p. 78; *b. Sanhedrin* 37a; *Cant. R* 7:5; Ginzberg, *Legends*, 1:12; 5:14-15, n. 39; 5:19, n. 55; 5:117-118, n. 109; 5:125-126, n. 137.

7.   Ginzberg, *Legends*, 1:349; 3:84; 6:32, n. 186; Eliade, *Sacred and Profane*, pp. 24-29. For additional examples of the sacred center as the source of cosmic perfection, order and harmony in the Bible see Michael A. Fishbane, "The Sacred Center: The Symbolic Structure of the Bible," in *Texts and Responses, Studies Presented to Nahum N. Glatzer*, ed. M. Fishbane and P. Flohr (Leiden: E. J. Brill, 1975), pp. 6-27. For examples from post biblical literature see Raphael Patai, *Man and Temple in Ancient Jewish Myth and Ritual* (New York: Ktav Publishing House, 1967), pp. 105-113. See also Robert L. Cohn, *The Shape of Sacred Space: Four Biblical Studies* (Chico, Ca.: Scholars Press, 1981), pp. 54-61 where a distinction is made

between the Hebrew Bible, where Mount Sinai and Mount Zion are never juxtaposed and the Apocrypha and the New Testament where they are juxtaposed. It is interesting to note that the vast majority of Israelite temples from the biblical period have been found concentrated in one continuous block between Shiloh and Arad. The chain of temples forms a kind of backbone along the mountainous massif in the southern part of the country. See Menahem Haran, *Temples and Temple Service in Ancient Israel* (Oxford: The Clarendon Press, 1978), pp. 41-42 and on temples and sites other than the Solomonic Temple in Jerusalem see Roland de Vaux, *Ancient Israel* (New York, Toronto: McGraw Hill Book Co., 1965) 2:302-308. There are to be sure, historical reasons for this phenomenon having to do with the nature of the earliest Israelite settlement in Canaan. Nevertheless, the deeper workings of the collective unconscious in which temples are connected to sacred mountains cannot be discounted as a factor in the location of these holy places.

8. Moses Buttenwieser, *The Psalms: Chronologically Treated With a New Translation* (Chicago: University of Chicago Press, 1938) 1:205-210; cf. *Anchor Bible, Psalms 1-50* introd., trans. and notes Mitchell Dahood S.J. (Garden City, NY: Doubleday, 1966), pp. 150-153.

9. In this context verse seven can be translated so that *olam* has a spatial as well as a temporal sense: "O gates lift up your heads! Up high you doors to the cosmos." Through this entrance passes the King of Glory, the transcendent God who becomes immanent. There is a suggestion of this entire symbolic complex in Ibn Ezra's comment on this psalm: "For there are places on earth that receive a divine energy such as indicated in the verse 'And this is the gateway to heaven' (Gen. 28:17). That is why the psalmist begins with 'The earth is the Lord's' because of 'the mountain of the lord.'" Cf. Commentary of Abraham Ibn Ezra to Ps. 24. It may be that the custom of chanting Ps. 24 on the first two nights of *Rosh Ha-Shanah* in the synagogue service of the neo-Sephardic (Hasidic) rite is an echo of the temple symbolism in which the sacred time commemorating the birthday of the world is celebrated in the sacred space, in the structure, which is itself a miniature world. See the discussion below in Sinai: Priestly Piety.

10. See below, Olympus section "Symbolism and Sacred Center" and notes 43-52.

11. Ginzberg, *Legends*, 1:65; 5:87, n. 39.

12. For an excellent summary and bibliography of structuralist interpretations, see Charles Segal, "The Raw and the Cooked in Greek Literature: Structures, Values, Metaphor," *Classical Journal* 69 (1974): 289-308.

13. See Rene Girard, *Violence and the Sacred,* trans. Patrick Gregory (Baltimore: Johns Hopkins University Press, 1977) for a presentation and development of this view.

14. For interpretations of Greek sacrifice, see below, Olympus section "General Practices of Piety" and notes 78-92. For a comparison of Greek and Hebrew sacrifice, see R. K. Yerkes, *Sacrifice in Greek and Roman Religion and Early Judaism* (New York: Scribners, 1952). In the Middle

Ages, Moses Maimonides explained the biblical sacrificial system as inculcating magnanimity and providing the background for a unique kind of God-man relationship on the one hand (*Yad ha-Hazakah, Hilkot Issure Mizbeah* 7:1). But on the other hand, he argued that sacrifices served as a gradualist pedagogical device to wean the Israelites from "the universal service" of paganism to a more exalted worship of the one God. See *The Guide of the Perplexed*, trans. with intro. and notes S. Pines (Chicago: University of Chicago Press, 1964), Part III, chs. 29-32, pp. 518-531. Cf. Isadore Twersky, *Introduction To The Code of Maimonides* (*Mishneh Torah*) Yale Judaica Series 12 (New Haven and London: Yale University Press, 1980), pp. 390-391; 432-433.

15. In fact, according to Mircea Eliade, sacrifice is connected in many cultures with the myth of the dying and reviving god. The god dies in keeping with the law of reciprocity but is reconstituted as part of nature and the rhythm of the universe. The recurring birth and death of the god is linked to the ebb and flow of nature and agriculture. By offering sacrifices human beings perpetuate the life of the divinity by participating in its drama to which they feel intimately related. The violence of the sacrifice parallels the violent act causing the death of the god but also the birth of nature. Since death is part of the rhythm leading to life, the individual must give something precious, i.e., his own blood or that of a prized animal or the first fruits of the field, in order to keep the cycle in motion, to experience its power and fecundity, to integrate the self with the foundations of the cosmos. See Mircea Eliade, *Myth and Reality*, trans. Willard R. Trask (New York: Harper and Row, 1963), p. 106f.

Sinai: Priestly Piety

As noted in the introductory remarks to the previous chapter sketching the contrasting perspectives of prophetic and priestly piety, the mistaken impression may be carried away that priestly religion is inferior to prophetic religion. But this is a modern conception unthinkable for the world of antiquity. In this world there was no real opposition seen between priest and prophet and it would not have occurred to anyone to deny the substantiality and validity of either. The prophet in Israel was universally recognized as the one who makes known the word of God and the priest was unanimously acknowledged as the servant of God. It is no accident that Moses the prophet and Aaron the high priest are both from the tribe of Levi. Aaron and his family were the first to accept the new direction in Hebrew religion revealed to Moses and they were followed by the whole Levite tribe.[1] In fact, we are told that Aaron served as a "prophet" for Moses to others (Exod. 7:1-2) and Moses and Aaron participated together in most of the signs and miracles in Pharaoh's court. Priest and prophet were not regarded as mutually exclusive; a priest could also be a prophet as was the case with Jeremiah and Ezekiel. If prophets sometimes engaged in bitter controversy against the priests it was only because the priests supported and benefited from a corrupt social establishment. This criticism must not be construed as a denial of the indispensability of God's servants and their service to an orderly society. To the contrary, in their messages of consolation the prophets envisage along with Israel's restoration the reinstitution of the temple service (e.g., Isa. 60:7; Ezek. 40-48). As noted above, it is true that the classical prophets placed ethics above the cult in their hierarchy of values but they did not repudiate the cult and in the preclassical prophetic books and in the Torah, ritual and ethical commandments are considered equally binding. On the other hand, there are a number of admonitions appearing in the Pentateuch originating in priestly circles that express a highly refined ethical consciousness (e.g., Lev. 19:17-18).

The connection between the priesthood and prophecy is symbolized by the two portable religious structures that accompanied the Israelites in their wilderness journey to the Promised Land, the Tent of Meeting (*'ohel moed*) and the Tabernacle (*mishkan*). Both institutions are rooted in the idea that no human being can see God. In both, the divine revelation takes the form of a cloud.[2] But unlike the Tabernacle, the Tent of Meeting is situated outside the Israelite camp. No cultic services or appurtenances are mentioned in connection with it, and instead of priests and Levites, Joshua is in constant attendance. The divine revelation in the Tent of Meeting appears to be of an occasional, not a regular character. Thus, the Tent of Meeting was an institution that took shape in prophetic circles, set aside for meditation, for concentration and for the sharpening of the worshipper's perceptions in preparation for the revelation of the divine presence. In contrast, the Tabernacle developed in priestly circles was the vehicle for making tangible through rite, symbol and ritual objects the transcendental concepts revealed in the Tent of Meeting. It was a cultic institution *par excellence*, housing the deity in its focal center.[3]

Function and Symbolism in Tabernacle and Temple

The various critical views of the Tabernacle in the wilderness[4] agree with the traditional view that in many respects the Tabernacle was a blueprint for the Temple. Both the Tabernacle and the Temple were, according to the Bible and tradition, earthly creations of a heavenly model revealed by God to Moses, to David and Solomon. Moses is instructed: "And let them make me a sanctuary that I may dwell among them. Exactly as I show you—the pattern of the Tabernacle and the pattern of all its furnishings—so shall you make it" (Exod. 25:8-9). "Note well, and follow the patterns for them, that are being shown you on the mountain" (Exod. 25:40). When David gave his son Solomon the plans for the Temple buildings, the tabernacle and all utensils, he assured him that "All this that the Lord made me understand by His hand on me, I give you in writing—the plan of all the work" (1 Chron. 28:19). Though this tradition is not recorded with regard to Solomon in the biblical text, we do find it in the post-biblical apocryphal work The Wisd. of Sol. 9:8: "You have commanded me to build a sanctuary on Your holy mountain, and an altar in the city of your habitation, a copy of the holy tabernacle which You have prepared from the beginning."[5]

Both the Tabernacle and the Temple were referred to in biblical Hebrew as "the house of God" and it is this concept of a divine residence that explains the intrinsic nature of the institution. The priests are the servants of God, the sacrifices are the food of the deity, the incense provides fragrance in the dwelling and the candelabra provides light. All the religions of the ancient Near East shared the view of the temple as a dwelling place of divinity, and as part of the pre-biblical heritage these conceptions were adapted to the monotheistic beliefs of ancient Israel. To be sure, even the pagan religions had long since ceased to conceive of their gods in such crudely anthropomorphic terms and clearly the biblical authors did not envisage their God as requiring daily food, incense and light. The entire complex of rites and rituals was only a symbolic means of making God accessible to humans, of reconciling divine transcendence with divine immanence. Thus, for example, the High Priest performed six regular rites inside the Tabernacle. He offered up the incense on the altar of gold (Exod. 30:7-8). He tended the lamps (Exod. 27:20; Lev. 24:2). He arranged twelve loaves of bread, in two rows of six each on the table of gold (Lev. 24:5-9). He carried the two onyx-stones on the shoulderpieces of the *ephod* and the twelve stones (engraved with the names of the twelve tribes) set in the breastpiece (the *Urim* and *Tumim*) for a reminder before the Lord (Exod. 28:29; cf. ibid. v. 12). When the high priest entered the Holy of Holies and when he came out, the bells on the skirts of the *ephod's* robe jingled (Exod. 28:35). The high priest also performed an act of ritual significance by wearing the diadem (Exod. 28:38). Taken together, these rites embrace almost all the human senses and cater, as it were, to all the individual's possible needs. The incense provides for the sense of smell, the lamps for the sense of sight and the loaves, a symbol for the need for food, the sense of taste. The bells attract the sense of hearing, the stones on the *ephod* and the breastpiece awaken the sense of memory and the diadem on the high priest's forehead evokes the sense of divine grace. There are signs that originally there was also a libation to correspond to the human need for drink.[6]

In the choice of construction plan, color scheme and exterior and interior furnishing, the Temple-Tabernacle gave expression to the idea that it was a cosmic structure at the center of the world from which everything else was created or, itself, a miniature world. With regard to furnishings, the metal "Sea" (*yam*) in the Temple courtyard (1 Kings 7:23-26) has been shown by archaeologists to be connected with the Mesopotamian *apsu*, the name of a basin of holy water in the Temple. But *apsu* is also the god of the subterranean freshwater ocean, one of the protagonists in some Mesopotamian cosmogonies, the counterpart of the Sea (*yam*) in some Hebrew creation stories. Thus the metal Sea in the Temple courtyard symbolized the act of Creation. In Ezekiel's vision of the Temple (Ezek. 43:13-17) the foundation of the altar is termed "bosom of the earth", a cosmic reference, and the name *har'el* in verse 15 of that context may mean "the mountain of God" (Hebrew), i.e., the cosmic mountain or the "underworld" (Akkadian *arallu*). Similarly, the platform (*kiyor*) upon which Solomon stood as he dedicated the

Temple (2 Chronicles 6:13) has been connected by scholars with the Akkadian *kiuru*, which may signify the earth or a sacred space. Finally, there are verbal parallels between the account of the completion of the world (Gen. 2:1-4) and the account of the completion of the Tabernacle (Exod. 39-40).[7]

As to color scheme, the first color mentioned among the materials requisitioned for the building of the sanctuary was the color blue or more accurately blue-purple (Exod. 25:4), regarded as the most expensive, then purple and crimson (both contain a mixture of blue) in a descending order of costliness. The curtain over the Ark was made of blue (or blue purple), purple and crimson (Exod. 26:31; 36:35), and a cloth of "pure blue" was placed over the Ark during journeys (Num. 4:6).[8] The *ephod* robe of the high priest was also of a pure blue color. As we saw in the previous chapter, blue is a cosmic color, for as the rabbis, explaining why the Ark was covered in blue pointed out, the Ark was the earthly equivalent of the throne of divine glory. Blue "resembles the sea and the sea resembles the sky and the sky resembles the throne of divine glory."[9]

There were three principles underlying the construction plan and material gradations in the Tabernacle and the Temple.

1) The more important the object the greater its cost and the greater its splendor. This principle is found in many religions and many temples all over the world whose grandeur testifies to the belief that the higher a ritual object is in the hierarchy of holiness, the greater the human effort to embellish it.

2) The Tabernacle and the Temple were built on an eastern axis so that all the entrances face east and the line traversing the Holy of Holies eastward is superior to all the rest of the corners of the compass. Thus the objects on the axis which enters the Holy of Holies from the east are more elaborate and important than others (i.e., the veil over the Ark, *paroket,* is superior to the inner curtains in quality and holiness). This symbolism is no doubt an outgrowth of pre-biblical traditions, possibly of rites connected with the Sun cult of ancient Egypt and Babylon, but retained in the monotheistic ambiance of the Tabernacle and the Temple out of a conservative adherence to convention. This explanation seems to be substantiated by the prophet Ezekiel who reports:

Then He (God) brought me into the inner court of the House
of the Lord, and there at the entrance to the Temple of the
Lord, between the portico and the altar were about twenty-
five men, their backs to the Temple of the Lord, and their
faces to the east; they were bowing low to the sun in the east
(Ezek. 8:16). [10]

The cosmic overtones are clear and so is the connection to creation,
for the Garden of Eden was in the east (Gen. 2:8).

3) The Tabernacle and Temple were constructed according to a
plan of concentric circles, with the throne of the cherubim in the
Holy of Holies at the very center and the sanctity and the value of a
ritual object progressively diminishing with its distance from the
center.[11]   This pattern of construction clearly demonstrates the
symbolism of the most sacred standing, as it were, at the center of
the world. The image is that of a wheel with the Holy of Holies at
its hub. The hallowing and illuminating presence of God discharges
its energy along the spokes.

Just as the plan of concentric circles in the Tabernacle and the
Temple established a progressively diminishing degree of holiness
from the center to the periphery, so did the same arrangement
provide for increasing degrees of taboo as one moved from the
periphery to the center.   The taboo consisted of three basic
prohibitions, touch, sight and approach, each one varying with the
ritual circles.   Thus, the Tabernacle and most of its court was
inaccessible to common people who may not look at, touch or
approach any piece of furniture, no matter how insignificant with
the exception of the sacrificial altar.[12]   The Levites are permitted to
come near the sacred furniture but only when it is covered. Only
priests may come into contact with the appurtenances of the
Tabernacle but even they may not look at the ark cover (*kapporet*),
which is concealed by the veil (*paroket*), turning the ark and its
cover into a place of mystery and concealment. Only the high
priest may enter here, and only on the Day of Atonement, when he
must change his garments to perform a special rite in which his
vision of the ark was blocked by a screen of smoke.[13]   The whole
system is intended to underscore the difference between profane
space that is neutral and homogenous, and sacred space that is
exquisitely graded and hallowed.[14]   Here Jonathan Z. Smith's
observation, correcting Eliade, is very much to the point, namely,
that the incongruity of sacred space and the ritual distinctions of the
hierarchy within the tabernacle and temple precincts reflects, to a
certain extent, similar incongruities of profane space in Israelite

territory and social and religious differentiation's in Hebrew society outside the tabernacle and the temple.

The taboo connected with the Tabernacle and its appurtenances operated from two poles of ritual holiness as conceived in antiquity. At one pole there was contagious sanctity. A non-priest or an unhallowed object that came in contact with any of the articles of the Tabernacle, or even with the priests while they are anointed with the holy oil or officiating near the Tabernacle furniture, contracted holiness and became consecrated. At the other end of the sacred spectrum was contagious defilement. Non-priests and unhallowed objects, as well as priests and sacred articles in the Tabernacle could be defiled, for example, by coming in contact with a human corpse. Contagious defilement had a remedy. The person or object could be purified and the contaminating substance thrust out of the community and into the desert. The purification rites of the Tabernacle on the Day of Atonement (Lev. 16) and the purification by means of the ashes of the red heifer (Num. 19) are based on this belief. But contagious sanctity had no remedy. There was no activity or rite that could remove it from an object or a person so that the object had to be destroyed and the person was liable to meet immediate death at the hands of heaven.[15] The fatal demonic nature of the divine wrath triggered by these cultic transgressions was devoid of moral considerations and made no distinction between deliberate or inadvertent action.[16]

We see here an excellent illustration of what Eliade has called the "ambivalence of the sacred." The sacred attracts and repels; it is at once sacred but its contagion is worse than defilement in that it has no remedy. Thus the holy is both beneficial and dangerous; it is a vehicle for immortality but also of mysterious death. Throughout the entire organism of the Tabernacle and the Temple, in which structure, ritual and belief system are all interwoven, the dialectic of paradox persists. The holy is accessible and inaccessible, unique and transcendent on the one hand (the Tabernacle and the Temple are made from a heavenly model), repeatable on the other hand (the Solomonic Temple is a duplicate of the Tabernacle).[17]

Sacrifice and Prayer

In its external form the sacrificial ritual of the Bible closely resembled Caananite and Greek rites. In all three religions, when an animal was sacrificed a portion of it or its totality was burnt upon an altar. Thus the Hebrew *zevah* is related to the Greek *thusia*, where a portion of the animal was burnt on the altar, a part given to the priests and a part eaten as a sacred meal. The Hebrew *Olah* corresponds to the Greek holocaust, in which the whole victim is burnt on the altar. The scholars speculate that these similar rites may have originated in a civilization that preceded both the Greeks and the Canaanites along the shores of the Eastern Mediterranean. Before the Israelites entered Canaan their sacrificial practice may have well been characterized by the offering of the Pascal lamb, in which no part of the animal was burnt, blood played a central role and the meat was eaten in a communal meal of the faithful. When the Israelites settled in Canaan, they adopted from the Canaanites the *olah* and the *zevah*, which were burnt on the altar, combining them with the ancient rites in the use of blood connected with the Pascal offering.[18]

We have discussed in the general introduction to this chapter various theories regarding the underlying motivation of the sacrificial rites in various cultures and religious traditions. It is quite possible that the sacrificial cult of pre-biblical Israel can be understood in terms of some of these theories. But monotheism endowed these rites with a transcendental significance in which they became a prayer acted out, a symbolic action accurately expressing the internal feeling of the person making the offering and God's response to it. As mentioned in the previous chapter, in the context of prophetic piety, sacrifice, like prayer, is a symbolic gesture of submission to the will of God. Like the human dialogue relationship on which it is modeled, the act depends on the morality and the sincerity of both parties that make possible their intimate exchange. In the absence of these, according to the Sinai belief system, sacrifice ceases to be a religious act.

This demand for perfect conformity between internal sincerity of intent and external ritual action is evident in the laws governing the sacrifice of expiation (the *asham*). The purpose of the offering was to break the vicious circle in which an exacting conscience, conscious of wrongdoing, inflicts an individual with guilt and fear of punishment. In the case of an individual who is suffering but has done no wrong, and is lacerated by a conscience interpreting the suffering as punishment for unknown or inadvertent sins, the sacrifice removes the torment of psychological guilt. But the sacrifice is ineffective if it is not accompanied by reparation and confession if the wrongdoing was deliberately done.[19] The view expressed by this requirement is that only after rectification has been made with man can it be sought with God. The idea that in matters of justice man takes priority over God became part of rabbinic law in the Second Temple period: "The Day of Atonement atones for the sins between man and God. But the Day of Atonement does not atone for the sins between man and his fellow until he has made restitution to his fellow."[20]   If the sin was involuntary the sacrifice and internal remorse was sufficient for expiation. The act of confession and internal remorse in the case of a deliberate sin, such as the taking of a false oath, converted it into an involuntary sin for which the sacrifice brings expiation. Thus the priestly code of the Book of Leviticus prepares the way for the prophetic doctrine of repentance by establishing a priestly doctrine of repentance; i.e., remorse and sacrifice obliterate inadvertent sins, remorse plus confession and sacrifice annul deliberate sins. The prophets, as we saw in chapter four, taught that repentance alone suffices to remove sin and neutralize the relentless effects of the doctrine of reciprocity. The priests insisted that repentance also requires sacrificial expiation.[21]

Among the deeper religious meanings which the Sinai tradition attached to the sacrificial system was the concept of sacrifice as a gift and as a quest for union with God. If the popular religion of Israel sometimes construed sacrifice as a gift to God that would benefit man, a kind of *do ut des* (Gen. 28:20-22), in its more exalted expressions it realized in the words of the prayer ascribed to David: "All is from You and it is Your gift that we have given to You" (1 Chron. 29:14; cf. Ps. 50:9-12). From this perspective it is right to render tribute to God as a subject pays tribute to a king. But more than tribute, it is a gift in which the giver symbolically gives part of his life and of himself, since the offerings are either domesticated animals or vegetable produce upon which human beings depend for life sustenance. The gift is irrevocable since it is wholly or partially destroyed; flour, bread and incense are burned; liquids are poured out and animals slaughtered and burned. In this way the gift is transferred into the realm of the invisible, the only way it can be given to God. These meanings are embedded in the Hebrew terms for sacrifice, *korban* coming from a root meaning "to bring near" and *olah* meaning "that which goes up." The idea of union with God through the eating of a divine victim was never part of the Israelite sacrificial symbolic system. But the Hebrews did conceive of union with God as a result of sharing: sharing the same possessions, sharing a common life and the sharing of hospitality. The sacrifice embodying this idea was the peace offering (*zevah shelamim*) in which both concepts of gift and communion were embodied. When God accepted His part of the offering on the altar, the sacrificers ate the rest in a joyful religious meal in which group solidarity and the solidarity between God and humans were cemented by all taking a meal together.[22]

Prayer was as prevalent as sacrifice in the Temple courts and it is no mere coincidence that the Temple is called a "house of prayer" (i.e., in Solomon's dedicatory prayer, 1 Kings 8:22-53 and in the post-exilic prophecy of Isa. 56:7). Nevertheless, prayer was considered a religious rite of secondary order in the Temple, a substitute for sacrifice and, in the case of an indigent, an offering of the poor. A visitor to the Temple was expected to bring a drink offering, a burnt, peace or grain offering, but if unable to do so he (or she) was at the very least expected to utter a prayer. The Book of Psalms which, as noted earlier, is a collection of stereotyped Temple prayers, reflects this reality as the worshipper asks that his prayer "be taken like incense" before the Lord and his "upraised hands" (i.e., palms raised as in a prayer gesture) "as an evening sacrifice" (Ps. 141:2). Elsewhere the individual who has come empty-handed to the Temple prays: "Accept O Lord the free will offerings of my mouth . . ." (Ps. 119:108). If the visitor to the Temple did not or could not say a prayer, as a sign of submission and respect to God he (or she) would make the minimal gesture of prostration, a practice still followed by the masses at the end of the Second Temple period. In the cultic activity within the Temple proper, prayer was peripheral, used by laymen (not priests) as liturgical formulas accompanying the bringing of the first fruits (Deut. 26:1-10), and the tithe of the third year (Deut. 26:13-15). The confession of the high priest on the Day of Atonement (Lev. 16:21) and his blessing of the people (Lev. 9:22f; Num. 6:23ff.) took place outside the Temple (in the Temple court) and was apart from the essence of the ritual performed inside. The priestly service in the First Temple period has been aptly described as "speechless worship."[23]

Festivals and Holy Days

According to the Bible (Deut. 16:16-17) it was incumbent on male Israelites to visit the Temple three times a year on the festivals of Passover, *Shavuot* (Pentecost) and *Sukkot* (Tabernacles) and to bring an offering, or as we have seen, to utter a prayer or, at the very least, to bow down before the Lord. It would take us too far afield to discuss in detail the feasts and holy days of the Hebrew liturgal calendar.[24] In this chapter the focus is on the religious pattern underlying these celebrations. I have already noted that the Hebrews historicized the agricultural celebrations of the ancient

Near East by linking them to events in the sacred history of Israel. But the festivals are not merely recollections of temporal history; they partake of the meta-historical, of sacred time. The Book of Leviticus introduces the discussion of the festivals by God's words to Moses rendered in the Buber-Rosenzweig translation of the Bible into German as follows: "Speak to the Israelite people and say to them: These are your appointments with God, which you shall proclaim as sacred occasions" (Lev. 23:2).

Our appointments with God, as distinguished from other appointments in our calendars, are in the category of sacred time. Sacred time, characteristic of Sabbaths and festivals, belongs to an eternal realm that is periodically reintegrated and made present by hallowed ritual. Thus sacred time is recoverable and repeatable. In contrast, the other appointments in our calendars are in the category of profane or secular time. They are characterized by one time experiences that have a beginning and an end, and even though they may continue year after year, like secular work, entertainment and celebration, since they are *not* linked to the eternal they are transitory and *no* experience is in essence identical with the one that preceded it and the one that will follow it. There is *n o* hallowed ritual that periodically reintegrates and makes present the experiences of the infinite. Thus profance time is *not* recoverable or repeatable.

A second characteristic of sacred time is that it represents a return to pristine beginnings, in many religions a return to the beginning of the cosmos and the origin of nature, a return to the creation of man and a return to the moment when the ancestor or civilizing hero brought the revelation of a new direction. It represents the human desire to live in the world as it came from the Creator's hands, fresh, pure, strong and hallowed. Every renewal of the individual, of society and of the cosmos is felt as a return to the unfragmented unity of God. Thus the rituals of the festival in pointing to renewal represent the human desire for *imitatio dei*, of patterning oneself on the divine model, in returning to the presence of God, where history gives way to eternity. As Eliade points out:

For it is no mere matter of a feast bringing "the eternal moment" of sacred time into profane succession; it is further. . . . the total annihilation of all the profane time that made up the cycle now coming to an end. In the wish to *start a new life in the midst of a new creation*—an aspiration clearly present in all the ceremonies for beginning one year and ending another—there also enters the paradoxical desire to attain to an historic existence, to be able to live only in sacred time.[25]

A quick survey of the Hebrew festivals reveals that in either the name of the festival, in its rites and liturgy, or in the interpretation they have been given by the Sinai tradition, the ideas associated with sacred time are interwoven. The New Year (*Rosh Hashanah*) celebrates the birth of the world and the birth of man.[26] The return to the first moment of Genesis and to the patriarchal inauguration of faith (the Torah reading for *Rosh Hashanah* deals with Abraham and Sarah) presages all the potential that will be realized with the birth of the New Year. The Day of Atonement with its rituals of purification, fasting and forgiveness marks a return of the individual to the unblemished spiritual state with which he (or she) entered the world. The confessional on the Day of Atonement, we are told, brings about a spiritual rebirth and the white garments worn on this day are in imitation of the celestial beings.[27] In a similar vein the ritual of the scapegoat, in which the high priest confesses the sins of the Israelites while placing his hands upon a live goat which is then dispatched to the wilderness with its burden of communal sin (Lev. 16:20-22) symbolizes the abolition of the past year and past time and the regeneration of the individual and the community with the New Year.

The symbolism of the return to origins can also be detected in the festival of *Sukkot* (Tabernacles). The return to the Exodus when Moses led the Israelites out of Egypt and to a new conception of their relationship to God is symbolized by the dwelling in booths (*sukkot*) for seven days (Lev. 23:43-43). The return to the desert sojourn also includes a recovery of the strong, pristine faith of the people that enabled them to follow Moses into the wilderness. The prophet Jeremiah, speaking for God, reminds a later generation: "I accounted to your favor, the devotion of your youth, your love as a bride (Israel is often depicted by the prophets as God's bride). How you followed me in the wilderness, in a land not sown." (Jer. 2:2).

The Passover festival combines rituals that celebrate the rebirth of nature and the renewal of life characterized by a spring festival (i.e., the green vegetable on the Seder plate, the recitation of the Song of Songs) as well as the return to the archetypal event of

Israel's sacred history, the Exodus. In this context the obligation spelled out by the Passover Haggadah is particularly illuminating: "In each generation every individual should feel as though he or she had actually been redeemed from Egypt."[28] According to the Bible, Passover is the beginning of the Hebrew year (Exod. 12:1) and in Second Temple and talmudic times it served as the beginning of the Hebrew year for certain purposes.[29] Rabbi Joshua maintained that the world was created in the Hebrew month of *Nisan*, the month in which Passover falls. It is the month when the grass, herb yielding seed and tree yielding fruit were created and it is still the month when the earth is full of grass and the trees begin to yield fruit. It is also the time when the springtime mating of the animal world takes place.[30]

The festival of *Shavuot (Pentecost)* represents the return to the second archetypal event to which the exodus from Egypt is linked— the revelation of the Torah on Mount Sinai. It is also significant that rabbinic tradition links the giving of the Torah on *Shavuot* with Creation (cf. Chapter 2 Sinai II: Creation Interpreted, note 5). In the bringing of an offering of the first fruits at *Shavuot*, as in the bringing of the barley offering at Passover, there is a return to that basic religious impulse of gratitude of creature to Creator displayed by the first generations, Adam, according to rabbinic tradition,[31] and Cain and Abel, according to the Bible. Finally, the Sabbath *is* a commemoration of the act of Creation (Exod. 31:12-71). Its observance is an act of *imitatio Dei*. Through it Israel replicates the pattern of the primordial act of rest participating continuously in a sacred rhythm that until Sinai had been observed by God alone (Gen. 2:13).

Dietary Laws and Sexual Code

The principles underlying the festivals of the Sinai tradition outlined above are also reflected in the dietary laws, the laws of the clean and unclean, and the sexual code of the Book of Leviticus. The prohibitions are a language of actions rather than words that express belief in a particular kind of cosmic order linked to God's holiness. Thus the catalogue of forbidden foods in Leviticus 11 is explicitly connected with the idea of Israel's being holy even as God is holy (Lev. 11:44). Holiness in the context of these laws has a number of connotations. Its root meaning is to "set apart," but it also implies unity, integrity, as well as perfection of the individual and the species. Applied to the dietary laws it means that clean animals conform fully to their class. Unclean animals are imperfect members of their class or their class itself confuses the scheme of creation and the order of the world. The pig does not conform to the perfect model of the domesticated meat-animal in a rural society because it is not a ruminant though it has cloven hoofs. The Book of Leviticus echoes the threefold classification unfolded in Creation: the earth, the waters, and the heavens. Creatures are classified as to how they live on the earth, in the water and in the air, with each element allotted its proper kind of creature life. Four-legged species hop, jump or walk on the earth. Scaly fish swim with fins in the water. Two legged fowls fly with wings in the air. Thus four-footed creatures which fly are unclean, as are species which have two legs and two hands and which go on all fours like quadrupeds. Amphibians and reptiles are the quintessential examples of the unclean because they belong to more than one element and because they exhibit an improper means of locomotion for their elements, neither swimming nor walking, but slithering and squirming. In addition, creatures that are also primarily predators seem to be excluded.

The priestly law code sought to separate not only entities that are generic opposites but even those that appeared dangerously close to each other. The biblical prohibition of boiling a kid in its mother's milk (Exod. 23:19; 34:26; Deut. 14:21) is related in this context to the incest taboo (Lev. 18:7) or, as one writer humorously and succinctly put it: "You shall not put a mother and her son into the same pot any more than into the same bed."[32] Such a combination in food or sex violates the fundamental principle of cosmic order: "upholding the separation between two classes or types of relationships."[33] The Hebrew mind had a horror of the hybrid whether it was an animal that seemed to straddle two groups (Lev. 11), a human transvestite (Deut. 22:5) or even a fabric woven of linen and wool (Deut. 22:11). This repugnance is expressed in the narrative of Genesis 6 concerning the sons of God who copulated with the daughters of man, begetting the giants in the earth (*nefilim*). The cross-bred progeny was not allowed to develop and served as a sign to God of man's continuing wickedness. It is this conception that underlies the powerful feeling against incest, homosexuality and bestiality (Lev. 18:7-16, 22-23) in the Sinai tradition.

As in the festival celebrations, so in the dietary laws and the sex regulations of the priestly code we are carried back to creation and the human aspiration to resemble God by becoming holy. The verb "to separate" appears prominently in the verses summing up the dietary laws (Lev. 11:46-47) and the laws of holiness (Lev. 20:25-

26) that include both dietary and sex regulations. The same verb is used in the first chapter of Genesis where the primordial acts of separation punctuate the process of creation. The implication is that as God brought order out of chaos, so must the human being, by using as food creatures that fit safely into clear categories of classification and avoiding the indeterminate and amorphous species that evoke echoes of primordial chaos. As God is a living God and His commandments confer life on those who observe them, so must humans forfeit as food creatures that are primarily predators. Finally, as God distinguished in His creation of the first humans between the heavenly beings and the earthbound couple Adam and Eve, between humans and animals, and between male and female among the humans, so must people manage their sexuality so that they do not return to the disorder that preceded the emergence of our world. The priestly law code is an extended meditation ritual on the "oneness purity and completeness of God"[34] replicated in the life of His people. As the native wise man quoted by Levi-Strauss put it: "All sacred things must have their place." To which Levi-Strauss adds:

> It could even be said that being in their place is what makes them sacred for if they were taken out of their place, even in thought, the entire order of the universe would be destroyed. Sacred objects (and in our context a sacred people) therefore contribute to the maintenance of the order of the universe by occupying the places (and in this context eating the food and choosing the sexual partners) allotted to them. (See also ch.. 4 Sinai: The Struggles of Theodicy, notes 20-23).[35]

How interesting, as Huston Smith has noted, that "our language retains the memory of this early insight. The sublime is what remains within its limits—*sub limen*."[36]

Functions of the Priests

In addition to the priestly functions mentioned above there were also the following: offering of the sacrifices (specifically, sprinkling the blood and burning the suet, Lev. 1:1-6): blessing the people (Deut. 10:8; 21:5; Num. 6:22-27); sounding the trumpets (Lev. 25:9; Num. 10:10) and carrying the ark (Deut. 10:8; 31:9, 25). There were also mantic functions carried out by the high priest. The priestly circles of ancient Israel absorbed and adapted the mantic and magical traditions of the ancient Near East discussed in the preceding chapter, without any theological pangs of conscience. These traditions were incorporated into the priestly codes and the instructional lore by which the priests were prepared for their office. Oracular consultation by means of the *ephod* and the *urim* and *Thumim* (Exod. 28:30; Lev. 8:8; 1 Sam. 2:28; 14:3; 21:10;, 13, 15, 18; 23:6,9; 28:6; 30:7) or by the sacred lots (Lev. 18:8-10; 33:54; 34:13; 36:2) are good examples of priestly adaptation of mantic practices to Israelite institutional forms. The consultation took place when it was necessary to decide between two alternatives and the answer came in terms of "yes" or "no". In more complicated situations, in matters of national importance such as the selection of Saul as the first king of Israel (1 Sam. 10:17-21) the lot (*goral*) was used.[37] The ordeal of the suspected adulteress (Num. 5:11-29) is a priestly adaptation of a ritual which merges mantic and magical practices while the ritual of the scapegoat (Lev. 16) is patently magical.

The difference between priestly and prophetic use of mantic power is that the priestly lot is a public ritual while prophetic divination is a spontaneous, private inflow of God's instruction into prophetic consciousness. The first and second kings of Israel were selected by Samuel. Samuel selected Saul by the priestly lot in a public ceremony before the Lord, i.e., in the Sanctuary court. The selection was made through a process of elimination in which the lots selected the tribe, the clan and then the individual. Samuel selected David through prophetic divination. God directed the prophet privately to the house of Jesse. Again, in a process of elimination in which Samuel, at first relying on his own judgment (he seeks out the son of Jesse who most closely resembles Saul, who was "a head taller than any of the people," 1 Sam. 9:2), is gently led by God to David (1 Sam. 6:6-13).

There is a similar distinction between priestly and prophetic healing. The priests were recipients of healing traditions in which there were systematic, graded approaches to the treatment of disease which was viewed as an impure spirit that invaded the human body or even inanimate objects. The therapeutic process consisted of diagnosis, quarantine and purification rites (Lev. 13-16; Num. 19). In the case of an emergency there were apotropaic rituals such as the burning of incense to ward off the plague (Num. 17:12-13). Prophetic healing was spontaneous, charismatic and miraculous. There was no recourse to accepted processes or systematic rites but only prayer and the waiting for divine instruction. Moses prayed for his sister Miriam (Num. 12:13). Here the seven day quarantine, though identical to priestly therapeutics

,is intended as a sign of shame (as v. 14 makes clear.), and Hezekiah prayed for himself (2 Kings 20:1-6). Elisha advised Naaman, the Aramean general, to bathe seven times in the Jordan (2 Kings 5:10). The prescription is practically identical to the priestly therapy of ablution, but in priestly healing, immersion is the end of a process of purification. Here it is independent of any process but only a symbol of the divine miracle.

Finally, the priests also served as judges and teachers. Though the elders and the heads of the clans generally served in this function, in the Temple centers the priests also participated. Eli, the priest of Shiloh, was one of the great judges of Israel (1 Sam. 4:18). The role of teacher was connected to that of judge, healer and supervisor of Temple ritual since in each of these functions the priests had to instruct the people. In addition, the priests were the guardians of the various scrolls (Deut. 31:9) combined in the Pentateuch in the time of Ezra. They were required to write a copy of the Torah for the king (Deut. 17:18) and to read it publicly to the people on the festival of *Sukkot* (Tabernacles, Deut. 31:10-13).

I began this section on priestly piety in the First Temple period by stating that it would be a mistake to conclude that priestly religion was inferior to prophetic religion. But we must also not lose sight of the fact that the priests saw God and His requirements of man through the prism of the Temple, the cult, the hereditary stratification of the priesthood into ordinary priests and high priests and the status quo of society which often conferred wealth, power and prestige, particularly on priests who served in royal sanctuaries. The priest was attached to a temple in a specific geographical area which tended to give him a static outlook on the world, He was essentially a functionary whose primary objective was to preserve traditions of the past and this tended to make him by instinct a conservative.

In their finest hours the priests protected the ancient heritage of Israel's cult from the influx of foreign religious influences and guarded the purity of God's dwelling from the defiling encroachments of pagan gods. But in their worst moments the priests were concerned only with jealously protecting the prerogatives of their office and guarding the jurisdiction of their shrines and temples. Inevitably the charismatic, itinerant, non-hereditary prophets, whose view of God, religion and society was dynamic and revolutionary, were bound to clash with such self-seeking priests. This clash is best exemplified in the meeting of Amos and Amaziah (Amos 9:10-17) in which the priest is oblivious to the nature of prophecy and the role of the prophet. Amaziah accuses Amos of preaching sedition, of trespassing on a royal sanctuary and seeking to deprive its priest of a livelihood. In his reply Amos affirms the non-hereditary character of prophecy, its independence of economic interests and its radical prediction that if ethics does not take primacy over the cult the state will be destroyed and its people exiled.[38]

Priestly Piety in the Second Temple and Talmudic Periods

The First and Second Temple Compared— So powerful was the impact of the Solomonic Temple on biblical religion that, with its destruction in 586 B.C.E., a void was created which the Judeans, exiled to Babylonia, were determined to fill as quickly as possible when the time of the Return from the Exile arrived. Through the permission granted in the Decree of Cyrus the Great (Ezra 1:2-6; 2 Chron. 36:22-23) and in the memorandum which was deposited in the archives of Ecbatana, the capital of Media (Ezra 6:3-12), the Second Temple was built on the site of the First Temple and became a direct successor of its Solomonic predecessor.

Nevertheless, there were important differences between the two institutions. The absence of the *Urim* and *Tumim* (the twelve precious stones on the breastplate of the High Priest that served as a divine oracle) removed the mantic function of the priesthood (Ezra 1:63, Neh. 1:65).[39] The First Temple played a critical role in the religious life of the Israelites but it did not embrace all its manifestations. It was, as we have seen, powerfully counterbalanced by prophecy. Moreover, it was not the first and only place where the service of God was conducted. Divine worship took place at open air altars for a long time before the cult was finally concentrated in and limited to the Temple. The Second Temple, however, at its inception was the focal point for all religious, social, and political activity. The ritual of the First Temple, as mentioned earlier, was in essence a speechless worship with the priests as protagonists and the lay people, for the most part, silent observers. Prayer, though not absent, was of secondary importance, a substitute for sacrifice. In contrast, in the Second Temple the emphasis began to shift to prayer, study, judicial decision and the conduct of public affairs. Sacrifice was not displaced but it was now surrounded by other forms of divine service. The First Temple was an elite institution of the priesthood. The Second Temple became a popular institution of the masses and thus a transition from the House of God in biblical times to the synagogue and the house of study in the Talmudic period. In the Temple, the individual's participation was vicarious. He or she brought occasional offerings (though not the daily *tamid* offering) but it was the priest who performed the sacrificial rites while the worshippers (particularly women) remained bystanders. In the synagogue, however, the individual Jew participated actively, reciting all the prayers (which in the case of the *Tefillah*, the nineteen silent blessings, are recited standing, and are repeated on behalf of everyone by the prayer leader). "The people themselves became both the performers and the bearers of the divine service."[40] In contrast to the temple, in the synagogue liturgy the priest had no real function. All his roles in the synagogue (priestly benediction, certain honors, redeeming the first born) were only ornamental touches reminiscent of the transitional phase in which the Second Temple prepared the way for the synagogue.[41]

From Temple to Synagogue— A brief survey of this evolution is in order. When Ezra and Nehemiah gathered the returned exiles from Babylonia in the court of the newly rebuilt Second Temple on the New Year (*Rosh Hashanah*) 445 B.C.E. to ratify their allegiance to the Mosiac law, Ezra read sections of the Torah to the assembled people and the Levites made the rounds elucidating and explaining the text (Neh. Ch. 8, 9, 13). Prayer was also included in this solemn assembly. Ezra continued to convoke such assemblies for specific purposes from time to time, originally on Sabbaths and Festivals, later during weekdays, and out of these gatherings the synagogue developed, an institution for public Torah reading, study and prayer.[42]

With the return from Babylonia and the rebuilding of the Second Temple there came about a change in the social and economic status of the priests. Their number reached several thousand and most of them lived in the towns outside Jerusalem where they tilled the soil for a livelihood. Though the new covenant ratified by the returnees in the Temple court included the obligation to bring priestly gifts, the people were not conscientious in bringing them and Nehemiah had to prod them periodically (Neh. 12:44-47; 13:10-13). The result was that the priests became economically independent of the Temple service until late into the Second Temple period, when, under the Hasmonean rulers, Herod and his successors, the priests became a privileged class. The new conditions of total cultic centralization, the increased number of priests and their decreased dependency on the priestly gifts, led to a regulation of the temple service among all the priests and Levites in the form of a rotating system of divisions or *mishmarot*. There were 24 divisions and every priestly division was allotted only two weeks per year for its service which was regarded partly as a privilege with material benefits and partly as a duty of service to God. Most important of all, there were lay people who accompanied the priests and Levites of each division in their Temple service. For, as the *Mishnah* expressed it: "How can an individual sacrifice be offered without him being present?"[43] The lay people assisted the priests in their service, served as liaisons between the priests and the public that thronged the Temple and gathered in the synagogue that existed on the Temple premises, to pray for the welfare of the people, for the pilgrims to Jerusalem, for pregnant and nursing women and their infants. Not all the lay people of a particular division (*mishmar*) came to Jerusalem. Those who could not do so assembled in the synagogues in their own town and read the story of creation from the Torah.[44]

The chamber of hewn stone in the Second Temple was also the seat of the supreme judicial body, the Great Court (*bet din ha-gadol*). The Temple was also a place of public education. It was not only officially recognized institutions that were in charge of educating the people and not only officially recognized scholars such as Rabbi Yohanan ben Zakkai, who could teach and preach in the Temple. Obscure sages and visionaries also taught and preached there along with public personalities. The Gospels tell us that Jesus taught the people daily in the Temple and even after his death the members of the Judeo-Christian apostolic community in Jerusalem would gather in the Temple to instruct the people (Matt. 21:23; 26:55; 14:49; Luke 20:1; 21:37; 18:20; Acts ch. 2-4).

The participation of lay people in the Temple service, the prayers and Torah reading that took place in the synagogue on Temple premises and in synagogues in the provinces, the judicial and educational functions, all were part of the embryonic development that led from Temple to synagogue. In addition there were liturgical rites developed in the Temple such as the use of palm branches and citrons (*lulav* and *etrog*) on the festival of *Sukkot*, the sounding of the ram's horn on the New Year, the chanting of the special "psalms of praise" (*Hallel*) on festivals and the priestly blessing of the people that in the course of time were extended into the service of the synagogue. Consequently, when the Second Temple was destroyed by the Romans in 70 C.E., Judaism could absorb the blow without collapsing. The Temple became an eschatological symbol to be resurrected at the end of days while for the ongoing daily life new frameworks of communal activity were established, apparently provisional but to all intents and purposes permanent, all of them revolving around the synagogue.[45]

Function and Symbolism of the Second Temple— The Second Temple, like its predecessor and the Tabernacle in the desert, was considered a true likeness of a heavenly original. According to rabbinic tradition, the lower Temple is set against the upper Temple, the heavenly Holy of Holies against the lower Holy of Holies, and the throne below, i.e., the Ark is set against the throne above, i.e., the throne of the Almighty.[46] Similarly, the services performed in both Temples correspond to each other and the spatial distance between the heavenly Temple and the earthly one in Jerusalem is only eighteen miles.[47]

The correspondence and proximity of the heavenly and earthly Temples suggest the concept that (as discussed earlier) underlies the symbolism of the Tabernacle and the Solomonic Temple, the Temple as a cosmic institution at the center of the world, or itself a microcosm. This symbolism is deeply embedded in the post-biblical literature describing the Temple. Josephus, the first century historian describes the veil over the Temple entrance as an *eikon*, an image, of the world and he goes on to describe the Temple furnishings and the vestments of the high priest in terms of cosmic symbols.[48] A succinct rabbinic saying sums up a detailed comparison between the Temple, the human body and the world: "The Temple corresponds to the whole world and to the creation of man who is a small world."[49]

The image of the sacred center, i.e., the Temple as the *axis mundi*, the middle of the world embodied in the construction plan of concentric circles in the Tabernacle and the Solomonic Temple, resurfaced in the Second Temple. But in the Second Temple the image reflected the change to a popular institution with pronounced lay participation so that the holiness in the center radiates in diminishing degrees far beyond the Temple proper to the entire Jewish world in the land of Israel and in the Diaspora. Thus the Mishna containing material from the Second Temple experience lists ten places with an ascending degree of sanctity. The land of Israel is holier than any other land. The walled cities in the land of Israel are still more holy in that lepers must be sent forth from their midst. Inside the walls of Jerusalem is still more holy. Only within these walls may the meat of those sacrifices possessing a lower degree of sanctity be eaten. The Temple Mount is still more holy, for no man or woman who has a flux, no menstruant, and no woman after childbirth may enter there. The Rampart is still more holy, for no Gentile (i.e., idolaters who are rendered impure by idol worship) may enter there and no one who has contracted contamination from a corpse. The Court of the Women is still more holy for none that has undergone immersion that day may enter there. The Court of the Israelites is still more holy, for no one whose atonement is incomplete may enter there. The Court of the Priests is still more holy, for Israelites may not enter therein except when bringing their sacrifices. The area between the Porch and the altar is still more holy, for no priest who has a blemish or whose hair is unloosed may enter there. The Sanctuary is still more holy, for no priest may enter therein without first washing his hands and feet. The Holy of Holies is still more holy, for no one may enter there at all except the High Priest on the Day of Atonement at the time of the service.[50]

But the Second Temple also gave birth to a second sacred center that would eventually supersede it, i.e., the Torah. The growing centrality of Torah teaching and dissemination as a sacred center in the Second Temple is underscored by the sessions of the Great Court held in the chamber of hewn stone. Indeed the rabbis explain the Temple Mount identified with Mount Moriah as the place from which instruction goes forth to Israel.[51]

The two elements connected with sacred time interwoven into the festival celebrations of the biblical period, its replication through ritual and the return to origins, particularly the return to creation, to the beginning of the cosmos, are also mirrored in the incremental rites contributed by the Second Temple to these celebrations. They are also to be found in the rites and symbolism of certain post-biblical holidays. It has already been noted that the lay people who did not accompany the *mishmarot* (the divisions) of priests, Levites and laymen to their respective two week duty in the Temple, gathered in their local synagogues and read from the Torah the story of creation. That this particular portion was chosen to be read at the time of the sacrifice in the Temple provides a clear indication of the link between Temple ritual and the return to creation.

During the Second Temple period rituals and prayers for rain became an increasingly important element in the Sukkot festival. They are a variation on the theme of the return to creation already encountered in the liturgy of the New Year (*Rosh Hashanah*) and Day of Atonement (*Yom Kippur*). It was a traditional belief that the fall of rain is matched by a corresponding rise of *Tehom*, the waters of the Deep separated by God from the waters above in the act of creation (Gen. 1:6-7). Thus we find Rabbi Levi saying: "It is the way of the world, rain descends and *Tehom* rises."[52] Rabbi Simeon ben Eleazar said: "There is no hand-breadth (of rain) that descends from above but it has two hand-breadths (of water) raised towards it by the earth.[53] Rabbi Eliezer said:

> When on the festival of Sukkot the water libations are carried out. Deep says unto Deep: "Let your waters spring forth, I hear the voice of two friends (i.e., the water and the wine poured on the altar).[54]

The holiday of *Simhat Torah*, the Rejoicing with the Torah, a post-biblical holiday celebrated at the conclusion of the *Sukkot* festival, is marked by the concluding of the reading of the Torah with the last chapter of Deuteronomy and the immediate return to the beginning of the Torah reading cycle with the reading of the first chapter of Genesis. Thus in the *Sukkot* festival there is a return to creation in nature and on the holiday of *Simhat Torah* a return to creation in the Torah.

The most spectacular and elaborate celebration in the Second Temple was connected with the festival of Sukkot. It was called the "Joy of the House of Water Drawing. "Combining all the elements of Second Temple worship, sacrifice, prayer, and study, the festivities reached their climax in the carnival like atmosphere of the ritual of the water libation, typifying Huizinga's contention that ritual is a form of play (see note 23 above). The festivities were heightened by the vast number of pilgrims who came to the Temple. The description of this festival contained in the Mishnah opens with these words: "Whoever has not seen the Joy of the House of Water-Drawing has never seen real joy in his life."[55] The lighting of the great candelabra at dusk was accompanied by the rising enthusiasm of the masses which eventually erupted into the ecstatic dancing of the "pious men" and "men of good deeds" who danced with burning torches in their hands. Even the venerable head of the Great Court, Rabban Shimon ben Gamaliel used to dance with eight golden burning torches; he threw them high up into the air and again caught them alternately, and so great was his skill that no torch ever touched another nor did any torch ever fall to the earth. The Levites sang, accompanying themselves with musical instruments, the priests sounded the trumpets at dawn and the crowd descended to the well of Siloam for the water libation.[56] The complex of rituals in this celebration have been shown to have their roots in rain-making symbols linked to biblical creation traditions discussed above.[57]

To conclude the survey of post-biblical festivals in which the motifs of sacred time are to be found, we turn to *Hanukkah*, the Feast of Lights. The name of the festival signifies "dedication" or better "re-dedication" of the altar and the Temple defiled by the idolatry of the Syrian Hellenists under Antiochus IV and their Jewish sympathizers. Thus the motif of a return to a pristine sanctity is already implied in the name of the holiday. Scholars, basing themselves on 2 Maccabbes, chapters one and two, are of the opinion that the eight days of the holiday were intended to be a delayed celebration of *Sukkot* (Tabernacles) since the Maccabees and their followers could not observe it at the proper time due to the war.[58] The central feature of the celebration is the kindling of lights in the eight branched candelabra (*Menorah*), reminiscent, according to the Talmud, of the miracle that occurred with the candelabra of the recaptured and cleansed Temple.[59] In 2 Maccabees there is a reference to fire that descended from heaven at the dedication of the altar in the days of Moses and at the sanctification of the Temple of Solomon. At the consecration of the altar in the time of Nehemiah and in the days of Judah Maccabee there was also a miracle of fire.[60] Josephus explains that the festival acquired its name because the right to serve God came to the people unexpectedly like a sudden light.[61]

The common denominator among these explanations is that the light is connected with a divine source; it is miraculous. In the legends woven around the Temple, the light emanating from the Temple is identified with the celestial light created on the first day of creation. Thus, the Temple situated at the center of the world illuminates the whole world.[62] Patai suggests that the lighting of the great candelabra at the annual "Joy of the House of Water Drawing" celebration on the *Sukkot* festival "may have represented the kindling anew of the cosmic light at its proper place, the Temple, the center and source of the light of the world."[63] I would suggest that the rekindling of the Temple candelabra on Hanukkah, originally a delayed *Sukkot* observance, assumed the same symbolism in the Hebrew imagination. It was held to be commemorative of God's creation of light at the *axis mundi*.

Some modern scholars maintain that the lighting of fires at the winter solstice (when the days are the shortest) is an observance with roots in ancient paganism. The gods who are believed to die with the approach of winter are searched out by their worshippers with lighted torch.[64] The Hebrews may very well have transformed the rite into a commemoration of the divine light piercing the primeval darkness at creation.

Even before the destruction of the Second Temple, Jewish ritual outside the Temple premises duplicated the morphology of the priestly cult—its concern for order, punctiliousness and repetition. The Pharisaic *havurot*, societies for the strict observance of the laws of ritual cleanliness and holy offerings, subscribed to the priestly doctrine that ritual purity is a matter of the highest importance in achieving holiness.[65]   With the destruction of the Temple the priestly cult was applied metaphorically to the daily life of the entire Jewish people and the individual Jew. The study of the sacrificial laws became a surrogate for the defunct Temple cult. Similarly, daily statutory prayers, according to the Talmud, were established to correspond to the (times of the) daily offerings in the Temple.[66]   The synagogue liturgy carries forward the cultic seasonal calendar with specific prayers and rites for each festival.   The blessings recited before eating are the equivalent of the gifts to God (through his agents the priests) in Temple times of the first fruits, the first born of the flock and the tithes. The blessing is an offering of words acknowledging gratitude to God.[67]

It was also in the architecture of the synagogue that the concept of the Torah as the sacred center of Israel was given the clearest expression.   Though the Torah shrine was usually on the wall facing Jerusalem, the *bema* (the pulpit) was in the very center of the hall, serving as a reader's platform from which the Torah was read as in the synagogue at Sardis, and the *diplostoon* at Alexandria.[68]   But the Torah is also a portable sacred center as the Ark of the Covenant was during Israel's sojourn in the wilderness. What is more it allows for a multiplicity of sacred centers which is characteristic of the Jewish tradition. It is the presence of a Torah scroll and a quorum for prayer that constitutes a synagogue which can be located almost anywhere.[69]   It is not only the presence of the Torah scroll that makes a sacred center but even the discussion of subjects relating to Torah constitutes a sacred center. "Rabbi Hananya ben Teradyon said: . . . Two people who sit together and do exchange words of the Torah-the Shekinah (i.e., the Divine Presence) is among them . . ."[70] It was the mobility of the Torah in the Second Temple period and afterward that made the periphery in the Diaspora and later in the exile a real alternative to the sacred center of the Jerusalem Temple.[71]

Notes

1. Menahem Haran, "Priests and Priesthood," *Encyclopedia Judaica* (Jerusalem: Keter Publishing House, 1972), 13:1083.

2. But as the names of the two structures indicate, there is a difference in the way in which the cloud appears and in the place where it rests. The Divine Presence, in the form of a cloud, descended to the entrance of the Tent of Meeting (not within it) in response to prophetic invocation. When the communion with Moses ended, the cloud disappeared from the entrance of the tent as a sign that the Divine Presence had left (Exod. 33:9-10; Num. 11:24-25; 12:5, 9-10; Deut. 31:15). In the Tabernacle the cloud appears upon the cherubim over the ark which is the place where God speaks to Moses (Exod. 25:22; Lev. 16:2; Num. 7:89).

3. On the various scholarly views regarding the identity of the two institutions and their relationship to each other see Israel Abrahams, "Tabernacle," *Encyclopedia Judaica* 15: 685-86. Recently there has been intriguing evidence that the Tabernacle was actually contained within the Solomonic Temple. See Richard Elliott Friedman, "The Tabernacle in the Temple," *Biblical Archeologist* 43 (1980): 241-248 and Yohanan Aharoni, "The Solomonic Temple, the Tabernacle, and the Arad Sanctuary," in *Orient and Occident: Cyrus Gordon Festschrift* ed. H. A. Hoffman Jr. (Neukirchen: Neukirchener, 1973), pp. 1-8. Cf. Menaham Haran, *Temples and Temple Service in Ancient Israel* (Oxford: The Clarendon Press, 1978), pp. 260-275.

4. Haran, *Temples and Temple Service in ancient Israel*, p. 46, p. 149. cf. Jon D. Levinson, "The Jerusalem Temple in Devotional and Visionary Experience," in *Jewish Spirituality*, pp. 32-34.

5. Philo, *De Vita Mosis* 2:15 (Loeb Classics ed.) 6:485-486, speaks of the incorporeal patterns according to which Moses was to make the furniture of the tabernacle and so do the rabbis (*Exodus R*. 35:6; Ginzberg, *Legends* 6, p. 62, n. 318. According to the rabbis, the heavenly pattern of the Tabernacle, that also served as the blueprint for the Temple, was handed down to Solomon through the long chain of tradition going back to Moses. See Ginzberg, *Legends* 6, p. 294, n. 57.

6. Haran, *Temples and Temple Service in Ancient Israel*, pp. 208-210; 213-218. The ancients conceived of memory and grace as manifestations of spiritual and even sensorial activity.

7. On *yam* and *apsu* see William F. Albright, *Archaeology and the Religion of Israel* (Baltimore, Md.: Johns Hopkins University Press, 1956; London: Oxford University Press, 1956); Frank M. Cross, *Caananite Myth and Hebrew Epic* (Cambridge, Mass.: Harvard University Press, 1973), pp. 112-144. On the foundation of the altar and Solomon's platform see Albright, *Archaeology and the Religion of Israel*, pp. 153-54 and Levinson, "The Jerusalem Temple in Devotional and Visionary Experience," in *Jewish Spirituality*, pp. 51-52, p. 60, notes 27-28 and *Creation and the Persistence of Evil* (San Francisco: Harper and Row, 1988), pp. 90-95.

8. On blue-purple see *The J.P.S. Torah Commentary Numbers* Commentary by Jacob Milgrom (Philadelphia and New York: The Jewish Publication Society of America, 1990), p.25 and Excursus 38, p. 411.

9. *Num. R.* to Num. 4:13,14; *Mishnat Rabbi Eliezer*, chap. 14. Modern scholarship has substantiated that the Ark and the cherubim were indeed conceived as the throne of the deity. See M. Haran, *Temples and Temple Service in Ancient Israel*, pp. 251-257. On the rabbinic interpretation of the cherubs and the Ark see *Baraita de Meleket ha-Mishkan*, (ed. Eisenstein) in *Ozar Midrashim*, p. 301; *Midrash Tadshe*, in A. Jellinek, *Bet Ha-Midrash* 3, 167; *b. Bava Batra* 99a; *Petiha* to *Lam. R.*, par. 9. Cf. Patai, *Man and Temple*, pp. 91-92.

10. During the Water-Drawing Celebration in the Second Temple, the participants on reaching the eastern Water-Gate, turned back toward the west facing the sanctuary and solemnly declared: "Our fathers who were on this place (stood) with their backs toward the Sanctuary and their faces towards the east, and they prostrated themselves eastwards to the sun. But as for us, our eyes are turned to the Lord." *M. Sukkah*, 5:4; *Tos. Sukkah*, 4,10 (ed. Zuckermandl), p. 199. Cf. F. I. Hollis, "The Sun Cult and the Temple at Jerusalem," in *Myth and Ritual*, ed. by S. H. Hooke (London: Oxford University Press, 1933), pp. 87-110. On the historical background of the utterances see J. Morgenstern, "The Gates of Righteousness," *Hebrew Union College Annual* 6 (1929): 1-37.

11. Haran, *Temples and Temple Service in Ancient Israel*, pp. 164-165.

12. Lay people could perform preliminary rites at the sacrificial altar because the altar did not become charged with sanctity until the blood of the sacrificial animal was sprinkled on it. See *Leviticus 1-16, The Anchor Bible* trans. with intro. and commentary Jacob Milgrom (New York, London, Toronto: Doubleday, 1991), pp. 443-44.

13. *Ibid.*, pp. 174, 178, 181.

14. Mircea Eliade, *The Sacred and the Profane*, trans. Willard R. Trask (New York: Harcourt Brace and Co., 1959), pp. 20-24.

15. Haran, *Temples and Temple Service in Ancient Israel*, pp. 176, 187-188. There was a lethal aura surrounding the holiness of the Tabernacle (and later the Temple) and numerous warnings are raised like red flags in the Pentateuch (Exod. 28:35; Lev. 16:2, 13 for the high priest; Exod. 28:43; 30:20-21; Lev. 10:6-7, 9; 22:9 for priests as a group; Num. 4:15, 19-20 for the family of Kohath; Num. 18:3 for all Levites; Num. 1:53; 8:19; 17:25; 18:5, 22 for Israelites).

16. Moses warned the priests that if they perform mourning rites when the anointing oil is on them, they will die and God's "anger will strike the community" (Lev. 10:6). The priests are also warned that the Levites must not officiate with the holy vessels "lest both they and you die." (Num. 18:3). cf. *The J.P.S. Torah Commentary Numbers* Excursus 5, pp. 342-43. Excursus 40, pp. 423-24. Rudolf Otto, *The Idea of the Holy* (New York: Oxford University Press, 1958), pp. 18-19 identifies the "wrath of God" that is devoid of morality as the *tremendum* itself.

17. Mircea Eliade, *Patterns in Comparative Religion* (Cleveland and New York: World Publishing Co., 1958), pp. 14-19: p. 384.

18. Roland de Vaux, *Ancient Israel* (New York, Toronto: McGraw Hill, 1965) 2: 440-441.

19. Jacob Milgrom, *Cult and Conscience: The Asham and the Priestly Doctrine of Repentance* (Leiden: E. J. Brill, 1976), pp. 106-110. Confession was also a requirement for sacrificial expiation in Hittite religion.

20. *M. Yoma*, 8:9. Cf. *M. Bava Kamma*, 9:5, 12; *b. Bava Kamma*, 103b; *Tos: Pesahim*, 3:1.

21. Milgrom, *Cult and Conscience*, pp. 126-127.

22. Roland de Vaux, *Ancient Israel* 2: 451-454.

23. Kaufmann, *The Religion of Israel*, pp. 303-304; Menahem Haran, "Priesthood, Temple, Divine Service," *Hebrew Annual Review* 7 (1983) *Biblical and Other Studies in Honor of Robert Gordis*, ed. by Reuben Aharoni, pp. 121-134.

24. The literature on the festivals is vast. The following are some of the significant works: Roland de Vaux, *Ancient Israel* 2, chs. 15-18; George Foote Moore, *Judaism* (Cambridge: Harvard University Press, 1950) 2: 21-69; Theodore H. Gaster, *Festivals of the Jewish Year* (New York: Sloane, 1953); H. Schauss, *Guide to Jewish Holy Days*, trans. S. Jaffe (New York: Schocken Books, 1962); Y. Vainstein, *The Cycle of the Jewish Year* (Jerusalem: World Zionist Organization, 1953). On specific festivals: Theodore H. Gaster, *Passover: Its History and Traditions* (New York: Henry Schuman, 1940); Louis Jacobs, *Guide to Rosh Hashanah* (London: Jewish Chronicle Publications, 1959); Louis Jacobs, *Guide to Yom Kippur* (London: Jewish Chronicle Publications, 1957).

25. Eliade, *Patterns in Comparative Religion*, p. 402 and pp. 388-405; Eliade, *The Sacred and the Profane*, pp. 68-100 and Eliade, *The Myth of the Eternal Return*, trans. by Willard R. Trask, Bollingen Series 46 (New York: Pantheon Books, 1954), p. 352. Sacred time and sacred space (discussed above in connection with the Tabernacle and the Temple) are two of the elements that, according to J. Huizinga, *Homo Ludens; A Study of the Play-Element in Culture*, trans. by. R. F. C. Hull (London: Routledge & Kegan Paul, Ltd., 1949), pp. 7-27, link religious ritual to play. Both play and religious ritual are activities which take place in a space hedged off from the rest of the world (the playground and the Temple) and in a specially designated time (play time and sacred time). Within these dimensions a temporarily real world of its own is created, the world of the game in which the individual exchanges his worldly identity for the identity of a player and the world of ritual activity in which the individual exchanges his normal identity for that of an actor in a sacred drama. These activities are given primacy to the exclusion of everything else. In both play and religious ritual, mirth and joy are prevalent, though both can be very serious as well. In both play and ritual there is a combination of strict rules to be obeyed, with ultimate human freedom to play or not to play the game, to practice or not to practice the rite.

26. *b. Rosh Ha-Shanah*, 10a: *Pesikta de Rav Kahana* 23:1 trans. William G. Braude and Israel J. Kapstein (Philadelphia: Jewish Publication Society of America, 1975), p. 352.

27. Samuel Joseph Agnon, *Days of Awe* (Hebrew) (Jerusalem and New York: Schocken Books, 1946), p. 302; *Shulhan Aruk, Orah Hayim*, par. 410, gloss of R. Moses Isserles. See also the daily morning prayer that begins with the words: "Oh my God Thou hast given to me a soul in purity." *The Prayer Book*, trans. and arranged by Ben Zion Bokser (New York: Hebrew Publishing Co., 1957), p. 5.

28. *Passover Haggadah: The Feast of Freedom*, ed. Rachel Anne Rabinowicz (New York: The Rabbinical Assembly, 1982), p. 67. Eliade, *Patterns of Comparative Religion*, pp. 321; 390-391 makes two valid points that are particularly relevant to Passover. 1) The symbol of nature is restricted to a single object (i.e., *karpas*, the green vegetable on the Seder plate) so that there is no mistaking a pantheistic adoration of nature. 2) Sacred time is arranged independently of nature's rhythms so that there is no mistaking the two realms. Thus the date of Passover, based on the adjusted lunar calendar will not always coincide with the onset of spring. Astronomical time and the signs of nature are but the signposts to a deeper, more encompassing truth-the renewal and recommencement of all things, the individual, society and the cosmos.

29. *M. Rosh Ha-Shanah* 1:1.

30. *b. Rosh Ha-Shanah*, 11a.

31. *b. Avodah Zarah*, 8a. Moshe Greenberg, "The Festival in Scripture and Sacred Time," (Hebrew) *Proceedings of the Rabbinical Assembly* 43 (Jerusalem, 1984), pp. 3-4.

32. Jean Soler, "The Dietary Prohibitions of the Hebrews," *The New York Review of Books* (June 14, 1979), pp. 24-30.

33. *Ibid.*

34. Mary Douglas, *Purity and Danger: An Analysis of Concepts of Pollution and Taboo* (London: Routledge and Kegan Paul, 1966), pp. 41-52. cf. Robert Alter, "A New Theory of Kashrut," *Commentary* 68, no. 2 (August, 1979): 46-52. The rabbinic extension of the dietary laws to include a total separation of meat from dairy foods involving separate dishes, silverware, and pots and pans clearly conforms to the blueprint of preventing the mingling of opposing realms.

35. Claude Levi Strauss, *The Savage Mind* (Chicago: The University of Chicago Press, 1966), p. 10.

36. Huston Smith, *Forgotten Truth* (New York: Harper & Row, 1976), p. 117, n. 28.

37. M. Haran, "Kehunah, Kohanim," *Enziklopedia Mikrait* (Jerusalem: Mosad Bialik, 1962) 4: 22-26. Other examples of the use of the *goral* are the apportionment of the land west of the Jordan to the tribes (Num. 26:55-56; Joshua 14-21; Judges, 1,3) the discovery of the man who took from the plunder dedicated to God, thus endangering the lives of all the Israelites (Josh. 7:13-18), the selection of the fighters who were to avenge the rape-murder of the concubine in Gibeah (Judges 20:9-10).

38. Shalom Spiegel, *Amos versus Amaziah* (New York: The Jewish Theological Seminary, 1958), pp. 1-24.

39. It is interesting that *M. Sotah* 9:12 links the disuse of the *Urim* and *Tumim* to the death of the early prophets suggesting, perhaps, that the priesthood became subservient to the prophets in all matters pertaining to divine inquiry.

40. Joseph Heinemann, *Prayer in the Talmud: Forms and Patterns*, p. 14.

41. S. Safrai, *Ha-Mikdash Bi-Tekufat Ha-Bayit Ha-Sheni* (Jerusalem: Jewish Agency, 1958), pp. 5-6; p. 11.

42. S. Safrai, "The Synagogue and its Worship," in *The World History of the Jewish People*: vol. 8, *Society and Religion in the Second Temple Period*, pp. 68-70. Talmudic tradition and many scholars in the older school of modern Jewish scholarship trace the origins of the Synagogue to the Babylonian Exile. But Philo, Josephus, the New Testament and another talmudic tradition as well as some nineteenth and twentieth century scholars trace it to the biblical period. *Ibid.*, pp. 68-69. cf. Louis I. Rabinowitz, "Synagogue," *Encyclopedia Judaice* 15: 579-583 and bibliography on p. 628; Wilhelm Bacher, "Synagogue," *Jewish Encyclopedia* 11: 619-628; Solomon Zeitlin, "The Origin of the Synagogue," *Proceedings of the American Academy for Jewish Research* (1931).

43. *M. Ta'anit* 4:1.

44. *M. Ta'anit* 4:2-3; *b. Ta'anit*, 27b.

45. S. Safrai, *Pilgrimage At The Time of The Second Temple* (Hebrew) (Jerusalem: Akadamon, 1986), pp. 8-9.

46. *Exod. R.* 35:6; 33:4; *The Midrash on Psalms* 30, trans. by William G. Braude (New Haven: Yale University Press, 1959), p. 386; *Gen. R.* 55:7 (ed. Theodor-Albeck), p. 591; A. Jellinek, *Bet Ha-Midrash* 5, p. 63; *Cant. R.* 3:10; 4:4 *Mekilta de Rabbi Ishmael*, *Beshallah*, (ed. Horowitz-Rabin), pp. 149-150.

47. *Num. R.* 4:13; *Gen. R.* 69:7 (ed. Theodor-Albeck), p. 797; *Midrash Sekel Tov*, p. 142; *Seder Arkin*, ed. Eisenstein, *Ozar Midrashim*, p. 70; Jellinek, *Bet Ha-Midrash* 5:63; *b. Hagigah*, 12b; *Yalkut Shimeoni*, *Vayishlah* 33, par. 132. cf. Patai, *Man and Temple*, pp. 130-132.

48. Josephus, *Wars of the Jews* 5,5,4; 5,5,5,; 5,5,7; *Antiquities* 3,7,5; 3,7,7, cf. *Wisdom of Solomon* 18:24. According to Philo, *Life of Moses* 3:21, trans: F. H. Colson, Loeb Classics Ed. p. 501, the candlestick is the symbol of heaven and the altar of incense is the symbol of things on earth.

49. *Midrash Tanhuma*, *Pekude*, par. 3. Cf. Raphael Patai, *Man and Earth in Jewish Custom, Belief and Legend* (Hebrew) (Jerusalem: Hebrew University Press, 1942) 1: 165ff.

50. *M. Kelim*, 1:6-9. There is less sanctity in the synagogue and the house of study (*bet ha-midrash*) which are sacred only when they are in use. When no longer used they may be sold for secular purposes. *b. Megillah*, 26a-b. Cf. Louis Jacobs, "Holy Places," *Conservative Judaism* 37, no. 3 (Spring, 1984): 8.

51. *Gen. R.* 55:2 (ed. Theodor-Albeck), p. 591 and Intro. to this chapter.

52. *Gen. R.* 32:7 (ed. Theodor-Albeck), p. 294.

53. *Gen. R.* 13:13 (ed. Theodor-Albeck), p. 122.

54. *b. Ta'anit*, 25b. The idea that there is a correspondence between the falling of rain and the rising of the Deep is also found in the Canaanite Ras Shamra texts. See Ivan Engnell, *Studies in Divine Kingship in the Ancient Near East* 2nd ed. (Oxford: Blackwell, 1967), pp. 11, 101. Cf. Patai, *Man and Temple*, pp. 59-60. The concept of a deluge that annihilates all flesh in order to prepare the way for a new and regenerated humanity, dramatically enacted in the Babylonian New Year ritual (see chapter 2 and Eliade, *The Myth of the Eternal Return*, pp. 55-58) is paralleled in the Sinai tradition by allusions to Noah and the biblical flood story in the prayers for rain on *Shemini Azeret* (the festival of Solemn Assembly). *Mahzor*, Part 2 (for festivals) (Sulzbach, 1853), pp. 84,90. The rain prayed for should come as a blessing and not as a curse (as in the days of Noah).

55. *M. Sukkah* 5:1. That the most joyous celebration of the Second Temple should fall on the festival of *Sukkot* is no accident. Of the three pilgrim festivals mentioned in Deut. 16, it is only of *Sukkot* (Tabernacles) that the Bible says "you shall have nothing but joy" (Deut. 16:15). A medieval Jewish Bible commentator explains it this way: "You shall hold a festival for the Lord your God seven days because you are now free to rejoice, for you have gathered everything (i.e., the entire harvest) . . . and you shall have nothing but joy" for your thoughts can now be entirely focused on rejoicing. Commentary of R. Joseph Bekor Shor to Deut. 16:15.

56. *M. Sukkah*, 5: 2-4; *Tos. Sukkah* 4:2; *b. Sukkah*, 52a-53a; *Yer. Sukkah* 5: 2-3.

57. Patai, *Man and Temple*, pp. 32-47.

58. Moshe David Herr, "Hanukkah," *Encyclopedia Judaica* 7: 1283-84. Solomon Zeitlin, *The First Book of Maccabees*, Dropsie College Edition, Jewish Apocryphal Series (New York: Harper & Row, 1950), pp. 53-54; Jonathan A. Goldstein, I Maccabees Anchor Bible 41 (Garden City, NY: Doubleday, 1976), p. 27.

59. *b. Shabbat*, 21a.

60. 2 Maccabees 1:18-36; 2:8-12,14; 10:3.

61. Josephus, *Antiquities* 12,7,7.

62. *Gen R.* 3:4 (ed. Theodor-Albeck), p. 20; *The Midrash on Psalms* 104 trans. William G. Braude, p. 196; *Tanhuma Bereshit* (ed. Buber), p. 112; *Pesikta de Rav Kahana* 21, trans. William G. Braude and Israel J. Kapstein (Philadelphia: The Jewish Publication Society of America, 1975), pp. 341-42; *Tanhuma Tezaveh* 6; *b. Menahot*, 86b; *Lev. R.* 31:7; *Cant. R.* 4:4; *Gen. R.* 55:7 (ed. Theodor-Albeck), p. 591.

63. Patai, *Man and Temple*, p. 85.

64. Solomon Grayzel, "Hanukkah and Its History," in *Hanukkah: The Feast of Lights* ed. by Emily Solis-Cohen Jr. (Philadelphia: Jewish Publication Society, 1955), p. 39.

65. On the Pharisaic Havurot see *b. Bekorot*, 30b; *M Demai*, 2:3; *Tos. Demai* 2:2-3; Jacob Neusner, *Fellowship in Judaism* (London: Valentine Mitchell, 1963).

66. *b. Berakot*, 26b.

67. *b. Berakot*, 35a; Richard S. Sarason "Religion and Worship: The Case of Judaism" in *Take Judaism for Example: Studies Toward the Comparison of Religions*, ed. J. Neusner (Chicago and London: University of Chicago Press, 1983). pp. 49-65.

68. *Toseftah Sukkah* 4:6 (ed. Lieberman), p. 273; *Yer Sukkah* 5:1; *b. Sukkah*, 51b; Saul Lieberman, *Tosefta Ki-Fshutah* (New York: Jewish Theological Seminary, 1962) 4:889-892; Andrew Seager, "The Architecture of the Dura and Sardis Synagogue" in *The Synagogue: Studies in Origins, Archaeology and Architecture*, ed. Joseph Gutman (New York: Ktav Publishing House, 1975), pp. 90, 179-180; Erwin R. Goodenough, *Jewish Symbols in the Greco-Roman Period*, Bollingen Series 37 (New York: Pantheon Books, 1965), pp. 191, 193.

69. See above note 50.

70. *M. Avot*, 3:3

71. In the Second Temple period and afterward we also get the transference of *Axis Mundi* symbolism from a sacred place and a sacred object to a sacred person, the *Zaddik* or holy man as a mobile center of the world. Honi the Circledrawer established himself as a sacred center when he fashioned a mandala-like circle in which he stood and commanded the rain to fall (see the discussion in chapter six). Of Rabbi Hanina ben Dosa (also discussed in chapter six) we are told: "The entire world is sustained for the sake of Hanina my son," *b. Berakot*, 17b. "What does the earth rest on? . . . Rabbi Elazar ben Shamua says: 'It rests on one pillar and *zaddik* is its name. Thus Scripture says: 'The Holy Man (*Zaddik*) is the foundation of the world' (Prov. 10:25), *b. Hagigah*, 12b. Cf. Arthur Green, "The Zaddiq as *Axis Mundi* in Later Judaism," *Journal of the American Academy of Religion*, 45, No. 3 (September, 1977): 332-347. For an extended treatment of the *zaddik* in rabbinic literature see Rudolph Mach, *Der Zaddik in Talmud und Midrasch* (Leiden: E. J. Brill, 1957). Cf. G. Scholem, "Three Types of Jewish Piety," *Eranos Jahrbuch* 38 (1969): 331-347 and *The Messianic Idea in Judaism* (New York: Schocken Books, 1971), pp. 251-56. See my article "From Sacred Space to Sacred Object to Sacred Person" *Shofar: An Interdisciplinary Journal of Jewish Studies* (Winter, 1994): 28-37.

Olympus: Piety in Action

Greek piety was primarily a matter of practice, of actions which acknowledged the gods, rather than an expression of a unified concept of deity or an organized system of beliefs.[1] The actions required by piety were as diverse as the types of gods and the individuals and communities who worshipped them. Instead of one temple viewed as the site of creation, there were countless sacred spaces scattered through cities and rural areas. No single hereditary priesthood supervised worship as a professional class with a common training, ideology, or function. Rather those who performed religious duties or guarded sacred tradition were ordinary citizens who obtained their positions in diverse ways, from inheritance to election to lot. The rites they supervised were also diverse. Although sacrifice was a typical element, communities established different ways of approaching and celebrating their divine patrons, with unique characteristics evolving sometimes out of revelation, but also from accretions of local myths and customs, or the political aspirations of public officials.

Because the Greeks believed that all their success depended on divine favor, acts of worship or propitiation permeated all areas of human endeavor. Religious and secular life were so closely intertwined that the Greeks did not even conceptualize religion as a separate category.[2] Political responsibilities often included religious duties on which the survival of the community depended. Every city-state established its own sacred calendar to worship the divine guardians of its public life, and state leaders invoked the divine presence at political actions by such religious devices as sacrifices, curses, and prayers. Every family, farm, tribe, and district conducted its own rites by and for its members, officiated by its own leaders, to communicate with its private divine patrons, solemnize its regular activities, or respond to extraordinary events affecting it. Individuals too worshipped individual gods, goddesses, or heroes as their personal patrons, according to their own age, status, profession, personality, or need, often adding private rites to general cult practice. Moreover, the entire Greek world joined together to honor its major common deities in great Panhellenic festivals, such as the Olympic games, which included activities considered secular today.

Many aspects of Greek worship can be traced back to the earliest common culture of the Mediterranean area.[3] Thus the Greeks and the Hebrews share several cult practices such as blood sacrifice and the fertility rites and rain magic (with the parading of tree branches, pelting with fruits, leaves, and grains, drawing and pouring of liquids, and dancing on the earth) which were vital activities of early farmers everywhere. Those geographical areas which later became Greek-speaking must have had their own local variations of common customs from the beginning.

Successive waves of Indo-European migrations, commercial contacts with the near East, and wide spread colonization added different conceptualizations of the divine and new religious activities. The Greek temple, for example, was a relatively late addition to the worship and does not seem to have appeared in Greece until the end of the Dark Ages.[4] Earlier archaeological sites have yielded remains of sacrificial altars, undifferentiated cult images, and houses which may have been shrines or dining halls for sacrificial meals. A monumental building, however, with stylistic devices such as column orders, constructed to contain the image of a highly individualized anthropomorphic deity, must have resulted from the diffusion of near Eastern and Egyptian culture, religion, science and technology which stimulated so many other aspects of Greek civilization.

The unique features of Greek religion are related to geographical and historical factors which fostered different political structures from those in the ancient Near East or Israel.[5] The areas populated by the Greeks consisted of isolated valleys separated by steep mountains, clusters of individual islands in the Aegean, and coastal regions of Asia Minor. The Greeks were never able to form a stable political union despite their common language, feelings of Panhellenism, and the occasional formation of leagues and alliances.

Although the separate communities developed differently, most followed the same general pattern. The earliest villages were ruled by kings who were believed to have special relationships with the gods. They functioned as both mediators for and representatives of the people, responsible for performing the rites necessary to the group's survival. The good king would bring prosperity to the land and its inhabitants; the gods would punish them all for his failures. Although the group itself may have had no religious role in the earliest rites, the linear B tablets from Pylos suggest that by the late Mycenaean period there were different kinds of religious functionaries and ceremonies in which the town or public played some part.[6]

After the Mycenaean kingdoms were destroyed (c.1200-1100 B.C.E.), kingship as such disappeared. At first communities were controlled by noble families who divided up the duties once performed by the king. Gradually the place where the nobles and commons met to market, muster for defense, or settle disputes developed an identity of its own which warranted loyalty and a divine protector. The city-state which emerged as the central authority retained most earlier institutions. In some places, temples to patron deities were built on the ruins of palaces of Mycenaean kings (e.g., Athens, Tiryns). The wealth once used to glorify kings, however, was now spent on houses and honors for the divinities identified with all members of the community.

Noble families usually kept control of the festivals and cults founded by their ancestors. In Sparta, hereditary kings functioned as priests in the developed state. In Athens, the archon basileus, the king archon elected for a one-year term, performed the oldest religious rites which may have once been the duty of the ancient kings. The city-state, as a community ruled by its citizens, also instituted its own new cults and festivals. In Athens, the archon eponymous, who gave his name to his year of office, regulated these as part of his many political duties. So long as the aristocracy controlled the state by monopolizing the archonships and the council of elders, the Areopagus, which conducted most of the state business, the aristocracy also probably controlled public religion. As the democracy developed in fifth century Athens, however, the people gained much more authority over religion by virtue of the power of the assembly (Ekklesia) and council (Boule) to oversee annual executives, control state finances, and maintain public safety. In religious matters, the *demos* followed the same general policy as in deliberative and legislative affairs, diffusing authority so that it was, in the words of Robert Garland, "shared out among a number of groups comprising amateurs as well as experts, priests as well as 'laity', with no one group [acting] wholly on its own initiative without reference to or consultation with at least one other group."[7]

The evolution from kingship to participatory government was replicated in changes in the actual practice of religion.[8] After the demise of the kings, there was no single human being who mediated between the gods and the common people. Leaders of various social or political groups—heads of families, magistrates of cities, generals of armies—all officiated at the rites of their respective organizations. In fact, anyone including women and slaves could perform a sacrifice or utter prayers, vows, and curses. The diverse public rites which developed involved the participation of all members of the community and promoted the unity of the different segments of society which had joined together to form the polis.[9]

Despite the fact that most Greek-speaking communities acknowledged the same major deities, defined, and organized into families by such Panhellenic poets as Homer and Hesiod, each separate place imbued the common pantheon with characteristics, legends, and cult practices important to its own locale. Moreover, individuals could choose to be initiated into mystery cults whose secret rituals provided some spiritual direction, dogma, and hope for an afterlife (see Chapter 10).

Such pluralism did not produce a monolithic religion supervised by a single religious leader or priesthood. Nor did it develop a clearly articulated tradition like the Bible or Talmud to spell out the rules for ritual correctness or interpret the symbolism behind cult actions and objects. Information about Greek practice is sporadic and derives from ancient art, artifacts, literature, and inscriptions which require interpretation and conjecture by modern scholars. From the immense and varied religious life suggested by such sources, we can present only a few general features of Greek piety in action for comparison with Hebrew patterns of worship.

Sacred People: Priests and Priestesses

There was no class or caste of priests in Greece corresponding to the Levite priesthood in Israel. There were, however, various individuals who were called *hiereis* or *hiereiai*, priests or priestesses, i.e., sacred men or women who, in Plato's words (*Statesman 290*), "according to law and custom know how to give the gods, by means of sacrifices, the gifts that please them for us and by prayers to ask for us the gain of good things from them".[10] They had no corporate identity, for they were associated only with specific cults and shrines, with their gender most often corresponding to the deity they served. Each person was known as the priest or priestess of _____ and had very narrowly defined functions related only to that particular deity and shrine, as the official intermediary between the god of that place and the people who came to pray and sacrifice there. Being a priest was a part time job, not a way of life. An official could occasionally hold more than one such office at one time.[11] The term of office varied according to the custom of the cult and could last a year, a festal cycle, or even a lifetime.[12]

Unlike the Levite priests and modern clergy, the priests and priestesses of Greece were neither teachers, judges, nor spiritual leaders. Rather they were the individuals who supervised the activities conducted at their particular sanctuary. It was their function to serve the god, that is, to take charge of the religious property and the religious rituals conducted there. They tended the statue which represented the deity, washing, clothing, and protecting it. They offered sacrifices on the community's behalf at regular intervals and assisted individuals who came there to sacrifice for themselves or as representatives of others. Although they sometimes had assistants such as professional immolators (*thuteis* or *hierothuteis*), the priests themselves had to vow the victim to sacrifice, and recite the prayer which accompanied the offering, as well as assure the exact observance of the ritual, on which the validity of the sacrifice depended.[13] There were various other kinds of attendants at the shrines, but not all of them seem to have had the status of priest or priestess.

Some sanctuaries were the sites of activities similar to those conducted by the priests of Israel. Oracles, discussed in chapter 6, were pronounced by certain priests or priestesses in special shrines such as Delphi where the god was believed to be literally present to respond through his prophet to questions posed by individuals or states. Divination by lot also occurred in these shrines, often with a priest or priestess officiating. In contrast to Israel, however, where only the High Priest used the lot he bore on his breastplate, knucklebones were commonly kept on holy tables in Greek temples to be thrown as lots by worshippers themselves.[14]

As in Israel, so in Greece, disease was attributed to supernatural causes and those servants of the gods who knew how to propitiate and purify were sought after by communities endangered by epidemics and individuals in need of healing. Greek tradition records the appearance of mantics associated with Apollo who were able to cure plague by means of purifications and rituals. The shrines of Asklepios, the son of Apollo, however, became the particular sanctuaries where the sick were treated when they came, purified themselves by ritual baths and sacrifices, and then slept overnight on sacred ground.[15] Here again the priests were responsible for the properties and the supervision of the rituals, with the assistance of a number of attendants. The priests also interpreted the dreams sent by the god as cures to the sleeping patients and effected the remedies indicated by the dreams, if the god himself or his servant did not miraculously heal the sufferer during the night. Often the priest had a colleague with some medical skill who administered the cure (surgery, drugs, applications of drugs or snakes, magnetism), while the priest attended to the proper observance of ritual. As medicine became more scientific, the physician gradually took over the actual healing, replacing the one-night miracle with extended treatments consisting of baths, exercise, diet, and relaxation. Grateful patients, throughout the history of the cult, left testimonials of their cures as offerings at the sanctuaries. Even when the doctors traveled from city to city or made house calls, they still associated themselves with the god and the temples, calling themselves Sons of Asklepios. The votive offerings and records of illnesses, cures, and remedies kept at the shrines contributed significantly to the training of doctors and the development of scientific medicine.

Priests and priestesses of the different cults were chosen in different ways. In some cases, the offices belonged to a particular *genos* or family. The priest of Erechtheus-Poseidon and the priestess of Athens Polias, who administered the main cults on the Athenian acropolis, always came from the family of the Eteoboutidae who traced their ancestry back to the brother of the first king Erechtheus. The Eumolpidae, descendants of Eumolpus, one of the mythical founders of the Eleusinian Mysteries, provided the hierophants (priest-teachers) of the cult at Eleusis, whereas the descendants of his son Keryx, the Kerykes, were eligible to become the torchbearer and the sacred herald of their festivals.[16] When Clisthenes in the late sixth century reorganized Athens, he left the old hereditary priesthoods of the four legendary tribes and ancient demes alone (as Plato's lawgiver would later recommend at *Laws* 759b). In such hereditary offices, the succession generally moved from the eldest brother to youngest and then sons of the eldest, although lot, which was believed to express divine will, was sometimes employed.[17]

If no family was associated with the ancient traditions, the priest was selected by different means. Plato, in *Laws* 759b, recommended both election and allotment from an approved slate of candidates. When Clisthenes created new cults for his ten new tribes, he made those new priestly offices annual and appointed by lot. Feaver suggests that Clisthenes' reforms removed the hereditary priesthoods from political power while opening the new priesthoods to all classes of Athenian citizens. This democratization of cult continued with the development of the democracy. The new priesthoods of the gods Bendis and Asklepios, adopted by Athens in the last quarter of the fifth century, were chosen by lot "from all the Athenians." The choice of the priest of Asklepios followed the democratic practice most closely; the allotment rotated from tribe to tribe according to the official order of tribes.[18] In Hellenistic times, more than fifty priesthoods were auctioned in Asia Minor. An inscription from the island of Chios the priesthood begins, "The man who purchases the priesthood shall purchase it for life, provided he continues to live in the city."[19]

There were few requirements for priesthood. The priests' knowledge, derived from custom and sacred law, could be easily learned from observation and participation. In fact, Isocrates remarked in *Nemean Oration* 7.23, "Any man is thought qualified to be a priest." Plato, however, advised (*Laws* 759) that no one under sixty should be considered capable of administering divine things. Although very few positions demanded life-long celibacy or real asceticism beyond the special initiation rites at installation or while officiating, every administrator of the sacred had to be as pure as the sanctuary itself. As "a kind of walking temple," the *hiereus* or *hiereia* had to be free from any physical defect, unpolluted personally, and from paternal and maternal households free from pollution such as homicide or other crimes against the divine.[20] In addition, he or she had to avoid contact with natural pollution related to birth and death. Inscriptions reveal what these restrictions meant in practice: e.g., at Cos a priest or priestess could not enter a house of birth, death or miscarriage for a prescribed period, and could neither ignore or touch the corpse of a suicide (a passerby had to be summoned.) As an intermediary between the community and the deity, he or she also had to be an outstanding representative of the group and a full citizen (for three generations, according to one inscription).[21]

The position of priest or priestess brought perquisites in the form of gifts and honors.[22] In accordance with ancient custom, the sacrificer received some kind of payment—food, skin of the sacrificed animal, coins left in a collection box, or even a salary. In early times, the priest's person was consecrated and his robes untouchable by profane hands. His appearance set him apart: long hair bound by a band, a garland, white or purple robes with a special waistband, a staff in his hand. In *Moralia* "Table Talk," 4.6 "Who the god of Jews is," Plutarch compares the robe of the priest of Dionysus to the High Priest of the Jews: each wears a mitre, a gold embroidered fawn skin, a gown reaching his ankles, and buskins, with bells attached to his clothes which ring as he walks (672).

Such a person deserved respect and reverence from the community. In legend all the Greeks suffered plague for Agamemnon's rejection of the priest of Apollo at Troy, whereas Odysseus received a valuable gift of wine for sparing the priest when he sacked Ismaros. Alexander the Great, after the capture of Thebes, protected its priests and priestesses from becoming part of the victors' spoils (Plutarch, *Alexander*, 11). At Athens, some priests received the same high honors granted to other officials: public maintenance in the Prytaneion, special seats in the theater, even crowns. But as the democracy developed, they were no longer sacrosanct; they were subject to the official public examination after their year of service and to the same kinds of litigation as other citizens.[23]

Some men were considered the guardians of religious tradition and customary sacred law. The hierophants at Eleusis taught the secrets of the mysteries to the initiates. At Athens there were people called exegetes, who, advised individuals enquiring about proper procedures for such matters as sacrifice, purification, or funeral rites.[24] In Plato's dialogue, Euthyphro's father inquired of one such interpreter about what to do with a slave who had killed a farmhand in a drunken brawl. Theophrastus' superstitious man (*Characters* 16.6) consulted an exegete every time a mouse, sacred to Apollo, nibbled through a bag of barley groats.

Traditions about three separate boards (*exegetai pythocrestoi, ex Eumolpidon*, and *ex eupatridon*) in Athens are confusing.[25] Most scholars agree, however, that: exegetes were not priests involved in the actual performance of ritual or service of a deity; they were not diviners or mantics interpreting the will of the gods from signs or oracles; and they were not "students of divinity," articulating the spiritual or intellectual aspects of pious behavior.[26] Jacoby doubts that the exegetes qua exegetes had any political influence or any secular legal expertise. For the evidence about the exegetes comes from the period when, in contrast to biblical law and the Hebrew priesthood's connection with it,

> [Greek] secular and sacred law were as widely separated as is altogether possible in an-ancient state: justice itself is secular; those who wish to do so can confine themselves to this secular law, while those who are pious are equally free to consult an exegetes when they find this desirable or necessary.[27]

Sacred Space

Temenos, Temple, and Image— Ancient Greece abounded with holy places, areas which were set aside as consecrated either because sacred acts were performed there or because the power of deity was sensed in the surroundings. Archaeological remains of sacrifices reveal that many places were considered holy long before they were connected with any particular deity and long before temples were built there.[28]   As in ancient Israel, so too in Greece, mountains were especially associated with the divine and rites were held either on their tops or in the shadows of their peaks. Caves too or the rounded tombs of ancestors (*tholoi*) were consecrated as homes of the spirits of the dead and the powers of the earth and underworld. Rivers and springs were also holy, as well as certain trees. As in the Israel of the patriarchs, pillars or stones glistening with oil served to mark a sacred center or a place of epiphany. Some sanctuaries have been found within Mycenaean palaces and a few Mycenaean buildings have been called temples because they appear to be religious complexes. Remains in the central hearth of both palaces and individual dwellings indicate its consecration as the sacred center of domestic life.

In historical times, three standard features articulated Greek sacred space: (1) the temenos with (2) an altar for burning sacrifices and (3) a temple to house a cult image.[29]   The temenos was an area "cut off" and marked as sacred and separated from its profane surroundings by a boundary stone or a high stone wall with only one entrance which was often gated. As holy ground it had to remain pure and free from pollution.[30]   Water basins were set up at its entrances so that worshippers could dip their hands in and sprinkle themselves before passing through. Normal activities of daily life were suspended within it. No one tainted by sexual intercourse, birth or death could enter. Hippolytus' description of the inviolate grove of Artemis depicts the sacred place as the physical representation of his patroness's chaste purity and the moral equivalent of his own pursuit of virtue.[31]

> No shepherd dares to feed his flock within it.
> No reaper plies a busy scythe within it.
> Only the bees in springtime harvest the inviolate meadow
> its gardener is the spirit Reverence who
> refreshes it with water from the river
> . . . in whose very soul the seed
> of Chastity toward all things alike
> nature has deeply rooted, they alone may
> gather flowers there: the wicked may not.
> (75-81, Grene, trans.)

Ritual cleansing was associated with spiritual purification. Hesiod, for example, warned those crossing a river to "wash wickedness and their hands" (*Works and Days*, 737-740) and Hippolytus, after hearing a proposition about incest, wants to wash his ears in a flowing stream (653).

The temenos often contained the same features which marked the sacred spot earlier.[32] The navel stone at Delphi is the most famous example of the rock as a sign, but there were many others, e.g., an unhewn rock at Eleusis. Trees associated with the deity and the place might also be found there; Apollo's sanctuary at Delos contained the palm tree on which it was said his mother leaned while giving birth to him. Often there was a whole grove of trees within or just outside the wall, as at Olympia where the temenos was called the Altis or Grove. Perhaps the rustling of the leaves, the songs of birds, and the protective shade suggested the presence of the supernatural. Antigone recognized the sanctity of the grove of the Eumenides:

> . . . it is clearly a holy place
> Shady with vines and olive trees and laurel
> A covert for the song and hush of nightingales
> In their snug wings. But rest on this rough stone.
> (Sophocles, *Oedipus at Colonus*, 16-19, Fitzgerald, Trans.)

Springs and fountains too were situated within or nearby. At Delphi, the Kassiotis spring flowed into the sanctuary while the Castilian fountain poured down the rocks just outside it.

The temenos' most essential element, however, was the altar on which the sacrificial fire was kindled.[33] In most places it remained the center of cult activity even if a temple and image were added. The altar could be made of natural rock, stones piled together, or just mounds of remains of ash and bones, as at the altar of Zeus at Olympia. Sometimes it was constructed of bricks or hewn stones, its sides decorated with volutes, and its center containing a metal tablet for the fire. Usually altars were rectangular, although irregular or round ones have been found. The larger ones were built on a podium and had steps for the priest to reach the top.

Often the temenos included a temple as well, behind the altar with a great tall doorway open to it so that the cult image within could watch the activities performed in its honor.[34] By the seventh century, the Greek temple achieved its standard form: a rectangular tile-roofed building about one hundred feet long, generally facing east, resting on a platform raised three steps. The center of the temple was the *naos* (room or *cella*) which contained the image set on a pedestal, an incense stand, a table of offerings, and sometimes an eternal flame. Some temples also contained altars for burnt offerings inside as well.[35] Most temples had a *pronaos* or front porch; some had an inner room or *adyton* with restricted access, and an *opisthodomos* or back porch. A colonnade surrounded the *naos*. The sculptural decorations on the pediments and friezes above and sometimes inside the colonnade were highlighted with red and blue paint to help worshippers perceive the details as they looked up from below. Differences in the space between the external columns and the *naos* and greater sculptural detail on some rear porches suggest that different kinds of activities took place within and just outside different temples.[36] The presence of ramps at some (e.g., Olympia, Delphi), for crowds moving in and out, indicate that the *naos* was used for more than just housing the image.

The images which looked out from within have no counterpart in Ancient Israel where idolatry was considered a sin. In Greece, the oldest and most sacred representatives of well-known duties were the *xoana*, so called because they were made of wood.[37] The first Hera at Samos and the Artemis at Icaros were simple wooden planks, but later ones were carved out as seated (e.g., the olive wood Athena Polias) or standing (e.g., the second Hera at Samos) anthropomorphic figures. Some were thought to have fallen from heaven (the Palladion, Athena Polias, the Artemis of Tauris) and great attention was paid to keeping them, their garments, and their temples pure.[38]

The image had some of the ambiguous powers associated with the ark in ancient Israel. The festival day when Athena Polias was moved to the sea for bathing was considered *apophras*, unlucky and impure, a day on which no other cult activity or serious business transpired. Scholars attribute the fear to various beliefs: either the image itself was in need of purification, or its protective power was leaving the city, or moving an image so fraught with divinity could be extremely dangerous.[39] According to Plutarch, when the image of Artemis of Pellene was moved by the priestess and carried about, all averted their eyes "for not only to mankind is its image awful and grievous, but even trees it causes to become barren and cast their fruit wherever it is carried" (*Aratus* 32).

As the technologies of casting bronze and sculpting marble developed, more elaborate statues were produced, either as votive gifts or as new cult images for new temples.[40] The Athena Parthenos and the Zeus of Olympia, both by Phidias, represented the zenith of the form. Their faces, arms, and feet were covered with ivory, their clothing plated with gold, and their eyes set with precious stones. The seated figure of Zeus was said to be so large that if he stood up from his throne, he would have broken through the roof (Strabo, 8.354). The throne itself was elaborately sculpted.

Such images were considered as works of talented men, *agalmata* (pleasing gifts) constructed to delight the gods, not as gods in themselves. According to Pausanias, Zeus showed his pleasure in Phidias' statue of him by flashing lightning in response to the sculptor's prayer as he finished the work. Pausanias had seen the bronze urn marking the spot where the lightning struck (5.11.9). The sight of such images gleaming in the darkened *naos* inspired the piety and reverence of those who had entered to admire or pray. Quintilian believed that the beauty of Phidias' Zeus "added something even to the awe (*religio*) with which the god was already regarded; so perfectly did the majesty of the work give the impression of godhead" (12.10.8-9).

From a simple temenos marked by an altar and a stone, tree, or spring some precincts developed into large sanctuaries with altars and temples to more than one Olympian deity and pits and hearths for the worship of chthonic powers and ancestors.[41]   By the end of the fifth century, the Athenian acropolis, for example, had altars to both Zeus and Athena, as well as two temples to Athena (the Parthenon and the Erechthion), a temple to Athena Nike (Victory) and a temple to Brauronian Artemis, and smaller walled precincts to Pandrosus and Erechthius, plus an Armory and a house for the Arrephoroi, the two young girs who served Athena for a year. From the Propylaea, the elaborate entrance to the sacred precinct, the worshippers' eyes would be drawn to the huge outdoor sculpture of Athena Promachos, also by Phidias, on the same axis as the altar of Athena, with her two temples forming the background for the activities conducted in the open air.

The major sanctuary was only one among many sacred places in any given area.[42]   In Athens, for example, the festival processions which moved through the city along the Sacred Way to the Acropolis would have passed by such spaces as a consecrated well, an altar to Aphrodite Urania and an altar to the Twelve Gods in the Agora, the Eleusinion, the hill where the cave of Apollo was situated under the Propylaea, and the Areopagus which contained altars to Ares, and the caves of the Eumenides, invited to guard Athens by Athena herself. Nor were these the only sacred spaces in the city where every deme and tribe had its own patrons and shrines, and every locale had its own groves to heroes (e.g., Academus, Lycus), nature divinities, and ancestors.

Symbolism and Sacred Center— The symbolism associated with the sacred place is not as clearly articulated as in the Sinai tradition. Certain mountains were important to the Greeks, whether they were viewed as homes of the gods, points of contact with them, or the breasts or mons of Mother Earth.[43]   Thus many sacred places were chosen in part because of their proximity to a mountain. The shrine of Delphi, for example, was built on a col of Mt. Parnassus.   Vincent Scully considers that Mt. Parnassus, with its rocky gorges, horned peaks, cloud-covered summits, and the caves, valleys, and rivers below, is a visual correlative to the myth of conflict between the Olympian and Chthonic gods expressed in Apollo' struggles with the Python and the Furies.[44]   Proximity to the seas on the other hand, determined the site of shrines to Poseidon; his temples, e.g., at Paestum or Sunium, were built on promontories overlooking the water.   Shrines to chthonic deities or heroes were more likely to be situated near caves or in man-made pits.

Natural features cannot explain everything, however.   An acropolis like the one at Athens offered a good position for the defense of an area.   Both Olympia, described as reflecting "absolute order and calm" and Delphi, with its more turbulent ambiance, probably developed into great panhellenic shrines as much because of their distance and independence from any of the powerful Greek city-states as because of a natural setting symbolically associated with the divine.[45]

Most sanctuaries appear to have grown in a haphazard way rather than according to a plan which permitted descending degrees of sanctity emanating from the holiest center.   The individual Greek sacred spaces took shape over centuries in which new cults were added to old and new buildings had to conform both to the particular natural features and the unique demands of traditional piety.   The Erechthion, for example, was built as the new home for the Athena Polias after its temple was destroyed by the Persians. Its position was moved slightly from the site of the old temple in order to be in balance with the location of the recently built Parthenon and Propylaea as well as the ancient Altar of Athena. Because the ground it was built on was so irregular and contained the shrines to Pandrosos and Erectheus, as well as the salt pool of Poseidon, and the sacred olive of Athena, the temple itself has a very irregular shape.[46]   Mt. Parnassus was so steep and its ledges so narrow that Delphi's development was determined by the shape of the open spaces.   Yet, wherever possible, the temples themselves seem to have been intentionally oriented toward the East, as in their Semitic counterparts, to face the rising sun on the dawn of the particular deity's feast day, according to Scully.[47]   The sacrificial altar faced the sun as well so that the participants looked to the east toward the open sky.   The background scenes of mountain peaks above and around and, often, sacred waters beyond and below, interacted with each of the man-made features to create an all encompassing divine ambiance[48]

Many of the sanctuaries embodied the same symbolism of the sacred center as the Jerusalem temple, albeit in different ways. The navel stone at Delphi marked not only the center of the shrine, but also the center of the earth. The geographical center of Athens was also a sacrificial center; distances within and outside the city were measured from the Altar of the Twelve Gods set up in the agora at the end of the sixth century. On the Acropolis at Athens both the sacred olive tree and a salt pool left open to the sky, legendary gifts of Athena and Poseidon, linked the spot with the heavens above, the earth, and the underworld and waters below.

The same kind of symbolism can be seen in the hearth fixed to the ground, but leading to the sky through an open lantern in the roof. This center of the family's life, where meals and major events such as birth, marriage, death, and kinship with strangers were consecrated, was personified as the goddess Hestia "and marked the axis through which all parts of the universe are joined. Many city-states, e.g., Delphi, Sparta, Athens, established community hearths, often in round buildings. In Athens, this *Hestia Koine* became the political center of the democracy, linking every hearth in the polis without elevating any one family in particular.[50]

Sometimes the sanctuary was linked to creation as well to the cosmos as a whole. In Athens in the sanctuary of the Olympian Earth, there was a chasm where it was said that the waters of Deucalion's flood had disappeared. At the Hydrophoria, or Water Drawing Festival, a procession of girls poured water down it to those who had died in the god-sent deluge which nearly destroyed the earth. According to Pausanias, the Athenians asserted that Deucalion had built the sanctuary of Olympian Zeus and exhibited the tomb of survivors of the flood nearby (1.18.78). Pisistratus chose this spot, with its symbolism of the new creation, for constructing his temple to Zeus (not completed until Roman times).

As in the Jerusalem temple, the embellishments without and within turned the temple into a miniature world. The colors suggested the sky and earth; tree like columns stretched heavenward from the ground. The sculpture linked the spot and the patron deity with the cosmos and creation. The throne of Phidias' Zeus, for example, was elaborately sculpted with important figures such as the sun and the moon, Hermes and Hestia, Aphrodite and Eros, and Amphitrite and Poseidon, connecting the chief gods with major powers in the macrocosm and microcosm while illustrating

Zeus' control over them. Phidias' Athena stands on a pedestal which depicts Pandora's release of misery and evil into the world, symbolizing the power of wisdom, daughter of Zeus, over the negative forces of creation.

But the Greek temple also illustrated the relationship of mortal and city to gods and cosmos by means of its sculpture. On the Parthenon, for example, metopes showing the Trojan War, the battle of the Lapiths and Centaurs, the fight between the Athenians and the Amazons, and the triumph of the gods over the giants link the city and its legendary heroes with the gods while symbolizing the Athenian victory over the Persians and the triumph of reason over barbarity. The West Pediment recreated the contest of Athena and Poseidon for the patronage of Athens, honoring the divine sources of the contemporary city's naval and commercial power. On the east pediment appeared the miraculous birth of Athena, symbolic of the birth of Athens as the leader of Greece. The frieze inside the colonnade was unusual in Greek religious sculpture, for it featured the inhabitants of Athens themselves, moving in their various ceremonial roles in a great religious processional, towards the gods who are themselves shown on the east frieze above the front entrance, watching their worshippers approach them. Here sacred time and present moment, mortal and immortal, sacred place and cosmos were linked together forever in the sculptural representation of the festival.[51]

The temples provided the opportunity for individual architects, sculptors and citizens to win personal glory for their talent or magnanimity. The names of Phidias, Polygnotus, and Ictinus are almost as well-known today as the names of the famous Greek playwrights and poets, and Pericles is nearly as closely associated with the Athenian Acropolis as Athena herself is. But these mortals achieved everlasting fame because their creations embodied the grandeur of the immortals they worshipped. Five hundred years later, Plutarch, admiring the temples and sculpture commissioned by Pericles, remarked

> A bloom of eternal freshness hovers over these works of his
> and preserves them from the touch of time, as if some
> unfading spirit of youth, some ageless vitality had been
> breathed into them. (*Pericles*, 13; Scott-Kilvert, trans.)[52]

Access and Taboo— The concept of *temenos* as an area "cut off" has been considered to derive as much from custom and law which protects one individual's honor, person, and property from another's as from beliefs in the absolute otherness of the divine or the complete separation of sacred from profane.[53] Therefore, unlike the Jerusalem temple, most Greek sanctuaries were open and public; although they were marked by a wall, they permitted access to indoor images and cult objects as well as outdoor events. The altar on which the sacrifice was burned remained the focus of the cult, and the sacrifices, whether indoors or outside the temple, required the presence and participation of the individuals offering the sacrifice, even though a priest officiated. The temples and the objects within were most often dedications, offerings made to please the gods. Therefore, they were not generally the hub of holiness separated off by taboos, as in the Jerusalem temple.

There were some degrees of sanctity associated with location in certain Greek sacred spaces, however. The Telesterion, or hall of imitation into the Eleusinian Mysteries, contained a smaller room, the Anaktoron, which only the hierophant (chief priest) could enter. It probably housed the old wooden image of Demeter and was important in the secret culminating initiation rite.[54] The temple of Apollo at Delphi also had an inner room, an *adyton*, reserved for the Pythian priestess.[55] There were also restrictions on access to some sanctuaries or the temples within them. *Abata* were places to which entry was absolutely forbidden, e.g., lands and tombs of people struck by lightning, the grove of the Eumenides at Colonus. The chorus in Sophocles' play describe their terror of such a place.

> . . . for he'd never
> dare to go in there
> in the inviolate thicket
> of those whom it's futile to fight,
> those whom we tremble to name.
>
> When we pass we avert our eyes -
> close our eyes!
> In silence, without conversation
> shaping our prayers with our lips
> (125-32, Fitzgerald, trans.)

Pausanias knew about a precinct of Lycaeon Zeus on Mount Lycaeon which no person was allowed to enter on pain of certain death within the year (8.36.6). Parker suggests that extreme restrictions derive more from "protection against the universe's destructive and avenging powers" than from the notion "that absolute holiness implies absolute inaccessibility."[56] The taboos on touch, sight, and sound protected the passer from attracting the divine energy, as in the Jerusalem temple.

Other kinds of restrictions have been separated into various categories by scholars.[57]   (1) In many places, admission or viewing was granted only on feast days.   Pausanias arrived at the sanctuary of Mother Dindymene in Thebes on the one day of the year it was open (9.25.3) whereas he missed seeing the shrine of Artemis at Hyampolis which was open only two days a year (10.35.4).   (2) In other cults, all but the sanctified few were excluded from the shrine; e.g., only a young woman who may never go with a man again and a virgin consecrated for a year could enter the sanctuary of Aphrodite at Sicyon.   (3) Certain shrines were open to those on special business only, e.g., the rite of *incubatio* (sleeping inside the Temple of a god like Asklepios) or consulting an oracle.   (4) Several temples granted admission according to sex; e.g., most cults of Ares were open to males only.   (5) Certain nationalities were excluded from others: e.g., Dorians from the temple of Athena in Athens.   Some exclusions were very specific: e.g., those who had eaten a certain food or were wearing certain garments.

Scholars can only speculate on the reasons for the taboos. Hewitt contends that some restrictions derive from cults that originated in the Near East and were connected to chthonic and fertility deities.[58] Parker notes that exclusions according to gender and class replicated the division of labor and status in society as a whole.[59] Some objects were forbidden out of a concern for purity, but context frequently affected this restriction.[60]   The pomegranate was taboo in one festival of Demeter and the focus of the rite in another. Alluring purple gowns were not in themselves impure, but were out of place in festivals requiring women to renounce sex (e.g., Peloponnesian cults of Demeter). From the very specificity of most of the categories, Corbett concludes that people in the right categories who arrived when a shrine was open were able to enter unchallenged.[61]

Breaking the rules was, of course, sacrilegious and dangerous. That which was polluted had to be purified and perpetrators were punished by the gods, their human agents, or the laws. The chorus gives Oedipus minute instructions on how to make expiation for his unwitting entrance into the grove of the Eumenides at Colonus (469-89).   Tradition records tales of violations that provoked instant reciprocity.[62]   Miltiades, for example, when in desperate need of money, was enticed to enter a shrine of Demeter, whose mysteries were forbidden to men. Retreating in terror before he reached the temple, he fell, injured his leg, and died from the wound (Herodotus 6.134-6).   The Persians' sack of the Athenian acropolis confirmed their impiety as well as their barbarity; their defeat was viewed as a punishment for their profanation.

The law also punished crimes against the gods and the things consecrated to them.[63] With so many valuables stored in the sanctuaries as offerings, temple robbing was a capital crime and citizens were forbidden burial in their native land. The felling of olive trees sacred to Athena was also punishable by death, even if those trees were growing on private property. Citizens could also be tried for impiety. The desecration of the Herms and the public parodying of the secret Eleusinian mysteries on the eve of the Sicilian expedition resulted in a witchhunt in Athens in which several defendants were executed and Alcibiades was condemned *in absentia*. Although certain politicians manipulated the situation, the people's anxiety was genuine; impiety and an impious leader could doom not only the expedition but the future of the polis.

All the prohibitions and punishments functioned to maintain the distinction between men and gods, as symbolic action equivalent to the tales of hubristic heroes who transgressed mortal limits.[64] The community believed that honoring the distinction was vital to its survival. It feared both the physical danger associated with divine wrath and the social chaos engendered by disrespect for the moral codes the gods upheld. Odysseus made the connection between piety and morality when he wondered about the Phaeacians: "Are they full of hubris and savage and unjust /Or kind to strangers with god fearing attitudes?"*(Od 6.120-21)*. Tragic sinners like Aeschylus' Xerxes and Agamemnon also polluted consecrated objects. That justice was exacted for violation of law and custom proved the existence of the gods and the efficacy of worship. The chorus of *Oedipus the King* prayed that the lawbreakers and the proud be punished for: " Where such deeds are held in honor/ Why should I honor the gods in dance?" (895-6, Grene, trans.)

Sacred Acts in Sacred Time

The Theban chorus' words, "honor the gods with dance", remind us that many acts which we now think of as secular and associate with Greek humanism or aesthetics, e.g., dance, music, poetry, drama, and athletics, were actually Greek forms of worship. As in Hebrew worship, they derived from the most ancient religious rituals surrounding the sacrifice, rain, and fertility magic, and the banishment of evil from the community. Other activities which have been excluded from our solemn religious ceremonies— obscenity, scatology, insult—were also part of the oldest ways to worship. Over time the Greeks transformed some of their rituals, which were precise and formulaic repetitions, into ever-new exhibitions of human physical, intellectual, and artistic skills to honor and entertain the gods and to provide, according to Aristotle, "pleasant relaxation for themselves" (*Nic. Eth* 8.1160.23-4).

The great festivals (called *synodoi* or goings-together; *panegyreis* or assemblies; *heortai* or holidays) were closely connected to the political and secular institutions of their founders.[65] Each city-state had its own festal calendar regulating the sequence of celebrations and separating out the sacred time. Civilian officials supervised preparations and events whereas citizens participated at all levels, marching in sacred processions, competing for prizes in various contests, or setting up business to accommodate those who attended. The city-states certainly used these occasions to engender feelings of harmony and patriotism. To a modern outsider, such celebrations might resemble our own secular holidays - the Rose Bowl on New Year's Day, the Fourth of July, or Labor Day Weekend.

To the Greeks, however, they were also holy days. The festivals took place in the sacred spaces reserved for the gods only during the sacred time set apart for their worship. Every festival included the same kinds of activities associated with priestly piety in Israel - sacrifice, offerings, prayers, processions, purification rituals, and rituals which commemorated events in the sacred past of myth and legend. In addition, "pleasant relaxation" was considered a gift from the gods and an *imitatio dei*, much as the Jewish Sabbath is both a required day of rest and an imitation of God's activity on the seventh day. As Plato explains,

> So taking pity on the suffering that is natural to the human race, the gods have ordained the change of holidays as times of rest from labor. They have given as fellow celebrants the Muses, with their leader Apollo, and Dionysus—in order that these divinities might set humans right again (Plato, *Laws* 2.653D, Pangle, trans.).

The Organization of Sacred Time— The religious activity of each community was regulated according to its own sacred calendar. The normal year was divided into twelve lunar months of 30 or 29 days alternately, beginning at the approximately time of the new moon, with an intercalary month inserted periodically to make the calendar year correspond with the solar year.[66] The holidays were distributed throughout the year on fixed dates, on the same day of the same month. Festivals were sometimes called *hieromenia* or "sacred months", a term which indicates that time, like space, people, and cult objects, was set apart as sacred.[67] During *hieromenia* communities restricted profane activities to insure that the religious obligations of the entire community could be fulfilled and that peace and harmony prevailed (v. Demosthenes 21. *Against Meidias*).[68] *Hieromenia* often prevented the Spartans from taking the field, whereas the Athenians conducted festivals at home while their armies and navies were away on campaigns. Sacred truces announced by heralds, like sacred spaces and priests, were generally respected by enemies, especially for panhellenic festivals, but surprise attacks during local festivals argue against a general ban on warfare during sacred occasion.[69]

In Athens, about which scholars have the most information, the sacred year began at midsummer with the new moon after the summer solstice, in the month called Hecatombion. Burkert analyzes the cluster of annual festivals at the end of the year and the first month of Hecatombian as forming a unit which cleansed, renewed and reconstituted the community, culminating in the Pan-Athenaia as the great New Year's festival, reminiscent of Near Eastern celebrations though lacking their cosmic dimensions.[70] By the end of the fifth century, the civil calendar corresponded to the religious calendar. On the last day of the last month, the citizens sacrificed to Zeus Savior and Athena Savior, the protectors of the city, and the archon basileus led the other magistrates and Council to a sacrifice thanking Zeus for preserving the city in their year of office and praying for the protection of next year's officials.[71] At the new year, the new archons took their oath of office.

Most scholars believe, however, that there was no special attention paid to the new year as such. Some consider the eight year cycle in which the lunar and solar years were brought into correspondence as an important unit which was referred to as the Great Year; after 776, the non-local festivals were organized on a 4-year cycle which halved the Great Years.[72] Others judge the month the most meaningful unit because there were several important monthly holidays. The new moon was marked by processions, banquets and private gifts of incense at the statues of the gods. The second day was sacred to the *agathos daimon*, a chthonic deity, and the third, fourth, sixth, seventh, and eighth honored the days of the month on which important gods and goddesses were born.[73] Parker views the turning points of the year and the month as significant times marked by ceremonies of purification and renewal.[74] During the month of Thargelion, at the beginning of summer and the harvest, the Athenians celebrated the Thargelia which included practices similar to the Hebrews: the marching around with tree branches and a scapegoat (*pharmakos*) ritual (found elsewhere in Greece) where disreputable men were selected and then driven out.[75] On the next day, new fire arrived from Delphi. In Maimakterion six months later, at the beginning of winter and ploughing, several lesser-known expulsion and renewal rites took place. Every new moon and the mid-month after it also occasioned such public and private purifications.

Almost every month also had an important annual festival.[76] Some corresponded to the actual activities of the agricultural year: e.g., a pre-plowing festival, *Proerosia*, a winter festival, the Haloa, on the threshing floor, with sacrifices to earth to promote growth, festivals of sprouting, shooting, and blossoming when the grain was growing, and the pre-harvest Thargelia. As in ancient Israel, many of the seasonal festivals also commemorated activities of gods and heroes in the sacred past; several rituals of the Anthesteria, or blossoming festival, refer back to the time when Dionysus introduced the grape to Athens. The city's largest and grandest festivals, the Panathenaia, the Eleusinian Mysteries, and the City Dionysia, were held after the periods of greatest labor when the citizens had the leisure to celebrate.

Although the festival year does not seem to trace an annual waxing, waning, and rebirth at the new year, many of the individual holidays contain the same pattern. At the Anthesteria the new wine from last year's grape harvest was drunk on the second day with rituals to ward off and appease the spirits of the dead which were connected to myths about guilt and atonement (i.e., Orestes and Ikarios). The third day began that night with a sacred marriage between the cult figure of Dionysus and the Archon basileus' wife and the events of the next day were merry; the community ate a stew commemorating the first meal of the survivors of the flood and celebrated the renewal with swinging contests. Burkert compares the sequence to Good Friday followed by Easter.[77] The movement from tragedy to comedy in the dramatic festival follows the same pattern.

General Practices of Piety— Sacrifices, as the most important way of honoring the gods, played a central role in every holy day as well as solemnizing significant secular activity. Although the rites differed according to occasion and place, all followed the same general pattern of events.[78] Participants representing both sexes, from different age groups and occupations, separated themselves from daily life by washing and putting on fresh clothes and an adornment such as a garland or fillet and then led the sacrifical victim to the sacred place, along a way which was itself sacred, carrying the necessary objects, e.g., baskets of grain, water jars, tools for the slaughter in a ceremonial procession. At the sacred spot, a circle was marked out to enclose the victim, the participants and the altar. After water was sprinkled on all present and the sacrificer recited a prayer, the group hurled groats or stones at the animal. The sacrificer first cut hairs from the victim's forehead and threw them on the fire before he cut the animal's throat or neck artery. The women screamed out a shrill cry as the animal was struck. The blood was gathered in a basin and poured over the altar and then the animal was skinned and butchered and its inner organs (*splanchna*) were roasted on the fire. When the innermost circle had tasted these entrails, the inedible parts (and sometimes edible pieces as well) were placed on the altar in some kind of symbolic order suggestive of reconstitution. Food offerings, e.g., cakes and broth, were also placed there; wine was poured on the fire and fanned the flame. Finally the meat meal was roasted or boiled and the community of participants shared the meal. Custom often dictated that all the meat be consumed in the sanctuary, as in the Passover regulations. The holocaust, where the entire animal was destroyed by fire without any human consumption, was rare in Greece and was enacted primarily in cults associated with the dead or in individual acts of expiation.[79]

The Greeks themselves were puzzled by their ritualized slaughter in which humans ate the meat of an animal as a gift for anthropomorphic gods who did not require food.[80] Hesiod's tale about Prometheus' deception of Zeus explained why humans traditionally ate the best parts, and, according to structuralists, mediated the distinctions between gods who don't eat, men who must eat to survive, but cook their food, and animals who devour meat raw.[81] Whatever the etiology and symbolic meaning of the blood sacrifice, the shared meal clearly brought mortals into fellowship with immortals. While the humans feasted on the meat, the inedible parts (the viscera, bones, and blood), the source of life, were transformed into smoke, or spiritualized, and sent heavenwards to the gods, the givers of life. Invited to the hearth or sanctuary by invocations or prayers, the gods became guest-friends of their hosts, sharing the consecration as well as the meal. In Book 14 of the *Odyssey*, Odysseus' pious swineheard tossed the forehead bristles of the boar into the flames as a first offering before killing it; cut flesh from every quarter and then floured it and cast it into the flames for the gods; then set apart a portion for his special patrons, the wood nymphs and Hermes, with proper prayers; and finally burned a piece for the gods and poured out some wine before sitting down to eat (422-429). In some city states, couches and tables were prepared and meals set out for the gods invited to the feast, e.g., the Dioscuri at Sparta and Athens. The Roman lectisternium probably derived from this Greek custom.[82]

Although the gods in no way needed the food and drink, the shared meal was both a gift and a sacrifice from the human perspective.[83] For the offerings were the first fruits of "men who eat bread," a common Homeric epithet, before it was clear there would be more, or of perfect domestic animals who were substitutes for man. Such offerings were symbolic actions which acknowledged that there was a higher order beyond the "desire to fill one's belly."[84] The renunciation, which Burkert terms "serene wastefulness" is a "surrender to a higher will," an act of faith or hope that the gods would provide more.[85]

In the blood sacrifice in particular, the spectators' experience of death, as they watched the life drain from the animal, brought them closer to the power of that higher will.[86] The ritualized encounter with death was a means of alleviating its terror. The meat meal and the god-given pleasures accompanying the feast reconfirmed the survival and goodness of human life. This movement from death to life replicated the movement from chaos to order in the first creation; it marked the transition from one season to the next in the agricultural year, and it reitified the passage of the individual from an old stage of life to a new one, as when the youth became a man and a maiden a wife, since all change could be assimilated to a death of the old order and birth of the new.[87] Many of the rituals and festivals which developed around the sacrifice contain this basic structure.

The activities of the sacrifice, whether family, state, or private, joined all the individual participants together into a fellowship with each other as well as with the gods. All parts of the group had their place and task in the sacred work. They shared in the slaughter by throwing barley or stones at the victim and tasting the *splanchna*. According to Burkert, it was this communally enacted aggression and shared guilt which created the solidarity.[88] But they all shared in the feast as well; in the great public festivals, rich and poor, powerful and weak participated, ate meat, and delighted together in activities which exalted mortals while honoring and pleasing the gods.

As in Ancient Israel, blood sacrifice was often accompanied by bloodless offerings. The first fruits mentioned above were presented by individuals and communities as a tithe of whatever the fields produced season by season.[89] The libation or liquid offering of honey, water, oil, or wine (*sponde*) was ubiquitous in Greek life, from the wine poured on the sacrificial altar to the solemnizing of a treaty (also *sponde*) to the drops poured out whenever wine was drunk, to the individual's private prayer.[90] Entreating Zeus on behalf of Patroclus, Achilles solemnly prepares a special goblet for his libation, washes his hands carefully, and finally pours out the wine as he looks up toward the god in the sky (*Il.* 16. 225-32). The Greeks had water libation ceremonies similar to the water rites of Sukkot in Jerusalem in their connection to the waters of creation and to rain magic.[91] At the Hydrophoriai in Athens, water for the dead who had been killed in the flood was poured into a cleft where the waters from Deucalion's flood had drained away. The Eleusinian mysteries concluded in a different water libation in which one jug was poured to the heavens with the cry *hye* (rain) while one was poured to the earth with the cry *kye* (conceive). The words suggest rain and fertility magic. The liquid offerings cannot be retrieved for the worshippers own benefit like first fruits or the animal's meat and skin. Therefore, Burkert considers it the "highest and purest form of renunciation". Its main purpose may then have been "raising to hope through serene wastefulness."[92]

Any individual or community could also present a gift of his own choosing to the gods. Xenophon, with the approval of Delphi, established a sanctuary with a temple to Artemis near Olympia and promised tithes as well as sacrifices and a festival (*Anabasis* 5.3.7-B). Literature and inscriptions describe many such votive offerings, accompanied by prayers and promising first fruits, slaves, herds, clothes, or artifacts in exchange for wishes such as health, victory in war, safe journeys, children, or good harvests.[93] Often the gift was placed in the sanctuary or hung up in the temple (*anathemata*).[94] Sometimes it was presented to mark a transition: a lock of hair by a boy or girl leaving childhood, a tool by a retiring artisan.

Sacrifice, libation and offerings were all accompanied by prayers.[95] In private as well as in the sanctuary, those who addressed their gods had to prepare themselves. Achilles washed his hands and his cup. Penelope changed her clothes as well before calling on Athena to save her son Telemachus (*Od.* 4.759-67). Rather than kneel, the petitioner usually stood with his arms stretched out, palms upward to the sky, or out to sea for sea gods. Praying in front of a cult image may have been especially effective.[96]   The words of the prayer had to be carefully chosen; the wrong name for the deity or the wrong sentiment expressed could cause harm instead of good. Eteocles, praying for the safety of Thebes, defined precisely the divinities he was addressing:

> Gods of the city, of this country gods,
> Lords of its fields, and its assembly places,
> Springs of Dirce, waters of Ismenus
> (Aeschylus, *Seven Against Thebes*, 271-3, Grene, trans.)

He ordered the anxious female chorus to stop their predictions of doom lest their words provoke the disaster; they must either be silent or pray a better prayer: "May the gods stand our allies" (266). His fear of the negative power of words reflects the ancient belief in curses familiar from Greek saga and the story of Balak and Balam (Numbers 22-24) as well as from the numerous Greek inscriptions invoking the power of the gods for the harm of personal enemies, a practice forbidden by the Hebrews.

Eteocles' own prayer ended with a vow of sacrifices and the dedication of the spoils of victory. There was no magical *do ut des* expected, however. The Greeks knew their prayers rested on the knees of gods who were not compelled to grant them. Zeus only answered half of Achilles' prayer for Patroclus. Athena turned her face away from the Trojan women's supplication (*Iliad* 6.311).

No formulaic prayers of the Greeks survive.[97]   There were ritualistic cries, however, as well as standard types of prayers and hymns which resemble Hebrew psalms (e.g., thanksgiving, processionals, supplications, hymns of praise), and a standard prayer form: an invocation which included the proper name and probable location of the deity, the reason for calling, proof of piety, examples of previous help, a clear statement of the request, and a vow. Not all prayers would have all pieces and more elaborate ones might include myths about the god and descriptions of his worship. Examples of such prayers abound in poetry and drama, but they are each one of a kind without any repetition from one to another. The complexity of the lyric, and the great variety of diction and imagery remind us that the prayers were composed by men, often for prizes in contests, and were performed in a religious setting as offerings as well as honors or supplications. The fear of boring the gods by sameness and the desire to please them with ever new songs led to the creation of great choral poetry and may account for the absence of collections of standardized hymns.[98]

Dancing was an integral part of the hymns and processions preceding the sacrifice and of the musical and dramatic events produced in the gods' honor.[99]   Whether it originated in rain or fertility magic or rites to wake the dead or attract the gods' attention, the dance clearly pleased the gods.[100]   Artemis, Apollo, and the muses and nymphs in particular delighted in dance, practiced it themselves, and were believed to join their dancing worshippers.   The wild dances of the followers of Dionysus brought them to a state of ecstasy where they experienced union with the powerful relaxer god.   There were special dances for particular deities and festivals.   The *pyrrhice*, for example, commemorated Athena's dance as she leapt from Zeus' head in full armor, and was danced at the Panathenaia.   There were types of dances, with special names and rhythms, but, like the prayers and hymns, the dance movements and their musical accompaniment were not fixed and formulaic and the choruses required training and rehearsal time before performances.   From the seventh century on, choruses grouped according to age and gender competed for the prize of presenting the best danced hymn at festivals.

Transformations From Ritual— Contests became an important part of many local festivals as well as the great panhellenic games. Scholars trace their origins to the belief that such competitions helped to "maintain the energies of nature, following a regular cycle," and relate them to rituals of initiation where youths symbolically die as children to be reborn as adults or rituals where the guilt or pain of real death can be assuaged by mock killing.[101] In both the loss of the contest was equivalent to death, the victory an affirmation of life.   Burkert connects both to the basic movement of the sacrifice; the transition from the bloody slaughter to the purifying fire.   The oldest event at Olympia, the footrace, was actually run from the altar of Pelops, where a black ram was sacrificed, to the altar of Zeus, where the consecrated parts of the oxen sacrificed to him were arranged for burning.   A priest signaled the start of the race with a torch.   The victor set fire to the consecrated parts, restoring the life to its giver in a spiritualized form while initiating the preparation of the feast which sustained the lives of men.   The Panathenaia had a similar torch-race in which the sacred fire was carried from the altar of Eros in the grove of Academus to the altar of Athena.

Footraces were not unknown to the Hebrews.   At the water drawing festival during Sukkot in the Second Temple, young priests and other celebrants competed as part of the joyous festivities prescribed for the holiday. The Greeks transformed their rite, however, into a cycle of four great panhellenic festivals, the Olympian, Pythian, Isthmian, and Nemean Games, which honored the gods and heroes with contests displaying physical strength and prowess by which man might be called god-like.[102] From their earliest beginnings at Olympia in the eleventh century to their traditional founding in 776 B.C.E. to the circuit of the four established by the sixth century and their popularity until their closing by the Christians, one can see increasing secularization. New athletic contests were added (e.g., wrestling, horse and chariot races); the military implications of athletics were developed; athletes became more professional; victors and victorious cities exploited the political benefits; and the sacred time was a commercial opportunity for innkeepers, vendors, prostitutes etc. But the religious aspects were never forgotten. Athletes prepared themselves for the contest at Olympia by a thirty day period of separation, sexual abstinence, and fasting on a vegetarian diet. On the opening day there were sacrifices, prayers, and dedications to Zeus and all participants swore on oath before the altar. There were also public sacrifices during the games, the most sacred day being the one after the new moon when the procession to the great ash altar and the footrace were held. In a solemn ceremony after the games, the victors were crowned at the temple of Zeus. They were treated like gods (and military heroes) when they returned home.

The myths and poetry associated with the games connected contemporary festivals to sacred time. According to legend, the games were all founded by gods or heroes in commemoration for a death, e.g., Apollo's slaughter of the Python or Pelops' compensation for the death of his father-in-law. Relics on display at Olympia and events such as the sacrifice of the black ram to Pelops or the chariot race correlate with myths about the legendary founder.[103] The victory odes performed at celebrations related this sacred past of warriors and gods to current winners and their cities in a juxtaposition which elevated the contemporary occasion while illustrating eternal truths about humanity and god. In *Olympia* I, for example, Pindar honors the victory of Syracuse and its tyrant Hieron by examining the legend of Pelops, their Dorian ancestor, through which he considers the true nature of the gods and uses Tantalus, Pelops' father, as an exemplar of divine punishment for excess (51-7). *Pythia* I compares Apollo's calming of Typhon, buried beneath Mt. Aetna, to the victor's recent founding of a city on the site. *Pythia* VIII connects a young boy wrestler's family with the divine and heroic protectors of his birthplace and alludes to his city's current troubles. The ending exalts his victory, but places his god granted fame in the context of the human condition and the city's danger.

> Man's life is a day. What is he?
> What is he not? A shadow in a dream
> is man: but when God sheds a brightness,
> Shining life is on earth
> And life is sweet as honey.
> Aigina dear mother,
> Keep this city in her voyage of freedom:
> You with Zeus and Lord Aiakos,
> Peleus, and noble Teleman, and Achilles
> (95-100, C. M. Bowra, trans.) [104]

The dramatic festivals at Athens provide another example of the transformation of ancient forms of worship. Although the origin of drama is obscure, it is clear that it arose out of the singing, dancing, animal mummery, masks, and contests between winter and spring which are part of age-old and world-wide fertility rites, and in Greece were particularly associated with Dionysus, the god of wine, liquid life, and relaxation.[105] Tradition however credited real human beings with creating the dramatic genre and the main festival, the city Dionysia, in mid sixth century Athens: Thespis the first actor who combined two earlier forms, choral lyric and poetic recitation, to make a play, and Pisistratus the tyrant who adopted this experimental form, unconnected to aristocratic entertainments, for new state festival in honor of Dionysus, the special god of the Attic peasants.[106]

The City Dionysia became both the product and the pride of the democratic union which it helped to shape.[107] Tragedy elevated the common man by placing him (as chorus) in the orchestra with the aristocratic heroes in plots which focused on the heroes' moments of defeat when they recognized their limits and commonalty with fellow mortals. All the citizens participated in the festival. Plays by citizen/poets were chosen by the archon eponymous, the wealthiest citizens were taxed to pay for the training and costumes of the citizen choruses, the population as a whole paraded in the great processions of revelers (*komoi*), shared the sacrifices to Dionysus, and watched the performances, and representatives chosen from the tribes selected the victorious playwrights and (later) first actors. Allies parading their tribute and relatives of the war dead marching together fostered patriotism as well as group solidarity.

The religious dimensions of the dramatic performances were as important as the social and political effects. Like the athletic contests, performances were held in the sacred precinct within sacred time. In the sacred procession, the image of the god was paraded through the city and brought into the theater to watch the sacrifices and dramas. The plays contained the same kinds of hymns, prayers, and dances as religious activities held outside the theater.[108] Choruses and actors repeated the moral lessons of myth: the dangers of sacrilege, hybris, and excess and the certainty of punishment from the gods.

But tragedy replaced the formulaic repetitions of ritual with creative manipulations of saga which kept the sacred past relevant to the ambiguous present by validating contemporary institutions and examining current problems in the light of mythic time.[109] In the *Oresteia* of 458, for example, Aeschylus added a new ending to the saga of the house of Atreus; to determine the guilt and just punishment of Orestes the matricide, Athena established the court of the Areopagus at Athens as a substitute for the blood vendetta of earlier generations of men and gods. Aeschylus' trilogy traced the movement from savagery to civilization, an evolution the Athenians felt they had passed through themselves with the guidance of their patron goddess. Although there were no topical allusions in the trilogy, Athena's presence in the third play and her founding of their current jury system directly connected the citizens with the gods and Athens' sacred past. But in 458, the Court of the Areopagus was the focus of a violent struggle between the aristocrats and the commons. Thus the conflict on the divine and heroic levels was directly relevant to the conflict in Athens. Aeschylus' resolution in which Athena persuaded the Furies to accept the court's verdict and become Beneficent Ones (*Eumenides*) provided a paradigm for peaceful compromise and cooperation in Athens.

In the words of translator and scholar Robert Maegher, such tragedies "broke hearts and opened minds", for it placed the social and political issues of the day *sub specie aeternitatis*, examining them in an ordered sequence and moral context in "the seeing place" (*theatron*) to produce an "insight."[110] Aristotle defined the effect as a catharsis of pity and fear, compassion for undeserved misfortune and recognition that it could happen to oneself (*Poetics* 1453a.1-10). Such insight into the human condition is effected, however, by playing out the inevitable pain, suffering, and death of the noble heroes of saga against the framework of a higher order.[111]

After 486, an old comedy followed the three tragedies and a satyr play on each day of dramatic presentations at the City Dionysia and was the central feature of the late winter festival, the Lenaea. This genre led to social harmony, psychological catharsis, and religious reverence by a different path. Its hero was the common man or woman, often with a name which suggests his political identity, e.g., Demos in *Knights* or Philocleon (I Love Cleon) in *Wasps*. The plot came from contemporary life, not myth; three plays, *Acharnians*, *Peace*, and *Lysistrata* derive from the realities of the Peloponnesian War and several have characters who are real Athenians, e.g., Lamachus the general in *Acharnians*, Socrates in *Clouds*. The fantastic plots violate the laws of probability and necessity in life as well as the inevitability of myth in such a way that the underdog hero defeats all the individuals, institutions, and natural limitations which oppresses him and ends up with all the power and pleasure he desires. Such a play produced a different kind of catharsis, "a relaxation, recovery, and recognition" according to Kenneth Reckford. For the ordinary citizen, restricted or made anxious and hostile by the laws and customs which regulated civilized life, was relaxed by the sacred release of comedy, with its childish dirty jokes and scatology, and outrageous freedom, and so recovered his good feeling and good will, and recognized the joys and possibilities of ordinary life.[112]

The joyousness of comedy may have been replicated in occasions such as the water drawing festival in the Second Temple. There are no counterparts to some of the features which produced it, however, for the sacred release permitted drunkenness, scatology, obscene and insulting speech (*aischrologia*), as well as the worship of sexuality *per se*.[113] In the Dionysiac festivals, drunken revelers paraded in the *komos* wearing masks or animal skins and smeared with wine leas. Some marchers (*ithyphalloi*) carried clay images of huge erect phalluses. Under their costumes and often visible, the comic actors wore inflatable phalluses attached to pieces suggesting pubic hair over tights representing naked skin. In both the *komos* and the comedies, as well as in the procession of initiates from Athens to Eleusis during the Greater Mysteries of the festival of Demeter, participants could lampoon powerful individuals and make obscene gestures and remarks. The gods themselves were prime targets. In *Birds*, the hero nearly raped Iris, ridiculed Zeus' lechery, conquered Olympus, and married into Zeus' family after outsmarting Heracles, Poseidon, and a barbarian god on the advice of a cowardly Prometheus. Dionysus himself was portrayed as a buffoon and butt in *Frogs*. Zeus did not appear in *Clouds*, but his existence was disapproved after ridicule of the antiquated belief that rain is caused by his pissing in a sieve.

Scatology and sexual innuendo were ubiquitous in the comedies. Most characters defecate, masturbate and get horny, and most plays end with an orgy or wedding.

The obscenity, scatology, insult, and sex may derive from magic rites to promote fertility or keep evil from the group. In the witty and humorous anarchy of the comedies, however, hostilities between sexes, age groups, classes and statuses are played out in uninhibited and fantastic ways which exorcise bad feeling, unite the audience through laughter, and lead them to the recognition of their commonalty as physical beings. Through the insult, sexuality, and fantasy too, anxieties about death and the mysterious higher order are reduced to manageable proportions. All the elements together effect a celebration of the good things of life - wine, women and song, food, festivals, and fellowship - and a reverence for life itself, represented by Dionysus and Demeter in particular, but also by the myriad divinities prayed to, praised, and even ridiculed in the plays.

Rules and Taboos— The regulations which governed behavior during sacred time varied according to cult or context. Public obscenity, scatology, and insult were acceptable only in times of festivals to appropriate deities and the sacred release itself was protected against unholy excess by custom and law.[114] Certain activities were forbidden at festival time because they were the exact opposite of what would insue or be prayed for.[115] Sexual abstinence, for example, was demanded at the various Thesmophoriai, celebrated in honor of Demeter, when the chief purpose was receiving the goddess' continuing blessing on reproduction. Fasting too was required in certain cults, perhaps as a preliminary renunciation in preparation for the great sacrificial feast to follow. In contrast to Ancient Israel, however, there were no categories of impure animals or foods which had to be universally avoided.[116] There were, however, temporary taboos at certain festivals. The pomegranate, eaten as part of the ritual at the Thesmophoria, was banned to the Eleusinian initiates, probably because it was the fruit Hades had used to trap Persephone into returning. Other banned foods included beans, apples, eggs, egg-laying animals, the meat of animals that had died naturally, and various kinds of fish and animals which ate dung or humans. The latter two categories might derive from beliefs that eating perpetrators of such savage and unclean acts could pollute the eaters, making them unclean. The taboo on beans was very ancient and has attracted many explanations ranging from its quality as a launching point of the soul to its association with sex, birth, and death, to its being poisonous to those with a particular enzyme deficiency.

The reasons for such temporary bans maybe unclear and related to context and cult. The existence of temporary taboos or releases, however, enhanced the movement into sacred time. Burkert suggests the distinctions "presuppose that the sacred does not constitute the entire world and does not lay infinite claims on men."[117] Some Greek individuals and groups, however, chose permanent abstentions which regulated their entire life in the ways which the dietary rules governed all Israel all the time.[118] The Pythagorean community in Southern Italy (c550-450) and the Orphic brotherhoods of the fifth century and later developed ascetic regimens which kept them physically and morally pure. Their practices were related to a belief in the transmigration of souls and an acceptance of suffering in this life as a punishment for evil in a previous life. They instituted food taboos and full or partial vegetarianism because they feared to eat anything which possessed a soul. Other elements of their regimen have been traced back as far as Homer and Hesiod as practices denoting purity and piety. Scholars have interpreted their whole way of life, however, as a means of setting themselves apart from the ordinary community and its religious and social behavior, by either rejecting its basic act (e.g., blood sacrifice by the Orphics after initiation throughout sacrifice) and by extending other temporary religious abstentions (e.g., food taboos, restrictions on sexual activities, vows of silence, wearing white garments).[119] Their aspirations toward holiness made their practices suspect; Theseus accuses Hippolytus of masking his lust with his Orphic pretensions (947-58). Their eschatological beliefs connected to sin and punishment had enormous influence, however.

Private Piety

These ascetic groups represent an extreme example of the personal choice permissible within Greek religion.[120] It was very possible and indeed prevalent to exercise private religious preferences and remain within the community at the same time. The best examples are the mystery religions which offered individuals who had passed through a secret initiation rite a special status and relationship to the deity which continued even after death. The Athenian government sponsored the Eleusinian Mysteries, which were part of the city's sacred calendar. The rites were conducted by two ancient families from Eleusis, and initiation was open to anyone, including women, slaves, and foreigners, so long as they could speak Greek and were not criminals. Their seriousness and popularity is attested by the reverential comments by such ancient authors as Sophocles and Cicero. Other mysteries developed into universal and privately incorporated clubs after the decline of the polis as the center of life in the Hellenistic world. Associations of members initiated into the mysteries of Isis and Osiris and Dionysus were ubiquitous. Apuleius' second century C.E. novel *The Golden Ass* expresses the change in life and status and the degree of piety the author achieved when Isis became his personal savior (see Book IX especially). Inscriptions of vows to individual deities indicate that choice was often based on profession; e.g., the herald selected Hermes, the fisherman Poseidon, the vintner Dionysus/Phales. Sometimes circumstances dictated the choice: young maidens belonged to Artemis, but moved to Demeter with marriage and motherhood. The sick took refuge in the shrines of Asklepios, resorting to incubation in his temple to dream their cures and offer themselves to his healing priests. The *Hieroi Logoi* of Aelius Aristides testify to the gratitude and piety felt by the sick toward the gods. The philosopher Socrates, struggling toward a new definition of god and piety, attended all the public festivals and remembered on his deathbed that he owed a thank offering to the healing god, a cock to Asklepios (*Phaedo* 118).

Notes

1.   See John Gould "On Making Sense of Greek Religion," pp. 1-33 in P. E. Easterling and J. V. Muir, eds., *Greek Religion and Society* (Cambridge: Cambridge University Press, 1985) as well as Robert Garland, "Priests and Power in Classical Athens," pp. 75-91 in Mary Beard and John North, eds., *Pagan Priests: Religion and Power in the Ancient World* (Ithaca: Cornell University Press, 1990), for discussions of the different conceptions of piety and the consequent problems of interpretation by modern scholars.

2.   Garland, p. 75 in Beard and North.

3.   For an excellent introduction to the sources for evaluating the prehistory as well as a survey of the aspects and development through the classical period plus a copious bibliography of the primary and secondary sources, see Walter Burkert, *Greek Religion,* trans. John Raffan (Cambridge: Cambridge University Press, 1985), pp. 10-19. This chapter is especially indebted to this book

4.   Burkert, *Greek Religion*, p. 88-89. For detailed studies of temple architecture and its development, see H. Berve and G. Gruben, *Greek Temples, Theatres and Shrines* (London: Thames and Hudson, 1963) and A. W. Lawrence, *Greek Architecture*, (London: Penguin, 1984). J. Sharwood

Smith, *Temples Priests and Worship* (London: George Allen and Unwin, 1975) offers a good brief introduction to the topic.

5. See N. G. L. Hamond, *A History of Greece to 322 B.C* (Oxford: Clarendon Press, 1967) for a history of the period covered here. *The Cambridge Ancient History*. Vols. 3-5 (Cambridge: Cambridge University Press, 1980-1988) contains articles on the political and social development of the entire area. See especially J. K. Davies, "Religion and the State", pp. 368-88 in vol. 4.

6. See James Hooker, "Cult-Personnel in the Linear B Texts from Pylos," pp. 159-173 in Beard and North for the texts and interpretation.

7. P. 90. The article argues for the shift in control discussed in the above paragraph.

8. See Jean Pierre Vernant, "Space and Political Organization in Ancient Greece" pp. 212-234 in *Myth and Thought Among the Greeks* (London: Routledge and Kegan Paul, 1983) for a structural analysis of the changes.

9. Burkert, *Greek Religion*, p. 53, discusses the uniqueness of the Greek sacrifice in which all the mortals are active participants.

10. Thomas Pangle defines *hieron* or sacred as "what is filled with the divine presence, what the gods reserve to themselves," as opposed to *hosion* or pious, which is "what they allocate to or require of humans," pp. 518-519, note 7 of his translation of "*The Laws of Plato*" (New York: Basic Books, 1980). See also Robert Parker *Miasma: Pollution and Purification in Early Greek Religion* (Oxford: Clarendon Press, 1983), p. 151 and Burkert, *Greek Religion*, pp. 268-271 for analysis of Greek terms associated with the sacred. The main ideas and information in the following discussion of priests and priestesses are taken from Burkert, *Greek Religion*, pp. 95-98. Garland, pp. 77-81 in Beard and North discusses the state's relations with the independent priesthoods in addition to other details about them.

11. According to an inscription which records arbitration between rival factions of the *genos* (family of the Salaminioi, the same individual should be a priest of two cults on Salamis. See David G. Rice and John E. Stambaugh, *Sources for the Study of Greek Religion* (Missoula: Scholars Press, 1979) p. 82 for a translation of the inscription. Leopold Sabourin, *Priesthood: A Comparative Study* (Leiden: E. J. Brill, 1973) p. 36 believes most only held one priestly office at a time, however.

12. Douglas Feaver, "Historical Developments in the Priesthoods of Athens," *Yale Classical Studies* 15 (1957): 137 quotes an inscription indicating that the priestess of Athena Nike was appointed or allotted for life. On p. 157, he notes that Lysimache, honored with a statue on the acropolis, had served as the priestess of Athena Polias for sixty-four years. At Delphi, however, the priest's term lasted only six months.

13. Sabourin, pp. 36-37.

14. According to the scholiast to Pindar *Pythian* 4.337, as noted in W. R. Halliday, *Greek Divination: A Study of its Methods and Principles* (Chicago: Argonaut, Inc., 1967), pp. 206-207.

15. For a complete discussion of the various shrines, their histories, practices, and extant texts, see Alice Walton, *The Cult of Asklepios*. Cornell Studies in Classical Philology (New York: Ginn & Co., 1894. Reprint: Johnson Reprint Corporation, 1965).

16. Feaver, p. 127.

17. The inscription about the *genos* of the Salaminioi indicates that lot was used for succession there. See Feaver, pp. 128-130 for an interpretation of the inscription, as well as Rice and Stambaugh, p. 81. Sabourin, p. 39, believes the movement through a *genos* from eldest brother down was more typical, although one priest of Poseidon at Athens was also chosen by lot among the members of the *genos*.

18. Feaver discusses this development on pp. 136-37.

19. See Rice and Stambaugh, pp. 128-129 for a translation of the inscription.

20. Parker, *Miasma*, pp. 175.

21. Parker, *Miasma*, pp. 52-53; 175, n. 177.

22. Burkert, *Greek Religion*, pp. 97-98, where he also suggests that priests and priestesses were often treated like deities.

23. Feaver, pp. 144-147.

24. Felix Jacoby, *Atthis: The Local Chronicles of Ancient Athens* (Oxford: Clarendon Press, 1949), pp. 44-45.

25. See Jacoby's discussion of the evidence, pp. 8-51, as well as a contrasting interpretation by James H. Oliver, *The Athenian Expounders of Sacred and Ancestral Law* (Baltimore: Johns Hopkins University Press, 1950), and a summary of both arguments in Herbert Bloch, "The Exegetes of Athens and the Prytaneion Decree," *American Journal of Philology* 74 (1953): 407-418. Garland also discusses the exegetes in Beard and North, pp. 81-82.

26. Jacoby, pp. 47-49.

27. P. 48. See chapter 8 for further discussion of this point.

28. See Burkert, *Greek Religion*, pp. 10-53 for a discussion of the remains and their relationship to practices of historical Greece.

29. Burkert, *Greek Religion*, p. 50.

30. See *Miasma* for a discussion of many aspects of this topic. The chapter on "Sacrilege", pp. 144-190 has been especially helpful for this section, but on pp. 19-22 he discusses lustration and on pp. 74-78 he discusses rules for the separation of religion and sexuality which are similar to Hebrew restrictions: e.g., washing or changing clothes after intercourse before entering sacred places; not making the gods unwitting witnesses to urination or nakedness.

31. Parker, *Miasma*, p. 164; 190. Translations of tragedies are quoted from David Grene and Richmond Lattimore, eds. *The Complete Greek Tragedies*. 4 vols. (Chicago: University of Chicago Press, 1959-60). Translators of individual plays are cited in the text.

32. Burkert, *Greek Religion*, pp. 84-87 for important features of the temenos.

33. Burkert, *Greek Religion* , pp. 87-88.

34. Burkert, *Greek Religion*, pp. 88-92. In addition to the sources listed in note 4 see J. N. Coldstream, "Greek Temples: Why and Where", pp. 67 - 97, and Martin Robinson, "Greek Art and Religion", pp. 155-190, in Easterling and Muir.

35. P. E. Corbett "Greek Temples and Greek Worshippers: The Literary and Archaeological Evidence", *Bulletin of the Institute of Classical Studies of University of London* 17(1978): 149-158 reviews the indications that various activities took place inside the temple.

36. Corbett, pp. 152-4.

37. Burkert, pp. 167, 187.

38. In Athens, two festivals were devoted to sweeping out the temple and bathing the image of Athena Polias, the Kallynteria and Plynteria, respectively. At the Panathenaea, the goddess was presented with a new gown (*peplos*). Similar festivals for deities were held all over Greece, Parker, *Miasma*, 26-28.

39. See John D. Mikalson, "Hemera Apophras", *American Journal of Philology*, 96 (1975): 19-27 for an examination of the meanings of the term, as well as Burkert, pp. 101, 228 and H. W. Parke, *Festivals of the Athenians* (London: Thames and Hudson, 1977), pp. 154-5.

40. For a general introduction to Greek sculpture, see Martin Robertson, *A Shorter History of Greek Art* (Cambridge: Cambridge University Press, 1985).

41. For detailed descriptions of major Greek sanctuaries and their development, see Vincent Scully, *The Earth the Temple and the Gods: Greek Sacred Architecture* (New Haven: Yale University Press, 1979) and R. A. Tomlinson, *Greek Sanctuaries* (London: Paul Elek, 1976).

42. As Pausanias' *Guide to Greece: Book 1. Attica* reveals, the discussion of sacred space in the Acropolis and city in no way exhausts the list of consecrated areas. For a fuller discussion, see the works cited in note 41 as well as Parke, *Festivals*, Erika Simon, *Festivals of Attica: An Archaelogical Commentary* (Madison: University of Wisconsin Press, 1983) and John M. Camp, *The Athenian Agora: Excanations in the Heart of Classical Athens* (London: Thames and Hudson, 1986), as well as Pausanias.

43. Scully, pp. 12-14.

44. Scully, p. 109.

45. Scully, p. 146, on the calm at Olympia.

46. Tomlinson, pp. 88-89.

47. Scully, p. 44 and Burkert, p. 92.

48. Scully emphasizes the interaction and its effect in his discussion of the Athenian acropolis, pp. 183-5.

49. For a structural analysis of the significance of the hearth and its relation to the *omphalos* or navel stone, see J. P. Vernant, "Hestia-Hermes: The Religious Expression of Space and Movement in Ancient Greece", pp. 127-175. The quote comes from p. 160 in *Myth and Thought*.

50. J. P. Vernant, *Myth and Thought*, p. 188 in the essay "Geometry and Spherical Astronomy in the first Greek Cosmology."

51. In addition to the works on art cited in notes 4, 34, and 40, see J. J. Pollitt, *Art and Experience in Classical Greece* (Cambridge: Cambridge University Press, 1972), pp. 71-110, Simon, *Festivals*, pp. 55-72, and Susan Woodford, *The Parthenon* (Cambridge: Cambridge University Press, 1981).

52. Translations of Plutarch are quoted from Ian Scott-Kilvert, *Plutarch: The Rise and Fall of Athens* (Penguin: New York, 1960).

53. Parker, *Miasma*, pp. 152-4. and pp. 160-166.

54. See works on major sanctuaries listed in note 41 as well as George E. Mylonas, *Eleusis and the Eleusinian Mysteries* (Princeton: Princeton University Press, 1961).

55. See chapter 6, note 21, as well as note 41 to this chapter.

56. Parker, *Miasma*, p 167.

57. Parker, *Miasma*, p. 177; Corbett, pp. 150-150; Joseph William Hewitt, "The Major Restrictions on Access to Greek Temples", *Transactions and Proceedings of the American Philological Association* 40 (1909): 83-92.

58. Hewitt examines the cults with restrictions for signs of oriental or chthonic origins in the article cited above.

59. Parker, *Miasma*, p. 177.

60. Parker, *Miasma*, pp. 144-5 and Appendix 4 "Animals and Food," pp. 356-65.

61. Corbett, pp. 151-2.

62. Parker, *Miasma*, p. 179, refers to a "popular subliterary genre of 'impiety instantly punished'" and gives Greek examples and parallels in note 193.

63. Parker, *Miasma*, pp. 170-171; 168-169 as well as Douglas M. MacDowell, *The Law in Classical Athens* (Ithaca, NY: Cornell University Press, 1978) pp. 135; 192-202.

64. Parker, *Miasma* pp. 189-90.

65. Cartledge, "The Greek Religious Festivals," pp. 98-103 in Easterling and Muir; Martin Nilsson, *Greek Folk Religion* (New York: Harper and Brothers, 1961), pp. 22-41; 84-101, as well as Parke, *Festivals* and Simon, *Festivals*.

66. Benjamin D. Meritt, *The Athenian Year* (Berkeley: University of California Press, 1961), pp. 17-18 contrasts the careful observation of the young crescent in Israel with the rule of convenience most probably used by the Athenians.

67 Parker, *Miasma*, pp. 154.

68. Jon D. Mikalson, *The Sacred and Civil Calendar of the Athenian Year* (Princeton: Princeton University Press, 1975), p. 203.

69. Parker, *Miasma*, pp. 155-158.

70. *Greek Religion*, pp. 227-234.

71. Parke, *Festivals*, pp. 29, 168-169.

72. Simon, *Festivals*, pp. 4-5.

73. Parke, *Festivals*, pp. 23-24; Mikalson, *Sacred and Civil Calendar*, pp. 13-24.

74. *Miasma*, pp. 23-31.

75. For descriptions of the Thargelia and other scapegoat rituals, see Parke, *Festivals*, pp. 146-155, Simon, *Festivals* and Burkert, *Greek Religion*, pp. 82-84.

76. See Parke, *Festivals*, and Simon, *Festivals*, pp. 76-79, as well as Nilsson for specific details about festivals mentioned.

77. *Greek Religion*, p. 237-242. See also his comments on sacred marriages on pp. 108-109.

78. Burkert, *Greek Religion*, pp. 54-57.

79. Burkert, *Greek Religion*, pp. 63.

80. Burkert, *Greek Religion*, pp. 57.

81. See J. P. Vernant, "Sacrifice and Alimentary Codes in Hesiod's Myth of Prometheus," reprinted in R. L. Gordon, ed. *Myth, Religion, and Society: Structuralist Essays* (Cambridge: Cambridge University Press, 1981), pp. 57-79.

82. Burkert, *Greek Religion*, p. 107.

83. Burkert, *Greek Religion*, pp. 66-73.

84. Burkert, *Greek Religion*, p. 66.

85. Burkert, *Greek Religion*, p. 72.

86. Burkert, *Greek Religion*, pp. 58, 65.

87. For a study of the relationship between sacrifice and creation, see Bruce Lincoln, *Myth, Cosmos, and Society: Indo-European Themes of Creation* (Cambridge: Harvard University Press, 1986). For its relation to tragedy, see Burkert's "Greek Tragedy and Sacrificial Ritual," *Greek Roman and Byzantine Studies* 7(166): 87-121.

88. Burkert, *Greek Religion*, pp. 58-59.

89. Burkert, *Greek Religion*, pp. 67.

90. Burkert, *Greek Religion*, pp. 70-72.

91. Burkert, *Greek Religion*, p. 73, as well as Parke, *Festivals*, Simon, *Festivals* and Mylonas. See Raphael Petai, *Man and Temple in Ancient Jewish Myth and Ritual* (New York: KTAV, 1967), pp. 24-41 for a description, analysis, and comparison of water drawing festivals.

92. Burkert, *Greek Religion*, p. 72.

93. See Rice and Stambaugh, pp. 150-151 for a selection of dedications and votive offerings from the Acropolis.

94. Burkert, *Greek Religion*, p. 79.

95. Burkert, *Greek Religion*, pp. 73-75.

96. Corbett, p. 151 provides several examples, including an ugly baby who became beautiful after her nurse prayed before a statue of Helen (Herodotus, 6.61).

97. Burkert, *Greek Religion*, p. 74. He mentions several cries: the women's shrill *ololyge* at sacrifice and birth, the Dionysian *Euhoi, thriambe, dithyrambe, Iakchos Iakhe*, in the Eleusinian procession, and the *ie ie paian* associated with Apollo.

98. Burkert, *Greek Religion*, p. 103.

99. Burkert, *Greek Religion*, pp. 102-103.

100. For theories of function and descriptions as well as comparisons of various Greek and Israelite Forms, see W. O. E. Oesterley, *The Sacred*

Dance: A Study in Comparative Folklore (Cambridge: Cambridge University Press, 1923). Reprinted Brooklyn: Dancy Horizons, Inc. For discussions of Greek dances see Lillian B. Lawler, *The Dance in Ancient Greece* (Middletown: Wesleyan University Press, 1965) and T. B. L. Webster, *The Greek Chorus* (London: Methuen, 1970).

101.   Cartledge, p. 107 in Easterling and Muir, as well as Burkert, *Greek Religion*, p. 105-107 and *Homo Necans; The Anthropology of Ancient Greek Sacrificial Ritual and Myth,* trans. Peter Bings (Berkeley: University of California Press, 1983), where he builds on the theory of K. Meuli, (on pg. 53, with bibliography) about the connection between funerals and competitive contests to analyze the relation of ritual killing to various myths and forms of worship. Gregory Nagy "Pindar's *Olympian* I and the Aetiology of the Olympic Games," *Transactions of the American Philological Associaton,* 116 (1986): 71-88, presents a detailed analysis of the relation of accrued myth and ritual to practice and poetry at the Olympics.

102.   For descriptions and history of the developments, see the bibliography provided by Cartledge in Easterling and Muir, pp. 223-225. Major works on the athletic contests are M. I. Finley, and H. W. Pleket, *The Olympic Games: The First Thousand Years* (New York: Viking, 1976); H. A. Harris, *Greek Athletes and Athletics* (Bloomington: Indiana University Press, 1966) and *Sport in Greece and Rome* (Ithaca: Cornell University Press 1972). Parke, *Festivals,* pp. 33-37, discusses the athletic contests at the Panathenaia.

103.   Burkert, *Homo Necans,* pp. 93-103 and Nagy.

104.   Quoted from *Pindar: The Odes* (New York: Penguin, 1969).

105.   See Kenneth Reckford's appendix A "From *Komos* to *Komoidia"* pp. 443-451 in *Aristophanes' Old and New Comedy. Vol. I Six Essays in Perspective* (Chapel Hill: University of North Carolina Press, 1987) as well as Arthur Picard-Cambridge, *Dithyramb, Tragedy, and Comedy,* 2nd ed. revised by T. B. L. Webster (Oxford: Clarendon Press, 1962).

106.   Gerald Else, *The Origin and Early Form of Greek Tragedy* (Cambridge: Harvard University Press for Oberlin College, 1965) emphasizes these aspects.

107.   For all aspects of the festival, see Arthur Picard - Cambridge, *Dramatic Festivals of Athens,* 2nd ed. revised by John Gould and P.M. Lewis (Oxford: Clarendon Press, 1968). Else, p. 76, comments on the elevation of the *demos* implicit in the Form.

108.   Gerald Else, "Ritual and Drama in Aischyleian Tragedy," *Illinois Classical Studies* 11 (1977): 70-87 examines the dramatist's use of prayers and laments.

109.   See Anthony J. Podlecki, *The Political Background of Aeschylean Tragedy* (Ann Arbor: University of Michigan Press, 1966) for an example of relations between myth-based drama and topical situations.

110.   At a series of Carolyn Benton Cockefaire Lectures at the University of Missouri-Kansas City in April, 1987, as well as *Mortal Vision: The Wisdom of Euripides* (New York: St. Martin's Press, 1989), pp. 33-52.

His book studies the power of drama to illuminate contemporary issues by comparison with traditional tales.

111.   For an analysis of the power and effect of tragedy, see also Reckford, p. 12 and Oliver Taplin, *Greek Tragedy in Action* (London: Methuen, 1978), pp. 168-70.

112.   Pp. 3-24.

113.   See Burkert, *Greek Religion*, pp. 103-105 and Reckford's appendixes C and D, "Dionysus and the Phallus", pp. 457-460, and "Aischrologia," pp. 461-467.

114.   See MacDowell, pp. 194-7 and Picard-Cambridge, *Dramatic Festivals* pp. 69-70.

115.   Parker, *Miasma*, pp. 81-86.

116.   Parker, *Miasma*, pp. 357-365, Appendix 4; Animals and Food. In studying these particular taboos, Parker refers to Greek classifications according to honor rather than ritual purity and cites sources which indicate that those plants and animals "lacking honor" were still considered edible.

117.   *Greek Religion*, p. 270.

118.   Chapter 6, note 68.

119.   Burkert, *Greek Religion*, pp. 303-4. On p. 304, he notes their association with he Essenes in later tradition.

120.   For a discussion of expressions of private choices, see André-Jean Festugière, *Personal Religion Among the Greeks* (Berkeley: University of California Press, 1954).

Conclusions and Comparisons

For both civilizations the cult was of critical importance because it opened up communication between the human and the divine and concretized the eternal models to be emulated in human life. Thus both the Hebrew and the Greek festivals represented an aspect of *imitatio dei*, in returning to the presence of divinity, where history gives way to eternity. The Hebrew and Greek sacrificial systems not only resembled one another in external rites but also in the deeper conception that sacrifice was a gift to the deity expressing human gratitude as well as the human quest for union with the deity or deities. The sacrifice of expiation was also part of both sacrificial systems, though much less predominant in Greece.

On Olympus as on Sinai sacred space was carefully designated with an eye to separating the holy from the profane. Hebrews and Greeks were very conscious of the ambiguous power of the deity which is both beneficial and dangerous, that confers immortality but also brings sudden and mysterious death. Therefore both civilizations had rules incorporating taboos and purifications intended to protect the purity of the sacred and the safety of the worshipper. Since the ambiguity of divine power was the source of both disease and cure, healing traditions and techniques were an integral part of the cult. In Israel the priestly therapeutic approach consisted of diagnosis, quarantine, purification rituals and in cases of emergency, apotropaic rituals such as the burning of incense to ward off plagues. In Greece worshippers could appeal for health to any divine patron they chose, but by the fifth century, the shrines of Asklepios became the centers for healing and the catalyst for the development of scientific medicine, usually associated with Hippocrates who was educated and practiced at the god's sanctuary in Kos.

In Israel the belief in one God was reflected in the cult. In the pre-Mosaic, patriarchal era the cultic structure was horizontal; sacrifices were offered by individual patriarchs on local altars and at regional shrines throughout the land of Israel. But from the time of Moses onward there was an increasing centralization of religion in which the cult was verticalized and a religious hierarchy established. The holy of holies in the Jerusalem Temple was the sacred center with sanctity emanating from it in degrees to various parts of the land of Israel and the Diaspora. The Sinaitic Revelation provided the authority for the organization of the sacred calendar, the rules for the cult and the supervision of the religious administration by the Levite priesthood. First Temple ritual was, for the most part, a speechless worship and the lay people were silent observers. Only the priests were permitted into the most sacred inner precincts to perform the ritual. In the Second Temple more activities were added which involved the participation of the laity. It was not until the destruction of the Second Temple, however, when the synagogues became mobile sacred centers, that the rabbis replaced the priests and the laity conducted the ritual. Despite the return to the horizontal in sacred space, the vertical authority of revelation and Scripture insured uniformity of worship.

Polytheism, by its very nature, produced a plurality of sacred places and cult practices to correspond to the variety of divinities worshipped. Despite the fact that the poets had described Zeus as the supreme authority, with his Olympian children and siblings as chief deities, Greek religion never developed the vertical structure of Hebrew monotheism. Although individuals and communities often sought authoritative advice at Panhellenic shrines such as Apollo's Delphi and Zeus' Dodona, the cultic structure of Greek religion was basically horizontal. Without any centralized political organization equivalent to the "holy nation" in the "promised land," no divinity was singled out as most important; rather respect was due to all, even if one was a particular personal patron (v. Euripides' *Hippolytus*, 88-107). Nor was there a unified and authoritative body of regulations for worship, which established one sacred center from which holiness emanated or a class which administered the sacred according to those regulations. Instead Greek-speaking communities worshipped the same gods in different ways, following their own local customs, and in different places, each with its own degrees of sanctity and different means for preserving it. Priests and priestesses had limited duties and responsibilities as administrators of individual shrines and supervisors of cult activities conducted there. Unlike the Hebrew priesthood, they were not united by heredity, training, belief, or rules. In fact, each group of worshippers had its own ancestral traditions of sacred law, and, in some cases, established its own new cults and cult practices.

Just as Greek cult structure, in contrast to the Hebrews, was horizontal rather than vertical, so Greek cult practice, in contrast to the Hebrews, was democratic rather than hierarchical. In expressing private piety, the Greek worshipper had a variety of personal choices among individual deities and shrines. He or she had many ways to take part in religious ritual, from processions, to actual sacrificing, to sharing the consecrated food with the officiating priest. Although some cults did restrict access and participation, Greek worship was generally conducted in public and the worshippers were more often actors than silent observers. In addition, as citizens of city-states, Greek men often selected religious officials, made laws to administer, enforce, and protect religious activities, and even introduced new gods and shrines.

Both societies separated out sacred times, space, and acts. Nevertheless, Hebrew worship retained a stronger adherence to the repetitive rituals that transport the individual and the group from the profane to the sacred, from the temporal to the eternal. On the other hand, in practice, Greek worship included a much broader spectrum of human activity now considered secular and was much more man centered than Hebrew worship. The anthropomorphic conception of deity permitted idolatry and the veneration of sexuality and nature. It also encouraged the glorification of physical beauty, athletic skills, artistic creativity, and intellectual endeavor as ways to please the gods, acknowledge their gifts to man, and manifest the godlike in human beings. Thus, forms which originated as religious activities, e.g., visual and performing arts, achieved high aesthetic levels and have been valued as such independent of their context as worship. Those individuals who excelled because of their prowess, talents, or wisdom immediately became famous in their own right although their exhibitions or creations were either presented to please the gods or exemplify divine power and mystery.

Many Greek rituals also drew spectators or participants into sacred time by means of repeated actions or connections to myths of origin or epochal events, as in Hebrew worship. Other Greek rituals, however, were transformed into unique and original performances or exhibitions in which the temporal events, places, and people were associated with the eternal. This juxtaposition both elevated the present human circumstance and made possible its examination in the light of eternity. But the deviation from repeated sacred patterns and the introduction of the topical constituted the beginning of desacralization and, in Huizinga's terms, the movement from sacred ritual to secular play.

It is true that both societies integrated the sacred and the secular to a much greater degree than we do today, solemnizing daily activity by oaths, prayers, libations, other offerings, and, among the Hebrews, obeying the regulations of the Torah and the oral law. Descralization is also exemplified, however, by the greater degree of state responsibility for the cult in Greece than in Israel. Religion was not identical with the state in either culture, but there was a far greater tendency to bend the secular to the sacred in Israel and to maintain a holy nation devoted to God and His service. In the city-states of Greece, worshipping the gods was just one (albeit a very important one) among many aspects of community life which the citizens governed for themselves.

Chapter 8

Public Life—Law and the State

Introduction

In his study of legal domination, in which the law becomes an instrument of the state subordinating the interests of individuals to the interests of the collectivity and the will of the government, Max Weber pointed out that every legal system must rest upon a belief in its legitimacy. But this belief in the legitimacy of legal authority, like the belief in the legitimacy of charismatic authority, has a circular quality. Thus charismatic authority rests on a belief in the holiness, the morality or the supernatural power of a person but this individual loses his or her authority as soon as those subject to it no longer believe in the extraordinary character or powers of the leader. The result is a question begging faith in which charismatic domination exists only as long as it proves itself and such proof is either accepted by the believers or rejected. Similarly, "any legal norm can be created or changed by a procedurally correct enactment. In other words, laws are legitimate if they have been enacted; and the enactment is legitimate if it has occurred in conformity with the laws prescribing the procedures to be followed."[1] Just as charismatic leadership can function whether the leader is a saint or a tyrant, so belief in the legitimacy of a legal order can be based on expediency (e.g., the usefulness of law

for the protection of life and property) or on some ultimate value
(from the most exalted, e.g., law as an emanation of God's will, to
the most depraved, e.g., law as an expression of a despot's will) or
on some combination of the two. In the modern era, ideologies
(e.g., Nazism and Communism) have become the ultimate value
legitimating the legal order even though, as in the case of Hitler
and Stalin, the ideology was only a mask for the dictator's will. The
Nazi and Communist totalitarian states of the twentieth century are
an interesting example of how the circular logic of charismatic
authority and legal domination are fused and reinforce one another.[2]

The Sinai and Olympus traditions avoided the dangers inherent in
the circular logic legitimating both charismatic and legal authority
by grounding this authority in divine revelation and natural law.
The legitimacy of the law in Israel rests on the divine revelation at
Mount Sinai and the covenant established between God and the
Israelites, not only those present at the revelation but all future
generations as well. Similarly, Moses' charismatic authority
derived primarily from God and only secondarily from the belief and
the assent of the Israelites. Since the moral and religious
prescriptions of the law are clearly spelled out, the prophet or ruler
who defies them or strays from them loses his or her authority and
can be deposed. At the same time the law of God contained in the
Torah is depicted as the most effective instrument in promoting the
physical and spiritual well being of the individual and the
community. As the rabbis continued to rationalize the oral law,
they insisted that like the written law it was revealed to Moses
(implicitly and made explicit in later generations) thus anchoring
its legitimacy in the Sinaitic Revelation.

In Greece, the legitimacy of the law was at first rooted in the
divine justice fostered by Zeus on Olympus. When the Greek city
states began to make their own specific laws and then belief in
traditional religion began to wane, the Greeks were confronted by
the inevitable problems of circularity described by Weber. The
Sophists, Thucydides, Xenophon and Plato who lived under the
radical democracy in Athens where the people both legislated and
judged, wrote about the issues relating to legal and political
legitimacy. Plato in particular, sought to ground the law and the
state on some higher principle. For him and later Greek
philosophers, the legitimating authority was the law of nature which
they saw as being in conformity with reason and expressing the
impulse for the good. Thus laws enacted by legislators must be
rational and lead human beings to that which is good. As Weber
notes: "Natural law has . . . been the collective term for those norms

which owe their legitimacy not to their origin from a legitimate lawgiver but to their immanent and teleological qualities."[3] He goes on to point out that the justification of a legal system by rooting it in natural law is the only remaining alternative (to avoid the dangers inherent in the circular reasoning by which law is legitimated) after beliefs in divine revelation and the sacredness of tradition have declined.

Weber not only examined how law was legitimated but also how it was rationalized in Western civilization. He suggested a theoretical model of four stages in which legal concepts and practices develop, each stage representing a progressive rationalization (and to a certain extent bureaucratization) of the law.

(1) Charismatic legal revelation through law prophets.

(2) Empirical creation and finding of law by legal notables.

(3) Imposition of law by secular or theocratic powers.

(4) The systematic elaboration of law and professionalized administration of justice by persons who have received their legal training in a learned and formally logical manner.[4] Weber acknowledged that in actuality the rationality of law progressed in many different sequences, not only in patterns like this. In addition, in some societies not all the stages have occurred, regardless of sequence. Weber's model corresponds very closely to the development of Jewish law but only his stage three, the imposition of law, describes the significant developments in the legal system of the Greek polis, although there are some similarities to stages one and two in the earliest periods of Greek history.

Charismatic Legal Revelation through Law Prophets

This once universal form of law-finding rested on the belief that law could *only* be revealed. Wherever the more primitive method of blood feuds and vengeance had been abandoned, legal disputes were decided by resorting to an oracle or an ordeal or both. Priests and law prophets increased their power by being called upon to interpret oracles and supervise trials by ordeal on a case by case basis. But since coercive power was in the hands of political authorities not the law prophets, law-finding was separate from law enforcement. In addition, law prophecy involved an elaborate ritual and adherence to certain formal procedures. Thus the separation of adjudication from enforcement and the formalization of legal procedure have their rudimentary origins in the institutions of legal revelation.

Empirical Creation and Finding of Law by Legal Notables

From charismatic law prophets called upon to find the law from case to case, there evolved legal notables who, in the course of time, became elected or appointed officials involved in empirical law-finding. They were usually descendants of distinguished families and their positions became hereditary, particularly where the families were regarded as endowed with charismatic gifts. The notables were responsible not only for adjudicating disputes but also for stating annually before the assembled community, the rules in accordance with which they would declare or "find" the law. This yearly declaration and report served a double purpose: to make the rules known to the public and to refresh the memory of the law prophet. In this stage we have the origin of adjudication by rules and the duty of their public disclosure. This kind of judge-made law results in the formation of legal norms and contributes to the further rationalization of the legal order.

Imposition of Law by Secular or Theocratic Powers

In this type of legal innovation laws may be enacted implicitly, although there is no conscious departure from tradition and legal revelation. Thus the assembled notables or the heads of tribes may attribute a special sanctity or superior authority to a certain interpretation of sacred tradition and so in effect enact a law, although, as was the case in the Sinai tradition, the enactors did not for a moment believe they were creating new laws. They were merely making explicit what had long been implicit in the Sinaitic Revelation. Another scenario is the proclamation by a prophet of a new principle received through revelation which is adopted by the assembly of the people and propagated accordingly. A secularized version of this scenario is the use of revelation as an ex post facto ratification of human law-finding. The end result of all these scenarios is the same: revelation is gradually superseded by lawmaking through initiative and consensus although there is no explicit abandonment of tradition or enactment of new laws.

The Greeks, however, separated sacred law from polis law early in their history, as they subordinated the interests of individuals or nobles to the interests of the collectivity. Through procedures established for correct enactment they made new laws for themselves but because of reverence for the gods and ancient human lawmakers they retained the legitimizing support of tradition. As noted above, when the divine basis for legal enactments became questionable, philosophers found new legitimation in nature and natural law.

Systematic Elaboration of Law and Professionalized Administration of Justice

Such systematization is favored by established authorities because it allows them the maximum flexibility for decision making on all substantive legal and political issues. In the Sinai tradition, as in most Asiatic civilizations, religious and ritualistic regulations were never clearly differentiated from secular rules. Moral exhortations and legal commands were intertwined. Thus Jewish law governs the relations between humans and God as well as the relations between human beings, and the Hebrew term designating this law, *halakah*, means "the way," the way in which a person shall go, a way of conduct analogous to "the Tao" of Confucianism. In keeping with an outlook that viewed all of life as governed by religion, it is not surprising that on Sinai the professional jurists who elaborated the *halakah* and administered it were rabbis. In Greek city states, however, the religious and ritualistic regulations were separated from secular rules. A class of priests and professional interpreters of sacred law did develop and was consulted by the state and individuals for specific questions requiring their expertise. But, because the rules of government were made by the consensus of the citizens themselves and the citizens judged each other case by case, no professional class of jurists ever developed.

What was true of law was also true of the state. In the Sinai tradition, where the covenant included everyone and every aspect of life, religion became highly relevant to the political and social organization of the community. The Hebrew word *am* denotes a salvational community that is the recipient of a divinely revealed law embracing all human institutions. These institutions are not immaterial to the religious life; they either express or do not express the will of God for humans and they are either conducive or not conducive to a life of true submission to God. In the Greek system, where law and adjudication became major functions of government and the rulers and the ruled exchanged positions regularly, it was the polis, the organization of the autonomous citizens of a small geographical area, which became the focus of all aspects of individual and community life and the central means through which both achieved goodness.

Notes

1.   Max Weber, *Staatssozialogie* (Berlin: Duncker & Humboldt, 1956), p. 99; Reinhard Bendix, *Max Weber: An Intellectual Portrait* with intro. by Guenther Roth (Berkeley, Los Angeles, London: University of California Press, 1977), p. 419.

2.   *Max Weber: The Theory of Social and Economic Organization*, trans. A. M. Henderson and Talcott Parsons, ed. with intro. Talcott Parsons (New York: Oxford University Press, 1947), pp. 155-56; 329-333; Bendix, *Max Weber: An Intellectual Portrait*, p. 419; Hannah Arendt, *The Origins of Totalitarianism* (Cleveland and New York: The World Publishing Co., 1958), pp. 341-388.

3.   *Max Weber on Law in Economy and Society* ed. with intro. and annotations Max Rheinstein, trans. Edward Shils and Max Rheinstein (Cambridge: Harvard University Press, 1954), pp. 287-88; Bendix, *Max Weber: An Intellectual Portrait*, p. 420.

4.   Bendix, *Max Weber: An Intellectual Portrait,* p. 392, n. 19 reduces Weber's four categories to three: charismatic legal revelation through law prophets, imposition of law by authority, and lawmaking by legal notables.

Sinai: Covenant and Polity

The Covenant

Like every other political tradition, the essence of the Hebraic political outlook is the concern with justice and power, justice as the expression of the legal system, power as characterizing the state. But unlike the classical Greek concept of politics which focused primarily on structure, in Israel the focus was on relationships. It was not so much the best structure that would result in the best regime but that the best government would reflect the proper relationships between justice and power, the governors and the governed, God and man. The term "covenant" best sums up this orientation since its very basis is the definition of relationships.

Simply put, a covenant is a general obligation involving two or more parties. Paradoxically, the root meaning of the word conveys two seemingly opposite actions, cutting and binding, that are, on deeper reflection on the concept, not at all mutually exclusive. Separation and linkage in covenant relationships suggests a bond between independent and not necessarily equal parties who assume mutual obligations and commitments, in an atmosphere of mutual respect, for a joint endeavor. Though our modern legal contracts are related to the covenant concept, a covenant goes beyond a mere agreement for mutual advantage. It demands a pledge of loyalty and ultimately a moral commitment among the parties that causes the development of a particular kind of community among them.[1]

The covenant par-excellence in the Bible is that established between God and Israel at the Sinaitic Revelation (Exod. 19-24) in which God elected Israel as His treasured people and Israel pledged itself to live by the divine law. But this agreement is steeped in paradox. God limited Himself in order to establish the covenant with a particular people, yet unlike all other treaty partners in the ancient world, God transcended His covenant. On the other hand, though Israel, through the freedom of will granted to all human beings, had freedom to break the covenant, God was bound in a way no human is bound, by His own forces which He Himself had created.[2] This did not mean that Israel suffered no consequences for breaking the covenant. The doctrine of reciprocity made that impossible and the Torah is quite explicit that to obey or not to obey the covenant could be a matter of life and death (Deut. 30:19-20). But it did mean that the covenant was *not* invalidated by the failure to comply on the part of Israel. They could always return to its commitments and a patient and forgiving deity was always ready to receive them as the prophets tirelessly taught. The basis for this reconciliation is the unconditional covenant with Abraham resulting from a mysterious decision of God (Gen. 12:1-7; Gen. 15:7; Exod. 2:23-24; Exod. 20:2; Deut. 7:8).

But though God's covenant with Israel at Sinai, like the revelation itself, was wrapped in mystery, the results of the covenant, like the content of the revelation, were absolutely clear. The Sinai covenant transformed the Israelites from a family of tribes into a body politic and the Torah, the teaching revealed at Sinai, eventually came to be regarded as the constitution of the nation. This constitution (developing, as we shall see, through the stages of legal rationalization described by Weber) spelled out the regulations that were to govern all aspects of life in the holy nation whose ultimate ruler and authority was God. What it did *not* dictate or establish was the organization of the regime. The assumption was that as long as the basic covenant was in place supplementary covenants would emerge (as they did) to establish the proper balance between God, the governors and the governed so that the structure of the government was immaterial. It would emerge as convenience and necessity determined.[3]

The Law

As S. N. Eisenstadt has noted, Weber's understanding of Jewish civilization hinged on his view of the Jews as a pariah people and this view, to some extent, influenced his very brief reference to Jewish law.[4] But Weber often conducted simultaneous lines of investigation on interdependent topics without attempting to clarify their connections or establish a consistent approach to their treatment throughout his writings.[5] Thus his theoretical framework for the development of law in various societies is, as noted above, strikingly congruent (though not in every respect) with the historical development of Jewish law as we have come to understand it today. This congruency was not mentioned by Weber himself or by his interpreters and stands independent of his view of the Jews as a pariah people.

Stages of Development—The revelation at Sinai, which contained the essence of the Hebrew law code, is paradigmatic of Weber's first stage of legal development and Moses is the prototype of the charismatic law prophet. The Bible makes clear that the law finding (as Weber described it) of this stage was on a case by case basis (Exod. 18:13-17). The frequent divine guidance given to Moses in legal matters typifies the role of the law prophet in interpreting oracles. The trial by ordeal, so characteristic of this stage, is also found in the Bible in the ritual of the *sotah*, the woman suspected of adultery by her husband (Num. 5:11-31). The beginning of bureaucratization and the development of formal procedures is evident from Exod. 18:13-17 and from the regulations governing judges, witnesses and crimes as well as other matters contained in the law codes of Exodus, Leviticus, Numbers, and Deuteronomy. The separation of adjudication from law enforcement originating in this early rationalization of the law is clearly expressed in Deut. 16:18: "You shall appoint magistrates and officials for your tribes . . ." On this verse the medieval Jewish Bible commentator, Rashi, comments: "*Shofetim* (magistrates) are the judges who pronounce sentence and *shoterim* (officials) are those who chastise the people at their (the judges) order, beating and binding the recalcitrant with a stick and a strap until he accepts the judge's sentence." Elsewhere in the Pentateuch we are told that the man who blasphemed God and the man who gathered wood on the Sabbath were placed in detention until Moses could determine what their punishment should be. God directed Moses to have the blasphemer and the man who violated the Sabbath stoned by the entire community (Lev. 24:10-14; Num. 15:32-36). Moses, who pronounced the judgment, was not to carry out the execution but the members of the community who hold the coercive power serve as the enforcers of the law.[6]

The two examples just mentioned underscore a unique element in the Hebrew legal system. Though Israel shared ancient legal traditions with the peoples of the Near East in which, as noted above, the organic blend of the juridical, moral and religious realms was integrated, in Israel this integration was far more complete than elsewhere. Like the Babylonia of Hammurabi, ancient Israel saw the purpose of the law as establishing justice, ensuring domestic tranquillity and promoting the general welfare, to paraphrase the constitution of the United States. But the law of Sinai had an additional purpose, to sanctify life, a purpose stemming from its divine authorship. In Mesopotamia the law, though corresponding to a cosmic ideal transcending even the gods, had a human author-the king. The difference in legal effect between the Hebraic and Mesopotamian system was that for the Hebrews certain crimes were also sins, a violation of God's will. Thus for the Babylonians, Assyrians and Hittites the procedure in the case of adultery was to leave it to the discretion of the offended husband to punish his wife or pardon her. If the wife was punished, so was the paramour. If the husband pardoned his wife, the paramour went free also. The husband's pardon wiped out the crime.

Not in biblical law. "If a man commits adultery with the wife of another man, both the adulterer and the adulteress must be put to death" (Lev. 20:10; Deut. 22:22-23). The husband has no right to mitigate or cancel the punishment because adultery is not only a wrong committed against the husband, it is a sin against God. Moreover, if the parties to the adultery go unpunished the community will suffer as well because of the doctrine of reciprocity and corporate or horizontal responsibility, not to speak of the social disruption that rampant adultery would bring to the group. To be sure, the oral tradition elaborated by the rabbis (to be discussed below) required two unimpeachable witnesses to have been present when the act was committed and they must clearly warn the participants of the consequences of their act before the death penalty could be imposed. Nevertheless, in essence the theoretical concept remained. Similarly, biblical law, unlike its Near Eastern counterparts, does not allow the family of a murdered man or woman to accept a monetary settlement in lieu of the death of the murderer; "the murderer must be put to death" (Num. 35:17), although here too the rabbinic law of witnesses made capital punishment for murder a rarity in Jewish courts. Conversely, the Hebrew concept of the sanctity of life prohibited capital punishment for crimes against property whereas Assyrian and Babylonian law enjoin it in certain cases.[7]

We turn now to the second stage of Max Weber's model of legal rationalization. The legal notables engaged in empirical law-finding most closely resemble the biblical priests. These priests were descended from distinguished families tracing their lineage back to Moses and Aaron and the charismatic power of these two leaders became attached to the hereditary priestly office. But the chief priests were also appointed to office by the kings of Judah and Israel who took advantage of the royal prerogative to select priests who were most politically advantageous to them. There was already present here a source of conflict that, as we shall see later, emerged among the several power centers of the Hebrew state. The previous chapter discussed the judicial function of the priest but the Bible also underscores their role in empirical law-finding.

> If a case is too baffling for you to decide, be it a controversy over homicide, civil law, or assault-matters of dispute in your courts-you shall promptly repair to the place that the Lord

your God will have chosen and appear before the levitical priests, or the magistrate in charge at the time, and present your problem. When they have announced to you the verdict in the case, you shall carry out the verdict that is announced to you from that place that the Lord chose, observing scrupulously all their instructions to you. You shall act in accordance with the instructions given you and the ruling handed down to you; you must not deviate from the verdict that they announce to you either to the right or to the left (Deut. 17:8-13).

These verses were taken to mean that the law should be determined by teachers (as noted in chapter 6 the function of the priests and levites was also to teach the people) and judges according to their human knowledge and understanding, i.e., empirically.[8] Finally, in their capacity as teachers the priests, like Weber's notables, made known to the community the rules in accordance with which they would decide the law in their capacity as judges. Moses set the pattern by orally communicating the laws to the people (Exod. 21:1;24:3-4) and the Bible seeking to insure the public communication of the law on a national scale ordained that every seven years the entire Israelite population including gentiles residing in the land be summoned to hear a public reading (and explanation) of the Torah (Deut. 31:10-13).

But prophets too engaged in empirical law-finding as already noted in chapter six. Ezekiel set forth the laws that were to govern the Temple, the altar and the priests (Ezek. 43:10-44:11) and Zechariah answered a legal inquiry addressed to the priests and prophets about weeping and practicing abstinence in the fifth month (*Av*) because of the destruction of the Temple and Jerusalem (Zech. 7:1-4). In fact, two prophets, Elisha and Jeremiah, in keeping with Weber's description of the notables' charismatic right to deviate from precedent, decreed rulings different from Torah law.[9]

Weber's third stage of legal development, the imposition of law by secular or theocratic powers, corresponds to two major turning points in the history of Jewish law:

1) the discovery of the book of the Torah (the book of Deuteronomy according to scholarly consensus) in the Temple during the reign of King Josiah (639-609 B.C.E.) when a covenant was concluded with the people to accept as binding the divine law contained in this book (2 Kings 22:8-23:3).

2) the renewal of the covenant by Ezra and Nehemiah with the returnees to Jerusalem when the Torah, the entire Pentateuch, became binding on the people on the New Year of 445 B.C.E. (Neh.

8:1-8; Neh. 10:1). In both instances the Torah book (Deuteronomy in the time of Josiah, the Pentateuch in the time of Ezra) became the constitution of the Jewish polity. Characteristic of both periods was the implicit enactment of laws without a conscious departure from legal revelation and tradition. The central feature of the Deuteronomic law code that inspired the covenant in the days of Josiah was the centralization of the Hebrew cult at one chosen site, at the Temple in Jerusalem and the abolition of local sanctuaries and shrines outside the Temple (Deut. 12:1-28). The older Mosaic law codes did not know of this requirement. The priests of Josiah's time simply attributed greater validity and superior authority to the law code of Deuteronomy over its predecessors.[10]

In the time of Ezra and Nehemiah when the Five Books of Moses had been canonized, the central task was to harmonize the various law codes by interpretation (*midrash*). Thus for example, the expulsion of the foreign wives to whom some of the Judeans were married was mandated by Ezra on the basis of an interpretation and a harmonization of the passages in the law codes dealing with the issue. Marriages to Canaanites are forbidden to Israelites for religious reasons (Exod. 34:15-16; Deut. 7:3). Marriages to Ammonites and Moabites are forbidden because of their ethnic hostility to Israel (Deut. 23:4-7). Marriages to Edomites and Egyptians are permitted after the third generation because the Edomites are kinsmen and the Israelites were initially welcomed as sojourners in Egypt (Deut. 23:8-9). But Ezra makes no distinction between these various groups. He lumps them all together and compares them to Canaanites (Ezra 9:1-2) who according to the levitical code (Lev. 18:24 ff.; 20:22) have defiled the land of Israel (cf. Ezra 9:11).[11] That interpretations such as this one were considered to be the meaning of the law and were accepted as part of the Torah constitution is evident from Neh. 8:7-8. There we are told that "the Levites *explained* the Teaching to the people, while the people stood in their places. They read from the scroll of the Teaching of God, translating it and *giving the sense*, so they understood the reading." The underlined words in these verses refer to the interpretations of Ezra and his priestly and levitical colleagues.

It is important to note that the reign of King Josiah, during which the Deuteronomic law code was made the law of the land, is the closest analogue in the Sinai tradition to Weber's concept of the imposition of law by secular power. Even the most idolatrous kings were conceived as subordinate in authority to God and His law. Prior to the Josianic reform, the Torah literature and law codes were a religious and moral ideal observed by some but not universally enforced. The day- to- day life of the people was conducted according to customary law and ancestral traditions regulating vast areas of human relationships. The Torah was a utopian yardstick by which the real life of the people was measured by the prophets. When they found the gap between the real and the ideal too great, they denounced the reigning standards of religion and morality. During Josiah's reign the ideal came very close to the real.[12] Similarly, the proclamation of the entire Pentateuch as the constitution of the Judean community of returned exiles by Ezra and Nehemiah and the covenant established with the returnees is an unambiguous example of the imposition of law by theocratic power. The Second Commonwealth, until the time of King Herod, was ruled by a priestly theocracy. Under this theocracy, as in the time of King Josiah, strenuous efforts were exerted to implement the ideal law of the Torah as the real law of the state.

With the emergence of the rabbinic academies and law courts we come to the fourth stage in Weber's model of legal rationalization: the systematic elaboration of law and the professionalized administration of justice by persons who have received their legal training in a learned and formally logical manner. According to Weber, the transition from stage three to stage four is marked by the evolution from a more substantive approach to justice or even political expediency to the formal, procedural and logical rationality of the law, which is combined with substantive justice. He explained the distinction between the substantive and formal approach as follows:

> Law . . . is formal to the extent that in both substantive and procedural matters, only unambiguous general characteristics of the facts of the case are taken into account. This formalism can again be of two different kinds. It is possible that the legally relevant characteristics are of a tangible nature, i.e., that they are perceptible as sense data. This *adherence to external characteristics* of the facts, for instance the utterance of certain words, the execution of a signature, or the performance of a certain symbolic act with a fixed meaning, represents the most rigorous type of legal formalism. The other type of formalistic law is found where the legally relevant characteristics of the facts are disclosed through the *logical analysis of meaning* and where, accordingly, definitely fixed legal concepts in the form of highly abstract rules are formulated and applied.[13]

Weber pointed out that this step in the rationalization of the law was far from simple since the most ancient and the most modern types of law and legal procedure contain various mixtures of the perennial elements of legal thought. Every legal system is involved in an effort of formalization and struggles to achieve substantive justice. The various directions the law will take as a result of the combination and recombination of these elements depends on the character of the trained professionals engaged in these endeavors. In Jewish law these professionals were the rabbis who developed the various forms of acquisition (*kinyanim*) corresponding to Weber's first example of the formal approach and the exegetical principles (*middot*) which correspond to Weber's second type of legal formalism, the logical analysis of meaning.

In their rationalization of Jewish law the rabbis were confronted by the dichotomy between ancient traditions which formed the basis of legal authority on the one hand and a logical, rational determination of law that would make the law relevant and applicable in their time. No law code explicitly includes all the possible cases. As society developed, new legal questions emerged that were not clearly discussed in the Bible; so that by the time of the rabbis (ca. first century B.C.E. to fifth century C.E.) there was a great need for special interpretation and rational deduction to derive new laws from the Torah or to find support in Scripture for old laws which had become part of public practice for centuries.

In solving this problem the rabbis learned from Greek rhetoric. Hillel the Elder drew on ancient rules of interpretation that had been systematized, defined and given definite form by Greek rhetoricians in their interpretations of law and their philosophical allegorizations of the works of Hesiod and Homer. Hillel demonstrated that the validity of ancient traditions rested not only on the hoary authority of the past but also on reason. He showed how these traditions could also be derived by means of hermeneutic rules and he then used these same rules to expand the interpretation of the Torah. There were two steps to the process. In the first step Hillel established a biblical basis for the hermeneutic rules. This enabled him to derive laws directly from the Torah reinforcing the authority of custom and tradition with Scriptural sanction. What was not contained in Scripture could now be derived through rational methods. The second step was to raise in status the results of the hermeneutically derived interpretations to the sanctity of the biblical text itself so that it could be regarded as divinely revealed.[14] This approach is summed up in the talmudic dictum: "Whatever a diligent student shall teach in the presence of his master has already been said to Moses on Sinai."[15] The interpretations of Hillel and his school, according to this view, were but a later unfolding of that which already existed *in potentia* in the revelation on Sinai. They were derived from that which was implicit in the words of the Torah but was not made explicit until their time. In this way the oral law and the written law were given the same rank, both products of the Sinaitic Revelation.

The following are some examples of Hillel the Elder's rules of interpretation that were also used by the Greek and Roman rhetoricians. The inference *a fortiori*, in Hebrew *kal va-homer* (the light and the weighty) i.e., from major to minor premise and from minor to major premise, argues that a law that operates under certain conditions will surely be operative in other situations where the same conditions are present in a more acute form. Thus Exod. 20:22 gives permission to build the Sanctuary altar of stone, brick or anything else. By means of a *kal va-homer* it is concluded that since the material may be chosen in the case of this most important ritual object of the Sanctuary, it may *a fortiori* be chosen for the other less important ritual objects as well.[16] One of the various inferences from analogy argues that just as the daily sacrifice, which the Bible says should be brought "at its appointed time" (Num. 28:2) is due even on a Sabbath, so the Passover lamb, which Scripture also demands at "its appointed time" (Num. 9:2) must be slaughtered even if Passover falls on a Sabbath.[17]

The rule of the general and the specific, *kelal u-perat*, states that if the range of a statute is indicated both by a wider and a narrower term, it is the one coming second that counts. This means that if the narrower term comes second, it restricts the wider one but if the wider one comes last it includes and adds to the narrower one. Lev. 1:2 commands that offerings be brought from animals, oxen and sheep. The general terms "animals" is restricted by the more specific "oxen and sheep" thus excluding wild animals.[18] On the other hand, Exod. 22:9-10 establishes the liability of an individual charged by another to watch his ass, ox or sheep or any animal. Since the specific terms "ass, "ox", "sheep" are mentioned and added to by the more general term "any animal" the regulation is extended to include wild animals as well.[19]

Finally, there is the rule that an ambiguity in the law may be settled by examining the context in which the law appears, *davar ha-lamed me'inyano*. The commandment "You shall not steal" (Exod. 20:13) is interpreted as referring to the theft of a person, i.e., kidnapping, not the theft of property which is mentioned in Lev. 19:11. The reason is that the prohibition against stealing appears together with other capital crimes against a person, namely murder and adultery.[20]

The impact of Greco-Roman law and literature on talmudic jurisprudence and lore is also evident in the fact that one of the major forms of rabbinic literary expression, the commentary, is of Greek origin. In addition, sages like R. Akiba successfully learned the methods of Epicurean philosophy (though adamantly opposing its teachings[21]), which were completely assimilated and transformed for the purpose of ordering the Jewish oral tradition.[22]

The Noahite Laws— Under the rubric of the Laws of the Sons of Noah rabbinic tradition gives juridical formulation to a Hebraic concept of natural law analogous to the Greco-Roman concept but also quite different from it. In chapters two and six we saw that the wisdom writings of Israel emphasize that the glory of God can be perceived in the divine order planted in the works of creation. This perception of God in nature that is the product of reason and life experience is also a revelatory experience, a wisdom counterpart of the Sinaitic Revelation. Basic to the biblical and rabbinic world view is the conviction of God's unity, in which the natural order and the moral order represent two sides of the same divine nature. Similarly, the perception of God through reason and experience is but the other side of the human coin in which God is encountered through the revelation of the Torah. In the Bible, gentiles are assumed to know of God in His capacity as creator of nature and author of morality through human reason and life experience. For this reason they are held accountable for breaking elementary moral laws though nowhere in the Bible is the ground for their responsibility set forth. The innate moral impulse of the gentiles, what we might call their conscience, derives in the biblical view from "godfearing" (*yirat elohim*), a human virtue that has no reference to knowledge of or revelation from God. Gentile "godfearing" keeps them from murder (Gen. 20:11), adultery (Gen. 39:9) and breach of faith (Gen. 39:8 f.; 42:18); lack of it accounts for Amalek's brutal attack on Israel's stragglers in the wilderness journey to the Promised Land (Deut. 25:18). The rabbis summed up this view of gentile morality stemming from reason and life experience as follows: "If someone tells you there is wisdom among the gentile nations, believe him; that there is Torah (the revealed teaching of Sinai) do not believe him."[23]

In the rabbinic conception of the Noahite Laws all human beings are commanded to observe seven fundamental religious and ethical principles: the prohibition of (1) idolatry, (2) murder, (3) blasphemy, (4) sexual immorality, (5) theft, (6) cruelty to animals (before the flesh of an animal is used for food the animal must be slaughtered)[24] and the positive injunction (7) to establish courts of justice. These principles represent the standard of a civilized society and are incumbent upon all non-Jews (and are enforceable on non-Jews living in a Jewish state), Jews being further obligated to observe the 613 commandments of the written and the oral Torah. Although rabbinic tradition claims that the Noahite Laws were a divine command first directed to Adam, after the flood it is Noah who stands for the whole human race, as Adam had done at the very beginning of creation. Thus Noah becomes the guarantor of mankind and for this reason rabbinic Hebrew prefers to speak of the seven commandments of the "children of Noah" (*bnei Noah*) when it refers to humanity as a moral entity.

In addition to the view of the Noahite Laws as a divine revelation to Adam, the dominant view in rabbinic literature, there is also the rabbinic tradition that the Patriarchs came to their belief in God and their observance of these commandments through their powers of reason.[25]   Philo identifies the Patriarch's observance of the pre-Mosaic laws with the Greek concept of natural law.[26]   Harry A. Wolfson[27] has pointed out that Philo adds three new elements from Jewish tradition to the Greek concept of natural law:

(1) The natural laws do not exist side by side with the written law but mark a stage in the history of the development of the written law.

(2) Philo associates the natural laws with some of the outstanding figures of the pre-Mosaic age-Enosh, Enoch and Noah, Abraham, Isaac and Jacob.

(3) Philo also uses the term natural law to mean the law implanted by God in nature at the creation of the world.

According to Philo, the Patriarchs lived perfectly virtuous lives in keeping with the natural law of their time, that is the law emerging from their own right instincts and reason and the law implanted by God in the universe at creation. This law was later incorporated in the Torah revealed at Sinai. Thus in post-biblical literature, the Noahite Laws represent the fusion of the Torah view of the divine revelation at Sinai as the source for human conduct and the wisdom view of reason and life experiences evidenced in creation as also a divine source for living the good life.

It is this latter view underlying the seven Noahite Laws which make them strikingly parallel to the Roman concept of the *jus gentium*, the law of the nations governing the transactions of foreigners living in Rome. The outstanding Roman jurists such as

Ulpian and Cicero and the great jurists of the Augustan and post-Augustan age, were trained in Greek philosophy. Reflecting on what they learned from Plato, Aristotle and the Stoics concerning a law of nature that is the same as the law of reason, the Roman jurists concluded that the *jus gentium* since it was based on the ideas and practices common to many nations, must owe its existence to that nature which the Greek philosophers claimed was the same as reason. Thus the *jus gentium* and natural law came to be identified. The Roman jurist Ulpian, a native of Phoenicia, whose literary activity coincides with the compilation of the *Mishnah* (200 C.E.) stated: "Natural law is that which all animals have been taught by nature; this law is not peculiar to humans; it is common to all animals which are produced on land and the sea and the fowls of the air as well. From it comes the union of man and woman called by us matrimony; and therewith the procreation and rearing of children; we find in fact that animals in general, the very wild beasts, are marked by acquaintance with this law."[28] Ulpian's explanation of natural law has its counterpart in the penetrating observation of the Palestinian Amora R. Johanan: "Had not the Torah been revealed to Israel, man would have learned modesty from the cat, honesty from the ant, chastity from the pigeon and manners from the rooster."[29] Both the Roman jurist and the rabbinic sage affirm that the instincts deeply rooted in our nature and shared by other creatures as well form the foundation of our moral codes and our legal institutions.

The Rabbinic Court System— There were courts of justice in every city. In towns with less than 120 inhabitants there was only a court of three judges, three being the minimum number, so that where opinions were divided a majority could prevail.[30] These courts exercised jurisdiction in cases of flagellation and in civil matters, i.e., contracts, debts and obligations including matters involving the imposition of fines. But their jurisdiction did not apply to severe civil cases such as robbery, assault and battery. Courts of three judges supervised divorce proceedings and cases of levirate marriage and a whole variety of ritual matters including the conversion of non-Jews. As business transactions multiplied and it became impossible to have a regular court of three ordained judges (the judges were ordained rabbis) in every Jewish settlement, one man, if a scholar and acknowledged by the people as such, had the right to pronounce judgment and even to force the parties to accept his decision. Three plain men, even if not scholars, had the same right to pronounce judgment and force the parties to appear. In all cases a single uncommissioned scholar and a three-member court of ordinary people had the same judiciary power.

In towns with 120 inhabitants or more, the law called for a court of twenty three judges designated as a small Sanhedrin (*Sanhedrin Ketanah*). These courts exercised jurisdiction in criminal matters generally, including capital cases as well as in quasi-criminal cases involving the destruction of animals. If a case originally dealt with civil matters but might in due course give rise to criminal sanctions, it was brought before a court of twenty three. If the criminal accusations were found to be groundless, the case would be referred to a court of three for civil judgment.

The court of seventy one judges, known in early rabbinic times as the Great Court (*Bet Din Ha-Gadol*) and later as the Great Sanhedrin, had practically unlimited judicial, legislative and administrative powers but certain judicial and administrative functions were reserved to it alone. The high priest, the head of a tribe and the president (*nasi*) of the Sanhedrin itself, if accused of a crime could only be tried by a court of seventy one. Crimes such as the uttering of false prophecy, a rebellious teaching (going contrary to the written and oral law) by an elder and the idolatrous subversion of a whole town or tribe were under the jurisdiction of the court of seventy one. Death penalties connected with the rebellious son (Deut. 21:18-21), the individual who persuades another to worship idols and false witnesses, had to be confirmed by the Great Sanhedrin. The ordeal of a woman suspected of adultery took place in the Temple court in Jerusalem, the seat of the Great Sanhedrin. Among the administrative functions of this court were the appointment of lesser tribunals, criminal as well as civil, the election of kings and high priests, the expansion of the precincts of the Temple and the city of Jerusalem, the offering of a sacrifice for the sin of the whole community and the appointment and control of priests serving in the Temple. But its chief function was that of an appellate and interpreting court.[31]

In addition to this three tier court system, there was a special court of priests that sat in the Temple and was charged with the supervision of Temple ritual and with civil matters concerning priests. There was also a court of levites with similar functions.[32]

Before the Maccabean revolt the high priest was the pontifical head of religion and the state. As head of the state the high priest was advised by a council, *gerousia*, made up of representatives of the Jewish aristocracy and modeled after that of the Greek cities. When the vital interests of the state were involved, the high priest would convene a Great Assembly. It was the Great Assembly (or the Great Synagogue as it is sometimes called) that ratified the Pentateuch as the constitution of the Jewish people in the time of Ezra and Nehemiah and that elected Simon the Hasmonean to the high priesthood over 300 years later. However, Simon was given authority only over the Temple and its services and not over the wider religious life of the people such as the observance, interpretation and imposition of penalties for the violation of religious law. These matters, as noted above, were under the jurisdiction of the *Bet Din Ha-Gadol* later known as the Great Sanhedrin.

The religious Sanhedrin had no jurisdiction over political offenders. Those who committed crimes against the state were punished by the civil rulers, the high priest, king or Roman procurator (when Judea became a Roman province), who convoked a political Sanhedrin (*synedrion*), a court of their advisers to decide the fate of such culprits. The difference between the religious Sanhedrin and the political Sanhedrin was that the religious Sanhedrin held its sessions in designated places at specific times, while the political Sanhedrin was summoned, like a Grand Jury, only in cases of emergency such as the interrogation of Jesus and the trial of Paul.[33]   After the destruction of the Second Temple, when R. Gamaliel II became head of the Sanhedrin in Yavneh in 80 C.E., to his inherited religious authority he added the office of political head of the Jews.

The State

Though the modern Hebrew term *medinah* is used today for politically sovereign states, in the Jewish political tradition "there is no state . . . in the sense of a reified political entity complete in and of itself."[34] From the Sinai perspective, the modern concept of state sovereignty and its implication of absolute independence is untenable. No state that is a human creation can be sovereign in this sense, since only God is sovereign and the state is subordinate to Him. In the Sinai tradition God "entrusts the exercise of his sovereign powers to the people as a whole, mediated through His Torah-as-constitution as provided through His covenant with Israel."[35] In turn, the people entrust the exercise of this sovereignty to their appointed leaders who are responsible to them and to God. The leaders' conduct in office and their management of the affairs of state are measured by the yardstick of the Torah.

The Sinai concept of the state is best described by the term "polity." This implies a covenantal relationship between the members who reach a consensus through negotiation and bargaining. A polity suggests a political-legal jurisdiction irrespective of size or structure. Thus the Judean community of returnees in Jerusalem under the leadership of Ezra and Nehemiah, though officially a province of the Persian empire, was no less a polity than the independent Judean and Israelite states or the united monarchy that preceded it. Finally, the term "polity" used in this context implies the lack of absolute sovereignty.

Within the Hebrew polity power was and is diffused. Again this reflects the covenantal system and its insistence that political omnipotence be permanently denied to human beings. The division of authority among the power centers of the Hebrew polity can be depicted by a well-known rabbinic statement: "R. Simeon said: 'There are three crowns, the crown of Torah, the crown of the priesthood, and the crown of kingship (or governance, *malkut*). But greater than all of these is the crown of a good name (*shem tov*).'"[36] The crown of Torah represents the authority of the bearers , teachers and interpreters of the constitutional Torah. The crown of priesthood denotes the authority of Aaron and his descendants and the other priestly houses who were responsible for the formal worship, shared rituals and symbolic expressions of the Hebrew faith. The crown of kingship represents the power center of civil authority which began with the elders (*zekenim*) and tribal leaders (*nesiim*) of the primitive democracy of ancient Israel, was given to the first three kings of Israel (Saul, David and Solomon) and with the division of the united monarchy after the death of Solomon was shared with non-Davidic kings. The fourth source of authority in the Hebrew polity was associated with the crown of the good name. This crown represents charismatic leadership in which the divine spirit is channeled through a living personality rather than through a constitutional Torah or an institutional priesthood or civil authority. As discussed in chapter six, such charismatic personalities make their impact on the masses through their moral perfection and their mystical intensity, or through the miracles associated with them.[37] Their authority and power derive from "the good name" they have attained among the populace. Moses derived his authority as much from the crown of a good name as from the crown of Torah. Prophets like Elijah and Elisha belong somewhat more to the crown of the good name than to the crown of Torah. The Rechabites of the First Temple period, the Essenes as well as Jesus and the disciples in the time of the Second Temple can be seen as offshoots of the crown of the good name. Honi ha-Ma'agel (the circle maker) discussed in chapter six belongs more to the crown of the good name than to the Pharisaic crown of Torah.

It is apparent from these examples that there was overlapping in these power centers. In certain individuals and groups there was a merging of two and sometimes three sources of authority. The judges of biblical times combined the authority of the crown of the good name and the crown of civil authority. Samuel, who possessed the crowns of charismatic and Torah authority was compelled by the people and the divine command to concede the crown of civil authority to Saul. The first three kings of Israel are portrayed as having charismatic authority as well as civil authority. Saul and David are charismatic war leaders; Saul prophesies under the spirit and David plays divine melodies while Solomon is clothed with divine wisdom. In the prophets Jeremiah and Ezekiel three sources of authority were combined, the crowns of charisma (*shem tov*), Torah and the priesthood. On the other hand, a single power center could be split between two factions such as the division in the priestly crown between the Aaronide and Zadokite priestly lines or the cleavage in the crown of civil authority between the kings of Israel and Judah and between the kings of each country and their opposition, the remnants of the ancient primitive democracy, the elders and the assembly of the people to be discussed below.

This division of authority among the crowns differs from conventional separation of power systems in that the crowns are primarily concerned with the source, character and purpose of authority, that is, orientation and only secondarily with functions (executive, legislative, judicial). In the ideal Jewish polity no power center has the constitutional right to encroach upon the domain of others to deprive them of their authority. Moreover, the ideal polity of Sinai cannot be complete unless all the power centers are represented in one form or another. The interdependence and the interaction of the four sources of power are what gives vitality to the system. But in reality inter-crown conflict was far more characteristic of public life on Sinai, and in certain periods of time some of the power centers were completely merged or disappeared altogether. Nevertheless, the basic elements of the ideal Jewish polity continued to reassert themselves, if not in one era then in a succeeding one. With this conceptual outline of the Jewish polity in mind, it is instructive to see how it functioned in two periods that fall within the chronological framework of this book.

Ancient Israel and the First Temple Period— The Hebrew polity of ancient Israel was a primitive democracy, a governmental form derived from Mesopotamia. The biblical terms *'edah*, the original technical term for "assembly": and *kahal*, referring to "the people" as a collective unit are strikingly parallel to the primitive democratic institution in Mesopotamia.[38] The *'edah* originated in the semi-nomadic society of early Israel (from the time of the Patriarchs until the beginning of the monarchy, ca. 1350-1020 B.C.E.) where a strong egalitarianism prevailed and where no hierarchy of rulers or complex governmental structure was permitted to arise. Here each member was as important as any other and had the right and opportunity of expressing his views at the "assembly." Of course, in this governing body the elders, who were presumed to have wisdom as well as age, played a dominant role, and their opinions carried great weight, particularly since no formal vote was taken but, rather a consensus was reached on issues confronting the group. As the supreme authority representing the entire people, the assembly had an important role to play in the allocation of land to the various tribes (Num. 32:2ff.; Josh. 22:12ff.) served as the judiciary (Num. 35:12, 24, 25) and exercised an executive function in making war, dividing the spoils and making treaties (Num. 31:26ff.; Josh. 9:15ff.)[39] Thus the *'edah* and the *kahal* epitomized the crown of governing authority (*keter malkut*).

In ancient Israel, as in Mesopotamia, there arose a charismatic leadership that was not intended to be permanent but only to deal with the particular crisis that had called it forth. The charismatic leader received a divine mandate which was ratified by the assembly. In Israel, Moses became the prototype of this kind of leader, aptly described by Yehezkel Kaufmann as an apostle prophet. His mandate from God (Exod. 3:10-12) was confirmed by the assembly of elders (Exod. 3:16; 4:29). Moses' leadership was called forth by the crisis of the exodus from Egypt and the sojourn in the desert and was ended prior to the Israelite entry into Canaan. Thus he epitomized the crown of the good name (*keter shem tov*, the Bible calls him the humblest man on earth Num. 12:3), charismatic authority par excellence. But he was also lawgiver and judge (Exod. 18-24) wearing the double crown of charismatic as well as constitutional authority (*keter torah*). The crown of priesthood (*keter kehunah*) went to Aaron and his sons (Exod. 28-29; Lev. 8-9).

From the time of Moses throughout the period of the Judges the four power centers were present and interacted with one another. At times, as noted earlier, there was a merging of sources of authority.

Significantly, during this era it is only the crown of priesthood that is handed down from father to son in dynastic fashion. The two attempts to make charismatic and Torah authority dynastic (one in which Abimelech, the son of Jerubaal-Gideon, sought to capitalize on his father's charisma and become king, Judges 9, and one in which Samuel sought to make his sons judges, 1 Sam. 8:1-5) ended in failure.

The instability of primitive democracy in Israel, as in Mesopotamia, led to the demand for the creation of the monarchy. As the result of the conquest, the territorial holdings of Israel increased in Palestine. The increase in land meant an increasing distance between the tribes and a difference in regional interests that splintered tribal cohesiveness and tribal consensus thus crippling the primitive democracy in its confrontation with frequent and repeated crises. Symptomatic was the fact that the judges, as charismatic leaders, rose to defend against attack one or more but never all the tribes, even though they were linked in a confederacy. The subjugation of Israelite territory by the Philistines toward the end of the period of the Judges (1045-1025 B.C.E.) necessitated a more permanent and comprehensive national leadership that could guarantee a settled life of peace and independence. The nations surrounding Israel established monarchies immediately after the conquest and settlement of their territory. Yet such was Israel's belief in its primitive democracy ruled by God, Who raised up leaders for His people in time of emergency, that it clung to tribal democracy long after it had conquered and settled the Promised Land. But this belief had to give way to the harsh realities of the times.[40]

Though there was opposition to the monarchy in Israel (the book of Samuel contains anti-monarchy and pro-monarchy traditions)[41], it was *not* based on the belief that the institution of kingship *per se* was a sin against God and a rebellion against His rule comparable to that of idolatry. The Deuteronomic law code (Deut. 17:14-20) permitted the selection of a king as long as he was a Hebrew and God's chosen and as long as he did not multiply wives, horses or silver and gold. Kingship is permitted as long as the king revered God and observed His commandments. Neither the prophets nor the historical books of the Bible ever demanded the abolition of the monarchy and the return to the primitive democracy. The fact that the first king, Saul, was designated by God to rule over Israel (his subsequent rejection by God presupposes a previous acceptance) and that the monarchy became a national ideal in the day-to-day life of the people and in its messianic hopes, is a clear indication that there was no fundamental religious opposition to the institution.

The anti-monarchy circles in ancient Israel were concerned about the historical continuity of the people and its covenant with God that was threatened by the transition from semi-nomadic existence in the years of desert wandering to settled urban life under a human king ruling as an absolute master.[42] They were worried that the king, using governmental authority, would squelch the other interdependent power centers. But these fears were unfounded. The other sources of power remained. From the time of the first king, Saul, throughout the First Temple period, during the united monarchy and after its division into the kingdoms of Judah and Israel, in order to become king and to maintain a stable rule a man had to have the tribal leaders' acceptance. These were the "elders" (*zekenim*) who along with the "assembly of the people" constituted the remnants of the primitive democracy that continued to survive under the monarchy and provided the critical leverage to offset some of the power of the king. After the death of Saul it was "the elders of Israel" who played the pivotal role in the jockeying for power between David and the house of Saul (2 Sam. 3:17). To become and remain king a man needed a supportive priesthood. It was Zadok, David's high priest of the south from Hebron who backed Solomon for the throne while Abiathar, David's high priest of the north from Shiloh, backed the rebellious Adonijah, David's other son, in his bid for kingship after David's death (1 Kings 1:19-40). Finally, from Saul down to the last monarchs of the northern and southern kingdom, no royal house was ever established or deposed without the authoritative word of the prophet.

This is not to say that the kings did not attempt to eliminate power centers, or factions within the power centers, that from their perspective overly limited or threatened their authority. Saul suspecting that the priests of Nob supported David massacred all of them. Abiathar was the sole survivor and continued as high priest under David (1 Sam. 22:16-23). But ultimately such attempts did not succeed. In David's reign, the supplanting of the institutions of tribal democracy by royal ones that excluded the traditional leadership of the assembly and elders, centralizing power in the monarchy, aroused an ever increasing resentment among the people. This resentment surfaced in the revolt of David's son Absalom, who sought his father's throne, and in the revolt of Sheba ben Bichri, who called for the overthrow of the House of David (2 Sam. 15-20). Both revolts were supported by the latent institutions of primitive democracy that survived after the advent of the monarchy, "the men of Israel" and "the elders of Israel."[43]

Solomon removed the chief priest of the northern tribes, Abiathar, because he supported Adonijah, Solomon's rival to the throne. Thus Zadok, the chief priest of the south remained the sole high priest in office. In addition, Solomon sought to destroy the latent infrastructure of the primitive democracy of the northern tribes that had survived into the monarchy. He established twelve administrative districts each of which was to provide food for the court in Jerusalem for one month of the year. The boundaries of these twelve new districts did not correspond to the existing boundaries of the twelve tribes and the administrative heads of each district were personally appointed by Solomon supplanting the tribal leaders and "people's assembly" of the northern tribes (the tribe of Judah from which the House of David came was not redistricted, 1 Kings 4). Anger over this power play, among other grievances, precipitated the division of the monarchy after Solomon's death in which the assembly of all Israel served as the power broker in rejecting Rehoboam, Solomon's son, and in enthroning Jeroboam I as king over the ten northern tribes (1 Kings 12).[44]

During the reign of King Ahab, his Phoenician wife, Jezebel, sought to eliminate charismatic and Torah authority embodied in the Hebrew prophets of the time by putting them to the sword (1 Kings 18:12-13). But the brutal policy ultimately failed. The house of Ahab was destroyed by the founder of a new dynasty anointed according to the authoritative word of the prophet Elisha (2 Kings 9).

The Second Temple Period— In 538 B.C.E. Cyrus the Great, the Persian conqueror of Babylonia issued a royal edict granting permission to the Jews to return to Jerusalem to rebuild the Temple. At the head of the returnees stood Zerubavel, a descendant of the Davidic line (representing the *keter malkut*, the crown of civil authority) assisted by Joshua, the High Priest representing the crown of priesthood. However, once the Temple was rebuilt Joshua sought to undermine the position of Zerubavel, despite the protests of the prophets (Zech. 3:6; 10:13), the bearers of charismatic and Torah authority. Joshua and his supporters succeeded because the returned exiles and their co-religionists who remained in Babylonia were afraid that Zerubavel might excite the suspicions of the Persians that the Jews were contemplating a revolt leading to an independent state and the reinstatement of the Davidic monarchy. The Persian policy of religious toleration would allow for a high priest but not for a Davidic king. This reality led to the creation of the priestly theocracy in the Second Commonwealth which represented a compromise between the ideal of an independent state governed by a Davidic king and the present reality in which Judea was a province of the Persian Empire.

Nevertheless, the ascendance of the priests to power did not eradicate the view that the new community should be headed by a secular leader from the House of David representing the crown of kingship rather than by a high priest wearing two crowns, priestly and civil authority. This view was widely held, particularly by those Jews who were not among the former exiles but who had remained in Judea, and among whom there may have been descendants of the royal family.[45] These opponents of priestly leadership were scornfully nicknamed *Perushim*, Pharisees, Separatists, by Joshua the High Priest and his followers. Later on, as the Pharisees developed a wide ranging oral interpretation of the Torah which gave them a life style distinguishing them more markedly from gentiles than did the life style of other Jews, the political origin of the name took on an additional religious significance.[46] Those who believed in the supremacy of the high priesthood called themselves *Zedukim*, Sadduccees, adherents of the family of Zadok, elevated to the position of sole high priest by Solomon as discussed above. That the Pharisees never completely accepted the merger of the crown of governmental power with the crown of the priesthood is evident from the Pharisaic author of 1 Maccabees. Describing the appointment of Simon the Maccabee he tells us that "the Jews and the priests were well pleased that Simon should be their leader and high priest forever until there should arise a faithful prophet (who would authorize the restoration of the Davidic monarchy). . . ."[47]

Throughout the Second Temple period those who favored a theocracy under a high priest and those who hoped for a restoration of the monarchy did not envision an absolutist form of government in which the interdependent power centers would be abolished. Thus Josephus, the Jewish historian of this period who was a Pharisee, looked upon the priestly theocracy as the ideal form of government. In fact Josephus coined the word *theocracy* and considered it the basis of the kingdom of God going back to Moses.[48] But, according to Josephus, Moses intended that the priestly theocracy share power with a people's council and should the people desire a monarchy it should be subordinate to the high priest and the council.[49] The Pharisaic author of I Maccabees also favored a government of a high priest and a people's council in the interim, until a Davidic king would be restored. He stated that among the various aspects of Roman rule that Judah Maccabee admired was the fact that "none of them did ever put on a diadem neither did they clothe themselves with purple to be magnified thereby; . . . they had made for themselves a senate house, and day by day three hundred and twenty men sat in council consulting always for the people . . . ."[50]

The rabbis debated the meaning of Deut. 17:14f. as to whether the monarchy was optional or obligatory.[51]   Though the prevailing Pharisaic ideal of government, a Davidic monarchy, remained the ideal of the rabbis, they were divided over the reality of the present. There were those who insisted on a Davidic ruler even in the present and therefore opposed the priestly rule of the Hasmonean family and there were those who felt that kingship in Israel need not be tied to the House of David.[52]

Throughout the Second Temple period the tension between the power centers was intense. The Essenes, representing charismatic and, to some extent, Torah authority repudiated the priesthood of the Jerusalem Temple and retreated to the Judean desert. The crown of civil authority governing internal Jewish communal affairs under Roman rule in Judea was torn with the house of Herod and the Sadducean high priests cooperating with the Romans, while three political divisions split the Pharisees. There was a radical group, the Zealots, fanatically dedicated to the violent overthrow of Rome and the Jewish puppets of Rome; a pacifistic group, disgusted by the bloodshed and willing to give up the Jewish state to Roman domination in order to secure peace; and a third group, faithful to the classical Pharisaic ideal of an independent Jewish state as necessary for Judaism but realistic about its implementation.[53] There was tension between Jesus and the disciples, themselves Pharisees but representing charismatic authority par excellence, and some Pharisaic leaders who saw them as a threat to the crown of Torah.

For a short term during the reign of the Hasmonean family and prior to the imposition of Roman rule in Judea, the crown of Torah authority was in the ascendance when the Pharisees were the political ruling class and as members of the Sanhedrin replaced the rule of the high priest, the theocracy, with government by law, a nomocracy. After the destruction of the Second Temple the crown of priestly authority was absorbed by the rabbinate. But the tension and struggle continued within the rabbinate itself and outside its ranks between Torah and charismatic authority and between these two power centers and the civil authority governing internal Jewish affairs now vested in Jewish communal lay leadership.[54]

Rabbinic Views of Political Office— Despite their attachment to an independent Jewish polity and to the Davidic monarchy, the rabbis held a dim view of the offices of communal and political leadership. The biblical narratives telling of the intrigues and assassinations surrounding all the kings of Israel and Judah, the bloody history of the political strife in the Second Temple period and their own experiences as leaders in the Jewish community led them to believe that the virtuous life was incompatible with public office. "Why did the dynasty of King Saul come to an early end?" asked the third century scholar Samuel. "Because it was not stained by misrule." For "no one is accepted as a public leader except one carrying a bag of reptiles on his shoulders," that is, a leader succeeds only if prepared to disregard the rule of ethics.[55] The rabbinic assertion that "office buries its holder" was exemplified by references to biblical passages where a prophet outlived four kings (Isa. 1:1; Jer. 1:1-3).[56] The rabbis composed a prayer, still part of the Jewish liturgy, praising "those faithfully attending to the needs of the community," and R. Ammi on his deathbed regretted not having taken part in communal life. His disciples and friends found that was precisely his greatest claim to honor: "Above all your other virtues you have avoided acting as a judge and have never permitted yourself to seek public office."[57]

In medieval Egypt, Moses Maimonides served as "Head of the Jews" without receiving remuneration for his services, earning his living as a physician. Referring to the officials of the Prince of the Diaspora, the assistants of the secular head of the Jewish community, who received remuneration for their labors, he wrote: "Most religious men lose fear of God when they gain authority. Earning one silver coin as an employee in tailoring, carpentry or weaving is preferable to the emoluments granted by the Prince of the Diaspora."[58]

Notes

1.   Daniel J. Elazar and Stuart A. Cohen, *The Jewish Polity: Jewish Political Organization from Biblical Times to the Present* (Bloomington: Indiana University Press, 1985), pp. 8-11; Moshe Weinfeld, "Covenant," *Encyclopedia Judaica* (Jerusalem: Keter Publishing House, 1972) 5: 1011-1022.

2.   Paul Ramsey, "Elements of a Biblical Political Theory," *Journal of Religion* 29, No. 4 (October, 1949): 265. On the dialectical nature of the covenant see Jon D. Levenson, *Creation and the Persistence of Evil* (San Francisco: Harper & Row, 1988), pp. 140-148.

3.   Gordon M. Freeman, *The Heavenly Kingdom: Aspects of Political Thought in the Talmud and Midrash* (Lanham, New York, London: University Press of America, 1986), p. 55.

4.   S. N. Eisenstadt, " 'ha-Yahadut ha-Kedumah' shel Weber u-Defus ha-Historiah ha-Yehudit," *Tarbiz* 49, No. 3-4 (1979-80): 384-421; *Max Weber on Law in Economy and Society*, p. 244.

5.   Bendix, *Max Weber: An Intellectual Portrait*, p. xlvii. This analysis of Weber's stages of legal development was arrived at independently and differs in a number of respects from that of M. Fishbane, *Biblical Interpretation in Ancient Israel* (Oxford: Oxford University Press, 1988), pp. 235-262.

6.   In the case of capital punishment by stoning, which as a survival of *vindicta publica* was characterized by the participation of the whole population (Lev. 24:16; Num. 15:35; Deut. 17:7), the Tannaitic Midrashim make a distinction between the two cases mentioned in the Torah.   In the case of the blasphemer (Lev. 24:14) the *Sifra, Emor* 19:1 (ed. Weiss), p. 104b includes the judges among those carrying out the execution. Since the verse says "all those that heard him" (i.e., his blasphemy) this includes the witnesses and the judges because the witnesses had to repeat the *ipsissima verba* (i.e., the blasphemous words) in the presence of the judges, *M. Sanhedrin*, 7:5.   But in the case of the man who gathered wood on the Sabbath (Num. 15:32-36), the *Sifre, Shelah* 114 (ed. Friedman), pp. 33b-34a includes the witnesses among those carrying out the stoning but not the judges.

7.   Moshe Greenberg, "Some Postulates of Biblical Criminal Law," in *The Jewish Expression*, ed. Judah Goldin (New York: Bantam Books, 1970), pp. 21-29 (reprinted from the *Yehezkel Kaufmann Jubilee Volume*, Jerusalem, 1960). See, however, the critique by B. Jackson, "Reflections on Biblical Criminal Law" in *Studies in Biblical Law* ed. David Daube (Oxford: The Clarendon Press, 1947): 25-63.

8.   *Sifre*, Deut. 153 (ed. Friedman), p. 104b; *The Principles of Jewish Law*, ed. Menachem Elon (Jerusalem: Keter Publishing House, 1975), p. 53.

9.   These deviations and others like them such as Elijah's offering a sacrifice on Mount Carmel in contradiction to the law requiring the centralization of the cult in the Jerusalem Temple are regarded as *hora'at sha'ah, Sifre, Shofetim* 175 (ed. Friedman), p. 107b; *Sifre Re'eh* 85 (ed.

Friedman), p. 92. The rabbis debated whether these law-findings of the prophets were the result of revelation or legal reasoning, *b. Temurah*, 16a. Cf. Ephraim E. Urbach, "Halakah U-Nevuah," *Tarbiz* 18 (1946-47): 5 ff. and above Chapter 6- Sinai IV: The Intellectual Piety of the rabbis, note 13.

10. Yehezkel Kaufmann, *The Religion of Israel*, trans. and abridged Moshe Greenberg (Chicago and London: The University of Chicago Press, 1960), pp. 176-184 and the other examples cited there.

11. Yehezkel Kaufmann, *Toledot ha-'Emunah ha-Yisraelit* (Jerusalem: Bialik Institute and Dvir Ltd., 1956) 8: 291-292.

12. Kaufmann, *The Religion of Israel*, p. 290; pp. 338-340; U. Cassuto, *A Commentary on the Book of Exodus* (Jerusalem: Magnes Press, 1967), pp. 178-220.

13. *Max Weber on Law in Economy and Society*, p. 63; Bendix, *Max Weber: An Intellectual Portrait*, pp. 398-99.

14. David Daube, "Rabbinic Methods of Interpretation and Hellenistic Rhetoric," *Hebrew Union College Annual* 22 (1949): 239-264 and notes 23-28; Saul Lieberman, *Hellenism in Jewish Palestine* (New York: The Jewish Theological Seminary of America, 1950), pp. 52-82. This procedure is already at work in the Bible itself. See M. Fishbane, *Biblical Interpretation in Ancient Israel*, 258-261.

15. *Yer. Berakot*, 2:8.

16. Daube, "Rabbinic Methods of Interpretation and Hellenistic Rhetoric:" 251 and sources cited there.

17. *Yer. Pesahim*, (ed. Krotoschin), p. 33a; *b. Pesahim*, 66a.

18. *Siphra* to Lev. 1:2 (ed. Weiss), p. 4b.

19. *Mekilta de Rabbi Ishmael* to Exod. 22:9-10, Tractate *Nezikin* 16 (ed. Lauterbach), 3:121.

20. *Mekilta de Rabbi Ishmael* to Exod. 20:13, Tractate *Bahodesh* (ed. Lauterbach) 2:261; *b. Sanhedrin*, 86a. For further discussion of rabbinic exegesis (*midrash*) see Ephraim E. Urbach, *The Halakah: Its Sources and Development* trans. Raphael Posner (Jerusalem-Tel-Aviv: Masada Ltd., 1986), pp. 95-105 and David Weiss Halivni, *Midrash, Mishnah, and Gemara: The Jewish Predilection for Justified Law* (Cambridge and London: Harvard University Press, 1986), pp. 9-65.

21. *M. Sanhedrin* 10:1.

22. Henry A. Fischel, *Rabbinic Literature and Greco-Roman Philosophy* (Leiden: E. J. Brill, 1973), p. 54; p. 89.

23. *Lam. R.* 2:13.

24. In this Noahite law prohibiting cruelty to animals the ethic concerned only with the relation of human beings to one another is transcended and ethical consciousness is given an enormously broader scope by being set within a cosmic framework that encompasses the non-human elements of nature, the lower animals and the plant and mineral kingdoms. The Noahite prohibition is related to two rabbinic concepts known as *za'ar ba'ale hayim*," the pain of living creatures," and *ba'al taschchit*, literally "do not destroy." These two concepts underscore that reverence for life includes not only the animals but also plants, trees, earth

and water. Cf. Elijah J. Schochet, *Animal Life in Jewish Tradition: Attitudes and Relationships* (New York: Ktav Publishing House, 1984).

25. *Pesikta Rabbati* 33 (ed. Friedman), p. 150a; *Num. R.* 14:2; *Seder Eliyahu Rabba* 7 (ed. Friedman), p. 35; *Gen. R.* 61:1 (ed. Theodor-Albeck), pp. 657-658; *Gen. R.* 95:3 (ed. Theodor-Albeck), p. 1188; *Tanhuma, Vayigash* 11. Cf. my "Two Views of the Patriarchs: Noahides and Pre-Sinai Israelites," in *Texts and Responses: Studies in Honor of Nahum Glatzer* (Leiden: E. J. Brill, 1975), p. 52. Marvin Fox, *The Philosophical Foundations of Jewish Ethics: Some Initial Reflections*, The Second Annual Feinberg Memorial Lecture (Cincinnati: Judaic Studies Program, March 29, 1979), p. 14, n. 33 ignores this rabbinic tradition and thus overstates the case for the revelational authority of these laws. Similarly, with the post-talmudic authorities though citing the dominant view of Maimonides (*Yad, Hilkot Melakim*, 8:11) that all men including gentiles must recognize the revelation at Sinai as the source of these laws, he ignores the view of R. Menahem Ha-Me'iri of fourteenth century Provence that gentiles who observe the Noahite laws do *not* have to believe these laws were divinely revealed. See Ha-Me'iri's commentary on *M. Avot*, ed. S. Stern, 1854, Introduction, pp. 3b ff. and *Bet HaBehirah* on *b. Avodah Zarah* (ed. A. Schreiber), p. 46. Cf. Jacob Katz, *Exclusiveness and Tolerance* (New York: Schocken Books, 1958), pp. 119-21.

26. *De Abrahamo* I, 3, 5-6; III, 16; XLVI, 275-276.

27. *Philo* 4th ed. revised (Cambridge: Harvard University Press, 1968) 2:180-187.

28. *Digest* 1.1.1.; *Institutes* 1.2.1.

29. *b. Eruvin*, 100b. The words "Had the Torah not been revealed . . . " imply that those who did not receive the Sinaitic Revelation, i.e., pre-Sinai Israelites such as the Patriarchs and gentiles could learn from nature and reason according to one rabbinic tradition cited above. The context of R. Johanan's observation is a discussion of the psychology and etiquette of human sexual relations, i.e., life experience. Nature, reason and life experience *are* vehicles of divine revelation for the wise which they feel duty-bound to follow, as biblical wisdom teaches. E. E. Urbach, *The Sages*, pp. 322-23 rightly sees no dichotomy between nature, reason and revelation in this statement.

30. *b. Sanhedrin*, 3b.

31. Meyer Waxman, "Civil and Criminal Procedures of Jewish Courts," in *Studies in Jewish Jurisprudence* ed. Edward Gershfield (New York: Hermon Press, 1971), pp. 188-195.

32. Haim H. Cohen, "Bet Din and Judges," *Encyclopedia Judaica* 4:722.

33. Solomon Zeitlin, *Who Crucified Jesus?* 4th ed. (New York: Bloch Publishing Co., 1964), pp. 76-83; 165-179; 193-207; Hugo Mantel, *Studies in the History of the Sanhedrin* (Cambridge: Harvard University Press, 1961), pp. 92-100; p. 282. Haim H. Cohn, *Reflections on the Trial and Death of Jesus* (Jerusalem: The Israel Law Review Association, 1977), pp. 19-33 argues that the purpose of the interrogation was to get Jesus to modify his stand so as to save him from crucifixion.

34. Elazar and Cohen, *The Jewish Polity*, p. 5.

35. *Ibid.*

36. *M. Avot* 4:13.

37. Elazar and Cohen, *The Jewish Polity*, pp. 16-17 speak of only three *ketarim*, crowns or power centers. In my essay-review of their book "The Republic of Moses," *Menorah Review* 12 (Winter, 1988): 5, I pointed out that the crucial element missing from their analysis was the fourth power center, the *keter shem tov*, the crown of the good name, i.e., charismatic authority.

38. Thorkild Jacobsen, *Toward the Image of Tammuz and Other Essays on Mesopotamian History and Culture*, ed. William Moran (Cambridge: Harvard University Press, 1970), pp. 132-140; 142-47; 150-56; 162-67.

39. Robert Gordis, "Democratic Origins in Ancient Israel-The Biblical 'Edah," in *Alexander Marx Jubilee Volume* (New York: Jewish Theological Seminary, 1950), pp. 369-88. Cf. C. U. Wolf, "Traces of Primitive Democracy in Ancient Israel," *Journal of Near Eastern Studies* 6 (1947): 98-108; J. L. McKenzie, "The Elders in the Old Testament," *Analecta Biblica* 10 (1959): 388-400; E. A. Speiser, "Background and Function of the Biblical *Nasi*," *Catholic Biblical Quarterly* 25 (1963): 111-17.

40. Yehezkel Kaufmann, *Toledot ha-'Emunah ha-Yisraelit* (Jerusalem and Tel-Aviv: Mosad Bialik, 1954) 1:3, 686 ff. (Chap. *Malkut 'Elohim*). This view is also shared by Martin Noth in his *History of Israel*, 2nd ed. (New York: Harper and Row, 1958), pp. 164-65.

41. Anti-monarchy: 1 Sam. 7:3-8, 22a; 10:18-25a; 12, 15. Pro-monarchy: 1 Sam. 9:1-10, 16; 11:1-11, 13-14 [with additions], 15. Cf. my *Judaism and the Gentile Faiths: Comparative Studies in Religion* (Rutherford, Madison, Teaneck NJ: Fairleigh Dickinson University Press, 1981), pp. 150-51.

42. J. Liver, "Kingship" in *Enziklopedia Mikrait* 4 (Jerusalem: Mosad Bialik, 1950), cols. 1086-87; 1089-90.

43. Hayim Tadmor, "The People and the Kingship in Ancient Israel: The Role of Political Institutions in the Biblical Period," in *Jewish Society Through the Ages*, ed. H. H. Ben Sasson and S. Ettinger (New York: Schocken Books, 1973), pp. 49-54. Tadmor sees in "the men of Israel" the people's army based on the family unit and in the "elders of Israel" the representatives of the people according to the patriarchal territorial structure.

44. Baruch Halpern, "Sectionalism and the Schism," Journal *of Biblical Literature* 93 (1974): 519-32.

45. Kaufmann, *Toledot ha-'Emunah ha-Yisraelit*, 1:3, 691 ff. The ideal of the Davidic monarchy is the central theme of the book of Chronicles, the product of this period.

46. Solomon Zeitlin, *The Rise and Fall of the Judean State* (Philadelphia: The Jewish Publication Society of America, 1962), 1:10-13. The tannaitic statement of the *Sifra* on Lev. 20:26 (ed. Weiss), p. 93d, "Just as I am a *Parush,* you shall be *Perushim.* If you are separated from the nations says the Lord, you belong to me; if not you belong to Nebuchadnezzer, the King of Babylon and his companions," has been understood as reflecting the

religious significance of the name Pharisee. Cf. Salo Baron, *A Social and Religious History of the Jews*, 2nd ed. (New York: Columbia University Press, 1952) 2:342. A later origin of the Pharisees in the Hasmonean period, a view held by many scholars, has been advocated by Louis Finkelstein, *The Pharisees: The Sociological Background of their Faith* (Philadelphia: The Jewish Publication Society of America, 1962). However, Finkelstein has now accepted an earlier origin for the Pharisees, cf. "The Origin of the Pharisees Reconsidered," *Conservative Judaism* (Winter, 1969), p. 25 and S. Zeitlin, "The Origin of the Pharisees Reaffirmed," *The Jewish Quarterly Review* 59 (1969): 255-267.

47. 1 Maccabees 14:41.

48. Josephus, *Contra Apion* 2, 17:21-23.

49. Josephus, *Antiquities* 4,8,17. Josephus took Deut. 17:14 f. as permitting not commanding the institution of kingship.

50. 1 Maccabees 8:14-15.

51. *Sifre*, Deut. 156 (ed. Friedmann), p. 105a; *Midrash Tannaim* on Deut. 17:14 (ed. Hoffman), pp. 103-4; *b. Sanhedrin*, 20b.

52. *Yer. Horayot* 3, 47a, 48a; *Yer. Sotah* 8, 25c; *Tos. Horayot* 2:5; *b. Horayot*, 13a; Maimonides, *Yad, Hilkot Melakim*, 1:8.

53. M. Stern, "The Political and Social History of Judea Under Roman Rule" in *A History of the Jewish People* ed. H. H. Ben Sasson (Cambridge: Harvard University Press, 1969), pp. 249-276.

54. Elazar and Cohen, *The Jewish Polity*, pp. 122 ff. with my addition, see above n. 37. On the tension between *keter Torah* and *keter shem tov*, between Torah and charismatic authority see Ephraim A. Urbach," Ha-Masoret al Torat ha-Sod Bitekufat ha-Tannaim," *Studies in Mysticism and Religion Presented to G. Scholem* (Jerusalem: Magnes Press, 1967), p. 24 ff. and my "Angelic Opposition to the Ascension of Moses and the Revelation of the Law," *Jewish Quarterly Review* N.S. 61 (July, 1971): 297-98 and more recently David J. Halperin, *The Faces of the Chariot* (Tubingen: J. C. B. Mohr (Paul Siebeck), 1988), pp. 440-443.

55. *b. Yoma, 22b.*

56. *b. Pesahim*, 87b.

57. *Tanhuma, Mishpatim*, 2.

58. Moses ben Maimon, *Responsa*, ed. D. H. Baneth (Jerusalem, 1946), p. 63.

Olympus: Polis and Participatory Government

The Greeks had no covenant with the one God which revealed the rules for daily life and subsumed all aspects of the community under His authority. Only in the earliest stages of Greek history, when societies were organized according to family and clan, did divine imperatives and religious institutions correspond with the political and judicial administration, for then ancestral law (*ta patria*) was the only law. In some respects, this period resembles Weber's stages one and two and the first two stages of Hebrew law because ancestral law was also sacred law (*ta hosia*).[1] Based on the moral and religious authority of Zeus, it was transmitted through an oral tradition of myths, legends, and maxims as well as revealed through oracles (*chresmoi*) later collected under the names of such charismatic figures as Orpheus and Musaeus or the Pythian priestess of Apollo at Delphi. These revelations contained not only enigmatic references to the future but also prescriptions for ritual piety and moral behavior. Nilsson compares the examples of *ta patria* in the maxims of Hesiod's *Works and Days* to the legalism of the Hebrew priests.[2] Rulers of families who traced their lineage back to the gods or founders of cults had the authority to interpret or apply the oral laws and oracles. Over the years special hereditary priesthoods developed to regulate the activities associated with their particular shrines and cults according to ancestral sacred law.[3] In these stages, legal notables were also religious notables.

As families and clans in a certain geographical area joined together to become a political unit, sacred law was gradually displaced as the source of community order. At first kings and ruling nobles had both political and religious authority, but as early as Homer and Hesiod the procedures for justice appear to have been independent of cults and priests.[4] As the new units became autonomous city-states (*poleis*) and passed law codes and new legislation on their own, they did not disturb the old cultic traditions and hereditary priesthoods, but neither did they enlarge the role of those religious leaders in the functioning of the state.[5] Rather the interpreters of sacred law were consulted by the government only for questions about obscure or disputed religious regulations or for interpretations of oracles pertaining to the future. Although Athens at first applied to these professionals (e.g., *chresmologoi*) ad hoc, by the fourth century the polis may have instituted the office of exegete (for Delphi, Eleusis, and other cults) open to citizens with the appropriate heredity and knowledge of sacred law.[6] Moreover, the state gradually became the vehicle for organizing sacred law (through official calendars of sacrifice) and even for legislating penalties and ensuring enforcement. The priests could make judgments about infringements of sacred law at public ceremonies and shrines, but they had no power to effect them on their own. Unpunished offenses against the gods, however, threatened the safety of the entire community. Therefore, individuals could be charged, brought to trial, and fined or punished through the judicial system of the polis.[7]

Because sacred law became separated from polis law, any discussion of the uniqueness of Greek public life must concentrate on stage three of Weber's model—the imposition of law by secular authorities—for the city-states of Greece (qua political organizations) evolved "through human initiative and consensus," selecting their own lawmakers and executives, and legislating for themselves by group decisions. In fact, Athens, where the jury courts were invented, never advanced to Weber's stage 4. Its democracy, which empowered ordinary citizens to govern, legislate, and judge their fellow citizens, did not foster either the development of a professionalized administration of justice by trained experts or the growth of legal precedents and a body of case law which would restrict each panel's decision. Therefore, the Athenian polis produced professional speechwriters and rhetoricians rather than the lawyers and jurisconsults of Rome or the learned rabbis of Israel.

Law and the state were inseparable aspects of Greek public life, for the polis made the laws by which it governed itself and maintained justice. Consequently, the Greeks esteemed the structure of government and the human art of governing far more highly than the Hebrews did, and grounded their legitimation of the state and its legal system, in Weber's terms, on both divine action and natural law. Humans, according to the philosophers, were by nature 'political animals' who required a community of fellow human beings not only for survival but also for achieving the best and most virtuous life. Justice (*dike*), bestowed by Zeus, separated human beings from the lower animals, for it prevented them "from devouring one another" like fish and fowl (Hesiod *Works and Days* 276-280).[8] Protagoras' myth, in Plato's dialogue about him, connects justice with the art of government. When, after creation and the gift of fire, humans began living in cities to protect themselves from wild animals and provide each other with the means of life, they so mistreated one another that Zeus sent Hermes to bring them mutual respect (*aidos*) and justice (*dike*) "to be the ordering principle of cities and the bonds of friendship and consideration." (322c). Aristotle explains, in *Politics* 1253a, that because of their unique capacity for reason and language and thus their ability to perceive and communicate what is just and unjust, or good and evil, human beings form associations based on a common perception of such things. He agrees that *dike* is the ordering principle of the association, so that the state functions to educate the citizens to be good and just as well as to prevent them from encroaching on one another.[9]

As the Greek states evolved toward their characteristic polis organization, their conception and legitimation of law also developed. To the gods they traced back their earliest custom law, which was common to most communities. New and unique practices, which were clearly the product of human reformers or group decisions, required new sources of legitimation. Whatever the form of the political association developed by men, however, its laws must be sovereign, "for where the laws are not sovereign, there is no *politeia*." (*Politics* 1292a30). To such philosophers as Plato and Aristotle, the connection of the best community with law and justice was predicated upon its connection to the divine order and the highest good.

> He who commands that law should rule may thus be regarded as commanding that God and reason alone should rule . . . . Law as the pure voice of God and reason may thus be defined as "reason free from all passion." (Aristotle *Politics*, 1287a5; Barker, trans.)

Such a community was more than a modern political entity. It was the center of the individual's social, cultural, and ethical life and the means through which he might achieve his highest human potential as a 'rational' as well as a 'political' animal.

Stages of the Legitimation of Law

The polytheistic Greeks began, like the Hebrews, by ascribing their concepts and procedures for justice to their gods. Justice has its origins in the Olympian pantheon, personified as Dike, the daughter of Zeus and Themis (Established Custom), who, with her siblings, the Seasons, Lawfulness (Eunomia), and Peace, "take care of the works of mortal men." (Hesiod *Theogony* 900-903). From the earliest time Dike and her mother were the nurturers and regulators of community life, Themis being associated with the elements of structure which give order to the group and Dike more with the places assigned to individuals within it. Together they represent the forces which keep human society intact, viewed as immutable, eternal, and suprahuman, and fostered and protected by Zeus.

As the Greek communities developed, Dike became the more prominent concept.[10] In *Works and Days* 256-62, Hesiod describes her function: she sits beside her father and tells him of men's wicked deeds so that they will pay for their perversions of justice.[11] According to a fragment from a lost tragedy by Aeschylus, Dike received her revered position after Zeus overcame his father by means of justice; i.e., after being attacked, he paid him back, not unjustly. Now, as the goddess herself explains, she rewards the just for their just life, but implants a prudent mind in the reckless by ensuring that they receive punishment.[12]   Thus Dike is closely associated with the doctrine of reciprocity discussed in chapter four as the principle which maintains the balance in the moral, natural, and social order of the cosmos.[13]

Justice is also concerned with the preservation of rights and property from the encroachment of others. The word *dike* probably derives from the verb *deiknumi*, meaning "I show," and thus may be related to the boundary mark or sign which divided two pieces of property, as its connection with adjectives like "crooked" and "straight" suggests.[14]   When a conflict develops over place or property, *dike* is the term applied to the procedures which separate the disputants and prevent violence. As such, it is connected to distributive justice, to the settling of disputes by the weighing of claims and counterclaims. According to the Homeric *Hymn to Hermes*, Zeus keeps scales of justice (*talanta dikes*) on Olympus where all the gods gather in assembly (324). When Apollo accuses Hermes of stealing his cattle, the two brothers go there to their father to submit the case to his judgment (*dos diken*, 312). Once the facts are clear, Hermes and Apollo effect a compromise sealed by an oath.

According to myth, Zeus gave *dike* to men. Zeus' mediation on Olympus provided the paradigm for mediation on earth. From him, legendary kings like Minos and Agamemnon received their authority to settle disputes, right wrongs, and establish laws (e.g., *Il.* 9.99; Aeschylus *Agamemnon* 41-43, 60-62; *Od.* 19.178-9; Plato *Laws* 624b-625a). As the state developed, the word *dike* was used for the more specific human procedures which effected retributive and distributive justice: e.g., law suits in general, claims of plaintiffs and defendants, decisions and punishments. H. D. Robertson summarizes the meanings implied in its uses. The goddess is the guiding principle of the universe upheld and followed by the supreme god, and the bond which holds society together, restrains lawless self-assertiveness, and makes civilized human life possible. Again, *dike*, as manifested among men, includes the broadest principles of equity and the principles underlying the most detailed provisions of statute law.[15]

Other children of Zeus were also associated with principles and procedures of justice and law. The Muses, the daughters of Zeus and Memory, provide "heaven nourished" kings with sweet words so that their true judgments will be persuasive and settle even a great quarrel without violence (Hesiod *Theogony* 81-93). Apollo, as the god of the oracle at Delphi, was concerned with the purification rituals by which reckless behavior might be compensated, the laws of homicide, rules governing slavery, procedures for emancipation, and charters for new cities or colonies whose foundation he recommended. From his Pythian priestess Lycurgus was reputed to have received the constitution of Sparta. Athena too, as the daughter of Zeus most clearly manifesting his persuasive wisdom backed by force, was connected to the making of laws (for Zaleucus of Western Locris) and the process of voluntary arbitration as well as the establishment of legal procedures and precedents for her patron city Athens.[16]

The whole body of custom law handed down by tradition as the normal order of things was also ascribed to the gods. Referred to as the *nomoi*, these customs were at first viewed as part of the way the universe was ordered and were considered eternal and valid for all time as the normative way of life.[17] As the chorus of *Oedipus the King* describes:

> May destiny ever find me
> pious in word and deed
> prescribed by the laws (*nomoi*) that live on high:
> laws begotten in the clear air of heaven,
> whose only father is Olympus;
> no mortal nature brought them to birth,
> no forgetfulness shall lull them to sleep;
> for God is great in them and grows not old.
> (863-71, Grene, trans.)[18]

In Xenophon's *Memorabilia* 4.19-25, Socrates and Hippias of Elis discuss the contents of the *nomoi*: e.g., worship of the gods, honor to parents, the prohibition against incest, and the custom of returning good for good. They also deduce that violations of such customs bring about their own punishment. Socrates and Hippias have already agreed that these *nomoi* must have come from the gods because they are observed in every country in the same way and yet all men cannot meet together and do not speak the same language.

But Socrates and Hippias are actually debating whether "just" and "lawful" mean the same thing, and they must qualify their term *nomoi* with the adjective *agraptoi* (unwritten) because they live in a polis which has a written law code attributed to a mortal man, Solon, at a particular moment in the unique history of Athens. For, by the mid-seventh century B.C.E., Greek communities were beginning to enact legislation concerning areas of life previously governed by traditional patterns of behavior deemed appropriate and binding on the group. From the inscriptional and literary evidence, scholars have determined that the earliest lawcodes have several features in common.[19] The impetus towards legislation begins in civic turmoil produced by such events as feuds between aristocratic families or clashes between rich and poor because of increased economic activity. When those in charge, whether tyrants, aristocrats, or peoples' assemblies, are unable to deal with the conflict by traditional means, they appoint an outsider to draw up clear procedures for settlement of such grievances and guidelines to control behaviors which led to the problems. The code is then enacted by the community and written down and placed on public view to be available to all. The legal inscriptions from Deros on Crete dated to the later part of the seventh century B.C.E., for example, begin with the words, "The city has thus decided." The examples indicate that written codes confirmed the authority of the polis, whatever its type of government, over the lives of its citizens and, in the words of Gagarin, "served the interest not of any single group or political party, but of all the citizens as incorporated in that unique institution . . . ."

Although the traditions about several famous Greek lawgivers fit the pattern (e.g., Zeleucis in Western Locris, Charondas at Catana, Lycurgus in Sparta [whose laws remained unwritten, however], Pittacus in Mytilene, and Demonax in Cyrene), our information on Athens provides the fullest example of the development.[20] Before there was a named legislator and a written code, the thesmothetes or lawgivers had already begun the practice of recording their decisions and setting them up in a public place so they could be used as precedents for settling future conflicts. Archons probably had at that time the power to settle disputes themselves on their own authority. In 621 B.C.E., Draco was appointed to draft a code, perhaps as archon and perhaps because the murder (in violation of an oath) of the supporters of Cylon's attempt at tyranny had provoked turmoil uncontrollable by normal means. Thus Draco became known as the first legislator in Athens. His legislation did not curb the conflict or prevent the development of a new crisis, however; increasing economic activity brought with it increasing struggles between the rich aristocratic landholders and the poor farmers who were being driven from their land and even into slavery for debts. In 594 B.C.E., the government elected Solon, a poet-philosopher from the rising merchant class, to be archon with extraordinary power to make a new law code (retaining only the homicide regulations of Draco) which the citizen body enacted, had inscribed and placed in a public site, and agreed to uphold. From then on until the end of the fifth century any new legislation that was passed was added to the code and the entire body was referred to as the laws of Solon.

All the literary traditions agree that written law was produced by a human agent, usually a single reformer or mediator, and/or enacted by the human community. Thus, unlike the *vomoi*, the written codes had no clear divine sanction. Interestingly enough, however, legends and myths accrued to the lawgivers which associated their codes directly with the gods (as in the case of Zaleucis, Lycurgus, and Minos, mentioned above) or provided them with famous philosophers as teachers and world-wide travels to places famous for their codes.[21] Solon, for example, visited Thales at Miletus, according to Plutarch. Thales, himself advisor on the formation of a common government center at Teos (Herodotus 1.170), was credited with teaching Zaleucas who in turn instructed Charondas. Although such tales cannot be true, they reveal the urge to find extraordinary legitimation for rules clearly made by ordinary men.

Moreover, the tales indicate the need to place the man-made laws beyond the reach of the temporal conditions which had made them necessary, and as eternally valid as the old custom law.[22] After the Athenians had sworn an oath to give Solon's laws a ten-year trial and not to alter them without him, Solon left the city to avoid having to repeal any (Herodotus 1.29). In Western Locris, anyone who wanted to introduce a new law or alter an old one had to present his proposal before the council with a noose around his neck. Since, if his argument failed he would be strangled, only one law was changed there in two hundred years (Demosthenes 24.139-41). Other stories make clear that the man-made law should remain more powerful than the men who made them.[23] Zaleucus and Charondas, for example, both suffered from punishments decreed in their own codes. Szegedy-Maszak concludes that, "when the legislator submits to punishment rather than exempt himself or change the law, it is clear that the code has become supreme." [24]

The co-existence of written and unwritten *nomoi*, of specific laws enacted by men, and rules embedded in the group's traditional way of life, created certain problems for the community which could not be obscured by the growth of legends sanctioning legislators and legislation. Pericles' Funeral Oration distinguishes between the two types of laws and emphasizes the Athenians' reverence for both: "those (*nomon*) which have been established (*keintai*) for the help of the injured (*adikoumenon*) and those which, although unwritten (*agraptoi*), bring disgrace which all acknowledge upon their transgressors" (Thucydides 2.37). But what if the laws which men establish conflict with the traditional unwritten norms? 'Just' and 'legal' might then diverge. Socrates' conversation with Hippias as well as Plato's continuing interest in the relationship between justice, law, and the state (e.g., *Republic, Statesman*, and *Laws*) reveal the philosophers' concern with this issue.

Sophocles' *Antigone* (dated to 442 B.C.E.) starkly dramatizes the conflict. When Creon announces a decree denying burial to the traitor Polynices, he offers a reasonable justification: his order will deter future civil war and thus protect the state and the lives of its citizens. But Antigone disobeys Creon's decree because her obligations to her family and the gods below require that she give her brother proper burial regardless of his crimes on earth. Her words reveal her willingness to die rather than put the laws of men above the laws of god:

> For me it was not Zeus who made that order.
> Nor did that Justice (*Dike*) who lives with the gods below
> mark out such laws (*nomous*) to hold among mankind.
> Nor did I think your orders were so strong
> that you, a mortal man, could over-run
> the gods' unwritten (*agrapta*) and unfailing laws (*nomima*).
> Not now, nor yesterdays', they always live,
> And no one knows their origin in time.
> So not through fear of any man's proud spirit
> would I be likely to neglect these laws,
> draw on myself the gods' sure punishment (*diken*).
> (450-59, Wycoff, trans.)

Her vocabulary exhibits the development of a new word *nomima* to distinguish the normative way of life passed on by tradition through behavior patterns, rituals, maxims, myths, and legends from the more recent rules which, though legally enacted and written down by the state, were also called *nomoi*.[25]

The awareness of the possible divergence of written law from traditional norms was complicated by the realization that other cultures, or even other Greek communities, had developed very different custom-laws. The increase in trade, travel, and colonization had brought Greeks into contact with peoples who had diverse patterns of behavior, institutions, and legal codes. The spread of reading and writing facilitated examination and comparison and resulted in the articulation of the idea that the old *vomoi* might not really be eternal or universally binding. Around the end of the sixth century, Heraclitus asserted that "all the laws (*nomoi*) of men are nourished by one law, the divine law" (KRS 250), as if it were, in Ostwald's words, "the fountain-head of norms which it issues . . . " or, in Kerferd's, the standard "from which to derive human laws, and in the process to justify some of them while rejecting others as not in accord with the higher law."[26]

Others, however, emphasized the relativity of local traditions. Herodotus, for example, reports on the variety of customs (relating to such aspects of life as marriage, death, and worship) among the nations participating in the Persian War. Although he frequently compares the most unusual barbarian practices with the Greek norms, he is rarely judgmental, for he believes that:

> If anyone, no matter who, were given the opportunity of choosing from amongst all the nations in the world the set of beliefs (*nomous*) which he thought best, he would inevitably, after careful consideration of their relative merits, choose that of his own country . . . . There is abundant evidence that this is the universal feeling(*nenomikasi*) about the ancient customs (*nomous*) of one's country. (3.38, de Selincourt, trans.)[27]

After relating Darius' anecdote about the Greeks' horror at Indians' eating their parents' dead bodies, and the Indians' corresponding refusal even to hear about Greeks' burning theirs, Herodotus concludes: "One can see by this what custom can do (*nenomistai*), and Pindar, in my opinion, was right when he called it king of all (*nomon panton Basilea*)".

Vomoi which vary from place to place may appear to be arbitrary conventions of men rather than eternally valid laws from the gods.[28] Protagoras' myth in fact implies that justice was not innate; the humans created by Epimetheus and Prometheus had everything they needed for survival but the art of living together (*poliken technen*) and so began to do wrong to one another (*adikein* at 322b). Later in Plato's dialogue Protagoras argues that, to prevent citizens from acting only in their own interest, the polis must educate them to learn the laws made by the lawgivers of old and to live accordingly, in the same way as writing teachers sketch out letters in their students' copybooks to compel them to write according to their guidelines (236).[29]

From one perspective, the laws made by men were a great advance because they prevented the strong from overpowering the weak. As Theseus explains to the herald from Thebes in Euripides' *Suppliant Women,*

> In earliest times, before there are common laws (*nomoi koinoi*),
> One man has power and makes the law (*nomon*) his own:
> Equality (*tod' ison*) is not yet. With written laws,
> (*gegrammenon ton vomon*)
> People of few resources and the rich
> Both have the same recourse to justice (*diken isen*).
> (430-434, Jones, trans.)

Such written laws were best obeyed because in the long run they preserved the community life which made survival possible.

But of course they were not always obeyed. The speaker in a fragment from the satyr play *Sisyphus,* ascribed to Critias at the end of the fifth century, argues that the laws made by men to curb their natural violence were such insufficient deterrents to evil that "some man, acute and wise in mind" invented the gods and fear of their punishments to restrain the savage nature of man.[30] For him, religion as well as law was a convention developed in the course of time for social reasons. Such passages as this one and the above speech quoted from Euripides indicate that the sanction accorded the *nomoi*, both written and unwritten, was also being undermined by speculation about the real nature of human beings.

For over a century the *physiologoi* had been looking to nature (*physis*) rather than the anthropomorphic gods for explanations of the origin and processes of the world around them (as discussed in chapters two and three). By the mid- fifth century, several theories had been posited which defined the primary substance or substances out of which the cosmos was generated and the laws of motion and change by which particular things came to be. Now similar terms were applied to human beings and society.[31] In a state of raw nature, unrestrained humans are part of the biological continuum and behave, like animals, according to the eternal laws of self-preservation. But because reason is unique to them, they can be restrained, by wise leaders, excellent *vomoi*, and good training. From this perspective, however, the *nomoi*, which arise by convention through the agreements of men, are bound to conflict with the eternal and universal laws of nature. And, when that happens, there is no good reason for obeying the *vomos* besides the avoidance of punishment.

When Aristophanes mocks the ethics, metaphysics, and rhetoric of contemporary philosophers, in *Clouds* in 423 B.C.E., he puts the following words into the mouth of the Unjust Argument who is trying to persuade the young hero Phidippides to study with him:

> Let me turn now to—the demands of Nature (*physeos anagkas*). Suppose you fall in love with a married woman—have a bit of fun—and get caught in the act. As you are now, without a tongue in your head, you're done for. But, if you come and learn from me, you can do what you like (*chro te physei*) and get away with it. (1075-78, Sommerstein, trans.)[32]

After Phidippides has passed his course, he is able to prove that it's not illegal for a son to beat his father, although the reverse is the universal practice (*vomizesthai*, 1416), because laws are made by men and he can easily persuade the people to change the law. He clinches his argument by an appeal to nature: "Look at the cocks and the other birds; they fight back against their fathers" (1426-7).

That Aristophanes' humorous exaggeration parodies a very serious examination of the relative value of *nomos* and *physis* is clear from the study of individual natures in plays such as Euripides' *Hippolytus* or Sophocles' *Philoctetes*, the fragment from *Sisyphus*, and the conversations of sophists like Callicles and Thrasymachus in Plato's *Gorgias* and *Republic* respectively.[33] The antithesis between concepts of justice and the universal laws of human nature occurs throughout Thucydides' *Peloponnesian Wars*.[34] In the Melian Dialogue, for example, when the neutral islanders argue that they will have the gods' favor because the Athenians are unjust (*ou dikaious*), the Athenian envoys reply:

> Of gods we believe, and of men we know, that by a necessary law of their nature (*physeos anagkaias*) they rule wherever they can. And it is not as if we were the first to make this law (*thentes nomon*), or to act upon it when made: we found it existing before us and shall leave it to exist ever after us. (5.105.2, Crawley, trans.)

Again and again the historian asserts that in bad times ideas of right and wrong or legal prohibitions are unable to restrain men's bad behavior (e.g., during the plague at 2.53 and the Corcyraean Revolution at 3.83-84), for, in the words of Diodotus during the Mitylenean Debate, "Only great simplicity can hope to prevent human nature (*anthropeias physeos*) doing what it has once set its mind upon, by force of law" (*nomon*, 3.45.7, Crawley, trans). Even beginning from a more positive view of human nature than Thucydides' history or the fragment from *Sisyphus*, Antiphon the Sophist argued that the laws and customs of men were inferior to nature because they inhibited actions beneficial to survival (e.g., retaliating when injured), and created artificial distinctions between human beings (e.g., aristocrats and base born; Greek and barbarian), when "we all breathe the air through our mouth and nostrils" (fragments from *On Truth*).[35]

The writers who participated in the 'Greek Enlightenment' of the fifth century B.C.E. had clearly uncovered contradictions in earlier assumptions about justice and law. If custom-law differed from place to place, it could not be universally valid. If men made laws which were improvements on the old ways of settling conflicts, then the old ways were neither timeless nor the best ways of doing things. But, if the natural world followed certain laws and human beings were a part of nature, weren't those laws superior to (or at least more beneficial or powerful than) man-made laws or customs? Why then should men obey the *nomoi*, whether written or unwritten? A speech ascribed to Demosthenes (25.16) in the fourth century summarizes the three basic reasons which had evolved with the development of the *vomoi*: 1) They are a discovery and gift of the gods; 2) They are decided upon by men of wisdom, and 3) They are established by common agreement of the city as that by which every citizen should regulate his life. The speaker, however, argues that Nature, in a raw state, is inferior to law because it is disorderly, corruptible, and varies with the individual, whereas laws aim at what is just, good, beneficial, and common to all, and apply equally and impartially.[36]

But the philosophers of the fourth century proposed a different view of nature, and human nature, which provided a more substantial legitimation of law. To the *physiologoi*'s concept of the developed cosmos as a harmonious and balanced whole governed by necessary laws of nature, Plato, Aristotle, and later the Stoics added the emphasis on reason and goodness as first principles of creation and movement. Thus nature was not only regular, but purposive, and provident.[37] The rational principle which governs the whole (*logos*) was equated with the mind of god because of its perfect order and goodness. Human beings, as parts of nature endowed with the unique qualities of god-like reason and speech, could achieve their highest potential only by living a life in conformity with divine natural law. In the words of the Stoic Chrysippus:

> for our individual natures (*physeis*) are part of the nature of the whole universe. And this is why the end may be defined as life in accordance with nature(*physei*) or, in other words, in accordance with our own human nature as well as that of the universe, a life in which we refrain from every action forbidden by the law common to all things (*nomos ho koinos*), that is to say, the right reason (*orthos logos*) which pervades all things and is identical with this Zeus, lord and ruler of all that is. (Diogenes Laertius *Zeno* 7.88, Hicks, trans.)[38]

From this perspective, there would be no conflict between *physis* and *nomos*, between natural law and the written and unwritten rules developed in the best communities or by the wisest legislators, for the higher reason which governs the universe sets the norm or pattern for positive law and man can apprehend that pattern by virtue of his possession of reason.[39] Thus Aristotle can define "two kinds of political justice, the natural (*physikon*) and the conventional (*nomikon*)," or "two kinds of laws, the particular (*idion*), both written and unwritten, and the general (*koinon*) in accordance with nature, and analyze the distinctions between them without necessarily impugning man-made law (e.g., *Ethics 1135a* and *Rhetoric 1373b*). So too could Cicero, selecting ideas from the major schools of Hellenistic philosophy, connect the *ius civile* applicable to Roman citizens to the *ius gentium* common to all peoples to the *ius naturale* and *ius caelestale*.[40] In this respect, there is a clear parallel to that rabbinic strand of the Noahite laws rooted in nature and human reason.

If Cicero and his predecessors are somewhat vague about what adherence to natural law means in practice, they make clear that it extends beyond the self-preservation, avoidance of injury, and care of the young common to other animals. Rule by right reason includes not only following the guidance of prudent moderation, but hurting no one, and giving everyone his own. In *de Legibus* Cicero adds reverence for the gods, duty to the fatherland, parents, and relatives, gratitude and readiness to forgive, respect for all who are superior in age, wisdom, or status, and truthfulness. The emphasis on kindness and respect for others derived from the Stoic idea that all individuals are citizens of the same cosmos sharing sparks of the same divine reason despite the artificial distinctions of nations, statuses, and even genders (e.g., *de Legibus* 1.24-35.). Many scholars believe that Stoic teachings about the cosmopolis of nature and the equality of all humans, as necessary parts of the provident whole, influenced the development of principles of equity in Roman positive law.[41]

Law conceived in these terms is more than the settling of conflicts or even the regulation of morality by legislation or unwritten norms. Tied to the laws of nature, which had been studied, systematized, and fit into a unified metaphysical theory, human law had achieved the legitimacy and sanctification once accorded the *nomoi* and *dike* bestowed by the anthropomorphic gods. Cicero, in *de Legibus* 2.8, called law "the primal and ultimate mind of God, whose reason directs all things either by compulsion or restraint . . . [and] that law which the gods have given to the race . . . the reason and mind of a wise lawgiver applied to command and prohibition" (Wood, trans.).[42] The laws of his *Republic* derive their validity from such a conception of nature in which human nature shares:

> True law is right reason in agreement with nature; it is of universal application, unchanging and ever-lasting; it summons to duty by its commands, and averts from wrongdoing by its prohibitions. And it does not lay its commands or prohibitions upon good men in vain, though neither have any effect on the wicked. It is a sin to try to alter this law, nor is it allowable to attempt to repeal any part of it, and it is impossible to abolish it entirely. We cannot be freed from its obligations by senate or people, and we need not look outside ourselves for an expounder or interpreter of it. And there will not be different laws at Rome and at Athens, or different laws now and in the future, but one eternal and unchangeable law will be valid for all nations and all times, and there will be one master and ruler, that is, God, over us all, for he is the author of this law, its promulgator, and its enforcing judge. Whoever is disobedient is fleeing from himself and his denying his human nature, and by reason of this very fact he will suffer the worst penalties, even if he escapes what is commonly considered punishment. (*de Republica* 3.33, Wood, trans.)[43]

Stages of Legal and Political Development

The evolution of Greek justice and law presents a marked contrast with the development of the Hebrew system, for the historical

Greeks did not generally believe that any god had revealed a specific substantive code of law to men. There were relatively few legends about divine revelation, and most seem to have developed much later than the written codes themselves. Moreover, the legends were often examined critically by their reporters (e.g., Herodotus 1.66 on Lycurgus). Plutarch accepts the plausibility of "the other account" of such ancient leaders and lawmakers as Zaleucus, Minos, Zoroaster, Numa, and Lycurgus:

> namely, that since they were managing headstrong and captious multitudes, and introducing great innovations in modes of government, they pretended to get sanction from the god, which sanction was the salvation of the very ones against whom it was contrived. (*Numa* 4.8, Perrin, trans.)[44]

Of course, Greek justice originated on Olympus and the divinities clearly provided models and support for human behaviors and procedures which would maintain justice and order on earth. Neither Zeus nor his pantheon were actual lawmakers, however, and their priests never developed into a professionalized caste responsible for effecting or interpreting a divine code. Greek laws, always associated with human lawmakers, were generally written and displayed in public, but they were not preserved as sacred scripture in the manner of Hebrew laws. Nor did the interpreters of Greek laws claim any divine inspiration which validated their adaptations of the original document and fostered the preservation of its continuous development in a form like the oral scripture and its method of Midrash (i.e., exegetical interpretation of the Bible).

Greek law and justice appear to have developed through time and chance in human history rather than to have been mandated from above through covenant, Torah, and Talmud. To trace its development, modern scholars must rely on evidence which is scant and tentative: the first literary texts, which are not in themselves legal or historical documents; fragments of codes, which have been randomly preserved and are difficult to interpret; comparisons with law in other early cultures; writers from the fifth century and later who included anachronisms or biases in their descriptions of earlier periods; speechwriters who interpreted law and legal history according to their clients' needs.[45] Despite the difficulty in reconstructing a precise history of Greek law, one fact remains indisputable: in most Greek communities the development of the legal system cannot be separated from the development of the political constitution, for in the words of Bonner and Smith, "In

Greek theory and practice, the administration of justice was always a very important function of government."[46] Moreover, although it is difficult for scholars to agree on precisely which lawmaker contributed what reform and when, they are able to outline the major stages in the development of government and justice.[47]

In the earliest times Greek communities were ruled by kings who traced their authority back to Zeus and inhabitants generally defended themselves and their property on their own, relying on family members for support, according to the method referred to as 'self help.' Gagarin refers to this stage as 'pre-legal.'[48] Gradually individuals began to voluntarily submit their disputes to selected arbitrators, whether kings, nobles, or respected elders, in order to avert the violence and damage self-help could engender. Gagarin calls this stage 'proto-legal' because the ad hoc procedures were both public and formal. Sometime in this period, monarchies were replaced by aristocracies in which noble families shared the king's power and functions by some mechanism. As mentioned above, these first two stages correspond in some ways to the first two stages of Weber's model because the kings and ruling nobles also had religious authority. (Even here, however, sacred law and the hereditary priesthoods became separated from the arbitrations conducted in public.)

The true 'legal' stage, according to Gagarin, (somewhat similar to stage three in Weber's model) begins with the development of written codes of law in which the government's interference in self-help becomes compulsory, the procedures become fixed, and substantive law, with prescribed penalties, replaces ad hoc decision-making. In Athens, about which scholars have the most information, this stage began with the first lawmakers Draco and Solon and evolved in tandem with a political constitution which moved toward democracy. By the end of the Pelponnesian War, the Athenian demos (common people) controlled all institutions of the polis, including both lawmaking and judging. After the devastating experiences of two bloody oligarchic revolutions and a humiliating military defeat, however, the Athenians revised their law code and set up new procedures for lawmaking which turned their democracy into a 'republic' where the law, not the majority, was revered as the ruler of all.[49]

Kings, Nobles, and Self-Help— Although the authority of the early kings may have originated in the power of the father in a family, by the period depicted in myth and epic, kings ruled by a divine right derived by descent from a god or hero.[50] They carried the scepter as a symbol of their authority, communed with the gods through rituals, and decided what was right and proper (*themis*) for the community and individuals. As human agents for the gods, they effected justice (*dike*) according to both inspiration and custom and their word was the law (*themistes*). In the *Iliad* and the *Odyssey*, Homer depicts many kings who in practice call on a council of peers before making important decisions and then summon a popular assembly, usually of those able to bear arms, to announce their plans. The king may disregard his assembled subjects' opinions, as Agamemnon does when he refuses to return the Trojan priest's daughter at the beginning of the *Iliad* (1.22- 25). But the wise king would try to accommodate the subjects he must lead into battle. So Agamemnon does give back the girl after all when the plague strikes his camp and he does apologize to Achilles when his best warrior's refusal to fight has demoralized and weakened his troops.

Although one may see the outline of democratic institutions here, in the executive, council, and assembly, only the king and his peers have any real power and the assembly itself is probably not made up of all the free people in the community. Moreover, none of the institutions except kingship is formalized and government business is conducted ad hoc, with the assembly meeting only at the whim of the king or noble. It is important to recognize, however, that Homer and Hesiod depict a world in which the sense of community is very strong and has the features associated with the later Greek polis, whatever its particular constitution: an autonomous and self-contained geographical community with a residence for its ruler and a public space for its assemblies, a center to which all the inhabitants looked for justice as well as defense.[51]

After the twelfth century, beginning with a period of disruption and immigration due to the Trojan War and the Dorian Invasion, a major change occurred in many Greek communities: the noble supporters of the king replaced monarchy with an aristocracy in which their families shared the functions of government once united in the authority of the sole ruler.[52] Over a period of time, Athens developed a system where the archon eponymous, who gave his name to the year and performed the king's political functions, the archon basileus, who took over the king's religious duties, and the polemarch, who led the troops, controlled the government as annual magistrates. As the duties of government increased, the nobles added six more thesmothetes, probably connected with giving judgments, so that they had a board of nine magistrates, all most likely selected by lot or election by the nobility themselves for a term of one year with reelection to the same office prohibited. In addition, there was an advisory council composed of ex-magistrates and perhaps the leaders of the hereditary tribes. The inhabitants able to assist in the community's defense would be called together in the agora to hear pronouncements and register their approval or disapproval. Although the king had disappeared, the noble families, who were once his advisors and were more like tribal chiefs, now controlled the community.

In the pre-legal period of the kings and early aristocracies, justice consisted primarily of self-defense, or, in legalistic terminology, self-help.[53]   When an individual sustained injury to his person, property, or honor, he was expected to retaliate or recoup his losses on his own. If the victim was killed, his family was expected to avenge his death. Victims backed by strong families were able to kill whomever or conquer whatever they could in order to retaliate. When Menelaos suffered the abduction of his wife Helen by the Trojan prince Paris, for example, his elder brother Agamemnon organized the other Greek princes to recover the woman and punish the insult by destroying Troy. Telemachus in Ithaca, however, had no relatives or powerful supporters to help him drive out the suitors of his mother who were destroying his patrimony in his father's absence (v. *Od.* 16.95-96). He and his father, both only sons, needed the help of Athena to restore order in their house. In such a system, there were no crimes or criminals per se.[54]   The homicide fleeing retaliation in his own community, for example, was generally accepted into other communities as an unfortunate suppliant protected by Zeus. Fear of retaliation as well as public approval or disapproval, based on the sense of what was right and proper, on *themistes* and *nomoi*, provided the major sanction against anarchy.

Scholars see several relics of self-help in the legal system which eventually developed.[55]   The later terms for the defendant, *pheugon* or 'flee-er,' and   plaintiff/prosecutor, *diokon* or 'pursuer,' probably derive from the victim's or his relatives' literal pursuit of the one who had done them an injury. Even when legal procedure became compulsory, there was no public prosecutor in the modern sense; it was up to the 'pursuer' or injured party to bring the charges. The fact that women had no legal status and were represented by a male guardian (*kurios*) has been traced to their physical inability to defend their claims by self help and thus their early reliance on male relatives to redress any injuries to them.[56]   Those caught in adultery or theft on the victim's property could be killed on the spot or led to the prison officials, with death as the prospective penalty, as if the state's authority to punish stopped at the individual's private property. The archon's oath, traced back to the end of the monarchy, guaranteed property rights to the people (Aristotelian *Athenian Constitution* 56.2).

Later homicide laws also suggest practices associated with self-help. Exile was probably the earliest legal penalty for homicide because in reality murderers had always run away as fast as they could, preferring the perils of separation from home to certain death at the hands of their victim's family.[57] Prosecution for homicide remained the responsibility of the victim's family, who could be prosecuted themselves, as well as disgraced, if they failed to act. And, even when the state supervised the punishment of the convicted murderer, the victim's family was permitted to watch the execution (Demosthenes 23.69).

But myth also dramatizes the problems that self-help causes for the family and the larger community. First of all, the sense of what is right and proper is too vague to provide adequate guidance in a complex situation. Agamemnon, for example, must choose between a Zeus-born king's duty to punish Paris' violation of the sacred guest-host relation and his obligation as head of his family to protect the lives of his children (v. Aeschylus *Agamemnon* 40-217). Moreover, the necessity of avenging the death of a relative places the avenger in a difficult position. At the end of the Odyssey , the suitors' families argue about whether they are obligated to retaliate for murders which were just punishments; some fear the consequences if they do not act as expected (24.432-434). In the second play of Aeschylus' trilogy, Orestes hesitates to become a matricide to avenge the death of his father, but Apollo threatens him with dire punishments for his refusal. Both myths end with just revenge escalating into a vendetta which threatens to wipe out the family and community. Only the intervention of Athena, with Zeus' approval, prevents disaster.

'Proto-legal' Procedures— In the period of the monarchies and early aristocracies, several ad hoc methods evolved to curb the dangers of self-help.[58] Homer records many incidents where the disputants attempt to effect a compromise among themselves. The quarrel between Agamemnon and Achilles begins when Agamemnon realizes he must return the priest's daughter and decides to take Achilles' war prize instead. Achilles' first instinct is to kill Agamemnon on the spot (*Il.* 189-191), but, with Athena's help, he decides to withdraw from the war to prove his superior value to the group and thus regain his damaged honor and his prize. When Agamemnon is forced to capitulate and offers Achilles the girl back plus many additional gifts, Achilles refuses what he views as a bribe. Ajax, begging Achilles to change his mind, argues that even the immediate family of a murder victim will accept a monetary compensation and give up their anger (*Il.* 9.632-6). Such 'blood money' was not permitted by later Athenian law, but in earlier times it did help to prevent the outbreak of a feud. The price was probably viewed as a compensation for the loss of the victim's contribution to his group as well as for the insult to its honor.[59]

Homer and Hesiod depict societies where such settlements most often take place in a community similar to the polis, where, according to Luce, "men were constrained to pay some heed to one another, where customary law was a force in their affairs, and where the citizens met from time to time to hear discussions of proposals in assembly."[60]   The Cyclopes who do not have such a community represent a lower level of civilization characterized by their lack of organization and custom-law:

> Giants, louts, without a law to bless them (*athemiston*) . . . .
> Kyklopes have no muster and no meeting,
> no consultation (*agorai boulephoroi*) or old tribal ways (*themistes*)
> but each one dwells in his own mountain cave
> dealing out rough justice (*themisteuei*) to wife and child,
> indifferent to what the others do.
> (*Od.* 9.106; 112-115, Fitzgerald, trans.)

To depict a scene of civilized life on the shield of Achilles, Homer selects a 'proto-legal' procedure where the community and its leaders function to peacefully settle a potentially violent disagreement. A circle of elders and an arbiter are listening to arguments about a reparation, with gold set out to be part of the verdict (*Il.* 497-508). Scholars dispute the precise meaning of the Greek text: what is the issue? - the amount of the blood price or whether it must be accepted at all; who is speaking?—the disputants or the elders suggesting a compromise; what is the gold for?—blood-money or a prize for the judge whose compromise is accepted by both.[61] All agree, however, that the scene describes a stage with public and formal procedures to prevent the excesses of self-help and that such practices were ubiquitous (e.g., v. *Il.* 1.138; *Od.* 11.186; *Od.* 12.4 39-440; *Theogony* 80-93).

This stage has been defined by Gagarin as 'proto-legal' because, although the society has established public and formal processes for settling disputes between its members, they remain voluntary, ad hoc, and customary, rather than compulsory and fixed in written procedural and substantive law.[62] The processes do not arise from law-breaking per se, that is, from any clear definition of tort or crime, or sin deriving from a higher morality which must be effected on earth. Anti-social people presumably would try to get away with as much as they could and would not be shamed into agreeing to arbitration by their peers although the threat of divine punishment for hubris always provided some sanction for those wise enough to learn without suffering. Nor does arbitration procedure arise from simple problems where the facts are indisputable and the solutions obvious. Rather it comes about because both sides are basically honest and have a valid case, frequently involving pride as well as life and property, so that the solution involves a compromise acceptable to both. Although voluntary, the arbitration would be encouraged by the group, because of the recognized dangers to all from an escalating grievance, and particularly by the arbitrator, because of the power and prestige arising from 'straight judgments.'[63]

The literary sources do not indicate that the arbitrators had any special knowledge or inspiration similar to those of the charismatic interpreters of Hebrew law. Although the king was once viewed as the mediator between the gods and his subjects and carried the scepter as the symbol of his authority to determine what was right and proper (*themis*) and to issue *themistes*, there is no suggestion in Homer or Hesiod that either he or his subjects considered his particular judgments inspired.[64] Moreover, the disputants were free to select arbitrators who were elders or wise citizens instead of kings. Individuals who developed a reputation for judicious decisions were evidently sought out by rival claimants, not only from their communities (e.g., simile in *Od.* 12.439-40), but also from neighboring groups (e.g., Herodotus 1.96-98). Such arbitrators satisfied their constituents and achieved their reputations because of their ability to structure compromises and their skills of persuasive speech. They did not rely on a body of oral law, preserved and passed on through the royal succession, or on the oral formulae and rules of a professionalized legal class.[65] Nor is there any sign that they decided their cases by conducting trials by ordeal, by wagers, or by oaths, although oaths would be offered as part of the evidence (and frequently declined) and may have been sworn by all as testimony to the honesty of the presenters and the impartiality of the judges.[66]

Although this stage marks a clear advance over unrestrained self-help, it could not satisfy all the needs of a developing Greek society.[67] Voluntary and ad hoc, it treated only those disputes which were referred to an outsider. Settlements which were reached may have conformed to customary ideas of what was right and proper, but they were too tied to the particulars of individual parties and their grievances to set precedents for future decisions. Moreover, despite the fact that anyone might have access to the process, a voice in the selection of his arbitrator, and perhaps a share in the approval of the best settlement, the quality of justice in the community depended in great part on the quality and motives of the rulers. And, unfortunately, unjust rulers were not unknown. "It's the justice (*dike*) of divine kings to love one man and hate another," Penelope says in praising Odysseus by contrasting him with his peers (*Od.* 4.690-693). In *Works and Days*, Hesiod rages against "bribe-devouring lords who love to judge such a case as theirs" (38-39) and threatens princes who pervert justice and give crooked judgments with certain punishment from Zeus and his daughter Dike (248-264). Indeed, the threat of divine retribution was the major sanction on the behavior of powerful and arrogant kings or nobles. Although Homer and Hesiod emphasize Zeus' wrath at those who " decide crooked judgments (*themistas*) by force in the agora/ and drive out *dike*, having no care for the gods" (*Il.* 16.387-388), the poor and powerless who lived in such a community were at the mercy of their betters and suffered from the crop-destroying storms and floods sent to punish their impious rulers.

The lyric poets in the age between Hesiod and Solon reflect the growing awareness that the perversion of justice disrupts the social order and prevents the state from prospering.[68] In this period of social turmoil, some landowners who were not well-born (eupatrid), but had become wealthy, wanted a share in the political order; other poor landowners, unable to compete with the wealthy, were being enslaved for debt; meanwhile the eupatrid families fought among themselves for the power and prestige of leadership. Lawless violence was the obvious danger and *eunomia* "justice and good order" was the rallying cry of political activity. At some point, arbitration became compulsory and some procedures were fixed by custom.[69] In Athens, the archons were the designated arbitrators and citizens would take their disputes to the appropriate one: e.g., the archon basileus for religion; the archon eponymous for family and inheritance; the polemarch for disputes involving aliens and military matters; the thesmothetes for other issues which came under their provenance. Perhaps the council of nobles assisted them on difficult decisions. As ex-archons and members for life, council members had the experience and prestige to "watch over the laws and administer the most and greatest of the city's affairs" (Aristotelian *Athenian Constitution 3.4*) Thus the eupatrid families controlled the annual offices and the council. The non-noble or poor landholders and artisans, even if they could afford to share the expense of community festivals or war, still had little share in the government or justice and probably had to depend on their kinship relationship to the wealthy nobles for protection.[70]

Law and the Growth of the Sovereignty of the People— The first substantive change, which initiated the 'legal stage,' seems to have been a response to a political, economic, and judicial crisis. In Athens, enslavement for debt and rivalry between ruling families created conditions in which, sometime after his Olympic victory in 640 B.C.E., Cylon attempted to establish a tyranny by seizing the Athenian acropolis. When the Cylonians failed and were promised protection as suppliants, they were murdered by the eupatrid Alcmeonidids as soon as they left the protecting image of the Zeus. These two terrible crimes, the attempt to establish tyranny and the murder of suppliants, added blood-feud to previous dissention and necessarily led to further civic disorder.

Draco and Homicide— Twenty years later, possibly because of conflicts resulting from the Cylonian conspiracy and its aftermath, the Athenians appointed Draco as a special commissioner with the authority to make laws and publish them.[71] The later Athenians referred to his code as a *thesmos*, a law imposed on them by a higher power.[72] There are no legends which suggest that Draco had any divine inspiration, however. Although scholars dispute the facts about Draco's code (and even his existence as a historical figure), it is probable that most of his substantive law was a writing down of customary practice (such as enslavement for debt and eupatrid control of government) which did not solve the problems of the community at the time.[73] As a result, his code gained a reputation for the harshness of its penalties; Plutarch records the saying that "it was written not in ink but in blood" (*Solon* 17). But a written code, published for all to see, with a clear statement of obligations, fixed penalties for disobedience, and compulsory procedures, represents a great advance for the community which values social order.[74] Now the government could prevent revenge from escalating into vendetta and limit the inconsistent or crooked judgments of the archons and council.

Sometime between Homer and Draco, however, homicide became a special category of custom and law, connected to the religious idea of pollution which descended on the killer and the people and land that harbored him. Thus only Draco's homicide law was preserved by Solon, according to tradition. When Athenian law was recodified at the end of the fifth century, the homicide laws, inscribed in 409-408 B.C.E. were attributed to Draco. If that surviving inscription actually records the earliest homicide code, it reveals a distinction between intentional and unintentional homicide, sets the penalty for unintentional homicide as exile, and establishes by whom and how pardon might be arranged, with attention to how the state should take over the pardoning process when the victim of unintentional homicide has left no relatives to negotiate pardon. A second section of the inscription establishes the procedures for prosecution which define the responsibilities of the victim's family, protect the accused before trial, and protect the community from pollution before and after the trial. It also names the ephetes as judges, and spells out situations in which homicide is justified and therefore not punishable. Gagarin considers these laws which protect the rights of all parties and fix elements such as which relative must act and what happens if not all agree to pardon are innovations of Draco's which not only prevent conflict and guarantee justice but also increase the state's ability to control families and individuals.[75]

Homicide became the one part of the developing legal system that was directly connected with the religion.[76] Although the family of the victim still had to initiate the prosecution, the archon basileus, the king archon, whose duties were primarily religious (e.g., supervising state sacrifices, festivals, sacred lands, legal cases concerning religious offenses or impiety), was the one who administered all phases of the trial. All the participants in the trial bound themselves with dreadful oaths sealed by specific ritual sacrifices called 'cut pieces' (v. Antiphon 6.6; Demosthenes 23.67-8). The courts which developed to try the various types of homicide all met in sacred spaces which had some connection with sacred lore about murder. The Areopagus, for example, the site for judgment of intentional homicide by the council of ex-archons which met there in the fifth and fourth centuries, not only was sacred to Ares, but also contained shrines to Athena Areia, and the Eumenides. The court of the Areopagus itself was connected in myth to the murder trial of Ares after he killed Poseidon's son, caught in the act of raping his daughter, as well as with the trials of Cephalus for killing Procris, Dedalus for killing Talus, and the more famous trial of Orestes for killing his mother. Cases of lawful homicide were held in the Delphinion, where there was a temple of Artemis and Apollo of Delphi, supposedly founded by Theseus after he went to Delphi to justify his slaying of the Pallantidai. Unintentional homicide was tried at the Palladium, the temple for Pallas Athena, built after the Argives were mistaken for enemies and killed. When the killer was unknown or not human (but had to be punished anyway to avoid pollution), the trial was held in the sacred hearth of the city, the Prytaneion. In all these cases, the trials were conducted in the open air to prevent the participants from sharing a roof with the accused and thus polluting themselves if he were judged guilty. There is some indication that there was even a court which met at the seashore so the judges could hear a man exiled for unintentional homicide defend himself against a new charge of intentional homicide while he pleaded his case from a boat so as not to pollute the land.[77]

The connection of killing with pollution from the gods had several implications for the development of the legal system. The conservatism of religion in general was added to the basic reluctance to view law as temporary and easily changed, so that the homicide laws were all remembered as ancient prescriptions of Draco to which very little had been added. The fear of pollution, however, meant that intentional homicide became a very dangerous crime which had to be punished with death and confiscation of property rather than left to the family to either avenge or negotiate compensation for. If the defendant left before the trial was complete, he condemned himself to permanent banishment. An unintentional homicide was also punished by exile, but, so long as he stayed away from Attica and prescribed public places, the killer was protected by Athenian law and his property was not confiscated. The family of his victim also had the right to grant him a pardon after a number of years.

In protecting the community from pollution and vendetta, the system of homicide laws and courts also ended up protecting, if not sanctifying, the life of the individual. Intentional homicide included planning a murder as well as executing it and intending to harm a person when it resulted in actual death. Nor was the trial of the defendant a hasty affair. After the family took their case to the archon basileus, he had to make a public proclamation about the accused, and conduct three pretrials each a month apart to determine the facts before supervising the actual trial in the jury-court (of the ephetes and later the Areopagus) another month later. So long as the defendant stayed away from the public places prescribed by law, he was protected from harm until the verdict of guilty was voted by the judges. And, although there was a wider range of situations where homicide was a lawful self defense of persons and property, the state did intervene and hold a trial to determine the facts which might justify a death.

Solon— Draco's homicide code may have been preserved with minor changes, but the rest of his laws failed to defuse the developing economic crisis. Again the Athenians appointed an individual with special powers to make them a new body of laws.[78] Again they did not develop any legends of divine inspiration to give his *thesmos* the religious authority which obligated their obedience. Solon's historicity is beyond doubt because he has left behind lyric poems explaining the problems in Athens and justifying his solutions. Although he sets his description within the framework of the divine moral order, placing the blame on the citizens' lawlessness and greed, he proclaims the solutions as his own. He defines the ideal for society as *eunomie*, 'good government based on good laws'(Diehl, Fragment 3). According to his own words (fragment 5), Solon tried to give each group its due, not allowing either side to win unjustly. Although he canceled debts and forbid enslavement of the debtor's person or the selling of children for debt, he seems to have left the earlier governmental structure nearly intact. But he set apart the functions of the various magistrates and the advisory council (Areopagus by now?), including provisions to insure that the magistrates obey the laws, and codified acceptable behavior in many areas of life (e.g., providing guidelines for tort law, and rules governing family, economic and political life as well as bringing diverse cult practices into a unified state 'calendar of sacrifices'). Thus he smoothed the path to *eunomie*.

Solon also introduced several innovations which smoothed the path to democracy. Before Solon, participation in government was based on a kind of divine right derived from noble birth. But Solon organized the population of Attica into classes based on a property qualification, and enabled those who were not eupatrids, but whose land produced enough wealth, to be eligible for the executive offices and thus membership in the council. Although the rich still controlled the machinery of government in Solon's day, the eupatrids lost some of their power and later politicians could open up offices to the lower property classes in the future.

Solon did three other things which the author of the Aristotelian *Constitution of Athens* singled out as being "most favorable to the common people" (*demotikotata*, 9.1). He considers the prohibition on loaning money on personal security, mentioned above, the most important, but he adds two other innovations which led the way to the elaborate jury/court system of the fifth and fourth centuries. In the first place, Solon made it possible for 'anyone who wanted ' to secure punishment on behalf of an injured party. He may have introduced this legislation in order to insure that those who were illegally enslaved or sold for debt could regain their rights. Once this mechanism was added to the procedures deriving from self-help, however, certain acts which were formerly grievances between individuals became crimes against the public at large.[79] Plutarch reports that Solon aimed for more that protecting the weak:

> . . . the lawgiver wisely accustomed the citizens as members of one body to feel and sympathize with one another's wrongs. We are also told of a saying of Solon's which echoes the spirit of this law . . . . [the best governed city was] 'The city where those who have not been wronged show themselves just as ready to punish the offender as those who have been.' (*Solon* 18, Scott-Culvert, trans.)

The introduction of the volunteer prosecutor, as well as the development of various related procedures for enabling the weak to claim redress, gave the common people a variety of ways to secure justice which matched their particular means and needs.[80]

Although Solon left the control of justice in the hands of the archons, thesmothetes, and ephetes, he added an element which the *Constitution of Athens* calls "the most important in strengthening the people," - "appeal to the court." Despite the difficulty in understanding all the terms referred to in the ancient sources and sorting out what is anacronistic, scholars generally agree that Solon gave the participants in a case the right to appeal the magistrate's decision to an assembly of citizens, which he termed the *heliaia*.[81] Their selection and their relationship to the popular assembly are unclear, for at this early time the common people still had little actual power. It is assumed, however, that the transformation from a court where a magistrate judges to a court where the magistrate only officiates and the dicasts decide began when Solon allowed the right of appeal to the people.

The Pisistratids— Neither Solon's laws against tyranny nor the general oaths of obedience to his code could prevent dissension from surfacing again, however, for the eupatrid families, threatened by wealthy landholders, still continued to fight among themselves, while the poor, released from slavery and debt, still had no way of obtaining land. When war with Megara complicated the situation, the victorious general Pisistratus established himself as tyrant in 546 after two earlier tries. He and his sons, Hipparchus and Hippias, ruled Attica for the next 36 years. Under their regime, the poor farmers and the landless made significant progress. Pisistratus rewarded some supporters by giving them land confiscated from banished eupatrids and advancing loans for its development. Others he settled in conquered lands outside Attica. He restored citizenship to landholders disenfranchised by slavery for debt, and admitted the landless to citizenship for the first time. The tyrants also kept the nobles under control in various ways. Pisistratus made sure his own supporters were elected to the chief offices, which enabled them then to become members of the Areopagus. To weaken the power of the nobles in rural areas, he appointed district judges to take over their hereditary functions as local arbitors. Although the tyranny itself was illegal and operated outside the law, the Pisistratids did retain much of Solon's code. Their cultural policies (e.g., new civic festivals, coinage with Athena and the owl as symbols, as well as their political and economic leveling, did much to strengthen and centralize the state, moving it forward from "the confederacy of dynasts that it was in Solon's day."[82]

The Reforms of Clisthenes— By 510, however, the tyranny of Pisistratus' son Hippias had been overthrown with the help of Sparta and the dynasts were again struggling for power. Clisthenes, leader of the Alcmeonid exiles responsible for Hippias' defeat, "politicized the demos, whom nobody had ever been interested in before," according to Herodotus 5.69. Although the details remain murky, the means and the effects of Clisthenes' victory are clear.[83] Despite the fact that he was not archon, he was able to get a majority in the popular assembly and pass reforms which were ratified by them and accepted as legitimate. Thus the assembly (*Ekklesia*) for the first time achieved power as an institution which could make policy and law. According to Ostwald, the term used for Clisthenes' reforms, *nomos*, indicates the different source for its authority; Draco's and Solon's laws were called *thesmoi* because they were imposed on the people by the lawmaker as a higher authority, but *nomos* implies that the people who live under it accept the law as valid and binding on their own without imposition from above.[84] With Clisthenes, the traditional prerogatives of the assembly were confirmed—e.g., final verdict in all cases involving the death penalty except homicide, final voice on peace, war, and alliance. And for the first time the *Ekklesia* met regularly and chose a probouletic Council of Five Hundred, the *Boule*, to prepare the agenda for its meetings.

The reforms Clisthenes passed in the *Ekklesia* were nothing short of a reorganization of the population of Attica so that citizenship and participation in government were based on membership in a deme, trittyes, and tribe rather than on the old kinship ties of genos, phratry, and the four ancient hereditary tribes. Although he did not eliminate the old divisions or interfere with their cults, he created ten new tribes to supersede them , naming them after Attic heroes chosen by the Priestess of Apollo at Delphi from a list he submitted. From then on, each Athenian citizen was registered as a member of a deme, a small traditional locale which now had its own local government of demarch, assembly, and minor officials to handle local administration and deme cults. The demes were grouped together into thirty larger units called trittyes organized according to the three major geographical divisions of Attica (inland, coast, and city). Each of the ten tribes contained one trittyes from each division, and, like the demes, had their own officers, meetings, and cults. Each tribe provided fifty members of the Boule annually, as well as a general for a board of ten generals and a military regiment when needed.[85] The reorganization actively promoted the unity of the population by discouraging regionalism and weakening kinship ties; more important, it gave the ordinary citizens experience in self- government at the local levels.

Democracy— Although Athens did not become a democracy over night, Herodotus considers Clisthenes the founder of popular government (*democratien*) in Athens (6.131), and dates its greatness and heroism in the Persian Wars to the freedom achieved after he became their leader (5.78). The rallying cry of Clisthenes and his supporters was *isonomia*, defined not only as equality under the law, but also as the equal participation of all citizens in the making, administering, and enforcing of law.[86] This kind of equality developed during and after the Persian Wars, when Athens saved itself (and the other Greeks) with its navy which required the lowest classes as rowers and therefore gave them a share in the government. By the last decade of the fifth century, Athens had instituted all of the features which the Greeks themselves considered distinctive of democracy or rule of the people: magistrates appointed by lot, by all and from all (although the lowest remained excluded by law but not in fact); with the length and number of terms limited, and their conduct in office subject to public examination according to regular and fixed procedures (the generals, who were eventually elected, and could hold office for an unlimited number of consecutive terms, had the greatest power, but they too were subject to examination); open debate of all questions, with the popular courts competent to decide most cases and the assembly sovereign in all matters; (v. Herodotus *Histories* 3.80; Aristotle *Politics* 1317a40-1318a7).[87]

The process probably began with the selection of archons by lot from a list submitted by the tribes, a change made official in 487/6. Sometime in the 450's the third property class was made eligible for the archonship. At the same time as participation in the executive offices was increased, however, the power of those officials was limited by the growing sovereignty of the popular bodies. In the early 460's, the reform of Ephialtes transferred most of the traditional probouletic, administrative, and judicial functions from the Areopagus to the *Ekklesia* and *Boule*, leaving the old aristocratic council with responsibility for only homicide and religious infractions. The change led to the development of popular courts called dikasteries, a widely representative *Boule* which in effect ran the government, and an assembly which decided all important issues. Sometime before the oligarchic revolution in 411, all citizens received payment for their participation in government, whether as archons, jurors, soldiers or sailors, or members of the *Boule*; early in the fourth century, they were paid as well for their attendance at the meetings of the *Ekklesia*.[88] This innovation was a necessary feature of the democracy, for it made *isonomia* not only constitutionally possible, but also economically feasible for the poorest citizens of Athens. Vlastos considers that this equalitarian distribution of political power ensured conformity to law; thus he defines *isonomia* also as 'equality as a guarantee of law.'[89]

The power of the people over the court system was a major aspect of their sovereignty.[90] Once Solon granted them the right of appeal from the magistrates' decisions and instituted the *heliaia* as their jury-court, that power grew gradually as more litigants chose to exercise that right. Its progress was hastened by the growth and complexity of the polis as it became more powerful and by the reforms of Ephialtes which reduced the jurisdictions of the Areopagus. Although minor cases were handled by demarchs or archons and later by compulsory arbitration as well, the increase in the number of important cases or appeals necessitated the splitting of the heliaia into separate jury-courts known as dicasteries. There the judges, called dicasts, heard the opposing arguments of the litigants and then cast their votes without help or instruction from the presiding magistrate and without consultation with each other. There was no appeal from the majority decision, nor did the magistrate himself act as judge; rather he officiated at a preliminary hearing to prepare the case for the judges, supervised the trial, and then announced the dicasts' decision.

The dicasteries were innovative in a variety of ways. In the first place, these public courts were almost entirely secular and civic, for, in the words of Richard Garner, "Like some exotic species, they evolved too late to share in the rich mythical cultural code which connected every traditional aspect of Greek life through generations of shifting and developing legend." [91] There were no tales of the gods' help in establishing the dicasteries nor were there divine or legendary models for trials by jury, with their archons or thesmothetes presiding, scribes recording, litigants presenting opposing cases according to fixed procedures, and dicasts voting as individuals to effect a majority verdict. Unlike the homicide courts, these new courts had no overt connection to gods and heroes and their sacred spaces; the names of the courts (e.g., Red, Greater, Triangular, Middle, New) reveal their separation from the religious life of the city. Although the trials were sanctified by oaths sworn in the name of gods such as Zeus, Apollo, Poseidon, and Demeter (v. Demosthenes 25.149-151 for the heliasts' oath), the procedures themselves were modeled on the more secular aspects of the very competitive Greek society—war, wrestling, poetry, music, and singing contests—where combatants faced off against each other in a balanced and symmetrical opposition. The trials were structured so that the plaintiff and defendant presented their cases in alternating speeches to a group of dicasts who voted, like an audience, for the best argument. The courts themselves were used not only to settle torts and prosecute crimes, but also as a way to retaliate against private or political enemies in order to uphold personal honor in community of fellow citizens.[92]

In the second place, the judges themselves were very different from the kings or nobles of the earlier 'proto-legal' stages who mediated disputes as if by a kind of divine right, or from the priests and rabbis of Israel. The dicasts of democratic Athens were ordinary citizens without any special expertise, rank, or office. They acted as non-professional representatives of the whole citizen body, since all citizens could not be present all the time for every case although the law guaranteed a hearing before the people.[93] Every year 6,000 citizens, whose only qualification was that they were over thirty and in full possession of citizens' rights, were chosen by lot from a pool of volunteers, swore an oath "to judge according to the laws and decrees of Athens and in matters where there are no laws, by the justest opinion," and then were allotted to the various courts in which the individual magistrates had jurisdiction. The size of the jury-courts differed according to the importance of the case, and the procedure for allotment changed over the years to avoid foreknowledge of who would sit in what trial. In general, however, the juries were much larger than our own, probably for two reasons: to prevent bribery and to provide the input of a larger mass in reaching the majority decision (v. Aristotle *Politics* 1286a20).

The same ordinary citizens were sovereign over the deliberative and legislative aspects of their government through the institutions of the *Ekklesia* and the *Boule*. All citizens over eighteen belonged to the popular assembly which met regularly and required a quorum of 6,000 for important decisions on such questions as ostracism, taxation, or war and peace. Every year five hundred citizens over thirty were chosen by lot, fifty from each tribe from a larger list submitted by the demes, to serve in the *Boule*, the Council of Five Hundred which prepared the agenda for assembly meetings, carried out the decisions of the assembly, and conducted the day to day business of government (e.g., diplomacy, financial administration, military affairs, certain types of trials and investigations of executives) in cooperation with the various magistrates and generals. The *Boule* was organized so that the council members of each tribe served as a select committee (prytany) for a tenth of the year, in an order determined by lot, with a new member of the prytany being chosen by lot each day to preside over the *Boule* and the *Ekklesia* if it met on that day. Because no citizen could be a member of the council more than twice in his lifetime, the responsibility for governing the polis was spread throughout the citizen body.

Although Draco and Solon laid down laws (*thesmoi*) for the people, the ordinary citizens legislated new laws for themselves in the democracy. Any citizen had the power to propose a new law to the council, and, if the council approved, the proposal could be brought before the assembly for discussion and amendment. If the proposal was passed by a vote of the majority of the citizens at the meeting, it became a law. The new laws of the democracy were generally called either *psephismata* (decrees) or *nomoi* (laws).[94] Although the terms are frequently interchangeable, the former more often referred to specific actions taken in particular cases, whereas the latter concerned more general and fundamental rules. Those *nomoi* intended to have permanent validity were inscribed on wood or stone and put up in public places where the citizens whom they concerned would be able to see them. These inscriptions were the official texts. Although the archons may have had copies of those laws which concerned their offices, there was probably no centralized collection until the end of the fifth century.

Toward the Sovereignty of Law— The system described above has been termed a radical democracy because the people controlled all aspects of government and guarded against their executives becoming too powerful by limiting terms to only one year, preventing the same individual from holding the same office more than once, and subjecting magistrates to official examinations of their conduct in office. In Pericles' Funeral Oration, Thucydides states the ideal upon which the system was founded: ordinary citizens were capable of judging, if not initiating public matters, and were considered useless if they did not participate in governing (2.40).

But the historian also notes that Pericles was an intelligent and incorruptible leader who "could exercise an independent control over the multitude . . . [so that] what was nominally a democracy became in his hands government by the first citizen" (2.65-66). Later leaders were more ambitious but much less disinterested and farsighted than Pericles. They derived their power either from their speaking ability by which they persuaded the majority, or from their military success which led to their reelection to the board of ten generals, the only continuous offices in the democracy. Thucydides traces their demagoguery as they conducted the Peloponnesian War more out of self-interest than patriotism and ended up catering to the whims of the people in order to remain on top.

In 404, after a series of political and military disasters, Athens was forced to surrender to Sparta. The victors established a provisional government by choosing thirty aristocrats whom they empowered to devise a new oligarchical constitution. Under the protection of a Spartan guard, these 'Thirty Tyrants,' who granted only 3,000 others full citizen rights, initiated a lawless period of arbitrary arrests, banishments, and confiscations. When some of the exiles attempted an overthrow and the Thirty fled the city, the Spartans negotiated a peace which restored the democracy.[95]

From the suspension of the laws in the oligarchic revolution and the reign of terror under the Thirty, the Athenians gained a new respect for their legal system and a new interest in preserving it in coherent form.[96] Already in 410, after the restoration of the democracy, they had appointed officials to collect copies of the laws of Solon and Draco and inscribe them on stone and set them up in front of the Stoa Basileos. The inscription considered to be Draco's code on homicide probably dates from this period. But there must have been so many obscurities and inconsistencies arising from new laws and decrees passed after Solon and so many problems resulting from the defeat by Sparta that it became necessary to establish procedures for the review and supplementation of the laws by the *Boule* and two boards of nomothetes or lawmakers.

The completion of the new code in 403/2 marked a new stage in Athenian law. No prosecution could be brought for offenses committed before 403/2 and no old law was considered valid if it did not appear in the new inscriptions made from 410-403/2. Thus there could be no appeal to 'unwritten law' or ancient principles and practices since this code was now acknowledged as the limit of legal memory.[97] At the same time, the sacred calendar was reinscribed on the back of the same stone walls as the law codes, presumably so that the people could have a clear and accessible statement of all the official rules. The government also established a central record office which kept laws, decrees, and other official documents, written on papyrus rather than on stone, so that official texts could be easily brought to court and read to the jury. MacDowell suggests that the adoption of the Ionic alphabet for these official inscriptions and documents "symbolized the determination to make a fresh start."[98]

During the first half of the fourth century, the democratic government also established new procedures for law-making which protected the democracy from its own excesses.[99] According to Xenophon's *Memorabilia* 1.42, Pericles had defined laws as "all those which the majority, after assembling and debating, enacts as to what should and should not be done," a classic statement of what Weber defines as circularity. But the assembly had been too quick to change its laws, reverse its decrees, and introduce innovations, as the jokes of Aristophanes (e.g., *Clouds* 1421- 24; *Ekklesiazousai* 812-829) and tragic common trial of the victorious generals after *Arginousai* (v. Xenophon *Hellenika* 1.7) indicate.

In the fourth century, the Athenians continued to pass decrees by the previous method, but they developed *nomothesia* as a new process for making new laws or amending the existing laws. If any citizen introduced such a proposal and the *Ekklesia* voted in favor of it, the law was referred to a board of nomothetes selected from those citizens who had taken the heliastic oath for that year and thus were considered representative of the whole people. The new law became valid only if the nomothetes, after detailed examination, voted in favor of its passage. To protect the integrity of the body of law, the proposer of a new law had to repeal the old law or make certain that the new one did not contradict a previous law or was an unsuitable law in itself. Otherwise he could be charged in court and fined if he lost his case. *Nomothesia* also included an annual review of all the laws before the assembly of the people on a fixed day. If the *Ekklesia* voted that any problems caused by inconsistencies or redundancies in the code were serious enough, they sent them to nomothetes for correction.

These new procedures meant that no one organ was in absolute control of the legislative process. The nomothetes could not initiate or draft proposals to change or amend the law, but once the *Ekklesia* voted to send a proposal to them, they, not the *Ekklesia*, had the final authority. *Nomothesia* was both conservative, in that it preserved the venerated law code traced back to Solon, and innovative, because it allowed for change according to careful procedures. Thus in the fourth century, Athenian law was protected from the whims of its makers and law itself was considered the ruler of all.[100]

New Developments in the Polis Culture

Toward Secularization— In the process of developing an orderly society based on law and participatory government, most Greek communities, according to J. K. Davies, experienced

> . . . a double movement: first, a gradual and partial emancipation of 'the state' from the rhythms and institutions of cult, and second, an equally gradual and partial reorientation and redefinition of cult activities and institutions in ways more convenient for civic organization.[101]

There are several reasons for this movement. In the first place, as the states themselves replaced monarchies or aristocracies ruled by divine right with illegitimate tyrannies, the new rulers strengthened the organization of the polis in order to weaken the power of the noble families and to broaden their own base of support. Colonization and increasing wealth also played a role in generating new ideas about community life. Moreover, both Greek geography and Greek religion militated against the kind of centralization which could result in a temple-state such as those found in the Near-East. Since Greek polytheism was so polymorphous and the Greek speaking communities never achieved a lasting political unity larger than the polis, no local deity identified with a powerful polis ever attained the singular status of God or Marduk.

Thus the Greek communities became secularized in so far as they became autonomous, ruling themselves and making their own laws without dependence on priests or divine codes requiring inspired interpretation.   It would be a mistake to consider the Greek communities as secular societies, however, for religion was so deeply imbedded into all levels of their life that 'church' and 'state' cannot be easily separated out.[102]   As the state became an autonomous entity, it did not disturb the ancient cults with their practices and hereditary priesthoods.   In fact, the Athenian archons took over and continued the traditional cultic responsibilities of the earlier kings.   Important deities earlier connected to places and people also came to be viewed as ancestors or patrons of the new civic organization.   In Athens, for example, the worship of Athena as protectress of the polis and of Apollo Patrous as mythical founder of the family of citizens has been traced back to the time of Solon.[103]

The developing state, however, applied its freedom to innovate to the sphere of religion.[104]   When Athens, for example, became the political center of Attica, it also connected itself to important rural shrines by building branch shrines within the city, as in the case of Artemis of Brauron or Demeter and Persephone of Eleusis, and introducing processions from the city to the local sacred spaces for traditional rites like the Eleusinian Mysteries.   The state also created new cults and priesthoods, as for the eponymous heroes of Clisthenes' new tribes (allowing the Priestess of Delphi to make the final selection), and established new festivals at public expense, such as the Panathenaea and the City Dionysia, which expressed the new identity as a political unit.   In addition, the state took over some of the administrative aspects of religion, appointing minor officials or electing new priests, inscribing the sacred calendar to bring all the public cultic regulations together for the citizens, and enforcing sacred law by trying certain violations in its secular courts.   These changes indicate a preference for spreading the participation in religion rather than extending the functions of the existing priesthoods or magistracies.[105]   Moreover, wealthy city-states and individuals devoted their surplus to building elaborate stone temples or treasuries to house their lavish gifts to the gods which became not only proofs of piety, but also symbols of civic power and pride.   Such innovations shifted the power away from religion per se and moved the state closer to secularization.

Yet ideas about the gods and the moral order they represented provided support for the ideals and practices of the developing state. Themis and Dike were personified as divinities and identified with the procedures for justice and order on earth.   The gods had always been overseers of the most basic social relations, as protectors of families, beggars, strangers, and suppliants. And oaths which made the gods witnesses of all significant human interactions transformed the dishonest citizen into an impious individual subject to punishment from the eternal as well as the temporal order. Particular deities, however, became associated with particular aspects of civic life. Both Zeus and Athena received the epithet 'Guardian of the Polis' (*polieus* and *polias*, respectively). Cities went to Apollo at Delphi to gain approval for colonization or new laws and cults. Although Solon accepted responsibility for his code, his piety went beyond his belief in the gods' justice or his special worship for Athena. The solutions he proposed to establish *eunomie*, which he defended in fragment 5,

> Thus would the people be best off, with the leaders they follow:
> neither given excessive freedom nor put to restraint;
> (Lattimore, trans).[106]

reflect the divine prescript "Nothing in excess" associated with Delphi. Later writers in Athens refer to Zeus by the democratic epithet *Agoraios*, `Guardian of the Popular Assemblies' (e.g., Aeschylus *Eumenides* 973; Herodotus 5.46).

The Athenian ideal of *isonomia* or *isotes* ('equality') was also related to the religious and philosophical ideas of cosmic order as a balance of power.[107] As early as *Il.* 15.186-195, Homer alluded to a tale in which Hades, Zeus, and Poseidon, the three sons of Cronus, had drawn lots to divide his domain into three equal portions. Hesiod too described a universe in which the earth was equidistant between the heavens and Hades (*Theogony* 720-721). Early philosophers like Anaximander associated cosmic order with the harmony which equal powers maintain by restraining each other or, like the Pythagoreans and Heraclitus, with the harmony created by the balance of opposites. All connected the self- regulating equilibrium established by natural law with ideas of justice and the good. For physicians like Alcmaeon of Croton and Hippocrates, the balance of equal powers represented the normal state of health; disease was defined as the predominance of any one element or quality. Alcmaeon, most probably a contemporary of Clisthenes, actually used the terms *isonomian* and *monarchian* to describe the two.[108] In Euripides' *Phoenissae* of 409 B.C.E., Jocasta, trying to dissuade Eteocles from refusing to share power with his brother, personifies Equality (*isotes*) as the divine source of humanity's true good and develops a moral argument for moderation based on the natural order, in which day and night willingly yield to each other (541-57).

Rhetoric, Not Jurisprudence— The democratic polis never attempted to establish economic equality, but it did take pride in its *isonomia* as equal participation in law and government. Because its legal administration depended on ordinary citizens rather than on experts, Athens did not develop either a class of lawyers and jurisconsults or the science of jurisprudence. In fact, according to Robert Bonner,

> Ever jealous of the expert, as democracy always is, the Athenians even tried to prevent the rise and development of a legal profession. The law required every man to plead his own case in court and permitted any man to prosecute. . . . The people actually administered justice, interpreting and applying the law in each case as they saw fit. No trained jurist on the bench balked the popular will by citing inconvenient precedents. In theory, a judicial decision rendered today could be reversed in a similar case tomorrow. [109]

Because each panel of dicasts represented the sovereign people, they were free to hear both sides, decide what the facts were, and then reach their own decision, bound only by the heliastic oath sworn at the beginning of their year of service. No higher authority such as a presiding magistrate or jurisconsult could intervene during the trial to offer counsel or interpretation of the law. Nor could the dicasts discuss the issues of the case together; after listening to the litigants' speeches, each dicast voted his opinion in secret and the majority decision constituted a verdict from which there was no appeal. The trials themselves did not produce official statements of the reasons behind any particular verdict. Bonner concludes, moreover, that the Athenians did not develop "a body of case law in equity or authoritative interpretations of statute law or binding precedents" or " experts like modern judges to instruct the jury in the law applicable to the matter at issue, fairly and impartially it may be, but authoritatively nevertheless" because these would have restricted the freedom of the sovereign panel to judge the individual case on their own.[110]

In place of jurists and jurisprudence, however, the Greeks developed oratory and rhetoric, expert speakers and the science of speechmaking, in order to guide both those who would have to persuade and those who would have to decide in the public arenas of the polis.[111] The Greeks had always valued the ability to argue effectively in defense of one's self and honor; a hero like Achilles had been taught "to be a speaker of words as well as a doer of deeds" (*Il.* 9.443). But the art of public speaking became extremely important in city states which chose their leaders and judges from among the ordinary citizens and gave their popular assemblies real power to debate and decide crucial issues. Any citizen could speak in the Athenian assembly and any citizen who heard the debate could vote his decision. The litigants in a case could not hire lawyers to speak for them (although they did use speechwriters and were allowed to introduce advocates to supplement their own speeches) nor could a dicast request clarification before he made up his mind. Thus the sophists provided a real service when they promised to teach ordinary citizens how to speak correctly and clearly, how to argue effectively, how to organize their speeches so that their listeners could follow their arguments, and how to use psychology to manipulate the audience.

Aristophanes might sum up their lessons as "making the weaker argument the stronger," as in *Clouds*, and Plato point out the dangers of clever speech unrelated to truth, as in *Gorgias*, *Protagoras*, and *Phaedrus*. But the democracy did not function day to day according to principles of absolute and abstract truth. Rather, its aims were more pragmatic—the best decision on a particular question—and its institutions were predicated on the belief that the citizens could decide only after thorough examination of all the issues or proposals as well as their causes and consequences.[112] In this context, the effective presentation of all sides of a given issue was not only not immoral, but was a necessary element of successful government. Therefore, fifth and fourth century Athens produced great teachers and speechwriters like Antiphon, whose practice speeches illustrate how to argue opposing sides of a question, Lysias, who was expert at assuming the litigant's character to develop the most persuasive argument for his case, and Isocrates and Demosthenes, who were as famous for their political positions as for their rhetorical abilities.[113]

Moreover, rhetoric became a serious branch of philosophy, a counterpart of dialectic and an art (*techne*) whose methods should be studied and taught, according to Aristotle's *Art of Rhetoric* 1354a. From his introduction to that work, it is clear that he has used and improved upon earlier manuals produced as guidelines to effective oratory. Aristotle defined the function of rhetoric as "not so much to persuade, as to find out in each case the existing means of persuasion" (1355b). In developing the best means of persuasion in the dicasteries, the speechwriters and rhetoricians developed analysis of evidence, motive, and character or state of mind of the litigants, as well as methods of logical reasoning.[114] Here they used and advocated arguments primarily based on probability and contradiction, which Aristotle examines and illustrates in Book 2. But, because they also looked for arguments based on the law itself, the science of interpreting the law began in the actual speeches presented at trials and the handbooks describing effective proofs.[115]

The speechmakers and rhetoricians used arguments based on the law in a variety of ways. Although the Athenian court was not bound by any precedents, speechwriters developed the practice of referring to issues and verdicts in earlier cases to bolster their own arguments. At *Rhetoric* 1.15.9-12, Aristotle recommends that, if the law is counter to a case, one should examine the law at issue to see if it contains equivocal language or contradicts other laws. Litigants also interpreted the intent of the lawmakers or insisted that the 'spirit' of the law must be considered. Aristotle, in discussing justice and law in *Rhetoric* I.13-15, defines the general principle of equity as "justice that goes beyond the written law," and explains why its application is necessary before he proceeds to show how it can be used for particular arguments. As discussed in detail in the section on Sinai, the Greeks' development of such principles of legal analysis as well as the rules of logical argument greatly influenced the rabbinic method of interpreting Scripture.

Political Science— The political life of the autonomous Greek city state also gave rise to political science.[116] The earliest literature displays a great interest in community relations. The heroes of myth and legend are all 'political animals' who exhibit their excellence and win their glory by competition with and leadership of others. The *Iliad*, for example, focuses on the conflict between individual will and community need, whereas the *Odyssey* presents a spectrum of possibilities for social, economic and political life, as Odysseus struggles to return from war and regain his position as king. When polis culture developed, lyric poets like Tyrtaeus, Alcaeus, and, of course, Solon, as well as early philosophers like Thales and Pythagoras, were actively involved in the lives of their cities. By the early fifth century, however, the writers of democratic Athens were particularly self-conscious about their new institutions.[117] From Pelasgus in Aeschylus' *Suppliants* to Theseus in Euripides' *Suppliant Women* and Sophocles' *Oedipus at Colonus*, the legendary good kings of tragedy behave like good Athenians and articulate as well as act on the principles of rule of the sovereign people and of law.[118] The historians too not only describe the polis directing its domestic and foreign affairs, but also include analyses of the principles underlying its government and comparisons with other systems. Herodotus, for example, introduces a debate about the best constitution into a meeting of the conspirators who have just killed the Persian Magi and prepared the way for Darius' rule. The men discuss the benefits and drawbacks of three types—monarchy, oligarchy, and democracy—before finally agreeing to select one of their group as king (3.80-84). According to Vlastos, the speaker in favor of democracy introduces "a revolutionary advance in man's understanding of the problem of government" for he bases the failure of monarchy on the unequal distribution of political privilege instead of on the personal immorality of the monarch.[119] Through the speeches of the various participants and his own analysis of leaders and events, Thucydides also examines the dynamics of both democratic and oligarchic societies in peace and war. He and the dramatists contemporary with him warn of the danger to democracy when persuasive speech is unrelated to reason or virtue. A political treatise authored by an Old Oligarch (ascribed to Xenophon) praises the Athenian system in practice at the same time as it rejects its basic assumption that the common people should rule instead of the best.

   In the fourth century, after the radical democracy had failed and the restored democracy had executed Socrates, Plato withdrew from active political life, but not from thinking about politics. His interest in developing the best leaders and the best constitution led him to speculate on the ideal and the real state in such dialogues as the *Republic*, the *Politicus* and the *Laws*. Aristotle analyzed politics from a more pragmatic perspective.[120] His school studied and collected constitutions from many city states and either he or one of his pupils wrote a history and description of the Athenian constitution. But, of course, he too was interested in the theoretical and examined such questions as the aim, origin, and nature of the state, the types of constitutions, the best rulers and governments, and the reasons for political disorder in his *Politics* and *Ethics*. And, for Aristotle, as for earlier Greeks, politics and ethics were intimately connected:

> Before we can undertake properly the investigation of our next theme—the nature of an ideal constitution—it is necessary for us to first determine the nature of the most desirable way of life (1323a14). . . . The best way of life, for individuals severally as well as for states collectively, is the

life of goodness duly equipped with such a store of requisites
(i.e., of external goods and of the goods of the body) as
makes it possible to share in the activities of goodness.
(1324b-1324a1 *Politics*, Barker, trans.)

Notes

1.   See James H. Oliver, *The Athenian Expounders of the Sacred and
Ancestral Law* (Baltimore: Johns Hopkins University Press, 1950) for a
detailed study of this type of law and its interpreters.   Pp. 43-52 define and
summarize Oliver's reconstruction of the stages of development.   His
appendices contain texts of references to the expounders.
2.   Martin Nilsson, *Greek Folk Religion* (New York: Harper and
Brothers, 1961), pp. 107.
3.   See chapter 6 and notes for discussion and bibliography.
4.   For specific information on practices during this period, see below.
Robert J. Bonner and Gertrude Smith, *The Administration of Justice from
Homer to Aristotle.* Vol. 1 (Chicago: University of Chicago Press, 1930), pp.
1-57; Michael Gagarin, *Early Greek Law* (Berkeley: University of
California Press, 1988), pp. 19- 50; Douglas M. MacDowell, *The Law in
Classical Athens* (Ithaca: Cornell University Press, 1978), pp. 1-23 discuss
this period in detail.
5.   J. K. Davies, "Religion and the State," *Cambridge Ancient History*
Vol. IV, sec. ed.   (Cambridge: Cambridge University Press, 1988) p. 375.
The entire article, pp. 368-388, examines the gradual shift in power from
religion to the state.
6.   Oliver traces the movement from the use of *chresmologoi*, whom he
argues derived prestige from their eupatrid descent, to exegetes as officials
of the state on pp. 1-46 and 105.   See Felix Jacoby, *Atthis; the Local
Chronicles of Athens* (Oxford: Clarendon Press, 1949), pp. 8 - 51, as well as
Herbert Bloch, "The Exegetes of Athens and the Prytaneion Decree,"
American Journal of Philology 74 (1953): 407 -418 for a different view of the
exegetes' relation to the chresmologues and skepticism about their official
status.
7.   MacDowell, *Law*, pp. 192-202.   Martin Ostwald, *From Popular
Sovereignty to the Sovereignty of Law: Law, Society, and Politics in Fifth
Century Athens* (Berkeley: University of California Press, 1986), pp. 525-
550, analyzes the information on the impiety trials. Davies, pp. 375-377,
cites inscriptions which indicate the state's legislating on cult matters.
8.   Translations from Hesiod are quoted from Hugh G. Evelyn-White,
Hesiod, the Homeric Hymns, and Homerica. Loeb Classical Library
(Cambridge,: Harvard University Press, 1970).
9.   See Ernest Barker, *The "Politics" of Aristotle, translated with an
Introduction Notes and Appendixes* (Oxford: Oxford University Press, 1958)
for a commentary on the passage as well as analyses of Aristotle's
conception of law, pp. liv-lv, his vocabulary of the concepts of law and
justice, pp. lxix-lxxii, and an appendix on justice, law, and equity in the

Ethics and *Rhetoric*, pp. 362-73. I have quoted Barker's translation of the *Politics* from this edition.

10. For a comparison and contrast of the uses of the terms *themis* and *dike*, see Martin Ostwald, "Ancient Greek Ideas of Law," *Dictionary of the History of Ideas: Studies in Selected Pivotal Ideas* (New York: Scribner, 1973), pp. 674-679.

11. For an analysis of the concept of *dike* in Hesiod, see Michael Gagarin, "*Dike* in the *Works and Days*," *Classical Philology* 68 (1973): 81-94.

12. See Hugh Lloyd-Jones' appendix to the second edition of volume 2 of Herbert Weir Smyth, *Aeschylus: Plays and Fragments with an English Translation*. Loeb Classical Library (Cambridge: Harvard University Press), pp. 576-581 for Lloyd-Jones' restoration of the text plus his comments and translation.

13. See Hans Kelson's analysis of this ideas and its appearance in a variety of cultures in *Society and Nature: Perspectives in Social Inquiry*. Classics Staples and Precursors in Sociology (1946; reprint, New York: Arno, 1974) as well as chapter 4 and notes.

14. L. R. Palmer, "The Indo-European Origins of Greek Justice," *Transactions of the Philological Society* (1950): 149-168. In fact, Palmer traces it back to the initial boundaries drawn by the apportionment of rights and functions among the deities in the organization of the cosmos (see chapter four) and connects the concepts and language with other Indo-European cultures.

15. H. G. Robertson, "*Dike* and *Hybris* in Aeschylus' *Suppliants*," *Classical Review* 50 (1936): 104. Many scholars argue that *dike* did not originally imply any moral concept of righteousness or goodness contained in our word 'justice'. Gagarin stresses the early emphasis on procedure in his 1973 article as well as his "*Dike* in Archaic Greek Thought," *Classical Philology* 69 (1974): 186-197; See also Hugh Lloyd Jones, *The Justice of Zeus* (Berkeley: University of California Press, 1971); E. A. Havelock, *The Greek Concept of Justice from its Shadow in Homer to its Substance in Plato* (Cambridge: Harvard University Press, 1978). For a summary of the major points of conflict and an excellent bibliography on the issue, see Richard Garner, *Law and Society in Classical Athens* (New York: St. Martins Press, 1987), pp. 4-10.

16. See M. L. West, *The "Hesiodic Catalogue of Women": Its Nature, Structure, and Origins* (Oxford: Clarendon Press, 1985), as well as Michael Gagarin, *Early Greek Law*, pp. 35-36, for text, interpretation, and bibliography of references to Athena as arbitrator in the Hesiodic *Catalogue of Women*.

17. For an examination of the variety of uses of this term, see Martin Ostwald, *Nomos and the Beginnings of the Athenian Democracy* (Oxford: Clarendon Press, 1969) pp. 20-54. See pp. 9-10 for a discussion and bibliography on the etymology of the word *nomos*. In *From Popular Sovereignty*, pp. 87-90, Ostwald summarizes developments of the term.

18. Translations of the Athenian tragedies are quoted from David Grene and Richmond Lattimore, eds., *The Complete Greek Tragedies*, 4 vols. (Chicago: University of Chicago Press, 1959-60). Translators of individual plays are cited in the text.

19. Gagarin, *Early Greek Law*, analyzes the remains of the codes as well as the literary evidence. He establishes the pattern in Chapter 6, "The Emergence of Written Law," pp. 121-141. The quote at the end of the paragraph appears on p. 141.

20. See Gagarin, *Early Greek Law*, pp. 51-80, for a survey of the literary evidence with bibliography of primary and secondary sources.

21. See Andrew Szegedy-Maszak, "Legends of the Greek Lawgivers," *Greek Roman and Byzantine Studies* 19 (1978): 199-209 for analysis of the legends with bibliography of primary and secondary sources. The author discusses the connections with places and people renowned for their law or intelligence on pp. 202-204.

22. See Szegedy-Maszak, pp. 207-208 for examples.

23. See Szegedy-Maszak, pp. 205-207.

24. P. 207.

25. Ostwald, *Popular Sovereignty*, pp. 94-107, examines new terms developed to distinguish between the two types of law and traces their evolution. Arthur W. H. Adkins, "Law versus Claims in Early Greek Religious Ethics," *History of Religions* 21 (1982): 232-233, argues that the *Antigone* passage reflects the conflicting claims of the gods of the city against the gods of the household rather than a conflict between the laws of men and the 'higher' laws of the gods.

26. Heraclitus is quoted from G. S. Kirk, J. E. Raven, and M. Schofield, *The Presocratic Philosophers: A Critical History with a Selection of Texts* (Cambridge: Cambridge University Press, 1983), p. 211; Ostwald, *Nomos*, p. 28; G. B. Kerferd, *The Sophistic Movement* (Cambridge: Cambridge University Press, 1981), p. 113.

27. Quotes from Herodotus are taken from Aubrey de Selincourt, trans., *Histories* (Baltimore: Penguin, 1954).

28. W. K. C. Guthrie, *A History of Greek Philosophy. Vol. III: The Fifth Century Enlightenment* (Cambridge: Cambridge University Press, 1969), pp. 55-134. Guthrie's Chapter IV "The *Nomos-Physis* Antithesis in Morals and Politics" traces the development of the issue, providing analyses and bibliography on primary sources illustrating major attitudes. See also Kerferd, Chapter 10 "The *Nomos-Physis* Controversy," pp. 111-130.

29. For a discussion of the views of the historical Protagoras as well as Plato's use of him, see Guthrie, pp. 63-68, 181-192; and Kerford, pp. 18-13, 42-44, 84- 93, 132-136, 142-148, where he discusses this myth, and 164-169.

30. See Jonathan Barnes, *The Presocratic Philosophers* (London: Routledge & Kegan Paul, 1982), pp. 451-460 for a translation and analysis of the passage.

31. Guthrie, pp. 60-68, 100-110.

32. The passage is quoted from *Aristophanes: "Lysistrata" "The Acharnians", "The Clouds"* (Middlesex, England: Penguin, 1973).

33.   The history of the use of these two terms has been examined by F. Heinimann. *'Nomos' und 'Physis': Herkunft und Bedeutung einer Antithese im griechischen   Denken des 5. Jahrhunderts*. Basel, 1945. Reprint 1965. Friedrich Solmsen, *Intellectual Experiments of the   Greek Enlightenment* (Princeton: Princeton University Press, 1975), concentrates on the interest in psychology.   In addition to works cited in notes 28-29, see Ernest Barker, *Greek Political Theory: Plato and   his Predecessors* (1918; reprint, New York: Barnes and Noble, 1960), pp. 63-98 for general statements on the sophists and Plato's use of them.

34.   Guthrie, pp. 84-88; Solmsen, pp. 127-32, 140-171. For further analysis of the way in which Thucydides views human nature, see chapter 9.   The translation below is quoted from *Thucydides: "The Peloponnesian War"* (New York: Modern Library, 1951).

35.   The translation comes from Barker, *Greek Political Theory*, p. 98. See pp. 95-98 for analysis of fragments of Antiphon's *On Truth*, as well as sources in notes 28-29, especially Kerford, pp. 115-117.

36.   Guthrie, pp. 75-76.

37.   See chapter 4 as well as both books by Barker cited above.   See also Paul Foriers and Chaim Perelman, "Natural Law and Natural Rights," *Dictionary of the History of Ideas; Studies in Selected Pivotal Ideas* (New York: Scribner, 1973), pp. 13-18.

38.   The passage is quoted from R. D. Hicks, *Diogenes Laertius: "Lives of the Eminent Philosophers"* 2.   Loeb Classical Library (Cambridge: Harvard University Press, 1950). For a detailed study of the development of the idea of the uniqueness of human beings, see Robert Renehan, "The Greek Anthropocentric View of Man," *Harvard Studies in Classical Philology* 85(1981): 239-259.

39.   For the development of these ideas in Plato, Aristotle, and Cicero, see Huntington Cairns, *Legal Philosophy from Plato to Hegel* (Baltimore: Johns Hopkins Press, 1949), pp. 29-44; 92-101; 127-150 respectively.

40.   For a study of Cicero's views, see Neal Wood, *Cicero's Social and Political Thought* (Berkeley: University of California Press, 1988), pp. 70-90 as well as Marcia Colish, *The Stoic Tradition from Antiquity to the Early Middle Ages. Vol. 1. Stoicism in Classical Latin   Literature* (Leiden: E. J. Brill, 1985), pp. 89-104.

41.   For an expression of this view, see Henry Sumner Maine, *Ancient Law: Its Connection with the Early History of Society and Its Relation to Modern Ideas* (1864; reprint, Tucson, 1986), pp. 50-65; Ernest Barker's translation and introduction to Otto Gierke, *Natural Law and the Theory of Society 1500-1800* (Cambridge: Cambridge University Press, 1934), pp. xxxiv- xxxvii; as well as Foriers and Perelman, pp. 16-17. Colish, however, argues, pp. 341-389, that Stoic theories had little real impact on the *responsa* of the Roman jurisconcults or the practices and prefaces of the Roman emperors.   She attributes legal developments to the Romans' pragmatic responses to changing social conditions rather than to philosophical ideals.

42.   P. 71.

43. Pp. 71-72.

44. Bernadotte Perrin, *Plutarch's Lives*. Vol. 1. Loeb Classical Library (New York: G. P. Putnam's Sons, 1928).

45. For a discussion and bibliography of the problems of evaluating the sources for constitutional history, see C. Hignett, *A History of the Athenian Constitution to the End of the Fifth Century B.C.* (Oxford: Clarendon Press, 1958), pp. 1-32; P. J. Rhodes, *A Commentary on the Aristotelian "Athenaion Politeia"* (Oxford: Clarendon Press, 1981), pp. 15-30, as well as notes on specific passages.

46. Bonner and Smith 1, p. 153.

47. I have relied primarily on Hignett, Rhodes, and Bonner and Smith 1 for my summaries. For a detailed analysis of Greek history, see also *Cambridge Ancient History*.

48. Gagarin, *Early Greek Law*, pp. 8-9, presents a three stage model for the development of law.

49. Raphael Sealey, *The Athenian Republic: Democracy or the Rule of Law?* (University Park, PA: The Pennsylvania State University Press, 1987), pp. 146-148.

50. For a discussion of kingship, see Bonner and Smith 1, pp. 1-57.

51. J. V. Luce, "The *Polis* in Homer and Hesiod," *Proceedings of the Royal Irish Academy* 78.c, 1 (1978):1-15 traces attitudes and institutions of later Greek communities back to Homer and Hesiod.

52. Hignett, pp. 38-85, traces the movement from monarchy to aristocracy in Athens and analyzes the early institutions.

53. For descriptions of self-help, see Bonner and Smith, pp. 11-19, 52, 61.

54. Bonner and Smith 1 make the point about homicide on pp. 16-17. George Calhoun, *The Growth of Criminal Law in Ancient Greece*, (1927; reprint, Westport, Conn.: Greenwood Press, 1974) traces its development out of private grievances or torts which were viewed as offences against the entire community and punished by public action.

55. See Calhoun, pp. 62-77, as well as Sealey, *Athenian Republic*, pp. 31-32, 75.

56. Raphael Sealey, *Women and Law in Classical Greecee,* (Chapel Hill: University of North Carolina Press, 1990), p. 152.

57. Gagarin argues for this interpretation of the reinscription of Draco's code, using incidents of murder narrated in Homer to support the practice. See *Early Greek Law*, pp. 32, 88, as well as his *Drakon and the Early Athenian Homicide Law* (New Haven: Yale University Press, 1981), pp. 6-10, 98-125; and Bonner and Smith, vol. 2,(1938), pp. 192-194, 201. For later homicide laws and procedures, see Bonner and Smith 2, pp. 198-231 and Douglas M. Macdowell, *Athenian Homicide Law in the Age of the Orators* (Manchester: University Press, 1963). On pp. 8-31, MacDowell summarizes the family's responsibilities.

58. Bonner and Smith 1 discuss ad hoc attempts at arbitration and compromise, pp. 29-56. See also Gagarin, *Early Greek Law*, pp. 19-50.

59. Sealey, *Athenian Republic*, p. 75.

60. Luce, p. 10.

61. See Gagarin, *Early Greek Law*, pp. 26-33, for a summary of the problems, bibliography, and interpretation.

62. Gagarin, *Early Greek Law*, pp. 40-47, summarizes the characteristics of this stage.

63. Bonner and Smith 1, pp. 42-43.

64. Bonner and Smith 1, pp. 9-10.

65. Gagarin, *Early Greek Law*, pp. 25-26, 45.

66. Although Bonner and Smith 1 give examples of wager, combat, and oath, pp. 26-28, Gagarin, *Early Greek Law*, p. 29, denies that these represent legal situations.

67. Gagarin, *Early Greek Law*, pp. 105-109, summarizes the inadequacies.

68. Calhoun, pp. 24-41.

69. Bonner and Smith 1, pp. 61-66.

70. Hignett, pp. 74-85, summarizes the aristocratic state before Solon.

71. Hignett, p. 87; Gagarin, *Drakon*, pp. 20-21.

72. Ostwald, *Nomos*, pp. 158-160.

73. That is, if Draco wrote down any laws other than homicide. See Hignett, pp. 84, 305-311; Bonner Smith 1, pp. 133-138.

74. Gagarin, *Early Greek Law*, pp. 78-79.

75. Gagarin, *Early Greek Law*, p. 139. I have used this book and *Drakon* extensively for my information on Draco and the homicide code. See *Drakon*, pp. xiv-xvii and 30-64 as well as *Early Greek Law*, pp. 86-89, for the text, translation, and analysis. *Drakon*, pp. 21-29 treats the question of the authenticity of the inscription. Gagarin disagrees, however, with the opinion that Draco's homicide laws indicate a religious concern with pollution (*Drakon*, pp. 164-167). See also MacDowell, *Law*, pp. 109-122, for a summary, or his *Athenian Homicide Law* for a detailed discussion of the code and its problems as well as its relation to religion.

76. Garner, *Law and Society*, pp. 35-39, discusses the connection of the homicide courts with religious traditions.

77. MacDowell, *Athenian Homicide Law*, pp. 82-84; *Law*, p. 117.

78. For the conditions in Athens before Solon's appointment and his reforms, see Bonner and Smith 1, pp. 149-186; Hignett, pp. 86-107; Gagarin, *Early Greek Law*; Calhoun, pp. 42-56.

79. Calhoun, p. 56, dates the enactment of true criminal law to this innovation.

80. Robin Osborne, "The Law in Action in Classical Athens," *Journal of Hellenic Studies* 105 (1985): 40-58 describes the variety of legal actions. I have not discussed the problems connected with abuse of volunteer prosecution, i.e., sycophancy. See MacDowell, *Law,* pp. 53-66; Bonner and Smith 2, pp. 39-74; as well as Robert Bonner, *Lawyers and Litigants in Ancient Athens: The Genesis of the Legal Profession* (Chicago: University of Chicago Press, 1927), pp. 59-71. The passage from Plutarch has been quoted from Ian Scott-Kilvert, *The Rise and Fall of Athens: Nine Greek Lives by Plutarch* (New York: Penguin, 1960).

81. See Rhodes, pp. 106, 160-162, and Mogens Herman Hansen, "The Athenian *HELIAIA* from Solon to Aristotle," *Classica et Mediaevalia* 33 (1981): 9-47, as well as Hignett, pp. 97-98, and Bonner and Smith 1, pp. 151-157.

82. The term is quoted from Hignett, p. 123. For details on the Pisistratids, see Hignett, pp. 108-123 and Bonner and Smith 1, pp. 181-186.

83. See Hignett, pp. 124-166; Bonner and Smith 1, pp. 187-250; Ostwald, *Nomos,* pp. 148-158; as well as Victor Ehrenberg, "Origins of Democracy," *Historia* 1 (1950): 537-548; D. M. Lewis, "Cleisthenes and Attica," *Historia* 12 (1963): 22-40; and A. Andrewes, "Kleisthenes' Reform Bill," *Classical Quarterly* 27 (1977): 241-248.

84. Ostwald, *Nomos,* p. 158.

85. See Hignett, pp. 244-250 for the selection of generals and their relationship to the tribes.

86. For an analysis of this term and the passages in which it occurs, see Ostwald, *Nomos,* pp. 96-147, and Ehrenberg, pp. 526-537, as well as Gregory Vlastos, "*ISONOMIA,*" *American Journal of Philology* 74 (1953): 337-366.

87. For details concerning these developments, see Hignett, pp. 159-251 and Bonner and Smith 1, pp. 251-278, as well as Ostwald, *Popular Sovereignty,* pp. 3-83.

88. Hignett, pp. 396-397.

89. Pp. 356-361.

90. For full descriptions of the jury courts, see Bonner and Smith 1, pp. 221-250, as well as *MacDowell,* Law, pp. 24-40. Although I have concentrated on the dicasteries, the Athenians also developed procedures for settling torts on the local level and through arbitration without trial. For further information, see Bonner and Smith 1, pp. 318-334, 346-354; Bonner and Smith 2, pp. 97-116; and MacDowell, *Law,* pp. 203-211.

91. The quote is from p. 47. Garner develops this idea in a section entitled "The Popular Courts and their Secular Nature," pp. 39-48. In his introduction to *Law and Society,* he summarizes the relation of justice and law to the values and forms of traditional competitive aspects of Greek society.

92. Garner, pp. 67-70.

93. Bonner and Smith 1, p. 226.

94. See MacDowell, *Law,* pp. 44-46, as well as Sealey, *Athenian Republic,* p. 33.

95. For a summary of the period, see Hignett, pp. 260-268; Bonner and Smith 1, pp. 323-334; and Ostwald, *Popular Sovereignty,* Part III. Peter Krentz, *The Thirty at Athens* (Ithaca: Cornell University Press, 1982), also discusses this period in detail.

96. MacDowell, *Law,* pp. 46-52, and Sealey, *Athenian Republic,* pp. 35-50.

97. Sealey, *Athenian Republic,* p. 37, considers this a sophisticated legal reform.

98. MacDowell, p. 47.

99.   See, in addition to MacDowell and Sealey, Douglas M. MacDowell, "Law-Making in Athens in the Fourth Century B.C.," *Journal of Hellenic Society* 95 (1975): 62-74 and P. J. Rhodes, "*NOMOTHESIA* in Fourth Century Athens," *Classical Quarterly* 35 (1984): 55-60.

100.   Sealey, *Athenian Republic*, pp. 50-52.

101.   Davies, p. 371. The entire article, pp. 368-88, is rich in details which illustrate the movements and makes the further argument that there were many other important aspects of religious life that never coincided with political life. I have summarized several of Davies' points in the following discussion.

102.   Davies, pp. 370-371, presents an excellent discussion of this point, explaining how the same group could function in various different capacities at different times- e.g., a tribe was an army regiment, a political entity, a lineage linked to a god or hero, and a cult group with its own sacred spaces and rituals. Robert Garland, "Priests and Power in Classical Athens," p. 75, in Mary Beard and John North, eds. *Pagan Priests: Religion and Power in the Ancient World* (Ithaca: Cornell University Press, 1990), notes that religion itself was not a separate concept for the Greeks and that the use of this category is a tool of modern scholars which often creates misunderstanding.

103.   Davies. pp. 379-80, shows how the cult of Athena Patrous unified all the various phratries under the one lineage, so that festivals in his honor marked important family and state occasions.

104.   In addition to Davies, see Martin P. Nilsson, *Cults, Myths, Oracles, and Politics in Ancient Greece* (Lund: C. W. K. Gleerup, 1951) for a detailed discussion of the relation between religious innovation and political events.

105.   Garland makes this point very forcefully on p. 90. The entire article analyses the diffusion of religious authority in democratic Athens.

106.   Lattimore's translation is quoted from *Greek Lyrics* (Chicago: University of Chicago Press, l960), pp. 22.

107.   See chapters 2, 3, and 4 as well as Gregory Vlastos, "Equality and Justice in Early Greek Cosmologies," *Classical Philology* 42 (1947):156-178 and Vlastos, *ISONOMIA*, pp. 361-365.

108.   Vlastos, *ISONOMIA*, pp. 363-365, analyzes the political terminology of the fragment and relates it to the events in Croton and Athens.

109.   Bonner, p. v. I have selected and rearranged sentences for this quotation.

110.   Pp. 74-75. See the whole chapter on "The Character of the Courts," pp. 72-95, for an elaboration of this view.

111.   For a general work on the topic, see George Kennedy, *The Art of Persuasion in Greece* (Princeton: Princeton University Press, 1963).

112.   Kennedy, pp. 13-17.

113.   See Bonner, pp. 1-25 for a summary of the careers of the ten orators of the Greek canon, or Kennedy for a more detailed introduction.

114.   Kennedy, pp. 88-103.

115.   Bonner, pp. 175-199, analyzes "tactics and technicalities."

116.   Barker, *Greek Political Theory*, traces major ideas about the state through Plato.   See also Cynthia Farrar, *The Origins of Democratic Thinking: The Invention of Politics in Classical Athens* (Cambridge: Cambridge University Press, 1988) for a detailed study of the ideas of Protagoras, Thucydides, and Democritus.

117.   See Ostwald, *Nomos* and *Popular Sovereignty*, as well as articles by Ehrenberg and Vlastos cited above.

118.   Ehrenberg analyzes Aeschylus' *Suppliants* as one of the earliest literary reflections of the ideals of democracy.

119.   *ISONOMIA*, p. 358.

120.   For a summary of Aristotle's ideas, see R. G. Mulgan, *Aristotle's Political Theory: An Introduction for Students of Political Theory* (Oxford: Clarendon Press, 1977), which contains a useful bibliography.

Conclusions and Comparisons

All law on Sinai is ultimately grounded in the divine revelation to Moses which has no real equivalent in the polis culture of Greece. This basic difference affects many aspects of the development of law and the state in the two traditions. In the first place, the Hebrews did not struggle with the problem of legitimation as the Greeks did because they maintained their belief in the divine authority of the law to the extent that they considered even legal innovations of a later age to be implicit in the revealed Torah. This belief dictated both the content of the law, in which the sacred and the secular were intertwined, and the form of legal development. The Hebrew law emerged through commentary and exegesis on the biblical text as well as through the responses to legal questions by continuing generations of sages who were formally trained jurists. Even latter day forms and procedures were anchored in the biblical text. The revealed law does provide for legislation by the sages but direct legislation accounted for a much smaller body of law than did exegesis, commentary and *responsa*.

In Greece the secular and sacred were also intertwined but the sacred law of religious regulations and general moral pronouncements did not serve the needs of the developing political organization. Therefore, lacking a divine revelation of casuistic and procedural law, the Greeks created their own laws, appointing citizens as lawmakers and legislating by consensus. At first the lawmaking was *ad hoc* as the need arose but later each polis instituted fixed procedures for correct enactment of legislation. These autonomous communities of citizen lawmakers never produced a professionally trained jurist class although they did produce comprehensive codes of law whose authority they elevated through tradition and philosophy as well as the sanctification of law itself.

The event at Sinai resulted not only in a revealed law but also in a covenanted community. This covenant with God determined the political organization of the Hebrews and colored their attitude toward public life. Consecrated and accepted for all succeeding generations by the Israelites before they entered the Promised Land, the covenant was not limited to citizens of a particular geographical area but embraced a community of believers through time, in both Hebrew commonwealths and in the Diaspora. In this Hebrew polity God entrusted a degree of his sovereignty to human rulers on the condition that political omnipotence not reside in a single person or group. The essential issue was the division of power and the proper relationship between the various centers of power, e.g., the four crowns, not the political vehicle through which the community was governed. The four crowns derived their authority from God to rule the people but with the exception of the crown of priesthood and the Davidic dynasty the crowns were open to any member of the community who possessed learning, ability or charisma and was chosen by God and ratified by the people's assembly. Although the Hebrews idealized the Davidic monarchy they were never bound to any particular governmental structure. Their polity embraced a primitive democracy, a monarchy limited by the law and the other centers of power, a theocracy and a nomocracy. Since the relationship with God was the focal point of the Hebrew polity, serving God was the highest vocation for the individual while political activity though necessary was not particularly esteemed.

The Greeks had a radically different approach to political life. The polis was never a secular society in the modern sense. The survival of the state depended on its right relationship with the gods and its institutions were protected by its various divine patrons. All serious activities were solemnized by oaths and sacrifices which turned violations into impieties as well as crimes. Nevertheless, the Greek polis did not conceive of itself as a covenanted community through time regulated by fixed laws from a transcendent authority. Rather the polis evolved *ad hoc* out of the unification of the inhabitants of a small geographical area at a specific time in their history. Each polis developed its own structure of government as it struggled to achieve order amidst the social and economic conflict accompanying the awakening from the dark ages. Thus the structure of government was extremely important in defining the functions and limitations of the various centers of power.

Long before Solon produced the first written code, there were fixed procedures for a regular exchange of magistrates and a clear definition of their separate spheres of authority. As the people gained more and more power, the procedures and functions of the institutions through which they operated, the assembly, council and courts, were also regulated by law. Thus by the end of the fifth century when the laws were recodified, Athens had in effect a political constitution. In fact, Aristotle was able to collect 158 such constitutions from various city-states of the Greek world. In contrast, the successive Hebrew types of government retained the fluidity of the early primitive democracy. Although procedures and institutions were inevitably introduced there was never the same concern for precise definitions of function. The Torah remained the only political document for the Hebrew polity down through the ages and even today, the State of Israel does not have a written constitution.

Moreover, the centers of political power were different in the two civilizations. In the Athenian polis as in the Hebrew polity it was the diffusion of power that became the best defense against civil disorder. But in the Greek democracy power was diffused throughout the citizen body by the people themselves rather than channeled through four crowns deriving their authority from God as in Israel. In Athenian practice, the Greek ideal of *isonomia* meant not only equality under the law but also equal opportunity to participate in the governing process; so that all citizens above the age of eighteen were members of the sovereign assembly for life and magistrates, councilmen and jurors relinquished their positions to other citizens each year. It is true that after the failure of the radical democracy in Athens, Plato and Aristotle argued against the assumption that the ordinary citizen could govern, judge and legislate. Both preferred the rule of the man or men who were best in terms of education and virtue. But recognizing the impossibility of finding a person such as a philosopher-king, they chose the mixed constitution which is based on good laws and which checks and balances the powers of the people, the magistrates and the council.

In contrast to ancient Israel, the Greeks never idealized monarchy except in utopian speculation. They were too suspicious of the corruption of men by power. Since power resided in all the people and the polis was the focal point of Greek life, they judged the non-participant a useless citizen. In fact, unlike the Hebrews, Greeks considered the political arena as one of the best places for an individual to demonstrate excellence and achieve honor.

The different structures of public life in Greece and Israel can be related to the different conceptions of the divine in the two traditions. Hebrew monotheism posited a transcendent God who created all things and is therefore the supreme authority. He delegated a portion of this authority to human leaders through the four crowns. As long as they submit to God's law, the people must submit to them. The result is a hierarchical and vertical flow of power. In marked difference, Greek polytheism posited a group of gods who were identified with the natural world at the same time that some of them developed anthropomorphic qualities and functions. No one of them was responsible for the entire creation; it emerged naturally. When Zeus achieved supreme authority through bargaining and compromise as well as through violence, the order he established was based on the distribution of power and privilege throughout the pantheon. The Greek political system is horizontal rather than vertical, reflecting the participation of the divine community in governing the universe. In the earthly counterpart of divine government on Olympus, the fixing of the boundaries which separated the areas of authority led to the political constitution embodied in the man-made law codes. The early nature philosophers also conceived of the natural order as a balance or harmony of diverse parts. But Plato, Aristotle and the Stoics viewed nature as a hierarchy. Plato in *The Republic* in particular, posited a hierarchical political system based on that model; this system derived its ultimate authority from the idea of the good.

Despite the differences between the Hebrews and the Greeks regarding the foundations of the community and the structures and channels of authority, the two cultures were very concerned about the welfare of the governed. Both idealized and attempted to reify the rule of law to keep it above human corruption. Early in their history each developed fixed procedures for adjudication and written codes of law which were made available to the general public. In Greece the codes were inscribed on wood or stone and placed outside for all to see. In Israel the priests instructed the people in the Torah and there were periodic public readings of it. The law codes of both societies were freely and voluntarily accepted by the populaces. The Book of Exodus describes the spontaneous response of the Israelites: "All that the Lord has spoken we will do." (Exod. 18:7-8). Not only did the Greek city states make their own law but according to Socrates (*Crito* 52) the citizen by living and participating in the state had accepted the entire body of law as binding. Either he must obey each provision, persuade his fellow citizens to change a law to which he objects, or leave the state and live elsewhere.

Moreover, each society provided safeguards against the exploitation of the populace by the ruler. The Hebrew charismatic leader or king was subordinate to the Mosaic Law and constrained by the people's assembly of the primitive democracy whose remnants remained even after the growth of the monarchy. The ideal leaders of the Hebrew polity such as Moses and Samuel were known to have never used their office for personal gain (Num. 16:15; 1 Sam. 8:3). The public officials of Athens were all subject to investigation of their conduct in office at the end of their term or in extraordinary circumstances during their service.

Both cultures valued the community as the means through which the individual achieves completeness. For the Israelites the polity provided the best setting in which the relationship to God and man could be worked out. The Greeks viewed humans as social beings by nature, unable to survive without community. The constitutions they developed to apportion authority were more than social contracts to prevent disorder. They provided the framework through which the individual could achieve his fullest potential as a virtuous and happy human being. Wisdom was the instrument for both cultures in attaining the highest objectives of group life. On Sinai the anchoring of political power in divine wisdom is ideally represented by King Solomon who at the beginning of his reign, was asked by God: "What shall I give you?" (1 Kings 3:5). Solomon chose wisdom which was exemplified in his inspired judgments and vast learning. For the rabbis this wisdom was embodied in the covenant of the written and the oral law and imparted to the people through the rabbinic academies, synagogues and schools.

Although the Greeks never developed a professional or learned class of rulers and judges, they did develop thinkers and teachers, from the Sophists who offered practical guidance to citizens, to the philosophers and ethicists who based their ideas of community on their knowledge of nature and natural law and who believed that virtue was knowledge. Both Plato and Aristotle held that education toward the good was a major function of the state. If Aristotle looked to the community's most virtuous men as models of the good, Plato's conception in *The Republic* is much closer to the Hebrew idea of covenant; his ideal, just state derives directly from a transcendental model and its hierarchical structure is consented to by the governed because knowledge resides in its governors.

In *The Republic* Plato described a utopian state in order to define justice. But in the harsh world of power politics, both the Hebrews and the Greeks struggled to achieve goodness and still survive as viable communities. In ancient Israel and Judah, confronted by superpowers to the north and south and enemies on every border, the political leaders resorted to geopolitical strategies. It was the prophets who saw beyond the crisis of the moment to the unfolding of God's larger plan for humanity in history. Without the conception of such an overarching divine program for history, the Greeks responded to each particular event as a particular problem to be solved. As they grappled with each issue they raised ultimate questions of justice and expediency, might and right. It was the rapid changes in fifth century Athens (its defeat of the Persian Empire, its attempt to maintain a democracy at home and an empire abroad) that led Herodotus and Thucydides to look for the general laws of cause and effect and thus begin the science of history.

Chapter 9

The Concepts and the Methods of History

Introduction

In archaic, agrarian societies where language had fully developed, there was a vivid conception of a temporal world of past, present and future. But this temporal conception, like the farming communities in which it arose, was harnessed to the seasonal cycle of nature. Embedded in the flow of winter to spring, to summer to fall, back to winter and then back again to spring and summer, time moved in circles like a merry-go-round without any destination in sight. It had motion but no meaning.

In these societies mythic time, the time of primeval beginnings validated all human activities. The historical present gained meaning and reality only when it was converted into mythic time through the repetition of a ritual or through the performances of mundane actions as reenactments of paradigmatic acts first performed in the period of origins and archetypes.[1] History as the chronicle of the events of a group did not exist at all. To ask an individual living in a realm governed by cyclical and mythic conceptions of time, "What is the history of your people?" would be like asking, "What is the history of winter?"

As human consciousness began to separate from and transcend the idea of the simple, natural cycles of seasonal time, a more linear conception of progressive temporality began to prevail. According to anthropologists, it is only in cultures where such temporal progression is prevalent that histories are kept. The evidence for the earliest forms of recorded history in the Mediterranean basin begins with such records as the Sumerian, Assyrian, and Egyptian king lists, some of which go back to the first half of the second millennium. By 1300 B.C.E. there were royal inscriptions on buildings, where the king usually gave his name and titles, lavished praise on his particular god or gods, noted the season and the circumstances when the building was started, and then described the building operation itself. Later these descriptions were expanded to include events immediately preceding the erection of the building as well as a summary of the king's past military exploits to date. In succeeding centuries the information was placed on monoliths and arranged systematically and chronologically, as in the records of the Assyrian rulers of the first millennium B.C.E. Eventually these annals extended beyond mere raw facts into statements of motives, criticism of actions, and appraisals of character.[2]

Inscriptions on buildings or annals, however, do not meet historian Chester Starr's definition of history "as explaining (one's) present condition by a disciplined factual description of (one's) past.[3] Starr has specified four strands of development which led to the writing of such history in Greece:

> first the development of a sense of space and the differentiation of peoples in this geographical framework; secondly the growing awareness of time as a continuous dimension within which human changes occur; thirdly, the consolidation of the city-state and the companion self-awareness of its citizens; and fourthly, the crystallization of intellectual processes in poetry and art as well as in philosophy.[4]

Although Starr is referring to the Greeks, these four strands were present in ancient Israel even earlier. Clearly the conception of a childless patriarch, chosen from the ethnic groups formed and dispersed after the failure of the tower of Babel and promised a distant land for a powerful nation in a future generation, reveals the requisite sense of space, uniqueness, group self-awareness, and human change over time. It was the "crystallization of intellectual processes" around the concepts of monotheism and covenant, however, that made the expanding past a constant condition by which the Hebrews understood the linear progression of all events in time—from 1800 B.C.E. to the moment of proud national consciousness, under David and Solomon, and continuing into the future.

The earliest Greek poets were not ahistorical.[5] Homer and Hesiod synthesized a vast amount of episodic myth into organized sequences. Hesiod even traced the succession of ages from the remote golden age through the more recent age of heroes down to his own grim iron age. But, although Hesiod's *Works and Days* is couched as a response to a recent quarrel with his brother, it does not record any specific contemporary events or agents or offer any chronology beyond the cyclical signs of the seasons.

In the period after Hesiod, however, many changes occurred which stimulated the kinds of developments Starr has posited as necessary for the writing of history. That the movement of Greeks east and west for trade and colonization and the later conquest of eastern Greeks by Lydia and Persia produced an awareness of geography and ethnic differences is clear from the fact that some individuals produced maps of the world (e.g., Anaximander) while others (e.g., Scylax of Caryanda, Euthymenes of Marseilles) collected descriptions of the natural features, peoples, and customs of non-Greek places. Because they chose to communicate in prose rather than the poetry or epic and reported stories (*logoi*), they were called the *logographoi* (story writers or tellers) by later writers.[6]

Contact with older civilizations such as Egypt, which could trace itself much further back and in a much more systematic way, may have been a catalyst not only for a more developed sense of time, but also for a more critical attitude toward Greek myths (v. Herodotus *Histories* 2.142-143).[7] The longer Egyptian chronologies seemed to place the oldest Greek stories in more recent times and to disprove the mingling of Greek gods with heroes. The *logographoi* generally accepted the major events and agents as real and even related them to the gods and heroes of the non-Greeks, but they realized that their own genealogies were confused and unsynchronized, and worse, that the poetic elaborations involving the gods were improbable. Some tried to systematize their material and correct the traditions according to their ideas of probability, to make them more credible. Others disregarded the old stories and looked to nature rather than the gods or heroes for explanations of origin and change. They developed new methods such as empirical analogy and deductive reasoning to ascertain and prove new theories about first principles and processes in nature and even about the evolution of human society and the psychology of human nature.

The "crystallization (and secularization) of intellectual process" is also related to the development of the city-state and the increasing self-awareness of citizens who began to make their own laws and select their own leaders. The social and political upheavals of the archaic age in Greece not only produced rapid changes, but also the consciousness of continuous change itself and the recognition of the citizens' own power as agents of change. Such perceptions increased the interest in the timely at the expense of the timeless. Lyric poetry from Tyrtaeus to Pindar and extant Athenian drama reflect that interest even when the subject matter is taken from myth. Greek cities began to keep chronological lists of their leaders-archons in Athens, kings in Sparta, priestesses in Argos—which Starr believes indicate a "belief that the present, itself a real condition, was the product of time in the past."[8] But as in Israel, so in Greece, the first real history was written in a time of great national pride and self-consciousness when the weak coalition of Greek city-states was able to repulse the invasion of the fabulously wealthy and powerful Persians.[9]

One of the most important motivations for writing history was the desire to confer a degree of immortality on particular events and people. But the impulse to remember was different on Sinai and Olympus. As Momigliano said of the Greek historian:

> He records, not what everybody knows, but what is in danger of being forgotten or has already been forgotten. History is to the Greeks and consequently to the Romans an operation against Time, the all destroying, in order to save the memory of the events worth being remembered. The fight against oblivion is sought by searching for the evidence.[10]

In ancient Israel, however, the injunction to remember became a religious imperative for an entire people (Deut. 25:17; Isa. 44:21; Mic. 6:5 and the ever insistent demand to "remember that you were slaves in Egypt . . ." scattered throughout the Pentateuch). The motivation was the continuing testimony to the greatness of God who revealed His will and purpose for humanity in history. The survival of individual or group activity was important only insofar as it bore witness to God and his eternal message. Personal or group immortality depended on this rather than on the "fight against oblivion." Nor did Hebrew history require the same kind of search for evidence since it contained a divine revelation which *ipso facto* made it unimpeachable.

Despite these differences, the first Hebrew and Greek historians used similar devices for ordering and recording their historical memories.[11] For both, chronology grew out of genealogy which connected the present group to its founding hero, linked that group with different ethnic groups and places, and often bestowed names on the group through eponymous ancestors.[12] On Sinai, for example, all post-diluvian generations traced their origin to Noah and his three sons. The Hellenes considered Hellen, also the son of the survivors of the flood, as the eponymous founder of them all, and his sons Dorus, Aeolus, and Xuthus, father of Ion and Achaeus, the founders of their major branches, but other more specific groups, even enemies like the Trojans, Argives, and Spartans, traced themselves back to common ancestors, e.g., Atlas. The Hebrew and Greek historians also made use of archival lists of kings, battles, priests (or priestesses), and official documents. Both employed these types of information to provide a chronological framework for the entire narrative as well as to link its individual segments.

These segments of Hebrew and Greek memory, however, were products of the oral tradition which the first historians were committing to writing for the first time. Therefore, they used the devices of story-telling—plot, character dialogues, type-scenes—to produce an imaginative reconstruction of the past. According to Immerwahr this "mimetic method . . . reaches into the smallest narrative details and tends to destroy the distinction between 'fact' and interpretation. This factor, more than any other, gives ancient historiography its unique character."[13] To the modern sensibility, such history may seem more like fiction than fact, for history is presented as the coming together of great individuals to effect great events rather than as the interaction of impersonal historical, social, economic, and political forces. Moreover, for the Hebrews and Herodotus, the first Greek historian, these great events in time are themselves linked to an overarching eternal order. The resulting Hebrew pattern was connected to the will of God and his design in history which meant the irruption of eternity into time. Although the Greeks saw no continuing plan in history, they did discern patterns in events. Thus recurrences reminiscent of cyclical conceptions were part of the linear history written by both the Hebrews and the Greeks.[14]

Notes

1. Mircea Eliade, *The Myth of the Eternal Return* (New York: Pantheon Books, 1954), pp. 34-48 and passim. See also B. A. Van Groningen, *In the Grip of the Past: Essay on an Aspect of Greek Thought* (Leiden: E. J. Brill, 1953) for a detailed examination of this phenomenon and its continuation beyond the Greek Archaic Age. For further discussion of various aspects of the cyclic view of time, as well as the distinctions between historical and philosophical time, see conclusion of this chapter and also the following chapter, 10: The End Time: Apocalypse and Eschatology.

2. J. Jaynes, *The Origin of Consciousness in the Breakdown of the Bicameral Mind* (Boston: Houghton Miflin, 1976), pp. 250-51; John Van Seters, *In Search of History: Historiography in the Ancient World and the Origins of Biblical History* (New Haven: Yale University Press, 1983), pp. 191-199; Baruch Halpern, *The First Historians: The Hebrew Bible and History* (San Francisco: Harper and Row, 1988), pp. 212-218.

3. Chester Starr, *The Awakening of the Greek Historical Spirit* (New York: Knopf, 1968), p. 3.

4. Ibid., p. 5.

5. In addition to Starr's chapter on epic and myth, pp. 12-36 see M. I.. Finley, "Myth, Memory, and History," *History and Theory* 4 (1965): 281-302; A. Cook, "Herodotus: The Act of Inquiry as a Liberation from Myth," *Helios* 3 (1976): 2-66; and Van Seters, pp. 9-54.

6. Starr discusses the development of the sense of space and awareness of ethnic differences, pp. 41-56 and the *logographoi* on pp. 114-117. Geography became a special branch of scientific study in Greece; see J. Oliver Thomson, *History of Ancient Geography* (Cambridge: Cambridge University Press, 1948). For a detailed study of the *logographoi*, see Lionel Pearson, *Early Ionian Historians* (Oxford: Clarendon Press, 1939). Pearson discusses the use of the term *logographoi* on pp. 5-7.

7. See Virginia Hunter, *Past and Process in Herodotus and Thucydides* (Princeton: Princeton University Press, 1982), pp. 50-92, for the effect of such knowledge on Herodotus. In 2.143, Herodotus recounts Hecataeus' comparison of his own genealogy with the Egyptian king lists. Hecataeus' words, quoted below, make clear his interest in and criticism of the poets' stories. See Pearson, pp. 97-98, as well as Robert Drews, *The Greek Accounts of Eastern History* (Washington: Center for Hellenic Studies [distributed by Harvard University Press], 1973) pp. 11-19.

8. Ibid., p. 72.

9. Drews emphasizes the effect of the 'great event' on the development of historiography; see especially pp. 35-37.

10. Arnaldo Momigliano, "Time in Ancient Historiography," *History and Theory*, Beiheft 6, (1966): 15, reprinted in *Essays in Ancient and Modern Historiography* (Middleton: Wesleyan University Press, 1977), p. 191.

11. Van Seters, pp. 8-54, especially 31, and 51ff. for summaries of points.

12. Van Seters, pp. 26-29, as well as Elias Bickerman, "Origines Gentium," *Classical Philology* 47 (1952): 56-81.

13. Henry Immerwahr, "Historiography," *Cambridge History of Classical Literature*. 1 (Cambridge: Cambridge University Press, 1982-5), p. 457-458.

14. For discussion of these concepts, see below, as well as G. E. Trompf, *The Idea of Historical Recurrence in Western Thought: From Antiquity to the Reformation* (Berkeley: University of California Press, 1979), and Momigliano's essay cited above.

Sinai I: Antiquarian Impulse
in Programmatic History

As in so many different facets of life surveyed in these pages , the biblical concept of the covenant between God and Israel was also crucial to the importance attached to history in the Sinai tradition. The shifting back and forth of the covenant language in the Bible between the singular of the individual and the plural of the group underscores the importance of the collective historical destiny which became a powerful motivating force in the writing and compiling of history. The divine factor in the covenant equation gave a programmatic cast to Hebrew history. There is a divine plan for humanity and the Bible selects from the undifferentiated mass of past events, those happenings that give us a glimpse of the implementation of this plan. But this programmatic history is not totally schematic or legendary but amazingly concrete and factual, anchored in historical realities. Chronology is by and large respected. There is no blurring of the events and characteristics of one age with those of another. Historical figures are portrayed in all their individuality. The editors who periodically redacted the sources at their disposal did not flatten them out completely.

The genuine antiquarian interest of the biblical historians derived from what Nicholas Berdayev called the passion for "justice . . . fulfillment and solution in this mortal and terrestrial life,"[1] or as the rabbis put it "to perfect the world under the dominion of God." Thus human actions and motivations must be analyzed, the changing configuration of nations and empires must be understood and the encounter between God and humanity and its dialectic of obedience and rebellion probed. The purpose of this enlightenment is not merely to satisfy the curiosity to know but to elevate human life.

The Torah History: From Creation to the Covenant

Although the Jewish and Christian traditions have held that the Pentateuch was written by Moses, except for the last passage describing Moses' death, there is no specific statement in the Pentateuch that this is indeed the case. The remark that Moses wrote "this torah" (this teaching) in Deut. 31:9 and 31:24 may refer only to the chapters immediately preceding this statement although in a wider sense much more of the content of these books goes back to the time of Moses. One of the basic conclusions of modern biblical scholarship, after intensive examination of internal textual and historical evidence, is that the Pentateuch was compiled from several prior sources brought together and edited considerably later than when they were first set down in writing. Duplicate versions of certain traditions were included in the final draft while alternative traditions were incorporated in some stories so as to leave traces of the constituent parts.

According to the documentary hypothesis, formulated in the nineteenth century but modified by continuing research down to the present, four prior documents. labeled J, E, P and D were the sources out of which the Five Books of Moses were constituted. The J or Yahwist sources, so called because of its preference for the divine name YHVH when relating pre-Mosaic traditions, is thought to date from as early as the time of Solomon or, according to some scholars, as late as 848-722 B.C.E. and its locale is Judea. The E or Elohist source (from the Hebrew Elohim, another name for God in the Pentateuch) avoids using YHVH for pre-Mosaic traditions in accordance with Exod. 6:3 which states that the Patriarchs had not known this divine name. The E source dates from somewhere between 922-722 B.C.E. and originated in the northern kingdom of Israel. After the fall of the northern kingdom of Israel to the Assyrians in 722 B.C.E. refugees from the north bearing the E source came to Judea. There the two documents, J and E, containing ancestral traditions of stories describing the earliest history of humanity, the Hebrew patriarchs, Moses and the Exodus and the wanderings of Israel in the wilderness were combined to form the foundation of the Pentateuch narrative.

The third or D source (the core of which is chapters 5-26 and chapter 28 of Deuteronomy) is linked to a specific event: the religious reforms carried out by King Josiah of Judea around 622 B.C.E. as a result of the discovery in the Jerusalem Temple of a "lost Torah of Moses." Scholarly consensus believes this book to be the book of Deuteronomy which, though containing many earlier traditions, was constituted as a unified source and canonized at that time (see chapter one).[2] The Deuteronomic writings closely resemble the literary style of the prophet Jeremiah who was born not later than 697 B.C.E. and thus was a young man when the Josianic reform took place in 622 B.C.E. It is likely that the Deuteronomic movement preceded the reign of Josiah by many years originating at the end of the preceding century during the reign of King Hezekiah and continued into the sixth century B.C.E. During this time several generations of scribes edited what has come to be known as the Deuteronomistic history, i.e., the sequence of historical books that follows the Pentateuch, Joshua, Judges, 1 and 2 Samuel and 1 and 2

Kings. The language of these post-Pentateuchal books is strikingly similar to that of Deuteronomy and the history that is unfolded in them seems to have its preamble in the Book of Deuteronomy.[3] Recent scholarship has suggested that the levitical priests of Shiloh from the line of Abiathar, one of whose descendants was the prophet Jeremiah, were the writers-editors of the Deuteronomistic history and possibly the book of Jeremiah or at least parts of it.[4]

The fourth strand of the Pentateuchal sources, P, is believed to have been compiled by a priestly group some time before the reign of King Hezekiah of Judea (715-697).[5] The interests of this group centered on the rituals, sacrificial laws and other cultic regulations contained in the Book of Leviticus, on the genealogical details, the life spans of individuals and other statistics as well as particular aspects of the narratives in Genesis, Exodus and Numbers.[6] The final redaction of the Pentateuch was, as noted in chapter one, accomplished by Ezra and a collegium of priests in Jerusalem during the early days of the Second Temple. It was far more than a mere compilation of received texts. It was a highly creative enterprise that gave birth to new narrative syntheses.[7]

Nineteenth century biblical scholars sought to place the four sources of the documentary hypothesis on the procrustean bed of a somewhat naive evolutionary theory, seeing the four documents as successive stages in a single line development of biblical ideas from the primitive to the advanced. Today it is recognized that the four sources most probably overlapped in time so that each source contains some of the earliest as well as the latest concepts in Hebrew religious thought.

Identifying the four sources of the Pentateuch does not lead to the origins of its content because the editors relied on historical, legal, folkloristic and theological materials transmitted orally for centuries before being committed to writing. To trace the origins of this material the form-critical method, introduced in the first decades of the twentieth century, seeks to isolate the types (forms) of composition that characterize the smallest units of tradition gathered in the four sources from which the Pentateuch was constituted. This method leads not only to literary understanding but also to the life settings of the earliest traditions, i.e., how they were used by the community in a concrete context while still independent oral units, as discussed in chapter one.

From this and other modes of analysis scholars have concluded that there were many links in the chain that led from the smallest units of oral tradition to the biblical text and that the relationship between the biblical narratives and the events on which they are based is complex and indirect. A variety of versions of the central biblical themes-primeval humanity, patriarchal wanderings, liberation from Egyptian slavery , the covenant at Sinai, settlement in the Promised Land, apostasy and return to God, the divine meaning behind catastrophes and destruction-were extant. These varying versions reflected different localities, tribes, groups of bards and storytellers, religious functionaries and lay intellectuals. As the biblical material was being elaborated and integrated in the course of the centuries, ancient Israel was developing those aspects of its religious outlook that had cosmic implications and whose validity transcended particular historical and social conditions. Thus the Hebrew Bible, beginning with the Pentateuch is an organic interweaving of particular antiquarian concerns with universal principles. The text in all its complexity emerged from an extensive and profound exploration by religious thinkers and historians in the Sinai tradition of the meaning of Hebrew identity from a cosmic perspective through an intense and forceful clarification of the divine will.

Even the most casual reader of the Bible is aware that biblical historiography is not factual in the modern sense. But neither is it fiction. The biblical historians, like other ancient and even modern historians, used dramatic and literary devices (e.g., speeches and dialogue) in the reconstruction of events. Nevertheless, the bottom line was history because the biblical historians like their modern successors aimed, in the famous formulation of Leopold Von Ranke, "to discover how it really was." The determining factor that separates fiction from history is the relation to evidence. The fiction writer has the freedom to imaginatively create characters, places and events out of whole cloth. But the historian (including the biblical historian) though utilizing fictional techniques was and is limited in his imaginative depiction by the evidence at his disposal. His intent to stay within the framework of that evidence is what makes him a writer of history and not a writer of romances.[8] In addition, poetry, epic, legend and folklore were considered by ancient peoples a necessary and legitimate form of historical perception and interpretation. These genres were not merely a more elevated form of discourse alongside prose, but were considered absolutely essential in making the past become present reality. Thus ancient historians approached the documents containing these materials as primary sources of the first order, invaluable for their historical reconstructions.[9]

The Song of the Sea— A classic illustration of the operation of all the factors discussed above, in the writing and compiling of the Torah history can be found in Exodus 14-15. Exodus 15 is known in biblical and post-biblical tradition as the Song of the Sea chanted by Moses and the Israelites after their miraculous escape from the pursuing Egyptians and their crossing of the Sea of Reeds. This is a lyrical account, impressionistic and episodic, of a major turning point in Israelite history. Exodus 14 is a historical prose rendering of the same event. The poetic version is dated approximately in the late twelfth or early eleventh century B.C.E.[10] But this approximate dating does not allow us to draw conclusions about the relationship of the parallel texts Exodus 14-15. Short of a secure dating the only other way to establish which version (the poetic or the prose) of the crossing of the Sea of Reeds is dependent on the other (i.e., is later than the other) is to note, if possible, several points of difference between them. These differences point to the conclusion that one text only could be derived from the other. This means, for all practical purposes, that the author of the derivative version must have interpreted the source in a way with which the modern investigator takes issue. If there is complete agreement between the sources there is no basis for deciding priority.

In Exodus 14-15 there are indeed differences between the poetic and prose accounts. The documentary hypothesis has established that the prose version of Exodus 14 is a combination of sources, the most pertinent for our purposes are the J and the P sources. Neither the J source nor the Song of the Sea in Exodus 15 speaks of the Israelites crossing the sea between walls of water or in any other fashion. As to the Egyptians we can only surmise that according to the Song of the Sea they were on barks or barges and were thrown from there into the stormy sea. But the P source in Exodus 14 does state that "the Israelites went into the sea on dry ground, the waters forming a wall for them on their right and on their left . . . Then the Lord said to Moses: 'Hold out your arm over the sea, that the waters may come back upon their chariots and upon their horsemen.'" (Exod. 14:22, 26). Thus the P account with its walls of water and an Israelite crossing on dry land is dependent on The Song of the Sea. The Song of the Sea with no walls of water and no Israelite crossing could not derive from the P source. This is also true of the relationship between the J source in Exodus 14 and the Song of the Sea. There are significant differences between them. Though both versions speak of a wind blowing, the timing and the effect are different. According to the J source the Egyptians are drowned when the wind *stops* blowing and the sea returns to its normal state

(Exod. 14:27). In the Song it is simply the divine wind that overthrows Pharaoh and his host (Exod. 15:10). Thus the poetic account is more naturalistic in its description than the J source which is derived from and dependent on it.

The editor-writers of the J and the P sources had the Song of the Sea in front of them and considered it a document of prime importance for their historical prose reconstruction of the crossing of the Sea of Reeds. Both had an antiquarian motivation, in Ranke's words of finding out exactly how it was. How did the Israelites cross the Sea of Reeds? The reconstruction of the J source suggests that an east wind blew driving the waters of the shallow sea back laying the dry ground bare. The reconstruction of the P source posits the sea split so that the Israelites marched through the sea on dry ground while towering walls of water rose to their right and their left.

The editor-writer of the P source based his reconstruction on three factors: 1) a bit of evidence gleaned from the Song of the Sea itself, the oldest extant document available, 2) an image from an ancient cosmogonic motif of the Sea's destruction by God, 3) an association with the tradition that the Israelites crossed the Jordan dry-shod (Josh. 3:14-4:11). The Song in Exod. 15:8 lyrically describes God's intervention as follows:

> At the blast of your nostrils the waters
> piled up.
> The floods stood straight like a wall;
> The deeps froze in the heart of the sea.

The heaped, congealed waters suggested to the P editor-writer a pathway through the sea. The splitting of the sea by God also was intended by the P editor-writer as an allusion to the vanquishing of the primordial ocean by the Creator when the earth and its inhabitants were brought into being. As we saw in chapter two, the dispersal of this aquatic chaos prior to creation represented the Hebrew reworking of the Mesopotamian combat myth. The power and the might of God exalted in the Song of the Sea has many literary allusions to the old cosmogonic myth.[11] The P source sought to preserve them in his prose reconstruction. The passage through the sea on dry land also served the P writer-editor as an allusion to the first entry of Israel into the Promised Land when the Jordan was dammed so that the Israelites in full battle dress could pass over on dry land.[12] The priestly tradent (i.e., a recorder and preserver of traditions) combined genuine antiquarian interest in a specific event with a transcendent view of Israel's programmatic history. From his perspective, the crossing of the Sea of Reeds in connection with the Exodus was an example of a recurring pattern of God's salvation in the here and now and as such should be linked to divine action in creation and in the fulfillment of divine promise in the conquest of Canaan.

The Deuteronomistic History—A Cultic Interpretation

As noted above, modern biblical scholarship has accepted the thesis that the Book of Deuteronomy and the Former Prophets (Joshua, Judges, 1 and 2 Samuel and 1 and 2 Kings) together constitute a single historical work. It is the work of an author, not just an editor, who treated his sources with utmost seriousness and though he selected from them, rarely departed from them.[13] Much of the history records literal fact such as the plundering of Jerusalem (1 Kings 14:25 f.; 2 Kings 12:18 f.; 14:13 f.). The history covering the Divided Monarchy has the greatest amount of documentation and is corroborated by external sources, Assyrian, Babylonian and Egyptian.

The Deuteronomist historian made use of topographical and physical data but also of folktales and poetry. His written sources included lists of Solomon's and David's officers, their conquests, texts displayed on sanctuaries, inscriptions on monuments, building and burial inscriptions as well as record books that may have existed in the temples of the northern kingdom of Israel in Dan and Beth El. He also used popular sources (history interlaced with legend) recounting the activities of the prophets, works that may very well have been entitled the Acts of Ahiya the Shileonite, the Acts of Elijah, the Acts of Elisha. Among the written sources mentioned in Kings are "the book of the transactions of Solomon"," the book of the chronicles of the kings of Judah," and "the book of the chronicles of the kings of Israel." These were not official memoirs of the kings but political histories dealings with the king's statecraft and the events of his public life. It is most unlikely that there was a continuous, official book of memoirs, particularly in the northern kingdom of Israel since the frequent revolts and assassinations that wiped out dynasties undoubtedly wiped out the records of those dynasties.[14]

Like all good historiography the Deuteronomistic history is based largely on antiquarian research and partly on historical imagination. But like every history it is inevitably interpretive offering a cultic interpretation of political history. The central theme is Israel's apostasy, a theme developed programmatically in the Pentateuch (Exod. 23:23 f.; 34:11-16; Num. 33:50-56; Deut. 6:14; 7:1-6, 16, 20-26; 18:9-14; 20:17 f. 31;16-20 and 12:2-4.) which traces it to the trap of Canaan's gods who are a mortal danger for the Hebrews. The history establishes this framework in the last chapter of the book of Joshua in which the Israelites, in a covenant made under Joshua, agree to put away the gods to which they were exposed in Mesopotamia, Egypt and Canaan and to worship the Lord alone. The covenant made under King Josiah (2 Kings 23:1-3) is the closing frame of this interpretation and all that transpires between these two covenants is judged from their perspective. There are, to be sure, gradations of cultic sinfulness. From the perspective of the Josianic reform and the centralization of the cult in the Jerusalem Temple, the toleration of external shrines and altars (*bamot*) even to the God of Israel is a deviation. Worse than that are shrines and altars dedicated to foreign gods and even more despicable is the introduction of these gods and their paraphernalia into Jerusalem, on the Temple mount and even into the Temple itself.

According to this interpretation, the internal anarchy and external foreign threat to the security of the nation, the dominant situation of the Book of Judges, was due to Israel's transgression of the covenant (Judges 2:11-23). During the monarchy, the length of a reign, its tranquillity and prosperity and its dynastic endurance, i.e., whether the king was succeeded by an heir or assassinated together with his entire family, were determined by fidelity to the covenant. Though heavily indebted to this religious doctrine, the Deuteronomist did not indiscriminately impose it on the historical evidence. He did not condemn as an apostate every king who suffered defeat or assassination. Nor did he make reformers of those monarchs with long reigns. He adhered to logical causation and provided a defensible evaluation of the events. For example, King Josiah of Judea, the pious and saintly king, the great hero of the Deuteronomistic history is slain in battle at Megiddo, we are told, when he tried to prevent Pharaoh Neco of Egypt, who was on a campaign against the Assyrians, from crossing his territory (2 Kings 23:28-30). On the other hand, Omri, the king of the northern kingdom of Israel who, according to the history, "did what was displeasing to the Lord, he was worse than all who preceded him" (1 Kings 16:25) died peacefully and established a dynasty that lasted four generations.

Cultic interpretation led to stylization which meant that the historian saw a pattern in events. The Book of Kings is organized by reign. Implicit in this scheme of organization is the historian's equation of nationhood with statehood and his belief that a national life without a monarchy is tantamount to exile. Explicit reference to the idea that a national life without proper governance (i.e., kingship) is a recipe for disaster is already found in the introduction to the Deuteronomistic history (Deut. 12:f.) and is echoed in the Book of Judges (Judges 17:6; 21:25 and see the discussion above in chapter 8). In the Book of Kings events are sandwiched in between accession and death formulas and here again, as already noted, the historian refrained from imposing a straitjacket of religious doctrine (i.e., good kings prosper, bad kings suffer) on his material.

The Deuteronomist's criteria of selection for his history was determined by the covenantal framework (Joshua to Josiah). Quite clearly it is not a global history since major political events are omitted. There is no discussion of economics and only a sparse treatment of domestic politics. Even in the field of foreign relations, of interest to the Deuteronomist, political ramifications are reported only incidentally and the import of developments is deliberately ignored. There is not a single account of a reign which gives the slightest hint that a king pursued an integrated political policy. Even those sections of the history devoted to the Temple do not deal with human causes and motivations.

How can we account for these gaps? Clearly, the covenantal focus makes many other subjects peripheral. Moreover, in this history the sources tend to dominate the narrative so that their concerns intersect with those of the historian. For example, the Elijah cycle of stories came to the Deuteronomist historian already formed as a primary source. The story of the sacrifice on Mount Carmel (1 Kings 18) does not censure an offering outside of the Jerusalem Temple as it should from a Josianic perspective. The Deuteronomist did not want to censure Elijah because God justified his action which undermined the claims of the Baal worshippers. The inconsistency in the text stems from a reverence toward the sources that transcends the central themes of the historian.

An additional factor limiting the scope of the Deuteronomistic history is the Hebrew aversion to the coherent analysis of complex political matters. The previous chapter discussed the Sinai attitude toward politics which was viewed as a corrupting force leading the people away from God. It was political expediency that induced Solomon and many of his successors in Judah and the northern kingdom of Israel to introduce foreign gods and cults into the sacred precincts of Hebrew ritual. The total subordination of the state and its institutions to God and the Torah is the Hebrew political ideal. This outlook had its impact on the Hebrew idea of history. Events may have overt causes that moderns recognize as historical but behind them is God. What need is there to minutely analyze human motivation when human interests are the agencies of God's activity manipulated in response to the nation's behavior? If Assyria is the agent of God's retribution directed against the nations that have violated His universal teachings (Isa. 10:5-15 and the discussion in chapter 4) then the need for detailed geopolitical analysis of Assyrian motives and activity in the Near East dwindles to the vanishing point.

The distaste for complex political analysis is not unique to the Hebrew historian. Assyrian and Babylonian texts present events in isolation not in interlock, nor do they conceive of policy as a grand strategy in which the hopes and fears embodied in that policy are evaluated. In these histories piety alone motivates a king to build a temple and provocation alone induces him to undertake military activity. In fact, the Deuteronomistic historian is more sophisticated than his Near Eastern contemporaries for he understands that human agents do not consciously carry out God's will. Rehoboam unwittingly acts out his role in the drama whose climax is the division of the United Monarchy (1 Kings 12:13-15) unaware that divine reciprocity is at work in recompense for the sins of Solomon. Between the divine plan and the unwitting human action there is still free will and opportunity for human causation leading to the interpretation of events based on sources and evidence. In sum, the Deuteronomistic history is programmed by metahistorical commitments as to its selection of historical material but not to the falsification or invention of the historical records.[15]

The Reconstruction of A Folk Hero's Exploit— One of the most potent implements in the tool box of the historian is the historical reconstruction that weds historical imagination to existing evidence. In Judg. 3:12-30, the Deuteronomist gave us such a reconstruction. Eglon, the corpulent king of Moab who occupied Jericho ("the city of palms"), is sent a tribute from the Israelites through Ehud ben Gera, a lefthanded Benjamite who concealed a short two edged sword on his right thigh. After delivering the tribute, Ehud started back home with his Israelite porters but then doubled back to the court. Asking to confer privately with the king on a secret message, Ehud secured the dismissal of the courtiers and entered the upper chamber where the king was sitting alone. There Ehud thrust his dagger deep into the fat Eglon's belly and the king expired as his anal sphincter exploded. After locking the doors of the upper chamber, Ehud stepped out into the corridor. When Eglon's servants returned, the locked doors of the chamber created the impression that the king desired some privacy and so they waited. When after a long interval the king did not appear, they got the key, unlocked the upper chamber and found Eglon dead. In the meantime, Ehud had the time to muster his troops from the hills and taking advantage of the confusion in the Moabite palace seized the fords of the Jordan and annihilated the Moabites.

The story is not part of a continuous narrative such as the Davidic court history but rather a short incident integrated into the episodic framework of the Book of Judges. The historian has condensed and extracted from a lengthy folkloristic hero-tale in the oral tradition a reconstruction of the events. The reconstruction revolves around two elements about which the historian assumes his readers have information-Ehud's lefthandedness and the layout of the Moabite king's palace. These two sources of information preclude the reader from inventing action not narrated by the historian.

The Hebrew term describing Ehud's lefthandedness is *'itter* coming from a root meaning "to bind," and implies that his right hand was impeded, i.e., he was schooled in the use of his left hand for combat. Righthanded combatants in hand-to-hand fighting or in the use of the sling find their martial repertoire and tactical training useless when they come up against a lefthander. In the pre-monarchic era Israel's farmer-soldiers fought on foot in hand-to-hand combat. In such a society lefthanded warriors undoubtedly enjoyed great prestige in the tribal armies. Ehud, we are told, was a Benjamite and from other sources we gather that the tribe of Benjamin specialized in producing lefthanded warriors (Judg. 20:16; 1 Chron. 12:2). Thus Ehud was the closest to a professional soldier that Israel had at that time. It is quite understandable that he should have been chosen to bring the tribute to Eglon and to carry out the cloak and dagger operation.

The building plan of the Moabite king's palace suggests how it was possible for Ehud to carry out the operation undetected. The upper room in which the king was slain was a throne platform overlooking and accessible from the audience chamber. It was a room atop wooden joists with a door that could be closed from the inside to give the king privacy when the elevated throne room doubled as an indoor toilet, i.e., it was a room with a commode. Ehud entered the room on the podium with his message while the dismissed servants waited in a portico off the audience hall. After killing Eglon (whose death was instantaneous with no seepage of blood, the only sign of violence was the king's bowel discharge onto the floor) Ehud fastened the doors of the throne chamber from within, and deftly swung down through the as yet unused privy opening through the floor to the level below. He exited from an adjoining room into the audience chamber and crossed deliberately to the door entering the portico where the king's servants saw him and concluded that his audience was at an end. As Ehud walked out to the courtyard unchallenged, the courtiers reentered the audience chamber. Concluding from the unsavory smell that the king was relieving himself, they waited an extended interval before unlocking the throne room from without and discovering the dead body.

The narrative economy and the logic driven reconstruction and presentation point to the historian's genuine antiquarian interest in composing Judg. 3:12-30. Confronting the no doubt epic proportions of the hero tale in the oral folk tradition, the Deuteronomist wanted to know precisely how Ehud carried out his mission and what his qualifications were. From his source and from the evidence known to him (i.e., the lefthanded warrior tradition and the design of palaces in his time) he drew the elements that were synthesized with his historical imagination.[16]

Prophetic History—A Moral Interpretation

It is a startling fact that in the Deuteronomistic history, with the sole exception of Isaiah, none of the classical prophets are mentioned.[17] But even in the case of Isaiah, the prophet is depicted in 1 Kings 19-20 as a clairvoyant, a healer and miracle worker without any reference to his role as a great spiritual teacher who introduced revolutionary concepts (including a concept of history) into the religion of Israel. The originality of Isaiah's historical vision is underscored by a comparison with the historical outlook of the Torah and the writings of the Deuteronomist. In the latter sources the history of humanity is divided into two periods:

1) The era prior to the division of the languages at the Tower of Babel was one of a united humanity worshipping God.

2) After the division of the human species nations came into existence with idolatry as their religion.

When God revealed Himself, first to the patriarchs and then to all of Israel in the time of Moses, the bifurcation of humanity continued through a separation of Israel from the nations. The people of Israel who recognized and accepted God became the subject of biblical history. The nations who did not recognize and accept Him stood outside that history. What happened to them was of consequence only insofar as it impinged on the destiny of Israel. Aside from this intersection with the Sinai tradition, the history of the nations had no divine meaning and was therefore of no interest to the biblical historian. This division between Israel and the nations was seen as perpetual. There was no expectation of a merger of destinies in the future.

In Isaiah's vision of the End of Days (Isa. 2:2-4) there is a return at the climax of human history to the worship of one God and the unity of the nations that once existed at the very beginning of that history. In this denouement of the drama of humanity, the nations all share the divine grace which until now had descended on Israel alone. The prophets Habakkuk and Jeremiah inserted an activist program in this scenario. Rather than just sit and wait for this to happen, Israel's mission is to combat idolatry to hasten the realization of the ideal of one humanity under God. Underlying the prophecies of the Second Isaiah (Isa. 40-66) is this belief in Israel's active role in the attainment of a universal history.

The classical prophets not only introduced a new concept of universal history not found in the Pentateuch and the Early Prophets, they also interpreted the history of Israel differently than the Torah and the Deuteronomist historian. As noted above, the Deuteronomist gave us a cultic interpretation of Israel's political history. This outlook is also present in the Torah. Both these strands of biblical literature see Israel's apostasy, the religious-cultic sin of idolatry as the determining factor that brought on the destruction of the two states (the kingdoms of northern Israel and Judah) and calamity upon their inhabitants. The restoration of national sovereignty will come as a result of religious-cultic repentance, the antidote to religious-cultic sin. There is not a word in these sources about the serious breach of social morality in Israel and Judah (the perversion of justice, the concentration of land, wealth and power in the hands of aristocrats and the rich who exploited and oppressed the poor, the widows and orphans) as a factor in the decline and fall of the state. That is not to say that the religious-ethical perspective is completely absent in the Torah and Early Prophets. They see God as not only commanding the cult but also justice and morality. God judges human beings for sins committed against one another as He judges them for sins committed against Him. The doctrine of reciprocity operates in both the realms of cult and ethics equally. But these sources see religious-ethical infractions as the sins of *individuals* for which they are accountable to be sure. These ethical violations are not, however, a continuing historical factor in the life of the *nation* leading to its destruction and the exile of its people. Thus the Book of Kings, explaining the destruction of the Kingdom of Judah says of King Menasseh that in addition to his religious-cultic outrages he also "put so many innocent people to death that he filled Jerusalem with blood from end to end" (2 Kings 21:16; cf. 24:4). That the Deuteronomist historian mentions this fact only *after* a detailed catalogue of King Menasseh's misdeeds and only *after* God decrees destruction for Jerusalem for its religious-cultic sins is highly instructive. It tells us that the religious-ethical factor is ancillary to the religious-cultic factor in the loss of national sovereignty.

Not for the classical prophets. They see apostasy and the breach of morality as equal in their effect in bringing down the state. But they go even further than the Torah and the Deuteronomist in contending that sins of morality outweigh even cultic sins in determining the fate of the nation. Amos, the first of the classical prophets, accuses Israel almost entirely for its violations of ethics and predicts that these sins alone will bring its demise.

The intense prophetic focus on the ethics of the day and the redemption of the End of Days led to a curious phenomenon-a complete lack of historical perspective in the classical prophets. There is not a single vision in which periods of time pass before the prophet's eyes in orderly succession. There is no chain of generations or events that unfold before him revealing the secrets of the time and the passing of kingdoms. Every prophecy envisions only one era, the one in which the prophet is living or the one at the end of history. Even where a classical prophet enumerates many events, they are only a framework for the word of God, not a signpost for changing times. The only major change toward which events point is in the distant future in the great upheaval that will usher in the Day of the Lord.

But there is not even a hint of all of this in the Deuteronomist history. From the Deuteronomist's almost total silence about the classical prophets, their stature as spiritual teachers of the first rank and their original views and interpretation of Israelite history, we can conclude that his history and that of the Torah emerged from a different school with a different *weltanschauung* than that of the classical prophets. Clearly the various writer-redactors of the Torah and the Deuteronomic history knew of the classical prophets and their views. These priestly editor-writers and their disciples, as mentioned earlier, had access to sources containing hero stories about the classical prophets similar to the Elijah-Elisha cycle of tales in the Books of Kings. From this literature the redactor of 2 Kings took a section about Isaiah which he included in the text. But as discussed at length in chapter seven and above, the priestly view of the Sinai tradition and Israelite historical destiny differed from the radical outlook of classical prophecy. The priests through their redaction of the Torah and the Deuteronomic history emphasized the concepts of Israelite popular religion-apostasy, cultic deviations, folk heroes and folk literature that are the foundation of the national-religious strand of Hebrew faith. Apostolic prophecy was part of this historical framework. The Deuteronomist's history is patterned in such a way as to indicate that in the beginning was the word of the prophet and in the end-the fulfillment of his prophecy. But the radical demands of the prophets and their original concepts of ethics, knowledge of God and universal history were seen as far too arcane for the people's understanding. From a priestly-pedagogical point of view it was sufficient to exhort the people to loyalty to God and cult. To ask for more was foolish and futile. Moreover, the priests themselves had a vested interest in excluding the prophetic view that morality took precedence over the cult in determining the destiny of the nation. These may have been the motives behind the studied silence about classical prophecy and its ideas in the Deuteronomist history. After the destruction of the First Temple in 586 B.C.E., however, and during and after the Babylonian exile, the classical prophets and their message assumed a new importance in the religious consciousness of the Jewish people. The final redactors of the Pentateuch and the Early Prophets began to gather the prophetic literature for eventual inclusion in the biblical canon.[18]

Ezra and Nehemiah—History as Autobiography

The third division of the Hebrew Bible known as "The Writings" (*Ketuvim*) contains a variety of historiographic genres. The Books of Ezra and Nehemiah covering the period 539-432 B.C.E. are in one sense a continuation of the Deuteronomist's history, picking up the thread of events with the return to Judea of the Babylonian exiles. But these post-exilic works are inferior in their scope, in their style and in their power of description and expression to the historiography of the Early Prophets. Ezra and Nehemiah are written partly in Aramaic and partly in Hebrew, a sign of the cultural assimilation of the exilic Jews.

The twenty three chapters of the two books are drawn from three main sources:

1) An Aramaic work about Zerubavel (a descendant of the Davidic dynasty and the second governor of the returning exiles in Judea) and the building of the Second Temple;

2) The autobiography of Ezra;
3) The autobiography of Nehemiah. The autobiographical form of Ezra and Nehemiah gives the two books the immediacy of contemporary history and distinguishes them from the impersonal account of the Chronicler to be discussed shortly. The first person narrative may have been influenced directly or indirectly by Babylonian, Egyptian or Persian models made accessible by translations. The similarity between these models and Ezra and Nehemiah is to be found in a motif common to both, the justification of the writer in the presence of the deity. Thus Nehemiah records in his memoirs: "O my God, remember to my credit all that I have done for this people!" (Neh. 5:19). But this verse also underscores the difference. In addition to God, Nehemiah was confronted with a people with its own will that reacted to the leaders' initiatives and in the end decided the issues. The Near Eastern potentates, supreme in power, were accountable to no human beings. Unlike the Near Eastern inscriptions of kings and princes who recounted their accomplishments in autobiographical form, in Ezra and Nehemiah the autobiographical style is put in service to a new purpose, to tell of "the formation of a community built not on autocratic foundations but on the principle of the pact between God and people through the intermediary of a reformer who paradoxically derives his powers from the King of Persia."[19] Instead of glorifying the individual, the first person narrative relates the birth of a theocratic community.

A second unique characteristic of the Books of Ezra and Nehemiah is the inclusion of formal documents of the Persian Kings Cyrus, Darius and Artaxerxes in their native language within the text. These documents attest to the rights given by the Persian monarchs to the Jewish exiles returning to Jerusalem. They are the first link in a historiographic chain leading from these autobiographical works to the Books of the Maccabees in the Apocrypha and to the history of Flavius Josephus in which the literature of privileges extended to the Jews and the Jewish state by gentile governors and governments are included in the historical account. A third characteristic that distinguishes the Books of Ezra and Nehemiah from the Deuteronomist's history is that unlike the latter they are not programmatically subordinated to a cultic interpretation of political history nor for that matter are they part of a religious-ethical framework imposed on the events of their time like the prophetic historical approach. The works are empirically written. No event is explained by the sinfulness or righteousness of the present generation. If there is any interpretive bias in these books it is past oriented. It is the sins of the past that have determined the course of Israel's history in the aftermath of the Temple's destruction and the people's exile.[20]

Chronicles—The Idealization of the Past

The Books of 1 and 2 Chronicles composed some time during the fourth century B.C.E. are a post-exilic account of the history of Israel up to the Edict of Cyrus permitting the rebuilding of the Second Temple and the return of the exiles to Jerusalem. The author of Chronicles was probably a levite since he expands the role of the levites extolling their virtues above those of the priests (2 Chron. 29:34), perhaps signaling the ascendance of levite religious authority confirmed under Ezra and Nehemiah (Neh. 8:7, 9, 11; 9:4 ff. cf. chapter 6, Sinai II, note 6). There are three focal points to the Chronicler's history: the tribe of Levi, Jerusalem and the Temple and the Davidic dynasty. His sources included the Torah and Deuteronomist histories as well as twenty other books to which he directs the reader to obtain more details. Among these books were twelve whose authors were prophets.[21]

The early history of Israel in 1 Chronicles is schematically presented in the form of genealogies. The history broadens out into narrative only at the beginning of the monarchy and this is the clue to the writer's point of view. He was not interested in beginnings, gropings and failures only in stability, permanence and continuity. The latter characteristics were embodied in Israel's monarchy and in the House of David in particular. The Chronicler glorified the Davidic dynasty, the only legitimate governing authority in his eyes, and suppressed its sins and failures. Thus David's sin with Bathsheba, the continuing turmoil in his family life, the revolts of Absalom and Sheba ben Bichri, the account of the famine and the struggle for succession to the throne at the end of David's life, all are eliminated from the historical record. In contrast the northern kingdom of Israel is portrayed as illegitimate. It was established through a revolt against God and the House of David and its perpetuation involved idolatry and unlawful forms of worship. In this respect Chronicles differs sharply from the far more realistic accounts in the Books of Samuel and Kings.

Another fundamental difference between the history of the Deuteronomist and the account of the Chronicler is that according to the Book of Kings the Deuteronomic laws were in force when Israel conquered the Promised Land but the people and their kings strayed from them, offering sacrifices on the high places outside the

Jerusalem Temple until the reforms of King Hezekiah and later King Josiah. According to Chronicles, the entire Five Books of Moses including the priestly code of Leviticus were observed throughout the First Temple period, most certainly during the reigns of the righteous kings. In Chronicles, the cult of the Second Temple period is projected back into the First Temple period. The Deuteronomist looking back from the perspective of the Deuteronomic law code and its morality saw cultic sin as a continuing factor in the destiny of the nation. Beginning with the sins of Solomon there was a precipitous religious decline, relieved only briefly by the reforms of Kings Hezekiah and Josiah, leading eventually to destruction and exile. The Chronicler surveying the past from the perspective of the Book of Leviticus and the entire Pentateuch saw merit and righteousness as the predominant factor determining the destiny of the nation. Beginning with Solomon the cultic faithfulness of the Kings of Judah were punctuated briefly by periods of sinfulness for which there was immediate retribution. This retribution and the repentance of even such incorrigibles as King Menasseh (2 Chron. 33:10-19) satisfied the demands of the doctrine of reciprocity. The destruction and the exile were the result of King Zedekiah (the last king of Judah) and his generation alone. The merit and righteousness of the nation caused a seventy year limit to be placed on the exile and were responsible for the Edict of Cyrus and the return to Jerusalem.

Even more than the Deuteronomist, the Chronicler assigned an important role in his work to the prophets. He depicted them as the writers of history who in each generation record the events of the period. But they also made history, serving as God's emissaries transmitting His message to kings and people, rebuking them for sins and warning them of retribution, encouraging faith and preaching repentance. A classical prophet like Jeremiah, omitted from the Deuteronomist's history is mentioned several times by the Chronicler (2 Chron. 35:25; 36;12, 21). Nevertheless, the classical prophetic ideas about universal history and the supremacy of morality over the cult in determining national destiny are as conspicuously absent in the Chronicler's work as in the Deuteronomist's account.

The Chronicler's history had a restorative messianic function, i.e., it was directed to a recreation of a past pictured by the historical imagination and the memory of the nation as ideal. From this perspective, the Davidic dynasty, the Jerusalem Temple and Hebrew prophecy represented the acme of ancient Israel's material and spiritual glory. But there was also a future messianic thrust and a utopian inspiration in the Books of Chronicles. In "the days of small things" in which the Chronicler and his generation were living, when Judea was only a remote province of the Persian Empire, he reminded his readers of God's promise of eternal rule for the House of David. The Books of Chronicles were also a blueprint for the historical outlook of the rabbis (to be discussed below) in which there was a projection backward into earlier generations of the religious doctrines and practices of their times and a restorative messianism idealizing the biblical period.[22]

Notes

1. Nicholas Berdyaev, *The Meaning of History* (Cleveland and New York: Meridian Books, The World Publishing Company, 1968), p. 88.

2. The evidence for this conclusion is twofold:

a). The abolition of local sanctuaries outside the Jerusalem Temple and the centralization of all cultic activity in the Temple is the first provision of the Deuteronomic code (Deut. 12: 1 ff.). This legalization is unique to Deuteronomy. Exod. 20:21 permits sacrifice at local shrines and altars. Lev. 17:1-8 regards all slaughtering outside the sanctuary as offering to the satyrs. Thus, it implies the existence of a multitude of sanctuaries. Sacrificing in these sanctuaries is forbidden but there is no word here about the abolition of the shrines themselves. It is only Deut. 16:1 ff. that requires that the Pascal sacrifice be made in the Temple. Exod. 12:1 ff. and 12:21 ff. do not know of this requirement. The Josianic reform, implemented on the basis of the "book of the Torah" found in the Temple, included the destruction of all altars and shrines outside of Jerusalem (2 Kings 23:9, 13, 15, 19-20; 2 Chron. 34:3-8).

b). The prohibition of the worship of the heavenly bodies is emphasized in Deut. 17:3 (cf. Deut. 4:19) as something "which I have not commanded." The Josianic reform included the destruction of the astral cults (2 Kings 23:4, 11) that had become a permanent fixture in the Temple during the 55 year reign of King Amon and the early years of King Josiah since he assumed the throne when he was eight years old (2 Kings 21:6). The special emphasis in Deuteronomy was most probably directed against this widespread worship of the heavenly bodies which were subsequently rooted out in the reform.

3. Martin Noth, *A History of Pentateuchal Traditions* (Englewood Cliffs, NJ: Prentice Hall, 1972), German edition, 1948. *Uberlieferungsgeschichtliche Studien* (Tubingen: Max Niemeyer Verlag, 1957), original edition, 1943. Pages 1-110 are in English translation as *The Deuteronomistic History* in the *Journal for the Study of Old Testament* supplement series (Sheffield, 1981).

4. Yehezkel Kaufmann, *The Religion of Israel* trans. and abridged Moshe Greenberg (Chicago and London: University of Chicago Press,

1960), pp. 161-174; 415-420. Cf. Richard Elliott Friedman *Who Wrote the Bible?* (New York: Summit Books, 1987), pp. 117-135.

5. Kaufmann, *The Religion of Israel*, p. 205, Friedman, *Who Wrote the Bible?*, 188-216.

6. The documentary hypothesis was not universally accepted by modern Jewish scholars particularly not by scholars of a traditional bent. David Hoffman (1843-1921) in his commentaries to the books of Leviticus and Deuteronomy rejected the documentary hypothesis of Julius Wellhausen but did not himself formulate an original method of biblical investigation. On the other hand, Benno Jacob (1862-1945) though he did not accept the Mosaic authorship of the Pentateuch nor the dogma of literal inspiration rejected both textual criticism and Higher Criticism with its Documentary Hypothesis. He developed a theory concerning the eternal rhythm of the Bible which is expressed by the repetition of key words in set numbers in the narratives of the Torah and its laws. His major exegetical works were: *Das erste Buch der Torah: Genesis uebersetzt und erklaert* (Berlin: Schoken, 1934) and *The Second Book of the Bible: Exodus* interpreted by Benno Jacob, trans. with an intro. Walter Jacob (New York: Ktav Publishing House, 1990). Similarly Umberto Cassuto (1883-1951) appreciated the scholarly basis of modern biblical criticism but rejected the Documentary Hypothesis. In its place he posited the existence of an oral tradition and a number of ancient poetic epics which were subsequently woven into the unitary texts of the Pentateuch and other biblical books. Cassuto's Ugaritic studies which throw considerable light on the literary structure and vocabulary of the Bible as well as his mastery of ancient Near Eastern literature powerfully reinforced his original unitary thesis. Cf. U. Cassuto, *Studies on the Bible and Ancient Orient* (Jerusalem: Magnes Press, Hebrew University, 1972-1979); *The Documentary Hypothesis and the Composition of the Pentateuch*, trans. Israel Abrahams (Jerusalem: Magnes Press, Hebrew University, 1983); *Biblical and Oriental Studies*, trans. Israel Abrahams (Jerusalem: Magnes Press, Hebrew University, 1978); *A Commentary on the Book of Exodus* trans. Israel Abrahams (Jerusalem: Magnes Press, Hebrew University, 1967).

7. Richard Elliott Friedman, "Sacred History and Theology: The Redaction of Torah", in *The Creation of Sacred Literature* ed. R. E. Friedman, *Near Eastern Studies* 22 (Berkeley, Los Angeles, London: University of California Press, 1981): 25-34.

8. Evidence is not the same as proof. History, unlike Euclidean geometry, is not susceptible to proof since it is impossible to obtain mathematical proof about the past. The past yields only facts that add up to evidence. Like a prosecutor or a defense attorney, the historian must persuade his readers and other historians who are his jury that the reconstruction of the past he or she proposes is reasonably accurate.

9. Baruch Halpern, *The First Historians: The Hebrew Bible and History* (San Francisco: Harper & Row, 1988): 8-13; Gerhard Von Rad, *Old Testament Theology* (Edinburgh and London: Oliver and Boyd) 1:109.

10. Frank M. Cross, *Canaanite Myth and Hebrew Epic: Essays in the History of the Religion of Israel* (Cambridge, Ma: Harvard University Press, 1973), p. 124.

11. U. Cassuto, *A Commentary on the Book of Exodus*, pp. 123-125.

12. Cross, *Canaanite Myth and Hebrew Epic*, pp. 125-144. On the Battle at the Sea, as part of a sequence of events in early Israelite epic narrative and the use of these early epic sources in later prose reconstructions see Frank M. Cross, "The Epic Traditions of Early Israelite Institutions," in *The Poet and the Historian: Essays in Literary and Historical Biblical Criticism* ed. R. E. Friedman, Harvard Semitic Studies 26 (Chico, Ca.: Scholars Press, 1983): 13-39 and particularly p. 27.

13. See above note 3.

14. Kaufmann, *Toledot ha-'Emunah ha-Yisraelit* 2(1), Vol. 4, pp. 293-298.

15. Halpern, *The First Historians*, pp. 207-235.

16. Ibid., pp. 39-75

17. 2 Kings 14:25 does mention Jonah ben Amitai but not Amos. 2 Kings 22:14 mentions Huldah but not Jeremiah.

18. Kaufmann, *The Religion of Israel*, 132-33; 358-59; *Toledot ha-'Emunah ha-Yisraelit* 1(1): 25-31 and n. 4. p. 26; 3(1): 16-17.

19. Arnaldo Momigliano, *Essays in Ancient and Modern Historiography* (Middletown, Ct.: Wesleyan University Press, 1977), p. 29.

20. Yehezkel Kaufmann, *Toledot ha-'Emunah ha-Yisraelit* 8: 451-453.

21. Sara Japhet, "Chronicles, Book of" *Encyclopedia Judaica* 5 (Jerusalem: Keter Publishing House, 1972): 527-531. Scholars have long held that the Chronicler was also the author of Ezra and Nehemiah but this view has been convincingly refuted by M. Z. Segal, "*Sifre Ezra U-Nehemiah*" *Tarbiz* 14, no. 3-4 (April-July, 1943): 81-103. B. Uffenheimer, *The Visions of Zechariah: From Prophecy to Apocalyptic* (Jerusalem: The Israel Society for Biblical Research and Kiryat Sepher, 1961), p. 175 argues that the main body of Chronicles 1 and 2 was formed close to the year 520 B.C.E.

22. Kaufmann, *Toledot ha-'Emunah ha-Yisraelit* 8:453-480; G. Scholem, *The Messianic Idea in Judaism* (New York: Schoken Books, 1971), pp. 3-4. Cf. J. Liver "*Historiah Ve-Historiografia be' Sefer Divre ha-Yamim,*" in *Sefer Biram* (Jerusalem: The Israel Society for Biblical Research, 1955) 2: 154 ff.

Olympus: Commemoration and Investigation of Human Achievements

History and Poetry

Our word 'history' comes from a Greek word *'historie'* which means 'inquiry' or 'research' and implies either *autopsis*, i.e., seeing for oneself, or learning from hearsay (*akoe*).[1] Democritus, the mid fifth century philosopher, used the word to describe his own activities:

> Of all the men of my time, it is I who have traveled over the greatest part of the earth, practicing *historie* to the fullest extent as I saw the greatest variety of climate and terrain and listened to the largest number of learned men.[2]

When recording the past became the subject of history per se, however, the word also included investigating the reports of eyewitnesses and subjecting all hearsay (*akoe*) to critical judgment (*gnome*) in order to determine what really happened.

Herodotus refers to his account of the Persian Wars as the result of his *histories* in the very first words of the work. As he briefly summarizes the earliest hostilities, he applies rational analysis to traditional legends and demythologizes them. For example, omitting Zeus from the tales, he reports that Phoenician merchant sailors abducted Io as she was viewing their goods and that Greek sailors later kidnapped Europa in retaliation (1- 2.1).

After summarizing the legendary causes for enmity between Greeks and Persians, however, Herodotus dismisses their significance to his *historie*.

> But I am not going to say that these things happened exactly this way or otherwise. Rather I am going to begin with the first person whom I myself know started the hostilities against the Hellenes and then move forward in my account (1.5.3).

He begins at 1.6.1. with Croesus, the King of Lydia, whom Cyrus the Persian conquered in 546 B.C.E. and ends his history in 479 B.C.E. after the Greeks, victorious at Plataea and Mycale, have forced the Persians out of Sestos and back into Asia. Thus his account of the Persian Wars focuses on more recent times, about which he himself can obtain reliable information, rather than on the legendary past, where the details of "how it really was" cannot be verified by *autopsis, akoe,* and/or *gnome.*

In his first sentence, Herodotus also proclaims that one of his purposes for his history is explaining why the Greeks and the Hellenes fought one another. His interest in causation, in the linking of one event to the next so that the unique moments in time can be seen as related to one another rather than as random happenings, is visible even in the series of legendary abductions and retaliations which he later dismisses as unverifiable. His attempt to be objective is made clear by his assertion that he intends to record the achievements of both Hellenes and barbarians (1.1.1.), and to talk about cities both great and small (1.5.3-4). He demonstrates his lack of bias by citing Persian and Phoenician as well as Greek tales about early hostilities. Thus Herodotus' proem, 1.1-5, defines him as a historian, i.e., an author about to describe and account for a past event as accurately and objectively as possible. Because of his attempt to record the truth, Cicero called him the 'Father of History' (*de Legibus* 1.5).

In the very same sentence, however, Cicero had to qualify his judgment because Herodotus also included so many incredible stories. For Herodotus, the first 'historian,' had the same impulse to commemorate as the earlier Greek poets and the Hebrews (although he was commemorating human actions rather than divine irruptions into human time).[3] His first sentence announces that he is presenting the results of his research "so that the achievements of men will not be forgotten in time and the great deeds, monuments, and natural wonders of both the Hellenes and the barbarians will not lack glory (*aklea*)." Many scholars have pointed out that the historian is alluding to the Homeric phrase *klea andron*, the glorious deeds of heroes, e.g., *Il.* 9.189, the singing of which gave rise to Greek epic.[4] As Drews has noted, "what epic had done for the heroes who lived "once upon a time," historiography would do for men who lived in the remembered past".[5]

The epic poet honored both the Greeks and their enemies, admiring their valor and sympathizing with their sufferings without bias. In the period between Homer and Herodotus, as the Greeks traveled and colonized the Mediterranean, they perceived different customs, learned foreign tales, and saw many natural wonders and monumental buildings, all of which stimulated their own intellectual, material, and cultural progress. The fifth century historian, extending the grace along with the aim of the epic poet, desired to preserve the memory of such admirable but heretofore unrecorded things as well as memorialize the glorious achievements of various peoples.

If Herodotus' commemorative purpose derives from epic, so too does his subject. Obviously he, following the poets, focuses on noteworthy actions of heroes, albeit those who have lived in the last hundred years or so. Like the *Iliad*, his *Histories* (and most Greek histories after it) centers on a great war which enables the participants to display their best and worst qualities, and to suffer and perhaps to learn (and exemplify for posterity) something about the limits to human ambition. Just as the poets of the epic cycle supplemented Homer's account with a beginning and end to the Trojan war, Herodotus tells the story from the first major aggression against the Asiatic Greeks by Croesus through the expansion of the Persian empire to the last major battle which drove the Persians out of Europe.

Other aspects of Herodotus' subject matter are also related to epic. His intent to explain the reason why the Hellenes and barbarians fought with one another resembles Homer's question in *Il.* 1.8: "Who of the gods sent the two [Agamemnon and Achilles] into contention to battle?" Herodotus' explanation is closer to the epic and tragic interaction of divine compulsion and human will (see below as well as chapter five) than later historians, who found different more secular responses to the question of causation. Herodotus' interest in cities great and small recalls the invocation to the *Odyssey* in which the poet says his hero "saw the cities of many men and learned their way of thinking" (1.3). Here too Herodotus, and later historians, expanded the depiction and analysis of political decision-making which were already present in the war council and assembly type-scenes of epic.

Many of the narrative techniques used by Herodotus and later historians derived from epic, and from Attic tragedy which dramatized episodes from myth. Just as Homer had to weave a connected story out of the separate pieces of the oral tradition, so Herodotus had to incorporate the new information he had about the Greeks and barbarians into his account of the hostility which culminated in the Persian Wars of 490-479 B.C.E. For his descriptions of the customs, wonders, and tales of the various nations conquered by Persia, he adapted the paratactic style of Homer to his prose narrative, stringing out the various pieces of knowledge side by side, one after the other, and using the same or similar phrase to introduce and conclude each piece ('ring composition'), to mark the unit or digression. To foreshadow significant events as well as to suggest the complexity of causation, he introduced the kinds of warning scenes and predictive oracles, omens, and dreams which had already appeared in epic and drama and were, of course, taken seriously by most of his fifth century readers (see chapter six).

In Herodotus' historical reconstructions of how the people acted and interacted, he used the devices of epic and tragedy to recreate credible dramatizations of what really happened. Following the poets, Herodotus and later historians built unique scenes out of dialogue, imagining private conversations, or reconstructed public speeches which they had not heard. Moreover, the historians highlighted incidents which have great human interest, particularly those which focus on decisions or physical or psychological suffering, as Homer and the tragedians did. And they constructed their major episodes, and perhaps even structured their entire sequence of events, like dramatic plots, so that there is a clear beginning, middle, and end, often with the reversal Aristotle preferred in tragedy.[6]

Modern readers consider such artistry as appropriate in narrative fiction, but not proper for historiography. The ancient critics, however, approved of historians who adorned the hard core of truth with inventive poetic arts so that their prose accounts imitated real life. Thus history could both teach and delight its readers by making them feel that they were present at the actual event. Waters notes that Herodotus, an early prose writer, made as great a leap forward in the "effectiveness and charm of his style" as he did in his "application of rational investigation into his recounting of the past."[7] The clear and unbiased presentation of the truth remained the distinguishing characteristic of history, however. Any stylistic adornment which distracted from or vitiated that high standard of accuracy was severely censured by serious historians and critics.[8]

Despite its debt to poetry, history conveyed a very different kind of truth. According to Aristotle's famous contrast at *Poetics* 1451b.5-7, poetry relates the universal, e.g., what may happen in conformity with the laws of probability and necessity and how certain types will speak and act. History, however, deals with the particular, with what has actually happened and with what real individuals like Alcibiades have spoken or done. Because history records events as they occur, in a chronological sequence, in all their uniqueness as particulars, history relates a far fuller and thus more complex truth, if it is faithful to what actually happened. As Immerwahr states after comparing Herodotus' dramatic use of the Hellespont with Aeschylus' in *Persians*,

> . . . the ultimate meaning of the flow of history cannot be as clear as the meaning of events which are chosen by the poet for their theological meaning . . . . Herodotus, though less vivid, is nevertheless closer to the event, for he sees it as a complex of human motivations and superhuman forces, a complex which is not intelligible to him under a simple theological scheme.[9]

The Development of Historie

The historiographer's question, "how did this come from that?," has often been applied to the invention of Greek history itself. By the beginning of the fifth century, the Greeks had the intellectual tools and the interest to preserve a credible account of the past and relate it to present realities. Within the next hundred years, the early prosewriters, the *logographoi* or *logopoioi*, had developed genealogy or mythography, which attempts to systematize the myths and legends, often by connecting present cities and peoples with heroic founders and ancestors; ethnography, which describes foreign lands with their geography, inhabitants, and customs; horography, which gives a year-by-year account of local history including information of all kinds; and chronology, which provides a system of time-reckoning by arranging events in sequence.[10] Concerning Herodotus' predecessors and contemporaries who wrote down these first prose records, the extant fragments and comments by later Greek and Roman historians preserve only sketchy information. Two names stand out from the list, however: Hecataeus of Miletus, whom Herodotus mentions (at 2.143, as a visitor to Egypt; at 5.36 & 125-6 as a participant in the Ionian revolt; and at 6.137 as a source for a story) and Hellanicus of Lesbos, a contemporary who probably published some of his writings later than Herodotus.[11]

Hecataeus the prosewriter (*logopoios*), as Herodotus calls him, was both a genealogist and an ethnographer. His prose travelogue, the *Perigesis* or *Periodos Ges* (*Circumnavigation of the Known World*) probably described his journey around the Mediterranean coast from Spain east to Asia and then back west again through Egypt to Libya. It included comments on the cities and peoples passed en route, with attention to native customs, natural wonders, origins, and part in ancient Greek legends. Hecataeus was particularly concerned to check the accuracy of the Greek legends with the natives, and attempted to connect unfamiliar places with familiar myths, e.g., by tracing the origins of place names to eponymous Greek gods and heroes.

Although there are fewer extant fragments of Hecataeus' other work, the *Genealogies*, its beginning is often quoted because he calls the tales of the Greeks "many and absurd" and promises to write "the truth as it seems to me." Thus he attempted to organize the heroic tradition so that the various genealogies would be not be incompatible or the stories contradictory. Although he reports many incredible details, some fragments reveal his critical and rationalizing spirit; reasoning from probability, for example, he concludes that Cerberus was a snake so deadly it was called the 'hound of hell'.

Despite the fact that he did retain many fantastic elements, historians of historiography consider him an important predecessor to Herodotus for several reasons. Because Herodotus cites him, it is clear that he consulted his works and probably used him as an unacknowledged source for other information.[12] But he is also important to the invention of history per se. Not only did he connect contemporary geography and ethnology with the mythic past and compare Greek and non-Greek, but his rationalizing tendencies undermined the heroic legends and made it easier to elevate recent men and their accomplishments.[13] More crucial for Herodotus' *Histories* was, in the words of Starr, Hecataeus' "insistence on recording his observation of physical reality . . . and his example . . . of "research" which sought to write "as it seems to me to be true." [14]

The writings of Hellanicus of Lesbos indicate the interests of the *logographoi* by the close of the fifth century. He was a mythographer and chronographer who worked out parallel genealogical trees for the Greek heroes, tracing them all the way back to the beginning: e.g., the Pelasgians originated from Phoroneus, one of the earliest post-diluvian humans, the branches of Hellenes from the eponymous sons of Deucalion, and the houses of Atreus and Aeneas both from Atlas. At least one work, the *Priestesses of Argos*, was an attempt to synchronize events according to an accepted list which went back further than any other. The book seems to have begun with mythical times and moved forward to the Peloponnesian War. He also wrote a local history of Athens, the *Atthis*, which was mythical, genealogical and chronological in that it began with the earliest times, and systematized the list of legendary kings, but also historical in that it brought the record up to the present, including events in the Peloponnesian War. In addition, he wrote ethnographical works dealing with the foundations of the Greek cities of Asia Minor and the customs and tales of the surrounding natives.

Perhaps his *Persica* and the closely contemporary *Persica* of Dionysius of Miletus and Charon of Lampsacus (and the *Lydiaca* of Xanthus of Lydia), were stimulated by the Persian War, for they covered not only the legendary ancestors and eponymous heroes of the peoples of the Persian empire, but also the kings from Cyrus to Darius and the events of the war itself. In fact, Drews conjectures that Greek historiography was "in a real sense, a result of history itself." i.e.,. a response to the contact with Persian culture, and a reaction to Persian expansion and defeat.[15] These writers of *Persica*, however, did not organize their information according to any unifying concepts that went beyond the geographical or chronological, nor did they provide much analysis or embellishment.

Herodotus, born in Halicarnassus in 484 B.C.E., was the first prose writer to concentrate on the recent past and to study it as an unfolding process. From internal references (e.g., 6.98; 7.235.2), scholars conclude that he completed the book by 425 B.C.E., when the Peloponnesian War was already in progress. Using much of the same information from oral sources as the *logographoi*, as well as autopsy and at least Hecataeus' works, Herodotus incorporated both the *logoi* of the barbarians and the oral histories of the recent Greeks into a rationally coherent account of the growth of the Persian empire and the Greek response to its aggressions. Thus, just around the same time as Ezra and his group were editing the Holy Scriptures, Herodotus produced the first, in Brown's words, "orderly account of past events and of the people who participated in them, with a reasoned explanation of why things happened as they did."[16]

Many have asked what prompted Herodotus to undertake such a massive task. Surely one answer is his own individual genius, for his prose style, considered so charming, effortless, and smooth by the ancients, separates him from the earlier and contemporary *logographoi*. Another must be his curiosity and critical spirit, for he points out the errors of predecessors and tries to get at the truth about so many details. But, as Drews has emphasized, the Greek defeat of the Persian empire, fabled in Greece for its enormous wealth, power, and marvels since the time of Croesus, generated such pride and such interest in all the participants that Herodotus felt that the information about them, primarily remembered through the oral tradition, must be written down, like epic, so that it would never be forgotten. The poets and dramatists of the early fifth century had already responded to the 'great event' with elegies, victory odes, and tragedies. But Herodotus, an Asiatic Greek himself, a sometime resident of Athens and Thurii, and a traveler interested in the tales and customs of both sides and all parts of each, had a much bigger story to tell: so many new as yet unsung heroes, achievements, and marvels to record for posterity. As Drews has written,

> What sets him apart from the writers of the early *Persica* is that which would henceforth be the fundamental characteristic of every Greek historian: the desire to tell that which has not been told before . . .it was Herodotus who both completed the story of the Great Event and won recognition for a new endeavor: enlarging the written record of men's deeds by applying *historie* to the past.[17]

Fornara suggests that Herodotus had a further motive for writing: warning his contemporaries about the dangers of the Archidamian War (431-421 B.C.E.).[18]   Herodotus, having researched the Greeks and barbarians, and the causes and conclusion of the Persian War, had discovered a pattern in history. Whatever his own development or his process of composing his *Histories*, he was writing while the Delian League-turned Athenian Empire became more aggressive and expansionist, and the threatened Peloponnesian League was forced to respond.[19]   Applying the lessons he learned from the Persian War, Herodotus could foresee disaster for the once victorious Greeks.   Earlier Aeschylus had warned his Athenian audience about hubris through the ghost of Darius in *Persians* (821 -831). Now Herodotus reported the details of the Persian expansion and defeat, showing how, in Fornara's words, "triumph brings a momentum leading to egoism and excess," to suggest that the Greeks were heading for a similar crisis.[20]

Herodotus' Histories

The *Histories* reflects both an antiquarian interest in how things were and the contemporary political consciousness aroused by the great events of the fifth century.[21]   Its content also exhibits the intellectual pursuits, attitudes, and methods of the Greek enlightenment, for Herodotus was a cosmopolitan investigator curious about many different kinds of knowledge. Like most of the early Greek thinkers, he wrote as a private individual without any special authority himself or connection to a single authoritative group. In both collecting material and selecting what he would write down, he was bound only by his own interests and what he judged would interest or inform his diverse Greek-speaking audience.

He gathered his information from different places and from many sources: from earlier writers like Hecataeus, from authoritative records at shrines like Delphi, from what he could see with his own eyes, from the myths and folk tales transmitted orally by the various peoples he visited or learned about, as well as from the oral histories of royal courts, Greek city-states, and powerful aristocratic families.[22]   Scholars speculate that Herodotus consulted or heard performances of professional storytellers (whom he called *logioi*) whose task it was to preserve important memories worthy of glory.[23] Thus Herodotus may have received much of his information already in story form. Most were probably free-floating pieces, however, unconnected to any long organized and programmatic narrative.

Out of such diverse materials, written and oral, the Hebrew Bible was edited into a connected prose history by anonymous authors. Herodotus, however, is a persona in his own *Histories*, who introduces himself by name and lets his readers know how and where he got his information.[24]   Sometimes he is a simple observer; at others he acts as an eyewitness investigator trying to confirm the truth of some detail; in more than five hundred places he critically evaluates his data.[25]   In 2.99, for example, he announces

> Up to this point the account is based on my own observation (*opsis*), and opinion (*gnome*), and research (*historie*), but now I come to the accounts which I heard (*ekouon*) from the Egyptians. Here too I will add something from my own observation (*opsis*).

Frequently he names the source, tries to cross-check his information (e.g., *logioi* of the Persians, Greeks, and Phoenicians, 1.1- 1.5.2) and records the questions he posed, as when he asked the Egyptian priests for the truth about Helen and the Trojan War (2.113-120). This first person account of his investigative process interrupts the third person narrative of the actual history so often that his method becomes part of his story.

Herodotus' procedure is as important as the results of his inquiry because he is unwilling to accept his sources without appraising their credibility. His Hebrew counterparts remained faithful to their old and sacred information while using their historical imaginations to recreate the past as it really was. Herodotus, however, applied the critical and intellectual tools of Greek philosophy and science to the oldest written and oral traditions, the opinions of earlier thinkers, and the oral accounts of relatively recent events alike in order to determine the accuracy of this material. Like the Hebrews, he records what has been handed down, but he is generally skeptical about his information unless he can verify it. As he remarks at 7.152, "I am obliged to report what was said, but I am not at all obliged to believe everything, and let this statement hold true for the whole work." (see also 2.123). From the beginning, when he makes a distinction between the mythic past and what he himself knows (see also 3.122), he judges what has been handed down to him, and he informs his readers of his reasons for acceptance, rejection, or doubt. Lloyd categorizes several types of arguments Herodotus employs in attempting to get at the truth: for example, 1) induction for scientific questions, indicating an understanding of scientific method, e.g., 2.22, 24-27, 104, and perhaps even the method of experiment at 2.5.10-14; 2) argument from probability (*eikos*), used by Hecataeus and already well developed by the teachers of forensic rhetoric; 3) archaeological proofs based on the existence of such objects as temples and stelae and the information contained on them; 4) arguments from analogy, so important in early Greek philosophy. Lloyd characterizes Herodotus' methods of argument as a "thorough-going empiricism. . . firmly rooted in his experience of men and the phenomenal world so that traditions which contradict this are firmly rejected."[26]

Nothing is sacred to the critical investigator as he tries to determine how it really was. Not only has his research in Egypt discredited Greek beliefs that the gods participated in the heroic age, but it has also led him to challenge the Greeks' very knowledge of their own gods. His corrections of Greek traditions were based partly on the *post hoc ergo propter hoc* fallacy; he traces many aspects of Greek cult (as well as other features of Greek civilization) to the older Egyptian, Pelasgian, and Libyan religions.[27] From this he concludes that Homer and Hesiod put together a synthesis and taught the Greeks about the gods only four hundred years ago (2.49-57). In his commentary, Lloyd notes the care with which Herodotus indicates his sources and builds his proofs, "doubtless through nervousness at offending religious scruples."[28]

Arguments from probability were also a valuable tool for getting at the truth behind a remote myth, for his experience of men and human life helped him reason out how another human being was likely to behave in a given situation and thus judge what accounts were incredible. To introduce such evidence, he often uses phrases like "it is probable" e.g., 3.38.2, or "reason persuades", e.g., 3.45.3, indicating that he has based his conclusion on his experience of human behavior. At 2.120, for example, after interrogating the Egyptian priests, he rejects Homer's version and places Helen in Egypt during the Trojan War, reasoning that if she had really been in Troy the Trojans would have surely returned her at some point in the war rather than risk their lives, children, and city.

This discussion with the priests reveals that Herodotus has not rejected all of the information about the events and people of the remote past. He accepts the Trojan War as an indisputable fact, just as he accepts the priests' assertion that they learned what really happened at Troy from Menelaos himself (2.118). In like manner, in the preface and at 3.122, he prefers to limit his account to the first men he knows, Croesus of Lydia, and Polycrates of Samos, respectively, but he does not deny the existence of the characters of myth, although he rationalizes their lives according to the criterion of probability. Nor does he ever reject the gods although he calls the poets' stories into question. In 2. 116, he conjectures that Homer knew Helen was in Egypt, but didn't use that version because it was not suitable to epic poetry. Faced with the problem that the war was fought despite Helen's absence from Troy, he states his belief that the Greeks refused to accept the truth because of divine providence so that men would know that great sins provoke great punishments from the gods (2.120.5).

Herodotus' quest for verification and accuracy also led him to test very different kinds of information. He investigated the descriptions and analyzed the theories of his predecessors in geography and geology, trying to account for such problems as the behavior and effect of the Nile on Egypt (2.15-34), and rejecting the map of the Ionians because of his own observation of the Nile delta (2.16). Despite his respect for Egypt and things Egyptian, however, he corrects Hecataeus' opinion that the Greek alphabet derived from Egypt, arguing from *opsis* as well as logic that Cadmus and his Phoenicians introduced writing to Greece (5.58-61). The facts behind events had to be set straight too. Reporting conflicting accounts, for example, Herodotus carefully explains his reasons for his emphatic judgment that Ephialtes was the traitor at Thermopylae, using as evidence the Amphictyones' condemnation of him, his subsequent flight into exile, and the honor Sparta accorded his killer (7.213- 214).

But Herodotus also recognizes limits to his research. In seeking the source of the Nile, he remarks that nobody I have spoken with, Egyptian, Libyan, or Greek, claimed to know anything, except the scribe of the temple treasury of Athena in the Egyptian city of Sais, but he seemed to make sport of me although he claimed to know accurately (2.28).

He went south as far as Elephantine to make his own observations (*autoptes*), but beyond that point he had to be content with hearsay (*akoe*, 2.29.1). In some passages he admits to a complete lack of information on a question, as at 7.60, where he can't provide a number count because no one has reported it, or at 9.84, where he can't say with certainty who removed Mardonius' body for burial. Such cross-checking, interrogation, and on site investigations, plus the ultimate rejection of some material, lead readers to understand the complexity of the truth and the difficulty of uncovering it at the same time as they are following the narrative. For this reason, Szegedy-Maszak compares the author's persona as an investigator of *logoi* to an Athenian dicast, "examining witnesses, collecting evidence, scrutinizing data on the basis of probability, and occasionally delivering a verdict."[29]

If the task of the researcher was to investigate the data in order to establish its accuracy, it was the task of the author to put the results together into a coherent whole. Like the Hebrews, Herodotus organized his information according to a linear and chronological principle, working from a systematic idea of what happened when based on the genealogies and mythographies then current among the Greeks, as well as Lydian, Persian, Egyptian, and Spartan King lists.[30] Into his sustained account of the political and military events which marked the expansion and defeat of the Persian empire, however, he wove his geographical, ethnological, and legendary materials, providing background about each new foreign group confronted as well as relevant information about Greek communities consulted for alliance or aid. Beginning with Croesus, King of Lydia, at the time of his confrontation with Cyrus, Herodotus moves back in time to the beginning of Croesus' reign and brings the history of Lydia and Croesus up to date, including what was going on at Athens, Sparta, and Delphi when he consulted with them, as well as details about Lydia worth preserving. When he moves on to the Persian conquest of Lydia, he goes back again in time to the birth and rise of Cyrus to the throne of Persia, before picking up his history with Cyrus' treatment of the Greeks who were the former subjects of Lydia and Cyrus' new conquests, noting details about campaigns, customs, and individuals he finds most interesting. When Cambyses, Cyrus' son, conquers Egypt, Herodotus devotes a full book to its marvels, natural, human, and historical, before moving on to the next Persian dynast and the next peoples conquered. Not until the end of book 6, after he has presented the background on the Ionian Greeks and their allies and narrated the revolt and its results, does he get to the actual Persian Wars and move his literal history forward more quickly. He uses the device of ring composition throughout, framing pieces of his background material with introductory phrases and conclusions which return the reader to the relevant point in the linear progression.

The *Histories* which results from such an organization is, according to Meier, a "multi-subjective, contingency oriented account" in which the sequence of political and military events is "caused by many different subjects which met by chance."[31] Unlike the Bible, it does not concentrate on one particular group or area, nor does it trace the ultimate source of all events since creation to the will of God. Rather, Herodotus, reporting military and political events from the time he knew something about for certain, perceived a sequence of particular actions performed by different groups or individuals for different reasons and in response to ever new situations. Meier compares him to an Ionian researcher in that "he needed to know everything about each novelty" in the historical process.[32] As the linear movement progresses, and new places, customs, leaders, and reasons for behavior accumulate, there is a kind of leveling so that no one group or leader emerges as hero and no one reason stands out as the ultimate cause for the sequence of events which Herodotus is tracing. Meier points out that the element of contingency is so strong in the *Histories* because it reflects the Greek perception of a cosmos and nature determined by laws beyond the control of any single human or godly force and not particularly responsible for military and political affairs (which since Solon were decided by the citizens in Athens).[33]

Yet Meier also notes the corollary that in the Greek view all individual elements in the cosmos are interrelated so that various particulars can only be interpreted in relation to others.[34] If the linear progress develops out of ever new events in time in new places and with new people, the historian has organized the information so that he can highlight certain themes he has found important, certain general causes for action, which he sees imbedded in the particular events, and even certain patterns in past history which suggest present dangers.

Out of so many different types of particulars, Herodotus has built up, according to Cook, a "network of interrelated analogies" and motifs which underline implicit themes.[35] For, in characterizing each new place as he traces the historical sequence, he repeatedly comments on the same types of information about participants: e.g., specific customs; political organization; relations with their neighbors; the way leaders obtained their positions; internal union or dissension; reasons for aggression or self defense. Each detail is unique in itself and Herodotus does not generally make explicit comparisons or contrasts. Yet as they accumulate, they draw attention to the central political issues of fifth century Greece: the importance of custom and tradition, the very real differences between nations and even Greek city-states, the advantages and disadvantages of the different kinds of polities, the dangers of internal strife or too much enforced unity, the particular problems engendered by success and power. The earlier Persian conquests set the stage for the comparison and contrast between Greece and Persia, as poor against rich, materialistic against spirited, weak against powerful, free against conquered, separatist against unified.[36] The earlier Asian contacts with Athens and Sparta in particular prepare readers to understand the problems and actions of those cities and their leaders in the reigns of Darius and Xerxes.[37]

As he presents his linear and contingent account of the political and military sequence, he uses his historical imagination to engage his readers and help them interpret the meaning of the events. Many of the tales he records must have already come to him in story form, e.g., how Croesus' ancestor Gyges attained the throne of Lydia by killing his predecessor Candaules and marrying his queen (1.7-13). Other scenes he probably set himself, to embed the explanation of an event in an account which imitated a credible real-life situation. At 3.134, for example, the historian presents the chief arguments for Darius' attack on Scythia and Greece as pillow talk between the king and his queen Atossa. So too, when Xerxes contemplates invading Greece, Herodotus stages a conference of leaders in which the motives for the expedition and the best strategies are carefully debated (7.8-11). Often Herodotus provides a warning scene in which a wise advisor, like a Hebrew prophet, suggests the best course of action and the reasons for it (e.g., Solon to Croesus; Croesus to Cyrus; Artabanus to Xerxes).[38]

As the history unfolds, the causes for events are dramatized by such encounters and the accumulations of analogous scenes. Herodotus himself provides further explications of cause as he comments on the validity of his source, reasons through the conflicting accounts, or adds his own assessment of motivation. Often the historian tries to distinguish the pretext from the real cause.[39] Moreover, because he presents the religious, the political, the psychological, and the ethnic all on the same linear and paratactic plane, his explication tends to level the secular with the sacred as an equally important explanation for events and their connection.[40] Thus, the search for cause becomes as complex and multilayered as the search for truth.[41]

The gods are certainly an important element in explaining the course of events, but their effect is somewhat ambiguous. For the *Histories*, like epic and contemporary tragedy, reflects the Greek belief that actions have a double motivation, a divine and human cause, expressing the interplay of necessity and choice in individual acts and decisions (see chapter five). Oracles of the gods seem to direct the action because they are constantly consulted by various individuals and nations. But their meaning depends on the way humans solve their riddles. Croesus' misinterpretation of the oracle of Delphi (1.53) lost him his own kingdom. Both Herodotus (1.34) and the Pythia (1.91) blame him for his fall. Yet his situation is complicated by the fact that, as the fifth descendant of Gyges, he is also doomed to lose the throne according to divine vertical reciprocity. Themistocles' interpretation of the "wooden walls" and "divine Salamis" in Delphi's oracle to the Athenians (7.141-143) led them toward their great naval victory, which is later ascribed by him to the gods.

Dreams too play a role in the movement of the action. Astyges, for example, has two dreams which foreshadow his grandson Cyrus' conquest of Asia (1.107-108), while Cyrus then dreams of Darius' succession and attempt to bridge Europe and Asia (1.209). When Xerxes hesitates to invade Greece, swayed by the arguments of Artabanus, the gods send him and then Artabanus dreams which urge them on toward the disaster (7.14-19).

The last example suggests that the gods represent a kind of necessity, a belief that things are fated to develop in a certain way. But the conversations which precede the dreams of Xerxes and Artabanus articulate human motives (e.g., glory and safety) for which the gods provide the culminating and correlative metaphysical explanation. Artabanus insists that "God does not allow anyone but himself to think great thoughts" (7.10e), that a new conquest would increase their hubris, and that it is "wrong to teach the soul always to seek more than it already has" (7.16a). Artabanus' arguments make clear that further Persian expansion into

Greece will be an act of hubris bound to attract punishment from the gods.

Herodotus himself asserts at 7.139 and 8.13 that the Greek victory had divine help; at 9.100, he reasons that several remarkable coincidences prove that the gods are active in human events. In 2. 120, he draws his own conclusion about the gods' moral purpose in permitting the Trojan War, but at 8.109.3 he allows Themistocles, the crafty hero of Salamis, to pronounce the pious interpretation of the victory as divine reciprocity

> We did not accomplish these deeds, but rather the gods and heroes, who begrudged that one man should rule both Europe and Asia, a man unholy and reckless who treated the holy and the profane in the same way.

It is not surprising that Herodotus, like the Deuteronomic historians, perceives divine retribution as an important element in human history. The doctrine of reciprocity is, according to the mythmakers and philosophers, the principle which maintains the cosmic order; the certainty that evil will be repaid with evil keeps everyone and everything operating justly within its own portion (*moira*) and prevents encroachments which destroy the balance of the harmonious whole (see chapter 4). Herodotus' acceptance of this fundamental principle is clear from his description of how Arabian snakes reproduce; the female, having killed the male as he releases the sperm, pays recompense (*tisin*) to him when her offspring kill her as they emerge from the womb (3.109).[42]

His Greek contemporaries also saw reciprocity at work in human lives and history. Herodotus reports, for example, that when the Spartan Cleomenes died by gruesome self-mutilation, most Greeks viewed his death as a punishment for earlier crimes, i.e., corrupting the Pythia to lie about Demaratus; violating the shrine at Eleusis; treachery and sacrilege in Argos (6.75). Since the Spartans ascribed his death to his own drunkenness, however, Herodotus opines that "Cleomenes paid the penalty (*tisis*) to Demaratus" (6.84.3).

Throughout the *Histories* Herodotus uses retribution, on the human and divine levels, as a means of both explaining the connection between events and providing a motive for them. His preface describes the first hostile contacts between Europe and Asia as a chain of reciprocal abductions. That the gods follow the same practice of avenging injustice is evident from the Delphic Oracle's response to the Lydians after Gyges has killed Candaules; the

Pythia said that revenge (*tisis*) would be granted in Gyges' fifth generation (1.13.2). The defeat of Croesus, his descendant, was fated as vertical reciprocity, which his patron Apollo could not avert, for, as the Pythia stated (1.91), "It is impossible even for a god to escape destiny (*moiran*)." Although she also blames Croesus' downfall on his misreading of the oracles, Herodotus has already used the terms of divine retribution to account for Croesus' misfortune: "Great punishment (*nemesis*) from god overtook Croesus, as is likely (*hos eikasai*), because he thought himself the most fortunate of all men" (1.34).

This revenge motif runs through the entire *Histories*. It affects so many incidents that De Romilly suggests Herodotus uses it partly as a device for introducing interesting anecdotes while Immerwahr describes it a principle of organization, a way of connecting one event to the next by providing *tisis* as a link.[43] Indeed, the great Persian expeditions into Greece are themselves explained in part as continuing links in the chain of retributions for injuries done by each side to the other, Darius' to punish Athens for her part in the Ionian revolt, and, ten years later, Xerxes' to avenge his father's defeat.

Other more clearly psychological and political explanations are also presented as part of the background to events. The fact that Croesus, for example, wanted to avenge Cyrus' treatment of his brother-in-law Astyges (1.73-74) provides an immediately intelligible motive for his attack on Persia as well as an opportunity for a good story. At 1.46, however, Herodotus has already given a political reason; Croesus feels threatened by the growth of Persia. Croesus himself has been an expansionist, subduing most of the peoples west of the river Halys, on any pretext great or small (1.26.3.). After Croesus consults Delphi about his plans, the historian summarizes his motives for attacking Persia, adding confidence in the oracles to his "wish to increase his own portion (*moiran*) in his desire for land" (1.73), before introducing revenge for Astyges.

As the chain of reciprocal attacks and counterattacks continues and the historian gets closer to the recent past, these political and psychological reasons receive more attention. Atossa is motivated to persuade Darius to invade Greece by her Greek doctor for his own very private reasons; he hopes to get home to Greece if there is a war. The arguments presented to Darius have nothing to do with reciprocity. The young king, having so much power, must either use it or appear weak to his subjects; he will prevent plots against himself by occupying and weakening his rivals (3.134). When the Scythians and their neighbors discuss their response to Darius' crossing into Europe, the Scythians suggest that Persian punishment of them for an old injury is only a pretext for Persian expansion, arguing that the Persians have enslaved all the nations on their way to Scythia instead of attacking only them (4.118). And Darius has already determined to invade Greece before Athens' participation in the Ionian Revolt gives him retribution as a motive.

The beginning of book 7 (1-20) provides an excellent summary of all the contingencies and causes of the climactic confrontation between the Greeks and the barbarians.[44] Xerxes' cousin Mardonius urges him to punish Athens for Marathon because it will add to the king's glory, prevent invasions of Persia, and enrich his empire. Herodotus notes that Mardonius also has personal reasons for encouraging the reluctant king: his eagerness for adventure and his desire to be governor of Greece. Then, at the same time as the ruling family of Thessaly invites Xerxes into Greece, the Pisistratid exiles in Susa urge him to attack, using the doctored oracles of Onomacritus as bait.

At the conference before the expedition, Xerxes adds his own reasons: the past history of Persia incites him to increase its glory and wealth; he must avenge the Ionian Revolt and his father; he plans to conquer all of Europe, enslaving the innocent and the guilty, as he makes the Persian boundaries equal to the heavens of Zeus (see also 7.157.1, where the Greek allies seeking aid from Syracuse argue that punishing Athens is just a Persian pretext for conquering all of Greece and moving west to Sicily). Mardonius' response emphasizes that the Persians, who have previously enslaved other nations without being greatly injured by them, cannot now allow a guilty nation to escape their punishment. Moreover, he is certain that superior Persian wealth and manpower will ensure victory. At first unswayed by Artabanus' rejoinder, Xerxes announces his decision to invade, summarizing

> It is no longer possible for either of us to retreat, but the battle lies before us to do injury or suffer it, so that all our possessions will be in the hands of the Greeks or all theirs will belong to us, for there is no middle ground for our enmity (7.11.3).

When Xerxes changes his mind, the dreams from the gods provide the external compulsion for the actions which derive from fear, greed, and ambition as well as the desire for revenge, the overconfidence that leads to hubris, and the irresistible force of expansionism. These aspects of human causation are presented by

Herodotus without any abstract analysis, through dialogue between characters or through his own brief comments.   As the ideas accumulate in incident after incident, however, they become an important part of the historian's research into the reasons for the war.

Herodotus' historical imagination enables him to suggest a general pattern as he presents the linear progression of particular incidents.[45] The outlines of the pattern are already intimated in the preface by the early chain of reciprocal injuries and the statement that he will discuss cities great and small because

> Most of the cities that were great long ago have become small; those which have become great in my own time were formerly small. Realizing that human good fortune never remains in the same place, I will preserve the memory of both (1.5.4).

Such a statement may suggest that human history is in fact cyclic; Croesus even tells Cyrus "there is a cycle in human affairs which, moving around, does not allow the same humans to always prosper" (1.207.2). The whole history illustrates this universal movement as powerful nations like Lydia, Egypt and Babylon are swallowed up by Persia as it grows to greatness and then Persia, having begun in poverty and weakness, is itself destroyed by the tenuous union of less rich and powerful Greek city-states, whose individual development is also described at various points. As in the cosmos, so in human history, reciprocity is restoring the balance over time so that eternal justice and harmony ultimately prevail.[46]

But the *Histories* tells a linear story which develops out of many particular individuals and nations coming together in unique situations with a multiplicity of motivations. The variety of actions possible in any one point on the line is emphasized by the arguments used by different speakers in the many debates or private talks which accompany the progression of events.   Herodotus' frequent use of scenes in which an adviser warns of the consequences of a wrong decision indicates how important free choice is, even when the wrong choice seems inevitable.[47] Immediately after mentioning the cycle, for example, Croesus suggests a strategy supported by so many good political and psychological arguments that Cyrus changes his mind about how to conquer the Massagetae (1.208.1). His defeat results in part from his choice of strategy, but also from the choices of Queen Tamyris, particularly after her son chose to commit suicide when a Persian prisoner (1. 213-214).

While presenting the particular causes for actions, the historian also uses certain scenes or anecdotes to indicate there is a positive program for happiness which human beings ignore at their peril.[48] He has, in fact, manipulated his theme of Persian expansion presented in chronological order to introduce Croesus before describing Cyrus' rise to the throne of Persia.[49] Not only can he thus begin with a colossal fall as a pattern for future reversals, but he can present a confrontation between Solon and Croesus (most probably fictitious) at the point when Sardis is at her zenith and Athens is just starting to develop. Solon is a wise adviser who tries to convince Croesus that the happiest of men is the one who dies happy after serving his state, his family, and his gods and receiving his due honor. The aged Athenian specifically rejects wealth as the determinant of good fortune, and applies his statement about individuals to nations as well (1.30-33). But Croesus, supposing he is the happiest of men, ignores Solon's warning. Before the king attacks Cappadocia, Sandanis the Lydian tries to dissuade him, arguing that Lydia's wealth is a danger to them because their poorer enemies will surely never stop trying to get their possessions, whereas they themselves have nothing to gain from their conquest.

The growth of wealth and power, the desire for more, the overconfidence which success breeds, and the disasters which result run through the history as a motif significant enough to be called a pattern which explains the rise and fall of individuals and nations. Herodotus ends the *Histories* with an anecdote about it, again placed out of the chronological sequence. Someone long ago had suggested to Cyrus that the Persians should move from their small and barren country to a better one now that they were masters of Asia. But Cyrus warned that they would have to be prepared to give up their rule and be ruled instead, "for soft countries produce soft men, nor is it possible for the same land to bear fine fruit and men good at war." Herodotus concludes his book by affirming that the early Persians chose "to dwell in their rugged land rather than cultivate rich plains and become slaves to other men" (9.122.3-4).

Herodotus suggests a different program which can bring more real good fortune than the quest for wealth and power. Piety and patriotism which go beyond self-interest are of course primary goods. But, as Herodotus' last words indicate, slavery is one of the worst evils and freedom is one of the most important possessions that individuals or nations should desire. In the Persian debate about the best type of state (3.80), Otanes compares the advantages of self-government to the dangers of monarchy, stressing the fact that the citizens make their own decisions and their governors are responsible to the governed. Herodotus praises the incentives of freedom himself when commenting on the significance of the Athenian expulsion of their tyrants; as slaves to other men, they were no better than their neighbors, but now each person desired to work hard for himself (5.78). The point is dramatized best in scenes in which Demaratus first insists to an uncomprehending Xerxes that Spartans will fight to the death rather than submit to slavery (7.102), and then reminds the king of his words when the outnumbered Spartans bravely stand their ground at Thermopylae against fleeing Persians who have to be whipped back into the battle (7.209-212).

Greek freedom is of course not unlimited, but it is restrained by valor made effective because of wisdom and strong law (7.102) rather than by the despot's whip. Much earlier, when Croesus was considering Athens and Sparta as allies, Herodotus connected Greece with the rule of law; he introduced Solon as the man who had made laws at the Athenians' request (1.29) and described the way in which Lycurgus established a well-ordered government by "changing the laws and insuring that they not be transgressed" (1.65). In the Persian debate, Otanes also acknowledges the importance of law; speaking in favor of democracy, he equates the rule of the people with the rule of law by calling it *isonomia* (see chapter eight). At 7.104.4-5, Demaratus tells Xerxes about the Spartans: "Law is their despot which they fear more than your subjects fear you," so much so that because it commands them to, they will never give ground in battle. But their quest for excellence and honor also spurs them to great achievements.[50] The Spartan behavior at Thermopylae confirms Demaratus' words, and Herodotus eulogizes their consummate valor (7.213-228).

If Herodotus has based his interpretation of the past on his own experience, he is also using that past to comment on the present. Many scholars have noted that he focuses on issues which were particularly relevant in the last quarter of the fifth century, e.g., *nomos, physis*; the influence of the place on a people. More important, his treatment of the Greeks as they respond to the Persian advance prefigures the current internal strife in the individual city-states (e.g., the rivalry between Demaratus and Cleomenes in Sparta, or Clisthenes and Isagoras in Athens), the inability to form a stable union to promote their common interest (as when some Medize or when only Themistocles' trick keeps the Peloponnesians together to fight at Salamis) and the struggle between the city-states for hegemony (as when the Syracusan Gelo refuses aid unless he can hold the supreme command or when the

Athenians and Tegeans argue over the honor of commanding a wing at Plataea).

Although Herodotus does not point out the parallels, he dramatizes incidents in ways which suggest contemporary events.[51] For example, at 5.90 - 93, after helping the Athenians to expel the Pisitratids has brought them no benefits, the Spartans call a conference which has the same motives, participants, and arguments as the council of the Peloponnesian League in Sparta in 432 just before the outbreak of the Archidamian War. Herodotus' account of their reasons for hoping to restore the despotic government to Athens resembles both the barbarians' arguments for attacking rivals, from Croesus through Xerxes, and Thucydides' description of the underlying reason for the Peloponnesian War (1.23.6)

> They saw the Athenians growing greater and no longer willing to obey them, and realizing that the Athenians, being free, would become a match for them . . . (5.91.1).

When the Corinthians argue from their own experience that despotism is terrible and "contrary to justice" (5.92.e5), Hippias swears that the Corinthians too will someday be grieved by the Athenians (5.93.1). No Greek reader could fail to recognize this allusion to one of the immediate causes of the outbreak of the conflict between the Athenian and Peloponnesian leagues. Indeed the terms the historian uses throughout to characterize the barbarian expansion, e.g., *arche* (empire), *polupragmonesis* (meddlesomeness), *pleonexia* (greediness), variations of *auxomai* (grow in power), are the very words the Greeks themselves were using to describe the Athenian movement from liberator to enslaver of Greece in old comedy (e.g., *Birds*) as well as in political oratory.[52]

According to Fornara, "Herodotus' intention was to make his listeners understand the crisis of the day in historical perspective."[53] The patterns perceived, on the individual, national, and divine levels, were more than literary motifs; they were realities relevant to his own time which had to be communicated. Herodotus does not abstract his message from his story or analyze the similarity between then and now, for he and his readers, as inheritors of epic and spectators of drama, could perceive the ideas embodied in the narrative and appreciate their relevance without conceptualizing them.[54] Characters like Solon and the Persian who comments before Platea, "Whatever necessity comes from the god man is powerless to avert" (9.16.4), reflect on the instability of human life and the necessity of disappointment and death. Yet the variety of paths taken to inevitable ends and the differences between Greek growth and Persian expansion indicate that history is not a repeatable cycle, and human agents, like epic and tragic heroes, are responsible for human events.

Thucydides' Histories

Thucydides was as much of a pioneer in the writing of history as his older contemporary.[55] First readers of Thucydides are struck by the differences between his book and Herodotus' *Histories*. Thucydides himself points out one major contrast: he will not, like the *logographoi*, compose in order to please at the expense of truth (1.21.1) and his work will not include the fabulous (*muthodes* at 1.22.4).

Not only has he abandoned story-telling and the dramatic scenes fictionalized to mimic life, but he has also eliminated the metaphysical framework (familiar from epic, drama, and Herodotus) as an explanation of the cause and course of the war. As a result, particular events proceed from human contingencies and necessities, without the foreshadowing provided by oracles, dreams, wise advisors, and exemplary stories, or the all-encompassing principle of human and divine retribution. Sealy comments that "By turning his attention from grievances to power politics, he made one of his major contributions to Greek political thought."[56]

The change is philosophical as well as artistic. More like the sophists than Herodotus was, Thucydides only uses empirical data from the sensible the world around him and interprets it critically on the basis of his reason and his own experiences, unencumbered by traditional explanations. Since the perceptible facts of history are not metaphysical, religion is introduced as a part of other more mundane aspects of military and political life. Thucydides reports, for example, that the Spartans inquired at Delphi for a favorable outcome before deciding to fight and then invoked an old curse against the Athenians in order to "have the greatest pretext for the war" (1.126.1). He notes that the plague-stricken Athenians stopped expecting any help from religion when they recognized the futility of supplications and divinations, and comments, in reference to a disputed recollection of an ancient prediction (famine or plague), that the Athenians' "memories conformed to their sufferings" (2.54.3). He judged Nicias, who delayed a vital retreat because of an eclipse of the moon (7.52.4), "too much inclined toward divination and such things."

Thucydides' analysis does not indicate any personal atheism.[57] If he describes the cynical exploitation of religion by some politicians and city-states, he also shows its observation by others. The pious Nicias encourages his men with statements reflecting the doctrine of reciprocity (7.77.2-3), whereas the soldiers' fear that rain and thunder were evil omens increased their despair during the last futile attempt to escape from Sicily (7.79.3). He also seems to have done research into religious history in order to give background on landmarks, customs, and institutions which play some role in the events and actually cites fifteen oracles. According to Jordan, Thucydides provides

> first rate insights into the psychology of religious people. For him religion is the underlying fabric which holds society together and he shows how a prolonged and vicious war gradually destroys that fabric as it destroys so much besides.[58]

Thucydides rejects more than the "fabulous" or metaphysical found in his predecessors. The absence of anecdotes and stories, as well as any geographical and ethnological information not immediately relevant to the event narrated, changes the nature of the work and limits the subject of his *historie*. As Thucydides says in his opening sentence, he, an Athenian, has written the history of the war between the Peloponnesians and the Athenians. He shows no interest in other kinds of achievements which are not connected to the war or in other non-Greek peoples except as their leaders (e.g., Tissaphernes in 8) or characteristics (e.g., the Odrysians of Thrace at 2.97) affect the course of military and political strategies. Thus, although he reports on all the Greek city-states involved from the same generally objective and detached perspective as Herodotus, his history of the Peloponnesian War is not "multi-subjective" in the way the *Histories* is.

Moreover, Thucydides is not interested in the past per se. Rather he is writing a contemporary history, which he began as soon as the war broke out because he believed it was the greatest yet and most worthy of recording (1.1). If his intention to commemorate and his choice of war as the subject are reminiscent of epic and Herodotus, the emphasis on the present is new. Thucydides was the heir of Herodotus' method of *historie* (which could only be applied to recent times) and its results (which provided a correct and complete record of the recent past), as well as its commemoration of noteworthy recent men and women. According to Drews,

"Thucydides recognized that politically active Greeks would find it worthwhile to read about events in which they themselves had participated."[59]   Before reporting on the Peloponnesian War, however, Thucydides brings the written record up to date. He fills in the last fifty years since the Persian Wars (Penteconteia, 1.89-118), beginning exactly where Herodotus ended, and completes the account of the careers of the two most important Greeks leaders at the end of the *Histories*, Themistocles and Pausanias (1.128-139).

Thucydides does delve back into the past occasionally, but only for very specific reasons. At 1.2-20, for example, he summarizes Greek history from the earliest times to the Persian Wars (called the Archaeology) to prove that no period could match the combined resources, power, or destruction that resulted from the present war. At 1.126, he reports the details of the Cylonian conspiracy, which happened long ago, to explain the curse the Spartans used as a pretext for the war, and then introduces Pausanias when Athenians respond with a counter-curse which involves his behavior. In other places, he corrects errors about the past preserved in the oral tradition, e.g., 1.20 or 6.54, where the information helps explain the Athenian overreaction to the sacrileges. At the beginning of Book 6, he surveys the habitation of Sicily from mythic times on, aware of the Athenians' ignorance of its size and peoples.

Thucydides is just as concerned to explain "how it really was" as the Hebrew historians and Herodotus were. In fact, he criticizes Hellanicus for inaccuracy at 1.97.2. Like Herodotus, he had few written records or documents and even fewer predecessors' written works. Like Herodotus too, he relied on Homer and the epic tradition for his information about the beginnings of Greece, accepting the facts, but remaining skeptical about poetic exaggeration (1.10.3). In contrast to Herodotus, however, Thucydides does not simply rationalize the myths and then dismiss them. Rather he uses his historical imagination to reconstruct the important truths embedded in the disconnected tradition according to his understanding of present realities.[60] At 1.5.2, for example, he infers that piracy was a pandemic and respectable profession from the honor with which it is still treated in some places, whereas at 1.6.2 he concludes that all the Greeks once went about armed for self-defense, using the fact that some still do as evidence. As he builds his argument, he draws inferences from Homer in several places, e.g., 1.3.2; 1.9.3; 1.10.3). He also uses archaeology to prove a point; Carian bodies found in the graves on Delos reveal the extent of pirate/islander migrations(1.8.1).

He leaves many of the details he asserts about the past unproven, however, because he is in fact hypothesizing. He has applied the general anthropocentric and evolutionary theories of the sophists of his day to the particulars of the historical process in earlier periods to demonstrate how human beings used their intelligence to gain control over their natural and social environment.[61] His thesis about the rise and fall of previous Greek powers is based on analogies with the present and uses all the terms of current political discourse found in later passages of his book. Indeed, his own grasp of contemporary political and military situations governs his entire presentation of the past, for he concentrates on the movement from weakness to power, why it occurred and what common expeditions it led to, and the internal and external problems which resulted.

For less distant events, both historians depended primarily on oral sources. Thucydides, of course, had his own eyewitness evidence as a person who lived through the entire course of the war.[62] He probably began keeping notes on the causes and progress of the war around 431 B.C.E., just about the time Herodotus was publishing his *Histories*. He was an active participant until his loss of Amphipolis in 424, as an elected general (4.104-107), resulted in exile from Athens for twenty years, so that he had the leisure and freedom to learn about the war from both sides (5.26). Although he knew how and when the war ended (see 2.65.12, 5.26.1, 6.15.3), he evidently did not live to complete his record of it. His *Histories* breaks off mid-sentence, in the twenty-first year, in the summer of 411, during the oligarchic revolution in Athens.

Before beginning his account of the specific causes of the present war, Thucydides gives his readers some insight into his methods of establishing the truth of his description.[63] In 1.22.3, he emphasizes that he has tried to be as accurate as possible in recording what was done in the war (*ta erga*), crosschecking accounts of participants or eyewitnesses because he knows that bias or faulty memory can produce differing versions of the same event. But the speeches, so important to the political life of the Greek city-states, presented a more difficult problem. It was hard for him to retain word-for-word even a speech (*logos*) that he heard himself. Therefore, he wrote what he thought the situation demanded while sticking as closely as possible to what was actually said (1.22.1) by the particular speaker.

Unlike Herodotus, Thucydides does not present his search for the truth as part of his history. Instead, having outlined his procedure in very general terms, he progresses through his account detail by detail without noting sources, or presenting contradictory versions and his reasons for choosing one over the other. Pearson suggests that because he was writing contemporary history, many of his facts must have been well-known. Thus his search for accuracy would have been less complicated than Herodotus'.[64]

But Thucydides presents his own interpretation of those facts, often abstracting his opinions and analysis from his linear story. Unlike Herodotus, he rarely gives reasons for such personal judgments which he often qualifies by phrases such as "it seems to me," "I think," or "as is likely." Pearson finds that he interjects such comments mainly on issues which "demanded critical expression of opinion," such as the quality of the leaders and the relative importance of the various events.[65] Moreover, because it is never clear how much of the speeches reflect what he thought the situation demanded, it is hard to gage the extent of his own interpretation of the issues debated. If his reason for judgment is not always specified, however, his "rationality" is evident throughout; according to Hunter, Thucydides, like Herodotus, displays skepticism, perception of contradictions, skillful argumentation, and, in addition, " a highly complex theoretical construct . . . , a unified, coherent and critically appraisable . . . model of reality."[66]

The Archaeology, though introduced to prove a point, is strategically placed at the beginning to present a new interpretation of the past which is vital to understanding the forthcoming history.[67] For this purpose, he starts much further back than Herodotus was willing to go. Rejecting, like some contemporary philosophers, the traditional Greek view of civilization's degeneration from a Golden Age, Thucydides posits an early historical stage where survival was precarious because of the lack of resources, stable communities, or unification.[68] He does not ascribe change to divine intervention, moral imperatives, or heroic deeds, in the manner of poets and storytellers. The few legendary heroes he does single out are not the traditional civilizers like Theseus, but those whose resources or plans made collective action possible, like Minos, Athens' legendary enemy who was the first to build a navy, clear the sea of pirates, and pile up wealth.[69] Because Thucydides focuses on strategies for survival and growth, he presents what Connor calls a "quite unsentimental" and "highly impersonal" survey of "the escape from instability and the gradual accumulation of power."[70] He in fact emphasizes those pragmatic elements, e.g., navies, walls, constitutions, and those psychological motives, e.g., fear, greed, ambition, which were embedded in Herodotus' stories and conversations. In his reasoned analysis, here and later in the book, De Romilly finds the discovery of the relationship between wealth and war.[71]

Hypothesizing about those periods when earlier wars occurred, Thucydides describes the growth of military power and political unity, and the collective achievements (i.e., war and expeditions) they lead to as communities become stable, secure, and wealthy, particularly if they have navies and can control the sea. Growth also leads to empire, since the weaker, either out of fear or desire for gain, attach themselves to the stronger and eventually become their subjects. Growth can also bring its own problems: internal, if individuals begin to act according to their own fears, greed and ambition and thus cause factionalism and disunity; or external, if that growth attracts the fear and envy of others and thus produces war. War is certainly a great human achievement, noteworthy for the number of men, resources, and leaders, and strategies involved. Yet, as the events of each successive period suggest, progress and victory bring changes which can result in the loss of power and wealth.

By the end of the Archaeology, Thucydides has introduced the major combatants of the Peloponnesian War and briefly characterized their development, according to the general pattern as well as the unique particulars. Before he reports on the specific events that initiated the actual war, he proclaims the real cause which forced them into fighting: the great growth of the Athenian empire frightened the Spartans (1.23.6).

Thucydides' Archaeology has outlined a process similar to the one described by Herodotus, in which the political and military responses to the accumulation of too much power and wealth lead to its disintegration and loss.[72] But the skeletal scheme provides only a general guide to Thucydides' meticulous report which exposes the complexity of the issues, personalities, strategies, interactions, and reversals of expectation out of which such a process might be extracted. Thucydides' organization of the *Histories* is almost always strictly chronological. He rarely deviates from his movement forward; when he does (as in his placement of the Pentecontaetia), he uses ring composition, like Herodotus, to bring his readers back to the main point.[73]

After the preliminaries to the war have been presented in Book 1, at the beginning of Book 2 he dates the actual outbreak of hostilities, synchronizing it with important events and major systems in the Greek world. He then announces his intention to follow the order of events as each occurred, year by year, according to summers and winters. Sometimes he uses such phrases as "when the corn was ripe" (e.g., 2.79.1), or "at the rising of Arcturus" (2.78.2), to relate the time of certain events to the daily lives of his readers.[74]   At 5.25, he dates the Peace of Nicias according to the Spartan Ephorate and Athenian Archonship, noting that it concluded ten years of war. He has fit all of the events into a larger framework of about seventy-five years, the fifty since the Persian War and the twenty-seven years of the Peloponnesian War in its three phases (5.26.1).

Having forsworn the obviously pleasurable devices of the oral style adapted by Herodotus, Thucydides tells his story by combining several different types of exposition: very detailed narrative of the specific facts, usually in a day by day account, political speeches of the participants, usually reported in direct discourse, and his own interpretations or opinions (e.g., of Pericles and his successors at 2.65).[75]   As he progresses, he highlights particular incidents which exemplify changes war brings, such as the plague and the Corcyrean revolution, or which illustrate recurrent problems, as the question of how to treat the rebellious Mityleneans shows both the fickleness of the people who can be persuaded by clever speaking, and the difficulties of a democracy in control of an empire.   The space devoted to the relatively unimportant takeover of Melos and then the two books which follow on the Sicilian expedition dramatize the aggressiveness and overconfidence of the Athenians. As the account of the war proceeds year by year, the repetition and development of particular words, themes, issues, actions, and motivations create a series of recurrences which, according to Connor, "represent the complexity of historical developments and the cumulative effects of changes that are individually almost infinitesimal."[76]

The events themselves are usually described in meticulous detail, including causes, participants, terrain or harbors, strategies and results. If some sections read more like military reports, most are very engaging and dramatic, partly because of the suspense as human beings use their intelligence to respond to changing situations, but also because of the emphasis on the suffering that occurs.[77]   The fact that Thucydides was himself a survivor of the plague and assesses its effect on the morals of the ravaged Athenian population makes his detailed description (2.47-2.54) all the more personal and involving.[78]   His horrifying account of the intensity of the Corcyraean revolution is followed by his even more disturbing analysis of the reasons why it happened the way it did and continued to happen in similar fashion throughout the Greek world (3.70-84). Books 6 and 7, which trace the Sicilian expedition from its exuberant launching to its catastrophic conclusion, are among the most emotional passages in all Greek literature.

To complement the action, Thucydides presents speeches in which the participants argue the issues and strategies at each point in the war. Debates, both public and private, were long a part of Greek literature, from Homer through contemporary drama to Herodotus' mimetic conversations and conferences. But for the historian of war, deliberative speeches are actually part of *ta erga*, political events, since the Greek city-states, oligarchic as well as democratic, rarely made important decisions before holding some sort of public discussion. Therefore, Thucydides reports them as part of the record, promising to be as accurate as possible.

He also uses his historical imagination, however, to make his speakers say what the situation demanded, and to position the speeches strategically to characterize the participants, as well as to interpret and aid the progress of events.[79] In book 1, for example, the speeches at the first congress in Sparta, where Corinth urges war against Athens, not only present the contrast between aggressive Athens and slow Sparta through the eyes of the Corinthians, but also enable the Athenian envoys to display their spirit while defending their acquisition of the empire. The Spartan King Archidamus' response assesses the difficulties involved, and suggests strategies for procrastination and preparation, while confirming the Corinthians' judgment of Spartan conservatism. In the second congress, the Corinthians again urge the vote for war, evaluating the resources of each side, the vulnerabilities of Athens, and the danger and disgrace which would result from Athens' attempt to enslave all Greece. The speeches of Pericles to the Athenian assembly respond to all these points, encouraging and planning for war because of its necessity. His Funeral Oration in particular seems placed just before the plague to characterize Athens at the height of her power, wealth, and culture, with the best leader, and the most innovative liberal society, committed to a firm belief in the intelligence and community spirit of the citizens (2.34-46).

Thucydides' speeches, which dramatize human reason in operation, reflect the rhetorical style and ideas generally attributed to the Sophists and tragedians of his day.[80] Very often he pairs antithetical speeches so that participants present opposing arguments, as when Cleon and Diodotus debate the treatments of the rebellious Mityleneans (3.36-3.49), when the Melians and the Athenians discuss whether the weaker neutrals should submit to Athens without a fight (5.85-111), or when Nicias and Alcibiades argue the benefits and risks of the Sicilian expedition (6.9-6.23). Most employ antitheses (e.g., "in word but not in deed") in vocabulary and syntax as well as idea. Some characterize the speaker by sentence construction, vocabulary, or biographical reference.[81]   The arguments themselves are based primarily on probability and center on questions of safety, advantage and interest. The particular situation or issue is often clarified or the argument defended by reference to a general law about human nature. For example, when the Melians protest that the gods will protect them from this unjust conquest, the Athenians respond,

> "About the gods we have the opinion, and about men we know clearly that, by a necessity of their nature (*phuseos anagkaias*), wherever they have power, they rule. We did not make this law (*nomon*), nor were we the first to use it, but taking it up as we found it, we will continue to use it in the future, knowing that you and everybody else having our power would do the same (5.105.2).

The examination of nature (*physis*), its laws, and its relation to custom law and man-made legal enactments (all *nomos*) was especially topical during the war (see chapter 8). Thucydides has applied current ideas about nature and human nature to history and developed a theory, expressed both in speeches and in his own analysis, which uses certain universal laws of human nature to explain the particular events of the Peloponnesian War.[82]   The Corinthians (1.68-71) recognize that the innovative Athenians are only doing what is natural - "it is necessary . . . that the new always prevail" (1.71.3). In defending themselves (1.73-78), the Athenians also claim that they have only done "what is the common practice of mankind, having conquered, not to let it go for the three greatest reasons, glory, fear, and profit, . . . since it's always been the rule that the weaker be controlled by the more powerful" (1.76.2).

Individuals act according to the same universal principles as cities. After the death of Pericles, Thucydides asserts (2.65) that the leaders who followed made policy for their own self interest according to private ambition and greed, surrendering to the people's whims, and thus ended up conducting the war less successfully and causing dissension in the city. As he describes the course of the war, he analyzes the behavior of leaders like Cleon, Nicias, Alcibiades, Pisander, and Phrynichus responding to particular situations out of self-interest or fear, the strategies of oligarchic and democratic factions struggling for control, and the actions of the crowd behaving "as the crowd loves to do" (e.g., 4.28.3).

Because human beings use their intelligence for their own survival and advantage, growth and progress can occur. Thucydides judges Pericles the best leader of Athens, not only because he was incorruptible and could control the crowd for their own good, but also because he had the foresight to propose a strategy for a limited and victorious war with Sparta, if his successors had only stuck to it. But Pericles himself (1.140.1) recognizes that events often turn out contrary to plan, and that men are wont to blame them on chance (*tuche*). The plague was one such unexpected event, which brought incredible suffering. But the unexpected or irrational is a necessary concommitant of war itself.[83]   The Sicilian expedition is in many ways a paradigm for the entire war because, despite all the strategies and counter-strategies, the Athenians err and suffer a total and unexpected reversal (7.75.7). Demosthenes' night attack on Epipolae (7.42-46), a surprise to the Syracusans, dramatizes the unpredictability of war and the inability of human intelligence to control its course. (Even in the daylight, the historian notes, nobody really knows what's going on, except right near himself.) The Athenians themselves were so confused by the darkness that all their plans went awry.   In fact there was so much disorder and perplexity that the historian had difficulty learning what happened from either side (7.44). The Syracusans were emboldened by their unexpected success and regained the initiative in the war.

Unexpected or irrational elements introduced into a rational and civilized society can produce an unexpected effect on its citizens. The plague, for example, changes the Athenian character, for with death so close, the citizens pursued pleasures without limit, undeterred by either law or piety.   War, like the plague, also introduces the unexpected or irrational into human life and can overwhelm all the reasonable restraints that led to progress. As Thucydides himself comments after he has reported on the details of the Corcyrean revolution (which is paradigmatic of all the other violent civil wars between oligarchic and democratic factions that took place during the war),

> In peace and better circumstances, cities and private citizens have better inclinations because they have not fallen into dire necessity, but war, taking away easy supply of daily wants, is a harsh teacher and makes many men's temperaments equal to their circumstances (3.82.2).

In the preceding sentence and again at 3.83.2, the response is attributed to a universal law of human nature,

> When life was so confounded by the crisis in the city, human nature, always eager to do wrong and act contrary to law,

now took control over the law, delighting to reveal an
uncontrollable temperament, stronger than justice, hostile to
all superiority.

If human nature operates in an expected way, even in response to
the irrational and unexpected, then one may ask whether
Thucydides is describing a cyclic rather than a linear process.[84] In
his introduction, he states that he expects his book to be a useful
possession for all time for those who wish to understand the past as
a guide to the future since human nature will remain the same
(1.22.4).[85]   And almost every major point about a particular
probability in the speeches, as well as judgments in the analysis,
can be bolstered by a general statement about universal human
nature in similar circumstances.   Yet each particular is different,
and from the Archaeology on, each example of the universal
process rises in a different way, develops power and wealth which is
superior to its predecessors, and thus is able to launch a grander
expedition leading to an even grander catastrophe.   Although the
Athenians expect the Spartans to preserve their gains in similar
ways from similar motives (1.76.1), the Spartans are so different in
temperament, resources, and government, that the particulars in that
process cannot be precisely the same. Thucydides himself suggests
the relationship between the cyclic pattern and the linear particular
when he distinguishes the Corcyrean revolution from those that
occurred after it:

> So the cities were disturbed by stasis and those to whom it
> came latest, from their knowledge of earlier ones, brought
> even more excess to devising new strategies both in the
> ingenuity of their attacks and the extraordinary nature of their
> revenges (3.82.3).

The relationship between the universal human nature and the
particular political manifestation, with its resulting sense of
inevitability, resembles the double motivation of epic, tragedy, and
the *Histories* of Herodotus.   For Thucydides' perspective is
ultimately tragic.[86] He begins with the two Greek city-states at the
height of their power and resources, finding good in both, but partial
to Athens for its spirited leadership against Persia and its belief in
intelligence. War between them is inevitable because the growth of
political and military power has a dynamic of its own.   That his
lucid political analysis is also passionately moral is clear from his
description of the way civil war reduced every customary civic and
private virtue to its exact opposite (3.83.3-7).[87] And the Athenians

were subject not only to the vicissitudes of wars, but also to plague and the death of Pericles, who was able to restrain their hubris (2.65.9). The Athenian historian traces the loss of the concord, patriotism, and faith in reason, by which Pericles had defined the city's greatness, at the same time as he reports how new leaders abandon his strategy and produce the inevitable stasis because of their own ambition, greed, and ability to use rhetoric to manipulate the overconfident and equally ambitious and greedy populace.

Of course, history is more complex than tragedy and Thucydides has applied reasoned analysis to the tragic dynamic of power politics. Yet perhaps the lessons of these two fifth-century Athenians genres are similar. Thucydides never explains what he meant by calling his history a useful possession for all time. After tracing the development of ideas as events proceed, Connor concludes that the *Histories* teaches not how to predict the future or control events, but rather the complexity of events and the consequent vulnerability of civilization and order; "it reminds us how easily men move from the illusion of control over events to being controlled by them - from action to *pathos*."[88]   Yet, as Hermocrates suggests at Gela (4.62), human beings, although unable to foresee all contingencies, must use their forethought in order to survive. Thus the tragic paradox of rational human beings, who push their most godlike but ultimately insufficient quality to its limits, is implicit in Thucydides' record of how the Peloponnesian War really was.

Later Greek Historiography: Xenophon to Polybius

In the next century, history and its related forms became a very popular branch of Greek literature.[89]   Scholars know of hundreds of authors, most of whose works survive only in brief references or quotes by other authors who use, criticize, and correct them in their own writings.[90]   From these sources, it is clear that Herodotus and Thucydides set standards for style and content, but that other older forms continued to develop and new forms evolved to satisfy new interests. Historians also became even more self-conscious about history as a genre than their pioneering predecessors, offering opinions about method, arguing about style, and making more explicit statements on the usefulness and moral purpose of history. They were influenced by the theory and practice of the rhetoricians, the professional teachers, writers, and orators of the fourth century and later, as well as by the professional philosophers, such as Plato and Aristotle, who not only examined the issues raised by the rise and fall of Athens, but also speculated about the origin of the state, its function, types of constitutions, reasons for changes in government, and the best way for the state to produce the best citizens.

Several of the older forms, such as geography, ethnology and chronology, continued to flourish or to be incorporated into the historical record going right up to contemporary events. Ctesias of Cnidus, a physician in the court of Artaxerxes II, wrote, among other works, a much read *Persica* as a supplement or correction to Herodotus.[91] Local chronicles, which recorded the major events of one city year by year from an early period to the author's own day, were very popular. Several such *Atthides*, modeled on the *Atthis* of Hellanicus, were written between 400 and 263 by individual Athenians.[92] Timaeus of Tauromenium (356-260), while in exile in Athens, wrote a history of Sicily from the beginning to the First Punic War, imitating the more severe style of Thucydides.[93] Ephorus (405-330) produced not only a local history of his native Cyme, but also a "universal history" which covered the cities of Greece and Asia Minor from the Return of the Heraclidae to 341 B.C.E. and included mythology, aetiology, geography and ethnology as well as political and military events.

New forms were also developed in the fourth century as a response to changing circumstances. The professionalization of various areas of endeavor gave rise not only to treatises on particular skills and their history, but also to biographies of founders or great exemplars.[94] Perhaps Xenophon's and Plato's love for Socrates began the trend toward preserving the life and teachings of the masters of the major schools of philosophy, e.g., Epicurus. But history itself can also explain the new interest in biography. As it became clear that monarchies would replace the communities of citizens as makers of great events, the personalities and motives of powerful individuals assumed even greater importance. Theopompus (b. 378) organized a fifty-eight book history around the career of Philip II of Macedon, starting with his accession, whereas Alexander the Great's contemporaries, Clitarchus, Ptolemy, and Callisthenes began the long list of his biographers, some of whom (e.g., Nearchus, Megasthenes) incorporated the romantic and fantastic elements present in oriental narrative.

Autobiography too became an important literary form, deriving its impetus from the growing emphasis on the individual's life as well as from rhetorical forms such as courtroom apologia. Philosophical speculation on types government produced both histories or descriptions of constitutions, e.g., the Aristotelian *Constitution of*

Athens, and utopias like Plato's *Republic*. A selected list of the writings of Xenophon of Athens indicates how broad the scope of history-related topics became: The *Anabasis*, an autobiographical account of his expedition into Persia as a mercenary for Cyrus the Younger; The *Cyropaideia*, an idealized, romantic, and utopian biography of Cyrus the Elder, which contains detailed instructions for military leaders; *The Constitution of the Spartans* (a *Constitution of the Athenians* was also ascribed to him); *Agesilaus*, a laudatory biography of the Spartan king who died in 360; and *Memorabilia*, a collection of memoirs about Socrates, as well as his version of Socrates' self-defense.

Xenophon of Athens (c.430-354) was also a historian in the Thucydidean sense of the word.[95] In fact, he (like the Oxyrhynchus Historian and Theopompus) began his *Hellenica* in 411 where the *Histories* broke off, opening with the statement, "after these things," as if it were a conscious continuation. Not only did he use Thucydides' annalistic organization to describe the rest of the war, but he also imitated his severe style and limited the subject matter to military and political events, saving different topics and more fictional embellishments for his other works. Like Thucydides, he included speeches and analyses of character and motives, as well as dramatic presentations of significant or paradigmatic events, e.g., the trials after the battle of Arginusai. Having been a professional soldier himself, he provided detailed information on such matters as discipline, weaponry, and troop organization. Because he was exiled from Athens after his service in Persia, he was able do *historie* in several places and get various perspectives. Although his other writings indicate great appreciation for Sparta, where he spent much of his adult life, his *Hellenica* is a generally objective account of the military and political events of Greece from 411 to 362.

Xenophon is not considered as astute a historian as either of his great predecessors, but it is clear that he absorbed their lessons about the pattern of events and their causes and applied them to the history of his own times.[96] As he traces politics and war from the fall of Athens through the hegemony of Sparta to its fall at the battle of Mantinea, he shows the continuation of the very elements - imperialism leading to tyranny; greed and ambition of individual leaders and rival cities causing factionalism at home and battles with neighbors - which led to the fall of Athens. Again there is the emphasis on the unexpected, the bad luck which confounds good plans, as well as the tragic awareness that the unexpected might have been avoided if leaders and cities had not been overconfident or blinded by their passions. Just as the particular events proceed as a series of unexpected reversals, so the entire account reveals the same general pattern. As Higgins points out, Xenophon underlines the joy with which Peloponnesian War ended in 404, when "everyone thought this day was the beginning of freedom for Greece (2.2.23)," only to comment after the battle to Mantinea in 362 :

> When these things were done, what had happened was just the opposite of what all men expected to happen . . . . Both side claimed the victory, but neither was any better off . . . before than after the battle. In fact, there was even more disorder and confusion in Greece afterwards than before (7.5.26-27).[97]

The fact that he ends the *Hellenica* here with the words, "Let this be written by me up to this point. What happens after will perhaps be a concern to someone else," suggests that he had a unified conception of the whole period and that he expected more events worthy of preservation and examination in the future.

Xenophon's traditional piety, so clear from his other works, permits him to suggest divine causation, in the Hebrew or Herodotean manner, for the course of the human events he has witnessed. At 5.4.1, he asserts

> One could list many examples from Greek and foreign history to show that the gods are not indifferent to irreligion or to evil doing. Here I shall mention only the case which occurs at this point in my narrative.

He summarizes the events he is about to report in detail according to the principles of the doctrine of reciprocity. The Spartans who had sworn they would be the liberators of Greece and then seized the Acropolis of Thebes were punished by the very men they had wronged. The Thebans who had brought in the Spartans for their own advantage were then driven out in turn by a few exiles. Like epic, tragedy, and Herodotus, Xenophon ascribes to the gods certain things which are otherwise inexplicable, such as extraordinary courage, folly, and weather. He also credits the gods with what Thucydides might call a universal law of human nature. "Perhaps god has arranged that the arrogant thoughts of men increase with their power," says a speaker warning against the growth of Olynthus (5.2.18).

But, if Xenophon describes the follies of men corrupted by the quest or attainment of power, he also suggests positive ways to avoid catastrophe. After the expulsion of the Thirty Tyrants, Thrasyboulos urges the Athenians, with the words of Delphi, to "know themselves," to recognize their limitations and faults, and be true to their sworn amnesty agreement, pointing out that adherence to their own laws would preserve their peace, order, and freedom (2.4.40-41). Higgins considers Xenophon's statement that the people stood by their oaths and still live together as fellow-citizens in his own day a proud confirmation of the rule of law in Athens.[98] Higgins also believes that Callistratus is expressing Xenophon's own ideas when he explicitly urges Athens and Sparta to learn from past mistakes "that self-aggrandizement is profitless and therefore be moderate in their friendship with one another (6.3.11)."[99]   The *Hellenica* as a whole, however, like Thucydides' *Histories*, emphasizes the both the futility and inevitability of power politics.

Xenophon is credited with being the first Greek historian to make an explicit statement about the usefulness of history.[100] At 5.1.4., he defends himself for pausing to describe the glorious homecoming of Teleutias, which does not concern resources, danger, or skill; he asserts that it is more important to consider how the Spartan commander had behaved which made his troops respect him so much. After Teleutias has been killed in an unsuccessful charge he ordered while enraged, the historian pauses to point out the moral:

> I say that from such disasters men learn that one must not punish even household slaves in anger. . . . Anger does not look ahead, whereas judgment thinks about avoiding harm oneself no less than inflicting it on the enemy (5.3.7).

Complementing, and perhaps influenced by, both philosophy's new emphasis on ethics and professionalized rhetoric's development of praise and blame as literary forms, history, from the fourth century on, had a clearly-stated moral and educative purpose. And historians, having chosen important subjects and imitated their well-respected predecessors, gave themselves the right to enunciate these lessons in their own voice. Philistius of Syracuse, as well as Xenophon, included specific praise and blame, but it was Ephorus, the pupil of the rhetorician Isocrates, who made such critical appraisals a part of history writing per se. Scholars believe he chose and manipulated his material in order to encourage virtue; to him is attributed the statement "history is philosophy by paradigm."[101]

The methods of history also changed as the list of practitioners grew. Although Herodotus and Thucydides depended on their own *historie* and judgment of oral sources, later historians had a whole series of written histories which they could cull for facts and materials.[102] Some, like Xenophon, Timaeus, and Polybius, clearly combined their own eyewitness and investigation of hearsay with their reading, but others became more like armchair historians, researching texts rather than places and people to get information on the past. To justify going over previously recorded subjects, many criticized their predecessors' facts or interpretations even as they used their material. Others wrote compilations of data gleaned from earlier histories or epitomes of popular works. Theopompus, for example, summarized Herodotus in two books and later his own work was epitomized in turn.

History, as a branch of literature, maintained its stylistic connections with rhetoric and poetry.[103] In fact, once rhetoric became professionalized, many potential historians were educated in the ways of producing clear and persuasive narrative as well as appraising character and motive. But some historians were criticized for striving to provide pleasure and arouse emotion at the expense of truth and seriousness. They were referred to as 'tragic' historians because they exploited the dramatic potential of such incidents as the deaths of notable men, cities being conquered, and battle scenes. Duris of Samos (c.340-260), for example, not only included subjects covered by Herodotus and overdone by Ctesias— anecdotes, portents, marvels, scandals—but also, according to Plutarch (*Pericles* 28), magnified the events of the conquest of Samos "into a tragedy," providing grim, and false, details of crucifixions and heads beaten in.

Although Polybius recognizes the mimetic purpose ascribed above to both Herodotus and Thucydides—"trying to bring things before the readers' eyes,"—he objects to the later emphasis on horror and catastrophe, calling it not only "ignoble and womanish ," but also "not proper and useful to history." His judgment of Phylarchus of Athens leads him to an analysis of the differences between history and poetry:

> A historical author should not try to thrill his readers by such exaggerated pictures, nor should he, like a tragic poet, try to imagine the probable utterances of his characters or reckon up all the consequences probably incidental to the occurrences with which he deals, but simply record what really happened and what really was said, however commonplace. For the object of tragedy is not the same as that of history . . . it is the task of the historian to instruct and to convince . . . serious students by the truth of the facts and the speeches (2.56.10-12)

He adds that because Phylarchus simply describes catastrophes without suggesting their causes or nature, he doesn't even arouse emotion properly. For it is impossible for readers to judge an act as good or evil unless they know the reasons and purposes of the doer. Polybius' criticism of Phylarchus reveals how self-conscious serious practitioners have become about defining history by its emphasis on truth and accuracy above all, its connection of what really happened with an explanation of why it happened, and its educative purpose.[104]

Like earlier historians of contemporary events, Polybius lived in interesting times.[105] A Megalopolite active in the Achaean League who was deported to Rome after the Greek defeat at Pydna in 168, he became a friend of Scipio Aemilianus and even accompanied him on campaigns to Spain and Africa. After the Romans destroyed Corinth, he participated in the settlement of Greece. Although he wrote a panegyric on Philopoemon, a book on military strategy, and an account of the Numantine War, he is best remembered for his *Histories* which he must have worked on during most of his life among the Romans.

As a military leader and politician himself and an eyewitness to Roman councils and wars, he is adamantly opposed to those historians who simply do research with texts and documents, or even from autopsy and oral informants, without ever having had any practical experience in military and political affairs.[106] Not only is such a historian bound to misunderstand his sources, but he is also very likely to ask the wrong questions because he won't know what's important. Only pragmatic knowledge of a subject will enable the historian to ascertain the true facts and comprehend their causes (e.g., 12.28).

Like his model Thucydides, Polybius recognized early in his career that something momentous was occurring.[107] He also realized that its magnitude required an expansion of the definition of history. As he states in his preface (1.3-4), before the 140th Olympiad (220), there had never been a unity of initiative, results, or place, but afterwards particular events in Italy, Libya, Europe, and Asia have all been connected, leading up to only one end, Rome's conquest of nearly the entire world. Since history has become an organic whole, he can no longer write a monograph on a single action or place, but must write a universal history which studies all the interconnections of events in order to understand the whole.[108]

His subject is no less than the rise of Rome, how and with what system of government it succeeded in overpowering nearly the whole inhabited world and putting it all under one Roman rule, something which had never been accomplished before (1.1.5). Aware of the complexity of his *Histories*, he provides his readers with a table of contents at 1.5-6, with background information, and again 3.1-5, with a brief summary of the remaining books. Often he begins a book with a brief precis of what just preceded and an introduction to what will follow. He also dates his material by the universal Greek system according to Olympiads as well as by using major events in different places as reference points.

He is so careful to facilitate understanding because he believes what he has to say is so important.[109] History is not simply a matter of recording successes and failures so that readers can assign praise or blame (3.34), although praise and blame are important and must be distributed impartially, truthfully, and with evidence to support judgments (10.21.8). History's pragmatic value is more important, however, for those who study history are able, in a systematic way to handle anything that happens (9.2.5). Not only do the reversals of others teach one how to bear changes of fortune (*tuches*) bravely (1.1.2), but the written record of events can sometimes prevent readers from repeating the same mistakes (e.g., 38.4.8). The practical lessons drawn from his record of events cover such topics as the best methods of fire-signaling (10.43-7), the proper preparation for attack (5.98), a condemnation of Mantinean treachery (2.5), and approval of Philip's clemency and moderation to Athens which gained him their cooperation instead of their hostility (5.9).

Indeed, according to De Romilly, Polybius considers such moderate behavior a major lesson of the *Histories*; he attributes Rome's rise to their early benevolence, a "practical opportunism" which led them, unlike the Greeks, to give a share in Roman power to subjects who could help them, and which produced goodwill between rulers and ruled.[110] Throughout he praises good leaders and rational strategies while calling attention to irrational policies or ideas driven by foolish passions. He devotes all of book 6 to political theory, with a specific study of the Roman constitution and military system in their prime, and a comparison with the Greek and Carthaginian systems because

> The greatest cause of success (*epituchian*) or its opposite in every matter is the constitution of the state, for from this fountain all plans and actions not only come forth, but also reach their consummation. (6.2.9-10).

Like his greatest predecessors, Polybius is deeply concerned with the cause of events, for it is only by adding cause to the statement of fact that "the practice of history becomes fruitful" (12..25b.2).[111] Elaborating on Thucydides' distinction of the pretext from the real reason (1.23.6), Polybius, at 3.6.6., separates out the beginning, i.e., the first attempt to execute a action, from the judgments and opinions, reasoning processes, and all the factors internal and external that contribute to a decision and plan. As an example, he analyses the reasons for Alexander's expedition against Persia, going back to Philip's perceptions of Persian weakness and wealth and the pretexts of Persian lawlessness Philip used to secure the goodwill of the Greeks. The fact that Alexander actually started the war by crossing into Asia was the least important level of explanation.

The example only suggests the complexity of the elements he analyzes as he records Rome's growth during the period he is covering: the military and political conditions of each participant; the state of mind and the character of groups and leaders; the intelligence of the plans themselves; and the immediate circumstances, psychological, geographical, and natural, which contribute to the action and its result. Understanding the cause of the things that happen demands such detailed scrutiny because "the greatest affairs often grow out of trifles and it is easiest to remedy the first conceptions and opinions" (3.6.7).

Such statements make clear that human beings have choices and therefore some control over the course of human events.[112] At 10.2, he exalts strategists over lucky leaders (*epituche*), using Lycurgus and Scipio as examples of men who made their own success by manipulating traditional religious ideas to obtain the support. Polybius acknowledges the social and political value of belief and practice among the masses (e.g., 6.56; 10.2.9-12), but he does not ascribe to the gods or chance things that men cause and can remedy by themselves, like the low birthrate discussed in 34.17.5-10.

Of course, Polybius knows that everything that happens cannot be attributed to human action. Some things are so inexplicable or random that they must be ascribed, if not to the will of the gods, at least to something superhuman. By the time of Polybius, chance or fortune (*tuche*), referred to by earlier historians as the unexpected element in human affairs, had achieved new stature as a philosophical and religious concept and was even personified as a goddess. Tuche represented the instability of good or bad fortune, which, in always moving from one person or place to the next, could account for the vicissitudes of history, while offering some reassurance that metaphysical order existed, even if it was beyond human comprehension. Thus, Tuche was useful to tragic historians like Duris and Phylarchus as a kind of *dea ex machina*. Polybius himself quoted from Demetrius of Phalerum's treatise on Tuche when reflecting on the fall of Macedon after it had destroyed Persia.

> Fortune, bound by no covenant with us in respect to our lives, always introducing new things beyond our calculation, demonstrating her power by things contrary to expectation (29.21.5).

Polybius employs fortune or related supernatural ideas as a historical cause in a variety of ways.[113] At 36.17.2, he says the action of god or chance (*tuchen*) may be used when the reason for things is impossible or difficult for man to understand, such as an extraordinary weather or disease. Although most human affairs have a human explanation, sometimes such irrational things happen that the reporter may say the event was heaven-sent and that madness from the gods had entered into the participants (36.17.15). In some places, Polybius sees Tuche operating to punish injustice according to the doctrine of reciprocity. At 15.20, for example, after describing the impiety, savagery, and greed of Philip and Antiochus against the infant son of Ptolemy, the historian points out that in this instance Tuche exacted from them the appropriate penalty and made them an example for future kings (v. 31.9.4; 32.15.4). At 29.27.12, he implies that Tuche can also be provident, having directed the affairs of Perseus and the Macedonians so that Egypt was saved.

In his introduction to the *Histories*, Polybius suggests that Tuche has had a goal or *telos* in the general course of events, directing all things toward one and the same aim (1.4.1), Roman hegemony. At 1.5.3, he calls this the most beneficent and beautiful activity of Tuche, who is always inventing new things and playing a role in the lives of men, but has never before accomplished so great a deed. This dramatic and rhetorical presentation justifies his composing a universal history (as well as perhaps his country's commitment to Rome in the Fourth Macedonian War). But the *Histories* does not demonstrate the overpowering role of fortune so much as it shows wise leaders of a stable government and brave generals of a courageous, well-organized army defeating lesser men and communities. Walbank suggests that the Rome's remarkable rise to world power led Polybius "to confuse what had happened with what was destined to happen and so to invest [it] with a teleological character." [114]

If the vicissitudes of history are so astounding that they bring to mind the mutability of fortune (e.g., 29.21, as power passes from Macedon to Rome and 38.21.3 as Scipio destroys Carthage), the shifts in power themselves follow a predictable pattern.[115] According to Polybius, who was present, Scipio quoted Hector's verses predicting that "sacred Ilion shall perish," as he viewed the ruins of Carthage, realizing that all the previous great empires had met their doom and fearing for his own country as well (38.22). The wanton destruction of Carthage in the Third Punic War may have suggested to Polybius that Scipio's fear was justified. For book six, in which Polybius praises Rome's constitution, also contains a general political theory which Polybius terms the "cycle of constitutions" (6.10.1.); states evolve according to nature, naturally develop from one form of government to the next until degenerating into mob rule and savagery which begin this process again (6.3-9).[116]	But the decline itself does not come about by chance; citizens in prosperous states bring it on themselves because they begin to fight with each other for more than their share of money, honor, and power (6.57).

The pragmatic historian makes clear that anyone who understands this will recognize the stage of growth or decline in any state (6.9.11; 6.57.4); Rome, having reached its acme, will have a change to the opposite in the future. The fragments of book 36, as well as other historians' accounts, suggest that the razing of Carthage manifested the signs of internal decay. For Polybius reports that some Greeks recognized in the Roman severity the same lust for domination that had afflicted Athens and Sparta, while others were surprised by the Roman deceit and fraud, more characteristic of a tyrant than a civilized state (36. 5.11).[117]

Notes

1.   For an examination of the use of the word, see F. Muller, *"De historiae vocabulo atque notione,"* *Mnemosyne* 56 (1926): 234-257. For a summary of its early uses as inquiry or investigation, see also Robert Drews, *The Greek Accounts of Eastern History* (Washington: Center for Hellenic Studies, 1973), pp. 14-15; Charles William Fornara, *The Nature of History in Ancient Greece and Rome* (Berkeley: University of California Press, 1983), pp. 47-51; and Alan B. Lloyd, *Herodotus Book II: Introduction* (Leiden: E. J. Brill, 1975), pp. 81-84. Two of the greatest recent scholars of Greek history and historiography have written, in addition to numerous articles and books on individual topics and authors, brief surveys to which I am particularly indebted for ideas and general information: Arnaldo Momigliano, "Greek Historiography," *History and Theory* 17 (1978): 1-28; and Henry Immerwahr, "Historiography," in *The Cambridge History of Classical Literature. 1* (Cambridge: Cambridge University Press, 1982), pp. 426-471.

2.   Taken from Clement of Alexandria, *Strom.* 1.15.69, as quoted and translated by Drews, p. 14.

3.   For the influence of poetry on history and the relation between the two, see John Finley, *Three Essays on Thucydides* (Cambridge: Harvard University Press, 1967); A. W. Gomme, *The Greek Attitude to Poetry and History* (Berkeley: University of California Press, 1954); and F. W. Walbank, "History and Tragedy," *Historia* 9 (1960): 216-234. Convenient summaries of relations appear in Fornara, *Nature*, pp. 31-31, 76-79, 96-97 and K. H. Waters, *Herodotus the Historian: His Problems, Methods and Originality* (London: Croom Helm, 1985), pp. 61-67.

4.   Henry Immerwahr, *"Ergon*: History as a Monument in Herodotus and Thucydides," *American Journal of Philology* 81 (1960): 261-290; Gregory Nagy, "Herodotus the *Logios,"* *Arethusa* 20 (1987) : 175-184; as well as Gomme, p. 78.

5.   Drews, p.19.

6.   Several scholars have analyzed particular sections to show how carefully Herodotus and Thucydides have selected and structured their material to elucidate a process in history which is essentially tragic. See, for example, F. M. Cornford, *Thucydides Mythistoricus* (London: Edward Arnold, 1907); Finley, *op. cit.*; Charles Willian Fornara, *Herodotus: An Interpretive Essay* (Oxford: Clarendon Press, 1971); Virginia Hunter, *Past and Process in Herodotus and Thucydides* (Princeton: Princeton University Press, 1982); Henry Immerwahr, "Historical Action in Herodotus," *Transactions and Proceedings of the American Philological Association* 85 (1954): 16-45 as well as his *Form and Thought in Herodotus.* APA Monograph 23 (Cleveland: Western Reserve University Press, 1982). For a summary, see Fornara, *Nature*, pp. 171-172.

7.   P. 21. Later Greek historians also objected to too much artistry at the expense of the truth.

8.   See Walbank, "History" and B. L. Ullman, "History and Tragedy," *Transactions and Proceedings of the American Philological Association* 73 (1942): 30-53, as well as the discussion of Polybius' historiography below.

9.   "Historical Action," p.30, after an analysis which begins on p.23.

10.   Fornara, *Nature*, pp. 1-29, defines the types of writing related to but different from 'history,' with examples.

11.   For a detailed study of both, with many fragments quoted, see respective chapters in Lionel Pearson, *Early Ionian Historians* (Oxford: Clarendon Press, 1939), from which most of the following information has been taken.

12.   Lloyd, pp. 127-129, examines the value of Hecataeus as a source, particularly for Book 2.

13.   Drews, pp. 11-19, argues against the position that Hecataeus was the true father of history, providing bibliography, but acknowledges the importance of his "diminishing the deeds of heroes," p.19.

14.   Chester Starr, *The Awakening of the Greek Historical Spirit* (New York: Knopf, 1968), p. 115.

15.   P. 43.

16.   "Herodotus and His Profession," *American Historical Review* 59 (1954): 830.

17.   Pp. 95-96. See as well his interesting chapter on the earliest Greek accounts, pp. 20-44, and his detailed analysis of Herodotus' presentation of eastern history to argue his point about the 'great event,' pp. 45-96.

18.   As argued in *Herodotus*.

19.   Many scholars have explained the invention of history as the result of the intellectual development of Herodotus, e.g., from geographer to ethnographer according to F. Jacoby, "Herodotus," *RE*, Suppl. 2 (Stuttgart, 1913): 205-520 and K. Von Fritz, "Herodotus and the Growth of Greek Historiography," *Transactions and Proceedings of the American Philological Society* 67 (1936): 315-340. This question requires an examination of the unity of the *Histories* and a reconstruction of how, when, and why Herodotus put the results of so many different kinds of inquiry into one book. For bibliographies and summaries of the various positions, see Fornara, *Herodotus*, pp. 1-23 and Hunter, appendix to chapter two, pp. 304-313.

20.   P. 90.

21.   In addition to works cited earlier, there are several other important studies of the *Histories*: S. Benerdete, *Herodotean Inquiries* (The Hague: Nijhoof, 1969); W. W. How and J. A. Wells, *A Commentary on Herodotus*. Two Volumes (Oxford: Clarendon Press, 1928); R. W. Macon, *Herodotus: The Fourth, Fifth, and Sixth Books* (London: Macmillan, 1895); and *The Seventh, Eighth, Ninth Books*. Two Volumes, 1908; Sir J. L. Myres, *Herodotus. The Father of History* (Oxford: Clarendon Press, 1953); J. E. Powell, *A Lexicon to Herodotus* (Cambridge: Cambridge University Press, 1938) and "*The History*" *of Herodotus*. Cambridge Classical Studies 4 (Cambridge: Cambridge University Press, 1939); as well as the collection of essays edited by D. Boedeker, *Herodotus and the Invention of History* in

Arethusa 20, 1 & 2 (1987), which contains a survey of the major scholarship. Waters includes an excellent bibliography arranged by topics.

22. Lloyd, *Introduction*, pp. 76-140, contains a detailed study of the sources for book 2 as well as many comments on his use of sources in general. See also O. Murray, "Herodotus and Oral History," in H. W. Am. Sansisi- Weerdenburg and A. Kuhrt (eds.), *Aechmenid History II: The Greek Sources* (Leiden: Nederlands Instituut voor Nabije Oosten, 1987), pp. 96 -115 for sources about the east; Rosalind Thomas, *Oral Tradition and Written Record in Classical Athens* (Cambridge: Cambridge University Press, 1989) for Athenian family traditions and the effects of writing on them; and S. West, "Herodotus' Epigraphical Interests," *Classical Quarterly* 35 (1985): 278-305.

23. It is possible that Herodotus himself was such a *logios* and gave public recitations of parts of the *Histories*. See Nagy, as well as Hunter, pp. 324 -325.

24. This phenomenon is studied in detail in two articles in the *Arethusa* 20 collection: Carolyn Dewald, "Narrative Surface and Authorial Voice in Herodotus' *Histories*," pp. 147-170, and John Marincola, "Herodotean Narrative and the Narrator's Presence," pp. 121-137. It must be noted, however, that some scholars, following Detlev Fehling, *Herodotus and His Sources: Citation, Invention and Narrative Art*, trans. J. G. Howie (Leeds: Francis Cairns, 1989), believe that Herodotus invented the persona and the sources in order to add credibility to his fictionalized narrative of events. See the refutation by Dewald and Marincola, pp. 26-32, as well as John Van Seters' summary and conclusions about the literary techniques and conventions of ancient historiography, pp. 43-51, in *In Search of History: Historiography in the Ancient World and the Origins of Biblical History* (New Haven: Yale University Press, 1983).

25. Dewald, pp. 154-163.

26. Quoted from *Introduction*, p. 163. Many critics discuss his intellectual debt to earlier philosophers and his methods of assessing his materials, e.g., Dewald, p. 162 and Hunter, pp. 59-65, 107-115, but Lloyd's chapter on his attitudes and intellectual affinities, esp. pp. 160-170, provides numerous examples, while his commentaries in the next two volumes analyze the arguments marshaled at specific passages.

27. Lloyd, *Introduction*, pp. 147-149.

28. Volume 2, p. 251, after detailed commentary on the section.

29. *Arethusa* 20, p. 173, in response to Dewald's article in which she compares Herodotus to a Homeric warrior describing his own heroic battle to find the truths hidden within a collection of *logoi* full of biases, falsehoods, and problems.

30. There are many problems related to Herodotus' reckoning by generations and coordination of the various lists he knew. See F. Mitchel, "Herodotus' Use of Genealogical Chronology," *Phoenix* 10 (1956): 48-69 and D. W. Prakken, *Studies in Greek Genealogical Chronology* (Lancaster, PA: Lancaster Press, 1943), as well as excellent summaries of problems and bibliography in Lloyd, *Introduction*, pp. 170-194 and Hunter, esp. pp.

253-257 and 331-332, within a study which analyzes chronology in relation to processes in history, and rationality as the intellectual tool for uncovering them.

31.   C. Meier, "Historical Answers to Historical Questions: The Origins of History in Ancient Greece," *Arethusa* 20 (1987): 41-57. The words quoted appear on p. 44.

32.   P. 48.

33.   Pp. 51 and esp. 56.

34.   P. 57. See above chapters two through four for our explication of this point in relation to creation, the origin of evil, and the moral order.

35.   A. Cook, "Herodotus: The Act of Inquiry as a Liberation from Myth," *Helios* 3 (1976), p. 35. Cook develops ideas from Myres and Benerdete to describe the "network" in order to explicate Herodotus' "liberation." Analogy in itself is a major method of reasoning in this period. See G. R. E. Lloyd, *Polarity and Analogy: Two Types of Argumentation in Early Greek Thought* (Cambridge: Cambridge University Press, 1966), as well as Hunter's discussion on pp. 112-113, 258-261, 323-324.

36.   D. Konstan analyzes the artistry with which Herodotus develops these contrasts through type-scenes in "Persians, Greeks, and Empires," in *Arethusa* 20 (1987): 59-73.

37.   D. Boedeker, "The Two Faces of Demaratus," *Arethusa* 20 (1987): 185-201, analyzes the way Herodotus develops the character of Demaratus in Sparta and in Persia, by analogy with other Greek exiles, to highlight contrasts and explore important issues "by suggestion and juxtaposition," p. 201. M. Lang responds on the following page that Herodotus treats other important characters in a similar way for similar reasons.

38.   R. Lattimore, "The Wise Advisor in Herodotus," *Classical Philology* 34 (1939): 24-35, studies this device and its effects in detail.

39.   See Immerwahr's analysis of the differences in meaning between *aitie* and *prophasis* and bibliography on the question in "Aspects of Historical Causation in Herodotus," *Transactions and Proceedings of the American Philological Association* 87 (1956): 242-247.

40.   As Cook concludes, p.61, after discussing the divine element in the *Histories*. He provides a good summary of the use of oracles and dreams and divine causation in general, pp. 57-62.

41.   Immerwahr in particular, in his articles and book, analyzes this complexity and the artistry by which it unfolds. In addition to more general works cited above, see also R. Sealy, "Herodotus and the Causes of War," *Classical Quarterly* 5 (1957): 1-12 and J. de Romilly, "La vengeance comme explication historique dans l'oevre d'Herodote," *Revue des Etudes Grecques* 84 (1971): 314-337, as well as her *The Rise and Fall of States according to Greek Authors* (Ann Arbor: University of Michigan Press, 1977).

42.   Sealy, pp. 4-7.

43.   de Romilly, "La vengeance," esp. pp. 317-323 and Immerwahr,"Aspects," p. 253.

44.   See Immerwahr, "Aspects," pp. 273-276, for analysis of 7.1-18.

45. Many scholars, such as Immerwahr, de Romilly, *Rise and Fall*, and Hunter, are very concerned with the pattern, which Hunter calls 'process', and its relation to causation in particular incidents. They deny, however, that pattern or process implies a cyclical rather than a linear perception. They point out that the time span covered by Greek historians (generally less than one hundred years) is in fact too short to be considered a cycle.

46. Immerwahr, "Aspects," pp. 249-250, and 262 with notes, as well as Meier (see notes 31 and 32).

47. See Lattimore, as well as Immerwahr, "Historical Action," pp. 38-45.

48. Cook, pp. 41-42, analyzes the way Herodotus uses the 'cautionary tale' to relate fact to explanation.

49. Immerwahr, "Aspects." pp. 254 ff., analyzes the scene in detail to illustrate the introduction of complex causation and pattern stories to come in the *Histories*. Waters, pp. 71-74, discusses other examples of 'deliberate structuring' and reasons for them.

50. Konstan contrasts the valor which is a 'state of mind' or 'interiority' with the Persian 'exteriority' symbolized by their materialism and tendency to quantify.

51. In addition to Fornara, *Herodotus*, see Kurt Raaflaub, "Herodotus, Political Thought and the Meaning of History," *Arethusa* 20 (1987): 221-248. I have taken examples cited from this article.

52. Raaflaub, pp. 224-248. De Romilly, Hunter, and others also note the terms used for expansion throughout both Herodotus and Thucydides.

53. *Herodotus*, p. 80.

54. Raaflaub, pp. 233-238.

55. In addition to Cornford, Hunter, Finley, and de Romilly, there are many studies of Thucydides, e.g.: Charles Norriss Cochrane, *Thucydides and the Science of History* (New York: Russell & Russell, 1965); W. Robert Connor, *Thucydides* (Princeton: Princeton University Press, 1984); Lowell Edmonds, *Chance and Intelligence in Thucydides* (Cambridge: Harvard University Press, 1975); Peter Pouncey, *The Necessities of War: The Pessimism of Thucydides* (Oxford: Basil Blackwell, 1980); H. R. Rawlings, *The Structure of Thucydides' History* (Princeton: Princeton University Press, 1981); Jacqueline de Romilly, *Histoire et Raison chez Thucydide* (Paris: Les Belles Lettres, 1956) and *Thucydides and Athenian Imperialism,* P. Thody, trans. (Oxford: Basil Blackwell, 1963); A. G. Woodhead, *Thucydides on the Nature of Power* (Cambridge: Harvard University Press, 1970); as well as E. A. Betant, *Lexicon Thucydideum*. Two Volumes, (1843-1847; reprint, Hildesheim: G. Olms, 1961) and A. W. Gomme, rev. & compl. by A. Andrewes and K. J. Dover, *A Historical Commentary on Thucydides* (Oxford: Clarendon Press, 1945-1981).

56. P. 12.

57. Borimir Jordan, "Religion in Thucydides," *Transactions and Proceedings of the American Philological Association* 116 (1986): 119-147 provides bibliography on those scholars who consider Thuccydides either disinterested in religion or an atheist, and marshals evidence to suggest

instead that Thucydides went out of his way to do research on religion and describe its effect on events. I have summarized his conclusions.

58.   P. 147.

59.   P. 98. Drews emphasizes that this was the only direction real *historie* could take, since the historians "were not custodians of the past," p. 96. See also p. 138.

60.   See Hunter's appendix, pp. 299-301, for bibliography on the Archaeology, with special reference to de Romilly's *Histoire*, as well as Hunter's own analysis and notes, pp. 17-43, where she is particularly concerned with his method of dealing with the past, in contrast to Herodotus'. See also pp. 32-39, 105-107, and n. 12, where she notes connections with earlier theories and provides bibliography. Connor, pp. 20-32, also discusses contemporary influences on ideas and method.

61.   In addition to Hunter, see A. Parry, "Thucydides' Historical Perspective," *Yale Classical Studies* 22 (1972): 47-61. Parry's analysis of Thucydides' diction, particularly *ergon* (deed) and *logos* (word or thought), leads him to conclude that Thucydides views civilization as the "successful imposition of intelligence on the brute matter of the outside world," p. 59, and "history as man's constant attempt to order the world about him by his intelligence," p. 57.

62.   As with Herodotus, so with Thucydides, much attention has been devoted to the historian's intellectual development, the question of when he wrote which portions, and the all important issue of the unity of his *Histories*. See de Romilly, *Thucydides*, pp. 3-10 for a summary of the problems and bibliography, and 370 -372 for her own response to new directions in scholarship twenty years later. See also Connor's introduction, pp. 3-19 and conclusion, 231-250, where he discusses the impact of new criticism and reader response theory on the questions of the author and the unity of the text.

63.   Connor, pp. 27-29, shows how Thucydides has separated his work from the inspiration of poetry and prophecy as well as from the early historians and speechwriters, while stylistically proclaiming his rhetorical and even poetic abilities. Lionel Pearson, "Thucydides as Reporter and Critic," *Transactions and Proceedings of the American Philological Association* 83 (1947): 37-60, discusses the passage, particularly the contrast between *erga* and *logoi*, and analyzes the way in which Thucydides actually proceeds from the Archeology on.

64.   "Thucydides," p. 59.

65.   "Thucydides," p. 60. He also notes that Thucydides' "willingness to do so distinguishes him from inferior later historians who substituted moralizing for the critical expression of opinion."

66.   P. 114, after analyzing the methods of both historians in relation to pre-Socratic philosophy to show that their use of logic and argumentation, and Thucydides' 'world picture' match the definition of scientific practice and 'rationality' posited by W. W. Wartofsky in *Conceptual Foundations of Scientific Thought: An Introduction to the Philosophy of Science.*

67.   Most scholars cited above analyze the placement as well as the themes and methods in the Archaeology. See especially Hunter, pp. 17-49 and Connor, pp. 20-32.

68.   Connor, pp. 22-24. For information on contemporary anthropologies, see E. A. Havelock, *The Liberal Temper in Greek Politics* (New Haven: Yale University Press, 1957).

69.   Connor, pp. 24-25.

70.   P.23.

71.   *Rise*, pp. 22-24.

72.   See, for example, Hunter, pp. 226-228, or de Romilly, pp. 7-8.

73.   See Connor, pp. 42-47, for an analysis of the artistic and thematic reasons for the placement of the Pentecontaetia.

74.   See Hunter, p. 167, as well as her appendix to chapter 4, pp. 316-319, for a summary of the difficulties of Thucydides' chronology, with bibliography.

75.   Pearson, "Thucydides," catalogues the various kinds of opinions offered.

76.   P. 235. See also his specific book by book analysis and his concluding summary of style as method which draws the reader into an awareness of the complexity and the constant transformation of ideas and thus creates the need for exercising judgment, e.g., p. 247.

77.   Connor judges the suffering generated by war as one of the major subjects, e.g., pp. 31-32, and, by the end of the Archaeology, its magnitude as the measure of the greatness of a war. See also Parry.

78.   Parry emphasizes the dramatic effect on readers of viewing the war through the perspective of someone who actually experienced it, i.e., through Thucydides' own eyes (p.48), so that for him, the account becomes 'intensely personal' and 'tragic,' p. 47.

79.   For bibliography on the questions raised by the speeches and criticism of the various approaches to them, see K. J. Dover, "Thucydides "As History" and "As Literature," *History and Theory* 22 (1983): 59-63. Both Hunter and Connor point out the integration of the action with the speeches. Connor emphasizes that these two elements together enable the historian to present the complexities without asserting his own opinion, e. g., p. 236.

80.   See especially Finley's chapter "On the Origins of "Thucydides' Style."

81.   See, for example, Daniel Thomkins, "Stylistic Characterization in Thucydides: Nicias and Alcibiades," *Yale Classical Studies* 22 (1972): 181-214.

82.   See Hunter's comments, pp. 152-162, on human nature as an explanation rather than a cause of the historical process.

83.   See Hunter, p. 135 with note 21 and appendix A to chapter 6, pp. 333-335, for a summary of the scholarship on *tuche* and its role in the historical process, as well as Edmonds, *Chance*, Connor, pp. 243- 244, and Fornara, *Nature*, 79n.

84.   See Hunter, pp. 241-262, for a discussion of the error of simplifying the historians' concept of time to these two opposites and the way in which the analogy is used to develop the detailed account of what she calls "processual time" so Thucydides and Herodotus " could see totality, to seek out interrelationships, and to perceive and depict multiplicity of movement and of time," p. 253.

85.   See Connor's discussion of this passage, pp. 29-30, as well as pp. 242-248, where he traces the progression of ideas in similar statements throughout the history.

86.   De Romilly, *Fall*, pp. 47-58, in the chapter entitled "Hybris in Politics," relates Thucydides' pattern to the religious pattern and analyzes the decline of morals which success brings in both, but notes that the historian "links this simple pattern with a lucid reflection on the very nature of power," p. 47.

87.   Lowell Edmonds, "Thucydides' Ethics as Reflected in the Description of Stasis (3.82 - 83)," *Harvard Studies in Classical Philology* 79 1975): 73-92, points out that this 'ethical inversion' reflects traditional belief, but that the historian's originality comes from the fact that he has analyzed it as "expressed in political action," p. 91, in general terms as well as in particular events.

88.   P. 247.

89.   For general ideas and information in this brief survey, I am indebted to Immerwahr's "Historiography," pp. 458 -471, as well as Fornara, *Nature*.

90.   For the collection, see Felix Jacoby, *Die Fragmente der Griechischen Historiker* (Berlin and Leiden: E. J. Brill, l923).

91.   See Drews, pp. 103 -116, for an evaluation of Ctesias.

92.   For detailed information, see Felix Jacoby, *Atthis: The Local Chronicles of Ancient Athens* (Oxford: Clarendon Press, 1949), and Lionel Pearson, *The Local Historians of Attica* (Philadelphia: Lancaster Press, 1942).

93.   See Arnaldo Momigliano, "Athens in the Third Century B.C.E. and the Discovery of Rome in the Histories of Timaeus of Tauromenium," pp. 37-65 in *Essays in Ancient Historiography* (Oxford: Basil Blackwell, 1977).

94.   For a thorough study of the genre, see Arnaldo Momigliano, *The Development of Greek Biography* (Cambridge: Harvard University Press, l977).

95.   For bibliography and detailed studies of Xenophon and his works, see J. K. Anderson, *Xenophon* (New York: Charles Scribner's Sons: 1974) and W. E. Higgins, *Xenophon the Athenian: The Problem of the Individual and the Society of the Polis* (Albany: State University of New York Press, 1977).

96.   Higgins' chapter, "History," pp. 99-127, summarizes the criticism and analyzes Xenophon's style and philosophy. I have quoted from his translations.

97.   P. 104.

98.   P. 123.

99.   P.123.

100. Fornara, *Nature*, p. 106, in a section entitled "History's Purpose," pp. 104-120, from which the following information has been summarized.

101. Fornara, *Nature*, p.109.

102. Drews, pp. 121-122.

103. See survey in Fornara, *Nature*, pp. 120-134, as well as Victor D'Huys, "How to Describe Violence in Historical Narrative: Reflections of the Ancient Greek Historians and their Critics," *Ancient Society* 18 (1987): 209- 250; B. L. Ullman, "History and Tragedy," *Transactions and Proceedings of the American Philological Association* 73 (1942): 30-53; and Walbank, "History."

104. For an examination of Polybius' historiographical statements, see Kenneth Sacks, *Polybius on the Writing of History*. Classical Studies 24 (Berkeley: University of California Press, 1981).

105. For detailed examination of Polybius' life and works, see Kurt Von Fritz, *The Theory of the Mixed Constitution in Antiquity: A Critical Analysis of Polybius' Ideas* (New York: Columbia University Press, 1954) and F. W. Walbank, *Polybius* (Berkeley: University of California Press, 1972), as well as Momigliano's review of Walbank's *Polybius*, "The Historian's Skin," reprinted from the *New York Review of Books* 21, 12, 18 July, 1974, in *Essays in Ancient Historiography* (Oxford: Basil Blackwell, 1977), pp. 67-77 and A. M. Eckstein, "Josephus and Polybius: A Reconsideration," *Classical Antiquity* 9.2 (1990): 175-208.

106. See especially historiographical proems to books 2 and 9. Eckstein, pp. 185-186, points out Polybius' similarities to Josephus in this respect.

107. Walbank, *Polybius*, emphasizes his debt to Thucydides. See especially pp. 40-42 and 66.

108. For the development of the concept of universal history, see Fornara, *Nature*, pp. 42-46 and Walbank, *Polybius*, pp. 66-68, as well as Sacks, pp. 108-118.

109. For an analysis of Polybius' term *pragmatike historia*, see Walbank's chapter, pp. 66-96 as well as pp. 56-57. For the utility of praise and blame. see pp. 27-28.

110. *Rise*, pp. 75-79.

111. See Walbank, *Polybius*, pp. 157-160, for a discussion of his statements on causality, their application and their relation to his view of Roman expansionism.

112. Walbank, *Polybius*, pp. 58-67, discusses the calculable and incalculable in history and Polybius' use of the term *tuche* for the latter. See Eckstein, pp. 196-198, for the emphasis on rationality and the destructive power of irrationality, and pp. 200 -202, for a summary of the uses of *tuche* with citations.

113. In addition to sources cited above, see Von Fritz, *Theory*, Appendix II.

114. *Polybius*, p. 65.

115. De Romilly, *Fall*, includes Polybius. The historian uses the biological metaphor as a guide to the general movement in various places, e. g., 6.4.11-13. See Walbank, *Polybius*, pp. 142-146.

116. Walbank, *Polybius*, devotes an entire chapter, pp. 130- 156, to book 6. See this as well as his article, "Polybius on the Roman Constitution," *Classical Quarterly* 37 (1943): 73-89, and Von Fritz, *Theory*, pp. 40-59, for an analysis of the theories, their philosophical antecedents, and Polybius' uses of them. De Romilly, *Rise*, p. 11, notes the limitation of the concept of the cycle to the evolution of constitutions; he is not suggesting that history itself is cyclic. Walbank too makes the distinction in "Polybius," pp. 86 -87, and *Polybius*, p. 146, where he suggests that the theory of a cycle of types of constitutions provides a framework for understanding the Roman constitution which is itself outside the cycle, since it is a mixture of types. Yet, according to nature, it too will decline.

117. Polybius does not give his own opinion nor does he answer his own question posed at 3.4: whether Roman rule is acceptable to her subjects and worthy of praise. Momigliano, "Historian's Skin," pp. 72-74, disagrees with Walbank's assessment, pp. 173-181, that the realistic historian sided with the Romans because he recognized that their success required the elimination of enemies.

Sinai II: Jewish Historiography in the Hellenistic World

Jewish historical writing of the Hellenistic era retained the basic programmatic orientation of the Bible but presented it using the methods developed by Greek poets, dramatists, chroniclers and historians. From the biblical book of Daniel to the books of Maccabees in the Apocrypha to the *Antiquities* and *Wars of the Jews* of Flavius Josephus there is an inspired interweaving of the techniques of Olympus with the content of Sinai.

Daniel

1-6: History as Entertainment— In ancient Near Eastern folklore Daniel was the prototype of the wise and righteous man (Ezek. 14:14; 20; 28:3). Accordingly, he served as the protagonist of a series of hero tales emanating from the exile. In these stories, contained in the first part of the book chapters one to six, Daniel and three Jewish friends served successively at the court of three kings, Nebuchadnezzer and Belshazzar the Babylonians and Darius the Mede. Daniel, as wise man, interpreted the visions and dreams of the kings. Denounced by jealous courtiers, Daniel and his friends stood steadfast in their faith and refused to worship foreign gods or living kings despite the threat of death. The miracles by which they were saved served to heighten respect for them and their religion. The central theme of these narratives is the triumph of Jews and Judaism in the exile. The moral lesson was that in spite of all it was possible to reconcile worldly success with the duties of pious Jews. The main text of Daniel 1-6 has been dated at approximately 304 B.C.E. with later additions and interpolations.[1]

The Daniel collection of chapters 1-6 was probably read and listened to for sheer pleasure. The narration of the stories follows the international style of folk tales with heros and villains clearly delineated. The Horatio Alger theme of the boy who, like Joseph in Pharaoh's court, against all odds, through sheer intelligence and moral goodness, achieved power, money and fame delighted the audience. The heavy emphasis on the Jewish loyalties of Daniel and his friends particularly impressed the Jewish listeners.

But did the editor-writer who compiled Daniel 1-6 out of five disparate hero tales have only the entertainment and moral uplift of his readers in mind? Or is there also embedded in the work historical intent? There are a number of clues that point to a historical motivation even though the form of these chapters borders on fiction. Clearly the existence of Jewish courtiers who remained devout Jews while holding important posts in the courts of the Babylonian and Persian kings was a well known historical fact as evidenced by the role of Nehemiah. The editor-writer of Daniel 1-6 made this fact the unifying theme of the primary sources that came down to him. Secondly, he gave chronological unity to his work.[2] Unlike the extensive embellishments and tangential elements introduced in a completely folkloristic or fictional account the anonymous editor-author narrated compactly and avoided digressions. The narrative goes straight to the climax and details serve the reconstruction of events. The inability of the Chaldean visionaries to interpret the king's dreams is contrasted with Daniel's art but their continued failure to solve other riddles is later stated simply with dramatization. This economy of treatment is a sign of historiographic intentionality.[3]

To establish historical reality the editor puts one of the tales about Belshazzar, the new king of Babylon (Dan. 2) in the form of a historical record and another in the form of a royal proclamation (Dan. 4). Similarly, the first revelation to Nebuchadnezzer is related as if it were a chronicle entry (Dan. 2) and the event is later recounted in a royal letter (Dan. 4). There is an awareness of the fact that "Babylonian scribes put their historical-and pious-novelettes into the form of royal inscriptions attributed to some bygone ruler."[4]

Even the dream of Nebuchadnezzer and Daniel's interpretation of it (Dan. 2) has historical significance. The king dreamt of a great image (the head of fine gold, breasts and arms of silver, belly and thighs of bronze, legs of iron and feet part iron and clay) that was shattered by a stone from heaven. In Daniel's interpretation, the different metals in the different parts of the statue each represent a universal monarchy and the monarchies are not concurrent but successive. The stone that destroys the statue is the divine power at work in history, that upon the ruins of the great image establishes the kingdom of God for eternity. We have here a Jewish adaptation of the Greek concept of a succession of world empires. The Greek poet Hesiod (8th century B.C.E.) contrasted a golden era of peace at the dawn of history with the age of iron and violence of his own time. But neither Hesiod or any other Greek source represents four empires by the four metals as does the editor-writer of Daniel chapter two. It is possible that he may have had in mind the Iranian concept that the divine sponsor of military power was also the patron of metals.[5] Another element that is unique to the editor-author of Daniel 1-6 is that he placed the doctrine of the four kingdoms in the framework of a universal history with an apocalyptic climax. The stone demolishes all the parts of the statue at the same time including the golden head. In place of all the kingdoms of the past rolled up into one pagan empire comes the kingdom of God.

7-12: History as Apocalyptic— It was the apocalyptic motif in Daniel 2 that attracted the attention of a later generation who were witnesses and victims of the internecine warfare that erupted over the succession to Alexander the Great's empire. The troubles and despair reached their culmination in the persecution of the Jews in the land of Israel by Antiochus IV in which the practices of Judaism were banned. Hellenization was encouraged causing a civil war among the Jews, a Jewish rebellion brutally crushed and paganization of the Temple implemented. In those dark days of suffering the anguished question was in the words of Isaiah: "Watchman, what of the night?" (Isa. 21:11). What consolation can prophecy offer us? But prophecy had ceased in Israel for a variety of reasons discussed in chapter six. Yet Daniel, the hero of the exile, had predicted the kingdom of the Greeks and also its fall to be replaced by the kingdom of God. In place of prophecy there emerged four apocalyptic writers who updated the Daniel stories that were well known in Jerusalem about 170 B.C.E. The first to be updated was the vision of the four kingdoms symbolized by the different metals in Daniel chapter 2. The updated version is Daniel chapter 7, where the four kingdoms are represented by four beasts symbolizing the four empires of Babylonia, Medea, Persia and Macedonia. The message of consolation was that the pagan empires will be destroyed and the kingdom of God will be established soon.

It is the fourth and last apocalyptic tract published under the name of Daniel (Dan. 10-12) that is the focus of this discussion. In these chapters an angel surveys the course of history from Cyrus the Great to Antiochus IV. The events are prefigured and thus predetermined by the celestial struggle between the guardian angels of Persia and Greece and the angel Gabriel who is supported by Michael, the heavenly patron of Israel. The Persian period of the distant past is dealt with briefly. After Alexander's death and the split of his empire, the history is confined to wars and pacts between the Seleucids of Syria and the Ptolemies of Egypt and sandwiched in between them, Judea and Jerusalem. The survey becomes more detailed as it approaches the author's own time, the reign and actions of Antiochus IV. He describes the paganization and pollution of the Temple and the persecution of the Jews. He refers to the first successes of the Maccabees as "a little help" that came to the Jews in their adversity (Dan. 11:34), thus indicating the tract was composed about the summer of 166 B.C.E.[6] At this point the angel's foreknowledge ends and Daniel begins his prophecy whose culmination is the establishment of the kingdom of God.

The concept of a prophet, who like a historian, surveys and describes the past as if it were the future before declaring his own original predictions (a style that distinguishes the apocalyptic from the prophetic approach to history) is derived from the Greeks. Greek poets and dramatists from Homer to Euripides as well as the historian Herodotus used techniques such as oracles, dreams and visions to recount specific events as if they were predictions.[7] What is unique to Daniel chapters 10-12 that places it squarely in the Sinai tradition is the divine determinism, i.e., history as revealing the purpose of the Creator. In contrast the Greeks did not see a divine plan in history.

The historiographical intent of the four editor-writers of Daniel 7-12 is clear throughout these chapters despite the cryptic apocalyptic language and symbolism that obscures the historical background. The main evidence is that they respected the chronological framework established by their predecessors in Daniel 1-6.[8] The revelations of Daniel communicating the visions he has seen, all come after King Nebuchadnezzer of Babylonia. Two visions (Dan. 7, 8) are placed under Belshazzar, the last Babylonian king according to the hero tales (Dan. 5). The vision of Daniel 9 is placed under an imaginary king, Darius the Mede, who according to Dan. 6:1 became king in Babylon after Belshazzar.[9] The final vision (Dan. 10-12) is said to have taken place under Cyrus the Persian who, according to Dan. 6:28 followed Darius the Mede on the throne.

The First and Second Books of Maccabees—History as Propaganda

The First and Second Books of Maccabees are part of the non-canonical literature of the post-biblical period included in the Apocrypha. Both books drew on a Seleucid chronicle and a Jewish common source and cover the events leading to the Maccabean Revolt of 168-165 B.C.E. and its aftermath. In this revolt, after initial setbacks, a guerrilla army of Jewish pietists under the leadership of Mattathias and Judah the Maccabee defeated the forces of the Seleucid ruler Antiochus IV Epiphanes and their Jewish sympathizers. The victorious Maccabees purified and reconsecrated the Jerusalem Temple that had been defiled by idolatry, lifted the ban on Jewish religious observances and founded a dynasty of theocratic rulers (high priest-kings) known as the Hasmoneans.

It is these events, largely ignored by the apocalyptic writer of Daniel, who as noted above, dismissed the Maccabees as only "a little help", that the author of One Maccabees sought to emphasize. He was a Jew in Judea who wrote his work about 90 B.C.E. in the elegant Hebrew style of the biblical books of Samuel (although the original Hebrew text was lost surviving only in a very literal Greek translation). In countering the view of the Maccabees expressed in Dan. 11:34, the author of One Maccabees intended to legitimize the Hasmonean dynasty as the books of Samuel proved the legitimacy of the Davidic line. Unlike Daniel chapters 7-12 One Maccabees denies the resurrection of the dead, to be discussed in the next chapter, and suggests that martyrdom can be in vain. These latter views were undoubtedly prompted by the necessity to overcome the apocalyptic resignation engendered by Daniel 7-12, which prompted many Jews to accept martyrdom rather than organize militarily to defeat their persecutors.

The sober narrative is not impartial but ardently nationalistic and partisan. Like the books of Samuel, First Maccabees is punctuated by bursts of passion in the form of poetic insertions that interrupt the flow of the narrative. In addition, Mattathias, one of the protagonist-heroes of the book (the other hero is his son Judah) is cast in the model of the biblical heroes Abraham, Joseph, Phineas, Joshua and David. But unlike the biblical histories, the author of First Maccabees abstained from the use of the biblical names of God deeming them too holy to be used.[10] The absence of prophecy and miracles also distinguishes First Maccabees from the biblical histories. The author accepts the doctrine that prophecy had ceased after Haggai, Zechariah and Malachi (see chapter 6) and was also keenly aware that certain of the apocalyptic prophecies of Daniel 7-12 did not materialize.

Scholars have been impressed with the general accuracy of First Maccabees as a historical work though there are several errors in the narrative. The author was well informed on Seleucid institutions and his work is remarkable for its geographic precision. Sites of battles and important events are almost always named and the author, following the model of the biblical histories, took great care to give his narrative a chronological framework. He expended great effort to find material (1 Macc. 9:22) and filled out the skeleton of bare facts with speeches, prayers and the rhetoric of propaganda.[11]

Second Maccabees is an abridgement by an anonymous author of a larger work of five books written around 86 B.C.E. by Jason of Cyrene. The abridgment was produced between the years 78-77 B.C.E. and 63 B.C.E. The author consciously wrote to refute the account of events and their interpretation in First Maccabees. If First Maccabees seeks to redress the slight to the Maccabees in Daniel 7-12 by a propagandistic legitimation of the Hasmonean dynasty, Second Maccabees seeks to uphold the view of events and their interpretation by the apocalyptic writers of Daniel 7-12. The protagonist-heroes of First Maccabees, Mattathias and Judah, retain their stature in Jason's account but Judah's brothers are shown to be ineffective and tainted by treason and sin. It was not the Hasmonean military prowess that brought victory, as in First Maccabees, but the martyrdom of the saints that won God's favor for Israel. Second Maccabees, like Daniel 7-12, upholds the belief in the resurrection of the dead.

For Second Maccabees chronological data are not an indispensable part of the history as they are for First Maccabees but rather a propagandistic device to discredit First Maccabees and vindicate the apocalypticists of Daniel. In contrast to First Maccabees, the abridged history is marked by geographical vagueness and there is evidence that Jason of Cyrene committed geographical blunders in the original work. But these blemishes are put in perspective when it becomes apparent that the author is not interested in conveying details, but rather in inspiring his readers. Second Maccabees is written in the popular style and narrative patterns of Hellenistic history. In these histories of mass appeal, the writers played strongly on the reader's emotions, with graphic portrayals of atrocities and heroism and heavy doses of dramatic language and rhetoric. The authors expressed strong moral judgments and even digressed from the narrative to preach to the reader. Nevertheless, a generally accurate description of the course of events was not precluded by this convention of literary license and Jason of Cyrene's work judged by this standard is in many ways a respectable history.[12]

Flavius Josephus—Pragmatic History

Josephus is the first great Jewish historian in the modern sense and his works represent the apex of Hellenistic-Jewish historiography. Rarely is a historian's life as dramatic and provocative as his history but in the case of Josephus', life and literature were but opposite sides of the same coin minted in the fires that led up to and encompassed the Roman-Jewish War of 66-70 C.E. and its aftermath. Born into a priestly family in Jerusalem and descended on his mother's side from the Hasmonean dynasty, Josephus claimed that in his youth he was renowned for his learning as well as his lineage. He became acquainted at first hand with the various religious groups of the Second Temple period, joined the Pharisees and at the age of twenty-six, because of his knowledge of Greek, was sent on a mission to Rome to secure the release of some priests accused by the Roman procurator of Judea. With the outbreak of the Jewish revolt against Rome, Josephus was appointed commander of the Jewish forces in the Galilee but his authority was disputed by a rival faction led by John of Gischala. Overcoming this challenge, Josephus managed to fortify the various cities of the region in preparation for the Roman attack. Despite these efforts, Jewish disunity and the overwhelming might of the Roman army under the command of Vespasian quickly put an end to the Jewish defenses. Josephus persuaded the men closest to him that suicide was preferable to captivity but he and a companion who were the last to remain alive surrendered to the Romans. Though at first held prisoner he was released when Vespasian was proclaimed emperor, Josephus having predicted the greatness in store for the Roman commander. Josephus accompanied Vespasian's son Titus on his successful campaign against Jerusalem and sought in vain to persuade the defenders to lay down their arms. He was an eyewitness to the subsequent sacking of the city and the burning of the Temple. Josephus settled in Rome where he enjoyed the privilege of Roman citizenship and an annual pension arranged for him by the emperor Vespasian who allowed him to live in the royal palace. On the other hand, Josephus was denounced by his fellow Jews as a traitor though he continued to identify with Judaism throughout his life and defend it against hostile detractors.

Josephus published *The Jewish War* in Aramaic sometime between 75 and 79 C.E. He wrote it most likely at the direction of Vespasian who had a double motive in commissioning the work: to glorify his accomplishments and those of his son Titus and to warn Babylonian Jews lest they also revolt against Rome. A Greek version was subsequently written and it is this one that has been preserved until the present. The *Jewish Antiquities* written around 93 C.E. is a larger work in length and in scope covering the history of the Jews from the Creation to the beginning of the Jewish revolt against Rome. Josephus wrote this work in order to explain Judaism to the Greco-Roman world and to evoke respect for it on the part of non-Jews. He emphasized the antiquity of Judaism because in the

Hellenistic world the more venerable the religion the greater its prestige.

The last two works of Josephus were his autobiography entitled *The Life* and a polemical-apologetic work *Against Apion* (or as it was originally titled *On the Antiquity of the Jews*). Josephus wrote his autobiography to refute the charges leveled against him by Justus of Tiberias, a Jewish councilor in a minor Greek city in Palestine, later a secretary to the Roman puppet king in Palestine, Agrippa II. Justus was the author of a limited historical work or works that have not survived but which included a description of the revolt against Rome. He accused Josephus of misconduct in the Galilee when he was commander of the region before the arrival of Vespasian.[13] In *Against Apion* Josephus, in the first part of the work, lashes out against various anti-Jewish accusers and their accusations with logical arguments and biting sarcasm. In the second part of the work he seeks to reveal the inner value of Judaism and its ethical superiority over the values of the Hellenistic world.

Josephus used a variety of sources for his histories. In his description of Herod's kingdom in *The Jewish War* (book 1) and in the *Jewish Antiquities* (books 15-17) Josephus was indebted to the work of Nicholas of Damascus. This outstanding Greek intellectual (he was not only a historian, a philosopher and a dramatist but also a statesman and an orator) who was King Herod's advisor composed a universal history in 144 books at Herod's instigation.[14] Josephus also used the memoirs or commentaries of the Roman generals Vespasian and Titus, his own abundant correspondence with his friend King Agrippa II, the testimony of deserters and his own knowledge as an eye-witness of a good many of the events which he describes.

The preservation of Josephus' works is due to the great interest he aroused in Christian circles of the early Church. His mention of numerous persons, places and occurrences known from the New Testament and his dramatically shocking account of the fall of Jerusalem that seemed to corroborate the prophecies of misfortune in the Gospels intrigued the early church theologians. But most important of all was the *Testimonium Flavianum*, the testimony concerning Jesus found in a famous paragraph of the *Jewish Antiquities* (books 18, 63-64) which scholarly consensus today considers a later interpolation. Nevertheless the testimony was of major importance for the Church in that it was considered reliable evidence for the divine nature and messiaship of Jesus.[15]

Paraphrase of Biblical History— In recounting the history of his people in biblical times, Josephus shaped the material in such a way as to make it understandable to Greco-Roman non-Jewish readers, to evoke sympathy for and even identity with the biblical characters but at the same time to underscore the truth of the biblical tradition and its religious outlook. Thus Josephus portrays Abraham, Moses, Joseph, Saul, David and Solomon as having the characteristics of Plato's philosopher-king, the Stoic sage and Thucydides' ideal statesman, Pericles.[16]   His description of Adam and Eve before the Fall as unblemished by any evil is strikingly reminiscent of the Stoic ideal of *Apatheia*.[17]   In explaining the ritual of the *lulav* (the palm branch used on the festival of *Sukkot*, Tabernacles, see ch. 7), Josephus identifies it with the *Eiresione*, the branch decorated with fruit that was held in Athenian festivals.[18] Josephus' tendency to subjectivize the actions of the biblical heroes and heroines and to moralize on them is unlike the Torah but very much like the historical books of the Bible, Kings and Chronicles. On the other hand, Josephus' description of the inner thoughts and life of the biblical characters has no parallel in the Bible or in post-biblical literature where actions are described without spelling out the inner dialogue that accompanies them.   However, this explicit psychological examination of protagonists is very characteristic of Greek literature and drama beginning with Homer.[19]

   Keeping in mind his readers' interests and his own apologetic purposes, Josephus omitted long lists of Semitic names, embarrassing incidents (Reuben's sleeping with Jacob's concubine Bilhah, Gen. 35:22; Tamar's impregnation by her father-in-law Judah, Gen. 38; the golden calf, Exod. 32; the complaint of Aaron and Miriam against Moses' wife, Num. 12:1) and condensed technical material and uninteresting details.   In treating miracles Josephus sought to achieve three objectives: to satisfy the curiosity of his Greek and Roman readers, to buttress his own belief in miracles by inserting a list of historians of antiquity both Greeks and barbarians, who had reported on similar events or facts (*Antiquities* 1, 107; 1, 348), and to ground miracles scientifically. All of this, of course, led to inconsistencies which are the hallmark of Josephus' work.[20]   Yet, these inconsistencies notwithstanding, Josephus' paraphrase of the Bible using Greek terms and motifs "transforms the genre of antiquarian, rhetorical historiography and succeeds in producing a Greek version of Jewish sacred history with specifically religious implications."[21]

Historiographic Method— When Josephus tells his readers in a number of places in his work that he intends to tell the truth of events without bias[22] he is expressing his aim in writing pragmatic history as Polybius conceived it, i.e., the history of events and political events in particular. Such a history eschews mythology but is characterized by "truth and accuracy and this is instructive to all who read it."[23]   But Josephus had other models as well beginning with Herodotus and Thucydides and including other Greeks such as Ctesias, Diodorus Siculus and Hecataeus of Abdera as well as Hellenized Orientals writing the history of their people for the Greeks like Berossus, Manetho and Philo of Byblus. Dionysius of Halicarnassus, the champion of rhetorical history, who argued the importance of style including the spacing and the laying out of the narrative to create balance and symmetry, and the use of pathos to rouse feelings, also had a profound impression on Josephus.

Like Thucydides, Josephus makes a distinction between real and apparent causes of historical events and the subjective and objective perceptions of historical figures. He also is as skilled as Thucydides in distinguishing the fundamental cause as well as the immediate concomitant and cumulative causes of war.   The fundamental cause of the Roman-Jewish War was the Jewish rejection of everything Roman.   The cumulative cause was the alliance between Judea and Rome in the time of the Maccabees which began with Roman aid but ended up becoming a debt which brought Roman occupation, domination, interference, suppression of liberties accompanied by contempt for Jewish nationalism and religion.   The concomitant causes which favored war were the worsening internal situation of the Roman Empire and the impetuous optimism of the Jewish revolutionary party which took advantage of the general upheaval to launch the insurrection.   This optimism was fueled by Messianic visions of redemption just around the corner in which the power of the pagan empire would be broken as foretold in the book of Daniel. The immediate causes of the war were the provocative acts of the Roman procurator Florus who goaded the Jews into taking up arms and the cessation of the sacrifices in honor of the Roman people in the Jerusalem Temple.[24]

Like the Greek historians, poets and rhetoricians Josephus uses proems and epilogues to introduce and conclude sections of this history.   In keeping with Greek historiography and the advice of Dionysios of Halicarnassus, he uses speeches to dramatically punctuate his narrative.   The speeches are both direct and indirect and the most well-known are: the speech of King Agrippa trying to persuade the Jews to give up the war against Rome, (*The Jewish*

War 2:345-401) Josephus' speech to the besieged combatants in Jerusalem urging surrender to the Romans (*The Jewish War* 5:362-419) and the two part speech of Elazar to the besieged fighters of Masada urging them to take their lives and the lives of their families rather than surrender to the Romans (*The Jewish War* 7:323-336; 341-388).[25]

With regard to chronology Josephus is meticulous in giving his readers the hour, the day, the month, the year, the Olympiad, the season, the reign, the consulship in terms of placing events in time. But on the other hand he is not above altering chronology for narrative flow (recommended by Dionysios of Halicarnassus in criticism of Thucydides) or apologetic purposes. Thus to explain his own earlier participation in the Roman-Jewish War and his later desertion to the Romans he created a period of moderation and legitimacy sandwiched between periods of terror and anarchy. Why after the initial victory of the Jewish revolutionaries against the Romans were generals like Josephus selected who had not participated in the earlier revolutionary activity? The answer was that Josephus was selected during the reign of the moderates who replaced the early extremists and tried to deal with the crisis initiated by the latter. When the moderates in turn were ousted by the extremists Josephus deserted to the Romans. By characterizing the first period as tyrannical and the second as legitimate and moderate Josephus was able to condemn the fomenters of the war and at the same time justify his own involvement.[26]

On the whole, however, Josephus was faithful to chronology and to his sources. He did not invent entirely new episodes or chronological frameworks without any basis in fact. But like all ancient historians he shaped his material to meet his own tendentious and literary aims. He organized his history as much around people as around events. He gives detailed information on institutions, holidays, religious sects, laws, Temple organizations and rites, military campaigns and battles. He is acutely sensitive to geography and his descriptions of scenery and topography represent some of his finest historical writing.

Though Josephus' work like that of his Greek counterparts eminently fits Leopold Von Rankes' description of the historian's antiquarian task discussed above, it also contains the biblical conception of programmatic history. Josephus never loses sight of the operation of the transcendent in his people's history. Despite his references to the Greek concepts of fate and fortune throughout his history, the contexts in which these remarks occur give evidence of his attachment to the Hebraic idea of Divine Providence and the biblical-apocalyptic view that empires come into being as part of the divine plan.[27]

Rabbinic Literature—The Interiorization of History

Classical rabbinic literature was never intended as historiography in the modern sense or for that matter even in the biblical sense of the term. Biblical history despite its cultic, ethical or apocalyptic tendencies had, as noted above, a specificity as to time and place and a genuine antiquarian interest. In contrast, the rabbis seem to revel in anachronisms in which Og, King of Bashan, is present at Isaac's circumcision, Job is a servant of Pharaoh and David is a rabbinic sage. Moreover the history of their own period cannot be written by relying only on the vast literature created by the rabbis. Rabbinic literature does not record historical events of prime importance or it mentions them in such a legendary or fragmentary fashion as to make even initial retrieval almost impossible.

Though these facts suggest a complete lack of rabbinic historical perspective we know from a number of rabbinic statements that the rabbis were able to recognize anachronisms when it suited their purposes. Commenting on Gen. 25:22 "She went to inquire of the Lord" (i.e., Rebecca sought divine guidance on the turmoil in her womb) the rabbis, assuming that such guidance is best found in synagogues and houses of study, logically ask: "And were there, then, synagogues and houses of study in those days?"[28]   That the rabbis were not totally oblivious to historical chronology is evidenced by the *Seder Olam Rabbah* (*The Greater Order of the World*) attributed to the second century Palestinian Rabbi Jose ben Halafta, a dry and somewhat rudimentary chronology of persons and events from Adam until Alexander the Great.[29]

The key to understanding this historiographical eclipse is, paradoxically, to be found in *the* event whose description by Josephus marks the watershed of Jewish historical writing in antiquity - the destruction of the Second Temple in 70 C.E. In the aftermath of the destruction, Rabban Yohanan ben Zakkai, a leader in the Pharisaic party of Jerusalem before 70, had made his peace with the Romans, even before the collapse of Jerusalem, and was permitted to conduct a rabbinic academy and court at Yavneh. At Yavneh R. Yohanan inaugurated the legal reformation of talmudic Judaism, by which he prepared the Jewish people to survive the Temple's destruction and insured that the synagogue and academy would inherit its prerogatives (see chapters 6 & 7).[30]   The task of reconstruction mandated an avoidance of reflection upon recent history for such a focus would only sink the survivors of the catastrophe deeper into despair and cause disillusionment with God, with Judaism and with the will to live. But historians not only look backward they look forward. In the ancient world the study of history was considered important because it might lead to a clearer idea of its ultimate direction. In the programmatic history of the Sinai tradition this direction led to the Messianic Age and the redemption of Israel and the rest of the world. Since the time of the Book of Daniel this cherished hope had become a deeply held principle of Jewish faith shared by the apocalypticists and the rabbis, as will be discussed in the next chapter. But as noted above, Messianic activism was responsible for the misplaced optimism of the Jewish revolutionaries who believed that divine help as well as the internal upheavals in the empire would insure victory over Rome. This attempt "to hasten the end" had ended in disaster but so powerful was the belief and the longing to act it out in the theater of current history that two additional uprisings against Rome with eschatological overtones occurred in the next century ending in Jewish death and destruction. No less an authority than Rabbi Akiba named Bar Kochba, the military leader of the revolt of 132 C.E., as the Messiah. To focus on the historical future was to play with millenarian fire and the disasters to which it could lead.

This is not to say that the pragmatic rabbis lost faith in the coming of the Messiah. They did not. But they counseled that the time of his arrival should be removed from human hands and left to heaven alone.[31]   R. Yohanan ben Zakkai and the Sages who followed him screened off the immediate past and the distant future concentrating the people's attention on the here and now. Similarly, they narrowed the spotlight of their attention to the inner world of Judaism, to law, ritual, prayer and meditation, ignoring the tumult in the rise and fall of gentile empires. It is for these reasons that the scholars of Yavneh did not produce historical works and it would be fifteen centuries and more until Jewish scholars would again return to the historian's craft.[32]

However, it was far more than the pragmatic concern for reconstruction and survival that conditioned the rabbinic attitude toward history. As masters of the Hebrew Bible the rabbis knew that its central message was the divine plan for the establishment of God's kingdom on earth in which the Jewish people had a central role as a result of its eternal covenant with God. In addition, they inherited from the Torah and the prophets a belief in a meta-historical plane that was more real than the historical world of power politics. For example, as discussed earlier, Assyria thought its victory over Israel was the result of superior might, the evidence of a superior civilization, not realizing that it had been only the instrument of divine reciprocity. Thus Assyrian arrogance as victimizer would also lead to Assyrian suffering as victim.

The meta-historical level which partakes of sacred time and eternity is characterized, as Eliade has noted (see Chapter 7) by the repetition of eternal symbols and in mundane historical terms, the rise and fall of civilizations. If therefore one has in mind the three central points in the divine plan which are also eternal archetypes, Creation, Revelation and Redemption there is no need for historical specificity because the details of the rise and fall of empires are ultimately unimportant. From this perspective all historical events are in one disguise or another recurrences underscoring perennial truths, a view akin not only to the Greek historians' views of recurrent patterns in history but also to the philosophers' ahistorical conceptions of time and eternity. As the rabbis saw it, given the frailty of human memory which is constantly forgetting these recurrences and the truths underlying them, it makes good sense to use the shorthand of allegory and symbolism to get at the truths rather than become bogged down in the historical details. Thus for example, it is possible to symbolize Rome as Esau-Edom without distinguishing between pagan Rome and Christian Rome or between the various emperors.[33] Similarly, from the vantage point of the meta-historical, time (as the Kabbalists were later to point out) is an illusion and so it can be compressed or expanded making it possible for Job to be a servant of Pharaoh and David to be a rabbinic sage. (In the case of David we also have a projection backward of rabbinic doctrines and practices, a restorative messianism idealizing the biblical period and its heroes, a tendency already found in the Books of Chronicles, as noted above). The perennial truths of the inability of the wicked to be influenced by their association with the righteous as in the case of Pharaoh and Job and the superiority of learning and piety to martial ability as in the case of David are important, not the particularities of time and place.[34] On the other hand, in their focus on the law and ritual of the present the rabbis were extremely conscious and careful of time sequences.[35]

In sum, though the rabbis did not write history, they had a profound historical awareness. They interiorized history but continued to shuttle back and forth between the pragmatic demands of profane time and the undimmed visions of sacred time, between the historical realities of the present and the meta-historical truths of eternity. Like the later Kabbalists, the rabbis did not offer direct representations of contemporary events but transformed them into vivid images of timeless symbols.

Notes

1. H. L. Ginsberg, "Daniel, Books Of" *Encyclopedia Judaica* 5:1283 and *Studies in Daniel* (New York: Jewish Theological Seminary of America, 1948): 5-40. The interpolation of verses 41-43 in chapter 2 was made after 246 B.C.E. by a sage of Jerusalem who witnessed and was a victim of the internecine struggle between Alexander's successors.

2. He deduced from Jeremiah 25:1 that Nebuchadnezzer's first year as conqueror of Jerusalem coincided with the fourth year of King Jehoiakim of Judah. Thus "the princes of Judah" including Daniel and his companions were brought to Babylon (Jer. 24:1) in the third year of Jehoiakim (Dan. 1:1). In the second year of Nebuchadnezzer (Dan. 2:1) two years later, Daniel interpreted the king's dream on the basis of a night vision. Daniel continued his interpretive work until the first year of Cyrus (Dan. 1:21) the date when the Jewish exiles returned to Jerusalem (2 Chron. 36:22). The chronological framework makes Daniel an exilic prophet.

3. See notes 8-9 in Sinai I: Antiquarian Impulse in Programmatic History.

4. Elias Bickerman, *Four Strange Books of the Bible: Jonah/Daniel/Koheleth/Esther* (New York: Schocken Books, 1967), p. 98.

5. Ibid., p. 67; A. Momigliano, "The Origins of Universal History" in *The Poet and the Historian* ed. Friedman, pp. 144-148.

6. The first to recognize that the Book of Daniel was a product of the time of Antiochus IV (Epiphanes) was the Neo-Platonic philosopher Porphyry in the twelfth book of his treatise *Against the Christians*. Of course, Porphyry was mistaken in attributing the *entire* book to an author who lived in Judea at the time of Antiochus IV since it is only Daniel 7-12 that can be so designated.

7. Bickerman, *Four Strange Books of the Bible* , p. 117-118; Kaufmann, *Toledot ha-'Emunah ha-Yisraelit*, 3(1), pp. 16-17.

8. See above note 2.

9. The editor writer of Daniel 1-6 relates that the incident of Daniel in the lion's den occurred under King Darius. But Persian kings named Darius reigned after Cyrus not before him. On the other hand, according to the doctrine of the four empires (Dan. 2) and biblical prophecies (Isa. 13:17; Jer. 51:11) Babylon was to be conquered by the king of the Medes. Thus the editor created an imaginary king, Darius the Mede, who succeeded Belshazzar, the last Babylonian king who was succeeded by Cyrus.

10. Still more extreme was the author of the book of Esther, who avoids all direct allusion to God, undoubtedly for the same reason.

11. *The Anchor Bible* , 1 Maccabees intro., trans. and commentary by Jonathan A. Goldstein (Garden City, NY: Doubleday & Company, 1976), pp. 6-8; 12-14; 21-22; p. 26; 84-85.

12. Ibid., pp. 33-34; p. 78; p. 82. *The Anchor Bible* 2 Maccabees, new trans. with intro. and commentary by Jonathan A. Goldstein (Garden City, NY: Doubleday & Co., 1983), p. 4; 12-13; 20-21; p. 83.

13. In particular, Justus accused him of being an enemy of Rome, belonging to the war party and suppressing the peace party in Tiberias, committing acts of brigandage and violating women. Cf. Tessa Rajak "Josephus and Justus of Tiberias" in *Josephus, Judaism and Christianity* ed. Louis H. Feldman and Gohei Hata (Detroit: Wayne State University Press, 1987), pp. 81-94.

14. Cf. Ben Zion Wacholder, *Nicholas of Damascus*, University of California Publications in History Vol. 75, (Berkeley: University of California Press, 1962).

15. Cf. Heinz Schreckenberg, "The Works of Josephus and the Early Christian Church", in *Josephus, Judaism and Christianity*, pp. 315-324; Zvi Barras, *"The Testimonium Flavianum* and the Martyrdom of James" in *Josephus, Judaism and Christianity*, pp. 338-348.

16. Louis H. Feldman, "Introduction" *Josephus, Judaism and Christianity*, p. 30. See also above chapter 5, note 8.

17. Louis H. Feldman, "Hellenizations in Josephus' Portrayal of Man's Decline" in *Religions in Antiquity: Essays in Memory of Erwin R. Goodenough* ed. Jacob Neusner (Leiden: E. J. Brill, 1968), p. 343.

18. *Jewish Antiquities* 3:245 trans. H. St. John Thackeray *The Loeb Classical Library* (London: William Heinemann LTD, New York: G. P. Putnam & Sons, 1930) 4:435.

19. Isaac Heinemann, *"Darko shel Yosefus b'teur Kadmoniot ha-Yehudim" Zion* 5 (July, 1940): 184-186; Pere Villalba I. Varneda, *The Historical Method of Flavius Josephus* (Leiden: E. J. Brill, 1966), pp. 69-88.

20. Among Josephus' inconsistencies in his biblical paraphrase are his inclusion of these embarrassing incidents (the kidnapping of Joseph, Gen. 37, and the revolt of Korah, Num. 16), fantastic miracles (Baalam's talking donkey, Num. 22: 28-29; Jonah and the fish) and technical matters (details of the Tabernacle and the priestly vestments, Exod. 25-30). But Josephus may have had both ulterior and literary motives for including these matters. The kidnapping of Joseph foreshadowed the plots against Josephus by his enemies and the revolt of Korah foreshadowed the division among the Jews and the irresponsibility of the Jewish revolutionaries in the Roman-Jewish War. The technical details of the Tabernacle and the priestly vestments is explained by Josephus' pride in his priestly lineage. Baalam's talking donkey is in line with what Josephus adds to the biblical narrative on the snake in Eden, i.e., that in the earliest period all animals spoke a common language (*Antiquities* 1, 1, 4) a widespread belief of antiquity. Thus the Greeks, like the Jews, accepted the idea of animals having the possibility of speech (Achilles' horse in Illiad 19 and Aesop's fables. See Dov Noy, "The Jewish Versions of the Animal Languages Folktale" in *Scripta Hierosolymitana* 22 *Studies in Aggada and Folk Literature* (Jerusalem, Magnes Press, 1971): 171-208. Jonah's deliverance from the belly of the fish to bring God's message of repentance to Ninveh foreshadowed Josephus'

miraculous deliverance from Roman captivity (he also considered himself as possessing prophetic gifts) to bring the message of surrender and peace to his embattled brethren.

21. Harold W. Attridge, *The Interpretation of Biblical History in the Antiquitates Judaicae of Flavius Josephus*, Harvard Dissertations in Religion 7 (Missoula, Montana: Scholars Press, 1976), p. 183.

22. *The Jewish War*, preface; *Jewish Antiquities*, Loeb Classical Library ed. trans. H. St. John Thackeray, 8:56.

23. Varneda, *The Historical Method of Flavius Josephus*, pp. 253-256.

24. Ibid., pp. 12-19.

25. Ibid., pp. 203-209; pp. 89-115.

26. Shaye J. D. Cohen, *Josephus in Galilee and Rome: His Vita and Development As A Historian* (Leiden: E. J. Brill, 1979), p. 100.

27. Varneda, *The Historical Method of Flavius Josephus*, pp. 39-43; 46-50; pp. 51-54. Josephus sometimes uses the word *epiphaneia* (epiphany) in the sense of a visible manifestation of divine guidance in history. Cf. *Jewish Antiquities* 1:255; 2:339; 3:310; 8:119; 9:60; 18:75 and Otto Betz, "Miracles in the Writings of Flavius Josephus," in Louis Feldman ed. *Josephus, Judaism and Christianity*, p. 214. For the extensive scholarly treatment of Josephus see Heinz Schreckenberg, *Bibliographie zu Flavius Josephus* (Leiden: E. J. Brill, 1968, 1969) and Louis H. Feldman, *Josephus: A Supplementary Bibliography* (New York: Garland Publications, 1986) which supplements Schreckenberg's work.

28. *Gen. R.* 63:6 (ed Theodor-Albeck), p. 684. Cf. *Gen. R.* 46:4 (ed. Theodor-Albeck), p. 461 on whether the hermeneutic principle of *gezerah shavah* (an analogy between two laws based on a verbal congruence, developed in the Second Temple period by Hillel the Elder, see chapter 8, Sinai notes 14-15) was already given to Abraham.

29. The term "Greater" in the title is used to distinguish this work from a later one entitled *Seder Olam Zuta*, or "Minor Order" See *Seder Olam Rabbah*, ed. A. Marx (Berlin, 1903).

30. Cf. Jacob Neusner, *Life of Rabban Yohanan ben Zakkai* (Leiden: E. J. Brill, 1962).

31. R. Samuel bar Nachmani declared: "Blasted be those who calculate the end, for they say that since the time has arrived and he (the Messiah) has not come, he will never come. Rather wait for him, as it is written, "Though he tarry, wait for him . . ." *b. Sanhedrin*, 97b.

32. Nahum M. Glatzer's *Untersuchungen Zur Geschichtslehre Der Tannaiten*, (Berlin: Schocken Verlag, 1933), is still the classic work on the rabbinic attitude toward history. Cf. Jacob Neusner, "The Religious Uses of History: Judaism in First Century C.E. Palestine and Third-Century Babylonia," *History and Theory* 5 (1966): 153-171 and Yosef Hayim Yerushalmi, *Zakhor: Jewish History and Memory* (Seattle and London: University of Washington Press, 1982), pp. 16-26.

33. The identification of Esau with Rome dates from rabbinic homilies after the Bar Kokhba rebellion of 132-135 C.E. See Moshe David Herr, "Esau" *Encyclopedia Judaica* 6:858-859.

34. On the literary technique of stretching time and its purpose in rabbinic literature see I. Heinemann, *Darkei Ha-Aggadah* 2nd ed. (Jerusalem: The Magnes Press, 1954), p. 27 ff. On historical recurrence and the removal of historical specificity in the Bible, in apocalyptic literature, in Philo and in rabbinic literature as well as the unique features of rabbinic midrash see James L. Kugel "Two Introductions to Midrash" in *Midrash and Literature* ed. Geoffrey H. Hartman and Sanford Budick (New Haven and London: Yale University Press, 1986), pp. 84-89 and notes 11-15, pp. 101-102. On the organic connection between kabbalistic concepts and symbolism and rabbinic midrash see Joseph Dan, "Midrash and the Dawn of Kabbalah" in *Midrash and Literature*, pp. 127-139 and Moshe Idel, "Infinities of Torah in Kabbalah" in *Midrash and Literature*, pp. 141-157 and Moshe Idel, *Kabbalah: New Perspectives* (New Haven and London: Yale University Press, 1988), pp. 31-32.

35. *M. Berakot*, 1:1-2; *M. Pesahim*, 1:4; 3:6.

Conclusions and Comparisons

From history to meta-history the Greek and Hebrew historians and thinkers traveled a similar, though not identical, path. Since all historical writing is by necessity selective, both the Hebrew and the Greek historians were constrained to limit their focus but they used different criteria. On Sinai, the covenant between God and Israel circumscribed biblical historiography. Though the first eleven chapters of Genesis deal with universal history, the focus is soon narrowed to Abraham and his descendants. Non-Hebrew history becomes peripheral, relevant only to the extent that it impacts on the people of Israel. Only in the prophetic conception of history at the End of Days is the focus widened to include all of humanity once again.

On Olympus, the selection was based on the quality of an event that made it worthy to be rescued from oblivion and the evidence available to substantiate it. For Herodotus, the great events of the fifth century B.C.E. involving the Greeks and the barbarians determined his subject and its scope. But they were also determined by the stories and information that he could validate by his own experience or discover by resorting to earlier writers, authoritative records, oral histories, and myths and old tales transmitted orally by various peoples. Thucydides limited himself to the Peloponnesian War and its political framework because it was a great event worth recording and its particular incidents demonstrated general principles of human behavior. Moreover, Thucydides and his fellow countrymen had participated in the war so that the historical evidence was fairly easy to obtain from eyewitness reports and accessible primary sources.

Like Herodotus and Thucydides, the Hebrew historians were antiquarians who wanted to "discover how it really was" and like them they too used first hand testimonies and a variety of secondary sources. Josephus argued that the Jews had better organized records than the Greeks (*Contra Apionem*, 1:1), but he does not mention that the Jews were less concerned than the Greeks about the reliability of their records (for reasons discussed in the introduction to this chapter).

On Sinai, the revelational-covenental framework, combined with a low estimation of political life, accounted for the biblical historians' aversion to coherent analysis of complex political matters and the minute examination of human motivations. In contrast, on Olympus the in-depth political analysis and the subtle examination of human impulses characteristic of Herodotus,

Thucydides, Polybius and their successors underscored an anthropocentric perspective in which the political arena is one of the best places to achieve human fulfillment.

The Greek concentration on checking and testing historical sources and on contemporaneity as a criterion in determining historical selection made for a present centered history. Though they admired duration in a people's history, they viewed the remote past as problematic and filled with ambiguity, possibly because the antiquity of other civilizations exceeded their own, and the higher achievements of their own civilization were not in the distant past but in their own time. Though the future did not play a major role in the historical concerns of the Greeks, most of the historians on Olympus wrote with the future in mind, hoping that the record of their own times would provide pragmatic, moral and political lessons for the leaders of generations to come.

For the Sinai historians, a continuous unfolding of events from creation to their own time, and beyond into the messianic future, was connected with the biblical idea of the irruption of eternity into time. Superficially seen, time and eternity are polar opposites. But from the Hebrew perspective, time has its roots in eternity and thus must encompass the distant past as well as the distant future. In contrast to the present centered Greek historians, Hebrew historiography viewed events of the present (which they recognized as unique) in the mirror of the past. They felt religiously impelled to connect contemporary occurrences to their past counterparts; the biblical-rabbinic typologies traced through time are the literary expression of this outlook. The biblical historian connected the exodus from Egypt, a truly unique phenomenon, with God's promise to Abraham (Gen. 15:13-14; Exod. 6:2-4) and the Passover Haggadah urges "that in every generation every individual should feel as if he or she had actually been redeemed from Egypt" citing Exod. 13:8. In this way, the covenental links were established in Israel's salvational history.

Both the Greek and Hebrew historians saw the moral order as impinging on events. In the early historical narratives of the Bible, the flouting of grave moral imperatives such as those enshrined in the ten commandments accounted for the great flood in the time of Noah and the destruction of the cities of Sodom and Gomorrah. Similarly, the transgression of the other commandments contained in the Torah would bring about natural disasters in the form of plagues, drought and destruction by enemies (Lev. 26:14-33). But the cardinal sin that would and (actually did) bring about the destruction of the Hebrew states and the exile of their citizens was, for the Torah and the Deuteronomist historian, the cultic sin of idolatry. In the prophetic view, the sins of social morality (perversion of justice and the exploitation of the poor and defenseless) outweigh even cultic sins in deciding the fate of the nation.

The Greek historians likewise viewed infractions of the moral order as determining the course of events. For Herodotus, eternity literally irrupts into human time to punish the sin of hubris through horizontal, corporate, and individual reciprocity even as human agents express and act out their own political and personal motivations. The Persian defeat, for example, was due as much to Xerxes' arrogant transgression of his limits (he sought to rule both Europe and Asia) and his sacrilegious acts (he shackled the sacred Hellespont and savaged Greek images and temples) as to Greek patriotism, strategy, and valor. Although Thucydides and later historians generally eliminated the anthropomorphic divine explanation from their record of human affairs, their analysis presupposes universal laws of human nature and a moral order in which actions motivated by excess greed and ambition lead to the demise of civilized community life as well as to defeat and the loss of power. Polybius praises the mixed constitution of the Romans and their benevolent treatment of subjects as a pragmatic alternative that might prevent the succession of falls which result from excess.

Behind all these conceptions is a pattern in the rise and fall of nations which reflects both the mutability of human life and the principles of a cosmic harmony based on a balance of portions. As Momigliano has noted, however, Greek historians did not write from the same moral and spiritual perspective as the authors of the Bible. Greek history was a separate and limited genre with a clear anthropocentric interest in reporting the truth about important human events. Religious or metaphysical realities as well as moral and social values were articulated by the poets and philosophers of Greece (see chapter six) not the historians.[1]

Both Hebrew and Greek historians use imaginative reconstruction not only to recreate the past but also to tell interesting stories embedded in a connected historical narrative. In the Hellenistic era, Hebrew historians like the author of the book of Daniel and the books of Maccabees drew on a repertoire of techniques garnered from Greek poets, dramatists and popular historians, such as the recounting of history in the guise of prophecy for the future, and the graphic portrayal of atrocities and heroism using the language of drama and rhetoric. The works of Flavius Josephus represent the culmination of this felicitous marriage between Greek style and Hebrew content. Here Greek stylistic devices are supplemented by critical analysis which distinguishes between real and apparent causes of events and between fundamental and cumulative and immediate antecedents to the outbreak of war, in the manner of Thucydides and Polybius.

The rabbis turned away from the historical enterprise. The destruction of the Second Temple mandated an avoidance of reflection on the recent past which would only depress the survivors even more, or, even worse, reflection on the future with its messianic overtones might ignite another disastrous rebellion against Rome. Moreover, the rabbis inherited from the Hebrew Bible a belief in a metahistorical plane which is more real than the historical realm. This higher plane which is a dimension of sacred time and eternity is characterized by the repetition of eternal symbols or, in historical terms, the rise and fall of civilizations. From this vantage point, historical events are masks for perennial truths that like a leitmotif with minor variations are replayed down through the centuries. If the truths are born in mind, there is no need to encumber oneself with historical details.

The Greek historians, on the other hand, remained concerned with just such details which exhibited the changes in human life in time. Examination of the sequence of events revealed a recurring pattern, but historians described a relatively short span of time (about 150 years at most), analyzed each particular, and occasionally suggested that, by understanding what really happened and why, leaders might actually change the future. The continuing rise and fall of empires or forms of governments does imply a kind of inevitability, which Starr attributes to the fact that historians are generally realists and therefore pessimists. But he notes that "pessimism does not force one into the squirrel cage of hopeless cycles."[2]

It is the Greek philosophers, not the historians, who developed metahistorical concepts similar to those of the rabbis.[3] The influence of the nature philosophers and the Sophists on the methods, ideas, and styles of the first great historians has been pointed out above. But Polybius, who also knew the works of later thinkers, acknowledges his debt to Plato and certain other philosophers (6.5.1) when discussing the cycle of constitutions. Men such as Plato, Aristotle, and the Stoics Panaetius and Posidonius, having lived through great events themselves, developed theories which accounted for change, analyzed the different types of governments, speculated on the origins of human society, and posited the best type of government and leader for producing the best and happiest citizens. They were not, however, interested in specific events and agents or in linear and chronological time per se. The philosophers' ideas provide only the abstract framework for Polybius' detailed description of the unique mixed constitution of Rome and his complex analysis of the details of Rome's rise and incipient internal decay.

Philosophy's aims and interest were different and were ultimately ahistorical. From its beginnings, philosophy had been seeking the unity behind the multiplicity and flux apparent in the sensible world. Especially after Parmenides, the unchanging and eternal principle posited as the source of the things that come into being and pass away was looked upon as the only thing truly permanent and therefore fully knowable. Thus, philosophy was basically metahistorical because it devalued the particular in favor of the universal and was more interested in the theory than in the data.

It is no accident that the abstract exposition of the theory of cycles in history came from the philosophers (e.g., Empedocles, the Pythagoreans, Plato, and the Stoics). The perfection of the eternal was associated with the sphere, as the most perfect, regular and comprehensive shape, whose proper motion was circular. Time itself was also connected to the circular movement associated with the heavens. Plato's *Timaeus* describes the sensible universe as a moving image of the eternal and posits that time came into being with the ordering of the universe according to number. Although movement (as well as matter) makes change possible and distinguishes the created world from its perfect and unchanging model, the universe too was ultimately immutable and everlasting, for the cycles of change that it went through were infinitely repeatable, as in the solar month or solar year (*Timaeus* 37-39d).[4]

Aristotle related the measure of movement (as motion and change in nature) to the past and the future so that time is linear (*Physics* 4.11), but Plato and the Stoics connected the circular conception of time to human history in an ahistorical way.[5] In Plato's myth in *Statesman* 268-274e, the moving image of eternity rotates forward in the half-cycle when God is in control, but reverses its direction and degenerates when he withdraws during the other half-cycle, only to resume the opposite forward motion when he returns. In the Stoic conception of Ekpyrosis, the cyclical conversion of the universe back into fire, the exact same events and people recur in cycle after cycle so that time itself, eternally returning, is timeless and there is no real history to study. Both of these constructs are metahistorical. Moreover, in both, the ends of the cycles are marked by cataclysms and catastrophes which resemble the Messianic Woes. Therefore, we move now away from history to our final chapter, "The End Time: Apocalypse and Afterlife."

Notes

1.   "Greek Historigoraphy," *History and Theory* 17 (1978): 22-23.
2.   "Historical and Philosophical Time," *History and Theory* Beiheft 6 (1966): 28.
3.   See Starr, *ibid.*, pp. 29-32, as well as the following general works on the development of the concept of time: John Callahan, *Four Views of Time in Ancient Philosophy* (Cambridge: Harvard University Press, 1948); G. W. Trompf, *The Idea of Historical Recurrence in Western Thought: From Antiquity to the Reformation* (Berkeley: University of California Press, 1979); and G. J. Whitrow, *Time in History: The Evolution of Our General Awareness of Time and Temporal Perspective* (New York: Oxford University Press, 1988). James Barr, *Biblical Words for Time* (London: SCM Press, 1962), p. 142 makes the important suggestion that the whole notion of the "cyclical view of time" has to be broken down into more specific categories, i.e., a) the circular movement of earthly existence, b) the circular movement of heavenly bodies which measure time, c) the application to time of circularity as in the example of uniform motion, d) time as a cyclical cosmic process, occurring once but returning to where it began, e) time as a cyclical cosmic process repeating itself infinitely and f) time as a temporal cycle in which all historical events recur as before.
4.   See Callahan, pp. 3-37, for Plato's conceptions of time.
5.   See Callahan, pp. 38-87 for Aristotle's ideas about time.

Chapter 10

The Endtime: Afterlife and Apocalypse

Introduction

As noted in the introduction to the last chapter ancient societies in their early stages of development know of primordial time that is renewed again and again through the rhythms of nature and the repetitions of ritual. Logically speaking, primordial time should have its correspondence in final time when the whole world comes to an end. But the people of these societies do not have a conception of eschatology in the strict sense of the word. They are aware of final time for individuals because they have experienced pain, suffering and death. But, in the earliest images of death and the afterlife, the world continues on its natural course although individual lives come to an end.

Like individual lives, the natural course of the world necessitates decline. In some cultures, this movement is envisioned as a degeneration from a high point of harmony between the divine, the human, and the natural, as is described in the biblical Eden and the Greek Golden Age. On both Sinai and Olympus, the first decline is punctuated by a cataclysmic flood which is then followed by a renewal of creation that imitates the cyclic pattern of nature.[1]

The early Hebrews and Greeks associated mortality with this cycle and thought that the dead returned to the netherworld from which they came. The Hebrew *Sheol* and the Greek Hades are both dark places under the earth connected to the fertility and creativity of nature. Although they are removed from the heavenly light, both are devoid of the demonic terrors feared by other Mediterranean cultures. Rather, *Sheol* and Hades are neutral if uninviting homes for those ordinary mortals whose span on earth is finished. Very early, however, these netherworlds also became the places of extraordinary punishment for extraordinary sinners. Moreover, a few outstanding mortals, distinguished for virtue or achievement, could escape the confines of a netherworld altogether.

Both cultures developed customs to ease the passage from life for the dead and their mourners, as well as to connect the living with the dead through memory and respect. Neither the Greeks or the Hebrews ever evolved elaborate funeral rituals or cults of the dead to protect against their hostility and power to harm. In fact, the Hebrews desacralized burial practices and emphasized the impurity of the dead in order to discourage such activities and beliefs about the afterlife, which were widespread among their neighbors. According to Plutarch, Lycurgus' laws for burial in Sparta had been instituted to dispel superstition and fear of the dead (*Lycurgus*, 27).

Although funeral procedures remained relatively constant over the ages, the conceptions about death evolved as the cultures developed. For both the Hebrews and the Greeks, who were intensely concerned with justice and moral order, the afterlife became the place of judgment and recompense. The netherworld was gradually differentiated geographically as well as morally, so that those blessed by cult or behavior on earth took separate paths from those whose lives on earth merited atonement or eternal punishment. After Greek philosophy and science posited the divinity of the heavenly bodies, the two pictures of the afterlife expanded even further; the good and pure returned to the heavenly realm high above the earth instead of remaining below for purification or torture.

Although life on earth was the central focus for both cultures, the Hebrews and Greeks also felt the widespread human need to escape the tribulation of the present and/or the impending disaster of the near future. Thus they began to envision an end of time. Their new ideas were responses to political and social crisis: the inability of the restored nation of Israel to regain the independence and power promised by God in the face of the succession of ever mightier empires; the concomitant failures of the polis, anthropomorphic polytheism, and nature philosophy to provide adequate moral and social guidance in fourth century Greece.

The two cultures emphasized different aspects of the end. Bound together as well as to God by their covenant and salvation history, of time. The Greeks, however, followed several paths, some of which led to a belief in individual immortality, associated with the divinity of the soul and its reincarnation into ever new mortal bodies.

The new ideas from Sinai and Olympus were couched in the language and symbolism of past beliefs. Just as Hebrew apocalyptic transposed Hebrew prophecy to a different plane, so too did Platonic myth incorporate and thereby transform earlier myths, cults and philosophies. Moreover, both cultures conveyed their eschatological descriptions in a similar way—as an otherworld journey or an out of body experience in which an extraordinary human being is privy to a vision of the hidden realities of the supernatural realm, which helps to clarify mundane problems. When he returns to his own world, he reports what he has learned about the destinies of human beings, individual and collective, as well as the destiny of the universe.

The otherworld journeys taken from Sinai and Olympus are themselves transformations of earlier religious and literary motifs. Certain figures such as Enoch and Elijah were believed to have ascended to heaven. Others such as Isaiah ascended in life to eavesdrop on the divine council. Greek heroes like Heracles and Odysseus journeyed beyond the limits of the earth to make contact with the netherworld. The different accounts of these voyages in the later literature are all variations of the central theme:

1). A deity or deities who live in a perfect realm usually called heaven.

2). Human beings who live in an extremely imperfect realm most often referred to as earth.

3). Since human beings have only a partitive knowledge of the perfect realm and communication between the two realms is limited, both can be extended through the movement of a mediator. The need for a mediator is triggered by the ever sharpening awareness of the distance separating the realms and the contradictions between earthly justice and divine justice, between temporal suffering and eternal reward, between the transitory, imperfect nature of life and knowledge in the mundane realm and the enduring perfection in the supernatural realm.

4). The message from the supernatural realm validates what the author believes to be the moral order below.

According to one pattern, the mediator is a divine agent who descends to offer a revelation. In the Sinai tradition it might be an angel, a divine word directly spoken to a prophet or sage and enshrined in a text, or, as in early Christianity, a divine savior incarnated in a human being. In the Olympus tradition, the gods frequently descend, often in human guise, to help and protect the heroes. It was Hermes' particular function to deliver messages from Olympus to the worlds of humans and lesser divinities but other deities could also descend to aid humans. In the

Odyssey, for example, Athena disguises herself as various individuals (e.g., as Mentor) to guide Odysseus home, Telemachus to manhood, Penelope to happiness and Ithaca to peace. In Sophocles' *Philoctetes* the deified Heracles comes down to reveal and thus change the future for warriors entrapped by circumstance or character. In another pattern, the mediator is a human hero who undergoes the experience of either descending to the netherworld or ascending to the heavens to receive the revelation of divine secrets. In some cases this is an out of body experience in which the soul of the visionary travels to the other realm while the body lies inert in trance or in a near death state. Whatever the mode of return to the protagonist's native realm, the main focus is on the first half of the journey and the vision or revelation.[2]

The Hebrew apocalyptic vision has been termed metahistorical, for it focused on the end of the universe as the conclusion to the salvation history. This eschatology validated the national hope by predicting that the conquerors would be destroyed in a final cataclysm directed by the plan and the power of God. The Messianic Age will erupt as suddenly as the prophetic Day of the Lord, with global warfare and suffering to punctuate the end of the world like an exclamation point at the end of a sentence. Or in an alternate scenario mentioned earlier, the process is more gradual with the old order progressively decaying and dying and a transitional generation leading up to the catastrophe and the birth of a new world. Although the new world will be a recapitulation of creation, a return to the pristine purity of peace, joy, light, and love that characterized the existence of the first mortals in the Garden of Eden, both happenings are viewed as unique one-time events that will take place at the end of history. Like every other happening on the linear scale that is Hebrew history, these Endtime events are unparalleled and irreversible because they contain the divine presence that gives them an intrinsic value. But though the dominant thrust of the Hebrew Endtime is linear, the cyclical motif is not absent. It is present in the Bible in Dan. 9:24-27. Its presence in the *eschaton* echoes Hebrew ritual that follows the cyclical rhythms of nature and the cosmos and Israel's history with its archetypal repetitions of exile and redemption (as discussed in Chapter Seven, Sinai: Priestly Piety, notes 24-31).

In contrast, Greek ideas about the end were ahistorical and metaphysical. The philosophers conceived of the divine universe as eternal and unchanging because of its never ending repetition of an ordered cycle of movement. Thus the mythmakers' or philosophers' vision of the destiny of the universe is not really eschatological because the universe has no *eschaton* or unique ending. Rather there are an infinite series of endings, some punctuated by great destruction, as in archetypal repetitions of exile and redemption (as discussed in Chapter Seven, Sinai: Priestly Piety, notes 24-31).

In contrast, Greek ideas about the end were ahistorical and metaphysical. The philosophers conceived of the divine universe as eternal and unchanging because of its never ending repetition of an ordered cycle of movement. Thus the mythmakers' or philosophers' vision of the destiny of the universe is not really eschatological because the universe has no *eschaton* or unique ending. Rather there are an infinite series of endings, some punctuated by great destruction, as in Phaethon's fall, or the catastrophe which swallowed up Atlantis and early Athens.[3] But even these are followed by new beginnings and slow growth to a height from which inevitable decline must lead to the next destruction, e.g., the Stoic *ekpyrosis*, the periodic great conflagration which returned the world to the original pure fire out of which it was created. So the later Greek conception of the Endtime retained the earlier cyclic pattern. That pattern, however, now became infused with the philosophical description of divine nature as both good and the source of the good. It was also inextricably related to the concept of the immortality of the individual human soul which was derived from the divine and capable of achieving the knowledge and virtue necessary for faring well in life and death.

Notes

1.   G. Van der Leeuw, "Primordial Time and Final Time" in *Man and Time: Papers From the Eranos Yearbooks*, Bollingen Series 30, Vol. 3 (New York: Pantheon Books, 1957): 337-349; Mircea Eliade, *Cosmos and History: The Myth of the Eternal Return* (New York: Harper & Row, 1959), pp. 60, 73, 86-89; 96-137.

2.   Alan F. Segal, "Heavenly Ascent in Hellenistic Judaism, Early Christianity and their Environment," in *Aufstieg und Niedergang Der Roemischen Welt: Geschichte und Kultur Roms Im Spiegel Der Neueren Forschung*, II, ed. Hildegard Temporini and Wolfgang Haase, *Principat*, vol. 23 (2) (Berlin, New York: Walter de Gruyter, 1980), pp. 1339-1341; Ioan Petru Culianu, *Psychonodia I-A Survey of the Evidence Concerning the Ascension of the Soul and its Relevance* (Leiden: E. J. Brill, 1983), pp. 6-8. A synthesis of the research of Segal and Culianu reveals the following additional details in the ascent-descent motif:

1). The hero who undergoes the experience of descending to earth or ascending to heaven is called to his/her mission, i.e., elected by reason of special merit.   But only in the ascent motif does the hero pursue an individual quest to obtain a revelation.

2). In both the ascent and descent patterns the savior/hero is either a supermundane entity or one who takes on a spiritual form temporarily.   In some descent motifs the savior/hero is a spiritual being who temporarily takes on a human form.

3). Both the descending and the ascending savior/heros disclose to their disciples and/or to the whole world hidden realities of the other world concerning the destiny of human beings, individual and collective, as well as the configuration and destiny of the universe. But whereas the ascending savior/hero must overcome the mortal limitations of the human condition to obtain this information from divine beings, the descending hero is one of the divine beings and as such is entitled to the secrets kept from mortals. On the pre-Hellenistic varieties of the ascension theme see G. Widengren, *The Ascension of the Apostle and the Heavenly Book* (King and Savior III) (Uppsala: Uppsala Universitets Arsskrift, 1950). On the heavenly ascent in Islam and in medieval Jewish mysticism see A. Altmann, "The Ladder of Ascension," in *Studies in Mysticism and Religion: Presented to Gershom G. Scholem on his Seventieth Birthday* (Jerusalem: The Magnes Press, 1967), pp. 1-32. For a fine analysis of medieval and modern accounts of near death experiences see Carol Zaleski, *Otherworld Journeys* (New York, Oxford: Oxford University Press, 1987). On the meaning of ascending as opposed to descending symbolism see Erich Kahler, "The Nature of the Symbol," in *Symbolism in Religion and Literature*, ed. Rollo May (New York, 1960), pp. 50-75.

3.   For a fascinating survey of the various references in world literature to this global catastrophe and the various scientific explanations that have been adduced for it up to our own time see John White, *Pole Shift: Predictions and Prophecies of the Ultimate Disaster* (Garden City, NY: Doubleday, 1980).

Sinai I: The Road to Redemption and the World to Come—The Afterlife

Biblical Conceptions

Every living culture, consciously and unconsciously, is always borrowing and adapting foreign elements to its own context. It has been argued that the real quality of any civilization is demonstrated less by its indigenous creations and more by the way it constantly assimilates new grafts to its own trunk "but resists with all its power their over-luxuriant growth."[1] The views of the afterlife in biblical Israel could hardly be divorced from those held by Canaanites, Mesopotamians and Egyptians. The afterlife cast a particularly large shadow on the religious outlook of Egypt and Mesopotamia, though more so in the former than in the latter. Thus it is not surprising that mourning customs in Israel resembled the practices followed by many peoples of the ancient Near East. Weeping, the rending of clothes and the donning of sackcloth (Gen. 23:2; 37:34; 2 Sam. 1:11), fasting, sitting and sleeping on the ground (1 Sam. 31:13; 2 Sam. 1:12; 13:31; Isa. 3:26), going bareheaded and barefoot with upper lip covered (Ezek. 24:17), inflicting wounds and baldness upon oneself (Jer. 16:6; Ezek. 7:18; Isa. 22:12), shaving the hair of the face (Jer. 41:5) are all to be found in the Mediterranean world. In fact the prohibitions against some of these practices in the Torah (Lev. 19:27 f.; 21:5; Deut. 14:1) are an indication that they were part of the pagan rites of surrounding cultures. But in biblical Israel they remained isolated practices and never became collectively rooted in a cult of the dead.[2]

Though the Torah transformed and assimilated the sacrificial cult of the Mediterranean world to the monotheistic religion of Israel (see above ch. 7, Sinai: Priestly Piety, notes 18-23), it had nothing to say about funerary rites, apart from the few prohibitions mentioned above. On the one hand, it desacralized funeral practices that fill an emotional need for the living, placing them in the context of universal human customs. Thus the Bible (Gen. 50:1 ff., 26) has no qualms about relating that Jacob and Joseph were mummified even though this rite was connected with the Osiris cult. On the other hand, the Torah sealed off the world of the dead by declaring the dead body to be the most virulent form of ritual impurity (Num. 19:11-17). It did this to counter the pagan religious outlook of Israel's neighbors who viewed death as a passage to the kingdom of the dead, an autonomous, divine-demonic realm with its own laws and its own deity. The dead who enter this kingdom become divine good or evil spirits. Osiris, the dying and reviving god was the model for the dead in Egypt and in Mesopotamia the dead were identified with Tammuz.[3] Though a remnant of these pagan views is to be found in the Hebrew folk belief that the spirit of the dead could be implored to reveal the future (1 Sam. 28:8-25), biblical religion never regarded this spirit as a god. The soul was only a shade.

The Psycho-Physical Unity of Body and Soul

What is the biblical conception of the soul? It is to be found in three key terms and their interrelationship: spirit (*ruah*), breath (*neshamah*), and soul (*nefesh*). The term spirit (*ruah*) is used in the Bible in two senses. There is the life-giving spirit of God which is the vital force pervading all creation (Ps. 104:30; Cf. Num. 16:22; 27:16; Gen. 45:27; Ezek. 37:14; Job 10:12; 17:1). When this vital energy is withdrawn, death ensues (Gen. 6:3; Pss. 104:29; 146:4; Job 34:14; Eccles. 3:19, 21; 12:7). It is clear that the spirit of God transcends the human being (Ezek. 2:2; 3:14; 11:5; 37:1, 5 f., 8-10; Zech. 12:1; Job 12:10) but also dwells within him/her. When there was a weakening of physical or psychic power it was attributed to the lessening of the spirit. Job complains of his debilitating illness: "My spirit is crushed, my days run out; The graveyard waits for me" (Job 17:1). The Book of Joshua relates that when the Canaanite kings heard how Israel crossed the Jordan as a result of God's intervention, "they lost heart and no spirit was left in them" (Josh. 5:1; Cf. 2 Sam. 13:39; Isa. 65:14; Pss. 143-147; Prov. 15:4). On the other hand, when there was a return of the spirit, physical and psychic strength was immediately enhanced. Samson, dangerously weakened by thirst, finds his spirit returning to him when God miraculously provides him with water (Judg. 15:19. Cf. 1 Sam. 30:12). Jacob was emotionally and spiritually depressed since the loss of his beloved son Joseph but his spirit revived on hearing from his sons that Joseph was alive, well and even prospering in Egypt (Gen. 45:25, 27). The linking of physical and psychic states in the understanding of this term was undoubtedly confirmed by the personal experience of feeling the flushed face, the pounding heart, the increased pulse rate and the tight stomach when intense joy and happiness or emotional upset was in progress. Gradually the word" spirit" (*ruah*) was generalized and limited to describe all psychic activity unique to the individual. But even when so denoted it never lost its connotation of a connection with the physical functioning of the body below and the spirit of God above.

The term breath (*neshamah*) is used in a collective sense as that which vitalizes all living things. "Let all that breathes praise the Lord" (Ps. 150:6; Cf. Deut. 20:16; Josh. 10:40; 11: 11,14; 1 Kings 15:29). It is directly connected to body processes. "The Lord, God formed man from the dust of the earth. He blew into his nostrils the breath of life and man became a living being" (Gen. 2:7; Cf. Gen. 7:22; Isa. 42:5; Job 26:4; 27:3). This verse also clearly implies that the term is used in reference to that which transcends the human being having its source in divinity. This idea is explicitly stated in Prov. 20:27: "The lifebreath of man is the lamp of the Lord, revealing all his inmost parts" (cf. Job 32:8; 33:4; 34:14).

Unlike the word spirit (*ruah*), the word soul (*nefesh*) means life intertwined with the body. In biblical physiology the blood is the conveyor of the soul (*nefesh*) so that it is possible for the Bible to say emphatically "for the blood is the *nefesh*" (Deut. 12:23) and to prohibit eating blood (Lev. 17:11-14) as it prohibits murder (Gen. 9:4-6). When the body dies the soul (*nefesh*) ceases to exist (Num. 23:10; Judges 16:30). If spirit (*ruah*) is the universal life force transcending the human being, emanating from God and present everywhere, the soul (*nefesh*) is the same vital element confined to the individual creature. Though the soul (*nefesh*) dies with the person, the universal spirit (*ruah*) transcends death. But biblical theology does not make hard and fast distinctions. There are biblical passages that imply that the soul (*nefesh*) leaves the human being at death. Of Rachel the Bible says that "*as her soul departed for she was dying, she named her newborn son Ben Oni* whom his father called Benjamin" (Gen. 35:18). Conversely, when Elijah resuscitated the child of the widow of Zarephath we are told that "the child's soul (*nefesh*) returned to his body and he revived" (1 Kings 17:21-22).

The identification of soul (*nefesh*) with the body to constitute the individual led to an extension of its meaning to include all physical wishes, desires and urges. Thus human life and vitality are synonymous with bodily impulses (e.g., Deut. 12:15, 20 f.; 1 Sam. 2:16; Mic. 7:1; Prov. 10:3; 12:10; 25:25; Ps. 107:9). The term "*nefesh*" was also taken to reflect the entire spectrum of emotions and moods, e.g., Hannah poured out her *nefesh* to God (1 Sam. 1:15) because she was of bitter soul (1 Sam. 1:10. Cf. grief, Ezek. 27:31; joy and peace, Pss. 86:4; 94:19, longing and love, Ps. 63:2; Gen. 34:3; 44:30; hatred and scorn, Isa. 1:41; Jer. 15:1; Ezek. 25:15; 36:5, loathing and weariness, Job 10:1; Jer. 6:8; Ezek. 23:17 f.). A further development led to spiritual feelings and yearnings (Pss. 25:1; 86:4; 143:8).

To sum up, there is clearly an overlap in the terms "spirit" (*ruah*), "breath" (*neshamah*) and "soul" (*nefesh*). They represent a biblical kaleidoscope of human nature perceived from different angles but sharing a common holism. The anchor in the physical life of the body is to be found in the word "spirit" (*ruah*) even though it is the most universal and transcendent of the terms. A spiritual connection and an implication that it may transcend the body is to be found in the word "soul" (*nefesh*) even though it is the most particular and corporeal of the terms.[4]

Sheol—The Biblical Netherworld

The previous discussion implies that for the ancient Hebrew death was not the end of life but the transition from one mode of existence to another, from earthly life to afterlife. The Bible generally designates the realm of the afterlife as *Sheol*, variously located under the earth (Num. 16:30 ff.) or at the bottom of the mountains (Jonah 2:7) or under the waters of the cosmic ocean (Job 26:5). Scholars have noted a number of descriptive similarities between *Sheol* and the Ugaritic god of death, Mot. Both *Sheol* and the realm of Mot are pictured as a watery pit or bog. In fact one of the synonyms for *Sheol* is *bor*, the Hebrew word for "pit".[5] When Sheol is personified in the Bible it takes on the aggressiveness and the voracious appetite of Mot (Pss. 89:49; 49:16; Hos. 13:14; Isa. 5:14; Hab. 2:5; Prov. 27:20; Prov. 30:16; Prov. 1:12).

The personification of death in the Ugaritic myth stemmed from the need to describe and hence to understand the primeval power operating in the universe. The mythographers translated their intuitive perceptions of the nature of this power into graphic, concrete images. But what aspect of death became the focus of these descriptions? Three lines of thought have evolved in answering this question. One view holds that seasonal conflict is the focal point in which Mot personified represents the arid heat of summer who struggles with Ba'al the god of rain and vegetation. A second view argues that the struggle between the gods is not related to the seasons but to the sabbatical cycle of seven years of alternating drought and fertility.[6] A third approach, the cosmogonic interpretation, though accepting the natural cycle as part of the myth of Mot and Ba'al, holds that the epic has a far wider scope that reflects the clash between the forces of life and existence and those of death and dissolution.[7]

These views differ primarily in emphasis. The seasonal interpretation conceives of death as part of the cycle of nature. The cosmogonic interpretation views death as a chaotic power whose destructive force encompasses all forms of life and is therefore more mysterious and more menacing (see Ch. 2 Sinai 1: Creation by the One, notes 7-8). In biblical texts dealing with death both of these motifs have been adjusted to a monotheistic framework. The view of death as part of the natural cycle of human existence is suggested by the statement that God made man from the dust of the earth and to dust he must return (Gen. 2:7; 3:19). Job too echoes this idea when he says: "Naked I came from my mother's womb and naked shall I return there" (Job 1:20) and in a more positive vein Eliphaz, Job's friend, paints a peaceful and natural end to human life: "You will come in full vigor to the grave; Like a sheaf of corn in its season" (Job 5:26). In this context the term "*erez*" which is used interchangeably with *Sheol* in denoting the abode of the dead[8] has certain positive aspects. It is fertile and from it streams the primordial river that waters the surface of the earth (Gen. 2:6). It is the womb from which the sea burst forth at the time of creation (Job 38:8). In the psalms and in postbiblical wisdom texts the cosmic netherworld is called "mother earth" because human life had its origin there as in a mother's womb (Ps. 139:15-16; Sira 40:1). This realm of the dead from which the living also originated is one of the component parts of the universe testifying to God's glory (Ps. 95:3-5) and rejoicing with the world as together they witness God's redemption of His people (Isa. 44:23). The denizens of the netherworld as well as the generations yet to come join in acclaiming God as absolute ruler (Pss. 22:30; 78:4; Cf. Isa. 44:23).

In this perspective death was not evil but "the way of all the earth" (Josh. 23:14; 1 Kings 2:2) provided it came at the end of a full life. A full life meant a happy and meaningful existence as in the case of Abraham who is described as "dying at a happy ripe age, old and full of years, he was gathered to his kin" (Gen. 25:8; Cf. Gen. 25:17; 35:29; 49:29,33: Num. 20:24; 27:13; 31:2; Deut. 32:50; Judg. 2:10). But it also meant that the length of days predestined by divine decree, a belief of the ancient Hebrews (Ps. 139:13-16) and their neighbors[9], had been fulfilled. Though fixed and recorded in heavenly ledgers an individual's length of days was at times subject to change, either to be extended or cut short (Isa. 38:10-12; Pss. 89:46; 102:24,25. Cf. Ch. 4: Sinai: The Struggles of Theodicy, notes 34-35). These biblical passages cited above range from a neutral view of the abode of the dead as an integral part of the universe and its rhythms to a more positive assessment in which the dead of the netherworld join in praise of God.

But at the negative end of the spectrum *Sheol*, in contrast to *erez*, most closely resembles the cosmogonic interpretation of death as a chaotic, destructive power current in Near Eastern mythology. Like the mythological creatures that had to be vanquished by the god in the Near Eastern combat myth (see above Ch. 2: Creation: Genesis or Theogony? Introduction) *Sheol* had to be placed under divine dominion and turned into cosmic space.[10] As mentioned above *sheol* personified has a voracious appetite like Mot. The destructiveness of the Ugaritic realm of death is echoed in the Bible's description of the frightening death of Korah and his cohorts who rebelled against Moses and Aaron. Moses admonishes the Israelites that if Korah and his followers die a normal death it is a sign that God has not sent Moses and he is, as Korah and his allies claimed, only a power hungry politician.

> But if the Lord brings about something unheard of (Heb. *briah*, creation, stressing the uniqueness of the event) so that the ground opens its mouth and swallows them up with all that belongs to them, and they go down alive into Sheol, you shall know that these men have spurned the Lord. Scarcely had he finished speaking all these words when the ground under them burst asunder and the earth opened its mouth and swallowed them up with their households, all Korah's people and their possessions. They went down alive into Sheol, with all that belonged to them; the earth closed over them and they vanished from the midst of the congregation (Num. 16:30-33).

This narrative has a number of interesting implications for our discussion.

(1) In addition to demonstrating the insatiable appetite of *Sheol* and chaotic destructive death, the passage is an adumbration of the apocalyptic scenario of Isa. 24:19-23 which becomes a blueprint for apocalyptic eschatology as will be discussed below.

(2) The editor-writer of this episode was acutely aware of the creation account in Genesis where death is part of the normal cycle of nature (Gen. 2:7; 3:19) and he alludes to this in Moses' admonition, "if these men die as all men do, if their lot be the common fate of all mankind" (Num. 16:29). He was also aware that the netherworld and its association with violent death is not mentioned in the creation account and was not considered an integral part of the cosmos. Thus the words "if the Lord brings about

something unheard-of (Heb. *'im briah yivrah ha-Shem*, lit. "if the Lord creates something new") is an attempt to make the netherworld, *Sheol*, a part of God's continuing creation. But the phrase reveals the struggle of the editor-writer in uniting the inherited Near Eastern conception of an independent, chaotic and destructive realm of the dead with the integrated, harmonious and natural functioning realm of Genesis. His emphasis on the opening up of the netherworld for a punitive purpose as an *ad hoc* creation by God represents a clear polemic against the Ugaritic Mot. The biblical *Sheol* is subject to God's control unlike the autonomous realm of the dead in the Ugaritic epics.[11] Elsewhere, however, as part of the negative description of *Sheol* in the Bible we are told that the dead can no longer praise God (Isa. 38:18; Pss. 6:5; 30:9; 115:7). It may be that in this view there is also an echo of the polemic against the autonomous realm in which the dead are deified.

(3) The Korah narrative implies that *Sheol* is a place for the wicked who are punished there and particularly for those wicked who suffer an untimely death. In Babylonian religion violent, sudden death and annihilation were not seen as accidental or the result of the mysterious capriciousness of the deity but as divine retribution for sin, a conception that echoes in the Bible (Pss. 30:3,4, 6, 9,10, 12; 55:24; 94:1-7, 13b; 103:3-4; Isa. 38:17; Job 9:29-32; 33:13-30).[12] Violent, sudden death was often associated in the Bible with the denial of a proper burial which also was a divine punishment for transgression (Isa. 14:4-21, the king of Babylon; 1 Kings 21:19-24, Ahab and Jezebel). Such an "evil death" resulted in separation from the resting place of kin, just the opposite of natural death.

Sheol is also the destination of those who die of an uncommon illness unrelated to natural causes (e.g., Hos. 7:5; Prov. 13:12) or old age (1 Kings 15:23; 2 Kings 13:14) both of which were considered tolerable (Jer. 10:19). Such an exceptional sickness differed from an illness of divine chastisement in which there was hope for reprieve and recovery because sin may have strained the relationship with God but did not sever it (2 Sam. 7:14; Job 33:19, 26, 29). The unnatural disease (Deut. 29:21; Jer. 14:18; 16:4; 2 Chron. 21:19; Ps. 103:3) sometimes qualified by the term "evil" (2 Chron. 21:19) was without cure. The biblical writers viewed it as a divine decree of retribution and suspected the sufferers of severing their relationship with God (Job 24:19; 21:13; Pss. 9:17-18; 31;18; 49:14-16; 55:16; Isa. 38:1-12).[13]

Overwhelming grief may be the cause of untimely death (Gen. 37:35; 42:38; 44:31; 44:29; Pss. 88:3; 31; 11, 18). In the Genesis texts, though Jacob himself is not evil his language reflects the cultural patterns and usage of his time and place.[14]

(4) A final implication arising from the Korah episode and related to *Sheol* as a place of punishment for the wicked, is the biblical concept of God as judge. The connection between divine judgment and the descent to *Sheol* is often found in the psalms in which a forensic terminology predominates.

> For you uphold my right and claim
> enthroned as righteous judge . . .
> But the Lord abides forever;
> He has set up His throne for judgment;
> it is He who judges the world with
> righteousness, rules the people with equity . . .
> The Lord has made Himself known
> He works judgment; . . .
> Let the wicked be in Sheol
> all the nations who ignore God!
> Let not men have power
> let the nations be judged in your presence
> (Ps. 9:5,8,9,17, 18,20).

Even where the protagonist in the psalms is harassed by human enemies who bring him to the gates of *Sheol*, it is implied that it was God's execution of judgment that made possible their success (Ps. 69:27-28). But judgment does not always mean condemnation for sin and assignation to *Sheol*. It can also mean forgiveness of sin and rescue from *Sheol*. A leitmotif in the Bible is the idea that "God brings down to Sheol and brings up from it" (1 Sam. 2:6) underscoring His righteousness as a judge (Cf. 2 Sam. 22:20-24; Ps. 43:1). Divine deliverance was expected in the morning hours because that is when both the heavenly and earthly tribunals convene (Pss. 5:4; 130:5,6; 143:8; Jer. 22:12; Zeph. 3:3). Also associated with the image of divine judgment is the notion that human deeds are recorded in divine ledgers (Mal. 3:16-17). Both in Israel and in Mesopotamia this divine bookkeeping was pictured as being executed with the protocol and precision of judicial proceedings.[15] To be written down in God's book spells forgiveness of sin and deliverance, to be erased from it is a sign of condemnation and consignment to the netherworld (Dan. 12:1; Ps. 69:27-28; Exod. 32:32,33; Jer. 17:13).

The image of God as judge, like the conception of *Sheol* as a place of punishment, was dictated by the ethical thrust of Hebrew monotheism. It substituted the flexible, rational relationship of God and man governed by clearly articulated and easily understood moral requirements for the chaotic, demonic and mysterious realm of the dead presided over by Mot, the Ugaritic god of death. Remnants of the pagan myth remained in the Bible as discussed above in chapters one and two but only in a demythologized form. They resurfaced, transmuted by biblical ethics and theology, in the apocalyptic scenarios to be discussed below. The image of the court of law borrowed from the Babylonian imagery of the religious ordeal focused attention on the status of the person assigned to *Sheol.* Would he/she be pardoned and redeemed from the netherworld or was the lack of merits so great that redemption was impossible? In this way attention was diverted from the bizarre and distorted descriptions of the netherworld itself found in surrounding civilizations. Since *Sheol* remained largely undefined, it became less of a locale and more of a condition of submission to divine justice.[16]

From Biblical to Apocalyptic Conceptions of the Afterlife

As we have seen earlier in another context (Ch. 4 Sinai: The Struggles of Theodicy, note 9) the Bible, unlike a treatise of systematic theology incorporated in its various texts conflicting views about the afterlife without attempting to reconcile them. On the one hand it emphasized the psycho-physical unity of body and soul even after death (exemplified by the word *nefesh*) so that what survived was not only a soul which had once been present in the living individual but the whole person. On the other hand, there are contexts that imply that the *nefesh* leaves the individual at death and the term *ruah*, denoting the universal spirit, clearly transcends the death of the person returning to its source in God. Thus the sage of the Book of Ecclesiastes (*Kohelet*) raises the skeptical question: "Who knows if a man's *ruah* does rise upward and if a beasts *ruah* does sink into the earth?" (Eccles. 3:21. Cf. 9:10-12; 12:7). Similarly, in its conception of the netherworld, the Bible embraced a spectrum of views ranging from a positive outlook in which "mother earth" is the source of fertility and creation linked to the cycle of nature with its births and its deaths to the pessimistic conception of *Sheol* as a place of punishment, the result of divine judgment. On the one hand, *Sheol* is the permanent abode of the dead but on the other hand there is redemption from *Sheol* for which the righteous pray and hope.

Bypassing the netherworld for eternal fellowship with God was exemplified by Enoch (Gen. 5:24) and Elijah (2 Kings 2:2-15) who

were taken bodily into heaven. Job, cognizant of such possibilities,
could hope for an analogous redemption.

> O that you would hide me in Sheol
> Conceal me until your anger passes,
> Set me a fixed time to attend to me.
> If a man dies, can he live again?
> All the time of my service I wait
> Until my replacement comes.
> You would call me and I would answer You.
> You would set your heart on your handiwork
> (Job 14:13-15).

But like the skeptical *Kohelet* (Ecclesiastes) he could not quite
believe it (Job 7:7-9).

The conception of the afterlife as eternal fellowship with God was
an outgrowth of the covenant relationship. The fullness of life
promised by Scripture for the fulfillment of the covenant's terms
transcended merely empirical goods (though these were in no way
discounted) to embrace the spiritual delight of living uprightly in
the constant presence of God. But if life lived within the framework
of the covenant brings both material and spiritual blessings how
does one explain the fate of the righteous carried off to an "evil
early death", to *Sheol*, which in the pessimistic version means
removal from fellowship with God? And even though rescue from
Sheol is possible it is not a common occurrence but a rare case of
divine intervention reserved for isolated individuals. The anguish
and dismay evoked by this agonizing question occasionally surfaced
in the early strata of the Bible (e.g., 2 Sam. 3:33) but for the most
part it was repressed by the resignation of the individual to his/her
lot and the comfort derived from the belief that the torn strands of
individual life are somehow woven into the fabric of the group that
continues to live on in covenant with God.

But as the individual became the focus of religious attention in
the wisdom texts of the Bible, particularly in Psalms, Proverbs,
Ecclesiastes and Job, the previously muted anguish became more
vocal. In the Second Temple period the struggle between the pagan
powers and the representatives of God centered on the individual
whose self-sacrifice became pivotal in establishing God's
sovereignty on earth. Thus Esther is asked to risk her life to thwart
Haman's plan of genocide for the Jews of Persia (Esther 4:7-14) and
Daniel and his contemporaries place themselves in mortal danger
by refusing to worship the gods of Babylon and Persia (Dan. 3:4-23;
6:7-18). If such a demand is placed on the individual, his or her

salvation could no longer be allowed to merge and thus disappear into the continuing life of the nation. Moreover, the partial consolation that the severed fellowship with God, postulated by the pessimistic conception of *Sheol*, would be picked up and continued by the group was shattered when the group itself was faced with annihilation. In the Babylonian exile when the Judean exiles confronted assimilation and religious-ethnic obliteration or in the episode recorded in the Book of Esther and in the persecutions that led to the Maccabean Revolt in the land of Israel, when the people as a whole faced physical destruction, the old beliefs concerning the afterlife were severely challenged.

The result was that the belief that death could be ultimately surmounted by both the individual and the nation became a tenet of Hebrew faith. The development took two directions. In the first, the alternative version of the netherworld as part of the cycle of nature, as a fruitful, creative place, the mother of all things, whose inhabitants join in praise of God and where the righteous continue the intense fellowship with God that they enjoyed in life persisted into the Second Temple period. It was enhanced by the legacy of Hebrew wisdom whose axiom, "that in direct encounter with God, life acquires an indestructible content"[17] silenced Job's thundering protest after the revelation in the whirlwind (Job 42:3-6) and enabled the psalmist to rise above his torment by finding a refuge in the divine presence (Ps. 73:23-28). The cyclical view of life and death and a netherworld conceived as a fruitful, creative place is found in this passage from the work of Joshua ben Sira.

> Great travail is created for every man
> And a heavy yoke is upon the sons of Adam,
> From the day of their coming forth from their mother's womb,
> Until the day for their burial in the mother of all things
> (Joshua ben Sira 40:1).

Confronted by the premature death and perhaps martyrdom of the devout and righteous, those who adhered to this conception of the afterlife denied any connection between untimely death and divine judgment and punishment. They emphatically sought to dissociate God and death.

> Because God made not death, Neither delighted He when the living perish, For He created all things that they may have being.
> (Wisdom of Solomon 1:13,14)

> But the righteous though he die before his time will be at rest, For honorable old age is not that which stands in length of time (Ibid. 4:7).

An echo of this view emerges later in the New Testament though in the context of a discussion of the resurrection: "He is not the God of the dead but of the living" (Mark 12:27).

The second path led to an elaboration of the eschatological conquest of death through resurrection, an idea whose seeds are in the Torah and the prophets. That God can revive the dead is one of His praises sung by the Deuteronomist historian (Deut. 32:39). As has already been discussed, even the pessimistic view of *Sheol* held out the hope of divine rescue from its oblivion. In the miracles associated with the prophetic ministries of Elijah and Elisha, both served as instruments for God's revival of the dead (1 Kings 17:17 ff.;2 Kings 4:18 ff.). In Isaiah 24-27, to be discussed more in detail below, there is a mini apocalypse which includes the resurrection of the dead (Isa. 26:19) in a context of world judgment though scholars are divided as to whether this is only a figurative image for the resuscitation of the people as a whole or a later concept.[18] The fact that the apocalyptic setting of redemption and renewal after the great catastrophe includes the promise of the destruction of death forever (Isa. 25:8) links both personal and group immortality to the utopian messianic motif of the Endtime to be discussed later in this chapter.[19] The resurrection of the dead as symbolic of the redemption of the nation is the theme of Ezekiel's vision of the Valley of Dry Bones:

> I am going to open your graves and lift you out of the graves, O my people, and bring you to the land of Israel. You shall know, O my people, that I am the Lord, when I have opened your graves and lifted you out of your graves. I will put my breath into you and you shall live again, and I will set you upon your own soil (Ezek. 37:12-14).

The last link in this chain of development whose outlines are barely visible because of the paucity of literary evidence is Dan. 12:1-3.

At that time the great prince, Michael, who stands beside the
sons of your people will appear. It will be a time of trouble,
the like of which has never been seen since the nation came
into being. At that time your people will be rescued, all who
are found inscribed in the book. Many of those that sleep in
the dust of the earth will awake, some to eternal life, others
to reproaches, to everlasting abhorrence. And the
knowledgeable will be radiant like the bright expanse of sky,
and those who lead the many to righteousness will be like the
stars forever and ever.

Here too, in this second direction taken in the evolution of the
afterlife idea in the exile and after the return in the Second Temple
period, in Ezekiel's vision of the Valley of Dry Bones and in the
Daniel passage, the dead are located in the grave (Ezekiel) and in
the earth/dust (Daniel). Both are resting places for all human
beings and in the biblical perspective, these abodes of the dead are
viewed in a neutral or a positive light as discussed earlier.
Conspicuously absent is any reference to *Sheol* as the specific place
of the wicked in connection with resurrection. This new belief that
demonstrated God's ultimate justice for the martyred saints could
not be associated only with a place of the wicked.[20]

Nevertheless, the aspect of judgment and reward and punishment
connected with *Sheol* is clearly underscored in the Daniel verses
(including the judicial image of the heavenly ledger) but is totally
absent from Ezekiel's vision. Another difference between the
Ezekiel and Daniel passages is that in Daniel the resurrection does
not encompass the entire corpus of the nation but is limited to an
indefinite number of individuals, thus opening the door to the belief
in resurrection as a gift of God for the righteous *individual*..[21]

The author of Dan. 12:1-3 also drew on the mini-apocalypse of Isa.
24-27 but there are significant differences between the two sources.
Isaiah refers only to a resurrection of the righteous while Daniel
conceives of a double resurrection, one for the righteous to eternal
life and one for the wicked to eternal contempt. But in the Daniel
text it is not a general resurrection of all human beings, only for the
protagonists in the religious persecution prior to the Maccabean
Revolt whose suffering in the case of the righteous dead

and whose prosperity in the case of the wicked dead challenged the writers religious sensibilities. In Isaiah the resurrection is an end in itself, God's justification of the righteous. In Daniel the resurrection is a means to the end of reward and punishment. In Isaiah 24 the judgment of God is cosmic in scope, in Daniel it is limited in time to the Antiochan persecution and in place to the land of Israel and surrounding countries. The conception of the resurrection in Daniel has moved beyond and become more specifically focused than the ideas of Ezekiel and Isaiah.[22]   But in Daniel the resurrection and reward and punishment remain peripheral, a spin-off of the main apocalyptic event to be discussed below. The dead saints are resurrected to witness the triumph of God's sovereignty and to enjoy a redeemed Israel in a new world order. The brevity of the Daniel verses suggests a widespread belief in the doctrine of resurrection (just prior to the Maccabean Rebellion) to which the author can laconically refer in painting his larger apocalyptic picture, certain that his readers fully understand his meaning.

In the concise reference to the resurrection in Daniel we find a perfect complement to earlier biblical views of the afterlife and an adumbration of themes to appear later in the literature of the apocrypha and pseudepigrapha. In the earlier texts of the Bible the dead "sleep" in the dust of the earth and in Daniel they "awake." In the earlier books the term "*nefesh*" in many of its contexts suggests that body and soul go down to the netherworld as an undivided unit. In Daniel an undivided psycho-physical entity is resurrected. Finally, the Daniel passage concludes with a promise that the wise will shine with a special brilliance like the stars. The verse can mean that in the renewed Israel their influence will be manifest. But it can also mean that they will ascend to the heavens either before death, immediately after death or at the time of the resurrection.[23]   Thus the Daniel passage sets the stage for linking the heavenly ascent, and immortality and resurrection, themes taken up by the apocalypses to be discussed below.

The Road Not Taken

In tracing the development of the doctrine of resurrection from the Bible to the apocalypses, it is worthwhile to briefly consider, in Robert Frost's memorable words, "the road not taken." The cult of the dying and rising god, discussed above, and the regeneration ceremonies of their worshipers so popular in the Nile and Tigris and Euphrates river valleys had their echoes in the late monarchy of biblical Israel (Ezek. 8:14; Isa. 17:10-11). There was a three day season between the death and rebirth of the gods marked by fasting rituals, mourning ceremonies and temple worship. It is quite possible that the three day interval was connected to the actual experience of seeing the facial features of corpses begin to decompose after that period. The ultimate goal of the cultic rites was to magically transfer the vital power of the god to his worshipers. In the aftermath of the disastrous civil war between the kingdoms of Judah and northern Israel (known as the Syro-Ephramitic War) the suffering survivors of the northern kingdom came to the temple seeking healing and revivification of the nation. But their religious framework was the regeneration cult of nature mysticism transferred to the God of Israel. In their conception God revealed Himself in a regular cycle in which there is punishment and destruction, paralleling the withering of vegetation in summer, that alternates with forgiveness and healing, corresponding to the return of vegetation in the fall and winter. All that was required was to restore the connection of vitality from deity to worshiper and the blessings follow automatically as the rains follow the drought. But the prophet Hosea rejected this kind of contrition because it lacked the indispensable moral element of *hesed*, loving-kindness, and the absolute sincerity that must be present in a covenant relationship with the God of Israel who can in no way be compared to the processes or deities of nature (see Ch. 6 Sinai I: Prophetic Piety, note 7).[24] Thus in Israel during the biblical period a sharp line of demarcation was drawn to separate the Hebrew concept of resurrection from any analogy to the cycle of nature. A faint echo of this analogy surfaces in Job's plaintive speech but only to be discarded in the end.

> There is hope for a tree;
> If it is cut down it will renew itself
> Its shoots will not cease.
> If its roots are old in the earth;
> And its stump dies in the ground
> At the scent of water it will bud
> And produce branches like a sapling.
> But mortals languish and die;
> Man expires, where is he?
> The waters of the sea fail,
> And the river dries up and is parched.
> So man lies down never to rise;
> He will awake only when the heavens are no more,
> Only then be aroused from his sleep (Job 14:7-12).

The Question of Persian Influence

Scholars are divided as to the extent of Persian influence on Jewish resurrection beliefs.[25] But there are weighty arguments against such influence at least in the first stage culminating in Dan. 12:1-3 though it cannot be ruled out completely in the later development of the idea.

1). In the Persian context there is a separation of body and soul immediately after death with the soul traveling to another realm while the body is exposed to destruction by animals or fire. This is completely at odds with the old Hebrew concept of the psycho-physical unity of body and soul and the fact that in Israel the worst fate, a sign of punishment, was to die and be abandoned to destruction without burial.

2). In the Persian conception of resurrection, reward and punishment for the soul begins immediately after death while in Daniel, as noted above, the netherworld is neutral and not a place of punishment. Moreover, in Daniel the resurrection and reward and punishment are subordinate to the apocalyptic scenario.

3). In the Persian belief system the savior, the *Saoshayant*, has the mission of raising the dead while in Daniel, and even in later Judaism, the Messiah does not participate directly in the resurrection. The resurrection is an act of God.

4). In the Zoroastrian religion all human beings are resurrected but in the book of Daniel resurrection is limited to a select group.[26]

Notes

1.   Hamilton Gibb, "The Influence of Islamic Culture on Medieval Europe," *John Rylands Library Bulletin* 38 (1955/56): 86, 87.

2.   Yehezkel Kaufmann, *The Religion of Israel*, trans. and abridged, Moshe Greenberg (Chicago: The University of Chicago Press, 1960), p. 313.

3.   Ibid, pp. 314-316; Nicholas J. Tromp, *Primitive Conceptions of Death and the Nether World in the Old Testament* (Rome: Pontifical Biblical Institute, 1969), p. 15.

4.   Jacob Licht, "Nefesh," "Neshamah," *Encyclopedia Biblica* (Jerusalem: Bialik Institute, 1968): 5, cols. 898-904; 930-931; Walther Eichrodt, *Theology of the Old Testament*, trans. J. A. Baker (Philadelphia: The Westminster Press, 1967), 2:131-150. The Kabbalists, beginning with the Zohar, adapted the psychological doctrines of Neoplatonism to the biblical-rabbinic tradition in designating three essentially different parts of the soul in an ascending order. *Nefesh* is to be found in every human and is the seat of animal vitality and psycho-physical functions as well as the human ego. *Ruah* is the *anima* of ethical consciousness that emerges when the human being evolves beyond the purely psycho-physical functions. *Neshamah, spiritus*, is animated by the religious life and opens up the mystical abilities of perceiving the Godhead and the secrets of the universe. Kabbalists after the Zohar added two higher rungs to the soul *hayyah* and *yehidah* representing the most exalted spiritual state of intuitive understanding attainable only by a few select individuals. Cf. Gershom Scholem, *Kabbalah* (New York: Quadrangle, and Jerusalem: Keter Publishing House, 1974), pp. 152-165. This conception of five elements of the soul derives from the rabbinic view that the soul possesses five different powers. *Gen. R.* 14:9 (ed. Theodor-Albeck), pp. 132-133. Cf. Ginzberg, *Legends* 3:56; 5:74, n. 18.

5.   Ruth Rosenberg, "The Concept of Biblical Sheol Within the Context of Ancient Near Eastern Beliefs," unpublished Ph.D. dissertation Harvard University, March, 1981, 74-86.

6.   For a complete discussion of these views and references and bibliography see J. C. de Moor, *The Seasonal Pattern in the Ugaritic Myth of Ba'lu According to the Version of I'limilku* in *Alter Orient und Altes Testament* 16 (Neukirchen: Vluhn, 1971), pp. 9-28.

7.   Umberto Cassuto, "Baal and Mot in the Ugaritic Texts," *Israel Exploration Journal* 12 (1962): 79, 86; Frank Cross, *Canaanite Myth and Hebrew Epic* (Cambridge: Harvard University Press, 1973), p. 116; Rosenberg, "The Concept of Biblical Sheol," pp. 22-27.

8.   Rosenberg, "The Concept of Biblical Sheol," p. 41.

9.   For Egyptian views see M. Morenz and D. Mueller, *Untersuchungen zur Rolle des Schicksals in der aegyptischen Religion* (Berlin, 1960) and for Babylonian views E. Reiner, "Fortune Telling in Mesopotamia," *Journal of Near Eastern Studies* 19 (1960), trans. 26, Text 32; M. Tsevat, "Studies in the Book of Samuel," *Hebrew Union College Annual* 32 (1961): 191-216; Rosenberg, "The Concept of Biblical Sheol," pp. 177-190.

10. Rosenberg, "The Concept of Biblical Sheol," pp. 48-51.

11. Ibid, pp. 38-39.

12. Ibid, pp. 59-66.

13. On Isaiah 38 see S. Talmon, "Textual Study of the Bible," *Qumran and the History of the Biblical Text* (Cambridge: Harvard University Press, 1975), pp. 330-331 and the application of this interpretation to Hos. 13:14; Pss. 6:5; 30:7-8; 31:7, 9-11; 88:8, 10, 15-18 where unnatural illness is implied. Cf. Rosenberg, "The Concept of Biblical Sheol," p. 89, n. 6.

14. Other exceptions that do not associate *Sheol* with evil death but as a place for all dead without moral distinction are Eccles. 9:10; Ps. 89:49; 1 Kings 2:5, 9; Isa. 14:9. Eccles. 9:10 is not a description of the general nature of *Sheol* but part of a larger world view of Ecclesiastes. Ps. 89:49 conveys the idea "that no short lived mortal can hope to elude death, nor any man created to sin whose destination is *Sheol*. The real meaning of Isa. 14:10 as explained by its commentary Ezek. 32 is "You too have been slain like us" i.e., the kings are those whose lives were ended prematurely and thus their place is *Sheol*. Cf. Rosenberg, "The Concept of Biblical Sheol," pp. 234-245.

15. E. A. Speiser, "Census and Ritual Expiation in Mari and Israel," in *Oriental and Biblical Studies*, ed. J. J. Finkelstein and M. Greenberg (Philadelphia: University of Pennsylvania Press, 1967), pp. 171-186.

16. Rosenberg, "The Concept of Biblical Sheol," pp. 11, 118, 144; 246-249.

17. See the discussion in Eichrodt, *Theology of the Old Testament* 2:517-526.

18. Moshe Greenberg, "Resurrection," *Encyclopedia Judaica* (Jerusalem: Keter Publishing House, 1971) 14:98.

19. See Isa. 13:6-13; Joel 1:15; 2:1; 3:4; 4:14 and the discussion that will follow below.

20. Rosenberg, "The Concept of Biblical Sheol," pp. 250-251.

21. The Book of Daniel, trans. with intro., notes and commentary by Louis F. Hartman and Alexander A. Di Lella, *The Anchor Bible* 23 (Garden City, NY.: Doubleday and Co., 1979): 307-8. The condition of the wicked is arrived at by the parallel in Isa. 66:24.

22. George W. E. Nickelsburg, *Resurrection, Immortality and Eternal Life in Intertestamental Judaism* Harvard Theological Studies 26 (Cambridge: Harvard University Press, 1972), pp. 19-23, 27.

23. Ibid, p. 82, n. 134.

24. Hosea 6; Shalom Spiegel, "A Prophetic Attestation of the Decalogue Hosea 6:5 With Some Observation on Pss. 15 and 24," *Harvard Theological Review* 27 (1934): 131-139; Mircea Eliade, *A History of Religious Ideas* (Chicago: The University of Chicago Press, 1978) 1:150, 159, 355.

25. Eichrodt, *Theology of the Old Testament* 2:516, n. 2.

26. Ibid, pp. 516-517. Cf. E. E. Herzfeld, *Zoroaster and His World* (Princeton, N.J.: Princeton University Press, 1947), 1:296-308; Gherardo Gnoli, "Saoshyant," *The Encyclopedia of Religion* ed. Mircea Eliade (New York: Collier-Macmillan, 1987), 13:69-70.

Sinai II: The Road to Redemption
and the World to Come—The Apocalypse

The Nature and Background of Apocalyptic Literature

Though the themes and images of apocalyptic literature have their seeds in the Hebrew Bible they have also grown and blossomed in the soil of Hellenistic culture which absorbed the nutrients of the Babylonian and Persian civilizations. The word "apocalypse" comes from a Greek term meaning "to uncover" and refers to the divine mysteries whose revelation is sought by the visionary. But the term apocalyptic has a popular connotation that describes a disastrous turn in human affairs when an ordered society becomes chaotic, forecasts for the future are filled with gloom and foreboding and catastrophe looms on the horizon. So bad are the conditions of the present and so corrupt are the inhabitants of the world that there is utter despair of perfecting the individual and improving society. The only hope is a direct divine intervention to establish a new order for human life. It is the nature and the timing of this intervention that the visionary seeks to "uncover" among the other secrets of heaven and this is what links the formal definition of apocalypse with the more popular usage. Both the precise meaning of the word "apocalypse" and its wider popular connotation are implied in this recent definition of an apocalypse as

> a genre of revelatory literature with a narrative framework, in which a revelation is mediated by an otherworldly being to a human recipient, disclosing a transcendent reality which is both temporal insofar as it envisages eschatological salvation, and spatial insofar as it involves another supernatural world.[1]

The content of the apocalypses are embraced by the temporal and spatial dimensions mentioned in this definition which fall basically into two categories: heavenly ascents (or otherworldly journeys) and historical reviews.[2] Another way of describing the contents of the apocalypses for our purposes is to paraphrase the four topics whose discussion is prohibited by the *Mishnah*: what is above, (i.e., the heavenly ascent), what is beneath (the nature of the world and the individual's lot in it drawing on the wisdom tradition of Israel), what was beforetime (the historical review up to the visionary's time) and what is to come (the last stages of the present age, the Messianic Age, the World to Come and the afterlife).[3] This content was elaborated in a vast literature extending from the Hebrew Bible to the pseudonymous underground prophecies of postbiblical visionaries contained in apocryphal and pseudepigraphic works, to the Qumran Dead Sea scrolls, to the New Testament, particularly the Book of Revelation, and to the esoteric writings of the talmudic rabbis.

Apocalyptic literature is highly symbolic and is permeated with cryptic allusions to ancient imagery in the Sinai tradition. There are allusions to pre-monotheistic Near Eastern motifs whose remnants are still found in the Bible, to the Torah, to Hebrew prophecy and to wisdom. The image of the beasts emerging from the sea in Daniel 7 is clearly an echo of the Mesopotamian and Canaanite combat myths discussed in chapter two. The last will and testament motif in the Testament of the Twelve Patriarchs echoes Jacob's blessing of his sons in Genesis 49; a classic example of the allusion to prophecy is the interpretation of Jeremiah's prophecy concerning the seventy year length of the exile (Jer. 29:4-11) in Daniel 9. The connections to wisdom will be discussed below.

Foreign influences can also be detected in the mosaic of allusions. The impact of Babylonian divination and dream interpretation is seen in 1 Enoch (Enoch is patterned after Enmeduranki, founder of the guild of Babylonian diviners) and in Daniel 1-6. Greek influences on the Book of Daniel were discussed in the previous chapter. In the Jewish monotheistic framework of the apocalypses there is evidence of the adaptation of Persian motifs connected with the heavenly journey, the periodization of history, the suffering at the Endtime, resurrection and the clash between the supernatural forces of good and evil. The heavenly ascent of the Jewish apocalypses has its parallels in Babylonia, in Greek antiquity and in the Hellenistic world.[4]

A basic assumption of the apocalypses is that prophecy had come to an end and will be renewed only at the end of days. But here a fundamental distinction must be made between the Apocrypha and the Pseudepigrapha. The term "Apocrypha" is used for a collection of books not included in the canon of the Hebrew Bible although they are incorporated in the canon of the Roman Catholic and Greek Orthodox churches. The Apocrypha, for the most part, are anonymous historical and ethical works. The books included in the Pseudepigrapha are not accepted in their entirety by any church, only individual books are considered sacred by the Eastern churches, particularly the Ethiopian Church. These are visionary works attributed to the ancients dealing with the heavenly ascent, the mysteries of creation and the conflict and the working out of good and evil.

The books in the Apocrypha deal mainly with the struggle against idolatry because their authors believed that prophecy had ceased.[5] The period of new revelations and new directions was over and now began the great organizing period, the time to bend all existing Hebrew culture into obedience to the highest religious ideas that were the legacy of Torah, prophecy and wisdom. With the loss of Hebrew political sovereignty and with the increasing influence of paganism, first Persian and then Greek, the writers of the Apocrypha saw as their main task the defense of monotheism. In contrast, the authors of the Pseudepigrapha were convinced that prophecy continued (see Ch. 6 Sinai II: The Charismatic Piety of the Second Temple and Talmudic Periods). Though not oblivious to paganism and its snares, their major focus was the making and interpretation of law through the still open prophetic channels (e.g., the Book of Jubilees and the Qumran Manual of Discipline) and the deciphering of the past and the future with the help of the still operating prophetic spirit. But though they considered themselves the inheritors of the prophetic mantle, albeit in a weaker form, this conviction was not shared by a majority of their generation whose regnant belief system held that prophecy had ended. Thus these visionaries of the Pseudepigrapha had to go underground and together with some of those who wrote the books of the Apocrypha attributed their works to ancients who lived in the time of prophecy. At other times the visionaries explained themselves as permitted to "interpret" the prophetic books, to reveal the true meaning of the Endtime, the period in which they lived.

On the one hand, the apocalyptic writers regarded their inspiration as weaker than that of their prophetic predecessors and hence they adopted the names and styles of the prophets and seers of the past. But on the other hand, they claimed that because of their proximity to the Endtime they understood the eschatological predictions in the prophetic books better than did the original authors. The choice of pseudonymity was also motivated by a belief of these apocalyptists in the correspondence of primal time and end time discussed in the introduction to this chapter. In the early eras, from Adam to Moses, God revealed the mysteries of heaven and earth to these giants of the spirit. But then the secret teachings were sealed from the unenlightened masses and communicated to only a few of the elect in succeeding generations. But now as the Endtime approached these teachings were being revealed to the pious (whose pseudonyms served to protect them from the hostility and scorn of unbelievers) in order to strengthen their faith (Dan. 8:26; 12:4,9; 1 Enoch 104:10-13; 4 Ezra 14:38 and 14:42-47). To this internal explanation of pseudepigraphy must be added an external factor: pseudepigraphy was a widespread phenomenon in the Hellenistic world.

What was the social background out of which the apocalypses came? The classical period of Jewish apocalypse, from the second century B.C.E. to the first century C.E. has been understood by scholars as a period of unremitting crisis, religious, cultural, social, economic and political. Greco-Roman civilization, like its modern Western counterpart, had the impact of a tidal wave on the traditional structures of less powerful religious and ethnic groups. Small peoples everywhere in antiquity, like technologically inferior societies in our own time, were faced with an agonizing choice. Either immerse oneself in the waters of the dominant culture and allow one's own distinctive religio-ethnic traditions to dissolve, or build dikes against the foreign tide thus retaining identity but remaining a cultural and social backwater. As discussed in chapter six, the social impact of Hellenism brought about the development of parties or sects among the Jews patterned after the non-official, non-state social and religious societies of the Hellenistic world. The new possibilities for trade and commerce opened up by the conquests of Alexander the Great and his successors created a relatively small and powerful upper class in the land of Israel and the Diaspora that had the support of its Greek and later Roman masters. Anxious to become integrated into the cosmopolitan world of the time, they confronted an urban proletariat and an agrarian peasantry led by a priestly theocracy recruited from the lower echelons of the priesthood and from the levites faithful to the Torah who opposed all efforts toward assimilation into the ruling culture. Aligned to this latter group were the visionaries who continued the prophetic tradition underground.[6] Open conflict was inevitable.

The civil war among the Jews that ignited the Maccabean Revolt continued to smolder and periodically take flame even under the Hasmonean dynasty. Fueled by Syrian Greek and later Roman oppression, this internecine war pitted class against class, party against party, group against group and major segments of Jewish society in the land of Israel and in parts of the Diaspora against the Greek and later Roman administrations and the non-Jewish populations of those areas. From the Maccabean Rebellion of 165 B.C.E. until the Bar Kokhba Rebellion of 135 C.E. the land of Israel and segments of the Diaspora were periodically devastated by continuing unrest, uprisings and bloody suppressions.

The disintegration of the life sustaining socio-religious structures and the belief systems that undergirded them created the climate for the apocalyptic movements and their literature. Sociologists have pointed out that when a community finds itself excluded from the majority culture and its symbolic universe, it deals with the resulting chaos and alienation by creating a new symbolic universe that replaces the one disavowed. Apocalyptic visionary writings enabled the community of believers to maintain a sense of identity and a faith in their ultimate vindication despite a historical reality that repudiated their identity and denied their faith. The writers of the apocalypses and their readers claimed that true identity came from God's redemptive acts carried out on the cosmic level, not from the forms and institutions of Second Temple Israel. The apocalyptic movements that crystallized around these writings in the period under discussion expressed their opposition to the people and institutions of their time in three main ways.

1). The Qumran community withdrew to the region of the Dead Sea and formed a new society based on a symbolic utopian universe. In this new environment they created a new set of assumptions about power and new rules for access to it. These rules were seen as a return to pure original traditions that had been corrupted by the priestly theocratic establishment in Jerusalem. Then a millenarian prophet, the Teacher of Righteousness of Qumran, legitimated the rules by virtue of a revelation he received. He also introduced new community regulations and rituals on the basis of that revelation.

2). A second group, for the most part Pharisees, remained within the mainstream of Jewish society in the Second Temple period but expressed their identity in underground writings depicting a symbolic subuniverse.

3). A third group, the Zealots, an offshoot of the Pharisees, responded with violence becoming a revolutionary community and developing a symbolic counter-universe.[7]

The circles that gathered around John the Baptist and Jesus of Nazareth came from all three groups.

Prophecy versus Apocalyptic

Though the visionaries who wrote the apocalypses considered themselves the continuation of the prophetic tradition, there are clear differences between their visions and biblical prophecy and their writings and the prophetic books. The hallmark of Hebrew prophecy in the Bible is its apostolic mission. The prophet is a messenger bringing the divine word to his people. The biblical prophet knows the divine mystery and reveals the probabilities of the future. He/she perceives divine manifestations and symbols but they are subordinate to the mission, an outer garment for the basic message which is clear and direct, pertaining to a specific situation of the time. The apocalyptic prophet, such as Enoch in the Slavonic Book of Enoch, also has the role of a messenger but unlike biblical prophecy the apostolic mission is overshadowed by the heavenly visions and symbols shown to the visionary. In addition, the essence of the message that Enoch brings back is that of the secrets and mysteries of the universe and the Endtime, not a rational, specific directive.[8] In biblical prophecy the highest type of revelation is that which takes place in the waking state. The Bible knows of dream prophecy but it is considered a lesser vehicle for conveying the divine message since it is more subject to distortion (Num. 12:6-8; Jer. 23:25-29; 27:9; 29:8). The revelation in the waking state leads to a strong internal association between the prophetic vision and the external realistic environment of the prophet (e.g., Jer. 1:11-12). It also conveys a sense of the immediacy of the divine presence even though the Bible goes to great lengths to emphasize God's transcendence. In apocalyptic prophecy the dream is a highly valued means of divine communication (Dan. 7:1 ff.). The dream state leads to a weakened association between the vision and the external realistic environment of the visionary. The tendency is toward a self-enclosed symbolic, internal universe divorced from earthly reality (Rev. 1:12 ff.). Moreover, the apocalyptic revelation often takes place through the agency of angels, conveying a sense of the distance between the visionary and the divine presence. This feeling of God's remoteness is linked to the impact of the dominant belief that prophecy had ended with the destruction of the First Temple, an outlook echoed in Ps. 74:9 and in Dan. 9:24.[9]

The biblical prophet does not actively seek his divine mission. To the contrary, it is seen as a strange task that has been thrust upon him by God's revelation. The initial reaction is one of disbelief and astonishment and in a number of instances there is an attempt to escape the responsibility (Moses, Exod. 3-4; Jonah 1; Gideon, Judg. 6:11-18; Jer. 1). It is the numinous effect of the divine presence that compels the prophet to undertake the mission. To enable the prophet to overcome this initial hesitation he/she is gradually initiated into the prophetic role by a divine-human dialogue, sometimes couched in the form of question and answer (Amos 7:8; 8:2; Jer. 1:11,13; 24:3). The purpose is not only to introduce the mission but also to direct the prophet's attention to its essential elements and to enlist his/her intellectual, emotional and spiritual resources in carrying it out. The apocalyptic prophet is closer to the mystic who actively seeks and prepares for the divine revelation (see Ch. 6 Sinai I: Prophetic Piety, notes 10-13). As exemplified by Moses (see Ch. 5 Sinai: Biblical-Rabbinic Typologies notes 25-28), a central aspect of the prophetic task is to serve as intercessor between God and humanity. The purpose is to influence events by entreating God on behalf of the people and warning and consoling the people on behalf of God. In apocalyptic prophecy the intercessory role is greatly diminished and even negligible, for as we shall see, the possibility of influencing events in the apocalyptic scenario has been reduced to the vanishing point. The major role of the apocalyptic prophet is to serve as a purveyor of cosmic secrets and divine mysteries.[10]

The differences in the nature and content of the prophecies are reflected in the differences in the style and content of the literature. The insignia of the apocalypse is the otherworldly journey in space (to various locales in this world and to the heavenly and subterranean realms) and the historical survey in time. The Slavonic book of Enoch is, for the most part, an example of an otherworldly journey: the biblical Book of Daniel is a representative of the historical survey while the Ethiopic book of Enoch combines both elements. The changing visions of time and place have the effect of a television documentary. According to Kaufmann such " visions in perspective" are not to be found in classical Hebrew prophecy. Some of these visions are connected with the out-of-body experience that takes place in conjunction with the heavenly ascent.[11] Finally, the difference between the strong bond linking the prophetic vision to external reality and the weak bond linking the apocalyptic vision to its external environment is mirrored in the clarity of the prophetic utterance and the cryptic, allegorical character of the apocalypses.

The Transition from Prophecy to Apocalyptic

Scholars have sought to trace the chain of development that led from Hebrew prophecy to apocalyptic literature and the consensus at the present time is that though many links in the chain are still missing some can be identified.[12] The first is a prophetic vision of a catastrophic scenario of the Endtime that shows some striking similarities to later apocalyptic writings.

> The earth is breaking, breaking;
> The earth is crumbling, crumbling.
> The earth is tottering, tottering;
> The earth is swaying like a drunkard;
> It is rocking to and fro like a hut.
> Its iniquity shall weigh it down,
> And it shall fall to rise no more.
>
> In that day, the Lord will punish
> The host of heaven in heaven
> And the kings of the earth on earth.
> They shall be gathered in a dungeon
> As captives are gathered;
> And shall be locked up in a prison.
> But after many days they shall be remembered.
>
> Then the moon shall be ashamed,
> And the sun shall be abashed.
> For the Lord of Hosts will reign
> On Mount Zion and in Jerusalem,
> And the Presence will be revealed to His elders.
> (Isa. 24:19-23).

There are three points to be made about this remarkable passage. The first is that the powerful evocation of a spreading earthquake with its attendant horrors has the authentic ring of a first hand encounter or the searing prophetic recall or forecast of a global catastrophe (the reference to the sun and moon in the last stanza may not be a metaphor but an indication of globality).[13] The second point is that the passage is an excellent example of prophetic poetry's technique of heightening, focusing, specifying and concretizing. But as the process intensifies from verset to verset, and from line to line, we find the concrete, realistic world background collapsing into the abyss, and history being transformed into the stuff of apocalypse.[14] A third observation has to do with the fact that if we combine the above verses with the banquet of the Endtime on Mount Zion in Isa. 25:6, and the resurrection and the final judgment found in Isa. 26:19 to Isa. 27:1 we have here, as in Joel 2:10f. and 3:18ff., a capsule version of apocalyptic eschatology with the destruction followed by the judgment and eternal peace and happiness for the surviving righteous.

But it is in the prophecies of the exilic and post-exilic prophets Ezekiel and Zechariah that the transition points from prophecy to apocalyptic are the clearest. As already noted in chapter six, Ezekiel is the first prophet to describe an out-of-body experience (though there is an allusion to it in Isaiah 6, it is not as explicit as in Ezekiel) and thus set the pattern for a standard apocalyptic theme.[15] In Ezekiel and Zechariah the gulf between Creator and creature, symbolized by the departure of the Divine Presence from Jerusalem (Ezek. 11:22-25) and by the indirect address to the prophet who is called "son of man," (in contrast to Amos and Jeremiah who are addressed by name, Amos 7:8; 8:2; Jer. 1:11; 24:3), is bridged by the angel. The angel guides the prophet in the visionary Temple (Ezek. 40-48) and explains to him the meaning of the visions. Zechariah, for the most part is not even a direct partner in the divine-prophetic dialogue except through the mediation of an angel. One of the hallmarks of apocalyptic is the angel as mediator between a distant transcendent deity and the visionary. Also strikingly reminiscent of the apocalypses are the dramatic visions with many scenes from the heavenly kingdom contained in Ezekiel's prophecies, in which angels of various ranks fulfill a variety of functions. Ezekiel also formulated the concept of divine protection from avenging angels (Ezek. 9:3-6), which is a central motif of apocalyptic demonology.

In the prophecies of Zechariah, the dream sequences become the major source of the divine message and in this respect Zechariah is closer to the apocalyptic dreams of Daniel than to classical Hebrew prophecy where dreams are played down. Moreover, the lack of clarity in the dream images, the sudden appearance and disappearance of fantastic symbols often divorced from human reality, and the replacement of the natural laws of the external world by an intuitive, internal, free association of symbols, all bear the earmarks of apocalyptic. As Zechariah strives to interpret these symbols, the initiative for the prophetic-divine encounter slowly but perceptibly passes from the mediating angel to the prophet himself who, like an apocalyptic visionary, becomes a decoder of divine secrets and a seeker of divine wisdom. In the Book of Zechariah there is already recognizable a scribal tradition, possibly connected with the canonization process, that was to reach a high point under Ezra and his collegium of priests. There are references to the "earlier prophets" (Zech. 1:4-6; 7:7,12) and Zechariah specifically mentions the seventy year exile in Babylonia as well as messianic allusions both traceable to Jeremiah (Zech. 1:12; 3:8; 6:12. Cf. Jer. 29:4-11; 23:5; 33:15).[16] In his vision of the Messianic Age Zechariah describes a time when prophecy will be in disrepute to such an extent that prophets will claim to be farmers and families will suppress even by death any sign of the visionary in their children (Zech. 13:2-6). Rowland rightly sees in this passage an echo of the declining faith in the efficacy of prophecy prevalent in the belief system of the early Second Temple period.[17] Thus Zechariah points to the end of classical prophecy and the beginning of underground prophecy or apocalyptic.

Ezekiel's Vision of the Merkavah *(Throne-Chariot)*

One of the most celebrated prophetic visions, whose theme forms the centerpiece of many apocalypses and talmudic esoteric literature, is found in the first chapter of the Book of Ezekiel, repeated with variations in chapter ten and referred to by Ezek. 43:1-4. The prophet describes how a stormy wind and a fiery cloud approaching from the north served as the prologue to a view of four incredible beings, each with four different faces, a human face, a lion face, an ox face and an eagle face.

Four wheels, each of them constructed like "a wheel within a wheel"(Ezek. 1:16) accompanied these beings. Above them was a platform like crystal and above the platform a human-like appearance of the Deity sitting on a lapis-lazuli throne.

Generations of Bible commentators from the ancient Jewish interpreters to modern space age readers have struggled to decode this cryptic vision which is a potent adumbration of apocalyptic.[18] For our purposes it is sufficient to summarize the findings of modern scholarship on those elements in the ancient Near East that are found in the mosaic of this vision. The divine figure seen by Ezekiel most closely approximates in its motion, rainbow colors and radiance (Ezek. 1:28) the flying god Ashur. The head and upper body of this Assyrian god seem to have been white with wing feathers yellow and blue; a double yellow ring is in his flaming nimbus and great flaming streamers fly back from him.[19] The fantastic beings who are composites of human, animal and bird forms are common in Egypt and Mesopotamia. The head, whether human, animal or bird, symbolized the qualities attributed to the god. In Mesopotamia, the lesser divinities and demons were portrayed in composite form including winged quadrupeds with human faces; this combination also expressed certain attributes of these divine attendants.[20]

There are also distinct Hebrew elements in the mosaic. Isaiah and Micaiah saw the Deity seated on a throne and surrounded by ministering angels (Isa. 6; 1 Kings 22:19). The cherubim over the ark were considered the divine throne in ancient Israel (1 Sam. 4:4; 2 Sam. 6:2; Ps. 80:2) but they also constituted a divine chariot. Each of the faces symbolizes dominion: the human, ruler of all living things (Gen. 1:26); the lion, king of the beasts; the ox or the bull, the strongest of the animals; and the eagle, king of the birds. In addition, the lion is the most violent of the beasts (Gen. 49:9; Num. 23:24; 24:9; Judg. 14:18; 2 Sam. 1:23; 17:10 etc.); the eagle, the swiftest and the most high flying of the birds (Deut. 28:49; 2 Sam. 1:23; Jer. 48:40; Lam. 4:19; Job 39:27); the bull or the ox the most useful and the most imposing of domestic animals (Deut. 33:17; Prov. 14:4; Job 21:10; Exod. 21:37). All of these animals or combinations of them are to be found as carriers of gods or pedestals of gods in ancient Near Eastern art.[21]

Finally, the number four which predominates in the image of the beings (four directions, four creatures, four faces, four wings, four hands, four wheels) as Kaufmann has pointed out, suggests cosmic symbolism, the division of the world into four parts (Isa. 11:12),the four directions (i.e., east, forward, *kedma*, west, seaward, *yamah*, north and south, Gen. 13:14; 28:14).[22] Taken together with the eyes with which the rims of the wheels were inlaid (Ezek. 1:18), the vision suggests divine omnipotence and omniscience.[23] This meaning is related to Zech. 4:10, where on seeing a vision of a gold candelabrum with seven lamps, the prophet is told that "those seven are the eyes of the Lord, ranging over the whole earth." In a similar vein, the seven golden lampstands of Rev. 1:12-20 and the seven stars that belong to them can be connected to the Hellenistic Jewish interpretation of the seven branched candelabrum in the desert sanctuary (Exod. 25:31-40) as a symbol of the God of the seven planetary spheres "who sees."[24] The number four had special significance in Babylonian literature and numerology[25] and Carl Jung, drawing heavily on Ezekiel 1, perceived four as an archetype representing a complete unity so that God is properly conceived as a perfect quaternity.[26] Thus most of the components of Ezekiel's vision can be traced either to Israelite tradition, to the iconography of the cultures surrounding ancient Israel or to universal archetypes found in every culture. But the specific combinations in this visionary ensemble, such as the four distinct faces, remain unique.

The Wisdom Strand of Apocalyptic

As mentioned earlier, the Book of Zechariah, which is one of the bridges leading from prophecy to apocalyptic, evidences a scribal tradition in which the prophet specifically mentions or alludes to the work of earlier prophets. This interpretive function is a hallmark of biblical wisdom and of apocalyptic literature. One branch of biblical wisdom discussed above in chapter six was the secular or humanistic school exemplified by the Book of Job. One of the central themes underscored by the author is that even the wisest of human beings can only attain partitive knowledge. Given the interconnectedness of the natural and the moral realms (discussed in chapter four) it is not surprising that the human inability to understand the mysteries of nature is paralleled by the human inability to understand the principles of God's justice. One of the mysteries of nature is the correct measurement and the right proportion of all phenomena, for without this exquisite balance there can be no natural order. But only God knows the precise relationship of all things to each other and thus only He can direct and regulate the totality of the world of nature (Job 28:25-26).

Similarly, though humans have a crude grasp of the doctrine of reciprocity, its subtle relationships and proportions are far beyond human understanding. These conceptions of the interweaving of the natural and the moral realms and the limitations of human partitive knowledge pass into the apocalypses. But here the view is diametrically opposite to that of the Book of Job. In Job humans are destined to live with their partial insight. In the apocalypses the ascending hero will receive a revelation of both the secrets of nature and the mysteries of the moral governance of the cosmos which he will bring back to instruct his generation. Once humans receive information about the principles of divine reciprocity there is no purpose in holding back from them the secrets of nature, including the angelic world and the divinity, because the realms are inseparable.[27]

The idea of order and balance as a principle of nature is also found in the Book of Daniel which bears the earmarks of Hebrew wisdom. Daniel has mantic wisdom and is simultaneously seer and wise man enabling him to surpass even the learned Chaldean wise men and astrologers (Dan. 2:1-13; 4:3f.; 5:7f). In Daniel the emphasis is on the order in history. Even pagan rule is part of God's overarching providential plan. Though God seems to establish and remove kings haphazardly, the way in which the four kingdoms follow one another demonstrates divine order and sequence. Thus the regularity in history points to a perfectly administered universe.[28]

For the biblical wisdom teachers of the humanistic school geography as well as history underscored the order, beauty and mystery of the cosmos. The author of the Book of Job shows a wide familiarity with various geographical locations, their climatic conditions and their inhabitants (Job 9:26; 28; 40:15; 40:25ff.). A similar inference regarding the order of the cosmos and its mystery is drawn in the geographical section of 1 Enoch 76-77. In his heavenly journey Enoch is shown a vast topographical spectrum which correlates with actual areas on earth and he receives information regarding the origins of the winds and the climatic conditions of different locales.

A second branch of biblical wisdom discussed above in chapter six was the religious wisdom school exemplified by the priestly interpretation of the Torah by Ezra and his colleagues. This exegetical activity was expanded into a new form of piety that viewed the Torah as a combination of law code (*halakah*), the book of Israel's covenant with God and the summation of divine wisdom. Some of the wisdom psalms in praise of the Torah in the Book of Psalms also exemplify the religious wisdom school. The Book of Jubilees is a notable example of how the traditions of this school passed into the apocalypses. Jubilees is an expanded paraphrase of Genesis and more briefly Exodus down to the Sinaitic Revelation. The work is presented as a revelation transmitted to Moses by the Angel of the Presence and the laws are said to be inscribed on heavenly tablets (Jub. 3:10,31; 4:5,32).[29] The focus of the work is on legal (*halakic*) matters regulating the Jewish way of life highlighted by the Sabbath in the account of creation (chap. 2) and the instructions for its observance (chap. 50). Similar attention is given to the festival cycle, to the rite of circumcision and in chapters seven and twenty there is an adumbration of what later will become the rabbinic Noahite Laws.[30] The importance attached to divine order in nature, found in the biblical Book of Job and in the books of Enoch, and the emphasis on order in history in the Book of Daniel carry over into Jubilees but in a different context. The focus here is on the divine order in sacred time and ritual as exemplified by the solar calendar ordained by the author of Jubilees. The solar calendar contained exactly fifty two weeks, each month containing thirty days except for the third, sixth, ninth and twelfth months which contained thirty one days. This solar calendar was also known from the book of Enoch and the Qumran Dead Sea Scrolls, leading scholars to believe that it was an Essene calendar opposed to the mainstream adjusted lunar calendar of the Pharisees.[31] The organizing principle of this calendar is not the normal agricultural cycle or even the historical events of Israel's history such as the exodus but rather the cosmic events that occurred at the time of the biblical flood in the era of Noah. The viewing of sacred time from the perspective of a cataclysm is a clear sign that Jubilees belongs in the apocalyptic genre.

The religious wisdom strand of apocalyptic literature is also to be found in the characteristic works of the Qumran sect which are not descriptions of revelations but rules (*Serekh*), hymns and *pesharim* (commentaries). The *pesharim* are not strictly apocalypses but rather interpretations of the historical experience of the Qumran community and of biblical texts. The connection to apocalyptic is in the source of these interpretations which are attributed to a mysterious revelation received by the Teacher of Righteousness, the religious leader of the Qumran community.[32]

In the wisdom strata of apocalyptic literature there is a merging of prophetic revelation, mystical experience and the learning acquired through wisdom, i.e., the study of texts sacred and secular, and the observation of nature and of human life. In this context the wise men living after the destruction of the First Temple acquired the characteristics of prophets, and the prophets of the biblical period as seen through the apocalyptic prism became inspired wise men. From Adam and Enoch to the last prophets and latter day apocalyptic visionaries the interweaving of revelation and observation, rational inquiry and intuitive understanding continued. This comprehensive striving for knowledge, human and divine, is best understood against the historical background of the Hellenistic age. The apocalyptic writers were profoundly influenced by the Greek reverence for knowledge as the most precious possession of human beings. But from their perspective the Greeks lacked revelation, divine knowledge, which can uncover the future and the secrets of the universe. This was the inheritance of Sinai on to which could be grafted the best branches taken from Olympus.

Martin Hengel points to three stages in the apocalyptic view of wisdom:

1). The apocalyptic writers absorbed from the Hebrew wisdom school the belief that only the righteous, i.e., those who observe the precepts of the Torah, can be wise. Understanding is withheld from the wicked (Dan. 12:10; 1 Enoch 99:10; 92; 94-104).

2). In the tribulations of the Endtime the secret knowledge revealed to the early saints and prophets, and then concealed from the masses of humanity, will once again be revealed to the pious visionaries to strengthen them in the time of distress and raise them above their unknowing and brutish environment. The revelation contains the explanation of the meaning of history and its

consummation as well as the nature of the heavenly world, judgment and eternal salvation. But even this will be only a partitive disclosure, provisional and imperfect.
3). Full and perfect understanding is a gift reserved for the salvational end of time (1 Enoch 5:8; 32:3-6; 90:35; 91;10; Similitudes of Enoch 48:1f.; 49:1ff.)[33]

The Apocalyptic View of History

As mentioned earlier, the prophetic view of history in which the focus is on the events of the prophet's time, with the End of Days serving as background, differs markedly from the apocalyptic historical perspective in which there is an unfolding of human history from era to era and through successive changes of world empires culminating in the apocalypse and the New Age.[34] A second difference arises from the prophetic belief that human beings, once they are made aware of their options, can change the course of events if they so will it. In contrast, the apocalyptic writers believed that human history had reached a point where human choice could rarely alter the course of events. So much in human affairs and in the natural functioning of the universe had become congealed by human corruption (see chapter four on the interconnectedness of the moral and the natural realms), that the future was already predetermined and individual options had dwindled to decisions affecting one's own life. Human freedom remained; people could determine their own destiny but they could not change the course of history. This apocalyptic conception of the narrowing of human options in the face of a predetermined future has its roots in the prophecies of Jeremiah and Ezekiel. Jeremiah's generation, the generation that suffered the destruction of the First Temple, the end of the Judean state and exile to Babylonia believed the prophet's warning of this impending disaster was illogical and unmerited. They believed that the reforms of King Josiah, still evident in their generation, were sufficient to insure the inviolability of the Temple and of Jerusalem in the face of a Babylonian juggernaut, even as the piety of King Hezekiah and his generation insured the safety of the Temple and Jerusalem in the siege by an Assyrian superpower according to the prophecies of Isaiah. But Jeremiah and Ezekiel argued that the reforms of King Josiah could not undo the terrible burden of sin accumulated during the reign of King Manasseh prior to the reforms, and this load of transgression was kept potent by the vestigial idolatry still present in the contemporaries of the two prophets. This burden of sin had narrowed the people's options. The Josianic reforms could save Judea from destruction if the people submitted to Babylonian rule. But it was not sufficient to prevent their destruction if they did not submit. Moreover, Jeremiah's counsel of submission was based on the new concept of a pagan world empire that had inherited the disciplining task that Isaiah had assigned to Assyria (see Chap. 4: Sinai: The Struggles of Theodicy, note 4). It was God's will that Babylonia achieve world dominion and its rise had been foreordained just as its duration had been predetermined.[35]

The apocalyptic writers carried these concepts even further by universalizing them. It would not be wide of the mark to paraphrase H. H. Rowley's oft quoted statement that the prophets foretold the future that should arise out of the present because they believed in the possibility of human choice affecting the future. The apocalyptists foretold the future that was already mortgaged to the present because they had little faith that human decision could beget the future.[36] These two differing perspectives on history engendered two distinct styles of historical writing. The prophetic depiction of events is concrete and realistic. People and empires are full bodied, portrayed in all their individuality and color. In the apocalyptic account people and events lose their individuality and are reduced (or inflated) to mythical symbols. The contrast is exemplified by Isaiah's description of the Syrian war against Judea (Isa. 7) and the description of another Syrian war against Judea 568 years later (during the Maccabean uprising 168-165 B.C.E.) by the apocalyptic author of the twelfth chapter of the Book of Daniel. In the Book of Isaiah the protagonists are portrayed in their full historical context; in Daniel chapter 12 they are nameless symbols.

The apocalyptic version of human history from creation to the apocalyptist's era is often depicted as an old decaying order drawing to a close, followed by a period of transition that culminates in the universal upheaval of the apocalypse. Out of the ashes of the catastrophe emerges the new order of the New Age (see figure below).

	Apocalypse	
Old Age Old World Order	Transition	New Age New World Order

This scenario is best summed up by a passage in the Syriac Apocalypse of Baruch (2 Baruch) 85:10:

> For the youth of this world is past and the strength of the creation already exhausted, and the advent of the times is very short. Yea, they have passed by and the pitcher is near the cistern, and the ship to port, and the course of the journey to the city, and life to its consummation (cf. 4 Ezra 4:50 and 1 Enoch 85-93).

The apocalyptist sees his/her own generation as situated toward the end of the transition period very close to the catastrophe. This endpoint is the culmination of a process that began with Adam's sin and continued downhill as humanity sank deeper and deeper into corruption (4 Ezra 3:7 and 7:68).

But this is not the only scenario reflected in the literature. There are texts to support G. Scholem's contention that "the redemption . . . is in no causal sense a result of previous history. It is precisely the lack of transition between history and the redemption which is always stressed by the prophets and apocalyptists."[37] The aspect of suddenness is reflected in the rabbinic statement that three things come unawares, the Messiah, a found article and a scorpion."[38] It is also suggested in Jesus' remark: "The time will come when you will long to see one of the days of the Son of Man . . . Men will say to you: 'Look! There he is!' or 'Look! Here he is!' Do not go off in pursuit of him, for just as when lightning flashes, it shines from one end of the sky to the other, that will be the way with the Son of Man . . . In the time of the Son of Man it will just as in the time of Noah . . . People went on eating, drinking, marrying, and being married up to the very day that Noah got into the ark and the flood came and destroyed them all . . . It will be like that on the day when the Son of Man appears" (Luke 17:22-24; 26-27, 30).

Within the framework of the two scenarios just outlined there are a variety of historical views expressed in the apocalyptic writings. As mentioned in the last chapter, one of the characteristic features of Daniel 7-12 is the *vaticinia ex eventu*, the description of past or present historical occurrences in the form of a prophecy revealed in earlier times to strengthen the convictions of the faithful in the apocalyptic message of a divinely predetermined history. The readers of these chapters are given to understand that their traumatic experiences of the present must be projected on to the larger screen of all of human history which is divided into three segments:

1). The period from the creation of the world to the destruction of the First Temple (586 B.C.E.) during which the national history of Israel is the focal point according to sacred tradition.

2). The time of the four kingdoms is represented in Nebuchadnezzer's dream by the statue of four metals declining in value (Dan. 2) and the vision of the four beasts each more fearsome than its predecessor (Dan. 7). The decline of the fourth empire in the king's dream (Dan. 2) inversely parallels the growing human arrogance which reaches its climax in the persecution of the faithful by Antiochus Epiphanes just prior to the Maccabean Revolt symbolized by the growing ferocity of the four beasts with the fourth the most frightening and arrogant of all.

3). The era of the "eternal kingdom" that follows the apocalypse. This is the time of the consummation of the divine plan when the saints are saved and the world is renewed.[39]

In addition to apocalyptic works like Daniel 7-12, 1 Enoch, the Book of Revelation and some of the Qumran writings which view human history as only a reflection of a cosmic struggle between good and evil, there are other apocalyptic writings in which the Deuteronomist historian's conceptions are evident. One such work is The Testament of Moses dating from the early years of the first century C.E. and reflecting the events prior to and following the Maccabean Revolt. Though pseudonymous and carrying the name of a venerable figure of the past, The Testament of Moses differs from the typical apocalypse in that it is a prophecy uttered by Moses and not a revelation given to him by an angel. It shares with other apocalypses the schematic historical review but it is far less deterministic than Daniel or the book of Enoch which view the course of history as set and human beings as capable of only reacting. The review of history in The Testament of Moses is an extension of a similar overview found in Deut. 32 and the testament as a whole is a loose rewriting of Deut. 31-34. It is not surprising then to find the Deuteronomist pattern of cultic history, i.e., history as a chronicle of sin and punishment in this work. Also characteristic of the Deuteronomist outlook is the belief that the unfolding of events can be affected by human intervention (in chapter four by the mediator, in chapter nine by Taxo) albeit indirectly by petitioning God.[40]

The Deuteronomist historian's axiom that salvation comes through membership in the community of Israel and requires observance of the law is also found in the Jewish Sibylline Oracles dating from the middle of the second century B.C.E. and coming from the Jewish-Hellenistic Diaspora in Egypt. In Sibylline Oracle 3, which was possibly used by Jews in the Diaspora to convince enlightened Gentiles of the truth of Judaism, the rise and fall of empires is determined by faithfulness to the one God and His teachings. It is particularly the sin of idolatry that ends the reign of a king or kingdom, a clear echo of the Deuteronomist thesis. But elsewhere in specifying the types of conduct that lead to destruction or deliverance the writer of Sibylline Oracle 3 does not emphasize the cultic aspects of Israel's religion stressed by the Deuteronomist, with the exception of idolatry and worship in the Jerusalem Temple, but the ethical norms of the Ten Commandments, the Holiness Code of Lev. 19 and Hebrew prophecy. For the author of this work addressed to Gentiles, faithfulness to the law means to the Hebrew counterpart of the Greek natural law tradition, i.e., the Noahite Laws (see Chap. 8: Sinai: Covenant and Polity, notes 23-29).[41]

In book 4 of the Sibylline Oracles that dates to around 80 C.E. human history ends when the universe is devastated by a cataclysmic fire that is strikingly analogous to the Stoic conception of a world conflagration that may have influenced the author of this apocalypse. But the Babylonian doctrine of the Great Year in which the universal cataclysm is one of both fire and water also penetrated both Greek and Jewish sources.[42] Thus in the apocryphal work the Life of Adam and Eve, Eve transmits the words of the angel Michael: "Our Lord will bring upon your race the anger of his judgment, first by water, the second time by fire; by these two will the Lord judge the whole human race."[43] Similarly, the rabbis picture Jethro as calming the fears of the pagan kings who on hearing the tumult of the universe caused by the Sinaitic Revelation (Exod. 19:14-19) feared the approach of another deluge. Said Jethro: "The Holy One Blessed be He has already sworn that He will not bring (another) flood upon the world." "Perhaps," they ventured, "He will not bring a flood of water, yet He will bring a flood of fire."[44] In the New Testament, the Day of the Lord is described as a time when the earth will go through alternating purgations of flood and fire (2 Peter 3: 5-7; 10-12).

Messianism

No treatment of the apocalyptic view of history would be complete without a discussion, however brief, of messianism in the Sinai tradition. In biblical Hebrew the term *mashuah* (anointed) was used of sanctified material objects (Gen. 31:13; Exod. 40:9) and the term *mashiah* (anointed one) of consecrated persons such as priests (Lev. 8:12) and kings (2 Sam. 12:7; 22:50-51), the title expressing divine sanction and unique inviolability. In exilic and postexilic usage the term "anointed" denoted anyone with a special mission from God-prophets, patriarchs, even Gentile kings. For example, the Persian King Cyrus who issued the Edict of Return in 538 B.C.E. allowing the exiled Jews to rebuild the Temple in Jerusalem is called God's "anointed one" (Isa. 45:1) and in the Jewish Sibylline Oracles 3 a Gentile king, the seventh in a Ptolemaic Hellenistic dynasty, is seen as a messianic redeemer, echoing Isa. 45:1 [45]

With due regard for the complexities in the evolution of messianism it is best understood as oscillating between two poles, a restorative pole and a utopian one. The restorative aspect seeks a return to the ancient glories as noted in the introduction to this chapter. It focused on this world, envisioning an amelioration and improvement of the present human condition. The utopian strand envisions apocalyptic, catastrophic changes that will usher in a future that will surpass everything in the present and everything that came before. Every messianic vision and movement in the Sinai civilization from the ancient to the contemporary combines both elements and it is the shifting balance and creative tension between the restorative and utopian poles that determines the character of a given vision or movement at a particular historical juncture.[46]

The Deuteronomist history established the doctrine that the Davidic dynasty had been divinely selected to rule over Israel until the end of time (2 Sam. 7; 23:1-3,5); if obedient to God it was to have dominion over foreign peoples (2 Sam. 22:44-51. Cf. Pss. 2 and 18:44-51). But when the United Kingdom of ancient Israel was divided after the death of Solomon and the fervor of Jewish nationalism kindled under David and Solomon was subjected to the shock and strain of repeated defeats, deportations and dispersals in succeeding centuries, the yearning for the restoration of the ancient glories of the golden age became intense. With the universalization of Hebrew history in the time of Isaiah and Micah (see Sinai I: Antiquarian Impulse in Programmatic History, notes 17-18), the restoration of the House of David and renewed Israelite sovereignty (Isa. 11:1-5; 10-14) were seen as the switch turning on the light of world peace and prosperity (Isa. 2:2-4; Mic. 4:1-4).

But the utopian motif is also prominent in the prophetic literature. The Day of the Lord, already mentioned, is clearly connected to the messianic idea. At some certain, though as yet unspecified time, God will destroy the corrupt society of the present through a great upheaval in which there will be much lamentation and darkness. But this period of cleansing suffering will bring about the triumph of justice and righteousness.[47]   The utopian salvation of the End of Days portrays the wolf dwelling with the lamb and the leopard lying down with the kid (Isa. 11:6-9). For the purpose of analysis I have separated the utopian vision of peace in Isa. 11 from the restorative image reflected in both Isa. 11 and Isa. 2, but in the vision of the prophet, as discussed in the introduction to chapter four, the two elements are organically intertwined and holistically balanced so that an improvement in one sphere is bound to lead to an improvement in the other sphere.

The high national hopes of the exiles who returned to Judea to build the Second Temple were reflected in the prophecies of Haggai and Zechariah, the prophets of the return, in whose restorative vision there were two messianic figures, the high priest and the messianic king (Zech. 6:9-16). The Chronicler's history, (see Sinai I: Antiquarian Impulse in Programmatic History, notes 21-22), is written almost entirely from the restorative perspective of an idealized Davidic dynasty.   The Book of Daniel contains both restorative and utopian elements.   Though Daniel 12 is silent about the nature of God's kingdom in the New Age, we can infer from Daniel 7 and 9 that life on earth continues.   This is an echo of the restorative vision of the prophetic End of Days in which life is elevated but otherwise remains normal (Isa. 2).   But on the other hand, there is the distinct impression, particularly in Daniel 7-12, that the affairs of this life are directed from a higher world and as a result of this direction monumental changes will take place in the conduct of life on earth, a concept that is a hallmark of utopian messianism.   The apocryphal books of Joshua ben Sira and the Psalms of Solomon revolve around the restorative pole of Jewish messianism as do the Ethiopic Enoch and the Assumption of Moses. The Parables of Enoch (chs. 37-71) follow the Book of Daniel except that in Daniel the term "son of man" does not have a messianic connotation.   In contrast, in this work the term is applied to the Messiah who is assumed to have been preexistent and to actually have come from heaven.[48]

The Qumran Dead Sea Scrolls combine the restorative and utopian motifs. Like the prophets Haggai and Zechariah of the early Second Temple period, the Qumran sect envisaged two Messiahs: a priestly Messiah of the House of Aaron and a royal Messiah of the House of David.   These restorative elements are portrayed against a utopian background of a great war conducted on earth and in heaven which concludes with the victory of the forces of good. This is followed by an end to the period of wickedness, glory for the elect, a messianic banquet (presided over by the two Messiahs) that ushers in the New

Age which includes worship at the eschatological Temple. After the destruction of the Second Temple the apocalyptic works of 2 Baruch and 4 Ezra reflected the despair and the messianic hope of the period in a melding of restorative and utopian themes.

Talmudic Judaism, in the time of the *Tannaim* in the Land of Israel and in the time of the *Amoraim* in both the land of Israel and in Babylonia, retained the restorative pole of Jewish messianism hoping for the rebuilding of Jerusalem and the Temple and the restoration of the Davidic monarchy . The rabbis disengaged from the utopian pole that led to the two failed revolts against Rome and the devastation of Israel (see Sinai II: Jewish Historiography in the Hellenistic World, notes 29-35). But the rabbis did not repudiate either aspect of the messianic vision. In fact the Babylonian *Amoraim*, removed in time and space from the two disasters in the land of Israel, reintroduced utopian messianic ideas. But in rabbinic sources the restorative and utopian poles become two different stages of the Endtime. The Messianic Era ushered in by an act of God would be a continuation of normal life on earth but with world peace and prosperity, the Jewish people restored from exile, a rebuilt Temple in a rebuilt Jerusalem, all like the prophetic End of Days. The third century Babylonian Amora Samuel characterized the period: "The only difference between this era and the Days of the Messiah is the subjection of Israel to the nations."[49] The more utopian elements were left for the World to Come after the final judgment (to be discussed below) in which there would be a total transformation of the natural and the human orders. A similar eschatological blueprint is found in 4 Ezra and the Syriac Apocalypse of Baruch which are contemporary with the generation of the *Tannaim*, the disciples of Rabbi Johanan ben Zakkai and their successors. The authors of these apocalypses undoubtedly reflect authentic rabbinic teachings on this subject.[50]

One explosive, utopian messianic element remained (aside from the resurrection of the dead to be discussed below). The rabbis inherited from Ezekiel 38-39 the war of the Lord against Gog of the land of Magog, the incarnation of evil in the Endtime. With the victory over this eschatological enemy, the Messianic Era will begin and, according to some sources, the Messiah will fight in the war and lead the victorious armies.[51] It is psychologically understandable why this final apocalyptic war was placed just prior to the advent of the golden Messianic Age. Given the terrible imperfections of the world when continuous wars engulfed the planet, it was possible for people to look at these catastrophes as representing the final wars of Gog and Magog, after which the

Messiah would come. Thus humanity's unquenchable hope and yearning for the promised End of Days could be kept alive even during catastrophic periods. But there was the danger that instead of leaving it to God, human beings would attempt to actively control and direct these wars believing that since the Endtime was here God would intervene to help them. This is what happened in the Roman-Jewish War of 66-70 C.E. and in the Bar Kokhba Rebellion of 132-135 C.E. In the wake of the first disaster the author of the Book of Revelation placed the apocalyptic war of Gog and Magog, or what came to be known in the Christian tradition as Armageddon, at the end of the Messianic Age, prior to the final judgment. Later Jewish tradition also adopted this arrangement.[52]

The rabbis, however, sought to retain the psychological advantage of placing the apocalyptic war of Gog and Magog at the beginning of the Messianic Age but attempted to defuse it. The bitter disillusionment and the dovish attitudes of the post-Bar Kokhba era raised the question: How can the instruments of war that killed Bar Kokhba and Rabbi Akiba also be the instruments of God's Messiah? The rabbis answered by creating two Messiahs and a division of messianic labor. The warrior Messiah of the House of Joseph will conduct the final battle against the heathen nations in which he will die. He will be succeeded by the triumphant Messiah of the House of David who will usher in the Kingdom of God and the reign of everlasting peace. Both of these events will take place at an unspecified time in the distant future.[53]

If the talmudic rabbis emphasized the restorative element of messianism and distanced themselves from the utopian strands, the opposite tendency is found in early Christianity. The Book of Revelation, following the utopian path, takes off in its visions where the Jewish apocalypses left off. Despite all the innovations in its utopian vision of the new heaven and the new earth, the Book of Revelation still contains a small element of restorative messianism. It still clings to the name and image of Jerusalem. It is a new Jerusalem to be sure, but its name evoked all the old associations of Jesus and the old Jerusalem. The new Jerusalem is a celestial city and in the New Testament utopian messianism is universalized so that the restorative elements are minimized and overshadowed by the interiorization and spiritualization of the millennium. In these sources there is a greater emphasis on the millennium as constituting the perfect time (i.e., the Second Coming of the crucified Messiah) in contrast to the rabbis' equal emphasis on the perfect space (i.e., the land of Israel, Jerusalem and the Temple mount). In separating from their Jewish roots, the founders of the

Church sought to sever the Christian attachments to the locale of Jewish messianic expectations.

> For it is written that Abraham had two sons, one by the handmaid and one by the free woman. Now the son by the handmaid is born after the flesh but the son by the free woman is born through the promise. Which things contain an allegory: for these two women are the two covenants; one from Mount Sinai bearing children into bondage which is Hagar. Now this Hagar is Mount Sinai in Arabia, and answers to the Jerusalem that now is: for she is in bondage with her children. But the Jerusalem that is above is free, which is our mother (Gal. 4:21-26).

In the third century, Origen (185-254 C.E.), the most influential of all the theologians of the ancient Church, went even further than the author of Galatians by interpreting the Kingdom of God as an event that would take place not in space or in time but only in the souls of believers. According to Augustine (354-430) in his *City of God*, the Book of Revelation was to be understood as a spiritual allegory.[54]

This discussion of messianism in the Sinai tradition can be summed up with the following general observations:

1). In all messianic movements and visions there is a drive toward concretization and realization of the messianic ideal. The drive is strongest in the utopian pole of messianism but it is not absent in the restorative pole. Even the tendency in early Christianity to universalize, spiritualize and interiorize the millennium could not prevent the restorative and utopian strains from asserting themselves in the drive toward historic actualization. The crusades to free Jerusalem and the Holy land from the infidels are a clear example of utopian and restorative messianism in action.[55]

2). The image of the Messiah reflects the historical conditions of the time. Even when the messianic movement fails to be realized in the context of history, the messianic vision and its metaphors remain intact through reinterpretation.[56] It is true that the expectations of a scion of the House of David as a messianic king is the dominant image in the Sinai tradition. But this royal image has been modified and supplemented. When the returnees from Babylonia came to rebuild the Second Temple, it became clear that Judea would remain only a backwater province of the Persian Empire, that this was the age of "small things," and that in the impoverished circumstances of the time the Temple edifice would be a pale counterpart of its Solomonic predecessor. Against this background Zechariah, the prophet of the time, pictured the

Messiah-King as humbly "riding an ass" (Zech. 9:9), an image which Jesus concretized on his entry to Jerusalem (Mark 13:24-37; Matt. 24:27-51).[57] After the crucifixion of Jesus, the disciples and the early Church interpreted the "suffering servant" motif in Isa. 50:4-9; 52:13-53:12 as referring to the suffering Messiah who died on the cross. Their conception of the Second Coming (*parousia*) kept them from despairing of messianic salvation after his death. The images of the Messiah son of Joseph and Messiah son of David that arose after the failed Bar-Kokhba rebellion and its legacy of suffering has already been discussed. The same circumstances are reflected in the rabbinic legend that pictures the Messiah as dwelling among the lepers and beggars at the gates of Rome.[58]

3). The texts that lavish minute details in the portrayal of the Messiah and the Messianic Age are motivated by a fear that a postponement of the Golden Age to an unspecified future date (a strategy adopted by the rabbis after the two failed revolts against Rome) is liable to damage the hope for historic realization. But paradoxically the increase of fantastic detail does detach the millenarian yearning from its realistic base in history.[59]

The Heavenly Ascent

The only unambiguous account of a heavenly ascent in the Hebrew Bible is Elijah's journey in a fiery chariot carried upward by a whirlwind (2 Kings 2:2-15). The focus in the narrative is not on the journey itself but on the prophet Elisha's succession to the prophetic mission of Elijah. To witness Elijah's ascension is a sign of divine favor and Elisha is granted a double portion of God's spirit. Nevertheless, the fact that the ascension takes place at the end of Elijah's earthly task links the heavenly ascent to death and immortality, a motif taken up by the apocalypses and examined below. It also opens the door for post biblical tradition to turn Elijah into a messenger of God who returns to earth periodically for specific assignments and most notably to announce the cataclysmic "Day of the Lord."[60] Taken together the biblical narrative and the post-biblical traditions concerning Elijah provide the ascent and descent patterns of the ascension hero discussed in the introduction.

Far less explicit is the case of Enoch, one of the pre-deluge heroes in Gen. 5:21-25 of whom the Bible says twice that he walked with God. Moreover, the biblical narrative reports that Enoch disappeared (" . . . he was no more, for God took him.") but fails to mention his death despite the fact that it mentions the death of all the other antedeluvians. This omission and the unusual references to Enoch's disappearance and his walking with God served as clues for the apocalyptic authors of the Books of Enoch pointing to his physical transportation to heaven before his death. The Books of Enoch are faithful to the ascent-descent pattern and, in keeping with one strand of this motif (possibly influenced by Gnostic conceptions), Enoch is transformed into an angelic being.[61] As mentioned above (see note 27) the revelations on the heavenly journey deal with the secrets of nature as well as the problem of evil and the moral order. Enoch's heavenly journey comes at a time of crisis on earth when the traditional understanding of the natural and moral orders has been questioned. His ascent, revelation and descent are intended as mediation between the perfect realm of heaven and the chaos on earth. He verifies that the earth's moral values are still valid though in a mysterious way not yet understood by humans. Though earth is in turmoil, God's heavenly plan for the planet will soon become clear.[62]

The mysterious description of Abraham's covenant with God (Gen. 15: 7-21), in which the patriarch, after cutting the sacrifices in two and placing them opposite one another falls into a deep sleep, suggested a trance and a heavenly journey to the author of the Apocalypse of Abraham. This work written after the destruction of the Second Temple pictures Abraham ascending to heaven with an angelic guide Yahoel who bears a striking resemblance to the angel Metatron in talmudic mysticism.[63] The revelation to Abraham deals with the problem of theodicy (a major Jewish concern after the destruction of the Second Temple) but through the medium of the historical review that extends from creation to the Endtime. In this review there are two kinds of restoration, an apocalyptic restoration of the earth after its destruction at the end of time, and a restoration of the righteous to the Garden of Eden, the heavenly paradise after their death. Here we have a clear link between the human fear of death, extinction of life on earth, theodicy, the heavenly journey and the concept of immortality. One of the purposes of the apocalypse is to assuage human anxieties about death by pointing to Abraham's confirmed experience that the righteous can expect immortality. Abraham returns to earth though not entirely satisfied that he has understood everything.[64] In this apocalypse both ascent and descent patterns are present with Yahoel, the angel bearing God's name, and Abraham serving as mediators.[65]

The heavenly ascent of Isaiah implied in Isaiah 6 also prompted apocalyptic speculation. As discussed above, the prophet who is eavesdropping on the divine council volunteers his services as a messenger and is sent back to deliver God's message to a reluctant people, foreshadowing the later apocalyptic refrain of human obtuseness, imminent destruction and the survival of a saving remnant. Here too we have an ascent-descent pattern as well as the divine commission to disclose future events to the prophet's generation. This skeleton of the ascension theme was fleshed out in the later apocalyptic work The Ascension of Isaiah.

In this Christian apocalypse dating probably from the second century C.E. we have one of the most detailed realistic accounts of the trance state preceding the heavenly journey. The apocalypse describes the prophet Isaiah's address to King Hezekiah of Judea, his courtiers and councilors, and forty prophets with their followers. It then continues,

> . . . And while he was speaking by the Holy Spirit in the hearing of all he (suddenly) became silent and his consciousness was taken from him and he saw no (more) the men who were standing before him; his eyes were open, but his mouth was silent and the consciousness in his body was taken from him; but his breath was (still) in him, for he saw a vision . . . . And the people who were standing around, with the exception of the circle of prophets did (not) think that the holy Isaiah had been taken up.[66]

Then follows Isaiah's journey through the seven heavens and his prophecy of the corresponding descent of Jesus, thus pointing to a descent-ascent pattern in addition to the ascent-descent of Isaiah. The facial description and the pointed emphasis of the text that though "his consciousness was taken from him . . . his breath was (still) in him" when taken together with the heavenly ascent that follows and the remark that a heavenly journey was in progress corresponds very well with the descriptions of out of body experiences in the literature.[67]

The heavenly ascent is also the central theme of a famous talmudic narrative and its parallel variants as well as of a genre of rabbinic mystical writings known as the *Hekalot* literature.[68] In this context it is sufficient for our purposes to note that the rabbinic visionaries who made the heavenly ascent were called *yorde merkavah*, "descenders to the Merkavah." To paraphrase the medieval Jewish Bible commentator Rashi (R. Solomon ben Isaac) this term pleads for explanation. The word *merkavah* refers to Ezekiel's vision of the throne-chariot discussed above which was the objective of those who made the heavenly ascent. But the paradox is that though the mystical process is described in images of ascent its practitioners are called descenders. The solution lies in understanding that though the heavenly ascent is a transcendent experience, in mysticism transcendence and immanence are two sides of the same coin. If language pictures them as polar opposites we must remember that language is finite while Spirit is infinite defying spatial categorization. God envisioned by human beings is external and distant as the Bible underscores (Isa. 6:1; Ps. 121:1). But the Bible also teaches that God's spirit infuses the individual (Gen. 2:7; Prov. 20:7) and God's word lies upon the human heart (Deut. 6:6; 30:14). In Huston Smith's felicitous rendering, "as microcosm mirrors macrocosm man mirrors the Infinite" and "that which man seeks externally in the highest heavens he seeks internally in the depths of his soul."[69] Thus to descend to the *Merkavah* was to sink into mystic trance and ascend the heavenly realms so that the term *yorde merkavah* incorporates the ascent-descent pattern.

Jesus and the disciples were also deeply involved in the ascent to heaven. Jesus is described as lecturing Nicodemus on baptism as a spiritual rebirth and seeing the disbelief of his listener assures him of his personal experience: "For nobody has gone up to heaven except he who has come down from heaven, the Son of man" (John 3:13). Here we have both the ascent-descent and the descent-ascent patterns with Jesus as mediator. The story of the transfiguration in which Jesus and three of his closest disciples Peter, James and John go up a high mountain and the clothes of Jesus become shining white is an echo of the apocalyptic Enoch who is transformed on his heavenly ascent (see above note 61).[70] The disciples reported Jesus' ascension after the resurrection (Acts 1; Phil. 2:9; John 20:17; Eph. 1:20; Col. 3:1; Heb. 7:26; 8:1; 9:24) and they hoped to do the same themselves. Some believed a heavenly ascension could take place only at the end of the world which they expected imminently while others believed it would immediately follow after their own deaths. Still others believed, in keeping with the ascension tradition already cited, that the heavenly ascent was not only a reward after death but was possible for exceptional individuals while they were still alive.[71]

Notes

1.   John J. Collins, The Apocalyptic Imagination: An Introduction to the Jewish Matrix of Christianity (New York: Crossroad, 1984), p.4.

2.   Ibid., p. 6. Collins further subdivides these categories into apocalypses containing cosmogony, primordial events, recollections of the past, *ex eventu* prophecy, persecution, other eschatological upheavals, judgment and destruction of the wicked, judgment and destruction of the world, judgment and destruction of otherworldly beings, cosmic transformation, resurrection and other forms of afterlife. See further J. J. Collins, "Introduction: Towards the Morphology of a Genre," *Semeia: An Experimental Journal for Biblical Criticism* 14 (Missoula, Montana: Scholars Press, 1979): 9-15 and J. J. Collins, "The Genre Apocalypse in Hellenistic Judaism," in *Apocalypticism in the Mediterranean World and the Near East*, ed. David Hellholm (Tubingen: J. C. B. Mohr [Paul Siebeck], 1983), pp. 531-548.

3.   M. Hagigah, 2:1; b. Hagigah, 16a. Christopher Rowland, *The Open Heaven: A Study of Apocalyptic in Judaism and Early Christianity* (New York: Crossroad, 1982), pp. 75-77. Rowland does not apply the last category to the afterlife (though the Talmud does so) which he does not discuss at all. I have followed the talmudic interpretation because it fits the conceptual framework of this chapter. The actual meaning of what is beneath is what is beneath the earth, perhaps an allusion to the Orphic journey downward to the realm of the dead. The intent of the Mishnah was to prohibit esoteric speculation in precisely those areas that so fascinated the apocalyptic visionaries. As noted in Chapter 1, Sinai: Unity and Prose, note 13, Rabbi Akiba prohibited the reading of apocalyptic-pseudepigraphic works.

4.   Collins, The Apocalyptic Imagination, pp. 14-28; 79-80.

5.   Judith 9-11. On the reasons for the belief in the cessation of prophecy and its impact on Second Temple Judaism see Chapter 6, Sinai: Prophetic Piety, notes 1-13.

6.   Martin Hengel, Judaism and Hellenism 2 vols. (Philadelphia: Fortress Press, 1974) 1:18-57.

7.   Paul Hanson, "Apocalypticism," in *Interpreters Dictionary of the Bible Supplement* (Nashville, Tenn., 1976): 30-31. Hanson drew on the sociological insights of Karl Mannheim and Max Weber which also applied to the early forms of apocalyptic in the Hebrew Bible. See his The Dawn of Apocalyptic (Philadelphia: Fortress Press, 1975). A similar approach is taken by Sheldon R. Isenberg, "Millenarism in Greco-Roman Palestine," *Religion* 4 (1974): 26-46. For a critique of these approaches see George W. E. Nickelsburg, "Social Aspects of Palestinian Jewish *Apocalypticism*" in *Apocalypticism in the Mediterranean World and the Near East*, p. 648. On the Zealots see William R. Farmer, *Maccabees, Zealots and Josephus* (New York: Columbia University Press, 1956), p. 175; Solomon Zeitlin, *The Rise and Fall of the Judean State* , 2 vols. (Philadelphia: The Jewish Publication Society of America, 1962), 2:131, 215-16; 241-43; 320 and Martin Hengel, *Die Zeloten* (Leiden: E. J. Brill, 1961).

8.   Yehezkel Kaufmann, *Toledot ha-'Emunah ha-Yisraelit* (Jerusalem-Tel-Aviv: Bialik Institute-Dvir, 1953) 3 (1): 15-16.

9.   Benjamin Uffenheimer, *The Visions of Zechariah: From Prophecy to Apocalyptic* (Hebrew) (Jerusalem: The Israel Society for Biblical Research and "Kiryat Sepher," 1961), pp. 139-145. Against this view Martha Himmelfarb, "The Apocalyptic Vision," in *The Oxford Study Bible* (New York: Oxford University Press, 1992), pp. 190-91 argues that rather than keeping humanity from God the ascent apocalypses with their multiplication of angels provide the channel for human beings to be in contact with God, in rare instances during life though usually after death. But this contact is clearly not "the mouth to mouth" contact of which the Bible speaks in the case of Moses nor is it the direct address to Amos and Isaiah. Only in Isaiah's initiation to prophecy is their mediation by an angel (Isa. 6: 6-7) but in all subsequent prophecies no angel is present. Ultimately, of course, nearness and distance from God, immanence and transcendence, are two sides of the same coin. Cf. Jer. 23:23 and 31:2.

10.   Ibid., 136-139; 150-52.

11.   Kaufmann, *Toledot*, p. 16.   B. Uffenheimer, The Visions of Zechariah, p. 155, n. 1 rightly argues that the vision in perspective is not a category of thought intrinsic to apocalyptic but a matter of style related to the psychological outlook of a people steeped in history. It is found in later Jewish circles that had no connection whatsoever with apocalyptic. But he misses the specific connection to the out of body experience which is influenced by cultural factors.

12.   Rowland, *The Open Heaven*, pp. 193-196.

13.   See note 3 of the introduction to this chapter.

14.   Robert Alter, *The Art of Biblical Poetry* (New York: Basic Books, 1985), pp. 152-157.

15.   Kaufmann, *Toledot* 3: 17, 547-48.

16.   Ibid., p. 547; Uffenheimer, *The Visions of Zechariah*, pp. 62, 84-90; 161-64.

17.   Rowland, *The Open Heaven*, p. 202.

18.   Donald H. Menzel, *Flying Saucers* (Cambridge: Harvard University Press, 1953), an astrophysicist suggests that Ezekiel saw an atmospheric phenomenon called "sundogs," while Arthur W. Orton, "The Four Faced Visitors of Ezekiel," *Analog Science Fact-Fiction* 67 (1) (March, 1961): 99-115 argues that this is the account of the actual landing of extraterrestrial beings reported by a painstaking, truthful and critical observer. Cf. Ronald Story, *The Space Gods Revealed: A Close Look at the Theories of Erich von Daniken* (New York: Harper & Row, 1976).

19.   J. B. Pritchard, *The Ancient Near East in Pictures*, 2nd ed. (Princeton: Princeton University Press, 1969) #536; W. Andrae, *Colored Ceramics from Ashur* (London: K. Paul Trench, Trubner & Co., 1925), plate 8, p. 127; reproduced in color in A. Parrot, *Ninveh and Babylon* (London: Thames and Hudson, 1961), fig. 282.

20. J. Cerny, *Ancient Egyptian Religion* (London, New York: Hutchinson's University Library, 1957), pp. 29-40; Pritchard, *The Ancient Near East in Pictures*, 2nd ed. #644-66.

21. Pritchard, *The Ancient Near East in Pictures*, 2nd ed. #472-74; 486, 830, 500, 501, 531, 835, 534, 537.

22. Kaufmann, *Toledot* 3(2), p. 545.

23. Ezekiel 1-20, *The Anchor Bible*, trans. with intro. and commentary, Moshe Greenberg (Garden City, NY.: Doubleday and Co., 1983), pp. 57-58.

24. Morton Smith, "The Image of God: Notes on the Hellenization of Judaism with Especial Reference to Goodenough's Work on Jewish Symbols, page 497," *Bulletin of the John Rylands Library* 40 (2) (1958): 473-512. David J. Halperin, *The Faces of the Chariot* (Tubingen: J. C. B. Mohr [Paul Siebeck], 1988), p. 90.

25. Ezekiel 1-20, *The Anchor Bible*, pp. 57-58.

26. Carl G. Jung, *The Collected Works*, 19 vols. + index vol., ed. Herbert Read and others, trans. by R. F. C. Hull and others (New York: Pantheon Books, 1953-1967; Princeton: Princeton University Press, 1967-1978) Bollingen Series 20, vol., 18: The Symbolic Life: Miscellaneous Writings, paragraphs 1584-1690; Avis M. Dry, *The Psychology of Jung: A Critical Interpretation* (London: Wiley and Methuen, 1961), pp. 203-208. According to Jung an "archetype" is a symbol that recurs independently in the dreams of different people and in the imagery of different cultures. It therefore comes from a common source in the unconscious on which all human beings draw. Claude Levi-Strauss argued that a certain universal composition of the human mind produces the structure of myth which he calls "deep structures." On the illuminating distinction between Levi-Strauss' view of deep structure and Jung's conception of the archetype see R. J. Z. Werblowksy, "Structure and Archetype," in *The Gaster Festschrift, The Journal of the Ancient Near Eastern Society of Columbia University* 5 (1973): 435-442.

Jung viewed the Christian trinity as an incomplete version of an original divine fourness. He was vague in describing the missing fourth member. Sometimes he identified it as the female aspect of divinity, the Virgin Mary of Catholicism. But he also viewed the missing element as the devil, the evil within God that was purged but at the price of leaving Him incomplete. See Carl G. Jung, *Psychology and Religion: West and East*, Bollingen Series 20 (New York: Pantheon Books, 1958), paragraphs 103-107, pp. 59-63; paragraphs 169-295, pp. 109-200. Cf. Halperin, *The Faces of the Chariot*, pp. 190-191 who applies Jung's quaternity concept to a rabbinic midrash on the Merkavah.

27. 1 Enoch (Ethiopic Enoch) 27-28; 22; 33-36; 41:1; 41;3 ff.; 43-44; 52; 59; 60:11 ff. 69; 71; 72-80; 93: 11-14 and the revelation of mysteries by the evil angels in 7, 65 and 69. 2 Enoch (Slavonic Enoch) 5-6; 11-16; 24-30; 40; 47-48. All references to apocryphal or pseudepigraphic works are from R. H. Charles, *Apocrypha and Pseudepigrapha of the Old Testament*, 2 vols. (Oxford: Clarendon Press, 1913) unless otherwise designated. 3 Enoch (Hebrew Enoch) ed. H. Odeberg with a Prolegomenon by J. C. Greenfield

(New York: Ktav Publishing House, 1973), 11; 13; 14; 17; 41-42; 48 (d). Hekalot Rabbati 9:5. Cf. 2 Baruch (Syriac Baruch) 48:2-14; 59:5-11. The old Mesopotamian emphasis on the importance of order and regularity in nature and the equation of disorder and wickedness, an emphasis that passes into the Hebrew Bible (see Chapter 2: Creation: Genesis or Theogony? Sinai I: Creation by the One, notes 7-8) and the New Testament is underscored in 1 Enoch chapters 1-5; 46:5; 72-80. The rabbis also pointed to the regularity of the natural order and the catastrophes that ensue when it is broken. See Louis Ginzberg, *The Legends of the Jews* (Philadelphia: The Jewish Publication Society of America, 1955) 5:34-36, note 100. Cf. Ithammar Gruenwald, *Apocalyptic and Merkavah Mysticism* (Leiden: E. J. Brill, 1980), pp. 5-16.

28. Collins, *The Apocalyptic Imagination*, p. 78.

29. R. H. Charles, *The Book of Jubilees or the Little Genesis* (London: Black, 1902), pp. 262-63.

30. See my discussion in "Two Views of the Patriarchs: Noahides and Pre-Sinai Israelites," in *Texts and Studies Presented to Nahum N. Glatzer* (Leiden: E. J. Brill, 1975), pp. 44-45.

31. S. Talmon, "The Calendar Reckoning of the Sect from the Judean Desert,: *Scripta Hierosolymitana (Aspects of the Dead Sea Scrolls)* ed. C. Rabin and Y. Yadin, 4 (1958): 162 ff.

32. Collins, *The Apocalyptic Imagination*, pp. 120-121.

33. Martin Hengel, *Judaism and Hellenism* (Philadelphia: Fortress Press, 1974) 1:207-208. Hengel acknowledges that the three stages are not disconnected since Torah and prophecy already contain the deeper meanings, God's commandments are in actuality observed only in the circle of saints, and the revelation of the mysteries is already a preparation and foreshadowing of perfect knowledge in the time of salvation.

34. See above note 11 and Kaufmann, *Toledot* 3 (1), p. 17.

35. Yehezkel Kaufmann, *The Religion of Israel*, trans. and abridged Moshe Greenberg (Chicago: The University of Chicago Press, 1960), pp. 420-423, 436. See above Chapter 4, Is There A Moral Order in the Universe? Sinai: The Struggles of Theodicy, note 8.

36. *The Relevance of Apocalyptic* (London: Lutterworth Press, 1944), p. 38 and Paul D. Hanson, *The Dawn of Apocalyptic*, pp. 9 ff. The actual quote is: "The prophets foretold the future that should arise out of the present while the apocalyptists foretold the future that should break into the present . . . The apocalyptists had little faith in the present to beget the future." But the prophetic "Day of the Lord" was also a future that broke into the present. For the critique of this distinction see Rowland, *The Open Heaven*, p. 29; B. Vawter, "Apocalyptic: Its Relation to Prophecy," *Catholic Biblical Quarterly* 22, no. 1 (Jan., 1960): 33-46 and G. E. Ladd, "Why Not Prophetic Apocalyptic?" *Journal of Biblical Literature* 76 (Sept., 1957): 192-200.

37. *The Messianic Idea in Judaism* (New York: Schocken Books, 1971), p. 11. Scholem's categorical statement echoing H. H. Rowley oversimplifies the issue making no allowance for the alternative versions just cited which also are found in the sources. See above note 36.

38. Cant. R. 6:10. However, the third century date of this statement raises the question as to whether it is a polemic aimed against those attempting to calculate the Endtime.

39. Hengel, *Judaism and Hellenism*, 1:183; 2:123.

40. Collins, *The Apocalyptic Imagination*, pp. 102-106 and more fully in J. J. Collins, "The Date and Provenance of the Testament of Moses," in *Studies on the Testament of Moses* ed. G. W. E. Nickelsburg (Missoula, Montana: Scholars Press, 1973), pp. 15-32.

41. Collins, *The Apocalyptic Imagination*, pp. 95-99. On the Sibylline Oracles as a proselytizing tract for Diaspora Judaism see my "Two Views of the Patriarchs: Noahides and Pre-Sinai Israelites," p. 56 ff. and the sources cited there.

42. Collins, *The Apocalyptic Imagination*, pp. 95-97.

43. *Apocrypha and Pseudepigrapha of the Old Testament*, ed. R. H. Charles, 2:141.

44. b. Zebahim, 116a.

45. See my *Judaism and the Gentile Faiths*, p. 212.

46. Gershom Scholem, *The Messianic Idea in Judaism*, pp. 1-36; Lawrence H. Schiffman, "The Concept of the Messiah in Second Temple and Rabbinic Literature," *Review and Expositor* 84, no. 1 (Winter, 1987): 235-246.

47. Isa. 13:6-13; Joel 1:15; 2:1; 3:4; 4:14; Amos 5:18-20; Obad. 15; Zeph. 1:17-18; Mal. 3:23. Cf. Isa. 2:12; Ezek. 30:3; Zech. 14:1-9.

48. Emil Schurer, *The History of the Jewish People in the Age of Jesus Christ*, rev. and ed. G. Vermes, F. Millar, M. Black (Edinburgh: T & T Clark, 1979) 2:502 ff. In the Gospels the term "son of man" is used in the same sense that it is used in Daniel but with a messianic connotation (Mark 14:61; Matt. 26:63 f.; Luke 22:67 f.). The connection of the term with the Messiah, unlike its use in Daniel, was undoubtedly quite widespread in Jewish circles before and after the time of Jesus. Cf. George Foot Moore, Judaism in the First Centuries of the Christian Era (Cambridge: Harvard University Press, 1950) 2:335-337.

49. b. Berakot, 34b; b. Sanhedrin, 99a; b. Shabbat, 63a and elsewhere. Cf. Urbach, *The Sages*, pp. 665-666; 672. Scholem, *The Messianic Idea in Judaism*, pp. 18-19 ff.

50. 4 Ezra 7: 26-44; 2 Baruch 4:2-7; 26-29. Moore, *Judaism*, 2:338-345.

51. Sifre, Numbers 76, Behaaloteka, (ed. Friedman), p. 19b Sifre, Deut. 343, Ve-Zot ha-Berakah, (ed. Finkelstein), p.398; b. Sanhedrin, 97b; 1 Enoch 56;5; 4 Ezra 13:5; Sibylline Oracles 3: 319, 512; Targum Yerushalmi to Num. 11:26.

52. Rev. 20; James Hastings, *Encyclopedia of Religion and Ethics* 3:596-98; Morton Enslin, *Christian Beginnings* (New York and London: Harper & Brothers, 1938), pp. 351-72. On the transposing of aggressive feelings from the present to the future see Adela Yarbro Collins, *Crisis and Catharsis: The Power of the Apocalypse* (Philadelphia: The Westminster Press, 1984), pp. 157 ff. On the later Jewish sources adopting this scheme see *Sefer Eliyahu*

in *Midreshe Geulah*, ed. Even Shemuel [J. Kaufman], (Tel Aviv: Mosad Bialik—Masada, 1942-43), pp. 32, 45-46.

53.   Scholars note that the first unambiguous mention of this doctrine occurs in tannaitic passages of uncertain date, i.e., b. Sukkah, 52a and the Targum Ps. Jonathan to Exod. 40:11. See Joseph Klausner, *The Messianic Idea in Israel*, 3rd ed. (London: George Allen & Unwin, 1956), pp. 483-501; Urbach, *The Sages*, pp. 686 ff.

54.   "Millennium and Millenarism," *The Catholic Encyclopedia* 10:309-10.

55.   See the discussion in my *Judaism and the Gentile Faiths*, pp. 220-221 and the sources cited there.

56.   Ithammar Gruenwald, "Mi-Zeriha li-Shekiyah, " in *The Messianic Idea in Jewish Thought: A Study Conference in Honor of the Eightieth Birthday of Gershom Scholem* (Hebrew) (Jerusalem: The Israel Academy of Sciences and Humanities, 1982), p. 25.

57.   It is also true that there is a biblical tradition of opposition to the power and perks of kingship which points up the inner contradiction in the term "messianic-king." Zechariah's image and later that of Jesus could well reflect this tradition. See Y. Jacovitz, "Ani ve-Rokev al Hamor, " in *The Messianic Idea in Jewish Thought*, pp. 16-17. There is also Zechariah's message from God to Zerubavel of the Davidic line who was seen as a potential messianic-king: "Not by might or by power (or by wealth as some translate it) but by my spirit says the Lord of Hosts" (Zech. 4:6).

58.   b. Sanhedrin, 98a. J. Klausner, *The Messianic Ideal in Israel*, pp. 405-7 points out that the idea of a "suffering Messiah" is found only in post-tannaitic sources.

59.   Gruenwald, "Mi-Zeriha Li-Shekiyah," p. 36.

60.   This conception is based on Mal. 3:23-24. See also the vast materials cited in Ginzberg's Legends 7 under Elijah.

61.   Secrets of Enoch 22:8-9; 3 Enoch (ed. Odeberg), 10:1.

62.   1 Enoch 14; *The Books of Enoch: Aramaic Fragments of Qumran Cave 4* ed. J. T. Milik with Matthew Black (Oxford: The Clarendon Press, 1976), Intro. pp. 15-22.

63.   The Apocalypse of Abraham, Chs. 9-10, ed. and trans. G. H. Box (New York, 1919), p. 46 f. Cf. 4 Ezra 3:14; Syriac Baruch 4:4 where the covenant of the pieces was supposed to be proof that Abraham was given not only precognition of the sojourn in Egypt but also a vision of the Endtime. On the development leading from Yahoel to Metatron see G. Scholem, *Jewish Gnosticism, Merkabah Mysticism and Talmudic Tradition* (New York: The Jewish Theological Seminary, 1960), pp. 41-42.

64.   The Apocalypse of Abraham, Chs. 21 and 30.

65.   Alan F. Segal, *"Heavenly Ascent etc."*, pp. 1362-1363.

66.   Ascension of Isaiah 6.

67.   The out of body experience usually occurs in the waking state as documented by Glen O. Gabbard and Stuart W. Twemlow, *With the Eyes of the Mind* (New York: Praeger, 1984), pp. 109-110.

68.   b. Hagigah, 15a-b; Tosefta Hagigah 2:3-6 (ed. Lieberman): 381-382; Yer. Hagigah 2:1; Cant. R. 1:4. There is a vast scholarly literature that has grown up around this narrative but the best treatment thus far is that of Yehudah Liebes, *The Sin of Elisha (ben Avuyah): Four Who Entered Pardes (the Garden) and the Nature of Talmudic Mysticism* (Hebrew) (Jerusalem: Academon, 1990). Building on Liebes's work is my own treatment to be found in a forthcoming article, "The Heavenly Ascent and the Out of Body Experience in Talmudic Mysticism." On the Hekalot literature see Peter Schafer (ed.), Synopse zur Hekhalot Literatur (Tubingen: J. C. B. Mohr [Paul Siebeck], 1981) and David J. Halperin, *The Faces of the Chariot*.

69.   *Forgotten Truth* (New York: Harper & Row, 1976), pp. 20-21.

70.   Mark 9:2-8; Matt. 17:1-8; Luke 9:28-36; 2 Pet. 1:16 ff. Cf. Morton Smith, "Ascent to the Heavens and the Beginning of Christianity," *Eranos Yearbook* 50 (1981): 420-21; 423-24. The transformation into angelic form, in some cases, seems to be common to both the in body and out of body heavenly journey. Cf. Ascension of Isaiah 7:25; Slavonic Enoch 37:1 f.; 2 Corinthians 3:18.

71.   Morton Smith, "Ascent to the Heavens and the Beginning of Christianity," pp. 416-418.

Olympus: Paths to the Eternal,
Personal and Cosmic

Overview of Major Ideas and Developments

The Greek views of the afterlife encompassed a wide spectrum of possibilities, extending from everlasting death all the way up to apotheosis. *Thanatos*, Death, is one of the earliest personifications in Hesiod's *Theogony* (211-212) and is as primary an aspect of the natural order to come as Night his mother and Day his sibling (123-125). In *Works and Days* 109-116, even the golden race of mortals, who lived like gods beyond all evils, had to die, albeit death covered them like sleep (another sibling of Death in *Theogony*) and they became pure spirits dwelling on earth (*daimones*).

In its simplest form, death is a part of the cycle of nature, in which the individual demise is submerged in the survival of the group. On the battlefield at Troy, Glaucus compares the generation of humans to the generation of leaves and connects their death in winter to the birth of new life in the spring (*Il.* 6. 145-49). Like the Hebrews, the Greeks conceived of the earth as the mother from which they were all born and to which they returned at death and burial. Thus the underworld home of the dead was also the source of life and fertility. To escape this impersonal cycle, a mortal had to perform deeds worthy of memory so that his glorious name might live forever in epic song (see chapter 5). All desired to leave children behind; thus the family would renew itself even as its individual members perished.

The idea that death was natural (and was not created as a punishment for sin) became an important aspect of Greek physics and eschatology. Many of the pre-Socratic nature philosophers conceived of the eternal cosmos as a unity based on the balanced exchange of opposites (see chapters 2, 3, and 4). At *Phaedo* 71-72, Socrates uses the argument that, life and death also being opposites, "the living come from the dead no less than the dead from the living" (72a), to construct a proof for a new idea—the immortality of the individual soul as the seat of intellect and will.

But the acceptance of death as the common fate of all and an inevitable part of group survival does not allay fear about what happens when a person dies. Like other cultures, the Greeks developed a set of burial customs to ease the transition from life to death for both the corpse and the survivors. Ritual activities and cults which focused on the graves of certain heroes suggest that some dead persons, renowned in life, did not suffer the same departure from life as ordinary people, but actually lived on within the tomb, using their additional potency to benefit their worshippers. Other more extraordinary mortals (e.g., Heracles) were, like Enoch and Elijah, able to escape death entirely and ascend to the heavenly realm.

But what about the ordinary dead? What did they experience once the life left the body or once the period of mourning was over? The various answers to such questions came from the two basic avenues of Greek thought—the myths of the poets about the gods, nature, and mortals; and the speculations of the philosophers who opposed, borrowed, or adapted them.

As in the Mesopotamian myths and their vestiges in the Bible, the realm of the dead developed in conjunction with the cosmic order. In the *Theogony*, Hesiod generated a personification of the place, "dark Tartarus in the depths of the earth" (119), directly out of Chaos. But this netherworld is part of the moral order which arose out of the succession drama (see chapter 2). The poet describes Tartarus after Zeus has imprisoned the rebellious Titans, those archetypes of hubris and disorder (see chapter 3), down there, "as far from earth as heaven is" (720). Tartarus is connected to chastisement as well as to the natural order by details such as the following: 1) it is surrounded by a gated bronze fence and triple line of night; 2) is guarded by the fierce dog Cerberus, who permits entrance but never exit; 3) and is the home of the powerful goddess Hecate, whose punishment of oath-breaking immortals reduces them to a deathlike state. In its earliest literary description, the netherworld is the place of final reciprocity for famous sinners against the gods (e.g., Tityus, Tantalus, and Sisyphus, (Hom. *Od.* 11.576-600).

According to *Works and Days* 152-155, the men of the bronze age, a violent race who destroyed each other, were the first mortals to be seized by black death; they left the light of the sun and went down to the grim house of icy Hades without any glory to live after them. These men died prematurely by their own hands, unlike Korah and his followers whom God caused to be swallowed down to untimely death.

Some mythical sinners, however, were thought to have been punished with a sudden death inflicted by a god. Capaneus, for example, was struck by Zeus' thunderbolt as soon as he boasted that not even Zeus himself could stop him from burning Thebes. Odysseus' men who ate the cattle of the Sun were also destroyed by Zeus' thunderbolt which raised the storm at sea. When Strepsiades asserts, however, that Zeus uses his thunderbolt to punish perjurers in Athenian courts, the comic Socrates disproves the idea as silly and old-fashioned (Aristophanes *Clouds* 397-402). For the early death of an ordinary person was not generally viewed as a divine punishment for sin among the Greeks.

The depiction of what happened to the individual after death comes mainly from the accounts of otherworldly journeys which resemble those described by the Hebrews. Odysseus is the first hero who reports on such a journey, a voyage to the ends of the earth to learn about his future from the dead seer Tiresias. After digging a pit and sacrificing, Odysseus was able to see long-dead shades, converse with recent dead reanimated by a sip of blood, and even penetrate into some of the mysteries of the afterlife. The details of Homer's narrative incorporate topics prohibited in the Mishnah but developed in Hebrew apocalyptic; through lucid (rather than symbolic and opaque) language and dialogue, Homer reveals, in temporal and spatial terms, the past, present, and future of humanity and the connection of death to the natural and moral order. Other authors added to Homer's picture, incorporating new details from new and sometimes foreign sources.

Although Odysseus' journey is not technically 'otherworldly,' later poets and thinkers developed the motif of the voyage beyond the outermost limit. Parmenides, for example, began his philosophical poem by describing how the daughters of the sun led him on a path away from the world of ordinary experience to an otherworldly place where he received a divine revelation both of the "unshakable heart of well-rounded truth" and of "mortal opinion" (29-30).[1] The vehicle of his voyage, a horse-drawn chariot, suggestive of Elijah's ascent and Ezekiel's vision (as well as the chariots of the Greek gods and Pegasus the mythical winged horse), became associated with Greek otherworldly journeys which were also ascents toward superhuman knowledge. In Aristophanes' *Peace*, for example, the comic hero flies up to Olympus on a dungbeetle and learns about Peace and War from Hermes. In Plato's *Phaedrus*, Socrates describes the human soul as a winged chariot moving through the heavens, following the revolutions of the gods' chariots and getting glimpses of the ultimate truth.

Some of these motifs may be derived from or related to the kinds of trances or out of body experiences mentioned above. Legends which accrued around such mysterious figures as Abaris of Croton and Aristeas of Proconnesus suggest that certain individuals were believed to have left their bodies to travel in time and space, communicated directly with the gods, performed miraculous cures, and even reappeared after death, like the shaman of other cultures.[2] Following another path of release, some groups, like the worshipers of Dionysus, were able to commune (if not communicate) with divine nature in a state of ecstasy induced through wine, wild music and dance, and orgiastic rites that freed them from the restrictions of their normal consciousness. Others aimed to achieve a state of fellowship, union, or perhaps reunion with the divine by means of purification rites, initiation rituals, and, sometimes, ascetic practices, (e.g., in the Eleusinian Mysteries, the Pythagorean and Orphic ways, and in the later mystery cults).

The roads converge and impact on ideas about death and the afterlife because of the development of the concept of the *psyche*. Homer used the word, whose root meaning is "breath," to refer to the part of the person which left the corpse and went to Hades.[3] But, in later literature and cult, *psyche* gradually took on new connotations for the living associated with our words 'soul' or 'self,' even as philosophers were hypothesizing that breathy elements like fire or air were the primary matter out of which the divine and eternal cosmos arose.

Pythagoras and Empedocles, whose real lives are obscured by legend, traveled all the paths.[4] They displayed religious fervor in expressing their belief that the soul was a separate and immortal element of humans, derived from the divine and seeking return to it. At the same time, however, they developed theories to explain the material origins and mechanical processes of the natural world which, though full of oppositions and flux, operated according to laws which produced a well-ordered, unchanging, eternal, and therefore divine whole.

It was Plato who synthesized the ideas of poetry, cult, and philosophy to produce a religious, metaphysical, and ethical eschatology of lasting influence. Plato built his proofs for the theory of Forms and the immortality of the soul through rational argument in several different dialogues. Often, however, he interjected myths which describe abstract points in human terms or express intuitions that extend beyond the reach of philosophical discourse.[5] This is particularly true of the dialogues which refer to the immortality of the soul and its natural tendency toward the eternal and good. From Plato, therefore, come vivid and influential descriptions of the realm of the dead, the last judgment, and the fate of individual souls (v. *Gorgias*, *Phaedo*) as well as the famous eschatological revelation Er received during his out of body experience (v. the end of the *Republic*).

Like the Jewish apocalyptists, Plato reshaped traditional elements of language, tale, and symbol drawn from earlier poetry or cult to express his new idea about the divine governance of the universe and the consequences of this truth for human beings. In contrast to Jewish eschatology, Platonic myth does not veil the details of the truth in opaque symbolism. Rather the philosopher uses myth to further define terms or to cap ideas reached (or nearly reached) through careful and reasoned dialogue. The revelation contained in the myth clarifies the abstract theory by placing it in human space, time, and action. Moreover, the revelation would be meaningless without the discursive conversation.

The Greeks did not connect the afterlife with a culmination of history or resurrection of the dead for a last judgment at the end of time. For them history was the investigation of the words and deeds associated with specific events. Although they found causes and patterns in the rise and fall of nations, they had no concept of a divine program for humanity comparable to the salvation history of the Hebrews (see chapter 9). Thus the political and military crises which destroyed the centrality and independence of the polis in the fourth century did not result in the kind of metahistory developed by the Jewish apocalyptists who despaired of the restoration of their earthly Davidic kingdom.

Some poets and philosophers did speculate about a cataclysmic end of the world as a degeneration from perfection in which all the laws of nature would break down and matter would be reduced to its primal state. But most often this was just one point on an eternal cycle; the world would be reborn anew and the cosmos be regenerated. According to the early Stoics, even the particular events of history would be repeated exactly. Such an eschatology is ahistorical and cyclical; the cosmos as a whole is immortal even though its individual parts move and change in time, for the visible world is, in Plato's words, "an image of eternity moving according to number" (*Timaeus* 37d).

It is difficult to determine how far these ideas penetrated into popular belief. It is clear, however, that as the emphasis on the individual developed in the period between Homer and Plato, so too did the vision of death become more individualized. Graves dated to the end of the fifth century reveal a greater variety of burial practices and a greater emphasis on domestic and personal interests. Moreover, epitaphs on funeral monuments for ordinary people announce their names and details of their lives to passersby, as if insure for them the kind of immortality accorded earlier to epic heroes or founders of great aristocratic houses. There are also indications that the dead hoped to be reunited with their loved ones in the next world or receive rewards for their piety after death. There are signs too that some chose to be initiated into cults, mysteries, and brotherhoods which promised them a special status among the dead. Like the Hebrews, the Greeks had to adjust their belief system to the realities of the changing political structure. In the Hellenistic period, when the importance of the public religion of the polis declined as power shifted to new imperial institutions, opportunities increased for private, more individualized choices among rites, beliefs and systems of metaphysics which assuaged the fear of death.

Transitions from Life to Death: Burial Customs

Like the Hebrews, the ancient Greeks viewed death not as an evil, but rather as the normal culmination of a full and meaningful life. Solon's description to Croesus of the most fortunate of men includes their good deaths as well as their good lives (Herodotus 1.30-31). He names Tellus the Athenian as the most blessed because he lived to see his grandchildren and then died defending his country. Solon considers seventy years as the normal life span, and the happy man the one who has good things, keeps them until the end, and dies a peaceful death.

In contrast to the Bible, the Greeks did not express any firm belief in a divinely fixed limit to the individual's life. Nor did they believe that early death was normally a punishment from the gods for evil. In the same passage from Herodotus, in fact, Solon calls the deaths of the young athletes Cleobis and Biton the "best end of life," for the pious brothers died in their sleep at the altar of Hera after their proud mother asked the goddess to grant them "the best thing to befall a mortal." The early death of the beautiful brave warrior/athlete or citizen/patriot was a good death which insured his eternal glory. The untimely deaths of the young, particularly children or maidens, evoked pity rather than blame. For the elderly, death was anticipated as a release from the inevitable decrepitude, disease, and despair of old age. Mimnermus at least preferred dying young to losing his youthful vigor.[6]

The Greeks viewed death as a process, a graduated move 'from here to over there,'(e.g., *Phaedo* 117c) rather than a single event. The interval between the moment of death and the integration into the next world placed the deceased in an abnormal and indeterminate situation, threatening to him and possibly to his survivors, who also had to deal with the economic and social problems engendered by the death. Therefore, the Greeks, like most other cultures, practiced various customs to insure a successful completion of this final *rite de passage*. Procedures differed from start to finish, according to the different historical periods and political contexts, the varying social positions of the dead, and the different circumstances of the death, e.g., untimely, as in the case of children, warriors, the unmarried, and those struck by lightning. Proper performance was important; exegetes could be consulted for complex situations.   The following description presents only a summary of general practices.[7]

It was up to the survivors to perform the customary rites for the dead, which did not require the supervision or services of professionals such as priests. The burial of the corpse was the most important obligation to the dead human and to the gods below. In general, communities felt obligated to bury even a stranger and to set up cenotaphs for those whose bodies were missing.

The first phase of the funeral process was the *prothesis*, the laying out of the body in the family's home. Activities such as emitting shrill cries, cutting hair, strewing ashes or filth on bodies, and wearing torn clothing resemble Hebrew customs. Burkert interprets them, however, as "marking the household's fall from the state of normality."[8] On the third day after the death came the *ekphora*, the carrying out of the body to the burial ground. After the body was interred, a banquet was held at the house, and, on the ninth day, meals for the deceased were offered at the tomb. Later still, perhaps on the thirtieth day, when they may have thought the body was fully decomposed, a repetition of the grave rites and a communal feast of the survivors marked the end of the mourning period.

The fact that purification rites occurred throughout the process implies a fear of pollution (*miasma*, see chapter 4). The corpse does not seem to have been abhorrent in itself or dangerous to survivors. How then to account for the taboos and pollution connected with death? Although recent scholars have emphasized that the corpse is a sacred object, which must be treated with caution because it is between worlds and "lacks a proper social identity," Garland offers a broader explanation:

> . . . The sentiments surrounding a corpse in the period between death and burial, a time when rapid changes are taking place in the body, are *ipso facto* more fluid and uncertain than those which attend the final condition of the dead when entry to the afterlife has been fully achieved. It seems inevitable that considerations of hygiene, fear of unknown powers and a sense of guilt should at least have

contributed to the suggestiveness of the taboo placed upon
the Greek corpse, which, judged overall, seems to have
aroused practical, rather than pathological, concern.[9]

The grave itself had a marker; hence the words *mnema*,
'memorial,' or *sema*, 'sign', for 'tomb.' By the end of the fifth
century, this marker had developed from a stone or pile of stones
into an artistic and expensive monument, called a stele, with an
inscription and often a relief or a painting. The epitaph frequently
addressed the passersby, as in the famous "Stranger, announce to
the Lacedaemonians that we lie here, obedient to their orders,"
inscribed on the columns set up over the grave of the Spartan
warriors killed at Thermopylae (Herodotus 7.128).

Sometimes the monument is a sculpture of the deceased which
describes itself: e.g., "I stand here in Parian marble in place of the
woman, a memorial to Bitte, a tearful grief to her mother." A relief
of a grandmother named Ampharete holding a child accompanies an
epitaph to both: "When, in life, we both beheld the rays of the sun, I
held her thus on my lap; and now, both dead, I hold her still."[10]
Scenes of banquets and handshakes indicate hope for continuing
connection between the living and the dead or for a joyous reunion
in the next life.[11]

Up to the middle fifth century, however, most epitaphs
emphasized the activities and virtues of the deceased while alive
rather than expectations about the afterlife. Farnell speculates that
the Greeks then " . . . were more closely attached to the civic and
social existence, less insistent on the individualistic soul-theory and
therefore more likely to look back than to look forward."[12] But
paintings on funeral offerings, tomb reliefs, and epitaphs sometimes
use figures from the mythopoetic depiction of the netherworld such
as Charon the ferryman, Hermes the guide of the dead, and
Persephone, Hades' queen. And gradually the signs of hope for
blessing from a special deity like Dionysus or Persephone began to
increase. In southern Italy, for example, there was a grave precinct
in Cumae which prohibited burial to those who had not celebrated
the Bacchic rites, and later grave steles at Lilybaeum were
decorated with the emblems of the mysteries. Some epitaphs also
connected a blessed afterlife with a pious life on earth; e.g., a
woman assures her beloved nurse, "I know that even in death, if the
virtuous have any higher privilege, thou wilt have the first place of
honor by Persephone and Plouton."[13]

Despite the frequency of the 'if' in such expressions and the
occasional denial of any existence after death on some inscriptions

(e.g., "There is nothing left, for nothing awakens the dead -except to afflict the souls of those who pass. Nothing else remains."), the memorials on the tombs of the Hellenistic period reveal an increasing optimism about a personalized future beyond the grave.[14] A Greek inscription from Italy in the second century C.E., for example, expresses the new eschatological hope in no uncertain terms: "The Soul is immortal, for it came from God . . . the body is the garment of the soul. Honor the God in me."[15]

The family did not ignore its dead once the *rite de passage* was over. After the official period of mourning, they then participated in the annual festivals in which the polis honored all its dead in common. They also might make private tomb visits where they decorated the steles, made offerings and brought special gifts to the dead. The satirist Lucian (second century C.E.) explained such gifts to the dead as ways of impressing the survivors' neighbors (*On Mourning* 15). But these activities, as well as food and drink offered at the grave (sometimes through feeding tubes in the ground) suggest that the dead were also conceived of as being present near the tomb and able to benefit from the meals as well as the honors. The stele has often been interpreted as a physical embodiment or symbol of the deceased, who retained some limited consciousness in its vicinity. Therefore, it was best to walk by a grave in silence, and it was considered impious, and even illegal, to dishonor one's dead relatives.

In venerating the dead, moreover, the survivors could expect rewards for their piety. According to Garland, this attitude indicates "the earliest stage of eschatological speculation," and, in addition, "re-inforced a view of the essential and enduring nature of family ties, of the reciprocity of obligation, and of our inalienable connections with those on the other side."[16] Scholars emphasize, however, that the goal was perpetual remembrance rather than ancestor worship. The monuments of the ordinary dead were retrospective and the entombed had no effect on their descendants.

There were also special cults connected with the special dead called heroes, whom Farnell defines as

> a person whose virtue, influence, and personality was so powerful in his lifetime or through the peculiar circumstances of his death that his spirit after death is regarded as a supernormal power, claiming to be reverenced and propitiated.[17]

The heroes were considered to retain their potency in the vicinity of their tombs, and therefore were worshipped at their graves (or supposed graves) with the same kinds of rites, offerings into the ground, sacrifices and meals as the dead and the underground or chthonic deities. In exchange, heroes conferred health, fertility, and sometimes knowledge of the future on their worshippers. If offended, they could also bring disaster upon them until appeased.

The development of hero cults around certain figures was connected to the development of city-states.[18] Burkert considers that by the end of the eighth century, when the polis culture replaced rule by the old aristocratic families, who had their own private ancestor cults, "the cult of the common heroes of the land becomes the expression of group solidarity."[19] As the city states grew, they added new cults of the recently dead to their roster of cults of legendary founding heroes: at first warriors like those who fought at Marathon and Thermopylae, but later poets, philosophers, and even athletes. Rohde judges that, although each new translation from a human to a hero was regarded as a miracle and did not reflect a general belief in immortality, the fact that individuals were still being raised up offered some optimism: "Death does not end all conscious existence nor does the gloom of Hades swallow up all life."[20]

The popularity of these cults through history can be attributed in part to their proximity. Unlike the gods on Olympus, the heroes were right there in their worshippers' midst, within or near the city. Although in their tombs, they could be expected to return to life to help their communities. The painting of the battle of Marathon in the Painted Porch in Athens depicted Theseus, the city's greatest hero, rising from the earth to aid the Athenians (Pausanias 1.15.4). Castor and Pollux, the Dioscuri, could appear suddenly to rescue worshippers from danger in battle or at sea, manifesting themselves as stars or St. Elmo's fire. Like Elijah at the seder, they were expected at feasts for the gods, where special places were set for them.[21]

Some men who, like Korah, were swallowed up by the earth became heroes. Amphiarus the Argive seer, for example, was saved by a thunderbolt from Zeus which split the earth and enabled him to escape his pursuers with his chariot, horse, and charioteer. But, unlike Korah, the vanished Amphiarus was regarded as still alive under the earth; the Greeks visited him at the site to ask questions about their futures.

Trophonius, the Orchomenian architect, was swallowed alive by the earth at Lebedaia while fleeing a king he had tricked and robbed. Like Amphiarus, he was visited at an oracle at the place where the earth received him. The procedure there, which Pausanias experienced and described (9.39), involved a *katabasis* (descent beneath the earth) resembling literary accounts of otherworldy journeys. After preliminaries such as purifications, sacrifices, ritual bathing, and drinking from springs called Forgetfulness and Memory, the inquirer made a literal descent into the earth, through a dark narrow chasm, where he either saw or heard the future. When he ascended, while still in a state of terror, he had to sit on the throne of Memory and reveal what he learned to the priests, before he returned to his senses. Like the messages of the ascending heroes in the apocalypses, his story was written out for posterity.

Heracles was the most popular hero. A son of Zeus with a human father as well, he lived an extraordinary life of interminable labor, including a *katabasis* into Hades to steal Cerberus and a quest for the golden apples, symbols of immortality. He also died an agonizing death, burning himself up on a pyre after terrible torment from a poisoned robe, an immolation that later came to be regarded as an ascension and apotheosis. He was honored as a trusted companion and helper, an averter of evil who protected his own with images on amulets or words such as these on the door: "The son of Zeus, the fair victorious Heracles dwells here. No evil may enter in." Burkert offers two reasons for his popularity: he is the exemplar of the good, divinely ordained ruler who "finds his fulfillment among the gods," and

> Secondly he is a model for the common man who may hope that after a life of drudgery, and through that very life, he too may enter into the company of gods . . . Here the divine is close at hand in human form, . . . as an inspiring prototype.[22]

The Mythopoetic Picture of the Afterlife Before Plato

Like Enoch in Genesis, certain other Greek heroes were translated from life to a god-like existence without ever suffering death. A few mortals, beloved of the gods, were allowed to dwell with them: e.g., Ganymede and Tithonus. Although Heracles is depicted as dying in Hom. *Il.* 18.117-119 and his image addresses Odysseus in Hades at *Od.* 11.600-627, the hero/god was later apotheosized in poetry and described as living among the gods on Olympus with Hebe as his wife (Hom. *Od.* 11.602-604 [considered a later insertion]; Hesiod *Theogony* 952).

Other legendary figures were believed to live on in a wonderland far away from both the gods and mortals. In *Od.* 4.348-570, Menelaos relates his own future, which he has learned about on an otherworldly journey to the caves of Proteus, the old man of the sea:

> . . . the gods intend for you Elysion
> with golden Rhadamanthus at the world's end,
> where all existence is a dream of ease,
> snowfall is never known there, neither long
> frost of winter, nor terrential rain,
> but only mild and lulling airs from ocean
> bearing refreshment for the souls of men —
> the West Wind always blowing.
> (4.561-569, Fitzgerald, trans.)[23]

Elysion resembles the description of Olympus, as in 6.43-45. Its name is related to the word *enelysion(os)*, the designation of a place (or person) struck by lightning, which signifies election as well as destruction, according to Burkert.[24] Although Menelaos has been elected because of his relationship to Helen rather than for any merit of his own, the two will live like gods for eternity. They were not considered gods, however, for they were never worshipped or prayed to, as Olympians, chthonic deities, and heroes were.

The poets of the epic cycle record other warriors who were restored to life and taken to isolated places. The allegory of the ages of man in Hesiod's *Works and Days* extends this grace of eternal life; part of the fourth generation placed between the violent bronze and even grimmer iron ages, "a godlike race of heroes who are called demi-gods(159)," were permitted to live at the ends of the earth, "with carefree heart in the Isles of the Blessed ones," where fruits can be harvested three times a year (167-73). Their blissful existence was later connected with the Golden Age, when Cronus or Saturn, the Roman fertility god who became his equivalent, ruled the first and golden race of men. West, in his commentary on the passage from Hesiod, attributes the newer myth to a "psychological unwillingness to accept that paradise is finally lost."[25]

Epic poetry also supplied the imaginative details about the afterlife of ordinary mortals. The earliest and fullest description comes from *Odyssey* 11, when Odysseus must journey to the entrance to the underworld to bring up Tiresias the seer, who lives among the dead with full consciousness. Although Odysseus does not technically descend into the underworld, his experience has many of the features of an otherworldly journey. The hero goes because he is in crisis, far from home and lost both geographically and spiritually. Circe, a divine guide, gives him his quest, to learn the way home, and directs him to the place of revelation. Once there, he performs the rituals appropriate to chthonic powers (prayers, vows, libations and sacrifices of black animals offered into a pit he has dug), which summon Tiresias who gives him both directions and facts about his future, including the manner of his death. But the blood attracts other dead as well, whom he sees or converses with. From these interactions, he receives knowledge and advice vital to his survival in Ithaca, and, perhaps more important, a revival of his will to live. He returns to Circe a changed man, eager to be on his way home to Ithaca despite the dangers he knows he must face. Thus, his otherworldly journey, by revealing details about death, supports the life-affirming values already established in the *Odyssey*. Moreover, he obtains a superhuman insight about things ordinarily hidden from mortals, which he then reveals to his Phaeacian listeners.

Odysseus is the first questor hero in Greek literature to see into the afterlife, but his pattern is repeated again and again: e.g., by Orpheus to bring back Eurydice, Theseus to abduct Persephone, Heracles to get Cerberus for Eurystheus, Dionysus to rescue Semele from death. The latter two were said to have been initiated into the Eleusinian Mysteries before their journeys, and, unlike Odysseus, Heracles and Semele were eventually welcomed into Olympus. Although the texts where these stories were told are no longer extant, Polygnotus' painting of Odysseus' descent into Hades, which Pausanius saw in the Lesche of the Cnidians at Delphi (10.28-31), contains many details missing from Homer which must have come from later epic and lyric accounts of such descents. In Aristophanes' *Frogs*, Dionysus gets directions and advice from Heracles before traveling to Hades to bring back Euripides. His trip is a real *katabasis* in which he fully experiences the transition from Athens to the home of the dead, rowing across the waters which divide the two realms. There he meets its inhabitants, including a procession of those who had been initiated into the Eleusinian Mysteries. There he also discovers a comic solution to the real crisis of 405 B.C.E.

Although the god Dionysus and the other questor heroes returned from their otherworldly journeys, most mortals could look forward only to the time when "the end of death hid them away" (*Works and Days* 166). The poets were vague about where the dead went and how they got there. At *Il.* 23.100-101, Patroclus' shade (*psyche*), after appearing to Achilles in a dream, went directly down into the earth (v. Pausanias 4.33.7; 9.5.8.). Circe told Odysseus, however, to go by sea to the rim of the ocean, to the grove of Persephone, where the rivers Periphlegethon (Fire) and Cocytus (Wailing), the branch of the Styx (Hate), flow into the Acherusian Lake (Woe) and a rock marks their confluence (10.507-515). Hermes, on the other hand, led the dead suitors past the Ocean, the white rock, the gates of the sun, and the people of dreams to the meadow of asphodel where the *psychai* dwell (24.9-14).

Wherever the precise location, the place the dead went was, like Sheol, clearly separated from the living, and from the light. For Homer, being alive meant seeing the light of the sun and death meant leaving that light and going into the dark.[26] When Odysseus arrived at the rim of the Ocean, he noted that the area was hidden in mist and cloud and never graced by the sun (11.14-19). The place was separated from the heavenly divinities; according to Homer, "the gods especially hate the mouldy things fearful to look on" which are kept hidden there (*Il.* 20.65). A triple fence and a great gate which provided entrance but not exit shut it off from far-distant earth and heaven. There is no single precise topography of the realm itself, but certain features reappear: a river which must be crossed, other rivers which flow within it (suggesting perhaps the fertility that comes from beneath the earth), a white rock, trees such as myrtle, poplars, willows and cypress, waters of Memory and Forgetfulness (Lethe), a meadow of asphodel, and an area where extraordinary sinners are tormented.

Unlike Sheol, this dark place beneath the earth, at the end of the world, was the realm of an important god. Hades, Zeus' brother, whose name may mean 'Invisible,' presided over the area and was sometimes called the other or subterranean Zeus. Hades was in no way an enemy of the Olympian order or a satanic rival and threat to Zeus. Nor did he represent the same kind of terrible evil for men that Mot did. At *Il.* 15.187-193, Poseidon explains that when the three brothers, Zeus, Hades, and himself, drew lots for their shares of the universe, Hades received the gloomy darkness under the earth, but that the three enjoy heaven and earth in common. Zeus is the ultimate ruler, however, and arbiter of all quarrels between them. After Hades abducted Persephone, the daughter of Demeter, for example, he willingly obeyed Zeus' order to give her back to the light for part of the year. The introduction of agriculture and the Eleusinian Mysteries are both traced back to this mythic event which connects the underworld/ afterlife with regeneration and the nature cycle.

Together Hades and his consort Persephone oversaw the region of the dead. As the poetic and artistic depictions of their realm increased, other divine beings became associated with them as assistants. Hermes was the most important, as the Olympian son of Zeus who, according to the Homeric Hymn in his honor, was the only appointed messenger to Hades (572). This divine herald and wayfarer who traveled all the paths above and on the earth was also the one who eased dying and with his golden wand led the dead *psychai* into the underworld. Among the other chthonic divinities who inhabited the realm, e.g., Night, Styx, Hecate, were Upnos ('Sleep') and his brother Thanatos, the personification of Death, depicted on vases as winged figure but described by Euripides as "black robed Thanatos, Lord of the Dead, drinking up the blood of the slaughtered animals" (*Alcestis* 843-845; 1141-1142). The old ferryman Charon took the shades of the buried dead across the Acheron. Cerberus, the fierce and ugly hound of Hades, guarded the entrance to the home of the king and queen, devouring whoever tried to get out of its gates.

Homer refers to the dead who reside in Hades' kingdom as *psychai* and *eidola*. *Psyche* seems to refer both to the life that is lost at death and to the shade which then dwells in Hades.[27] Recent scholars have interpreted the *psyche* in Homer, which appears only in sleep, swoons, and at dying, as similar to the "free soul" of other cultures, "an unencumbered soul representing the individuality of a person and active during unconsciousness."[28] When death occurs, the free soul leaves the body, which has its own thinking feeling soul during its conscious life, and, in Homer, goes to the underworld as a shade or *psyche*. At *Il.* 16. 855-857, for example, the poet describes the death of Patroclus:

> The end of death covered him as he spoke. His *psyche*, flying from his limbs, went to Hades lamenting its fate, leaving youth and manhood behind.

The life fleeing his body resembles the *nefesh* departing from Rachel at her death (Gen. 35.18). A *psyche* appears to the observer as an *eidolon*, a crystalline image of the person as he lived, and sometimes bearing the scars of violent death. Odysseus, for example, sees the wounds and bloody gear of those slain in battle (*Od.* 11.40) whereas Clytemnestra's ghost displays the gashes from the matricide (Aeschylus *Eumenides*, 103). Achilles recognizes the *psyche* of Patroclus which appears to him at *Il.* 23.65; when it goes underground like smoke as he tries to embrace it, Achilles exclaims, "Oh wonder, there is a *psyche* and an *eidolon* even in the house of Hades, but with no real life (*phrenes*) in it (103-104). When Odysseus begs his mother's *psyche* to embrace and mourn with him, angry at her frustrating *eidolon* (*Od.* 11.211-214), Anticlea responds (218-222)

> the same law exists for all mortals when they die. No powerful sinews hold the flesh and bones together for the strength of the funeral pyre destroys all and the life force (*thumos*) leaves the white bones but the *psyche* flitting off like smoke flies away.

The shades in Hades are pitiable rather than menacing, for, lacking the *phrenes* and *thumos* of the living, they are powerless and witless. Only sipping the blood restores temporary consciousness so that Odysseus can converse with them. Both Patroclus and Elpinor are miserable until they are buried and dependent on the living to get them through the gate of Hades. Once over there, they seem to cluster together with similar *psychai* (e.g., the wives and daughters of illustrious men, the warriors who fell at Troy), and to do the same things they did in life. Odysseus saw Minos settling disputes among the dead, Orion among the animals he hunted, and Heracles with his bow and arrow. Polygnotus' painting shows the dead enjoying such things as playing dice, and listening to Orpheus' music. Aristophanes' *Frogs* 771-776 places the audience of thieves and rascals who enjoyed Euripides' dramas in Athens approving his performances down in Hades.

There is no indication in Homer or in cult that the dead needed elaborate supplies for the afterlife, or that most of the dead suffered any torture or were terrified by horrible monsters. Thus the Homeric depiction of the afterlife is somewhat optimistic. The kingdom of Hades was not demonic, chaotic, and mysterious like Mot's. The heroic dead of the *Odyssey* had little to fear after life and even retained some semblance of their individuality in Hades.

Yet it is quite clear that for the life-loving Greeks the kingdom of Hades held no attractions. Cut off from the living, they are also separated from life in time.[29] Without the sip of blood they do not recognize Odysseus, for they have no memory. Without a past or future, there can be no meaningful activity. Odysseus' mother hastened him back to the light, and Achilles, when Odysseus suggested that his glory among the living and dead compensated for his early death, responded

> Don't you try to tell me anything about death. I would rather
> be a serf hired out to a nobody with not much of anything
> than to be lord over all the dead and gone. (*Od.* 11.488-491)

In Homer, punishments for sin and error, including death, occurred
in life. Aegisthus was killed by Orestes, the rebellious suitors by
Odysseus; even the foolish crew who ate the cattle of the Sun died
in a storm. Only the greatest sinners against the gods suffered any
torture after death. Odysseus saw Tityus' liver being plucked by
vultures for his attempt to rape Leto, Sisyphus forever pushing his
rock and Tantalus being tantalized. Later writers added others to
the list: Ixion stretched on a wheel, sometimes fiery, for kindred
murder and the attempt to rape Hera; the Danaids condemned to
carry water in leaky vessels for the murder of their bridegrooms, all
futile endeavors which emphasize their timeless state. But ordinary
mortals, even minor criminals, could expect a neutral if static
existence in Hades.

There are suggestions in the literature between Homer and Plato,
however, that a belief in reward and punishment after death was
developing within certain contexts. The Homeric Hymn to Demeter
makes clear that those who had been initiated into the Eleusinian
Mysteries would be more fortunate than the uninitiated in the life to
come (480-482). Both Pindar and Sophocles allude to its blessings
for the initiated after death: "Blessed is he who goes under the earth
after seeing these things: He knows the consummation of life; he
knows its Zeus-given beginnings." and "to them alone is it given to
live there; to others everything is evil," respectively.[30]
Aristophanes' *Frogs* depicts the initiated worshipping Demeter in
Hades and proclaiming "For us alone the sun and its holy blaze
exist, who have experienced initiation and have treated strangers
and private individuals piously" (454-459). In Polygnotus' painting,
the uninitiated were grouped together near Sisyphus and carried
water in broken jars (perhaps symbolic of disdain for purification
rites). Pausanias notes that the Athenians of Polygnotus' time "paid
more honor to the Eleusinian Mystery than to any other kind of
piety" (10.31.2).

The gold tablet found in a grave at Hipponion in Southern Italy
and dated to the end of the fifth century also suggests that initiation
into the mysteries (here most likely Dionysiac) could insure a
special status in the underworld.[31] The text contains specific
instructions for the dead about the passage into Hades: avoid
drinking from the spring by the white cypress, but instead answer
the questions of the guards of the lake of memory and drink the cool

water from there, for that will permit walking the sacred way which other initiated also walk. This text and similar ones indicate that those who participated in the secret ceremonies (mysteries) and experienced religious insight and ecstasy have gained a special knowledge which identifies them with their divine patron and promises them a blessed status in the afterlife. Perhaps the ability to avoid forgetfulness (*lethe*) and retain memory after death, non-forgetfulness or truth (*a-lethe-ia*), connected the timelessness of these special dead with the timeless conscious existence of the gods.[32]   Indeed a later tablet found at Thurii tells the dead person "Fortunate and most blessed (*makariste*, a word which usually refers to deities), you will become a god instead of a mortal."[33]

Polygnotus' painting reveals that by the end of the fifth century ordinary mortals who harmed their fellow mortals or insulted the gods could expect punishment after death.   On Charon's boat he depicted a man being strangled by the father he'd mistreated and a sacrilegious thief being punished by a painful poison. Above them is Eurynomos, a blue-black monster who eats away the flesh of the dead and leaves them only their bones. According to Pausanias, this vengeful spirit, unmentioned in epic, was known to the officials at Delphi (10.28).

The early literature also contains some hints of the concept of a judgment after death.   Homer refers to Zeus and Helios punishing dead men who have sworn false oaths (*Il.* 3.276-279). In Hesiod's *Works and Days*, Justice (Dike), sits by her father Zeus' side, informing him of the wickedness of mortals so that they may pay the penalty (256-262). Aeschylus, in a fragment from a lost play, describes Justice in an image which suggests the divine ledgers of Israel and Mesopotamia; she is "writing their offenses on the tablet of Zeus" so that they can be punished at the proper time.[34]   Pindar, at *Olympian* 2.55-60, and Aeschylus, at *Suppliants* 228-231, mention an actual judgment of sinners by gods beneath the earth. Aeschylus' *Eumenides* is even more specific.   The Erinyes (Furies), chasing Orestes to exact his blood for the matricide, proclaim that in Hades he will see those who harmed god, guest or parent, "each suffering a penalty to fit the crime, for great Hades is an examiner of mortals beneath the earth who oversees all things with a recording mind" (269-275).

It is Plato in the next century, however, who gives us the fullest picture of judgment and reward and punishment after death. His myths are related to his new idea about the nature of the *psyche*, that Homeric shade which took on new meaning in cult, philosophy and literature in the period after Homer.[35]

The Soul: Separation and Immortality

At first glance, the Greeks' concept of the soul appears to be radically different from the Hebrews'. From Homer on, there was a separation between the body and soul at death. At *Il.* 1, the wrath of Achilles "hurled many mighty *psychas* of heroes to Hades, but the bodies themselves became carrion for dogs and birds" (3-5). The pseudo-Hesiodic *Shield of Heracles* is even more specific about the dichotomy: while the *psychai* go down under the earth to Hades, the bones and skin rot away on the dark earth (151-153).

In the early literature, the *psyche*, linguistically related, like *neshamah*, to 'breath,' only appears in swoons or at the point of death. Although it signifies 'life,' it has nothing to do with the living and conscious individual. Other terms correspond to the Hebrew *nefesh* as the life force intertwined with the body which ceases to exist when the body dies: *thumos* (which, like *neshamah* and *psyche*, is sometimes identified with the breath) and *menos* for strong emotions and will, *noos* and *phren* for thoughts and intellect.[36] Like *ruah*, these words are related to the physical effects of intense feelings, and are often associated with the chest area, the seat of the heart and lungs, the part of the body where "these impulses are thought to manifest themselves;" *thumos*, probably the most important Homeric word for aspects of consciousness, for example, is connected to words for smoke (Latin *fumus*) and sacrifice (Greek *thuo*), and, according to Jaeger, "suggests a hot welling-up of blood."[37] While alive, the mortal is a psycho-physical unity, with a holistic life or body soul, albeit the basic life forces of emotion and intellect are described by different terms associated with different body parts in different circumstances.[38]

The conception of two souls, one a body soul endowing a living individual with life, consciousness, and feeling, and the other a free soul representing the individual personality able to wander outside the body in dreams and swoons (which corresponds to Homer's *psyche*) has many parallels in other cultures.[39] That this idea remained a part of the Greek conception is clear from later references in poetry and drama to the *psyche* as a shade as well as in prose passages which discuss its freedom and superior insight in sleep, e.g., Xenophon, *Cyropaideia* 8.7.21.[40] To this kind of dualism, Bremmer traces Greek legends about out of body experiences which have been attributed to shamanistic tendencies or influences by other scholars.[41]

After Homer and Hesiod, however, *psyche* also became more closely associated with the living person and began to take on many of the emotional and noetic qualities of the life or body soul. Claus suggests that in fact the word *psyche* may have always had 'life force' connotations in the popular mind but that Homer reserved it exclusively for the concept of the 'shade' because he was defining terms and conditions to an audience eager for specific information about the afterlife. Once the *psyche/eidolon* had become part of the popular imagination, poets could refer to that concept in context, but also use the life force associations of the word *psyche* in reference to the consciousness, vitality, and emotions of living beings.[42] As the meaning of *psyche* was broadened, some of the other early words disappeared (e.g., *menos, ker*) or declined in range (e.g., *thumos*), while others such as *noos* and *phren* became more closely associated with reason and moral choice respectively.[43]

Although the archaic poets use *psyche* for physical satisfaction and strong emotion, the full development of this concept is most clearly seen in fifth century Athenian drama, where a complex of terms which includes *psyche* (e.g., *noos* and *phren*) defines the inner life of a character.[44] From the many examples, a few will be chosen to illustrate new aspects which relate *psyche* to the fullness of being alive implicit in *nefesh*. Its connection with the body's erotic impulses is most clear in Euripides' *Hippolytus* where the power of *eros* in or over the *psyche* is mentioned several times (504-505, 525-527) and implied in Hippolytus' defense against the charge of incest—he has a virgin *psychen* (1006). Its associations with strong emotions are ubiquitous: with violence at Sophocles' *Electra* 219; with courage at Euripides *Hecuba* 579-80; with cowardice at Aeschylus *Agamemnon* 1643-1646; with grief for oneself (e.g., Sophocles' *Oedipus Tyrannus* 64, Euripides *Ion* 876-877); with sympathy for others at Aeschylus *Prometheus Bound*, 690-692 or Aeschylus *Choephori* 743-750; even with hope about the afterlife, as at Euripides *Alcestis* 604-605. Other passages associate *psyche* with thought and knowledge, even if they do not attribute those activities to the *psyche* itself, e.g., Sophocles *Antigone* 176, 225, 708-91. Moreover, Euripides fragment 388, which defines the love for a *psyche* which is just, moderate, and good and leads the wise to love the pious, suggests that *psyche* may also have moral connotations.

As the *psyche* took on similar qualities to *nefesh* in relation to the living individual, it also became connected to the world outside the living body by extensions which relate it to the Hebrew concept of *ruah*. For, like the Hebrews, the Greeks conceived of the universe as an organic whole, with all parts akin to one another, either because they were derived from the same divinity and subject to the same divine order or because they arose from the same material and were subject to natural law (see chapter 4).

Very early conceptions related the soul to air or its most pure and fiery ether (*aither*). According to comparativists, the body soul was itself divided into an ego soul denoting individual living consciousness and a life soul identified with the breath, which was, like the free soul, insubstantial and unstable. They see a process by which "the original free soul becomes absorbed by the breath soul that, in turn, develops into a unitary soul." Bremmer tentatively posits that, by the time of Homer, *psyche*, the breath soul of the living, had replaced earlier terms for the free soul and had already "absorbed the role of the free soul as the soul of the dead. . . but had not yet lost all of its connections with its original function as breath."[45] As *psyche* developed into a unitary soul of the living, following the pattern in other early cultures, it also became joined to Greek ideas about the connection of breath, life, and air. The epitaph of the warriors who fell at Potidaea in 432 B.C.E.: "*Aither* received their *psychas*, the earth their bodies (*somata*)." indicates such a relationship.[46]

When the early philosophers looked to nature for explanations of the universe, they transferred qualities attributed to the divine order to the matter and processes of the physical world. Thales, for example, is reported to have said "all things are full of gods," and thought that soul was intermingled through the universe as a 'life force' which, because of its permanence and power to move, might be called divine.[47] Some philosophers posited air, *aither*, or fire as the first principle and connected the airy or breathy element in living humans with that substance out of which all things arose. Anaximenes is credited by later Greek philosophers and commentators with introducing the parallel, equating the *psyche*, as the air in us, with the wind (*pneuma*) or air which permeates the whole universe.[48]

Behind the flux of the natural world, Heraclitus perceived an eternal order and balance caused by fire, the common matter of all things, which he also called *logos*. The too soul was composed of fire and thus related to the cosmic fire and to *logos*. The soul, the seat of intelligence and motion for the body, drew in the *logos* by breathing. To keep the soul hottest, driest, and therefore most effective, human beings needed knowledge of the underlying order, that is, "the way all things are steered through all."[49] This principle of orderly change he called both wisdom and Zeus. His statements about the soul contained some eschatological ideas as well; although human souls participate in the cycle of orderly change, the most fiery, which may be equated with the virtuous, escape the colder, moister bodies to become *daimones* (spirits) and then to rejoin the cosmos for a time. But this fiery element which was once a soul remains a part of the natural world nonetheless and probably returns to it.[50]

The ideas of Diogenes of Apollonia, which Aristophanes parodied in *Clouds* in 423 B.C.E., present a composite of the features attributed to the air and the breath soul by the Presocratic nature philosophers. Air is first of all the basic substance out of which all things arise and to which they eventually return. Its primary characteristic is intelligence, for it has disposed itself "in the best way possible." It is the life principle (*psyche*) and faculty for intelligence (*noesis*) in all living things; its absence is a clear sign of death. Moreover, it is divine:

> And it seems to me that which has intelligence is what men call air (*aer*), and that all men are steered by this and that it has power over all things. For this very thing seems to me to be a god (*theos*) and to have reached everywhere and to dispose all things and to be in everything . . . .[51]

The philosophers discussed above seem to accept the belief in the sympathy of nature; all things derive from the same source and are subject to the same processes, albeit they are differentiated by the different matter or qualities that develop out of it according to such variables as temperature and motion. The air or fire which permeates and enlivens all things connects them, according to principles of holistic balance. There is no radical split between the soul and the body or the rest of the natural world. If the purest souls are the most intelligent or virtuous because their substance is most akin to the divine basic substance, they still participate in the cycle of balanced changes and differentiations which constitutes the natural order.

Pythagoras, Pindar, and Empedocles, however, had different conceptions of the soul which were much closer to religion, particularly to the mysteries associated with Demeter, Dionysus, and Orpheus. Whatever the origin of their ideas (Scythia, Thrace, and northern shamanism, or India), southern Italy and Sicily were the places in which they were first formulated in the late sixth century and from which they had spread to other areas of Greece by the end of the fifth. To these men, E. R. Dodds attributes a "fateful contribution:"

> by crediting man with an occult self of divine origin, and thus setting the soul and body at odds, it introduced into European culture a new interpretation of human existence, the interpretation which we call puritanical.[52]

From them comes the idea the body is an alien home for a *psyche* which has fallen from its divine origin and can return only by purifying itself, through ascetic practice, ritual, or knowledge, while imprisoned in its earthly existence. Eschatology is a very important aspect of their belief system. Not only do they describe judgment and reward and punishment after death, but they also posit metempsychosis, or reincarnation, the belief that the individual soul passes from one body to another. The development of this idea has been viewed as a logical consequence of the belief in immortality posited by the reason-loving Greeks; since the soul is immortal, it must have existed before birth into a particular body and must continue somewhere after that body's death. But metempsychosis is also very much connected to theodicy. As E. R. Dodds points out, judgment after death only insures that the wicked will finally be punished and exploits the horrors of Hades as a deterrent to wickedness.

> But the post-mortem punishment did not explain why the gods tolerated so much human suffering, and in particular the unmerited suffering of the innocent. Reincarnation did. On that view no human soul was innocent.[53]

The cycle of rebirths and the troubles in life were looked upon as punishments for former sins. By living the proper life and remembering former states of existence, in life and death, however, the individual soul might hope for an end to the cycle and the reunion with the divine for which it yearned.[54]

Pythagoras, generally accepted as the first to introduce these new ideas, was a late sixth-century sage who moved from Ionia to Croton in South Italy where he was active in politics, established a community, and posited number as the source of the universe and its order. Although Pythagoras never wrote anything himself, he was widely acclaimed for his wisdom, miraculous powers of healing and bilocation, and his ascetic practices which became a way of life for his followers. Interestingly enough, an other world journey is included in the stories about him. Burkert has pieced together the disparate details from late sources to reconstruct a *katabasis* in which, after fasting, he went down into Hades to receive a message related to the doctrine of immortality and rebirth.[55]

Pythagorean ideas about the soul and the afterlife must be construed from the fragmentary references in later writers.[56] Because he was said to have recognized the soul (*psyche*) of a friend in a dog's bark and to have remembered his own previous reincarnations as well as the events of 1,000 years, Pythagoras probably believed that the soul had a self or personality which continued after death. Later Pythagoreans described the soul as motes in the air, self-moving and the source of motion, like the divine, or a harmony or attunement of opposites. According to Herodotus 2.123, they thought the soul passed from humans into animals, fish, and birds before returning to human bodies. After 3,000 years its cycle was completed.

To attain blessedness for the soul after death, the Pythagoreans not only had special burial practices, but also developed a set of rules for life, passed on as maxims in the form of riddles, called *akousmata* or *sumbola*, a term which suggests passwords memorized for use in this world and the next.[57] Although many of the requirements derive from primitive superstition or indicate ritualistic purity, others provide for an orderly daily life and some demand exceptional piety and virtue.[58] Iamblichus' *Life of Pythagoras* (137, 135) emphasizes their belief in the gods and the requirement to live according to the gods' laws. One of the *akousmata* mentions the Isles of the Blessed, which they located on the sun and the moon; perhaps they hoped that souls, when they completed the cycle, retired there.

The Pythagoreans are reported to have taught that "Pleasure is in all circumstances bad, for we came here to be punished and we ought to be punished," and that "men brought sufferings upon themselves." An *akousma* asks, "What is the truest thing said? The response is, "That men are wicked."[59] Pythagoras' vision must have included some sort of subterranean Hades as well, for Aristotle reports that he traced earthquakes to the concourse of the dead and thought thunder was meant to frighten those in Tartarus.[60]

Pindar, the professional poet who alluded to the beliefs of his patrons in his victory odes, hymns, and dirges, reflects some of these new eschatological ideas. A fragment on the *psyche* describes the soul like a free soul, as in Homer, but now clearly divine, "alone from the gods," and capable of revealing the "coming judgment of delightful things and hard" to sleeping men in dreams.[61] *Olympian* 2, composed in 476 to celebrate the victory of a Sicilian patron, Theron of Acragas, provides more details. Lines 56-77 describe reward and punishment, a cycle of reincarnation, and then a path which leads to an eternal 'golden age' in the company of the gods. It is important to note, however, that there is a moral component; the good are defined as keeping oaths and the souls must be pure from all deeds of wrong. In fact, Pindar introduces these lines to illustrate that wealth is no benefit to a man unless he has virtue and knows about the future. Plato quotes from Pindar at *Meno* 81bc to support his contention that the immortality of the soul makes it imperative to live a virtuous life:

> in the ninth year Persephone sends back to the sun above the souls of those from whom she has received ancient woe's atonement, and from those very souls grow up glorious kings and men swift and strong and great sages, and at last they are called pure heroes by men.

As Long emphasizes, in the doctrine of metempsychosis "sin must be punished; atonement is part of the order of nature; the possibility of a blessed life in the other world is held out to man as an inducement to righteous living."[62]

Empedocles, the fifth century philosopher from Acragas, also connected sin with a cycle of transmigrations.[63]   In the *Purifications*, he proclaimed that the divine portion in humans, which he called a *daimon* instead of a *psyche*, was an exile from the heavenly Sphere perfected by Love because it had "trusted in raving Strife" and disturbed the harmony of the Sphere, perhaps by shedding blood in kindred murder and sacrifice. Therefore, the *daimon* was "clothed in an alien garment of flesh," and forced to suffer repeated rebirths. Empedocles explained how the *daimon* ascends through a series of cycles from lowest to highest plants, then animals, then men, "exchanging one hard path for another," until it finally achieves apotheosis, "sharing with the other immortals their hearth and table, without part in human sorrows and misery." To prepare for this blessed state, one must purify oneself, abstaining from all bloodshed and violence, meat eating, and perhaps even all sex relations.[64]

Empedocles also announced that he himself had already experienced the cycle. He claimed to be "once a boy and a girl, a bush and a bird and a leaping journeying fish," and opened *Purifications* with the statement that he had become "an immortal god, mortal no more," sought out by those seeking profit, prophecy, and healing.[65]   Several fragments describe a descent into Hades where he saw the personifications of horrors such as Murder, Anger, and Diseases wandering over the Meadow of Doom, as well as opposites like Beauty and Ugliness, Discord and Harmony, and Truth and Obscurity which together make up the mortal world. It is not clear whether this is a *katabasis* which describes punishments between reincarnations or a metaphorical description of exile into mortal existence, derived from earlier eschatological myths.[66]

Empedocles was also a nature philosopher who, according to O'Brien, was the first to provide "a place for this otherworldliness within a fully philosophical system."[67] In *On Nature*, he posited a cosmos composed of the four elements whose being and changes derive from interaction with two force-like elements, Love and Strife. Whether or how the two works are related is uncertain. Love and Strife play a part in both, the cycles in nature as a whole somewhat resemble the cycles of the *daimon*, and both emphasize the power of knowledge and thought. It is apparent, however, that Empedocles presented both works as religious revelations, for he composed in dactylic hexameter, the verse of epic, Delphic oracles, and Parmenides, and he began *On Nature* with the imagery of otherworldly mediation, by asking a Muse "to drive forth your well-reigned chariot from Piety's Hall."[68]

The eschatological ideas of Pythagoras, Pindar, and Empedocles not only resemble each other, but also were connected by the Greeks with the poetry of the mythic singer Orpheus, and the interrelated Orphic, Bacchic, and Eleusinian mysteries (e.g., Herodotus 2.81; 4.79).[69] Orpheus came from Thrace, a region familiar with shamanistic ideas, and the legends about him show their influence. With his unusual musical gifts, he was able to charm nature, and descend into Hades to win his wife Euridyce's release. When his head was cut off by Thracian women, it continued to sing. To Orpheus were attributed a number of poems, the earliest related to his shamanistic activities (e.g., a description of what he saw in his descent into Hades), but gradually more concerned with revelation about the soul and its destiny and the history of the divine cosmos itself. By the end of the fifth century, Orpheus was associated with a theogony/cosmogony (as in the Derveni Papyrus) and an anthropology which traced the origin of humans to the ashes of the Titans who had tried to kill Dionysus, the son of Zeus and Persephone. He was also connected with the following: 1) the Bacchic mysteries (e.g., Euripides *Hippolytus* 952-955); 2) Eleusis; 3) the bone plates found at Olbia which suggest a revelation to initiates about the soul and life after death; and 4) mendicant priests who used his books to bring purifications and sacraments which absolved wrongdoing and delivered from punishment in the next world (e.g., Plato *Republic* 364-66; *Protagoras* 316d).

Plato called 'Orphic' the idea that the soul was imprisoned in the body as a punishment for some sin (*Cratylus* 400c). The texts on gold leaves found in fourth century graves mounds in Thurii indicate that at least some people accepted these ideas. The soul of one of the deceased addresses Persephone: "I come pure, from the pure, Queen of the chthonic deities; . . .I am proud to be of your blessed race . . . I have paid penance for works not just." In another, the soul elaborates that Fate overcame it, but she has now stepped from the circle of grief to the circle of joy; then the soul is addressed in turn, "Blessed and fortunate one, thou shalt be god instead of mortal."[70]

It is difficult to separate 'Orphic' from Pythagorean and Bacchic or to know whether the cults and sects actually went as far as the poets and philosophers in positing reincarnation. There are several important elements, however, which the mysteries contributed to the Presocratic mix of ideas about the afterlife and the soul. First of all, there is the idea of special status in the next world which goes back to the Eleusinian Mysteries. Mystery means secret. Individuals chose to participate in sacrifices, fasting, purifications, processions, secret rituals and actions which culminated in revelations for their eyes only. According to Burkert, the Eleusinian and Bacchic Mysteries, which acknowledged the suffering and triumph over death of Demeter, Persephone, and Dionysus, both provoked and dispelled deadly terror. Thus the rites anticipated and overcame the terror of death. The one who was initiated, the *mystes*, is imagined as having a blessed afterlife, celebrating the mysteries he experienced in life.[71] Those who chose not to be initiated were doomed to cheerless futile lives in the next world; Polygnotus painted them carrying water in broken pots (Pausanias 10.31).

Because the rites were secret, it is not known exactly what happened, particularly at the moment of revelation. But it is clear that through various means, e.g., wine, music, dance, chanting, plays of light and dark, the participants were brought to a state of religious exaltation. At Eleusis, *mystai* and the fully initiated may have watched from the dark telesterion as the heirophant in the Anaktoron, which only he could enter, called up Persephone from Hades into a blaze of light and then cut an ear of corn. Burkert connects this culmination to John 12.24 and fragments from Euripides which relate harvesting grain to bringing forth life, and considers the acceptance of death as a good to be a "deeper level of worldly piety than that attained by vows and sacrifice."[72]

Bacchic rites in particular brought the *mystai* to a blessed state of orgiastic frenzy in which they could free themselves from their own inhibitions and from the limitations of polis life. Meeting at night in a cave or mountain, and stimulated by wine, music and dance, and worship of the *phallos*, the *mystai* achieved a kind of group ecstasy that brought them in touch with each other, nature, and the gods. To describe the experience, the chorus of Euripides' *Bacchae* 75 uses the phrase *thiaseuetai psychan* which Verrall translates as "congregationalizes his soul."[73] At *Phaedrus* 244d-e, Plato calls this madness which comes from the gods more perfect and valuable than sanity. Using terms which refer to the Dionysiac mysteries (which he names in the summary at 265b), he notes that through the very insanity and possession brought on by the proper prayers, purifications, and worship, the sufferer can find release from his troubles. This divine madness which is ecstasy, literally standing 'outside the self,' has much in common with the idea of the out of body experience and the soul that is free to wander. The goal, the insight into or experience of another realm of being, normally hidden from mortals, is similar to the purpose of the other world journey. The exaltation and the consequent yearning for union or communion with the beloved divine also relates the mysteries to the later phenomenon of mysticism.

Purification is an important aspect of both the cults and the philosophies. The preparation for the rites certainly involved literal washing, even bathing in the sea in the case of Eleusinian Mysteries. The chorus of *Bacchae* refers to the "life of holy service" and the purifications (*katharmoisi*, 74-78). There are indications that the ritual purity had an extended moral meaning. In the Homeric Hymn to Demeter, Hades promises Persephone that those who are unjust or irreverent toward her will suffer eternal recompense (367-369). Statements about initiates note their obligation of "piety to foreigners and ordinary people" (Aristophanes *Frogs* 459), and their duty "to honor parents, glorify the gods with fruits, and not to harm animals" (Porphyry, *On Abstinence* 42.2).[74] Cicero claims that the Eleusinian Mysteries have raised human beings from a rough and savage life to a state of civilized humanity (*De legibus* 2.14.36). And certainly the purity of the soul was most important to those who believed it was immortal, separate from the body, and subject to punishment and reincarnation. Empedocles entitled his work *Katharmoi* and the soul in the tomb at Thurii calls itself *ek katharon kathara*, "Pure from the pure."

To mark their special status and to insure their purity, members followed certain ascetic practices such as dietary prohibitions, fasting, silence, and sexual abstinence. For some, the strict way of life was in part a punishment; pleasures are evil since the soul has been sent here to suffer in atonement for crime. Vegetarianism was particularly associated with the Orphic sects (v. Euripides *Hippolytus* 952-953; Aristophanes *Frogs* 1032; Plato *Laws* 6.782c), some Pythagoreans, and Empedocles, as well as the Cretan Mystery cults. Dodds attributes this as much to the horror of shedding blood as to the fear that a human soul inhabited the animal; Alderink emphasizes the need to avoid imitating the Titans' behavior and to identify with Dionysus instead by preserving life.[75]

Seeing, knowing, and remembering were also important to the initiates and the philosophers. *Theoria* as viewing was a technical term for the 'vision' at the mysteries.[76] The *mystai* saw something holy which so changed them emotionally that they could be happy in this life and in the next (*Hymn to Demeter* 480-482). The chorus of *Bacchae* says, "O blessed is he who by happy favor knowing the sacraments of the gods," which Dodds interprets as a "potent kind of knowledge" (in his commentary to 72-75). Certainly the texts found in tombs indicate that the deceased possessed esoteric wisdom which directed them toward their special status in the afterlife. To them, as to those who clearly believed in reincarnation, recollection (*anamnesis*) was a very important aspect of their salvation. The Lake of Memory figures in the mythic eschatology, while the sages of metempsychosis remember their former lives.

To Pythagoras, however, Scolnicov attributes the the theme of "the moral value of intellectual activity." For he is the one who first called his ideas *philosophia*, uniting the *theoria* of Ionian inquiry, which aimed to comprehend the cosmos, with the *theoria* that led to the soul's purification and salvation.[77] All these phenomena related to religion and philosophy indicate the growth of individualism among the Greeks, for they represent the range of options possible as a matter of private choice. The Eleusinian Mysteries, even when the Athenian polis took over their supervision, never became a polis cult to which one belonged by virtue of his citizenship. Initiation was open to all who could speak Greek and were unpolluted by murder, but was required of none. Although the Bacchic cults promoted group ecstasy, they were not tied to any one particular place or shrine. The Pythagoreans established a brotherhood or community to follow their way of life together, but the Orphic priests may have been mendicants attracting followers one by one. Citizens of the polis, by definition rulers of their own communities, were generally free to select other kinds of religious experiences to supplement the public forms.

With increasing individualism and the weakening of the corporate center of kinship or polis, death became more of a personal problem, to which both the mysteries and the philosophies responded. The increase in literacy affected the range of choices. Not only were the ideas of the philosophers being disseminated in books for assessment by individual readers, but the cults and the wandering priests had their own sacred texts, *Hieroi Logoi*, to guide them on their special path to blessedness. In the late fifth century, under the pressures of plague and war, the Athenians became more interested in superstitions, cults, religious revelations, and things Pythagorean and Orphic.[78]

Plato: Soul and Afterlife

The political and intellectual situation in Greece in Plato's lifetime effected a change in his focus as radical as the Hebrew movement from prophecy to apocalyptic.[79] He was born in Athens around 428 B.C.E., early in the Peloponnesian War. As a member of an illustrious family which traced its descent back to Solon and the early kings, Plato expected to become a political leader himself.

Athens was the cultural center of Greece, the host to philosophers, rhetoricians, historians, and doctors, whose new interest in nature (*physis*) and human nature threatened to replace traditional beliefs, customs, and laws (*nomos*) and whose new ideas and their effects were examined in the tragedies and satirized in the comedies. Dodds summarizes this 'Enlightenment' as creating among the group in which Plato grew up not only a propensity for "settling all questions before the bar of reason," but also "the habit of interpreting all human behavior in terms of rational self-interest," . . . and "the belief that "virtue," *arete*, consisted essentially in a technique of rational living."[80]

As he grew to manhood, however, Plato lived through a period of degenerate democracy, oligarchic revolution, lawlessness, military defeat, the tyranny of the thirty, and, finally, a counter revolution, all of which led him to conclude that contemporary politics could not be compatible with virtue. When the new leaders condemned and executed Socrates in 399 B.C.E., on "a charge which was most unholy and which Socrates least of all deserved" (*Epistle* 7.325b), he decided to withdraw from public affairs and to pursue philosophy in order "to discern all kinds of justice political and private"

(*Epistle* 7.326a). Eventually he founded the Academy in order to train a new generation of leaders according to principles derived from the pursuit of truth rather than enlightened self-interest.

Like the apocalyptic writers, Plato was the heir to a long tradition, as polymorphous as polytheism and including not only religious beliefs, symbols, poetry, and cult, but also various theories about nature, and, from the time of Parmenides, a new concern with a realm of being beyond plurality and change. Like the Hebrews, Plato transposed the ideas and expressions of the past to offer a new explanation of the world which, if not metahistorical, was certainly metaphysical. And like them too, he developed a new literary form out of older ones to both convey and embody his message.

The catalyst for his new direction was clearly Socrates, a public figure who wrote nothing himself, but who was written about by Aristophanes and Xenophon as well as Plato. Most scholars agree that Socrates introduced into the prevalent conceptions of *psyche* the idea of 'the care for the soul' as the seat of intellect and will and therefore the true self or best part of an individual.

Socrates' development of the *psyche* was moral rather than pragmatic or metaphysical.[81] He went beyond the contemporary medical practitioners or theorists who viewed the soul as the psychsomatic *physis* which could be trained to direct the individual toward health and physical well- being.[82] Although once attracted to nature philosophy, he was disappointed by its failure to explain why or what was best (*Phaedo* 98a-b). Nor did Socrates speculate about the nature or origin of the soul, as Plato later would. Rather he cared and directed others to care "about wisdom and truth" and "how the soul shall be best" (*Apology* 29c; cf. 30a), urging Athenians to consider "only whether they do just or unjust things, the actions of good or bad men" (*Apology* 28c). He made an emphatic connection between virtue and knowledge, which the *psyche*, as the life force and waking consciousness of the individual, could discover and implement.

Socrates believed, according to Scolnicov, that "the salvation of the soul is in continuous inquiry," and that "although the endeavor may go on forever, the aim remains to point the way."[83] The earliest dialogues of Plato reflect Socrates' attempts to force citizens to examine their lives; his conversations reveal how confused their thinking is about things they take for granted, but fail to provide clear answers as substitutes. In the *Apology*, Socrates reveals his own humility. He interprets Apollo's oracle to mean Socrates is the wisest human because he knows what he does not know. He is very confident, however, that his activities have been worth the risk:

no greater good can happen to a man than to discuss human excellence each day and other things which you have heard me arguing (*dialogomenou*) and examining myself and others about—for the unexamined life is not worth living" (38a).

Socrates lived and died for this principle, to which he attached religious significance. He took the oracle of Apollo as a call to become a gadfly to Athens, like the Hebrew prophets, and would not abandon his mission. He believed himself to be directed through life by some intermediate divinity, which he called his *daimon*, whose lead he followed, even to his trial. Judged guilty, he submitted to the death penalty rather than commit an impiety against the body of law which he viewed as a holy covenant.

Although drawing on Socrates, Plato's own philosophy is also considered a synthesis of the previous contradictory theories about nature. To accommodate Parmenides' thesis that only the indivisible, unchanging, and eternal could be truly knowable, he posited a metaphysical realm of Being, composed of pure essences, Forms or Ideas, as the model and source of the objects and concepts in our sensible world of flux and plurality. His analysis of the natural world, which he called Becoming, was dependent on the earlier philosophers' theories of matter and process, and particularly on the later Pythagorean ideas about the relation between mathematics and order in the cosmos.

The soul was the element which linked the two realms. Out of earlier meanings, Plato forged a synthesis and a new conception of the *psyche* as belonging to Being, but born into Becoming and capable of directing the person toward knowledge and consequently toward the good. For, stimulated by objects and qualities perceived in the sensible world, the soul was able to recollect the knowledge obtained between incarnations, if encouraged and trained to move beyond the senses to rigorous intellectual endeavors.

Dodds notes that Plato has "cross-fertilized the tradition of Greek rationalism with earlier magico-religious ideas . . . ".[84] Taking over their mythical conception of the *psyche* as the hidden self, divine, separate, and guilty, he reinterpreted it as Socrates' rational *psyche*, and transformed the out of body experience into the kind of trance for which Socrates was famous (*Symposium* 174d-175c; 220cd), signifying "the practice of mental withdrawal and concentration which purifies the rational soul." The special knowledge derived from the out of body experience developed into a vision of the metaphysical truth also perceived through reason. As conveyed through the myth of Er, the voyager to the other world sees a confirmation of the older beliefs in reincarnation and the recollection of previous lives. Proved through rational argument as well as revelation, recollection (*anamnesis*) became the basis of Plato's new epistemology in which the soul recognizes imitations of the metaphysical Forms in the sensible world and is thus led toward true knowledge.

Plato's synthesis has also been called a 'transposition' which raised the entire tradition to a higher level. Quasi-magical ideas about the soul, its purification, and its destiny became attached to the soul as the individual's moral and spiritual self. The religious ecstasy of the mystery or orgy which impels toward communion with divinity was transposed from the lowest levels of eroticism and frenzy to intellectual exaltation, for the vision culminates in contemplation. In the *Symposium* and *Phaedrus* in particular older ideas about the sexual and even cosmic aspects of Eros have been reinterpreted as the love for wisdom. Plato thus brought together the scientific and religious traditions of Greece. According to Despland, by uniting "the rational contemplation of the truth . . ." with "the religious contemplation of the good, Plato transposed both . . . and in the process made a grander claim for the knowledge to which man can rise."[85]

Although Plato is often judged the first philosopher "to try to construct an integral system of philosophy," he did not present his new ideas to the general public in a systematic way.[86] Rather, he chose to develop a new form for exploring his new metaphysics and epistemology, the philosophical drama, which replicated the arguing, examining, and exposure of falsehood that Socrates practiced without any conviction that he had arrived at a complete and final truth. Usually called a dialogue, it is itself a synthesis, binding together the language and forms of philosophy, poetry, and religion.[87] Like the drama, the dialogue imitates conversation among a variety of characters, each with his own age, personality, education, interests, and convictions. The real topic for examination usually develops out of a real life situation. The clash of individuals expressing different ideas produces not only new insights, but also anger and pain at ignorance exposed and zeal for uncovering truth. The discussion occurs outside the public arena of court or assembly, in a private context where all ideas and assumptions can be introduced, including myths, religious beliefs, and practices.

The rational discourse of philosophy and science is primary, however. The philosophical drama is not only written in lucid prose, but also employs the devices of speechmaking and the techniques of logic, which Plato has refined into dialectic. Points are analyzed by the conversationalists according to an agreed upon definition of terms and the rule that statements must be consistent with the hypothesis.

It is difficult to abstract a clear and absolute definition of the soul from Plato's corpus of dialogues. Each one discusses a different issue, and draws on arguments from his whole theory only as they relate to the topic at hand.[88] In the *Phaedo*, where Socrates is facing death and concerned to prove the immortality of the soul, Plato emphasizes its separation from the body and its need to purify itself of earthly desires, stressing the Puritanism which became explicit in later doctrines of the divinity of the soul. In other dialogues, however, the soul cannot be directed toward Being without first feeling passion for objects in the sensible world; the senses stimulate the recollection which leads souls to the quest for and love of the higher reality. Moreover, the embodied soul which has attained wisdom or at least glimpsed at the vision cannot maintain the separation; the philosopher king of the *Republic* must descend to the sensible world to effect the Good in his state. The correspondence between the state and the individual in the *Republic* may have shaped Plato's definition of the soul as tri-partite. In other dialogues, however, the soul is more clearly a unity composed of rational and affective powers.

Some scholars attribute the form of the philosophical drama and the difficulty of extracting a dogma from it to the fact that Plato himself was refusing to be dogmatic. According to Dodds, Plato was certainly a rationalist in the fifth-century Greek sense: he believed that reason, not the senses, must provide the principles of scientific knowledge; that the world and man were governed by reason and a rational plan; and that using reason would lead to higher material, intellectual, and moral achievement.[89] But he came to realize that reason alone was an insufficient means to achieve the goal of true knowledge. First of all, he recognized that the path to knowledge was extremely difficult and that very few men had the affinity for following its demanding curriculum, as spelled out in the *Republic*, and described in *Epistle* 7 340cd. Moreover, he came to acknowledge the power of the irrational; it could prevent a person from recognizing the truth or acting on it, but it also it might lead the person without knowledge to an intuitive grasp of spiritual realities beyond the sensible world. If passion could direct one toward knowledge and the comprehension of its impact on human life, once achieved, knowledge of the Forms suggested an even higher level that went beyond them and Being itself, but was unreachable by reason alone.[90]

In *Epistle* 7, Plato despaired of anyone, even himself, being able to explain this experience:

> for it does not admit of verbal expression like other studies, but, as a result of continued application to the subject itself and communion therewith, it is brought to birth in the soul on a sudden, as light that is kindled by a leaping spark, and thereafter nourishes itself. (341cd, Bury, trans.)[91]

To communicate to the public, Plato developed a form which both replicated the difficulty of the endeavor and stimulated the emotions necessary for the quest. The form, moreover, discouraged dogma because it introduced the insufficiency of rational argument into the rational examination itself, by representing philosophy as an on-going process, with partitive goals for each encounter, and by using myth and religion as a complement to argument.

Plato often calls attention to his use of myth. The creation of the world described in *Timaeus*, for example, is introduced as a 'likely story' (*eikota mython*, 29d), which is necessary because the difference between Being and Becoming necessitates that the statements about them will be different in kind. Plato's ideas about the afterlife are presented primarily through myth.[92] Often these tales express abstract truths that philosophers can reach by reason but cannot communicate to others without placing the ideas in the world of human experience through devices of character, plot, setting, and language. And occasionally the myths go beyond the *logos* to express truths that are beyond the reach of reason but are none the less at least glimpsed at as true, like the Idea of the Good which is perceived beyond the Forms.

The myths only complement or supplement the truth which the dialectic has revealed. At *Phaedo* 61b4, for example, Socrates distinguishes between *mythos* and *logos*, the fiction of poets and the facts of rational analysis, and denies that he is a *mythologikos*, an inventor of myths. Shortly after (61e2), however, he agrees to *mythologein*, 'to tell tales,' about the journey into the afterlife, on which he is about to embark. As Burnet points out, the immortality of the soul can be proven, but the details about the afterlife cannot.[93] Once Socrates has completed the dialectical proofs, he can offer a 'beautiful myth' (110b1) to describe the World of Forms and the soul's journey to it. When he concludes, he reminds his listeners that the myth cannot be true in every detail, but that, since the soul truly is immortal, one must believe its nature and its dwelling place are something like he has described (114d1).

Although Plato alludes to mythical ideas about the afterlife and religious beliefs about reincarnation in a variety of dialogues, he presents the fullest picture in the long eschatological myths which conclude the *Gorgias, Phaedo*, and *Republic*.[94]   Each has a major philosophical issue to explore which is examined through dialectic. Each also introduces earlier tales about death as the arguments proceed. By the end, the earlier ideas are transformed by their new connection with the quest for virtue and truth. At the same time, the point reached through reason is elevated by its expression in terms which are clearly related to older definitions of piety and belief.

Gorgias begins as a discussion of rhetoric, but moves forward from what the rhetoricians purport to teach, i.e., success and therefore happiness, to a search for what the good life really is. Socrates is able to disprove that hedonism and injustice can produce happiness. As the conversation develops, Socrates casually introduces eschatological beliefs which raise the stakes of the argument. When Callicles argues that if lack of desire, which is contrary to nature (492c5), created happiness, the dead would be happiest of all, Socrates repeats an idea he's heard, that we are in fact dead, that the body (*soma*) is a tomb (*sema*) for the soul. He then recounts the interpretation, attributed to a wise Sicilian or Italian, of a myth about Hades; the leaky vessels of the uninitiated water carriers are really the souls of the foolish, who are untrustworthy and forgetful (492e7-493d4). Although Callicles rejects these ideas, as well as much of the later argument, the eschatological allusions have prepared for the major myth at the end which will emphasize Socrates' moral and intellectual imperatives.

When Callicles warns him of the danger of caring for his soul and pursuing wisdom, anticipating the charges and trial which actually occurred, Socrates proclaims his certainty that the soul must fear evil far more than death. He then offers to tell a true tale to prove the point, twice calling it a *logon*, although Callicles might consider it a *mython* (522d5- 523a1). According to Dodds, Plato emphasized *logos* because he believed the tale "expresses in imaginative terms 'a truth of religion,' (cf. *Epistle* 7 335a2)"[95]

The tale, portending the city's judgment against Socrates, focuses on the divine judgment after death. Socrates begins with allusions to Homer, the Olympian gods, and the division of the afterlife into the Islands of the Blessed for the pious and Tartarus for sinners. But, fusing these older features to the Empedoclean image of the body as an alien tunic, Socrates adds new elements which elevate the moral dimensions of the tradition. Once, he says, the trial took place just before death, when a person and his judges were both alive and clothed, and the wicked soul was covered by signs of earthly success which influenced the judges. Therefore, Zeus postponed the judgment until after death, made his own sons Minos, Rhadymanthus, and Aeacus judges, and had the dead proceed naked to the Meadow at the crossroads for trial. These changes enabled the final judgment to be as just as possible because the naked soul, separated from the body at death, retains the scars of its sinfulness, just as the body retains the signs of its former life and death. Only the sins are visible, for the earthly identity which used to influence the judges has been removed with the soul's clothing.

The judgment is therefore impartial and is based only on the questions of whether a sin has been committed, and if so, whether the sin is curable or not. Those who can learn from suffering and fear so that they will become better through punishment are given a mark to indicate that they are curable before being sent to the prison of Tartarus. Those who have committed so many injustices that they are judged incurable are marked and sent to Tartarus to serve as examples. (Archelaus the tyrant whose success Polus has just envied is placed there with the traditional sinners from Homer.) But the soul which has lived in holiness, truth, and justice is sent on to the Islands of the Blessed. Socrates emphasizes that politicians face the greatest danger of corruption in life and therefore punishment after death whereas philosophers have the greatest hope. He concludes by acknowledging that his listeners might condemn this as a myth and an old wives' tale, but that in fact their searching has produced nothing better or truer (527a5). He urges them to spend their lives in the pursuit and practice of virtue if they want to be happy in life and death, as if the process of philosophizing is as virtuous as the actual attainment of philosophical truth.

The eschatological myth in the *Phaedo* places the judgment of the soul after death into a broader philosophical context.[96] The dialogue, which reports Socrates' last conversation, focuses on his proof that the soul is immortal to justify his confidence that he has nothing to fear from the death of his body. To support his arguments that the soul has lived before and will survive death, Socrates introduces new ideas such as the related doctrines of recollection and reincarnation (unmentioned in *Gorgias* but alluded to in *Meno* 81) and the Theory of Forms. The concluding myth expresses these abstract concepts in the human terms and concrete images of life on earth.

As the conversation unfolds, Socrates draws upon earlier eschatological ideas which will develop new meaning from his conceptual analysis. He ascribes his hope for the future, for example, to the age old saying that the dead have some kind of existence after death which is better for the good than for the wicked (69c). To explain why suicide is wrong he repeats the contention of those in the mysteries that we are in a prison from which we must not free ourselves (62b). When discussing the philosophers' attempt to purify themselves from the demands of the body, he again refers to the mysteries and their myth that the uninitiated in Hades lie in the mud while the purified initiated dwell with the gods. But Socrates has defined the philosophers as the truly purified and inspired, the *bacchoi*, and the purification has been shifted from the rites themselves to the four virtues, temperance, justice, courage, and the most important of all, wisdom (69cd).

Socrates introduces the question of whether the souls exist in the next world by repeating an ancient *logos* that souls are reborn from dead souls again and again (70c). Once he has proven by rational analysis that souls are born from the dead and exist after death as akin to the divine (drawing upon recollection and the Forms to support his hypotheses) Socrates rejects the conventional idea that the soul perishes when it leaves the body and substitutes a modification of the cycle of reincarnation. The purified souls go away to Hades to the invisible divine, immortal, and wise, to whom they are akin, and dwell there forever, as the initiated are reported to do. But the impure, who have been devoted to and corrupted by their bodies, are weighed down by their earthly burden, hang around their graves and tombs, and are actually visible as ghosts, since they are too impure for the invisible world of Hades. They are compelled to wander there as punishment until they are imprisoned again in bodies of animals with habits like their own. Socrates completes his account by reiterating the prison metaphor, emphasizing that the senses and the sensible world captivate the soul which does not value knowledge and thus doom it to captivity (80d- 83a).

When he has completed his proof that the soul is immortal, imperishable, and existent in the next world, he caps his argument by urging his listeners to take care of their souls to make them as perfect and wise as possible in preparation for the journey to the next world. The first part of the eschatological myth focuses on the journey itself on which Socrates must soon embark. The philosopher contradicts the tradition that the path is simple; rather it has so many branches and wanderings that the dead person needs a guide, the same *daimon* which led him through life, to lead him to judgment and bring him back again after many revolutions. The orderly soul wisely follows the guide, but the corrupted soul struggles to stay with the body and must be dragged to judgment and punishment, shunned by all because of its stain of evil.

When Socrates proceeds to explain where the purified souls go to dwell with the gods, he places the belief in the immortality of the soul within the context of the Theory of Forms in an imaginative way (*mython*, 110b). For although we now live in an equivalent of a hollow in the earth, full of sediment, the purified soul will go to the true earth above, where everything is purer and more beautiful than our things which are subject to decay.

Our earth is not the only hollow, however. Among others is the large and deep Tartarus, into which all the major traditional rivers flow. Here the dead are led for judgment and divided into groups. Those who are neither very good or bad go the Acheron where they are punished for crime and purified, as well as rewarded for merit. The greatest sinners are judged incurable and hurled down to Tartarus forever. Great but repentant sinners who have been punished at Cocytus and Periphlegethon are given the opportunity to entreat their victims for release; their punishment must continue, however, until their victims relent. Presumably, almost all are eventually reborn. Although Socrates does not repeat what he said earlier about reincarnation, one group of the purified souls, the philosophers, live forever without bodies in an even more beautiful place above the real earth (107c-114c).

The *Republic*, a longer and more comprehensive dialogue, places eschatological myth into a more cosmic and metaphysical context.[97] The conversation arises out of Cephalus' joy that his wealth has enabled him to be honest and just all his life. For, although he used to scoff at the old myths that those who do wrong here must pay the penalty in Hades (330d), in his old age he has begun to fear that myths may be true. Socrates cannot accept the current meanings of justice proposed by his companions nor can he agree that people are just only because it profits them in life and protects them after death. Therefore, finding the ultimate meaning of justice becomes the central quest of the dialogue.

Only when the arguments (*logos*, 612a, 614a) have proven that justice is the best thing for the soul, which should do what is right regardless of the consequences, does Socrates reintroduce the question of rewards. The company confirms the benefits of justice in this life from their own experience, agreeing that the righteous man who suffers may be paying for some injustice in a former life and that any other seeming evil will be good for him in the end (613a). Rewards after death, however, can only be described through myth (*mythos*, 621b).

The myth of Er (613e-end) is an account of a near death experience. In the twelve day interval between Er's death in battle and preparation for the cremation of his body at home, the soul of Er journeyed forth into the next world. He was not brought up for judgment like the other dead souls; instead the judges told him he was to be a messenger (*aggelos*) to men about the things there and ordered him to observe and listen to everything in the place. At the end of the twelve days, Er was not allowed to drink from the river of forgetfulness with the souls about to be reborn. He could not explain how he got back to his body; he only knew he found himself on his pyre when he opened his eyes and came back to life. Thus the myth was saved.

In Er's revelation, Plato uses current ideas about the afterlife in a new way to place the meaning of justice in human life within a cosmos which includes the Forms and the Idea of the Good. Socrates invites comparison to other beliefs by contrasting Er's tale with Odysseus' long account (*apologon*) of the underworld to Alcinous (614b). The marvelous place (614c) Er visits has familiar elements like a meadow, a plain, different paths, and waters of forgetfulness. The configuration is entirely new, however. On the left of the judges are two holes in the earth; on the right are two in the sky. After the judgment, which takes place between them, the unjust are sent down for punishment through one of the holes in the earth, with tokens on their backs to mark their sins, while the just are sent upward through one of the openings in the sky. At the same time, other souls are coming back up from beneath or down from above through the other openings on either side. As they gather in the meadow and discuss their joys or sufferings, Er learns about the ten-fold punishment for every sin and the equal reward for every just and kind act. He hears that the wicked tyrant of his own city was denied release and, with other like sinners, had been dragged away, flayed with thorns, and hurled down to Tartarus forever.

Having rested in the meadow, the souls then moved on to another place where they saw a shaft of light from above heaven to the earth below, connecting all parts of the revolving firmament like a chain, and a model of the universe as a spindle resting on the lap of the goddess Necessity, and turned by her daughters the three Fates.

The details of the spindle (which pull together the subjects to be learned by rulers) emphasize the perfect mathematical arrangement of the universe. The harmony of the spheres is replicated in the harmony of the Sirens, each of whom sits on one of the eight whorls and sings her own note. Thus the universe is a cosmos, for all the parts move together on the shaft of Necessity's spindle. And the universe is also just, for each whorl also moves in its own direction and rotation at the same time, performing its own special function within the whole, like the parts of the soul of a just individual and the parts of a just state.

The vision of this spindle of Necessity reveals that human life on earth is part of the good and just order of the cosmos. Now the souls which have completed the judgments for their past lives are ready to choose new ones, and be reborn, with the guidance of the Three Fates and an interpreter. The choice has an element of necessity, which is built into the cosmos as a whole. Souls must select their next lives in an allotted order. There are, however, more than enough choices, and, although some lives are more difficult than others, the interpreter (*prophates*) makes clear that human beings are responsible for the way they live:

> virtue has no master. As a man honors or dishonors her, so each shall have more or less of her. The blame belongs to the one who chooses. God is blameless. (617e)

Once the souls have chosen their lives, they proceed in their allotted order to the three Fates in turn; Lachesis gives them the *daimon* of the life selected, which then leads them to Clotho to ratify the portion as she turns the spindle, and next to Atropos to spin the irreversible thread of destiny. Finally they have to drink water from the River of Unmindfulness (*Ameles*) on the hot dry Plain of Forgetfulness (*Lethe*). Some do not have the wisdom to drink only the necessary measure of the water (621a); presumably they forget more of what they have learned and have a harder time recollecting.

The myth's focus on the choice reiterates the emphasis on reason as the ruling element of the individual soul, the state, and the universe. Before Er reports on the various choices made, some funny and some tragic, Socrates interrupts the tale to point out how important it is to pursue the knowledge which will enable one to distinguish the good life from the bad, and thus be happy here and forever. He ends the dialogue with the hope that the tale may 'save' (*soseien*, 621c) all his listeners after their deaths. Thus the myth, which now expresses metaphysical knowledge as well as its import, has become the means of salvation. In fact, Socrates insists that the very process of philosophy, of pursuing justice with wisdom, will always keep his listeners on the upward path, dear to themselves and to the gods, here in this world and on their long journey in the next (621cd).

The *Republic* emphasizes scientific knowledge gained by conceptual analysis and study as the path to salvation. But there is an additional dimension to the philosopher's path; the philosopher is, by definition, a lover of wisdom and his journey is an emotional as well as an intellectual quest. In the *Symposium*, Socrates introduced this idea as a *logon* of the mantic Diotima (201d) who describes the process as an ascent in stages, like going up steps (211c). His reported conversation with her, composed of myth and dialectic, elevates the group's understanding of Eros from physical desire to desire for knowledge of true Beauty.

The emotional aspect of the quest is more fully developed in the *Phaedrus* where the definition of rhetoric is examined through the examples of three different speeches on the madness of love and its benefits for the beloved.[98] To Lysias' speech contending that a youth is better off with a non-lover, Socrates opposes his own speech, which defines the terms and examines both sides in a more orderly and analytical way. He stops abruptly, however, for his speech so far has been impious, since Love is divine and cannot be responsible for any evil. His second speech, therefore, redefines love as a divine madness sent by the gods for the benefit of lover and beloved alike.

He begins by carefully defining other familiar kinds of divine madness which have benefited humanity, e.g., the prophetic, the ecstatic, and the poetic, before moving to the divine madness of love. To prove his point about it, however, he must first define the nature of the soul, for it is that element in us which moves the body. He can easily argue that the soul is self-moving, and therefore uncreated and immortal. To tell what its form really is, he can only use resemblances, in a human and lesser way (246a). Therefore he describes the soul and its contact with the divine in the imaginative terms of myth and allegory, so that he can define divine love and its benefits. Once he completes his speech, which is primarily the myth and its analysis, he and Phaedrus can analyze the features of good writing and speaking, which must now necessarily include being an inspired lover of wisdom.

Socrates' myth employs the traditional imagery of the otherworldly ascent toward revelation to describe the human soul's place in the cosmos. Human and divine souls, as the self movers which cause motion in lifeless objects, both resemble chariots, with the charioteer dominating two winged horses whose natural motion is to soar upward. The goal is the vision of the highest realms which offers both knowledge and joy; the region beyond the heavens serves as the model for the gods and the gods are in turn models for humans.

In divine souls, the horses and charioteers are in harmony; perfect and fully winged, they are able to perform their function of ordering the universe in accord with the model. As Zeus and the other gods lead their chariots around their proper orbits, they can also observe heaven's outer limits. When at rest, they mount the steep ascent to the vault of heaven to see and feast on that place beyond (247c), where Being itself lives, indescribable in human terms and visible only to reason (247c). Thus the gods experience direct and pure knowledge in regular revolutions and find joy in its contemplation before returning again to their duties.

Human souls are akin to divine souls and try to follow the gods in their orbits. The two winged horses of their chariots are different, however: one good and beautiful, the other ugly and insolent, so that the human charioteers have a harder job regulating them. Although they are all eager to get that glimpse of reality which also nourishes their best part, in the struggle and confusion, some have their wings broken and never see much of anything real. By a decree of destiny (248c), those who have seen a truth are free from harm until the next revolution. But those who lose their wings (through mischance, forgetfulness, or heaviness) fall to earth and are placed in human bodies according to the amount of reality they perceived i.e., nine types of lives from philosopher down to tyrant. It takes 10,000 years for the soul to regain its wings, going from life to life, with reward and punishment in between. Only the philosopher, whose search for love has involved the pursuit of wisdom, can free himself from the cycle and return, after choosing this life three times in succession.

Madness develops when one sees beauty in this world and is reminded of the journey his soul once made with a god. Then he begins to sprout wings and, if only the charioteer can control the wicked horse, he can lead himself and his beautiful love object toward knowledge of the divine and *imitatio dei*, "taking their manner and way of life from the god, as much as it is possible for a human" (253a). Only this will lead to true happiness for both, since they will have subdued the source of evil in the soul and set free the source of goodness. Even if they do not become fully winged the first time, those who have tasted the love madness have begun the journey to heaven and will never pass down to the darkness beneath the earth.

Socrates' speech in the *Phaedrus* contains many of the same eschatological elements as the other myths: the soul's divine origin, its fall and incarnation, judgment with reward and punishment, the cycle of reincarnations, the paradox of necessity and choice in human life, a scale of lives, and the possibility of early release for the wise and virtuous. In focusing on the heavens before a soul has fallen to earth, however, the myth transposes current religious ideas in a different way. In the first place, Being itself, the ultimate intangible indescribable reality, visible only to reason, the governor of the soul (247c), has the highest place in the hierarchy. The Olympian gods are relegated to a second rank administrating the cosmos with the knowledge gained from their direct vision of Being. Vision itself, so important in the rites of the mysteries, is also used and changed by the new myth. For the soul's vision of Being, and of the god it followed in the ascent, is recollected when the soul sees a beautiful human beloved. The right use of the objects seen leads the lover toward knowledge of Being, keeps one always being initiated and perfected, and though seemingly mad, possessed by god (249). But the things seen, the *hiera* or holy objects (250a), are justice, temperance, and knowledge (247d), not the holy objects of the mystery cults. The terms associated with the exaltation and frenzy aroused by the mysteries and divine possession recur throughout the dialogue (e.g., 234d, 238d, 243a), but by the end they too have been transposed by association with the ecstasy of the vision and the way it is communicated between lovers (253a). Moreover, the whole idea of divine inspiration has been transposed. The divine madness which directs the souls of lover and beloved to remember Being is called the best and highest of all forms of divine madness (249d-e), as if philosophy has replaced oracles, mysteries, and poetry as diviner, conveyer, and communicator of truth.[99]

It is clear that Plato's eschatological myths support his metaphysical hypotheses by couching them as revelations of a supermundane reality. In the dialogues, most of his metaphysics is achieved through conceptual analysis and rational discourse. But the *Phaedrus*, even more than the other dialogues which introduce myths, calls attention to the limitations of human knowledge and communication. Early in the dialogue Socrates refuses to commit himself to believing or disbelieving in the tale about Boreas' seduction of a Nymph, called a *mythologema*, 229c. Although he rejects the current rationalizing and allegorizing of myth as simple-minded, Socrates prefers to dispense with the question until he has completed the task assigned by the Delphic commandment 'know thyself.' His speech about the soul, his true self, is in effect a transposition of myth-making so that it reflects the truth about the essential goodness of man, god, and the universe. At 265bc, he assesses the paradoxical validity of his myth as an expression of complex reality and of piety;

> We have somehow described the passion of love by using a comparison, perhaps touching upon a part of the truth, but going astray as well. Blending a not entirely untrustworthy speech (*logon*) we have sung a mythic playful (*mythikon*) hymn moderately and reverently.

He is careful to note that the philosopher can be called only a lover of wisdom; the term 'wise' seems appropriate for god alone (278d; cf. *Symposium* 204a). But Plato, like the Hebrew apocalyptic prophets, uses the vision of the world beyond as the intuitive ladder leading to fuller comprehension. Like them too, the recipient of the radiance of the vision has the obligation to share his knowledge. At the end of the *Phaedrus*, both Phaedrus and Socrates are eager to announce (*exaggello*, 279b) their new understanding of love to their respected beloveds.

Endtime: Decline, Destruction, and Palingenesis

The Greek vision of the afterlife is not connected to the end of days, as a culmination of the history of one nation or of all nations and the world at large. Each individual dies and goes on to the next world in his own time, according to his own lot in life. There are no accounts of a collective judgment or an awakening of all the dead for final judgment at the end of time.

For the Greeks, unlike the Hebrews, did not really conceive of an absolute end of time. They were not future- oriented, either in culture or philosophy; they considered the future "unknown and unknowable."[100]   As mythmakers, they were interested in beginnings, in the sacred time in which the world order and the customs for maintaining human life in society were established. Although the major divinities have stories about their births, once they reach their essential personalities and functions, they remain eternally themselves: e.g., Hermes, Dionysus, and Apollo ever youths; Zeus, Hades, and Poseidon always in their prime. The myths about their interactions with humans describe responses to immediate situations; even their prophesies concern short-term issues. There is never any overarching plan of Zeus, such as God's promise to Abraham or David, which provides the context for all the myths or points forward to a goal.

Only when Polybius recognized the inevitability of the Roman conquest did Greco-Roman historiography begin to remotely resemble the teleological salvation history of the Hebrews (see chapter nine). The Romans of Virgil's day could look upon their miraculous conquest of the Mediterranean world as a divine program or Stoic providence (e.g., Virgil's *Aeneid*). As the Babylonian concept of the catastrophic Great Year moved west, they also feared a time when Rome was fated for destruction; therefore, in crises the government consulted the collection of prophecies known as the Sibylline Books to identify and avert or mitigate predicted catastrophes.

Virgil, the poet of the transition from the republic to the principate, resembles the writers of Hebrew apocalyptic in that his *Aeneid* uses the past to validate the present. Although Virgil infused prophesies of Rome's future history into the story of its mythic founding, his predictions really narrate Rome's historical past, a *vaticina ex eventu* like most of Daniel 7 -12. The mythic Aeneas' otherworldly journey to the afterlife reveals the imminent reincarnation of souls into the bodies of the real leaders of the defunct republic. On one level, the revelation of Rome's future should validate the present hope for peace now that the civil war has ended and Augustus is the sole leader. Scholars suggest, however, that the ambiguities in the epic, and particularly in its prophecies, expose the ambivalence and anxiety of Virgil and his contemporaries: "the age's hope for the peace of a Golden Age under Augustus, and its fear that the hope might be deceptive and illusory."[101]

Thus Virgil's epic may arise from the same kind of historical despair as Hebrew apocalyptic. But it does not elevate Roman history to a metahistorical level. Although history has become cosmic, resting with Jupiter and Fate, it has no goal beyond Augustus' success. The scroll Jupiter reads to Venus about Aeneas and his progeny may resemble the Book of Truth in Dan. 10:21-11.2, but the prophecy ends with Augustus Caesar alone received in heaven after his victory brings peace on earth (1.257-296). All history and individual life do not culminate in the divinely effected *eschaton* described in Dan. 12:1-3 and elaborated on in Rev. 20:11-21:4. Rather the divine plan for history is interpreted in cyclic terms as the destruction of the old Trojan world and the birth of a new Roman civilization.

Because the Greek concept of the beginning was different, they were not really able to conceive of the end in the way the Hebrews did.[102] Their world was not created out of nothing, as in Genesis, but out of some primary eternal 'stuff' which Hesiod mythologizes as Chaos, but which the nature philosophers define as various kinds of matter. Natural processes, not one God who could destroy as well as create, imposed the order which made the cosmos. The processes might also produce disorder or reordering, but they could not destroy the matrix from which the world developed (see chapters two and three).

Greek philosophers, particularly after Parmenides, developed the distinction between the sensible world of constant flux, and an underlying or supramundane reality which was eternal and unchanging. Because sense perception of changing objects could not give truth, they placed a higher value on the more fully knowable eternal principle which governed the change, whether it was *logos* and fire for Heraclitus, number and harmony for the Pythagoreans, or the Forms in the Realm of Being for Plato. Thus, Greek philosophy was ontological, more interested in the general unchanging reality, without any real beginning or end, than in the particular developments of the natural or social world.

To explain how abstract and timeless Being effects and affects Becoming, Plato tells stories which put the eternal and unchanging into the terms of human time and experience. In the *Timaeus*, for example, Plato describes how the demiurge creates the cosmos out of a preexisting receptacle according to the model provided by the Forms. The speaker Timaeus makes clear that they, as human beings, cannot render an exact account of Being and must be content with 'a likely story (29cd).' According to Aristotle, his contemporaries at the Academy believed that in describing generation

> . . . they are doing as a geometer does in constructing a figure, not implying that the universe ever really came into existence, but for purposes of exposition facilitating understanding by exhibiting the object, like the figure, in process of formation. (*de caelo* 279b-280a; Cornford, trans.)[103]

The analogy from the geometer suggests a further reason why the Greeks did not posit an absolute end. They were always attracted to the circle and the sphere as the perfect shapes.[104] The development of mathematics and astronomy in Plato's lifetime, particularly among the Pythagoreans and Eudoxus, increased their awareness of the orderly revolutions of the spherical heavenly bodies. Thus, when the demiurge in *Timaeus* creates the planets, he also creates Time, which is the measure of their movements. Because their movements are orderly and eternal revolutions, the created world is a moving likeness of eternity (37d). Although the specific events and things of Becoming wax, wane, and change, the total movement of the whole is as like the demiurge's model as possible and "has been, is, and shall be perpetually throughout all time" (38bc, Cornford, trans.). The Great Year is here defined as "the moment when the relative speeds of all the eight revolutions have accomplished their courses together and reached their consummation, as measured by the circle of the Same and uniformly moving" (39d, Cornford, trans.). Not only is there no catastrophe, but, as Cornford notes, the concepts of beginning and end occur "only because the myth speaks as if time and its instruments had been created at some moment . . . ."[105]

Although the Greeks viewed the universe as ultimately indestructible, they, like the Hebrews, were conscious of degeneration and looked back to the beginning of human time when men were closer to the gods and life was easy. Aristophanes' comic myth in *Symposium* 189c-193d depicts an idyllic period when the human race had superior movement, strength, and pleasure, being round, two-sided, and divided into three sexes. When they tried to attack the gods, however, Zeus separated them in half. Aristophanes defines love as the yearning of the separated halves for their original partners and the restoration of their earliest nature, like a yearning for their former paradise.

Hesiod's myth of the Golden Age more closely resembles the Hebrew descriptions of the lost Eden and the Messianic Age and New Jerusalem to come. The 'golden race of men' who lived in the time of Cronus did not have to labor for food or suffer the pains of the aging process. Loved by the gods and dwelling in peace, they died as if overcome by sleep and then became protective *daimones* on earth (*Works and Days* 108-126).

This picture of the golden age became a powerful symbol of an ideal human society at peace with the gods, fellow humans, and nature. Plato used it in the long myth in *Statesman* (268d-275b) in order to help make clear the nature of the king. The Stranger describes the earliest period of the cosmos as being like the mythical reign of Cronus, using details similar to Paradise and the Messianic age (271d- 272e). Then "no creature was wild, nor did they eat one another and there was no war or strife among them" (271e). They had no need of states, families, labor for food, or even clothes and furniture, for the climate was temperate and the grass provided soft bedding. Gods ruled men directly while *daimones* ruled the animals, each caring for his charges like shepherds for their flocks.

In *Timaeus* and *Critas*, Plato looks backward to the lost continent of Atlantis and the earliest Athenian polis as functioning governments most similar to the ideal state described in the *Republic* . Four centuries later Virgil combined the political hope for a new Rome with the myth of the Golden Age. In the Fourth Eclogue, which is often called 'Messianic,' he used the birth of a child as a symbol of the inauguration of an age of peace. Here, as in Isa. 11 celebrating the rise of a Davidic king, the political change has cosmic implications: all nature lives in harmony, all human needs, spiritual as well as material, are satisfied, the age predicted by the Sibyl is complete, the virgin Justice has returned, and the Iron race has been replaced by the Gold.

But, in 40 B.C.E., when the poem was written, ostensibly to celebrate the consulship of Pollio or the anticipated birth of a child, the Romans were on the brink of yet another civil war and trying to patch Antony and Octavian together by creating a family tie through a political marriage. Eclogue 4 contains only one direct historical allusion, to Pollio the consul (11-12); the rest of the symbolism is as opaque as Isa. 7:14. Commenting that by this time the apocalyptic writings of the Jews were known in the West, Griffin notes that " . . . the messianic parallels are real. . . . The Fourth Eclogue is . . . the work of a mind which in despair at the situation on earth takes refuge in hopes and fantasies of another order. These are the circumstances in which messianic literature is normally produced."[106]

The idealizing of a golden age in the past presupposes a period of degeneration which has led to the imperfections of the present. Hesiod's myth comparing the decline of human races to ever baser metals from gold to silver to bronze to iron (*Works and Days* 106-201) resembles Nebuchanezzer's dream of the decline of empires in Dan. 2.[107] The Greek tale also predicts a future in which sin and suffering will only increase (180-206), but there is no apocalyptic hope for the defeat of evil by a god. Nor does Virgil's 'Messianic Eclogue' predict a cataclysmic end to the universe. Rather the Iron Age of the century of Roman revolution will cease and the golden race spring up (8-9) now that the new firstborn is being sent down from high heaven (7).

The Greeks did not lack tales about catastrophes which threatened to destroy the earth. Like the Hebrews, they told a flood story in which only a virtuous couple, Deucalion and Pyrrha, survived to repopulate the world. Plato interpreted the myth of Phaethon, child of the Sun who couldn't control his father's horses, as reflecting a truth about a great conflagration (*Timaeus* 22cd). And his own story about Atlantis and ancient Athens ends in the destruction of both civilizations when, in a time of terrible earthquakes and floods, Athens was swallowed up by the earth and Atlantis vanished into the sea forever (*Timaeus* 24cd).

For the Greeks such destruction was periodic or localized; something always survived somewhere so that renewal eventually followed destruction.[108] In *Timaeus*, Plato attributed the Phaethon myth to a deviation of the bodies revolving in the heavens which destroyed areas closest to the sun, whereas he traced flood stories to gods who cleansed the earth with water but left remnants of humans living on the high mountains. Egypt, untouched by either catastrophe, was able to endure the longest and keep records of those civilizations which had risen and perished periodically (22c-23). In *Laws*, the Athenian supposes that many civilizations have come and gone in the countless catastrophes and that all the tools and institutions which perished with them were only gradually rediscovered (677a- 678b). For Aristotle these disasters were part of the normal operations of nature, but they produced the same result: "each art and science has often been developed as far as possible and has again perished" (*Metaphysics* 1074b, cf. 993b; *Politics* 1329b).

Civilizations may wax and wane, due to external catastrophes or to general laws which types of governments follow in their specific events of growth and decay. The world as a whole is also subject to natural processes and the reordering of its elements over time. But most of the philosophers were more interested in the beginning than the end, in the first principle or *arche* out of which everything arose and the way sensible things developed and continue to maintain themselves.

Those who did speculate on an actual end linked it to a new beginning as part of a cycle of death and regeneration in the cosmos as a whole. Empedocles, for example, postulated a four-phased cycle: 1) an initial period of absolute unity and perfection when Love was in control; 2) a period when Strife entered and broke up the unity into combinations which make up the sensible world; 3) a period when Strife rules and no unification is possible; and 4) a final period when Love reenters and asserts the harmony which makes the compounding of the elements possible. These four stages alternate in an endless cycle, life being possible only when Love and Strife are both operative. Some Stoics too posited periodic total destruction and renewal: an end of the world when the fire out of which everything had developed resolved itself once again into pure fire, called *ekpyrosis*, and then a regeneration of the identical universe. Because they believed all human life was predetermined, history as well as nature was infinitely repeatable. As Nemesius wrote in the fourth century C.E.,

> Socrates and Plato will live again, with the same friends and fellow citizens. They will go through the same experiences and the same activities. Every village and field will be restored just as it was. And this restoration of the universe takes place not once, but over and over again—indeed to all eternity without end.[109]

Plato's myth in *Statesman* provides the most vivid picture of the cosmic cycle.[110] Again it is important to note that the stranger presents it as a myth, an amusement in the middle of their difficult task of finding the essential definition by means of eliminating part after part (268de). But he also presents it as something which will help them reach their ultimate object, for his story places human leadership in its cosmic context and expresses, in terms of human space, time, and experience, both the abstract eternal pattern and the deviations from it caused by matter and change in the sensible world. Here too as in his descriptions of the afterlife, Plato, like the Hebrew apocalyptists, uses older myths and symbols to introduce and develop his new ideas in a new tale. Thus the stranger recalls the way in which the heavenly bodies changed their course to show their favor of Atreus over Thyestes and the tales about the age of Cronus and the earthborn men before he explains the real source of all such stories.

The myth describes a universe which God guides for one part of its revolving course, but then lets go when the cycles have reached their allotted measure so that the universe turns backward in the opposite direction. The first age when God was at the helm is remembered as the age of Cronus, with all its perfection and pleasure. When by necessity He let go and the world turned and reversed itself by its own motion, there was a great shock, as the beginning and end rushed in opposite directions (273a). Although it gradually became more orderly by practicing the teachings of its divine guide, yet the disorder of its primeval nature finally prevailed. Before it sank into catastrophe, however, God resumed the helm. Strange things happen at the points of reversal; e.g., those alive at the time become younger and younger and return to earth (271ab). Because those deprived of the deities' care became enemies of animals, the earth, and each other, gods like Prometheus and Athena bestowed the information necessary for survival, i.e., fire, crafts, agriculture (274).

The stranger connects the periodic disordering and reordering of the universe with the cycle of individual deaths and rebirths in a manner reminiscent of Hebrew apocalyptic. The end of the age of Cronus corresponded with the end of the cycle of regeneration; "When every soul fulfilled all its births by falling into the earth as seed the prescribed number of times, then the helmsman of the universe dropped the tiller and withdrew . . ." (272e). When growth reverses its direction and all become young and return to the earth, the new generation must come from the dead and thus be earth-born, as legend tells, for the process of birth is reversed along with the reversal of the world's revolution (271b). After Plato tells all of this in a blend of old myth with new, he analyzes his story to bring out the similarities and differences between the God/shepherd and the mortal statesman. The myth of periodic destruction and palingenesis is only a different path to a higher level of philosophical examination (268d).

Eschatological Footnotes to Plato

Plato's dialogues have had an enormous influence on the history of literature, philosophy, and religion. His vivid myths about the afterlife have captured the imaginations of many later writers who, like him, transposed the tradition by infusing it with new ideas. Virgil, for example, is clearly imitating Homer when, in Book 6 of the *Aeneid*, he sends his hero on a literal *katabasis* to visit his father Anchises in Hades. But the underworld kingdom, so much more carefully described, has the geographical features of Platonic myth: e.g., the rivers, the path with clear divisions between Tartarus and Elysium, and the gathering of the souls to drink from Lethe.

Moreover, Virgil's Aeneas learns what Homer could not reveal— the metaphysical and ethical truths which govern the cosmos. As they pass Tartarus, the Sibyl, a guide similar to the *daimones* who lead the souls in *Phaedo*, tells him about the judgment by Rhadamanthus, lists the sins against society which warrant the terrible punishments described (608-627), and summarizes the lesson: "Learn justice, be warned, and do not scorn the gods" (620). Later (723-751) Aeneas' father explains that the whole heaven and earth are infused with spirit (*spiritus*, 726) and that the human mind is part of that fiery energy from which the whole cosmos derives. Because that immortal part is stained with the evils of its bodily prison, every impure soul must be cleansed by wind, water, or fire. The pure souls of the virtuous go directly to the blessed fields around Elysium. When a cosmic cycle is completed, they are reborn into new bodies.

Aeneas' questions about the souls standing near Lethe add a new historical dimension to reincarnation. So far the hero has received numerous prophecies of the great new nation fated to be founded by him and to reach its zenith under Augustus Caesar. This otherworld journey enables Aeneas to see his great progeny for himself, for Anchises reveals the names and achievements of the future Romans waiting to be born, from Aeneas' legendary son Silvius to the historical Augustus and Marcellus his heir who had just in fact died (756-886). Anchises' revelation "inflames his spirit with love of future glory" (889) and increases his willingness to suffer for Rome. Thus has the poet enriched old eschatological myth with the belief system of his age which combined Roman patriotism with an eclectic neo-Pythagorean/Platonic/Stoic philosophy.[111]

The same combination is also present in the earlier Dream of Scipio which concludes Cicero's *Republic* as a conscious imitation of the Myth of Er.[112] Cicero wrote it in the midst of a great political crisis, between 55 and 51 B.C.E., when the First Triumvirate was falling apart. His dialogue, like Plato's, is set in an earlier period and dramatizes a conversation, between Scipio Africanus the Younger and his associates, about the ideal state (the mixed Roman constitution) and justice. At the end of the discussion, Scipio relates his dream (Book 6). Macrobius comments that Cicero purposely changed the 'myth' to a dream because philosophers such as the Epicureans had ridiculed Plato's use of fiction to portray what he asserted was truth (*in somn. Scip.* 1.1.8-1.2.5).[113]

Cicero, like Plato, uses the revelation to place the state and the best ruler within a cosmic context where the eternal order of the universe and the fate of the soul support the conclusions reached through the discussion. Scipio's dead relative, Africanus the Elder, appears to him in a dream, warns him about his future, and, in response to his questions about other dead relatives, explains about the imprisonment of the immortal soul, drawn from the celestial fires, in the earthly body, and the return of the just souls to their celestial home. He assures the younger man that in time all patriots are assigned a special life of eternal bliss in heaven because the gods are most pleased by states united by law and right.

From a lofty vantage point, both are able to view the heavens and hear the celestial harmonies. They look out on a cosmos composed of eight concentric circles revolving around the earth which is fixed in the center. The outermost ring is the heaven of the fixed stars, then come the seven planetary spheres, Saturn, Jupiter, Mars, the sun, Venus, Mercury, and finally the moon. Everything below the moon is mortal and transitory except human souls.

As the elder Scipio explains the order and movement of the universe, he emphasizes the insignificance of earth and its pleasures, and the importance of keeping the soul free from impurity and injustice. Although many of his words resemble Platonic passages, the tone is Roman and Stoic. The revelation confirms the younger Scipio's resolve to aim for eternal rewards rather than give in to temporal political expediencies, a conclusion which calls to mind Cicero's own attempts to maintain his integrity and preserve the republic despite temptations and dangers.

The revelation to Scipio contains a Platonic idea which became one of the most important features of Hellenistic religion and philosophy—astral theology and its eschatology.[114] Several of Plato's myths about the afterlife suggest the return of all souls to a supramundane region and the reward of good souls in a higher region before reincarnation. In the *Timaeus*, after the demiurge has created the heavens as a moving image of eternity, he creates the heavenly gods as intelligent souls with voluntary motion and places them on the stars, planets, and earth as "living beings divine and everlasting, which abide forever" (40b). Both Plato and Aristotle (e.g., *Laws* 886b; *de caelo* 1.9; 2.3) use the eternal and regular revolution of the heavens to prove the existence of the gods.

To these visible divinities, more orderly and just than the older deities of myth, the Hellenistic world transferred its piety and its belief in the gods' relation to human life. Already the *Epinomis*, written by Plato or a follower, stated the connection:

> And since the heaven is completely filled with living beings, let us say that all of these bring word of everything to one another and to the gods in the highest regions, since the middle forms of living beings move with easy flight both to the earth and to the whole heaven. (985b, Nilsson, trans.)[115]

The universe was still viewed as an organic whole with all parts connected to each other, but now the fixed movements of the heavens fixed events on earth. *Heimarmene*, the Fate imposed by the inevitable courses of the planetary spheres, predetermined all aspects of human life. The most common manifestation of the change was the popularity of astrology among all classes and levels of education. Stoic fatalism, with its deterministic universe developed out of the purest heavenly fire by a necessary nexus of causes, gave a metaphysical foundation to the Stoic ethical demand to live according to nature and reason; the same pure fire was present in human souls as the spark igniting the body.[116]

For the Stoics, neo-Pythagoreans, and middle Platonists, astral theology also made the study of the heavens and development of mathematics and astronomy a religious pursuit, and the contemplation of the stars a mystic experience. As Claudius Ptolemy, who codified Greek astronomy in the second century C.E., wrote:

> Mortal as I am, I know that I am born for a day, but when I follow the serried multitude of the stars in their circular course, my feet no longer touch the earth; I ascend to Zeus himself to feast me on ambrosia, the food of the gods. (Palatine Anthology, 9.77)[117]

Astral theology certainly affected the view of the afterlife for those who believed in the immortality of the soul and its divine origin. Now the soul clearly originated in the heavens and its goal was to return to its celestial home, whether forever or during its period of rest between reincarnations. Its journey home was depicted as an astronomical path through dangerous sublunar space which was full of demonic powers that could help or harm, then upward from the lowest planets to the highest stars, with the soul gradually being purified of its earthly stains and sins by elements such as the winds closest to the earth, the water from the clouds, and finally the fiery heat of heaven. The Stoics, whose philosophy was ultimately earth centered and emphasized the cultivation of virtue and performance of duty in one's fated life, argued whether the virtuous soul retained its individuality in death until *ekpyrosis* or was simply reabsorbed into the cosmic fire.

Catasterism, an old belief that the great were translated into stars, became very popular.[118] In Scipio Africanus the Younger's dream, he learns that the souls of the just and loyal inhabit the milky way when their lives are over (16). At *Tusculan Disputations* 1.12.28, written the year his beloved daughter died, Cicero asks, "Isn't the whole heaven full of mankind?" On a Greek epitaph also from the first century B.C.E. a dead youth consoles his mother: "Mother, do not weep for me. What's the use? You ought rather to reverence me, for I have become an evening star among the gods."[119] Roman political myth, which asserted that Romulus and Julius Caesar were taken up to the heavens at death and became stars, was made manifest when the Romans began to release eagles at the emperor's funeral as signs of his soul's ascent (v. Herodian *History* 4.2), and to depict departed rulers seated in chariots with the gods on their way up to the heavens. In a copy of an official proclamation from Egypt, the god Phoebus Apollo, in announcing Trajan's death and the accession of Hadrian, says, "In white-horsed chariot have I now mounted with Trajan to the heavens. . . ."[120] Mithraism offered ordinary men of the Greco-Roman world a similar path of ascent toward immortality.[121] As a private association with rites promising a privileged afterlife, Mithraism was related to other Hellenistic mystery cults. It differed, however, because it was an astral cult with a heavenly savior god less connected to earth and its subterranean fertility than such popular mystery cult figures as Isis, Serapis, Dionysus, or Cybele. Mithra, whatever his Persian origins, became worshipped as a god of light who, after a miraculous birth from a rock, saved creation from darkness by slaying a bull. The god of the sun then allied himself with Mithra (e.g., clasped his hand and shared a banquet with him), and carried him up into the highest heavens in his chariot. The slaying of the bull had astrological significance, for its iconography corresponds in some way to the constellations, and the *mystes* had to pass through seven grades of initiation connected to an ascent through the seven planetary spheres, which was symbolized by a ladder with seven rungs.

Mithraism has been called "a new cult defined out of and wholly in terms of Hellenistic cosmic structure."[122] Ulansey interprets it as the response of Stoicizing intellectuals to Hipparchus' discovery (c. 128 B.C.E.) of the slow movement of the celestial equator, which is known as the precession of the equinoxes. His finding made clear that the entire cosmic structure moved in a way previously unknown and that the spring equinox had earlier occurred in the region of Taurus the Bull instead of Aries. According to Ulansey, Mithra, related to Perseus as both hero and constellation, personified the divine power behind the change. The cosmic movement itself was associated iconographically with the symbolism of world cycles (e.g., Saturn transferring power to Jupiter; Phaethon, whom the Stoics connected with the *ekpyrosis*).[123] This new cult fused old rites, e.g., purification by water, old symbols of connection between gods and humans, e.g., meals shared, light, and ladders, and old vehicles for the out of body experience or otherworldly journey, e.g., chariot and ladder, with the new astronomy and astral theology.

Now every initiate, identified with Mithra through the initiation and cult practice, would likewise be able to ascend the upward path to immortality in the chariot of the sun.

Astral theology moved the location of the afterlife.[124] If the stars were divinities to whom pure souls hoped to return, then the Elysian Fields, the abode of the blessed, and the home of the gods now belonged in the superlunar heavens, much further away from humans on the earth. The netherworld, the old kingdom of Hades, no longer had a clearly defined place. To some, it was life on earth itself, where the sufferer was either atoning for the sins of his previous existence or being tortured by his own vices, with the old rivers Cocytus, Acheron, Periphlegethon, and Styx now symbolizing passions like anger, remorse, sadness and hate. Others located Hades in the Southern Hemisphere, the lower half of the known earth, or in the celestial hemisphere below the earth, with Tartarus at its lowest point, opposite Olympus at its highest. Once divided into separate spaces along different paths, the netherworld became the abode of only the incurably polluted souls of sinners. More than dark and gloomy, it was also malevolent, full of terror, torture, and terrible torturers. The lower atmosphere, as the place where the curable souls might be purified, functioned as a kind of purgatory where they moved about and suffered until they could ascend. Yet the popular depiction of Hades passed on by the poets and the mysteries persisted despite the attempts to tailor it to the new astronomy. It is this blend which Dante adapted for his Divine Comedy, using Virgil as his guide through the Inferno and Purgatory and adding later horrors and demons to classical images while he transposed both classicism and medieval Christianity by fusing them with references to contemporary Italian life.

The demand to keep the soul pure in preparation for its journey after death led to an increasing asceticism and rejection of earthly life.[125] Plato and his predecessors had already described the body as an alien garment, a tomb or prison of the soul. The *Phaedo* particularly emphasized the philosopher's desire to separate his true self as much as possible from his fleshly needs and desires. Plato's metaphysics, moreover, emphasized the defects in matter and granted the highest reality to the Forms. Thus the older idea of ritual purification became more and more associated with moral purification and with its external signs: chastity, sobriety, and all forms of physical self-denial, as well as with integrity and virtue.

Yet Plato acknowledged the essential goodness of the imperfect world, the value of sensible objects as reminders of Being, and the need to make Becoming approximate the divine model as closely as possible. Orphism, according to Alderink, understood the body as temporal in contrast with the immortal soul, rather than as evil in contrast with good. Therefore, he considers Orphic asceticism and vegetarianism as actions "in conformity with the rule and nature of Zeus by protecting and generating new life," rather than as rejections of the physical world.[126] The Stoics also stressed the need to tend to the soul rather than the body and to cultivate virtue, but their model was nature and their virtue involved obligation to earthly responsibilities.

Other circles, associated with the term Gnostics, however, did reject the visible universe and looked even higher for the source of their being and true divinity.[127] Gnostic ideas are not associated with any one cult or philosophy; rather they appear in a variety of texts, Jewish, pagan, and Christian, among proponents and opponents, from the first century B.C.E. on. Some scholars trace the development, like Mithraism, to Hipparchus' discovery of the celestial movements associated with the precession of the equinoxes, as discussed above; the knowledge that the fixed stars were really in motion challenged the fixed and limited cosmos of astral theology.[128] But Platonic influence is also clear, since Plato's model for the visible world, including the celestial divinities, was certainly a supra-natural Being. Moreover, the Gnostic cosmogony attributed the creation of the universe to a demiurge, a kind of divine man, perhaps based on the Form for Man posited in post-Platonic circles.[129]

Gnostic myths taught that our world is evil; it originated from the sin of that demiurge, who fell in love with the material world he was supposed to create and thus assumed a material body. Therefore, the world must be transcended. Although human beings are mortal, they also have an immortal part and can be redeemed if only they 'know' about their original and true self. Clement of Alexandria quotes the definition of true *gnosis* (knowledge):

> the knowledge of who we were, and what we have become,
> where we were or where we were placed, whither we hasten,
> from what we are redeemed, what birth is and what rebirth.
> (*Excerpts of Theodotus*, 78.2)[130]

Such *gnosis* does not derive from intellect or from philosophy, which is considered a human tradition of this world. Rather it is a secret knowledge which comes through revelation, often by means of a redeemer, a spiritual figure sent down from the highest realm to offer salvation to the true seekers. In the Corpus Hermeticum, a collection from the second century C.E., for example, the messenger from above is generally Hermes Trismegistus (Thrice-Great), identified with the Egyptian god Thoth. In Tractate 1, the revelation is couched as the out of body experience of a sleeper whose soul was awake (1.1; 1.30). A giant named Poimandres, the Mind of the Absolute, calls to him and presents an opaque vision which requires interpretation. The explication Poimandres offers includes a cosmogony, an anthropology explaining the dual nature of humans, and a description of the ascent by which humans lose their material bodies, their bodily senses, and then their seven irrational feelings and passions as they pass through the seven zones of heaven. At the eighth, they join others who have reached this purely spiritual state, and then, hearing the music of the powers above, they ascend as powers themselves and enter into God, for "this is the good end of those who have obtained knowledge, to become God," (26).[131] The recipient of this supreme vision is, like the apocalyptic Enoch and Er, charged with the mission to become a messenger himself, to dispel the ignorance which draws others toward death on earth and to lead them to the knowledge of god which will bring salvation (cf., 10.15).

Gnosticism was only one among many competing beliefs. In the pluralistic and basically tolerant Hellenistic world, many Greeks even denied that there was any afterlife or hope for salvation. The Epicureans, for example, developed the atomic theory to disprove the immortality of the soul and thus dispel fears of judgment after death which prevented enjoyment of life on earth. Pliny the Elder (23-79 C.E.) considered many of the beliefs we have discussed as "childish gibberish . . . of men greedy for everlasting life, and death Nature's particular boon" (*Natural History*, 7.188). In the second century C.E., Lucian could ridicule eschatological myth and philosophy in his *Dialogues of the Dead* and *Trip to Hades*. But Tacitus (c. 55-116 C.E.) expresses the feeling of the 'If. . .' inscriptions on tombs, as well as the hopes of many even today, in his eulogy for his father in law Agricola:

> If there is any place for the spirits of the just; if, as the wise believe, great souls do not perish with the body, may you rest in peace (*Agricola* 46).

Notes

1.   See Alexander P. D. Mourelatos, *The Route of Parmenides: A Study of Word, Image, and Argument in the Fragments* (New Haven: Yale University Press, 1970), pp. 12-46 for an analysis of the otherworldly journey motif and its relation to both revelation and speculation.

2.   The influence of shamanism on Greek thought has been much discussed by classical scholars. Jan Bremmer, *The Early Greek Concept of the Soul* (Princeton: Princeton University Press, 1983), pp. 25-48, summarizes and critiques the evidence.   See also Mircea Eliade, *Shamanism: Archaic Techniques of Ecstacy*, Trask, trans. (Pantheon: New York, 1964) for a general study of the phenomenon, and for an examination of the Greek evidence, see J. D. P. Bolton, *Aristeas of Proconnesus* (Oxford: Clarendon Press, 1962) as well as E. R. Dodds, *The Greeks and the Irrational* (Berkeley: University of California Press, 1959), pp. 140-147.

3.   For a summary and bibliography on the etymology of *psyche*, see David B. Claus, *Toward the Soul: An Inquiry into the Meaning of Psyche before Plato* (New Haven: Yale University Press, 1981), p. 93, n3 as well as Bremmer, pp. 21-22, esp. n21.

4.   Walter Burkert, *Lore and Science in Ancient Pythagoreanism*, trans. Minar (Cambridge: Harvard University Press, 1972), pp. 136-165, discusses Pythagoras and shamanism. Charles Kahn, "Religion and Natural Philosophy in Empedocles' Doctrine of the Soul," *Archiv fur Geschichteder Philosophie* 42 (1960): 3-35, considers whether Empedocles can be called a shaman, pp. 30-35.

5.   There are many   analyses of Plato's use of myth in general and of specific myths in their contexts.   For a summary with bibliography, see Michael Despland, *The Education of Desire: Plato and the Philosophy of Religion* (Toronto: University of Toronto Press, 1985), pp. 175-186 and references to myth in his index, as well as ns92-94 below.

6.   S. C. Humphreys, *The Family, Women and Death: Comparative Studies* (London: Routledge and Kegan Paul, 1983), pp. 144-146.   For discussions of the Greek attitude toward death and the concept of the good death, see Humphreys and Ian Morris, "Attitudes toward Death in Archaic Greece," *Classical Antiquity* 9 (1989): 296-320.

7.   Robert G. Garland, *The Greek Way of Death* (Ithaca: Cornell University Press, 1985), presents a general introduction to all aspects of death and the afterlife. See Donna C. Kurtz and John Boardman, *Greek Burial Customs* (Ithaca: Cornell University Press, 1971) for practices in different periods and places; Humphreys as well as Ian Morris, *Burial and Ancient Society: The Rise of the Greek City State* (Cambridge: Cambridge University Press, 1987) and *Death-Ritual and Social Structure in Classical Antiquity* (Cambridge: Cambridge University Press, 1992) for the relation of burial practices to political life and social structure; and Emily Vermeule, *Aspects of Death in Early Greek Art and Poetry* (Berkeley: University of California Press, 1979).

8.   Walter Burkert, *Greek Religion*, trans. Raffan (Cambridge: Harvard University Press, 1985), p. 192.

9.   P. 47. Pp. 41ff and ns, pp. 146-149, summarize the rites and taboos and their various interpretations. See Robert Parker, *Miasma: Pollution and Purification in Early Greek Religion* (Oxford: Clarendon Press, 1983), pp. 32- 63 for examination of attitudes and practices relating to birth and death. Pages 53-66 discuss theories of interpretation and explications of death as a rite of passage. See also Morris, Death-Ritual, pp. 9-10 for summary and bibliography.

10.   Both epitaphs are quoted from Kurtz and Boardman, 262. See Richmond Lattimore, *Themes in Greek and Latin Epitaphs* (Urbana: University of Illinois Press, 1942) for other epitaphs.

11.   See Garland, pp. 67-71 and notes for pictures, primary sources, and interpretations.

12.   Louis Richard Farnell, *Greek Hero Cults and Ideas of Immortality* (Oxford: Clarendon Press, 1921), pp. 397-398.

13.   Farnell, p. 399.

14.   Quoted from Lattimore, p. 77. Erwin Rohde, *Psyche: The Cult of Souls and Belief in Immortality among the Ancient Greeks*, trans. Hillis (1925; reprint, Chicago: Ares 1987), p. 543, refers to the "dubious "If"" and gives examples in n157.

15.   Quoted from Farnell, p. 401. For other examples, see 390ff. as well as Lattimore.

16.   Quoted from pp. 119 and 120 respectively. Pp. 114-120 and their notes present and interpret the evidence about offerings at the tomb. See also Burkert, *Greek Religion*, pp. 191-194 and notes, as well as Humphreys, pp. 153- 157 and Morris, *Death-Ritual*.

17.   P.243. His book surveys the entire phenomenon from its beginning, distinguishing the types and examining examples in detail. See also Rohde's chapter, pp. 115-155, as well as Burkert, *Greek Religion*, pp. 203- 208.

18.   See Farnell, p. 15; Rohde, pp. 117-121, for speculation on origins.

19.   *Greek Religion*, p.204.

20.   P. 138.

21.   Burkert, *Greek Religion*, p. 213, notes the similarity.

22.   *Greek Religion*, p. 211.

23.   Cited translations from the *Odyssey* are quoted from Robert Fitzgerald, *Homer: "The Odyssey"* (Garden City: Doubleday, 1963). Uncited ones are my own.

24.   *Greek Religion*, pp. 198 and 427, n36.

25.   Translation is quoted from M. L. West, *Hesiod: "Theogony"; "Works and Days"* (New York; Oxford Press, 1988), pp. 41-42. See his note on the passage, p. 76, as well as his commentary to the lines in his edition of *Works and Days* (Oxford: Clarendon Press, 1978), pp. 192-196. The last quote appears on p. 195.

26.   Jasper Griffin, *Homer on Life and Death* (Oxford: Clarendon Press, 1980), p. 90, n25, cites Homeric passages and bibliography on the poets'

derivation of Hades from *a-ides* ('unseen'). R. Renehan, "On the Greek Origins of the Concepts of Incorporeality and Immortality," *Greek Roman and Byzantine Studies* 2 (1980): 109 connects *aides* with the dead's separation from the living which rendered them 'invisible' to those on earth. He notes that the cap of Hades makes the wearer invisible in Homer, e.g., *Il.* 5.845.

27. See Claus, pp. 1, 61, 92 n1, for evidence and bibliography on other interpretations and their refutation.

28. Quoted from Bremmer, p. 9. See pp. 3-12 for an explanation and bibliography on similar dualistic conceptions of a free soul and a body soul in other early cultures. Among the comparative studies of this dualistic conception, Bremmer cites E. Arbman, "Untersuchungen zur primativen Seelen vor stellungen mit besonderer Rucksicht auf Indien, I," *Le Monde Oriental* 20 (1926): 85-222; A. Hultkrantz, *Conceptions of the Soul among North American Indians* (Stockholm: Ethnological Museum of Sweden, 1953); Janos Lang, "The Concept of the *Psyche*: Its Genesis and Evolution," *Acta Ethnographica Academiae Scientiarum Hungaricae* 22,1-2 (1973): 177-97, esp. 188ff. Bremmer, pp. 66-69, however, notes that Greek soul belief might best be characterized as "multiple" rather than dualistic since the Homeric body soul or life force is more complex than the dualistic conception of the body soul (as ego and breath) in other early cultures or the unified center of consciousness that the *psyche* later became.

29. Humphreys, p. 161. She remarks that their timeless state is symbolized by the forgetfulness induced by Lethe, the futility of the sinners' punishments, and even the unnatural abundance of three growing seasons on the Isle of the Blessed.

30. Fragments 137 Snell and 837 Pearson, as quoted in David G. Rice and John E. Stambaugh, *Sources for the Study of Greek Religion* (Missoula: Scholars Press, 1979), p. 191.

31. Susan Guettel Cole, "New Evidence for the Mysteries of Dionysus," *Greek Roman and Byzantine Studies* 2 (1980): 223-238.

32. Humphreys, p. 161, with reference to Vernant, Detienne, and Gernet.

33. Translated from Cole's citation, pp. 233-234.

34. For text, translation, and interpretation, see Hugh Lloyd-Jones' appendix to the 2nd edition of volume 2 of Herbert Weir Smyth, *Aeschylus: Plays and Fragments with an English Translation* (Cambridge: Harvard University Press, 1963), pp. 576-581.

35. There have been many important studies of this development. The fullest account and the one which has generated the most scholarly response is Rhohde's *Psyche*. See also J. Burnet, "The Socratic Doctrine of the Soul," *Essays and Addresses* (London: Chatto & Windus: 1929), pp. 126-162; Burkert, *Greek Religion*, pp. 195-196, 300-301, 319-321; Claus; Dodds, *Greeks and the Irrational*, pp. 137-206, 213-235; W. K. C. Guthrie, *In The Beginning: Some Greek Views on the Origins of Life and the Early State of Man* (Ithaca: Cornell University Press, 1957), pp. 46-62; Werner Jaeger, *The Theology of the Early Greek Philosophers*, trans. Robinson. (Oxford: Clarendon Press, 1936), pp. 73-89; and Renehan.

36. See Bremmer, pp. 53-69 for summary and Claus, pp. 11-60, for detailed analysis of these terms in their contexts.

37. Quoted from Lang, p. 193 and Jaeger, p. 82 respectively. See Claus, pp. 13-15, and Bremmer, pp. 53-63, for refutations of theories that terms in Homer are connected to specific physical functions, organs, fluids, or gases. Renehan, p. 111, connects *psyche* with *nephesh*, and *thumos* with an original blood-soul, citing Rose OCD2; he comments that "The expelled breath is easily conceived as continuing to exist after death, whereas blood, tangible and visible, can now be seen to have become lifeless."

38. Claus, especially pp. 45-46.

39. See n28 above.

40. Claus, pp. 66-68, collects and assesses later references to *psyche* as a shade.

41. Pp. 25-53.

42. Pp. 98-99.

43. Claus, p. 100, charts the different uses of these terms in Homer and Euripides.

44. Examples have been culled from Claus' analysis, pp. 69-89.

45. Quoted from pp. 23-24. He quotes and summarizes Arbman and Hultkranz. See n28

46. Lattimore, p. 45.

47. G. S. Kirk, J. E. Raven, and M. Schofield, (abb. KRS) *The Presocratic Philosophers: A Critical History with a Selection of Texts* (Cambridge: Cambridge University Press, 1983), pp. 95-99. All translations of the Presocratics are quoted from this book and referred to by their KRS fragment numbers unless otherwise noted. For an examination of the origins of and philosophical problems associated with Greek natural theology, see L. P. Gerson, *Gods and Greek Philosophy: Studies in the Early History of Natural Philosophy* (London: Routledge, 1990).

48. KRS, pp. 158-161.

49. KRS, p. 202, fragment 227.

50. KRS, pp. 203-208.

51. KRS, pp. 440-445. The quotations come from KRS fragments 602, and 603 respectively.

52. *Greeks and the Irrational*, p. 139.

53. *Greeks and the Irrational*, p. 151. On p. 150, and n99, Dodds discusses Nilsson's view of the doctrine of rebirth as "pure logic."

54. See Herbert Strainge Long, "A Study of the Doctrine of Metempsychosis in Greece from Pythagoras to Plato" (Ph.D. diss., Princeton University, 1948) for a detailed examination.

55. Burkert, *Lore and Science*, pp. 155-165.

56. See Burkert, *Lore and Science*, pp. 133-147, and Long's chapter, pp. 13-28, as well as KRS, pp. 219-222, 236-238. The reference to *psyche* is cited from KRS p. 216, fragment 260. For a collection of sources, see Kenneth Guthrie et. al, *The Pythagorean Sourcebook and Library; An Anthology of Ancient Writings which relate to Pythagoras and Pythagorean Philosophy* (Grand Rapids: Phanes, 1987).

57. Burkert, *Lore and Science*, p. 176; KRS p. 229.

58. Burkert, *Lore and Science*, p. 185. See pp. 166-192 for a list and interpretation of the *akousmata*.

59. Quoted from KRS p. 232, fragment 277.

60. In a fragment and passage cited by KRS pp. 235-6 as fragments 282 and 283 respectively.

61. C. M. Bowra, *Pindar* (Oxford; Clarendon Press, 1964), p. 94. See also Long's chapter on Pindar, pp. 29-44.

62. The translation of fragment 33 is quoted from Long p. 39. Long's words are quoted from p. 43. He gives bibliography for the interpretation of the phrase "ancient woe's atonement" as reciprocity for some kind of original sin, e.g., the Titans' dismemberment of Persephone's son Zagreus/Dionysus, but himself considers the suffering as recompense for sins in the first sojourn on earth. Larry Alderink, *Creation and Salvation in Ancient Orphism* (Chico, Calif.: Scholars Press, 1981), pp. 72-74, however, interprets the passage to show that humans must pay a penalty for an event which transpired among the gods prior to their creation, for they were created because of the Titans' rebellion against Zeus, symbolized by the death and dismemberment of Dionysus. He connects human sin, which is judged and punished after death, with imitating Titanic behavior by indulging in rebellion and bloodshed instead of behaving piously.

63. For Empedocles' ideas, see Kahn; Long's chapter, pp. 45-62; D. O'Brien, *Empedocles' Cosmic Cycles: A Reconstruction from the Fragments and Secondary Sources* (Cambridge: Cambridge University Press, 1969); G. Zuntz, *Persephone: Three Essays on Religion and Thought in Magna Graecia* (Oxford: Clarendon Press, 1971), pp. 181-276; as well as KRS, pp. 313-317.

64. KRS fragments 407, 401, and 409, pp. 315-17, are cited in the preceding sentence. Dodds, *Greeks and the Irrational*, pp. 154-155 and n123, accepts the tradition which makes Empedocles the most puritan of all.

65. KRS fragments 417 and 399 respectively, pp. pp. 319 and 313.

66. Long p. 59 suggests the former, KRS p.316 the latter.

67. P. 250.

68. Kahn, pp. 6-7, quotes the text and emphasizes this point.

69. Alderink summarizes the bibliography and examines the texts and passages related to the cosmogony and anthropology. On p. 87 he characterizes Orphism as a "mood" or "an attitude" or a "structure of thought fluid enough to incorporate external elements . . . and to lend its own elements to other religious forms and movements." M. L. West, *The Orphic Poems* (Oxford: Clarendon Press, 1983), examines the historical development of Orphism.

70. See Zuntz, 302ff, for text and commentary. Burkert, *Greek Religion*, p. 295, and West, *Orphic Poems*, pp. 22-23, also discuss these texts. Alderink, pp. 59-65, examining passages from Plato, emphasizes that the Orphics clearly separated the body and the soul, but that nothing indicates that the body itself was the source of evil.

71. Burkert, *Greek Religion*, pp. 276-278. See George E. Mylonas, *Eleusis and the Eleusinian Mysteries* (Princeton: Princeton University Press, 1961), as well as Cole and Zuntz. For a information, bibliography, and texts relating to mystery religions, see Marvin W. Meyer, ed., *The Ancient Mysteries: A Sourcebook* (San Franciso: Harper and Row, 1987); and Kurt Rudolf, "Mystery Religions," in *Religions of Antiquity: Religion, History and Culture Selections from the Encyclopedia of Religion*, Robert Seltzer, ed. (New York: Macmillan, 1987), pp. 272-85..

72. *Greek Religion*, pp. 289-290.

73. E. R. Dodds cites Verrall's translation in his commentary to line 75 in *Euripides' "Bacchae"* (Oxford: Clarendon Press, 1944). His introduction to this edition, esp. ix- xxxv, is a classic statement of the nature of Dionysiac religion.

74. Porphyry's words are quoted from Rice and Stambaugh, p. 190.

75. Dodds, *Greeks and Irrational*, p. 154 and n121; Alderink, pp. 80-82.

76. Samuel Scolnicov, "Reason and Passion in the Platonic Soul," *Dionysius* 2 (1978): 37-38.

77. P.39.

78. Dodds, *Greeks and the Irrational*, pp. 188-195, discusses the reaction against the enlightenment. West, *Orphic Poems*, p. 20, connects it specifically with the war and plague.

79. There is an enormous bibliography of scholarship on Plato's life and the development of his ideas. See Despland's list. I have particularly consulted Paul Friedlander, *Plato*. 3 vols., trans. Meyerhoff (New York: Pantheon, 1958-1969), as well as Despland.

80. *Greeks and Irrational*, p. 208.

81. Claus, pp. 156-180, examines the evidence for Socrates' use of the term.

82. Claus, pp. 141-155, 175-180, examines the use of the term and the soul/body pair in Demosthenes, the medical texts, and Plato's *Gorgias*. See also Dodds, *Greeks and Irrational*, p. 209 and n4.

83. P.39.

84. *Greeks and Irrational*, p. 209f. The paragraph below summarizes and quotes from p. 210.

85. Despland, p. 204. Despland is summarizing and using the terms of A. Dies, *Autour de Platon* 2 (Paris: Beauchesne, 1927), pp. 400-449 and A. J. Festugiere, *Contemplation et vie contemplative selon Platon*, (1935; reprint, Paris: Vrin, 1967), pp. 75- 370. For further information on Plato's use of the terms of the mysteries, see G. J. De Vries, "Mystery Terminology in Aristophanes and Plato," *Mnemosyne* 26 (1973): 1-8; I. M. Linforth, "The Corybantic Rites in Plato, " *University of California Publications in Classical Philology* 13.5 (1946): 121-162 and "Telesic Madness in Plato, *Phaedrus* 244DE," *University of California Publications in Classical Philology* 13.6 (1946): 163-172.

86. As quoted from Bruno Snell, *The Discovery of the Mind; The Origins of European Thought*, trans. Rosenmeyer (New York: Harper Torchbooks, 1960), p. 223.

87. Despland, pp. 78-84; 164-165; 198-199; 223-230. He emphasizes the interplay of *mythos* and *logos*. See also Friedlander 1, pp. 154-170 and Scolnicov, pp. 44-45.

88. Platonic scholars generally agree on a division of the dialogues into three major groups, but it is difficult to establish a precise chronology within the groups. Therefore, scholars debate whether contradictions between dialogues are related to the concentration of each on the issue at hand or are actually products of a development of Plato's ideas. See T. M. Robinson, *Plato's Psychology* (Toronto: University of Toronto Press, 1970) for a detailed examination of Plato's ideas about the soul.

89. In "Plato and the Irrational," *Journal of Hellenic Studies* 65 (1945): 16-17. The discussion below is based primarily on his assessment, pp. 16-45.

90. Friedlander 1, pp. 46-69, discusses the erotic as a path to the intellectual vision, and what lies beyond it.

91. Quoted from R. G. Bury, *Plato, with an English Translation*. v. 7. Loeb Classical Library (Cambridge: Harvard University Press, 1952), pp. 530-531.

92. Despland discusses myth and Platonic myth, pp. 175-180, citing primarily W. Hirsch, *Plato's Weg zum Mythos* (Berlin: Walter de Gruyter, 1971). See also Friedlander 1, pp. 171-210, as well as G. R. F. Ferrari, *Listening to the Cicadas: A Study of Plato's "Phaedrus"* (Cambridge: Cambridge University Press, 1987), pp. 11-12, 32-34, 113-139; J. A. Stewart, *The Myths of Plato* (London: Centaur Press, 1960); and Robert Zaslavsky, *Platonic Myth and Platonic Writing* (Washington: University Press of America, 1981).

93. John Burnet, *Plato's "Phaedo"* (Oxford: Clarendon Press, 1911), p. 19. Although all the authors listed above discuss *mythos* and *logos*, Zaslovsky surveys their uses in context and concludes that Plato employs both terms to refer to accounts that are more or less true and that the distinction has more to do with the type of account: e.g., *logos*, when used in a narrow sense, is a "descriptive and/or classificatory and/or diairetic account," and *mythos* "a genetic and/or originally and/or synagogic account" (p. 219). David White, *Myth and Metaphysics in Plato's "Phaedo"* (London: Associated University Press, 1989), p. 284, suggests too that "the metaphysics is only provisional," and that the dialogue presents a vision of the philosophic life, with its interplay of reason and imagination, metaphysics and myth, as a model to emulate which produces a good happy life and a good death.

94. For general discussions of the eschatological myths, see Friedlander, pp. 180-190, Despland, pp. 179-80, Long, pp. 63-92. On p. 199, Friedlander notes how the divine cosmos becomes more important in each eschatological myth.

95. In his commentary on the passage in *Plato: "Gorgias"* (Oxford: Clarendon Press, 1959), p. 377. See this commentary, Stewart, pp. 133-145, and Zaslavsly, pp. 195-198, as well as works listed in notes 92 and 94 above for discussions of the myths of the *Gorgias*.

96. See Burnet's commentary, Stewart, pp. 103-132, and White for detailed analysis of myths and references to earlier ideas.

97. See Stewart, pp. 146-178, Zaslavsky, pp. 141-194, as well as Francis MacDonald Cornford, *"The Republic" of Plato* (New York: Oxford University Press, 1945), pp. 348-359.

98. See R. Hackforth's commentary, *Plato's "Phaedrus"* (Cambridge: Cambridge University Press, 1952); Ferrari, Stewart, pp. 381-357, and Zaslavsky, pp. 55-139, as well as works listed in note 85 above, for detailed analysis of myths in context.

99. Despland, pp. 154-157; Friedlander, pp. 52-55.

100. B. A. Van Groningen, *In the Grip of the Past: Essay on an Aspect of Greek Thought* (Leiden: E. J. Brill, 1953), p. 108. General ideas presented below are drawn especially from chapter 9, "Counterargument: the Future," pp. 90-120. Van Groningen contrasts the Greek and Judaeo-Christian views on p. 120 and on p. 115 notes that ancient Greece did not know the word "eschatology" or conceive of anything which "looks to the most remote future and nothing else."

101. Quoted from James J. O'Hara, *Death and the Optimistic Prophecy in Vergil's "Aeneid"* (Princeton: Princeton University Press, 1990), p.6. See this work for detailed analysis of the prophecies in relation to Vergil's audience's knowledge of the actual events. For ambiguities and devices which dramatize the age's conflict between hope and fear, see Susan Ford Wiltshire, *Public and Private in Vergil's "Aeneid"* (Amhurst: University of Massachusetts Press, 1989).

102. Van Groningen, pp. 62-79, esp. p. 68. He examines the tension between *initium* and *principium* in this chapter on philosophy. Gerson, pp. 5-13, discusses the concept of *arche* and traces "the attempts to show how a cause can be a principle as well" as marking "the stages in the development of Greek philosophical theology" (p. 7). See also Thorlief Boman, *Hebrew Thought compared with Greek*, trans. Moreau (Philadelphia: Westminster Press, 1960), pp. 27-33; 123-183 and Chester Starr, "Historical and Philosophical Time," *History and Theory* Beiheft 6 (1966): 30-32.

103. Quoted by Francis MacDonald Cornford, *Plato's Cosmology: "The Timaeus" of Plato translated with a Running Commentary* (London: Routledge & Kegan Paul, 1937), p. 26. Cornford asserts as he goes through the *Timaeus* that since the Demiurge is "mythical," and "was not really a 'maker,' there was no moment of creation" (p. 26). Boman, p. 174, emphasizes that Plato's *Timaeus* is giving a metaphysical and religious account of creation "where it is a matter of the relation of the world and man to God, not the physical and natural one Aristotle was looking for."

104. Burkert, *Lore and Science*, pp. 322-332, summarizes the Greek ideas about the circle, particularly in relation to geometry and astronomy. He refers to the 'sacred circle' at *Il.* 18.504, a Pythagorean *akousma* which names the circle and the sphere as most beautiful, and passages of Plato on circular planetary movement, with bibliography. Cornford, *Cosmology*, pp.

103-104, notes the connection of the circle with the cycle of natural and human life, from birth to death to rebirth.

105. P. 117. For Greek views of time, in addition to Cornford's commentary on the passage, see John F. Callahan, *Four Views of Time in Ancient Philosophy* (1948; reprint, New York: Greenwood, 1968), pp. 3-87. and J. G. Whitrow, *Time in History* (New York: Oxford University Press, 1988), pp. 37-51. Burkert, *Lore and Science*, pp. 314-315 and esp. n86, discusses Greek ideas related to the Great Year. Boman, pp. 123-153, contrasts Greek and Hebrew views.

106. Jasper Griffin, *Virgil* (Oxford: Oxford University Press, 1986), pp. 28-29. He notes the unhappy results of the marriage (daughters and desertion for Cleopatra) as well as the number of traditional materials (Catullus, Greek myth, pastoral, prophetic books) Virgil used in this unusual eclogue. For detailed analysis and bibliography, see John Van Sickle, *A Reading of Virgil's Messianic Eclogue* (New York: Garland, 1992), as well as Paul Alpers, *The Singer of the Eclogues: A Study of Virgilian Pastoral* (Berkeley: University of California Press, 1979), pp. 157-190; Eleanor Windsor Leach, *Vergil's Eclogues: Landscapes of Experience* (Ithaca: Cornell University Press, 1974), pp. 216-231; M. Owen Lee, *Death and Rebirth in Virgil's Arcadia* (Albany: State University of New York Press, 1989), pp. 77-89.

107. West, in his commentary on the passage, notes the similarities, p.175, considers the sources, and provides bibliography on later Greek uses of the myth, p.177.

108. See G. W. Trompf, *The Idea of Historical Recurrence in Western Thought: From Antiquity to the Reformation* (Berkeley: University of California Press, 1979), pp. 7-13 for a summary of Greek catastrophe theory with primary sources and bibliography, as well as Guthrie 63-79.

109. As quoted by Whitrow, p.43. For Stoic conceptions of *ekpyrosis*, see Michael Lapidge, "Stoic cosmology," pp. 161- 185 in John M. Rist, ed., *The Stoics* (Berkeley: University of California Press, 1978), and J. Mansfield, "Providence and the Destruction of the Universe in early Stoic Thought with some remarks on the "Mysteries of Philosophy," pp. 129-188 in M. J. Vermaseren, ed., *Studies in Hellenistic Religion* (Leiden: E. J. Brill, 1979). Fragments related to *ekpyrosis* are collected in Ioannes ab Arnim, *Stoicorum Veterum Fragmenta* (Stuttgart: Teubner, 1964).

110. For discussions of the myth, see Cornford, *Cosmology*, pp. 206-208, Friedlander 1, pp. 204-207, Guthrie pp. 71-71, Stewart, pp. 192-207, and Trompf, p.11.

111. For an analysis of the disappointments and fears, as well as the hopes, see works cited in n101.

112. For translation and commentary on this fragmentary work, see George Holland Sabine and Stanley Barney Smith, *"On the Commonwealth"*. *Marcus Tullius Cicero* (Columbus: Ohio State University Press, 1929).

113. Sabine and Smith, pp. 254-255, translate this passage from Macrobius.

114.   For a detailed analysis of this development, see Martin P. Nilsson, "The Origin of Belief among the Greeks in the Divinity of the Heavenly Bodies," *Harvard Theological Review* 33 (1940): 1-8; Pierre Boyance, "La Religion Astrale de Platon a Ciceron," *Revue des etudes grecques* 65 (1952): 312-350; Franz Cumont, *Afterlife in Roman Paganism.* (1922; reprint, New York: Dover, 1959) and *Astrology and Religion among the Greeks and Romans* (1912; reprint, New York: Dover, 1960). Luther Martin, *Hellenistic Religions: An Introduction* (New York: Oxford University Press, 1987), pp. 6-10 gives a succinct statement of what was in effect a 'paradigm shift' in ancient cosmology.

115.   As translated by Nilsson, p. 5.

116.   For a definition of *Heimarmene* and its relation to divination, see S. Sambursky, *Physics of the Stoics* (London: Routledge & Kegan Paul, 1959), pp. 57-71. Cumont, *Astrology*, pp. 30-56, traces the movement from east to west; he emphasizes that the developments in Greece are post-Platonic and, noting the congruence of Chaldean determinism and Stoic *heimarmene*, attributes the spread to the Hellenistic Stoic teachers with eastern backgrounds, as well as to the discoveries of astronomy. For a summary with primary sources, see George Luck, *Magic and Occult in the Greek and Roman World* (Baltimore: Johns Hopkins University Press, 1985), pp. 309-358. See J. M. Rist, *Stoic Philosophy* (Cambridge: Cambridge University Press, 1969), pp. 112-132 and the articles in Rist, *Stoics*, Margaret E. Reesor, "Necessity and Fate in Stoic Philosophy," pp. 187-202, and Charlotte Stough, "Stoic Determinism and Moral Responsibility," pp. 203-232, for moral problems associated with Fate. See also Martin's summary, pp. 38-44.

117.   As quoted in Cumont, *Astrology*, p. 81. Cumont devotes two chapters to this phenomenon.

118.   Cumont, *Afterlife*, traces this development, pp. 103-107, 112-115.

119.   Lattimore, p.35. On pp. 311-312, he notes Christian parallels.

120.   Quoted from Ramsey MacMullen and Eugene Lane, eds., *Paganism and Christianity 100- 425 C.E.: A Sourcebook* (Minneapolis: Fortress, 1992), p. 77.

121.   For detailed examinations and interpretations of the evidence, which is mainly iconographical, see Roger Beck, "Mithraism since Franz Cumont," *Aufsteig und Nierdergang der Romischen Welt* II, 17.4 (Berlin: Walter der Gruyter, 1984); Ugo Bianchi, ed., *Mysteria Mythrae* (Leiden: E. J. Brill, 1979); Franz Cumont, *The Mysteries of Mithra,* 2nd ed. revised by T. McCormack (New York: Dover, 1956); David Ulansey, *The Origins of the Mithraic Mysteries: Cosmology and Salvation in the Ancient World* (Oxford: Oxford University Press, 1989); and M. J. Vermaseren, *Mithras. The Secret God*, trans. T. & V. Magaw (New York: Barnes and Noble, 1963); as well as Martin's summary, pp. 113-118.

122.   Martin, p. 117.

123.   Pp. 76-87 for Hipparchus' discovery and its effect on astral religion; pp. 98-103 for iconography of world cycles. Ulansey interprets

Mithra as the equivalent of both the hero Perseus and the constellation closest to Taurus the Bull.

124.　Cumont, *Afterlife*, pp. 76-77.

125.　Cumont, *Astrology*, pp. 82-84.

126.　Pp. 80-83. The words are quoted from p. 83.

127.　See summaries in Martin, pp. 134-154 and Gilles Quispel, "Gnosticism," pp. 259-271 in Seltzer. For recent studies, see Werner Foerster, *Gnosis; a Selection of Gnostic Texts, I. Patristic Evidence*, trans. Wilson (Oxford: Clarendon Press, 1972) and Kurt Rudolph, *Gnosis: The Nature and History of Gnosticism*, trans. Wilson (San Francisco; Harper and Row, 1983). Rudolph, p. 60, contrasts the "procosmic dualism" of Greek philosophy with "anti cosmic" developments in gnosticism.

128.　Martin, pp. 135-136.

129.　Quispel, p.261.

130.　As quoted by Martin, 141.

131.　Foerster, pp. 333-334. He translates the entire tractate, pp. 328-335, and comments in the introduction, pp. 326-328, that this pagan Gnostic writing has a more positive picture of nature than other examples of gnosticism from Christian circles.

Sinai III: The Road to Redemption
and the World to Come—The Afterlife

The Afterlife in the Apocrypha and the Pseudepigrapha

Later Hebrew conceptions of the afterlife represent a confluence of earlier Hebrew traditions with Greek and Persian ideas. The richness and diversity of the afterlife scenarios reflect the openness of Second Temple Judaism which in turn reflected the pluralism of the Hellenistic world. The resurrection scenario of Dan. 12:1-3 with its earlier biblical overtones became the central plot with a variety of subplots. The old biblical conception of judgment that takes place in the netherworld and is also a feature of the resurrection in Dan. 12:1-3 is found throughout the apocalyptic literature but with some variations. The heavenly book appears in some descriptions (Testament of Judah 20) but not in others (i.e., The Book of Jubilees and the Assumption of Moses). In the Book of Enoch the heavenly book is connected with Israel's angelic advocate who is also its scribe (1 Enoch 89:61-65, 68-71, 76 f.; 90:17,20). The image of a heavenly prosecutor and defense attorney connected to the judgment scene though standard in the apocalypses (Jub. 17:15-18; 12; 48:2-4; Testament of Levi 5:6 f.; Testament of Dan 6:1-5) has its roots in the Hebrew Bible (Zech. 1:12; 3:1-2; Job 1:6-12). In Dan. 12:1 the reference to Michael "who stands" connotes standing in a disputation in a court of law (cf. Deut. 19:17; Josh. 20:6; Ezek. 44:24; Isa. 50:8).[1]

In the Testament of the Twelve Patriarchs two angels who serve as an individual's guides during life assume a judicial function as advocate and accuser at the time of death during the review of the lifetime. The angel of peace then leads the soul of the departed righteous into eternal life (Testament of Asher 1:3, 8, 9; 3:2; 6:4,5,6; Testament of Benjamin 6:1. Cf. 1 Enoch 40:8; 53:4; 54:4; 56:2 for the angel of peace as a heavenly guide). Plato also speaks of a daimon who guides the individual in life and who after death leads the soul to the place where the dead are congregated and where judgment is pronounced.[2] Quite possibly Greek influence and biblical tradition are interwoven in this apocalyptic text.

For the author of Dan. 12:1-3 judgment is directed at a specific, unjust, historical persecution limited in scope, in time and in place and is part of the climax of an apocalypse. But in 1 Enoch 22, 102-104 and in the Testament of Judah 25 judgment is no longer tied to a specific situation but has become generalized and globalized. In the Testament of Judah 25 judgment is disconnected from the apocalyptic climax. The text in Daniel refers to a select group of the knowledgeable who will merit ascension to heaven but the Assumption of Moses 10:9 speaks of all the righteous of Israel ascending to heaven.

Who are the wicked and what happens to them? In the Daniel apocalypse they are specified in a cryptic manner as the forces of Antiochus Epiphanes and the Jewish Hellenizers assisting him in the persecution of the Jewish pietists loyal to the covenant.[3] But in 1 Enoch 102-104 they are generalized to include all the disbelieving wealthy and powerful whose religious practice spans the spectrum from idolatry to concern for the Torah but whose hypocritical, lawless, immoral conduct is strengthened by their denial of reward and punishment in the afterlife. In their own eyes they are pillars of righteousness because they interpret the theology of the Deuteronomist historian as equating good fortune in this world with covenantal loyalty and moral rectitude. In the Wisdom of Solomon the wicked are in a state of spiritual non-existence even in their lifetime and this death in life is confirmed with the demise of the body when they go to their eternal destruction. Conversely, the immortality of the righteous is inherent while they are still alive. Thus for the author of this work reward and immortality, punishment and destruction are a continuum traversing life and death; for this reason he has no eschatological schedule for the afterlife.

In contrast the apocalyptic authors of 1 Enoch 22 and the Psalms of Solomon made a distinction between sinners on whom judgment has been executed in their lifetime and those who in their earthly lives did not experience the full working out of the law of reciprocity. The former remain in *Sheol* when the apocalyptic judgment ensues but the latter are resurrected to receive the full measure of recompense for their deeds. In these sources judgment also means a resurrection of the righteous who are rewarded. Thus in apocalyptic works such as 1 Enoch 22, the Psalms of Solomon and 4 Ezra 7, the specificity of judgment in Dan. 12:1-3 is considerably broadened with 4 Ezra 7 envisioning a universal resurrection and judgment. The author of 1 Enoch 22:1-14 conceived of some of the wicked remaining in *Sheol*, which, in Dan. 12:1-3, 2 Macc. 7:9,11,14, and 1 Enoch 102:4 f., is also the domicile of the righteous. Thus *Sheol* in these sources is viewed in a neutral light. Unlike some of the earlier texts of the Bible it is no longer associated exclusively with the wicked dead but is an undifferentiated resting place for righteous and wicked.

In 1 Enoch 22:1-14 we find for the first time *Sheol* separated into four divisions in which the following dwell after death:

1). The righteous who have died a natural death.
2). The righteous who have been martyred.
3). Sinners upon whom judgment has not been executed in their lifetime.
4). Sinners upon whom judgment has been executed in their lifetime.[4]

Like the Hebrew *Sheol*, the Greek Hades was also undifferentiated as a universal resting place for good and evil and later became compartmentalized for individuals of differing fate. Since the Greek development took place much earlier than 1 Enoch 22:1-14, the possibility of Greek influence cannot be denied.

As in the case of divine judgment, a similar broadening of the concept of resurrection is evident in the development leading from Daniel to the apocalypses. In Daniel the resurrection is intended as a just reward for the righteous whose untimely death as martyrs prevented them from witnessing and enjoying the blessings of the new and redeemed world. In 1 Enoch the resurrection is intended not only for martyrs but for all who have suffered unjustly. Moreover, in Enoch the resurrection is not only a solution to a problem of theodicy involving unjust and violent death. It is a wider solution to the theological quandary of suffering and oppression in general that does not necessarily lead to death. In Daniel, the Wisdom of Solomon and 2 Maccabees 7 the resurrection is a vindication of the deeds of the saints who have actually been condemned to death for their behavior. In Enoch the scene shifts from the experience of martyrs to the victims of unbelief and immorality. The resurrection is intended to vindicate the saints as a demonstration to lawless skeptics who argue that righteousness is unrewarded.[5]

As to the nature of the resurrection, the laconic brevity of Daniel that omits all details is expanded by the literal minded author of the Syriac Apocalypse of Baruch who questions whether the resurrected body will suffer the physical ailments and deficiencies that characterized life in this world. The dead he concludes must be raised with their former bodies so that the living can recognize them and thus be convinced of the miracle of resurrection (2 Baruch 49-51). Far more philosophical is the author of Book IV of the Sibylline Oracles. As in Daniel, divine judgment and the resurrection are but aspects of the apocalyptic destruction of all life. The last lines of the book imply a cyclical return to creation particularly since resurrection is described in the following scenario:

"God Himself will *again* form the bones and ashes of men" (Sibylline Oracles 4:181). Platonic and Stoic cosmological theories about the renewal of the universe may be combined here with the Hebrew resurrection concept.

Another example of the merging of Greek philosophical concepts and Hebrew biblical tradition may be found in those apocalyptic works that *do not* envision a resurrection of the body. These texts speak only of the spirits of the righteous enjoying the bliss of heaven (Jub. 23:29-30; 1 Enoch 22:9), a resurrection of the *spirits* of the sinful for punishment (1 Enoch 22:11,13), immortality of the soul (Wisdom of Solomon 1:15; 5:15) and immediate ascension to heaven (4 Macc. 9:22; 13:17; 16:25; 17:18 f.) for eternal life and immortality (4 Macc. 7:3; 9:22; 14:5 f.; 15:3; 16:13; 17:12).[6] It is clear that ascension to heaven and immortality immediately upon death are outgrowths of the biblical traditions of Enoch and Elijah and apocalyptic ascension texts. Eternal life and immortality can be traced to the conception inherent in the covenant relationship and enhanced by Hebrew wisdom that fellowship with God is the highest good. The righteous already enjoy this blessing in their lifetime and that continues after death so that for them resurrection is not relevant. The immortality of the soul is clearly a Greek concept but as noted above it is not entirely absent from the Hebrew Bible. Similarly, the resurrection of the spirit derives equally from Greek and Hebrew ideas of immortality of the soul and the belief in resurrection.

These views of the immortality of the soul without a bodily resurrection held by Hellenistic Diaspora Jews influenced Jews in the land of Israel who retained a belief in a bodily resurrection. As noted above, in 1 Enoch 22:14 we find for the first time divisions in *Sheol* for the righteous and the wicked. For the righteous, however, it is only a temporary domicile until the resurrection and their final reward. A second stage of this development elevated the intermediary state of the righteous from *Sheol* to heaven where they await the resurrection. Josephus expresses the older view of the intermediate state of the righteous in *Sheol* (*Antiquities* 18, 1, 3) but also the newer view of the temporary residence of the righteous in heaven (*Wars of the Jews* 3,8,5). Similarly, the dominant outlook of the rabbis located the intermediate state of the righteous in the heavenly Garden of Eden.[7] But the older conception persisted as a minority view. Thus the third century C.E. Amora R. Johanan commenting on Ps. 22:30 implied that after a preliminary vision of God the souls of the righteous and the wicked descend to *Sheol* to await the resurrection.[8] In Greek tradition, in poetry and in philosophy, we find a similar elevation of the righteous from an intermediate state in Hades to a more blessed temporary residence in the heavens.[9]

There is no mention of resurrection in 1 Maccabees for two reasons. First, as noted in the previous chapter this work suggests that martyrdom can be in vain and the belief in resurrection could prompt Jews to accept martyrdom rather than organize militarily to defeat their oppressors. Secondly, as Nickelsburg points out, the work is a Hasmonean court history written at a time when the Hasmonean dynasty was at the pinnacle of its success. The persecution that inspired the belief in resurrection and divine judgment in Dan. 12:1-3 had long since passed; the new rich and powerful class ruling Judea, who may be the same as the sinners of 1 Enoch 94-104, would not espouse a theology that questioned their success in this world and their salvation in the next world.[10]

The Qumran Dead Sea Scrolls also do not mention resurrection. Nickelsburg argues that though the community had suffered persecution it had not led to death, so that the motivation of Dan. 12:1-3 was absent. Moreover, the eschatological immediacy and the strong predestinarian orientation of the Qumran community gave its members the sense that they were already part of the new world and the new life, so there was no need to contemplate future death and resurrection.[11] But it seems to me that there is a much more compelling reason for the absence of resurrection from the Scrolls. Recent scholarship has pointed to the fact that the Qumran community's ritual-legal (*halakic*) practices are at odds with Pharisaic and later talmudic Judaism but are almost identical with those of the Sadducees. Thus it is now apparent that we must revise our monolithic view of the Qumran community and its belief system. The community consisted of Essenes to be sure, but Essenes who practiced a Sadducean *halakah* and quite possibly held Sadducean beliefs in certain areas.[12] We know from Josephus and the New Testament that the Sadducees denied the doctrine of the resurrection of the body and the immortality of the soul.[13] Thus the absence of references to resurrection in the Qumran Scrolls reflects, to a certain extent, Sadducean doctrine. As to the immortality of the soul the Scrolls speak of eternal life but it does not begin after death for it is already present during the lifetime of the individual. This is an echo of the wisdom idea of eternal fellowship with God that traverses life and death discussed above. Such a view dovetails well with the predestinarian theology of the Qumran community who believed that the people predestined for eternal life (i.e., the members of the sect) are already living that life.[14]

The views of divine judgment and the resurrection as part of the end of days scenario in Dan. 12:1-3 were an *ad hoc* solution to an existential crisis of theodicy triggered by the persecutions of the Maccabean period. While some of the later apocalypses retain the specific historical persecution framework, others generalize and universalize divine judgment and the resurrection as a result of the internal religious needs of Second Temple Judaism and Persian influence. But there were those apocalyptic writers who clung to the old biblical tradition, now globalized, of immediate ascension to heaven of all the righteous while the wicked remained in the netherworld. As a result of possible Greek influence combined with the biblical idea of the soul's survival of death, there were other visionaries who did not believe in a resurrection of the body but speak only of immortality for the souls of the righteous, and still others who believed in a resurrection of the spirits of the wicked for due recompense. Thus in the Second Temple period there was no single Jewish belief system with regard to the mode of and the individuals destined for resurrection, immortality, and eternal life, but a spectrum of views reflecting the rich diversity and fermentation of religious life.

Philo on the Afterlife

Philo, steeped in Greek philosophy, spoke of an irrational and a rational soul in human beings. He conceived of the irrational soul as corporeal and two of his various suggestions about its composition pertain directly to this discussion. He said that the rational soul is blood and links it directly to the Bible by stating that the law of Moses considers the blood to be the essence of the soul.[15] He also suggested that the soul is composed of breath (a Stoic term connoting something corporeal) which Philo calls air.[16] This emphasis on corporeality echoes the biblical term *nefesh*. But, as Harry Wolfson has pointed out, these views also reflect Greek philosophy; the conception of the soul as blood can be traced to Critias and the idea that it is air to Diogenes.[17] With regard to the rational soul, Philo, following Plato in the *Timaeus*, held that it was created by God but, unlike Plato, he argued that the human mind, the rational soul, a fragment of the divine, was created after an idea of mind and soul both created by God on what the Bible calls the first day of creation.[18] Philo maintained that the rational soul is incorporeal with no tinge of matter and thus gives evidence of its divine nature.[19] The rational and the irrational soul work cooperatively for the benefit of the individual. With regard to the rational soul, Philo also used the term "breath" but in the biblical sense meaning something incorporeal. He had in mind the biblical word *"neshamah"* and he even cited the verse "and God blew into his nostrils the breath of life" (Gen. 2:7).[20]

According to Philo, again echoing Plato in the *Timaeus* the irrational soul is mortal while the rational soul of the individual is immortal and gains eternal life as a distinct entity. Like his Jewish counterparts in the land of Israel and in the Greek Diaspora Philo sought to ground his belief concerning the afterlife in a biblical proof-text. Speaking of the immortality of the soul he cites Gen. 15:15,

> You shall go to your fathers in peace;
> You shall be buried at a ripe old age.

In his interpretation this verse points to the immortality of the soul returning to its source from which it originally entered the body.[21]

The Hellenistic Jews in Philo's time held three views of the soul's abode in eternity:

1) The soul's dwelling place is with the sun, moon and stars and particularly the stars which, according to Chrysippus the Stoic, contain the same elements as the souls of the wise who alone receive the blessing of immortality, a view echoed in Dan. 12:3; 2 Baruch 51:10; 4 Ezra 7:97; 1 Enoch 104:2.

2) The soul's permanent abode after death is in the realm of ideas.

3) The soul at death is reabsorbed into the primary elements of the world, earth, air, fire and water that constitute a universal ether.

Philo held that the soul on separating from the body returns to heaven and is reunited with the souls of angels that have never descended into human bodies, a conception that echoes Plato and is also found in apocalyptic literature (2 Baruch 51:10; 1 Enoch 104:6). But not all souls go to the same place. Though the souls of Abraham and Elijah went to heaven to be among the angels, the souls of Isaac and Enoch went to dwell in the intelligible world of incorporeal ideas, and finally the soul of Moses advanced beyond the realm of incorporeal ideas and beyond the realm of angels to the very presence of God.

Philo's conception of the afterlife centered on the immortality of the soul and he interpreted all the references to the resurrection of the body in the contemporary literature as figures of speech pointing to the soul's immortality. Merging Platonic and traditional Jewish views of the hereafter, Philo asserted that immortality is bestowed on the wise and the pious. But Philo parted company with Plato and the Stoics in his view of what happens to the wicked. Following in the footsteps of the Jewish beliefs of his day in individual providence and individual reward and punishment, Philo asserted that the wicked are denied immortality. He speaks of the "true Hades," the term used by the Septuagint in its translation of the Hebrew *Sheol*, as being the tortured conscience of the sinner in this world. But this is only the preamble to the wicked individual's loss of immortality in the afterlife. Though the individual sinner does not survive death, his/her essence is absorbed in the universal archetype of humanity that is immortal.[22]

Rabbinic Views of the Afterlife

The talmudic period that began before the year 70 C.E. but reached its apogee in the six centuries following the destruction of the Second Temple was the great organizing era in the history of Judaism. The rabbis sifted all existing Hebrew culture and structured it in accordance with the highest religious ideas as they conceived them. They received the variegated conceptions about the afterlife from biblical and Second Temple sources, that had already absorbed Persian and Greek influences, and sought to bend them into a unified framework. They established the belief in the resurrection of the dead as a dogma and enshrined it as the second blessing of the *Amidah* prayer (the eighteen benedictions).[23] In keeping with the biblical outlook of the psycho-physical unity of the human being and in opposition to Gnostic dualism and certain Greek schools of thought, the rabbis insisted on the resurrection of body and soul. The conflict between their view and that of the dualistic Greco-Roman schools is epitomized by the dialogue between R. Judah the Prince and the Roman ruler Antoninus. Said Antoninus: "On Judgment Day the body will plead that it was the soul which sinned and the soul will blame the body." R. Judah replied with the following parable:

> A farmer appointed a lame man and a blind man to guard his
> orchard, thinking that because of their defects each one
> would be incapable of any mischief. However, the two
> guardians contrived by means of the lame man sitting on the
> shoulders of the blind one, to steal and eat the fruit.
> When accused each pleaded his innocence, the one pointing to
> his inability to see and the other to his inability to walk.
> The farmer put the lame man on the blind man's shoulders and
> passed judgment on them. In a similar manner, on Judgment

Day God will bring the body and soul together and pass
judgment on them both. [24]

By the time of the rabbis internal developments and Persian
influence had solidified the belief in a universal resurrection but as
part of a national revival associated with the Messianic Age. After
Israel's return to its homeland as a result of the messianic
ingathering of the exiles the resurrection of the dead would take
place. Connected with the resurrection at the End of Days was the
idea of reward and retribution, since Second Temple Judaism from
the time of Dan. 12:1-3 considered resurrection as a gift of God
reserved for the righteous. But such a view clearly contradicts a
universal resurrection. Similarly, as a result of internal
development and Greek influence the belief in the immortality of
the individual soul which appealed to the human yearning for
survival after death became implanted in Jewish belief. But like
the resurrection, immortality of the soul was also conceived as a
divine blessing bestowed on the righteous. In addition, there seems
to be some confusion in the talmudic-midrashic sources with regard
to the sequence of the eschatological events, the Messianic Age,
the resurrection and the World to Come. Certain sources suggest
that the resurrection is the last stage of the Endtime identical with
the World to Come. Other sources speak of a resurrection that
precedes the last stage of the redemption which is the World to
Come and still other sources place the World to Come as a stage
before the resurrection.

It is clear that trying to encompass within one rabbinic system
various views of the afterlife from very different contexts would
inevitably produce internal contradictions. Two modern scholars
have sought to resolve these contradictions by seeking to
reconstruct the evolution of Jewish eschatology in two different
ways. George Foot Moore argued that in the earliest stage "the
days of the Messiah," "the World to Come," and "the coming
future" (*atid lavo*) all refer to the same time-the last chapter of
human history. During this period the righteous dead (only of Israel)
are resurrected to enjoy the blessings of the Messianic Age in the
land of Israel. The rabbinic homilies that picture the World to
Come in purely materialistic terms belong to this stage. In the
second stage, the various terms describing the Endtime are sorted
out and assigned to different time slots. The "Days of the Messiah,"
the golden age of Jewish redemption, is now only a preliminary
stage. At the end of the messianic era there will be a universal
resurrection of all the dead who must stand in the Final Judgment.

At the conclusion of the Final Judgment, the World to Come will ensue in which the righteous will live on in immortality while the wicked receive their retribution all in keeping with the doctrine of reciprocity (see Ch. 4 Is There A Moral Order in the Universe? Sinai: The Struggles of Theodicy).[25]

A different reconstruction of the conflicting rabbinic sources is suggested by Louis Finkelstein.[26] He pinpointed the essence of the conflict in the interval between death and resurrection and argued that from the earliest times two schools of thought were in controversy over this stage. One school asserted that the soul upon dying goes into *Sheol* and remains inactive there until the resurrection. The other school held that immediately upon death souls arise to divine judgment. In the view of the first school "the World to Come" means the resurrection. In the perspective of the second school "the World to Come" means the existence between death and resurrection. According to Finkelstein, the term "World to Come" was purposely left ambiguous by the rabbis so as not to decide between the two schools. In rabbinic literature the two opposing views surfaced in the debate between the schools of Shammai and Hillel. The school of Shammai held that after death souls are either in *Sheol* itself or in a designated divine "treasury" until the Messianic Age when the righteous are rewarded with resurrection. This corresponds to Moore's earliest stage. The school of Hillel asserted that immediately after death the souls are judged: those suffering retribution are in hell; those receiving reward are in heaven. At the end of human history all are resurrected for a review of the verdict.[27]

If we combine the interpretations of Moore and Finkelstein we can postulate a possible rabbinic scenario of the afterlife which is divided into three stages. The first stage is the state of the soul of the righteous in heaven, a view discussed above which may derive from Greek influence. The souls of the wicked remain in *Sheol*. In the second stage the righteous of Israel are resurrected to enjoy the blessings of the Messianic Age which include the redemption of the nation. The wicked continue in *Sheol*. In the third stage at the end of the Messianic Age, there is a second universal resurrection of the righteous and the wicked of all nations. The righteous are blessed with immortality in the World to Come and the wicked are dispatched to hell (*Gehinnom*).

Whether the result of purposeful ambiguity or the impossibility of totally reconciling divergent views of the afterlife, the rabbinic sources contributed to the debate over the afterlife among medieval Jewish thinkers. The most controversial was Moses Maimonides

who, following Philo (though not knowingly), emphasized the
immortality of the soul but not the resurrection of the body.[28]
Attacked on this point he sought to clarify his views by stating that
of course there would be a physical resurrection which would take
place on earth some time after the coming of the Messiah.   The
resurrected would then die again and the righteous would be
rewarded by immortality of the soul but not the body in the World to
Come.[29]   This view is unique to Maimonides.   In defending
Maimonides against his critics one commentator pointed out that
the critics thought that Maimonides held that the resurrection and
the World to Come are identical but in reality Maimonides held
that the resurrection and the World to Come are two distinct
entities;[30] thus the commentator echoes the original problem in the
rabbinic texts.

Within the theological framework outlined above a vast variety of
rabbinic views concerning the afterlife are to be found.   Some have
their analogies in Greco-Roman literature and law.[31]   Others have
their echoes in Philo and in apocalyptic-pseudepigraphic literature.
A rabbinic counterpart to one of the views discussed above is the
announcement by the ministering angels of the arrival of the
righteous after their death.   God then sends them forth to escort the
newcomers so that they may enter into heavenly peace. In the
celestial realm they dwell in the seventh heaven together with the
various orders of angels or they serve the Creator.[32]   In contrast, the
wicked are consigned to hell (*Gehinnom*).

The biblical *Sheol* evolved into the rabbinic *Gehinnom*. *Sheol* is
conceived in the Bible as a pit or a bog, damp, dank and miry,
characteristics found in the Greek Hades. In 1 Enoch 1-36, as noted
above, *Sheol* is separated into divisions. Finally the rabbis took the
various terms describing *Sheol* and turned them into seven levels of
hell, the netherworld counterpart of the seven levels of heaven, in
keeping with the principle as above so below.[33] But *Sheol* in some
conceptions is the resting place of wicked and righteous alike while
the true hell (*Gehinnom*) of early Judaism is only for the wicked.
The term *Gehinnom* was derived from an earthly place, the valley of
Hinnom outside Jerusalem where the apostate Jerusalemites
sacrificed their children as burnt offerings to the god Moloch (Jer.
7:30-34). In Enoch 27:1 ff. the phrase "accursed valley", an oblique
reference to the valley of Hinnom, is used to describe the place
where the wicked will be judged and punished. Thus in contrast to
the watery character of *Sheol* is the fiery nature of *Gehinnom* since
in the Bible conflagration is the image describing God's
chastisement of Israel (Isa. 1:7; Jer. 11:16; Amos 2:5; Lam. 4:11),

His retribution against the wicked Gentile nations (Gen. 19:24; Isa. 30:27,30; Amos 1,4,7,10,12,14; Obad. 1:18) and His final apocalypse (Isa. 66:24; Joel 2:1-3). The fiery valley of Hinnom has its analogue in the Greek description of a vast region consumed by fiery lakes and streams with boiling mud and water.

The rabbis, like the author of 1 Enoch 22, distinguished between classes of the wicked. The exceptionally wicked not only have no share in the World to Come but the *Mishnah* says of them "nor shall they stand in the judgment,"[34] i.e., they are never resurrected but remain in *Gehinnom*. The ordinary wicked are resurrected and have a chance for acquittal in the final judgment. There is a striking similarity here to Plato's teaching that the incurably evil like Aridaeus remain in the underworld though others less wicked leave it.[35] Early and even later rabbinic statements about *Gehinnom* seem to view it as a place of purgation for the ordinary sinner as well as a place of punishment. The *Mishnah* states: "The judgment of the wicked in *Gehinnom* is twelve months."[36] In this connection one thinks of Plato's view that those who had committed major offenses for which there could still be some rectification spend a year in Tartarus and then move on to other forms of purgative discipline (Plato, Phaedo 114). The fiery *Gehinnom* has its parallel in the purifying fires of the Greco-Roman afterlife scenarios.

The punishments for those who remained in hell were based on the doctrine of reciprocity and in some instances they were projections into the afterlife of actual tortures of living people or the mutilation and dishonor of dead bodies.[37] But in medieval times Moses Maimonides argued that Paradise and Hell were but figures of speech. Heaven meant the joy of communion with God. Hell meant to be deprived of eternal life.[38]

Just as repentance can change the outcome of the doctrine of reciprocity (see Ch. 4 Is There A Moral Order in the Universe? Sinai: The Struggles of Theodicy, note 7) so does the death of a wicked person, even one who has caused the name of God to be profaned, wipe out his/her guilt, provided the individual has repented. Thus according to talmudic law, when a criminal approached the site of execution he or she was urged to confess in the following words: "May my death be an expiation for all my wickedness."[39] Such a confession enabled the criminal to acquire a share in the World to Come. Moreover, the rabbis had a concept of expiation that stood in marked contrast to the view of Babylonian religion and some biblical texts that violent, premature death or lack of burial was a sign of very serious transgression. They held that in the case of the ordinary sinner, who in thought and way of life did not despise God and His teachings, such suffering and degradation could serve as an atonement and enable the individual to attain his or her rightful portion in the World to Come. [40]

George Foot Moore's words of caution are most appropriate in closing this discussion: "Any attempt to systematize the Jewish notions of the hereafter imposes upon them an order and consistency which does not exist in them. As has already been remarked their religious significance lies in the definitive establishment of the doctrine of retribution after death, not in the variety of ways in which men imagined it."[41]

Notes

1. George W. E. Nickelsburg, *Resurrection, Immortality and Eternal Life in Intertestamental Judaism*, Harvard Theological Studies 26 (Cambridge: Harvard University Press, London: Oxford University Press, 1972), pp. 11-14.

2. *Phaedo* 107D-108C. Myth of Er in *The Republic* 10, 614 ff. Nickelsburg, *Resurrection, Immortality* etc. , p. 162.

3. Dan. 11:30-33; Victor Tcherikover, *Hellenistic Civilization and the Jews* (Philadelphia: The Jewish Publication Society of America, Jerusalem: The Magnes Press, The Hebrew University, 1959), pp. 175-200.

4. T. Francis Glasson, *Greek Influence in Jewish Eschatology* (London: S.P.C.K. Biblical Monographs, 1961), pp. 12-19; Nickelsburg, *Resurrection, Immortality* etc. pp. 134-140; 142-43.

5. Nickelsburg, *Resurrection, Immortality* etc. , p. 124.

6. Ibid., pp. 40, 88, 110, 123, 136. Cf. Robert H. Pfeiffer, *History of New Testament Times with an Introduction to the Apocrypha* (New York: Harper & Brothers, 1949), pp. 336-340; James M. Reese, "Hellenistic Influence on the Book of Wisdom and its Consequences," *Analecta Biblica* 41 (Rome: Biblical Institute Press, 1970), pp. 62-71.

7. *Sifre* Numbers 139, *Pinhas*, (ed. Friedman), p. 52a; *Sifre* Numbers 40, *Naso*, (ed. Friedman), p. 12a.; *b. Shabbat*, 152b. This view is embedded in the Hebrew prayer book in the memorial prayer for the dead. See J. H. Hertz, *Daily Prayer Book*, rev. ed. (New York: Bloch Publishing Co., 1952), p. 1072.

8. *The Midrash on Psalms* 22:32, trans. William G. Braude, Yale Judaica Series 13 (New Haven: Yale University Press, 1959), pp. 325-269.

9. T. Francis Glasson, *Greek Influence in Jewish Eschatology*, pp. 33-37.

10. Nickelsburg, *Resurrection, Immortality* etc., pp. 120-30.

11. Ibid., pp. 151, 155-56; 166-67.

12. Yaakov Sussman, "*Heker Toledot ha-Halakah u-Megillot Midbar Yehudah*," *Tarbiz* 59 (1990): 11-76 and particularly pp. 36,62 where the possibility of difference in beliefs and theology is acknowledged.

13. Flavius Josephus, *Antiquities of the Jews* 18, 1, 4; *The Wars of the Jews* 2,8, 14; Matt. 22:23; Mark 22:18; Luke 20:27; Acts 23:8. Cf. Benedict T. Viviano, O. P. and Justin Taylor, S. M., "Sadducees, Angels and Resurrection (Acts 23:8-9)," *Journal of Biblical Literature* 3, no. 3 (Fall, 1992):496-98.

14. Nickelsburg, *Resurrection, Immortality* etc., p. 166.

15. Citations of Philo's works are from the Colson and Whitaker translation in the Loeb Classical Library. *Quod Deterius Potiori Insidiari Soleat* 22, 80; *Quis Rerum Divinarum Heres* 11, 55; *De Specialibus Legibus* IV, 23, 123.

16. *De Somniis* I, 22, 136. Philo's comparison of nature, animals and humans exhibits the universal element the Bible sees in *ruah*.

17. Harry A. Wolfson, *Philo: Foundations of Religious Philosophy in Judaism, Christianity and Islam* 4th ed. (Cambridge: Harvard University Press, 1968) 1:388.

18. *De Opificio Mundi* 7,29; *Legum Allegoria* I,13, 42; *De Decalogo* 25,134; *Quod Deterius Potiori Insidiari Soleat* 24, 90; Wolfson, *Philo* 1:390.

19. Wolfson, *Philo* 1:393. The idea that there is a divine spark in the human soul is to be found in Jewish thought beginning with Philo, continuing in the writings of the medieval Jewish poet-philosopher, Solomon Ibn Gabirol and finally emerging in kabbalistic doctrine. See Louis Jacobs, "The Doctrine of the 'Divine Spark in Man' in Jewish Sources" in *Studies in Rationalism, Judaism and Universalism* ed. Raphael Loewe (London: Routledge and Kegan Paul, 1966): 87-103. It was, however, the *Habad* branch of Hasidism that developed this idea into an entire metaphysical system at whose center stands the doctrine of the two souls in humans, the animal soul and the divine soul. Cf. Louis Jacobs, *Seeker of Unity* (New York: Basic Books, 1966) and more recently Rachel Elior, *The Paradoxical Ascent to God: The Kabbalistic Theosophy of Habad Hasidism* trans. Jeffrey M. Green (Albany, NY.: State University New York Press, 1992).

20. Wolfson, *Philo* 1:394.

21. *Quaestiones et Solutiones in Genesin*, III, 11. Cf. 4 Maccabees 18:23.

22. Wolfson, *Philo* 1:398-413 and the sources cited there.

23. *M. Sanhedrin*, 10:1; J. H. Hertz, *Daily Prayer Book*, pp. 133-34.

24. *b. Sanhedrin*, 91a; *Tanhuma, Vayikra*, 12.

25. *Judaism: In the First Centuries of the Christian Era*, 6th ed. (Cambridge: Harvard University Press, 1950) 2:378-392. Moore points out that in rabbinic literature "the resurrection of the dead" used without qualification refers to the universal resurrection before the Final Judgment. When the term 'World to Come' is used as a state preceding the resurrection it refers to the transition period between death and the Messianic Age when the souls of the righteous are in heaven and the wicked are in *Sheol* or in hell (*Gehinnom*). Ibid, pp. 380, 391.

26. *Mavo le-Massekhtot Avot ve-Avot de Rabbi Natan* (New York: Jewish Theological Seminary of America, 1950), Introduction, pp. xxxii-xxxv.

27. Ibid., pp. 217-220. The idea that the World to Come precedes and is separate from the resurrection is found in the Sabbath prayer: " There is none to be compared to You O Lord our God in this world neither is there any beside You O our king, in the life of the World to Come; there is none but You, our Redeemer, for the days of the Messiah; neither is there any like You O our Savior, for the revival of the dead." See J. H. Hertz, *Daily Prayer Book*, p. 42. On the other hand, *Sifre*, Deut. 6, Vaethanan, (ed. Finkelstein), p. 62 reads: "'In your going he will lead you' refers to this world, and 'in your lying down He will watch over you' refers to the hour of death, and 'in waking up' refers to the days of the Messiah, 'it will make you speak' refers to the World to Come." In this source the World to Come is clearly after the resurrection.

28. *Yad ha-Hazakah*, 8:2-3.

29. Moses Maimonides, *The Essay on Resurrection* , ed. with an intro. by J. Finkel, *Proceedings of the American Academy of Jewish Research* 9(1939): 61-105.

30. Commentary of *Lehem Mishneh* (Abraham di Boton, d. 1609). Cf. Isadore Twersky, *Introduction to the Code of Maimonides (Mishneh Torah)* (New Haven and London: Yale University Press, 1980), pp. 43, 502-3. For an interesting survey of the entire conception of resurrection and immortality from the Bible to the modern period see Louis Jacobs, *Principles of the Jewish Faith* 2nd ed. (London and Northvale, N.J.: Jason Aronson Inc., 1988): 398-454.

31. See Saul Lieberman, "Some Aspects of After Life in Early Rabbinic Literature," *Harry Austryn Wolfson Jubilee Volume*, English section (Jerusalem: American Academy for Jewish Research, 1965) 2:495-530.

32. *b. Ketubot*, 104a; *b. Hagigah*, 12b; *Midrash ha-Gadol* on Gen. 50:26. See Arthur Darby Nock, "Postscript," *Harvard Theological Review* 34 (1941): 101-109 on parallels to this rabbinic conception in the early Christian tradition. The number seven has a pivotal significance in all of Hebrew literature biblical and postbiblical. See Ginzberg, *Legends* 5:9, note 21 and Joshua Trachtenberg, *Jewish Magic and Superstition* 2nd ed. (New York: Atheneum, 1974), p. 119. A plurality of heavens was derived from an exegesis of the words "the heaven and heaven of heavens" and similar expressions (Deut. 10:14; 1 Kings 8:27; Ps. 68:34) and the number seven as a result of astronomical and astrological influences. Cf. Ginzberg, *Legends* 5:10-11, note 22; Moore, *Judaism* 1:368.

33. Ginzberg, *Legends* 5:11, note 25 and the sources cited there.

34. *M. Sanhedrin* 10:3; *Tosefta Sanhedrin* 10:3.

35. T. Francis Glasson, *Greek Influence in Jewish Eschatology*, p. 18.

36. *M. Eduyot* 2:10. Cf. *Midrash Mishle* 27:1. The temporary sojourn in *Gehinnom* of certain individuals was due to the fact that intercession was made for them by the living and their sins were atoned. Cf. *Pesikta Rabbati* 20 (ed. Friedman), p. 95b.

37. Martha Himmelfarb, *Tours of Hell* (Philadelphia: University of Pennsylvania Press, 1983), pp. 106-109. Cf. Saul Lieberman, "On Sins and their Punishments," and "Roman Legal Institutions in Early Rabbinics and in the Acta Martyrum" in *Texts and Studies* (New York: Ktav, 1974).

38. *Yad ha-Hazakah, Hilkot Teshuvah*, 8:5.

39. *M. Sanhedrin*, 6:2; *Tosefta Sanhedrin* 9:5.

40. *Sifre*, Numbers 112 (ed. Horovitz), pp. 121-122; *b. Sanhedrin*, 47a-b.

41. *Judaism* 2:389.

Conclusions and Comparisons

The extinction of life is so mysterious and perplexing that there can be no consistency in any culture's ideas about it. Thus both Sinai and Olympus explained the inevitable in a multiplicity of ways, some contradictory, and expanded their pictures as their civilizations changed. Yet a single energizing motivation underlies their conception of death at every stage: the confirmation of the justice of the divine cosmos, with the doctrine of reciprocity as its principle of order. From the earliest times, death was closely connected to the natural order of seasonal balance and exchange and was also the instrument of moral reciprocity, being itself the punishment for major sins and the place where the wicked who escaped retribution in life finally paid eternal recompense.

At first moral reciprocity was limited to extraordinary individuals. The greatest sinners were killed instantly; only a few of the most virtuous or excellent could escape death entirely. Ordinary mortals simply descended to a neutral netherworld where they would remain forever. Group identity, corporate responsibility, and reciprocity over time could explain away examples of unmerited reward or suffering in life.

The merging of the individual into the group afterlife was modified over time for two major reasons. First, as the legal systems focused on individual responsibility, this emphasis was projected into the afterlife. But, since flawed human justice obviously did not effect perfect reciprocity on earth, judgment which was truly unsullied could only be promised after death. Secondly, with the weakening or collapse of political systems which provided the framework for group identity, the emphasis shifted toward more individualized solutions to life's problems. The impact of both factors contributed to a conception of the afterlife which satisfied the demand for perfect reciprocity on an individual basis. New ideas such as resurrection, immortality of the soul, and reincarnation transformed death from a final ending to a transitional stage which confirmed individual and group participation in the just divine plan.

The connection of death with the natural order has both positive and negative implications. At the positive end of the spectrum the netherworld to which the dead descend is identified as mother earth, the source of fertility and divine and human creativity. In this perspective death is part of the cycle of nature, "the way of all the earth." The Hebrew texts sharing this outlook see *Sheol* as part of

God's universe and the inhabitants of *Sheol* as not separated from the deity but joining with living creatures in His praise.

The Greek underworld is also connected to fertility; it is the home of the grain goddess' daughter Persephone who returns to the upper world annually at the same time as the new crops sprout from the earth. Positive too is the view of some philosophers who considered the eternal cosmos a unity based on a balanced exchange of opposites. Heraclitus, for example, defined the world order "which always was, is, and will be," as "everlasting fire kindling in measures and going out in measures."[1] Later in Plato's *Phaedo* 70-72, Socrates bases a proof for the immortality of the soul on the cyclical argument that everything, including life and death, is generated from its opposite.

At the negative end of the spectrum the netherworld is a dark, dank, somewhat threatening space, the common gathering place of the dead who have no hope of escape. In some Hebrew texts sharing this view there is the suggestion that the dead are removed from God and cannot praise Him (Ps. 115:17). Hesiod in the *Theogony* places the Greek netherworld "as far from earth as heaven is" implying that the realm of the dead is doubly removed from the heavenly realm. The gods of the upper world do not like to look into its moldering darkness. In fact, the absence of light and the futility of its inhabitants' existence may symbolize death's separation from time which gives meaning to human activity.

There are, however, significant differences between the netherworlds of Sinai and Olympus. For the Hebrews there is no god of the netherworld and the suggestion that the dead are removed from God may be a possible polemic against the Ugaritic god of the dead, Mot. But the Greek netherworld is the kingdom of Hades who is himself a god and the brother of Zeus; it is also inhabited by other important deities like Persephone and Hecate. Moreover, the Greek cultic belief that some of the renowned dead actually lived on within the tomb, using their added potency to benefit their worshipers, has no Hebrew equivalent. The closest the Bible comes to this very ancient folk belief of the Mediterranean world is in the story of the witch of Endor who raised the spirit of Samuel for Saul (1 Sam. 28:7-25). But in this narrative Samuel is only a ghost; he has not continued in life in the grave. He brings no benefit to Saul, only a prophecy of defeat and death at the hands of the Philistines. Accentuating the Hebrew rejection of life in the grave and divinity of the netherworld is the concept of the dead body as conveying the most virulent form of ritual impurity (Num. 19:11-22).

The early Hebrews believed in a divinely fixed limit to human life and viewed early death as a sign of divine displeasure, a view which was modified by the talmudic rabbis.[2] The Greeks certainly had exemplars from myth who were struck down for hubris (e.g., Niobe), and sometimes interpreted early or sudden death as possible reciprocity for an ancestor's sin (e.g., Euripides *Hippolytus*, 820 1380). In general, however, they did not connect untimely death with punishment. More often they pitied those who died young, like children and maidens, and even envied the brave warriors who fell in battle before having to suffer painful old age or an ignominious death.

Among the Greeks it was believed that fame achieved in life conferred a kind of immortality after death. Homeric warriors like Sarpedon are spurred on to fight and die by the hope for eternal glory (*Il.* 21.322-28). This attitude continued through the centuries. Ordinary citizen hoplites fighting to defend their *poleis* were immortalized in verses and on tombs; the epitaphs of private persons too proclaim their desire to be remembered even by strangers.

In contrast, the Bible viewed fame as an illusion dispelled completely by death. As the Psalmist pointed out, "Man does not abide in honor; he is like the beasts that perish" (Ps. 49:13) and as Ecclesiastes noted in his melancholy reflection " . . . the wise man just like the fool, is not remembered forever; for as the succeeding days roll by, both are forgotten" (Eccles. 2:16). Nevertheless, the Bible does have a concept of immortality in which the psycho-physical unity of soul and body survives death. The Hebrew terms "*ruah*" (spirit), "*neshamah*" (breath) and "*nefesh*" (soul), though clearly suggesting an anchor in the body, also have a spiritual connection that implies the transcendence of the body. It is interesting that when the Hebrew Bible speaks of wisdom it connects it to the spirit of God (*ruah*, Exod. 31:2) but generally locates it in the human heart (Exod. 31:6; 1 Kings 3:9) rather than in the mind or soul.

The Greeks, however, put much more emphasis on the separation of the soul from the body and on the soul's capacity for rational thought. The concept of the *psyche*, the analogue of the Hebrew terms, developed from the part which fled the corpse and descended to Hades into the psycho-intellectual center of the living individual. For some philosophies and religions, the *psyche* was not only separable from the body and survived it, but possessed a divine origin and nature. As the divine rational and intellectual element in living humans it was capable of learning and choosing the best life and the best path to its source after death. This concept became the vehicle for new ideas about the afterlife.

On Sinai and on Olympus external political, social and economic upheavals combined with internal changes of perspective to pose serious challenges to the views of death inherited from the past. In ancient Israel, the exile and the loss of national sovereignty was accompanied by a shift in focus from the travail and redemption of the nation to the suffering and salvation of the individual. It was the latter issue that preoccupied the wisdom books of the Hebrew Bible. The loss of national sovereignty was coupled with a belief in the loss of prophecy among the Hebrews. But since the absence of divine guidance was intolerable to the Hebrew mind, this belief was mitigated by imaging an increase in distance between divinity and humanity, but not a complete break. The distance was bridged by the apocalyptic visionaries who spoke in enigmatic, symbolic language because they no longer possessed the clear and direct communication with God enjoyed by the biblical prophets who were close to the divine presence.

The increasing importance of the individual and the distancing of the deity made death far more of a problem than it had been earlier in biblical Israel. In addition, the law's insistence on individual responsibility and the postbiblical assumption that the individual, like Esther and Daniel, must assume the obligation of preserving the nation, even to the point of self-sacrifice, sharpened the demand for an answer to the problem of theodicy raised by the Book of Job. The oppression and martyrdom prior to the Maccabean Rebellion and the yearning for national redemption that it engendered were the catalysts combining many elements in the Hebrew belief system into a new solution to the problems of the individual and the problem of the nation.

In Greece too, political events and intellectual developments produced both an increase in individualism and an expansion of the old ideas about the afterlife and cosmic justice. Thucydides' description of the Corcyrean revolution (3. 70-85) epitomizes the breakdown of political consensus in the Greek *poleis* during the late fifth century, at the same time as new intellectual interests in nature (*physis*) and human nature weakened traditional beliefs, and custom/laws (*nomos*). Although the city-state system survived the Peloponnesian War, the citizens' fervor for their public life declined in the fourth century. New private religious options supplemented city worship. Comedy, the invention of the democracy, gradually eliminated its chorus, the voice of the citizens, and concentrated on slices of private life rather than political issues. Plato became a teacher rather than a politician. In his lifetime, mathematics and astronomy began to change the map of the cosmos from a three tiered universe (heaven, earth and Hades) to the geocentric Ptolemaic system, moving the gods from nearby Mount Olympus to the far distant stars at the outer limits. By the next century, political power also moved further away, to the cities of the East from which Alexander's successors ruled. In the midst of such changes, new beliefs, new rites, and new systems of metaphysics arose which helped individuals lost in the larger cosmos and cosmopolis to find peace and hope.

In Israel and in Greece the solution to the anxieties connected with death was the expansion of the arena of reciprocity for reward and punishment into the afterlife. What one does in this life affects what one experiences after death. Thus there is an interweaving of the scenarios of life and death.

The challenge of theodicy was answered in two ways during the Second Temple period in Israel. The first answer continued the earlier corporate view of the netherworld as the gathering place for all flesh but emphasized its positive image as a fruitful, creative place whose inhabitants praise God. The righteous who, though they suffered, had an intense fellowship with God in life were reassured that this fellowship would continue after death without the suffering that accompanies earthly existence. Though divine judgment was not denied by those holding this view of the hereafter it was peripheral, confined largely to life on earth.

Far more influential and ultimately triumphant was the answer offered by the doctrine of resurrection, whose embryonic form is in the Torah and prophets but whose full birth is in Dan. 12:1-3. Here divine judgment results in the resurrection of the righteous to the reward of eternal life and the wicked to the punishment of eternal reproach. The problem of theodicy is solved in a much more direct fashion than in the first approach mentioned above. Moreover, the first answer, though reassuring the righteous of their continued existence with God after death, was extremely vague as to the state of the wicked in the afterlife. The author of Dan. 12:1-3 is explicit about the punishment of the wicked. But the Daniel passage limits the resurrection in scope, time and place to the protagonists of the Maccabean Revolt in the land of Israel. In addition, the resurrection and reward and punishment are only one act in the far larger drama of the apocalyptic end of history and world upheaval leading to God's sovereignty in a redeemed and reunited Israel in a new world order. Later apocalyptic writings globalized the resurrection in place and universalized it in scope and in time.

Hellenistic Jewish writers under Greek influence emphasized the immortality of the soul but not the body while the rabbis, in systematizing the variety of afterlife scenarios that reached them, reiterated the psycho-physical unity of body and soul implied by the resurrection.

On Olympus as on Sinai the world beyond the grave was globalized and universalized. Here too there was a transition from a corporate to an individual afterlife in which self-identity remains, and everyone is judged on the basis of his or her actions in life. Some individuals chose to join a special cult which promised that participation in secret rites and identification with particular deities would guarantee them a joyful existence in a special place after death. Others believed that the soul had an immortal nature and would ultimately return to its divine source, led toward it either through cult or philosophy. Some among them posited reincarnation as a solution to the dilemmas of divine justice, human suffering, and death. Plato's imaginative descriptions of the soul's journeys back and forth, the trials, the punishments, the rewards, and the glimpses into Being have reverberated through the history of Western culture. But, like the author of Daniel, who describes the afterlife as only one small part of his larger apocalyptic vision of history, so too the Greek philosopher presents his myths about reincarnation not as ends in themselves, but as complements to philosophical discourse. Like the doctrine of the resurrection in Israel, reincarnation explicitly countered the challenge to theodicy by explaining that the cycle of rebirths and the troubles of life were punishments for sins in former lifetimes, all in keeping with the law of reciprocity. But the individual soul could hope for an end to the cycle and reunion with the divine if it remembered its former states of existence in life and in death and determined to live uprightly in its present lifetime. Combined with judgment after death and the punishments of the netherworld that served as a deterrent to wickedness, the concept fulfilled the needs of society and the yearnings of the individual. Plato not only synthesized previous concepts but introduced new and current ideas about the afterlife that focused on what happens between reincarnations.

In both reincarnation and the resurrection human free will and choice in this life are crucial to one's destiny in the afterlife. In Plato's Myth of Er at the end of the *Republic*, the souls choose the kinds of life they will live prior to their birth into human bodies. But the rabbis, like the Stoics, viewed the soul's choice as more circumscribed. They pictured the angel in charge of human conception as taking the drop that has not yet formed into an embryo and presenting it to God with the questions: "What shall be the fate of this drop? Shall it produce a strong person or a weak person, a wise human being or a fool, a rich individual or a poor one?" But regarding its righteousness or wickedness the angel does not ask because, according to the rabbinic axiom, only in the moral and religious realm is a human being a free agent, everything else is determined by God.[3] Though the soul is then given an overview of its life and death, as in the Myth of Er, the implication is that these have, to some extent, already been determined.[4] The rabbis portray the soul of the embryo as knowing and seeing everything but, prior to its emergence from the womb, its guardian angel taps it above the mouth causing it to forget all that it has seen and learned. As earlier scholars have already noted, we have here the Platonic doctrine of anamnesis; in the Myth of Er memory is also diminished by drinking the waters of forgetfulness.[5]

Despite certain rabbinic analogues to the Myth of Er, there is no reference to the doctrine of reincarnation in the Bible or the Talmud.[6] The rabbis must have been aware of it, for the doctrine was prevalent in the Near East from the second century onward among some Gnostic sects, especially among Manichaeans, in the Platonic and Neoplatonic schools, in several circles in the Christian Church, perhaps even in the beliefs of the Church Father Origen.[7] We know from other instances that biblical and rabbinic silence is often a sign of opposition, and it is quite possible that this is the case with reincarnation. It has been noted in this chapter that the prophet Hosea rejected the contrition of the people who sought to transfer the regeneration cult of nature mysticism to the God of Israel. The biblical writers and the rabbis opposed the doctrine of reincarnation because it too closely resembled pagan conceptions of gods dying and returning to life in countless cycles of death and life. This widespread belief was at the very center of the religious life of the ancient Near East and engendered the hope that perhaps mortals too could achieve an endlessly renewed life.[8]

Earlier conceptions of the relations between humans and gods facilitated the introduction of such ideas in Greece. Mortals and immortals were generated from the same mother earth, some heroes were engendered by gods (e.g., Sarpedon, Achilles), and sometimes gods disguised themselves as humans to move about the earth. Moreover, there were also *daimones*, intermediate between mortals and immortals, whom Hesiod first described as the spirits of the deceased golden race who remained active on earth after death to protect the living (*Works and Days* 121-125). The fact that a rare mortal had actually ascended to Olympus to live forever among the gods (e.g., Tithonus, Ganymede, Heracles, and, later, deified monarchs) increased the possibility that *imitatio dei* might take the form of imitating divine immortality after death. Some cults identified the initiate with a dying and returning divinity and promised eternal memory patterned after divine timelessness rather than the forgetful futility of human death. Some of these, as well as certain philosophies, focused on the reunion of the divine element in humans, soul or spirit, with its suprahuman source. Certain groups posited reincarnation. They hoped, however, not for cycles of endlessly renewed life, but rather for a culmination in the everlasting and blissful reunification with the source of their being.

Josephus, in explaining the Pharisaic belief in resurrection to his Greco-Roman audience, Hellenized the concept so that it could be understood in terms of reincarnation.[9] As we have seen, Philo interpreted all references to the resurrection of the body as referring to the immortality of the soul alone and, according to Urbach, this logically led him, like the Greek philosophers, to the belief in reincarnation.[10] In the Middle Ages, with the pagan drama of dying and reborn nature gods now a forgotten relic of a bygone era, and with new persecutions sharpening once again the questions of theodicy, the Kabbalists reintroduced reincarnation, or *gilgul* as they termed it, into the Jewish belief system giving it a distinctive cast of their own.[11]

Both the Hebrews and the Greeks extrapolated from the life and death of the individual to the life and death of the world. In Israel the conception of the covenant that linked reciprocity on the individual level to reciprocity in the life of the group was globalized as a result of universal conceptions of the Endtime in the Bible and in postbiblical literature. The Endtime embraced both the temporal and the spatial but on Sinai it is more becoming than being. It represented the consummation of history when the dead will be resurrected as well as the messianic ingathering of the exiles with Jerusalem as the center from which peace radiates to all parts of the cosmos. The End of Days represented the descent of the wicked into the apocalyptic abyss and the ascent of the righteous beyond the great cataclysm into the new world order. For the Greek philosophers the vision of the end was ontological rather than historical. Just as the individual soul is eternal and may have its cycles of reincarnations connected to the law of reciprocity so was the cosmos eternal and subject to cycles of destruction and rebirth, sometimes related to cosmic justice (e.g., Phaethon; the flood). In Greece the afterlife was not connected with a culmination of history or a resurrection of the dead for a last judgment at the end of time.

On Sinai and Olympus the doctrines of the resurrection and reincarnation clarified the mystery of the life and death of the individual and the world, thus removing some of the anxiety. But there remained a continuing human need for the validation of these teachings from on high and for the closing of the increasing gap between Creator and creature. In both civilizations mediators appeared who served as bridges and ladders to the heavenly realm, reassuring humanity of the care and love of divinity, of ultimate justice and the validity of God's order here and in the world beyond. For the Hebrew visionaries, the vehicle of mediation was the otherworldly journey in which a revelation was given to an ascending hero who must relay it to his generation. The message has both horizontal and vertical motifs. The horizontal motif is that the cumulative weight of human sin and corruption over time has brought history to an impasse that limits human options. The vertical motif is the appearance of the savior designated by the deity to usher in the reign of peace and the new world order after the upheaval. In the book of Daniel it is the angel Michael; in the book of Revelation it is Jesus the Lamb of God. A second strand of the vertical motif is the confirmation of the resurrection which Enoch brings back from the celestial region.

The Greeks and Romans also developed ways to close the gap and validate their beliefs from on high. The immortal soul that travels back and forth between reincarnations mediates between the realms. *Daimones* act like divine agents, guiding an individual, like Socrates, through life and leading the dead along the paths of judgment and reciprocity. In their otherworldly journeys Er, Scipio the Younger, and Aeneas receive revelations which both confirm cosmic order and justice and the ethical and political values on earth supported by metaphysics. Virgil and Horace, writing at the time of the bloody transition from republic to principate, adopt some of the same language as the Jews to express the nadir of moral and historical degeneration their society has reached. Both poets too hope for some kind of supernatural mediation to change the world. Virgil's Messianic Eclogue uses the birth of the divine child as the symbol of the better times to come, but Horace, in Ode 1.2, invokes a divine savior, Mercury in the guise of Augustus Caesar (41-52), as "Jove's choice for redeemer from sin" (29-30).[12] Although such words became conventional and indeed faint praise by the time of Lucan's eulogy to Nero at *Pharsalia* 1.33-66, the need only increased as the hope for political solutions diminished. Thus initiations like the Mithraic ascents, mediators like the gnostic Hermes and Poimandres, and philosophies like Neoplatonism appeared to provide the necessary reassurance of reunion with the divine in the better world beyond.

It is ironic that the Hebrew prophets and Plato envisioned far more options open for human choice than their successors. The Hellenistic world gave more scope to human opportunity and to religious pluralism (e.g., the mystery cults of Isis and Serapis, Mithraism and Gnosticism and the explosion of sectarian Judaism) than the era immediately preceding it. Yet apocalyptic, astrology and Stoicism, though acknowledging that free will still operates, saw it as more circumscribed, whether because of Stoic *Heimarmene* or the disorientation, moral corruption, oppression and powerlessness that was still part of the human experience. It is quite possible, as sociologists have pointed out, that for the Jews during the Second Jewish Commonwealth, the relative deprivation of the Hellenistic world, which raised expectations that could be fulfilled only by a privileged elite, was felt more keenly than the absolute deprivation of the exile.[13] In any case it is interesting to note that the assurance of control from a higher realm offered by Hebrew apocalyptic and its Greek analogues lessens the responsibility for suffering though not for sin and error. Thus Greek slaves are not responsible for their lot and Israel living under oppression is not to blame for its circumstances. Both slaves and chosen people are fulfilling a role assigned to them by a higher providence. But this condition is not permanent; salvation is assured to the faithful, the virtuous and the seekers of wisdom.

Notes

1. KRS, p. 197-198, (Fragment 217).

2. For the rabbis an early death, if accompanied by repentance, held no stigma at all. In the words of Rabbi Judah the Prince: "One may acquire eternal life after many years, another (person) may acquire it in an hour." Cf. *b. Avodah Zarah*, 17a.

3. *b. Niddah*, 16b. R. Hanina, the author of this view, admits that even in the moral and religious realm there are those who are by nature more inclined to piety and those who are less inclined. Cf. *Maharsha* (R. Samuel Edels, d. 1631) *Hiddushe Halakot Va-Aggadot* to b. Berakot, 33b, and Rashi to *b. Megillah*, 25a.

4. Ginzberg, *Legends* 3:58; 5:75-76, notes 19-20. But as discussed earlier in Ch. 4, Sinai: The Struggles of Theodicy, notes 34-37, the rabbis also held that God's will determines only certain elements in human life, our health, our wealth, our intelligence and our span of years; in most other things the individual bears the responsibility for his or her own welfare. Cf.

Yer. Shabbat 14:3; *Tosafot* to *b. Megillah*, 26a, s.v. *Hakol*; *Tosafot* to *b. Niddah*, 16b, s.v. *Hakol*; *Tosafot* to *b. Avodah Zarah*, 3b, s.v. *Shomer*.

5.   Ginzberg, *Legends* 5: 77, n. 20.

6.   Saul Lieberman, "Some Aspects of After Life in Early Rabbinic Literature," *Harry Austryn Wolfson Jubilee Volume* (Jerusalem: American Academy of Jewish Research, 1965) 2:501, n. 41.

7.   "Transmigration of Souls," *Catholic Encyclopedia*, 14:258.

8.   H. L. Ginsberg, "The North Caananite Myth of Anath and Aqhat," *Bulletin of the American Schools of Oriental Research* 97-98 (1945): 3-10; 15-23.

9.   *The Antiquities of the Jews*, 18,1,3 and *The Jewish Wars* 2,8,14. Cf. Nickelsburg, *Resurrection, Immortality and Eternal Life in Intertestamental Judaism*, p. 168 and T. Francis Glasson, *Greek Influence in Jewish Eschatology*, pp. 30-31.

10.   Ephraim E. Urbach, *The Sages: Their Concepts and Beliefs*, trans. Israel Abrahams, (Cambridge. and London: Harvard University Press, 1987), p. 235.

11.   Gershom Scholem, *On the Mystical Shape of the Godhead: Basic Concepts in the Kabbalah* trans. Joachim Neugroschel (New York: Schocken Books, 1991), pp. 197-250 and my *Judaism and the Gentile Faiths*, pp. 129-137. The Kabbalists viewed reincarnation as an outgrowth of God's love for His creatures in seeking to give them an opportunity to perfect all facets of the soul, something which is impossible within a single lifetime.

12.   The translation comes from Joseph P. Clancy, *"The Odes" and "Epodes" of Horace* (Chicago: University of Chicago Press, 1960), p. 26. James Michie, *"The Odes" of Horace: "The Centennial Hymn,"* intro. Rex Warner (Indianapolis: Bobbs-Merrill, 1963-1965), p. 8, translates the same phrase as "instrument of our atonement." For evidence that Horace was expressing ideas prevalent in the East and connected with Augustus, see R. G. M. Nisbet and Margaret Hubbard, *A Commentary on Horace: "Odes, Book I"* (Oxford: Clarendon Press, 1970), pp. 34-36.

13.   A. Stouffer et. al., *The American Soldier* (Princeton, N.J.: Princeton University Press, 1949), were the first to examine the central role of relative deprivation. Cf. Robert K. Merton, *Social Theory and Social Structure* rev. ed. (Glencoe, Il.: The Free Press, 1957), chap. 8; W. G. Runciman, *Relative Deprivation and Social Justice* (London: University of California Press, 1966), p. 3; David F. Aberle, *The Peyote Religion Among the Navaho* (Chicago: Aldine Publishing Co., 1966), pp. 323-29; Charles Y. Glock and Rodney Stark, *Religion and Society in Tension* (Chicago: Rand McNally, 1965), p. 246.

Select Bibliography

Introductions, Conclusions and Comparisons

Books

Alter, Robert. *The Art of Biblical Narrative*. New York: Basic Books, 1981.

Barr, James. *Biblical Words for Time*. London: SCM Press, 1962.

Bendix, Reinhard. *Max Weber: An Intellectual Portrait*. Berkeley: University of California Press, 1977.

Boman, Thorlief. *Hebrew Thought compared with Greek*. Translated by Jules L. Moreau. Philadelphia: Westminster Press, 1960.

Campbell, Joseph. *The Masks of God: Occidental Mythology*. New York: The Viking Press, 1972.

Cohn, Robert L. *The Shape of Sacred Space: Four Biblical Studies*. Chico, Calif.: Scholars Press, 1981.

Culianu, Ioan Petru. *Psychonodia I—A Survey of the Evidence Concerning the Ascension of the Soul and its Relevance*. Leiden: E. J. Brill, 1983.

Douglas, Mary. *Purity and Danger: An Analysis of Concepts of Pollution and Taboo*. London: Routledge & Kegan Paul, 1966.

Eliade, Mircea. *The Myth of the Eternal Return*. Translated by Willard R. Trask. Bollingen Series 46. New York; Pantheon Books, 1954.

——— · *Myth and Reality*. Translated by W. R. Trask. New York: Harper and Row, 1963.

Hadas, Moses, and Morton Smith. *Heroes and Gods: Spiritual Biographies in Antiquity.* New York: Harper and Row, 1965.

Harris, William V. *Ancient Literacy.* Cambridge: Harvard University Press, 1989.

Hays, H. R. *The Dangerous Sex: The Myth of Feminine Evil.* New York: Putnam, 1964.

Huizinga, J. *Homo Ludens:A Study of the Play Element in Culture.* Translated by R. F. C. Hull. London: Routledge & Kegan Paul, 1949.

Jacobsen, Thorkild. *The Treasures of Darkness.* New Haven: Yale University Press, 1976.

Jung, C. G. *Psychology and Religion: West and East.* Translated by R. C. F. Hull. Bollingen Series XX. New York: Pantheon Books, 1958.

————· *Collected Works of C. G. Jung.* 2nd edition. Princeton: Princeton University Press, 1968.

Kelson, Hans. *Society and Nature: Perspectives in Social Inquiry.* Classics. Staples and Precursors in Sociology. 1946. Reprint. New York: Arno, 1974.

Levi Strauss, Claude. *The Savage Mind.* Chicago: University of Chicago Press, 1966.

Neumann, Eric. *The Origins and History of Consciousness.* Princeton, N.J.: Princeton University Press, 1973.

Momigliano, Arnaldo. *Essays in Ancient Historiography.* Oxford: Basil Blackwell, 1977.

O'Brien, Joan, and Wilfred Major. *In the Beginning: Creation Myths from Mesopotamia, Ancient Israel and Greece.* Chico, Calif.: Scholars Press, 1982.

Otto, Rudolf. *The Idea of the Holy.* Translated by John W. Harvey. New York: Oxford University Press, 1958.

Phillips, John A. *Eve: The History of An Idea.* New York: Harper & Row, 1984.

Pritchard, James B., editor. *Ancient Near Eastern Texts Relating to the Old Testament.* 3rd edition. Princeton: Princeton University Press, 1969.

Rheinstein, Max, editor. *Max Weber on Law in Economy and Society.* Translated by Edward Shils and Max Rheinstein. Cambridge: Harvard University Press, 1954.

Russell, Jeffrey Burton. *The Devil: Perceptions of Evil from Antiquity to Primitive Christianity.* Ithaca: Cornell University Press, 1977.

Smith, Huston. *Forgotten Truth.* New York: Harper & Row, 1976.

Smith, Jonathan Z. *Imagining Religion: From Babylon to Jonestown.*
Chicago: The University of Chicago Press, 1982.

Starr, Chester. *The Awakening of the Greek Historical Spirit.* New
York: Knopf, 1968.

Sternberg, Meir. *The Poetics of Biblical Narrative: Ideological
Literature and the Drama of Reading.* Bloomington: Indiana
University Press, 1987.

Trompf, G. W. *The Idea of Historical Recurrence in Western
Thought: From Antiquity to the Reformation.* Berkeley:
University of California Press, 1979.

Van Groningen, Bernhard Abraham. *In the Grip of the Past: Essay on
an Aspect of Greek Thought.* Leiden: E. J. Brill, 1953.

Van Seters, John. *In Search of History: Historiography in the Ancient
World and the Origins of Biblical History.* New Haven: Yale
University Press, 1983.

Whitrow, G. J. *Time in History: The Evolution of Our General
Awareness of Time and Temporal Perspective.* New York:
Oxford University Press, 1988.

Widengren, G. *The Ascension of the Apostle and the Heavenly Book.*
King and Savior III. Uppsala: Uppsala Universitets Arsskrift,
1950.

Yerkes, R. K. *Sacrifice in Greek and Roman Religion and Early
Judaism.* New York: Scribners, 1952.

Zaleski, Carol. *Otherworld Journeys.* New York: Oxford University
Press, 1987.

Articles and Essays

Alter, Robert. "Introduction to the Old Testament." In *The Literary
Guide to the Bible.* Edited by Robert Alter and Frank Kermod.
Cambridge: Harvard University Press, 1987.

Bickerman, Elias. "Origines Gentium." *Classical Philology* 47
(1952): 56-81.

Fishbane, Michael A. "The Sacred Center: The Symbolic Structure
of the Bible." In *Texts and Responses, Studies Presented to
Nahum N. Glatzer.* Edited by M. Fishbane and P. Flohr. Leiden:
E. J. Brill, 1975.

Gould, John. "On Making Sense of Greek Religion." In *Greek
Religion and Society.* Edited by P. E. Esterling and J. V. Muir.
Cambridge: Cambridge University Press, 1985.

Immerwahr, Henry. "Historiography." In *Cambridge History of
Classical Literature.* Vol. 1. Cambridge: Cambridge University
Press, 1982-5.

Jacobs, Louis. "The Doctrine of the 'Divine Spark in Man' in Jewish Sources." In *Studies in Rationalism, Judaism and Universalism.* Edited by Raphael Loewe. London: Routledge and Kegan Paul, 1966.

Kahler, Erich. "The Nature of the Symbol." In *Symbolism in Religion and Literature.* Edited by Rollo May. New York: G. Braziller, 1960 50-75.

Momigliano, Arnaldo. "Time in Ancient Historiography." *History and Theory,* Beiheft 6, (1966): 15. Reprinted in *Essays in Ancient and Modern Historiography.* Middleton, Conn.: Wesleyan University Press, 1977.

Noy, Dov. "The Jewish Theodicy Legend." In *Fields of Offerings: Studies in Honor of Raphael Patai.* Edited by Victor D. Sanua. New York: Herzl Press, 1984.

Segal, Alan F. "Heavenly Ascent in Hellenistic Judaism, Early Christianity and their Environment." In *Aufstieg und Niedergang Der Roemischen Welt: Geschichte und Kultur Roms Im Spiegel Der Neueren Forschung II.* Edited by Hildegard Temporini and Wolfgang Haase. *Principat.* vol. 23 (2). Berlin, New York: Walter de Gruyter, 1980.

Van der Leeuw, G. "Primordial Time and Final Time." In *Man and Time: Papers From the Eranos Yearbooks.* Bollingen Series 30. vol. 3. New York: Pantheon Books, 1957.

Sinai: Primary Sources

These primary sources are generally listed chronologically and according to their relationship to one another.

Bible and Bible Commentaries

Tanakh: A New Translation of the Holy Scriptures According to the Traditional Hebrew Text. Philadelphia: The Jewish Publication Society, 1985.

The JPS Torah Commentary, Numbers. Commentary by Jacob Milgrom. Philadelphia. Jewish Publication Society of America, 1990.

Mikraot Gedolot. Hebrew Text of the Bible with Targum and Commentaries of Rashi, Ibn Ezra, Ramban and Sforno. New York: Pardes Publishing, 1951.

The *Anchor Bible* Series. Introductions, translations and notes. Garden City, N.Y.: Doubleday, 1964-.

Post-Biblical Pre-Talmudic Works

Apocrypha annd Pseudepigrapha of the Old Testament. Edited by R.
H. Charles. 2 vols. Oxford: Clarendon Press, 1913.
Brownlee, William H., translator. *The Dead Sea Manual of
Discipline.* New Haven: American Schools of Oriental
Research, 1951.
Megillat ha-Serakim. Edited by Jacob Licht. Jerusalem: Bialik
Institute, 1963.

Talmudic-Midrashic and Post-Talmudic Works

Mishnah. Introduction and commentary by Hanoch Albeck.
Jerusalem and Tel Aviv: Bialik Institute and Dvir, 1959-1974.
Babylonian Talmud (with commentaries of *Rashi* and *Tosafot*).
Vilna: Romm, 1895.
Maharsha (Edels, Samuel). *Hiddushe Halakhot Va-Aggadot.*
Palestinian Talmud. Vilna: Romm, 1922.
———· Krotoschin, 1866.
Tosefta. Edited by M. S. Zuckermandel with supplement by Saul
Lieberman. New York, 1970.
———· Edited with commentary by Saul Lieberman. 4 vols. New
York: Jewish Theological Seminary, 1955.
Avot de Rabbi Natan. Edited by S. Schechter. New York: Philipp
Feldheim, 1945.
The Fathers According to Rabbi Nathan. Translated by Judah Goldin.
New Haven: Yale University Press, 1955.
Mekhilta de Rabbi Ishmael. Edited with English translation by J.
Lauterbach. 3 vols. Philadelphia: Jewish Publication Society,
1949.
Mekhilta de Rabbi Simeon bar Yohai. Edited by J. N. Epstein and E.
Z. Melamed. Jerusalem: Mekize Nirdamim, 1955.
Seder Olam Rabba. Edited by Alexander Marx. Berlin, 1903.
Sifra. Edited by I. H. Weiss. Vienna, 1864.
Sifre de be Rav. Edited by Louis Finkelstein. 5 vols. New York:
Jewish Theological Seminary, 1983-1991.
Sefer Yezirah, The Book of Creation. Edited with an introduction
and commentary by Aryeh Kaplan. York Beach, Maine:
Samuel Weiser, 1990.
Midrash Tannaim. Edited with an introduction by David Hoffman. 2
vols. Berlin: Z. H. Isaacovsky, 1908-09.
Midrash Rabbah. Vilna: Romm, 1921.
Genesis Rabbah. Edited by J. Theodor and C. Albeck. 3 vols.
Jerusalem: Wahrmann Books, 1965.

Midrash Tanhuma. Edited by S. Buber. New York, 1946.

————· Jerusalem: Lewin-Epstein, 1967.

Midrash Ha-Gadol, Genesis. Edited by S. Schechter. Cambridge, England, 1902.

Midrash Mishle. Edited with an introduction by Burton L. Visotzky. New York: Jewish Theological Seminary, 1990.

Midrash Tehillim. Edited by S. Buber. New York: Om Publishing, 1947.

The Midrash on Psalms. Translated by William G. Braude. 2 vols. New Haven: Yale University Press, 1959.

Pesikta De-Rab Kahana. Translated by William G. Braude and Israel J. Kapstein. Philadelphia: The Jewish Publication Society of America, 1975.

Pesikta Rabbati. Edited by M. Friedman. Tel Aviv, 1963.

Mishnat Rabbi Eliezer. Edited by H. Enelow. New York: Bloch Publishing, 1934.

Tanna d'vei Eliyahu. Edited by M. Friedman. Vienna, 1902.

Bet Ha-Midrash. Edited by Adolf Jellinek. 6 vols. Jerusalem, 1938.

Ozar Midrashim. Edited by J. Eisenstein. 2 vols. New York, 1915.

Midreshe Geulah. Edited with an introduction by Even Shemuel (J. Kaufman). Tel Aviv: Mosad Bialik-Masada, 1942-43.

Ozar Ha-Meshalim Ve-Ha-Pitgamim. Edited by Israel Davidson. 2 vols. Jerusalem: Mosad Ha-Rav Kook, 1957.

Yalkut. Vilna, 1898.

Maimonides, Moses. *The Guide of the Perplexed.* Translated and Introduced by S. Pines. Chicago: University of Chicago Press, 1963.

————· *Mishneh Torah (Yad Ha-Hazakah).* Jerusalem: Mosad Ha-Rav Kook, 1965-66.

————· *The Essay on Resurrection.* Edited with an introduction by J. Finkel. *Proceedings of the American Academy of Jewish Research.* 9 (1939): 61-105.

Rabbi Moses ben Nahman (Nahmanides). *Commentary on the Torah.* Edited by C. B. Chavel. Jerusalem: Mosad Ha-Rav Kook, 1962.

Zohar. Edited by Reuben Margoliot. 5 vols. Jerusalem: Mosad Ha-Rav Kook, 1960.

Mahzor for Festivals. Sulzbach, 1853.

Daily Prayer Book. Translated with commentary and notes by Joseph H. Hertz. Revised Edition. New York: Bloch Publishing Co., 1952.

Secondary Sources—Books

Albright, William F. *Archaeology and the Religion of Israel.*
Baltimore: Johns Hopkins University Press, 1956.
Baron, Salo W. *A Social and Religious History of the Jews.* 18 vols.
New York: Columbia University Press, 1952-1983.
Bickerman, Elias J. *Four Strange Books of the Bible*:
Jonah/Daniel/Koheleth/Esther. New York: Schocken Books,
1967.
Buchler, Adolf. *Types of Jewish Palestinian Piety: From 70 B.C.E. to
70 C.E.-The Ancient Pious Men.* New York: Ktav, 1968.
Cassuto, Umberto. *From Adam to Noah.* Jerusalem: The Magnes
Press, 1953.
———. *The Documentary Hypothesis and the Composition of the
Pentateuch.* Translated by Israel Abrahams. Jerusalem:
Magnes Press, 1983.
Cohen, Shaye J.D. *Josephus in Galilee and Rome: His Vita and
Development As A Historian.* Leiden: E. J. Brill, 1979.
Collins, John J. *The Apocalyptic Imagination: An Introduction to the
Jewish Matrix of Christianity.* New York: Crossroad, 1984.
Cross, Frank Moore. *Canaanite Myth and Hebrew Epic.* Cambridge:
Harvard University Press, 1973.
Daube, David. *The New Testament and Rabbinic Judaism.* London:
Athlone Press, 1956.
———. *Collaboration With Tyranny in Rabbinic Law.* London:
Oxford University Press, 1965.
Eichrodt, Walther. *Theology of the Old Testament.* 2 vols.
Translated by J. A. Baker. Philadelphia: The Westminster
Press, 1967.
Elazar, Daniel J. and Cohen, Stuart A. *The Jewish Polity: Jewish
Political Organization from Biblical Times to the Present.*
Bloomington: Indiana University Press, 1985.
Enslin, Morton. *Christian Beginnings.* New York: Harper &
Brothers, 1938.
Feldman, Louis H. *Josephus: A Supplementary Bibliography.* New
York: Garland Publications, 1986.
Finkelstein, Louis. *The Pharisees.* Philadelphia: Jewish
Publication Society of America, 1940.
Fischel, Henry A. *Rabbinic Literature and Greco-Roman Philosophy.*
Leiden: E. J. Brill, 1973.
Fishbane, Michael. *Biblical Interpretation in Ancient Israel.*
Oxford: Oxford University Press, 1988.

Freeman, Gordon M. *The Heavenly Kingdom: Aspects of Political Thought in the Talmud and Midrash.* Lanham, MD: University Press of America, 1986.

Friedman, Richard E. *Who Wrote the Bible?* New York: Summit Books, 1987.

Ginsberg, H. L. *Studies In Daniel.* New York: Jewish Theological Seminary of America, 1948.

Ginzberg, Louis. *The Legends of the Jews.* 7 vols. Philadelphia: Jewish Publication Society of America, 1946-1954.

Glasson, T. Francis. *Greek Influence in Jewish Eschatology.* London: S.P.C.K. Biblical Monographs, 1961.

Gordis, Robert. *The Book of God and Man.* Chicago and London: University of Chicago Press, 1965.

———. *Koheleth—The Man and His World.* New York: The Jewish Theological Seminary of America, 1951.

Greenberg, Moshe. *Biblical Prose Prayer: As A Window to the Popular Religion of Ancient Israel.* Berkeley: University of California Press, 1983.

Gruenwald, Ithammar. *Apocalyptic and Merkavah Mysticism.* Leiden: E. J. Brill, 1980.

Halpern, Baruch. *The First Historians: The Hebrew Bible and History.* San Francisco: Harper and Row, 1988.

Hammer, Robert A. "Hasidut in Early Rabbinic Literature: A Study of the Pharisaic Concept of Piety." Ph.D. diss., Jewish Theological Seminary of America, 1969

Haran, Menahem. *Temples and Temple Service in Ancient Israel.* Oxford: The Clarendon Press, 1978.

Heschel, Abraham J. *The Prophets.* New York and Philadelphia: Jewish Publication Society of America and Harper & Row, 1963.

Himmelfarb, Martha. *Tours of Hell.* Philadelphia: University of Pennsylvania Press, 1983.

Jacobsen, Thorkild. *Toward the Image of Tammuz and Other Essays on Mesopotamian History and Culture.* Edited by William Moran. Cambridge: Harvard University Press, 1970.

Kaufmann, Yehezkel. *The Religion of Israel.* Translated and abridged by Moshe Greenberg. Chicago: University of Chicago Press, 1960.

———. *Toledot ha-Emunah ha-Yisraelit.* 8 vols. Jerusalem, Tel-Aviv: Mosad Bialik, 1953.

Klausner, Joseph. *The Messianic Idea in Israel.* 3rd edition. London: George Allen & Unwin, 1956.

Leiman, Sid Z. *The Canonization of Hebrew Scripture: The Talmudic and Midrashic Evidence.* Hamden, Conn.: The Connecticut Academy of Arts and Sciences, Archon Books, 1976.

Levinson, Jon D. *Creation and the Persistence of Evil.* San Francisco: Harper & Row, 1988.

Lieberman, Saul. *Hellenism in Jewish Palestine.* New York: The Jewish Theological Seminary of America, 1950.

—————. "Some Aspects of After Life in Early Rabbinic Literature." *Harry Austryn Wolfson Jubilee Volume.* 2 vols. English Section. Jerusalem: American Academy for Jewish Research, 1965.

Mantel, Hugo. *Studies in the History of the Sanhedrin.* Cambridge: Harvard University Press, 1961.

Milgrom, Jacob. *Cult and Conscience: The Asham and the Priestly Doctrine of Repentance.* Leiden: E. J. Brill, 1976.

Moore, George Foot. *Judaism: In the First Centuries of the Christian Era.* 3 vols. Cambridge: Harvard University Press,1950.

Muffs, Yochanan. *Love & Joy: Law, Language and Religion in Ancient Israel.* New York: The Jewish Theological Seminary of America, 1992.

Neusner, Jacob. *Life of Rabban Yohanan ben Zakkai.* Leiden: E. J. Brill, 1962.

Nickelsburg, George W. E. *Resurrection, Immortality and Eternal Life in Intertestamental Judaism.* Harvard Theological Studies 26. Cambridge: Harvard University Press, 1972.

Orlinsky, Harry. *Essays in Biblical Culture and Bible Translation.* New York: Ktav Publishing House, 1974.

Patai, Raphael. *Man and Temple in Ancient Jewish Myth and Ritual.* New York: Ktav Publishing House, 1967.

Rad, Gerhard von. *Wisdom in Israel.* Nashville: Abingdon Press, 1972.

Rosenberg, Ruth. "The Concept of Biblical Sheol Within the Context of Ancient Near Eastern Beliefs." Ph.D. diss., Harvard University, March, 1981.

Rowland, Christopher. *The Open Heaven: A Study of Apocalyptic in Judaism and Early Christianity.* New York: Crossroad, 1982.

Scholem, Gershom. *The Messianic Idea in Judaism.* New York: Schocken Books, 1971.

—————. *Jewish Gnosticism, Merkabah Mysticism and Talmudic Tradition.* New York: Jewish Theological Seminary of America, 1960.

Schultz, Joseph P. *Judaism and the Gentile Faiths: Comparative Studies in Religion.* Rutherford, N.J.: Fairleigh Dickinson University Press, 1981.

Scott, R. B. Y. *The Way of Wisdom in the Old Testament.* New York: Macmillan, 1971.

Smith, Morton. *Tannaitic Parallels to the Gospels.* Philadelphia: Society of Biblical Literature, 1951.

————· *The Secret Gospel.* New York: Harper & Row, 1973.

Steinsaltz, Adin. *Biblical Images.* New York: Basic Books, 1989.

Stern, Menahem, editor. *Greek and Latin Authors on Jews and Judaism.* Jerusalem: Israel Academy of Sciences and Humanities, 1974.

Tromp, Nicholas J. *Primitive Conceptions of Death and the Nether World in the Old Testament.* Rome: Pontifical Biblical Institute, 1969.

Uffenheimer, Benjamin. *The Visions of Zechariah: From Prophecy to Apocalyptic* (Hebrew). Jerusalem: The Israel Society for Biblical Research and *Kiryat Sepher*, 1961.

Urbach, Ephraim E. *The Sages: Their Concepts and Beliefs.* Translated by Israel Abrahams. Cambridge: Harvard University Press, 1987.

Varneda, Pere Villalba I. *The Historical Method of Flavius Josephus.* Leiden: E. J. Brill, 1966.

Wolfson, Harry A. *Philo:Foundations of Religious Philosophy in Judaism, Christianity and Islam.* 4th edition, revised. Cambridge: Harvard University Press, 1968.

Zeitlin, Solomon. *The Rise and Fall of the Judean State.* 2 vols. Philadelphia: Jewish Publication Society of America, 1962.

Secondary Sources—Articles and Essays

Cross, Frank M. "The Epic Tradition of Early Israelite Institutions." In *The Poet and the Historian: Essays in Literary and Historical Biblical Criticism.* Edited by Richard E. Friedman. Harvard Semitic Series 26. Chico, Calif.: Scholars Press, 1983.

Daube, David. "Concessions to Sinfulness in Jewish Law." *Journal of Jewish Studies* 10 (1959): 1-16.

————· "Rabbinic Methods of Interpretation and Hellenistic Rhetoric." *Hebrew Union College Annual* 22 (1949): 239-264.

Feldman, Louis H. "Hellenizations in Josephus' Portrayal of Man's Decline." In *Religions in Antiquity: Essays in Memory of Erwin R. Goodenough.* Edited by Jacob Neusner. Leiden: E. J. Brill, 1968.

Friedman, Richard E. "The Tabernacle in the Temple." *Biblical Archeologist* 43 (1980): 241-248.

——. "Sacred History and Theology: The Redaction of Torah." In *The Creation of Sacred Literature.* Edited by R.E. Friedman. *Near Eastern Studies* 22 (Berkeley: University of California Press, 1981): 25-34.

Glatzer, Nahum. "A Study of the Talmudic Interpretation of Prophecy." *The Review of Religion.* (January, 1946): 116-127.

Gordis, Robert. "Democratic Origins in Ancient Israel: The Biblical Edah." In *Alexander Marx Jubilee Volume.* New York: Jewish Theological Seminary, 1950.

Levinson, Jon D. "The Jerusalem Temple in Devotional and Visionary Experience." In *Jewish Spirituality: From the Bible Through the Middle Ages.* Edited by Arthur Green. World Spirituality: An Encyclopedic History of the Religious Quest 13. New York: Crossroad, 1986.

Licht, Jacob. *"Nefesh"* and *"Neshamah."* In *Encyclopedia Biblica.* Jerusalem: Bialik Institute, 1968.

Mantel, Hugo. "The Development of the Oral Law During the Second Temple Period." In *The World History of the Jewish People.* Edited by Michael Avi Yonah and Zvi Barras. vol. 8: *Society and Religion in the Second Temple Period.* Jerusalem: Masada Publishing Co., 1977.

——. "The Nature of the Great Synagogue." *Harvard Theological Review* 60 (1967): 75-91.

Neusner, Jacob. "The Religious Uses of History: Judaism in First Century A.D. Palestine and Third-Century Babylonia." *History and Theory* 5 (1966): 153-171.

Parzen, Herbert. "The Ruah ha-Kodesh in Tannaitic Literature." *Jewish Quarterly Review* N.S. 20 (July, 1929): 51-76.

Porter, Frank C. "The Yecer Hara, A Study in the Jewish Doctrine of Sin." In *Biblical and Semitic Studies.* New York: Charles Scribners & Sons, 1901.

Ramsey, Paul. "Elements of a Biblical Political Theory." *Journal of Religion* 29:4 (October,1949): 265-272.

Safrai, Samuel. "The Synagogue and its Worship." In *The World History of the Jewish People.* Edited by Michael Avi Yonah and Zvi Barras. vol. 8. *Society and Religion in the Second Temple Period.* Jerusalem: Masada, 1977.

Schiffman, Lawrence. "The Concept of the Messiah in Second Temple and Rabbinic Literature." *Review and Expositor* 84:1 (Winter, 1987): 235-246.

Schultz, Joseph P. "Two Views of the Patriarchs: Noahides or Pre-Sinai Israelites. In *Texts and Responses: Studies in Honor of Nahum Glatzer*. Edited by M. Fishbane and P. Flohr. Leiden: E. J. Brill, 1975.

————. "Angelic Opposition to the Ascension of Moses and the Revelation of the Law." *Jewish Quarterly Review* 61 (July 1971): 282-307.

Smith, Morton. "Ascent to the Heavens and the Beginning of Christianity." *Eranos Yearbook* 50 (1981): 403-429.

Spiegel, Shalom. "A Prophetic Attestation of the Decalogue, Hosea 6:5 With Some Observations on Psalms 15 and 24." *Harvard Theological Review* 27 (1934): 131-139.

Stern, Menahem. "The Period of the Second Temple." In *A History of the Jewish People*. Edited by H. H. Ben Sasson. Cambridge: Harvard University Press, 1976.

Urbach, Ephraim E. "Ascesis and Suffering in Talmudic and Midrashic Sources" (Hebrew). In *Yitzhak Baer Jubilee Volume*. Edited by S. W. Baron, B. Dinur, S. Ettinger, I. Halpern. Jerusalem: The Historical Society of Israel, 1960.

————. "*Halakhah U-Nevuah*." *Tarbiz* 18 (1946-47): 1-27.

————. "*Matay Paskah ha-Nevuah?*" *Tarbiz* 17 (1946): 1-11.

Zeitlin, Solomon. "The Origin of the Synagogue." *Proceedings of the American Academy for Jewish Research* (1931).

Olympus Sources

For further references to Greek primary sources, see notes to Olympus sections as well as the index.

Books

Adkins, A. W. H. *Merit and Responsibility: A Study in Greek Values*. New York: Oxford University Press, 1960.

Alderink, Larry. *Creation and Salvation in Ancient Orphism*. Chico, CA: Scholars Press, 1981.

Allen, R. E., editor. *Studies in Plato's Metaphysics*. New York: Humanities Press, 1965.

Anderson, J. K. *Xenophon*. New York: Charles Scribner's Sons: 1974.

André-Jean Festugière. *Personal Religion Among the Greeks*. Berkeley: University of California Press, 1954.

Barker, Ernest. *Greek Political Theory: Plato and his Predecessors*. 1918. Reprint. New York: Barnes and Noble, 1960.

————. *The "Politics" of Aristotle, translated with an Introduction, Notes and Appendixes*. Oxford: Oxford University Press, 1952.

Barnes, Jonathan. *The Presocratic Philosophers*. London, Boston: Routledge & Kegan Paul, 1982.

Boedeker, D., editor. *Herodotus and the Invention of History*. *Arethusa* 20, 1 & 2, 1987.

Bonner, Robert J. *Lawyers and Litigants in Ancient Athens: The Genesis of the Legal Profession*. Chicago: University of Chicago Press, 1927.

Bonner, Robert J., and Gertrude Smith. *The Administration of Justice from Homer to Aristotle*. Vol. 1. Chicago: University of Chicago Press, 1930.

Bowra, C. M. *Pindar*. Oxford: Clarendon Press, 1964.

Bremmer, Jan. *Hamartia: Tragic Error in the "Poetics" of Aristotle and in Greek Tragedy*. Amsterdam: Adolf M. Hakkert, 1969.

———. *The Early Greek Concept of the Soul*. Princeton: Princeton University Press, 1983.

Brown, Norman O. *Hesiod; "Theogony", translated with an Introduction*. Indianapolis: Bobbs-Merrill, 1953.

Brown, Andrew. *A New Companion to Greek Tragedy*. Totowa, N J: Barnes and Noble, 1983.

Burkert, Walter. *Lore and Science in Ancient Pythagoreanism*. Translated by Edwin L. Minar, Jr. Cambridge: Harvard University Press, 1972.

———. *Greek Religion*. Translated by John Raffan. Cambridge: Harvard University Press, 1985.

———. *Homo Necans; The Anthropology of Ancient Greek Sacrificial Ritual and Myth*. Translated by Peter Bings. Berkeley: University of California Press, 1983.

Calhoun, George. *The Growth of Criminal Law in Ancient Greece*. 1927. Reprint. Westport, Conn.: Greenwood Press, 1974.

Callahan, John F. *Four Views of Time in Ancient Philosophy*. 1948. Reprint. New York: Greenwood, 1968.

Claus, David B. *Toward the Soul: An Inquiry into the Meaning of Psyche before Plato*. New Haven: Yale University Press, 1981.

Cornford, Francis M. *Plato and Parmenides: Parmenides' "Way of Truth" and Plato's "Parmenides," translated with an Introduction and Running Commentary*. New York: Liberal Arts Press, 1957.

———. *Plato's Cosmology: "The Timaeus" of Plato translated with a Running Commentary*. London: Routledge and Kegan Paul, 1957.

———. *Principium Sapientiae: The Origins of Greek Philosophic Thought*. Cambridge: Cambridge University Press, 1952.

Cumont, Franz. *Afterlife in Roman Paganism*. 1922. Reprint. New York: Dover, 1959.

————· *Astrology and Religion among the Greeks and Romans.*
1912. Reprint. New York: Dover, 1960.
David J. Furley and R. E. Allen, editors. *Studies in Presocratic
Philosophy, Vol. 1, The Beginnings of Philosophy.* New York:
Humanities Press, 1970.
de Romilly, J. *The Rise and Fall of States according to Greek
Authors.* Ann Arbor: University of Michigan Press, 1977.
Despland, Michael. *The Education of Desire: Plato and the
Philosophy of Religion.* Toronto: University of Toronto Press,
1985.
Dodds, E. R. *The Greeks and the Irrational.* Berkeley: University of
California Press, 1959.
————· *The Ancient Concept of Progress and Other Essays.* Oxford:
Clarendon Press, 1973.
————· *Euripides' "Bacchae."* Oxford: Clarendon Press, 1944.
————· *Plato: "Gorgias."* Oxford: Clarendon Press, 1959.
Drews, Robert. *The Greek Accounts of Eastern History.* Washington:
Center for Hellenic Studies, 1973.
Easterling, P. E., and J. V. Muir, editors. *Greek Religion and
Society.* Cambridge: Cambridge University Press, 1985.
Farnell, Louis Richard. *Greek Hero Cults and Ideas of Immortality.*
Oxford: Clarendon Press, 1921.
Farrar, Cynthia. *The Origins of Democratic Thinking: The Invention
of Politics in Classical Athens.* Cambridge: Cambridge
University Press, 1988.
Finley, M. I., and H. W. Pleket. *The Olympic Games: The First
Thousand Years.* New York: Viking, 1976.
Fontenrose, Joseph. *The Delphic Oracle: Its Responses and
Operation.* Berkeley: University of California Press, 1978.
Fornara, Charles William. *The Nature of History in Ancient Greece
and Rome.* Berkeley: University of California Press, 1983.
Gagarin, Michael. *Early Greek Law.* Berkeley: University of
California Press, 1988.
————· *Drakon and the Early Athenian Homicide Law.* New Haven:
Yale University Press, 1981.
Garland, Robert G. *The Greek Way of Death.* Ithaca: Cornell
University Press, 1985.
Garner, Richard. *Law and Society in Classical Athens.* New York:
St. Martins Press, 1987.
Gomme, A. W. *The Greek Attitude to Poetry and History.* Berkeley:
University of California Press, 1954.

Gordon, R. D., editor. *Myth, Religion, and Society: Structuralist Essays by M. Detienne, L. Gernet, J. P. Vernant, and P. Vidal Naquet.* Cambridge: Cambridge University Press, 1981.

Greene, W. C. *Moira: Fate, Good, and Evil in Greek Philosophy.* Cambridge: Harvard University Press, 1944.

Guthrie, W. K. G. *A History of Greek Philosophy I-III.* Cambridge: Cambridge University Press, 1962-1969.

————. *In the Beginning: Some Greek Views of the Origins of Life and the Early State of Man.* Ithaca, NY: Cornell University Press.

Havelock, E. A. *The Greek Concept of Justice from Its Shadow in Homer to Its Substance in Plato.* Cambridge: Harvard University Press, 1978.

Higgins, W. E. *Xenophon the Athenian: The Problem of the Individual and the Society of the Polis.* Albany: State University of New York Press, 1977.

Hignett, C. *A History of the Athenian Constitution to the End of the Fifth Century B.C.* Oxford: Clarendon Press, 1958.

Humphreys, S. C. *Anthropology and the Greeks.* London: Routledge and Kegan Paul, 1978.

Hunter, Virginia. *Past and Process in Herodotus and Thucydides.* Princeton: Princeton University Press, 1982

Jaeger, Werner. *Paideia: The Ideals of Greek Culture,* 3 vols. Translated by G. Highet. New York: Oxford University Press, 1960.

————. *The Theology of the Early Greek Philosophers.* Translated by E. S. Robinson. Oxford: Oxford University Press, 1947.

Kahn, Charles H. *Anaximander and the Origins of Greek Cosmology.* Philadelphia: Centrum, 1985.

————. *The Art and Thought of Heraclitus: An Edition of the Fragments with Translation and Commentary.* Cambridge: Cambridge University Press, 1979.

Kennedy, George, editor. *Cambridge History of Literary Criticism, Vol. 1: Classical Criticism.* Cambridge: Harvard University Press, 1989.

Kennedy, George. *The Art of Persuasion in Greece.* Princeton: Princeton University Press, 1963.

Kerford, G. B. *The Sophistic Movement.* Cambridge: Cambridge University Press, 1981.

Kirk, G. S., J. E. Raven, and M. Schofield. *The Presocratic Philosophers: A Critical History with a Selection of Texts.* 2nd edition. Cambridge: Cambridge University Press, 1983.

Lattimore, Richmond. *Themes in Greek and Latin Epitaphs.* Urbana: University of Illinois Press, 1942.

Lloyd, G. E. R. *The Revolutions of Wisdom: Studies in the Claims and Practice of Ancient Greek Science.* Berkeley: University of California Press, 1987.

———· *Early Greek Science from Thales to Aristotle.* New York: W. W. Norton, 1970.

———· *Polarity and Analogy: Two Types of Argumentation in Early Greek Thought.* Cambridge: Cambridge University Press, 1966.

Lloyd-Jones, H. *The Justice of Zeus.* Berkeley: University of California Press, 1971.

Long, A. A., editor. *Problems in Stoicism.* London: Athlone, 1971.

Long, Herbert Strainge. "A Study of the Doctrine of Metempsychosis in Greece from Pythagoras to Plato." Ph.D. diss., Princeton University, 1948.

MacDowell, Douglas M. *The Law in Classical Athens.* Ithaca: Cornell University Press, 1978.

———· *Athenian Homicide Law in the Age of the Orators.* Manchester: University Press, 1963.

Martin, Luther. *Hellenistic Religions: An Introduction.* New York: Oxford University Press, 1987.

Mikalson, Jon D. *Athenian Popular Religion.* Chapel Hill, NC: University of North Carolina Press, 1983.

———· *The Sacred and Civil Calendar of the Athenian Year.* Princeton: Princeton University Press, 1975.

Miller, D. Gary. *Improvisation, Typology, Culture, and the 'New Orthodoxy': How 'Oral' is Homer?* Washington DC.: University Press of America, 1982.

Mulgan, R. G. *Aristotle's Political Theory: An Introduction for Students of Political Theory.* Oxford: Clarendon Press, 1977.

Mylonas, George E. *Eleusis and the Eleusinian Mysteries.* Princeton: Princeton University Press, 1961.

Nagy, Gregory. *The Best of the Achaeans: Concepts of the Hero in Archaic Greek Poetry.* Baltimore: Johns Hopkins University Press, 1979.

———· *Greek Mythology and Poetics.* Ithaca: Cornell University Press, 1990.

Nilsson, Martin. *Greek Folk Religion.* New York: Harper and Brothers, 1961.

Nussbaum, Martha C. *The Fragility of Goodness: Luck and Ethics in Greek Tragedy and Philosophy.* Cambridge: Cambridge University Press, 1986.

Ostwald, Martin. *From Popular Sovereignty to the Sovereignty of Law: Law, Society, and Politics in Fifth Century Athens.* Berkeley: University of California Press, 1986.

———· *Nomos and the Beginnings of the Athenian Democracy.* Oxford: Clarendon Press, 1969.

Parke, H. W., and D. E. Wormell. *The Delphic Oracle.* Vol I. *The History.* Oxford: Basil Blackwell, 1956.

Parke, H. W. *Festivals of the Athenians.* London: Thames and Hudson, 1977.

Parker, Robert. *Miasma: Pollution and Purification in Early Greek Religion.* Oxford: Clarendon Press, 1983.

Pearson, Lionel. *Early Ionian Historians.* Oxford: Clarendon Press, 1939.

Picard-Cambridge, Arthur. *Dithyramb, Tragedy, and Comedy.* 2nd edition. Revised by T. B. L. Webster. Oxford: Clarendon Press, 1962.

———· *Dramatic Festivals of Athens.* 2nd edition. Revised by John Gould and P.M. Lewis. Oxford: Clarendon Press, 1968.

Pollitt, J. J. *Art and Experience in Classical Greece.* Cambridge: Cambridge University Press, 1972.

Reckford, Kenneth. *Aristophanes' Old and New Comedy. Vol. I Six Essays in Perspective.* Chapel Hill: University of North Carolina Press, 1987.

Rhodes, P. J. *A Commentary on the Aristotelian "Athenaion Politeia."* Oxford: Clarendon Press, 1981.

Rist, John, editor. *The Stoics.* Berkeley: University of California Press, 1978.

Robinson, T. M. *Plato's Psychology.* Toronto: University of Toronto Press, 1970.

Rohde, Erwin. *Psyche: The Cult of Souls and Belief in Immortality among the Ancient Greeks.* Translated by W. B. Hillis. 1925. Reprint. Chicago: Ares, 1987.

Rudolph, Kurt. *Gnosis: The Nature and History of Gnosticism.* Translated by Robert McLachlan Wilson. San Francisco: Harper and Row, 1983.

Scully, Vincent. *The Earth the Temple and the Gods: Greek Sacred Architecture.* New Haven: Yale University Press, 1979.

Sealey, Raphael. *The Athenian Republic: Democracy or the Rule of Law?* University Park, PA: The Pennsylvania State University Press, 1987.

———· *Women and Law in Classical Greece.* Chapel Hill: University of North Carolina Press, 1990.

Seltzer, Robert, editor. *Religions of Antiquity: Religion, History and Culture Selections from the Encyclopedia of Religion.* New York: Macmillan, 1987.

Simon, Erika. *Festivals of Attica: An Archaelogical Commentary.* Madison: University of Wisconsin Press, 1983.

Snell, Bruno. *The Discovery of the Mind: The Greek Origins of European Thought.* Translated by T. G. Rosenmeyer. New York: Harper & Brothers, 1960.

Snodgrass, A. M. *The Dark Ages of Greece: An Archaeological Survey of the Eleventh to the Eighth Centuries B.C.E.* Edinburgh: Edinburgh University Press, 1971.

Starr, Chester G. *The Origins of Greek Civilization, 1100-650 B.C.* New York: Alfred A. Knopf, 1961.

Taplin, Oliver. *Greek Tragedy in Action.* London: Methuen, 1978.

Thalmann, William G. *Conventions of Form and Thought in Early Greek Epic Poetry.* Baltimore: The John Hopkins University Press, 1984.

Tomlinson, R.A. *Greek Sanctuaries.* London: Paul Elek, 1976.

Tyrrell, Wm. Blake, and Frieda S. Brown. *Athenian Myths and Institutions: Words in Action.* Oxford: Oxford University Press, 1991.

Ulansey, David. *The Origins of the Mithraic Mysteries: Cosmology and Salvation in the Ancient World.* Oxford: Oxford University Press, 1989.

Vermaseren, M. J., editor. *Studies in Hellenistic Religion.* Leiden: E. J. Brill, 1979.

Vermaseren, M. J. *Mithras. The Secret God.* Translated by T. & V. Magaw. New York: Barnes and Noble, 1963.

Vernant, Jean Pierre. *Myth and Thought Among the Greeks.* Translated from the French. London: Routledge and Kegan Paul, 1983.

Wace, A. J. B., and F. Stubbings. *A Companion to Homer.* London: Macmillan, 1962.

Walbank, F. W. *Polybius.* Berkeley: University of California Press, 1972.

Walcot, Peter. *Hesiod and the Ancient Near East.* Cardiff: University of Wales, 1966.

Waters, K. H. *Herodotus the Historian: His Problems, Methods and Originality.* London: Croom Helm, 1985.

West, M. L. *Hesiod: "Theogony."* Oxford: Oxford University Press, 1966.

———. *Hesiod: "Works and Days."* Oxford: Oxford University Press, 1978.

———· *Early Greek Philosophy and the Orient.* Oxford: Clarendon Press, 1971.

———· *The Orphic Poems.* Oxford: Clarendon Press, 1983.

Wood, Neal. *Cicero's Social and Political Thought.* Berkeley: University of California Press, 1988.

Zuntz, G. *Persephone: Three Essays on Religion and Thought in Magna Graecia.* Oxford: Clarendon Press, 1971.

Articles and Essays

Boyance, Pierre. "La Religion Astrale de Platon a Ciceron." *Revue des etudes grecques* 65 (1952): 312-350.

Cole, Susan Guettel. "New Evidence for the Mysteries of Dionysus." *Greek Roman and Byzantine Studies* 2 (1980): 223-238.

Davies, J. K. "Religion and the State." *The Cambridge Ancient History.* Vol. 4. Cambridge: Cambridge University Press, 1980-1988. pp. 368-88.

Dawe, R. D. "Some Reflections on *Ate* and *Hamartia*." *Proceedings of the Cambridge Philological Society* 186 (1960): 19-31.

Ehrenberg, Victor. "Origins of Democracy." *Historia* 1 (1950): 537-548.

Fisher, N. R. E. "Hybris and Dishonor." *Greece and Rome* 23 (1976): 177-93 and 26 (1979): 32-47.

Gagarin, Michael. "*Dike* in Archaic Greek Thought." *Classical Philology* 69 (1974): 186-197.

Garland, Robert. "Priests and Power in Classical Athens." *Pagan Priests: Religion and Power in the Ancient World.* Edited by Mary Beard and John North. Ithaca: Cornell University Press, 1990. pp. 75-91.

Immerwahr, Henry. "Historiography." *The Cambridge History of Classical Literature. 1.* Cambridge: Cambridge University Press, 1982.

Kahn, C. H. "Religion and Natural Philosophy in Empedocles' Doctrine of the Soul." *Archiv fur Geschichte der Philosophie* 42 (1960): 3-35.

Lesky, Albin. "Decision and Responsibility in the Tragedy of Aeschylus." *Journal of Hellenic Studies* 86 (1966).

Momigliano, Arnaldo. "Greek Historiography." *History and Theory* 17 (1978): 1-28.

Morris, Ian. "Attitudes toward Death in Archaic Greece." *Classical Antiquity* 9 (1989): 296-320.

Nagy, Gregory. "Pindar's *Olympian* I and the Aetiology of the Olympic Games." *Transactions of the American Philological Association* 116 (1986): 71-88.

Nilsson, Martin P. "The Origin of Belief among the Greeks in the
    Divinity of the Heavenly Bodies." *Harvard Theological Review*
    33 (1940): 1-8.
Osborne, Robin. "The Law in Action in Classical Athens." *Journal
    of Hellenic Studies* 105 (1985): 40-58.
Renehan, R. "On the Greek Origins of the Concepts of Incorporeality
    and Immortality." *Greek Roman and Byzantine Studies* 2 (1980):
    105-138.
Scolnicov, Samuel. "Reason and Passion in the Platonic Soul."
    Dionysius 2 (1978): 35-49.
Szegedy-Maszak, Andrew. "Legends of the Greek Lawgivers."
    Greek Roman and Byzantine Studies 19 (1978): 199-209.
Vlastos, Gregory. "Equality and Justice in Early Greek
    Cosmologies." *Classical Philology* 42 (1947): 156-78.
———. "ISONOMIA." *American Journal of Philology* 74 (1953):
    337-366.

Select Index

About the Authors

Dr. Lois Settler Spatz was graduated from Goucher College as a Phi Beta Kappa with Honors in Classics. She received an M.A.T. from The Johns Hopkins University and an M.A. and Ph.D. in Classics from Indiana University. She is the author of *Aeschylus* and *Aristophanes* for the Twayne World Authors Series, as well as articles and reviews for publications in classics. After working at Brooklyn College and Park College, she is now a Professor of English at the University of Missouri-Kansas City, where she specializes in ancient literature in translation, drama, and mythology, as well as teaching advanced Greek and Latin. She is the former director of the UMKC Cluster Program: Interdisciplinary Courses in the Humanities and co-coordinates the Classical and Ancient Studies Program, which she founded.

Dr. Joseph P. Schultz was graduated from Yeshiva College with a B.A. *cum laude* in English Literature. He received his Master of Hebrew Literature and his rabbinic ordination from the Jewish Theological Seminary of America and his Ph.D. in Near Eastern and Judaic Studies from Brandeis University. He is the author of *Judaism and the Gentile Faiths* and *Mid-America's Promise: A Profile of Kansas City Jewry*, among other books and articles. He founded the Judaic Studies Programs at Boston University and at the University of Missouri-Kansas City, where he is now Oppenstein Brothers Distinguished Professor of Judaic Studies and Professor of History. He specializes in the comparative study of religion, particularly in the area of mysticism.

Professors Schultz and Spatz teach several interdisciplinary courses together at the undergraduate and graduate levels. *Sinai & Olympus: A Comparative Study* developed out of their first joint endeavor.